AMERICAN POLITICAL THOUGHT

AMERICAN POLITICAL THOUGHT

READINGS AND MATERIALS

Keith E. Whittington
PRINCETON UNIVERSITY

NEW YORK OXFORD
OXFORD UNIVERSITY PRESS

Oxford University Press is a department of the University of Oxford.
It furthers the University's objective of excellence in research,
scholarship, and education by publishing worldwide.

Oxford New York
Auckland Cape Town Dar es Salaam Hong Kong Karachi
Kuala Lumpur Madrid Melbourne Mexico City Nairobi
New Delhi Shanghai Taipei Toronto

With offices in
Argentina Austria Brazil Chile Czech Republic France Greece
Guatemala Hungary Italy Japan Poland Portugal Singapore
South Korea Switzerland Thailand Turkey Ukraine Vietnam

For titles covered by Section 112 of the US Higher Education Opportunity Act, please visit www.oup.com/us/he for the latest information about pricing and alternate formats.

Published by Oxford University Press
198 Madison Avenue, New York, New York 10016
http://www.oup.com

Library of Congress Cataloging-in-Publication Data

Names: Whittington, Keith E., author.
Title: American political thought : readings and materials / Keith E. Whittington.
Description: New York : Oxford University Press, [2017]
Identifiers: LCCN 2015043123 | ISBN 9780199338863 (pbk.)
Subjects: LCSH: Political science--United States--History. | United States--Politics and government.
Classification: LCC JA84.U5 W485 2017 | DDC 320.0973--dc23 LC record available at http://lccn.loc.gov/2015043123

Printing number: 9 8 7 6 5 4 3 2 1

Printed in the United States of America
on acid-free paper

BRIEF CONTENTS

CONTENTS

TOPICAL OUTLINE OF VOLUME

1. **Democracy and Liberty**

Roger Williams, *The Bloudy Tenent of Persecution* (1644)
John Cotton, *An Exposition upon the 13th Chapter of the Revelations* (1644)
John Winthrop, *Little Speech on Liberty* (1645)
John Wise, *A Vindication of the Government of New England Churches* (1717)
Thomas Paine, *Common Sense* (1776)
John Adams, *Thoughts on Government* (1776)
Carter Braxton, *An Address to the Convention of the Colony* (1776)
Thomas Jefferson, *An Act for Establishing Religious Freedom* (1777)
Alexander Hamilton, *Federalist Papers* (1787)
James Madison, *Federalist Papers* (1787)
Brutus Essays (1787)
Letters from the Federal Farmer (1787)
Thomas Jefferson and James Madison, *Correspondence on a Bill of Rights* (1787–1789)
Thomas Jefferson, *Kentucky Resolutions* (1798)
Fisher Ames, *The Mire of Democracy* (1805)
Thomas Jefferson, *Letter to a Committee of the Danbury Baptists* (1802)
John Marshall, *Marbury v. Madison* (1803)
Lyman Beecher, *Practicability of Suppressing Vice* (1803)
Thomas Jefferson, *Letter to Samuel Kercheval* (1816)
James Kent and David Buel, Jr., *Debate at the New York Constitutional Convention* (1821)
George Bancroft, *The Office of the People in Art, Government, and Religion* (1835)
Henry David Thoreau, *Civil Disobedience* (1849)
John C. Calhoun, *A Disquisition on Government* (1850)
Theodore Parker, *Law of God and the Statutes of Men* (1854)

Hans J. Morgenthau, *In Defense of the National Interest* (1952)
James Burnham, *Containment or Liberation?* (1953)
J. William Fulbright, *The Arrogance of Power* (1966)
Jeane J. Kirkpatrick, *Dictatorships and Double Standards* (1979)
Samuel P. Huntington, *The Clash of Civilizations?* (1993)
Noam Chomsky, *Understanding Power* (2002)

FIGURES AND BOXES

PREFACE

This textbook takes a new approach to the study of American political thought. The target audience consists of professors, students, and readers interested in researching, teaching, and learning about the intellectual history and the history of political thought in the United States. The work focuses on those questions of politics and society of concern to all Americans and provides readers with the materials necessary for thinking intelligently about these issues. The book provides an introduction to the ideas that have affected, shaped, and transformed American politics and an appreciation of the controversies and disputes that have mobilized Americans since the first European settlements in North America.

American political thought sits at the intersection of political theory and American politics. With that in mind, this text highlights four important features of this material:

- The *full range of American political thought*
- The *interaction of American political thought and politics*
- The *struggle over American values*
- The central role of *history and historical development*

The teaching of American political thought has traditionally served a variety of purposes. It provides an entry point for studying American political history broadly. The debates that make up the central sources of American political thought trace the history of American politics and policymaking. Key political and policy innovations and significant challenges to American success have been accompanied by new thinking about what values are most central to American politics and how they should be applied, extended, or modified to help chart the path ahead.

American political thought provides an angle for better understanding American society and politics. The history of American political thought is the record of the struggle to define the fundamental principles that should guide political decision making. Contemporary politics rests on an inheritance of political traditions and values that have been built up (and sometimes torn down) across generations. American political thought exposes the choices that have been made over time and the rationales that underwrite political action.

The study of American political thought is the study of a particular kind of intellectual history. American political thought focuses on the ideas associated with different stages of society and politics, the contesting ideologies that motivate, legitimate, and guide political action. Unlike some other primary documents associated with historical study, the materials of American political thought do not simply show what happened and how people lived. They show how people have thought about the world in which they lived and how they sought to explain it, rationalize it, or change it.

An appreciation for American political thought complements the study of political theory as such. American political thought is concerned with ideas in action. It engages with the fundamental questions of political life, but it does so within immediate contexts and with foreseeable consequences. Participants in the American political tradition have sought to extrapolate basic commitments and lessons from the American political experience but have then made use of those lessons to advocate concrete action within the political realm. The study of American political thought serves as a bridge between the discussion of abstract principles and value systems and the examination of how politics works in practice.

FULL RANGE OF AMERICAN POLITICAL THOUGHT

This text covers the full range of American political thought. Many texts artificially truncate the subject, either by restricting the range of voices that have contributed to public debates in American history or by narrowing the scope of the subject matter to a few particular themes. This text takes an expansive approach to the subject matter, exposing readers to the full spectrum of political debate and challenging them to think about all the key issues that have informed and been informed by enduring American political values.

The text takes a comprehensive approach to understanding American political thought. The thinkers, writers, and speakers represented in these pages include scholars, intellectuals, politicians, judges, journalists, ministers, and political activists of all stripes. The debate over political values has not taken place in the seminar room, but neither has it been restricted to the loftiest seats of political power. The key consideration for inclusion is whether the speaker or writer was insightful, reflected significant political sentiments and concerns, and was influential in public debates. In those debates, presidents and senators rub elbows with labor organizers and escaped slaves. This text seeks to capture American political thought in all its richness, giving due consideration to those who spoke from the pulpit or the lectern, for the marginalized and for the privileged, on behalf of an America that had been inherited and of an America that was being imagined.

As part of the effort to broaden the scope of what is traditionally considered within the rubric of American political thought, the text also expands the field of issues under consideration. Each chapter is divided into five parts: democracy and liberty, citizenship and community, equality and status, political economy, and America and the world. These are overlapping categories, and even within a single speech or pamphlet a thinker may range over and connect several of these issues. Nonetheless, these divisions usefully capture some recurring debates within American political thought. Debates over democracy and liberty have revolved around such questions as how political authority is grounded, what popular government implies, how liberty can best be preserved, and what rights should be recognized. Debates over citizenship and community ask what it means to be an American, why and how the American political community is tied together, what are the bonds that hold the community together, and what are the privileges and duties of a citizen. Debates over equality and status consider what one of the axiomatic principles of the United States—that all men are created equal—might mean, what are the tensions between equality and liberty, how status and privilege can be reconciled with republican community, and on what terms different races, ethnicities, classes, and sexes work together in a common political and social space. Debates over political economy investigate the relationship between the material world and the political, between public policy and the public welfare, between labor and capital and the basic ordering of the social and economic world. Debates over America and the world try to identify how the United States can and should position itself on the international stage and what American foreign policy says about the values and identity of the United States, and how American values should shape American behavior abroad.

Such themes are broad, but they are regularly played out in particular contexts, motivated by specific public problems and concerned with distinct policies. These readings are chosen because the writer is able to rise above the details of a particular policy debate and illuminate broader concerns. These particular debates are an occasion for thinking about enduring features of American politics and recurrent aspirations, ideals, and concerns. They are of interest not because we seek to replay the legislative debates surrounding the construction of the Maysville Road or the occupation and governance of the Philippines, but because those debates open for inspection conflicting ideas about basic American commitments.

INTERACTION OF AMERICAN POLITICAL THOUGHT AND POLITICS

A central theme of the study of American political thought is that political action and political ideas are intertwined. *American Political Thought* presents readers with materials for evaluating the extent to which politics influences ideas and vice versa. Every historical chapter begins with an introduction that outlines the political, social, and intellectual circumstances of the period. These introductions provide an understanding of the most important political coalitions of that period, their platforms, major political personalities, the most important policy disputes, the social conditions and cleavages, and predominant social and political ideas. This information enables students to determine for themselves whether American political values are timeless or time-bound, whether the expression of political ideas operates on a separate track from the pursuit of political interests, or whether ideas and interests work in concert.

American political thought can be viewed primarily from the perspective of political philosophy, with American theorists contributing to timeless and universal debates over the deep foundations and eternal questions of political life. This book provides the resources for approaching American political thought in this way. The readings include substantial excerpts from the most profound political thinkers in American history—the *Federalist Papers* on constitutionalism, Thoreau on political resistance, Calhoun on majoritarianism, Lincoln on nationalism and equality, Dewey on democracy—and background discussion of the international philosophical debates within which they participated. The excerpts included in this volume address timeless themes and eternal questions of political life, and these thinkers can readily be put in dialogue with each other and with debates and concerns of today.

But the American contribution to the long tradition of Western political philosophy is limited. American political writers have been more practical and concrete in their concerns than theoretical and abstract. Over time, the United States has produced more statesmen and lawyers than political philosophers. Understanding what motivated these writers, how they intervened in political events, and what they sought to accomplish requires some appreciation for their surroundings, the problems they faced, the intellectual and political resources they possessed, and the conversations in which they were involved. These materials reveal the *political* in American political thought and the connections between public policy, political action, and political thought. They reveal the political ideals that inspired and puzzled political entrepreneurs.

STRUGGLE OVER AMERICAN VALUES

American political history is replete with disagreements over American political identity and ideals. *American Political Thought* details the struggle over American values and national ideals. The materials in the book demonstrate the range of arguments, actors, and political movements that have roiled the American political landscape. The book canvasses a diverse set of writers and political actors who have contributed to the American political conversation. The book illuminates the extent to which disputes within American political thought have been resolved, while also indicating the extent to which debates over ideas and practice have evolved across time and reemerged over time.

These materials help illuminate a specifically American political tradition. They illustrate the values and concerns that have moved generations of Americans in politics. They show how Americans have struggled with the fundamental questions of governance and political life. The answers they have offered have not always been persuasive, but they have influenced how American political institutions and political culture have developed and provide insights into the kinds of problems they have tried to solve.

This volume can also help dispel easy assumptions that Americans have always agreed about the political fundamentals and have primarily fought over resources rather than ideas. Although there has been substantial agreement over many basic issues—the divine right of kings has gained little traction in the United States—these areas of agreement can obscure substantial areas of disagreement. While Americans have almost universally endorsed popular government, for example, there have been heated disagreements over what popular government requires. Participants in those debates have approached these questions from a wide range of perspectives—religious and secular, liberal and conservative, egalitarian and inegalitarian. This volume gives space to those disparate voices, avoiding the crackpot and outlandish but including the diverse array of figures who have wielded some influence over public opinion and political movements over the course of American history.

HISTORY AND HISTORICAL DEVELOPMENT

Contemporary American political thought is the product of numerous arguments and decisions made by historical actors working within the political, legal, and intellectual constraints of their political eras. *American Political Thought* is organized historically so as to better reveal the nature of those constraints and how they have evolved over time. The historical organization highlights the connections between different types of disputes and arguments, as well as the terms of debate between opposing parties. The thematic organization within chapters helps tie together arguments across time and shows how conversations evolve over time and build on what has come before.

The historical institutionalist turn within the study of American political thought, and American politics more broadly, has focused our attention on the ways in which ideas and actions are connected and the extent to which American politics is characterized by critical junctures and path dependencies that help structure political thinking at any given moment. This book is sensitive to these historical intersections, revealing the distinctive quality of contemporary political ideas and developing an appreciation for alternative conceptions of the political future.

The volume divides the history of American political thought into several distinct chapters organized by time period. The chapters encompass the colonial period (before 1776), the founding (1776–1791), the early republic (1792–1828), the Jacksonian Era (1829–1860), the Civil War and Reconstruction period (1861–1876), the Gilded Age (1877–1900), the Progressive Era (1901–1932), the New Deal (1933–1950), the civil rights era (1951–1980), and recent politics (1981–present). The separation of these periods is certainly not hard and fast, but they serve to break American history into more digestible portions and highlight the intertwined debates that are distinctive to different historical eras. The historical approach highlights the fact that Elizabeth Cady Stanton was in dialogue with Frederick Douglass and Horace Greeley rather than Gloria Steinem, and Herbert Croly was in conversation with William Graham Sumner and Theodore Roosevelt rather than Milton Friedman. Later writers have had much to learn from earlier ones, but they also worked within their own intellectual and cultural milieu and responded to their own distinctive political problems and constraints.

PEDAGOGICAL FRAMEWORK

Most readers in American political thought have been not much more than anthologies, providing little of the additional content that is now common for texts designed for classroom use and offering minimal guidance for a student being tossed into an unknown sea. While emphasizing the excerpted text from the primary sources, this book tries to offer some additional context. The text presents a consistent pedagogical framework across the chapters:

- An opening chapter introduces the study of American political thought and highlights some general themes and vocabulary that make a frequent appearance in the literature.
- Each substantive chapter is divided into a consistent set of topical sections.
- Each chapter begins with a brief introduction to the political, social, and intellectual context of the period. Sections within each chapter summarize major themes, with a bulleted list of major developments for ease of reference.
- All readings are prefaced with explanatory headnotes, which contextualize the reading, indicate its importance, and provide questions for consideration as the student reads the material.
- Period illustrations help provide further context for the materials.
- Timelines throughout the volume summarize major events in the period and place source materials relative to those events.
- All chapters end with guidance for primary readings for further study and suggested readings in the secondary literature.

For ease of use, the readings in the text are modernized (except where the writer was intentionally archaic in his or her language). Footnotes appearing in the excerpts are from the original source, unless otherwise indicated. The sources from which the readings are drawn are consolidated in a section at the end of the book.

SUPPLEMENTS

We live in a time in which a wider range of once-difficult-to-find source materials in American political thought are now more readily available to students and researchers. Nonetheless, even amidst this plenty, some important works are hard to find. More fundamentally, confronted with such a vast sea of information, even experts can easily become lost. The value of a text of this sort is that it can bring together the familiar and the less familiar, separate the wheat from the chaff, reduce long texts to their core components, and provide necessary contextualization to help readers make sense of what is before them.

I have made every effort to produce a one-volume text that is flexible enough to support a range of teaching approaches and emphases while compact enough to be easily useable. Nonetheless, these pages only sample the richness of the many contributions to American political thought—a sample that I hope will be illuminating, thought-provoking, and captivating. I have made many more readings, similarly edited and introduced, available on a supplemental website. For those who want to read more deeply or to find a particular item that could not be included in the text, I hope that those materials will open the door to the wide range of contributions to American political thought. The website also includes useful tools for both instructors and students, including sample syllabi and self-study quizzes.

ACKNOWLEDGMENTS

I would not have embarked on this project without the inspiration provided by many valued teachers and students, some perhaps more distant than others. My eyes were first opened to American political thought by a second-hand copy of Alpheus Mason's pioneering *Free Government in the Making*,[1] and I hope this volume does justice to the tradition that he did so much to initiate. Happily, I found further encouragement in the field as an undergraduate studying with J. Budziszewski at the University of Texas and managed to wander into a graduate program at Yale that was filled with lively discussions at the intersections of political theory and American political history and a supportive community for American political thought. Perhaps less obviously, I am grateful to Howard Gillman and Mark Graber, who have not only been invaluable in their writing and conversations on American constitutional history but who also suffered with me through the process of learning how to produce a book of this sort. Without the experience with *American Constitutionalism*,[2] I am not sure that I would have attempted this book. My editor at Oxford University Press, Jennifer Carpenter, with the able assistance of Matt Rohal, was suitably encouraging in starting this project and appropriately stern in bringing it to more-or-less timely completion. At Princeton, James Sasso was particularly helpful in bringing this book to fruition. I thank the James Madison Program in American Ideals and Institutions for financial support that helped make this book possible.

As always, I appreciate the patience and love of Tracey and Taylor, who were willing to forgive me for starting another project amidst other obligations.

1 Alpheus Thomas Mason, *Free Government in the Making: Readings in American Political Thought* (New York: Oxford University Press, 1949).

2 Howard Gillman, Mark A. Graber, and Keith E. Whittington, *American Constitutionalism*, 2 vols. (New York: Oxford University Press, 2013).

CHAPTER 1

INTRODUCTION TO AMERICAN POLITICAL THOUGHT

INTRODUCTION

Modern political science has not generally had much room for ideas. Early in the twentieth century, Harold Laswell helped launch a more "realistic" political science by contending that politics is simply "who gets what, when, how," and the study of politics is best understood to be the study of the "influential," "those who get the most of what there is to get."[1] A generation earlier, the great sociologist Max Weber would have lodged a partial dissent:

> Not ideas, but material and ideal interests, directly govern men's conduct. Yet very frequently the "world images" that have been created by "ideas" have, like switchmen, determined the tracks along which action has been pushed by the dynamic of interest.[2]

Material interests matter, but beliefs about those interests and how they could best be advanced are determined by ideas. Ideas have consequences.

The study of American political thought is premised on the notion that ideas matter in politics. There is little doubt that ideas are not *all* that matter in politics, but one can hardly look over the political terrain and dismiss ideas as irrelevant, the mere playthings of cloistered intellectuals. For many generations of Americans, the story of American political thought served as inspiration. The political ideas that unfolded over time on the North American continent helped constitute the American people and formed a national identity. The American political tradition linked the rising generation to those of the past and created a community whose members might be separated by time and space. Such narratives have become more difficult to sustain over time. American society seems more fragmented, ideas more contested. But that has not made American intellectual life irrelevant, only more vibrant. New stories, new traditions, will be built from the old, taking account of where American politics has been

1 Harold D. Laswell, *Politics: Who Gets, What, When, How* (New York: McGraw-Hill, 1936), 3.

2 Max Weber, "The Social Psychology of the World Religions," in *From Max Weber*, eds. Hans H. Gerth and C. Wright Mills (New York: Oxford University Press, 1946), 280.

and seeking to fathom where it should go. The history of American political thought provides the raw materials for constructing an understanding of the world we inhabit and a vision of the one that we seek to bring into being.

The study of American political thought can be approached from a number of disciplinary perspectives. From the perspective of political philosophy, American writers are part of a "grand conversation" that extends from the ancients through the American founders. At their best, American political thinkers advance our understanding of what the political good is and how we can best secure it. American thinkers are valuable to the extent that they address fundamental questions regarding the foundations of political authority, the proper relationship between the individual and the state, and the requirements of freedom and justice. For purposes of thinking about the history of political theory, the substantive arguments that Americans have been able to offer regarding those fundamental questions are what matters.

From the perspective of American politics, the arguments articulated by political actors are an important aspect of American political development. The study of American political development is centrally concerned with the evolution of American political institutions and practices over time and the forces that channel, obstruct, stifle, and facilitate political change. Ideas can be a critical part of that larger context that structures day-to-day politics. It is a routine feature of politics that ideas "guide political conduct," including ideas about "notions of human identities; conceptions of interests, including but not limited to economic interests; ideologies and philosophies of how the world works and should work; and hopes and fears."[3] Political actors struggle over ideas, and ideas shape how (and what) political questions are contested. Understanding American political thought is a valuable tool for understanding how American politics has played and is playing itself out.

From the perspective of intellectual history, American political thought is a rich source of materials for understanding political and social movements and the shifting contexts within which politics takes place. "Political theory is born out of the conflicts in a society or between societies, out of the struggle between the 'is' and the 'ought to be.' It is politics—the contest for authority—distilled and articulated into systematic thought." The words and actions of particular individuals operate with a larger "climate of opinion, the prevailing the belief systems" of the time, and the fully appreciating political actions and arguments requires some understanding of the intellectual environment within which they are made.[4] Moreover, the intellectual historian would emphasize the pervasive importance of ideas, the extent to which meaning is intrinsic to human action. Ideas "are the means by which we perceive, understand, judge, or manipulate" social and physical reality. Ideas are themselves a form of "expressive action," and understanding the work that they do in particular social and political contexts is essential to understanding society and politics as such.[5]

---

3 Rogers M. Smith, "Ideas and the Spiral of Politics: The Place of American Political Thought in American Political Development," *American Political Thought* 3 (2014): 130.

4 Alan Pendleton Grimes, *American Political Thought*, Rev. Ed. (New York: Holt, Rinehart and Winston, 1960), viii.

5 Gordon S. Wood, "Intellectual History and the Social Sciences," in *New Directions in American Intellectual History*, eds. John Higham and Paul K. Conkin (Baltimore: Johns Hopkins University Press, 1979), 32, 34.

WHAT IS AMERICAN POLITICAL THOUGHT?

The subject matter of American political thought is itself subject to uncertainty and disagreement. The topic stands somewhat awkwardly at the intersection of several scholarly fields of inquiry, and scholars of American political thought have often felt the need to present their subject with some apologies for the fact that it is not rather different.

WHAT IS *AMERICAN* IN AMERICAN POLITICAL THOUGHT?

It is not unusual to organize the teaching of political thought by geographic region. Classes in "continental political thought" (or perhaps, more usually, "political philosophy"), examining the works of European political writers, are common. Less common, but not unknown, are classes on such diverse topics as Asian, British, or German political thought. And, of course, the venerable "Western political thought" continues to demand a place on the college curriculum. The field of political philosophy is crowded, and some division into discrete classes is a necessary convenience. But there is a logic to dividing the territory geographically rather than topically or temporally. The study of American political thought is no different.

At heart, all such divisions depend on the notion that their subject matter is distinctive, if not exceptional. American political thought can be treated separately, and perhaps even demands to be treated separately, because its subject is distinct from and cannot be readily reduced to the currents of political ideas that have been developed elsewhere. If American thinkers have drawn from and made use of the English John Locke, the French Jean-Jacques Rousseau, or the German Immanuel Kant, they nonetheless have created a distinctive tradition of their own.

But what is the unity that overcomes the diversity of American political thinkers? One alluring answer is that American political thought "has at its center a tradition of constitutionalism."[6] The implications are manifold. A commitment to constitutionalism suggests a commitment to certain principles and values, but principles that are hardly set in stone. Modern constitutionalism seeks to limit the power of government officials, secure the rights of individuals, and promote good government. Yet the history of American constitutionalism has been a history of contestation over its meaning, a history of disagreements and debates over the content of those principles and how they are to be balanced against one another.[7] American electoral and policy debates reflect a sustained engagement with the meaning of America itself. The most celebrated contributions to those debates not only reflect but remake what we take America to mean. But American political thought is also distinctly particular and pragmatic. American political thinkers have not traditionally preoccupied themselves with abstractions and ideals. Their concerns have been with details of American institutions, practices, and habits. Their orientation has

6 Donald S. Lutz, *A Preface to American Political Theory* (Lawrence: University Press of Kansas, 1992), 28.

7 See Howard Gillman, Mark A. Graber, and Keith E. Whittington, *American Constitutionalism: Powers, Rights, and Liberties* (New York: Oxford University Press, 2015). The study of American constitutionalism overlaps with but is distinct from the study of American political thought. The detailed debates over constitutional law fall to the former, while debates over politics and policy fall to the former.

been practical and flexible. American political thought has been dominated by the "man of action" more than the man of contemplation. "The role of philosophy in American politics has been essentially that of a servant, the tool of statesmanship."[8] Political theory has been an instrument, not an end in itself.

American political thought revolves around distinctly American themes, but it is also the product of American authors. American political thought would not be very interesting if the contributors to it shared little more than a common citizenship. Their contribution to a shared national tradition of thinking about politics and American identity gives the subject its richness and coherence. At the same time, this is a tradition characterized by Americans thinking about what it means to be an American and what characterizes the United States as a nation. The American political identity has always been up for grabs, but it is a conversation among the members of the community that shapes that identity for them. Outsiders may have their own ideas about what America stands for in the world, but American political thought is primarily interested in how Americans think about themselves and their shared political project.[9] Even so, the United States has always been a land of immigrants and itinerants, and what it means to be "an American" for this purpose is itself a subject of contestation. Few figures are as canonical to American political thought as the revolutionary writer Thomas Paine, but Paine grew up in England, wrote some of his most influential work while an activist in the French Revolution of the 1790s, and gained international fame as a pamphleteer during the less than a decade that he spent in Revolutionary America. The escaped slave Frederick Douglass became one of the most important orators and political activists of the antebellum period, but many of his contemporaries, including Chief Justice Roger Taney, would have doubted that Douglass was or could be a full-fledged member of the American political community. The boundaries of the American community have always been porous.

WHAT IS *POLITICAL* IN AMERICAN POLITICAL THOUGHT?

The field has long been ecumenical about the scope of American political thought. The "political" has generally been broadly construed, to include arguments over national identity and the organization of American social and economic systems and institutions as well as over governmental policymaking and office holding. As the feminist slogan of the 1960s observed, "the personal is the political." Individual consciousness and personal situations have political implications, and writers in American political thought have ranged from discussions of public affairs in the classic sense of public policy to the intimate intersections between the private sphere and personal arrangements to the public sphere and the structure of society. The mid-twentieth-century sociologist C. Wright Mills insisted that it is the "political task of the social scientist—as of any liberal educator—continually to translate

8 Alpheus Thomas Mason, *Free Government in the Making* (New York: Oxford University Press, 1949), ix.

9 There is little point in denying the influence, however, of close observers of the American scene who did not call America home. The French nobleman Alexis de Tocqueville in the nineteenth century and the Swedish economist Gunnar Myrdal in the twentieth century are among those who intervened from the outside to make lasting contributions to the internal discourse of American political thought.

personal troubles into public issues, and public issues into the terms of their human meaning for a variety of individuals."[10] But this type of "sociological imagination" is not the exclusive purview of the social scientist. Rather it is the common coin of the social activist, the political writer, and the policy entrepreneur.

If the subject matter of American political thought ranges widely over the social landscape, it also looks to abstract from the ceaseless flow of the political debates of the moment. The study of American political thought does not seek to track the political news cycle. The momentary preoccupations of what British journalists have dubbed the chattering classes might quickly disappear without a trace, and without being particularly informative of deeper political values and assumptions. The study of American political thought seeks to separate enduring statements of political principle from the minutiae of particular policy debates or electoral posturing. Separating the wheat from the chaff is no easy task. Even texts that are now regarded as great works of statesmanship or American writing might in their own time have been marginalized or derided. Manifestoes that were taken to be important by contemporaries might soon fade from public memory. One of the complications of a tradition of political oratory and writing that is so closely intertwined with politics itself is that the informative and insightful sits cheek to jowl with the superficial and the transitory.[11]

WHAT DOES *THOUGHT* SIGNIFY IN AMERICAN POLITICAL THOUGHT?

"American political thought" is the conventional name for the field, but some have preferred the more elevated terms of "philosophy" or "theory" to "thought." From that perspective, it would be something of an embarrassment that mere politicians, journalists, and political activists rub shoulders with *bona fide* scholars and philosophers. Is there room for a Henry Clay or Theodore Roosevelt alongside a James Madison and Abraham Lincoln, or for a William Lloyd Garrison or Jane Addams alongside a Ralph Waldo Emerson and John Dewey? It is certainly true that a class in continental political philosophy would focus its attention on such authors of great works as G. W. F. Hegel and Jürgen Habermas and would not make room for speeches by political leaders or the opinions of jurists. A course in contemporary political philosophy would similarly sample such careful and systematic thinkers as John Rawls and Michael Walzer. The focus of American political thought is somewhat different.

The study of American political thought is oriented toward ideas in politics, and as such sits between politics and philosophy. This orientation has several implications. It makes room for both politicians and scholars. The most analytically astute philosopher might make barely a ripple in the intellectual currents of the mainstream, but similarly the average political officeholder is unlikely to advance particularly influential or enduring ideas. The orientation of American political thought is to bring under consideration those

10 C. Wright Mills, *The Sociological Imagination* (New York: Oxford University Press, 1959), 187.

11 Similarly, American political thought is focused on works that contribute to American public life, but the boundary between the public and the private can be obscure. Public orations by significant political figures might be heard by only a few. Private correspondence might circulate widely. Technical scholarship might influence a privileged few, and yet be largely inaccessible to lay audiences and veil its political assumptions and implications.

who shape the American political tradition, for good or for ill. If American political thought attempts to balance influence and insight, it also seeks to balance the innovative with the exemplary. Some actors on the American political stage are particularly original, advancing new ideas and distinctive arguments, while others are notable primarily because they give eloquent expression to ideas that are the common currency of the age. Both the groundbreaker and the disciple are of interest.

"Thought" is used somewhat advisedly in this context. The German émigré Leo Strauss emphasized that "political philosophy ought to be distinguished from political thought in general." Political thought indicated simply "reflection on, or the exposition of, political ideas," but political philosophy sought to distinguish between true knowledge and mere opinion, between the eternal truth and the locally conventional.[12] There is little doubt that some of the contributors to American political thought seek to identify and express the truth in this sense, but our interest in them is not measured entirely by how close we judge them to be reaching that standard. We study political philosophy in order to come to a better understanding of the fundamental nature of politics and society. We study American political thought for those reasons, but for other reasons as well.

Ideas in politics are sometimes derided as "ideology." Marxists would observe that the "ideas of the ruling class are in every epoch the ruling ideas."[13] Social, economic, and political dominance is rationalized and legitimated through the production and dissemination of compatible systems of belief. As such, ideologies are always deceptive, a distraction from the real conflict. Social scientists have been inclined to broaden the concept and shed its distinctively pejorative aspects. We might instead think of ideology as a system of beliefs organized to make sense of the world, to give it meaning, and to inspire action.[14] It was closer to this sense that the intellectual historian Richard Hofstadter had in mind with his classic "studies in the ideology of statesmanship," the "political traditions" that linked the beliefs and values of "practical politicians" with the "common climate of American opinion."[15]

RECURRENT THEMES

There are a number of recurrent themes in American political thought and in the study of American political thought. While the many contributors to American political debates have been focused on their own particular substantive disagreements and immediate political concerns, their arguments illuminate more abstract features of the American political tradition. Each debate may revolve around its own particular components, but the disputants draw on a reservoir of political values and assumptions. Political writers and thinkers draw from that

12 Leo Strauss, *What is Political Philosophy? And Other Studies* (New York: Free Press, 1959), 12.

13 Karl Marx, "The German Ideology: Part I," in *The Marx-Engels Reader*, 2nd ed., ed. Robert C. Tucker (New York: W.W. Norton, 1978), 172.

14 See, e.g., Daniel Bell, *The End of Ideology*, rev. ed. (New York: Free Press, 1962), 400; Clifford Geertz, "Ideology as a Cultural System," in *The Interpretation of Cultures* (New York: Basic Books, 1973).

15 Hofstadter, *The American Political Tradition and the Men Who Made It* (New York: Alfred A. Knopf, 1948), xxxvi.

well to help defend their immediate political claims and construct justifications for their favored actions. Such debates both make use of and help reconstruct inherited ideas. Understanding those concepts can help reveal the deeper meaning of American political debates.

AMERICAN EXCEPTIONALISM

From before the United States was a nation, inhabitants of the European settlements of North America claimed that America was unique. America was part of a "New World" that promised that its inhabitants could shed themselves of Old World afflictions. The vast virgin wilderness allowed pioneers a fresh start, leaving the crowded cities of Europe behind. Life on the global frontier stripped away many of the old customs and prerogatives. The barest pauper could seek his fortune and claim an equal status with the well-bred. Whether religious outcasts seeking refuge or economic migrants pursuing wealth and comfort, the new Americans were lured by the promise that things were different on the far side of the Atlantic. America was the exception to the global norms. Both foreign visitors in the United States and Americans abroad have often marveled at the differences between the Americans and even their closest cousins in Europe.

American exceptionalism has taken a myriad of forms over time. In its more secular form, American exceptionalism might assert the uniqueness of the land, people, culture, or circumstances of the United States. In its more religious form, American exceptionalism might posit that Americans are God's chosen and have a divine mission in the world. Sometimes exceptionalism helps underwrite missionary forays abroad; at other times, exceptionalism has helped justify withdrawing from a corrupt world. The particular features of the American landscape that make the country unique have likewise been various. The United States might be regarded as distinctly prosperous, especially religious, or particularly committed to liberty and democracy.

One prominent strand of American exceptionalism has emphasized the especially ideological nature of the United States. The intellectual historian Richard Hofstadter famously remarked, "it had been our fate as a nation not to have ideologies but to be one."[16] On the one hand, Americans showed an aversion to explicit political ideologies. Rather than battling over grand visions of society, Americans had traditionally favored "compromise and plain dealing, a preference for hard work and common sense."[17] "Isms" were derided as foreign and impractical, whether socialism, anarchism, fascism, or imperialism; Americans were said to resist such appeals to abstractions. On the other hand, American identity has long been defined by ideological commitment. A nation of immigrants, the United States has (to some degree) resisted efforts to understand its national identity by reference to a common ethnicity or religious creed. On the opening of World War I, with the nation still struggling to absorb millions of new immigrants, William Tyler Page won a national contest to draft "An American's Creed." His short affirmation of "the basic principles of American political faith" was quickly embraced as a totem of American patriotism, recited

16 Richard Hofstadter, *Anti-Intellectualism in American Life* (New York: Alfred A. Knopf, 1962), 43.

17 *Ibid.*

by schoolchildren and promoted by Congress.[18] As one publisher admonished, all Americans should "know your American's Creed as you do your daily prayers."[19] To be a good American was to believe in certain political ideals: popular government, "a sovereign nation of many sovereign states," freedom, and equality. Americans were defined not by their shared heritage, but by their shared ideology.[20]

LIBERALISM

In the 1950s, the political historian Louis Hartz penned one of the most influential accounts of American political thought. Hartz provocatively argued that "what might be called the storybook truth" about the United States is that "the American community is a liberal community."[21] Hartz himself was not uncritical of this feature of American life, but he thought there was little question that, broadly speaking, the American political tradition was univocally—perhaps even inescapably—liberal.

By "liberal," Hartz did not mean the conventional division of American politics into liberals and conservatives. His reference point was the liberal philosophical tradition, a tradition encompassing such varied writers as John Locke and John Stuart Mill, Baron de Montesquieu and Immanuel Kant. This Lockean tradition emphasizes a number of fundamental propositions, including the priority of individual liberty, equality in the moral worth of individuals, toleration of different beliefs and private actions, the need to justify government action, the rule of law, and private property.[22] From this perspective, the mainstream of American politics operated within a small corner of the range of political possibilities. The United States, Hartz contended, had no genuinely revolutionary tradition that spurred anarchist and socialist movements, but also no serious reactionary tradition that might give rise to fascist or feudalist movements. Institutions like judicial review "flourished on the corpse of philosophy in America"; pragmatism and compromise were the watchwords of the "moral unanimity of a liberal society."[23]

---

18 Matthew Page Andrews, *The American's Creed and Its Meaning* (Garden City, NY: Doubleday, Page & Co., 1919), 21.

19 "Let Every American Know His Creed; Teach It to the Children; Spread it Throughout the United States; Now is the Time," *Baltimore* 11 (August 1918): 34.

20 Authors have differed, however, on the precise content of the American Creed. In his accounting, William Tyler Page drew from such varied sources as the Declaration of Independence, the Gettysburg Address, and a War Department brochure on flag etiquette. More recent scholars have pointed to such overlapping values as "liberty, equality, justice, and fair opportunity for everybody," "liberty, egalitarianism, individualism, populism, and laissez-faire," and "equality, liberty, individualism, constitutionalism, democracy." Gunnar Myrdal, *An American Dilemma* (New York: Harper & Row, 1944), xiviii; Seymour Martin Lipset, *American Exceptionalism* (New York: W.W. Norton, 1996), 19; Samuel P. Huntington, *American Politics* (Cambridge: Harvard University Press, 1981), 33.

21 Louis Hartz, *The Liberal Tradition in America* (New York: Harcourt, Brace & World, 1955), 3.

22 The liberal tradition is often subdivided into two strands, with a "classical" tradition emphasizing individualism, private property, and freedom *from* government coercion and a "modern" tradition emphasizing social justice and an effective freedom *to* pursue one's favored goals.

23 Hartz, 10.

REPUBLICANISM

In the 1960s, some scholars such as the colonial historian Bernard Bailyn began to emphasize a different philosophical tradition that also had influence in American political thought.[24] Republicanism (sometimes, civil or classical republicanism) is a closely related tradition to liberalism but has a variety of distinctive characteristics that separates it from, and sometimes puts it in antagonism with, standard liberal tropes. Scholars have pointed to a lengthy tradition of political writers extending from Niccolò Machiavelli's work on the Florentine Republic at the turn of the sixteenth century to seventeenth-century critics of the English monarchy like James Harrington and Algernon Sidney and backwards to ancient writers like Cicero, Aristotle, and Polybius who developed ideas of popular government that found fertile ground in the United States.

Republicanism and liberalism share some features, but differ on others. They share, for example, a concern with constitutionalism. Republicanism has usually been understood to emphasize somewhat different aspects of liberty than liberalism. "Republican liberty" might be thought of broadly as emphasizing self-government. In a directly political sense, self-government might mean active participation in the governance of the community; to be self-governing is to be actively engaged in civic life. Alternatively, self-government might mean "independent," to be free from the arbitrary will of others. Liberty in this sense might be quite consistent with substantial governmental interference with private life, including laws that would make liberals uncomfortable.[25]

Civic republicanism has also emphasized some more distinctive political concerns. The Latin *res publica* is commonly translated as "public business," or simply commonwealth, and highlights the shared or public aspect of politics. In keeping with that priority, writers in the republican tradition have often emphasized what they saw as the preconditions for a public-minded model of governance. Civic, or public, virtue focused on patriotism, a willingness to engage in self-sacrifice, and a commitment to advancing the public good even at the expense of private goods and self-interest. "Corruption," or the loss of civic virtue, was an ever-present threat to the stability and longevity of republics. Small, homogeneous communities were often understood to be the best environment for promoting this kind of public engagement and other-regarding behavior. If private individuals are at the heart of liberalism, citizens are at the heart of republicanism.

CONSERVATIVES AND RADICALS

The Hartzian account of American political culture marginalized the importance of alternatives to liberalism. To the extent that he recognized their occasional appearance on the American scene, he tended to suggest that they were fleeting and feeble. Hartz began his book with a quote from the French commentator on American democracy, Alexis de Tocqueville. Still living in the shadow of the French Revolution and the convulsions that

24 Bernard Bailyn, *The Ideological Origins of the American Revolution* (Cambridge: Harvard University Press, 1967).

25 See, e.g., Quentin Skinner, *Hobbes and Republican Liberty* (New York: Cambridge University Press, 2008).

followed, Tocqueville thought "Americans have this great advantage, that they have attained democracy without the sufferings of a democratic revolution and that they were born equal instead of becoming so."[26] America was the land of the middle class, neither needing nor tolerating revolutionaries working to elevate the downtrodden or conservatives pining for aristocratic order. American radicals and conservatives, on this reading, are pale imitations of the real thing, advocating merely another flavor of liberalism.

The question that the Hartzian narrative raises, of course, is whether there is after all a robust radical or conservative tradition in America. Historians like Staughton Lynd and Howard Zinn, motivated by feelings of "shame and distrust toward the Founding Fathers," have looked to recover an alternative history of "American radicalism" that, from the 1760s to the 1960s, has been concerned with exposing and resisting domestic oppression.[27] Similarly, conservative writers like Russell Kirk and Pat Buchanan have sought to identify a lineage of "thinkers who have stood by tradition and old establishments" and resisted "radical theories and social transformation" from the American founding forward.[28] Having experienced neither a monarchy nor a socialist revolution, can the United States truly be said to have had either conservatives or radicals?

RACE AND GENDER

The discussion of liberalism, radicalism, and conservatism is often grounded in ideas about socioeconomic class. To what degree does American political thought revolve around the idea of a classless society, and to what degree does it build on ideas of class and hierarchy? But class is not the only driver of political conflict, and disputes over race and gender have often been prominent features of American political debate. Such debates generate conflicting ideas about what politics means and how individuals should be understood to fit within the community.

It has been easy to set aside such disputes as politically and socially important but ideologically impotent. The Swedish sociologist Gunnar Myrdal influentially argued that when it came to race, the ideals and values of the American Creed were too often sacrificed to "interests," "jealousies," "prejudice," and "habits."[29] There was a gap between American political thought and American political practice, but Myrdal was among those who thought that a renewed embrace of accepted moral values could eventually overcome mere prejudice and eventually close that gap. But we might think that such immutable personal characteristics as race have instead been the subject of thought and contestation. Racial and other categories might have been defended, justified, and legitimated—and not just overlooked—by value systems. Rather than marking a falling away from the American Creed, these alternative traditions would mark a challenge to the dominance of that political catechism, a vision of America that prioritized native birth or white skin over egalitarianism and individualism.[30]

---

26 Alexis de Tocqueville, *Democracy in America*, trans. George Lawrence (New York: Harper & Row, 1969), 509.

27 Staughton Lynd, *Intellectual Origins of American Radicalism* (New York: Pantheon, 1968), v.

28 Russell Kirk, *The Conservative Mind* (Washington, D.C.: Regnery, 1953), 5, 3.

29 Myrdal, xlvii.

30 See, e.g., Rogers M. Smith, *Civic Ideals* (New Haven: Yale University Press, 1999).

RELIGION

Liberalism is often portrayed as a rather secular ideology. Religion is relegated to a private sphere, where different religious beliefs—or even the lack of belief—can be safely tolerated. The American Creed of such political goods as liberty and equality replaces the diverse religious creeds of a fractious nation. But this vision of American political thought might be distorted.

Religion has been a powerful force in American life. Religion, like race, has often been a source of social and political conflict, and conflict is always a fertile ground for fostering new political ideas and for challenging political actors to consider new applications of old ideas. Religious believers have taken a lead in political movements, and religious ideas have been a source of inspiration for social and political struggle. "Moral dreams define the nation's ideals," and "a godly people" has been an "all-American answer" to the question of national identity.[31]

DEMOCRACY AND CONSTITUTIONALISM

From its beginnings, American political thought took for granted two fundamental but not always complementary commitments: a commitment to democracy and popular government on the one hand, and a commitment to individualism and limited government on the other. A great deal of the American political tradition has consisted of an effort to rework and reconsider these twin commitments, to adjust how they are to be reconciled and what they are taken to require.

During the ratification debates, James Madison emphasized the "republican" character of the American constitutional experiment, as against a "pure democracy." A republic was governed by elected representatives, he insisted, whereas a democracy allowed the people to rule directly through large popular assemblies.[32] For Madison, and his contemporaries, there was no question of whether American government would be a popular government, a government of, by, and for the people. The challenge for the founding generation, as it has been for subsequent generations, was how to make popular government the best that it can be, of how best to ensure that republican politics would be consistent with free government. On the eve of the Second World War, the intellectual historian Ralph Henry Gabriel observed that democracy had "two different but interrelated connotations" for Americans. "Realistic democracy" recognized the logrolling, the campaigning, and the lobbying that were central to American political practice, but "romantic democracy" pointed to "a cluster of ideas which made up a national faith and which, though unrecognized as such, had the power of a State religion."[33] The "democratic faith" was central to the American identity. At the same time, the U.S. Constitution has provided "a fixed point of reference" for the study

---

31 James A. Morone, *Hellfire Nation* (New Haven: Yale University Press, 2003), 3.

32 James Madison, "No. 10," in *The Federalist Papers*, ed. Clinton Rossiter (New York: New American Library, 1961), 81.

33 Ralph Henry Gabriel, *The Course of American Democratic Thought* (New York: Ronald Press Company, 1940), 13.

of American political thought. While the Constitution embodies a commitment to popular government, importantly it is centrally occupied with the "processes and institutions by which the people, acting in their constitutive capacity, have consented to be governed."[34] The celebration, examination, and critique of the detailed mechanisms by which the democratic will was to be identified—and restrained—have always been at the heart of American political thought. The history of American political debate has been, to a significant degree, a history of debate over the meaning of American constitutionalism.

SUGGESTED READINGS

Carey, George W. *A Student's Guide to American Political Thought* (Wilmington, DE: Intercollegiate Studies Institute Books, 2004).

Commager, Henry Steele. *The American Mind: An Interpretation of American Thought and Character Since the 1880s* (New Haven, CT: Yale University Press, 1950).

Curti, Merle. *The Growth of American Thought* (New York: Harper & Row, 1943).

Hanson, Russell L. *The Democratic Imagination in America: Conversations with Our Past* (Princeton, NJ: Princeton University Press, 1985).

Hartz, Louis. *The Liberal Tradition in America: An Interpretation of American Political Thought Since the Revolution* (New York: Harcourt, Brace, and World, 1955).

Higham, John, and Paul K. Conkin, eds. *New Directions in American Intellectual History* (Baltimore, MD: Johns Hopkins University Press, 1979).

Hofstadter, Richard. *The American Political Tradition and the Men Who Made It* (New York: Alfred A. Knopf, 1948).

Hofstadter, Richard. *Anti-Intellectualism in American Life* (New York: Alfred A. Knopf, 1962).

Kammen, Michael. *Mystic Chords of Memory: The Transformation of Tradition in American Culture* (New York: Alfred A. Knopf, 1991).

Kersh, Rogan. *Dreams of a More Perfect Union* (Ithaca, NY: Cornell University Press, 2001).

Lipset, Seymour Martin. *American Exceptionalism: A Double-Edged Sword* (New York: W.W. Norton, 1996).

Lutz, Donald S. *A Preface to American Political Theory* (Lawrence: University Press of Kansas, 1992).

Merriam, Charles Edward. *A History of American Political Theories* (New York: Macmillan, 1903).

Miller, Perry. *The Life of the Mind in America: From the Revolution to the Civil War* (New York: Harcourt, Brace, and World, 1965).

Parrington, Vernon Louis. *Main Currents in American Thought*, 3 vols. (New York: Harcourt, Brace, and World, 1930).

Perry, Lewis. *Intellectual Life in America: A History* (Chicago, IL: University of Chicago Press, 1984).

Peterson, Merrill D. *The Jefferson Image in the American Mind* (New York: Oxford University Press, 1960).

Potter, David M. *People of Plenty: Economic Abundance and the American Character* (Chicago, IL: University of Chicago Press, 1954).

Shklar, Judith N. *Redeeming American Political Thought* (Chicago, IL: University of Chicago Press, 1998).

Smith, Rogers M. *Civic Ideals: Conflicting Visions of Citizenship in U.S. History* (New Haven, CT: Yale University Press, 1997).

---

34 George W. Carey, *A Student's Guide to American Political Thought* (Wilmington, DE: Intercollegiate Studies Institute Books, 2004), 8.

CHAPTER 2

THE COLONIAL ERA, BEFORE 1776

I. INTRODUCTION

The colonial period, the pre-history of the United States of America, was long and complex. The small group of Pilgrims who landed at Plymouth on the *Mayflower* was as far removed from the Sons of Liberty who launched the American Revolution as we are from the generation that fought the Civil War. The Pilgrims departed from England in 1620 just a few years after the death of William Shakespeare and the introduction of the King James Bible, and they were very much products of the still ongoing Protestant Reformation that was marked by Martin Luther's rejection of the Catholic Church and King Henry VIII's separation of the Church of England from the Roman Church. In language, dress, and ideas, they were far removed from the Patriots who were part of the Age of Enlightenment and were raised on the philosophers David Hume, John Locke, and Jean-Jacques Rousseau and were contemporaries with the economist Adam Smith and the philosopher Immanuel Kant. The population of the colonies had grown from 50,000 people clustered in a few coastal towns in 1650 to over two million on the eve of the Revolution, stretching from Cape Elizabeth in modern Maine to Savannah, Georgia.

The colonies also differed dramatically among themselves. The national memory focuses on the Pilgrims at Plymouth, but not all the colonists traced their roots to the *Mayflower*. The Puritans who settled New England had fled religious persecution in England and hoped to establish more faithful communities in the New World. The Quakers who settled Pennsylvania were religious dissenters in their own right, but as likely to be rejected by the Massachusetts Puritans as the English Anglicans. But the settlement of other colonies was driven by more material motives. At the same time that the Pilgrims were establishing a self-governing settlement at the Massachusetts Bay, Jamestown was being established by the Virginia Company on the Chesapeake Bay with an explicit goal of turning a profit. The southern plantations were business ventures intended to enrich both the colonists and the investors back home in England. The Dutch colony along the valley of the Hudson River was designed to exploit the lucrative fur trade before eventually being turned over to England and renamed New York.

Although each colony was bound by legal, political, economic and social ties to England, there were no formal connections among them. The colonists were involved in a robust global trading system, but much of their commercial traffic flowed across the ocean rather than among the colonies. Each colony was individually governed by England, though the forms of colonial rule differed. Proposals were frequently made to organize the colonies to advance common economic and security goals, but they never got very far. Most famously, Benjamin Franklin proposed a plan for union to a congress of colonial delegates that met in Albany, New York, in 1754. The pressure of the French and Indian War had encouraged the colonies to call the convention, but neither the colonial governments nor London was willing to accept the creation of a continental government.

The New England colonies dominate the history of American political thought during this period. Their relative political independence and religious traditions gave rise to a robust culture of arguing in print about political, social, and religious arrangements. Early Massachusetts lawyers and ministers frequently took up the pen to explain their actions and to exhort and instruct others. By contrast, southern politicians were more likely to distinguish themselves with oratories that left no written trace, and southern planters left more telling observations in personal journals than published pamphlets.

Disagreements were often the provocation for developing extended political and theoretical arguments in the colonies. The long-serving Massachusetts Bay governor John Winthrop found himself frequently writing to try to mollify critics of his extensive powers and how he used them. The influential Puritan minister Cotton Mather took to print to advance his favored theological and social positions, trading barbs with the dissenter Roger Williams among others. The increasing clashes between the colonists and their imperial governors in the years leading up to the Declaration of Independence in 1776 generated a wealth of writing meant to persuade both the English colonists living in North America and the English governors in London of conflicting views about how imperial affairs should be conducted. As a result, exemplary writings in American political thought during this period can primarily be found in the early days of the colonies and their last years before independence.

Politics. The politics of the American colonies was deeply caught up in the politics of England. The Massachusetts Bay Colony covered much of modern New England. Although based on a land grant given by Catholic-sympathizing King Charles I, the colony from its outset was more focused on providing a refuge for Puritans fleeing persecution in England than turning a profit for its investors. The Puritans were a relatively extreme sect of Calvinist Protestants, who often argued in England that the Church of England had not gone far enough in distancing itself from Catholic doctrines and rituals. When King Charles dissolved the British Parliament in 1629, the investors agreed to emigrate to New England, securing local rule for the colony—but only male, church members were granted a vote. The long-serving colonial governor John Winthrop and the influential Puritan minister John Cotton

FIGURE 2-1 TIMELINE OF THE COLONIAL ERA

Events	Year	American Writings
Jamestown Settlement founded in Virginia	1607	
Plymouth Settlement founded in Massachusetts	1620	
	1620	Mayflower Compact
John Williams exiled from Massachusetts Colony	1636	
	1641	Massachusetts Body of Liberties
	1644	Roger Williams' The Bloudy Tenent
King Charles I executed	1649	
Parliament installed William and Mary on the English throne in the Glorious Revolution	1689	
John Locke's Second Treatise of Government	1689	
	1701	Cotton Mather's A Christian at his Calling
	1732	Benjamin Franklin's Poor Richard's Almanack begins publication
Montesquieu's On the Spirit of the Laws	1748	
Albany Congress	1754	
Jean Jacques Rousseau's On Civil Liberty	1762	
Treaty of Paris ending French-Indian War	1763	
	1764	James Otis's Rights of the British Colonies
Stamp Act adopted by Parliament	1765	
Boston Massacre	1770	
Boston Tea Party	1774	
First Continental Congress convened	1774	
Parliament suspends Massachusetts colonial government	1774	
	1775	Patrick Henry's Give Me Liberty Speech
Battle of Bunker Hill	1775	
Adam Smith's The Wealth of Nations	1776	Declaration of Independence
	1776	Thomas Paine's Common Sense

were among those migrating to the colony amidst the crisis in England. Growth in population soon brought internal divisions over the correct path for the colony and for the Puritan religion, and splinter groups soon fled or were exiled from Massachusetts and established new colonial outposts of their own—including Connecticut, Rhode Island, and New Hampshire. The Puritans sided with Parliament in the English Civil War of the 1640s, and as a consequence when the monarchy was reestablished under King Charles II the Massachusetts Bay charter (and home rule) was revoked. When a charter for Massachusetts was reestablished in 1691, a royal governor was installed, appointed by the king and answerable to London. The colonists were allowed only to elect the members of the General Court, the colonial legislature, but suffrage was no longer restricted to church members.

The early self-government established in Massachusetts Bay was the exception, not the rule. The model of royal governors predominated throughout the American colonies. Even as Puritan opponents to the monarchy migrated to New England, supporters of the Crown migrated to the southern colonies. As in Massachusetts, the Virginians elected a legislature, which could make policy and impose taxes but which was subject to an absolute veto by the royal governor and had to contend with royally appointed judges. Governors and legislatures were generally able to figure out ways of working together to solve local problems. The legislature's power of the purse, including the ability to set the governor's salary, helped overcome the governor's unchecked appointment and veto power. Even so, tensions routinely arose between the interests of the colonists as reflected in the legislature and the interests of the imperial government as reflected in the governor. When European wars spilled over into the North American continent with the French and Indian War of the 1750s, the colonists chafed at the imposition. While young colonists like George Washington were able to win some fame in the military conflicts on the western frontier, the end of the war eliminated the French threat on the continent, cleared the way for more aggressive western settlement, and left England with a massive debt that it tried to relieve in part by imposing new taxes on the colonies. Tax measures like the Stamp Act of 1765 and the Townshend Revenue Act of 1767 soon put the British Parliament and the royal governors charged with enforcing imperial policies at loggerheads with colonial legislatures. In Massachusetts, the conflict led to the dissolution of the General Court and the imposition of martial law, which eventually gave way to the Revolution and American independence.

The process of moving from protest to revolution was not a rapid one. The taxes themselves, though sweeping, were relatively modest. Many of the more conservative colonists argued that the new revenue measures were a reasonable response to the cost of waging a war that, in part, helped advance the interests of the English colonists. Others argued that the taxes may be excessive, but that political negotiation with British officials would likely produce some appropriate accommodation. But many charged that the imposition of taxes on the English colonists by the British Parliament was a violation of longstanding constitutional principles. The colonists did not, and as a practical matter could not, elect any members of Parliament, and they contended that Parliament, therefore, did not have the authority to tax them. Rather, the colonists elected colonial assemblies that did have the power to tax the colonists—to satisfy local governmental needs. The complex system of imperial trade regulation was the appropriate mechanism by which British interests were enriched by the economic activities in the colonies. As the colonists threatened not to comply with the tax measures and to obstruct their collection, the British government further asserted its complete authority over colonial affairs. With King George III supporting parliamentary authority, and the British military being increasingly used to enforce parliamentary directives, the colonial "patriots" eventually gave up on finding a *modus vivendi* with the British government and instead renounced their loyalty to the Crown and declared their independence. Loyalists generally fled the country.

Society. The economic and social life of the colonies had a similarly ambivalent relationship with England. Throughout the colonial era, the large majority of immigration came from the British Isles, with the next two largest contingents hailing from Africa and the German states. Migration to the colonies was actively encouraged over these decades, feeding rapid population growth and geographic expansion of settlements up and down the Atlantic coast and farther west into the interior of the continent. While some revolutionaries could trace their familial roots back to the first European settlements, most had arrived on American shores more recently. The oldest colonies—Massachusetts, Virginia, Pennsylvania, New York—also became the largest.

The new arrivals huddled close to the Atlantic. The primary seaports became the largest cities—Philadelphia, New York, Boston, Charleston—but even those were relatively small. The largest colonial city, Philadelphia, had less than 30,000 inhabitants, when London's population was approaching one million. Small towns and plantations (especially in the South) predominated. Life on the coast was not only safer and easier than life in the wilderness, but it also helped connect the colonists to a global economy. The American colonies exported a diverse array of raw materials and agricultural products, while importing manufactured goods and more exotic consumer goods like tea and spices. Even relatively self-sufficient, and isolated, farmers enjoyed access to such consumer goods. Those who were able often sent their children back to England to enrich their education and professional training. Colonists made trips to Europe for business and political reasons. Americans published in England and read the latest works produced in Europe.

The place of the colonies within a global economic web highlighted their continued dependence on the mother country. As revolutionary sentiment increased, economic boycotts of English-made goods and a movement to favor "homespun" clothing sought to assert American economic independence from England and leverage English economic interests in the American market for political purposes. But homespun goods were an inadequate substitute for the more polished goods that could be purchased from Europe, and many large-scale exporters relied on access to foreign markets. The British countered American protests by cracking down on smuggling, trying to force the colonists to buy government-approved and taxable goods. As Americans contemplated independence, English trade regulations restricting American commerce seemed more grating, but the importance of American access to English markets also seemed undeniable.

Ideas. The seventeenth and eighteenth centuries was a fertile time for ideas, and the Americans participated in that lively intellectual environment—even if they were more often consumers than producers of the ideas that were being discussed in Europe.

One crucial source of ideas in colonial America was religion. The colonists were overwhelmingly Protestant Christians, but within that general orientation there was a wide range of views, from the radical to the conservative. The American Puritans were a Calvinist sect that generally embraced separation from the irredeemable Church of England. Puritan thought, as it developed in England and was carried to and enriched in the colonies, emphasized the fallen nature of mankind. Individuals obtained salvation only through grace, and while grace is unearned the elect who have been saved were obliged to attempt to fulfill Biblical command. Failure and sin were unavoidable, but the saved demonstrated their status by strictly following God's law. The Quakers (or "Friends") who fled to William Penn's colony were likewise dissenters from the Church of England. Their theology emphasized the direct communication between God and believers and the obligation of adherents to bear witness to God's truth through good works. The Quakers embraced equality and pacifism, which sometimes put them at odds with the government. When Roger Williams fell out with religious authorities in Massachusetts, he fled to the wilderness of Rhode Island and founded the first Baptist church in North America. The Baptist dissenters, who also established a beachhead in the southern colonies, became vocal advocates of religious toleration, individual conversion, and the formation of voluntary communities of believers. While the more mainstream Anglican churches that predominated farther south benefited from religious establishment and government support, they also tended to accept the primacy of the Bible and personal access to revelation. The First Great Awakening of the 1730s and 1740s saw Protestant evangelicalism flourish, with popular revivals promoting a more emotional and accessible form of Christianity. This milieu was one that favored religious controversy, but one that also fostered debates over individualism, rights, and equality.

A second source of influence on colonists' thought came from their English heritage. The seventeenth century was a time of political ferment in Great Britain. The early days of the colonies corresponded to the outbreak of the English Civil War between Parliament and the monarchy, the execution of King Charles I in 1649, the rise of the republican Oliver Cromwell, and the Glorious Revolution of 1688 that overthrew the Catholic King James II and established a limited monarchy under the Protestant William and Mary. These conflicts spurred the development of new political ideas. The philosopher John Locke was one of many writers who lent intellectual support to the Parliamentarians by elaborating theories of the social contract, individual rights, legislative supremacy, and a right of revolution against tyrants. In the early eighteenth century, republican writers achieved influence in both England and the American colonies. Led by the publication of John Trenchard and Thomas Gordon's *Cato's Letters*, these writers helped popularize Locke's political theory, while introducing a greater emphasis on religious freedom, freedom of the press, the importance of civic virtue, and fear of aristocratic conspiracies. The Americans inherited English political institutions and legal frameworks, and William

Blackstone's 1766 treatise, *Commentaries on the Laws of England*, became an essential reference for understanding the common law.

A third influence came from the Enlightenment philosophy that was sweeping Europe in the eighteenth century. Scottish philosophers, historians, and political economists like David Hume, Thomas Reid, and Adam Smith linked moral philosophy with empirical investigations. For many figures in the Scottish Enlightenment movement, principles of "common sense" informed both our perception of the world and our moral sensibility. The French Enlightenment similarly featured both sociological studies and examinations of first principles. Baron de Montesquieu's 1748 study, *The Spirit of the Laws*, became a frequently cited guide to English constitutional principles, republican government, and the idea of the separation of powers. Jean-Jacques Rousseau's more speculative 1762 work, *On the Social Contract*, celebrated a relatively pure form of democratic government, while writers like Voltaire explored the boundaries of skepticism and intellectual freedom.

II. DEMOCRACY AND LIBERTY

Major Developments

- The formation of self-governing colonies
- The adoption of governing colonial charters
- The struggle over religious liberty in New England

The American colonies had substantial experience with popular government and claims of individual liberty by the time of the American Revolution. All of the colonies featured a popularly elected legislative assembly, which made laws, imposed taxes, appropriated public funds, and voiced the concerns of the electorate. In the beginning, residents of the Massachusetts Bay Colony enjoyed the right to elect their own governor as well. The more common model of colonial governance allowed the local population to elect only the lower chamber of the colonial legislature. The governor was normally appointed in England, and the governor in turn filled most of the colonial offices, including the judges and a governor's council or upper legislative chamber. Despite this modicum of local rule, however, some crucial policy decisions were made in England. Parliament laid down the rules regarding trade, and the King's Privy Council held a veto over colonial laws. Individual towns often had their own governing bodies that were subject to election.

Democratic practice was also limited by election rules. Suffrage was routinely restricted by age, sex, race, and property. Only adult, white males had the prospect of voting to fill some government offices. Generally, those men also needed to be local freeholders—that is, local residents who owned land within the jurisdiction. In some cases, voters also needed to be members in good standing in the preferred church.

The colonial charters—the legal documents granting the settlers the right to establish a colony in a designated area of land claimed by the English government—routinely guaranteed the settlers the ordinary rights of Englishmen. The king's subjects would not give up their legal protections when they left the homeland and moved to the new colonies. The colonists could not vote for the British House of Commons, but they had similar voting rights for colonial legislatures as they would have possessed in England (though land ownership was far more widespread in the colonies, effectively expanding the electorate). They were entitled to the same property rights and criminal justice protections that they would have enjoyed at home.

But ideas about political and legal rights did not stand still in the colonies. When the Pilgrims sought safe harbor in Massachusetts rather than their original destination of Virginia, they set about establishing a government of their own. Part of that process was the adoption of the Massachusetts Body of Liberties, declaring that the Massachusetts colonists would enjoy a wide variety of legal protections from abusive government officials. Even so, the Massachusetts colonists did not always agree on what good government entailed. Roger Williams fell out with the leaders of the Massachusetts Bay Colony and fled to the wilds of Rhode Island, from which he called for greater religious liberty. Massachusetts minister John Cotton defended a more restricted view of religious tolerance against dissenters like Williams. Massachusetts governor John Winthrop found himself having to justify his political authority and explain the limits of liberty to dissenters. As the seventeenth century turned into the eighteenth century, theories of natural law gained ground in the American colonies and played a more prominent role not only in internal religious and political disputes but eventually in colonial struggles with the British government.

ROGER WILLIAMS

THE BLOUDY TENENT OF PERSECUTION (1644)

Apprenticed by the famed English jurist Edward Coke and educated at Cambridge University, Roger Williams joined the Puritan faith and followed others to the colony of Massachusetts in 1631, settling in Salem. Though himself a radical Puritan minister, Williams soon found himself disputing with the religious and political leadership in the colony. In contrast to the Massachusetts founders, Williams contended that the state could only enforce those Biblical commandments that imposed duties among individuals but not those that imposed duties to God. Tipped off by the Massachusetts governor John Winthrop that he was about to be arrested and deported, Williams fled the colony and took refuge among the Native Americans on Narragansett Bay. There he founded a settlement of other dissenters and established a Baptist church, and in 1644 he received an English charter for a separate colony of Rhode Island.

His most important publication was *The Bloudy Tenent*, initially published in London just as Williams was returning to America with his new colonial charter. The treatise offered a bold defense of the freedom of individual religious conscience against both secular and religious authorities (the "bloody tenent," or doctrine, being the suppression or exclusion of religious dissent). Rooted in the Puritan tradition, the argument was framed as commentaries on Scripture. Much of the work was posed as a debate with John Cotton, the leading minister in Boston. Cotton and Williams continued their exchange across multiple pamphlets. Williams's radical beliefs eventually led him to withdraw from all religious congregations, but his writings offered one of the earliest defenses of religious liberty in America.

Does Williams have anything to offer to secular thinkers? Is his argument for toleration of religious dissenters consistent with the goals of a Puritan colony? Is his defense of individual conscience consistent with the maintenance of organized religion? Does his attack on "persecution" apply equally well to religious and secular authorities? Is it persecution for religious authorities to exclude dissenters from the faith? Is it appropriate for John Cotton to exclude Williams from the Puritan congregations of Massachusetts? How far must civil authorities tolerate disruptive religious preaching?

First, that the blood of so many hundred thousand souls of Protestants and Papists, split into the wars of present and former ages, for their respective consciences, is not required nor accepted by Jesus Christ the Prince of Peace.

Secondly, pregnant scriptures and arguments are throughout the work proposed against the doctrine of persecution for cause of conscience.

Thirdly, satisfactory answers are given to scripture and objections produced by Mr. Calvin, Beza, Mr. Cotton; and the ministers of the New England Church and others former and later, tending to prove the doctrine of persecution for cause of conscience.

Fourthly, the doctrine of persecution for cause of conscience, is proved guilty of all the blood of the souls crying for vengeance under the altar.

Fifthly, all civil states, with their offices of justice, in their respective constitutions and administrations, are proved essentially civil, and therefore not judges, governors, or defenders of the spiritual, or Christian, state and worship.

Sixthly, it is the will and command of God that, since the coming of his Son the Lord Jesus, a permission of the most Paganish, Jewish, Turkish, or anti-Christian conscience and worships be granted to all men in all nations and countries; and they are only to be fought against with that sword which is only, in soul matters, able to conquer; to wit, the sword of God's Spirit, the word of God.

Seventhly, the state of the land of Israel, the kings and people thereof, in peace and war, is proved figurative and ceremonial, and no pattern nor precedent for any kingdom or civil state in the world to follow.

Eighthly, God requires not a uniformity of religion to be enacted and enforced in any civil state; which enforced uniformity, sooner or later, is the greatest occasion of civil war, ravishing the conscience, persecution of Christ Jesus in his servants and the hypocrisy and destruction of millions of souls.

Ninthly, in holding an enforced uniformity of religion in a civil state, we must necessarily disclaim our duties and hopes of the Jews' conversion to Christ.

Tenthly, an enforced uniformity of religion throughout a nation or civil state, confounds the civil and religious, denies the principles of Christianity and civility, and that Jesus Christ is come in the flesh.

Eleventhly, the permission of other consciences and worships than a state professes, only can, according to God, procure a firm and lasting peace; good assurance being taken, according to the wisdom of the civil state, for uniformity of civil obedience from all sorts.

Twelfthly, lastly, true civility and Christianity may both flourish in a state or kingdom, notwithstanding the permission of diverse and contrary consciences, either of Jew or Gentile.

. . .

If Paul, if Jesus Christ were present here at London, and the question were proposed what religion would they approve of: The Papists, Prelatists, Presbyterians, Independents, etc. would each say, Of mine, of mine.

But put the second question, if one of the several sorts should by major vote attain the sword of steel: what weapons does Christ Jesus authorize them to fight with in His cause? Do not all men hate the persecutor, and every conscience true or false complain of cruelty, tyranny?

. . .

. . . [I]n the middle of all these civil and spiritual wars (I hope we shall agree in these particulars.)

First, however the proud . . . overlook the poor and cry out . . . *heretics*, shall blasphemers and seducers escape unpunished? [T]here is a surer punishment in the Gospel for defiling of Christ. . . . He that believeth not shall be damned, *Mark* 16.16.

Secondly, whatever worship, ministry, ministration, the best and purest are practiced without faith and true persuasion that they are the true intentions of God, they are sin, sinful worships, ministries, etc. And however in civil things we may be servants unto men, yet in divine and spiritual things the poorest person must disdain the service of the highest prince: Be ye not the servants of men 1 *Cor.* 14.

Thirdly, without search and trial no man attains this faith and right persuasion. 1 *Thessal.* 5.21. Try all things.

In vain have English Parliaments permitted English Bibles in the poorest English houses, and the simplest man or woman to search the Scriptures, if yet against their souls persuasion from the Scripture, they should be forced . . . to believe as the Church believes.

Fourthly, having tried, we must hold fast, 1 *Thessal.* 5.21. . . . [H]aving brought the Truth dear, we must not sell it cheap. . . . Least of all for . . . a little puff of credit and reputation from the changeable breath of uncertain sons of men.

. . .

[F]or civil peace, what is it but *pax civitatis*, the peace of the City, whether an English City, Scotch, or Irish City, or further abroad, French, Spanish, Turkish City, etc.

Thus it pleased the Father of Lights to define it, *Jeremiah* 29.7. Pray for the peace of the City; which peace of the City, or citizens, so compacted in a civil way of union, may be entire, unbroken, safe, etc. . . . The peace of the City or Kingdom, being a far different peace from the peace of the religion or spiritual worship, maintained and professed of the citizens. This peace of their worship (which worship also in some cities being various) being a false peace, God's people were and ought to be nonconformitants, not daring either to be restrained from the true, or constrained to false worship, and yet without breach of the civil or city-peace, properly so called.

[H]ence it is that so many glorious and flourishing cities of the world maintain their civil peace. . . .

. . .

. . . God's witnesses in all ages and generations of men, have been charged with arrogance, impetuousness, etc. and yet the God of Heaven, and Judge of all men, has graciously discharged them from such crimes and maintained and avowed them for his faithful and peaceable servants.

. . .

God's people by their preaching, disputing, etc. have been (though not the cause) yet accidentally the occasion of great contentions and divisions, yea tumults and uproars in towns and cities where they have lived and come, and yet neither their doctrine nor themselves arrogant nor impetuous, however so charged: For thus the Lord Jesus discovered men's false and secure suppositions, *Luke* 12.51. *Suppose ye that I am come to give peace on earth? I tell you nay, but rather division, for from hence forth shall there be five in one house divided, three against two, and two against three, the father shall be divided against the son, and the son against the father, etc.* . . .

. . .

It will be said, whence then arises civil dissensions and uproars about matters of religion?

I answer: When a kingdom or state, town or family, lies and lives in the guilt of a false God, false Christ, false worship: no wonder if sore eyes be troubled at the appearance of the light, be it never so sweet. . . .

[B]reach of civil peace may arise, when false and idolatrous practices are held forth, yet no breach of civil peace from the doctrine or practice, or the manner of holding forth, but from that wrong and preposterous way of suppressing, preventing, and extinguishing such doctrines by weapons, banishment, death, etc. by which men commonly are persuaded to convert. . . .

Hence the town is in an uproar, and the country takes the alarm to expel that fog or mist of error, heresy, blasphemy (as is supposed) with swords and guns; whereas the light alone, even light from the bright shining sun of righteousness, which is able, in the souls and consciences of men to dispel and scatter such fogs and darkness.

. . .

. . . [A] civil government is an ordinance of God, to conserve the civil peace of people, so far as concerns their bodies and goods. . . .

But from this grant I infer . . . that the sovereign, original, and foundation of civil power lies in the people. . . . And if so, that a people may erect and establish what form of government seems to them most meet for their civil condition: It is evident that such governments as are by them erected and established, have no more power, nor for no longer time, than the civil power of people consenting and agreeing shall betrust them with. . . .

And if so, that the magistrates receive their power of governing the church, from the people; undeniably it follows, that a people, as a people, naturally considered . . . have fundamentally and originally, as men, a power to govern the church, to see her do her duty, to correct her, to redress, reform, establish, etc. And if this be not to pull God and Christ, and Spirit out of Heaven, and subject them unto natural, sinful, inconstant men, and so consequently to Satan himself . . . let Heaven and Earth judge.

. . .

• Government forced religion will homogenize the society and cause less problems

JOHN COTTON

AN EXPOSITION UPON THE 13TH CHAPTER OF THE REVELATIONS (1644)

A prominent and politically savvy Puritan preacher in England, John Cotton fled to Boston, Massachusetts, in 1633 to evade the growing persecution of the noncomforming Puritans by the Anglican authorities. He immediately established himself as one of the leading religious figures in the New England colonies in the mid-seventeenth century. He became an advocate of the "New England Way" of Congregationalism, which decentralized the church and allowed individual congregations to govern themselves independently. Cotton was a defender of the rule that allowed only church members in good standing to vote and hold office in the colonial government and condemned the idea of democracy in which policy decisions were made in popular assemblies. "Purity, preserved in the church, will preserve well ordered liberty in the people, and both of them establish well-balanced authority in the magistrates."[1]

His commentary on the Biblical book of Revelation offers the then-common Protestant view that the Pope is the Beast of the Sea that is allowed to deceive the faithful, speak blasphemies, and say "great" or "arrogant" things. In that context, Cotton condemns earthly governments for their willingness to tolerate and empower the blasphemies of the Beast. The broader political lesson, however, is one of the corrupting influence of power and the grasping nature of man. It was both fruitless and problematic to fail to recognize the true "liberty" appropriate to each office (whether religious, civil, or familial), but it was dangerous to give discretionary power beyond those bounds since such excessive power would be abused.

Why did Cotton think that power corrupts? Is all power corrupting and subject to abuse, according to Cotton? How might we distinguish proper liberty from improper license? Is the danger of excessive power limited to religious "arrogance" and the pronouncement of false doctrines? Would this argument suggest that it would be dangerous to allow religious officials to serve as government officials, or should the church control the state? What might be the connection between these views on power and his advocacy of Congregationalism?

This may serve to teach us the danger of allowing to any mortal man an inordinate measure of power to speak great things, to allow to any man uncontrollableness of speech, you see the desperate danger of it. Let all the world learn to give mortal men no greater power than they are content they shall use, for use it they will: and unless they be better taught of God, they will use it ever and anon, it may be make it the passage of their proceeding to speak what they will. And they that have liberty to speak great things, you will find it to be true, they will speak great blasphemies. No man would think what desperate deceit and wickedness there is In the hearts of men. And that was the reason why the Beast did speak such great things, he might speak, and nobody might control him. What, sayeth the Lord in *Jer.* 3.5. *Thou hast spoken and done evil things as thou couldst.* If a Church or head of a Church could have done worse, he would have done it. This is one of the strains of nature, it affects boundless liberty, and to run to the utmost extent. Whatever power he hath received, he hath a corrupt nature that will improve it in one thing or other; if he have liberty, he will think why may he not use it. Set up the Pope as Lord Paramount over kings and princes, and they shall know that he has power over them, he will take liberty to depose one, and set up another. Give him power to make laws, and he will approve, and disprove as he list; what he approves is canonical, what he disproves is rejected. Give him that power, and he will so order it at length, he will make such a state of religion, that he that so

1 John Cotton, "Letter to Lord Say and Seal in the Year 1636," in Thomas Hutchinson, *The History of the Colony of Massachusetts-Bay*, vol. 1 (Boston, MA: Thomas and John Fleet, 1764), 500.

lives and dies shall never be saved, and all this springs from the vast power that is given to him, and from the deep depravation of nature. He will open his mouth, *His tongue is his own, who is Lord over him, Psal.* 12.3.4. It is therefore most wholesome for magistrates and officers in Church and Commonwealth, never to affect more liberty and authority than will do them good, and the People good; for whatever transcendent power is given, will certainly overrun those that give it, and those that receive it. There is a strain in a man's heart that will sometime or other run out of excess, unless the Lord restrain it, but it is not good to venture it. It is necessary therefore, that all power that is on earth be limited, Church-power or other. If there be power given to speak great things, then look for great blasphemies, look for a licentious abuse of it. It is counted a matter of danger to the state to limit prerogatives; but it is a further danger, not to have them limited. They will be like a tempest, if they be not limited. A prince himself cannot tell where he will confine himself, nor can the people tell. But if he have liberty to speak great things, then he will make and unmake, say and unsay, and undertake such things as are neither for his own honor, nor for the safety of the state. It is therefore fit for every man to be studious of the bounds which the Lord hath set: and for the People, in whom fundamentally all power lies, to give as much power as God in his word gives to men. And it is meet that magistrates in the commonwealth, and of officers in churches should desire to know the utmost bounds of their own powers, and it is safe for both. All entrenchment upon the bounds which God hath not given, they are not enlargements, but burdens and snares. They will certainly lead the spirit of a man out of his way sooner or later. It is wholesome and safe to be dealt withall as God deals with the vast Sea; *Hitherto shalt thou come, but there shalt thou stay thy proud waves*. And therefore if they be but banks of simple sand, they will be good enough to check the vast roaring sea. And so for imperial monarchies, it is safe to know how far their power extends; and then if it be but banks of sand, which is most slippery, it will serve, as well as any brazen wall. If you pinch the sea of its liberty, though it be walls of stone or brass, it will beat them down. So it is with magistrates, stint them where God hath not stinted them, and if they were walls of brass, they would beat them down, and it is a meet they should. But give them the liberty God allows, and if it be but a wall of sand it will keep them. . . . So let there be due bounds set, and I may apply it to families; it is good for the wife to acknowledge all power and authority to the husband, and for the husband to acknowledge honor to the wife, but still give them that which God hath given them, and no more nor less. Give them the full latitude that God hath given, else you will find you dig pits, and lay snares, and cumber their spirits, if you give them less. There is never peace where full liberty is not given, nor never stable peace where more than full liberty is granted. Let them be duly observed, and give men no more liberty than God does, nor women, for they will abuse it. The Devil will draw them, and God's providence leads them thereunto, therefore give them no more than God gives. And so for children; and servants, or any others you are to deal with, given them the liberty and authority you would have them use, and beyond that stretch not the tether, it will not tend to their good nor yours. And also from hence gather, and go home with this meditation: That certainly here is this distemper in our natures, that we cannot tell how to use liberty, but we shall very readily corrupt ourselves. Oh the bottomless depth of sandy earth! Of a corrupt spirit, that breaks over all bounds, and loves inordinate vastness; that is it we ought to be careful of.

. . .

JOHN WINTHROP

LITTLE SPEECH ON LIBERTY (1645)

A founder of the Massachusetts Bay Colony, John Winthrop served as its first governor and was repeatedly reelected to that office until his death in 1649. As governor, Winthrop exercised expansive, discretionary power, which was sometimes resisted by the voters. Over the course of the 1630s, Winthrop battled with the lower house of the colonial legislature (the deputies) over how much discretion should be left in the hands of magistrates (including Winthrop), especially in the months when the legislature was out of session. The legislators wanted to enact a detailed system of positive law, including prescribed sentences for violations of the law. Winthrop favored a legal system built on custom and precedent, and a political system that preserved substantial discretion "when necessary occasions call for action" and "no particular express law" was provided. The adoption of the Massachusetts Body of Liberties in 1641 was part of the process of trying to specify the rights of the inhabitants of the colony and tie the hands of the magistrates.

The deputies continued to push for a more robust legal code, however, and in the summer of 1644 (as he was being demoted to deputy governor) Winthrop defended the colonial authority from charges that it was an arbitrary government. The deputies issued a brief critique of Winthrop's discourse on arbitrary government, which spurred another response from Winthrop. In that response, Winthrop clarified that statutes were often useful but that he meant to endorse the value of the English common law and traditional moral law. He distanced himself from the idea that "judges should have liberty to do what they may," but reemphasized that rules do not need to appear in the statute books in order to provide sufficient guidance to judges. That fall, a council of church elders led by John Cotton gave their support to magisterial discretion. The following spring, Winthrop was put on trial for exceeding his authority as a justice of the peace. His acquittal on those charges put to rest his conflict with the lower house, and he resumed the office of governor in 1646. His "Little Speech on Liberty" was delivered to the General Court as part of his defense to those charges.

What are the possible causes of error on the part of government officials, according to Winthrop? Why are some failures more forgivable than others? How tolerant should citizens be of mistakes by their elected leaders? What is the difference between natural liberty and civil liberty? What is the relationship between liberty and restraint? Does good government limit true freedom? Does liberty need to be sacrificed in order to achieve order? Under what conditions is it proper to challenge authority?

. . . The great questions that have troubled the country, are about the authority of the magistrates and the liberty of the people. It is yourselves who have called us to this office, and being called by you, we have our authority from God, in way of an ordinance, such as has the image of God eminently stamped upon it, the contempt and violation whereof has been vindicated with examples of divine vengeance. I entreat you to consider, that when you choose magistrates, you take them from among yourselves, men subject to the passions as you are. Therefore when you see infirmities in us, you should reflect upon your own, and that would make you bear the more with us, and not be severe censures of the failings of your magistrates, when you have continual experience of the like infirmities in yourselves and others. We account him a good servant, who breaks not his covenant. The covenant between you and us is the oath you have taken of us, which is to this purpose, that we shall govern you and judge your causes by the rules of God's laws and our own, according to our best skill. When you agree with a workman to build you a ship or house etc. he undertakes as well for his skill as for his faithfulness, for it is his profession, and you pay him for both. But when you call one to be a magistrate, he does not profess nor undertake to have sufficient skill for that office, nor can you furnish him with gifts etc. therefore you must run the hazard of his skill and ability. But if he fail in faithfulness, which by his oath he is bound unto, that he must answer for. If it fall out that the case be clear to common apprehension, and the rule clear also, if he transgress here, the error is not in the skill, but in the evil of the will: it must be required of him. But if the cause be doubtful, or the rule doubtful, to men of such understanding and parts as your magistrates are, if your magistrates should err here, yourselves must bear it.

For the other point concerning liberty, I observe a great mistake in the country about that. There is a twofold liberty, natural (I mean as our nature is now corrupt) and civil or federal. The first is common to man with beasts and other creatures. By this, man, as he stands in relation to man simply, has liberty to do what he lists; it is a liberty to evil as well as to good. This liberty is incompatible and inconsistent with authority, and cannot endure the least restraint of the most just authority. The exercise and maintaining of this liberty makes men grow more evil, and in time to be worse than brute beasts: *omnes sumus licentia deteriores* [we are all the worse for licentiousness]. This is that great enemy of truth and peace, that wild beast, which all the ordinances of God are bent against to restrain and subdue it. The other kind of liberty I call civil or federal, it may also be termed moral, in reference to the covenant between God and man, in the moral law, and the politic covenants and constitutions, among men themselves. This liberty is the proper end and object of authority, and cannot subsist without it; and it is a liberty to that only which is good, just and honest. This liberty you are to stand for, with the hazard (not only of your goods, but) of your lives, if need be. Whatsoever crosses this, is not authority, but a distemper thereof. This liberty is maintained and exercised in a way of subjection to authority; it is of the same kind of liberty wherewith Christ hath made us free. The woman's own choice makes such a man her husband; yet being so chosen, he is our lord, and she is to be subject to him, yet in a way of liberty, not of bondage; and a true wife accounts her subjection her honor and freedom, and would not think her condition safe and free, but in her subjection to her husband's authority. Such is the liberty of the church under the authority of Christ, her king and husband; his yoke is so easy and sweet to her as a bride's ornaments; and if through forwardness or wantonness etc. she shake it off, at any time, she is at no rest in her spirit, until she take it up again; and whether her lord smiles upon her, and embraces her in his arms, or whether he frowns, or rebukes, or smites her, she apprehends the sweetness of his love in all, and is refreshed, supported and instructed by every such dispensation of his authority over her. On the other side, you know who they are that complain of this yoke and say, let us break their bands etc. we will not have this man to rule over us. Even so, brethren, it will be between you and your magistrates. If you stand for your natural corrupt liberties, and will do what is good in your own eyes, you will not endure the least weight of authority, but will murmur, and oppose, and be always striving to shake off that yoke; but if you will be satisfied to enjoy such civil and lawful liberties, such as Christ allows you, then will you quietly and cheerfully submit unto that authority which is set over you, in all the administrations of it, for your good. Wherein, if we fail at any time, we hope we shall be willing (by God's assistance) to hearken to good advice from any of you, or in any other way of God; so shall your liberties be preserved, in upholding the honor and power of authority amongst you.

JOHN WISE

A VINDICATION OF THE GOVERNMENT OF NEW ENGLAND CHURCHES (1717)

John Wise was a native of Massachusetts and a Congregational minister. He spent most of his life in Ipswich, Massachusetts, where he was once arrested for organizing resistance to the collection of taxes that had been imposed by the royal governor who was installed after the charter for the Massachusetts Bay Colony was revoked. After a revolt displaced the royal governor in 1692, Wise participated in the effort to reorganize the government under the principles of the old charter.

In the first two decades of the eighteenth century, Wise engaged in an extended debate with Increase and Cotton Mather over the organization of the New England churches. The Mathers proposed that the individual congregations be brought under the authority of a single association. Wise rejected this centralizing impulse, and argued on behalf of the traditional structure of voluntary, self-governing congregations. Drawing on the natural law theories of the German philosopher Samuel Pufendorf, Wise took a democratic approach to understanding and adhering to the natural law. Although his immediate target was church governance, Wise's defense of local democracy had increasing resonance in the political arguments that helped justify the American Revolution.

What does man's natural sociability mean for Wise? How important is a sociable impulse for Wise's conclusions about the civil state? What is the basis of the equality of man? How supportive of democracy is Wise? What does he see as its advantages and disadvantages? Does he provide a basis for supporting political revolutions?

I shall consider Man in a state of Nature Being, as a Free-Born Subject under the Crown of Heaven, and owing Homage to none but God himself. It is certain Civil Government in General, is a very Admirable Result of Providence, and an Incomparable Benefit of Mankind, yet much needs be acknowledged to be the Effect of Human Free-Compacts and not of Divine Institution; it is the Produce of Man's Reason, of Human and Rational Combinations, and not from any direct Orders of Infinite Wisdom, in any positive Law wherein is drawn up this or that Scheme of Civil Government. Government . . . is necessary—in that no Society of Men can subsist without it; and that Particular Form of Government is necessary which best suits the Temper and Inclination of a People. Nothing can be God's Ordinance, but what he has particularly Declared to be such; there is no particular Form of Civil Government described in God's Word, neither does Nature prompt it. . . . Government is not formed by Nature. . . ; if it were, it would be the same in all Countries; because Nature keeps the same Method, in the same thing, in all Climates. . . .

The Prime Immunity in Man's State, is that he is most properly the Subject of the Law of Nature. He is the Favorite Animal on Earth; in that this Part of God's Image, *viz.* Reason is Congenate with his Nature, wherein by a Law Immutable, Enstamped upon his Frame, God has provided a Rule for Men in all their Actions, obliging each one to the performance of that which is Right, not only as to Justice, but likewise as to all other Moral Virtues, the which is nothing but the Dictate of Reason founded in the soul. . . . That which is to be drawn from Man's Reason, flowing from the true Current of that Faculty, when unperverted, may be said to be the Law of Nature; on which account, the Holy Scriptures declare is written on Men's hearts. . . . The way to discover the Law of Nature in our own state, is by a narrow Watch, and accurate Contemplation of our Natural Condition, and propensions. Others say that this is the way to find out the Law of Nature. *Scil.* If a Man any ways doubts, whether what he is going to do to another Man be agreeable to the Law of Nature, then let him suppose himself to be in that other Man's Room; And by this Rule effectually Executed] . . . [I]n pursuing our Condition for the discovery of the Law of Nature, this is very obvious to view, *viz.*

1. A Principle of Self-Love, and Self-Preservation, is very predominant in Man's Being.

2. A Sociable Disposition.

3. An Affection or Love to Mankind in General. . . . Man is a Creature extremely desirous of his own Preservation; of himself he is plainly Exposed to many Wants, unable to secure his own safety, and Maintenance without the Assistance of his fellows; and he is also able of returning Kindness by the furtherance of mutual Good; But yet Man is often found to be Malicious, Insolent and easily Provoked, and as powerful in Effecting mischief, as he is ready in designating it. Now that such a Creature may be Preserved, it is necessary that he be Sociable; that is, that he be capable and disposed to unite himself to those of his own species, and to Regulate himself towards them, that they may have no fair Reason to do him harm; but rather incline to promote his Interests, and secure his Rights and Concerns. This then is a Fundamental Law of Nature, that every Man as far as in him lies, do maintain a Sociableness with others, agreeable with the main end and disposition of human Nature in general. For this is very apparent, that Reason and Society render Man the most potent of all Creatures. And Finally, from the Principles of Sociableness, it follows as a fundamental Law of Nature, that Man is not so Wedded to his own Interest, but that he can make the Common good the mark of his Aim: And hence he becomes Capacitated to enter into a Civil State by the Law of Nature; for without this property in Nature, viz. Sociableness, which is for Cementing of parts, every Government would soon molder and dissolve.

The Second Great Immunity of Man is an Original Liberty Enstamped upon his Rational Nature. He that intrudes upon his Liberty, Violates the Law of Nature. . . . For as to his Dominion, the whole frame of the Lower Part of the Universe is devoted to his use, and at his Command; and his Liberty under the Conduct of Right Reason, is equal with his trust. Which Liberty may be briefly Considered, Internally as to his Mind, and Externally as to his Person.

1. The Internal Native Liberty of Man's Nature in general implies, a faculty of Doing or Omitting things according to the Direction of his Judgment. But in a more special meaning, this Liberty does not consist in a loose and ungovernable Freedom, or in an unbounded License of Acting. Such License is disagreeing with the condition and dignity of Man, and would make Man of a lower and meaner Constitution than Brute Creatures. . . .

2. Man's External, Personal, Natural Liberty, Antecedent to all Human parts, or Alliances must also be considered. And so every Man must be conceived to be perfectly in his own Power and disposal, and not to be controlled by the Authority of any other. And thus every Man, must be acknowledged equal to every Man, since all Subjection and all Command are equally banished on both sides; and considering all Men thus at Liberty, every Man has a Prerogative to judge for himself, *viz.* What shall be most for the Behoof, Happiness and Well-being.

3. The Third Capital Immunity belonging to Man's Nature, is an equality among Men; Which is not to be denied by the Law of Nature, till Man has Refigured himself with all his Rights for the sake of a Civil State; and then his Personal Liberty and Equality is to be cherished, and preserved to the highest degree, as will consist with all just distinctions among Men of Honor, and shall be agreeable with the public Good. For Man has a high valuation of himself, and the passion seems to lay its first foundation (not in Pride, but) really in the high and admirable Frame and Constitution of Human Nature. . . . It follows as a Command of the Law of Nature, that every Man Esteem and treat another as one who is naturally his Equal, or who is a Man as well as he. There be many popular, or plausible Reasons that greatly Illustrate this Equality, viz. that we all Derive our Being from one stock, the same Common Father of human Race. . . .

And also that our Bodies are Composed of matter, frail, brittle, and liable to be destroyed by thousand Accidents; we all owe our Existence to the same Method of propagation. The Noblest Mortal in his Entrance on to the Stage of Life, is not distinguished by any pomp or of passage from the lowest of

Mankind; and our Life hastens to the same General Mark: Death observes no Ceremony, but Knocks as loud at the Barriers of the Court, as at the Door of the Cottage. This Equality being admitted, bears a very great force in maintaining Peace and Friendship among Men. For that he who would use the Alliance of others, in promoting his own Advantage, ought as freely to be at their service, when they want his help on the like Occasions. *One Good turn Requires another*, is the Common Proverb; for otherwise he must need esteem others unequal to himself, who constantly demands their Aid, and as constantly denies his own. And whoever is of this Insolent Temper, cannot but highly displease those about him, and soon give Occasion of the Breach of the Common Peace. . . .

. . . . [I]t would be the greatest absurdity to believe, that Nature actually invests the Wise with a Sovereignty over the weak; or with a Right of forcing them against their Wills; for that no Sovereignty can be Established, unless some Human Deed, or Covenant Precede. Nor does Natural fitness for Government make a Man presently Governor over another; for that as *Ulpian* says, *by a Natural Right all Men are born free*; and Nature having set all Men upon a Level and made them Equals, no Servitude or Subjection can be conceived without inequality; and this cannot be made without Usurpation or Force in others, or Voluntary Compliance in those who Resign their freedom, and give away their degree of Natural Being. . . .

1. Every Man considered in a Natural State, must be allowed to be Free, and at his own dispose; yet to suit Man's Inclinations to Society; And in a peculiar manner to gratify the necessity he is in of public Rule and Order, he is Impelled to enter into a Civil Community; and Divest himself of his Natural Freedom, and puts himself under Government; which amongst other things Comprehends the Power of Life and Death over Him; together with Authority to enjoin him some things to which he has an utter Aversion, and to prohibit him other things, for which he may have as strong an Inclination; so that he may be often under this Authority, obliged to Sacrifice his Private for the Public Good. So that though Man is inclined to Society, yet he is driven to a Combination by great necessity. For that the true and leading Cause of forming Governments, and yielding up Natural Liberty, and throwing Man's Equality into a Common Pile to be new Cast by the Rules of fellowship; was really and truly to guard themselves against the Injuries Men were liable to Interchangeably; for none so Good to Man, as Man, and yet none a greater Enemy. So that,

2. The first Human Subject and Original of Civil Power is the People. For as they have a Power every Man over himself in a Natural State, so upon a Combination they can and do, bequeath this Power unto others; and settle it according as their united discretion shall Determine. For that this is very plain, that when the Subject of Sovereign Power is quite Extinct, that Power returns to the People again. And when they are free, they may set up what species of Government they please; or if they rather incline to it, they may subside into a State of Natural Being, if it be plainly for the best. . . .

3. The formal Reason of Government is the Will of a Community, yielded up and surrendered to some other Subject, either of one particular person, or more, Conveyed in the following manner.

Let us conceive in our Mind a multitude of Men, all Naturally Free and Equal; going about voluntarily, to Erect themselves into a new Commonwealth. Now their Condition being such, to bring themselves into a Political Body, they must needs Enter into diverse Covenants.

. . .

. . . A Civil State is a Compound Moral Person, whose Will . . . is the Will of all; to the end it may Use, and Apply the strength and riches of Private Persons towards maintaining the Common Peace, Security, and Wellbeing of all. . . .

. . .

In General concerning Rebellion against Government, for Particular Subjects to break in upon Regular Communities duly Established, is from the premises to Violate the Law of Nature; and is a high Usurpation upon the first grand Immunities of Mankind. Such Rebels in the States, and Usurpers in Church affront the World, with a presumption that the Best of the Brotherhood are a Company of Fools, and that themselves have fairly Monopolized all the Reason of Human Nature. Yea, they take upon them the Boldness to assume a Prerogative of trampling underfoot the natural original Equality and Liberty of their Fellows; for to push the Proprietors of Settlements out of possession of their old, and impose new Schemes upon them, is virtually to declare them in a state of Vassalage, or that they were Born to; and therefore will the Usurper be so gracious as to insure them they shall not be Sold at the next Market. . . .

In Special I shall now proceed to Enquire, Whether any of the aforesaid Species of regular, unmixed Governments, can with any good show of Reason be predictable of the Church of Christ on Earth. If the Churches of Christ, as Churches, are either the Object or Subject of a Sovereign Power entrusted in the hands of Man, then most certainly one of the fore-cited Schemes of perfect Government will be applicable to it.

. . .

I shall begin with a Monarchy. Its certain, his Holiness, either by reasonable Pleas, or powerful Cheats, has assumed an absolute and universal Sovereignty. . . . But the sad Enquiry is, Whether this sort of Government has not plainly subverted the Design of the Gospels, and the end for which Christ's Government was Ordained, *viz.* the Moral, Spiritual, and Eternal Happiness of Men?

But I have no occasion to pursue this Remark with tedious Demonstrations. It's very plain, it's written with Blood in Capital Letters . . . That the Government of this Ecclesiastical Monarch has instead of Sanctifying, absolutely Debauched the World, and subverted all good Christianity in it. So that without the least show of any vain presumption, we may infer, That God and wife Nature were never Propitious to the Birth of this Monster.

An Aristocracy which places the Supreme Power in a Select Company of choice Persons. . . . This Government might do to support the Church in its most valuable Rights, etc. If we could be assured they would make the Scripture, and not their private Will, the Rule of their Personal and Ministerial Actions. . . .

It is very plain . . . the Primitive Constitution of the Churches was a Democracy. . . .

. . .

. . . But to abbreviate; it seems most agreeable with the Light of Nature, that if there by any of the Regular Government settled in the Church of God it must needs be.

A Democracy. This is a form of Government, which the Light of Nature does highly value and often directs to as most agreeable to the Just and Natural Prerogatives of Human Beings. This was of great account, in the early times of the World. And not only so, but on the Experience of several Thousand years, after the World had been tumbled, and tossed from one Species of Government to another, at a great Expense of Blood and Treasure, many of the wise Nations of the World have sheltered themselves under it again; or at least have blended and balanced their Government with it.

It is certainly a great Truth that Man's Original Liberty after it is Resigned (yet under due Restriction) ought to be Cherished in all wise Governments; or otherwise a man in making himself a Subject, he alters himself from a Freeman, into a Slave, which to do is Repugnant to the Law of Nature. Also the Natural Equality of Men among Men must be duly favored; in that Government was never Established by God or Nature to give one Man a Prerogative to insult over another; therefore in a Civil, as well as in a Natural State of Being, a just Equality is to be indulged so far as that every Man, which is agreeable both with Nature and Religion. . . . The End of all good Government is to Cultivate Humanity, and Promote the happiness of all, and the good of every Man in all his Rights, his Life, Liberty, Estate, Honor, etc. without injury or abuse done to any. Then certainly it cannot easily be thought, that a company of Men, that shall enter into a voluntary Compact, to hold all Power in their own hands, thereby to use and improve their united force, wisdom, riches, and strength for the Common and Patriotic good of every Member, as is the Nature of a Democracy; I say it cannot be that this sort of Constitution, will so readily furnish those in Government with an appetite, or disposition to pretty upon each other, or embezzle the common Stock; as some Particular Persons may be apt to do when set off, and Entrusted with the same Power. And moreover this appears very Natural, that when the aforesaid Government or Power, settled in all, when they have Elected certain capable Persons to Minister in their affairs, and the said Ministers remain accountable to the Assembly; these Officers must needs be under the influence of many wise cautions from their own thoughts . . . in their whole Administration. And from thence it must needs follow that they will be more apt, and inclined to steer Right for the main Point, *viz.* The peculiar good, and benefit of the whole, and every particular Member fairly and sincerely. And why may not these stand for very Rational Pleas in Church Order?

For certainly if Christ has settled any form of Power in his Church he has done it for his Church's safety, and for the Benefit of every Member. Then he must needs be presumed to have made choice of that Government as should least Expose his People to Hazard, either from the fraud, or Arbitrary measures of particular Men. And it is as plain as daylight, there is no Species of Government like a Democracy to attain this End. There is but about two steps from an Aristocracy, to a Monarchy, and from thence but one to a Tyranny; an able standing force, and an Ill-Nature, *ipso facto,* turns an absolute Monarch into a Tyrant; this is obvious among the Roman *Caesars,* and through the World. And all these direful Transmutations are easier in Church affairs (from the different Qualities of things) then in Civil States. For what is it that cunning and learned Men can't make the World swallow as an Article of their Creed, if they are once invested with an Uncontrollable Power, and are to be the standing Orators to Mankind in matters of Faith and Obedience? . . .

THOMAS PAINE

COMMON SENSE (1776)

Thomas Paine was an English Quaker who took the advice of Benjamin Franklin, whom he met in London, that he should emigrate to America to seek his fortune. Paine arrived in Philadelphia in 1774 and launched a new career as a writer and editor. His first pamphlet was an attack on the institution of slavery. His short book setting out commonsense reasons for American independence was an immediate sensation, and he was thrust into the center of the debate over the American separation from England and the establishment of a purely republican form of government in the United States. While in England looking for investors for a bridge-building project, the French Revolution broke out and Paine adopted the cause as his own. In 1791, he published a defense of the French Revolution against conservative critics such as the English politician Edmund Burke. That book, *Rights of Man*, was banned in England for its hostility to a monarchical form of government, but won him fame in revolutionary France. He briefly served in the revolutionary government, but eventually fell out with Robespierre and was imprisoned. He returned to the United States in 1802 at the urging of Thomas Jefferson, but by then he was known as much for his radicalism and atheism as for his earlier support for the American Revolution.

Why does Paine begin by considering the origins of government? What does he consider to be the most natural form of government? What does he see as the problem with monarchies? What is the case for independence? To what extent is the case for independence connected to the case for democracy? Would it be possible to adopt political reforms that would render independence unnecessary or undesirable? Does Paine's understanding of government differ from Wise's?

On the Origin and Design of Government in General, with Concise Remarks on the English Constitution.

Some writers have so confounded society with government, as to leave little or no distinction between them; whereas they are not only different, but have different origins. Society is produced by our wants, and government by our wickedness; the former promotes our happiness *positively* by uniting our affections, the latter *negatively* by restraining our vices. The one encourages intercourse, the other creates distinctions. The first is a patron, the last a punisher.

Society in every state is a blessing, but Government, even in its best state, is but a necessary evil; in its worst state an intolerable one: for when we suffer, or are exposed to the same miseries *by a Government*, which we might expect in a country *without Government*, our calamity is heightened by reflecting that we furnish the means by which we suffer. Government, like dress, is the badge of lost innocence; the palaces of kings are built upon the ruins of the bowers of paradise. For were the impulses of conscience clear, uniform and irresistibly obeyed, man would need no other law-giver; but that not being the case, he finds it necessary to surrender up a part of his property to furnish means for the protection of the rest; and this he is induced to do by the same prudence which in every other case advises him, out of two evils to choose the least. Wherefore, security being the true design and end of government, it unanswerably follows that whatever form thereof appears most likely to ensure it to us, with the least expense and greatest benefit, is preferable to all others.

In order to gain a clear and just idea of the design and end of government, let us suppose a small number of persons settled in some sequestered part of the earth, unconnected with the rest; they will then represent the first peopling of any country, or of the world. In this state of natural liberty, society will be their first thought. A thousand motives will excite them thereto; the strength of one man is so unequal to his wants, and his mind so unfitted for perpetual solitude, that he is soon obliged to seek assistance and relief of another, who in his turn requires the same. Four or five united would be able to raise a tolerable dwelling in the midst of a wilderness, but one man might labor out the common period of life without accomplishing anything; when he had felled his timber he could not remove it, nor erect it after it was removed; hunger in the meantime would urge him to quit his work, and every different want would call him a different way. Disease, nay even misfortune, would be death; for though neither might be mortal, yet either would disable him from living, and reduce him to a state in which he might rather be said to perish than to die.

Thus necessity, like a gravitating power, would soon form our newly arrived emigrants into society, the reciprocal blessings of which would supersede, and render the obligations of law and government unnecessary while they remained perfectly just to each other; but as nothing but Heaven is impregnable to vice, it will unavoidably happen that in proportion as they surmount the first difficulties of emigration, which bound them together in a common cause, they will begin to relax in their duty and attachment to each other: and this remissness will point out the necessity of establishing some form of government to supply the defect of moral virtue.

Some convenient tree will afford them a State House, under the branches of which the whole Colony may assemble to deliberate on public matters. It is more than probable that their first laws will have the title only of Regulations and be enforced by no other penalty than public disesteem. In this first parliament every man by natural right will have a seat.

But as the Colony increases, the public concerns will increase likewise, and the distance at which the members may be separated, will render it too inconvenient for all of them to meet on every occasion as at first, when their number was small, their habitations near, and the public concerns few and trifling. This will point out the convenience of their consenting to leave the legislative part to be managed by a select number chosen from the whole body, who are supposed to have the same concerns at stake which those have who appointed them, and who will act in the same manner as the whole body would act were they present. If the colony continue increasing, it will become necessary to augment the number of representatives, and that the interest of every part of the colony may be attended to, it will be found best to divide the whole into convenient parts, each part sending its proper number: and that the *elected* might never form to themselves an interest separate from the *electors*, prudence will point out the propriety of having elections often: because as the *elected* might by that means return and mix again with the general body of the *electors* in a few months, their fidelity to the public will be secured by the prudent reflection of not making a rod for themselves. And as this frequent interchange will establish a common interest with every part of the community, they will mutually and naturally support each other, and on this, (not on the unmeaning name of king,) depends the *strength of government, and the happiness of the governed.*

Here then is the origin and rise of government; namely, a mode rendered necessary by the inability of moral virtue to govern the world; here too is the design and end of government, viz. Freedom and security. And however our eyes may be dazzled with show, or our ears deceived by sound; however prejudice may warp our wills, or interest darken our understanding, the simple voice of nature and reason will say, it is right.

I draw my idea of the form of government from a principle in nature which no art can overturn, viz. that the more simple any thing is, the less liable it is to be disordered, and the easier repaired when disordered; and with this maxim in view I offer a few remarks on the so much boasted constitution of England. That it was noble for the dark and slavish times in which it was erected, is granted. When the world was overrun with tyranny the least remove therefrom was a glorious rescue. But that it is imperfect, subject to convulsions, and incapable of producing what it seems to promise, is easily demonstrated.

Absolute governments, (though the disgrace of human nature) have this advantage with them, they are simple; if the people suffer, they know the head from which their suffering springs; know likewise the remedy; and are not bewildered by a variety of causes and cures. But the constitution of England is so exceedingly complex, that the nation may suffer for years together without being able to discover in which part the fault lies; some will say in one and some in another, and every political physician will advise a different medicine.

I know it is difficult to get over local or long standing prejudices, yet if we will suffer ourselves to examine the component parts of the English constitution, we shall find them to be the base remains of two ancient tyrannies, compounded with some new Republican materials.

First.—The remains of Monarchical tyranny in the person of the King.

Secondly.—The remains of aristocratic tyranny in the persons of the Peers.

Thirdly.—The new Republican materials, in the persons of the Commons, on whose virtue depends the freedom of England.

The two first, by being hereditary, are independent of the People; wherefore in a *constitutional sense* they contribute nothing towards the freedom of the State.

To say that the constitution of England is an *union* of three powers, reciprocally *checking* each other, is farcical; either the words have no meaning, or they are flat contradictions.

To say that the Commons is a check upon the King, presupposes two things.

First.—That the King is not to be trusted without being looked after, or in other words, that a thirst for absolute power is the natural disease of monarchy.

Secondly.—That the Commons, by being appointed for that purpose, are either wiser or more worthy of confidence than the Crown.

But as the same constitution which gives the Commons a power to check the King by withholding the supplies, gives afterwards the King a power to check the Commons, by empowering him to reject their other bills; it again supposes that the King is wiser than those whom it has already supposed to be wiser than him. A mere absurdity!

There is something exceedingly ridiculous in the composition of Monarchy; it first excludes a man from the means of information, yet empowers him to act in cases where the highest judgment is required. The state of a king shuts him from the World, yet the business of a king requires him to know it thoroughly; wherefore the different parts, by unnaturally opposing and destroying each other, prove the whole character to be absurd and useless.

. . .

Wherefore, laying aside all national pride and prejudice in favor of modes and forms, the plain truth is that *it is wholly owing to the constitution of the people, and not to the constitution of the government* that the crown is not as oppressive in England as in Turkey.

. . .

Of Monarchy and Hereditary Succession

Mankind being originally equals in the order of creation, the equality could only be destroyed by some subsequent circumstance: the distinctions of rich and poor may in a great measure be accounted for, and that without having recourse to the harsh ill-sounding names of oppression and avarice. Oppression is often the *consequence*, but seldom or never the *means* of riches; and though avarice will preserve a man from being necessitously poor, it generally makes him too timorous to be wealthy.

But there is another and greater distinction for which no truly natural or religious reason can be assigned, and that is the distinction of men into KINGS and SUBJECTS. Male and female are the distinctions of nature, good and bad the distinctions of Heaven; but how a race of men came into the world so exalted above the rest, and distinguished like some new species, is worth inquiring into, and whether they are the means of happiness or of misery to mankind.

. . .

To the evil of monarchy we have added that of hereditary succession; and as the first is a degradation and lessening of ourselves, so the second, claimed as a matter of right, is an insult and imposition on posterity. For all men being originally equals, no one by birth could have a right to set up his own family in perpetual preference to all others for ever, and though himself might deserve some decent degree of honors of his contemporaries, yet his descendants might be far too unworthy to inherit them. One of the strongest natural proofs of the folly of hereditary right in Kings, is that nature disapproves it, otherwise she would not so frequently turn it into ridicule, by giving mankind an *Ass for a Lion*.

Secondly, as no man at first could possess any other public honors than were bestowed upon him, so the givers of those honors could have no power to give away the right of posterity, and though they might say "We choose you for our head," they could not without manifest injustice to their children say "that your children and your children's children shall reign over ours forever." Because such an unwise, unjust, unnatural compact might (perhaps) in the next succession put them under the government of a rogue or a fool. Most wise men in their private sentiments have ever treated hereditary right with contempt; yet it is one of those evils which when once established is not easily removed: many submit from fear, others from superstition, and the more powerful part shares with the king the plunder of the rest.

This is supposing the present race of kings in the world to have had an honorable origin: whereas it is more than probable, that, could we take off the dark covering of antiquity and trace them to their first rise, we should find the first of them nothing better than the principal ruffian of some restless gang, whose savage manners or pre-eminence in subtly obtained him the title of chief among plunderers: and who by increasing in power and extending his depredations, overawed the quiet and defenseless to purchase their safety by frequent contributions. . . .

. . .

But it is not so much the absurdity as the evil of hereditary succession which concerns mankind. Did it ensure a race of good and wise men it would have the seal of divine authority, but as it opens a door to the *foolish*, the *wicked*, and the *improper*, it hath in it the nature of oppression. Men who look upon themselves born to reign, and others to obey, soon grow insolent. Selected from the rest of mankind, their minds are early poisoned by importance; and the world they act in differs so materially from the world at large, that they have but little opportunity of knowing its true interests, and when they succeed to the government are frequently the most ignorant and unfit of any throughout the dominions.

. . .

If we enquire into the business of a King, we shall find that in some countries they may have none; and after sauntering away their lives without pleasure to themselves or advantage to the nation, withdraw from the scene, and leave their successors to tread the same idle round. In absolute monarchies the whole weight of business civil and military lies on the King; the children of Israel in their request for a king urged this plea, "that he may judge us, and go out before us and fight our battles." But in countries where he is neither a Judge nor a General, as in England, a man would be puzzled to know what *is* his business.

. . .

In England a King hath little more to do than to make war and give away places; which, in plain terms, is to impoverish the nation and set it together by the ears. A pretty business indeed for a man to be allowed eight hundred thousand sterling a year for, and worshipped into the bargain! Of more worth is one honest man to society, and in the sight of God, than all the crowned ruffians that ever lived.

Thoughts on the Present State of American Affairs

In the following pages I offer nothing more than simple facts, plain arguments, and common sense: and have no other preliminaries to settle with the reader, than that he will divest himself of prejudice and prepossession, and suffer his reason and his feelings to determine for themselves: that he will put on, or rather that he will not put off, the true character of a man, and generously enlarge his views beyond the present day.

Volumes have been written on the subject of the struggle between England and America. Men of all ranks have embarked in the controversy, from different motives, and with various designs; but all have been ineffectual, and the period of debate is closed. Arms as the last resource decide the contest; the appeal was the choice of the King, and the Continent has accepted the challenge.

. . .

The Sun never shined on a cause of greater worth. It's not the affair of a City, a County, a Province, or a Kingdom; but of a Continent—of at least one eighth part of the habitable Globe. It's not the concern of a day, a year, or an age; posterity are virtually involved in the contest, and will be more or less affected even to the end of time, by the proceedings now. Now is the seed-time of Continental union, faith and honor. The least fracture now will be like a name engraved with the point of a pin on the tender rind of a young oak; the wound would enlarge with the tree, and posterity read it in full grown characters.

By referring the matter from argument to arms, a new era for politics is struck—a new method of thinking hath arisen. All plans, proposals, etc. prior to the nineteenth of April, *i.e.* to the commencement of hostilities, are like the almanacs of the last year; which though proper then, are superseded and useless now. Whatever was advanced by the advocates on either side of the question then, terminated in one and the same point, viz. a union with Great Britain; the only difference between the parties was the method of effecting it; the one proposing force, the other friendship; but it hath so far happened that the first hath failed, and the second hath withdrawn her influence.

As much hath been said of the advantages of reconciliation, which, like an agreeable dream, hath passed away and left us as we were, it is but right that we should examine the contrary side of the argument, and enquire into some of the many material injuries which these Colonies sustain, and always will sustain, by being connected with and dependent on Great-Britain. To examine that connection and dependence, on the principles of nature and common sense, to see what we have to trust to, if separated, and what we are to expect, if dependent.

. . .

I challenge the warmest advocate for reconciliation to show a single advantage that this continent can reap by being connected with Great Britain. I repeat the challenge; not a single advantage is derived. Our corn will fetch its price in any market in Europe, and our imported goods must be paid for buy them where we will.

But the injuries and disadvantages which we sustain by that connection, are without number; and our duty to mankind at large, as well as to ourselves, instruct us to renounce the alliance: because, any submission to, or dependence on, Great Britain, tends directly to involve this Continent in European wars and quarrels, and set us at variance with nations who would otherwise seek our friendship, and against whom we have neither anger nor complaint. As Europe is our market for trade, we ought to form no partial connection with any part of it. It is the true interest of America to steer clear of European contentions, which she never can do, while, by her dependence on Britain, she is made the make-weight in the scale of British politics.

Europe is too thickly planted with Kingdoms to be long at peace, and whenever a war breaks out between England and any foreign power, the trade of America goes to ruin, *because of her connection with Britain.* The next war may not turn out like the last, and should it not, the advocates for reconciliation now will be wishing for separation then, because neutrality in that case would be a safer convoy than a man of war. Everything that is right or reasonable pleads for separation. The blood of the slain, the weeping voice of nature cries, IT IS TIME TO PART. . .

. . .

Men of passive tempers look somewhat lightly over the offences of Great Britain, and, still hoping for the best, are apt to call out, *Come, come, we shall be friends again for all this.* But examine the passions and feelings of mankind: bring the doctrine of reconciliation to the touchstone of nature, and then tell me whether you can hereafter love, honor, and faithfully serve the power that hath carried fire and sword into your land? If you cannot do all these, then are you only deceiving yourselves, and by your delay bringing ruin upon posterity. Your future connection with Britain, whom you can neither love nor honor, will be forced and unnatural, and being formed only on the plan of present convenience, will in a little time fall into a relapse more wretched than the first. But if you say, you can still pass the violations over, then I ask, hath your house been burnt? Hath your property been destroyed before your face? Are your wife and children destitute of a bed to lie on, or bread to live on? Have you lost a parent or a child by their hands, and yourself the ruined and wretched survivor? If you have not, then are you not a judge of those who have. But if you have, and can still shake hands with the murderers, then are you unworthy the name of husband, father, friend, or lover, and whatever may be your rank or title in life, you have the heart of a coward, and the spirit of a sycophant.

. . .

But the most powerful of all arguments is, that nothing but independence, *i.e.* a Continental form of government, can keep the peace of the Continent and preserve it inviolate from civil wars. I dread the event of a reconciliation with Britain now, as it is more than probable that it will be followed by a revolt somewhere or other, the consequences of which may be far more fatal than all the malice of Britain.

. . .

Where there are no distinctions there can be no superiority; perfect equality affords no temptation. The Republics of Europe are all (and we may say always) in peace. Holland and Switzerland are without wars, foreign or domestic: Monarchical governments, it is true, are never long at rest: the crown itself is a temptation to enterprising ruffians at home; and that degree of pride and insolence ever attendant on regal authority, swells into a rupture with foreign powers in instances where a republican government, by being formed on more natural principles, would negotiate the mistake.

. . .

A government of our own is our natural right: and when a man seriously reflects on the precariousness of human affairs, he will become convinced, that it is infinitely wiser and safer, to form a constitution of our own in a cool deliberate manner, while we have it in our power, than to trust such an interesting event to time and chance. If we omit it now, some Massanello may hereafter arise, who, laying hold of popular disquietudes, may collect together the desperate and the discontented, and by assuming to themselves the powers of government, finally sweep away the liberties of the Continent like a deluge. Should the government of America return again into the hands of Britain, the tottering situation of things will be a temptation for some desperate adventurer to try his fortune; and in such a case, what relief can Britain give? Ere she could hear the news, the fatal business might be done; and ourselves suffering like the wretched Britons under the oppression of the Conqueror. Ye that oppose independence now, ye know not what ye do: ye are opening a door to eternal tyranny, by keeping vacant the seat of government. There are thousands and tens of thousands, who would think it glorious to expel from the Continent, that barbarous and hellish power, which hath stirred up the Indians and the Negroes to destroy us; the cruelty hath a double guilt, it is dealing brutally by us, and treacherously by them.

To talk of friendship with those in whom our reason forbids us to have faith, and our affections wounded thro' a thousand pores instruct us to detest, is madness and folly. Every day wears out the little remains of kindred between us and them; and can there be any reason to hope, that as the relationship expires, the affection will increase, or that we shall agree better when we have ten times more and greater concerns to quarrel over than ever?

You that tell us of harmony and reconciliation, can ye restore to us the time that is past? Can you give to prostitution its former innocence? Neither can ye reconcile Britain and America. The last cord now is broken, the people of England are presenting addresses against us. There are injuries which nature cannot forgive; she would cease to be nature if she did. As well can the lover forgive the ravisher of his mistress, as the Continent forgive the murders of Britain. The Almighty hath implanted in us these inextinguishable feelings for good and wise purposes. They are the Guardians of his Image in our hearts. They distinguish us from the herd of common animals. The social compact would dissolve, and justice be extirpated from the earth, or have only a casual existence were we callous to the touches of affection. The robber and the murderer would often escape unpunished, did not the injuries which our tempers sustain, provoke us into justice.

O! ye that love mankind! Ye that dare oppose not only the tyranny but the tyrant, stand forth! Every spot of the old world is overrun with oppression. Freedom hath been hunted round the Globe. Asia and Africa have long expelled her. Europe regards her like a stranger, and England hath given her warning to depart. O! receive the fugitive, and prepare in time an asylum for mankind.

. . .

III. CITIZENSHIP AND COMMUNITY

Major Developments

- The formation of separate colonies under British authority
- The grounding of political communities in consent of the governed
- The formation of factions within the colonies

The colonists were all the subjects of the British Crown, which claimed sovereignty over the colonies until the end of the American Revolution. Judge Edward Coke had declared in 1608 that anyone "born within the King's power or protection, is no Alien."[2] The colonists were English by birthright.

But the political and social foundations for the society that was being carved out of the North American wilderness could not always be taken for granted. Many of the colonists had emigrated from England in order to start a new life, free from the restrictions and burdens that limited them back home. Upon his arrival in America, Massachusetts Governor John Winthrop reminded his fellow colonists that although they might have their differences, they should stand united by "bonds of brotherly affection."[3] They would have to huddle together for protection and safety and sacrifice for each other in order to secure the success of the whole.

Winthrop's call for unity was not always easy to realize in practice. Winthrop himself battled dissenters from his administration of the Massachusetts Bay Colony and from the version of Puritanism that the Massachusetts leadership endorsed, eventually splintering New England into separate colonies. As the decades wore on, leadership struggles erupted across the colonies, sometimes dividing the political elite into separate camps. Ideologically driven political parties were largely unknown in the colonies, but parties or factions organized around personalities and patronage were common. As tensions with England grew in the mid-eighteenth century, the colonists began to question the degree to which they formed a single community with the distant motherland. Political and social authority could not be taken for granted, and the foundations of a well-ordered society sometimes seemed under siege.

2 *Calvin's Case*, 7 Co. Rep. 25a (1608).
3 John Winthrop, "A Modell of Christian Charity" (1630).

MAYFLOWER COMPACT (1620)

The Mayflower Compact was signed aboard the ship *Mayflower* by the heads of the households that were traveling to settle in the New World. The ship had originally been destined for Virginia, which already had a locally elected assembly and a royal charter, and where the Pilgrims had been authorized to settle. The *Mayflower* was forced by bad weather to make port in Massachusetts, however, and the passengers decided to make a "covenant" among themselves to establish a civil government in the new territory. The Compact was the first colonial charter to be written by the colonists themselves and helped launch a largely self-governing colony in New England.

How does the Mayflower Compact differ from a constitution? What bases for political authority are implied by the Compact? Why make a covenant at all? Is the Compact a sufficient basis on which to form a society and government and settle the new territory in New England? Could a signer of the Compact reasonably refuse to obey future colonial directives or contribute to colonial projects in the future? Is a signer of the Compact positioned any differently relative to the community and the government than a passenger who refused to sign? What rights and duties would a non-signer have in the Plymouth colony? Should the settlers who arrived on the ship *Fortune* in 1621 been asked to sign the Compact as well?

In the name of God, Amen. We whose names are under-written, the loyal subjects of our dread sovereign Lord, King James, by the grace of God, of Great Britain, France, and Ireland King, Defender of the Faith, etc.

Having undertaken, for the glory of God, and advancement of the Christian faith, and honor of our King and Country, a voyage to plant the first colony in the northern parts of Virginia, do by these presents solemnly and mutually, in the presence of God, and one of another, covenant and combine our selves together into a civil body politic, for our better ordering and preservation and furtherance of the ends aforesaid; and by virtue hereof to enact, constitute, and frame such just and equal laws, ordinances, acts, constitutions and offices, from time to time, as shall be thought most meet and convenient for the general good of the Colony, unto which we promise all due submission and obedience.

In witness whereof we have hereunder subscribed our names at Cape Cod, the eleventh of November, in the year of the reign of our sovereign lord, King James, of England, France, and Ireland, the eighteenth, and of Scotland the fifty-fourth. Anno Dom. 1620.

JONATHAN MAYHEW

A DISCOURSE CONCERNING UNLIMITED SUBMISSION AND NON-RESISTANCE TO THE HIGHER POWERS (1750)

By the 1750s, Jonathan Mayhew was a prominent Boston minister. He preached a number of influential political sermons, and he was an early advocate of American colonial rights against the British government. On the hundredth anniversary of the execution of King Charles I, Mayhew delivered this sermon on "unlimited submission." Resisting efforts by monarchists to portray Charles as a martyr, Mayhew insisted that Charles had been a tyrant and that his violation of traditional English liberties justified rebellion and the king's eventual execution. The sermon was reprinted in both America and London and widely read, and he frequently found himself in political and theological controversies with his fellow ministers in both countries. He continued to preach against British tyranny throughout his tenure at Boston's West Church. He was credited with inciting riots against the Stamp Act in 1765. He died at a relatively young age in 1766.

What is the target of Mayhew's sermon? Does Christianity require unlimited submission to civil government? Does Christianity require that its believers refuse to submit at all to civil government? Under what conditions is resistance to government an affront to God? Does Mayhew's analysis of the duties of submission depend on what form government takes, whether it is monarchical or republican? What are the obligations of a political subject or citizen?

Rom. XIII. 1, 8.

1. Let every soul be subject unto the higher powers. For there is no power but of God; the powers that be, are ordained by God.
2. Whoever therefore resisteth the power, resisteth the ordinance of God; and they that resist, shall receive to themselves damnation.
3. For rulers are not a terror to good works, but to the evil. Will thou then not be afraid of the power? Do that which is good, and thou shalt have praise of the same.
4. For he is the minister of God to thee for good. But if thou do that which is evil, be afraid; for he beareth not the sword in vain. For he is the minister of God, a revenger to execute wrath upon him that doth evil.
5. Wherefore ye must needs be subject, not only for wrath, but also for conscience sake.
6. For, for this cause pay you tribute also: for they are God's ministers, attending continually upon this very thing.
7. Render therefore to all their dues: tribute to whom tribute is due; custom, to whom custom; fear, to whom fear; honor to whom honor.

It is evident that the affair of civil government may properly fall under a moral and religious consideration, at least so far forth as it relates to the general nature and end of magistracy and to the grounds and extent of that submission which persons of a private character ought to yield to those who are vested with authority. This must be allowed by all who acknowledge the divine original of Christianity. For although there be a sense, and a very plain and important sense, in which Christ's *kingdom is not of this world*, his inspired apostles have, nevertheless, laid down some general principles concerning the office of civil rulers and the duty of subjects, together with the reason and obligation of that duty. . . .

The Apostle's doctrine . . . may be summed up in the following observations, viz.

That the end of magistracy is the good of civil society, *as such*:

That civil rulers, as such, are the ordinance and ministers of God, it being by his permission and providence that any bear rule, and agreeable to his will that there should be *some persons* vested with authority in society, for the well-being of it.

That which is here said concerning civil rulers extends to all of them in common: it relates indifferently to monarchical, republican, and aristocratical government, and to all other forms which truly answer the sole end of government, the happiness of society; and to all the different degrees of authority in any particular state, to inferior officers no less than to the supreme.

That disobedience to civil rulers in the due exercise of their authority is not merely a *political sin* but an heinous *offense against God and religion*.

That the true ground and reason of our obligation to be subject to the higher powers is the usefulness of magistracy (when properly exercised) to human society and its subservience to the general welfare.

That obedience to civil rulers is here equally required under all forms of government which answer the sole end of all government, the good of society; and to every degree of authority in any state, whether supreme or subordinate.

(From whence it follows, That if unlimited obedience and non-resistance, be here required as a duty under any one form of government, it is also required as a duty under all other forms; and as a duty to subordinate rulers as well as to the supreme.)

And lastly, that those civil rulers to whom the Apostle enjoins subjection are the persons *in possession; the powers that be*, those who are actually vested with authority.

There is one very important and interesting point which remains to be inquired into; namely, the *extent* of that subjection *to the higher powers* which is here enjoined as a duty upon all Christians. Some have thought it warrantable and glorious to disobey the civil powers in certain circumstances, and, in cases of very great and general oppression when humble remonstrances fail of having any effect, and when the public welfare cannot be otherwise provided for and secured, to rise unanimously even against the sovereign himself in order to redress their grievances, to vindicate their natural and legal rights, to break the yoke of tyranny, and free themselves and posterity from inglorious servitude and ruin. It is upon this principle that many royal oppressors have been driven from their thrones into banishment, and many slain by the hands of their subjects. . . . But, in opposition to this principle, it has often been asserted that the Scripture in general (and the passage under consideration in particular) makes all resistance to princes a crime, in any case whatever.—If they turn tyrants and become the common oppressors of those whose welfare they ought to regard with a paternal affection, we must not pretend to right ourselves unless it be by prayers and tears and humble entreaties; and if these methods fail of procuring redress we must not have recourse to any other, but all suffer ourselves to be robbed and butchered at the pleasure of the *Lord's anointed*, lest we should incur the sin of rebellion and the punishment of damnation. For he has God's authority and commission to bear him out in the worst of crimes, so far that he may not be withstood or controlled. Now whether we are obliged to yield such an absolute submission to our prince, or whether disobedience and resistance may not be justifiable in some cases notwithstanding anything in the passage before us, is an inquiry in which we are all concerned; and this is the inquiry which is the main design of the present discourse.

Now there does not seem to be any necessity of supposing that an absolute, unlimited obedience, whether active or passive, is here enjoined merely for this reason, that the precept is delivered in *absolute terms*, without any *exception* or *limitation* expressly mentioned. We are enjoined (ver. I) to be *subject to the higher powers*, and (ver. 5) to be *subject for conscience sake*. And because these expressions are absolute and unlimited (or, more properly, general), some have inferred that the subjection required in them must be absolute and unlimited also, at least so far forth as to make passive obedience and nonresistance a duty in all cases whatever, if not active obedience likewise. Though, by the way, there is here no distinction made betwixt active and passive obedience; and if either of them be required in an unlimited sense, the other must be required in the same sense also by virtue of the present argument, because the expressions are equally absolute with respect to both. But that unlimited obedience of any sort cannot be argued merely from the indefinite expressions in which obedience is enjoined appears from hence, that expressions of the same nature frequently occur in Scripture, upon which it is confessed on all hands that no such absolute and unlimited sense ought to be put. For example, *Love not the world; neither the things that are in the world. Lay not up for yourselves treasures upon earth; Take therefore no thought for the morrow*; are precepts expressed in at least equally absolute and unlimited terms: but it is generally allowed that they are to be understood with certain restrictions and limitations, some degree of love to the world and the things of it being allowable. Nor, indeed, do the *Right Reverend Fathers in God* and other *dignified clergymen* of the established church seem to be altogether averse to admitting of restrictions in the latter case, how warm sever any of them may be against restrictions and limitations in the case of submission to authority, whether civil or ecclesiastical. It is worth remarking, also, that patience and submission under private injuries are enjoined in much more peremptory and absolute terms than any that are used with regard to submission to the injustice and oppression of civil rulers. Thus, *I say unto you, that ye resist not evil; but whosoever shall smite thee on the right cheek, turn to him the other also. And if any man will sue thee at the law, and take away thy coat, let him have thy cloak also. And whosoever shall compel thee to go a mile with him, go with him twain*. Any man may be defied to produce such strong expressions in favor of a passive and tame submission to unjust, tyrannical rulers as are here used to enforce submission to private injuries. But how few are there that understand those expressions literally? And the reason why they do not is because (with submission to the *Quakers*) common sense shows that they were not intended to be so understood.

. . .

There is, indeed, one passage in the New Testament where it may seem, at first view, that an unlimited submission to civil rulers is enjoined: *Submit yourselves to every ordinance of man for the Lord's sake.—To every ordinance of man*.—However, this expression is no stronger than that before taken notice of with relation to the duty of wives: *So let thine wives be subject to their own husbands*—IN EVERYTHING. But the true solution of this difficulty (if it be one) is *this*: by *every ordinance of man* is not meant every command of the civil magistrate without exception, *but every order of magistrates appointed by man, whether superior or inferior*; for so the Apostle explains himself in the very next words: *Whether it be to the king as supreme, or to governors, as unto then that are sent*, etc. But although the Apostle had not subjoined any such explanation, the reason of the thing itself would have obliged us to limit the expression *every ordinance of man* to such human ordinances and commands as are not inconsistent with the ordinances and commands of God, the supreme lawgiver, or with any other higher and antecedent obligations.

. . .

And if we attend to the nature of the argument with which the Apostle here enforces the duty of submission to *the higher powers*, we shall find it to be such an one as concludes not in favor of submission to all who bear the *title* of rulers in common, but only to those who *actually* perform the duty of rulers by exercising a reasonable and just authority for the good of human society. . . .

. . .

. . . It is obvious, then, in general that the civil rulers whom the Apostle here speaks of, and obedience to whom he presses upon Christians as a duty, are *good rulers*; such as are, in the exercise of their office and power, benefactors to society. Such they are described to be throughout this passage. Thus it is said that they are not a *terror to good works but to the evil*; that they are *God's ministers for good, revengers to execute wrath upon him that doth evil; and that they attend continually upon this very thing*. St. Peter gives the same account of rulers they are *for a praise to them that do well, and the punishment of evildoers*. It is manifest that this character and description of rulers agrees only to such as are rulers in fact as well as in name to such as govern well and act agreeably to their office. And the Apostle's argument for submission to rulers is wholly built and grounded upon a presumption that they do in fact answer this character, and is of no force at all upon supposition to the contrary. *If rulers are a terror to good works and not to the evil; if they are not ministers for good to society* but for evil and distress by violence and oppression; if they *execute wrath upon* sober, peaceable persons who do their duty as members of society, and suffer rich and honorable knaves to escape with impunity; if, instead of *attending continually upon* the good work of advancing the public welfare, they *attend* only upon the gratification of their own lust and pride and ambition to the destruction of the public welfare—if this be the case, it is plain that the Apostle's argument for submission does not reach them; they are not the same but different persons from those whom he characterizes and who must be obeyed according to his reasoning. . . . If those who bear the title of civil rulers do not perform the duty of civil rulers but act directly counter to the sole end and design of their office; if they injure and oppress their subjects instead of defending their rights doing them good, they have not the least pretense to be honored, obeyed, and rewarded according to the Apostle's argument. For his reasoning, in order to show the duty of subjection to the *higher powers*, is, as was before observed, built wholly upon the supposition that they do *in fact* perform the duty of rulers.

. . .

I now add, farther, that the Apostle's argument is so far from proving it to be the duty of people to obey and submit to such rulers as act in contradiction to the public good and so to the design of their office, that it proves *the direct contrary*. For, please to observe, that if the end of all civil government be the good of society, if this be the thing that is aimed at in constituting civil rulers, and if the motive and argument for submission to government be taken from the apparent usefulness of civil authority, it follows that when no such good end can be answered by submission there remains no argument or motive to enforce it; and if instead of this good end's being brought about by submission, a *contrary end* is brought about and the ruin and misery of society effected by it, here is a plain and positive reason against submission in all such cases, should they ever happen. And therefore, in such cases a regard to the public welfare ought to make us withhold from our rulers that obedience and subjection which it would, otherwise, be our duty to render to them. If it be our duty, for example, to obey our King merely for this reason, that he rules for the public welfare (which is the only argument the Apostle makes use of, it follows by a parity of reason that when he turns tyrant and makes his subjects his prey to devour and to destroy instead of his charge to defend and cherish, we are bound to throw of our allegiance to him and to resist, and that according to the tenor of the Apostle's argument in this passage. Not to discontinue our allegiance, in this case, would be to join with the sovereign in promoting the slavery and misery of that society the welfare of which we ourselves as well as our sovereign are indispensably obliged to secure and promote as far as in us lies. It is true the Apostle puts no case of such a tyrannical prince; but by his grounding his argument for submission wholly upon the good of civil society it is plain he implicitly authorizes and even requires us to make resistance whenever this shall be necessary to the public safety and happiness. Let me make use of this easy and familiar *similitude* to illustrate the point in hand. Suppose God requires a family of children to obey their father and not to resist him, and enforces his command with this argument that the superintendence and care and authority of a just and kind parent will contribute to the happiness of the whole family so that they ought to obey him for their own sakes more than for his. Suppose this parent at length runs distracted, and attempts, in his mad fit, to cut all his children's throats. Now, in this case, is not the reason before assigned why these children should obey their parent while he continued of a sound mind, namely, *their common good*, a reason equally conclusive for disobeying and resisting him since he is become delirious and attempts their ruin? It makes no alteration in the argument, whether this parent properly speaking loses his reason, or does, while he retains his understanding, that which is as fatal in its consequences as anything he could do were he really deprived of it. This similitude needs no formal application. . . .

Thus it appears that the common argument, grounded upon this passage, in favor of universal and passive obedience really overthrows itself by proving too much, if it proves anything at all; namely, that no civil officer is, in any case whatever, to be resisted, though acting in express contradiction to the design of his office; which no man in his senses ever did or can assert.

If we calmly consider the nature of the thing itself, nothing can well be imagined more directly contrary to common sense than to suppose that *millions* of people should be subjected to the arbitrary, precarious pleasure of *one single man* (who has *naturally* no superiority over them in point of authority) so that their estates, and everything that is valuable in life, and even their lives also shall be absolutely at his disposal, if he happens to be wanton and capricious enough to demand them. "What unprejudiced man can think that God made ALL to be thus subservient to the lawless pleasure and frenzy of ONE so that it shall always be a sin to resist him! Nothing but the most plain and express revelation from Heaven could make a sober impartial man believe such a monstrous, unaccountable doctrine; and, indeed, the thing itself appears so shocking—so out of all *proportion*, that it may be questioned whether all the *miracles* that ever were wrought could make it credible that this doctrine *really* came from God. At present, there is not the least syllable in Scripture which gives any countenance to it. The hereditary, indefeasible, divine right of kings, and the doctrine of nonresistance, which is built" upon the supposition of such a right, are altogether as fabulous and chimerical as transubstantiation or any of the most absurd reveries of ancient or modern visionaries. These notions are fetched neither from divine revelation nor human reason; and if they are derived from neither of those sources, it is not much matter from *whence they come, or hither they go*. Only it is a pity that such doctrines should be propagated in society, to raise factions and rebellions, as we see they have in fact been, both in the *last* and in the present REIGN.

. . . We may very safely assert these two things in general without undermining government: One is that no civil rulers are to be obeyed when they enjoin things that are inconsistent with the commands of God. All such disobedience is lawful and glorious, particularly if persons refuse to comply with any *legal establishment of religion*, because it is a gross perversion and corruption (as to doctrine, worship, and discipline) of a pure and divine religion brought from heaven to earth by the *Son of God* (the only King and Head of the *Christian* church) and propagated through the world by his inspired apostles. All commands running counter to the declared will of the Supreme Legislator of heathen and earth are null and void: and therefore disobedience to them is a duty, not a crime. Another thing that may be asserted with equal truth and safety is that no government is to be submitted to at the *expense* of that which is the *sole end* of all government the common good and safety of society. Because to submit in this case, if it should ever happen, would evidently be to set up the *means* as more valuable and above the *end*, than which there cannot be a greater solecism and contradiction. The only reason of the institution of civil government, and the only rational ground of submission to it, is the common safety and utility. If, therefore, in any case the common safety and utility would not be promoted by submission to government but the contrary, there is no ground or motive for obedience and submission, but for the contrary.

Whoever considers the nature of civil government must, indeed, be sensible that a great degree of *implicit confidence* must unavoidably be placed in those that bear rule. This is implied in the very notion of authority's being originally a trust, committed by the people to those who are vested with it as all just and righteous authority is; all besides is mere lawless force and usurpation, neither God nor nature having given any man a right of dominion over any society independently of that society's approbation and consent to be governed by him—Now as all men are fallible it cannot be supposed that the public affairs of any state should be always administered in the best manner possible, even by persons of the greatest wisdom and integrity. Nor is it sufficient to legitimate disobedience to the *higher* powers that they are not so administered, or that they are in some instances very ill-managed; for upon this principle it is scarcely supposable that any government at all could be supported or subsist. Such a principle manifestly tends to the dissolution of government, and to throw all things into confusion and anarchy—But it is equally evident, upon the other hand, that those in authority may abuse their *trust* and power *to such a degree* that neither the law of reason nor of religion requires that any obedience or submission should be paid to them; but, on the contrary, that they should be totally *discarded* and the authority which they were before vested with transferred to others, who may exercise it more to those good purposes for which it is given. Nor is this principle, that resistance to the *higher powers* is, in some extraordinary cases, justifiable, so liable to abuse as many persons seem to apprehend it. For although there will be always some petulant, querulous men in every state—men of factious, turbulent, and carping dispositions—glad to lay hold of any trifle to justify and legitimate their caballing against their rulers and other seditious practices; yet there are, comparatively speaking, but few men of this *contemptible character*. It does not appear but that mankind ill general have a disposition to be as submissive and passive and tame under government as they ought to be—witness a great, if not the greatest, part of the known world, who are now groaning, but not murmuring, under the heavy yoke of tyranny! While those who govern do it with any tolerable degree of moderation and justice and, in any good measure, act up to their office and character by being public benefactors, the people will generally be easy and peaceable, and be rather inclined to flatter and adore than to insult and resist them. Nor was there ever any *general* complaint against any administration *which lasted long* but what there was good reason for. Till people find themselves greatly abused and oppressed by their governors, they are not apt to complain; and whenever they do, in fact, find themselves thus abused and oppressed, they must be stupid not to complain. To say that subjects in general are not proper judges when their governors oppress them and play the tyrant and when they defend their rights, administer justice impartially, and promote the public welfare, is as great *treason* as ever man uttered 'tis treason not against one *single* man but the state—against the whole body politic; 'tis treason against mankind; 'tis treason against common sense; 'tis treason against God. And this impious principle lays the foundation for justifying all the tyranny and oppression that ever any prince was guilty of. The people know for what end they set up and maintain their go errors; and they are the proper judges when they execute their *trust* as they ought to do it—when their prince exercises an equitable and paternal authority over them; when from a prince and common father he exalts himself into a tyrant; when from subjects and children he degrades them into the class of slaves, plunders them makes them his prey, and unnaturally sports himself with their lives and fortunes.

. . .

To conclude, Let us all learn to be *free* and to be *loyal*. Let us not profess ourselves vassals to the lawless pleasure of any man on earth. But let us remember, at the same time, government is sacred and not to be *trifled* with. It is our happiness to live under the government of a PRINCE who is satisfied with ruling according to law, as every other *good prince* will. We enjoy under his administration all the liberty that is proper and expedient for us. It becomes us, therefore, to be contented and dutiful subjects. Let us prize our freedom but not *use our liberty for a cloak of maliciousness*. There are men who strike at *liberty* under the term *licentiousness*. There are others who aim at *popularity* under the disguise of *patriotism*. Be aware of both. *Extremes* are dangerous. There is at present amongst *us*, perhaps, more danger of the *latter* than of the *former*. For which reason I would exhort you to pay all due regard to the government over us, to the KING and all in authority, and to lead a *quiet and peaceable* life. And while I am speaking of loyalty to our *earthly prince*, suffer me just to put you in mind to be loyal also to the supreme RULER of the universe, *by whom kings reign and princes decree justice*. To which King eternal, immortal, invisible, even to the ONLY WISE GOD be all honor and praise, DOMINION and thanksgiving, through JESUS CHRIST our LORD. AMEN.

WILLIAM LIVINGSTON

OF PARTY DIVISIONS (1753)

The precocious William Livingston graduated from Yale University at the early age of eighteen and apprenticed with one of the leading lawyers in New York. For a single year he published a highly influential weekly magazine on politics and society, *The Independent Reflector*, until one of the political figures he skewered had it shut down. By the time of the American Revolution, Livingston had moved to New Jersey and served in the Continental Congress. He left military service with the New Jersey militia to become the wartime governor of the state. Near the end of his life, he led the New Jersey delegation to the federal constitutional convention, where he advocated for the interest of the small states. His essay on party divisions reflected an eighteenth-century hostility to parties, or factions. At this point, parties primarily referred to coalitions of elite political actors, rather than the mass political parties that emerged to mobilize voters a century later, but these divisions were often seen as subversive of public virtue and threatening to the public welfare.

What reasons does Livingston offer for opposing party divisions? What does he see as the primary alternative to party spirit? Is there a tension between the majority of his essay and his last paragraph? How can they be reconciled? Should we be equally distrustful of political parties? Do his concerns still ring true? Are parties necessarily divisive? Do they necessarily seek the partial, rather than the common, good?

. . .

From the moment that Men give themselves wholly up to a party, they abandon their *reason*, and are led captive by their *passions*. The cause they espouse, presents such bewitching charms, as dazzle the judgment; and the side they oppose, such imaginary deformity, that no opposition appears too violent; nor any arts to blacken and ruin it, incapable of a specious varnish. They follow their leaders with an implicit faith, and, like a company of dragoons, obey the word of command without hesitation. Though perhaps they originally embarked in the cause with a view to the public welfare; the calm deliberation of reason are imperceptibly fermented into passion; and their zeal for the common good, gradually extinguished by the predominant fervor of faction. A disinterested love for their country, is succeeded by an intemperate ardor; which naturally swells into a political enthusiasm; and from that, easy is the transition to perfect frenzy. As the religious enthusiast fathers the wild ravings of his heated imagination, on the spirit of God; and is ready to knock down every man who doubts his divine inspiration; so the political visionary miscalls his party-rage the perfection of patriotism; and curses the rational lover of his country, for his unseasonable tepidity. The former may be reduced to his senses, by shaving, purging, and letting of blood; as the latter is only to be reclaimed by time or preferment.

Next to the duty we owe the Supreme Being, we lie under the most indispensable obligation, to promote the welfare of our country. Nor ought we to be destitute of a becoming zeal and fortitude, in so glorious a cause. We should show ourselves in earnest, resolute and intrepid. We cannot engage in a nobler undertaking; and scandalous would be our languor and timidity, where the sacrifice of our lives, is no extravagant oblation. . . . But in vain does party-spirit veil itself with the splendid covering, of disinterested patriotism. In vain usurp the robe of honor, to conceal its latent motives. The disguise may fascinate the multitude; but appears transparent to the unprejudiced and judicious. . . .

When I see a man warm in so important an affair as the common interest, I either suspend my judgment, or pass it in his favor. But when I find him misrepresenting and vilifying his adversaries, I take it for a shrewd sign, that 'tis something more than the laudable motive he pretends, which impels him with such impetuosity and violence.

. . .

A man of this turn, is not half so intent upon reforming the abuses of his own party, as discerning the errors of his enemies. To view the virtues of the side he espouses, he uses the magnifying end of the perspective; but inverts the tube, when he surveys those of his adversaries. Instead of an impartial examination of the principles he acts upon, or the regularity of his progress, he contents himself with exclaiming against the real or suppositious faults of his antagonists. In short, 'tis not so much the goodness of his own cause, as the exaggerated badness of the other, that attaches him to his leaders, and confirms him in his delirium. Like a set of pagans, he makes the spots in the sun, a reason for adoring the moon.

. . .

. . . Unspeakably calamitous have been the consequences of party divisions. It has occasioned deluges of blood, and subverted kingdoms. It always introduces a decay of public spirit, with the extinction of every noble and generous sentiment. The very names of things are perverted. . . .

. . .

[A]s the designing party man always appears in the mask of public spirit conceals the most selfish and riotous disposition, under the venerable pretext of asserting liberty, and defending his country; so the ministerial scribbler, taking advantage of this frequent prostitution, gives a sinister turn to the most laudable views, and stigmatizes every man who opposes the encroachments of the Court. Hence the necessity of our greatest caution in siding either party, till by a watchful observation in the conduct of both, we have plainly discovered the true patriot from the false pretender.

. . .

. . . To conclude, should a future governor give into measures subversive of our liberties, I hope he will meet with proper opposition and control. But should a faction be formed against him, without law or reason, may the authors be branded with suitable infamy.

IV. EQUALITY AND STATUS

Major Developments

- The establishment of African-American slavery in the colonies
- The rise of antislavery sentiment
- Popular challenges to elite rule

Colonial Americans were familiar with inequality. Women were legally, socially, and economically distinguished from men. Native Americans were understood to exist outside the society created by the Europeans in a quasi-state of nature. Africans had been brought to British North America in chains and were kept in a distinct form of servitude. Some men and families were fabulously wealthy, owning vast tracts of land and operating flourishing businesses. Others occupied a lower social, economic, and legal status. In some cases, membership in favored churches carried political rights that were denied to those of different faiths.

At the same time, the colonies held open the promise of extraordinary upward mobility. The colonists had fled European societies riven by sharp religious cleavages, rigid class structures, and sometimes desperate economic conditions. In America, land was plentiful, geographic mobility was possible, and class structures were fluid. Religious dissenters, social reformers, and political leaders were often willing to challenge traditional assumptions about how society should be organized.

The revolutionary period of the 1760s and 1770s was a particularly turbulent time for the inherited social order. Arguments about natural rights and philosophical first principles called into question the significance of tradition, social convention, and long-settled political arrangements. Revolutionary leaders sought to justify their actions, and their personal status as new political leaders, by making new appeals to the fundamental political and legal equality of men. The colonists, they insisted, were the equals to any English subject. Local popular leaders were as good as the British elite. Conservatives feared that revolutionary ideas were threatening to break down the social order and throw the colonies into social, as well as political, anarchy. Some reformers sought to push ideas of equality farther than many revolutionary leaders were prepared to go.

William Henry Drayton and Jonathan Boucher reflected those more conservative sensibilities. To them, claims of natural equality were calling into question the kind of political and social authority that was necessary to maintain a smooth-functioning society—and ultimately liberty itself. The petition of a group of Massachusetts slaves illustrates more radical opinions. The Quakers had long argued for the natural equality of man and the implication that slavery was immoral. The Revolution encouraged some to amplify that message.

WILLIAM HENRY DRAYTON

THE LETTERS OF FREEMAN (1769)

William Henry Drayton was a conservative lawyer and plantation owner in South Carolina. As a young lawyer, he published a series of essays under the pseudonym "Freeman" protesting against the American agitation over Parliamentary taxes. Like many Loyalists, he denounced the patriots as mere partisans and frustrated office seekers hoping to shift government policy to benefit themselves. His loyalty was rewarded with a gubernatorial appointment to the upper house in the South Carolina colony. Just a few years later, he was horrified by what he took to be British overreaching in Massachusetts in the 1770s and joined the patriots in denouncing the English government with another letter from Freeman addressed to the Continental Congress. He joined the revolutionary government in the colony and became the chief justice of the state Supreme Court during the war and served in the Continental Congress. He died while serving in that office in Philadelphia. The later Freeman letters enumerated the violations of traditional English liberties that were taking place in the colonies. The early letters objected to the popular call for a boycott on British goods and the public ostracism of those who did not comply. Drayton insisted that his political scruples would not be bound by mob rule.

Is there education or training that is particularly valuable for making public policy? Is there a virtue to our legislatures being more populated by lawyers than plumbers? Is there a problem with self-appointed popular "committees" announcing rules that are to be enforced through shaming and boycotts? Is a popular committee calling for trade boycotts consistent with the authority and legitimacy of an elected legislature endorsing the continuation of such trade? Is there any rule that a popular committee could not legitimately make and try to enforce through private action? In what sense were Drayton's "rights" violated by being named as unpatriotic and being made the subject of a secondary boycott?

. . .

The *profanum vulgus* [vulgar mob], is a species of mankind which I respect as I ought,—it is *humani generis* [the human race]. But, I see no reason, why I should allow my opinion to be controlled by theirs. I think, I am at least as capable to think and judge for myself, as those gentry are for themselves. And I must further say, that I will admit of no encroachments upon my rights.

A man, who can "boast of having received a liberal education," and men who have read a little, whether their knowledge is acquired from compendiums, or the embellishments of a map, it matters not; I say, I think such men should make a proper use of such advantages, and not have consulted *de arduis reipublicae* [about difficult public affairs], with men who never were in a way to study, or to advise upon any points, but rules how to cut up a beast in the market to the best advantage, to cobble an old shoe in the nearest manner, or to build a necessary house. Nature never intended that such men should be profound politicians, or able statesmen; and unless a man makes a proper use of his reading, he is but upon a level with those who never did read. From which reasoning I conclude, that in point of knowledge, all the members of the committee are upon a level with each other. A learned body of statesmen truly! Will a man in his right senses, be directed by an illiterate person in the persecution of a lawsuit? Or, when a ship is in a storm, and near the rocks, who, but a fool, would put the helm into the hand of a landsman?

Having delivered some of my sentiments, concerning the above committee of respectable and learned personages, I shall now touch upon their proceedings; pull the masks from their faces; and see what kind of figures they will then cut. This treatment, I suppose, will occasion one to hang his lip, another to take a pinch of snuff, not knowing where to look or what to say in their vindication, and every one to buzz this review of their conduct like wasps, because I attack them in return, for their having taken liberties with me, contrary to all right and justice. In these cases I am no respecter of persons.

. . .

This committee has violated the first principles of liberty. Its members act in a despotic and unjust manner. They have, agreeable to the constitution, exercised a liberty to do, or not to do, the act of signing the resolution. But they have exercised that liberty in a selfish manner; for they have assumed a power, unknown to the constitution, to compel great numbers, and to endeavor to intimidate freemen, to make a painful surrender of that liberty and right, which they themselves have exercised in the most ample manner, the liberty and right of thinking, judging, and acting for themselves. Have not I a right of liberty in this country, equal to the right of any one man in it? Have I committed any act against the laws of the land, to forfeit my birthright? . . . And, because I exercise my liberty, agreeable to the constitution of my country, must my name be printed and dispersed through *North America*, with designs to prejudice my countrymen against me?

If these proceedings are not arbitrary and unjust, I confess, that I am ignorant of the idea which those epithets convey. Is this a land of liberty? Who ought to be called lovers of liberty? Those who violate its first principles? Or those who religiously maintain them?

. . .

The industrious mechanic, I always considered as a useful and necessary part of society; so necessary, that a society cannot subsist without that class of people. But, friends! Every man to his trade: a carpenter would find himself somewhat at a loss in handling a smith's tools, and he would find himself but in an awkward situation upon a cobbler's bench. When a man acts in his own sphere, he is useful in the community, but when he steps out of it, and sets up a for a statesman! Believe me, he is in a fair way to expose himself to ridicule, and his family to distress, by neglecting his private business. Such men are often converted into cat's paws, and made to serve a turn. I love my country! I have every inducement that any one man can have—But I venerate the constitution of my country; and to show that I do, I will always make the most vigorous efforts to exercise my liberty agreeable to the laws, notwithstanding any abuse which has been, or shall be thrown out against me. I will not be intimidated from my duty; and interest herself . . . shall not bribe me to a compliance to derogate from the dignity of the name, Freeman.

. . .

That body [the popular committee calling for a boycott] is, in effect, the legislative, whose rules and laws are put in execution, and required to be obeyed. When other laws are set up, and other rules pretended or enforced, than what the legislative, constituted by society, have enacted, it is plain that the legislative is changed. And, whoever introduces new laws, not being authorized by the fundamental appointment of the society; or subverts the old, disowns, and overturns the power by which they were made, and to set up a new legislative. . . .

. . .

. . . [The people] must grant, either that the general assembly, is still the supreme legislative; that, it is not lawful for the people to assume the reins of government, at this juncture; and therefore, that the last resolution, which subverted and invalidated the liberty allowed by general assembly, is illegal, and the authors thereof, guilty of a breach in the law; which is so far of a treasonable nature, as, that it tends to the subversion of a fundamental principle in the *British* constitution. Or, that the people, agreeable to revolution principles, have actually assumed to themselves, the supreme legislative proper, and therefore, that the last resolution is illegal, and of course, as the people are possessed of such supreme power, and to make a law, to invalidate a privilege allowed by general assembly, that the authority of that body is thereby annihilated, *in toto*.

. . .

SLAVES' PETITION TO MASSACHUSETTS GOVERNOR THOMAS GAGE (1774)

African slaves were introduced into the American colonies early in the seventeenth century. Many immigrants also arrived in the colonies as indentured servants, who had contracted for a period of labor to repay the debt from their Atlantic passage, but Africans were quickly differentiated from indentured servants and subjected to more onerous conditions of servitude that extended across their lives and extended to their children. By the end of the seventeenth century, slave labor had become an important aspect of the colonial economy and society, and their numbers grew rapidly over the course of the century. Though slavery extended across the British colonies, slaves were more numerous in the southern colonies.

Slavery was less prevalent in Massachusetts and New England than in more southern colonies, and free blacks were better positioned. In 1772, the King's Bench in England declared that chattel slavery was not consistent with the English common law and could only be supported by local statute. In 1783, Massachusetts became the only state to end slavery through judicial decision. As revolutionary fervor grew in the 1770s, slaves took note of the increased appeals to natural rights. With the elected legislature suspended in Massachusetts and British troops occupying Boston, a group of slaves directed an appeal to the English colonial governor, General Thomas Gage, asking for their general emancipation. Although the threat of emancipation was later made by British officials during the Revolutionary War, in 1774 Gage was not yet ready to issue such an emancipation proclamation.

What is the basis for the slaves' call for emancipation? How does their rhetoric compare with other political discourse of the period? Are their arguments more or less radical than the arguments made by the revolutionaries? What role does religion play in their argument? Does the petition reinforce the contention of some slaveholders that the slaves should not be converted to Christianity?

The Petition of a Great Number of Blacks of this Province who by Divine Permission are Held in a State of Slavery within the Bowels of a Free and Christian Country

Humbly showing

That your Petitioners apprehend we have in common with all other men a natural right to our freedoms without being deprived of them by our fellow men as we are a freeborn People and have never forfeited this Blessing by any compact or agreement whatever. But we were unjustly dragged by the cruel hand of power from our dearest friends, and some of us stolen from the bosoms of our tender parents and from a populous, pleasant and plentiful country, and brought here to be made slaves for life in a Christian land. Thus are we deprived of everything that has a tendency to make life even tolerable, the endearing ties of husband and wife we are strangers to [us], for we are no longer man and wife than our masters or mistresses think proper married or unmarried. Our children are also taken from us by force and sent many miles from us, where we seldom or ever see them again, there to be made slaves of for life, which sometimes is very short by reason of being dragged from their mother's breast. Thus, our lives are embittered to us on these accounts. By our deplorable situation we are rendered incapable of showing our obedience to Almighty God. How can a slave perform the duties of a husband to a wife or parent to his child? How can a husband leave master and work and cleave to his wife? How can the wife submit themselves to their husbands in all things? How can the child obey their parents in all things? There is a great number of us [who are] sincere . . . members of the Church of Christ. How can the master and the slave be said to fulfill that command "live in love, let brotherly love continue and abound, bear yea one another's burdens"? How can the master be said to bear my burden when he bears me down with the heavy chains of slavery and oppression against my will, and how can we fulfill our part of duty to him while in this condition, and as we cannot serve our God as we ought while in this situation. Neither can we reap an equal benefit from the law of the land, which does not justify but condemns slavery; or, if there had been any law to hold us in bondage, we are humbly of the opinion there never was any to enslave our children for life when born in a free country. We therefore beg your Excellency and Honors will give this its due weight and consideration, and that you will accordingly cause an act of the legislative to be passed that we may obtain our natural right [and] our freedoms, and our children be set at liberty at the year of twenty one for whose sakes more particularly your petitioners is in duty ever to pray.

*Similiar to John Lockes idea of a consensual centralized gov't

JONATHAN BOUCHER

ON CIVIL LIBERTY, PASSIVE OBEDIENCE, AND NON-RESISTANCE (1775)

A Loyalist, Jonathan Boucher used his post as an Anglican minister in Virginia and Maryland in the 1770s to urge his fellow Americans to try to resolve their grievances with Britain peacefully and, if their petitions for redress failed, to accept the inconvenience of a bad government policy patiently. With the outbreak of the American Revolution, Boucher fled to England (he delivered his final sermon in America with a pistol at hand). He later published his American sermons as a book dedicated to his friend, former President George Washington, who might, Boucher hoped, "train the people around you to a love of order and subordination; and, above all, to a love of peace." Boucher thought it was evident that the "American revolt" was triggered by trivial disagreements blown out of proportion by "partisans" and "conspirators" who wished to obtain political power for themselves and shed themselves of British debt. Boucher was horrified but not surprised that the "revolutionary spirit" was spreading beyond the American shores, which would be to the ultimate regret of those caught in the tumult. Boucher had preached obedience to the accepted order and acceptance of social and political hierarchies. Against those who argued for the fundamental equality of individuals, Boucher suggested that the world was always divided between those who would govern and those would be governed, and the belief in political equality only invited incessant discord.

How can we distinguish between utopian fantasies and credible efforts at change and reform? Is Boucher right to worry that revolutionary ideas cannot be readily contained and will tend to destabilize any government? What political disagreements would justify armed revolution? Were grievances over Parliamentary taxes on the North American colonies sufficient to justify war? Are potential revolutionaries liable to be too optimistic about the costs associated with mounting a rebellion? Are arguments about liberty and democracy just tools that would-be leaders use to gain political power?

Galatians, ch. V, ver. I. Stand fast, therefore, in the liberty wherewith Christ has made us free.

. . .

[T]here is a sense in which politics, properly understood, form an essential branch of Christian duty. These politics take in a very principal part, if not the whole, of the second table of the Decalogue, which contains our duty to our neighbor.

It is from this second table that the compilers of our Catechism have very properly deduced the great duty *of honoring and obeying the king*, and all that are put in authority under him. Reverently to submit ourselves to *all our governors, teachers, spiritual pastors, and masters*, is indeed a duty so essential to the peace and happiness of the world, that St. Paul think no Christian could be ignorant of it. . . . I do no more than St. Paul enjoined. All I pretend to, all I aim at, is to *put you in mind* only of your *duty to your neighbor*.

. . .

. . . Every sinner is, literally, a slave; *for his servants, ye are, to whom ye obey*. And the only true liberty is the liberty of being the servants of God; for, *his service is perfect freedom*. The passage cannot, without infinite perversion and torture, be made to refer to any other kind of liberty; much less to that liberty of which every man now talks, though few understand it. . . . Let a minister of God, then, stand excused if (taught by him who knows what is fit and good for us better than we ourselves, and is *wont also to give use more than either we desire or deserve*) he seeks not to amuse you by any flowery panegyrics on liberty. Such panegyrics are the productions of ancient heathens and modern patriots; nothing of the kind is to be met with in the Bible, nor in the Statute Book. The word *liberty*, as meaning civil liberty, does not, I believe, occur in all the Scriptures. . . . The only circumstance relative to government, for which the Scriptures seem to be particularly solicitous, is in inculcating obedience to lawful governors, as well knowing where the true danger lies. . . .

It has just been observed, that the liberty inculcated in the Scriptures . . . is wholly of the spiritual or religious kind. This liberty was the natural result of the new religion in which mankind were then instructed; which certainly gave them no new civil privileges. They remained subject to the governments under which they lived, just as they had been before they became Christians, and just as others were who never became Christians; with this difference only, that the duty of submission and obedience to Government was enjoined on the converts to Christianity with new and stronger sanctions. The doctrines of the Gospel make no manner of alteration in the nature or form of Civil Government; but enforce afresh, upon all Christians, that obedience which is due to the respective Constitutions of every nation in which they may happen to live. Be the supreme power lodged in one or in many, be the kind of government established in any country absolute or limited, this is not the concern of the Gospels. Its single object, with respect to these public duties, is to enjoin obedience to the laws of every country, in every kind or form of government.

. . .

. . . If the form of government under which the good providence of God has been pleased to place us be mild and free, it is our duty to enjoy it with gratitude and with thankfulness; and, in particular, to be careful not to abuse it by licentiousness. If it be less indulgent and less liberal than in reason it ought to be, still it is our duty not to disturb and destroy the peace of the community, by becoming refractory and rebellious subjects, and *resisting the ordinances of God*. However humiliating such acquiescence may seem to men of warm and eager minds, the wisdom of God in having made it our duty is manifest. . . .

. . . To respect the laws, is to respect liberty in the only rational sense in which the term can be used; for liberty consists in a subserviency to law. "Where there is no law," says Mr. Locke, "there is no freedom." The mere man of nature (if such a one there ever was) has no freedom: *all his lifetime he is subject to bondage*. It is by being included within the pale of civil polity and government that he takes his rank in society as a free man.

. . .

True liberty, then, is a liberty to do everything that is right, and the being restrained from doing anything that is wrong. So far from our having the right to do everything that we please, under a notion of liberty, liberty itself is limited and confined—but limited and confined only by laws which are at the same time both its foundation and its support.

. . .

The popular notion, that government was originally formed by the consent or by a compact of the people, rests on, and is supported by, another familiar notion, not less popular, nor better founded. This other notion is, that the whole human race is born equal; and that no man is naturally inferior, or, in any respect, subjected to another. . . . Man differs from man in everything that can be supposed to lead to supremacy and subjection, *as one star differs from another star in glory*. It was the purpose of the Creator, that man should be social. But, without government, there can be no society; nor, without some relative inferiority and superiority, can there be any government. A musical instrument composed of chords, keys, or pipes, all perfectly equal in size and power, might as well be expected to produce harmony, as a society composed of members all perfectly equal to be productive of order and peace. . . . On the principle of equality, neither his parents, nor even the vote of a majority of the society . . . can have any . . . authority over any man. Neither can it be maintained that acquiescence implies consent; because acquiescence may have been extorted from impotence or incapacity. Even an explicit consent can bind a man no longer than he chooses to be bound. . . .

Any attempt, therefore, to introduce this fantastic system into practice, would reduce the whole business of social life to the wearisome, confused, and useless task of mankind's first expressing, and then withdrawing, their consent to an endless succession of schemes of government. Governments, though always forming, would never be completely formed: for, the majority today, might be the minority tomorrow; and, of course, that which is now fixed might and would be soon unfixed. . . .

It is indeed impossible to carry into effect any government which, even by compact, might be framed with this reserved right of resistance. Accordingly there is no record that any such government ever was so formed. If there had, it must have carried the seeds of its decay in its very constitution. . . .

. . .

. . . We are, indeed, so disorderly and unmanageable, that, were it not for the restraints and the terrors of human laws, it would not be possible for us to dwell together. But as men were clearly formed for society, and to dwell together, which yet they cannot do so without the restraints of law, or, in other words, without government, it is fair to infer that government was also the original intention of God. . . . Accordingly, when man was made, his Maker did not turn him adrift into a shoreless ocean, without star or compass to steer by. As soon as there were some to be governed, there were also some to govern. And the first men, by virtue of that paternal claim, on which all subsequent governments have been founded, was first invested with the power of government. . . .

. . .

When it is asserted that Christianity made no alteration in the civil affairs of the world, the assertion should neither be made, nor understood, without some qualification. The injunction to *render unto Caesar the things that are Caesar's*, is no doubt very comprehensive; implying that unless we are good Subjects, we cannot be good Christians. But then we are to *render unto Caesar*, or the supreme magistrate, that obedience only to which God has given him a just claim. Our paramount duty is to God, to whom we are to render *the things that are God's*. If, therefore, in the course of human affairs, a case should occur . . . in which the performance of both these obligations becomes incompatible, we cannot long be at a loss in determining that it is our duty to obey God rather than men. . . . In Mahometan countries, a plurality of wives is allowed by law. In many countries still Pagan, the worship of images is enjoined by the State. In several parts of Africa, parents who are past labor are, by the laws of the land, exposed by their children to be torn in pieces by wild beasts. And even in so civilized a country as China, children are thus exposed by their parents, with the sanction and authority of the laws. Would Christianity endure such shocking outrages against all that is humane, moral, or pious, though supported by Government? It certainly would not. . . .

. . .

[E]very man who is a subject must necessarily owe to the government under which he lives an obedience either active or passive: active, where the duty enjoined may be performed without offending God; and passive, (that is to say, patiently to submit to the penalties annexed to disobedience,) where that which is commanded by man is forbidden by God. . . . Resolute not to disobey God, a man of good principles determines, in cases of competition, as the lesser evil, to disobey man: but he knows that he should also disobey God, were he not, at the same time, patiently to submit to any penalties incurred by his disobedience to man.

. . .

V. POLITICAL ECONOMY

Major Developments

- Promotion of colonies as economic enterprises
- Disagreements over consistency of wealth and religious duty
- The promotion of personal virtue as the path to economic prosperity

Conditions were harsh in the new colonies, but they represented an opportunity for a fresh start. For some, the fresh start was communal. The New World was virgin land upon which a new, more just society could be built. But building a new society required sacrifices, as individuals dedicated themselves to caring for each other and themselves. Massachusetts Bay Colony founder John Winthrop warned his fellow settlers that a "community of perils calls for extraordinary liberality" in treating neighbors as brothers. The Christian Pilgrims must be prepared to make an example of themselves, to become a model for the world. The moral reformer Thomas Tryon saw the possibility that God's children could walk in this new land unburdened by "those outward cares, vexations and turmoils" that so bedeviled the people of the Old World.[4]

For others, the fresh start was personal. The New World offered an unprecedented bounty for enterprising adventurers who were willing to take advantage of it. Captain John Smith publicized the endless possibilities to his fellow Englishmen. "No place," he gushed, "is more convenient for pleasure, profit, and man's sustenance."[5] Decades later, publicists continued to assure Europeans that in Virginia "nobody is poor enough to beg, or want food, though they have abundance of people that are lazy enough to deserve it." America was "the best poor man's country in the world."[6]

America was supposed to be profitable to those who remained in the mother country as well as to those who made the journey across the Atlantic. Most of the colonies were established by investors who hoped that the fruits of the New World would be shipped back to England. More broadly, the economic theory of mercantilism held that a favorable balance of trade was the key to national wealth. Trade regulations were designed to keep the colonies as consumers of finished goods produced in Europe and producers of agricultural goods and raw materials that could be imported to England. The colonists sometimes chafed at the restriction on their ability to buy cheaper goods elsewhere or sell their own goods at the most lucrative markets. Smugglers maintained a flourishing business. But most colonists accepted the basic logic of the mercantilist system and their role within the British empire. British trade regulations at least guaranteed ready access to English markets, and there were few examples of international free trade that suggested another option to the system of colonial trade regulations. The American colonies sometimes suffered from an undeveloped manufacturing sector and inadequate currency reserves. Paper currency sometimes seemed like a means for overcoming both of those problems, but presented its own problems by inflating prices and discouraging credit.

---

4 Thomas Tryon, *The Planter's Speech to his Neighbors and Countrymen of Pennsylvania, East and West Jersey* (London: Andrew Sowle, 1684), 3.

5 John Smith, *A True Relation of Such Occurrences and Accidents of Note as Have Happened in Virginia* (London: John Tappe, 1608), 60.

6 Robert Beverley, *The History and Present State of Virginia* (London: R. Parker, 1705), 223.

JOHN WINTHROP

A MODELL OF CHRISTIAN CHARITY (1630)

John Winthrop came from a rising family and worked as a minor official and attorney in England. As a Puritan convert, however, he was increasingly isolated by the policies of King Charles I. In 1629, he emigrated to America with the charter for the Massachusetts Bay Colony in his pocket. He was repeatedly elected as governor and became one of the most influential figures in New England. But he was also an increasingly controversial one, as schisms in Massachusetts led to the settlement of separate colonies in the region.

His sermon on Christian charity was prepared on the voyage and delivered upon his arrival. It became perhaps his best-known work. In the sermon, he called on his fellow colonists to overcome their differences, come together as a community, and work to advance the common good. He warned that the "eyes of all people are upon us," but together they could create a "city upon a hill" that would give glory to God and serve as an example to others.

Does Winthrop expect his model community to eliminate divisions and differences? What prevents the "rich and mighty" from "eat[ing] up the poor"? Is Winthrop utopian? Does he have anything to offer to nonbelievers? If religion is critical to constraining "the wicked," is a just polity possible in a secular society? How far must individuals embrace others as brothers, as members of the same body? Does his call to "bear one another's burdens" apply outside the conditions of an isolated settlement in the wilderness?

GOD ALMIGHTY in His most holy and wise providence, has so disposed of the condition of mankind, as in all times some must be rich, some poor, some high and eminent in power and dignity; others mean and in submission.

The Reason hereof.

1. *Reason.* First to hold conformity with the rest of His world, being delighted to show forth the glory of his wisdom in the variety and difference of the creatures, and the glory of His power in ordering all these differences for the preservation and good of the whole, and the glory of His greatness, that as it is the glory of princes to have many officers, so this great king will have many stewards, counting himself more honored in dispensing his gifts to man by man, than if he did it by his own immediate hands.

2. *Reason.* Secondly, that He might have the more occasion to manifest the work of his Spirit: first upon the wicked in moderating and restraining them, so that the rich and mighty should not eat up the poor, nor the poor and despised rise up against and shake off their yoke. Secondly, in the regenerate, in exercising His graces in them, as in the great ones, their love, mercy, gentleness, temperance etc., and in the poor and inferior sort, their faith, patience, obedience, etc.

3. *Reason.* Thirdly, that every man might have need of others, and from hence they might be all knit more nearly together in the bonds of brotherly affection. From hence it appears plainly that no man is made more honorable than another or more wealthy, etc., out of any particular and singular respect to himself, but for the glory of his Creator and the common good of the creature, man. Therefore God still reserves the property of these gifts to Himself as *Ezek.* 16:17, He there calls wealth, *His gold and His silver*, and *Prov.* 3:9, He claims their service as His due, *Honor the Lord with thy riches*, etc.—All men being thus (by divine providence) ranked into two sorts, rich and poor; under the first are comprehended all such as are able to live comfortably by their own means duly improved; and all others are poor according to the former distribution. There are two rules whereby we are to walk one towards another: Justice and Mercy. These are always distinguished in their act and in their object, yet may they both concur in the same subject in each respect; as sometimes there may be an occasion of showing mercy to a rich man in some

sudden danger or distress, and also doing of mere justice to a poor man in regard of some particular contract, etc. There is likewise a double Law by which we are regulated in our conversation towards another. In both the former respects, the Law of Nature and the Law of Grace (that is, the moral law or the law of the gospel) to omit the rule of justice as not properly belonging to this purpose otherwise than it may fall into consideration in some particular cases. By the first of these laws, man as he was enabled so withal is commanded to love his neighbor as himself. Upon this ground stands all the precepts of the moral law, which concerns our dealings with men.

To apply this to the works of mercy, this law requires two things. First, that every man afford his help to another in every want or distress. Secondly, that he perform this out of the same affection which makes him careful of his own goods, according to the words of our Savior (*Matt.* 7:12), *whatsoever ye would that men should do to you. . . .*

. . .

This law of the Gospel propounds likewise a difference of seasons and occasions. There is a time when a Christian must sell all and give to the poor, as they did in the Apostles' times. There is a time also when Christians (though they give not all yet) must give beyond their ability, as they of Macedonia (2 *Cor.* 8). Likewise, community of perils calls for extraordinary liberality, and so doth community in some special service for the church.

Lastly, when there is no other means whereby our Christian brother may be relieved in his distress, we must help him beyond our ability rather than tempt God in putting him upon help by miraculous or extraordinary means. This duty of mercy is exercised in the kinds: giving, lending and forgiving.

Question: What rule shall a man observe in giving in respect of the measure?

Answer: If the time and occasion be ordinary he is to give out of his abundance. . . .

. . .

Question: What rule must we observe and walk by in cause of community in peril?

Answer: The same as before, but with more enlargement towards others and less respect towards ourselves and our own right. . . .

The definition which the Scripture gives us of love is this: *Love is the bond of perfection.* First it is a bond or ligament. Secondly, it makes the work perfect. There is no body but consists of parts and that which knits these parts together, gives the body its perfection, because it makes each part so contiguous to others as thereby they do mutually participate with each other, both in strength and infirmity, in pleasure and pain. To instance in the most perfect of all bodies: Christ and his Church make one body. The several parts of this body considered a part before they were united, were as disproportionate and as much disordering as so many contrary qualities or elements, but when Christ comes, and by his spirit and love knits all these parts to himself and each to other, it is become the most perfect and best proportioned body in the world (*Eph.* 4:16). *Christ, by whom all the body being knit together by every joint for the furniture thereof, according to the effectual power which is in the measure of every perfection of parts, a glorious body without spot or wrinkle*; the ligaments hereof being Christ, or his love, for Christ is love (1 *John* 4:8). So this definition is right. *Love is the bond of perfection.*

From hence we may frame these conclusions:

First of all, true Christians are of one body in Christ (1 *Cor.* 12). *Ye are the body of Christ and members of their part.*

Secondly, the ligaments of this body which knit together are love.

Thirdly, nobody can be perfect which wants its proper ligament.

Fourthly, All the parts of this body being thus united are made so contiguous in a special relation as they must needs partake of each other's strength and infirmity, joy and sorrow, weal and woe. (1 *Cor.* 12:26) *If one member suffers, all suffer with it; if one be in honor, all rejoice with it.*

Fifthly, this sensitivity and sympathy of each other's conditions will necessarily infuse into each part a native desire and endeavor, to strengthen, defend, preserve and comfort the other. To insist a little on this conclusion being the product of all the former, the truth hereof will appear both by precept and pattern. 1 *John* 3:16, *Ye ought to lay down our lives for the brethren. Gal.* 6:2, *Bear ye one another's burdens and so fulfill the law of Christ.*

. . .

It rests now to make some application of this discourse. . . .

First, for *the persons*. We are a company professing ourselves fellow members of Christ, in which respect only, though we were absent from each other many miles, and had our employments as far distant, yet we ought to account ourselves knit together by this bond of love and live in the exercise of it, if we would have comfort of our being in Christ. . . .

Secondly for the *work* we have in hand. It is by a mutual consent, through a special overvaluing providence and a more than an ordinary approbation of the churches of Christ, to seek out a place of cohabitation and consortship under a due form of government both civil and ecclesiastical. In such cases as this, the care of the public must oversway all private respects, by which, not only conscience, but mere civil policy, does bind us. For it is a true rule that particular estates cannot subsist in the ruin of the public.

Thirdly, the *end* is to improve our lives to do more service to the Lord; the comfort and increase of the body of Christ, whereof we are members, that ourselves and posterity may be the better preserved from the common corruptions of this evil world, to serve the Lord and work out our salvation under the power and purity of his holy ordinances.

Fourthly, for the *means* whereby this must be effected. They are twofold, a conformity with the work and end we aim at. These we see are extraordinary, therefore we must not content ourselves with usual ordinary means. Whatsoever we did, or ought to have done, when we lived in England, the same must we do, and more also, where we go. That which the most in their churches maintain as truth in profession only, we must bring into familiar and constant practice; as in this duty of love, we must love brotherly without dissimulation, we must love one another with a pure heart fervently. We must bear one another's burdens. We must not look only on our own things, but also on the things of our brethren. Neither must we think that the Lord will bear with such failings at our hands as he doth from those among whom we have lived. . . .

. . .

[W]hen God gives a special commission He looks to have it strictly observed in every article. . . . We are entered into covenant with Him for this work. We have taken out a commission. The Lord has given us leave to draw our own articles. We have professed to enterprise these and those accounts, upon these and those ends. We have hereupon besought Him of favor and blessing. Now if the Lord shall please to hear us, and bring us in peace to the place we desire, then has He ratified this covenant and sealed our commission, and will expect a strict performance of the articles contained in it; but if we shall neglect the observation of these articles which are the ends we have propounded, and, dissembling with our God, shall fall to embrace this present world and prosecute our carnal intentions, seeking great things for ourselves and our posterity, the Lord will surely break out in wrath against us, and be revenged of such a people, and make us know the price of the breach of such a covenant.

Now the only way to avoid this shipwreck, and to provide for our posterity, is to follow the counsel of Micah, *to do justly, to love mercy, to walk humbly with our God*. For this end, we must be knit together, in this work, as one man. We must entertain each other in brotherly affection. We must be willing to abridge ourselves of our superfluities, for the supply of other's necessities. We must uphold a familiar commerce together in all meekness, gentleness, patience and liberality. We must delight in each other; make other's conditions our own; rejoice together, mourn together, labor and suffer together, always having before our eyes our commission and community in the work, as members of the same body. So shall we *keep the unity of the spirit in the bond of peace*. The Lord will be our God, and delight to dwell among us, as His own people, and will command a blessing upon us in all our ways. So that we shall see much more of His wisdom, power, goodness and truth, than formerly we have been acquainted with. We shall find that the God of Israel is among us, when ten of us shall be able to resist a thousand of our enemies; when He shall make us a praise and glory that men shall say of succeeding plantations, "may the Lord make it like that of *New England*." For we must consider that we shall be as a city upon a hill. The eyes of all people are upon us. So that if we shall deal falsely with our God in this work we have undertaken, and so cause Him to withdraw His present help from us, we shall be made a story and a by-word through the world. We shall open the mouths of enemies to speak evil of the ways of God, and all professors for God's sake. We shall shame the faces of many of God's worthy servants, and cause their prayers to be turned into curses upon us till we be consumed out of the good land whither we are going.

I shall shut up this discourse with that exhortation of Moses, that faithful servant of the Lord, in his last farewell to Israel, *Deut.* 30. *Beloved, there is now set before us life and good, Death and evil, in that we are commanded this day to love the Lord our God, and to love one another, to walk in his ways and to keep his Commandments and his ordinance and his laws,* and the articles of our Covenant with Him, that *we may live and be multiplied, and that the Lord our God may bless us in the land whither we go to possess it. But if our hearts shall turn away, so that we will not obey, but shall be seduced, and worship and serve other Gods,* our pleasure and profits, *and serve them;* it is propounded unto us this day, *we shall surely perish out of the good land whither we pass over this vast sea to possess it;*

Therefore let us choose life,
that we, and our seed
may live, by obeying His
voice and cleaving to Him,
for He is our life and
our prosperity.

COTTON MATHER

A CHRISTIAN AT HIS CALLING (1701)

Cotton Mather was the grandson of famed Puritan minister John Cotton and the son of the minister Increase Mather. He quickly became a Boston pastor in his own right. From that perch, he became the leading theologian in New England, writing hundreds of books and essays that became central texts in New England intellectual circles well into the nineteenth century. His interests were wide-ranging. He was an early advocate of smallpox inoculations but also became infamous for endorsing the Salem witch trials at the end of the seventeenth century.

Among his more popular works was his writing on good works, which influenced Benjamin Franklin, among others. Puritan theology held that salvation could not be achieved by good works in the world, but Mather argued, "Let no man pretend unto the name of a *Christian*, who does not approve the proposal of a *perpetual endeavor to do good in the world*."[7] Man has an obligation to resist selfishness, avoid idleness, and help his neighbors. In his essay on the Christian's two callings, he emphasized that the Christian had material as well as spiritual obligations.

What is the basis for thinking that there are material obligations? Are those obligations primarily to others? Do those considerations apply only to Christians? To what extent is Mather calling for self-sacrifice? Is Mather just reflecting a particularly frontier mentality? Does his message still resonate today?

Gen. 47.3. *What is your OCCUPATION?*

. . .

There are *two callings* to be minded by all Christians. Every Christian has a general calling; which is, to serve the Lord Jesus Christ, and save his own soul. . . . But then, every Christian has also a personal calling; or, a *particular employment*, by which its *usefulness* in his neighborhood, is distinguished. God has made man a *sociable* creature. We expect benefits from *human society*. It is but equal, that *human society* should receive benefits from *us*. . . .

. . .

A Christian should be able to give this account, *that he has an occupation*. . . . That is to say, there should be some *special business* . . . where a Christian should for the most part spend the most of his time; and this, that so he may glorify God, by doing of *good* for *others*, and getting of *good* for *himself*. . . . It's not *honest*, nor *Christian*, that a *Christian* should have no *business* to do. . . . Can anything be more express, than that command of God? *Exod.* 20.9. *Six days thou shalt labor*. . . . Emphatical are the words of the apostle, *Eph.* 4.28. *Let him that stole, steal no more, but rather let him labor*. . . . Our apostle seems to make it a law of *Ephesians* too, that if men that could *labor*, would *not*, there should be a degree of *stealing* chargeable upon them. . . . Yea, a *calling* is not only our duty, but also our *safety*. Men will ordinarily fall into horrible *snares*, and infinite *sins*, if they have not a *calling*, to be their *preservative*. . . . The temptations of the *devil* are best resisted by those that are least at *leisure* to receive them. . . .

There are *gentlemen*, it's true, who live upon their *means*; and some in their *age* retire to eat the pleasant fruit of their *labor*, which they underwent in their *youth*. But yet it well becomes the best *gentlemen* to study some way of being *serviceable* in the world, and employ themselves in some good *business*. . . . *Idle gentlemen* have done as much hurt in the world as *idle beggars*. And pardon me, if I say, any *honest mechanics* really are more honorable than *idle* and useless *men of honor*. Every man ordinarily should be able to say, *I have something wherein I am occupied for the good of other men*.

. . .

---

7 Cotton Mather, *Bonifacius* (Boston: B. Green, 1710).

. . . As it is not lawful ordinarily to live without a calling, so a Christian must live by no calling, but what shall be a lawful one. . . . [T]he *wrath* of God will cleave to all the *gain* gotten by a *calling* that shall be forbidden by the *word* of God. . . . All of the works of our *occupation* are *ill works*, if they be not for *allowable uses;* and we don't *profess honest trades*, if they be not for *profitable uses*. Nor should we take up a *business*, whereof we may own, *there is no need at all of any such business in the world*.

Every *calling*, whereby God will be dishonored; every *calling* whereby none but the lusts of men are nourished; every *calling* whereby men are damnified in any of their true interests; every such *calling* is to be rejected. . . .

. . .

A Christian should follow his *occupation* with *industry*. . . . By *slothfulness* men bring upon themselves, what? But poverty, but misery, but all sorts of confusion. . . . We find *Prov*. 10.4, *He becomes poor, who deals with a slack hand but the hand of the diligent makes rich*. . . . Would a man *rise by* his business? I say, then let him *rise to* his business. . . . I tell you, with *diligence* a man may do marvelous things. *Young* man, *work hard* while you are *young*. You'll reap the effects of it, when you are *old*. . . .

. . . Laudable *recreations* may be used now and then. But, I beseech you, let those *recreations* be used for *sauce*, but not for *meat*. . . . *Thou wicked and slothful person*, reform your ways, or you are not far from *outer darkness*. . . . Is it nothing to you, that you are contracting the character of a *vagabond* and a *prodigal*? Do you not find the *alehouse* to be the very suburbs of *Hell*. . . ?

A Christian should follow his occupation with discretion. . . . It was among the maxims of wisdom given of old, *Be thou diligent for to know the state of thy flocks;* that is to say, often examine the condition of your *business*, to see whether you go forward or backward, and learn how to order your concerns accordingly. . . .

A Christian should follow his *occupation* with *honesty* . . . A Christian in all his *business* ought so altogether justly to do everything that he should be able to say with him, *Act*. 23.1. *Men and Brethren, I have lived in all good conscience*. . . . It is *uncharitable*, it is *disingenuous*, it is *inhumane*, for one man to prey upon the *weakness* of another. . . . Let a principle of *honesty*, cause you carefully to pay the *debts*, which in your *business* must fall upon you. Run into *debt*, as *little* as you may, though *something* men commonly *must*. But being in *debt*, be as ready to get *out of it*, as ever you were to get *into it*. . . . Let a principle of *honesty* cause you to keep your *word*, in all your *business*. You sometimes give your *word;* let that *word* then be as good as your *bond*. . . .

A Christian should follow his *occupation* with *contentment*. . . . That one man has a spirit formed and fitted for *one occupation*, and another man for another, this is from the operation of that God, who *forms the spirit of man within him*. . . . Count not your *business* to be your *burden* or your *blemish*. Let not a *proud heart* make you ashamed of that *business* wherein you may be a *blessing*. For my part, I can't see an honest man hard at work in the way of his *occupation*, be it never so mean . . . but I find my heart sensibly touched with respects for such a man. It's possible, you may see others in some greater and richer *business;* and you may think, that you might be yourselves greater and richer, if you were in some other *business*. Yea, but has not the God of Heaven cast you into that business, which now takes you up? . . . Your *occupation* well followed will doubtless furnish you with *food* and *raiment*. Well, and now what says the apostle of the Lord upon it? 1 *Tim*. 6.8 *Having food and raiment, let us be therewith content*. . . .

. . .

. . . Don't imagine that your *hands* will be *sufficient* for you, without the *help of God*. And with the *help of God*, never fear, but your *hands* will be sufficient for you. Stick to your *business*, and leave it with God, how you shall succeed in your *business*. . . . I say to you as the Psalmist once, *Trust in the Lord, and do good, and in truth thou shalt be fed*.

. . .

BENJAMIN FRANKLIN

THE WAY TO WEALTH (1758)

For twenty-five years, Benjamin Franklin published an annual almanac that included pithy advice from the fictional Richard Saunders, or Poor Richard. The almanac was wildly successful, and Poor Richard became a celebrated literary figure. As Franklin concluded the publication of his almanac, he looked to collect Poor Richard's aphorisms on financial well-being into a single pamphlet. This essay was framed as the advice that the wise old "Father Abraham" offered to a gathering of men who were waiting for the start of an auction and were spending the time bemoaning the "badness of the times." Abraham's monologue is largely a collection of aphorisms from "Poor Richard" on how to become wealthy.

How does Franklin's advice compare to Mather's? Is Franklin counseling passivity in the face of bad government policies? Does Franklin's emphasis on individual effort overlook other factors affecting individual prosperity? What personal virtues does Franklin value, and why does he value them? Are they valuable for their own sake, or is personal character merely an instrumental good?

. . .

"Friends," says he, "the taxes are indeed very heavy; and if those laid on by the government were the only ones we had to pay, we might more easily discharge them; but we have many others, and much more grievous to some of us. We are taxed twice as much by our idleness, three times as much by our pride, and four times as much by our folly; and from those taxes the commissioners cannot ease or deliver us by allowing an abatement. However, let us harken to good advice, and something may be done for us; 'God helps them that help themselves,' as Poor Richard says.

"I. It would be thought a hard government that should tax its people one-tenth part of their time to be employed in its service; but idleness taxes many of us much more; sloth by bringing on diseases, absolutely shortens life.

. . .

"If time be of all things the most precious, wasting time must be," as Poor Richard says, 'the greatest prodigality!' since, as he elsewhere tells us, 'Lost time is never found again; and what we call time enough always proves little enough.' Let us, then, up and be doing, and doing to the purpose: so by diligence shall we do more with less perplexity. "Sloth makes all things difficult, but industry all easy; and he that rises late, must trot all day, and shall scarce overtake his business at night: while laziness travels so slowly, that poverty soon overtakes him. Drive your business, let not that drive you; and early to bed, and early to rise, makes a man healthy, wealthy, and wise," as Poor Richard says.

". . . 'He that has a trade, has an estate; and he that has a calling, has an office of profit and honor,' as Poor Richard says; but then the trade must be worked at, and the calling well followed, or neither the estate nor the office will enable us to pay our taxes. If we are industrious, we shall never starve; for 'at the working man's house hunger looks in, but dares not enter.' Nor will the bailiff or constable enter; for, 'industry pays debts, while despair increases them.' What, though you have found no treasure, nor has any rich relation left you a legacy, 'Diligence is the mother of good luck, and God gives all things to industry. Then plough deep while sluggards sleep, and you shall have corn to sell and to keep." . . . 'One today is worth two tomorrow,' as Poor Richard says; and farther, "Never leave that till tomorrow, which you can do today." . . .

"Methinks I hear some of you say, 'Must a man afford himself no leisure?" I will tell thee, my friend, what Poor Richard says: 'Employ your time well, if you mean to gain leisure; and, since you are not sure of a minute, throw not away an hour." Leisure is time for doing something useful: this leisure the diligent man will obtain, but the lazy man never." . . .

"II. But with our industry, we must likewise be steady, settled, and careful, and oversee our own affairs with our own eyes, and not trust too much to others. . . . "Want of care does us more damage than want of knowledge;' and again, 'Not to oversee workmen, is to leave them your purse open."

"Trusting too much to other's care is the ruin of many; for, 'In the affairs of this world, men are saved, not by faith, but by the want of it;" but a man's own care is profitable; for if you would have a faithful servant, and one that you like—serve yourself. A little neglect may breed great mischief; for want of a nail the shoe was lost; for want of a shoe the horse was lost; and for want of a horse the rider was lost; being overtaken and slain by the enemy; all for want of a little care about a horse-shoe nail."

"III. So much for industry, my friends, and attention to one's own business: but to these we must add frugality, if we would make our industry more certainly successful. . . . 'If you would be wealthy, think of saving as well as of getting'. . . .

"Away then with your expensive follies, and you will not then have so much cause to complain of hard times, heavy taxes, and chargeable families; for, 'Women and wine, game and deceit, make the wealth small, and the want great.' And farther, 'What maintains one vice, would bring up two children.' . . . Beware of little expenses; 'A small leak will sink a great ship,' as Poor Richard says. . . . Here you are all got together to this sale of fineries and knick-knacks. You call them goods; but, if you do not take care, they will prove evils to some of you. . . . Remember what Poor Richard says, 'Buy what you have no need of, and ere long you shall sell your necessaries.' . . . Many a one, for the sake of finery on the back has gone with a hungry belly, and half starved their families. . . . 'A ploughman on his legs, is higher than a gentleman on his knees," as Poor Richard says. . . . 'If you would know the value of money, go and try to borrow some; for he that goes a borrowing, goes a sorrowing,' as Poor Richard says. . . . Poor Dick says, 'It is easier to suppress the first desire, than to satisfy all that follow it. And it is as truly folly for the poor to ape the rich, as for the frog to swell, in order to equal the ox.' 'Vessels large may venture more, but little boats should keep near shore.'. . .

. . .

"IV. This doctrine, my friends, is reason and wisdom: but after all, do not depend too much upon your own industry, and frugality, and prudence, though excellent things; for they may all be blasted without the blessing of Heaven; and, therefore, ask that blessing humbly, and be not uncharitable to those that at present seem to want it, but comfort and help them. Remember, Job suffered, and was afterwards prosperous.

"And now, to conclude, 'Experience keeps a dear school, but fools will learn in no other,' as Poor Richard says, and scarce in that; for it is true, 'We may give advice, but we cannot give conduct.' However, remember this, 'They that will not be counseled cannot be helped.' . . ."

Thus the old gentleman ended his harangue. The people heard it, and approved the doctrine, and immediately practiced the contrary, just as if it had been a common sermon; for the auction opened, and they began to buy extravagantly. . . .

• In America you must work hard to get anywhere in life - All time is precious for raising your status/stability in life.

VI. AMERICA AND THE WORLD

Major Developments

- Colonization of eastern seaboard of North American continent
- Negotiations and wars with Native American populations
- Tensions with England and revolutionary break

The United States began on the periphery. The center—of power, of politics, of culture—was back in Europe. Those who traveled to and settled in North America were voyaging to the frontier. They were building a new society that bore a distinct but frayed relationship to the one they had left. In sailing to the New World, they did not leave the Old World behind, but they did mark themselves as different.

The reasons for migrating to the United States were various. For some, the motive was economic. For others, the motive was religious. For others, the voyage was involuntary. These various motives both shaped the North American colonies themselves and helped influence how those colonies looked upon the broader world.

For some, the settlements in the New World offered the possibility of a new start on how to build a society and a model for the rest of the world. From this perspective, the settlers bore a profound burden. They held the hope that change was possible. They aspired to clear a path that could be followed by others, whether they struggled in pursuit of freedom or virtue.

The colonists were well aware that they lived in a large and complex world. They may have been physically isolated on the shores of the North American continent, but their apparent isolation made them all the more vulnerable and dependent. They were self-consciously part of a global community. Europe was simultaneously distant and always close at hand.

Most notably, they were *colonists* within a global empire. The debate over whether those colonists identified themselves as Americans or as English increasingly occupied their attention on the eve of the American Revolution, but the answer was not at all obvious even by 1776. The fate of the colonies was deeply intertwined with the actions of the great European powers. Their economies and governments were deeply enmeshed in that of the British empire. Their trade and domestic security were shaped by the machinations of French and Spanish empires. Their intellectual community spread across the Atlantic and embraced all of Europe.

But they were also settlers on the frontier of the New World. The land that they occupied may not have been as crowded as the cities of Europe, but it most certainly was not empty. The western frontier was at their doorstep, and held both promise and threat. The frontier offered opportunity and escape, offering the space for developing new customs, new relationships, and new ways of thought. The frontier was also threatening. The European foothold in North America was tenuous and the colonies were still fragile. The native populations were geographically closer to the colonists than the European powers, and the distance between claiming territory and holding territory was obvious. The American Indians were both allies and antagonists, and they themselves modeled a different way of life that could be both enticing and frightening to the transplanted Europeans.

The global environment was not as great of a consideration early in the colonial era as it was in the years leading up to the American Revolution. When the war between France and England spilled over into North America, and Native American tribes were recruited as proxies for the great powers, security and America's place in the world became more pressing concerns. Joseph Doddridge reflected the security concerns of western settlers, who sometimes questioned which, if any, government could best protect their interests. The newspaper essays of John Dickinson and Daniel Leonard played out the worries of more conservative colonists as tensions between England and the colonies escalated. Was independence a serious option, or was the real question simply which empire would best serve the interest of the colonies? The Declaration of Independence committed the colonies to the path of independence while offering a public justification accepting the United States into the family of nations.

JOSEPH DODDRIDGE

NOTES ON THE SETTLEMENT AND INDIAN WARS (1824)

Joseph Doddridge was born in Pennsylvania and lived from a young age on the western frontier of that state in the years surrounding the American Revolution. Upon coming of age, he became an itinerant preacher along the Appalachians before settling in western Virginia and studying medicine. His memoir and account of the western frontier in the 1760s and 1770s was widely celebrated in nineteenth-century America. Doddridge's notes were first prepared for publication in the 1820s, and undoubtedly incorporated his perspective as an adult in the Jeffersonian era, but they were taken to be one of the best available accounts of the views and experiences of the first settlers of what had then been the western frontier of the United States. Members of his own family had been killed and captured on the Pennsylvania frontier, and Doddridge sought to convey both the pervasive fear and the everyday pleasures of life in that contested territory, where the Revolutionary War was experienced primarily as just one episode in a long-running war of extermination between Native Americans and white settlers. By the end of his own life, Doddridge could see that the Native Americans of the Appalachian regions were "a subjugated people," whose "national character" was destined to fade into nostalgic memory. But his memories were of a series of wars, in which the Indians "fought for their native country" with "patriotic motives" and the white settlers battled to claim territory for the benefit of their own posterity. Doddridge hoped to capture that desperate struggle, because the way of life of neither the Native American tribes nor the white frontiersmen was likely to endure much longer.

Doddridge thinks that both sides were engaged in a "war of extermination." Why would he think that? How did the situation of the settlers differ from the situation of the inhabitants of Boston or Philadelphia during the Revolutionary War? Did the Americans ever face the possibility of "subjugation" during these conflicts? Doddridge compared the nature of the war between the Indians and the settlers to wars between the Romans and the Jews, the Greeks and the Turks, and the Irish and the British. Why did he think the ferocity shown by the settlers was justified? Would Doddridge have similarly justified adopting such measures against the British in Canada, who had allied with Native American tribes? Why does he think that there was no alternative to extermination or subjugation in the wars on the western frontier, but that other options were possible in the conflict with Britain?

. . .

My reader will understand by this term [fort], not only a place of defense, but the residence of a small number of families belonging to the same neighborhood. As the Indian mode of warfare was an indiscriminate slaughter of all ages, and both sexes, it was as requisite to provide for the safety of the women and children as for that of the men.

. . .

The necessary labors of the farms along the frontiers, were performed with every danger and difficulty imaginable. The whole population of the frontiers huddled together in their little forts, left the country with every appearance of a deserted region. . . .

. . .

The early settlers on the frontiers of this country were like Arabs of the desert of Africa, in at least two respects: every man was a soldier, and from early in the spring, till late in the fall, was almost continually in arms. Their work was often carried on by parties, each one of whom had his rifle and everything else belonging to his war dress. These were deposited in some central place in the field. A sentinel was stationed on the outside of the fence, so that on the least alarm the whole company repaired to their arms, and were ready for the combat in a moment. . . .

In military affairs, when everyone concerned is left to his own will, matters are sure to be but badly managed. The whole frontiers of Pennsylvania and Virginia presented a succession of military camps or forts. We had military officers . . . but they, in many respects, were only nominally such. They could advise but not command. Those who chose to follow their advice did so, to such an extent as suited their fancy, or interest. . . . Public odium was the only punishment for their laziness or cowardice. There was no compulsion to the performance of military duties, and no pecuniary reward when they were performed.

It is but doing justice to the first settlers of this country to say, that instances of disobedience of families and individuals to the advice of our officers, were by no means numerous. The greater number cheerfully submitted to their directions with a prompt and faithful obedience.

. . .

The history of man is, for the most part, one continued detail of bloodshed, battles and devastations. War has been, from the earliest periods of history, the almost constant employment of individuals, clans, tribes and nations. Fame, one of the most potent objects of human ambition, has at all items been the delusive but costly reward of military achievements. . . .

. . . In his primitive state man knows no object in his wars, but that of the extermination of his enemies, either by death or captivity.

. . .

It is, to be sure, much to be regretted that our people so often followed the cruel examples of the Indians in the slaughter of prisoners, and sometimes women and children; yet let them receive a candid hearing at the bar of reason and justice, before they are condemned, as barbarians, equally with the Indians themselves. History scarcely presents an example of a civilized nation carrying on a war with barbarians without adopting the mode of warfare of the barbarous nation. . . .

. . .

Our revolutionary war has a double aspect; on the one hand, we carried on a war with the English, in which we observed the maxims of civilized warfare with the utmost strictness; but the brave, the potent, the magnanimous nation of our forefathers had associated with themselves, as auxiliaries, the murderous tomahawk and scalping knife of the Indian nations around our defenseless frontiers, leaving those barbarous sons of the forest to their own savage mode of warfare, to the full indulgence of all their native thirst for human blood. On them, then, be the blame of all the horrid features of this war between civilized and savage men, in which the former were compelled, by every principle of self-defense, to adopt the Indian mode of warfare in all its revolting and destructive features.

Were those who engaged in the war against the Indians less humane than those who carried on the war against their English allies? No. They were not. Both parties carried on the war on the same principle of reciprocity of advantages and disadvantages. . . .

. . .

How is a war of extermination, and accompanied with such acts of atrocious cruelty, to be met by those on whom it is inflicted? Must it be met by the lenient maxims of civilized warfare? Must the Indian captive be spared his life? What advantage would be gained by this course? . . .

Philosophy shudders at the destructive aspect of war in any shape; Christianity, by teaching the religion of the good Samaritan, altogether forbids it; but the original settlers of the western regions, like the great part of the world, were neither philosophers nor saints. They were "men of like passion with others," and therefore adopted the Indian mode of warfare from necessity, and a motive of revenge. . . .

. . . If mercy may be associated with the carnage and devastation of war, that mercy must be reciprocal; but a war of utter extermination must be met by a war of the same character; or an overwhelming force which may put an end to it, without a sacrifice of the helpless and unoffending part of hostile nations; such a force was not at the command of the first inhabitants of this country. The sequel of the Indian war goes to show that in a war with savages, the choice lies between extermination and subjugation. Our government has wisely and humanely pursued the latter course.

. . .

JOHN DICKINSON

LETTERS FROM A FARMER IN PENNSYLVANIA (1768)

John Dickinson was a philosophically attuned lawyer and politician in Philadelphia. Though a defender of the proprietary government of Pennsylvania against critics such as Benjamin Franklin, he was an early and influential critic of Parliamentary taxation of the colonies. He was slow to embrace the call for American independence, but he became a key drafter of the first federal constitution after independence, the Articles of Confederation. These newspaper articles, published pseudonymously as "Letters from a Farmer," were particularly concerned with the Townshend Act. In this letter, Dickinson addresses the issue of whether the taxes were too small to justify the level of protest that was building in the colonies.

When can constitutional limitations be overlooked? What are the consequences of accepting a constitutional violation? Was it in American interests for Parliament to be able to make laws for the colonists? Is it viable to maintain an empire in which Parliament was restricted to regulating external affairs?

. . .

With a good deal of surprise I have observed, that little notice has been taken of an act of parliament, as injurious in its principle to the liberties of these colonies, as the *Stamp Act* was: I mean the act for suspending the legislation of *New York.*

The assembly of that government complied with a former act of parliament, requiring certain provisions to be made for the troops in *America,* in every particular, I think, except the articles of salt, pepper and vinegar. In my opinion they acted imprudently. . . . But my dislike of their conduct in that instance, has not blinded me so much, that I cannot plainly perceive, that they have been punished in a manner pernicious to *American* freedom, and justly alarming to all the colonies.

If the *British* parliament has legal authority to issue an order, that we shall furnish a single article for the troops here, and to compel obedience to *that* order, they have the same right to issue an order for us to supply those troops with arms, clothes, and every necessary; and to compel obedience to *that* order also; in short, to lay *any burthens* they please upon us. What is this but *taxing* us at a *certain sum,* and leaving to us only the *manner* of raising it? How is this mode more tolerable than the *Stamp Act?* Would that act have appeared more pleasing to *Americans,* if being ordered thereby to raise the sum total of the taxes, the mighty privilege had been left to them, of saying how much should be paid for an instrument of writing on paper, and how much for another on parchment?

. . .

The matter being thus stated, the assembly of *New York* either had, or had not, a right to refuse submission to that act. If they had, and I imagine no *American* will say they had not, then the parliament had *no right* to compel them to execute it. If they had not *this right,* they had *no right* to punish them for not executing it; and therefore *no right* to suspend their legislation, which is a punishment. In fact, if the people of *New York* cannot be legally taxed but by their own representatives, they cannot be legally deprived of the privilege of legislation, only for insisting on that exclusive privilege of taxation. . . .

. . .

There is another late act of parliament, which appears to me to be unconstitutional, and as destructive to the liberty of these colonies, as that mentioned in my last letter; that is, the act for granting the duties on paper, glass, etc.

The parliament unquestionably possesses a legal authority to *regulate* the trade of *Great Britain,* and all her colonies. Such an authority is essential to the relation between a mother country and her colonies; and necessary for the common good of all. He who considers these provinces as states distinct from the *British Empire,* has very slender notions of *justice,* or of their *interests.* We are but parts of a *whole;* and therefore there must exist a power somewhere, to preside, and preserve the connection in due order. This power is lodged in the parliament; and we are as much dependent on *Great Britain,* as a perfectly free people can be on another.

I have looked over *every statute* relating to these colonies, from their first settlement to this time; and I find every one of them founded on this principle, till the *Stamp Act* administration. *All before,* are calculated to regulate trade, and preserve or promote a mutually beneficial intercourse between the several constituent parts of the empire; and though many of them imposed duties on trade, yet those duties were always imposed *with design* to restrain the commerce of one part, that was injurious to another, and thus to promote the general welfare. The raising of a revenue thereby was never intended. . . .

. . .

Here we may observe an authority *expressly* claimed and exerted to impose duties on these colonies; not for the regulation of trade; not for the preservation or promotion of a mutually beneficial intercourse between the several constituent parts of the empire, heretofore the *sole objects* of parliamentary institutions; *but for the single purpose of levying money upon us.*

This I call an innovation; and a most dangerous innovation. . . .

. . .

Here then, my dear countrymen, rouse yourselves, and behold the ruin hanging over your heads. If you ONCE admit, that *Great Britain* may lay duties upon her exportations to us, *for the purpose of levying money on us only,* she then will have nothing to do, but to lay those duties on the articles which she prohibits us to manufacture—and the tragedy of *American* liberty is finished. . . .

. . .

Upon the whole, the single question is, whether the parliament can legally impose duties to be paid *by the people of these colonies only,* for the sole purpose of raising a revenue, *on commodities which she obliges us to take from her alone,* or, in other words, whether the parliament can legally take money out of our pockets, without our consent. If they can, our boasted liberty is but *vox et praeterea nihil* [a sound and nothing else].

. . .

Every government at some time or other falls into wrong measures. These may proceed from mistake or passion. But every such measure does not dissolve the obligation between the governors and the governed. The mistake may be corrected; the passion may subside. It is the duty of the governed to endeavor to rectify the mistake, and to appease the passion. They have not at first any other right, than to represent their grievances, and to pray for redress, unless an emergency is so pressing as not to allow time for receiving an answer to their applications, which rarely happens. If their applications are disregarded, then that kind of *opposition* becomes justifiable which can be made without breaking the laws or disturbing the public peace. This conflicts in the *prevention of the oppressors reaping advantage from their oppressions,* and not in their punishment. For experience may teach them what reason did not; and harsh methods cannot be proper until milder ones have failed.

If at length it becomes undoubted that an inveterate resolution is formed to annihilate the liberties of the governed, the *English* history affords frequent examples of resistance by force. What particular circumstances will in any future case justify such resistance can never be ascertained till they happen. Perhaps it may be allowable to say generally, that it never can be justifiable until the people are fully convinced that any further submission will be destructive to their happiness.

. . .

The *nature* of any impositions laid by parliament on these colonies, must determine the *design* in laying them. It may not be easy in every instance to discover that design. Whenever it is doubtful, I think submission cannot be dangerous; nay, it must be right, for, in my opinion, there is no privilege these colonies claim, which they ought in *duty* and *prudence* more earnestly to maintain and defend, than the authority of the

British parliament to regulate the trade of all her dominions. Without this authority, the benefits she enjoys from our commerce, must be lost to her: The blessings we enjoy from our dependence upon her, must be lost to us. Her strength must decay; her glory vanish; and she cannot suffer without our partaking in her misfortune. *Let us therefore cherish her interests as our own, and give her everything, that it becomes* FREEMEN *to give or to receive.*

The *nature* of any impositions she may lay upon us may, in general, be known, by considering how far they relate to the preserving, in due order, at the connection between the several parts of the *British* empire. One thing we may be assured of, which is this—Whenever she imposes duties on commodities, to be paid only upon their exportation from *Great Britain* to these colonies, it is not a regulation of trade, but a design to raise a revenue upon us. Other instances may happen, which it may not be necessary at present to dwell on. I hope these colonies will never, to their latest existence, want understanding sufficient to discover the intentions of those who rule over them, nor the resolution necessary for asserting their interests. They will always have the same rights, that all free states have, of judging when their privileges are invaded, and of using all prudent measures for preserving them.

. . .

These duties, which will inevitably be levied upon us—which are now levying upon us—are *expressly* laid FOR THE SOLE PURPOSE OF TAKING MONEY. This is the true definition of "*taxes.*" They are therefore *taxes.* This money is to be taken from *us. We* are therefore taxed. *Those* who are *taxed* without their own consent, expressed by themselves or their representatives, are *slaves. We are taxed* without our own consent, expressed by ourselves or our representatives. *We* are therefore—SLAVES.

. . .

No free people ever existed, or can ever exist, without keeping, to use a common, but strong expression, "the purse strings," in their own hands. Where this is the case, *they* have a *constitutional check* upon the administration, which may thereby be brought into order *without violence:* But where such a power is not lodged in the *people,* oppression proceeds uncontrolled in its career, till the governed, transported into rage, seek redress in the midst of blood and confusion.

. . .

What shall we now think when, upon looking into the late act, we find the assemblies of these provinces thereby stripped of their authority *on these several heads?* The *declared* intention of the act is, "that a revenue should be raised IN HIS MAJESTY'S DOMINIONS IN AMERICA, for making a more certain and adequate provision *for defraying the charge of* THE ADMINISTRATION OF JUSTICE, and *the support of* CIVIL GOVERNMENT in such provinces where it shall be found necessary, and *toward further defraying the expenses of* DEFENDING, PROTECTING AND SECURING THE SAID DOMINIONS."

Let the reader pause here one moment—and reflect—whether the colony in which *he* lives, has not made such "certain and adequate provision" *for these purposes,* as is *by the colony judged suitable to its abilities, and all other circumstances.* Then let him reflect—whether if this act takes place, money is not to be raised on *that* colony *without its consent,* to make "provision" *for these purposes,* which *it does not judge to be suitable to its abilities, and all other circumstances.* Lastly, let him reflect—whether the people of that country are not in a state of the most abject slavery, *whose property may be taken from them* under the notion of right, *when they have refused to give it.*

. . .

. . . Is it possible to form an idea of a slavery more *complete,* more *miserable,* more *disgraceful,* than that of a people, where *justice is administered, government exercised,* and a *standing army maintained,* AT THE EXPENSE OF THE PEOPLE, and yet WITHOUT THE LEAST DEPENDENCE UPON THEM? . . .

. . .

A perpetual *jealousy,* respecting liberty, is absolutely requisite in all free states. The very texture of their constitution, in *mixed* governments, demands it. For the *cautions* with which power is distributed among the several orders, *imply,* that *each* has that share which is proper for the general welfare, and therefore that any further acquisition must be pernicious. *Machiavelli* employs a whole chapter in his discourses, to prove that a state, to be long lived, must be frequently corrected, and reduced to its first principles. But of all states that have existed, there never was any, in which this jealousy could be more proper than in these colonies. For the government here is not only *mixed,* but *dependent,* which circumstance occasions *a peculiarity in its form,* of a very delicate nature.

Two reasons induce me to desire, that this spirit of apprehension may be always kept up among us, in its utmost vigilance. The first is this—that as the happiness of these provinces indubitably consists in their connection with *Great Britain,* any separation between them is less likely to be occasioned by civil discords, if every disgusting measure is opposed singly, and *while it is new:* For in this manner of proceeding, every such measure is most likely to be rectified. On the other hand, oppressions and dissatisfactions being permitted to accumulate—*if ever* the governed throw off the load, *they will do more.* A people does not reform with moderation. . . .

. . .

When an act injurious to freedom has been *once* done, and the people *bear* it, the *repetition* of it is most likely to meet with submission. For as the *mischief* of the one was found to be tolerable, they will hope that of the second will prove so too; and they will not regard the *infamy* of the last, because they are stained with that of the first.

. . .

From these reflections I conclude, that every free state should incessantly watch, and instantly take alarm on any addition being made to the power exercised over them. . . .

. . .

DANIEL LEONARD

MASSACHUSETTENSIS (1775)

Daniel Leonard was a successful Boston lawyer. His vocal support for British authorities in the wake of the Boston Tea Party eventually led to his being run out of his home by an angry mob. In the winter and spring of 1774 and 1775, he published a series of essays in a Loyalist newspaper under the pseudonym "Massachusettensis." The essays were immediately recognized as one of the best defenses of the Loyalist cause by an American, and John Adams published a response to the essays under his own pseudonym, "Novanglus." When British troops evacuated Boston in 1776, Leonard left with them. His property in America was confiscated, and he accepted a judicial position in the British colony of Bermuda. He eventually moved permanently to England.

Is it reasonable for Britain to tax the colonies to help defray the costs of defending the empire? Is it plausible that colonial assemblies could perform all the governmental functions as Parliament? Can a political system operate effectively with fully autonomous local assemblies? Did the obligations of the English colonists to the Parliament lessen when they moved to North America? If the constitutional form of a government seems desirable, do citizens have a duty to be patient and work within the system when bad policies are adopted? Was Leonard right to worry about the risks of creating independent governments in America free from the checks and balances of the British constitution? Was there greater safety from being a part of the British empire? Under what conditions is it better to be part of a larger political system than be an independent state?

. . .

At the conclusion of the late war, Great-Britain found, that, though she had humbled her enemies, and greatly enlarged her own empire, that the national debt amounted to almost one hundred and fifty millions, and that the annual expense of keeping her extended dominions in a state of defense, which good policy dictates no less in a time of peace than war, was increased in proportion to the new acquisitions. Heavy taxes and duties were already laid, not only upon the luxuries and conveniences, but even the necessaries of life in Great-Britain and Ireland. She knew, that the colonies were as much benefited by the conquests in the late war, as any part of the empire, and indeed more so, as their continental foes were subdued, and they might now extend their settlements not only to Canada, but even to the western ocean—The greatest opening was given to agriculture, the natural livelihood of the country, that ever was known in the history of the world, and their trade was protected by the British navy. The revenue to the crown, from America, amounted to but little more than the charges of collecting it.—She thought it as reasonable, that the colonies should bear a part of the national burden, as that they should share in the national benefit. For this purpose, the stamp-act was passed. . . . At first we did not dream of denying the *authority* of parliament to tax us, much less to legislate for us. We had always considered ourselves, as a part of the British empire, and the parliament, as the supreme legislature of the whole. Acts of parliament for regulating our internal polity were familiar. We had paid postage, agreeable to act of parliament for establishing a post-office, duties imposed for regulating trade, and even for raising a revenue to the crown, without questioning the right, though we closely adverted to the rate or quantum. We knew that, in all those acts of government, the good of the whole had been consulted, and, whenever through want of information anything grievous had been ordained, we were sure of obtaining redress by a proper representation of it. We were happy in our subordination; but in an evil hour, under the influence of some malignant planet, the design was formed of opposing the stamp-act by a denial of the right of parliament to make it. . . .

. . .

Perhaps the whole story of empire does not furnish another instance of a forcible opposition to government with so much specious and so little real cause, with such apparent probability without any possibility of success. . . .

. . . An Englishman glories in being subject to and protected by such a government. The colonies are a part of the British empire. The best writers upon the laws of nations tell us, that when a nation takes possession of a distant country, and settles there, that country, though separated from the principal establishment or mother-country, naturally becomes a part of the state, equal with its ancient possessions. Two supreme or independent authorities cannot exist in the same state. It would be what is called *imperium in imperio,* and the height of political absurdity. The analogy between the political and human body is great. Two independent authorities in a state would be like two distinct principles of volition and action in the human body, dissenting, opposing, and destroying each other. If then we are a part of the British empire, we must be subject to the supreme power of the state, which is vested in the estates of parliament, notwithstanding each of the colonies have legislative and executive powers of their own, delegated or granted to them for the purposes of regulating their own internal police, which are subordinate, and must necessarily be subject, to the checks, control and regulation of the supreme authority.

This doctrine is not new; but the denial of it is. It is beyond a doubt that it was the sense both of the parent country and our ancestors, that they were to remain subject to parliament; it is evident from the charter itself, and this authority has been exercised by parliament, from time to time, almost ever since the first settlement of the country, and has been expressly acknowledged by our provincial legislatures. It is not less our interest than our duty to continue subject to the authority of parliament. . . . [W]here shall we find the British constitution, that we all agree we are entitled to? We shall seek for it in vain in our provincial assemblies. They are but faint sketches of the estates of parliament. The houses of representatives or burgesses have not all the powers of the house of commons: in the charter governments they have no more than what is expressly granted by their several charters. The first charters, granted to this province, did not empower the assembly to tax the people at all. . . . [T]he supposition of our being independent states, or exempt from the authority of parliament, destroys the very idea of our having a British constitution. The provincial constitutions, considered as subordinate, are generally well adapted to those purposes of government, for which they were intended, that is, to regulate the internal police of the several colonies; but, having no principle of stability within themselves, tho' they may support themselves in moderate times, they would be merged by the violence of turbulent ones. The several colonies would become wholly monarchical or wholly republican, were it not for the checks, controls, regulations and supports, of the supreme authority of the empire. Thus, the argument that is drawn from their first principle of our being entitled to English liberties, destroys the principle itself; it deprives us of the bill of rights, and all the benefits resulting from the revolution, of English laws, and of the British constitution.

. . .

Let us now suppose the colonies united and molded into some form of government. Think one moment of the revenue necessary both to support this government and to provide for even the appearance of defense. Conceive yourselves in a manner exhausted by the conflict with Great-Britain, now staggering and sinking under the load of your own taxes, and the weight of your own government. Consider further, that to render government operative and salutary, *subordination* is necessary. This our patriots need not be told of; and when once they had mounted the steed, and found themselves so well seated as to run no risk of being thrown from the saddle, the severity of their discipline to restore subordination, would be in proportion to their former treachery in destroying it. We have already seen specimens of their tyranny, in their inhuman treatment of persons guilty of no crime, except that of differing in sentiment from themselves. What then must we expect from such scourges of mankind, when supported by imperial power?

To elude the difficulty, resulting from our defenseless situation, we are told, that the colonies would open a free trade with all the world, and all nations would join in protecting their common mart. A very little reflection will convince us that this is chimerical. American trade, however beneficial to Great-Britain, while she can command it, would be but as a drop of the bucket, or the light dust of the balance, to all the commercial states of Europe. Besides, were British fleets and armies no longer destined to our protection, in a very short time France and Spain would recover possession of those territories, that were torn, reluctant and bleeding from them, in the last war, by the superior strength of Britain. . . .

Great-Britain aside, what earthly power could stretch out the compassionate arm to shield us from those powers, that have long beheld us with the sharp, piercing eyes of avidity, and have heretofore bled freely and expended their millions to obtain us? . . . Which state would you prefer being annexed to, France, Spain, or Holland? I suppose the latter, as it is a republic: but are you sure, that the other powers of Europe would be idle spectators, content to suffer the Dutch to engross the American colonies or their trade? And what figure would the Dutch probably make in the unequal contest? Their sword has been long since sheathed in commerce. . . .

. . .

The end or design of government, as has been already observed, is the security of the people from internal violence and rapacity, and from foreign invasion. The supreme power of a state must necessarily be so extensive and ample as to answer those purposes; otherwise it is constituted in vain, and degenerates into empty parade and mere ostentatious pageantry. These purposes cannot be answered, without a power to raise a revenue; for without it neither the laws can be executed nor the state defended. This revenue ought, in national concerns, to be apportioned throughout the whole empire according to the abilities of the several parts; as the claim of each to protection is equal: a refusal to yield the former is as unjust as the withholding the latter. . . . If the proportion of each part was to be determined only by itself in a separate legislature; it would not only involve it in the absurdity of *imperium in imperio,* but the perpetual contention arising from the predominant principle of self-interest in each, without having any common arbiter between them, would render the disjointed, discordant, torn and dismembered state incapable of collecting or conducting its force and energy, for the preservation of the whole, as emergencies might require. A government thus constituted would contain the seeds of dissolution in its first principles, and must soon destroy itself.

. . .

From what source has the *wealth* of the colonies flowed? Whence is it derived? Not from agriculture only. Exclusive of commerce, the colonists would this day have been a poor people, possessed of little more than the necessaries for supporting life; of course their numbers would be few; for population always keeps pace with the ability of maintaining a family: there would have been but little or no resort of strangers here; the arts and sciences would have made but small progress; the inhabitants would rather have degenerated into a state of ignorance and barbarity. Or had Great-Britain laid such restrictions upon our trade, as our patriots would induce us to believe, that is, had we been pouring the fruits of all our labor into the lap of our parent, and been enriching her by the sweat of our brow, without receiving an equivalent; the patrimony derived from our ancestors must have dwindled from little to less, till their posterity should have suffered a general bankruptcy.

But how different are the effects of our connection with, and subordination to Britain? They are too strongly marked to escape the most careless observer. Our merchants are opulent, and our yeomanry in easier circumstances than the noblesse of some states: Population is so rapid as to double the number of inhabitants in the short period of twenty-five years: Cities are springing up in the depths of the wilderness: Schools, colleges, and even universities, are interspersed through the continent: Our country abounds with foreign refinements, and flows with exotic luxuries. These are infallible marks, not only of *opulence,* but of *freedom*. . . .

. . .

THOMAS JEFFERSON

DECLARATION OF INDEPENDENCE (1776)

In 1774, the First Continental Congress assembled to develop a collective response in the colonies to Parliament's imposition of the Coercive, or Intolerable, Acts, suspending self-government in Massachusetts. A boycott of British goods proved ineffective, and violence escalated in Boston. In 1775, the Second Continental Congress appointed George Washington to lead a continental army. By 1776, the American public had given up on reconciling with Britain, and Congress appointed a committee to draft the Declaration of Independence. Thomas Jefferson took the lead in drafting the document, and a final version was approved on July 4, 1776, and individually signed by the members of Congress. The Declaration was widely publicized, and the date of its adoption was immediately embraced as Independence Day. The Declaration was endorsed by local colonial assemblies. The Declaration of Independence adopted on July 4 was only one of numerous documents produced by Congress, colonial assemblies, town meetings, and the like that both announced a political separation from Britain and justified the actions that the colonists were taking. Jefferson's own draft of the Declaration drew not only on broad philosophical sources but also on earlier protests of British policy, including his own 1774 pamphlet elaborating the rights of the colonies and the abuses of the British government. The finished document helped shape public and international opinion on the revolutionary movement, and after the war it became a key touchstone of the American political creed.

What might the claim that "all men are created equal" mean? What are "unalienable rights"? Does the Declaration provide any reasons for believing these claims? Under what conditions can a people legitimately "abolish" the existing government? Does the Declaration make a persuasive case that those conditions had been satisfied? Who are "the governed" and "the people" who give and withhold consent to the government, and how can they be identified? Could the Continental Congress reasonably speak on behalf of the people? How could the people voice their desire to alter or abolish the government today?

. . .

We hold these truths to be self-evident, that all men are created equal, that they are endowed by their Creator with certain unalienable rights, that among these are life, liberty and the pursuit of happiness. That to secure these rights, governments are instituted among men, deriving their just powers from the consent of the governed. That whenever any form of government becomes destructive to these ends, it is the right of the people to alter or to abolish it, and to institute new government, laying its foundation on such principles and organizing its powers in such form, as to them shall seem most likely to effect their safety and happiness. . . . The history of the present King of Great Britain is a history of repeated injuries and usurpations, all having in direct object the establishment of an absolute tyranny over these states. To prove this, let facts be submitted to a candid world.

. . .

He has dissolved representative houses repeatedly, for opposing with manly firmness his invasions on the rights of the people.

. . .

He has made judges dependent on his will alone, for the tenure of their offices, and the amount and payment of their salaries.

He has erected a multitude of new offices, and sent hither swarms of officers to harass our people, and eat out their substance.

He has kept among us, in times of peace, standing armies without the consent of our legislature.

. . .

He has combined with others [Parliament] to subject us to a jurisdiction foreign to our constitution, and unacknowledged by our laws; giving his assent to their acts of pretended legislation:

For quartering large bodies of armed troops among us:

. . .

For imposing taxes on us without our consent:

For depriving us in many cases, of the benefits of trial by jury:

. . .

For suspending our own legislatures, and declaring themselves invested with power to legislate for us in all cases whatsoever.

. . . He has excited domestic insurrections amongst us, and has endeavored to bring on the inhabitants of our frontiers, the merciless Indian savages, whose known rule of warfare, is undistinguished destruction of all ages, sexes and conditions.[8]

. . .

Nor have we been wanting in attention to our British brethren. We have warned them from time to time of attempts by their legislature to extend an unwarrantable jurisdiction over us. We have reminded them of the circumstances of our emigration and settlement here. We have appealed to their native justice and magnanimity, and we have conjured them by the ties of our common kindred to disavow these usurpations, which, would inevitably interrupt our connections and correspondence. They too have been deaf to the voice of justice and of consanguinity. We must, therefore, acquiesce in the necessity, which denounces our separation, and hold them, as we hold the rest of mankind, enemies in war, in peace friends.

We, therefore, the representatives of the United States of America, in General Congress, assembled, appealing to the Supreme Judge of the world for the rectitude of our intentions, do, in the name, and by the authority of the good people of these colonies, solemnly publish and declare, that these united colonies are, and of right ought to be free and independent states; that they are absolved from all allegiance to the British Crown, and that all political connection between them and the state of Great Britain, is and ought to be totally dissolved. . . .

8 At this point, Jefferson penned an attack on the international slave trade. "[H]e has waged cruel war against human nature itself, violating its most sacred rights of life & liberty in the persons of a distant people who never offended him, captivating & carrying them to slavery in another hemisphere, or to incur miserable death in their transportations thither. This piratical warfare, the opprobrium of infidel powers, is the warfare of the Christian king of Great Britain. Determined to keep open a market where MEN should be bought & sold, he has prostituted his negative for suppressing every legislative attempt to prohibit or to restrain this execrable commerce and that this assemblage of horrors might want no fact of distinguished die, he is now exciting those very people to rise in arms against us, and to purchase that liberty of which he has deprived them, by murdering the people upon whom he also obtruded them; thus paying off former crimes which he urges them to commit against the lives of another." Congress voted to delete this passage.

FOR FURTHER STUDY

Adams, John. *John Adams: Revolutionary Writings*, ed. Gordon Wood (New York: Library of America, 2011).

Bailyn, Bernard, ed. *Pamphlets of the American Revolution, 1750–1776* (Cambridge, MA: Harvard University Press, 1965).

Franklin, Benjamin. *Franklin: The Autobiography and Other Writings on Politics, Economics and Virtue*, ed. Alan Houston (New York: Cambridge University Press, 2004).

Hyneman, Charles S., and Donald S. Lutz, eds. *American Political Writings during the Founding Era, 1760–1805* (Indianapolis, IN: Liberty Fund, 1983).

Lutz, Donald S., ed. *Colonial Origins of the American Constitution: A Documentary History* (Indianapolis, IN: Liberty Fund, 1998).

Merrill, Jensen, ed. *Tracts of the American Revolution, 1763–1776* (Indianapolis, IN: Bobbs-Merrill, 1967).

Morgan, Edmund S. *Puritan Political Ideas, 1558–1794* (Indianapolis, IN: Bobbs-Merrill, 1965).

Paine, Thomas. *Paine: Political Writings*, ed. Bruce Kuklick (New York: Cambridge University Press, 2000).

Sandoz, Ellis, ed. *Political Sermons of the American Founding Era, 1730–1805* (Indianapolis, IN: Liberty Fund, 1991).

Vaughan, Alden, ed. *The Puritan Tradition in America, 1620–1730* (Hanover, NH: University Press of New England, 1997).

SUGGESTED READINGS

Bailyn, Bernard. *The Ideological Origins of the American Revolution* (Cambridge, MA: Harvard University Press, 1967).

Becker, Carl. *The Declaration of Independence: A Study in the History of Political Ideas* (New York: Random House, 1958).

Bercovitch, Sacvan. *The American Jeremiad* (Madison: University of Wisconsin Press, 1978).

Breen, T. H. *American Insurgents, American Patriots: The Revolution of the People* (New York: Hill and Wang, 2010).

Colbourn, Trevor. *The Lamp of Experience: Whig History and the Intellectual Origins of the American Revolution* (Chapel Hill: University of North Carolina Press, 1965).

Greene, Jack P. *Peripheries and Center: Constitutional Development in the Extended Polities of British Empire and the United States, 1607–1788* (Athens: University of Georgia Press, 1986).

Greene, Jack P. *The Constitutional Origins of the American Revolution* (New York: Cambridge University Press, 2010).

Kammen, Michael G. *Deputyes and Libertyes: The Origins of Representative Government in Colonial America* (New York: Knopf, 1969).

Kerber, Linda. *Women of the Republic: Intellect and Ideology in Revolutionary America* (Chapel Hill: University of North Carolina Press, 1980).

Kramnick, Isaac. *Republicanism and Bourgeois Radicalism: Political Ideology in Late Eighteenth-Century England and America* (Ithaca, NY: Cornell University Press, 1990).

LaCroix, Alison L. *The Ideological Origins of American Federalism* (Cambridge, MA: Harvard University Press, 2010).

Lutz, Donald S. *Popular Consent and Popular Control: Whig Political Theory in the Early State Constitutions* (Baton Rouge: Louisiana State University Press, 1988).

Maier, Pauline. *American Scripture: Making the Declaration of Independence* (New York: Vintage, 1997).

Maloy, J. S. *The Colonial American Origins of Modern Democratic Thought* (New York: Cambridge University Press, 2010).

McConville, Brendan. *The King's Three Faces: The Rise and Fall of Royal America, 1688–1776* (Chapel Hill: University of North Carolina Press, 2007).

McIlwain, Charles Howard. *The American Revolution: A Constitutional Interpretation* (New York: Macmillan, 1923).

McLaughlin, Andrew C. *The Foundations of American Constitutionalism* (New York: New York University Press, 1932).

McWilliams, Wilson Carey. *The Idea of Fraternity in America* (Berkeley: University of California Press, 1973).

Miller, Perry. *Errand into the Wilderness* (Cambridge, MA: Harvard University Press, 1964).

Morgan, Edmund S. *Visible Saints: The History of a Puritan Ideal* (Ithaca, NY: Cornell University Press, 1965).

Nash, Gary B. *The Unknown American Revolution: The Unruly Birth of Democracy and the Struggle to Create America* (New York: Viking, 2005).

Nelson, Eric. *The Royalist Revolution: Monarchy and the American Founding* (Cambridge, MA: Harvard University Press, 2014).

Perry, Lewis. *Intellectual Life in America: A History* (Chicago, IL: University of Chicago Press, 1989).

Pocock, J. G. A., ed. *Three British Revolutions: 1641, 1688, 1776* (Princeton, NJ: Princeton University Press, 1980).

Potter, Janice. *The Liberty We Seek: Loyalist Ideology in Colonial New York and Massachusetts* (Cambridge, MA: Harvard University Press, 1983).

Reid, Thomas Phillip. *The Constitutional History of the American Revolution*, four volumes (Madison: University of Wisconsin Press, 1986–1993).

Rossiter, Clinton L. *Seedtime of the Republic* (New York: Harcourt, 1953).

Stoner, James R. *The Common Law and Liberal Theory: Coke, Hobbes, and the Origins of American Constitutionalism* (Lawrence: University Press of Kansas, 1992).

White, Morton G. *The Philosophy of the American Revolution* (New York: Oxford University Press, 1978).

Wood, Gordon S. *The Radicalism of the American Revolution* (New York: Vintage, 1991).

Yirush, Craig. *Settlers, Liberty, and Empire: The Roots of Early American Political Theory, 1675–1775* (New York: Cambridge University Press, 2011).

CHAPTER 3

THE FOUNDING ERA, 1776–1791

I. INTRODUCTION

Novus Ordo Seclorum—A New Order of the Ages—declares the reverse of the seal of the United States. The project of founding a new order began even before the colonists declared their independence from Great Britain. The English authorities had disrupted the established colonial governments, and the revolutionaries were forced to establish alternative forms of political organization that could mobilize opposition to the English and coordinate plans. Establishing those forms of governance was necessarily fluid in a rapidly evolving situation. Popularly elected revolutionary assemblies both governed and drafted constitutions, leading Thomas Jefferson to worry that the state constitutions were not sufficiently entrenched as a higher law that would stand separate and supreme to the legislature. The state governments in turn sent delegates to the Continental Congress, which drafted Articles of Confederation to serve as a federal constitution. But the Articles languished for years before the state legislatures bothered to ratify it. No doubt the states thought Congress was sufficiently restrained, since its membership was all under the direct control of the state legislatures.

Political innovation and experimentation was the order of the day. The revolutionary constitutions reacted against the perceived abuses of the colonial governors. Legislatures—the voice of the people—reigned supreme. Legislators were to be held accountable through frequent elections. But the people soon tired of their legislatures. Often without any mechanism for amending the constitution, constitutional drafters would simply have to start over, throwing out the old constitution and adopting an entirely new one. When towns in Massachusetts objected to a new constitution, they insisted on a ratification vote as a way to place a check on constitutional drafters. The new constitutions adopted more robust systems of checks and balances, complicating notions of popular government.

The era of new constitutional foundings drew to a close with the meeting of a constitutional convention in Philadelphia in the summer of 1787 to consider amending the Articles of Confederation. James Madison quickly shifted the agenda of the convention by drafting

FIGURE 3-1 TIMELINE OF THE FOUNDING ERA

Events	Year	Writings
George Washington crosses the Delaware River	1776	
	1776	Virginia Declaration of Rights adopted
	1776	John Adams's Thoughts on Government
	1777	Articles of Confederation drafted
	1777	Thomas Jefferson's Bill Establishing Religious Freedom
France recognizes American independence	1778	
Pennsylvania first state to abolish slavery	1780	
Massachusetts Constitution ratified	1780	
British surrender at Yorktown	1781	
Articles of Confederation ratified	1781	
Treaty of Paris ending American Revolution	1783	
Shay's Rebellion begins	1786	
Annapolis Convention	1786	
Constitutional Convention in Philadelphia	1787	
	1787	U.S. Constitution drafted
	1787	Brutus essays published in New York newspapers
	1787	Federalist Papers published in New York newspapers
	1787	Thomas Jefferson's Notes on the State of Virginia
U.S. Constitution ratified	1788	
George Washington inaugurated as president	1789	
	1789	James Madison introduces the federal Bill of Rights in Congress
French Declaration of the Rights of Man	1789	
Rhode Island last of original states to ratify U.S. Constitution	1790	
Edmund Burke's Reflections on the Revolution of France	1790	
Federal Bill of Rights ratified	1791	

the Virginia Plan, which proposed abandoning the Articles and replacing it with a new federal constitution. The U.S. Constitution would grant expansive new powers to the federal government to achieve national objectives and impose new limits on the state governments. It shifted power and authority away from a confederation of equal states and toward popular, national majorities. It replaced a single legislative chamber with no enforcement powers and controlled by states with a bicameral legislature situated within a three-branch system of government. The battle for ratification was hard-fought, with anti-Federalists objecting to the creation of a more powerful, distant central government with insufficient limits. The Bill of Rights marked a modest concession to anti-Federalist objections, carefully designed to mollify the opposition to the new government while not interfering with its objectives.

Politics. The years under the Articles of Confederation were once characterized as the "critical period."[1] These seemed like critical days in which the future of the union and of republican government was tested. The possibility that the nation might fail the test seemed real, with economic conditions less than ideal and political dysfunction apparently rampant. More recently, the Confederation period has been painted in brighter colors. Democracy seemed to blossom with the Declaration of Independence. The people were given new control over government, and the colonial checks on popular decision making were taken off. But democratic practices were still rudimentary. Annual elections and term limits were common. But legislative seats were distributed by convenience, often centered around towns but not necessarily adjusted to reflect changing patterns of population growth and western migration. Voice voting, rather than written ballots, in public meetings under the watchful eyes of local elites was routine in many jurisdictions.

The division between Federalists and anti-Federalists built on local political factions. The Federalists favored ratification of the U.S. Constitution and a stronger national government capable of advancing national interests. The anti-Federalists opposed ratification, preferring to keep most political power in the hands of the state governments. These were marriages of convenience. The Federalists were often drawn from the ranks of politicians who had held national office under the Articles of Confederation and who had ties to commercial interests with a more national and international orientation. The anti-Federalists had fewer national ties, grounded as they were in state-level officials and local economic and social interests. The Federalists John Jay and Alexander Hamilton were local rivals of New York governor George Clinton, who opposed ratification. The Federalist James Madison was an architect of the U.S. Constitution, but was under constant pressure from the powerful and more senior Patrick Henry, who dominated Virginia politics. Anti-Federalists like Clinton and Henry did little to coordinate their actions, while Madison and Hamilton had not only worked together to organize the constitutional convention in Philadelphia but continued to work together to get the Constitution adopted.

---

1 See John Fiske, *The Critical Period in American History, 1783–1789* (Cambridge, MA: Riverside Press, 1898).

Society. The Confederation period was a time of social unrest. The old social order threatened to dissolve along with the old political order. Ordinary soldiers in the Continental Army demanded new political power and social status. Farmers found their hold over their land threatened by debt and fluctuations in the market, and they sought ways to recover their position. Most famously, Shay's Rebellion broke out in 1786 in western Massachusetts and lasted for months as hundreds of farmers closed courthouses and blocked sheriffs to prevent foreclosures on farms for failure to pay taxes before being put down by the state militia. Both colonial and British forces recruited slaves to fight as soldiers in exchange for their freedom, but the Continental Army stopped the practice out of concern for the stability of the larger slave system. With peace came new attention to the antislavery cause and new demands from slaves and free blacks for greater freedoms of their own. The northern states moved to end slavery within their borders, creating a stark divide in the union between states committed to freedom and those who retained slavery.

The place of women in the emerging society likewise had to be negotiated. War had disrupted many family relations, and the struggle for independence had mobilized many women to play visible roles in public affairs. Republican ideas and the new emphasis on liberty and equality called into question old assumptions about the social order. A prominent response was the development of what modern historians have called the idea of "republican motherhood."[2] Women were praised as playing an essential role in creating and maintaining republican government, but they did so through their work in the domestic sphere rather than participating in the political arena. Republican government was understood to require a virtuous and patriotic citizenry, and women bore the primary responsibility for instilling those qualities in the next generation. Nonetheless, the thought that women might do more and participate directly in the public sphere was now being raised.

Ideas. American thought in the founding period revolved around the proper organization of government. The Americans were now responsible for creating governments of their own, and there at least seemed to be the possibility that they could start with a clean slate. All agreed that good government would be popular government. How best to instantiate popular government was the question.

In the late eighteenth century, a serious education was a classical education. The men who debated how best to found an American republic knew their Greeks and Romans, and more modern commentaries on them. Thomas Jefferson's reading list for his teenage nephew began with "a course of antient history, reading every thing in the original and not in translations."[3] Plutarch, Thucydides, Plato, and Cicero were familiar names. As James Madison prepared his proposals for constitutional reform, he ransacked his library (and the two trunks of books that Thomas Jefferson shipped to him from Europe) with a

---

2 See Linda K. Kerber, *Women of the Republic* (Chapel Hill: University of North Carolina Press, 1980).

3 Thomas Jefferson, *Memoir, Correspondence, and Miscellanies*, ed. Thomas Jefferson Randolph, vol. 1 (Charlottesville, VA: F. Carr, 1829), 286.

particular interest in possible parallels between historical confederacies and republics and the American Confederation. Especially when viewed through the prism of more modern commentators, they often drew the lesson that a well-ordered state sought to protect liberty, but that demagogues and turmoil were a constant threat in democracies and confederacies were prone to internal strains from antagonistic interests.

Modern republican thinkers gave the founders some confidence that they benefitted from "a new science of politics," as James Madison put it in the *Federalist Papers*. A growing body of work in political philosophy was placing emphasis on the need for polities to counterbalance interests to avoid the eventual subversion of the state. As Montesquieu concluded, "every man invested with power is apt to abuse it. . . . To prevent this abuse, it is necessary from the very nature of things that power should be a check to power."[4] But modern writers were also elaborating the social and economic conditions of free societies and the moral foundations of good government. The Scottish writer Adam Ferguson warned that "where fortune constitutes rank . . . [they] lead men through the practice of sordid and mercenary arts to the possession of a supposed elevation and dignity." A "dutiful" citizenry and "upright" government officials were essential to block such corrupting influences.[5] The Massachusetts Federalist Jonathan Mason declared that after the revolution, "we are now in the possession of those rights and privileges attendant upon the original state of nature, with the opportunity of establishing a government for ourselves," but Americans had the unique advantage having "the experience of ages to copy from."[6]

II. DEMOCRACY AND LIBERTY

Major Developments

- Debate over the requirements of republican government
- The development of the idea of checks and balances
- The formation of complex republican constitutions

By 1776, the American colonists had been gradually moving toward independence for over a decade. But the publication of Tom Paine's *Common Sense* in the same year as the signing of the Declaration of Independence irreversibly linked the cause of American independence with the cause of popular government. Paine made a mockery of the "mixed constitution" of England, contending monarchies had done nothing but lay "the world in blood and ashes." In England, "a king hath little more to do than to make war and give away places; which in plain terms, is to impoverish the nation and set it together by the ears." Good government had no place for "crowned ruffians."[7] The American Revolution was fought to throw off monarchy as well as British imperialism. It announced a change in the form of government as well as a change in its location.

---

4 Montesquieu, *The Spirit of the Laws*, 4th ed., vol. 1 (London: J. Nourse and P. Vaillant, 1766), 220.

5 Adam Ferguson, *An Essay on the History of Civil Society* (Dublin: Boulter Grierson, 1767), 240.

6 Jonathan Mason, "Oration at Boston, 1780," in *Principles and Acts of the Revolution in America*, ed. Hezekiah Niles (Baltimore, MD: William Ogden Niles, 1822), 46.

7 Thomas Paine, *Common Sense* (Philadelphia, PA: W. and T. Bradford, 1776), 29, 31.

After 1776, there was widespread agreement that the United States would be a republic. What republican government required was less certain. There were few models of purely popular governments that could provide much guidance. Ancient democracies seemed to threaten liberty more than advance it—mob rule by another name. More modern republics were incomplete and unstable. Massachusetts judge James Sullivan suggested that "The poor and the rich are alike interested in that important part of government called legislation," and proposed the adoption of universal manhood suffrage. His friend John Adams was appalled. Sullivan had taken the principle that the legitimacy of government is derived from the consent of the governed too far. If taken too literally, then how "arises the Right of the Majority to govern, and the Obligation of the Minority to obey?" Why not extend the franchise to women and children as well, since they too were subject to the laws? Adams argued instead that only the well qualified should hold the important public office of elector. Only "when the Understanding and Will of Men . . . is fit to be trusted by the Public" should they be given access to a ballot. Property holding was a crucial marker of independent and sober judgment. The proper goal for establishing a secure republican government was not to open up the franchise, but rather to "make the Acquisition of Land easy to every Member of Society."[8] How best to preserve both liberty and popular government was the challenge for those trying to found new governments in the midst of the Revolution. As Samuel Adams, John's cousin, reminded a correspondent, "The Commonwealth of England last twelve years, and then the exiled King was restored with all the Rage & Madness of Royalty!" The Americans would have to be zealous in practicing "the moral and political Virtues upon which the very Existence of a Commonwealth depends."[9]

The quest to establish a republican form of government in the United States that was consistent with liberty occupied much of the attention of political leaders in the first several years of independence. John Adams in Massachusetts and Carter Braxton in Virginia offered relatively conservative advice on founding revolutionary governments. Thomas Jefferson successfully proposed separating government from organized religion in Virginia. The transition from the Articles of Confederation to the U.S. Constitution prompted an extended debate between Federalists and anti-Federalists over how constitutional government should be organized.

8 John Adams, *The Papers of John Adams*, ed. Robert Joseph Taylor, vol. 4 (Cambridge, MA: Harvard University Press, 1979), 211, 213.

9 Samuel Adams, *The Writings of Samuel Adams*, ed. Harry Alonzo Cushing, vol. 4 (New York: G.P. Putnam's Sons, 1908), 312.

JOHN ADAMS

THOUGHTS ON GOVERNMENT (1776)

John Adams was one of the most influential lawyers in revolutionary America. He quickly rose to a leading role among the Massachusetts patriots in the 1760s and 1770s and developed sharp legal and political attacks on British claims to authority. He was thus a natural choice to represent the colony at the Continental Congress, where he helped draft the Declaration of Independence and oversee the war effort. After the war, he drafted the influential Massachusetts Constitution of 1780 before serving as the primary American diplomat in Europe. Upon returning to the United States, he was elected vice president and then president of the United States.

His "Thoughts on Government" was published as a pamphlet by a close ally, the Virginian Richard Henry Lee. The pamphlet reflected the advice that Adams was offering to politicians in various states who were drafting new constitutions after the start of the war. Adams urged the creation of republican governments, drawing on the extensive literature on constitutionalism and popular government that had been produced in Europe over the past century, as well as more classical thought. Adams advocated for the creation of a "mixed government" that incorporated a natural aristocracy to help balance and moderate democratic tendencies.

What is republican government for Adams? Why does Adams favor a mixed government? Is a mixed government consistent with republicanism? How do his constitutional suggestions in 1776 differ from the design of the U.S. Constitution? Are all of his ideas about a properly constructed constitutional government still in favor?

. . .

We ought to consider what is the end of government, before we determine which is the best form. Upon this point all speculative politicians will agree, that the happiness of society is the end of government, as all divines and moral philosophers will agree that the happiness of the individual is the end of man. From this principle it will follow, that the form of government which communicates ease, comfort, security, or, in one word, happiness, to the greatest number of persons, and in the greatest degree, is the best.

All sober inquirers after truth, ancient and modern, pagan and Christian, have declared that the happiness of man, as well as his dignity, consists in virtue. . . .

. . .

Fear is the foundation of most governments; but it is so sordid and brutal a passion, and renders men in whose breasts it predominates so stupid and miserable, that Americans will not be likely to approve of any political institution which is founded on it.

Honor is truly sacred, but holds a lower rank in the scale of moral excellence than virtue. Indeed, the former is but a part of the latter, and consequently has not equal pretensions to support a frame of government productive of human happiness.

The foundation of every government is some principle or passion in the minds of the people. The noblest principles and most generous affections in our nature, then, have the fairest chance to support the noblest and most generous models of government.

. . [T]here is no good government but what is republican. That the only valuable part of the British constitution is so; because the very definition of a republic is "an empire of laws, and not of men." That, as a republic is the best form of governments, so that particular arrangement of the powers of society, or, in other words, that form of government which is best contrived to secure an impartial and exact execution of the laws, is the best of republics.

. . .

As good government is an empire of laws, how shall your laws be made? In a large society, inhabiting an extensive country, it is impossible that the whole should assemble to make laws. The first necessary step, then, is to depute power from the many to a few of the most wise and good. . . .

The principal difficulty lies, and the greatest care should be employed, in constituting this representative assembly. It should be in miniature an exact portrait of the people at large. It should think, feel, reason, and act like them. That it may be the interest of this assembly to do strict justice at all times, it should be an equal representation, or, in other words, equal interests among the people should have equal interests in it. Great care should be taken to effect this, and to prevent unfair, partial, and corrupt elections. Such regulations, however, may be better made in times of greater tranquility than the present; and they will spring up themselves naturally, when all the powers of government come to be in the hands of the people's friends. At present, it will be safest to proceed in all established modes, to which the people have been familiarized by habit.

. . . I think a people cannot be long free, nor ever happy, whose government is in one assembly. My reasons for this opinion are as follow:—

1. A single assembly is liable to all the vices, follies, and frailties of an individual; subject to fits of humor, starts of passion, flights of enthusiasm, partialities, or prejudices, and consequently productive of hasty results and absurd judgments. . . .

2. A single assembly is apt to be avaricious, and in times will not scruple to exempt itself from burdens. . . .

3. A single assembly is apt to grow ambitious, and after a time will not hesitate to vote itself perpetual. . . .

4. A representative assembly, although extremely well qualified, and absolutely necessary, as a branch of the legislative, is unfit to exercise the executive power, for want of two essential properties, secrecy and dispatch.

5. A representative assembly is still less qualified for the judicial power, because it is too numerous, too slow, and too little skilled in the laws.

6. Because a single assembly, possessed of all the powers of government, would make arbitrary laws for their own interest, execute all laws arbitrarily for their own interest, and adjudge all controversies in their own favor.

But shall the whole power of legislation rest in one assembly? Most of the foregoing reasons apply equally to prove that the legislative power ought to be more complex; to which we may add, that if the legislative power is wholly in one assembly, and the executive in another, or in a single person, these two powers will oppose and encroach upon each other, until the contest shall end in war, and the whole power, legislative and executive, be usurped by the strongest.

The judicial power, in such case, could not mediate, or hold the balance between the two contending powers, because the legislative would undermine it. And this shows the necessity, too, of giving the executive power a negative upon the legislative, otherwise this will be continually encroaching upon that.

To avoid these dangers, let a distinct assembly be constituted, as a mediator between the two extreme branches of the legislature, that which represents the people, and that which is vested with the executive power.

Let the representative assembly then elect by ballot, from among themselves or their constituents, or both, a distinct assembly, which, for the sake of perspicuity, we will call a council. It may consist of any number you please, say twenty or thirty, and should have a free and independent exercise of its judgment, and consequently a negative voice in the legislature.

These two bodies, thus constituted, and made integral parts of the legislature, let them unite, and by joint ballot choose a governor, who, after being stripped of most of those badges of domination, called prerogatives, should have a free and independent exercise of his judgment, and be made also an integral part of the legislature. This, I know, is liable to objections; and, if you please, you may make him only president of the council, as in Connecticut. But as the governor is to be invested with the executive power, with consent of council, I think he ought to have a negative upon the legislative. If he is annually elective, as he ought to be, he will always have so much reverence and affection for the people, their representatives and counselors, that, although you give him an independent exercise of his judgment, he will seldom use it in opposition to the two houses, except in cases the public utility of which would be conspicuous. . . .

. . . And these and all other elections . . . should be annual, there not being in the whole circle of the sciences a maxim more infallible than this, "where annual elections end, there slavery begins."

. . . This will teach them the great political virtues of humility, patience, and moderation, without which every man in power becomes a ravenous beast of prey.

This mode of constituting the great offices of state will answer very well for the present; but if by experiment it should be found inconvenient, the legislature may, at its leisure, devise other methods of creating them, by elections of the people at large . . . or it may change the term for which they shall be chosen to seven years, or three years, or for life, or make any other alterations which the society shall find productive. . . .

A rotation of all offices . . . has many advocates. . . . It would be attended, no doubt, with many advantages; and if the society has a sufficient number of suitable characters to supply the great number of vacancies which would be made by such a rotation, I can see no objection to it. These persons may be allowed to serve for three years, and then be excluded three years, or for any longer or shorter term.

. . .

Judges, justices, and all other officers, civil and military, should be nominated and appointed by the governor, with the advice and consent of council, unless you choose to have a government more popular; if you do, all officers, civil and military, may be chosen by joint ballot of both houses; or, in order to preserve the independence and importance of each house, by ballot of one house, concurred in by the other. Sheriffs should be chosen by the freeholders of counties; so should registers of deeds and clerks of counties.

. . .

. . . [T]he judicial power ought to be distinct from both the legislative and executive, and independent upon both, that so it may be a check upon both, as both should be checks upon that. The judges, therefore, should be always men of learning and experience in the laws, of exemplary morals, great patience, calmness, coolness, and attention. Their minds should not be distracted with jarring interests; they should not be dependent upon any man, or body of men. To these ends, they should hold estates for life in their offices; or, in other words, their commissions should be during good behavior. . . . For misbehavior, the grand inquest of the colony, the house of representatives, should impeach them. . . .

A militia law, requiring all men, or with very few exceptions besides cases of conscience, to be provided with arms and ammunition, to be trained at certain seasons . . . is always a wise institution, and, in the present circumstances of our country, indispensable.

Laws for the liberal education of youth, especially of the lower class of people, are so extremely wise and useful, that, to a humane and generous mind, no expense for this purpose would be thought extravagant.

The very mention of sumptuary laws will excite a smile. Whether our countrymen have wisdom and virtue enough to submit to them, I know not; but the happiness of the people might be greatly promoted by them, and a revenue saved sufficient to carry on this war forever. Frugality is a great revenue, besides curing us of vanities, levities, and fopperies, which are real antidotes to all great, manly, and warlike virtues.

. . .

A constitution founded on these principles introduces knowledge among the people, and inspires them with a conscious dignity becoming freemen; a general emulation takes place, which causes good humor, sociability, good manners, and good morals to be general. That elevation of sentiment inspired by such a government, makes the common people brave and enterprising. That ambition which is inspired by it makes them sober, industrious, and frugal. You will find among them some elegance, perhaps, but more solidity; a little pleasure, but a great deal of business; some politeness, but more civility. If you compare such a country with the regions of domination, whether monarchical or aristocratical, you will fancy yourself in Arcadia or Elysium.

. . .

CARTER BRAXTON

AN ADDRESS TO THE CONVENTION OF THE COLONY (1776)

Carter Braxton was the scion of one of the first families of Virginia and in the years before the American Revolution was a prominent planter and politician. He quickly embraced the American cause, helped finance the war effort, and was elected to serve in the Continental Congress, where he signed the Declaration of Independence.

In 1776, he published a pamphlet under the pen name "A Native of That Colony" directed to the members of the Virginia revolutionary assembly. Braxton urged the delegates to quickly establish a new government to stave off the threat of anarchy and outlined his thoughts on how such a government might be structured. He rejected a purely republican government as unrealistic and impermanent, and instead advocated a modified version of the English government. Members of the lower house of the legislature should stand for election every three years and be barred from holding any other government office. They in turn would select a governor to serve during good behavior and the members of an upper legislative chamber (the Council of State), who would hold office for life.

How do Braxton's ideas compare to Adams's? To what extent does Braxton embrace republicanism? What lessons does he draw from England? What does he mean by "virtue," and what is its significance? How essential is virtue for popular government?

. . .

Government is generally divided into two parts, its *mode or form of constitution*, and the *principle* intended to direct it.

The simple forms of government are despotism, monarchy, aristocracy, and democracy. One of these an infinite variety of combinations may be deduced. The absolute unlimited control of one man describes *despotism*, whereas *monarchy* compels the sovereign to rule agreeable to certain fundamental laws. *Aristocracy* vests the sovereignty of a state in a few nobles, and *democracy* allows it to reside in the body of the people, and is thence called a popular government.

Each of these forms are actuated by different *principles*. The subjects of an unlimited despotic Prince, whose will is their only rule of conduct, are influenced by the principle of *fear*. In a monarchy limited by laws, the people are insensibly led to the pursuit of *honor*, they feel an interest in the greatness of their Princes, and inspired by a desire for glory, rank and promotion, unite in giving strength and energy to the whole machine. Aristocracy and democracy claim for their principle *public virtue*, or a regard for the public good independent of private interest.

. . .

What has been the government of Virginia, and in a revolution, how is its spirit to be preserved; are important questions. The better to discuss these points, we should take a view of the constitution of England; because by that model ours was constructed, and under it we have enjoyed tranquility and security.

Our ancestors the English, after contemplating the various forms of government, and experiencing as well as perceiving the defects of each, wisely refused to resign their liberties either to the single man, the few, or the many. They determined to make a compound of each the foundation of their government; and of the most valuable parts of them all, to build a superstructure that should surpass all others, and bid defiance to time to injure, or anything, except national degeneracy and corruption to demolish.

. . .

If the independence of the Commons could be secured, and the dignity of the Lords preserved, how can a government be better formed for the preservation of freedom? And is there anything more easy than this? If placemen and pensioners were excluded a seat in either house, and elections made triennial, what danger could be apprehended from prerogative. I have the best authority for asserting, that with these improvements, added to the suppression of boroughs and giving the people an equal and adequate representation, England would have remained a land of liberty to the latest ages.

Judge of the *principle* of this constitution by the great effects it has produced. Their code of laws, the boast of Englishmen and of freedoms; the rapid progress they have made in trade, in arts and sciences, and respect they commanded from their neighbors, then gaining the empire of the sea, are all powerful arguments of the wisdom of that constitution. . . .

. . . The same principles which led the English to greatness, animates us. To that principle our laws, our customs, and our manners are adapted, and it would be perverting all order, to oblige us, by a novel government, to give up our laws, our cultures, and our manners.

. . .

It is well known that *private* and *public* virtue are materially different. The happiness and dignity of man I admit consists in the practice of *private* virtues, and to this he is stimulated by the rewards promised to such conduct. In this he acts for himself, and with a view of promoting his own particular welfare.

Public virtue, on the other hand, means a disinterested attachment to the public good, exclusive and independent of all private and selfish interest, and which, though sometimes possessed by a few individuals, never characterized the mass of the people in any state. And this is said to be the principle of democratic governments, and to influence every subject of it to pursue such measures as conduce to the prosperity of the whole. A man therefore, to qualify himself for a member of such a community, must divest himself of all interested motives, and engage in no pursuits which do not ultimately redound to the benefit of society. . . .

. . . But [such principles] can never meet with a favorable reception from people who inhabit a country to which providence has been more bountiful. They will always claim a right of using and enjoying the fruits of their honest industry, unrestrained by any ideal principles of government, and will gather estates for themselves and children without regarding the whimsical impropriety of being richer than their neighbors. These are rights which freemen will never consent to relinquish. . . .

. . .

. . . I do not recollect a single instance of a nation who supported this form of government for any length of time, or with any degree of greatness; which convinces me, as it has many others, that the principle contended for is ideal, and a mere creature of a warm imagination.

One of the first staples of our country, you know, is esteemed by many to be one of the greatest luxuries in the world, and I fancy it will be no easy matter to draw you into measures that would exclude its culture and deprive you of the wealth resulting from its exportation.

. . .

The Governor [of the proposed government] will have dignity to command necessary respect and authority, to enable him to execute the laws, without being deterred by the fear of giving offense; and yet be amenable to the other branches of the legislature for every violation of the rights of the people. If this great officer was exposed to the uncertain issue of frequent elections, he would be induced to relax and abate the vigorous execution of the laws whenever such conduct would increase his popularity. . . . Hence it would follow, that the apprehensions of losing his election would frequently induce him to court the favor of the great, at the expense of the duties of his station and the public good. For these, and a variety of other reasons, this office should be held during good behavior.

The Council of State who are to constitute the second branch of the legislature should be for life. They ought to be well informed of the policy and laws of other states, and therefore should be induced by the permanence of their appointment to devote their time to such studies as they best qualify them for that station. They will acquire firmness from their independence, and wisdom from their reflection and experience, and appropriate both to the good of the state. . . .

The Representatives of the people will be under no temptation to swerve from the design of their institution by bribery or corruption; all lucrative posts being denied them. And should they on any occasion be influenced by improper motives, the short period of their duration will give their constituents an opportunity of depriving them of power to do injury. . . .

. . .

THOMAS JEFFERSON

AN ACT FOR ESTABLISHING RELIGIOUS FREEDOM (1777)

Thomas Jefferson did not share the traditional religious faith of most of his countrymen and was more secular than most. He saw the Revolution as an opportunity to weaken the hold of organized religion on society and politics, and drafted an act for establishing religious freedom with the hopes that it would be adopted in Virginia. The bill did not win immediate support, and Jefferson eventually departed the state to serve as the American envoy to France.

Jefferson's proposal gained new life a decade later. In 1784, Patrick Henry proposed to institute a state tax to support Christian teachers. The proposal was liberal in the sense that it allowed individuals to designate the church they wished to support, rather than simply directing all funds to the Anglican Church, which had enjoyed a privileged place in the Virginia colony. James Madison rallied opposition with a pamphlet arguing against religious assessments, observing that if the state had the authority to favor Christianity then it equally had the authority to favor particular sects within the Christian faith, raising the fears of the minority Baptists. After Henry's proposal was defeated, the legislature passed Jefferson's statute in 1786.

Does Jefferson rely on secular or religious arguments to reject an established religion? Why might Jefferson's proposal be preferable to Henry's proposal of taxpayer choice? Is Jefferson's policy essential to religious liberty? As a practical matter, does Jefferson's bill benefit Christians, or are the real beneficiaries those who do not accept the Christian faith?

Well aware that Almighty God hath created the mind free; that all attempts to influence it by temporal punishments or burdens, or by civil incapacitations, tend only to beget habits of hypocrisy and meanness, and are a departure from the plan of the Holy Author of our religion, who being Lord both of body and mind, yet chose not to propagate it by coercions on either, as was in his Almighty power to do; that the impious presumption of legislators and rulers, civil as well as ecclesiastical, who, being themselves but fallible and uninspired men, have assumed dominion over the faith of others, setting up their own opinions and modes of thinking as the only true and infallible, and as such endeavoring to impose them on others, hath established and maintained false religions over the greatest part of the world, and through all time; that to compel a man to furnish contributions of money for the propagation of opinions which he disbelieves, is sinful and tyrannical; that even the forcing him to support this or that teacher of his own religious persuasion, is depriving him of the comfortable liberty of giving his contributions to the particular pastor whose morals he would make his pattern, and whose powers he feels most persuasive to righteousness, and is withdrawing from the ministry those temporal rewards, which proceeding from an approbation of their personal conduct, are an additional incitement to earnest and unremitting labors for the instruction of mankind; that our civil rights have no dependence on our religious opinions, more than our opinions in physics or geometry; that, therefore, the proscribing any citizen as unworthy the public confidence by laying upon him an incapacity of being called to the offices of trust and emolument, unless he profess or renounce this or that religious opinion, is depriving him injuriously of those privileges and advantages to which in common with his fellow citizens he has a natural right; that it tends also to corrupt the principles of that very religion it is meant to encourage, by bribing, with a monopoly of worldly honors and emoluments, those who will externally profess and conform to it; that though indeed these are criminal who do not withstand such temptation, yet neither are those innocent who lay the bait in their way; that to suffer the civil magistrate to intrude his powers into the field of opinion and to restrain the profession or propagation of principles, on the supposition of their ill tendency, is a dangerous fallacy, which at once destroys all religious liberty, because he being of course judge of that tendency, will make his opinions the rule of judgment, and approve or condemn the sentiments of others only as they shall square with or differ from his own; that it is time enough for the rightful purposes of civil government, for its officers to interfere when principles break out into overt acts against peace and good order; and finally, that truth is great and will prevail if left to herself, that she is the proper and sufficient antagonist to error, and has nothing to fear from the conflict, unless by human interposition disarmed of her natural weapons, free argument and debate, errors ceasing to be dangerous when it is permitted freely to contradict them.

Be it therefore enacted by the General Assembly, That no man shall be compelled to frequent or support any religious worship, place, or ministry whatsoever, nor shall be enforced, restrained, molested, or burdened in his body or goods, nor shall otherwise suffer on account of his religious opinions or belief; but that all men shall be free to profess, and by argument to maintain, their opinions in matters of religion, and that the same shall in nowise diminish, enlarge, or affect their civil capacities.

And though we well know this Assembly, elected by the people for the ordinary purposes of legislation only, have no powers equal to our own and that therefore to declare this act irrevocable would be of no effect in law, yet we are free to declare, and do declare, that the rights hereby asserted are of the natural rights of mankind, and that if any act shall be hereafter passed to repeal the present or to narrow its operation, such act will be an infringement of natural right.

*Stresses the ideas of argument and debate

ALEXANDER HAMILTON

FEDERALIST PAPERS (1787)

The debate over the ratification of the U.S. Constitution was fought not only in state conventions but also in newspapers, pamphlets, and barrooms. Several states quickly ratified the Constitution with little debate and little opposition. New York and Virginia were two of the largest states in the Confederation, and they were also slow to hold ratification conventions. The Federalists who supported the Constitution did not win firm majorities in the elections for either convention; they needed to swing some anti-Federalist delegates to their side in order to secure ratification.

Two New Yorkers, Alexander Hamilton and John Jay, planned a series of newspaper essays under the pseudonym "Publius" that would respond to public arguments against the Constitution and help build support for ratification. John Jay soon fell ill, and Hamilton recruited James Madison to join the project. The collection was published in two volumes in 1788 with eight essays that had not previously appeared in print. The New York convention met and narrowly ratified the Constitution shortly after the publication of the second volume. The essays were written as documents in a political campaign, and in many instances offered arguments that were primarily designed to win over opponents but did not necessarily reflect the true views of the author. The essays were quickly recognized both as outstanding commentaries on the new Constitution and as significant contributions to political philosophy. Historians did not reach an agreement on the individual authorship of specific essays in the collection until the twentieth century. Many of Hamilton's contributions to the series focused on the enhanced powers of the national government and the addition of the presidency and the judiciary to the federal structure.

What does Hamilton view as the crucial problems with the Confederation? How plausible are his objections to the form of government established by the Articles? Does he favor limited government? Why does he believe that the new federal government will not be a threat to liberty? What are the virtues of the presidency? Why is the judiciary the "least dangerous branch"? Did Hamilton correctly forecast how those institutions would operate?

NO. 1

After an unequivocal experience of the inefficiency of the subsisting federal government, you are called upon to deliberate on a new Constitution for the United States of America. The subject speaks its own importance; comprehending in its consequences nothing less than the existence of the UNION, the safety and welfare of the parts of which it is composed, the fate of an empire in many respects the most interesting in the world. It has been frequently remarked that it seems to have been reserved to the people of this country, by their conduct and example, to decide the important question, whether societies of men are really capable or not of establishing good government from reflection and choice, or whether they are forever destined to depend for their political constitutions on accident and force. If there be any truth in the remark, the crisis at which we are arrived may with propriety be regarded as the era in which that decision is to be made; and a wrong election of the part we shall act may, in this view, deserve to be considered as the general misfortune of mankind. This idea will add the inducements of philanthropy to those of patriotism, to heighten the solicitude which all considerate and good men must feel for the event. Happy will it be if our choice should be directed by a judicious estimate of our true interests, unperplexed and unbiased by considerations not connected with the public good. But this is a thing more ardently to be wished than seriously to be expected. The plan offered to our deliberations affects too many particular interests, innovates upon too many local institutions, not to involve in its discussion a variety of objects foreign to its merits, and of views, passions and prejudices little favorable to the discovery of truth.

. . .

NO. 9

A firm Union will be of the utmost moment to the peace and liberty of the States, as a barrier against domestic faction and insurrection. It is impossible to read the history of the petty republics of Greece and Italy without feeling sensations of horror and disgust at the distractions with which they were continually agitated, and at the rapid succession of revolutions by which they were kept in a state of perpetual vibration between the extremes of tyranny and anarchy. If they exhibit occasional calms, these only serve as short-lived contrast to the furious storms that are to succeed. . . .

From the disorders that disfigure the annals of those republics the advocates of despotism have drawn arguments, not only against the forms of republican government, but against the very principles of civil liberty. They have decried all free government as inconsistent with the order of society, and have indulged themselves in malicious exultation over its friends and partisans. Happily for mankind, stupendous fabrics reared on the basis of liberty, which have flourished for ages, have, in a few glorious instances, refuted their gloomy sophisms. And, I trust, America will be the broad and solid foundation of other edifices, not less magnificent, which will be equally permanent monuments of their errors.

But it is not to be denied that the portraits they have sketched of republican government were too just copies of the originals from which they were taken. If it had been found impracticable to have devised models of a more perfect structure, the enlightened friends to liberty would have been obliged to abandon the cause of that species of government as indefensible. The science of politics, however, like most other sciences, has received great improvement. The efficacy of various principles is now well understood, which were either not known at all, or imperfectly known to the ancients. The regular distribution of power into distinct departments; the introduction of legislative balances and checks; the institution of courts composed of judges holding their offices during good behavior; the representation of the people in the legislature by deputies of their own election: these are wholly new discoveries, or have made their principal progress towards perfection in modern times. They are means, and powerful means, by which the excellences of republican government may be retained and its imperfections lessened or avoided. To this catalogue of circumstances that tend to the amelioration of popular systems of civil government, I shall venture, however novel it may appear to some, to add one more, on a principle which has been made the foundation of an objection to the new Constitution; I mean the ENLARGEMENT of the ORBIT within which such systems are to revolve, either in respect to the dimensions of a single State or to the consolidation of several smaller States into one great Confederacy. . . .

. . .

. . . So long as the separate organization of the members be not abolished; so long as it exists, by a constitutional necessity, for local purposes; though it should be in perfect subordination to the general authority of the union, it would still be, in fact and in theory, an association of states, or a confederacy. The proposed Constitution, so far from implying an abolition of the State governments, makes them constituent parts of the national sovereignty, by allowing them a direct representation in the Senate, and leaves in their possession certain exclusive and very important portions of sovereign power. . . .

NO. 15

. . .

There is nothing absurd or impracticable in the idea of a league or alliance between independent nations for certain defined purposes precisely stated in a treaty regulating all the details of time, place, circumstance, and quantity; leaving nothing to future discretion; and depending for its execution on the good faith of the parties. . . .

If the particular States in this country are disposed to stand in a similar relation to each other, and to drop the project of a general DISCRETIONARY SUPERINTENDENCE, the scheme would indeed be pernicious, and would entail upon us all the mischiefs which have been enumerated under the first head; but it would have the merit of being, at least, consistent and practicable. Abandoning all views towards a confederate government, this would bring us to a simple alliance offensive and defensive; and would place us in a situation to be alternate friends and enemies of each other, as our mutual jealousies and rivalships, nourished by the intrigues of foreign nations, should prescribe to us.

But if we are unwilling to be placed in this perilous situation; if we still will adhere to the design of a national government, or, which is the same thing, of a superintending power, under the direction of a common council, we must resolve to incorporate into our plan those ingredients which may be considered as forming the characteristic difference between a league and a government; we must extend the authority of the Union to the persons of the citizens the only proper objects of government.

Government implies the power of making laws. It is essential to the idea of a law, that it be attended with a sanction; or, in other words, a penalty or punishment for disobedience. If there be no penalty annexed to disobedience, the resolutions or commands which pretend to be laws will, in fact, amount to nothing more than advice or recommendation. . . .

. . . Why has government been instituted at all? Because the passions of men will not conform to the dictates of reason and justice, without constraint. Has it been found that bodies of men act with more rectitude or greater disinterestedness than individuals? The contrary of this has been inferred by all accurate observers of the conduct of mankind; and the inference is founded upon obvious reasons. . . .

NO. 17

It may be said that it would tend to render the government of the Union too powerful, and to enable it to absorb those residuary authorities, which it might be judged proper to leave with the States for local purposes. Allowing the utmost latitude to the love of power which any reasonable man can require, I confess I am at a loss to discover what temptation the persons entrusted with the administration of the general government could ever feel to divest the States of the authorities of that description. The regulation of the mere domestic police of a State appears to me to hold out slender allurements to ambition. Commerce, finance, negotiation, and war seem to comprehend all the objects which have charms for minds governed by that passion; and all the powers necessary to those objects ought, in the first instance, to be lodged in the national depository. The administration of private justice between the citizens of the same State, the supervision of agriculture and of other concerns of a similar nature, all those things, in short, which are proper to be provided for by local legislation, can never be desirable cares of a general jurisdiction. It is therefore improbable that there should exist a disposition in the federal councils to usurp the powers with which they are connected; because the attempt to exercise those powers would be as troublesome as it would be nugatory; and the possession of them, for that reason, would contribute nothing to the dignity, to the importance, or to the splendor of the national government.

But let it be admitted, for argument's sake, that mere wantonness and lust of domination would be sufficient to beget that disposition; still it may be safely affirmed, that the sense of the constituent body of the national representatives, or, in other words, the people of the several States, would control the indulgence of so extravagant an appetite. It will always be far more easy for the State governments to encroach upon the national authorities than for the national government to encroach upon the State authorities. The proof of this proposition turns upon the greater degree of influence which the State governments if they administer their affairs with uprightness and prudence, will generally possess over the people; a circumstance which at the same time teaches us that there is an inherent and intrinsic weakness in all federal constitutions; and that too much pains cannot be taken in their organization, to give them all the force which is compatible with the principles of liberty.

. . .

NO. 23

. . .

The principal purposes to be answered by union are these: the common defense of the members; the preservation of the public peace as well against internal convulsions as external attacks; the regulation of commerce with other nations and between the States; the superintendence of our intercourse, political and commercial, with foreign countries.

The authorities essential to the common defense are these: to raise armies; to build and equip fleets; to prescribe rules for the government of both; to direct their operations; to provide for their support. These powers ought to exist without limitation, BECAUSE IT IS IMPOSSIBLE TO FORESEE OR DEFINE THE EXTENT AND VARIETY OF NATIONAL EXIGENCIES, OR THE CORRESPONDENT EXTENT AND VARIETY OF THE MEANS WHICH MAY BE NECESSARY TO SATISFY THEM. The circumstances that endanger the safety of nations are infinite, and for this reason no constitutional shackles can wisely be imposed on the power to which the care of it is committed. This power ought to be coextensive with all the possible combinations of such circumstances; and ought to be under the direction of the same councils which are appointed to preside over the common defense.

. . . The MEANS ought to be proportioned to the END; the persons, from whose agency the attainment of any END is expected, ought to possess the MEANS by which it is to be attained.

. . .

Who is likely to make suitable provisions for the public defense, as that body to which the guardianship of the public safety is confided; which, as the centre of information, will best understand the extent and urgency of the dangers that threaten; as the representative of the WHOLE, will feel itself most deeply interested in the preservation of every part; which, from the responsibility implied in the duty assigned to it, will be most sensibly impressed with the necessity of proper exertions; and which, by the extension of its authority throughout the States, can alone establish uniformity and concert in the plans and measures by which the common safety is to be secured? . . .

NO. 70

There is an idea, which is not without its advocates, that a vigorous Executive is inconsistent with the genius of republican government. The enlightened well-wishers to this species of government must at least hope that the supposition is destitute of foundation; since they can never admit its truth, without at the same time admitting the condemnation of their own principles. Energy in the Executive is a leading character in the definition of good government. It is essential to the protection of the community against foreign attacks; it is not less essential to the steady administration of the laws; to the protection of property against those irregular and high-handed combinations which sometimes interrupt the ordinary course of justice; to the security of liberty against the enterprises and assaults of ambition, of faction, and of anarchy. . . .

. . .

The ingredients which constitute energy in the Executive are, first, unity; secondly, duration; thirdly, an adequate provision for its support; fourthly, competent powers.

The ingredients which constitute safety in the republican sense are, first, a due dependence on the people, secondly, a due responsibility.

. . .

That unity is conducive to energy will not be disputed. Decision, activity, secrecy, and dispatch will generally characterize the proceedings of one man in a much more eminent degree than the proceedings of any greater number; and in proportion as the number is increased, these qualities will be diminished.

This unity may be destroyed in two ways: either by vesting the power in two or more magistrates of equal dignity and authority; or by vesting it ostensibly in one man, subject, in whole or in part, to the control and co-operation of others, in the capacity of counsellors to him. . . .

. . .

NO. 78

. . .

Whoever attentively considers the different departments of power must perceive, that, in a government in which they are separated from each other, the judiciary, from the nature of its functions, will always be the least dangerous to the political rights of the Constitution; because it will be least in a capacity to annoy or injure them. The Executive not only dispenses the honors, but holds the sword of the community. The legislature not only commands the purse, but prescribes the rules by which the duties and rights of every citizen are to be regulated. The judiciary, on the contrary, has no influence over either the sword or the purse; no direction either of the strength or of the wealth of the society; and can take no active resolution whatever. It may truly be said to have neither FORCE nor WILL, but merely judgment; and must ultimately depend upon the aid of the executive arm even for the efficacy of its judgments.

This simple view of the matter suggests several important consequences. It proves incontestably, that the judiciary is beyond comparison the weakest of the three departments of power; that it can never attack with success either of the other two; and that all possible care is requisite to enable it to defend itself against their attacks. It equally proves, that though individual oppression may now and then proceed from the courts of justice, the general liberty of the people can never be endangered from that quarter; I mean so long as the judiciary remains truly distinct from both the legislature and the Executive. For I agree, that "there is no liberty, if the power of judging be not separated from the legislative and executive powers." And it proves, in the last place, that as liberty can have nothing to fear from the judiciary alone, but would have everything to fear from its union with either of the other departments; that as all the effects of such a union must ensue from a dependence of the former on the latter, notwithstanding a nominal and apparent separation; that as, from the natural feebleness of the judiciary, it is in continual jeopardy of being overpowered, awed, or influenced by its co-ordinate branches; and that as nothing can contribute so much to its firmness and independence as permanency in office, this quality may therefore be justly regarded as an indispensable ingredient in its constitution, and, in a great measure, as the citadel of the public justice and the public security.

The complete independence of the courts of justice is peculiarly essential in a limited Constitution. By a limited Constitution, I understand one which contains certain specified exceptions to the legislative authority; such, for instance, as that it shall pass no bills of attainder, no ex-post-facto laws, and the like. Limitations of this kind can be preserved in practice no other way than through the medium of courts of justice, whose duty it must be to declare all acts contrary to the manifest tenor of the Constitution void. Without this, all the reservations of particular rights or privileges would amount to nothing.

. . .

There is no position which depends on clearer principles, than that every act of a delegated authority, contrary to the tenor of the commission under which it is exercised, is void. No legislative act, therefore, contrary to the Constitution, can be valid. To deny this, would be to affirm, that the deputy is greater than his principal; that the servant is above his master; that the representatives of the people are superior to the people themselves; that men acting by virtue of powers, may do not only what their powers do not authorize, but what they forbid.

If it be said that the legislative body are themselves the constitutional judges of their own powers, and that the construction they put upon them is conclusive upon the other departments, it may be answered, that this cannot be the natural presumption, where it is not to be collected from any particular provisions in the Constitution. It is not otherwise to be supposed, that the Constitution could intend to enable the representatives of the people to substitute their WILL to that of their constituents. It is far more rational to suppose, that the courts were designed to be an intermediate body between the people and the legislature, in order, among other things, to keep the latter within the limits assigned to their authority. The interpretation of the laws is the proper and peculiar province of the courts. A constitution is, in fact, and must be regarded by the judges, as a fundamental law. It therefore belongs to them to ascertain its meaning, as well as the meaning of any particular act proceeding from the legislative body. If there should happen to be an irreconcilable variance between the two, that which has the superior obligation and validity ought, of course, to be preferred; or, in other words, the Constitution ought to be preferred to the statute, the intention of the people to the intention of their agents.

Nor does this conclusion by any means suppose a superiority of the judicial to the legislative power. It only supposes that the power of the people is superior to both; and that where the will of the legislature, declared in its statutes, stands in opposition to that of the people, declared in the Constitution, the judges ought to be governed by the latter rather than the former. They ought to regulate their decisions by the fundamental laws, rather than by those which are not fundamental.

. . .

This independence of the judges is equally requisite to guard the Constitution and the rights of individuals from the effects of those ill humors, which the arts of designing men, or the influence of particular conjunctures, sometimes disseminate among the people themselves, and which, though they speedily give place to better information, and more deliberate reflection, have a tendency, in the meantime, to occasion dangerous innovations in the government, and serious oppressions of the minor party in the community. Though I trust the friends of the proposed Constitution will never concur with its enemies, in questioning that fundamental principle of republican government, which admits the right of the people to alter or abolish the established Constitution, whenever they find it inconsistent with their happiness, yet it is not to be inferred from this principle, that the representatives of the people, whenever a momentary inclination happens to lay hold of a majority of their constituents, incompatible with the provisions in the existing Constitution, would, on that account, be justifiable in a violation of those provisions; or that the courts would be under a greater obligation to connive at infractions in this shape, than when they had proceeded wholly from the cabals of the representative body. Until the people have, by some solemn and authoritative act, annulled or changed the established form, it is binding upon themselves collectively, as well as individually; and no presumption, or even knowledge, of their sentiments, can warrant their representatives in a departure from it, prior to such an act. But it is easy to see, that it would require an uncommon portion of fortitude in the judges to do their duty as faithful guardians of the Constitution, where legislative invasions of it had been instigated by the major voice of the community.

. . .

BOX 3-1 THE TWO JAMES MADISONS

One persistent debate within the study of American political thought is whether there are "two James Madisons." Of course, there is no question of whether the historical figure of James Madison was a single individual. The "problem" is one of interpreting his ideas and whether he had a consistent political philosophy that guided his writing and actions throughout his career or whether he made a sharp break in his later life from his early political ideas.

The "early" Madison is the best known. It was in this guise, in the 1780s, that he earned his historical reputation as the "Father of the Constitution." In those years after the Revolution and under the Confederation government, Madison was known as a strong nationalist. He called for constitutional reform that would put more political power in the hands of the national political leaders and the federal government. He denounced the abuses of the state leaders and local governments. He insisted on weakening the power of the states in national councils and increasing the ability of the federal government to rein in errant state governments. As he left the Philadelphia Convention of 1787, he thought his fellow delegates had made a terrible mistake by agreeing to the "Connecticut Compromise" that created the U.S. Senate with equal state representation and rejecting his own proposal for giving Congress an unqualified veto over state laws. The James Madison of the 1780s seemed like a natural ally to New York's Alexander Hamilton and Massachusetts's John Adams.

The "late" Madison is perhaps less remembered today but was equally important to American political history. The Madison of the 1790s was a leading critic of the presidential administrations of George Washington and John Adams and the political program of Secretary of Treasury Alexander Hamilton and argued that the delegated powers of the national government should be strictly construed. In this guise, Madison helped develop the intellectual underpinnings of the "states' rights" movement that continues to reverberate in political and constitutional debates today. He argued that the U.S. Constitution should be understood as a "compact" of the states and that the states had the authority to evaluate the constitutionality of the federal government's actions. He allied with such antagonists of federal power as Thomas Jefferson to create the Democratic-Republican Party that rode to victory in the elections of 1800 under the banner of limited federal power.

Some Jeffersonians never fully trusted Madison because of his early nationalism, leading them to favor his fellow Virginian, James Monroe, who had been an anti-Federalist during the constitutional ratification debates. Some Federalists such as Alexander Hamilton could never understand why Madison would abandon them to join forces with Jefferson. Some historians have found it impossible to reconcile the nationalism of the early Madison and the states' rights advocacy of the later Madison. To them, Madison had changed. Others have argued that Madison was basically consistent across his career; it was the nation and politics that had changed around him. A single political philosophy can explain both Madison's drafting of the Virginia Plan of 1787 and his authorship of the Virginia Resolution of 1798.

Is there a "Madison problem" in American political thought? Did Madison change his tune across the last two decades of the eighteenth century, or was he always guided by a consistent and coherent political philosophy?

JAMES MADISON

FEDERALIST PAPERS (1787)

James Madison had been a key architect of the effort at constitutional reform. His thoughts on the vices of the Confederation and his outline for a new constitutional system laid the foundations for the work of the Philadelphia convention. Nonetheless, Madison was disappointed by the results of the convention, which had rejected his proposal for a congressional veto over state laws and for a legislature based entirely on the popular vote. When he left Philadelphia, he was convinced that the new Constitution would ultimately fail to solve the problems facing the nation. But he remained committed to winning ratification of a document that he still thought preferable to the Articles of Confederation. He played a leading role in moving the Virginia convention to a favorable ratification vote. Despite their differences, he readily joined Hamilton in the project of trying to win ratification in New York. His essays gave particular attention to the proposed federal system, the design of the new Congress, and the system of the separation of powers.

Was Madison correct to swallow his doubts about the Constitution? What does he see as the virtue of an "extended republic"? Can Congress be trusted more than the state legislatures to protect liberty and advance the public good? Is equal state representation in the Senate a fatal flaw in the Constitution? Does bicameralism serve any useful function in a republican government? Why does Madison object to "parchment barriers"? To what extent does the Constitution rely on them?

NO. 10

Among the numerous advantages promised by a well-constructed Union, none deserves to be more accurately developed than its tendency to break and control the violence of faction. The friend of popular governments never finds himself so much alarmed for their character and fate, as when he contemplates their propensity to this dangerous vice. He will not fail, therefore, to set a due value on any plan which, without violating the principles to which he is attached, provides a proper cure for it. The instability, injustice, and confusion introduced into the public councils, have, in truth, been the mortal diseases under which popular governments have everywhere perished; as they continue to be the favorite and fruitful topics from which the adversaries to liberty derive their most specious declamations. The valuable improvements made by the American constitutions on the popular models, both ancient and modern, cannot certainly be too much admired; but it would be an unwarrantable partiality, to contend that they have as effectually obviated the danger on this side, as was wished and expected. Complaints are everywhere heard from our most considerate and virtuous citizens, equally the friends of public and private faith, and of public and personal liberty, that our governments are too unstable, that the public good is disregarded in the conflicts of rival parties, and that measures are too often decided, not according to the rules of justice and the rights of the minor party, but by the superior force of an interested and overbearing majority. . . .

By a faction, I understand a number of citizens, whether amounting to a majority or a minority of the whole, who are united and actuated by some common impulse of passion, or of interest, adversed to the rights of other citizens, or to the permanent and aggregate interests of the community.

There are two methods of curing the mischiefs of faction: the one, by removing its causes; the other, by controlling its effects.

There are again two methods of removing the causes of faction: the one, by destroying the liberty which is essential to its existence; the other, by giving to every citizen the same opinions, the same passions, and the same interests.

It could never be more truly said than of the first remedy, that it was worse than the disease. Liberty is to faction what air is to fire, an aliment without which it instantly expires. But it could not be less folly to abolish liberty, which is essential to political life, because it nourishes faction, than it would be to wish the annihilation of air, which is essential to animal life, because it imparts to fire its destructive agency.

The second expedient is as impracticable as the first would be unwise. As long as the reason of man continues fallible, and he is at liberty to exercise it, different opinions will be formed. As long as the connection subsists between his reason and his self-love, his opinions and his passions will have a reciprocal influence on each other; and the former will be objects to which the latter will attach themselves. The diversity in the faculties of men, from which the rights of property originate, is not less an insuperable obstacle to a uniformity of interests. The protection of these faculties is the first object of government. From the protection of different and unequal faculties of acquiring property, the possession of different degrees and kinds of property immediately results; and from the influence of these on the sentiments and views of the respective proprietors, ensues a division of the society into different interests and parties.

The latent causes of faction are thus sown in the nature of man; and we see them everywhere brought into different degrees of activity, according to the different circumstances of civil society. A zeal for different opinions concerning religion, concerning government, and many other points, as well of speculation as of practice; an attachment to different leaders ambitiously contending for pre-eminence and power; or to persons of other descriptions whose fortunes have been interesting to the human passions, have, in turn, divided mankind into parties, inflamed them with mutual animosity, and rendered them much more disposed to vex and oppress each other than to co-operate for their common good. So strong is this propensity of mankind to fall into mutual animosities, that where no substantial occasion presents itself, the most frivolous and fanciful distinctions have been sufficient to kindle their unfriendly passions and excite their most violent conflicts. But the most common and durable source of factions has been the various and unequal distribution of property. Those who hold and those who are without property have ever formed distinct interests in society. Those who are creditors, and those who are debtors, fall under a like discrimination. A landed interest, a manufacturing interest, a mercantile interest, a moneyed interest, with many lesser interests, grow up of necessity in civilized nations, and divide them into different classes, actuated by different sentiments and views. The regulation of these various and interfering interests forms the principal task of modern legislation, and involves the spirit of party and faction in the necessary and ordinary operations of the government.

. . .

It is in vain to say that enlightened statesmen will be able to adjust these clashing interests, and render them all subservient to the public good. Enlightened statesmen will not always be at the helm. Nor, in many cases, can such an adjustment be made at all without taking into view indirect and remote considerations, which will rarely prevail over the immediate interest which one party may find in disregarding the rights of another or the good of the whole.

The inference to which we are brought is, that the CAUSES of faction cannot be removed, and that relief is only to be sought in the means of controlling its EFFECTS.

If a faction consists of less than a majority, relief is supplied by the republican principle, which enables the majority to defeat its sinister views by regular vote. It may clog the administration, it may convulse the society; but it will be unable to execute and mask its violence under the forms of the Constitution. When a majority is included in a faction, the form of popular government, on the other hand, enables it to sacrifice to its ruling passion or interest both the public good and the rights of other citizens. To secure the public good and private rights against the danger of such a faction, and at the same time to preserve the spirit and the form of popular government, is then the great object to which our inquiries are directed. Let me add that it is the great desideratum by which this form of government can be rescued from the opprobrium under which it has so long labored, and be recommended to the esteem and adoption of mankind.

By what means is this object attainable? Evidently by one of two only. Either the existence of the same passion or interest in a majority at the same time must be prevented, or the majority, having such coexistent passion or interest, must be rendered, by their number and local situation, unable to concert and carry into effect schemes of oppression. If the impulse and the opportunity be suffered to coincide, we well know that neither moral nor religious motives can be relied on as an adequate control. They are not found to be such on the injustice and violence of individuals, and lose their efficacy in proportion to the number combined together, that is, in proportion as their efficacy becomes needful.

From this view of the subject it may be concluded that a pure democracy, by which I mean a society consisting of a small number of citizens, who assemble and administer the government in person, can admit of no cure for the mischiefs of faction. . . . Hence it is that such democracies have ever been spectacles of turbulence and contention; have ever been found incompatible with personal security or the rights of property; and have in general been as short in their lives as they have been violent in their deaths. Theoretic politicians, who have patronized this species of government, have erroneously supposed that by reducing mankind to a perfect equality in their political rights, they would, at the same time, be perfectly equalized and assimilated in their possessions, their opinions, and their passions.

A republic, by which I mean a government in which the scheme of representation takes place, opens a different prospect, and promises the cure for which we are seeking. Let us examine the points in which it varies from pure democracy, and we shall comprehend both the nature of the cure and the efficacy which it must derive from the Union.

The two great points of difference between a democracy and a republic are: first, the delegation of the government, in the latter, to a small number of citizens elected by the rest; secondly, the greater number of citizens, and greater sphere of country, over which the latter may be extended.

The effect of the first difference is, on the one hand, to refine and enlarge the public views, by passing them through the medium of a chosen body of citizens, whose wisdom may best discern the true interest of their country, and whose patriotism and love of justice will be least likely to sacrifice it to temporary or partial considerations. Under such a regulation, it may well happen that the public voice, pronounced by the representatives of the people, will be more consonant to the public good than if pronounced by the people themselves, convened for the purpose. On the other hand, the effect may be inverted. Men of factious tempers, of local prejudices, or of sinister designs, may, by intrigue, by corruption, or by other means, first obtain the suffrages, and then betray the interests, of the people. The question resulting is, whether small or extensive republics are more favorable to the election of proper guardians of the public weal; and it is clearly decided in favor of the latter by two obvious considerations:

In the first place, it is to be remarked that, however small the republic may be, the representatives must be raised to a certain number, in order to guard against the cabals of a few; and that, however large it may be, they must be limited to a certain number, in order to guard against the confusion of a multitude. . . .

In the next place, as each representative will be chosen by a greater number of citizens in the large than in the small republic, it will be more difficult for unworthy candidates to practice with success the vicious arts by which elections are too often carried; and the suffrages of the people being more free, will be more likely to center in men who possess the most attractive merit and the most diffusive and established characters.

. . . The federal Constitution forms a happy combination in this respect; the great and aggregate interests being referred to the national, the local and particular to the State legislatures.

The other point of difference is, the greater number of citizens and extent of territory which may be brought within the compass of republican than of democratic government; and it is this circumstance principally which renders factious combinations less to be dreaded in the former than in the latter. The smaller the society, the fewer probably will be the distinct parties and interests composing it; the fewer the distinct parties and interests, the more frequently will a majority be found of the same party; and the smaller the number of individuals composing a majority, and the smaller the compass within which they are placed, the more easily will they concert and execute their plans of oppression. Extend the sphere, and you take in a greater variety of parties and interests; you make it less probable that a majority of the whole will have a common motive to invade the rights of other citizens; or if such a common motive exists, it will be more difficult for all who feel it to discover their own strength, and to act in unison with each other. Besides other impediments, it may be remarked that, where there is a consciousness of unjust or dishonorable purposes, communication is always checked by distrust in proportion to the number whose concurrence is necessary.

. . .

The influence of factious leaders may kindle a flame within their particular States, but will be unable to spread a general conflagration through the other States. A religious sect may degenerate into a political faction in a part of the Confederacy; but the variety of sects dispersed over the entire face of it must secure the national councils against any danger from that source. A rage for paper money, for an abolition of debts, for an equal division of property, or for any other improper or wicked project, will be less apt to pervade the whole body of the Union than a particular member of it; in the same proportion as such a malady is more likely to taint a particular county or district, than an entire State.

In the extent and proper structure of the Union, therefore, we behold a republican remedy for the diseases most incident to republican government. And according to the degree of pleasure and pride we feel in being republicans, ought to be our zeal in cherishing the spirit and supporting the character of Federalists.

NO. 39

The first question that offers itself is, whether the general form and aspect of the government be strictly republican. It is evident that no other form would be reconcilable with the genius of the people of America; with the fundamental principles of the Revolution; or with that honorable determination which animates every votary of freedom, to rest all our political experiments on the capacity of mankind for self-government. If the plan of the convention, therefore, be found to depart from the republican character, its advocates must abandon it as no longer defensible.

What, then, are the distinctive characters of the republican form? Were an answer to this question to be sought, not by recurring to principles, but in the application of the term by political writers, to the constitution of different States, no satisfactory one would ever be found. Holland, in which no particle of the supreme authority is derived from the people, has passed almost universally under the denomination of a republic. . . .

If we resort for a criterion to the different principles on which different forms of government are established, we may define a republic to be, or at least may bestow that name on, a government which derives all its powers directly or indirectly from the great body of the people, and is administered by persons holding their offices during pleasure, for a limited period, or during good behavior. It is ESSENTIAL to such a government that it be derived from the great body of the society, not from an inconsiderable proportion, or a favored class of it; otherwise a handful of tyrannical nobles, exercising their oppressions by a delegation of their powers, might aspire to the rank of republicans, and claim for their government the honorable title of republic. It is SUFFICIENT for such a government that the persons administering it be appointed, either directly or indirectly, by the people; and that they hold their appointments by either of the tenures just specified; otherwise every government in the United States, as well as every other popular government that has been or can be well organized or well executed, would be degraded from the republican character. According to the constitution of every State in the Union, some or other of the officers of government are appointed indirectly only by the people. According to most of them, the chief magistrate himself is so appointed. And according to one, this mode of appointment is extended to one of the co-ordinate branches of the legislature. According to all the constitutions, also, the tenure of the highest offices is extended to a definite period, and in many instances, both within the legislative and executive departments, to a period of years. According to the provisions of most of the constitutions, again, as well as according to the most respectable and received opinions on the subject, the members of the judiciary department are to retain their offices by the firm tenure of good behavior.

On comparing the Constitution planned by the convention with the standard here fixed, we perceive at once that it is, in the most rigid sense, conformable to it. The House of Representatives, like that of one branch at least of all the State legislatures, is elected immediately by the great body of the people. The Senate, like the present Congress, and the Senate of Maryland, derives its appointment indirectly from the people. The President is indirectly derived from the choice of the people, according to the example in most of the States. Even the judges, with all other officers of the Union, will, as in the several States, be the choice, though a remote choice, of the people themselves, the duration of the appointments is equally conformable to the republican standard, and to the model of State constitutions. . . .

Could any further proof be required of the republican complexion of this system, the most decisive one might be found in its absolute prohibition of titles of nobility, both under the federal and the State governments; and in its express guaranty of the republican form to each of the latter.

. . .

First. In order to ascertain the real character of the government, it may be considered in relation to the foundation on which it is to be established; to the sources from which its ordinary powers are to be drawn; to the operation of those powers; to the extent of them; and to the authority by which future changes in the government are to be introduced.

On examining the first relation, it appears, on one hand, that the Constitution is to be founded on the assent and ratification of the people of America, given by deputies elected for the special purpose; but, on the other, that this assent and ratification is to be given by the people, not as individuals composing one entire nation, but as composing the distinct and independent States to which they respectively belong. It is to be the assent and ratification of the several States, derived from the supreme authority in each State, the authority of the people themselves. The act, therefore, establishing the Constitution, will not be a NATIONAL, but a FEDERAL act.

That it will be a federal and not a national act, as these terms are understood by the objectors; the act of the people, as forming so many independent States, not as forming one aggregate nation, is obvious from this single consideration, that it is to result neither from the decision of a MAJORITY of the people of the Union, nor from that of a MAJORITY of the States. It must result from the UNANIMOUS assent of the several States that are parties to it, differing no otherwise from their ordinary assent than in its being expressed, not by the legislative authority, but by that of the people themselves. Were the people regarded in this transaction as forming one nation, the will of the majority of the whole people of the United States would bind the minority, in the same manner as the majority in each State must bind the minority; and the will of the majority must be determined either by a comparison of the individual votes, or by considering the will of the majority of the States as evidence of the will of a majority of the people of the United States. Neither of these rules have been adopted. Each State, in ratifying the Constitution, is considered as a sovereign body, independent of all others, and only to be bound by its own voluntary act. In this relation, then, the new Constitution will, if established, be a FEDERAL, and not a NATIONAL constitution.

The next relation is, to the sources from which the ordinary powers of government are to be derived. The House of Representatives will derive its powers from the people of America; and the people will be represented in the same proportion, and on the same principle, as they are in the legislature of a particular State. So far the government is NATIONAL, not FEDERAL. The Senate, on the other hand, will derive its powers from the States, as political and coequal societies; and these will be represented on the principle of equality in the Senate, as they now are in the existing Congress. So far the government is FEDERAL, not NATIONAL. The executive power will be derived from a very compound source. The immediate election of the President is to be made by the States in their political characters.

The votes allotted to them are in a compound ratio, which considers them partly as distinct and coequal societies, partly as unequal members of the same society. The eventual election, again, is to be made by that branch of the legislature which consists of the national representatives; but in this particular act they are to be thrown into the form of individual delegations, from so many distinct and coequal bodies politic. From this aspect of the government it appears to be of a mixed character, presenting at least as many FEDERAL as NATIONAL features.

The difference between a federal and national government, as it relates to the OPERATION OF THE GOVERNMENT, is supposed to consist in this, that in the former the powers operate on the political bodies composing the Confederacy, in their political capacities; in the latter, on the individual citizens composing the nation, in their individual capacities. On trying the Constitution by this criterion, it falls under the NATIONAL, not the FEDERAL character; though perhaps not so completely as has been understood. . . .

But if the government be national with regard to the OPERATION of its powers, it changes its aspect again when we contemplate it in relation to the EXTENT of its powers. The idea of a national government involves in it, not only an authority over the individual citizens, but an indefinite supremacy over all persons and things, so far as they are objects of lawful government. Among a people consolidated into one nation, this supremacy is completely vested in the national legislature. Among communities united for particular purposes, it is vested partly in the general and partly in the municipal legislatures. In the former case, all local authorities are subordinate to the supreme; and may be controlled, directed, or abolished by it at pleasure. In the latter, the local or municipal authorities form distinct and independent portions of the supremacy, no more subject, within their respective spheres, to the general authority, than the general authority is subject to them, within its own sphere. In this relation, then, the proposed government cannot be deemed a NATIONAL one; since its jurisdiction extends to certain enumerated objects only, and leaves to the several States a residuary and inviolable sovereignty over all other objects. It is true that in controversies relating to the boundary between the two jurisdictions, the tribunal which is ultimately to decide, is to be established under the general government. But this does not change the principle of the case. The decision is to be impartially made, according to the rules of the Constitution; and all the usual and most effectual precautions are taken to secure this impartiality. Some such tribunal is clearly essential to prevent an appeal to the sword and a dissolution of the compact; and that it ought to be established under the general rather than under the local governments, or, to speak more properly, that it could be safely established under the first alone, is a position not likely to be combated.

If we try the Constitution by its last relation to the authority by which amendments are to be made, we find it neither wholly NATIONAL nor wholly FEDERAL. Were it wholly national, the supreme and ultimate authority would reside in the MAJORITY of the people of the Union; and this authority would be competent at all times, like that of a majority of every national society, to alter or abolish its established government. Were it wholly federal, on the other hand, the concurrence of each State in the Union would be essential to every alteration that would be binding on all. The mode provided by the plan of the convention is not founded on either of these principles. In requiring more than a majority, and principles. In requiring more than a majority, and particularly in computing the proportion by STATES, not by CITIZENS, it departs from the NATIONAL and advances towards the FEDERAL character; in rendering the concurrence of less than the whole number of States sufficient, it loses again the FEDERAL and partakes of the NATIONAL character.

The proposed Constitution, therefore, is, in strictness, neither a national nor a federal Constitution, but a composition of both. In its foundation it is federal, not national; in the sources from which the ordinary powers of the government are drawn, it is partly federal and partly national; in the operation of these powers, it is national, not federal; in the extent of them, again, it is federal, not national; and, finally, in the authoritative mode of introducing amendments, it is neither wholly federal nor wholly national.

NO. 46

. . .

Were it admitted, however, that the Federal government may feel an equal disposition with the State governments to extend its power beyond the due limits, the latter would still have the advantage in the means of defeating such encroachments. If an act of a particular State, though unfriendly to the national government, be generally popular in that State and should not too grossly violate the oaths of the State officers, it is executed immediately and, of course, by means on the spot and depending on the State alone. The opposition of the federal government, or the interposition of federal officers, would but inflame the zeal of all parties on the side of the State, and the evil could not be prevented or repaired, if at all, without the employment of means which must always be resorted to with reluctance and difficulty.

On the other hand, should an unwarrantable measure of the federal government be unpopular in particular States, which would seldom fail to be the case, or even a warrantable measure be so, which may sometimes be the case, the means of opposition to it are powerful and at hand. The disquietude of the people; their repugnance and, perhaps, refusal to cooperate with the officers of the Union; the frowns of the executive magistracy of the State; the embarrassments created by legislative devices, which would often be added on such occasions, would oppose, in any State, difficulties not to be despised; would form, in a large State, very serious impediments; and where the sentiments of several adjoining States happened to be in unison, would present obstructions which the federal government would hardly be willing to encounter. But ambitious encroachments of the federal government, on the authority of the State governments, would not excite the opposition of a single State, or of a few States only. They would be signals of general alarm. Every government would espouse the common cause. A correspondence would be opened. Plans of resistance would be concerted. One spirit would animate and conduct the whole. The same combinations, in short, would result from an apprehension of the federal, as was produced by the dread of a foreign, yoke; and unless the projected innovations should be voluntarily renounced, the same appeal to a trial of force would be made in the one case as was made in the other. But what degree of madness could ever drive the federal government to such an extremity. . . .

. . . The argument under the present head may be put into a very concise form, which appears altogether conclusive. Either the mode in which the federal government is to be constructed will render it sufficiently dependent on the people, or it will not. On the first supposition, it will be restrained by that dependence from forming schemes obnoxious to their constituents. On the other supposition, it will not possess the confidence of the people, and its schemes of usurpation will be easily defeated by the State governments, who will be supported by the people. On summing up the considerations stated in this and the last paper, they seem to amount to the most convincing evidence, that the powers proposed to be lodged in the federal government are as little formidable to those reserved to the individual States, as they are indispensably necessary to accomplish the purposes of the Union; and that all those alarms which have been sounded, of a meditated and consequential annihilation of the State governments, must, on the most favorable interpretation, be ascribed to the chimerical fears of the authors of them.

NO. 48

. . . It is agreed on all sides, that the powers properly belonging to one of the departments ought not to be directly and completely administered by either of the other departments. It is equally evident, that none of them ought to possess, directly or indirectly, an overruling influence over the others, in the administration of their respective powers. It will not be denied, that power is of an encroaching nature, and that it ought to be effectually restrained from passing the limits assigned to it. After discriminating, therefore, in theory, the several classes of power, as they may in their nature be legislative, executive, or judiciary, the next and most difficult task is to provide some practical security for each, against the invasion of the others.

What this security ought to be, is the great problem to be solved. Will it be sufficient to mark, with precision, the boundaries of these departments, in the constitution of the government, and to trust to these parchment barriers against the encroaching spirit of power? This is the security which appears to have been principally relied on by the compilers of most of the American constitutions. But experience assures us, that the efficacy of the provision has been greatly overrated; and that some more adequate defense is indispensably necessary for the more feeble, against the more powerful, members of the government. The legislative department is everywhere extending the sphere of its activity, and drawing all power into its impetuous vortex. The founders of our republics have so much merit for the wisdom which they have displayed, that no task can be less pleasing than that of pointing out the errors into which they have fallen. A respect for truth, however, obliges us to remark, that they seem never for a moment to have turned their eyes from the danger to liberty from the overgrown and all-grasping prerogative of an hereditary magistrate, supported and fortified by an hereditary branch of the legislative authority. They seem never to have recollected the danger from legislative usurpations, which, by assembling all power in the same hands, must lead to the same tyranny as is threatened by executive usurpations. In a government where numerous and extensive prerogatives are placed in the hands of an hereditary monarch, the executive department is very justly regarded as the source of danger, and watched with all the jealousy which a zeal for liberty ought to inspire. In a democracy, where a multitude of people exercise in person the legislative functions, and are continually exposed, by their incapacity for regular deliberation and concerted measures, to the ambitious intrigues of their executive magistrates, tyranny may well be apprehended, on some favorable emergency, to start up in the same quarter. But in a representative republic, where the executive magistracy is carefully limited; both in the extent and the duration of its power; and where the legislative power is exercised by an assembly, which is inspired, by a supposed influence over the people, with an intrepid confidence in its own strength; which is sufficiently numerous to feel all the passions which actuate a multitude, yet not so numerous as to be incapable of pursuing the objects of its passions, by means which reason prescribes; it is against the enterprising ambition of this department that the people ought to indulge all their jealousy and exhaust all their precautions. The legislative department derives a superiority in our governments from other circumstances. Its constitutional powers being at once more extensive, and less susceptible of precise limits, it can, with the greater facility, mask, under complicated and indirect measures, the encroachments which it makes on the co-ordinate departments. It is not unfrequently a question of real nicety in legislative bodies, whether the operation of a particular measure will, or will not, extend beyond the legislative sphere.

On the other side, the executive power being restrained within a narrower compass, and being more simple in its nature, and the judiciary being described by landmarks still less uncertain, projects of usurpation by either of these departments would immediately betray and defeat themselves. Nor is this all: as the legislative department alone has access to the pockets of the people, and has in some constitutions full discretion, and in all a prevailing influence, over the pecuniary rewards of those who fill the other departments, a dependence is thus created in the latter, which gives still greater facility to encroachments of the former. I have appealed to our own experience for the truth of what I advance on this subject. . . .

. . .

The conclusion which I am warranted in drawing from these observations is, that a mere demarcation on parchment of the constitutional limits of the several departments, is not a sufficient guard against those encroachments which lead to a tyrannical concentration of all the powers of government in the same hands.

NO. 51

To what expedient, then, shall we finally resort, for maintaining in practice the necessary partition of power among the several departments, as laid down in the Constitution? The only answer that can be given is, that as all these exterior provisions are found to be inadequate, the defect must be supplied, by so contriving the interior structure of the government as that its several constituent parts may, by their mutual relations, be the means of keeping each other in their proper places. Without presuming to undertake a full development of this important idea, I will hazard a few general observations, which may perhaps place it in a clearer light, and enable us to form a more correct judgment of the principles and structure of the government planned by the convention.

In order to lay a due foundation for that separate and distinct exercise of the different powers of government, which to a certain extent is admitted on all hands to be essential to the preservation of liberty, it is evident that each department should have a will of its own; and consequently should be so constituted that the members of each should have as little agency as possible in the appointment of the members of the others. Were this principle rigorously adhered to, it would require that all the appointments for the supreme executive, legislative, and judiciary magistracies should be drawn from the same fountain of authority, the people, through channels having no communication whatever with one another. Perhaps such a plan of constructing the several departments would be less difficult in practice than it may in contemplation appear. Some difficulties, however, and some additional expense would attend the execution of it. Some deviations, therefore, from the principle must be admitted. In the constitution of the judiciary department in particular, it might be inexpedient to insist rigorously on the principle: first, because peculiar qualifications being essential in the members, the primary consideration ought to be to select that mode of choice which best secures these qualifications; secondly, because the permanent tenure by which the appointments are held in that department, must soon destroy all sense of dependence on the authority conferring them.

It is equally evident, that the members of each department should be as little dependent as possible on those of the others, for the emoluments annexed to their offices. Were the executive magistrate, or the judges, not independent of the legislature in this particular, their independence in every other would be merely nominal. But the great security against a gradual concentration of the several powers in the same department, consists in giving to those who administer each department the necessary constitutional means and personal motives to resist encroachments of the others. The provision for defense must in this, as in all other cases, be made commensurate to the danger of attack. Ambition must be made to counteract ambition. The interest of the man must be connected with the constitutional rights of the place. It may be a reflection on human nature, that such devices should be necessary to control the abuses of government. But what is government itself, but the greatest of all reflections on human nature? If men were angels, no government would be necessary. If angels were to govern men, neither external nor internal controls on government would be necessary. In framing a government which is to be administered by men over men, the great difficulty lies in this: you must first enable the government to control the governed; and in the next place oblige it to control itself.

A dependence on the people is, no doubt, the primary control on the government; but experience has taught mankind the necessity of auxiliary precautions. This policy of supplying, by opposite and rival interests, the defect of better motives, might be traced through the whole system of human affairs, private as well as public. We see it particularly displayed in all the subordinate distributions of power, where the constant aim is to divide and arrange the several offices in such a manner as that each may be a check on the other that the private interest of every individual may be a sentinel over the public rights. These inventions of prudence cannot be less requisite in the distribution of the supreme powers of the State. But it is not possible to give to each department an equal power of self-defense. In republican government, the legislative authority necessarily predominates. The remedy for this inconveniency is to divide the legislature into different branches; and to render them, by different modes of election and different principles of action, as little connected with each other as the nature of their common functions and their common dependence on the society will admit. It may even be necessary to guard against dangerous encroachments by still further precautions. As the weight of the legislative authority requires that it should be thus divided, the weakness of the executive may require, on the other hand, that it should be fortified.

An absolute negative on the legislature appears, at first view, to be the natural defense with which the executive magistrate should be armed. But perhaps it would be neither altogether safe nor alone sufficient. On ordinary occasions it might not be exerted with the requisite firmness, and on extraordinary occasions it might be perfidiously abused. May not this defect of an absolute negative be supplied by some qualified connection between this weaker department and the weaker branch of the stronger department, by which the latter may be led to support the constitutional rights of the former, without being too much detached from the rights of its own department? . . .

There are, moreover, two considerations particularly applicable to the federal system of America, which place that system in a very interesting point of view. First. In a single republic, all the power surrendered by the people is submitted to the administration of a single government; and the usurpations are guarded against by a division of the government into distinct and separate departments. In the compound republic of America, the power surrendered by the people is first divided between two distinct governments, and then the portion allotted to each subdivided among distinct and separate departments. Hence a double security arises to the rights of the people. The different governments will control each other, at the same time that each will be controlled by itself. Second. It is of great importance in a republic not only to guard the society against the oppression of its rulers, but to guard one part of the society against the injustice of the other part. Different interests necessarily exist in different classes of citizens. If a majority be united by a common interest, the rights of the minority will be insecure.

There are but two methods of providing against this evil: the one by creating a will in the community independent of the majority that is, of the society itself; the other, by comprehending in the society so many separate descriptions of citizens as will render an unjust combination of a majority of the whole very improbable, if not impracticable. The first method prevails in all governments possessing an hereditary or self-appointed authority. This, at best, is but a precarious security; because a power independent of the society may as well espouse the unjust views of the major, as the rightful interests of the minor party, and may possibly be turned against both parties. The second method will be exemplified in the federal republic of the United States. Whilst all authority in it will be derived from and dependent on the society, the society itself will be broken into so many parts, interests, and classes of citizens, that the rights of individuals, or of the minority, will be in little danger from interested combinations of the majority.

In a free government the security for civil rights must be the same as that for religious rights. It consists in the one case in the multiplicity of interests, and in the other in the multiplicity of sects. The degree of security in both cases will depend on the number of interests and sects; and this may be presumed to depend on the extent of country and number of people comprehended under the same government. This view of the subject must particularly recommend a proper federal system to all the sincere and considerate friends of republican government, since it shows that in exact proportion as the territory of the Union may be formed into more circumscribed Confederacies, or States oppressive combinations of a majority will be facilitated: the best security, under the republican forms, for the rights of every class of citizens, will be diminished: and consequently the stability and independence of some member of the government, the only other security, must be proportionately increased. Justice is the end of government. It is the end of civil society. It ever has been and ever will be pursued until it be obtained, or until liberty be lost in the pursuit. In a society under the forms of which the stronger faction can readily unite and oppress the weaker, anarchy may as truly be said to reign as in a state of nature, where the weaker individual is not secured against the violence of the stronger; and as, in the latter state, even the stronger individuals are prompted, by the uncertainty of their condition, to submit to a government which may protect the weak as well as themselves; so, in the former state, will the more powerful factions or parties be gradually induced, by a like motive, to wish for a government which will protect all parties, the weaker as well as the more powerful.

It can be little doubted that if the State of Rhode Island was separated from the Confederacy and left to itself, the insecurity of rights under the popular form of government within such narrow limits would be displayed by such reiterated oppressions of factious majorities that some power altogether independent of the people would soon be called for by the voice of the very factions whose misrule had proved the necessity of it. In the extended republic of the United States, and among the great variety of interests, parties, and sects which it embraces, a coalition of a majority of the whole society could seldom take place on any other principles than those of justice and the general good; whilst there being thus less danger to a minor from the will of a major party, there must be less pretext, also, to provide for the security of the former, by introducing into the government a will not dependent on the latter, or, in other words, a will independent of the society itself. It is no less certain than it is important, notwithstanding the contrary opinions which have been entertained, that the larger the society, provided it lie within a practical sphere, the more duly capable it will be of self-government. And happily for the REPUBLICAN CAUSE, the practicable sphere may be carried to a very great extent, by a judicious modification and mixture of the FEDERAL PRINCIPLE.

BRUTUS ESSAYS (1787)

Long attributed to the New York judge Robert Yates, the true authorship of the Brutus essays remains a source of controversy.[10] There is far greater agreement on the status of these essays as among the most incisive of the anti-Federalist writings. Published in the New York newspapers during the ratification debate under the pseudonym "Brutus," these essays raised a wide range of doubts about the proposed Constitution. The quality of the arguments in the Brutus essays helped spur Alexander Hamilton to begin the Publius essays to help rally public opinion and convention delegate support to the cause of ratification.

Is there an overarching objection to the proposed Constitution in the Brutus essays? Does Brutus think a republic can be maintained under the Constitution? Is there an alternative to the Constitution in Brutus's account? Is he right that the Constitution created a "consolidated" government? How does Brutus differ from Publius? Do they disagree about how the Constitution will work, or about what the aims of the government should be?

NO. 1

When the public is called to investigate and decide upon a question in which not only the present members of the community are deeply interested, but upon which the happiness and misery of generations yet unborn is in great measure suspended, the benevolent mind cannot help feeling itself peculiarly interested in the results.

. . .

Perhaps this country never saw so critical a period in their political concerns. We have felt the feebleness of the ties by which these United States are held together, and the want of sufficient energy in our present Confederation, to manage, in some instances, our general concerns. Various expedients have been proposed to remedy these evils, but none have succeeded. At length a Convention of the States has been assembled, they have formed a Constitution which will now, probably, be submitted to the people to ratify or reject, who are the foundation of all power, to whom alone it of right belongs to make or unmake constitutions or forms of government, at their pleasure. The most important question that was ever proposed to the decision of any people under heaven, is before you, and you are to decide upon it by men of your own election, chosen specially for this purpose. If the Constitution, offered to your acceptance, be a wise one, calculated to preserve the invaluable blessings of liberty, to secure the inestimable rights of mankind, and promote human happiness, then, if you accept it, you will lay a lasting foundation of happiness for millions yet unborn; generations to come will rise up and call you blessed. You may rejoice in the prospects of this vast extended continent becoming filled with freemen, who will assert the dignity of human nature. You may solace yourselves with the idea, that society, in this favored land, will fast advance to the highest point of perfection; the human mind will expand in knowledge and virtue, and the golden age be, in some measure, realized. But if, on the other hand, this form of government contains principles that will lead to the subversion of liberty—if it tends to establish a despotism, or, what is worse, a tyrannic aristocracy; then, if you adopt it, this only remaining asylum for liberty will be shut up, and posterity will execrate your memory.

. . . It is insisted, indeed, that this Constitution must be received, be it ever so imperfect. If it has its defects, it is said, they can be best amended when they

10 For a summary of the evidence regarding the authorship of a number of anti-Federalist essays, see Michael P. Zuckert and Derek A. Webb, *The Anti-Federalist Writings of the Melancton Smith Circle* (Indianapolis, IN: Liberty Fund, 2009).

are experienced. But remember, when the people once part with power, they can seldom or never resume it again but by force. Many instances can be produced in which the people have voluntarily increased the powers of their rulers; but few, if any, in which rulers have willingly abridged their authority. This is sufficient reason to induce you to be careful, in the first instance, how you deposit the powers of government.

With these few introductory remarks, I shall proceed to a consideration of this Constitution.

The first question that presents itself on the subject is, whether a confederated government be the best for the United States or not? Or in other words, whether the thirteen United States should be reduced to one great republic, governed by one legislature, and under the direction of one executive and judiciary; or whether they should continue thirteen confederated republics, under the direction and control of a supreme Federal head for certain defined, national purposes only?

This inquiry is important, because, although the government reported by the Convention does not go to a perfect and entire consolidation, yet it approaches so near to it, that it must, if executed, certainly and infallibly terminate in it.

This government is to possess absolute and uncontrollable powers, legislative, executive and judicial, with respect to every object to which it extends, for by the last clause of section eighth, article first, it is declared, that the Congress shall have power "to make all laws which shall be necessary and proper for carrying into execution the foregoing powers, and all other powers vested by the Constitution in the government of the United States, or in any department or office thereof." And by the sixth article, it is declared, "that this Constitution, and the laws of the United States, which shall be made in pursuance thereof, and the treaties made, or which shall be made, under the authority of the United States, shall be the supreme law of the land; and the judges in every State shall be bound thereby, anything in the Constitution or law of any State to the contrary notwithstanding." It appears for these articles, that there is no need of any intervention of the State governments, between the Congress and the people, to execute any one power vested in the general government, and that the Constitution and laws of every State are nullified and declared void, so far as they are or shall be inconsistent with this Constitution, or the laws made in pursuance of it, or with treaties made under the authority of the United States. The government, then, so far as it extends, is a complete one, and not a confederation. It is as much one complete government as that of New York or Massachusetts; has as absolute and perfect powers to make and execute all laws, to appoint officers, institute courts, declare offenses, and annex penalties, with respect to every object to which it extends, as any other in the world. So far, therefore, as its powers reach, all ideas of confederation are given up and lost. It is true this government is limited to certain objects, or to speak more properly, some small degree of power is still left to the states, but a little attention to the powers vested in the general government, will convince every candid man, that if it is capable of being executed, all that is reserved for the individual states must very soon be annihilated, except so far as they are barely necessary to the organization of the general government. The powers of the general legislature extend to every case that is of the least importance. . . . It has authority to make laws which will affect the lives, the liberty, and property of every man in the United States; nor can the constitution or laws of any state, in any way prevent or impede the full and complete execution of every power given. The legislative power is competent to lay taxes, duties, imposts, and excises;—there is no limitation to this power, unless it be said that the clause which directs the use to which those taxes, and duties shall be applied, may be said to be a limitation: but this is no restriction of the power at all, for by this clause they are to be applied to pay the debts and provide for the common defense and general welfare of the United States; but the legislature have authority to contract debts at their discretion; they are the sole judges of what is necessary to provide for the common defense, and they only are to determine what is for the general welfare; this power therefore is neither more nor less, than a power to lay and collect taxes, imposts, and excises, at their pleasure; not only [is] the power to lay taxes unlimited, as to the amount they may require, but it is perfect and absolute to raise them in any mode they please. No state legislature, or any power in the state governments, have any more to do in carrying this into effect, than the authority of one state has to do with that of another. In the business therefore of laying and collecting taxes, the idea of confederation is totally lost, and that of one entire republic is embraced. It is proper here to remark, that the authority to lay and collect taxes is the most important of any power that can be granted; it connects with it almost all other powers, or at least will in process of time draw all other after it; it is the great mean of protection, security, and defense, in a good government, and the great engine of oppression and tyranny in a bad one. . . . Everyone who has thought on the subject, must be convinced that but small sums of money can be collected in any country, by direct tax; when the federal government begins to exercise the right of taxation in all its parts, the legislatures of the several states will find it impossible to raise monies to support their governments. Without money they cannot be supported, and they must dwindle away, and, as before observed, their powers absorbed in that of the general government.

. . .

The judicial power of the United States is to be vested in a supreme court, and in such inferior courts as Congress may from time to time ordain and establish. The powers of these courts are very extensive; their jurisdiction comprehends all civil causes, except such as arise between citizens of the same state; and it extends to all cases in law and equity arising under the constitution. One inferior court must be established, I presume, in each state, at least, with the necessary executive officers appendant thereto. It is easy to see, that in the common course of things, these courts will eclipse the dignity, and take away from the respectability, of the state courts. These courts will be, in themselves, totally independent of the states, deriving their authority from the United States, and receiving from them fixed salaries; and in the course of human events it is to be expected, that they will swallow up all the powers of the courts in the respective states.

How far the clause in the 8th section of the 1st article may operate to do away all idea of confederated states, and to effect an entire consolidation of the whole into one general government, it is impossible to say. The powers given by this article are very general and comprehensive, and it may receive a construction to justify the passing almost any law. A power to make all laws, which shall be *necessary and proper*, for carrying into execution, all powers vested by the constitution in the government of the United States, or any department or officer thereof, is a power very comprehensive and definite, and may, for ought I know, be exercised in such manner as entirely to abolish the state legislatures. Suppose the legislature of a state should pass a law to raise money to support their government and pay the state debt, may the Congress repeal this law, because it may prevent the collection of a tax which they may think proper and necessary to lay, to provide for the general welfare of the United States? For all laws made, in pursuance of this constitution, are the supreme law of the land, and the judges in every state shall be bound thereby, anything in the constitution or laws of the different states to the contrary notwithstanding.—By such a law, the government of a particular state might be overturned at one stroke, and thereby be deprived of every means of its support.

. . . And if they may do it, it is pretty certain they will; for it will be found that the power retained by individual states, small as it is, will be a clog upon the wheels of the government of the United States; the latter therefore will be naturally inclined to remove it out of the way. Besides, it is a truth confirmed by the unerring experience of ages, that every man, and every body of men, invested with power, are ever disposed to increase it, and to acquire a superiority over everything that stands in their way. This disposition, which is implanted in human nature, will operate in the federal legislature to lessen and ultimately to subvert the state authority. . . .

Let us now proceed to enquire, as I at first proposed, whether it be best the thirteen United States should be reduced to one great republic, or not? It is here taken for granted, that all agree in this, that whatever government we adopt, it ought to be a free one; that it should be so framed as to secure the liberty of the citizens of America, and such an one as to admit of a full, fair, and equal representation of the people. The question then will be, whether a government thus constituted, and founded on such principles, is practicable, and can be exercised over the whole United States, reduced into one state?

. . .

History furnishes no example of a free republic, anything like the extent of the United States. The Grecian republics were of small extent; so also was that of the Romans. Both of these, it is true, in process of time, extended their conquests over large territories of country; and the consequence was, that their governments were changed from that of free governments to those of the most tyrannical that ever existed in the world.

. . . In every government, the will of the sovereign is the law. In despotic governments, the supreme authority being lodged in one, his will is law, and can be as easily expressed to a large extensive territory as to a small one. In a pure democracy the people are the sovereign, and their will is declared by themselves; for this purpose they must all come together to deliberate, and decide. This kind of government cannot be exercised, therefore, over a country of any considerable extent; it must be confined to a single city, or at least limited to such bounds as that the people can conveniently assemble, be able to debate, understand the subject submitted to them, and declare their opinion concerning it.

In a free republic, although all laws are derived from the consent of the people, yet the people do not declare their consent by themselves in person, but by representatives, chosen by them, who are supposed to know the minds of their constituents, and to be possessed of integrity to declare this mind.

In every free government, the people must give their assent to the laws by which they are governed. This is the true criterion between a free government and an arbitrary one. . . . If the people are to give their assent to the laws, by persons chosen and appointed by them, the manner of the choice and the number chosen, must be such, as to possess, be disposed, and consequently qualified to declare the sentiments of the people; for if they do not know, or are not disposed to speak the sentiments of the people, the people do not govern, but the sovereignty is in a few. Now, in a large extended country, it is impossible to have a representation, possessing the sentiments, and of integrity, to declare the minds of the people, without having it so numerous and unwieldy, as to be subject in great measure to the inconveniency of a democratic government.

The territory of the United States is of vast extent; it now contains near three millions of souls, and is capable of containing much more than ten times that number. Is it practicable for a country, so large and so numerous as they will soon become, to elect a representation, that will speak their sentiments, without their becoming so numerous as to be incapable of transacting public business? It certainly is not.

In a republic, the manners, sentiments, and interests of the people should be similar. If this be not the case, there will be a constant clashing of opinions; and the representatives of one part will be continually striving against those of the other. This will retard the operations of government, and prevent such conclusions as will promote the public good. If we apply this remark to the condition of the United States, we shall be convinced that it forbids that we should be one government. The United States includes a variety of climates. The productions of the different parts of the union are very variant, and their interests, of consequence, diverse. Their manners and habits differ as much as their climates and productions; and their sentiments are by no means coincident. The laws and customs of the several states are, in many respects, very diverse, and in some opposite; each would be in favor of its own interests and customs, and, of consequence, a legislature, formed of representatives from the respective parts, would not only be too numerous to act with any care or decision, but would be composed of such heterogeneous and discordant principles, as would constantly be contending with each other.

The laws cannot be executed in a republic, of an extent equal to that of the United States, with promptitude.

The magistrates in every government must be supported in the execution of the laws, either by an armed force, maintained at the public expense for that purpose; or by the people turning out to aid the magistrate upon his command, in case of resistance.

In despotic governments, as well as in all the monarchies of Europe, standing armies are kept up to execute the commands of the prince or the magistrate, and are employed for this purpose when occasion requires: But they have always proved the destruction of liberty, and [are] abhorrent to the spirit of a free republic. . . .

A free republic will never keep a standing army to execute its laws. It must depend upon the support of its citizens. But when a government is to receive its support from the aid of the citizens, it must be so constructed as to have the confidence, respect, and affection of the people. . . . The confidence which the people have in their rulers, in a free republic, arises from their knowing them, from their being responsible to them for their conduct, and from the power they have of displacing them when they misbehave: but in a republic of the extent of this continent, the people in general would be acquainted with very few of their rulers: the people at large would know little of their proceedings, and it would be extremely difficult to change them. The people in Georgia and New-Hampshire would not know one another's mind, and therefore could not act in concert to enable them to effect a general change of representatives. The different parts of so extensive a country could not possibly be made acquainted with the conduct of their representatives, nor be informed of the reasons upon which measures were founded. The consequence will be, they will have no confidence in their legislature, suspect them of ambitious views, be jealous of every measure they adopt, and will not support the laws they pass. Hence the government will be nerveless and inefficient, and no way will be left to render it otherwise, but by establishing an armed force to execute the laws at the point of the bayonet—a government of all others the most to be dreaded.

In a republic of such vast extent as the United-States, the legislature cannot attend to the various concerns and wants of its different parts. It cannot be sufficiently numerous to be acquainted with the local condition and wants of the different districts, and if it could, it is impossible it should have sufficient time to attend to and provide for all the variety of cases of this nature, that would be continually arising.

In so extensive a republic, the great officers of government would soon become above the control of the people, and abuse their power to the purpose of aggrandizing themselves, and oppressing them. The trust committed to the executive offices, in a country of the extent of the United-States, must be various and of magnitude. . . . They will use the power, when they have acquired it, to the purposes of gratifying their own interest and ambition, and it is scarcely possible, in a very large republic, to call them to account for their misconduct, or to prevent their abuse of power.

These are some of the reasons by which it appears, that a free republic cannot long subsist over a country of the great extent of these states. If then this new constitution is calculated to consolidate the thirteen states into one, as it evidently is, it ought not to be adopted.

. . .

NO. 2

I flatter myself that my last address established this position, that to reduce the Thirteen States into one government, would prove the destruction of your liberties.

But lest this truth should be doubted by some, I will now proceed to consider its merits.

. . . When a building is to be erected which is intended to stand for ages, the foundation should be firmly laid. The constitution proposed to your acceptance, is designed not for yourselves alone, but for generations yet unborn. The principles, therefore, upon which the social compact is founded, ought to have been clearly and precisely stated, and the most express and full declaration of rights to have been made—But on this subject there is almost an entire silence.

If we may collect the sentiments of the people of America, from their own most solemn declarations, they hold this truth as self evident, that all men are by nature free. No one man, therefore, or any class of men, have a right, by the law of nature, or of God, to assume or exercise authority over their fellows. The origin of society then is to be sought, not in any natural right which one man has to exercise authority over another, but in the united consent of those who associate. The mutual wants of men, at first dictated the propriety of forming societies; and when they were established, protection and defense pointed out the necessity of instituting government. . . . The common good, therefore, is the end of civil government, and common consent, the foundation on which it is established. To effect this end, it was necessary that a certain portion of natural liberty should be surrendered, in order, that what remained should be preserved: how great a proportion of natural freedom is necessary to be yielded by individuals, when they submit to government, I shall not now enquire. So much, however, must be given up, as will be sufficient to enable those, to whom the administration of the government is committed, to establish laws for the promoting the happiness of the community, and to carry those laws into effect. But it is not necessary, for this purpose, that individuals should relinquish all their natural rights. Some are of such a nature that they cannot be surrendered. Of this kind are the rights of conscience, the right of enjoying and defending life, etc. Others are not necessary to be resigned, in order to attain the end for which government is instituted, these therefore ought not to be given up. To surrender them, would counteract the very end of government, to wit, the common good. From these observations it appears, that in forming a government on its true principles, the foundation should be laid in the manner I before stated, by expressly reserving to the people such of their essential natural rights, as are not necessary to be parted with. . . . It was because one part exercised fraud, oppression, and violence on the other, that men came together, and agreed that certain rules should be formed, to regulate the conduct of all, and the power of the whole community lodged in the hands of rulers to enforce an obedience to them. But rulers have the same propensities as other men; they are as likely to use the power with which they are vested for private purposes, and to the injury and oppression of those over whom they are placed, as individuals in a state of nature are to injure and oppress one another. It is therefore as proper that bounds should be set to their authority, as that government should have at first been instituted to restrain private injuries.

This principle, which seems so evidently founded in the reason and nature of things, is confirmed by universal experience. Those who have governed, have been found in all ages ever active to enlarge their powers and abridge the public liberty. This has induced the people in all countries, where any sense of freedom remained, to fix barriers against the encroachments of their rulers. . . . I need say no more, I presume, to an American, than, that this principle is a fundamental one, in all the constitutions of our own states; there is not one of them but what is either founded on a declaration or bill of rights, or has certain express reservation of rights interwoven in the body of them. From this it appears, that at a time when the pulse of liberty beat high and when an appeal was made to the people to form constitutions for the government of themselves, it was their universal sense, that such declarations should make a part of their frames of government. It is therefore the more astonishing, that this grand security, to the rights of the people, is not to be found in this constitution.

It has been said, in answer to this objection, that such declaration[s] of rights, however requisite they might be in the constitutions of the states, are not necessary in the general constitution, because, "in the former case, everything which is not reserved is given, but in the latter the reverse of the proposition prevails, and everything which is not given is reserved." It requires but little attention to discover, that this mode of reasoning is rather specious than solid. The powers, rights, and authority, granted to the general government by this constitution, are as complete, with respect to every object to which they extend, as that of any state government—It reaches to everything which concerns human happiness—Life, liberty, and property, are under its control. There is the same reason, therefore, that the exercise of power, in this case, should be restrained within proper limits, as in that of the state governments. To set this matter in a clear light, permit me to instance some of the articles of the bills of rights of the individual states, and apply them to the case in question.

For the security of life, in criminal prosecutions, the bills of rights of most of the states have declared, that no man shall be held to answer for a crime until he is made fully acquainted with the charge brought against him; he shall not be compelled to accuse, or furnish evidence against himself—The witnesses against him shall be brought face to face, and he shall be fully heard by himself or counsel. That it is essential to the security of life and liberty, that trial of facts be in the vicinity where they happen. Are not provisions of this kind as necessary in the general government, as in that of a particular state? The powers vested in the new Congress extend in many cases to life; they are authorized to provide for the punishment of a variety of capital crimes, and no restraint is laid upon them in its exercise, save only, that "the trial of all crimes, except in cases of impeachment, shall be by jury; and such trial shall be in the state where the said crimes shall have been committed." . . .

For the security of liberty it has been declared, "that excessive bail should not be required, nor excessive fines imposed, nor cruel or unusual punishments inflicted—That all warrants, without oath or affirmation, to search suspected places, or seize any person, his papers or property, are grievous and oppressive."

These provisions are as necessary under the general government as under that of the individual states; for the power of the former is as complete to the purpose of requiring bail, imposing fines, inflicting punishments, granting search warrants, and seizing persons, papers, or property, in certain cases, as the other.

For the purpose of securing the property of the citizens, it is declared by all the states, "that in all controversies at law, respecting property, the ancient mode of trial by jury is one of the best securities of the rights of the people, and ought to remain sacred and inviolable."

Does not the same necessity exist of reserving this right, under this national compact, as in that of these states? Yet nothing is said respecting it. In the bills of rights of the states it is declared, that a well regulated militia is the proper and natural defense of a free government—That as standing armies in time of peace are dangerous, they are not to be kept up, and that the military should be kept under strict subordination to, and controlled by the civil power.

The same security is as necessary in this constitution, and much more so; for the general government will have the sole power to raise and to pay armies, and are under no control in the exercise of it; yet nothing of this is to be found in this new system.

I might proceed to instance a number of other rights, which were as necessary to be reserved, such as, that elections should be free, that the liberty of the press should be held sacred; but the instances adduced, are sufficient to prove, that this argument is without foundation.—Besides, it is evident, that the reason here assigned was not the true one, why the framers of this constitution omitted a bill of rights; if it had been, they would not have made certain reservations, while they totally omitted others of more importance. We find they have, in the 9th section of the 1st article, declared, that the writ of habeas corpus shall not be suspended, unless in cases of rebellion—that no bill of attainder, or ex post facto law, shall be passed—that no title of nobility shall be granted by the United States, etc. If everything which is not given is reserved, what propriety is there in these exceptions? Does this constitution anywhere grant the power of suspending the habeas corpus, to make ex post facto laws, pass bills of attainder, or grant titles of nobility? It certainly does not in express terms. The only answer that can be given is, that these are implied in the general powers granted. With equal truth it may be said, that all the powers, which the bills of right, guard against the abuse of, are contained or implied in the general ones granted by this constitution.

So far it is from being true, that a bill of rights is less necessary in the general constitution than in those of the states, the contrary is evidently the fact.—This system, if it is possible for the people of America to accede to it, will be an original compact: and being the last, will, in the nature of things, vacate every former agreement inconsistent with it. For it being a plan of government received and ratified by the whole people, all other forms, which are in existence at the time of its adoption, must yield to it. This is expressed in positive and unequivocal terms, in the 6th article, "That this constitution and the laws of the United States, which shall be made in pursuance thereof, and all treaties made, or which shall be made, under the authority of the United States, shall be the supreme law of the land; and the judges in every state shall be bound thereby, anything in the *constitution*, or laws of any state, *to the contrary* notwithstanding."

"The senators and representatives before-mentioned, and the members of the several state legislatures, and all executive and judicial officers, both of the United

States, and of the several states, shall be bound, by oath or affirmation, to support this constitution."

It is therefore not only necessarily implied thereby, but positively expressed, that the different state constitutions are repealed and entirely done away, so far as they are inconsistent with this, with the laws which shall be made in pursuance thereof, or with treaties made, or which shall be made, under the authority of the United States; of what avail will the constitutions of the respective states be to preserve the rights of its citizens? Should they be plead, the answer would be, the constitution of the United States, and the laws made in pursuance thereof, is the supreme law, and all legislatures and judicial officers, whether of the general or state governments, are bound by oath to support it. No privilege, reserved by the bills of rights, or secured by the state government, can limit the power granted by this, or restrain any laws made in pursuance of it. It stands therefore on its own bottom, and must receive a construction by itself without any reference to any other—And hence it was of the highest importance, that the most precise and express declarations and reservations of rights should have been made.

This will appear the more necessary, when it is considered, that not only the constitution and laws made in pursuance thereof, but all treaties made, or which shall be made, under the authority of the United States, are the supreme law of the land, and supersede the constitutions of all the states. The power to make treaties, is vested in the president, by and with the advice and consent of two thirds of the senate. I do not find any limitation, or restriction, to the exercise of this power. The most important article in any constitution may therefore be repealed, even without a legislative act. Ought not a government, vested with such extensive and indefinite authority to have been restricted by a declaration of rights? It certainly ought.

So clear a point is this, that I cannot help suspecting, that persons who attempt to persuade people, that such reservations were less necessary under this constitution than under those of the states, are willfully endeavoring to deceive, and to lead you into an absolute state of vassalage.

LETTERS FROM THE FEDERAL FARMER (1787)

Although long attributed to the Virginia anti-Federalist Richard Henry Lee, the authorship of the "Federal Farmer" essays remains uncertain. The essays, originally published as pamphlets in the fall of 1787, were widely circulated in the northern states, particularly in New York, where anti-Federalist sentiment was strong. Alexander Hamilton identified Federal Farmer as one of the most persuasive of the anti-Federalist writers. The Federal Farmer essays argued that a more centralized system would eventually reduce the states to insignificance, but that such a large national system could not maintain a republican form of government.

Are the concerns of the Federal Farmer still relevant? Has history proven him wrong or right? Would anything be lost if the state governments were transformed into administrative extensions of the national government? What are the preconditions for a viable republican government? Could republican government be maintained if a supranational government were established for all of North America?

NO. 1

. . .

The first principal question that occurs, is, Whether, considering our situation, we ought to precipitate the adoption of the proposed constitution? If we remain cool and temperate, we are in no immediate danger of any commotions; we are in a state of perfect peace, and in no danger of invasions; the state governments are in the full exercise of their powers; and our governments answer all present exigencies, except the regulation of trade, securing credit, in some cases, and providing for the interest, in some instances, of the public debts; and whether we adopt a change three or nine months hence, can make but little odds with the private circumstances of individuals; their happiness and prosperity, after all, depend principally upon their own exertions. . . .

. . . It is natural for men, who wish to hasten the adoption of a measure, to tell us, now is the crisis—now is the critical moment which must be seized, or all will be lost: and to shut the door against free enquiry, whenever conscious the thing presented has defects in it, which time and investigation will probably discover. This has been the custom of tyrants and their dependents in all ages. If it is true, what has been so often said, that the people of this country cannot change their condition for the worse, I presume it still behooves them to endeavor deliberately to change it for the better. The fickle and ardent, in any community, are the proper tools for establishing despotic government. But it is deliberate and thinking men, who must establish and secure governments on free principles. Before they decide on the plan proposed, they will inquire whether it will probably be a blessing or a curse to this people.

. . .

To have a just idea of the government before us, and to show that a consolidated one is the object in view, it is necessary not only to examine the plan, but also its history, and the politics of its particular friends.

The confederation was formed when great confidence was placed in the voluntary exertions of individuals, and of the respective states; and the framers of it, to guard against usurpation, so limited and checked the powers, that, in many respects, they are inadequate to the exigencies of the union. We find, therefore, members of congress urging alterations in the federal system almost as soon as it was adopted. . . . We expected too much from the return of peace, and of course we have been disappointed. Our governments have been new and unsettled; and several legislatures, by making tender, suspension, and paper money laws, have given just cause of uneasiness to creditors. By these and other causes, several orders of men in the community have been prepared, by degrees, for a change of government; and this very abuse of power in the legislatures, which, in some cases, has been charged upon the democratic part of the community, has furnished aristocratical men with those very weapons, and those very means, with which, in great measure, they are rapidly effecting their favorite object. And should an oppressive government be the consequence of the proposed change, posterity may reproach not only a few overbearing unprincipled men, but those parties in the states which have misused their powers.

. . .

The plan proposed appears to be partly federal, but principally, however, calculated ultimately to make the states one consolidated government.

The first interesting question, therefore suggested, is, how far the states can be consolidated into one entire government on free principles. In considering this question extensive objects are to be taken into view, and important changes in the forms of government to be carefully attended to in all their consequences. The happiness of the people at large must be the great object with every honest statesman, and he will direct every movement to this point. If we are so situated as a people, as not to be able to enjoy equal happiness and advantages under one government, the consolidation of the states cannot be admitted.

. . .

. . . [O]ne government and general legislation alone, never can extend equal benefits to all parts of the United States: Different laws, customs, and opinions exist in the different states, which by a uniform system of laws would be unreasonably invaded. The United States contain about a million of square miles, and in half a century will, probably, contain ten millions of people; and from the center to the extremes is about 800 miles.

. . .

NO. 2

. . .

There are certain inalienable and fundamental rights, which in forming the social compact, ought to be explicitly ascertained and fixed—a free and enlightened people, in forming this compact, will not resign all their rights to those who govern, and they will fix limits to their legislators and rulers, which will soon be plainly seen by those who are governed, as well as by those who govern: and the latter will know they cannot be passed unperceived by the former, and without giving a general alarm—These rights should be made the basis of every constitution; and if a people be so situated, or have such different opinions that they cannot agree in ascertaining and fixing them, it is a very strong argument against their attempting to form one entire society, to live under one system of laws only. . . .

. . .

NO. 3

. . . .

First. As to the organization—the house of representatives, the democrative branch, as it is called, is to consist of 65 members: that is, about one representative for fifty thousand inhabitants, to be chosen biennially—the federal legislature may increase this number to one for each thirty thousand inhabitants, abating fractional numbers in each state. Thirty-three representatives will make a quorum for doing business, and a majority of those present determine the sense of the house. I have no idea that the interests, feelings, and opinions of three or four millions of people, especially touching internal taxation, can be collected in such a house. In the nature of things, nine times in ten, men of the elevated classes in the community only can be chosen. . . . The people of this country, in one sense, may all be democratic; but if we make the proper distinction between the few men of wealth and abilities, and consider them, as we ought, as the natural aristocracy of the country, and the great body of the people, the middle and lower classes, as the democracy, this federal representative branch will have but very little democracy in it, even this small representation is not secured on proper principles. The branches of the legislature are essential parts of the fundamental compact and ought to be so fixed by the people, that the legislature cannot alter itself by modifying the elections of its own members. . . . [I]n making the constitution, we ought to provide for dividing each state into a proper number of districts, and for confining the electors in each district to the choice of some men, who shall have a permanent interest and residence in it; and also for this essential object, that the representative elected shall have a majority of the votes of those electors who shall attend and give their votes.

. . .

[The house of representatives is on the plan of consolidation, but the senate is entirely on the federal plan;] and Delaware will have as much constitutional influence in the senate, as the largest state in the union: and in this senate are lodged legislative, executive and judicial powers: Ten states in this union urge that they are small states, nine of which were present in the convention. They were interested in collecting large powers into the hands of the senate, in which each state still will have its equal share of power. I suppose it was impracticable for the three large states, as they were called, to get the senate formed on any other principles: But this only proves, that we cannot form one general government on equal and just principles. . . .

. . .

In the second place it is necessary, therefore, to examine the extent, and the probable operations of some of those extensive powers proposed to be vested in this government. These powers, legislative, executive, and judicial, respect internal as well as external objects. Those respecting external objects, as all foreign concerns, commerce, imposts, all causes arising on the seas, peace and war, and Indian affairs, can be lodged nowhere else, with any propriety, but in this government. Many powers that respect internal objects ought clearly to be lodged in it; as those to regulate trade between the states, weights and measures, the coin or current monies, post offices, naturalization, etc. These powers may be exercised without essentially affecting the internal police of the respective states: But powers to levy and collect internal taxes, to form the militia, to make bankrupt laws, and to decide on appeals, questions arising on the internal laws of the respective states, are of a very serious nature, and carry with them almost all other powers. These taken in connection with the others, and powers to raise armies and build navies, proposed to be lodged in this government, appear to me to comprehend all the essential powers in the community, and those which will be left to the states will be of no great importance.

. . .

When I recollect how lately congress, conventions, legislatures, and people contended in the cause of liberty, and carefully weighed the importance of taxation, I can scarcely believe we are serious in proposing to vest the powers of laying and collecting internal taxes in a government so imperfectly organized for such purposes. . . . I am aware it is said, that the representation proposed by the new constitution is sufficiently numerous; it may be for many purposes; but to suppose that this branch is sufficiently numerous to guard the rights of the people in the administration of the government, in which the purse and sword are placed, seems to argue that we have forgotten what the true meaning of representation is. I am sensible also, that it is said that congress will not attempt to lay and collect internal taxes; that it is necessary for them to have the power, though it cannot probably be exercised. I admit that it is not probable that any prudent congress will attempt to lay and collect internal taxes, especially direct taxes: but this only proves that the power would be improperly lodged in congress, and that it might be abused by imprudent and designing men.

. . .

NO. 4

. . .

Third. There appears to me to be not only a premature deposit of some important powers in the general government—but many of those deposited there are undefined, and may be used to good or bad purposes as honest or designing men shall prevail. . . .

. . .

4th. There are certain rights which we have always held sacred in the United States, and recognized in all our constitutions, and which, by the adoption of the new constitution in its present form, will be left unsecured. . . .

. . .

It is proper the national laws should be supreme, and superior to state or district laws: but then the national laws ought to yield to inalienable or fundamental rights—and national laws, made by a few men, should extend only to a few national objects. This will not be the case with the laws of congress. . . .

. . . But the general presumption being, that men who govern, will, in doubtful cases, construe laws and constitutions most favorably for increasing their own powers; all wise and prudent people, in forming constitutions, have drawn the line, and carefully described the powers parted with and the powers reserved. By the state constitutions, certain rights have been reserved in the people; or rather, they have been recognized and established in such a manner, that state legislatures are bound to respect them, and to make no laws infringing upon them. . . .

It is true, we are not disposed to differ much, at present, about religion; but when we are making a constitution, it is to be hoped, for ages and millions yet unborn, why not establish the free exercise of religion, as a part of the national compact. There are other essential rights, which we have justly understood to be the rights of freemen. . . .

. . .

It may also be worthy our examination, how far the provision for amending this plan, when it shall be adopted, is of any importance. No measures can be taken towards amendments, unless two-thirds of the congress, or two-thirds of the legislatures of the several states shall agree—While power is in the hands of the people, or democratic part of the community, more especially as at present, it is easy, according to the general course of human affairs, for the few influential men in the community, to obtain conventions, alterations in government, and to persuade the common people they may change for the better, and to get from them a part of the power: But when power is once transferred from the many to the few, all changes become extremely difficult; the government, in this case, being beneficial to the few, they will be exceedingly artful and adroit in preventing any measures which may lead to a change; and nothing will produce it, but great exertions and severe struggles on the part of the common people. Every man of reflection must see, that the change now proposed, is a transfer of power from the many to the few, and the probability is, the artful and ever active aristocracy, will prevent all peaceable measures for changes, unless when they shall discover some favorable moment to increase their own influence. . . .

NO. 5

. . .

There are, however, in my opinion, many good things in the proposed system. It is founded on elective principles, and the deposits of powers in different hands, is essentially right. The guards against those evils we have experienced in some states in legislation are valuable indeed; but the value of every feature in this system is vastly lessened for the want of that one important feature in a free government, a representation of the people. Because we have sometimes abused democracy, I am not among those men who think a democratic branch a nuisance; which branch shall be sufficiently numerous to admit some of the best informed men of each order in the community into the administration of government.

. . .

. . . It is true there may be danger in delay; but there is danger in adopting the system in its present form; and I see the danger in either case will arise principally from the conduct and views of two very unprincipled parties in the United States—two fires, between which the honest and substantial people have long found themselves situated. One party is composed of little insurgents, men in debt, who want no law, and who want a share of the property of others; these are called levellers, Shayites, etc. The other party is composed of a few, but more dangerous men, with their servile dependents; these avariciously grasp at all power and property; you may discover in all the actions of these men, an evident dislike to free and equal government, and they will go systematically to work to change, essentially, the forms of government in this country; these are called aristocrats, Morrisites, etc. Between these two parties is the weight of the community; the men of middling property, men not in debt on the one hand, and men, on the other, content with republican governments, and not aiming at immense fortunes, offices, and power. . . . Men who wish the people of this country to determine for themselves, and deliberately to fit the government to their situation, must feel some degree of indignation at those attempts to hurry the adoption of a system, and to shut the door against examination. The very attempts create suspicions, that those who make them have secret views, or see some defects in the system, which, in the hurry of affairs, they expect will escape the eye of a free people.

. . .

THOMAS JEFFERSON AND JAMES MADISON

CORRESPONDENCE ON A BILL OF RIGHTS (1787–1789)

Thomas Jefferson was in France during the Philadelphia convention and the subsequent ratification debate, and as a consequence did not have to take a public stand on the ratification question. Jefferson did keep an active correspondence with his close friend James Madison and expressed some doubts about the document that emerged from the convention. Among his concerns was the lack of a Bill of Rights. Declarations of rights were common in the state constitutions that had been drafted during the Revolution. Madison was unconcerned, and worried that the proposals to amend the Constitution were just a tactic designed to derail ratification entirely. Madison thought that many of the amendments that were being proposed in the ratification conventions would gut the proposed Constitution. Nonetheless, he eventually gave in to political pressure and promised that amendments would be considered after ratification was secured. When Madison was elected to the House of Representatives for the first Congress, he took up the task of drafting a series of constitutional amendments that would not damage the original constitutional design. Ten of the twelve amendments that Congress passed were quickly ratified by the states and became known as the Bill of Rights.

Why does Madison not want a Bill of Rights? What advantages does Jefferson see from such amendments? Is there reason to think that Jefferson or Madison better assessed the situation? Would the Constitution have been as successful without the Bill of Rights? Is a bill of rights more or less useful in a republican government?

THOMAS JEFFERSON, LETTER TO JAMES MADISON, DECEMBER 20, 1787

. . . I will now add what I do not like. First the omission of a bill of rights providing clearly, and without the aid of sophism, for freedom of religion, freedom of the press, protection against standing armies, restriction of monopolies, the eternal and unremitting force of the habeas corpus laws, and trials by jury in all matters of fact triable by the laws of the land, and not by the law of nations. To say, as Mr. Wilson does, that a bill of rights was not necessary because all is reserved in the case of the general government which is not given, while in the particular ones all is given which is not reserved, might do for the audience to whom it was addressed, but is surely . . . opposed by strong inferences from the body of the instrument, as well as from the omission of the clause of our present Confederation, which had made the reservation in express terms. . . . Let me add, that a bill of rights is what the people are entitled to against every government on earth, general or particular; and what no just government should refuse, or rest on inference. . . .

JAMES MADISON, LETTER TO THOMAS JEFFERSON, OCTOBER 17, 1788

. . . My own opinion has always been in favor of a bill of rights, provided that it be so framed as not to imply powers not meant to be included in the enumeration. At the same time I have never thought the omission a material defect, nor been anxious to supply it even by *subsequent* amendment, for any other reason than that it is anxiously desired by others. I have favored it because I suppose it might be of use, and if properly executed, could not be of disservice.

I have not viewed it in an important light— 1. Because I conceive that in a certain degree . . . the rights in question are reserved by the manner in which the federal powers are granted. 2. Because there is great reason to fear that a positive declaration of some of the most essential rights could not be obtained in the requisite latitude. I am sure that the rights of conscience in particular, if submitted to public definition would be narrowed much more than they are ever likely to be by an assumed power. . . . 3. Because the limited powers of the federal Government, and the jealousy of the subordinate Governments, afford a security which has not existed in the case of the State Governments, and exists in no other. 4. Because experience proves the inefficiency of a bill of rights on those occasions when its control is most needed. Repeated violations of these parchment barriers have been committed by overbearing majorities in every State.

In Virginia, I have seen the bill of rights violated in every instance where it has been opposed to a popular current. Notwithstanding the explicit provision contained in that instrument for the rights of conscience, it is well known that a religious establishment would have taken place in that State, if the Legislative majority had found, as they expected, a majority of the people in favor of the measure; and I am persuaded that if a majority of the people were now of one sect, the measure would still take place. . . .

Wherever the real power in a Government lies, there is the danger of oppression. In our Governments the real power lies in the majority of the community, and the invasion of private rights is *chiefly* to be apprehended, not from acts of Government contrary to the sense of its constituents, but from acts in which the Government is the mere instrument of the major number of the Constituents. . . . Wherever there is an interest and power to do wrong, wrong will generally be done. . . .

The difference, so far as it relates to the point in question—the efficacy of a bill of rights in controlling abuses of power—lies in this: that in a monarchy the latent force of the nation is superior to that of the Sovereign, and a solemn charter of popular rights must have a great effect, as a standard for trying the validity of public acts, and a signal for rousing and uniting the superior force of the community; whereas, in a popular Government, the political and physical power may be considered as vested in the same hands, that is, in a majority of the people, and, consequently, the tyrannical will of the Sovereign is not to be controlled by the dread of an appeal to any other force within the community.

What use, then, it may be asked, can a bill of rights serve in popular Governments? I answer, the two following, which, though less essential than in other Governments, sufficiently recommend the precaution: 1. The political truths declared in that solemn manner acquire by degrees the character of fundamental maxims of free Government, and as they become incorporated with the National sentiment, counteract the impulses of interest and passion. 2. Although it be generally true, as above stated, that the danger of oppression lies in the interested majorities of the people rather than in usurped acts of the Government, yet there may be occasions on which the evil may spring from the latter source; and on such, a bill of rights will be good ground for an appeal to the sense of the community. . . .

Supposing a bill of rights to be proper. . . . I am inclined to think that *absolute* restrictions in cases that are doubtful, or where emergencies may overrule them, ought to be avoided. The restrictions, however strongly marked on paper, will never be regarded when opposed to the decided sense of the public; and after repeated violations, in extraordinary cases they will lose even their ordinary efficacy. Should a Rebellion or insurrection alarm the people as well as the Government, and a suspension of the Habeas Corpus be dictated by the alarm, no written prohibitions on earth would prevent the measure. . . .

THOMAS JEFFERSON, LETTER TO JAMES MADISON, MARCH 15, 1789

. . .

In the arguments in favor of a declaration of rights, you omit one which has a great weight with me: the legal check which it puts into the hands of the judiciary. This is a body, which, if rendered independent, and kept strictly to their own department, merits great confidence for their learning and integrity. . . . I cannot refrain from making short answers to the objections which your letter states to have been raised. 1. That the rights in question are reserved, by the manner in which the federal powers are granted. Answer. . . . [A] constitutive act which leaves some precious article unnoticed, and raises implications against others, a declaration of rights becomes necessary, by way of supplement. This is the case of our new federal constitution. This instrument forms us into one State as to certain objects, and gives us a legislative and executive body for these objects. It should, therefore, guard us against their abuses of power, within the field submitted to them. 2. A positive declaration of some essential rights could not be obtained in the requisite latitude. Answer. Half a loaf is better than no bread. If we cannot secure all our rights, let us secure what we can. 3. The limited powers of the federal government, and jealousy of the subordinate governments, afford a security which exists in no other instance. Answer. The first member of this seems resolvable into the first objection before stated. The jealousy of the subordinate governments is a precious reliance. But observe that those governments are only agents. They must have principles furnished them, whereon to found their opposition. The declaration of rights will be the text, whereby they will try all the acts of the federal government. In this view, it is necessary to the federal government also; as by the same text, they may try the opposition of the subordinate governments. 4. Experience proves the inefficacy of a bill of rights. True. But though it is not absolutely efficacious under all circumstances, it is of great potency always, and rarely inefficacious. A brace the more will often keep up the building which would have fallen, with that brace the less. There is a remarkable difference between the characters of the inconveniencies which attend a declaration of rights, and those which attend the want of it. The inconveniences of the declaration are, that it may cramp government in its useful exertions. But the evil of this is short-lived, moderate, and reparable. The inconveniencies of the want of a declaration are permanent, afflicting and irreparable. They are in constant progression from bad to worse. The executive, in our governments, is not the sole, it is scarcely the principal object of my jealousy. The tyranny of the legislatures is the most formidable dread at present, and will be for many years. . . .

III. CITIZENSHIP AND COMMUNITY

Major Developments

- Struggle over establishing American identity distinct from Britain
- Beginning of effort to define what it means to be an American
- Uncertainty over what united the states in a single country

Americans believed themselves to be both the same as and different from the English. They insisted that they had the same rights and shared the same heritage as their fellow British across the Atlantic. But they also accepted the belief that those who were living in the New World were exceptional, free from the corruption and burdensome customs of Europe. In urging New York to declare independence, Gouverneur Morris pointed out that "by degrees we are getting beyond the utmost pale of English government."[11] Independence had arrived, whether it was formally declared or not.

The U.S. Constitution announced that it was seeking to establish a "more perfect union," but establishing union across such large space and such diverse communities was no easy task. The putative Americans were more likely to view themselves as from Virginia or Massachusetts than from the United States, and their social and economic interests did not always converge. Morris's words about independence carried a warning. The western frontier was rapidly extending outward, and those "inhabitants acknowledge no authority but their own." The colonials who resided on the "small strip of land along the sea coasts" could either join those frontiersmen in their practical independence, or prepare "to build a huge wall against them." Did the residents of Boston or Charleston have more in common with those who lived in London or with those who were crossing the Appalachians? The answer was not always obvious.

The transplanted Frenchman John Hector St. John de Crevecoeur thought he knew the answer. European society, he thought, was divided between the "great lords" and the "herd of people who have nothing." A European became a "new man" in America, setting aside old distinctions of class and nationality. John Jay had a somewhat different take in urging the country to ratify the U.S. Constitution and solidify the union. He suggested that Americans were naturally "one people," sharing the same ancestors, the same language, and the same religion. It was only natural that they would join together as a whole.

11 Jared Sparks, *The Life of Gouverneur Morris*, vol. 1 (Boston, MA: Gray & Bowen, 1832), 104.

J. HECTOR ST. JOHN DE CREVECOEUR,

LETTERS FROM AN AMERICAN FARMER (1782)

Michel Guillaume Jean de Crevecoeur was the son of a minor nobleman in France. After the death of his first fiancé Crevecoeur emigrated to French Canada and worked as a surveyor for the French army before settling in New York in 1759, anglicizing his name to John Hector St. John, naturalizing to the status of British subject, marrying a local woman, and establishing a farm. His loyalties during the American Revolution were somewhat fluid, but after the war he became a vocal patriot. In 1780, he returned to France with his son and published his most successful work, *Letters from an American Farmer*. He largely remained in France until his death in 1813, serving some time as the French consul to New York.

The *Letters* are framed as the correspondence of a fictional Pennsylvania farmer directed to a friend in England providing a description of the North American colonies and their inhabitants. The book was more popular in Europe than in the United States, but was subsequently embraced as an important early work of American literature. The book opens with a celebratory account of the American melting pot and the centrality of personal industry and social and economic equality to the American identity, but concludes with a dark picture of the "horrors of slavery" in the South.

What is an American, according to Crevecoeur? What is the appeal of America? Does Crevecoeur's view of America still ring true? Are these qualities uniquely American? What makes a citizen?

. . .

. . . [America] is not composed, as in Europe, of great lords who possess everything and of a herd of people who have nothing. Here are no aristocratical families, no courts, no kings, no bishops, no ecclesiastical dominion, no invisible power giving to a few a very visible one; no great manufacturers employing thousands, no great refinements of luxury. The rich and the poor are not so far removed from each other as they are in Europe. Some few towns excepted, we are all tillers of the earth, from Nova Scotia to West Florida. We are a people of cultivators, scattered over an immense territory communicating with each other by means of good roads and navigable rivers, united by the silken bands of mild government, all respecting the laws, without dreading their power, because they are equitable. We are all animated with the spirit of an industry which is unfettered and unrestrained, because each person works for himself. If [a foreign visitor] travels through our rural districts he views not the hostile castle, and the haughty mansion, contrasted with the clay-built hut and miserable cabin, where cattle and men help to keep each other warm, and dwell in meanness, smoke, and indigence. A pleasing uniformity of decent competence appears throughout our habitations. . . . We have no princes, for whom we toil, starve, and bleed: we are the most perfect society now existing in the world. Here man is free; as he ought to be; nor is this pleasing equality so transitory as many others are. Many ages will not see the shores of our great lakes replenished with inland nations, nor the unknown bounds of North America entirely peopled. . . .

In this great American asylum, the poor of Europe have by some means met together, and in consequence of various causes; to what purpose should they ask one another what countrymen they are? Alas, two thirds of them had no country. Can a wretch who wanders about, who works and starves, whose life is a continual scene of sore affliction or pinching penury; can that man call England or any other kingdom his country? A country that had no bread for him, whose fields procured him no harvest, who met with nothing but the frowns of the rich, the severity of the laws, with jails and punishments; who owned not a single foot of the extensive surface of this planet? No! Urged by a variety of motives, here they came. Everything has tended to regenerate them; new laws, a new mode of living, a new social system; here they are become men: in Europe they were as so many useless plants, wanting vegetative mold, and refreshing showers; they withered, and were mowed down by want, hunger, and war; but now by the power of transplantation, like all other plants they have taken root and flourished! Formerly they were not numbered in any civil lists of their country, except in those of the poor; here they rank as citizens. By what invisible power has this surprising metamorphosis been performed? By that of the laws and that of their industry. The laws, the indulgent laws, protect them as they arrive, stamping on them the symbol of adoption; they receive ample rewards for their labors; these accumulated rewards procure them lands; those lands confer on them the title of freemen, and to that title every benefit is affixed which men can possibly require. This is the great operation daily performed by our laws. From whence proceed these laws? From our government. Whence the government? It is derived from the original genius and strong desire of the people ratified and confirmed by the crown. This is the great chain which links us all, this is the picture which every province exhibits. . . .

. . . What then is the American, this new man? He is either an European, or the descendant of an European, hence that strange mixture of blood, which you will find in no other country. I could point out to you a family whose grandfather was an Englishman, whose wife was Dutch, whose son married a French woman, and whose present four sons have now four wives of different nations. *He* is an American, who leaving behind him all his ancient prejudices and manners, receives new ones from the new mode of life he has embraced, the new government he obeys, and the new rank he holds. He becomes an American by being received in the broad lap of our great *Alma Mater*. Here individuals of all nations are melted into a new race of men, whose labors and posterity will one day cause great changes in the world. Americans are the western pilgrims, who are carrying along with them that great mass of arts, sciences, vigor, and industry which began long since in the east; they will finish the great circle. The Americans were once scattered all over Europe; here they are incorporated into one of the finest systems of population which has ever appeared, and which will hereafter become distinct by the power of the different climates they inhabit. The American ought therefore to love this country much better than that wherein either he or his forefathers were born. Here the rewards of his industry follow with equal steps the progress of his labor; his labor is founded on the basis of nature, *self-interest*; can it want a stronger allurement? Wives and children, who before in vain demanded of him a morsel of bread, now, fat and frolicsome, gladly help their father to clear those fields whence exuberant crops are to arise to feed and to clothe them all; without any part being claimed, either by a despotic prince, a rich abbot, or a mighty lord. . . . The American is a new man, who acts upon new principles; he must therefore entertain new ideas, and form new opinions. From involuntary idleness, servile dependence, penury, and useless labor, he has passed to toils of a very different nature, rewarded by ample subsistence.—This is an American.

. . .

As I have endeavored to show you how Europeans become Americans; it may not be disagreeable to show you likewise how the various Christian sects introduced, wear out, and how religious indifference becomes prevalent. When any considerable number of a particular sect happen to dwell contiguous to each other, they immediately erect a temple, and there worship the Divinity agreeably to their own peculiar ideas. Nobody disturbs them. If any new sect springs up in Europe, it may happen that many of its professors will come and settle in America. As they bring their zeal with them, they are at liberty to make proselytes if they can, and to build a meeting and to follow the dictates of their consciences; for neither the government nor any other power interferes. If they are peaceable subjects, and are industrious, what is it to their neighbors how and in what manner they think fit to address their prayers to the Supreme Being? But if the sectaries are not settled close together, if they are mixed with other denominations, their zeal will cool for want of fuel, and will be extinguished in a little time. Then the Americans become as to religion, what they are as to country, allied to all. In them the name of Englishman, Frenchman, and European is lost, and in like manner, the strict modes of Christianity as practiced in Europe are lost also. . . .

. . .

JOHN JAY

FEDERALIST PAPERS (1787)

John Jay was a relatively conservative supporter of the American Revolution. He represented New York in the Continental Congress (where he was elected president), drafted the New York state constitution of 1777, and served as the chief justice of the state supreme court for two years. He stepped down from the court in order to serve as an American diplomat in Europe, and he was a lead negotiator of the peace treaty with England. He later served as the first chief justice of the United States, but resigned in order to accept the office of governor of New York. While still chief justice, he traveled to England to negotiate what became known as the Jay Treaty, which settled remaining issues arising from the American Revolution and helped secure the continued peace.

Jay was a leading Federalist in New York, and Alexander Hamilton recruited him to help write a series of newspaper essays under the pseudonym "Publius" to encourage the state to ratify the proposed U.S. Constitution. But Jay became ill and completed only a handful of essays, leading Hamilton to turn to James Madison to complete the project. In this essay, Jay emphasized that the various states belonged to a single community and should naturally wish to form a closer union.

What does Jay see as the basis for an American nation? How does he leverage the experience of the Revolution to support the Constitution? Is he persuasive about the essential unity of the United States? Would his argument in favor of union become more or less powerful as time passed? Was there any reason for the people of the various states to not want a stronger union? If the colony of Quebec had wanted to join the United States in 1787, would Jay's argument lend support to forming a union with Quebec? Does Jay's argument give hope or raise problems for the future of the European Union?

NO. 2

. . . It is well worthy of consideration therefore, whether it would conduce more to the interest of the people of America that they should, to all general purposes, be one nation, under one federal government, or that they should divide themselves into separate confederacies, and give to the head of each the same kind of powers which they are advised to place in one national government.

It has until lately been a received and uncontradicted opinion that the prosperity of the people of America depended on their continuing firmly united, and the wishes, prayers, and efforts of our best and wisest citizens have been constantly directed to that object. But politicians now appear, who insist that this opinion is erroneous, and that instead of looking for safety and happiness in union, we ought to seek it in a division of the States into distinct confederacies or sovereignties. . . .

It has often given me pleasure to observe that independent America was not composed of detached and distant territories, but that one connected, fertile, widespreading country was the portion of our western sons of liberty. Providence has in a particular manner blessed it with a variety of soils and productions, and watered it with innumerable streams, for the delight and accommodation of its inhabitants. A succession of navigable waters forms a kind of chain round its borders, as if to bind it together; while the most noble rivers in the world, running at convenient distances, present them with highways for the easy communication of friendly aids, and the mutual transportation and exchange of their various commodities.

With equal pleasure I have as often taken notice that Providence has been pleased to give this one connected country to one united people—a people descended from the same ancestors, speaking the same language, professing the same religion, attached to the same principles of government, very similar in their manners and customs, and who, by their joint counsels, arms, and efforts, fighting side by side throughout a long and bloody war, have nobly established general liberty and independence.

This country and this people seem to have been made for each other, and it appears as if it was the design of Providence, that an inheritance so proper and convenient for a band of brethren, united to each other by the strongest ties, should never be split into a number of unsocial, jealous, and alien sovereignties.

Similar sentiments have hitherto prevailed among all orders and denominations of men among us. To all general purposes we have uniformly been one people each individual citizen everywhere enjoying the same national rights, privileges, and protection. As a nation we have made peace and war; as a nation we have vanquished our common enemies; as a nation we have formed alliances, and made treaties, and entered into various compacts and conventions with foreign states.

. . .

IV. EQUALITY AND STATUS

Major Developments

- Uncertainty over implications of revolutionary spirit for status of women
- Uncertainty over implications of revolutionary spirit for slavery

The Revolution upset traditional hierarchies. Thomas Paine had declared in his electrifying pamphlet, *Common Sense,* "We have it in our power to begin the world over again." The Americans were presented with an opportunity that had "not happened since the days of Noah until now."[12] The fire of revolution and the idea of natural rights were abroad in the land.

The Declaration of Independence proclaimed that all men are created equal. What did that mean? For many revolutionary leaders, it simply meant that Englishmen living in the colonies held the same political rights as Englishmen living in the British Isles. For some women, it was time to emphasize to American men that "our souls are by nature *equal* to yours."[13] For some ordinary soldiers, George Mason concluded, "the same Principles which attach them to the American Cause will incline them to resist Injustice or Oppression."[14] Antislavery advocates concluded, "Liberty is the right of every human creature, as soon as he breathes the vital air. And no human law can deprive him of that right, which he derives from the right of nature."[15]

As the wife of a leading revolutionary lawyer and politician, Abigail Adams was particularly well positioned to voice the concerns of women. She prompted John Adams to consider whether subjecting women to the "absolute power" of men was consistent with liberal ideals, though to limited effect. Thomas Jefferson reflected the dual face of revolutionary ideas as they applied to race and slavery. Jefferson was among the more radical of the leading revolutionaries in his embrace of new ideas of liberty and equality, but he accepted many of the racist views that were common to his generation, which helped him reconcile himself to the continued existence of slavery.

---

12 Thomas Paine, *Common Sense* (Philadelphia, PA: W. and T. Bradford, 1776), 87.

13 Judith Sargent Murray, "On the Equality of the Sexes," *The Massachusetts Magazine* 2 (1790): 135.

14 Quoted in Michael A. McDonnell, "'The Spirit of Levelling': James Cleveland, Edward Wright, and the Militiamen's Struggle for Equality in Revolutionary Virginia," in *Revolutionary Founders: Rebels, Radicals, and Reformers in the Making of the Nation*, eds. Alfred F. Young, Gary B. Nash, and Ray Raphael (New York: Alfred A. Knopf, 2011), 153.

15 Anthony Benezet, quoted in Maurice Jackson, "Anthony Benezet: America's Finest Eighteenth-Century Antislavery Advocate," in *The Human Tradition in Colonial America*, eds. Nancy L. Rhoden and Ian K. Steele (Wilmington, DE: Scholarly Resources, 2000), 10.

ABIGAIL ADAMS AND JOHN ADAMS

CORRESPONDENCE ON WOMEN'S RIGHTS (1776)

John Adams was one of the leading lawyers in the revolutionary movement in Massachusetts and the primary drafter of the state constitution of 1780. As a politician and diplomat, he was often away from his home and family. During these absences, he maintained a lengthy and rich correspondence with his wife, Abigail Adams. Abagail Adams was known as an active political presence, and when John Adams was elected president in 1796 she became a visible presence in the White House. As First Lady, she tried to be more cautious about expressing her opinions, but nonetheless in an increasingly polarized capital she became a target of the Jeffersonians, who called her "Mrs. President, not of the United States but of a faction." Her prodding to her husband that the revolutionaries should "remember the ladies" when seeking to expand liberty in America has become particularly famous.

Is Abigail Adams correct to link the revolutionary cause to the cause of women? Are her concerns primarily political? What would remembering the ladies entail? How receptive is John Adams to her concerns?

Abigail Adams wants women to be more recognized in society

ABIGAIL ADAMS TO JOHN ADAMS, MARCH 31, 1776

. . . [W]hat sort of defense Virginia can make against our common enemy . . . [?] Are not the gentry lords, and the common people vassals? Are they not like the uncivilized vassals Britain represents us to be? . . .

I have sometimes been ready to think that the passion for liberty cannot be equally strong in the breasts of those who have been accustomed to deprive their fellow creatures of theirs. Of this I am certain that it is not founded upon that generous and Christian principal [sic] of doing to others as we would that others should do unto us.

. . .

I long to hear that you have declared an independency. And, by the way in the new code of laws which I suppose it will be necessary for you to make, I desire you would remember the ladies, and be more generous and favorable to them than your ancestors. Do not put such unlimited power into the hands of the husbands. Remember, all men would be tyrants if they could. If particular care and attention is not paid to the ladies, we are determined to foment a rebellion, and will not hold ourselves bound by any laws in which we have no voice or representation.

That your sex are naturally tyrannical is a truth so thoroughly established as to admit of no dispute; but such of you as wish to be happy willingly give up the harsh title of master for the more tender and endearing one of friend. Why, then, not put it out of the power of the vicious and the lawless to use us with cruelty and indignity with impunity? Men of sense in all ages abhor those customs which treat us only as the vassals of your sex; regard us then as beings placed by Providence under your protection, and in imitation of the Supreme Being make use of that power only for our happiness.

JOHN ADAMS TO ABIGAIL ADAMS, APRIL 14, 1776

. . . North Carolina, which is a warlike colony . . . are ready to assist [Virginia], and they are in very good spirits and seem determined to make a brave resistance. The gentry are very rich, and the common people very poor. This inequality of property gives an aristocratical turn to all their proceedings, and occasions a strong aversion in their patricians to [Thomas Paine's] "Common Sense." But the spirit of these Barons is coming down, and it must submit. . . .

. . .

As to your extraordinary code of laws, I cannot but laugh. We have been told that our struggle has loosened the bonds of government everywhere; that children and apprentices were disobedient; that schools and colleges were grown turbulent; that Indians slighted their guardians, and negroes grew insolent to their masters. But your letter was the first intimation that another tribe, more numerous and powerful than all the rest, were grown discontented. This is rather too coarse a compliment, but you are so saucy, I won't blot it out. Depend upon it, we know better than to repeal our masculine systems. Although they are in full force, you know they are little more than theory. We dare not exert our power in its full latitude. We are obliged to go fair and softly, and, in practice, you know we are the subjects. We have only the name of masters, and rather than give up this, which would completely subject us to the despotism of the petticoat, I hope General Washington and all our brave heroes would fight; I am sure every good politician would plot, as long as he would against despotism, empire, monarchy, aristocracy, oligarchy, or ochlocracy. A fine story, indeed! I begin to think the ministry as deep as they are wicked. After stirring up Tories, land-jobbers, trimmers, bigots, Canadians, Indians, negroes, Hanoverians, Hessians, Russians, Irish Roman Catholics, Scotch renegadoes, at last they have stimulated the ladies to demand new privileges and threaten to rebel.

ABIGAIL ADAMS TO JOHN ADAMS, MAY 7, 1776

. . .

I cannot say that I think you are very generous to the ladies; for, whilst you are proclaiming peace and goodwill to men, emancipating all nations, you insist upon retaining an absolute power over wives. But you must remember that arbitrary power is like most other things which are very hard, very liable to be broken; and, notwithstanding all your wise laws and maxims, we have it in our power, not only to free ourselves, but to subdue our masters, and, without violence, throw both your natural and legal authority at your feet;—"Charm by accepting, by submitting sway, Yet have our humor most when we obey."

. . .

THOMAS JEFFERSON

NOTES ON THE STATE OF VIRGINIA (1787)

Thomas Jefferson took an active interest in the sciences, including the emerging European work in the human sciences. His political and scientific interests sometimes merged. He was particularly engaged with the French world of ideas. What began as an effort to explain the condition in Virginia to a French envoy after the American Revolution soon developed into a complete book that was first published anonymously in Paris and then printed in London. The book is wide-ranging, surveying not only the politics of the state but its social and economic condition, its natural environment, and its people. Jefferson readily mixed his observations on the situation in Virginia with his own views and speculations. His discussion of race and slavery in the book has proven particularly memorable and became an object of commentary in abolitionist debates.

How much influence does Jefferson think the environment has on humans? How much are differences among people attributable to inherent features? Does he analyze Native Americans and African-Americans in the same way? To what extent does Jefferson believe racial differences justify slavery? Why is he pessimistic about the possibility of a multiracial republic? Toward the end of his life, he worried that white Americans "have the wolf by the ear" and would not be able to successfully unwind the system of slavery. Was he right to worry about how the transition from slavery to freedom could be made?

. . .

The Indian of North America being more within our reach, I can speak of him somewhat from my own knowledge, but more from the information of others better acquainted with him, and on whose truth and judgment I can rely. From these sources I am able to say, in contradiction to this representation, that he is neither more defective in ardor, nor more impotent with his female, than the white reduced to the same diet and exercise: that he is brave, when an enterprise depends on bravery; education with him making the point of honor consist in the destruction of an enemy by stratagem, and in the preservation of his own person free from injury; or perhaps this is nature; while it is education which teaches us to honor force more than finesse; that he will defend himself against an host of enemies, always choosing to be killed, rather than to surrender, though it be to the whites, who he knows will treat him well: that in other situations also he meets death with more deliberation, and endures tortures with a firmness unknown almost to religious enthusiasm with us: that he is affectionate to his children, careful of them, and indulgent in the extreme: that his affections comprehend his other connections,

* Jefferson believes eventually the N. A. will be able to live among us.

weakening, as with us, from circle to circle, as they recede from the center: that his friendships are strong and faithful to the uttermost extremity: that his sensibility is keen, even the warriors weeping most bitterly on the loss of their children, though in general they endeavor to appear superior to human events: that his vivacity and activity of mind is equal to ours in the same situation; hence his eagerness for hunting, and for games of chance.

The women are submitted to unjust drudgery. This I believe is the case with every barbarous people. With such, force is law. The stronger sex therefore imposes on the weaker. It is civilization alone which replaces women in the enjoyment of their natural equality. That first teaches us to subdue the selfish passions, and to respect those rights in others which we value in ourselves. Were we in equal barbarism, our females would be equal drudges. The man with them is less strong than with us, but their woman stronger than ours; and both for the same obvious reason; because our man and their woman is habituated to labor, and formed by it. With both races the sex which is indulged with ease is least athletic. An Indian man is small in the hand and wrist for the same reason for which a sailor is large and strong in the arms and shoulders, and a porter in the legs and thighs. They raise fewer children than we do. The causes of this are to be found, not in a difference of nature, but of circumstance. The women very frequently attending the men in their parties of war and of hunting, child-bearing becomes extremely inconvenient to them. It is said, therefore, that they have learnt the practice of procuring abortion by the use of some vegetable; and that it even extends to prevent conception for a considerable time after. During these parties they are exposed to numerous hazards, to excessive exertions, to the greatest extremities of hunger. Even at their homes the nation depends for food, through a certain part of every year, on the gleanings of the forest: that is, they experience a famine once in every year. With all animals, if the female be badly fed, or not fed at all, her young perish: and if both male and female be reduced to like want, generation becomes less active, less productive. . . . The same Indian women, when married to white traders, who feed them and their children plentifully and regularly, who exempt them from excessive drudgery, who keep them stationary and unexposed to accident, produce and raise as many children as the white women. Instances are known, under these circumstances, of their rearing a dozen children.

. . . [T]o form a just estimate of their genius and mental powers, more facts are wanting, and great allowance to be made for those circumstances of their situation which call for a display of particular talents only. This done, we shall probably find that they are formed in mind as well as in body, on the same module with the '*Homo sapiens Europaeus*.' The principles of their society forbidding all compulsion, they are to be led to duty and to enterprise by personal influence and persuasion. Hence eloquence in council, bravery and address in war, become the foundations of all consequence with them. To these acquirements all their faculties are directed. Of their bravery and address in war we have multiplied proofs, because we have been the subjects on which they were exercised. Of their eminence in oratory we have fewer examples, because it is displayed chiefly in their own councils. Some, however, we have of very superior luster. . . .

. . .

. . . I do not mean to deny, that there are varieties in the race of man, distinguished by their powers both of body and mind. I believe there are, as I see to be the case in the races of other animals. I only mean to suggest a doubt, whether the bulk and faculties of animals depend on the side of the Atlantic on which their food happens to grow, or which furnishes the elements of which they are compounded? . . .

. . .

. . . It will probably be asked, Why not retain and incorporate the blacks into the state, and thus save the expense of supplying, by importation of white settlers, the vacancies they will leave? Deep rooted prejudices entertained by the whites; ten thousand recollections, by the blacks, of the injuries they have sustained; new provocations; the real distinctions which nature has made; and many other circumstances, will divide us into parties, and produce convulsions which will probably never end but in the extermination of the one or the other race. To these objections, which are political, may be added others, which are physical and moral. The first difference which strikes us is that of color. Whether the black of the negro resides in the reticular membrane between the skin and scarf-skin, or in the scarf-skin itself; whether it proceeds from the color of the blood, the color of the bile, or from that of some other secretion, the difference is fixed in nature, and is as real as if its seat and cause were better known to us. And is this difference of no importance? Is it not the foundation of a greater or less share of beauty in the two races? Are not the fine mixtures of red and white, the expressions of every passion by greater or less suffusions of color in the one, preferable to that eternal monotony, which reigns in the countenances, that immoveable veil of black which covers all the emotions of the other race? Add to these, flowing hair, a more elegant symmetry of form, their own judgment in favor of the whites, declared by their preference of them, as uniformly as is the preference of the Oranootan for the black women over those of his own species. The circumstance of superior beauty, is thought worthy attention in the propagation of our horses, dogs, and other domestic animals; why not in that of man? Besides those of color, figure, and hair, there are other physical distinctions proving a difference of race. They have less hair on the face and body. They secrete less by the kidneys, and more by the glands of the skin, which gives them a very strong and disagreeable odor. This greater degree of transpiration renders them more tolerant of heat, and less so of cold, than the whites. . . . They seem to require less sleep. A black, after hard labor through the day, will be induced by the slightest amusements to sit up till midnight, or later, though knowing he must be out with the first dawn of the morning. They are at least as brave, and more adventuresome. But this may perhaps proceed from a want of forethought, which prevents their seeing a danger till it be present. When present, they do not go through it with more coolness or steadiness than the whites. They are more ardent after their female: but love seems with them to be more an eager desire, than a tender delicate mixture of sentiment and sensation. Their griefs are transient. Those numberless afflictions, which render it doubtful whether heaven has given life to us in mercy or in wrath, are less felt, and sooner forgotten with them. In general, their existence appears to participate more of sensation than reflection. . . . Comparing them by their faculties of memory, reason, and imagination, it appears to me, that in memory they are equal to the whites; in reason much inferior, as I think one could scarcely be found capable of tracing and comprehending the investigations of Euclid; and that in imagination they are dull, tasteless, and anomalous. . . . Many millions of them have been brought to, and born in America. Most of them indeed have been confined to tillage, to their own homes, and their own society: yet many have been so situated, that they might have availed themselves of the conversation of their masters; many have been brought up to the handicraft arts, and from that circumstance have always been associated with the whites. Some have been liberally educated, and all have lived in countries where the arts and sciences are cultivated to a considerable degree, and have had before their eyes samples of the best works from abroad. The Indians, with no advantages of this kind, will often carve figures on their pipes not destitute of design and merit. They will crayon out an animal, a plant, or a country, so as to prove the existence of a germ in their minds which only wants cultivation. They astonish you with strokes of the most sublime oratory; such as prove their reason and sentiment strong, their imagination glowing and elevated. But never yet could I find that a black had uttered a thought above the level of plain narration; never see even an elementary trait of painting or sculpture. In music they are more generally gifted than the whites with accurate ears fortune and time. . . .

. . . Whether further observation will or will not verify the conjecture, that nature has been less bountiful to them in the endowments of the head, I believe that in those of the heart she will be found to have done them justice. That disposition to theft with which they have been branded, must be ascribed to their situation, and not to any depravity of the moral sense. The man, in whose favor no laws of property exist, probably feels himself less bound to respect those made in favor of others. When arguing for ourselves, we lay it down as a fundamental, that laws, to be just, must give a reciprocation of right: that, without this, they are mere arbitrary rules of conduct, founded in force, and not in conscience: and it is a problem which I give to the master to solve, whether the religious precepts against the violation of property were not framed for him as well as his slave? And whether the slave may not as justifiably take a little from one, who has taken all from him, as he may slay one who would slay him? That a change in the relations in which a man is placed should change his ideas of moral right and wrong, is neither new, nor peculiar to the color of the blacks. . . .

. . . Notwithstanding these considerations which must weaken their respect for the laws of property, we find among them numerous instances of the most rigid integrity, and as many as among their better instructed masters, of benevolence, gratitude, and unshaken fidelity. The opinion, that they are inferior in the faculties of reason and imagination, must be hazarded with great diffidence. To justify a general conclusion, requires many observations, even where the subject may be submitted to the Anatomical knife, to Optical glasses, to analysis by fire, or by solvents. How much more then where it is a faculty, not a substance, we are examining; where it eludes the research of all the senses; where the conditions of its existence are various and variously combined; where the effects of those which are present or absent bid defiance to calculation; let me add too, as a circumstance of great tenderness, where our conclusion would degrade a whole race of men from the rank in the scale of beings which their Creator may perhaps have given them. To our reproach it must be said, that though for a century and a half we have had under our eyes the races of black and of red men, they have never yet been viewed by us as subjects of natural history. I advance it therefore as a suspicion only, that the blacks, whether originally a distinct race, or made distinct by time and circumstances, are inferior to the whites in the endowments both of body and mind. It is not against experience to suppose, that different species of the same genus, or varieties of the same species, may possess different qualifications. Will not a lover of natural history then, one who views the gradations in all the races of animals with the eye of philosophy, excuse an effort to keep those in the department of man as distinct as nature has formed them? This unfortunate difference of color, and perhaps of faculty, is a powerful obstacle to the emancipation of these people. Many of their advocates, while they wish to vindicate the liberty of human nature, are anxious also to preserve its dignity and beauty. Some of these, embarrassed by the question 'What further is to be done with them?' join themselves in opposition with those who are actuated by sordid avarice only. Among the Romans emancipation required but one effort. The slave, when made free, might mix with, without staining the blood of his master. But with us a second is necessary, unknown to history. When freed, he is to be removed beyond the reach of mixture.

. . .

BENJAMIN BANNEKER AND THOMAS JEFFERSON

CORRESPONDENCE ON SLAVERY (1791)

Benjamin Banneker was born a free black in colonial America. He lived and worked most of his life on his family's farm near Baltimore. Despite limited formal education, he proved to be skilled with numbers and mechanics. In time, he became an avid astronomer and calculated his own almanac, earning some local fame in the process. Banneker sent a handwritten copy of his first published almanac to Secretary of State Thomas Jefferson, who was himself keenly interested in natural history and information pertinent to farming in the Chesapeake area.

Banneker's race was as much noted as his accomplishments. The Baltimore publishers of his almanac promoted his work as "an extraordinary effort of genius . . . by a sable descendant of Africa," and urged readers "in this enlightened era" to support the work "not only on account of its intrinsic merits" but also for "controverting the long established illiberal prejudice against the blacks."[16] Banneker himself took the opportunity, when sending the manuscript to Jefferson, to invite him to a dialogue on the implications of the first words of the Declaration of Independence for the black inhabitants of America. Jefferson's *Notes on the State of Virginia* would suggest that blacks possessed less reasoning capacity than whites. Banneker offered up his own work as a counterexample, contradicting the common prejudice that blacks were "rather brutish" and "scarcely capable of mental endowments." Jefferson's response was brief, ducking the political implications of Banneker's letter but indicating that the Secretary of State would forward the almanac to the same French scientific establishment that would be the audience for Jefferson's observations on Virginia. Banneker published the exchange of letters in the next edition of his almanac, which was widely circulated in antislavery circles in both the United States and England.

Is Jefferson's response to Banneker consistent with what he wrote in the *Notes*? Does Banneker's example have political implications? Why might political and legal equality turn on the quality of scientific accomplishments? What use does Banneker make of revolutionary ideology? Does the argument of the Declaration of Independence have direct relevance for the slavery question? Is Banneker right to think that combating racism is a necessary step toward ending slavery?

BENJAMIN BANNEKER, LETTER TO THOMAS JEFFERSON (AUGUST 19, 1791)

I am fully sensible of the greatness of that freedom, which I take with you on the present occasion, a liberty which seemed to me scarcely allowable, when I reflected on that distinguished and dignified station in which you stand, and the almost general prejudice and prepossession which is so prevalent in the world against those of my complexion.

I suppose it is a truth too well attested to you, to need a proof here, that we are a race of beings who have long labored under the abuse and censure of the world, that we have long been considered rather brutish than human, and scarcely capable of mental endowments.

Sir, I hope I may admit, in consequence of that report which has reached me, that you are a man far less inflexible in sentiments of this nature than many others, that you are measurably friendly and well disposed towards us, and that you are ready and willing to lend your aid and assistance to our relief, from those many distressed and numerous calamities, to which we are reduced.

Now, sir, if this is foolish in truth, I apprehend you will readily embrace every opportunity to eradicate that train of absurd and false ideas and opinions, which so generally prevails with respect to us, and that your sentiments are concurrent with mine, which are that one universal father has given being to us all, and that he has not only made us all of one flesh, but

16 Quoted in John H. B. Latrobe, *Memoir of Benjamin Banneker* (Baltimore, MD: John D. Troy, 1845), 9.

that he has also without partiality afforded us all the same sensations, and endued us all with the same faculties, and that however variable we may be in society or religion, however diversified in situation or color, we are all of the same family, and stand in the same relation to him.

Sir, if these are sentiments of which you are fully persuaded, I hope you cannot but acknowledge, that it is the indispensable duty of those who maintain for themselves the rights of human nature, and who profess the obligation of Christianity, to extend their power and influence to the relief of every part of the human race, from whatever burden or oppression they may unjustly labor under, and this I apprehend a full conviction of the truth and obligation of these principles should lead all to.

Sir, I have long been convinced, that if your love for yourselves and for those inestimable laws, which preserve to you the rights of human nature, was founded on sincerity, you could not but be solicitous that every individual of whatever rank or distinction, might with you equally enjoy the blessings thereof, neither could you rest satisfied, short of the most active diffusion of your exertions, in order, to their promotion from any state of degradation, to which the unjustifiable cruelty and barbarism of men may have reduced them.

Sir, I freely and cheerfully acknowledge that I am of the African race, and in that color which is natural to them of the deepest dye, and it is under a sense of the most profound gratitude to the supreme ruler of the Universe, that I now confess to you, that I am not under that state of tyrannical thralldom, and inhuman captivity, to which too many of my brethren are doomed, but that I have abundantly tasted of the fruition of those blessings, which proceed from that free and unequalled liberty, with which you are favored, and which, I hope you will willingly allow, you have received from the immediate hand of that being, from whom proceeds every good and perfect gift.

Sir, suffer me to recall to your mind that time in which the arms and tyranny of the British crown were exerted with every powerful effort in order to reduce you to a state of servitude; look back, I entreat you, on the variety of dangers to which you were exposed; reflect on that time in which every human aid appeared unavailable, and in which even hope and fortitude wore the aspect of inability to the conflict, and you cannot but be led to a serious and grateful sense of your miraculous and providential preservation; you cannot but acknowledge, that the present freedom and tranquility which you enjoy, you have mercifully received, and that it is the peculiar blessing of heaven.

This, sir, was a time in which you clearly saw into the injustice of a state of slavery, and in which you had the apprehension of the horrors of its condition, it was now, sir, that your abhorrence thereof was so excited, that you publicly held forth this true and invaluable doctrine, which is worthy to be recorded and remembered in all succeeding ages. "We hold these truths to be self-evident, that all men are created equal, and that they are endowed by their creator with certain inalienable rights, that among these are life, liberty and the pursuit of happiness."

Here, sir, was a time in which your tender feelings for yourselves had engaged you thus to declare, you were then impressed with proper ideas of the great valuation of liberty, and the free possession of those blessings to which you were entitled by nature; but, sir, how pitiable is to reflect that although you were so fully convinced of the benevolence of the Father of mankind, and of his equal and impartial distribution of those rights and privileges which he had conferred upon them, that you should at the same time counteract his mercies, in detaining by fraud and violence so numerous a part of my brethren, under groaning captivity and cruel oppression, that you should at the same time be found guilty of that most criminal act, which you professedly detested in others with respect to yourselves.

Sir, I suppose that your knowledge of the situation of my brethren, is too extensive to need a recital here; neither shall I presume to prescribe methods by which they may be relieved, otherwise than by recommending to you and all others, to wean yourselves from those narrow prejudices which you have imbibed with respect to them, and as Job proposed to his friends, "put your souls in their souls stead," thus shall your hearts be enlarged with kindness and benevolence towards them, and thus shall you need neither the direction of myself nor others, in what manner to proceed therein.

. . .

THOMAS JEFFERSON, LETTER TO BENJAMIN BANNEKER (AUGUST 30, 1791)

I thank you sincerely for your letter of the 19th instant, and for the Almanac it contained. Nobody wishes more than I do to see such proofs as you exhibit, that nature has given to our black brethren, talents equal to those of the other colors of men, and that the appearance of a want of them is owing merely to the degraded condition of their existence, both in Africa and America. I can add with truth, that nobody wishes more ardently to see a good system commenced for raising the condition both of their body and mind to what it ought to be, as fast as the imbecility of their present existence, and other circumstances which cannot be neglected, will admit. . . .

V. POLITICAL ECONOMY

Major Developments

- Tensions between debtors and creditors
- Struggle over interstate trade
- Debate over federal taxation power

The Confederation period was a time of substantial economic uncertainty. The colonial economy had revolved around trade with Great Britain, but the Revolution disrupted those ties without laying out a clear alternative path. The war created large private and public debts. Wartime confiscation had thrown some property rights into disarray. Hard currency was at a premium, and paper money created spurts of inflation. Farms and workshops had been neglected, and sometimes damaged, during the war. Debtors resisted paying their creditors, sometimes violently. States refused to restore property to Loyalists. New taxes fell heavily on a population with limited means to pay them. State governments refused to forward needed funds to the Confederation government.

Economic turmoil did not bode well for the Articles of Confederation. Rightly or wrongly, the new political system often took the blame for economic distress. At the same time, the newfound political freedom created new expectations. How many of the old fetters had been thrown off? Did debts to the English really need to be paid? Could democratic government be used to improve the conditions of the least well off? The Philadelphia merchant Pelatiah Webster expressed shock and shame at the sight of American "men like children" blubbering that they could not pay the taxes that were needed to defend the United States from its enemies.[17]

James Madison and Thomas Jefferson were much engaged by the changing economic climate, but they had somewhat different reactions to it. For both, economics were inexorably tied up with politics. Republican government needed a firm material foundation to be successful. Madison worried that the newly independent democratic governments were abusing their powers and undermining trust in the possibility of republicanism. Jefferson reflected a purer commitment to agrarianism than Madison did. Farmers were God's chosen people, and America was fortunate not to be cursed with the destitute and unruly mobs of the great cities of Europe.

17 Pelatiah Webster, *Political Essays* (Philadelphia, PA: Joseph Crukshank, 1791), 98.

JAMES MADISON

VICES OF THE POLITICAL SYSTEM OF THE UNITED STATES (1787)

In preparation for the Philadelphia Constitutional Convention, James Madison drafted a series of notes outlining what he thought were the major problems with the American political system under the Articles of Confederation. He saw a large number of problems with the system of government that had emerged out of the American Revolution. The relationship between the state and national governments, the design of the national government, and the behavior of the states were all faulty. A simple constitutional amendment would not be adequate to fix the problems; comprehensive constitutional reform was necessary if the experiment in republican government were to be saved. These talking points helped justify shifting the Philadelphia convention from the modest task of drafting possible amendments to the Articles to the more radical task of drafting an entirely new federal constitution.

To what extent are the problems that Madison identifies ones of institutional design? Does the proposed U.S. Constitution address all of these problems? Were there other ways to address these problems? Are Madison's concerns ones that everyone can agree on, or does he require controversial assumptions to be made? Are these flaws in the system, or is Madison just not winning all the political battles? When does "common interest" require a "concert of action"? What does Madison see as being in the common interest? What does he regard as an injustice? Could a similar list of vices be drawn up regarding the state of politics today? When does the diagnosis of political problems suggest the need for constitutional solutions?

1. FAILURE OF THE STATES TO COMPLY WITH THE CONSTITUTIONAL REQUISITIONS.

This evil has been so fully experienced both during the war and since the peace, results so naturally from the number and independent authority of the States and has been so uniformly exemplified in every similar Confederacy, that it may be considered as not less radically and permanently inherent in, than it is fatal to the object of, the present System.

2. ENCROACHMENTS BY THE STATES ON THE FEDERAL AUTHORITY.

Examples of this are numerous and repetitions may be foreseen in almost every case where any favorite object of a State shall present a temptation. Among these examples are the wars and Treaties of Georgia with the Indians—The unlicensed compacts between Virginia and Maryland, and between Pena. & N. Jersey—the troops raised and to be kept up by Massachusetts.

3. VIOLATIONS OF THE LAW OF NATIONS AND OF TREATIES.

From the number of Legislatures, the sphere of life from which most of their members are taken, and the circumstances under which their legislative business is carried on, irregularities of this kind must frequently happen. Accordingly not a year has passed without instances of them in some one or other of the States. The Treaty of peace—the treaty with France—the treaty with Holland have each been violated. The causes of these irregularities must necessarily produce frequent violations of the law of nations in other respects.

. . .

4. TRESPASSES OF THE STATES ON THE RIGHTS OF EACH OTHER.

. . . See the law of Virginia restricting foreign vessels to certain ports—of Maryland in favor of vessels belonging to her own citizens—of N. York in favor of the same.

Paper money, installments of debts, occlusion of Courts, making property a legal tender, may likewise be deemed aggressions on the rights of other States. As the Citizens of every State aggregately taken stand more or less in the relation of Creditors or debtors, to the Citizens of every other States, Acts of the debtor State in favor of debtors, affect the Creditor State, in the same manner, as they do its own citizens who are relatively creditors towards other citizens. . . . If the exclusive regulation of the value and alloy of coin was properly delegated to the federal authority, the policy of it equally requires a control on the States in the cases above mentioned. It must have been meant 1. to preserve uniformity in the circulating medium throughout the nation. 2. to prevent those frauds on the citizens of other States, and the subjects of foreign powers, which might disturb the tranquility at home, or involve the Union in foreign contests.

The practice of many States in restricting the commercial intercourse with other States, and putting their productions and manufactures on the same footing with those of foreign nations, though not contrary to the federal articles, is certainly adverse to the spirit of the Union, and tends to beget retaliating regulations, not less expensive & vexatious in themselves, than they are destructive of the general harmony.

5. WANT OF CONCERT IN MATTERS WHERE COMMON INTEREST REQUIRES IT.

. . . Instances of inferior moment are the want of uniformity in the laws concerning naturalization & literary property; of provision for national seminaries, for grants of incorporation for national purposes, for canals and other works of general utility, which may at present be defeated by the perverseness of particular States whose concurrence is necessary.

6. WANT OF GUARANTY TO THE STATES OF THEIR CONSTITUTIONS & LAWS AGAINST INTERNAL VIOLENCE.

The confederation is silent on this point and therefore by the second article the hands of the federal authority are tied. According to Republican Theory, Right and power being both vested in the majority, are held to be synonymous. According to fact and experience a minority may in an appeal to force, be an overmatch for the majority. 1. If the minority happen to include all such as possess the skill and habits of military life, & such as possess the great pecuniary resources, one third only may conquer the remaining two thirds. 2. One third of those who participate in the choice of the rulers, may be rendered a majority by the accession of those whose poverty excludes them from a right of suffrage, and who for obvious reasons will be more likely to join the standard of sedition than that of the established Government. 3. Where slavery exists the republican Theory becomes still more fallacious.

7. WANT OF SANCTION TO THE LAWS, AND OF COERCION IN THE GOVERNMENT OF THE CONFEDERACY.

A sanction is essential to the idea of law, as coercion is to that of Government. The federal system being destitute of both, wants the great vital principles of a Political Constitution. Under the form of such a Constitution, it is in fact nothing more than a treaty of amity of commerce and of alliance, between so many independent and Sovereign States. From what cause could so fatal an omission have happened in the articles of Confederation? from a mistaken confidence that the justice, the good faith, the honor, the sound policy, of the several legislative assemblies would render superfluous any appeal to the ordinary motives by which the laws secure the obedience of individuals: a confidence which does honor to the enthusiastic virtue of the compilers, as much as the inexperience of the crisis apologizes for their errors. The time which has since elapsed has had the double effect, of increasing the light, and tempering the warmth, with which the arduous work may be revised. It is no longer doubted that a unanimous and punctual obedience of 13 independent bodies, to the acts of the federal Government, ought not be calculated on. . . . How indeed could it be otherwise? In the first place, Every general act of the Union must necessarily bear unequally hard on some particular member or members of it. Secondly the partiality of the members to their own interests and rights, a partiality which will be fostered by the Courtiers of popularity, will naturally exaggerate the inequality where it exists, and even suspect it where it has no existence. Thirdly a distrust of the voluntary compliance of each other may prevent the compliance of any, although it should be the latent disposition of all. . . .

8. WANT OF RATIFICATION BY THE PEOPLE OF THE ARTICLES OF CONFEDERATION.

In some of the States the Confederation is recognized by, and forms a part of the constitution. In others however it has received no other sanction than that of the Legislative authority. From this defect two evils result: 1. Whenever a law of a State happens to be repugnant to an act of Congress, particularly when the latter is of posterior date to the former, it will be at least questionable whether the latter must not prevail; and as the question must be decided by the Tribunals of the State, they will be most likely to lean on the side of the State. 2. As far as the Union of the States is to be regarded as a league of sovereign powers, and not as a political Constitution by virtue of which they are become one sovereign power, so far it seems to follow from the doctrine of compacts, that a breach of any of the articles of the confederation by any of the parties to it, absolves the other parties from their respective obligations, and gives them a right if they choose to exert it, of dissolving the Union altogether.

9. MULTIPLICITY OF LAWS IN THE SEVERAL STATES.

In developing the evils which vitiate the political system of the U.S. it is proper to include those which are found within the States individually, as well as those which directly affect the States collectively, since the former class have an indirect influence on the general malady and must not be overlooked in forming a complete remedy. Among the evils then of our situation may well be ranked the multiplicity of laws from which no State is exempt. . . . Try the Codes of the several States by this test, and what a luxuriancy of legislation do they present. The short period of independency has filled as many pages as the century which preceded it. Every year, almost every session, adds a new volume. . . . A review of the several codes will show that every necessary and useful part of the least voluminous of them might be compressed into one tenth of the compass, and at the same time be rendered tenfold as perspicuous.

10. MUTABILITY OF THE LAWS OF THE STATES.

. . . We daily see laws repealed or superseded, before any trial can have been made of their merits: and even before a knowledge of them can have reached the remoter districts within which they were to operate. . . .

11. INJUSTICE OF THE LAWS OF STATES.

If the multiplicity and mutability of laws prove a want of wisdom, their injustice betrays a defect still more alarming: more alarming not merely because it is a greater evil in itself, but because it brings more into question the fundamental principle of republican Government, that the majority who rule in such Governments, are the safest Guardians both of public Good and of private rights. To what causes is this evil to be ascribed?

These causes lie 1. in the Representative bodies. 2. in the people themselves.

1. Representative appointments are sought from 3 motives. 1. ambition 2. personal interest. 3. public good. Unhappily the two first are proved by experience to be most prevalent. Hence the candidates who feel them, particularly, the second, are most industrious, and most successful in pursuing their object: and forming often a majority in the legislative Councils, with interested views, contrary to the interest, and views, of their Constituents, join in a perfidious sacrifice of the latter to the former. A succeeding election it might be supposed, would displace the offenders, and repair the mischief. But how easily are base and selfish measures, masked by pretexts of public good and apparent expediency? How frequently will a repetition of the same arts and industry which succeeded in the first instance, again prevail on the unwary to misplace their confidence?

How frequently too will the honest but unenlightened representative be the dupe of a favorite leader, veiling his selfish views under the professions of public good, and varnishing his sophistical arguments with the glowing colors of popular eloquence?

2. A still more fatal if not more frequent cause lies among the people themselves. All civilized societies are divided into different interests and factions, as they happen to be creditors or debtors—Rich or poor—husbandmen, merchants or manufacturers—members of different religious sects—followers of different political leaders—inhabitants of different districts—owners of different kinds of property &c &c. In republican Government the majority however composed, ultimately give the law. Whenever therefore an apparent interest or common passion unites a majority what is to restrain them from unjust violations of the rights and interests of the minority, or of individuals? Three motives only 1. a prudent regard to their own good as involved in the general and permanent good of the Community. This consideration although of decisive weight in itself, is found by experience to be too often unheeded. It is too often forgotten, by nations as well as by individuals that honesty is the best policy. 2dly. respect for character. However strong this motive may be in individuals, it is considered as very insufficient to restrain them from injustice. In a multitude its efficacy is diminished in proportion to the number which is to share the praise or the blame. Besides, as it has reference to public opinion, which within a particular Society, is the opinion of the majority, the standard is fixed by those whose conduct is to be measured by it. . . . 3dly. will Religion the only remaining motive be a sufficient restraint? It is not pretended to be such on men individually considered. Will its effect be greater on them considered in an aggregate view? quite the reverse. The conduct of every popular assembly acting on oath, the strongest of religious Ties, proves that individuals join without remorse in acts, against which their consciences would revolt if proposed to them under the like sanction, separately in their closets. When indeed Religion is kindled into enthusiasm, its force like that of other passions, is increased by the sympathy of a multitude. . . . Place three individuals in a situation wherein the interest of each depends on the voice of the others, and give to two of them an interest opposed to the rights of the third? Will the latter be secure? The prudence of every man would shun the danger. The rules & forms of justice suppose & guard against it. Will two thousand in a like situation be less likely to encroach on the rights of one thousand? The contrary is witnessed by the notorious factions & oppressions which take place in corporate towns limited as the opportunities are, and in little republics when uncontrolled by apprehensions of external danger. If an enlargement of the sphere is found to lessen the insecurity of private rights, it is not because the impulse of a common interest or passion is less predominant in this case with the majority; but because a common interest or passion is less apt to be felt and the requisite combinations less easy to be formed by a great than by a small number. The Society becomes broken into a greater variety of interests, of pursuits, of passions, which check each other, whilst those who may feel a common sentiment have less opportunity of communication and concert. It may be inferred that the inconveniences of popular States contrary to the prevailing Theory, are in proportion not to the extent, but to the narrowness of their limits.

The great desideratum in Government is such a modification of the Sovereignty as will render it sufficiently neutral between the different interests and factions, to control one part of the Society from invading the rights of another, and at the same time sufficiently controlled itself, from setting up an interest adverse to that of the whole Society. . . . As a limited Monarchy tempers the evils of an absolute one; so an extensive Republic meliorates the administration of a small Republic.

An auxiliary desideratum for the melioration of the Republican form is such a process of elections as will most certainly extract from the mass of the Society the purest and noblest characters which it contains; such as will at once feel most strongly the proper motives to pursue the end of their appointment, and be most capable to devise the proper means of attaining it.

12. Impotence of the laws of the States

THOMAS JEFFERSON

NOTES ON THE STATE OF VIRGINIA (1787)

What began as an effort to explain the condition in Virginia to a French envoy after the American Revolution soon developed into a complete book that was first published anonymously in Paris and then printed in London. Jefferson's examination of his home state is wide-ranging, surveying not only the politics of the state but its social and economic condition, its natural environment, and its people. Jefferson readily mixed his observations on the situation in Virginia with his own views and speculations. Among his comments was an assessment of the social and economic conditions most favorable to republican citizenship. There Jefferson gave classic voice to a persistent strand of American political thought, agrarianism. Like many in the late eighteenth century, Jefferson thought that the crowded cities and emerging manufacturers in Europe were inimical to free government. The life of the independent small farmer, Jefferson thought, was perfectly suited to sustaining republicanism.

Why might there be a connection between socioeconomic conditions and a free society? Are employees too dependent to be good citizens? Are there forms of labor that undermine the capacity of citizens? Does farming have the virtues that Jefferson attributes to it? Is farming uniquely virtuous? Is the life of an entrepreneur or small business owner the modern equivalent to Jefferson's family farms? Are the small family farms of New England better suited to republican government than the plantation system of the South? Do Jefferson's observations have relevance for thinking about the political significance of political inequality?

. . .

We never had an interior trade of any importance. Our exterior commerce has suffered very much from the beginning of the present contest. During this time we have manufactured within our families the most necessary articles of clothing. Those of cotton will bear some comparison with the same kinds of manufacture in Europe; but those of wool, flax and hemp are very coarse, unsightly, and unpleasant: and such is our attachment to agriculture, and such our preference for foreign manufactures, that be it wise or unwise, our people will certainly return as soon as they can, to the raising raw materials, and exchanging them for finer manufactures than they are able to execute themselves.

The political economists of Europe have established it as a principle that every state should endeavor to manufacture for itself: and this principle, like many others, we transfer to America, without calculating the difference of circumstance which should often produce a difference of result. In Europe the lands are either cultivated, or locked up against the cultivator. Manufacture must therefore be resorted to of necessity not of choice, to support the surplus of their people. But we have an immensity of land courting the industry of the husbandman. Is it best then that all our citizens should be employed in its improvement, or that one half should be called off from that to exercise manufactures and handicraft arts for the other? Those who labor in the earth are the chosen people of God, if ever he had a chosen people, whose breasts he has made his peculiar deposit for substantial and genuine virtue. It is the focus in which he keeps alive that sacred fire, which otherwise might escape from the face of the earth. Corruption of morals in the mass of cultivators is a phenomenon of which no age nor nation has furnished an example. It is the mark set on those, who not looking up to heaven, to their own soil and industry, as does the husbandman, for their subsistence, depend for it on the casualties and caprice of customers. Dependence begets subservience and venality, suffocates the germ of virtue, and prepares fit tools for the designs of ambition. This, the natural progress and consequence of the arts, has sometimes perhaps been retarded by accidental circumstances: but, generally speaking, the proportion which the aggregate of the other classes of citizens bears in any state to that of its husbandmen, is the proportion of its unsound to its healthy parts, and is a good-enough barometer whereby to measure its degree of corruption. While we have land to labor then, let us never wish to see our citizens occupied at a work-bench, or twirling a distaff. Carpenters, masons, smiths, are wanting in husbandry: but, for the general operations of manufacture, let our work-shops remain in Europe. It is better to carry provisions and materials to workmen there, than bring them to the provisions and materials, and with them their manners and principles. The loss by the transportation of commodities across the Atlantic will be made up in happiness and permanence of government. The mobs of great cities add just so much to the support of pure government, as sores do to the strength of the human body. It is the manners and spirit of a people which preserve a republic in vigor. A degeneracy in these is a canker which soon eats to the heart of its laws and constitution.

. . .

VI. AMERICA AND THE WORLD

Major Developments

- Establishment of an independent country
- Creation of internal security
- Uncertainty over relations with neighboring Native American tribes

There were three primary challenges to America's place in the world during the founding period. The first and most pressing was winning and maintaining national independence from Britain. The American colonies declared independence in 1776, but British forces did not leave American territory and England did not recognize the United States as an independent nation for over five years. Despite the fact that the British empire was fighting to keep colonies half a world away, winning independence was no easy task. Even after the signing of the Treaty of Paris in 1783, the peace was precarious. The Confederation Congress could do little more than "earnestly recommend" that the state governments would resolve the property claims of Loyalists, and Britain did not quickly withdraw from the territory in the northwest. As Samuel Adams warned Richard Henry Lee after peace was declared, Britain "appears to be not a cordial friend."[18] Disputed issues between the two countries were not resolved until the negotiation of the Jay Treaty a decade later.

The second challenge was securing the territorial borders of the new nation—and extending them outward. France and Spain claimed territory to the south and west, and Britain was slow to accept the northern boundaries. The more persistent problem was the presence of Native American tribes along the frontier. In some cases, the tribes had allied with Britain during the war, generating lasting hostilities. In other cases, the tribes had not been overtly hostile to the United States, but the pressures of new settlement created growing tensions.

The third challenge arose from the relationship among the states themselves. The Articles of Confederation declared a "mutual friendship and intercourse among the people of the different States in this Union," but the relationship among the states was not completely harmonious even in the midst of the war for independence. The nightmare scenario for some of the more nationalist-minded revolutionaries was that the union that had sustained the states through the war would fall apart during peacetime. The United States might break into several distinct countries, perhaps with some allying with European powers. Rather than being insulated by wilderness and oceans, the United States might come to look more like Europe, with rival states on each other's doorstep.

---

18 Samuel Adams, *The Writings of Samuel Adams*, ed. Harry Alonzo Cushing, vol. 4 (New York: G.P. Putnam's Sons, 1908), 311.

CORN TASSEL (ONITOSITAH)

REPLY TO THE AMERICAN COMMISSIONERS (1777)

The western border of the British colonies had long been a subject of tension. By the time of the American Revolution, some progress had been made in settling the boundaries of the northwest, but in the southwest the competing claims of the Cherokees and the colonial settlers remained up in the air, often leading to armed skirmishes between the two sides. The area near the modern borders of Virginia and Tennessee was a site of strategic importance and had been contested by the Cherokee, the British, and the revolutionaries. A treaty negotiated at Long Island on the Holston River between a number of Cherokee leaders and representatives from the southern American states ceded much of eastern Tennessee to the Americans.

Corn Tassel, known by a variety of names, was a key figure in peace negotiations in eastern Tennessee. A notable warrior, he acted on behalf of his chief in 1777, but in later years he spoke as a chief himself. In 1786, he was forced at gunpoint to cede additional land to the settlers, and in 1788 he was among a group of chiefs murdered by a local militia while attending peace talks. His speeches were translated and recorded by American officials at these meetings.[19] His relationship with the commissioners at Long Island was tense, and he had already accused them of lying to the Cherokees to manipulate tribal alliances in the war. When the commissioners at Long Island insisted that the tribes should give up all claim to any territory where white settlements had been established, Corn Tassel objected.

Are Corn Tassel's arguments within the tradition of American political thought, or is he arguing from outside the American tradition? What might be the basis for American claims to the territory in what is now Tennessee? Does the farmer have superior claims to land than the hunter-gatherer? What is required to establish property rights in land? What would be required to establish American political authority over native tribes?

It is not a little surprising, that when we enter into treaties with our brothers, the whites, their whole cry is *more land*! Indeed, formerly, it seemed to be a mere matter of formality with them to demand what they knew we durst not refuse. But on the principles of fairness, of which we have received assurances, during the conducting of the present treaty, and in the name of free will and equality, I must reject your demand.

Suppose, in considering the nature of your claim, (and in justice to my nation I shall and will do it fully,) I were to ask one of you, my brother warriors, under what kind of authority, by what law, or on what pretense he makes this exorbitant demand of nearly all the lands we hold between your settlements and our towns, as the cement and consideration of our peace.

Would he tell me it is by right of conquest? No! If he did, I should retort to him, that *we* had last *marched* over his territory; even up to this very place which he has *fortified* so far within his former limits; nay, that some of our young warriors . . . are still in the woods, and continue to keep his people in fear, and that it was but till very lately that these identical walls were your strongholds, out of which you durst scarcely advance.

If, therefore, a bare march, or reconnoitering a country is sufficient reason to ground a claim to it,

19 A speech with overlapping themes by "Old Tassel" at the meeting was reported in Archibald Henderson, "Treaty of Long Island of Holston," *North Carolina Historical Review* 8:1 (1931): 90–91. As with many Native American speeches, the records of this speech are sketchy, given problems of translation, overlapping names, and faithful reporting. This excerpt is taken from a memorandum prepared by William Tatham, who served as secretary to the American commissioners.

we shall insist on transposing the demand, and your relinquishing your settlements on the western waters, and removing one hundred miles back towards the east, whither some of our warriors advanced against you in the course of last year's campaign.

Let us examine the facts of your present irruption, into our country; and we shall discover your pretensions on that ground. What did you do? You marched into our territories with a superior force; our vigilance gave us timely notice of your maneuvers; your numbers far exceeded us, and we fled to the strongholds of our extensive woods, there to secure our women and children.

Thus, you marched into our towns; they were left to your mercy; you killed a few scattered and defenseless individuals; spread fire and desolation wherever you pleased; and returned again to your own habitations. If you want this, indeed, as a conquest, you omitted the most essential point; you should have fortified the junction of the Holston and Tennessee rivers, and have, thereby, conquered all the waters above you. But, as all are fair advantages during the existence of a state of war, it is now too late for us to suffer for your mishap of generalship!

Again, were we to enquire by what law or authority you set up a claim; I answer, *none*! Your laws extend not into our country, nor ever did; you talk of the law of nature and the law of nations, and they are both against you.

Indeed much has been advanced on the want of, what you term, civilization among the Indians; and many proposals have been made to us to adopt your laws, your religion, your manners, and your customs. But, we confess, we do not yet see the propriety or practicality of such a reformation; and should be better pleased with beholding the good effects of these doctrines on your own practice, then with hearing you talk about them, or reading your papers to us upon such subjects.

You say, *"Why do not the Indian till the ground, and live as we do?"* May we not with equal propriety, ask *why the White people do not hunt and live as we do?* You profess to think it no injustice towards us to kill a cow or hog for their sustenance, when they happen to be on your lands. We wish, however, to be at peace with you; and, to do as we would be done by. We do not quarrel with you for killing an occasional buffalo, bear, or deer on our lands when you need one to eat; but you go much farther; your people hunt to gain a livelihood by it; they kill all our game; our young men resent the injury; and, it is followed by bloodshed and war.

This is not a mere affected injury; it is a grievance which we equitably complain of, and it demands a permanent address.

The great God of Nature has placed us in different situations. It is true, he has endowed you with many superior advantages; but he has not created us to be your slaves: *We are a separate people!* He has given each their lands, under distinct considerations and circumstances; he has stocked yours with the cow, ours with the buffalo; yours with the hog; ours with the bear; yours with the sheep, ours with the deer. He has, indeed, given you an advantage in this, that your cattle are tame and domestic, while ours are wild, and demand not only a larger space for range, but art to hunt and kill them; they are, nevertheless, as much our property as other animals are yours; and ought not to be taken away without our consent, and for something equivalent.

ALEXANDER HAMILTON

LETTER TO JAMES DUANE (1780)

James Duane was a member of the New York delegation to the Continental Congress, later serving as mayor of New York City until accepting a position as federal district court judge. Alexander Hamilton spent the war as the captain of an artillery company and aide-de-camp to General George Washington. The problems of war were very much on Hamilton's mind during the Confederation period. Hamilton's experience with the politics surrounding the army even in the midst of the revolutionary crisis convinced him that the Confederation government was ill prepared to adequately provide for the national security of the newly independent country. The demands of national security drove his interest in constitutional reform. In a letter to Duane in 1780, while still serving on Washington's staff, Hamilton outlined what he saw as the deficiencies with the American government and the dangers that they created.

How does Hamilton's analysis of the vices of the Confederacy differ from Madison's? To what extent does the U.S. Constitution address Hamilton's concerns? How important are national security considerations to evaluating a political system? What does Hamilton mean by an "excess of the spirit of liberty"? Does Hamilton think that there are intrinsic tensions between republican government and national security?

Agreeably to your request, and my promise, I sit down to give you my ideas of the defects of our present system, and the changes necessary to save us from ruin. . . .

The fundamental defect is a want of power in Congress. It is hardly worthwhile to show in what this consists, as it seems to be universally acknowledged; or to point out how it has happened, as the only question is how to remedy it. It may, however, be said, that it has originated from three causes: An excess of the spirit of liberty, which has made the particular States show a jealousy of all power not in their own hands; and this power has led them to exercise a right of judging in the last resort of the measures recommended by Congress, and of acting according to their own opinions of their propriety, or necessity; a diffidence, in Congress, of their own powers, by which they have been timid and indecisive in their resolutions; constantly making concessions to the States, till they have scarcely left themselves the shadow of power; a want of sufficient means at their disposal to answer the public exigencies, and of vigor to draw forth those means; which have occasioned them to depend on the States individually, to fulfill their engagements with the army; the consequence of which, has been to ruin their influence and credit with the army, to establish its dependence on each State separately, rather than *on them*, that is, rather than on the whole collectively.

It may be pleaded that Congress had never any definitive powers granted them, and of course could exercise none, could do nothing more than recommend. The manner in which Congress was appointed would warrant, and the public good required that they should have considered themselves as vested with full power to *preserve the republic from harm*. They have done many of the highest acts of sovereignty, which were always cheerfully submitted to: The Declaration of Independence, the declaration of war, the levying of an army, creating a navy, emitting money, making alliances with foreign powers, appointing a dictator, etc. All these implications of a complete sovereignty were never disputed, and ought to have been a standard for the whole conduct of administration. Undefined powers are discretionary powers, limited only by the object for which they were given; in the present case the independence and freedom of America. . . .

But the Confederation itself is defective, and requires to be altered. It is neither fit for war nor peace. The idea of an uncontrollable sovereignty in each

State over its internal police will defeat the other powers given to Congress, and make our union feeble and precarious. . . .

The Confederation gives the States, individually, too much influence in the affairs of the army. They should have nothing to do with it. The entire formation and disposal of our military forces ought to belong to Congress. It is an essential cement of the union; and it ought to be the policy of Congress to destroy all ideas of State attachments in the army, and make it look up wholly to them. For this purpose all appointments, promotions, and provisions whatsoever, ought to be made by them. It may be apprehended that this may be dangerous to liberty. But nothing appears more evident to me than that we run much greater risk of having a weak and disunited federal government, than one which will be able to usurp upon the rights of the people.

. . .

The forms of our State constitutions must always give them great weight in our affairs, and will make it too difficult to bend them to the pursuit of a common interest, too easy to oppose whatever they do not like, and to form partial combinations subversive of the general one. There is a wide difference between our situation and that of an empire under one simple form of government. . . . [T]he danger [of an empire under one simple form of government] is that the sovereign will have too much power, and oppress the parts of which it is composed. In our case, that of an empire composed of confederated States each with a government completely organized within itself, having all the means to draw its subjects to a close dependence on itself, the danger is directly the reverse. It is that the common sovereign will not have power sufficient to unite the different members together, and direct the common forces to the interest and happiness of the whole.

The leagues among the old Grecian republics are a proof of this. They were continually at war with each other, and for want of union fell a prey to their neighbors. They frequently held general councils; but their resolutions were not further observed than as they suited the interests and inclinations of all the parties, and at length they sank entirely into contempt.

. . . [A] little time hence some of the States will be powerful empires; and we are so remote from other nations, that we shall have all the leisure and opportunity we can wish to cut each other's throats.

. . .

The Confederation, too, gives the power of the purse too entirely to the State Legislatures. It should provide perpetual funds, in the disposal of Congress, by a land tax, poll tax, or the like. All imposts upon commerce ought to be laid by Congress and appropriated to their use. For without certain revenues, a government can have no power. That power which holds the purse-strings absolutely, must rule. . . .

Another defect in our system is want of method and energy in the administration. . . . Congress have kept the power too much in their own hands, and have meddled too much with details of every sort. Congress is, properly, a deliberative corps, and it forgets itself when it attempts to play the executive. It is impossible such a body, numerous as it is, constantly fluctuating, can ever act with sufficient decision or with system. . . . The variety of business must distract, and the proneness of every assembly to debate must at all times delay.

. . .

I fear a little vanity has stood in the way of these arrangements, as though they would lessen the importance of Congress and leave them nothing to do. But they would have precisely the same rights and powers as heretofore, happily disencumbered of the detail. They would have to inspect the conduct of their ministers, deliberate upon their plans, originate others for the public good; only observing this rule: that they ought to consult their ministers, and get all the information and advice they could from them, before they entered into any new measures or made changes in the old.

A third defect is the fluctuating constitution of our army. This has been a pregnant source of evil; all our military misfortunes, three fourths of our civil embarrassments, are to be ascribed to it. . . .

The imperfect and unequal provision made for the army is a fourth defect. . . . Without a speedy change the army must dissolve. It is now a mob, rather than an army; without clothing, without pay, without provision, without morals, without discipline. We begin to hate the country for its neglect of us. The country begins to hate us for our oppressions of them. Congress have long been jealous of us. We have now lost all confidence in them, and give the worst construction to all they do. Held together by the slenderest ties, we are ripening for a dissolution.

. . .

The Confederation in my opinion, should give Congress complete sovereignty, except as to that part of internal police which relates to the rights of property and life among individuals, and to raising money by internal taxes. It is necessary that everything belonging to this should be regulated by the State Legislatures. Congress should have complete sovereignty in all that relates to war, peace, trade, finance; and to the management of foreign affairs; the right of declaring war; of raising armies, officering, paying them, directing their motions in every respect; of equipping fleets, and doing the same with them; of building fortifications, arsenals, magazines, etc.; of making peace on such conditions as they think proper; of regulating trade, determining with what countries it shall be carried on; granting indulgencies; laying prohibitions on all the articles of export or import; imposing duties; granting bounties and premiums for raising, exporting importing . . . ; instituting Admiralty Courts, etc.; of coining money; establishing banks on such terms, and with such privileges as they think proper; appropriating funds, and doing whatever else relates to the operations of finance; transacting everything with foreign nations; making alliances, offensive and defensive, treaties of commerce, etc.

The Confederation should provide certain perpetual revenues, productive and easy of collection; a land tax, poll tax, or the like; which, together with the duties on trade, and the unlocated lands, would give Congress a substantial existence, and a stable foundation for their schemes of finance. What more supplies were necessary should occasionally demanded of the States, in the present mode of quotas.

. . .

The advantages of securing the attachment of the army to Congress, and binding them to the service by substantial ties, are immense. We should then have discipline,—an army in reality as well as in name. Congress would then have a solid basis of authority and consequence; for, to me, it is an axiom, that in our constitution an army is essential to the American Union.

. . .

. . . There are epochs in human affairs when novelty even is useful. If a general opinion prevails that the old way is bad, whether true or false, and this obstructs or relaxes the operations of the public service, a change is necessary, if it be but for the sake of change. This is exactly the case now. It is a universal sentiment that our present system is a bad one, and that things do not go right on this account. The measure of a Convention would revive the hopes of the people and give a new direction to their passions. . . .

. . .

GEORGE WASHINGTON

CIRCULAR LETTER TO THE STATE GOVERNORS (1783)

In 1781, the British General Cornwallis surrendered at Yorktown, Virginia, and the next year the Americans and the British reached a peace agreement, which was formalized as the Treaty of Paris in the summer of 1783. With the final withdrawal of British troops that fall, George Washington resigned as general of the American forces. As his role as military commander was winding down, he prepared a set of recommendations for the American political leaders on the organization of military affairs moving forward. He sent his "Sentiments on a Peace Establishment" to Congress, proposing that a standing army be stationed at the frontier, that the militia be made uniform across the country, that an adequate arsenal be established, and that military academies be founded. These proposals were narrowly defeated. In his circular letter to the governors of the various states, Washington warned that the Americans must seize the opportunity to place their independence on a firmer foundation.

How much does Washington think the Americans will benefit from having no immediate neighbors? Why does he think Americans enjoy a particularly fortuitous environment for founding a new nation? What does he see as the chief threats to the American future? Are his fears credible? How important was the maintenance of a firm union of the states to the prosperity of the country? Could the American experiment have been as successful if the states had formed separate confederacies after the war? How does Washington's perception of the future security threats to the United States compare with Hamilton's?

The great object for which I had the honor to hold an appointment in the service of my country being accomplished, I am now preparing to resign it into the hands of Congress, and to return to that domestic retirement which it is well known I left with the greatest reluctance. . . .

. . .

The citizens of America, placed in the most enviable condition, as the sole lords and proprietors of a vast tract of continent comprehending all the various soils and climates of the world, and abounding with all the necessaries and conveniences of life, are now by the late satisfactory pacification acknowledged to be possessed of absolute freedom and independency. They are from this period to be considered as the actors on a most conspicuous theatre, which seems to be peculiarly designated by Providence for the display of human greatness and felicity. Here they are not only surrounded by everything which can contribute to the completion of private and domestic enjoyment but Heaven has crowned all its other blessings, by giving a fairer opportunity for political happiness, than any other nation has ever been favored with. . . . The foundation of our empire was not laid in the gloomy age of ignorance and superstition; but at an epocha when the rights of mankind were better understood and more clearly defined, than at any former period. . . . At this auspicious period, the United States came into existence as a nation; and, if their citizens should not be completely free and happy, the fault will be entirely their own.

Such is our situation and such are our prospects; but, notwithstanding the cup of blessing is thus reached out to us; notwithstanding happiness is ours, if we have a disposition to seize the occasion and make it our own; yet it appears to me there is an option still left the United States of America, that it rests in their choice, and depends upon their conduct, whether they will be respectable and prosperous, or contemptible and miserable, as a nation. This is the time of their political probation; this is the moment when the eyes of the whole world are turned upon them; this is the moment to establish or ruin their national character forever; this is the favorable moment to give such a tone to our federal Government, as will enable it to answer the ends of its institution, or this may be the ill-fated moment for relaxing the powers of the Union, annihilating the cement of the confederation, and exposing us to become the sport of European politics, which may play one State against another, to prevent their growing importance, and to serve their own interested purposes. For, according to the system of policy the States shall adopt at this moment, they will stand or fall; and by their confirmation or lapse it is yet to be decided whether the resolution is ultimately to be considered as a blessing or a curse; a blessing or a curse, not to the present age alone, for with our fate will the destiny of unborn millions be involved.

. . .

There are four things, which I humbly conceive, are essential to the well-being, I may even venture to say, to the very existence of the United States as an independent power.

First. An indissoluble union of the States under one federal head.

Second. A sacred regard to public justice.

Third. The adoption of a proper peace establishment; and,

Fourth. The prevalence of that pacific and friendly disposition among the people of the United States, which will induce them to forget their local prejudices and policies; to make those mutual concessions, which are requisite to the general prosperity; and, in some instances, to sacrifice their individual advantages to the interest of the community.

These are the pillars on which the glorious fabric of our independency and national character must be supported. Liberty is the basis and whoever would dare to sap the foundation, or overturn the structure under whatever specious presence he may attempt it will merit the bitterest execrations and the severest punishment which can be inflicted by his injured country.

. . .

Under the first head, although it may not be necessary or proper for me, in this place, to enter into the particular disquisition of the principles of the Union, and to take up the great question which has been frequently agitated, whether it be expedient and requisite for the States to delegate a larger proportion of power to Congress, or not; yet it will be a part of my duty, and that of every true patriot, to assert without reserve, and to insist, upon the following positions. That, unless the States will suffer Congress to exercise those prerogatives they are undoubtedly vested with by the constitution, everything must very rapidly tend to anarchy and confusion. That it is indispensable to the happiness of the individual States, that there should be somewhere lodged a supreme power to regulate and govern the general concerns of confederated republic, without which the Union cannot be of long duration. That there must be a faithful and pointed compliance on the part of every State, with the late proposals and demands of Congress, or the most fatal consequences will ensue. That whatever measures have tendency to dissolve the Union or violate or lessen the Sovereign authority, ought to be considered as hostile to the liberty and independency of America, and the authors of them treated accordingly. And lastly, that unless we can be enabled by the concurrence of the States, to participate in the fruits of resolution, and enjoy the essential benefits of civil society, under a form of government so free and uncorrupted, so happily guarded against the danger of oppression, as has been devised and adopted by the articles of confederation, it will be a subject of regret, that so much blood and treasure have been lavished to no purpose, that so many sufferings have been encountered without a compensation, and that so many sacrifices have been made in vain.

Many other considerations might be here adduced to prove that without an entire conformity to the spirit of the Union, we cannot exist as an independent power. It will be sufficient for my purpose to mention but one or two, which seem to me of the greatest importance. It is only in our united character, as an empire, that our Independence is acknowledged, that our power can be regarded or our credit supported among foreign nations. The treaties of the European powers with the United States of America will have no validity on a dissolution of the Union. We shall be left nearly in a state of nature; or we may find, by our own unhappy experience, that there is a natural and necessary progression from extreme anarchy to extreme tyranny, and that arbitrary power is most easily established on the ruins of liberty, abused to licentiousness.

As to the second article, which respects the performance of public justice, Congress have, in their late address to the United States, almost exhausted the subject; they have explained their Ideas so fully, and have enforced the obligation of the States are under, to render complete justice to the public creditors, with so much dignity and energy, that, in my opinion, no real friend to honor and Independency of America can hesitate a single moment, respecting the propriety of complying with the Just and honorable measures proposed. If their arguments do not produce conviction, I know of nothing that will have greater influence; especially when we recollect that the system referred to, being the result of the collected wisdom of the continent, must be esteemed, if not perfect, certainly the least objectionable of any that could be devised; and that, if it shall not be carried into immediate execution, bankruptcy with all its deplorable consequences, will take place, before any different plan can possibly be proposed and adopted. So pressing are the present circumstances, and such is the alternative now offered to the States.

. . .

If, after all, a spirit of disunion, or a temper of obstinacy and perverseness should manifest itself in any of the States; if such an ungracious disposition should attempt to frustrate all the happy effects that might be expected to flow from the Union; if there should be a refusal to comply with the requisitions of Congress for funds to discharge the annual Interest of the public debts; and if that refusal should revive again all those jealousies, and produce all those evils, which are now happily removed, Congress, who have in all their transactions, shown a great degree of magnanimity and justice, will stand Justified in the sight of God and man; and the State alone, which puts itself in opposition to the aggregate wisdom of the continent, and follows such mistaken and pernicious counsels, will be responsible for all the consequences.

. . .

It is necessary to say but a few words on the third topic, which was proposed, and which regards particularly the defense of the republic; as there can be little doubt that Congress will recommend a proper peace establishment for the United States, in which a due attention will be paid to the importance of placing the militia of the Union upon a regular and respectable footing. If this should be the case, I would beg to urge the great advantage of it in the strongest terms. The militia of this country must be considered as the palladium of our security, and the first effectual resort in case of hostility. It is essential, therefore, that the same system should pervade the whole; that the formation and discipline of the militia of the continent should be absolutely uniform, and that the same species of arms, accoutrements, and military apparatus, should be introduced in every part of the United States. No one, who has not learned it from experience, can conceive the difficulty expense and confusion which result from a contrary system, or the vague arrangements which have hitherto prevailed. . . .

. . .

I now make it my earnest prayer, that God would have you, and the State over which you preside, in his holy protection; that he would incline the hearts of the citizens to cultivate a spirit of subordination and obedience to government; to entertain a brotherly affection and love for one another, for their fellow citizens of the United States at large, and particularly for their brethren who have served in the field; and finally, that he would most graciously be pleased to dispose us all to do justice, to love mercy, and to demean ourselves with that charity, humility, and pacific temper of mind, which were the characteristics of the Divine Author of our blessed religion, and without an humble imitation of whose example in these things, we can never hope to be a happy nation.

FOR FURTHER STUDY

Cogan, Neil H., ed. *The Complete Bill of Rights: The Drafts, Debates, Sources, and Origins* (New York: Oxford University Press, 1997).

Friedrich, Carl J., and Robert G. McCloskey, eds. *From the Declaration of Independence to the Constitution: The Roots of American Constitutionalism* (New York: Liberal Arts Press, 1954).

Hamilton, Alexander, James Madison, and John Jay, *The Federalist Papers*, ed. Clinton Rossiter (New York: New American Library, 1961).

Jefferson, Thomas. *Thomas Jefferson: Political Writings*, eds. Joyce Appleby and Terence Ball (New York: Cambridge University Press, 1999).

Lloyd, Gordon, and Margie Lloyd, eds. *The Essential Bill of Rights: Original Arguments and Fundamental Documents* (Lanham, MD: University Press of America, 1998).

Madison, James. *Selected Writings of James Madison*, ed. Ralph Ketcham (Indianapolis, IN: Hackett Publishers, 2006).

Sheehan, Colleen A., and Gary L. McDowell, eds. *Friends of the Constitution: Writings of the "Other" Federalists, 1787–1788* (Indianapolis, IN: Liberty Fund, 1998).

Storing, Herbert, ed. *The Anti-Federalist: An Abridgement by Murray Dry* (Chicago, IL: University of Chicago Press, 1985).

Zuckert, Michael P., and Derek A. Webb, eds. *The Anti-Federalist Writings of the Melancton Smith Circle* (Indianapolis, IN: Liberty Fund, 2009).

SUGGESTED READINGS

Adair, Douglass. *Fame and the Founding Fathers* (New York: W.W. Norton, 1974).

Adams, Willi Paul. *The First American Constitutions: Republican Ideology and the Making of the State Constitutions in the Revolutionary Era* (Chapel Hill: University of North Carolina Press, 1980).

Banning, Lance. *The Sacred Fire of Liberty: James Madison and the Founding of the Federal Republic* (Ithaca, NY: Cornell University Press, 1995).

Beard, Charles. *An Economic Interpretation of the Constitution of the United States* (New York: Free Press, 1913).

Carey, George W. *The Federalist: Design for a Constitutional Republic* (Urbana: University of Illinois Press, 1989).

Cornell, Saul. *The Other Founders: Anti-Federalism and the Dissenting Tradition in America, 1788–1828* (Chapel Hill: University of North Carolina Press, 1999).

Diamond, Martin. *As Far as Republican Principles Will Admit: Essays* (Washington, D.C.: AEI Press, 1991).

Edling, Max M. *The Revolution in Favor of Government: Origins of the U.S. Constitution and the Making of the American State* (New York: Oxford University Press, 2003).

Epstein, David F. *The Political Theory of the Federalist* (Chicago, IL: University of Chicago Press, 1984).

Gibson, Alan Ray. *Interpreting the Founding: Guide to the Enduring Debates over the Origins and Foundations of the American Republic* (Lawrence: University Press of Kansas, 2006).

Hendrickson, David C. *Peace Pact: The Lost World of the American Founding* (Lawrence: University Press of Kansas, 2006).

Kramer, Larry D. *The People Themselves: Popular Constitutionalism and Judicial Review* (New York: Oxford University Press, 2004).

Kruman, Marc W. *Between Liberty and Authority: State Constitution Making in Revolutionary America* (Chapel Hill: University of North Carolina Press, 1997).

Lienesch, Michael. *New Order of the Ages: Time, the Constitution, and the Making of Modern American Political Thought* (Princeton, NJ: Princeton University Press, 1988).

Lutz, Donald S. *Popular Consent and Popular Control: Whig Political Theory in the Early State Constitutions* (Baton Rouge: Louisiana State University Press, 1988).

Lynd, Staughton. *Intellectual Origins of American Radicalism*, new ed. (New York: Cambridge University Press, 2009).

McDonald, Forrest. *Novus Ordo Seclorum: The Intellectual Origins of the Constitution* (Lawrence: University Press of Kansas, 1985).

Maier, Pauline. *Ratification: The People Debate the Constitution, 1787–1788* (New York: Simon & Schuster, 2011).

Mansfield, Harvey C., Jr. *Taming the Prince: The Ambivalence of Modern Executive Power* (Baltimore, MD: Johns Hopkins University Press, 1989).

Morgan, Edmund S. *Inventing the People: The Rise of Popular Sovereignty in America* (New York: W.W. Norton, 1988).

Pangle, Thomas L. *The Spirit of Modern Republicanism: The Moral Vision of the American Founders and the Philosophy of John Locke* (Chicago, IL: University of Chicago Press, 1990).

Pocock, J. G. A. *The Machiavellian Moment: Florentine Political Thought and the Atlantic Republican Tradition* (Princeton, NJ: Princeton University Press, 1975).

Rakove, Jack N. *Original Meanings: Politics and Ideas in the Making of the Constitution* (New York: Vintage, 1997).

Robertson, David Brian. *The Original Compromise: What the Constitution's Framers Were Really Thinking* (New York: Oxford University Press, 2013).

Rosen, Gary. *American Compact: James Madison and the Problem of Founding* (Lawrence: University Press of Kansas, 1999).

Sheehan, Colleen. *James Madison and the Spirit of Republican Self-Government* (New York: Cambridge University Press, 2009).

Siemers, David J. *Ratifying the Republic: Antifederalist and Federalists in Constitutional Time* (Stanford, CA: Stanford University Press, 2002).

Storing, Herbert J. *What the Anti-Federalists Were For* (Chicago, IL: University of Chicago Press, 1981).

White, Morton G. *Philosophy, The Federalist, and the Constitution* (New York: Oxford University Press, 1987).

Wills, Garry. *Explaining America: The Federalist* (Garden City, NY: Doubleday, 1981).

Wood, Gordon S. *The Creation of the American Republic, 1776–1787* (Chapel Hill: University of North Carolina Press, 1969).

Zuckert, Michael P. *Natural Rights and the New Republicanism* (Princeton, NJ: Princeton University Press, 1998).

CHAPTER 4

THE EARLY NATIONAL ERA, 1792–1828

I. INTRODUCTION

"In every act of my administration, I have sought the happiness of my fellow citizens. My system for the attainment of this object has uniformly been to overlook all personal, local, and partial considerations; to contemplate the United States as one great whole. . . ."[1] George Washington's signal achievement as president was to convey a sense of stability, fidelity, and unity. The nation had passed through the struggles of revolution and founding. It now sought solidity. James Madison had hoped that that the Constitution would achieve some level of "veneration" and "reverence," and the country seemed to be on its way toward embracing the new constitutional government.[2] Politicians started to argue within the confines of the Constitution rather than arguing against it.

The terms of union were still unsettled, however. Economic and social interests across the nation diverged significantly. Debates over national economic policy and how to respond to the war between France and England split both political elites and the general populace in the 1790s. Thomas Jefferson's victory in 1800 promised lower taxes, smaller government, and greater deference to the states, but only aroused fear among those who had been most supportive of President Washington. To them, the Jeffersonian movement echoed anti-Federalist arguments against the Constitution itself and gave free rein to a dangerous democratic impulse.

Politics. The early republic witnessed more than one transformation in the structure of politics. The founders had no real experience with organized political parties, and they were quite skeptical of them. James Madison was typical in denouncing a politics

1 George Washington, *The Writings of George Washington*, ed. Jared Sparks, vol. 11 (Boston: Russell, Shattuck, and Williams, 1836), 42.

2 Alexander Hamilton, James Madison, and John Jay, *The Federalist Papers* (New York: Signet, 1961), 315.

FIGURE 4-1 TIMELINE OF THE EARLY NATIONAL ERA

Events	Year	Writings
	1790	Alexander Hamilton's First Report on Public Credit
Establishment of First Bank of the United States	1791	
Mary Wollstonecraft's Vindication of the Rights of Women	1792	
French King Louis XVI executed	1793	
Ratification of Jay Treaty with Britain	1794	
Federal troops put down the Whiskey Rebellion	1794	
Immanuel Kant's Perpetual Peace	1795	
	1796	George Washington's Farewell Address
Congress passes Alien and Sedition Acts	1798	
	1798	Kentucky and Virginia Resolutions
Napoleon Bonaparte seizes power in France	1799	
Thomas Jefferson defeats President John Adams	1800	
	1801	Thomas Jefferson's Inaugural Address

"violently heated and distracted by the rage of party."[3] Nonetheless, party divisions soon developed. As secretary of treasury under President George Washington, Alexander Hamilton not only developed much of the administration's domestic program but also led efforts to organize political support for the president, his policies, and his supporters. Hamilton's efforts were needed in part because Congressman James Madison was doing the same for the opposition. Both sides saw their efforts as temporary measures to get through a crisis. The Federalists saw the crisis being the Jeffersonian threat to a stable constitutional republic; the Jeffersonians saw the crisis being the Federalist subversion of republican commitments. With the decisive Jeffersonian victory in the elections of 1800, the Federalists were in retreat, a retreat from which they never recovered. The Federalist support dwindled, and they gradually withdrew into their core base of support, New England. When the Federalists were seen as engaging in an almost treasonous effort to pursue peace with Britain during the War of 1812, their support finally collapsed.

The Federalist–Republican divide set a pattern for the nineteenth century, at least. Looking back from the end of that century, the British observer James Bryce noted,

> The distinction which began in those early days has never since vanished. There has always been a party professing itself disposed to favor the central government, and

3 *Ibid.*, 317.

Events	Year	Writings
	1803	John Marshall's opinion in Marbury v. Madison
Louisiana Purchase	1803	
Battle of Tippecanoe launches the War of 1812	1811	
British troops burn the White House	1814	
Andrew Jackson wins Battle of New Orleans	1815	
American Colonization Society founded	1817	
	1819	John Marshall's opinion in McCulloch v. Maryland
President James Monroe wins reelection unopposed	1820	
New York Constitutional Convention	1821	
	1823	Announcement of Monroe Doctrine
John Quincy Adams wins presidency by congressional ballot	1824	
American Temperance Society founded	1825	

> therefore a party of broad construction [of the Constitution]. There has always been a party claiming that it aimed at protecting the rights of the States, and therefore a party of strict construction.[4]

Even with the collapse of the Federalists, this basic divide reasserted itself. The "Era of Good Feelings" under James Monroe allowed the former Federalists to reconcile with the Republican administration and for the nation to heal from the wounds of the war. Monroe ran unopposed for reelection in 1820. But a young generation of National Republicans like Kentucky's Henry Clay and Massachusetts's John Quincy Adams emerged after the War of 1812 calling for greater federal powers. With no obvious choice of a successor to Monroe and no parties to help organize the field of candidates, the presidential vote in 1824 splintered among multiple candidates, including Georgia's William Crawford (who had the backing of the old Jeffersonians), the National Republicans Adams and Clay, and the military hero and political novice Andrew Jackson. Adams won the White House through a vote in the U.S. House of Representatives, but Jackson served as a rallying point for states' rights Republicans, setting the stage for the emergence of a second party system in the 1830s.

4 James Bryce, *The American Commonwealth*, vol. 1 (London: Macmillan and Co., 1888), 379.

Society. Almost as soon as the Constitution was ratified, the eyes of the nation turned west. In 1803, President Jefferson commissioned Meriwether Lewis and William Clark to seek out a water route across the continent that would connect the Atlantic and Pacific. Settlers from the northern states moved into the Northwest Territory, organizing such new states as Ohio, Indiana, and Illinois. Citizens of the southern states did the same with the southwest territories, creating Kentucky, Tennessee, and Alabama. The Louisiana Purchase from France in 1803 and the smaller acquisition of Florida from Spain in 1819 vastly increased the size of the United States and established a secure American presence on the Mississippi River and the Gulf of Mexico.

The period also saw the emergence of the Second Great Awakening, a time of Protestant revivalism that gave new significance to more evangelical denominations like the Baptists and the Methodists. Itinerant ministers crisscrossed the frontier, hosting outdoor revival meetings. Unlike many of the better-educated, more upper-class ministers in the established towns and cities, the revival preachers had more populist roots and featured a more charismatic, emotional style. This new breed of Protestant preachers anticipated the near arrival of the millennium, when Christ's reign of peace would be established on earth. Moral reformation and social purification were essential steps in preparing the way for the Savior's return.

Positions on slavery began to harden in these years. In organizing the Northwest Territory, Congress prohibited slavery there. The first state to be carved out of those territories, Ohio, banned slavery in its constitution, and Congress criminalized American involvement in the international slave trade. The states north of Maryland and Delaware all adopted some form of emancipation. At the same time, the increasing profitability of cotton created new economic incentives for maintaining slavery and discouraged the diversification of the southern economy. The states south of Pennsylvania resisted emancipation, made individual manumission increasingly difficult, and imposed new legal restrictions on both slaves and free blacks. Unlike Ohio, new southern states like Alabama embraced slavery. The 1820 debate over the admission of Mississippi formalized the national division, prohibiting slavery in northern territories but allowing it in southern territories. The founding of the American Colonization Society in New Jersey in 1817 evidenced both the continued reformist impulse that favored abolition and the recognition of the growing hostility to a large free-black population within the United States.

Ideas. Religious ideas were in upheaval during the early republic, with implications for American political thought. Many were swept up in evangelical fervor. Traveling ministers rallied western settlers with tent revivals. The new faiths often urged a return to religious fundamentals, shedding the trappings of more traditional denominations, and called for a purification of both individuals and society in preparation for a second coming of Christ.

In New England, Unitarianism had an outsized influence. Harriet Beecher Stowe, the author of *Uncle Tom's Cabin*, claimed that "all the literary men of Massachusetts were

Unitarians . . . All the elite of wealth and fashion crowded Unitarian Churches."[5] Its advocates emphasized the value of reason, the moral goodness of God, and the intrinsic morality of mankind. The Unitarian commitment to reason intermingled with other intellectual currents of the period. Thomas Jefferson was not alone in thinking that the heart of Christianity was a moral code that could be squared with the conclusions of reason.

A repeated observation of the period was that the new nation was obsessed with the practical. Benjamin Franklin's stove and lightning rod, Eli Whitney's cotton gin, Robert Fulton's steamship, Samuel Morse's telegraph, and New York's Erie Canal spurred the imagination and marked American achievement. Budding politician Edward Everett complained about the relative lack of literary development in the United States, but chalked the apparent lack of interest to the American "demand for political services . . . and the necessity of rendering them."[6] Progress and opportunity, both technological and political, were deeply rooted in the American spirit.

II. DEMOCRACY AND LIBERTY

Major Developments

- Reaction to the French Revolution
- Experience with competitive elections
- Entrenchment of constitutional checks on legislatures
- Growth of religious disestablishment movement
- Rise of universal manhood suffrage

In 1778, France declared war against Great Britain and offered its aid to the American revolutionaries. In 1789, mobs stormed the infamous French prison the Bastille, and the legislature was reconstituted as the National Assembly and adopted the Declaration of the Rights of Man and of the Citizen. In 1792, King Louis XVI was arrested, and months later he was put to death by guillotine. In 1799, a *coup d'état* brought Napoleon Bonaparte to power in France.

In America, the French Revolution was at first seen by many as the dawning of a new era. Republican governments were blossoming, and monarchs were giving up their dictatorial powers. But as events turned sour in France, first with the execution of the king and the rise of the Reign of Terror and later with the end of the republican experiment, the fragility and dangers of popular government were brought home. The founders were well aware of classical examples of democratic governments that too often gave way to demagogues and tyrants, but the news from France highlighted the lesson. French radicalism had doomed the republican experiment in Europe, and many Americans worried that it

---

5 Quoted in Thomas H. O'Connor, *The Athens of America* (Amherst: University of Massachusetts Press, 2006), 11.

6 Edward Everett, *An Oration Pronounced at Cambridge before the Society of Phi Beta Kappa* (New York: J.W. Palmer & Co., 1824), 12.

would doom the republican experiment in the United States as well. John Quincy Adams later informed Alexis de Tocqueville, "[T]he crimes of the French Revolution have made a strong impression on us; there has been a reaction of feeling, and this impulse still makes itself felt."[7]

Domestic events seemed to give some cause for pessimism as well. Remarkably, the noisy and closely contested struggle over the ratification of the U.S. Constitution was quickly put into the past. Leading anti-Federalists accepted the legitimacy of the new federal government and either retired from politics or accommodated themselves to the new constitutional order. George Washington's presidency was universally welcomed. But cracks soon appeared in the façade. James Madison and Alexander Hamilton, former allies during the ratification debates, became heated rivals when it came time to make economic and foreign policy under the new U.S. Constitution. Washington met tax protests in western Pennsylvania with federal troops and worried that rebellion was afoot. As Jeffersonian criticism of the Federalist administration intensified, the Federalists suspected that France was plotting to bring down the American government. The classic cycle of democracy giving way to charismatic leaders and mob rule before collapsing into tyranny seem poised to play out in North America as it had in France.

The United States managed to survive these birthing pangs. There was a peaceful transition of power from the Federalists to the Jeffersonians after the elections of 1800. Judicial review and other constitutional checks of political power were exercised and accepted as legitimate. The United States emerged out of the War of 1812 whole, even if the Federalist Party did not. The Era of Good Feelings after the war seemed to briefly promise the arrival of the kind of consensus politics that the founders had imagined, even as democratic participation in politics expanded.

These readings survey the range of these events and debates. After beating the Federalists at the polls, Jefferson sought both to reconcile them to the transfer of power and to recover what he thought to be the true spirit of the Constitution, while arch-Federalist Fisher Ames saw the United States teetering on the edge of mob rule. Chief Justice John Marshall explained the inevitability of the power of judicial review in a constitutional republic. State constitutional conventions debated and adopted new rules for voting qualifications, expanding suffrage to include almost all adult, white males.

---

7 George Wilson Pierson, *Tocqueville in America* (New York: Oxford University Press, 1938), 420.

THOMAS JEFFERSON

KENTUCKY RESOLUTIONS (1798)

In 1798, the Federalist Congress adopted the Alien and Sedition Acts, which authorized the president to deport aliens and prohibited speech that tended to bring the government into contempt. The legislation responded in part to the increasing tensions with France and the threat of a possible war, and in part to the growing criticism of the administration by the Jeffersonian Republicans. Sedition Act prosecutions were launched against several Jeffersonian newspaper editors and politicians. The Jeffersonians responded by launching a public campaign against the statutes and the Federalists who backed them, and public opinion turned in favor of those who were being prosecuted.

The most visible and significant protests against the Alien and Sedition Acts came in a series of resolutions passed by the Virginia and Kentucky state legislatures in 1798. Those were the only two legislatures completely controlled by the Jeffersonians, and James Madison composed a draft of resolutions to be introduced in Virginia and Thomas Jefferson composed a draft for Kentucky. Several states responded with resolutions of their own denouncing the Virginia and Kentucky resolutions, and Madison left Congress for a seat in the state legislature, where he drafted the Virginia Report of 1799 defending the right of the states to evaluate the constitutionality of federal laws and advocating for a broad right to free speech. The resolutions and report were published together as a pamphlet by the Virginia legislature and widely distributed as campaign documents for the elections of 1800.

There were small, but important, differences between the resolutions drafted by Madison and Jefferson, and between Jefferson's draft and the version of the resolutions adopted by the Kentucky legislature. Most notably, the Virginia Resolutions called on the other states to join Virginia in protesting against the federal laws, while the Kentucky Resolutions hoped that the other states would join Kentucky in declaring the acts "void, and of no force." Jefferson's own draft put less emphasis on rallying the other states and stated that "nullification" was the rightful remedy to constitutional violations by Congress. State legislative protests of congressional actions were not uncommon in early American history, but the Virginia and Kentucky resolutions were particularly notable for their constitutional argument and visible role in mobilizing opposition to the Federalist Party. John C. Calhoun and the state of South Carolina laid claim to the legacy of the Kentucky Resolutions in particular when they advocated state nullification of the protectionist tariff in 1832, though an elderly James Madison publicly argued that the South Carolinians were misusing the resolutions of 1798.

Is there a difference between a state observing that unconstitutional laws are "void, and of no force" and a court doing so? Are laws unauthoritative and void because they violate the Constitution or because they have been declared void by a judge? How does Jefferson understand the relationship between the states and the federal government? Are state governments particular guardians of the liberty of citizens? What are the advantages to positioning state governments as "sentinels" guarding against federal constitutional violations? What are the disadvantages? Should states be able to identify and publicize federal constitutional violations at all?

---

1. *Resolved*, That the several states composing the United States of America, are not united on the principle of unlimited submission to their general government; but that by compact, under the style and title of a Constitution for the United States, and of amendments thereto, they constituted a general government for special purposes, delegated to that government certain definite powers, reserving, each state to itself the residuary mass of right to their own self-government; and that whensoever the general government assumes undelegated powers, its acts are unauthoritative, void, and of no force: That to this compact each state acceded as a state, and is an integral party, its co-states forming as to itself, the other party: That the government created by this compact was not made the exclusive or final judge of the extent of the powers delegated to itself; since that would have made its discretion, and not the Constitution, the measure of its powers; but that, as in all other cases of compact among parties having

no common judge, each party has an equal right to judge for itself, as well of infractions, as of the mode and measure of redress.

. . .

3. *Resolved*, That it is true as a general principle, and is also expressly declared by one of the amendments to the Constitution, that "the powers not delegated to the United States by the Constitution, nor prohibited by it to the states, are reserved to the states respectively, or to the people;" and that no power over the freedom of religion, freedom of speech, or freedom of the press, being delegated to the United States by the Constitution, nor prohibited by it to the states, all lawful powers respecting the same did of right remain, and were reserved to the states, or to the people; that thus was manifested their determination to retain to themselves the right of judging how far the licentiousness of speech and of the press may be abridged without lessening their useful freedom, and how far those abuses which cannot be separated from their use, should be tolerated rather than the use be destroyed; . . . and that in addition to this general principle and express declaration, another and more special provision has been made by one of the amendments to the Constitution, which expressly declares, that "Congress shall make no law respecting an establishment of religion, or prohibiting the free exercise thereof, or abridging the freedom of speech, or of the press," . . . therefore the act of the Congress of the United States, passed on the 14th day of July, 1798, entitled, "an act in addition to the act for the punishment of certain crimes against the United States," which does abridge the freedom of the press, is not law, but is altogether void, and of no force.

. . .

8. *Resolved*, lastly, That a committee of conference and correspondence be appointed, who shall have in charge to communicate the preceding resolutions to the legislatures of the several states; to assure them that this commonwealth continues in the same esteem of their friendship and union which it has manifested from that moment at which a common danger first suggested a common union; that it considers union, for specified national purposes, and particularly for those specified in their late federal compact, to be friendly to the peace, happiness, and prosperity of all the states: that, faithful to that compact, according to the plain intent and meaning in which it was understood and acceded to by the several parties, it is sincerely anxious for its preservation: that it does also believe, that to take from the states all the powers of self-government, and transfer them to a general and consolidated government, without regard to the special obligations and reservations solemnly agreed to in that compact, is not for the peace, happiness or prosperity of these states: and that therefore, this commonwealth is determined, as it doubts not its co-states are, tamely to submit to undelegated and consequently unlimited powers in no man or body of men on earth: that in cases of an abuse of the delegated powers, the members of the General Government, being chosen by the people, a change by the people would be the constitutional remedy; but, where powers are assumed which have not been delegated, a nullification of the act is the rightful remedy: that every State has a natural right in cases not within the compact, (*casus non foederis*), to nullify of their own authority all assumptions of power by others within their limits: that without this right, they would be under the dominion, absolute and unlimited, of whosoever might exercise this right of judgment for them: that nevertheless, this commonwealth, from motives of regard and respect for its co-states, has wished to communicate with them on the subject: that with them alone it is proper to communicate, they alone being parties to the compact, and solely authorized to judge in the last resort of the powers exercised under it, Congress being not a party, but merely the creature of the compact, and subject as to its assumptions of power to the final judgment of those by whom, and for whose use itself and its powers were all created and modified: that if the acts before specified should stand, these conclusions would flow from them[8] . . . that these and successive acts of the same character, unless arrested on the threshold, may tend to drive these states into

8 Among the changes in the adopted version, the legislature deleted his passage indicating that "nullification" was the rightful remedy to constitutional abuses by the federal government, which was merely a "creature of the compact."

revolution and blood, and will furnish new calumnies against republican governments, and new pretexts for those who wish it to be believed, that man cannot be governed but by a rod of iron: that it would be a dangerous delusion were a confidence in the men of our choice to silence our fears for the safety of our rights: that confidence is everywhere the parent of despotism—free government is founded in jealousy, and not in confidence; it is jealousy and not confidence which prescribes limited constitutions to bind down those whom we are obliged to trust with power: that our Constitution has accordingly fixed the limits to which, and no further, our confidence may go; and let the honest advocate of confidence read the alien and sedition acts, and say if the Constitution has not been wise in fixing limits to the government it created, and whether we should be wise in destroying those limits. . . . In questions of power, then, let no more be heard of confidence in man, but bind him down from mischief, by the chains of the Constitution. That this commonwealth does, therefore, call on its co-states for an expression of their sentiments on the acts concerning aliens, and for the punishment of certain crimes herein before specified, plainly declaring whether these acts are or are not authorized by the Federal compact. And it doubts not that their sense will be so announced, as to prove their attachment unaltered to limited government, whether general or particular, and that the rights and liberties of their co-states, will be exposed to no dangers by remaining embarked on a common bottom with their own: That they will concur with this commonwealth in considering the said acts as so palpably against the Constitution, as to amount to an undisguised declaration, that the compact is not meant to be the measure of the powers of the general government, but that it will proceed in the exercise over these states of all powers whatsoever: That they will view this as seizing the rights of the states, and consolidating them in the hands of the general government with a power assumed to bind the states, not merely in cases made federal . . . but in all cases whatsoever, by laws made, not with their consent, but by others against their consent: That this would be to surrender the form of government we have chosen, and to live under one deriving its powers from its own will, and not from our authority; and that the co-states, recurring to their natural right in cases not made federal, will concur in declaring these acts void, and of no force, and will each take measures of its own for providing that neither these acts, nor any others of the General Government not plainly and intentionally authorized by the Constitution, shall be exercised within their respective territories.[9]

9 Among the changes in the adopted version, the legislature changed the last line of this resolution to "and will each unite with this commonwealth, in requesting their repeal at the next session of Congress." The legislature added a new 8th resolution, stating "That the preceding resolutions be transmitted to the senators and representatives in Congress from this commonwealth, who are hereby enjoined to present the same to their respective houses, and to use their best endeavours to procure, at the next session of Congress, a repeal of the aforesaid unconstitutional and obnoxious acts."

FISHER AMES

THE MIRE OF DEMOCRACY (1805)

Fisher Ames was a conservative Federalist from Massachusetts. In running for a seat to the first meeting of the U.S. House of Representatives, he defeated the revolutionary leader Samuel Adams, who had become an anti-Federalist during the ratification debates. He served in Congress through Washington's tenure as president, and then returned to Massachusetts. Failing health forced him to decline the presidency of Harvard University, and he died at a relatively young age.

Ames was known as one of the great orators of his time. As the Jeffersonian movement grew and the monarchy fell in France, Ames became increasingly concerned about the excesses of democracy. He turned to speeches and writings to warn the people against the influence of demagogues. As Jefferson neared the end of his first term as president, Ames feared that the republic was nearing its end as well. The United States was "too democratic for liberty," and the voice of the people was treated as if it were the voice of God.[10] After Jefferson's reelection, he published an essay reminding his fellow Federalists that "every democracy" eventually falls prey to demagogues and is transformed into a tyranny.

Is public opinion a protector of liberty or threat to liberty for Ames? Can Ames's argument be reconciled with any view of popular government? Are constitutional checks sufficient to prevent the United States from suffering the usual fate of democracy? Why are demagogues the greatest threat to democracy? What does Ames mean by "vanity" is the "parent of our errors"?

It has been said that every man may be flattered. . . . There are opinions, which every man wishes every other man to entertain of his merit, temper, or capacity, and he is sure to be pleased when he discovers, that his skillful flatterer really entertains them. He indulges a complacency and kindness towards him, who puts him at peace and in good humor with himself. But to flatter the ignorant and inexperienced requires no skill, it scarcely requires anything more than a disposition to flatter; for with that class of people the very disposition is accepted as an evidence of kindness. It is still easier to make flattery grateful to a multitude, and especially an assembled multitude of such men. No arts are too gross, no topics of praise disgusting. Popular vanity comes hungry to an election ground, and claims flattery as its proper food. In democracies the people are the depositories of political power. It is impossible they should exercise it themselves. In such states therefore it is a thing inevitable, that the people should be beset by unworthy flatterers and intoxicated with their filters. Sudden, blind, and violent in all their impulses, they cannot heap power enough on their favorites, nor make their vengeance as prompt and terrible as their wrath against those, whom genius and virtue have qualified to be their friends and unfitted to be their flatterers. The most skillful sort of flattery is that, which exalts a man in his own estimation by ascribing to his character those qualities, which he is most solicitous to be thought to possess. . . . When therefore a demagogue invites the ignorant multitude to dwell on the contemplation of their sovereignty, to consider princes as their equals, their own magistrates as their servants and their flatterers, however otherwise distinguished in the world as their slaves, is it to be supposed that aristocratic good sense will be permitted to disturb their feast or to dishonor their triumph? Accordingly, we know from history, and we might know if we would from a scrutiny into the human heart, that every democracy, in the very infancy of its vicious and troubled life, is delivered bound hand and foot into the keeping of ambitious demagogues. Their ambition will soon make them rivals, and their bloody discords will surely make one of them a tyrant.

. . . .

10 Fisher Ames, *The Works of Fisher Ames* (Boston: T.B. Wait, 1809), 483.

[Popular opinions] will all be such as the multitude have an interest, or which is the same thing a pleasure, in believing. Of these, one of the dearest and most delusive is, that the power of the people is their liberty. Yet they can have no liberty without many strong and obnoxious restraints upon their power.

To break down these restraints, to remove these courts and judges, these senates and constitutions, which are insolently as well as artfully raised above the people's heads to keep them out of their reach, will always be the interested counsel of demagogues and the welcome labor of the multitude. The actual state of popular opinion will be ever hostile to the real and efficient securities of the public liberty. The spirit of '76 is yet invoked by the democrats, because they, erroneously enough, understand it as a spirit to subvert an old government, and not to preserve old rights. Of all the flattery, the grossest (gross indeed to blasphemy) is, that the voice of the people is the voice of God; that the opinion of a majority like that of the Pope, is infallible. Hence it is, that the public tranquility has, and the democrats say ought to have, no more stable basis than popular caprice; hence compacts and constitutions are deemed binding only so long as they are liked by a majority. The temple of the public liberty has no better foundation, than the shifting sands of the desert. It is apparent then that pleasing delusions must become popular creeds. After habit has made praise one of the wants of vanity, it cannot be expected that reproof will be sought or endured, a stomach spoiled by sweets will loath its medicines. Prudence and duty will be silent.

. . . .

. . . . It may be admitted that no ordinary pressure of grievances would impel a people to rise against government, when that government is possessed of great strength, and is administered with vigor. It cannot be supposed that men conscious of their weakness will attack a superior power. Yet oppression may at length make a whole nation mad, and when it is perceived that the physical strength is all on one side the political authority will inspire no terror.

But surely there is no analogy between such a government and a democracy. As the force of this latter depends on opinion, and that opinion shifts with every current of caprice, it will not be pretended that the propensity to change is produced only by the vices of the magistrates or the rigor of the laws, that the people can do no wrong when they respect no right, and that the authority of their doings, whether they act for good cause or no cause at all but their own arbitrary pleasure, is a new foundation of right, the more sacred for being new.

To guard against this experienced and always fatal propensity of republics to change and destroy, our sages in the great Convention devised the best distribution of power into separate departments, that circumstances permitted them to select. They intended our government should be a *republic*, which differs more widely from a democracy than a democracy from a despotism. The rigors of a despotism often, perhaps most frequently, oppress only a few, but it is of the very essence and nature of a democracy, for a faction claiming to be a majority to oppress a minority, and that minority the chief owners of the property and the truest lovers of their country. Already the views of the framers of the Constitution are disappointed. The Judiciary is prostrate. Amendments are familiarly resorted to for the purpose of an election, or to wreak the vengeance of an angry demagogue upon the senate. We are sliding down into the mire of a democracy, which pollutes the morals of the citizens before it swallows up their liberties. Our vanity is the parent of our errors, and these, now grown vices, will be the artificers of our fate.

THOMAS JEFFERSON

LETTER TO A COMMITTEE OF THE DANBURY BAPTISTS (1802)

Thomas Jefferson was not particularly fond of organized religion. He was even more critical of those who sought to control the opinions of others, and he had a great deal of faith in the virtues of a free exchange of ideas. In 1777, he had drafted a bill for the Virginia state legislature that would have declared "that all men shall be free to profess, and by argument to maintain, their opinions in matters of religion" without legal penalties. His act for establishing religious freedom was finally adopted in 1786. His faith in the efficacy of robust debate was reflected in his oft-repeated celebration of the free press. As he wrote to one correspondent in 1787, "were it left to me to decide whether we should have a government without newspapers or newspapers without a government, I should not hesitate to prefer the latter."[11]

Although the movement against established churches had gained some ground, Jefferson still feared that the major religious denominations were angling to extend religious establishments across all the states. He knew those church leaders regarded his possible election as president as an impediment to their aspirations, and he thought they were right to do so for he had "sworn upon the altar of God, eternal hostility against every form of tyranny over the mind of man."[12] The Baptists were a persecuted minority in several states, and Jefferson took the occasion of his election to the presidency to express his support for the Baptist congregation in Danbury, Connecticut. There he contended that religion was a private matter and that the civil state concerned itself only with actions, not opinions. In the twentieth century the letter became famous for the metaphor of "a wall of separation between Church and State," which the U.S. Supreme Court used to characterize the meaning of the First Amendment.

Does Jefferson regard matters of religious conscience any differently than thoughts on any other subject? Are Jefferson's views consistent with religion being a collective enterprise? Does religious freedom for Jefferson include religious practices or only religious beliefs? What does he mean by a "wall of separation between Church and State"? Why might Jefferson believe that natural rights and social duties are fully compatible?

. . . . [M]y duties dictate a faithful and zealous pursuit of the interests of my constituents, & in proportion as they are persuaded of my fidelity to those duties, the discharge of them becomes more and more pleasing.

Believing with you that religion is a matter which lies solely between Man and his God, that he owes account to none other for his faith or his worship, that the legitimate powers of government reach actions only, and not opinions, I contemplate with sovereign reverence that act of the whole American people which declared that their legislature should "make no law respecting an establishment of religion, or prohibiting the free exercise thereof," thus building a wall of separation between church and state. Adhering to this expression of the supreme will of the nation in behalf of the rights of conscience, I shall see with sincere satisfaction the progress of those sentiments which tend to restore to man all his natural rights, convinced he has no natural right in opposition to his social duties.

. . . .

11 Thomas Jefferson, *The Writings of Thomas Jefferson*, ed. Henry A. Washington, vol. 2 (New York: John C. Riker, 1853), 100.

12 *Ibid.*, 4:336.

JOHN MARSHALL

MARBURY V. MADISON (1803)

The lame-duck Federalist Congress was busy after the elections of 1800. In addition to passing the Judiciary Act of 1801, it also passed a law organizing the District of Columbia. Section 11 of that statute authorized the president to appoint an unspecified number of justices of the peace. John Adams nominated William Marbury to one of those new justiceships. The Senate confirmed his appointment the day before the Jeffersonians took control of the national government.

Marbury's commission was signed and sealed, but not delivered during the haste and confusion that marked the last hours of the Adams administration. Such tasks fell to Adams's secretary of state, John Marshall, who in turn employed his brother, James, to make the deliveries. (Obviously Marshall thus knew the situation well.) Thomas Jefferson, outraged by these last-minute appointments, ordered that the leftover commissions remain undelivered. Determined to hold office, Marbury in December 1801 asked the Supreme Court for a writ of mandamus ordering Jefferson's secretary of state, James Madison, to deliver his commission. The administration refused to recognize the Court's jurisdiction in the matter. In fact, it declined to send an attorney to argue the case or to even admit that a commission for Marbury had ever existed.

The central issue of the Marbury litigation was thought to be whether the justices could order the executive to deliver the commission. Whether the justices had the power to declare laws unconstitutional was not as clearly at issue. To most people, a more pressing test of that power might involve the law repealing the Judiciary Act of 1801. The Court heard a challenge to that repeal at about the same time in *Stuart v. Laird* (1803). Federalists failed to preserve their circuit court justiceships or secure Marbury his office. They neither persuaded elected officials to restore the Judiciary Act of 1801, nor convinced the Supreme Court to declare the repeal unconstitutional. Marbury never obtained his commission.

At the end of his opinion, Marshall determined that a provision of the Judiciary Act of 1789 that purported to give the U.S. Supreme Court jurisdiction over Marbury's case was unconstitutional. Marshall contended that the justices could not take their guidance from an unconstitutional statute but must instead follow the requirements of the Constitution. In doing so, Marshall avoided issuing an order restoring Marbury's commission, an order the Jefferson administration was likely to ignore, while simultaneously affirming the Court's power to declare congressional statutes null and void.

Marshall's argument in *Marbury* became the canonical defense of judicial review in the United States. The argument in defense of the power of judicial review was neither surprising nor original by 1803. Nevertheless, *Marbury* was the first time the U.S. Supreme Court had fully defended the right to declare federal laws unconstitutional. As you read, consider how persuasive Marshall's argument is. How else might judicial review be defended? What exactly is the power that Marshall is defending? Is the power outlined in *Marbury* limited to laws that are clearly unconstitutional? Is it limited to laws affecting the judiciary, or could the Court strike down any type of law? Are the other branches of government obliged to follow the conclusions about constitutional meaning that the Court reaches, or do those conclusions only guide the actions of the judges?

CHIEF JUSTICE MARSHALL delivered the opinion of the Court.

. . .

The authority, therefore, given to the Supreme Court by the act establishing the judicial courts of the United States to issue writs of mandamus to public officers appears not to be warranted by the Constitution, and it becomes necessary to inquire whether a jurisdiction so conferred can be exercised.

The question, whether an act, repugnant to the constitution, can become the law of the land, is a question deeply interesting to the United States; but, happily, not of an intricacy proportioned to its interest. It seems only necessary to recognize certain principles, supposed to have been long and well established, to decide it.

That the people have an original right to establish, for their future government, such principles as, in their opinion, shall most conduce to their own happiness, is the basis, on which the whole American fabric has been erected. The exercise of this original right is a very great exertion; nor can it, nor ought it to be frequently repeated. The principles, therefore, so established, are deemed fundamental. And as the authority, from which they proceed, is supreme, and can seldom act, they are designed to be permanent.

This original and supreme will organizes the government, and assigns, to different departments, their respective powers. It may either stop here; or establish certain limits not to be transcended by those departments.

The government of the United States is of the latter description. The powers of the legislature are defined, and limited; and that those limits may not be mistaken, or forgotten, the constitution is written. To what purpose are powers limited, and to what purpose is that limitation committed to writing, if these limits may, at any time, be passed by those intended to be restrained? The distinction, between a government with limited and unlimited powers, is abolished, if those limits do not confine the persons on whom they are imposed, and if acts prohibited and acts allowed, are of equal obligation. It is a proposition too plain to be contested, that the constitution controls any legislative act repugnant to it; or, that the legislature may alter the constitution by an ordinary act.

Between these alternatives there is no middle ground. The constitution is either a superior, paramount law, unchangeable by ordinary means, or it is on a level with ordinary legislative acts, and like other acts, is alterable when the legislature shall please to alter it.

If the former part of the alternative be true, then a legislative act contrary to the constitution is not law: if the latter part be true, then written constitutions are absurd attempts, on the part of the people, to limit a power, in its own nature illimitable.

Certainly all those who have framed written constitutions contemplate them as forming the fundamental and paramount law of the nation, and consequently the theory of every such government must be, that an act of the legislature, repugnant to the constitution, is void.

This theory is essentially attached to a written constitution, and is consequently to be considered, by this court, as one of the fundamental principles of our society. It is not therefore to be lost sight of in the further consideration of this subject.

If an act of the legislature, repugnant to the constitution, is void, does it, notwithstanding its invalidity, bind the courts, and oblige them to give it effect? Or, in other words, though it be not law, does it constitute a rule as operative as if it was a law? This would be to overthrow in fact what was established in theory; and would seem, at first view, an absurdity too gross to be insisted on. It shall, however, receive a more attentive consideration.

It is emphatically the province and duty of the judicial department to say what the law is. Those who apply the rule to particular cases, must of necessity expound and interpret that rule. If two laws conflict with each other, the courts must decide on the operation of each.

So if a law be in opposition to the constitution; if both the law and the constitution apply to a particular case, so that the court must either decide that case conformably to the law, disregarding the constitution; or conformably to the constitution, disregarding the law; the court must determine which of these conflicting rules governs the case. This is of the very essence of judicial duty.

If then the courts are to regard the constitution; and the constitution is superior to any ordinary act of the legislature; the constitution, and not such ordinary act, must govern the case to which they both apply.

Those then who controvert the principle that the constitution is to be considered, in court, as a paramount law, are reduced to the necessity of maintaining that courts must close their eyes on the constitution, and see only the law.

This doctrine would subvert the very foundation of all written constitutions. It would declare that an act, which, according to the principles and theory of our government, is entirely void; is yet, in practice, completely obligatory. It would declare, that if the legislature shall do what is expressly forbidden, such act, notwithstanding the express prohibition, is in reality effectual. It would be giving to the legislature a practical and real omnipotence, with the same breath which professes to restrict their powers within narrow limits. It is prescribing limits, and declaring that those limits may be passed at pleasure.

That it thus reduces to nothing what we have deemed the greatest improvement on political institutions—a written constitution—would of itself be sufficient, in America, where written constitutions have been viewed with so much reverence, for rejecting the construction. But the peculiar expressions of the constitution of the United States furnish additional arguments in favor of its rejection.

The judicial power of the United States is extended to all cases arising under the constitution.

Could it be the intention of those who gave this power, to say that, in using it, the constitution should not be looked into? That a case arising under the constitution should be decided without examining the instrument under which it arises?

This is too extravagant to be maintained.

In some cases then, the constitution must be looked into by the judges. And if they can open it at all, what part of it are they forbidden to read, or to obey?

There are many other parts of the constitution which serve to illustrate this subject.

It is declared that "no tax or duty shall be laid on articles exported from any state."

Suppose a duty on the export of cotton, of tobacco, or of flour; and a suit instituted to recover it. Ought judgment to be rendered in such a case? Ought the judges to close their eyes on the constitution, and only see the law?

The constitution declares that "no bill of attainder or ex post facto law shall be passed."

If, however, such a bill should be passed and a person should be prosecuted under it; must the court condemn to death those victims whom the constitution endeavors to preserve?

"No person," says the constitution, "shall be convicted of treason unless on the testimony of two witnesses to the fame overt act, or on confession in open court."

Here the language of the constitution is addressed especially to the courts. It prescribes, directly for them, a rule of evidence not to be departed from. If the legislature should change that rule, and declare one witness, or a confession out of court, sufficient for conviction, must the constitutional principle yield to the legislative act?

From these, and many other selections which might be made, it is apparent, that the framers of the constitution contemplated that instrument, as a rule for the government of courts, as well as of the legislature.

Why otherwise does it direct the judges to take an oath to support it? This oath certainly applies, in an especial manner, to their conduct in their official character. How immoral to impose it on them, if they were to be used as the instruments, and the knowing instruments, for violating what they swear to support!

The oath of office, too, imposed by the legislature, is completely demonstrative of the legislative opinion on the subject. It is in these words, "I do solemnly swear that I will administer justice without respect to persons, and do equal right to the poor and to the rich; and that I will faithfully and impartially discharge all the duties incumbent on me as according to the best of my abilities and understanding, agreeably to the constitution, and laws of the United States."

Why does a judge swear to discharge his duties agreeably to the constitution of the United States, if that constitution forms no rule for his government? If it is closed upon him, and cannot be inspected by him?

If such be the real state of things, this is worse than solemn mockery. To prescribe, or to take this oath, becomes equally a crime.

It is also not entirely unworthy of observation, that in declaring what shall be the supreme law of the land, the constitution itself is first mentioned; and not the laws of the United States generally, but those only which shall be made in pursuance of the constitution, have that rank.

Thus, the particular phraseology of the constitution of the United States confirms and strengthens the principle, supposed to be essential to all written constitutions, that a law repugnant to the constitution is void; and that courts, as well as other departments, are bound by that instrument.

The rule must be discharged.

LYMAN BEECHER

PRACTICABILITY OF SUPPRESSING VICE (1803)

Lyman Beecher was a prominent Presbyterian minister and seminary leader. Although the father of Harriet Beecher Stowe (the author of *Uncle Tom's Cabin*), Beecher opposed abolitionism and refused to teach African-American students. Beecher's reform causes were evangelicalism, temperance, and nativism. His anti-Catholic sermon in Boston in 1834 helped spur the burning of a convent in that city.

Beecher was an early leader in encouraging the social and political mobilization of Christian activists to fight a variety of social evils. Religious fervor helped spark a myriad of social reform movements in the early nineteenth century that took on perceived vices from drunkenness to prostitution, gambling to slave-holding, irreligion to indolence. Individual vices were widely understood to cause not only such social ills as poverty and domestic violence but also political damage to the foundations of republican government. Beecher was among those who traced the root cause of vice to inadequate or improper religious training, and urged Protestant evangelism as a part of any cure to such social diseases. But he was also notably practical in his approach to suppressing sin, proposing institutional solutions to what had often been viewed as personal failings. The formation of moral reform societies, the creation of religious schools, and the legal regulation of vice were all offered as more effective in curbing sin than simple preaching. Such large-scale, and often female-dominated, organizations as the Female Moral Reform Society (anti-prostitution), American Temperance Society (anti-alcohol), the American Bible Society (promotion of Christian piety), and the Society for the Relief of Poor Widows with Small Children (charitable) became central features of the early nineteenth-century American landscape.

Is the suppression of vice a public good? Does the tolerance of vice create costs for others in society? Can the language of vice and sin be stripped away from Beecher's argument without damaging it? Is there any objection to mobilizing public opinion to discourage individual behaviors? How do we use public opinion to suppress vice today? Are there any rights at stake in the construction of Beecher's moral society? Why does Beecher think that there is a connection between a moral society and republican government? How far must the virtuous tolerate vice?

. . .

The only question important to be at this time discussed, will be—Is the suppression of vice and promotion of virtue, by means of societies instituted for that particular purpose, a *practicable thing*? . . .

1. Why the influence of union should be less efficacious in reference to the suppression of vice, than in reference to any other object?

Is the superior strength and efficacy of united efforts, experienced, and acknowledged in all other cases, and shall the principle fail in its application to the most important of all objects? . . .

2. . . . In the natural world, God has provided remedies for most of the diseases, and various evils incident to life; in the moral world also, remedies are provided; and it seems to be a maxim of the divine government, that the evils of sin shall not be indispensable, but the effects of our own negligence and folly.

. . .

3. . . . Why is it that sin is always enabled to gain the ascendancy? . . . The majority are in the beginning moral. They have the power, and if awake, the inclination, to limit the prevalence of vice. But they are stupid. They do not consider. Sin is deceitful. In its commencement, while feeble, it hides its deformed visage, its growing strength, and deadly influence, beneath the cover of a name. It calls its indulgences innocent, puts bitter for sweet, and darkness for light. Hence the beginnings of sin pass often unnoticed. . . .

. . . [L]eave society in its natural inconsiderateness, the monster grows unseen, diffuses contagion, and enervates the body, until himself becomes a giant, and society a feeble infant, a helpless victim at his feet.

What then better calculated to answer this salutary needed purpose of keeping awake the attention of the community, than societies of the description we are considering, where every member is a soldier, every soldier a sentinel: and when it becomes the particular duty of a select number, to mark existing vices, to strip them of their disguise, to point out their origin, their consequences, and to prescribe the remedy.

To inconsideration as a circumstance facilitating the progress of sin, may be added indolence and fear. The effort necessary in an individual to reprove a neighbor, or prevent an evil practice, is too great to be undertaken. If the evil be not a personal injury, if it be only of a general nature, graduate and remote, it may rise to a great height, before an individual will volunteer to prevent it. . . .

How easy too, in view of these difficulties, to persuade ourselves that our attempts will be fruitless. Indeed in many cases the persuasion will be just. Our interference would but inflame and increase the evil. How obvious in this case, the necessity and utility of union. Two are better than one, for they have a good reward for their labor; and if one prevail against him, two shall withstand him; and a threefold cord is not quickly broken. What the individual could not do in that he was weak, many individuals combined can do with ease, because they are strong. . . .

4. A society of the description we are considering, is calculated to do good, from the influence it may have in the formation of public opinion.

Public opinion, has in society a singular influence; if vice can in any way instance enlist that opinion on its side, it triumphs. But let the weight of that opinion be laid upon any vicious practice, and it will most inevitably sink under it. Hence it becomes a matter of great importance, that public opinion should in all cases be correct; and be arranged with its whole influence on the side of virtue. . . .

. . . An association of the sober, virtuous part of the community, if that union become extensive, will have irresistible influence to stigmatize crimes, and to form correctly that opinion which is known to possess such influence over the minds of men. The good which is done in this way is exceedingly great; is effected silently; provokes no opposition, requires no expense, and but little exertion.

5. . . . Are any influenced less by the fear of God and the principle of duty, than by a regard to character and the public opinion? These societies contribute to correct that opinion, to array it on the side of virtue, and to make the doing good, indispensable to the enjoyment of a good character. . . .
6. That moral society may do much good, by turning their attention to the rising generation, to schools and private families, and by circulating moral and religious tracts, and by appointing in each school, small premiums, the rewards of good behavior and laudable progress. . . . A religious education forms children to habits of early industry, fixes the moral principle, fortifies against temptation, and prepares them, as they rise to years of discretion, to fill usefully the spheres in which they are called to move. . . .

. . .

Will it be suggested that such institutions may create dissensions in society? . . . Did not the gospel, heaven's greatest blessing, in its progress create dissension, and in the language of its enemies turn the world upside down? The question is, admitting such societies would produce some difficulty, will not the unrestrained progress of vice produce more. . . .

But the idea is fallacious. The suppression of vice by means of societies instituted for the purpose, is the most peaceful, and probably the most effectual method that can be devised; and, the only question is, shall vice have its own course, or shall we unite to limit its influence, to diffuse the blessings of piety and virtue, and to preserve to a good old age, the health and happiness of our nation. . . .

Two considerations render, to us, the preservation of religion and morals, peculiarly important. The first is, the nature of our government; the second, the circumstances in which we commenced our national existence. The iron rod may, in arbitrary governments, supply in some degree, the defect of moral restraint; but in a republic, the virtue of the citizens is the life of the government. In proportion as the fear of God is effaced, crimes will abound, and the arm of power must be strengthened to suppress them; until the nature of the government becomes essentially different.

THOMAS JEFFERSON

LETTER TO SAMUEL KERCHEVAL (1816)

In 1816, Samuel Kercheval asked Thomas Jefferson to endorse his call for a constitutional convention to draft a new constitution for the state of Virginia. Kercheval's effort was part of a recurrent debate in Virginia during the Jeffersonian era over whether the state constitution should be revised so as to make the government more democratic and to give more legislative seats to the western part of the state. Nonetheless, the state legislators successfully resisted the call for a constitutional convention until finally giving in to public pressure in 1829. Jefferson would not live to see the meeting of that convention. Wary of exerting undue influence over public affairs as a consequence of his stature as a former president, Jefferson was reluctant to speak publicly on the convention issue. He was willing to share his thoughts privately, however, and in doing so reemphasized his longstanding belief that constitutional forms should be as democratic as possible and that the constitutions themselves should be subject to frequent revision. It was a point on which he and his close friend James Madison had long disagreed. Although he specifically criticized certain features of the Virginia state constitution, many of those features were shared by the U.S. Constitution as well.

What does Jefferson mean when he says that a government is republican insofar "as every member composing it has his equal voice in the direction of its concerns"? Is he right that this is the measure of democracy? How important is the historical experience with democratic government to determining how extensive the suffrage ought to be? If more democratic governments were found to be less respectful of rights or less economically productive than less democratic governments, would this be a mark against them? Does Jefferson want to maximize democracy? Are there other political values that should be maximized, or traded off against democratic values? Are entrenched constitutions inconsistent with democracy? Are old constitutions likely to be worse than newer ones? Should constitutions automatically expire after some period of time?

. . .

. . . [L]et it be agreed that a government is republican in proportion as every member composing it has his equal voice in the direction of its concerns (not indeed in person, which would be impracticable beyond the limits of a city, or small township, but) by representatives chosen by himself, and responsible to him at short periods, and let us bring to the test of this canon every branch of our constitution.

In the legislature, the House of Representatives is chosen by less than half the people, and not at all in proportion to those who do choose. The Senate are still more disproportionate, and for long terms of irresponsibility. In the Executive, the Governor [who is chosen by the legislature] is entirely independent of the choice of the people, and of their control; his Council equally so, and at best but a fifth wheel to a wagon. In the Judiciary, the judges of the highest courts are dependent on none but themselves. In England, where judges were named and removable at the will of an hereditary executive, from which branch most misrule was feared, and has flowed, it was a great point gained, by fixing them for life, to make them independent of that executive. But in a government founded on the public will, this principle operates in an opposite direction, and against that will. . . .

But it will be said, it is easier to find faults than to amend them. I do not think their amendment so difficult as is pretended. Only lay down true principles, and adhere to them inflexibly. Do not be frightened into their surrender by the alarms of the timid, or the croakings of wealth against the ascendency of the people. If experience be called for, appeal to that of our fifteen or twenty governments for forty years, and show me where the people have done half the mischief in these forty years, that a single despot would have done in a single year; or show half the riots and rebellions, the crimes and the punishments, which have taken place in any single nation, under kingly government, during the same period. The true foundation of republican government is the equal right of every citizen, in his person and property, and in their management. Try by this, as a tally, every provision of our constitution, and see if it hangs directly on the will of the people. Reduce your legislature to a convenient number for full, but orderly discussion. Let every man who fights or pays, exercise his just and equal right in their election. Submit them to approbation or rejection at short intervals. Let the executive be chosen in the same way, and for the same term, by those whose agent he is to be; and leave no screen of a council behind which to skulk from responsibility. It has been thought that the people are not competent electors of judges *learned in the law.* But I do not know that this is true, and, if doubtful, we should follow principle. In this, as in many other elections, they would be guided by reputation, which would not err oftener, perhaps, than the present mode of appointment. . . .

. . . I am not among those who fear the people. . . .

Some men look at constitutions with sanctimonious reverence, and deem them like the arc of the covenant, too sacred to be touched. They ascribe to the men of the preceding age a wisdom more than human, and suppose what they did to be beyond amendment. I knew that age well; I belonged to it, and labored with it. It deserved well of its country. It was very like the present, but without the experience of the present; and forty years of experience in government is worth a century of book-reading; and this they would say themselves, were they to rise from the dead. I am certainly not an advocate for frequent and untried changes in laws and constitutions. I think moderate imperfections had better be borne with; because, when once known, we accommodate ourselves to them, and find practical means of correcting their ill effects. But I know also, that laws and institutions must go hand in hand with the progress of the human mind. As that becomes more developed, more enlightened, as new discoveries are made, new truths disclosed, and manners and opinions change with the change of circumstances, institutions must advance also, and keep pace with the times. We might as well require a man to wear still the coat which fitted him when a boy, as civilized society to remain ever under the regimen of their barbarous ancestors. It is this preposterous idea which has lately deluged Europe in blood. Their monarchs, instead of wisely yielding to the gradual change of circumstances, of favoring progressive accommodation to progressive improvement, have clung to old abuses, entrenched themselves behind steady habits, and obliged their subjects to seek through blood and violence rash and ruinous innovations, which, had they been referred to the peaceful deliberations and collected wisdom of the nation, would have been put into acceptable and salutary forms. Let us follow no such examples, nor weakly believe that one generation is not as capable as another of taking care of itself, and of ordering its own affairs. Let us, as our sister States have done, avail ourselves of our reason and experience, to correct the crude essays of our first and unexperienced, although wise, virtuous, and well-meaning councils. And lastly, let us provide in our constitution for its revision at stated periods. What these periods should be, nature herself indicates. By the European tables of mortality, of the adults living at any one moment of time, a majority will be dead in about nineteen years. At the end of that period, then, a new majority is come into place; or, in other words, a new generation. Each generation is as independent as the one preceding, as that was of all which had gone before. It has then, like them, a right to choose for itself the form of government it believes most promotive of its own happiness; consequently, to accommodate to the circumstances in which it finds itself, that received from its predecessors; and it is for the peace and good of mankind, that a solemn opportunity of doing this every nineteen or twenty years, should be provided by the constitution; so that it may be handed on, with periodical repairs, from generation to generation. . . . [T]he dead have no rights. They are nothing; and nothing cannot own something. . . . This corporeal globe, and everything upon it, belong to its present corporeal inhabitants, during their generation. They alone have a right to direct what is the concern of themselves alone, and to declare the law of that direction; and this declaration can only be made by their majority. That majority, then, has a right to depute representatives to a convention, and to make the constitution what they think will be the best for themselves. . . .

. . .

JAMES KENT AND DAVID BUEL, JR.

DEBATE AT THE NEW YORK CONSTITUTIONAL CONVENTION (1821)

The end of the Jeffersonian era was the beginning of a wave of constitutional reform at the state level. Territories applying for statehood called popular conventions to draft new constitutions, and existing states used conventions to revisit and reform their inherited constitutions. From Alabama in 1819 and Massachusetts in 1820 to New York in 1821 and Virginia in 1829, states debated the fundamentals of their political systems. Among the major issues at these conventions was the scope and nature of elections. A desire to reapportion the legislature and change the rules of suffrage so as to redistribute political power often spurred the call for constitutional change in the first place. As Figure 4-2 indicates, the property qualifications on voting that were once common came under assault in the Jeffersonian period and were largely abandoned during the Jacksonian era.

The debate in New York was reflective of the forces abroad in the land in these years. The New York state constitution of 1777 granted the right to vote in elections to the lower chamber of the legislature to adult, male residents who owned land or paid property taxes. The property requirement was much higher for voters in state senate and gubernatorial elections. The state constitution adopted in 1821 required only taxpaying and militia service, and even those requirements were eliminated by constitutional amendment a few years later. New York, like most other states, had moved to universal, white, manhood suffrage.

Universal suffrage was not adopted without controversy. In New York, Chancellor James Kent was a leading voice in the constitutional convention. A conservative Federalist, the highest judicial officer in the state, and one of the most esteemed lawyers in the country, Kent argued forcefully against extending the franchise for fear that it would threaten property rights and subvert good government. David Buel, Jr., was among his most thoughtful opponents. An upstate lawyer who was then serving as a county judge, Buel would later become a Jacksonian Democrat. Buel pointed to the trend of expanding suffrage that was increasingly noticeable as western states joined the union and the apparent safety of those democracies.

What is the logic for having different suffrage requirements for different elected offices? Is an aspect of checks and balances lost if the upper and lower chambers of the legislature are chosen by the same electorate? Are property qualifications for voting consistent with the principles of republican government? Does it matter how low the property qualifications are? In a modern context, would democracy suffer if those who paid no federal income tax (most individuals with an annual income below around $30,000, or about a quarter of the population) were not allowed to vote? Would public policy likely be any different? Is voting a right, or is it a tool to achieve better government?

CHANCELLOR KENT. . .

. . . I cannot but think that the considerate men who have studied the history of republics or are read in the lessons of experience, must look with concern upon our apparent disposition to vibrate from a well balanced government, to the extremes of the democratic doctrine. . . .

. . .

The senate has hitherto been elected by the farmers of the state—by the free and independent lords of the soil, worth at least $250 in freehold estate, over and above all debts charged thereon. The governor has been chosen by the same electors, and we have hitherto elected citizens of elevated rank and character. Our assembly has been chosen by freeholders, possessing a freehold of the value of $50, or by persons renting a tenement of the yearly value of $50, and who have been rated and actually paid taxes to the state. By the report before us, we propose to annihilate, at one stroke, all those property distinctions and to bow before the idol of universal suffrage. That extreme democratic principle, when applied to the legislative and executive departments of government, has been regarded with terror, by the wise men of every age, because in every European republic ancient and modern, in which it has been tried, it has terminated disastrously, and been productive of corruption, injustice, violence, and tyranny. And dare we flatter ourselves that we are a peculiar people, who can run the career of history, exempted from the passions which have disturbed and corrupted the rest of mankind? . . .

It is not my purpose at present to interfere with the report of the committee, so far as respect the qualifications of electors for governor and members of assembly. I feel grateful if we may be permitted to retain the stability and security of a senate, bottomed upon the freehold property of the state. Such a body, so constituted, may prove a sheet anchor amidst the future faction and storms of the republic. The great and leading governing interest of this state, is, at present, the agricultural; and what madness would it be to commit that interest to the winds. The great body of the people, are now the owners and actual cultivators of the soil. With that wholesome population we can always expect to find moderation, frugality, order, honesty, and a due sense of independence, liberty, and justice. . . . Their habits sympathies, and employments, necessarily inspire them with a correct spirit of freedom and justice; they are the safest guardians of property and the laws. We certainly cannot too highly appreciate the value of the agricultural interest. It is the foundation of national wealth and power. . . .

. . .

. . . The tendency of universal suffrage, is to jeopardize the rights of property, and the principles of liberty. . . . [T]here is a tendency in the poor to covet and to share the plunder of the rich; in the debtor to relax or avoid the obligation of contracts; in the majority to tyrannize over the minority, and trample down their rights; in the indolent and profligate, to cast the whole burdens of society upon the industrious and virtuous; and *there is a tendency in ambitious and wicked men, to inflame these combustible materials.* It requires a vigilant government, and a firm administration of justice, to counteract that tendency. . . .

. . . Society is an association for the protection of property as well as for life, and the individual who contributes only one cent to the common stock, ought not to have the same power and influence in directing the property concerns of the partnership, as he who contributes his thousands. He will not have the same inducements to care, and diligence, and fidelity. . . .

Liberty, rightly understood, is an inestimable blessing, but liberty without wisdom and without justice, is no better than wild and savage licentiousness. The danger which we have hereafter to apprehend, is not the want, but the abuse, of liberty. We have to apprehend the oppression of minorities, and a disposition to encroach on private right—to disturb chartered privileges—and to weaken and degrade, and overawe the administration of justice; we have to apprehend the establishment of unequal, and consequently, unjust systems of taxation, and all the mischiefs of a crude and mutable legislation. A stable senate, exempted from the influence of universal suffrage, will powerfully check these dangerous propensities. . . .

. . .

DAVID BUEL, JR. . . . The question whether it is safe and proper to extend the right of suffrage to other classes of our citizens, besides landholders, is decided as I think, by the sober sense and deliberate acts of the great American people. . . . An examination of the constitutions of the different states, will show us that those enlightened bodies of statesmen and patriots who have from time to time been assembled for the grave and important purpose of forming and reforming the constitution of the states—have sanctioned and established as a maxim, the opinion that there is no danger in confiding the most extensive right of suffrage to the intelligent population of these United States.

Of the twenty-four states which compose this union, twelve states require only a certain time of residence as a qualification to vote for all their elective officers—eight require in addition to residency the payment of taxes or the performance of militia duty—four states only *require* a freehold qualification. . . .

. . .

The progressive extension of the right of suffrage by the reformations which have taken place in several of the state constitutions, adds to the force of the authority. . . .

It is said by those who contend that the right of voting for senators should be confined to the landholders, that the framers of our constitution were wise and practical men, and that they deemed this distinction essential to the security of the landed property; and that we have not encountered any evils from it during the forty years' experience we have had. To this I answer, that if the restriction of the right of suffrage has produced no positive evil, it cannot be shown to have produced any good results.

The qualifications for assembly voters, under the existing constitution, are as liberal as any which will probably be adopted by this Convention. Is it pretended that the assembly, during the forty-three years' experience which we have enjoyed under our constitution, has been, in any respect, inferior to the senate? Has the senate, although elected exclusively by freeholders, been composed of men of more talents, or greater probity, than the assembly? Have the rights o property, generally, or of the landed interest in particular, been more vigilantly watched, and more carefully protected by the senate than by the assembly? . . . May we not . . . without the least derogation from the wisdom and good intentions of the framers of our constitution, ascribe the provision in question to circumstances which then influenced them, but which no longer ought to have weight?

. . . The notions of our ancestors, in regard to real property, were all derived from England. . . . But since that period, by the operation of wider laws, and by the prevalence of juster principles, an entire revolution has taken place in regard to real property. . . .

. . . It is supposed, however, by the honorable member before me (Chancellor Kent) that landed property will become insecure under the proposed extension of the right of suffrage, by the influx of a more dangerous population. That gentleman has drawn a picture from the existing state of society in European kingdoms, which would be indeed appalling, if we could suppose such a state of society could exist here. . . .

. . . The real property [in New York] will be in the hands of the many. But in England, and other European kingdoms, it is the policy of the aristocracy to keep the lands in a few hands. . . . Hence we find in Europe, the landed estates possessed by a few rich men; and the great bulk of the population poor, and without that attachment to the government which is found among the owners of the soil. Hence, also, the poor envy and hate the rich, and mobs and insurrections sometimes render property insecure. Did I believe that our population could degenerate into such a state, I should, with the advocates for the amendment, hesitate in extending the right of suffrage; but I confess I have no such fears. . . .

There are in my judgment, many circumstances which will forever preserve the people of this state

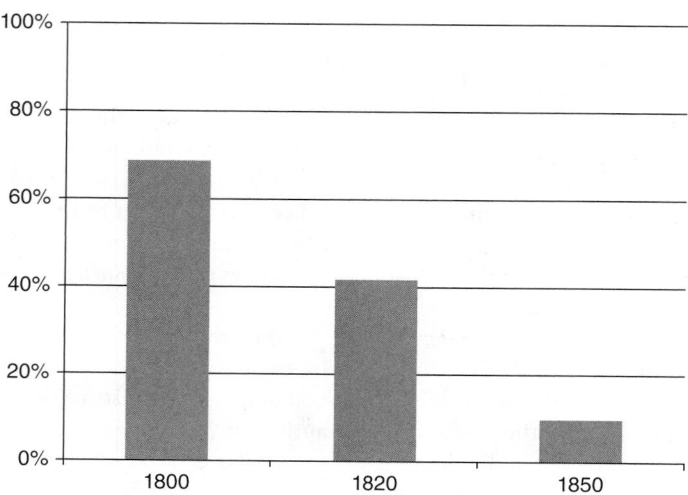

FIGURE 4-2 Percentage of States with Property Qualifications on Voting.

from the vices and the degradation of European population, beside those which I have already taken notice of. . . . The universal diffusion of information will forever distinguish our population from that of Europe. Virtue and intelligence are the true basis on which every republican government must rest. When these are lost, freedom will no longer exist. The diffusion of education is the only sure means of establishing these pillars of freedom. . . . [A] d I feel no apprehension, for myself, or my posterity, in confiding the right of suffrage to the great mass of such a population as I believe ours will always be. The farmers in this country will always outnumber all other portions of our population. . . . The city population will never be able to depress that of the country. . . .

. . .

I contend, that by the true principle of our government, property, as such, is not the basis of representation. Our community is an association of persons—of human beings—not a partnership founded on property. . . . Property, it is admitted, is one of the rights to be protected and secured; and although the protection of life and liberty is the highest object of attention, it is certainly true, that the security of property is a most interesting and important object in every free government. . . .

The truth is, that both wealth and talents will ever have a great influence; and without the aid of exclusive privileges, you will always find the influence of both wealth and talents predominant in our halls of legislation.

III. CITIZENSHIP AND COMMUNITY

Major Developments

- Emergence of political parties
- Development of states' rights theories of the U.S. Constitution
- Uncertainty over deference and elitism in a republic

The leaders of the early republic worried a great deal about community. Classic republican theory suggested that a free society necessitated that individuals subordinate their private interests to the public good of the group, a possibility that might only be realized in small, homogeneous communities. As the French philosopher Jean-Jacques Rousseau described the goal, "each individual believes himself no longer one but part of the unity and no longer feels except within the whole."[13] But the United States did not look like Athens or Sparta, or even Geneva. Was republican government possible within such a large, diverse country?

Every threat to unity foretold the possible end of the republican experiment. For George Washington and Thomas Jefferson, partisan divisions were particularly salient. Washington denounced partisan polarization as a forerunner to rebellion; Jefferson hoped to overcome partisan splits with good government. For John Marshall, regional divisions were particularly salient, and he worried that advocates of states' rights and a strict construction of the federal constitution were subverting the vigor and viability of national government and the instruments of the people of the nation. For Thomas Jefferson and others influenced by the republican tradition, differences of wealth and status called into question how far the American republic had departed from European aristocracies. For a later generation of utopian social reformers, traditional social and economic arrangements would always frustrate man's quest for community, and true progress required radical change that could be modeled in experimental socialist communities.

13 Jean-Jacques Rousseau, *Emile, or On Education*, trans. Allan Bloom (New York: Basic Books, 1979), 40.

GEORGE WASHINGTON

FAREWELL ADDRESS (1796)

Expecting George Washington to step down from the presidency after just one term of office, James Madison prepared the draft of a farewell address for him to deliver as his valedictory to the nation. But Washington decided to serve two terms, by which time Thomas Jefferson and James Madison had become estranged from his administration. Washington and Alexander Hamilton, Washington's former secretary of treasury, significantly revised Madison's original draft. The "address" was not delivered orally but was instead published as a letter in the daily newspaper in Philadelphia. From there it was widely reprinted and published separately as a small pamphlet.

In the mid-1790s, the Washington administration was beset by "Democratic-Republican Societies" that had sprung up across the country. The societies had a range of concerns, but they were all deeply critical of the administration and its policies and opposed the reelection of his congressional supporters. The Federalists suspected that the societies were front groups for the government of France and worried that they would instigate a rebellion against the new federal government. In an address to Congress, Washington denounced "certain self-created societies" for encouraging resistance to federal authority, and privately worried that nothing could be "more pernicious to the peace of society, than for self-created bodies" to take it upon themselves to criticize the actions of the elected representatives of the people.[14] In his farewell address he urged the people to rally around the "unity of government" and resist all "internal and external enemies" to it.

Is Washington right to worry about the fragility of republican government in 1796? Is his advice consistent with or inconsistent with the functioning of democracy? How can citizens simultaneously "concentrate [their] affections" on the government and support "different parties"? Is partisanship necessarily dangerous to free government? How can one distinguish between the "loyal opposition" and the disloyal faction? Does the distinction matter?

. . .

The unity of government which constitutes you one people is also now dear to you. It is justly so, for it is a main pillar in the edifice of your real independence, the support of your tranquility at home, your peace abroad; of your safety; of your prosperity; of that very liberty which you so highly prize. But as it is easy to foresee that, from different causes and from different quarters, much pains will be taken, many artifices employed to weaken in your minds the conviction of this truth; as this is the point in your political fortress against which the batteries of internal and external enemies will be most constantly and actively (though often covertly and insidiously) directed, it is of infinite moment that you should properly estimate the immense value of your national union to your collective and individual happiness; that you should cherish a cordial, habitual, and immovable attachment to it; accustoming yourselves to think and speak of it as of the palladium of your political safety and prosperity; watching for its preservation with jealous anxiety; discountenancing whatever may suggest even a suspicion that it can in any event be abandoned; and indignantly frowning upon the first dawning of every attempt to alienate any portion of our country from the rest, or to enfeeble the sacred ties which now link together the various parts.

For this you have every inducement of sympathy and interest. Citizens, by birth or choice, of a common country, that country has a right to concentrate your affections. The name of American, which belongs to you in your national capacity, must always exalt the just pride of patriotism more than any appellation derived from local discriminations. With slight shades

14 George Washington, *The Writings of George Washington*, ed. Jared Sparks, vol. 12 (Boston: Ferdinand Andrews, 1838), 45, and vol. 10, 437.

of difference, you have the same religion, manners, habits, and political principles. You have in a common cause fought and triumphed together; the independence and liberty you possess are the work of joint counsels, and joint efforts of common dangers, sufferings, and successes.

. . .

While, then, every part of our country thus feels an immediate and particular interest in union, all the parts combined cannot fail to find in the united mass of means and efforts greater strength, greater resource, proportionably greater security from external danger, a less frequent interruption of their peace by foreign nations; and, what is of inestimable value, they must derive from union an exemption from those broils and wars between themselves, which so frequently afflict neighboring countries not tied together by the same governments, which their own rival ships alone would be sufficient to produce, but which opposite foreign alliances, attachments, and intrigues would stimulate and embitter. Hence, likewise, they will avoid the necessity of those overgrown military establishments which, under any form of government, are inauspicious to liberty, and which are to be regarded as particularly hostile to republican liberty. In this sense it is that your union ought to be considered as a main prop of your liberty, and that the love of the one ought to endear to you the preservation of the other.

. . .

In contemplating the causes which may disturb our Union, it occurs as matter of serious concern that any ground should have been furnished for characterizing parties by geographical discriminations, Northern and Southern, Atlantic and Western; whence designing men may endeavor to excite a belief that there is a real difference of local interests and views. One of the expedients of party to acquire influence within particular districts is to misrepresent the opinions and aims of other districts. You cannot shield yourselves too much against the jealousies and heartburnings which spring from these misrepresentations; they tend to render alien to each other those who ought to be bound together by fraternal affection. . . .

. . . The very idea of the power and the right of the people to establish government presupposes the duty of every individual to obey the established government.

All obstructions to the execution of the laws, all combinations and associations, under whatever plausible character, with the real design to direct, control, counteract, or awe the regular deliberation and action of the constituted authorities, are destructive of this fundamental principle, and of fatal tendency. They serve to organize faction, to give it an artificial and extraordinary force; to put, in the place of the delegated will of the nation the will of a party, often a small but artful and enterprising minority of the community; and, according to the alternate triumphs of different parties, to make the public administration the mirror of the ill-concerted and incongruous projects of faction, rather than the organ of consistent and wholesome plans digested by common counsels and modified by mutual interests.

However combinations or associations of the above description may now and then answer popular ends, they are likely, in the course of time and things, to become potent engines, by which cunning, ambitious, and unprincipled men will be enabled to subvert the power of the people and to usurp for themselves the reins of government, destroying afterwards the very engines which have lifted them to unjust dominion.

Towards the preservation of your government, and the permanency of your present happy state, it is requisite, not only that you steadily discountenance irregular oppositions to its acknowledged authority, but also that you resist with care the spirit of innovation upon its principles, however specious the pretexts. . . .

I have already intimated to you the danger of parties in the State, with particular reference to the founding of them on geographical discriminations. Let me now take a more comprehensive view, and warn you in the most solemn manner against the baneful effects of the spirit of party generally.

This spirit, unfortunately, is inseparable from our nature, having its root in the strongest passions of the human mind. It exists under different shapes in all governments, more or less stifled, controlled, or repressed; but, in those of the popular form, it is seen in its greatest rankness, and is truly their worst enemy.

The alternate domination of one faction over another, sharpened by the spirit of revenge, natural to party dissension, which in different ages and countries has perpetrated the most horrid enormities, is itself a frightful despotism. But this leads at length to a more formal and permanent despotism. The disorders and miseries which result gradually incline the minds of men to seek security and repose in the absolute power of an individual; and sooner or later the chief of some prevailing faction, more able or more fortunate than his competitors, turns this disposition to the purposes of his own elevation, on the ruins of public liberty.

Without looking forward to an extremity of this kind (which nevertheless ought not to be entirely out of sight), the common and continual mischiefs of the spirit of party are sufficient to make it the interest and duty of a wise people to discourage and restrain it.

It serves always to distract the public councils and enfeeble the public administration. It agitates the community with ill-founded jealousies and false alarms, kindles the animosity of one part against another, foments occasionally riot and insurrection. It opens the door to foreign influence and corruption, which finds a facilitated access to the government itself through the channels of party passions. Thus the policy and the will of one country are subjected to the policy and will of another.

There is an opinion that parties in free countries are useful checks upon the administration of the government and serve to keep alive the spirit of liberty. This within certain limits is probably true; and in governments of a monarchical cast, patriotism may look with indulgence, if not with favor, upon the spirit of party. But in those of the popular character, in governments purely elective, it is a spirit not to be encouraged. From their natural tendency, it is certain there will always be enough of that spirit for every salutary purpose. And there being constant danger of excess, the effort ought to be by force of public opinion, to mitigate and assuage it. A fire not to be quenched, it demands a uniform vigilance to prevent its bursting into a flame, lest, instead of warming, it should consume.

It is important, likewise, that the habits of thinking in a free country should inspire caution in those entrusted with its administration, to confine themselves within their respective constitutional spheres, avoiding in the exercise of the powers of one department to encroach upon another. The spirit of encroachment tends to consolidate the powers of all the departments in one, and thus to create, whatever the form of government, a real despotism. A just estimate of that love of power, and proneness to abuse it, which predominates in the human heart, is sufficient to satisfy us of the truth of this position. . . .

THOMAS JEFFERSON

FIRST INAUGURAL ADDRESS (1801)

The 1790s were a decade of growing partisan polarization and political strife. The Federalists who controlled the federal government went so far as to adopt the Alien and Sedition Acts of 1798 to muzzle their Jeffersonian critics. When Thomas Jefferson emerged victorious over the Federalist incumbent, John Adams, in the presidential election of 1800, dark forces loomed. Jefferson swept both the popular vote and the Electoral College, but the New England-based Federalists complained that Jefferson's numbers were inflated by the inclusion of slaves in the distribution of electoral votes to the states. Worse, the original U.S. Constitution specified that the runner-up in the presidential contest would become the vice president. Jefferson's electors had also all cast their ballots for his running mate, Aaron Burr, resulting in a tie. The Federalists who controlled Congress in 1800 held up the results as they debated how to resolve the tie vote. Some Federalists favored giving the White House to Burr; others suggested declaring the presidency vacant and installing a Federalist. As Jeffersonian governors readied their militias to storm the capital if needed, Alexander Hamilton persuaded cooler heads in the Federalist Party to recognize Jefferson as the victor. As a result, the world saw the first peaceful transfer of power from one democratically elected head of government to another.[15]

Jefferson's supporters saw the "Revolution of 1800" as a mandate for a change in governing principles, not just a change of government personnel. The supporters of Adams thought the same thing, but were less happy about it. Jefferson faced the daunting task of using his inaugural address to simultaneously lay out his controversial philosophy of government and to pull the nation together after the hard-fought electoral contest. How to rally his supporters without alienating his opponents? As one communications scholar has pointed out, the special challenge of the inaugural address is to "construct a single people out of partisan division," and few inaugurals have felt that challenge as strongly as Jefferson's first inaugural.[16]

How does Jefferson try to overcome partisanship? How does Jefferson display partisanship? In what sense is he "partisan" in the first inaugural? Does Jefferson offer a coherent philosophy of government to guide his administration? Is this a particularly "democratic" vision of government? Is it consistent with the Constitution, or is the philosophy he articulates here fundamentally "anti-Federalist," as some of his critics have charged?

Called upon to undertake the duties of the first executive office of our country, I avail myself of the presence of that portion of my fellow-citizens which is here assembled to express my grateful thanks for the favor with which they have been pleased to look toward me, to declare a sincere consciousness that the task is above my talents, and that I approach it with those anxious and awful presentiments which the greatness of the charge and the weakness of my powers so justly inspire. A rising nation, spread over a wide and fruitful land, traversing all the seas with the rich productions of their industry, engaged in commerce with nations who feel power and forget right, advancing rapidly to destinies beyond the reach of mortal eye—when I contemplate these transcendent objects, and see the honor, the happiness, and the hopes of this beloved country committed to the issue and the auspices of this day, I shrink from the contemplation, and humble myself before the magnitude of the undertaking. Utterly, indeed, should I despair did not the presence of many whom I here see remind me that in the other high authorities provided by our Constitution I shall find resources of wisdom, of virtue, and of zeal on which to rely under all difficulties. To you, then, gentlemen, who are charged with the sovereign functions of legislation, and to those associated with you, I look with encouragement for that guidance and support which may enable us to steer with

15 See Bruce Ackerman, *The Failure of the Founding Fathers* (Cambridge, MA: Harvard University Press, 2005).

16 Karyln Kohrs Campbell and Kathleen Hall Jamieson, "Inaugurating the Presidency," *Presidential Studies Quarterly* 15 (1985): 396.

safety the vessel in which we are all embarked amidst the conflicting elements of a troubled world.

During the contest of opinion through which we have passed the animation of discussions and of exertions has sometimes worn an aspect which might impose on strangers unused to think freely and to speak and to write what they think; but this being now decided by the voice of the nation, announced according to the rules of the Constitution, all will, of course, arrange themselves under the will of the law, and unite in common efforts for the common good. All, too, will bear in mind this sacred principle, that though the will of the majority is in all cases to prevail, that will to be rightful must be reasonable; that the minority possess their equal rights, which equal law must protect, and to violate would be oppression. Let us, then, fellow-citizens, unite with one heart and one mind. Let us restore to social intercourse that harmony and affection without which liberty and even life itself are but dreary things. And let us reflect that, having banished from our land that religious intolerance under which mankind so long bled and suffered, we have yet gained little if we countenance a political intolerance as despotic, as wicked, and capable of as bitter and bloody persecutions. During the throes and convulsions of the ancient world, during the agonizing spasms of infuriated man, seeking through blood and slaughter his long-lost liberty, it was not wonderful that the agitation of the billows should reach even this distant and peaceful shore; that this should be more felt and feared by some and less by others, and should divide opinions as to measures of safety. But every difference of opinion is not a difference of principle. We have called by different names brethren of the same principle. We are all Republicans, we are all Federalists. If there be any among us who would wish to dissolve this Union or to change its republican form, let them stand undisturbed as monuments of the safety with which error of opinion may be tolerated where reason is left free to combat it. I know, indeed, that some honest men fear that a republican government cannot be strong, that this Government is not strong enough; but would the honest patriot, in the full tide of successful experiment, abandon a government which has so far kept us free and firm on the theoretic and visionary fear that this Government, the world's best hope, may by possibility want energy to preserve itself? I trust not. I believe this, on the contrary, the strongest Government on earth. I believe it the only one where every man, at the call of the law, would fly to the standard of the law, and would meet invasions of the public order as his own personal concern. Sometimes it is said that man cannot be trusted with the government of himself. Can he, then, be trusted with the government of others? Or have we found angels in the forms of kings to govern him? Let history answer this question.

Let us, then, with courage and confidence pursue our own Federal and Republican principles, our attachment to union and representative government. Kindly separated by nature and a wide ocean from the exterminating havoc of one quarter of the globe; too high-minded to endure the degradations of the others; possessing a chosen country, with room enough for our descendants to the thousandth and thousandth generation; entertaining a due sense of our equal right to the use of our own faculties, to the acquisitions of our own industry, to honor and confidence from our fellow-citizens, resulting not from birth, but from our actions and their sense of them; enlightened by a benign religion, professed, indeed, and practiced in various forms, yet all of them inculcating honesty, truth, temperance, gratitude, and the love of man; acknowledging and adoring an overruling Providence, which by all its dispensations proves that it delights in the happiness of man here and his greater happiness hereafter—with all these blessings, what more is necessary to make us a happy and a prosperous people? Still one thing more, fellow-citizens—a wise and frugal Government, which shall restrain men from injuring one another, shall leave them otherwise free to regulate their own pursuits of industry and improvement, and shall not take from the mouth of labor the bread it has earned. This is the sum of good government, and this is necessary to close the circle of our felicities.

. . .

THOMAS JEFFERSON

LETTER TO JOHN ADAMS (1813)

In 1787, John Adams published a dense historical and theoretical analysis of constitutional governments. In that work, he objected to the argument of a French economist that republican governments should have only unicameral legislatures because the "equality of all the citizens" meant that there was no need for multiple chambers to represent different orders of society. Adams insisted that "in every state, in the Massachusetts for example, there are inequalities which God and nature have planted there, and which no human legislator ever can eradicate." In a republic there may be "a moral and political equality of rights and duties" and an absence of "artificial inequalities of condition" created by titles of nobility, but there were myriad other relevant inequalities, including wealth, birth, and talent. This "natural aristocracy among mankind" could either be the "brightest ornament and glory of the nation" or "the most dangerous" to public liberty, depending on how their skills and ambitions were managed.[17] Allowing the natural aristocracy to vent their ambitions in a senate chamber may be most beneficial to a republic.

Nearly three decades later, the Jeffersonian writer John Taylor dusted off Adams's work in order to take him to task for being too sympathetic to the mixed constitution of Great Britain and insufficiently appreciative of the principles of republican government. Among Taylor's complaints was that Adams felt the need to make room in every viable political system for "a natural and unavoidable aristocracy."[18] Taylor preferred to reason from the fundamental moral equality of man, but thought Adams was too inclined to see inequalities rooted in nature itself. Adams wrote to Taylor to object to his interpretation of the text. Adams insisted that there was "a natural aristocracy of virtues and talents in every nation," but that this observation was not contrary to "moral equality of all mankind" and that the purpose of government was "securing to all men equal laws and equal rights."[19] Adams grumbled to Jefferson that he would not argue with Taylor over the point "that an aristocracy of bank paper is as bad as the nobility of France or England."[20] Jefferson in turn replied to Adams, agreeing that "there is a natural aristocracy among men," but Jefferson gently noted that the two disagreed over the political implications of that fact. Jefferson, like Taylor, thought Adams's solution of politically empowering and harnessing the natural aristocracy would only lead to trouble.

Is the idea of a "natural aristocracy" consistent with the principles of republicanism? Is Adams right to think that a natural aristocracy is unavoidable in any society? If divisions in society are natural, what is the best way politically to address this fact? Jefferson reframes the problem as largely one of wealth; is he right to think that the wealthy have enough political advantages even in a democracy to not need special constitutional protections? Is Jefferson too quick to dismiss the classical theory (on which Adams relied) that different classes or groups in society should be played off one another within the political system so as to achieve an overall balance?

. . .

. . . I agree with you that there is a natural aristocracy among men. The grounds of this are virtue and talents. Formerly, bodily powers gave place among the aristoi. But since the invention of gunpowder has armed the weak as well as the strong with missile death, bodily strength, like beauty, good humor, politeness and other accomplishments, has become but an auxiliary ground for distinction. There is also an

17 John Adams, *A Defence of the Constitutions of the Government of the United States of America* (Philadelphia, PA: Hall and Sellers, 1787), 108, 109, 116. On his title page, Adams identified himself as "a Member of the Academy of Arts and Sciences at Boston."

18 John Taylor, *An Inquiry into the Principles and Policy of the Government of the United States* (Fredericksburg, VA: Green and Cady, 1814), 9. On his title page, Taylor identified himself simply as "of Caroline County, Virginia."

19 John Adams, *The Works of John Adams*, ed. Charles Francis Adams, vol. 6 (Boston, MA: Charles C. Little and James Brown, 1851), 451, 458.

20 Thomas Jefferson, *The Writings of Thomas Jefferson*, ed. Henry Augustine Washington, vol. 6 (Washington, D.C.: Taylor & Maury, 1854), 209.

artificial aristocracy, founded on wealth and birth, without either virtue or talents; for with these it would belong to the first class. The natural aristocracy I consider as the most precious gift of nature, for the instruction, the trusts, and government of society. And indeed, it would have been inconsistent in creation to have formed man for the social state, and not to have provided virtue and wisdom enough to manage the concerns of the society. May we not even say, that the form of government is the best, which provides the most effectually for a pure selection of these natural aristoi into the offices of government? The artificial aristocracy is a mischievous ingredient in government, and provision should be made to prevent its ascendancy. On the question, what is the best provision, you and I differ; but we differ as rational friends, using the free exercise of our own reason, and mutually indulging its errors. You think it best to put the pseudo-aristoi into a separate chamber of legislation, where they may be hindered from doing mischief by their coordinate branches, and where, also, they may be a protection to wealth against the Agrarian and plundering enterprises of the majority of the people. I think that to give them power in order to prevent them from doing mischief, is arming them for it, and increasing instead of remedying the evil. For if the coordinate branches can arrest their action, so may they that of the coordinates. Mischief may be done negatively as well as positively. Of this, a cabal in the Senate of the United States has furnished many proofs. Nor do I believe them necessary to protect the wealthy; because enough of these will find their way into every branch of legislation, to protect themselves. From fifteen to twenty legislature of our own, in action for thirty years past, have proved that no fears of an equalization of property are to be apprehended from them. I think the best remedy is exactly that provided by all our constitutions, to leave to the citizens the free election and the separation of the aristoi from the pseudo-aristoi, of the wheat from the chaff. In general they will elect the really good and wise. In some instances, wealth may corrupt, and birth blind them; but not in sufficient degree to endanger the society.

It is probable that our differences of opinion may, in some measure be produced by a difference of character in those among whom we live. From what I have seen of Massachusetts and Connecticut . . . there seems to be in those two States a traditionary reverence for certain families, which has rendered the offices of the government nearly hereditary in those families. I presume that from an early period in your history, members of those families happening to possess virtue and talents, have honestly exercised the for the good of the people, and by their services have endeared their names to them. . . . But although this hereditary succession to office with you, may, in some degree, be founded in real family merit, yet in a much higher degree, it has proceeded from your strict alliance of Church and State. These families are canonized in the eyes of the people on common principles, "you tickle me, and I will tickle you." In Virginia we have nothing of this. Our clergy, before the revolution, having been secured against rivalship by fixed salaries, did not give themselves the trouble of acquiring influence over the people. Of wealth, there were great accumulations in particular families, handed down from generation to generation. . . . But the only object of ambition for the wealthy was a seat in the King's Council. . . . Hence they were unpopular; and that unpopularity continues attached to their names. . . . At the first session of our legislature after the Declaration of Independence, we passed a law abolishing entails. And this was followed by one abolishing the privilege of primogeniture, and dividing the lands of intestates equally among all their children, or other representatives. These laws, drawn by myself, laid the ax to the foot of pseudo-aristocracy. And had another which I prepared been adopted by the legislature, our work would have been complete. It was a bill for the more general diffusion of learning . . . to provide in each ward a free school for reading, writing and common arithmetic . . . and from these district schools to select a certain number of the most promising subjects, to be completed at an University, where all the useful sciences should be taught. Worth and genius would thus have been sought out from every condition of life, and completely prepared by education for defeating the competition of wealth and birth for public trusts. . . . The law of religious freedom, which made a part of this system, having put down the aristocracy of the clergy, and restored to the citizens the freedom of the mind, and those of entails and descents nurturing an equality of condition among them, this on education would have raised the mass of the people to the high ground of moral respectability necessary to their own safety, and to orderly government; and would have completed the great object of qualifying them to select the veritable aristoi, for the trusts of government, to the exclusion of the pseudalists. . . .

With respect to aristocracy, we should further consider, that before the establishment of the American States, nothing was known to history but the man of the old world, crowded within limits either small or overcharged, and steeped in the vices which that situation generates. A government adapted to such men would be one thing; but a very different one, that for the man of these States. Here every one may have land to labor for himself, if he chooses; or, preferring the exercise of any other industry, may exact for it such compensation as not only to afford a comfortable subsistence, but wherewith to provide for a cessation of labor in old age. Every one, by his property, or by his satisfactory situation, is interested in the support of law and order. And such men may safely and advantageously reserve to themselves a wholesome control over their public affairs, and a degree of freedom, which in the hands of the *canaille* [the common people] of the cities of Europe, would be instantly perverted to the demolition and destruction of everything public and private. . . .

But even in Europe a change has sensibly taken place in the mind of man. Science had liberated the ideas of those who read and reflect, and the American example had kindled feelings of right in the people. An insurrection has consequently begun, of science, talents, and courage, against rank and birth, which have fallen into contempt. . . .

. . .

JOHN MARSHALL

McCULLOCH V. MARYLAND (1819)

James McCulloch was the cashier of the Baltimore branch of the Bank of the United States. The Maryland state legislature imposed a tax on the notes of any bank not incorporated by the state of Maryland. When McCulloch refused to pay, Maryland brought suit in state court to collect the unpaid taxes. The Maryland government won at trial, and the ruling was affirmed by the Maryland supreme court. As expected, McCulloch then appealed to the U.S. Supreme Court.

The case received extensive newspaper coverage, and the courtroom was jammed. The bank's legal team was led by the rising legal and political star, Daniel Webster. U.S. Attorney General William Wirt also argued on behalf of the bank. They argued that Maryland's tax was an unconstitutional interference with the policies of the federal government. Maryland's legal team included Luther Martin, the elderly state attorney general and a delegate to the Philadelphia Constitutional Convention. They argued that the bank itself was unconstitutional, and the states had full authority to tax any business operating within their borders. The federal bank could hardly expect to compete with state banks while contributing nothing to state coffers.

Oral argument lasted for days. There was little doubt, however, about how the Court would rule. Chief Justice John Marshall's views on the subject were well known, and there was no reason to believe that a majority of his brethren on the Court disagreed with him. While the Supreme Court was hearing oral arguments in the McCulloch case, the Republican House overwhelmingly voted down resolutions to revoke the bank's charter. Shortly thereafter, the Supreme Court unanimously upheld the constitutionality of the bank charter and struck down the state tax as unconstitutional.

The opinion that Marshall wrote for the Court was more surprising. Marshall was not content to declare that the bank was constitutional. His unanimous opinion asserted that the necessary and proper clause permitted the national government to pass any reasonable means to secure a legitimate constitutional end. Marshall also indicated that any state effort to interfere with the national bank would be unconstitutional. "The power to tax," he declared, "involves the power to destroy." Under this ruling, even a tax aimed at all banks might be unconstitutional. Former President Madison complained that this broad interpretation of the necessary and proper clause and the implied powers of Congress obliterated "the landmarks intended by a specification of the powers of Congress." He hoped that "sound arguments & conciliatory expostulations addressed both to Congress & to their Constituents" might yet keep Congress within its original constitutional bounds. Such arguments might cause Congress to "abstain" from the powers that the Court was attempting to give it.[21]

Some states initially remained resistant to the bank and to the Court's decision. Ohio, for example, forcibly entered the bank's vaults and seized the money owed under taxes of the same sort that the Court had struck down in McCulloch. The bank sued, and the Ohio legislature eventually backed down, appropriating money to repay the bank for what the state government had confiscated.[22]

McCulloch v. Maryland is one of the most important constitutional decisions in American history. Marshall's analysis of implied powers and the meaning of the necessary and proper clause had enormous influence. How does Marshall understand the constitutional meaning of necessary and proper? What is the constitutional foundation for that understanding? Is he correct that a "stricter" construction would make government in the United States unworkable? The law incorporating the national bank did not forbid (or sanction) state taxes on that institution. Marshall nevertheless declared the Maryland tax unconstitutional. On what basis did he do so? Why did he assert that a state tax on a national bank is particularly constitutionally problematic?

CHIEF JUSTICE MARSHALL delivered the opinion of the Court.

In the case now to be determined, the defendant, a sovereign state, denies the obligation of a law enacted by the legislature of the Union, and the plaintiff, on his part, contests the validity of an act which has been passed by the legislature of that state.

21 Quoted in Keith E. Whittington, "The Road Not Taken: Dred Scott, Judicial Authority, and Political Questions," *Journal of Politics* 63 (2001): 373.

22 On the background and aftermath of McCulloch, see Mark R. Killenbeck, *M'Culloch v. Maryland* (Lawrence: University Press of Kansas, 2006); Richard E. Ellis, *Aggressive Nationalism* (New York: Oxford University Press, 2007).

The constitution of our country, in its most interesting and vital parts, is to be considered; the conflicting powers of the government of the Union and of its members, as marked in that constitution, are to be discussed; and an opinion given, which may essentially influence the great operations of the government. No tribunal can approach such a question without a deep sense of its importance, and of the awful responsibility involved in its decision. But it must be decided peacefully, or remain a source of hostile legislation, perhaps, of hostility of a still more serious nature; and if it is to be so decided, by this tribunal alone can the decision be made. On the supreme court of the United States has the constitution of our country devolved this important duty.

The first question made in the cause is, has Congress power to incorporate a bank? It has been truly said, that this can scarcely be considered as an open question, entirely unprejudiced by the former proceedings of the nation respecting it.. . .

. . .

In discussing this question, the counsel for the State of Maryland have deemed it of some importance, in the construction of the Constitution, to consider that instrument not as emanating from the people, but as the act of sovereign and independent States. The powers of the General Government, it has been said, are delegated by the States, who alone are truly sovereign, and must be exercised in subordination to the States, who alone possess supreme dominion.

It would be difficult to sustain this proposition. The convention which framed the Constitution was indeed elected by the State legislatures. But the instrument, when it came from their hands, was a mere proposal, without obligation or pretensions to it. It was reported to the then existing Congress of the United States with a request that it might be submitted to a convention of delegates, chosen in each State by the people thereof, under the recommendation of its legislature, for their assent and ratification. This mode of proceeding was adopted, and by the convention, by Congress, and by the State legislatures, the instrument was submitted to the people. They acted upon it in the only manner in which they can act safely, effectively and wisely, on such a subject—by assembling in convention. It is true, they assembled in their several States—and where else should they have assembled? No political dreamer was ever wild enough to think of breaking down the lines which separate the States, and of compounding the American people into one common mass. Of consequence, when they act, they act in their States. But the measures they adopt do not, on that account, cease to be the measures of the people themselves, or become the measures of the State governments.

From these conventions the Constitution derives its whole authority. The government proceeds directly from the people; is "ordained and established" in the name of the people, and is declared to be ordained, "in order to form a more perfect union, establish justice, insure domestic tranquility, and secure the blessings of liberty to themselves and to their posterity." The assent of the States in their sovereign capacity is implied in calling a convention, and thus submitting that instrument to the people. But the people were at perfect liberty to accept or reject it, and their act was final. It required not the affirmance, and could not be negatived, by the State Governments. The Constitution, when thus adopted, was of complete obligation, and bound the State sovereignties.

It has been said that the people had already surrendered all their powers to the State sovereignties, and had nothing more to give. But surely the question whether they may resume and modify the powers granted to Government does not remain to be settled in this country. Much more might the legitimacy of the General Government be doubted had it been created by the States. The powers delegated to the State sovereignties were to be exercised by themselves, not by a distinct and independent sovereignty created by themselves. To the formation of a league such as was the Confederation, the State sovereignties were certainly competent. But when, "in order to form a more perfect union," it was deemed necessary to change this alliance into an effective Government, possessing great and sovereign powers and acting directly on the people, the necessity of referring it to the people, and of deriving its powers directly from them, was felt and acknowledged by all. The Government of the Union then (whatever may be the influence of this fact on the case) is, emphatically and truly, a Government of the people. In form and in substance, it emanates from them. Its powers are granted by them, and are to be exercised directly on them, and for their benefit.

This government is acknowledged by all to be one of enumerated powers. The principle, that it can exercise only the powers granted to it, would seem too apparent to have required to be enforced by all those arguments which its enlightened friends, while it was depending before the people, found it necessary to urge. That principle is now universally admitted. But the question respecting the extent of the powers actually granted, is perpetually arising, and will probably continue to arise, as long as our system shall exist. . . .

If anyone proposition could command the universal assent of mankind, we might expect it would be this—that the Government of the Union, though limited in its powers, is supreme within its sphere of action. This would seem to result necessarily from its nature. It is the Government of all; its powers are delegated by all; it represents all, and acts for all. Though any one State may be willing to control its operations, no State is willing to allow others to control them. The nation, on those subjects on which it can act, must necessarily bind its component parts. But this question is not left to mere reason; the people have, in express terms, decided it by saying, "this Constitution, and the laws of the United States, which shall be made in pursuance thereof," "shall be the supreme law of the land," and by requiring that the members of the State legislatures and the officers of the executive and judicial departments of the States shall take the oath of fidelity to it. . . .

Among the enumerated powers, we do not find that of establishing a bank or creating a corporation. But there is no phrase in the instrument which, like the Articles of Confederation, excludes incidental or implied powers; and which requires that every thing granted shall be expressly and minutely described. Even the 10th amendment, which was framed for the purpose of quieting the excessive jealousies which had been excited, omits the word "expressly." . . . The men who drew and adopted this amendment had experienced the embarrassments resulting from the insertion of this word in the articles of confederation, and probably omitted it to avoid those embarrassments. A constitution, to contain an accurate detail of all the subdivisions of which its great powers will admit, and of all the means by which they may be carried into execution, would partake of the prolixity of a legal code, and could scarcely be embraced by the human mind. It would probably never be understood by the public. Its nature, therefore, requires, that only its great outlines should be marked, its important objects designated, and the minor ingredients which compose those objects be deduced from the nature of the objects themselves. . . . In considering this question, then, we must never forget, that it is a constitution we are expounding.

Although, among the enumerated powers of government, we do not find the word "bank" or "incorporation," we find the great powers to lay and collect taxes; to borrow money; to regulate commerce; to declare and conduct a war; and to raise and support armies and navies. The sword and the purse, all the external relations, and no inconsiderable portion of the industry of the nation, are entrusted to its government. It can never be pretended that these vast powers draw after them others of inferior importance, merely because they are inferior. Such an idea can never be advanced. But it may with great reason be contended, that a government, entrusted with such ample powers, on the due execution of which the happiness and prosperity of the nation so vitally depends, must also be entrusted with ample means for their execution. The power being given, it is the interest of the nation to facilitate its execution. The power being given, it is the interest of the Nation to facilitate its execution. It can never be their interest, and cannot be presumed to have been their intention, to clog and embarrass its execution by withholding the most appropriate means. . . .

. . .

. . . Congress is not empowered by it to make all laws, which may have relation to the powers conferred on the government, but such only as may be "necessary and proper" for carrying them into execution. The word "necessary," is considered as controlling the whole sentence, and as limiting the right to pass laws for the execution of the granted powers, to such as are indispensable, and without which the power would be nugatory. That it excludes the choice of means, and leaves to Congress, in each case, that only which is most direct and simple.

Is it true, that this is the sense in which the word "necessary" is always used? Does it always import an absolute physical necessity, so strong, that one thing, to which another may be termed necessary, cannot exist without that other? We think it does not. If reference be had to its use, in the common affairs of the world, or in approved authors, we find that it frequently imports no more than that one thing is convenient, or useful, or essential to another. To employ the means necessary to an end, is generally understood as employing any means calculated to produce the end. . . . The word "necessary" . . . has not a fixed character peculiar to itself. It admits of all degrees of comparison; and is often connected with other words, which increase or diminish the impression the mind receives of the urgency it imports. A thing may be necessary, very necessary, absolutely or indispensably necessary. . . . This comment on the word is well illustrated, by the passage cited at the bar, from the 10th section of the 1st article of the constitution. It is, we think, impossible to compare the sentence which prohibits a State from laying "imposts, or duties on imports or exports, except what may be absolutely necessary for executing its inspection laws," with that which authorizes Congress "to make all laws which shall be necessary and proper for carrying into execution" the powers of the general government, without feeling a conviction that the convention understood itself to change materially the meaning of the word "necessary," by prefixing the word "absolutely." This word, then, like others, is used in various senses; and, in its construction, the subject, the context, the intention of the person using them, are all to be taken into view.

Let this be done in the case under consideration. The subject is the execution of those great powers on which the welfare of a nation essentially depends. It must have been the intention of those who gave these powers, to insure, as far as human prudence could insure, their beneficial execution. This could not be done by confining the choice of means to such narrow limits as not to leave it in the power of Congress to adopt any which might be appropriate, and which were conducive to the end. This provision is made in a constitution intended to endure for ages to come, and, consequently, to be adapted to the various crises of human affairs. To have prescribed the means by which government should, in all future time, execute its powers, would have been to change, entirely, the character of the instrument, and give it the properties of a legal code. It would have been an unwise attempt to provide, by immutable rules, for exigencies which, if foreseen at all, must have been seen dimly, and which can be best provided for as they occur. To have declared that the best means shall not be used, but those alone without which the power given would be nugatory, would have been to deprive the legislature of the capacity to avail itself of experience, to exercise its reason, and to accommodate its legislation to circumstances. If we apply this principle of construction to any of the powers of the Government, we shall find it so pernicious in its operation that we shall be compelled to discard it. . . .

. . .

We admit, as all must admit, that the powers of the government are limited, and that its limits are not to be transcended. But we think the sound construction of the constitution must allow to the national legislature that discretion, with respect to the means by which the powers it confers are to be carried into execution, which will enable that body to perform the high duties assigned to it, in the manner most beneficial to the people. Let the end be legitimate, let it be within the scope of the constitution, and all means which are appropriate, which are plainly adapted to that end, which are not prohibited, but consist with the letter and spirit of the constitution, are constitutional.

. . .

. . . Should Congress, in the execution of its powers, adopt measures which are prohibited by the constitution; or should Congress, under the pretext of executing its powers, pass laws for the accomplishment of objects not entrusted to the government; it would become the painful duty of this tribunal, should a case requiring such a decision come before it, to say that such an act was not the law of the land. But where the law is not prohibited, and is really calculated to effect any of the objects entrusted to the government, to undertake here to inquire into the degree of its necessity, would be to pass the line which circumscribes the judicial department, and to tread on legislative ground. This court disclaims all pretensions to such a power.

. . .

It being the opinion of the Court, that the act incorporating the bank is constitutional; and that the power of establishing a branch in the State of Maryland might be properly exercised by the bank itself, we proceed to inquire—

2. Whether the State of Maryland may, without violating the constitution, tax that branch?

. . .

[T]he constitution and the laws made in pursuance thereof are supreme; . . . they control the constitution and laws of the respective States, and cannot be controlled by them. From this, which may be almost termed an axiom, other propositions are deduced as corollaries. . . . These are, 1st. that a power to create implies a power to preserve. 2nd. That a power to destroy, if wielded by a different hand, is hostile to, and incompatible with these powers to create and to preserve. 3d. That where this repugnancy exists, that authority which is supreme must control, not yield to that over which it is supreme.

. . .

. . . It is admitted that the power of taxing the people and their property is essential to the very existence of government, and may be legitimately exercised on the objects to which it is applicable, to the utmost extent to which the government may choose to carry it. The only security against the abuse of this power, is found in the structure of the government itself. In imposing a tax the legislature acts upon its constituents. This is in general a sufficient security against erroneous and oppressive taxation.

The people of a State, therefore, give to their government a right of taxing themselves and their property, and as the exigencies of government cannot be limited, they prescribe no limits to the exercise of this right, resting confidently on the interest of the legislator, and on the influence of the constituents over their representative, to guard then against its abuse. But the means employed by the government of the Union have no such security, nor is the right of a State to tax them sustained by the same theory. . . .

. . .

If we measure the power of taxation residing in a State, by the extent of sovereignty which the people of a single State possess, and can confer on its government, we have an intelligible standard, applicable to every case to which the power may be applied. We have a principle which leaves the power of taxing the people and property of a State unimpaired; which leaves to a State the command of all its resources, and which places beyond its reach, all those powers which are conferred by the people of the United States on the government of the Union, and all those means which are given for the purpose of carrying those powers into execution. We have a principle which is safe for the States, and safe for the Union. . . .

We find, then, on just theory, a total failure of this original right to tax the means employed by the government of the Union, for the execution of its powers. The right never existed, and the question whether it has been surrendered, cannot arise.

. . .

That the power to tax involves the power to destroy; that the power to destroy may defeat and render useless the power to create; that there is a plain repugnance, in conferring on one government a power to control the constitutional measures of another, which other, with respect to those very measures, is declared to be supreme over that which exerts the control, are propositions not to be denied. But all inconsistencies are to be reconciled by the magic of the word CONFIDENCE. Taxation, it is said, does not necessarily and unavoidably destroy. To carry it to the excess of destruction would be an abuse, to presume which, would banish that confidence which is essential to all government.

But is this a case of confidence? Would the people of any one State trust those of another with a power to control the most insignificant operations of their State government? We know they would not. Why, then, should we suppose that the people of any one State should be willing to trust those of another with a power to control the operations of a government to which they have confided their most important and most valuable interests? In the legislature of the Union alone, are all represented. The legislature of the Union alone, therefore, can be trusted by the people with the power of controlling measures which concern all, in the confidence that it will not be abused. This, then, is not a case of confidence, and we must consider it as it really is.

If we apply the principle for which the state of Maryland contends, to the constitution, generally, we shall find it capable of changing totally the character of that instrument. We shall find it capable of arresting all the measures of the government, and of prostrating it at the foot of the states. The American people have declared their constitution and the laws made in pursuance thereof, to be supreme; but this principle would transfer the supremacy, in fact, to the states. If the states may tax one instrument, employed by the government in the execution of its powers, they may tax any and every other instrument. They may tax the mail; they may tax the mint. . . they may tax all the means employed by the government, to an excess which would defeat all the ends of government. This was not intended by the American people. They did not design to make their government dependent on the states.

. . .

It has also been insisted, that, as the power of taxation in the general and State governments is acknowledged to be concurrent, every argument which would sustain the right of the general government to tax banks chartered by the States, will equally sustain the right of the States to tax banks chartered by the general government.

But the two cases are not on the same reason. The people of all the States have created the general government, and have conferred upon it the general power of taxation. The people of all the States, and the States themselves, are represented in Congress, and, by their representatives, exercise this power. When they tax the chartered institutions of the States, they tax their constituents; and these taxes must be uniform. But, when a State taxes the operations of the government of the United States, it acts upon institutions created, not by their own constituents, but by people over whom they claim no control. It acts upon the measures of a government created by others as well as themselves, for the benefit of others in common with themselves. The difference is that which always exists, and always must exist, between the action of the whole on a part, and the action of a part on the whole—between the laws of a government declared to be supreme, and those of a government which, when in opposition to those laws, is not supreme.

. . .

We are unanimously of opinion, that the law passed by the legislature of Maryland, imposing a tax on the Bank of the United States, is unconstitutional and void.

This opinion does not deprive the States of any resources which they originally possessed. It does not extend to a tax paid by the real property of the bank, in common with the other real property within the State, nor to a tax imposed on the interest which the citizens of Maryland may hold in this institution, in common with other property of the same description throughout the State. But this is a tax on the operations of the bank, and is, consequently, a tax on the operation of an instrument employed by the government of the Union to carry its powers into execution. Such a tax must be unconstitutional.

IV. EQUALITY AND STATUS

Major Developments

- Growing concerns over American "aristocracy"
- Growing concerns about "leveling" tendencies of American democracy
- Founding of American Colonization Society
- Retrenchment on women's rights

The Americans in the early republic struggled to reconcile their ideals of republican equality with their social and political practices. One historian characterized Virginia politics in the early republic as one in which there was a "firm attachment to government of the rich, the well-born, and the able."[23] The Republican Thomas Jefferson assured the Federalist John Adams in 1813 that "I agree with you that there is a natural aristocracy among men. The grounds of this are virtue and talents," and this natural aristocracy was "the most precious gift of nature" to the possibility of republican government.[24] But often the idea of "the able" ran together with the fact of the "well-born." The ranks of the rich were often assumed to be where the natural aristocracy of virtue and talent could be found that should lead politics and society. The virtue of republican government was often seen as its ability to weed out the well-born ne'er-do-wells who were tolerated and given free rein in aristocratic and monarchical government but who were made to sit on the sidelines in a popular government with real political accountability. John Adams had concluded that "inequalities are a part of the natural history of man." The key to good government was to avoid an "artificial aristocracy" whose status and influence was propped up by the law rather than supported by real talent and virtue.[25]

The idea of a natural aristocracy did not seem to do all the needed work of reconciling the realities of political leadership with the ideals of popular government. John Adams sometimes favored the trappings of the British monarchy in order to lend dignity and weight to government. By contrast, the more democratic-minded Thomas Jefferson liked to wear homespun clothing and set aside his powdered wig. Even the Democratic-Republican Party led by Jefferson did not go very far toward mobilizing a popular vote or extending the franchise beyond those who owned land, but at the same time political observers worried that the pressures facing the new polity had "plunged us into a premature struggle with all our infirmities . . . [and] roused into the utmost possible activity all the unruly passions of our democracy."[26] The newfound freedom that some women experienced in the war was withdrawn as politics settled into more normal routines. In the years after the Revolution, the momentum for the emancipation of African slaves slowed to a crawl, and

---

23 Charles S. Snyder, *Gentlemen Freeholders* (Chapel Hill: University of North Carolina, 1952), 3.

24 Thomas Jefferson, *Memoir, Correspondence, and Miscellanies*, ed. Thomas Jefferson Randolph, vol. 3 (Charlottesville, VA: F. Carr, 1829), 227.

25 John Adams, *The Works of John Adams*, ed. Charles Francis Adams, vol. 6 (Boston, MA: Charles C. Little and James Brown, 1851), 451.

26 Robert Walsh, "Introduction," in *The American Register*, vol. 2 (Philadelphia, PA: Thomas Dobson and Son, 1817), xv.

then reversed. Free blacks found themselves isolated and increasingly restricted by both law and social norms.

Federalists such as Judith Sargent Murray were more likely to express hostility to the democratic impulse. Jeffersonian Democrats might sometimes deride the majoritarian government and prefer checks and balances, but Federalists were more likely to emphasize the need for social hierarchies and deference to the views of social and political elites. For those who doubted the possibility of a multiracial republic, African colonization was one prominent way to deal with free blacks. The debate over emancipation and colonization was primarily a debate among whites, but free blacks throughout the North and border states joined the debate in public assemblies and in print.

JUDITH SARGENT MURRAY

THE NECESSITY OF SUBORDINATION (1798)

Judith Sargent Murray is best known as an early feminist writer, generally focusing on the equal abilities of men and women. But she also wrote on political subjects, and was particularly provoked in the 1790s by the French Revolution and the emergence of the Jeffersonian opposition to the Federalist administration in the United States. She hailed from a wealthy merchant family in Massachusetts. Her younger brother was an active Federalist, with a distinguished military career and stints administering western territories. He was dismissed from his post as governor of the Mississippi territory when Thomas Jefferson assumed the presidency. Murray dedicated her book to President John Adams, and she did all she could to help save her brother's career from "the Jacobins" who had swept the elections of 1800. As she lamented to a sympathetic congressman, the United States had "fallen upon evil times."[27]

Are Murray's arguments consistent with republican government? Is her objection to the franchise or to other aspects of democratic politics? Can her complaint here that American society was failing to acknowledge superiors be reconciled with a position supporting the equality of the sexes? How does Murray understand the relationship between equality and liberty?

. . .

. . . Surely, that state must be fruitful of calamities, which admits not an acknowledged superior; where every person has, in every respect, an absolute and uncontrollable right to consult his own feelings, submitting himself to no other empire than that of his wayward passions.

It is not, in every sense, true, that Nature is equal in her productions. The same plastic hand that formed a Newton, lends existence to an oyster. . . .

. . . The degrees of intellect, if we may judge by effects, are very unequally proportioned. Now a luminous genius darts through the complicated arrangements of nature. . . . But the natal place of this luminary, the same village, perhaps the same family, ushered into being the unfortunate idiot; whose faculties are scarcely adequate to the absolute calls of existence. . . . Is it just to refuse to merit its unquestionable dues? Is it equitable to deny to virtue the palm of honor? Or, ought we to hesitate in doing reverence to a superiority indubitable and decided?

Where is *unvaried equality to be found*? Not in heaven, *for there are principalities and powers*: Not, certainly, in any of the distributions we have traced on earth; for it is unquestionable, that *variety* constitutes one of the principal beauties in the arrangements of nature. . . .

. . .

There is no calculating the disorders which may result from relaxing the series of subordinations. . . . If licentiousness is successful in her imposture; if, assuming the mask of liberty, she completes her deception; if we prostrate before this baleful destroyer, where, I demand, is my safety? What security can I have, that my neighbor, whose sinewy arm can bear away the prize of strength, will not snatch from me that patrimony, which, descending from a virtuous line of ancestors, I have preserved, at the expense of laborious days, and many a self-denying conflict? . . .

. . . Yes, Liberty, sacred and genuine Liberty, draws with precision the line, nor will she permit a litigation of the inherent Rights of Man. She allows no imaginary claims; she is fearful or disturbing the regular succession of order; she is fond of the necessary arrangement of civil subordination; and she dreads that tumultuous and uprooting hurricane,

27 Quoted in Sheila L. Skemp, *First Lady of Letters* (Philadelphia: University of Pennsylvania Press, 2011), 311.

which, in mingling the various classes of mankind, destroys the beautiful gradation and series of harmony, again restoring all that wild uproar, resulting from the rude and misshapen domination of chaos. Yes . . . that people, that nation, that tribe or family, which is destitute of legislation, regulation, and officers of government, must unquestionably be in a deplorable situation. The strong will invariably oppress the weak; to the lusty arm of athletic guilt, imbecile innocence will fall a prey, and there is no power to redress! . . .

. . .

This party fury harrows up the soul!
The whirlwind of the passions tears the breast!
Let sovereign Reason each debate control,
Of calm investigating powers possess.

. . .

It will ever remain an incontrovertible fact, that, while the understandings of men are dissimilar, they can never contemplate persons or things in the same point of view; and, if they would learn to dissent with moderation, and discard from their vocabulary a language, for which, madness only can apologize, this world of ours would be a much more tolerable place of residence, than, in the present disposition of party, it is likely to become.

It is true, I cannot regard a *pure unmixed democracy* as that precise form of government, which is, in *all its parts*, the most friendly to the best interests of mankind. I cannot think that the *art* of legislation is within the knowledge of *every man*. He whose mind is *filled* with agricultural or commercial pursuits, whose education and subsequent occupation has been *principally* directed to a particular business or profession, cannot, I have conceived, obtain sufficient leisure to investigate, with the requisite attention, the great *art of government*; and, as I have regarded power, in *unsteady* and *unskillful* hands, as a great evil, so I have called that man misguided, and an invader of public peace who . . . has inflated the fanciful and superficial with erroneous ideas of retaining prerogatives, which, by their own free suffrages, they had voluntarily relinquished. He who violently or insidiously destroys the unquestionably necessary series of subordination, who produces the various classes of mankind as usurpers on those orders, which, in the scale of being, take rank above them, must inevitably throw a nation or a state into strong convulsions; nor, will reason authorize such an attempt, save in the last extremity. When the officers of government are chosen—when they are legally inaugurated, and have, in due form, taken their appropriate places, I am free to confess that I adopt, in an unqualified sense, the sentiment which Homer has put into the mouth of his Pylian sage; and at least until a *succeeding election*, I would say,

"Be silent, friends, and think not here allowed,
That worst of tyrants, an *usurping crowd*."

. . .

MEMORIAL OF THE FREE PEOPLE OF COLOR TO THE CITIZENS OF BALTIMORE (1826)

African colonization was a popular policy among whites looking for a solution to the continuation of African slavery in the United States. Many leading reformers of the early republic joined the American Colonization Society and other such movements that were committed to removing freed slaves to Africa (primarily the new country of Liberia). Colonization was thought to solve the perceived social and political problem of what to do about the large number of free blacks that a general policy of emancipation would create, and as a consequence to encourage private individuals to be more willing to free their own slaves and facilitate slaveholding state governments in adopting policies liberalizing emancipation.

There were many free blacks already residing in the United States by the 1820s, particularly in more northern states. Their opinion of African colonization was divided. For some, such as those who participated in a public meeting in Baltimore in 1826 and wrote a petition to Congress, colonization was a means of escaping the racist conditions in the American states and extending the aspirations of freedom and republican nation-building to Africa. For others, such as those who participated in a public meeting in Philadelphia in 1817, colonization meant "cast[ing] into the savage wilds of Africa the free people of color" who had already helped to build America and had established ties of affection and interest with Americans (including the population still enslaved).[28]

Do the Baltimore petitioners seem to regard themselves as Americans? Do they appeal primarily to American values in advocating colonization, or do they argue from outside the American political tradition? To what degree are their arguments strategic, designed to appeal to a white audience? Are these black advocates of colonization "pushed" out of the United States, or "pulled" into the promise of founding a new nation? To what extent does this call for colonization echo the European calls for colonization of North America two centuries earlier?

We have hitherto beheld in silence, but with the intensest interest, the efforts of the wise and philanthropic in our behalf. If it became us to be silent, it became us also to feel the liveliest anxiety and gratitude. The time has now arrived, as we believe, in which your work and our happiness may be promoted by the expression of our opinions. We have therefore assembled for that purpose, from every quarter of the city, and every denomination, to offer you this respectful address, with all the weight and influence which our number, character, and cause, can lend it.

We reside among you, and yet are strangers; natives, and yet not citizens; surrounded by the freest people and most republican institutions in the world, and yet enjoying none of the immunities of freedom. This singularity in our condition has not failed to strike us, as well as you, but we know it is irremediable here. Our difference of color, the servitude of many and most of our brethren, and the prejudices which those circumstances have naturally occasioned, will not allow us to hope, even if we could desire, to mingle with you one day, in the benefits of citizenship. As long as we remain among you, we must (and shall) be content to be a distinct race, exposed to the indignities and dangers physical and moral, to which our situation makes us liable. All that we may expect, is to merit, by our peaceable and orderly behavior, your consideration and the protection of your laws.

It is not to be imputed to you that we are here. Your ancestors remonstrated against the introduction of the first of our race, who were brought amongst you; and it was the mother country that insisted on their admission, that her colonies and she might profit, as she thought, by their compulsory labor. But the gift was a

28 William Lloyd Garrison, *Thoughts on Colonization*, part 2 (Boston, MA: Garrison and Knapp, 1832), 9.

curse to them, without being an advantage to herself. The colonies, grown to womanhood, burst from her dominion; and if they have an angry recollection of their union and rupture, it must be at the sight of the baneful institution which she has entailed upon them.

How much you regret its existence among you, is shown by the severe laws you have enacted against the slave-trade, and by your employment of a naval force for its suppression. You have gone still further. Not content with checking the increase of the already too growing evil, you have deliberated how you might best exterminate the evil itself. This delicate and important subject has produced a great variety of opinions; but we find, even in that diversity, a consolatory proof of the interest with which you regard the subject, and of your readiness to adopt that scheme which may appear to be the best.

Leaving out all considerations of generosity, humanity, and benevolence, you have the strongest reasons to favor and facilitate the withdrawal from among you of such as wish to remove. It ill consists, in the first place, with your republican principles, and with the health and moral sense of the body politic, that there should be in the midst of you, an extraneous mass of men, united to you only by soil and climate, and irrevocably excluded from your institutions. Nor is it less for your advantage in another point of view. Our places might, in our opinion, be better occupied by men of your own color, who would increase the strength of your country. In the pursuit of livelihood, and the exercise of industrious habits, we necessarily exclude from employment many of the whites, your fellow-citizens, who would find it easier, in proportion as we depart, to provide for themselves and their families.

But if *you* have every reason to wish for our removal, how much greater are *our* inducements to remove! Though we are not slaves, we are hot free. We do not, and never shall, participate in the enviable privileges which we continually witness. Beyond a mere subsistence, and the impulse of religion, there is nothing to arouse us to the exercise of our faculties, or excite us to the attainment of eminence. Though, under the shield of your laws, we are partially protected, not totally oppressed; nevertheless, our situation will and must inevitably have the effect of crushing, not developing, the capacities that God has given us. We are, besides, of opinion that our absence will accelerate the liberation of such of our brethren as are in bondage, by the permission of Providence. When such of us as wish, and may be able, shall have gone before to open and lead the way, a channel will be left, through which may be poured such as hereafter receive their freedom from the kindness or interest of their masters, or by public opinion and legislative enactment, and are willing to join those who have preceded them. As a white population comes in to fill our void, the situation of our brethren will be nearer to liberty, for their value must decrease and disappear before the superior advantages of free labor, with which their's can hold no competition.

Of the many schemes that have been proposed, we most approve of that of *African colonization*. If we were able, and at liberty to go whithersoever we would, the greater number, willing to leave this community, would prefer *Liberia*, on the coast of Africa. Others, no doubt, would turn them towards some other regions; the world is wide. Already established there, in the settlement of the American Colonization Society, are many of our brethren, the pioneers of African restoration, who encourage us to join them. . . . In Africa we shall be freemen indeed, and republicans, after the model of this republic. We shall carry your language, your customs, your opinions and Christianity to that now desolate shore, and thence they will gradually spread, with our growth, far into the continent. The slave-trade, both external and internal, can be abolished only by settlements on the coast. Africa, if destined to be ever civilized and converted, can be civilized and converted by that means only.

We foresee that difficulties and dangers await those who emigrate, such as every infant establishment must encounter and endure; such as your fathers suffered, when first they landed on this now happy shore. . . . [But] a foothold has been obtained, and the principle obstacles are overcome. The foundations of a nation have been laid, of which they are to be the fathers.

The portion of comforts which they may lose, they will cheerfully abandon. Human happiness does not consist in meat and drink, nor in costly raiment, nor in stately habitations. To contribute to it even, they must be joined with equal rights, and respectability, and it often exists in a high degree without them. If the sufferings and privations to which the emigrants would be exposed were even greater than we imagine, still they would not hesitate to sacrifice their own personal and temporary case, for the permanent advantage of their race, and the future prosperity and dignified existence of their children.

. . .

We have ventured these remarks, because we know that you take a kind concern in the subject to which they relate, and because we think they may assist you in the prosecution of your designs. If we were doubtful of your good will and benevolent intentions, we would remind you of the time when you were in a situation similar to ours, and when your forefathers were driven, by religious persecution, to a distant and inhospitable shore. We are not so persecuted; but we, too, leave our homes, and seek a distant and inhospitable shore. An empire may be the result of our emigration, as of theirs. The protection, kindness, and assistance which you would have desired for yourselves under such circumstances, now extend to us: — so may you be rewarded by the riddance of the stain and evil of slavery, the extension of civilization and the Gospel, and the blessings of our common Creator!

V. POLITICAL ECONOMY

Major Developments

- Establishment of a viable fiscal system for the national government
- Establishment of a national bank
- Adoption of a federal system of protective tariffs and economic subsidies
- Launch of a federal system of internal improvements

The U.S. government was born out of an economic crisis. The inability of the national government to impose its own taxes in order to repay its debts and finance its activities had become unbearable by the time of the Philadelphia Convention of 1787, and the key feature of the U.S. Constitution was the provision of a taxation power for the federal government. How the federal government might use its newfound powers was a source of uncertainty and controversy. During the struggle over ratification, the anti-Federalists had imagined that the federal government might impose such high taxes that the state governments would be crushed and the citizenry would be driven into subjection. The actual battles over fiscal policy that emerged with the establishment of the new government were perhaps more mundane but no less contentious.

The economic policies of the 1790s were largely set by Secretary of Treasury Alexander Hamilton, and immediately served to divide Hamilton from his earlier ally, James Madison, and helped spur the creation of a rival political party led by Madison and Thomas Jefferson. The new U.S. government started with a looming public debt that was not rivaled (in relative terms) until the Civil War. The immediate goal of federal fiscal policy was to draw down the debt through a system of tariffs on imports, excise taxes on the production and sale of certain goods, and sales of public land. Hamilton also favored using fiscal policy to encourage the growth and development of manufacturers and to provide a long-term stable currency, while establishing a Bank of the United States to coordinate federal borrowing and provide capital for private endeavors. The emerging Jeffersonian party generally opposed those innovations and favored free trade, little direct federal intervention in the economy, and fiscal "economy" (balanced budgets and low spending).

The divisions of the 1790s over economic policy laid the foundations for the arguments of the Jeffersonian era that followed. Although skeptical of manufacturing, the Jeffersonians generally made their peace with industrialization. The War of 1812 also exposed the problematic consequences of an inadequate industrial base and financial system, and a younger generation of Republican politicians like Henry Clay and John Quincy Adams pushed not only for the continuation of the Bank of the United States but also for a more expansive system of protectionist tariffs, federal economic subsidies, and "internal improvements" (the construction of roads, canals, and railways).

Alexander Hamilton in the treasury department and James Madison in the U.S. House of Representatives squared off over the foundations of American economic policy in George Washington's first term as president. Hamilton generally won those battles in Congress, and eventually Madison and his allies were forced to accommodate themselves to some of Hamilton's policies (as president, Madison signed the charter establishing the Second Bank of the United States). Hamilton's reports on public credit and manufactures laid out the core of Federalist fiscal policy. John Taylor of Caroline was among the most vocal critics of Hamiltonian economic policies in the early nineteenth century, including those that were being adopted and extended by other putative Republicans.

ALEXANDER HAMILTON

FIRST REPORT ON PUBLIC CREDIT (1790)

Before the election of George Washington to be the first president under the U.S. Constitution, Alexander Hamilton had primarily made his reputation as a lawyer and soldier. He had been a senior aide to Washington during the Revolutionary War and had worked as a lawyer and New York politician during the Confederation period. He had been a leading Federalist in New York, and his skills as a political organizer and publicist were crucial to the ratification of the U.S. Constitution. Much of his focus as a constitutional designer was on matters of national security. As a New York lawyer, he was pivotal in the founding of the Bank of New York, and it was that experience that might have led Washington to pick Hamilton as his secretary of treasury. Hamilton quickly established himself as Washington's chief political lieutenant and an ambitious economic reformer.

Congress moved quickly to impose a system of taxes to fund the federal government. Hamilton's first order of business as secretary of treasury was to devise a plan for dealing with the public debt inherited from the war and the Confederation and establishing the United States as creditworthy for the future. The main bone of contention was how to treat the greatly devalued government notes that were then outstanding. In many cases, the initial creditors (e.g., soldiers who had accepted notes as wages, those who helped finance the war effort) had sold their notes for cash to speculators who paid pennies on the dollar. Many objected to paying face value on the notes to these speculators, preferring either to repudiate the debt or discriminate between the initial creditors and subsequent holders of the notes. Hamilton successfully advocated that all of the outstanding debt be redeemed at full face value, while also urging a system of rotating debt that would allow government notes to be used as a kind of circulating currency but that would commit the government to permanent debtor status (though one with a good credit rating).

Why did Hamilton prefer repaying all debt in full? Is it fair that financial speculators received the full value of the debt while many ordinary citizens received a fraction of what they were owed? Are there ever circumstances in which the public debt should be repudiated? What are the obligations of a new government—or even a new generation—regarding inherited debts? Could politicians in 2050 reasonably repudiate the public debt incurred by politicians in 2010?

. . .

In the opinion of the Secretary, the wisdom of the House, in giving their explicit sanction to the proposition which has been stated, cannot but be applauded by all who will seriously consider and trace, through their obvious consequences, these plain and undeniable truths:

That exigencies are to be expected to occur, in the affairs of nations, in which there will be a necessity for borrowing.

That loans in time of public danger, especially from foreign war, are found an indispensable resource, even to the wealthiest of them.

And that, in a country which, like this, is possessed of little active wealth, or, in other words, little moneyed capital, the necessity for that resource must, in such emergencies, be proportionably urgent.

And as, on the one hand, the necessity for borrowing in particular emergencies cannot be doubted, so, on the other, it is equally evident that, to be able to borrow upon good terms, it is essential that the credit of a nation should be well established.

. . .

If the maintenance of public credit, then, be truly so important, the next inquiry which suggests itself is: By what means is it to be effected? The ready answer to which question is, by good faith; by a punctual performance of contracts. State, like individuals, who observe their engagements are respected and trusted, while the reverse is the fate of those who pursue an opposite conduct.

Every breach of the public engagements, whether from choice or necessity, is, in different degrees, hurtful to public credit. When such a necessity does truly exist, the evils of it are only to be palliated by a scrupulous attention, on the part of the Government, to carry the violation no further than the necessity absolutely requires, and to manifest, if the nature of the case admit of it, a sincere disposition to make reparation whenever circumstances shall permit. But, with every possible mitigation, credit must suffer, and numerous mischiefs ensue. It is, therefore, highly important, when an appearance of necessity seems to press upon the public councils, that they should examine well its reality, and be perfectly assured that there is no method of escaping from it, before they yield to its suggestions. . . .

While the observance of that good faith, which is the basis of public credit, is recommended by the strongest inducements of political expediency, it is enforced by considerations of still greater authority. There are arguments for it which rest on the immutable principles of moral obligation. And in proportion as the mind is disposed to contemplate, in the order of Providence, an intimate connection between public virtue and public happiness, will be its repugnancy to a violation of those principles.

This reflection derives additional strength from the nature of the debt of the United States. It was the price of liberty. The faith of America has been repeatedly pledged for it, and with solemnities that give peculiar force to the obligation. There is, indeed, reason to regret that it has not hitherto been kept; that the necessities of the war, conspiring with inexperience in the subjects of finance, produced direct infractions; and that the subsequent period has been a continued scene of negative violation or non-compliance. But a diminution of this regret arises from the reflection, that the last seven years have exhibited an earnest and uniform effort, on the part of the Government of the Union, to retrieve the national credit, by doing justice to the creditors of the nation; and that the embarrassments of a defective Constitution, which defeated this laudable effort, have ceased.

From this evidence of a favorable disposition given by the former Government, the institution of a new one, clothed with powers competent to calling forth the resources of the community, has excited correspondent expectations. A general belief accordingly prevails, that the credit of the United States will quickly be established on the firm foundation of an effectual provision for the existing debt. The influence which this has had at home is witnessed by the rapid increase that has taken place in the market value of the public securities. From January to November, they rose thirty-three and a third per cent; and, from that period to this time, they have risen fifty per cent more; and the intelligence from abroad announces effects proportionally favorable to our national credit and consequence.

It cannot but merit particular attention, that, among ourselves, the most enlightened friends of good government are those whose expectations are the highest.

To justify and preserve their confidence; to promote the increasing respectability of the American name; to answer the calls of justice; to restore landed property to its due value; to furnish new resources, both to agriculture and commerce; to cement more closely the union of the States; to add to their security against foreign attack; to establish public order on the basis of an upright and liberal policy;—these are the great and invaluable ends to be secured by a proper and adequate provision, at the present period, for the support of public credit.

To this provision we are invited, not only by the general considerations which have been noticed, but by others of a more particular nature. It will procure, to every class of the community, some important advantages, and remove some no less important disadvantages.

The advantage to the public creditors, from the increased value of that part of their property which constitutes the public debt, needs no explanation.

But there is a consequence of this, less obvious, though not less true, in which every other citizen is interested. It is a well-known fact, that, in countries in which the national debt is properly funded, and an object of established confidence, it answers most of the purposes of money. Transfers of stock or public debt are there equivalent to payments in specie; or, in other words, stock, in the principal transactions of business, passes current as specie. The same thing would, in all probability, happen here under the like circumstances.

The benefits of this are various and obvious:

First.—Trade is extended by it, because there is a larger capital to carry it on, and the merchant can, at the same time, afford to trade for smaller profits; as his stock, which, when unemployed, brings him an interest from the Government, serves him also as money when he has a call for it in his commercial operations.

Secondly.—Agriculture and manufactures are also promoted by it, for the like reason, that more capital can be commanded to be employed in both; and because the merchant, whose enterprise in foreign trade gives to them activity and extension, has greater means for enterprise.

Thirdly.—The interest of money will be lowered by it; for this is always in a ratio to the quantity of money, and to the quickness of circulation. This circumstance will enable both the public and individuals to borrow on easier and cheaper terms.

And from the combination of these effects, additional aids will be furnished to labor, to industry, and to arts of every kind. . . .

. . .

Having now taken a concise view of the inducements to a proper provision for the public debt, the next inquiry which presents itself is: What ought to be the nature of such a provision? This requires some preliminary discussions.

. . .

The Secretary has too much deference for the opinions of every part of the community not to have observed one, which has more than once made its appearance in the public prints, and which is occasionally to be met with in conversation. It involves this question: Whether a discrimination ought not to be made between original holders of the public securities, and present possessors, by purchase? . . .

In favor of this scheme it is alleged that it would be unreasonable to pay twenty shillings in the pound to one who had not given more for it than three or four. And it is added that it would be hard to aggravate the misfortune of the first owner, who, probably through necessity, parted with his property at so great a loss, by obliging him to contribute to the profit of the person who had speculated on his distresses.

The Secretary, after the most mature reflection on the force of this argument, is induced to reject the doctrine it contains, as equally unjust and impolitic; as highly injurious, even to the original holders of public securities; as ruinous to public credit.

It is inconsistent with justice, because, in the first place, it is a breach of contract—a violation of the rights of a fair purchaser.

The nature of the contract, in its origin, is that the public will pay the sum expressed in the security, to the first holder or his assignee. The intent in making the security assignable is, that the proprietor may be able to make use of his property, by selling it for as much as it may be worth in the market, and that the buyer may be safe in the purchase.

Every buyer, therefore, stands exactly in the place of the seller; has the same right with him to the identical sum expressed in the security; and, having acquired that right by fair purchase and in conformity to the original agreement and intention of the Government, his claim cannot be disputed without manifest injustice.

That he is to be considered as a fair purchaser, results from this: whatever necessity the seller may have been under, was occasioned by the Government, in not making a proper provision for its debts. The buyer had no agency in it, and therefore ought not to suffer. He is not even chargeable with having taken an undue advantage. He paid what the commodity was worth in the market, and took the risks of reimbursement upon himself. He, of course, gave a fair equivalent, and ought to reap the benefit of his hazard—a hazard which was far from inconsiderable, and which, perhaps, turned on little less than a revolution in government.

That the case of those who parted with their securities from necessity is a hard one, cannot be denied. But, whatever complaint of injury, or claim of redress, they may have, respects the Government solely. . . .

. . .

The impolicy of a discrimination results from two considerations: one, that it proceeds upon a principle destructive of that quality of the public debt, or the stock of the nation, which is essential to its capacity for answering the purposes of money—that is, the security of transfer; the other, that, as well on this account as because it includes a breach of faith, it renders property in the funds less valuable, consequently induces lenders to demand a higher premium for what they lend, and produces every other inconvenience of a bad state of public credit.

It will be perceived, at first sight, that the transferable quality of stock is essential to its operation as money, and that this depends on the idea of complete security to the transferee, and a firm persuasion that no distinction can, in any circumstances, be made between him and the original proprietor.

The precedent of an invasion of this fundamental principle would, of course, tend to deprive the community of an advantage with which no temporary saving could bear the least comparison.

And it will as readily be perceived that the same cause would operate a diminution of the value of stock in the hands of the first as well as of every other holder. The price which any man who should incline to purchase would be willing to give for it, would be in a compound ratio to the immediate profit it afforded, and the chance of the continuance of his profit. If there was supposed to be any hazard of the latter, the risk would be taken into the calculation, and either there would be no purchase at all, or it would be at a proportionally less price.

. . .

But there is still a point of view, in which it will appear perhaps even more exceptionable than in either of the former. It would be repugnant to an express provision of the Constitution of the United States. This provision is that "all debts contracted and engagements entered into before the adoption of that Constitution, shall be as valid against the United States under it as under the Confederation"; which amounts to a constitutional ratification of the contracts respecting the debt in the state in which they existed under the Confederation. And, resorting to that standard, there can be no doubt that the rights of assignees and original holders must be considered as equal. . . .

. . .

Deeply impressed, as the Secretary is, with a full and deliberate conviction that the establishment of the public credit, upon the basis of a satisfactory provision for the public debt, is, under the present circumstances of this country, the true desideratum toward relief from individual and national embarrassments; that without it these embarrassments will be likely to press still more severely upon the community; he cannot but indulge an anxious wish that an effectual plan for that purpose may during the present session be the result of the united wisdom of the Legislature.

. . .

ALEXANDER HAMILTON

REPORT ON MANUFACTURES (1791)

The Report on Manufactures is the third major report by Secretary of Treasury Alexander Hamilton to the U.S. Congress. In 1790, Hamilton had reported on the public credit (advocating redemption at full face value) and the national bank (advocating the establishment of the Bank of the United States), and in 1791 he reported on the mint (advocating the establishment of a national mint) and manufactures (advocating a system of public support for manufacturers).

The Report on Manufactures urged the adoption of a system of protectionist tariffs and fiscal subsidies to manufacturers and selected other industries and provided the intellectual lynchpin for the economic policies of the Federalists, the Whigs, and ultimately the Republican Party of the late nineteenth century. Hamilton's central concern was to protect "infant industries" and a "home market" for American-made manufactured goods and to shift the American economy away from its reliance on agriculture and toward industrial development. The relatively modest policies proposed by Hamilton were soon adopted, but the core principle that the federal government should actively favor and subsidize particular economic interests and activities was much more controversial.

Why did American manufacturers need government support in the 1790s? Are government subsidies for particular industries justifiable as a temporary measure? Under what conditions? Is there a rationale for providing permanent government support for some economic activities? Does Hamilton fairly represent his critics? Are all of his goals for his policies equally attractive? Was there reason to oppose the artificial development of any manufacturing at this point in the Industrial Revolution? Could the nation have been successful if natural economic incentives had never led to the development of an extensive industrial base?

. . .

The expediency of encouraging manufactures in the United States, which was not long since deemed very questionable, appears at this time to be pretty generally admitted. The embarrassments which have obstructed the progress of our external trade, have led to serious reflections on the necessity of enlarging the sphere of our domestic commerce. The restrictive regulations, which, in foreign markets, abridge the vent of the increasing surplus of our agricultural produce, serve to beget an earnest desire that a more extensive demand for that surplus may be created at home; and the complete success which has rewarded manufacturing enterprise in some valuable branches, conspiring with the promising symptoms which attend some less mature essays in others, justify a hope that the obstacles to the growth of this species of industry are less formidable than they were apprehended to be, and that it is not difficult to find, in its further extension, a full indemnification for any external disadvantages, which are or may be experienced, as well as an accession of resources, favorable to national independence and safety.

There are still, nevertheless, respectable patrons of opinions unfriendly to the encouragement of manufactures. The following are, substantially, the arguments by which these opinions are defended:

"In every country (say those who entertain them) agriculture is the most beneficial and productive object of human industry. . . . Nothing can afford so advantageous an employment for capital and labor, as the conversion of this extensive wilderness into cultivated farms. Nothing, equally with this, can contribute to the population, strength, and real riches of the country.

"To endeavor, by the extraordinary patronage of government, to accelerate the growth of manufactures, is, in fact, to endeavor, by force and art, to transfer the natural current of industry from a more to a less beneficial channel. Whatever has such a tendency, must necessarily be unwise; indeed, it can hardly ever be wise in a government to attempt to give a direction to the industry of its citizens. This, under the quick-sighted guidance of private interest, will, if left to itself, infallibly find its own way to the most profitable employment; and it is by such employment, that the public prosperity will be most effectually promoted. To leave industry to itself, therefore, is, in almost every case, the soundest as well as the simplest policy.

"This policy is not only recommended to the United States, by considerations which affect all nations; it is, in a manner, dictated to them by the imperious force of a very peculiar situation. The smallness of their population compared with their territory; the constant allurements to emigration from the settled to the unsettled parts of the country; the facility with which the less independent condition of an artisan can be exchanged for the more independent condition of a farmer;—these, and similar causes, conspire to produce, and, for a length of time, must continue to occasion, a scarcity of hands for manufacturing occupation, and dearness of labor generally. . . .

"If, contrary to the natural course of things, an unseasonable and premature spring can be given to certain fabrics, by heavy duties, prohibitions, bounties, or by other forced expedients, this will only be to sacrifice the interests of the community to those of particular classes. Besides the misdirection of labor, a virtual monopoly will be given to the persons employed on such fabrics; and an enhancement of price, the inevitable consequence of every monopoly, must be defrayed at the expense of the other parts of society. It is far preferable, that those persons should be engaged in the cultivation of the earth, and that we should procure, in exchange for its productions, the commodities with which foreigners are able to supply us in greater perfection and upon better terms."

. . .

It ought readily be conceded that the cultivation of the earth, as the primary and most certain source of national supply, as the immediate and chief source of subsistence to a man, as the principal source of those materials which constitute the nutriment of other kinds of labor, as including a state most favorable to the freedom and independence of the human mind—one, perhaps, most conducive to the multiplication of the human species, has intrinsically a strong claim to pre-eminence over every other kind of industry.

But, that it has a title to anything like an exclusive predilection, in any country, ought to be admitted with great caution; that it is even more productive than every other branch of industry, requires more evidence than has yet been given in support of the position. That its real interests, precious and important as, without the help of exaggeration, they truly are, will be advanced, rather than injured, by the due encouragement of manufactures, may, it is believed, be satisfactorily demonstrated. . . .

. . .

It is now proper . . . to enumerate the principal circumstances from which it may be inferred that manufacturing establishments not only occasion a positive augmentation of the produce and revenue of the society, but that they contribute essentially to rendering them greater than they could possibly be without such establishments. These circumstances are:

1. The division of labor.
2. An extension of the use of machinery.
3. Additional employment to classes of the community not ordinarily engaged in the business.
4. The promoting of emigration from foreign countries.
5. The furnishing greater scope for the diversity of talents and dispositions, which discriminate men from each other.
6. The affording a more ample and various field for enterprise.
7. The creating, in some instances, a new, and securing, in all, a more certain and steady demand for the surplus produce of the soil.

. . .

1. *As to the division of labor*

It has justly been observed, that there is scarcely any thing of greater moment in the economy of a nation than the proper division of labor. The separation of occupations causes each to be carried to a much greater perfection than it could possibly acquire if they were blended. This arises principally from three circumstances:

1st. The greater skill and dexterity naturally resulting from a constant and undivided application to a single object. . . .

2d. The economy of time, by avoiding the loss of it, incident to a frequent transition from one operation to another of a different nature. . . .

3d. An extension of the use of machinery. A man occupied on a single object will have it more in his power, and will be more naturally led to exert his imagination, in devising methods to facilitate and abridge labor, than if he were perplexed by a variety of independent and dissimilar operations. . . .

And from these causes united, the mere separation of the occupation of the cultivator from that of the artificer, has the effect of augmenting the productive powers of labor, and with them, the total mass of the produce or revenue of a country. In this single view of the subject, therefore, the utility of artificers or manufacturers, towards producing an increase of productive industry, is apparent.

2. *As to an extension of the use of machinery, a point which, though partly anticipated, requires to be placed in one or two additional lights*

The employment of machinery forms an item of great importance in the general mass of national industry. It is an artificial force brought in aid of the natural force of man; and, to all the purposes of labor, is an increase of hands, an accession of strength, unencumbered too by the expense of maintaining the laborer. May it not, therefore, be fairly inferred, that those occupations which give greatest scope to the use of this auxiliary, contribute most to the general stock of industrious effort, and, in consequence, to the general product of industry?

. . .

3. *As to the additional employment of classes of the community not originally engaged in the particular business*

This is not among the least valuable of the means by which manufacturing institutions contribute to augment the general stock of industry and production. In places where those institutions prevail, besides the persons regularly engaged in them, they afford occasional and extra employment to industrious individuals and families, who are willing to devote the leisure resulting from the intermissions of their ordinary pursuits to collateral labors, as a resource for multiplying their acquisitions or their enjoyments. The husbandman himself experiences a new source of profit and support from the increased industry of his wife and daughters, invited and stimulated by the demands of the neighboring manufactories.

Besides this advantage of occasional employment to classes having different occupations, there is another, of a nature allied to it, and of a similar tendency. This is the employment of persons who would otherwise be idle, and in many cases a burthen on the community, either from the bias of temper, habit, infirmity of body, or some other cause, indisposing or disqualifying them for the toils of the country. It is worthy of particular remark that, in general, women and children are rendered more useful, and the latter more early useful, by manufacturing establishments, than they would otherwise be. Of the number of persons employed in the cotton manufactories of Great Britain, it is computed that four sevenths, nearly, are women and children, of whom the greatest proportion are children, and many of them of a tender age.

And thus it appears to be one of the attributes of manufactures, and one of no small consequence, to give occasion to the exertion of a greater quantity of industry, even by the same number of persons, where they happen to prevail, than would exist if there were no such establishments.

4. *As to the promoting of emigration from foreign countries*

. . . Manufacturers who, listening to the powerful invitations of a better price for their fabrics or their labor, of greater cheapness of provisions and raw materials, of an exemption from the chief part of the taxes, burthens, and restraints which they endure in the Old World, of greater personal independence and consequence, under the operation of a more equal government, and of what is far more precious than mere religious toleration, a perfect equality of religious privileges, would probably flock from Europe to the United States, to pursue their own trades or professions, if they were once made sensible of the advantages they would enjoy, and were inspired with an assurance of encouragement and employment, will, with difficulty, be induced to transplant themselves, with a view to becoming cultivators of land.

. . .

5. *As to the furnishing greater scope for the diversity of talents and dispositions, which discriminate men from each other*

This is a much more powerful means of augmenting the fund of national industry, than may at first sight appear. It is a just observation, that minds of the strongest and most active powers for their proper objects, fall below mediocrity, and labor without effect, if confined to uncongenial pursuits. And it is thence to be inferred, that the results of human exertion may be immensely increased by diversifying its objects. When all the different kinds of industry obtain in a community, each individual can find his proper element, and can call into activity the whole vigor of his nature. And the community is benefited by the services of its respective members, in the manner in which each can serve it with most effect.

. . .

6. *As to the affording a more ample and various field for enterprise*

This also is of greater consequence in the general scale of national exertion than might, perhaps, on a superficial view be supposed, and has effects not altogether dissimilar from those of the circumstance last noticed. To cherish and stimulate the activity of the human mind, by multiplying the objects of enterprise, is not among the least considerable of the expedients by which the wealth of a nation may be promoted. Even things in themselves not positively advantageous sometimes become so, by their tendency to provoke exertion. Every new scene which is opened to the busy nature of man to rouse and exert itself, is the addition of a new energy to the general stock of effort.

The spirit of enterprise, useful and prolific as it is, must necessarily be contracted or expanded, in proportion to the simplicity or variety of the occupations and productions which are to be found in a society. It must be less in a nation of mere cultivators, than in a nation of cultivators and merchants; less in a nation of cultivators and merchants, than in a nation of cultivators, artificers, and merchants.

7. *As to the creating, in some instances, a new, and securing, in all, a more certain and steady demand for the surplus produce of the soil*

This is among the most important of the circumstances which have been indicated. It is a principal means by which the establishment of manufactures contributes to an augmentation of the produce or revenue of a country, and has an immediate and direct relation to the prosperity of agriculture.

It is evident that the exertions of the husbandman will be steady or fluctuating, vigorous or feeble, in proportion to the steadiness or fluctuation, adequateness or inadequateness, of the markets on which he must depend for the vent of the surplus which may be produced by his labor; and that such surplus, in the ordinary course of things, will be greater or less in the same proportion.

For the purpose of this vent, a domestic market is greatly to be preferred to a foreign one; because it is, in the nature of things, far more to be relied upon.

It is a primary object of the policy of nations, to be able to supply themselves with subsistence from their own soils; and manufacturing nations, as far as circumstances permit, endeavor to procure from the same source the raw materials necessary for their own fabrics. . . .

. . .

To secure such a market there is no other expedient than to promote manufacturing establishments. Manufacturers, who constitute the most numerous class, after the cultivators of land, are for that reason the principal consumers of the surplus of their labor.

. . .

The remaining objections to a particular encouragement of manufactures in the United States now require to be examined.

One of these turns on the proposition, that industry, if left to itself, will naturally find its way to the most useful and profitable employment. Whence it is inferred that manufactures, without the aid of government, will grow up as soon and as fast as the natural state of things and the interest of the community may require.

. . .

Experience teaches, that men are often so much governed by what they are accustomed to see and practice, that the simplest and most obvious improvements, in the most ordinary occupations, are adopted with hesitation, reluctance, and by slow gradations. The spontaneous transition to new pursuits, in a community long habituated to different ones, may be expected to be attended with proportionally greater difficulty. When former occupations ceased to yield a profit adequate to the subsistence of their followers, or when there was an absolute deficiency of employment in them, owing to the superabundance of hands, changes would ensue; but these changes would be likely to be more tardy than might consist with the interest either of individuals or of the society. . . .

. . .

The superiority antecedently enjoyed by nations who have preoccupied and perfected a branch of industry, constitutes a more formidable obstacle than either of those which have been mentioned, to the introduction of the same branch into a country in which it did not before exist. To maintain, between the recent establishments of one country, and the long-matured establishments of another country, a competition upon equal terms, both as to quality and price, is, in most cases, impracticable. The disparity, in the one, or in the other, or in both, must necessarily be so considerable, as to forbid a successful rivalship, without the extraordinary aid and protection of government.

But the greatest obstacle of all to the successful prosecution of a new branch of industry in a country in which it was before unknown, consists, as far as the instances apply, in the bounties, premiums, and other aids which are granted, in a variety of cases, by the nations in which the establishments to be imitated are previously introduced. It is well known . . . that certain nations grant bounties on the exportation of particular commodities, to enable their own workmen to undersell and supplant all competitors in the countries to which those commodities are sent. Hence the undertakers of a new manufacture have to contend, not only with the natural disadvantages of a new undertaking, but with the gratuities and remunerations which other governments bestow. To be enabled to contend with success, it is evident that the interference and aid of their own governments are indispensable.

. . .

Whatever room there may be for an expectation that the industry of a people, under the direction of private interest, will, upon equal terms, find out the most beneficial employment for itself, there is none for a reliance that it will struggle against the force of unequal terms, or will, of itself, surmount all the adventitious barriers to a successful competition which may have been erected, either by the advantages naturally acquired from practice and previous possession of the ground, or by those which may have sprung from positive regulations and an artificial policy. . . .

The objections to the pursuit of manufactures in the United States which next present themselves to discussion, represent an impracticability of success, arising from three causes: scarcity of hands, dearness of labor, want of capital.

With regard to scarcity of hands, the fact itself must be applied with no small qualification to certain parts of the United States. There are large districts which may be considered as pretty fully peopled; and which, notwithstanding a continual drain for distant settlement, are thickly interspersed with flourishing and increasing towns. If these districts have not already reached the point at which the complaint of scarcity of hands ceases, they are not remote from it, and are approaching fast towards it; and having, perhaps, fewer attractions to agriculture than some other parts of the Union, they exhibit a proportionally stronger tendency towards other kinds of industry. In these districts may be discerned no inconsiderable maturity for manufacturing establishments.

But there are circumstances which have been already noticed, with another view, that materially diminish, everywhere, the effect of a scarcity of hands. These circumstances are: the great use which can be made of women and children, on which point a very pregnant and instructive fact has been mentioned—the vast extension given by late improvements to the employment of machines—which, substituting the agency of fire and water, has prodigiously lessened the necessity for manual labor; the employment of persons ordinarily engaged in other occupations, during the seasons or hours of leisure, which, besides giving occasion to the exertion of a greater quantity of labor, by the same number of persons, and thereby increasing the general stock of labor as has been elsewhere remarked, may also be taken into the calculation, as a resource for obviating the scarcity of hands; lastly, the attraction of foreign emigrants. . . .

It may be affirmed, therefore, in respect to hands for carrying on manufactures, that we shall in a great measure, trade upon a foreign stock, reserving our own for the cultivation of our lands and the manning of our ships, as far as character and circumstances shall incline. . . .

. . .

The following considerations are of a nature to remove all inquietude on the score of the want of capital:

The introduction of banks, as has been shown on another occasion, has a powerful tendency to extend the active capital of a country. Experience of the utility of these institutions is multiplying them in the United States. It is probable that they will be established wherever they can exist with advantage; and wherever they can be supported, if administered with prudence, they will add new energies to all pecuniary operations.

The aid of foreign capital may safely, and with considerable latitude, be taken into calculation. . . .

It is not impossible, that there may be persons disposed to look, with a jealous eye, on the introduction of foreign capital, as if it were an instrument to deprive our own citizens of the profits of our own industry; but, perhaps, there never could be a more unreasonable jealousy. Instead of being viewed as a rival, it ought to be considered as a most valuable auxiliary, conducing to put in motion a greater quantity of productive labor, and a greater portion of useful enterprise, than could exist without it. . . .

But, while there are circumstances sufficiently strong to authorize a considerable degree of reliance on the aid of foreign capital, towards the attainment of the object in view, it is satisfactory to have good grounds of assurance, that there are domestic resources, of themselves adequate to it. It happens that there is a species of capital, actually existing with the United States, which relieves from all inquietude on the score of want of capital. This is the funded debt.

. . .

There remains to be noticed an objection to the encouragement of manufactures, of a nature different from those which question the probability of success. This is derived from its supposed tendency to give a monopoly of advantages to particular classes, at the expense of the rest of the community, who, it is affirmed, would be able to procure the requisite supplies of manufactured articles on better terms from foreigners than from our own citizens; and who, it is alleged, are reduced to the necessity of paying an enhanced price for whatever they want, by every measure which obstructs the free competition of foreign commodities.

It is not an unreasonable supposition, that measures which serve to abridge the free competition of foreign articles, have a tendency to occasion an enhancement of prices. . . .

But, though it were true that the immediate and certain effect of regulations controlling the competition of foreign with domestic fabrics was an increase of price, it is universally true that the contrary is the ultimate effect with every successful manufacture. . . . The internal competition which takes place soon does away with everything like monopoly, and by degrees reduces the price of the article to the minimum of a reasonable profit on the capital employed. This accords with the reason of the thing, and with experience.

Whence it follows, that it is the interest of a community, with a view to eventual and permanent economy, to encourage the growth of manufactures. In a national view, a temporary enhancement of price must always be well compensated by a permanent reduction of it.

. . .

Not only the wealth but the independence and security of a country appear to be materially connected with the prosperity of manufactures. Every nation, with a view to those great objects, ought to endeavor to possess within itself, all the essentials of national supply. These comprise the means of subsistence, habitation, clothing, and defense.

The possession of these is necessary to the perfection of the body politic; to the safety as well as to the welfare of the society. The want of either is the want of an important organ of political life and motion; and in the various crises which await a state, it must severely feel the effects of any such deficiency. The extreme embarrassments of the United States during the late war, from an incapacity of supplying themselves, are still matter of keen recollection; a future war might be expected again to exemplify the mischiefs and dangers of a situation to which that incapacity is still, in too great a degree, applicable, unless changed by timely and vigorous exertion. To effect this change, as fast as shall be prudent, merits all the attention and all the zeal of our public councils: 'tis the next great work to be accomplished.

. . .

A question has been made concerning the constitutional right of the Government of the United States to apply this species of encouragement, but there is certainly no good foundation for such a question. The National Legislature has express authority "to lay and collect taxes, duties, imposts, and excises, to pay the debts, and provide for the common defense and general welfare," with no other qualifications than that "all duties, imposts, and excises shall be uniform throughout the United States; and that no capitation or other direct tax shall be laid, unless in proportion to numbers ascertained by a census or enumeration, taken on the principles prescribed in the Constitution," and that "no tax or duty shall be laid on articles exported from any State."

These three qualifications excepted, the power to raise money is plenary and indefinite, and the objects to which it may be appropriated are no less comprehensive than the payment of the public debts, and the providing for the common defense and general welfare. The terms "general welfare" were doubtless intended to signify more than was expressed or imported in those which preceded; otherwise, numerous exigencies incident to the affairs of a nation would have been left without a provision. The phrase is as comprehensive as any that could have been used, because it was not fit that the constitutional authority of the Union to appropriate its revenues should have been restricted within narrower limits than the "general welfare," and because this necessarily embraces a vast variety of particulars, which are susceptible neither of specification nor of definition.

It is, therefore, of necessity, left to the discretion of the National Legislature to pronounce upon the objects which concern the general welfare, and for which, under that description, an appropriation of money is requisite and proper. And there seems to be no room for a doubt that whatever concerns the general interests of learning, of agriculture, of manufactures, and of commerce, are within the sphere of the national councils, as far as regards an application of money.

The only qualification of the generality of the phrase in question, which seems to be admissible, is this: That the object to which an appropriation of money is to be made be general, and not local; its operation extending in fact or by possibility throughout the Union, and not being confined to a particular spot.

No objection ought to arise to this construction, from a supposition that it would imply a power to do whatever else should appear to Congress conducive to the general welfare. A power to appropriate money with this latitude, which is granted, too, in express terms, would not carry a power to do any other thing not authorized in the Constitution, either expressly or by fair implication.

. . .

In countries where there is great private wealth, much may be effected by the voluntary contributions of patriotic individuals; but in a community situated like that of the United States, the public purse must supply the deficiency of private resource. In what can it be so useful, as in prompting and improving the efforts of industry?

. . .

JOHN TAYLOR

TYRANNY UNMASKED (1822)

John Taylor of Caroline was a Virginia politician of the doctrinaire Jeffersonian variety. He was the legislative sponsor of the Virginia Resolutions of 1798 that helped mobilize the Jeffersonians for the 1800 elections. He served three short stints in the U.S. Senate, but his main contribution to the politics of the early republic was as a writer. A harsh critic of Federalist and Whig policies and philosophies, he was perhaps the most significant political theorist in the United States in the first three decades of the nineteenth century. He was a staunch critic of John Marshall's nationalist constitutional philosophy, an advocate of states' rights, and a skeptic of majoritarian democracy. In the realm of political economy, he was a proponent of agrarianism and free trade, and a critic of the national bank and federal intervention in the economy through taxing and spending. The book *Tyranny Unmasked* was one of his last works and was particularly concerned with the system of protective tariffs that was being built by nationalists after the War of 1812 and that southern farmers thought primarily redistributed wealth from the agriculture-exporting sections of the country to the manufacturing sections of the country.

What does Taylor mean by "monopoly"? Why does he regard protectionist tariffs as "tyranny"? Would his critique of what we would call special-interest legislation be reduced if those policies could be shown to have benefits for the general public? Is there a problem with private actors seeking to use the political process to advance their particular economic interests? Are individuals or identifiable groups who are net tax contributors to the government being exploited by those who are net beneficiaries of government spending? Is a fiscal system that relies on an income tax more or less fair than one that relies on tariffs on imported goods to fund the government's budget?

. . .

Tyranny is wonderfully ingenious in the art of inventing specious phrases to spread over its nefarious designs. "Divine right, kings can do no wrong, parliamentary supremacy, the holy alliance," are instances of it in Europe. "Common defense, general welfare, federal supremacy and political economy," are impressed into the same service here. When the delusion of one phrase is past, another is adopted to work out the same ends as its predecessor. Political economy is represented as a complicated system of deprivations and compensations, or of getting and giving back money. In the multitude of transactions implied by this notion of political economy, will none of it stick to the fingers through which it passes? Will the privileged bands of brokers get nothing by this economical traffic? Will the officers necessary to enforce this species of political economy, require no salaries? An economy exposed to endless frauds, and incomputable expenses. The pretense "that though it inflicts deprivations, it bestows compensations," is one of those gross impositions upon the credulity of mankind, believed upon no better grounds than the stories of ghosts and apparitions. In the history of the world, there is no instance of a political economy bottomed upon exclusive privileges, having made any compensation for the deprivations it inflicts. . . .

. . .

. . . Laws for creating exclusive privileges and monopolies corrupt governments, interests, and individuals; and substitute patronage, adulation, and favor, for industry, as the road to wealth. . . .

. . .

The promise of future compensation for present wealth is the cunning offer made by the capitalists to the farmers. Build factories and give bounties to us now, and we will restore to you the blessing of free exchanges the moment we can no longer extort from you an enhanced price for our fabrics. Such is the basis of their arguments, and such the boon by which they are endeavoring to bribe the farmers, without paying any respect to other occupations. Is there any man in his senses who would make such a bargain with another man? No day of payment is prescribed. No security for performance is proposed. After all other interests have enriched the capitalist interest, it may break its promise, cease even to manufacture, and retain the wealth acquired by its bounties. . . . Vast estates are purchased by a promise, and no obligation to pay anything for them is incurred. Indeed no payment can ever be made for them, except a restoration of free exchanges and fair competition, suspended to bestow them. The utmost compensation to be expected is that of taking off the suspension. Why then put it on? To take away a social right, in order to restore the same social right, is worse than nothing, by the amount of the intermediate loss incurred by the suspension. Whilst the business of building factories is made lucrative by bounties, the capitalists will pursue it; when it ceases to be so, they will give it up. If other occupations should escape from their toils and become profitable, by receiving either patronage or justice, the capitalists will transfer their wealth from the worn out, to the new patronage, or at worst, employ it in free and fair exchanges upon equal ground with other wealth. Money emigrates without difficulty from one exclusive privilege, or from one occupation to another; it is neither nailed to the soil, nor to a factory; it follows the scent of profit; and the cry of capitalists upon the track of exclusive privileges, like hounds in pursuit of game, grows louder as the scent grows stronger. . . .

. . .

A passion for carnage, is the tyranny of savages. Ambition and avarice are the passions which produce civilized tyranny. A policy for encouraging the latter passions, is like one for training savage nations to become bloodhounds. If ambition is cultivated by feeding it with excessive power, it extorts from industry the fruits of its labor; if avarice is cultivated by feeding it with excessive wealth, it acquires political power to pillage industry also. Enormous political power invariably accumulates enormous wealth, and enormous wealth invariably accumulates enormous political power. Either constitutes a tyranny, because the acquisitions of both are losses of liberty and property to nations.

. . .

. . . Experience has demonstrated over and over again, that a free government cannot subsist in union with extravagance, heavy taxation, exclusive privileges, or with any established process by which a great amount of property is annually transferred to unproductive employments. Such a system is tyranny. How then can it harmonize or live in the same country with liberty? . . .

Taxation disguised in any way, is disguised tyranny, so far as it exceeds the genuine necessities of a good government. It is disguised by giving different names to different taxes, because capitation taxes are allowed to be highly oppressive. But in fact, all taxes are capitation. In every form they are paid by individuals, and ultimately fall on heads. . . .

In about twenty years the French revolutionary government passed, it is said, between seven and eight thousand laws; of which, about one hundred now remain in force. I know not a better proof of bad government than a perpetual flood of time-serving laws. To this flood of legislation is justly ascribed much of the concurrent dissatisfaction which subverted theory after theory, and terminated in an impetuous recurrence to a military despotism. In the United States about four thousand laws are annually passed, amounting in forty-five years to one hundred and eighty thousand. When there were fewer States, the annual number of our laws may have been less, but now it is probably more. In future, if the rage for legislation continues, the number of laws will considerably exceed this computation. A great majority of these laws are passed for the purpose of transferring property from the people to patronized individuals or combinations. They are annually shaving and shaving the fruits of industry, and have greatly contributed towards reducing it down to its present state. It is at length nearly drowned by this deluge of legislation. . . .

. . .

. . . Those who gain more by banking, by the protecting-duty monopoly, or by loaning to the government, than they lose by these property-transferring machines, constitute no exception to the fact, that the property-transferring policy invariably impoverishes all laboring and productive classes. A few individuals are enriched by every species of tyranny, as its essence in civilized countries consists of transferring property by laws. If the general good is the end of self-government, and if the property-transferring policy defeats the general good, it also defeats self-government. Therefore the United States cannot fulfil the great purpose to which they seem almost to have been destined, except by a degree of sagacity sufficient to discern, that the property-transferring policy in all its forms, however disguised, is a tyrannical imposition, only sustainable by the same species of political idolatry, which has blinded mankind to their interest, and is yet enslaving most or all civilized nations.

. . .

Let us no longer "sow our seed for the fowls to devour." Is it better to be governed by the costly pageants of the property-transferring policy, than by the free animating principle of fair exchanges and unplundered industry?

VI. AMERICA AND THE WORLD

Major Developments

- Secured independence with War of 1812
- Pursued territorial acquisition through negotiation and purchase
- Pacified frontier through assimilationist policies and war
- Announced Monroe Doctrine of protecting Western Hemisphere from Europe

Independence did not immediately establish American security. The Treaty of Paris formalizing the end of the American Revolution did not settle all issues, and Britain was slow to withdraw from its forts in the northwest. Some immediate issues were resolved by the unpopular Jay Treaty, but the ongoing conflicts between Britain and France threatened to draw the United States into the European fight. President Washington took it upon himself to proclaim American neutrality in the European war, despite the memory of French aid during the Revolution. The growing domestic rifts within the United States over what to do about the conflicts between Britain and France exhausted and frustrated President Washington. In his Farewell Address, he urged his fellow citizens to keep their distance from Europe and avoid entangling alliances.

The United States was on a near-war footing from the 1790s on, but the American government managed to avoid war until 1812. Provocations like the kidnapping of American seamen and the encouragement of tribal resistance to the United States in the northwest finally led to direct conflict, with embarrassing results (including the burning of the White House) and internal division (the Federalist-led Hartford Convention suggested that New England should seek a separate peace with Britain) but eventual success.

As wars expanded in Europe, the Spanish monarchy fell to France's Napoleon. The Spanish colonies in Latin America were thrown into disarray, with independence movements throwing off colonial governments. The American administration was under pressure to recognize the newly independent nations but hesitated before President James Monroe finally announced the Monroe Doctrine in 1823, extending diplomatic recognition to the new governments and declaring that any European intervention against them would be regarded as an attack on American interests.

GEORGE WASHINGTON

FAREWELL ADDRESS (1796)

As he prepared to step down after his second term as president, George Washington published a widely reprinted farewell address. Part of the address warned against the emerging partisanship of American politics (see above). Near the end of the open letter "to the people of America," President Washington turned to the relationship of the United States to the rest of the world. Having struggled to maintain American neutrality between France and England, Washington urged his fellow Americans to stay that course. There he famously warned against "entangling alliances" that would bind the fate of the United States to the turbulent international politics of Europe. This warning was often referenced as a touchstone for American isolationism and a policy of noninvolvement with the affairs of other countries and a refusal to make long-term security commitments that could draw the United States into unwanted wars.

What is Washington's concern about Europe? Is his warning against alliances a temporary measure or an enduring principle? How far does the concern with entangling alliances extend? How might the goal of observing "good faith and justice towards all nations" conflict with "passionate attachment to others"? Is Washington motivated by narrow security concerns or broader concerns about public morality? Why might Washington regard "commercial relations" as less dangerous than "political connections" with other countries?

. . .

Observe good faith and justice towards all nations; cultivate peace and harmony with all. Religion and morality enjoin this conduct; and can it be, that good policy does not equally enjoin it—It will be worthy of a free, enlightened, and at no distant period, a great nation, to give to mankind the magnanimous and too novel example of a people always guided by an exalted justice and benevolence. Who can doubt that, in the course of time and things, the fruits of such a plan would richly repay any temporary advantages which might be lost by a steady adherence to it? Can it be that Providence has not connected the permanent felicity of a nation with its virtue ? . . .

In the execution of such a plan, nothing is more essential than that permanent, inveterate antipathies against particular nations, and passionate attachments for others, should be excluded; and that, in place of them, just and amicable feelings towards all should be cultivated. The nation which indulges towards another a habitual hatred or a habitual fondness is in some degree a slave. It is a slave to its animosity or to its affection, either of which is sufficient to lead it astray from its duty and its interest. Antipathy in one nation against another disposes each more readily to offer insult and injury, to lay hold of slight causes of umbrage, and to be haughty and intractable, when accidental or trifling occasions of dispute occur. Hence, frequent collisions, obstinate, envenomed, and bloody contests. The nation, prompted by ill-will and resentment, sometimes impels to war the government, contrary to the best calculations of policy. The government sometimes participates in the national propensity, and adopts through passion what reason would reject; at other times it makes the animosity of the nation subservient to projects of hostility instigated by pride, ambition, and other sinister and pernicious motives. The peace often, sometimes perhaps the liberty, of nations, has been the victim.

So likewise, a passionate attachment of one nation for another produces a variety of evils. Sympathy for the favorite nation, facilitating the illusion of an imaginary common interest in cases where no real common interest exists, and infusing into one the enmities of the other, betrays the former into a participation in the quarrels and wars of the latter without adequate inducement or justification. It leads also to concessions to the favorite nation of privileges denied to others which is apt doubly to injure the nation making the concessions; by unnecessarily parting with what ought to have been retained, and by exciting jealousy, ill-will, and a disposition to retaliate, in the parties from whom equal privileges are withheld. And it gives to ambitious, corrupted, or deluded citizens (who devote themselves to the favorite nation), facility to betray or sacrifice the interests of their own country, without odium, sometimes even with popularity; gilding, with the appearances of a virtuous sense of obligation, a commendable deference for public opinion, or a laudable zeal for public good, the base or foolish compliances of ambition, corruption, or infatuation.

. . .

Against the insidious wiles of foreign influence (I conjure you to believe me, fellow-citizens) the jealousy of a free people ought to be constantly awake, since history and experience prove that foreign influence is one of the most baneful foes of republican government. But that jealousy to be useful must be impartial; else it becomes the instrument of the very influence to be avoided, instead of a defense against it. Excessive partiality for one foreign nation and excessive dislike of another cause those whom they actuate to see danger only on one side, and serve to veil and even second the arts of influence on the other. Real patriots who may resist the intrigues of the favorite are liable to become suspected and odious, while its tools and dupes usurp the applause and confidence of the people, to surrender their interests.

The great rule of conduct for us in regard to foreign nations is in extending our commercial relations, to have with them as little political connection as possible. So far as we have already formed engagements, let them be fulfilled with perfect good faith. Here let us stop. Europe has a set of primary interests which to us have none; or a very remote relation. Hence she must be engaged in frequent controversies, the causes of which are essentially foreign to our concerns. Hence, therefore, it must be unwise in us to implicate ourselves by artificial ties in the ordinary vicissitudes of her politics, or the ordinary combinations and collisions of her friendships or enmities.

. . .

Why forego the advantages of so peculiar a situation? Why quit our own to stand upon foreign ground? Why, by interweaving our destiny with that of any part of Europe, entangle our peace and prosperity in the toils of European ambition, rivalship, interest, humor or caprice?

It is our true policy to steer clear of permanent alliances with any portion of the foreign world. . . .

Taking care always to keep ourselves by suitable establishments on a respectable defensive posture, we may safely trust to temporary alliances for extraordinary emergencies.

. . .

THOMAS JEFFERSON

LETTER TO WILLIAM HENRY HARRISON (1803)

With the establishment of American independence, the United States was partly sheltered from Europe by the Atlantic Ocean. Nonetheless, European powers held colonial territory to the immediate north and south of the United States, and the Native American tribes throughout the American interior had been used as proxies in European wars for decades. The Jefferson administration's Indian policy was guided by two goals: to build ties of common interest between the Native American tribes and the United States and to "civilize" the tribes and set them on the path toward reaching the social, economic, and political conditions of the Europeans. The policy had mixed results. Some tribes embraced the civilization program and took up farming and, in many cases, Christianity. Others joined an inter-tribal resistance movement that hoped to contain the American frontier close to the Atlantic seaboard.

President Jefferson outlined his Indian policy in a letter to William Henry Harrison. Harrison was a native of Virginia, but his father's death left his family in poor financial condition. Harrison left his medical studies and joined the army, where he fought in the Indian wars in the Northwest Territory in the early 1790s. At the age of 28, he was appointed to be the governor of the newly created Indiana territory just west of the state of Ohio. Harrison served in that position for a dozen years, capping it with a defeat of Chief Tecumseh's forces at the Battle of Tippecanoe in 1811. Harrison resigned the governorship to become general of the northwest army in the War of 1812, and later used those military exploits to win the White House in 1840.

How does Jefferson propose to use trade as a tool of foreign policy? Jefferson was familiar with the consequences of debt; how does he intend to use debt as a tool of foreign policy? Is it reasonable for the United States to seek to acquire new land through purchases? Is a policy of purchasing land ultimately preferable to a policy of *acquiring* land through military conquest? Is purchasing land more consistent with American values? How does Jefferson's policy as president relate to his views of Native Americans expressed in his *Notes on the State of Virginia in Chapter* 3?

. . .

. . . Our system is to live in perpetual peace with the Indians, to cultivate an affectionate attachment from them, by everything just and liberal which we can do for them within the bounds of reason, and by giving them effectual protection against wrongs from our own people. The decrease of game rendering their subsistence by hunting insufficient, we wish to draw them to agriculture, to spinning and weaving. The latter branches they take up with great readiness, because they fall to the women, who gain by quitting the labors of the field for those which are exercised within doors. When they withdraw themselves to the culture of a small piece of land, they will perceive how useless to them are their extensive forests, and will be willing to pare them off from time to time in exchange for necessaries for their farms and families. To promote this disposition to exchange lands, which they have to spare and we want, for necessaries, which we have to spare and they want, we shall push our trading uses, and be glad to see the good and influential individuals among them run in debt, because we observe that when these debts get beyond what the individuals can pay, they become willing to lop them off by a cession of lands. At our trading house, too, we mean to sell so low as merely to repay us cost and charges, so as neither to lessen or enlarge our capital. This is what private traders cannot do, for they must gain; they will consequently retire from the competition, and we shall thus get clear of this pest without giving offense or umbrage to the Indians. In this way our settlements will gradually circumscribe and approach the Indians, and they will in time either incorporate with us as citizens of the United States, or remove beyond the Mississippi. The former is certainly the termination of their history most happy for themselves; but, in the whole course of this, it is essential to cultivate their love. As to their fear, we presume that our strength and their weakness is now so visible that they must see we have only to shut our hand to crush them, and that all our liberalities to them proceed from motives of pure humanity only. Should any tribe be fool-hardy enough to take up the hatchet at any time, the seizing of the whole country of that tribe, and driving them across the Mississippi, as the only condition of peace, would be an example to others, and a furtherance of our final consolidation.

Combined with these views, and to be prepared against the occupation of Louisiana by a powerful and enterprising people, it is important that, setting less value on interior extension of purchases from the Indians, we bend our whole views to the purchase and settlement of the country on the Mississippi, from its mouth to its northern regions, that we may be able to present as strong a front on our western as on our eastern border, and plant on the Mississippi itself the means of its own defense. . . . The Kaskaskias being reduced to a few families, I presume we may purchase their whole country for what would place every individual of them at his ease, and be a small price to us,—say by laying off for each family, whenever they would choose it, as much rich land as they could cultivate, adjacent to each other, enclosing the whole in a single fence, and giving them such an annuity in money or goods forever as would place them in happiness; and we might take them also under the protection of the United States. . . . I have given you this view of the system which we suppose will best promote the interests of the Indians and ourselves, and finally consolidate our whole country to one nation only. . . . The occupation of New Orleans, hourly expected, by the French, is already felt like a light breeze by the Indians. You know the sentiments they entertain of that nation; under the hope of their protection they will immediately stiffen against cessions of lands to us. We had better, therefore, do at once what can now be done.

JOHN QUINCY ADAMS

SPEECH ON INDEPENDENCE DAY (1821)

The position of secretary of state was traditionally the leading member of the president's Cabinet. Under the Virginia Dynasty, the position had been something of a stepping stone to the presidency, with James Madison serving as Thomas Jefferson's only secretary of state and James Monroe serving as James Madison's primary secretary of state. John Quincy Adams was the son of former president John Adams and the first New Englander to hold the office since the Federalists' defeat in the 1800 elections. Adams was not initially seen as a likely presidential prospect, but he proved to be an influential secretary of state and a savvy politician.

Adams was a voice of caution within the Monroe administration as independence movements broke out in the Latin American colonies. Adams favored delay in extending diplomatic recognition to the revolutionary Latin American states so as to avoid dangerous entangling alliances that might pull the United States into war with the European powers. But when Britain proposed a joint announcement recognizing the southern nations, Adams argued for unilateral action, in part because it would help keep open the option of American acquisition of Cuba and Texas without necessarily opposing England (Jefferson advised Monroe to ally with England in part because he thought the American acquisition of Cuba would be too costly and the United States could instead join England in seeking Cuban independence from Spain). In his Fourth of July address to the U.S. House of Representatives, the secretary of state warned against the United States involving itself in the affairs of others.

Why does Adams oppose allying the United States with the Latin American states? Does he see interests and values of the United States and the Latin American countries as being linked? How far might his policy of nonintervention extend? Does the revolutionary legacy of the United States suggest that the United States should be supportive of revolutionary movements elsewhere? Is the United States hypocritical in its unwillingness to assist the emerging nations of Latin America in throwing off colonial rule? Is Adams's warning resonant beyond the circumstances of the early nineteenth century?

. . .

Fellow citizens, I am speaking of days long past. Ever faithful to the sentiment proclaimed in the paper [the Declaration of Independence], which I am about to present once more to your memory of the past and to your forecast of the future, you will hold the people of Britain as you hold the rest of mankind,—Enemies in war—in peace, Friends. The conflict for independence is now itself but a record of history. The resentments of that age may be buried in oblivion. The stoutest hearts, which then supported the tug of war, are cold under the clod of the valley. My purpose is to rekindle no angry passion from its embers: but this annual solemn perusal of the instrument, which proclaimed to the world the causes of your existence as a nation, is not without its just and useful purpose.

. . .

The interest, which in this paper has survived the occasion upon which it was issued; the interest which is of every age and every clime; the interest which quickens with the lapse of years, spreads as it grows old, and brightens as it recedes, is in the principles which it proclaims. It was the first solemn declaration by a nation of the only legitimate foundation of civil government. It was the corner stone of a new fabric, destined to cover the surface of the globe. It demolished at a stroke the lawfulness of all governments founded upon conquest. It swept away all the rubbish of accumulated centuries of servitude. It announced in practical form to the world the transcendent truth of the unalienable sovereignty of the people. It proved that the social compact was no figment of the imagination; but a real, solid, and sacred bond of the social union. From the day of this declaration, the people of North America were no longer the fragment of a distant empire, imploring justice and mercy from an inexorable master in another hemisphere. They were no longer children appealing in vain to the sympathies of a heartless mother; no longer subjects leaning upon the shattered columns of royal promises, and invoking the faith of parchment to secure their rights. They were a nation, asserting as of right, and maintaining by war, its own existence. A nation was born in a day.

. . .

[W]hat has America done for the benefit of mankind? Let our answer be this—America, with the same voice which spoke herself into existence as a nation, proclaimed to mankind the inextinguishable rights of human nature, and the only lawful foundations of government. America, in the assembly of nations, since her admission among them, has invariably, though often fruitlessly, held forth to them the hand of honest friendship, of equal freedom, of generous reciprocity. She has uniformly spoken among them, though often to heedless and often to disdainful ears, the language of equal liberty, equal justice, and equal rights. She has, in the lapse of nearly half a century, without a single exception, respected the independence of other nations, while asserting and maintaining her own. She has abstained from interference in the concerns of others, even when the conflict has been for principles to which she clings, as to the last vital drop that visits the heart. She has seen that probably for centuries to come, all the contests of that Aceldama, the European World, will be contests between inveterate power, and emerging right. Wherever the standard of freedom and independence has been or shall be unfurled, there will her heart, her benedictions and her prayers be. But she goes not abroad in search of monsters to destroy. She is the well-wisher to the freedom and independence of all. She is the champion and vindicator only of her own. She will recommend the general cause, by the countenance of her voice, and the benignant sympathy of her example. She well knows that by once enlisting under other banners than her own, were they even the banners of foreign independence, she would involve herself, beyond the power of extrication, in all the wars of interest and intrigue, of individual avarice, envy, and ambition, which assume the colors and usurp the standard of freedom. The fundamental maxims of her policy would insensibly change from liberty to force. The frontlet upon her brows would no longer beam with the ineffable splendor of freedom and independence; but in its stead would soon be substituted an imperial diadem, flashing in false and tarnished luster the murky radiance of dominion and power. She might become the dictatress of the world: she would be no longer the ruler of her own spirit.

. . . Her glory is not dominion, but liberty. Her march is the march of mind. She has a spear and a shield; but the motto upon her shield is Freedom, Independence, Peace. This has been her declaration: this has been, as far as her necessary intercourse with the rest of mankind would permit, her practice.

My countrymen, fellow-citizens, and friends; could that Spirit, which dictated the Declaration we have this day read, that Spirit, which "prefers before all temples the upright heart and pure," at this moment descend from his habitation in the skies, and within this hall, in language audible to mortal ears, address each one of us, here assembled, our beloved country, Britannia ruler of the waves, and every individual among the sceptered lords of humankind; his words would be, "Go thou and do likewise!"

JAMES MONROE

SEVENTH ANNUAL MESSAGE (1823)

In the 1810s and 1820s, the colonies in Latin America broke away from the European empires. With Napoleon Bonaparte's conquest of Spain in 1808, the Spanish colonial governments in the Western Hemisphere were disrupted. Starting with Chile, Columbia, and Mexico in 1810, the Spanish and Portuguese lost control of their American colonies in rapid succession. The government of the United States was uncertain how best to respond. While the United States welcomed colonial independence, the commitment of the new countries to the south to republicanism was uncertain and the Americans still worried about offending Spain. Britain hoped to benefit from the disruption of the European empires and offered to join with the United States in discouraging European intervention in Latin America. Finally, the United States decided to announce a policy of its own and to recognize the Latin American states as independent nations. President James Monroe announced the "Monroe Doctrine" in his 1823 annual message to Congress, declaring that the United States would view any European intervention in the newly independent states in the Western Hemisphere as an act of aggression against American interests.

What justifications does Monroe offer for extending American protection to the Latin American countries? Does the Monroe Doctrine necessarily imply that the United States is allied with the countries to the south? Is Monroe committed to aiding independence movements in Latin America? Would the United States take the same view of a Canadian independence movement against Britain in the 1820s? Why should the United States look on the states in the Western Hemisphere any differently than states elsewhere in the world? Is the American protectorate just another form of imperialism?

. . .

The people being with us exclusively the sovereign, it is indispensable that full information be laid before them on all important subjects, to enable them to exercise that high power with complete effect. If kept in the dark, they must be incompetent to it. We are all liable to error, and those who are engaged in the management of public affairs are more subject to excitement and to be led astray by their particular interests and passions than the great body of our constituents, who, living at home in the pursuit of their ordinary avocations, are calm but deeply interested spectators of events and of the conduct of those who are parties to them.

To the people every department of the Government and every individual in each are responsible, and the more full their information the better they can judge of the wisdom of the policy pursued and of the conduct of each in regard to it. . . .

A precise knowledge of our relations with foreign powers as respects our negotiations and transactions with each is thought to be particularly necessary. Equally necessary is it that we should for a just estimate of our resources, revenue, and progress in every kind of improvement connected with the national prosperity and public defense. It is by rendering justice to other nations that we may expect it from them. It is by our ability to resent injuries and redress wrongs that we may avoid them.

. . .

. . . Of events in that quarter of the globe, with which we have so much intercourse and from which we derive our origin, we have always been anxious and interested spectators.

The citizens of the United States cherish sentiments the most friendly in favor of the liberty and happiness of their fellow men on that side of the Atlantic. In the wars of the European powers in matters relating to themselves we have never taken any part, nor does it comport with our policy so to do.

It is only when our rights are invaded or seriously menaced that we resent injuries or make preparation for our defense. With the movements in this hemisphere we are of necessity more immediately connected, and by causes which must be obvious to all enlightened and impartial observers.

The political system of the allied powers is essentially different in this respect from that of America. This difference proceeds from that which exists in their respective Governments; and to the defense of our own, which has been achieved by the loss of so much blood and treasure, and matured by the wisdom of their most enlightened citizens, and under which we have enjoyed unexampled felicity, this whole nation is devoted.

We owe it, therefore, to candor and to the amicable relations existing between the United States and those powers to declare that we should consider any attempt on their part to extend their system to any portion of this hemisphere as dangerous to our peace and safety. With the existing colonies or dependencies of any European power we have not interfered and shall not interfere, but with the Governments who have declared their independence and maintained it, and whose independence we have, on great consideration and on just principles, acknowledged, we could not view any interposition for the purpose of oppressing them, or controlling in any other manner their destiny, by any European power in any other light than as the manifestation of an unfriendly disposition toward the United States.

In the war between those new Governments and Spain we declared our neutrality at the time of their recognition, and to this we have adhered, and shall continue to adhere, provided no change shall occur which, in the judgment of the competent authorities of this Government, shall make a corresponding change on the part of the United States indispensable to their security.

. . .

Our policy in regard to Europe, which was adopted at an early stage of the wars which have so long agitated that quarter of the globe, nevertheless remains the same, which is, not to interfere in the internal concerns of any of its powers; to consider the government de facto as the legitimate government for us; to cultivate friendly relations with it, and to preserve those relations by a frank, firm, and manly policy, meeting in all instances the just claims of every power, submitting to injuries from none.

But in regard to those continents circumstances are eminently and conspicuously different. It is impossible that the allied powers should extend their political system to any portion of either continent without endangering our peace and happiness; nor can anyone believe that our southern brethren, if left to themselves, would adopt it of their own accord. It is equally impossible, therefore, that we should behold such interposition in any form with indifference. If we look to the comparative strength and resources of Spain and those new Governments, and their distance from each other, it must be obvious that she can never subdue them. It is still the true policy of the United States to leave the parties to themselves, in the hope that other powers will pursue the same course.

. . .

FOR FURTHER STUDY

Ames, Fisher. *The Works of Fisher Ames*, ed. W. B. Allen (Indianapolis, IN: Liberty Fund, 1983).

Foner, Philip S., ed. *The Democratic-Republican Societies, 1790–1800: A Documentary Sourcebook of Constitutions, Declarations, Addresses, Resolutions and Toasts* (Westport, CT: Greenwood Press, 1976).

Gallatin, Albert. *Selected Writings*, ed. Elmer James Ferguson (Indianapolis, IN: Bobbs-Merrill, 1967).

Hamilton, Alexander, and James Madison. *The Pacificus–Helvidius Debates of 1793–1794: Toward the Completion of the American Founding*, ed. Morton J. Frisch (Indianapolis, IN: Liberty Fund, 2007).

Marshall, John. *Writings*, ed. Charles F. Hobson (New York: Library of America, 2010).

Peterson, Merrill, ed. *Democracy, Liberty, and Property: The State Constitutional Conventions of the 1820s* (Indianapolis, IN: Liberty Fund, 2010).

Taylor, John. *An Inquiry into the Principles and Policy of the Government of the United States*, ed. Loren Baritz (Indianapolis, IN: Bobbs-Merrill, 1969).

Washington, George. *George Washington: Selected Writings*, ed. Ron Chernow (New York: Library of America, 2011).

SUGGESTED READINGS

Bailey, Jeremy D. *Thomas Jefferson and Executive Power* (New York: Cambridge University Press, 2007).

Banning, Lance. *The Jeffersonian Persuasion: Evolution of a Party Ideology* (Ithaca, NY: Cornell University Press, 1978).

Beeman, Richard, Stephen Botein, and Edward C. Carter II, eds. *Beyond Confederation: Origins of the Constitution and American National Identity* (Chapel Hill: University of North Carolina Press, 1987).

Bradburn, Douglas. *The Citizenship Revolution: Politics and the Creation of the American Union, 1774–1804* (Charlottesville: University of Virginia Press, 2009).

Davis, David Brion. *The Problem of Slavery in the Age of Revolution, 1770–1823* (Ithaca, NY: Cornell University Press, 1975).

Elkins, Stanley, and Eric McKitrick. *The Age of Federalism: The Early American Republic, 1788–1800* (New York: Oxford University Press, 1995).

Hatch, Nathan O. *The Democratization of American Christianity* (New Haven, CT: Yale University Press, 1991).

Hofstadter, Richard. *The Idea of a Party System: The Rise of Legitimate Opposition in the United States, 1780–1840* (Berkeley: University of California Press, 1970).

Kerber, Linda K. *Federalists in Dissent: Imagery and Ideology in Jeffersonian America* (Ithaca, NY: Cornell University Press, 1970).

McCoy, Drew R. *The Elusive Republic: Political Economy in Jeffersonian America* (Chapel Hill: University of North Carolina Press, 1980).

Miller, Perry. *The Life of the Mind in America: From the Revolution to the Civil War* (New York: Harcourt, Brace and World, 1965).

Nelson, John R., Jr. *Liberty and Property: Political Economy and Policymaking in the New Nation, 1789–1812* (Baltimore, MD: Johns Hopkins University Press, 1987).

Newmeyer, R. Kent. *John Marshall and the Heroic Age of the Supreme Court* (Baton Rouge: Louisiana State University Press, 2002).

Onuf, Peter S. *Jefferson's Empire: The Language of American Nationhood* (Charlottesville: University of Virginia Press, 2000).

Read, James H. *Power Versus Liberty: Madison, Hamilton, Wilson, and Jefferson* (Charlottesville: University of Virginia Press, 2000).

Risjord, Norman K. *The Old Republicans: Southern Conservatism in the Age of Jefferson* (New York: Columbia University Press, 1965).

Slotkin, Richard. *Regeneration Through Violence: The Mythology of the American Frontier, 1600–1860* (Middletown, CT: Wesleyan University Press, 1973).

Stourzh, Gerald. *Alexander Hamilton and the Idea of Republican Government* (Stanford, CA: Stanford University Press, 1970).

Thompson, C. Bradley. *John Adams and the Spirit of Liberty* (Lawrence: University Press of Kansas, 2002).

Tise, Larry E. *Proslavery: A History of the Defense of Slavery in America, 1701–1840* (Athens: University of Georgia Press, 2004).

Walling, Karl-Friedrich. *Republican Empire: Alexander Hamilton on War and Free Government* (Lawrence: University Press of Kansas, 1999).

Weiner, Greg. *The Constitution, Majority Rule, and the Tempo of American Politics* (Lawrence: University Press of Kansas, 2012).

Yarbrough, Jean M. *American Virtues: Thomas Jefferson on the Character of a Free People* (Lawrence: University Press of Kansas, 2009).

Zagarri, Rosemarie. *Revolutionary Backlash: Women and Politics in the Early American Republic* (Philadelphia: University of Pennsylvania Press, 2008).

CHAPTER 5

THE JACKSONIAN ERA, 1829–1860

I. INTRODUCTION

At his first inaugural, President Andrew Jackson declared "as long as our Government is administered for the good of the people, and is regulated by their will; as long as it secures to us the rights of person and of property, liberty of conscience and of the press, it will be worth defending."[1] Andrew Jackson was the first "outsider" candidate for president, and perhaps the first truly popular candidate since George Washington. His political career had been brief; his fame was based on his exploits as a military leader, which generated genuine popular enthusiasm for him as an individual. He rode that charismatic appeal to the presidency. Jackson never doubted his title to the White House. He thought the election of 1824 had been stolen from him by a "corrupt bargain" between John Quincy Adams (who became president) and Henry Clay (who became secretary of state).[2] His resounding victory at the polls in 1828 was, therefore, a vindication. It was a vindication, he was sure, not only for himself, but for the American people.

The Jacksonian Era marked a blossoming of a new generation of political and social leaders. They received their inheritance from the founders with some trepidation, but they sought to leave a legacy of their own. A young Abraham Lincoln expressed the anxiety in a speech to the Young Men's Lyceum. The "now lamented and departed race of ancestors" had left as a legacy "a political edifice of liberty and equal rights," and the first obligation

1 Andrew Jackson, *The Papers of Andrew Jackson*, eds. Daniel Feller, et al., vol. 7 (Knoxville: University of Tennessee Press, 2007), 79. The full passage in Jackson's first inaugural address argues that such a government would be voluntarily defended by state militias and would not require a standing national army to sustain itself.

2 The electoral vote in the 1824 presidential election was split among four candidates, including Adams, Jackson, and Clay. Jackson received the most popular and electoral votes, but well short of a majority. Without an electoral majority, the contest was determined by a vote in the U.S. House of Representatives, where supporters of Adams held a majority.

was to hand these down in turn, "unprofaned."[3] They confronted a new set of political, economic, and social challenges, and worked through those challenges by modifying some old ideas and developing some new ones.

Politics. A stable two-party system emerged for the first time in the Jacksonian Era. The divide between the Federalists and Jeffersonian Republicans was seen by both sides as a temporary expedient, and Jeffersonian dominance soon reduced the Federalists to insignificance. By contrast, the divide between the Jacksonian Democrats and the Whigs was soon entrenched. Neither side could banish the other, and both came to accept political parties and party competition as beneficial aspects of a working democracy. Though the Democrats tended to dominate national politics during these years, the Whigs were persistent and serious competitors and were able to win control of state and local governments across the country. Though the Whigs disintegrated over the slavery issue in the 1850s, the emergence of a successor party seemed natural.

Like the Republicans and Federalists, the Democrats and Whigs divided over constitutional ideology, public policy, and personalities. Unlike the Republicans and Federalists, the Democrats and Whigs developed deep roots in the mass electorate and mobilized large portions of the population to go to the polls. The Democrats grew up around the towering presence of President Andrew Jackson, with lesser figures like Martin Van Buren building a party apparatus that could sustain the general's legacy. The Whigs too grew up around Jackson, but in their case in opposition to him and his policies with presidential aspirants like Henry Clay and Daniel Webster casting their lot with others who were offended by the apparent crassness and recklessness of Jackson. The Jacksonians took on many of the substantive commitments of the old Jeffersonians, including a desire for frugal governments, states' rights, and a more laissez-faire attitude toward the economy and society. The Whigs were a direct outgrowth of the national Republicans of the 1810s and 1820s, with leaders like Clay and Webster advancing the more nationalist, interventionist vision that Chief Justice John Marshall had defended from the bench and that Clay had long pursued in Congress. Although the two parties divided on a range of social issues—from temperance to immigration—they agreed to compromise on the slavery issue. Although the Democrats may have leaned more toward the slave interests, both parties accepted the legitimacy of slavery and were able to compete on both sides of the Mason-Dixon line.

Society. The American population went through more than just a generational change during the Jacksonian Era. Immigration surged, with the United States adding more than two million foreign-born residents to its population in the antebellum years. The new arrivals in turn sparked a political reaction. Anti-Catholic and anti-immigrant nativist movements sprung up along the east coast. The Native American Party emerged in the mid-Atlantic states in the 1840s, achieving some local success, and was replaced in the

3 Abraham Lincoln, *Abraham Lincoln: His Speeches and Writings*, ed. Roy P. Basler (Cleveland, OH: World Pub. Co., 1946), 77.

FIGURE 5-1 TIMELINE OF THE JACKSONIAN ERA

Events	Year	Writings
Election of President Andrew Jackson	1828	
Virginia Constitutional Convention	1830	
William Lloyd Garrison founded The Liberator	1831	
Beginning of forcible removal of Native American tribes from southern states	1831	
	1832	Andrew Jackson's veto of Bank bill
American Anti-Slavery Society founded	1833	
Nullification crisis in South Carolina	1833	
Alexis de Tocqueville's Democracy in America	1835	
Hopedale Community founded in Massachusetts	1842	
Anti-Catholic riots in Philadelphia	1844	
Congress declares war on Mexico	1846	
Frederick Douglass founded The North Star	1847	
Seneca Falls Convention	1848	
Karl Marx and Friedrich Engel's Communist Manifesto	1848	
	1849	Horace Mann's The Massachusetts System of Common Schools
	1849	Henry David Thoreau's Civil Disobedience
Fugitive Slave Act of 1850	1850	
Herbert Spencer's Social Statics	1851	
	1852	Harriet Beecher Stowe's Uncle Tom's Cabin
	1857	Roger Taney's opinion in Dred Scott v. Sandford
	1857	George Fitzhugh's Cannibals All!
	1858	Lincoln-Douglas Debates in Illinois
John Stuart Mill's On Liberty	1859	
Charles Darwin's On the Origin of Species	1859	

1850s by the American Party (or "Know-Nothings"), which had a national reach and won presidential elector votes in 1856 before its collapse.

Despite the great expansion in available American territory during these decades, the country moved onto the path of urbanization. The United States had largely consisted of farms and small towns through its entire existence, but things began to change noticeably in the 1830s. Fed in part by the new immigration, the towns and cities of the northeastern states began to grow significantly. By the time of the Civil War, more than a third of the northeastern population lived in cities. The process of urbanization took hold elsewhere in the nation as well, but at a much slower pace. The growth of cities was accompanied by a growth in manufacturing, as men, women, and children found employment in the developing mills and factories of the northeast.

The moral reform movements that had begun in the late Jeffersonian period flourished in the Jacksonian Era. The American Temperance Society was founded in Boston in 1825 and claimed well over a million members by the end of Jackson's presidency; the American Anti-Slavery Society was founded in 1833 and claimed nearly a quarter of a million members within a decade; the anti-prostitution New York Female Moral Reform Society soon opened chapters in cities throughout the country. Such organizations were often dominated by women and fueled by (Protestant) religious fervor. Such engagement with social issues encouraged attention to women's rights as well, and the Seneca Falls Convention of 1848 was the first of many meetings to call for female suffrage and enhanced legal rights for women.

Ideas. The Jacksonian Era proved to be a hospitable environment for the development of new ideas. Although the scope of intellectual discourse in the antebellum South was sharply restricted by the slavery issue (antislavery arguments that were tolerated at the beginning of the nineteenth century were sharply censored in later decades), intellectual innovation flourished even there. As myriad antislavery arguments were being developed in New England, a host of proslavery arguments were developed in response in the South. The slavery issue was the starting point for a broader intellectual ferment in the North and the South. In the South, writers, politicians, and activists began to focus on developing a distinctly regional identity with a mythology, history, and culture all its own. Meanwhile, in the North, writers worked to construct an American identity that was distinctly Northern in its orientation.

New, often utopian, ideologies emerged. Some were explicitly religious, as with the founding of the Latter-day Saints, which posited new divine revelations in the United States. or the Adventist movement, which anticipated the imminent return of Jesus Christ. Others blurred the boundaries of philosophy and theology, as with the Transcendentalists, who thought that "true Christianity" meant sharing Christ's faith "in the infinitude of man."[4] Others were purely secular, such as the socialist communities advanced by reformers such as Robert Dale Owen and Albert Brisbane.

---

4 Ralph Waldo Emerson, *The Complete Works of Ralph Waldo Emerson*, vol. 1 (Boston, MA: Houghton, Mifflin and Company, 1904), 144.

II. DEMOCRACY AND LIBERTY

Major Developments

- Extension of suffrage to most white males
- Creation of mass political parties
- Expansion of constitutional restrictions on legislatures

Democratic ideas and practices took two different, but related, turns during the Jacksonian Era. The first was a democratization of American politics, which advanced along several dimensions. The most obvious feature of these democratizing trends was the acceleration of the extension of voting rights. The extension of the franchise had already begun in the Jeffersonian Era, but it came to its most immediate completion—universal, white, male suffrage—in the antebellum years. Constitutional conventions continued to meet in the original states as well as the new states, often voting to reduce voting qualifications. North Carolina was the last state to repeal property qualifications for voting in 1856, though taxpayer qualifications remained in some states until after the Civil War. The set of government officers subject to election expanded as well. Most notably, after New York adopted judicial elections in 1846, the practice rapidly spread to other states. At the presidential level, Andrew Jackson read election results as policy mandates and used evidence of popular support to enhance his authority. The Jacksonian Democrats were also the first to organize mass political parties. An important feature of the development of parties in the nineteenth century was to reduce the significance of individual candidates for office. Voters supported the party, not the person. As a result, less familiar candidates with lowly origins could rise to high office. The rise to the presidency of the Democrat Martin Van Buren, the son of a Dutch-speaking tavern keeper in small-town New York, exemplified the new political possibilities.

The second turn was toward greater constitutional checks on popular majorities. The same state constitutional conventions that extended voting rights to a larger share of the population also tended to impose more restrictions on state legislatures. Newly concerned about the fiscal irresponsibility of state legislatures, Jacksonian constitutions included new limits on legislative taxing and spending powers. Convention delegates hoped that elected judiciaries would be more independent from the politicians in the other branches and as a consequence more willing to exercise judicial review. The antislavery movement developed new ideas about individual rights and the problems associated with democratic majorities. At the same time, the proslavery movement had its own concerns about popular majorities (especially national majorities), and explored new constitutional checks on their powers.

George Bancroft expressed a distinctly partisan, Democratic view about the organization and purposes of democratic politics. South Carolina's John C. Calhoun offered a new diagnosis of democratic failings and new constitutional mechanisms to address them. From an antislavery perspective, Henry David Thoreau and Theodore Parker made the case for recognizing moral limits on democratic authority and the possibilities of individual resistance.

GEORGE BANCROFT

THE OFFICE OF THE PEOPLE IN ART, GOVERNMENT, AND RELIGION (1835)

George Bancroft was perhaps the greatest American historian of his day, but like many writers during the period he made his living through other work. A native of Massachusetts, he was an active Democrat, entering political service as the customs collector in Boston (where he gave jobs to other writers) and eventually rising to be acting secretary of war. Coming from modest means himself, his sympathies were with the labor groups that were also aligning with the emerging Democratic Party. In the last years before the Civil War, he switched his allegiance to the Republican Party and became an admirer of Abraham Lincoln. His speech on the "office of the people" at Williams College summarized some of the themes of the first volume of his comprehensive history of the United States, emphasizing the equality of man and the importance of public opinion.

What is the relationship for Bancroft between democracy and the capacity to reason? Why is the "common judgment" the nearest thing on earth to infallibility? Is Bancroft right in his assumption about mankind? Why is he not worried about bias and passion? Why might the mass be better than the individual? If some individuals, by nature or training, were shown to be more consistently right about policy questions, would democracy still be justified?

. . .

The intellectual function, by which relations are perceived, are the common endowments of the race. The differences are apparent, not real. The eye in one person may be dull, in another quick, in one distorted, and in another tranquil and clear; yet the relation of the eye to the light is in all men the same. Just so judgment may be liable in individual mind to the bias of passion, and yet its relation to truth is immutable and is universal.

In questions of practical duty. conscience is God's umpire, whose light illuminates every heart. There is nothing in books which had not first and has not still its life within us. Religion itself is a dead letter wherever its truths are not renewed in the soul. Individual conscience may be corrupted by interest or debauched by pride, yet the rule of morality is distinctly marked. . . . Duty, like death, enters every abode and delivers its message. Conscience, like reason and judgment, is universal.

. . .

If it be true that the gifts of mind and heart are universally diffused, if the sentiment of truth, justice, love, and beauty exists in every one then it follows, as a necessary consequence, that the common judgment in taste, politics, and religion is the highest authority on earth and the nearest possible approach to an infallible decision. From the consideration of individual powers I turn to the action of the human mind in masses.

If reason is a universal faculty, the universal decision is the nearest criterion of truth. The common mind winnows opinions; it is the sieve which separates error from certainty. The exercise by many of the same faculty on the same subject would naturally lead to the same conclusions. But if not, the very differences of opinion that arise prove the supreme judgment of the general mind. . . .

If wrong opinions have often been cherished by the masses, the cause always lies in the complexity of the ideas presented. Error finds its way into the soul of a nation only through the channel of truth. It is to a truth that men listen; and if they accept error also, it is only because the error is for the time so closely interwoven with the truth that the one cannot readily be separated from the other.

. . . There never was a school of philosophy nor a clan in the realm of opinion but carried along with it some important truth. And therefore every sect that has ever flourished has benefited Humanity, for the errors of a sect pass away and are forgotten; its truths are received into the common inheritance. . . .

In like manner the best government rests on the people and not on the few, on persons and not on property, on the free development of public opinion and not on authority; because the munificent Author of our being has conferred the gifts of mind upon every member of the human race without distinction of outward circumstances. Whatever of other possessions may be engrossed, mind asserts its own independence. . . . A government of equal rights must, therefore, rest upon mind; not wealth, not brute force, the sum of the moral intelligence of the community should rule the State. Prescription can no more assume to be a valid plea for political injustice. Society studies to eradicate established abuses and to bring social institutions and laws into harmony with moral right, not dismayed by the natural and necessary imperfections of all human effort, and not giving way to despair, because every hope does not at once ripen into fruit.

The public happiness is the true object of legislation, and can be secured only by the masses of mankind themselves awakening to the knowledge and the care of their own interests. Our free institutions have reversed the false and ignoble distinctions between men; and refusing to gratify the pride of caste, have acknowledged the common mind to be the true material for a commonwealth. . . . The world can advance only through the culture of the moral and intellectual powers of the people. To accomplish this end by means of the people themselves is the highest purpose of government. If it be the duty of the individual to strive after a perfection like the perfection of God, how much more ought a nation to be the image of Deity. . . . The duty of America is to secure the culture and the happiness of the masses by their reliance on themselves.

. . . Freedom of mind and of conscience, freedom of the seas, freedom of industry, equality of franchises—each great truth is firmly grasped, comprehended, and enforced; for the multitude is neither rash nor fickle. In truth, it is less fickle than those who profess to be its guides. Its natural dialectics surpass the logic of the schools. Political action has never been so consistent and so unwavering as when it results from a feeling or a principle diffused through society. The people is firm and tranquil in its movements, and necessarily acts with moderation, because it becomes but slowly impregnated with new ideas; and effects no changes except in harmony with the knowledge which it has acquired. . . .

Such is the political system which rests on reason, reflection, and the free expression of deliberate choice. There may be those who scoff at the suggestion that the decision of the whole is to be preferred to the judgment of the enlightened few. They say in their hearts that the masses are ignorant; that farmers know nothing of legislation; that mechanics should not quit their workshops to join in forming public opinion. But true political science does indeed venerate the masses. It maintains, not as has been perversely asserted, that "the people can make right," but that the people can discern right. Individuals are but shadows, too often engrossed by the pursuit of shadows; the race is immortal. Individuals are of limited sagacity; the common mind is infinite in its experience. Individuals are languid and blind; the many are ever wakeful. Individuals are corrupt; the race has been redeemed. Individuals are time-serving; the masses are fearless. Individuals may be false; the masses are ingenuous and sincere. Individuals claim the divine sanction of truth for the deceitful conceptions of their own fancies; the Spirit of God breathes through the combined intelligence of the people. . . . The decrees of the universal conscience are the nearest approach to the presence of God in the soul of man.

. . .

It is the uniform tendency of the popular element to elevate and bless humanity. The exact measure of the progress of civilization is the degree in which the intelligence of the common mind has prevailed over wealth and brute force; in other words, the measure of the progress of civilization is the progress of the people. Every great object connected with the benevolent exertions of the day has reference to the culture of those powers which are alone the common inheritance. . . .

. . .

. . . The movement of the species is upward, irresistibly upward. The individual is often lost; Providence never disowns the race. No principle once promulgated has ever been forgotten. No "timely tramp" of a despot's foot ever trod out one idea. The world cannot retrograde; the dark ages cannot return. Dynasties perish; cities are buried; nations have been victims to error or martyrs for right; humanity has always been on the advance, gaining maturity, universality, and power.

. . .

HENRY DAVID THOREAU

CIVIL DISOBEDIENCE (1849)

Henry David Thoreau was a central figure in the Transcendentalist movement and published a wide range of writing. He was best known to his contemporaries as a naturalist, and his meditation on his two years in isolation at a cabin on Walden Pond was one of his better-known works during his lifetime. His political activities attracted less attention from the general public, but he was deeply engaged in radical abolitionist circles in New England (Thoreau defended John Brown's attempt to initiate a slave uprising). It was his political activism that led him to refuse to pay the Massachusetts head tax, for he regarded all American governments as deeply unjust. He was briefly jailed for failure to pay his taxes but was freed when a benefactor covered his debt. His essay on "Resistance to Civil Government," more popularly known as "Civil Disobedience," was written to justify and explain his actions regarding the taxes. In it Thoreau develops an argument for individual passive resistance to unjust governments and laws. The essay received little attention at the time but ultimately became extremely influential as an approach to thinking about the limits of political authority and the possibilities of individual response to unjust government action.

Is Thoreau a Jeffersonian? Is he a democrat? Does he underestimate what government does? Was anarchism more realistic as a political philosophy at the time that Thoreau was writing? What does Thoreau accept as his obligation within society? What are the differences between how Thoreau thinks about human moral capacities and how Bancroft thinks about them? Under what conditions does Thoreau justify resistance to the state? What type(s) of resistance does his theory support? Would it be consistent with his theory to take collective action, or does this theory only justify individual actions? Does Thoreau support political efforts to change bad policies? Is it possible to support a right to revolution and not to support a right to civil disobedience? What does a "right" mean in this context?

I heartily accept the motto, "That government is best which governs least"; and I should like to see it acted up to more rapidly and systematically. Carried out, it finally amounts to this, which also I believe—"That government is best which governs not at all"; and when men are prepared for it, that will be the kind of government which they will have. Government is at best but an expedient; but most governments are usually, and all governments are sometimes, inexpedient. The objections which have been brought against a standing army, and they are many and weighty, and deserve to prevail, may also at last be brought against a standing government. The standing army is only an arm of the standing government. The government itself, which is only the mode which the people have chosen to execute their will, is equally liable to be abused and perverted before the people can act through it. Witness the present Mexican war, the work of comparatively a few individuals using the standing government as their tool; for, in the outset, the people would not have consented to this measure.

This American government—what is it but a tradition, though a recent one, endeavoring to transmit itself unimpaired to posterity, but each instant losing some of its integrity? . . . It is excellent, we must all allow. Yet this government never of itself furthered any enterprise, but by the alacrity with which it got out of its way. *It* does not keep the country free. It does not settle the West. *It* does not educate. The character inherent in the American people has done all that has been accomplished; and it would have done somewhat more, if the government had not sometimes got in its way. For government is an expedient by which men would fain succeed in letting one another alone; and, as has been said, when it is most expedient, the governed are most let alone by it. Trade and commerce, if they were not made of india-rubber, would never manage to bounce over the obstacles which legislators are continually putting in their way; and, if one were to judge these men wholly by the effects of their actions and not partly by their intentions, they would deserve to be classed and punished with those mischievous persons who put obstructions on the railroads.

But, to speak practically and as a citizen, unlike those who call themselves no-government men, I ask for, not *at once* no government, but at once a better government. Let every man make known what kind of government would command his respect, and that will be one step toward obtaining it.

After all, the practical reason why, when the power is once in the hands of the people, a majority are permitted, and for a long period continue, to rule is not because they are most likely to be in the right, nor because this seems fairest to the minority, but because they are physically the strongest. But a government in which the majority rule in all cases cannot be based on justice, even as far as men understand it. Can there not be a government in which majorities do not virtually decide right and wrong, but conscience?—in which majorities decide only those questions to which the rule of expediency is applicable? Must the citizen ever for a moment, or in the least degree, resign his conscience to the legislation? Why has every man a conscience, then? I think that we should be men first, and subjects afterward. It is not desirable to cultivate a respect for the law, so much as for the right. The only obligation which I have a right to assume is to do at any time what I think right. It is truly enough said that a corporation has no conscience; but a corporation of conscientious men is a corporation with a conscience. Law never made men a whit more just; and, by means of their respect for it, even the well-disposed are daily made the agents of injustice. A common and natural result of an undue respect for law is, that you may see a file of soldiers, colonel, captain, corporal, privates, powder-monkeys, and all, marching in admirable order over hill and dale to the wars, against their wills, ay, against their common sense and consciences, which makes it very steep marching indeed, and produces a palpitation of the heart. They have no doubt that it is a damnable business in which they are concerned; they are all peaceably inclined. Now, what are they? Men at all? or small movable forts and magazines, at the service of some unscrupulous man in power? . . .

The mass of men serve the state thus, not as men mainly, but as machines, with their bodies. They are the standing army, and the militia, jailers, constables, posse comitatus, etc. In most cases there is no free exercise whatever of the judgment or of the moral sense; but they put themselves on a level with wood and earth and stones; and wooden men can perhaps be manufactured that will serve the purpose as well. Such command no more respect than men of straw or a lump of dirt. They have the same sort of worth only as horses and dogs. Yet such as these even are commonly esteemed good citizens. Others—as most legislators, politicians, lawyers, ministers, and office-holders—serve the state chiefly with their heads; and, as they rarely make any moral distinctions, they are as likely to serve the devil, without *intending* it, as God. A very few—as heroes, patriots, martyrs, reformers in the great sense, and *men*—serve the state with their consciences also, and so necessarily resist it for the most part; and they are commonly treated as enemies by it. . . .

How does it become a man to behave toward this American government today? I answer, that he cannot without disgrace be associated with it. I cannot for an instant recognize that political organization as my government which is the slave's government also.

All men recognize the right of revolution; that is, the right to refuse allegiance to, and to resist, the government, when its tyranny or its inefficiency are great and unendurable. But almost all say that such is not the case now. But such was the case, they think, in the Revolution of '75. If one were to tell me that this was a bad government because it taxed certain foreign commodities brought to its ports, it is most probable that I should not make an ado about it, for I can do without them. All machines have their friction; and possibly this does enough good to counterbalance the evil. At any rate, it is a great evil to make a stir about it. But when the friction comes to have its machine, and oppression and robbery are organized, I say, let us not have such a machine any longer. In other words, when a sixth of the population of a nation which has undertaken to be the refuge of liberty are slaves, and a whole country is unjustly overrun and conquered by a foreign army, and subjected to military law, I think that it is not too soon for honest men to rebel and revolutionize. What makes this duty the more urgent is the fact that the country so overrun is not our own, but ours is the invading army.

. . .

All voting is a sort of gaming, like checkers or backgammon, with a slight moral tinge to it, a playing with right and wrong, with moral questions; and betting naturally accompanies it. The character of the voters is not staked. I cast my vote, perchance, as I think right; but I am not vitally concerned that that right should prevail. I am willing to leave it to the majority. Its obligation, therefore, never exceeds that of expediency. Even voting for the right is doing nothing for it. It is only expressing to men feebly your desire that it should prevail. A wise man will not leave the right to the mercy of chance, nor wish it to prevail through the power of the majority. There is but little virtue in the action of masses of men. When the majority shall at length vote for the abolition of slavery, it will be because they are indifferent to slavery, or because there is but little slavery left to be abolished by their vote. They will then be the only slaves. Only his vote can hasten the abolition of slavery who asserts his own freedom by his vote.

. . .

It is not a man's duty, as a matter of course, to devote himself to the eradication of any, even the most enormous, wrong; he may still properly have other concerns to engage him; but it is his duty, at least, to wash his hands of it, and, if he gives it no thought longer, not to give it practically his support. If I devote myself to other pursuits and contemplations, I must first see, at least, that I do not pursue them sitting upon another man's shoulders. I must get off him first, that he may pursue his contemplations too. . . .

. . .

Unjust laws exist: shall we be content to obey them, or shall we endeavor to amend them, and obey them until we have succeeded, or shall we transgress them at once? Men generally, under such a government as this, think that they ought to wait until they have persuaded the majority to alter them. They think that, if they should resist, the remedy would be worse than the evil. But it is the fault of the government itself that the remedy is worse than the evil. *It* makes it worse. Why is it not more apt to anticipate and provide for reform? Why does it not cherish its wise minority? Why does it cry and resist before it is hurt? Why does it not encourage its citizens to be on the alert to point out its faults, and do better than it would have them? Why does it always crucify Christ, and excommunicate Copernicus and Luther, and pronounce Washington and Franklin rebels?

. . .

As for adopting the ways which the State has provided for remedying the evil, I know not of such ways. They take too much time, and a man's life will be gone. I have other affairs to attend to. I came into this world, not chiefly to make this a good place to live in, but to live in it, be it good or bad. A man has not everything to do, but something; and because he cannot do everything, it is not necessary that he should do something wrong. . . .

I do not hesitate to say, that those who call themselves Abolitionists should at once effectually withdraw their support, both in person and property, from the government of Massachusetts, and not wait till they constitute a majority of one, before they suffer the right to prevail through them. I think that it is enough if they have God on their side, without waiting for that other one. Moreover, any man more right than his neighbors constitutes a majority of one already.

I meet this American government, or its representative, the State government, directly, and face to face, once a year—no more—in the person of its tax-gatherer; this is the only mode in which a man situated as I am necessarily meets it; and it then says distinctly, Recognize me; and the simplest, the most effectual, and, in the present posture of affairs, the indispensablest mode of treating with it on this head, of expressing your little satisfaction with and love for it, is to deny it then. My civil neighbor, the tax-gatherer, is the very man I have to deal with- for it is, after all, with men and not with parchment that I quarrel—and he has voluntarily chosen to be an agent of the government. How shall he ever know well what he is and does as an officer of the government, or as a man, until he is obliged to consider whether he shall treat me, his neighbor, for whom he has respect, as a neighbor and well-disposed man, or as a maniac and disturber of the peace, and see if he can get over this obstruction to his neighborliness without a ruder and more impetuous thought or speech corresponding with his action. I know this well, that if one thousand, if one hundred, if ten men whom I could name—if ten honest men only—ay, if one HONEST man, in this State of Massachusetts, ceasing to hold slaves, were actually to withdraw from this copartnership, and be locked up in the county jail therefor, it would be the abolition of slavery in America. For it matters not how small the beginning may seem to be: what is once well done is done forever. . . .

Under a government which imprisons any unjustly, the true place for a just man is also a prison. The proper place today, the only place which Massachusetts has provided for her freer and less desponding spirits, is in her prisons, to be put out and locked out of the State by her own act, as they have already put themselves out by their principles. It is there that the fugitive slave, and the Mexican prisoner on parole, and the Indian come to plead the wrongs of his race should find them; on that separate, but more free and honorable, ground, where the State places those who are not with her, but against her—the only house in a slave State in which a free man can abide with honor. If any think that their influence would be lost there, and their voices no longer afflict the ear of the State, that they would not be as an enemy within its walls, they do not know by how much truth is stronger than error, nor how much more eloquently and effectively he can combat injustice who has experienced a little in his own person. Cast your whole vote, not a strip of paper merely, but your whole influence. A minority is powerless while it conforms to the majority; it is not even a minority then; but it is irresistible when it clogs by its whole weight. If the alternative is to keep all just men in prison, or give up war and slavery, the State will not hesitate which to choose. If a thousand men were not to pay their tax-bills this year, that would not be a violent and bloody measure, as it would be to pay them, and enable the State to commit violence and shed innocent blood. This is, in fact, the definition of a peaceable revolution, if any such is possible. If the tax-gatherer, or any other public officer, asks me, as one has done, "But what shall I do?" my answer is, "If you really wish to do anything, resign your office." When the subject has refused allegiance, and the officer has resigned his office, then the revolution is accomplished. But even suppose blood should flow. Is there not a sort of blood shed when the conscience is wounded? Through this wound a man's real manhood and immortality flow out, and he bleeds to an everlasting death. I see this blood flowing now.

. . .

I have paid no poll-tax for six years. I was put into a jail once on this account, for one night; and, as I stood considering the walls of solid stone, two or three feet thick, the door of wood and iron, a foot thick, and the iron grating which strained the light, I could not help being struck with the foolishness of that institution which treated me as if I were mere flesh and blood and bones, to be locked up. I wondered that it should have concluded at length that this was the best use it could put me to, and had never thought to avail itself of my services in some way. I saw that, if there was a wall of stone between me and my townsmen, there was a still more difficult one to climb or break through before they could get to be as free as I was. I did not for a moment feel confined, and the walls seemed a great waste of stone and mortar. Ifelt as if I alone of all my townsmen had paid my tax. They plainly did not know how to treat me, but behaved like persons who are underbred. In every threat and in every compliment there was a blunder; for they thought that my chief desire was to stand the other side of that stone wall. I could not but smile to see how industriously they locked the door on my meditations, which followed them out again without let or hindrance, and *they* were really all that was dangerous. As they could not reach me, they had resolved to punish my body; just as boys, if they cannot come at some person against whom they have a spite, will abuse his dog. I saw that the State was half-witted, that it was timid as a lone woman with her silver spoons, and that it did not know its friends from its foes, and I lost all my remaining respect for it, and pitied it.

Thus the State never intentionally confronts a man's sense, intellectual or moral, but only his body, his senses. It is not armed with superior wit or honesty, but with superior physical strength. I was not born to be forced. I will breathe after my own fashion. Let us see who is the strongest. What force has a multitude? They only can force me who obey a higher law than I. They force me to become like themselves. I do not hear of *men* being *forced* to have this way or that by masses of men. What sort of life were that to live? When I meet a government which says to me, "Your money or your life," why should I be in haste to give it my money? It may be in a great strait, and not know what to do: I cannot help that. It must help itself; do as I do. It is not worth the while to snivel about it. I am not responsible for the successful working of the machinery of society. I am not the son of the engineer. I perceive that, when an acorn and a chestnut fall side by side, the one does not remain inert to make way for the other, but both obey their own laws, and spring and grow and flourish as best they can, till one, perchance, overshadows and destroys the other. If a plant cannot live according to its nature, it dies; and so a man.

. . .

I have never declined paying the highway tax, because I am as desirous of being a good neighbor as I am of being a bad subject; and as for supporting schools, I am doing my part to educate my fellow-countrymen now. It is for no particular item in the tax-bill that I refuse to pay it. I simply wish to refuse allegiance to the State, to withdraw and stand aloof from it effectually. I do not care to trace the course of my dollar, if I could, till it buys a man or a musket to shoot one with—the dollar is innocent—but I am concerned to trace the effects of my allegiance. In fact, I quietly declare war with the State, after my fashion, though I will still make what use and get what advantage of her I can, as is usual in such cases.

. . .

The authority of government, even such as I am willing to submit to—for I will cheerfully obey those who know and can do better than I, and in many things even those who neither know nor can do so well—is still an impure one: to be strictly just, it must have the sanction and consent of the governed. It can have no pure right over my person and property but what I concede to it. The progress from an absolute to a limited monarchy, from a limited monarchy to a democracy, is a progress toward a true respect for the individual. Even the Chinese philosopher was wise enough to regard the individual as the basis of the empire. Is a democracy, such as we know it, the last improvement possible in government? Is it not possible to take a step further towards recognizing and organizing the rights of man? There will never be a really free and enlightened State until the State comes to recognize the individual as a higher and independent power, from which all its own power and authority are derived, and treats him accordingly. I please myself with imagining a State at least which can afford to be just to all men, and to treat the individual with respect as a neighbor; which even would not think it inconsistent with its own repose if a few were to live aloof from it, not meddling with it, nor embraced by it, who fulfilled all the duties of neighbors and fellow-men. A State which bore this kind of fruit, and suffered it to drop off as fast as it ripened, would prepare the way for a still more perfect and glorious State, which also I have imagined, but not yet anywhere seen.

JOHN C. CALHOUN

A DISQUISITION ON GOVERNMENT (1850)

South Carolina's John C. Calhoun entered politics as a nationalist-minded "War Hawk" during the War of 1812. By the 1820s, his home state was moving in a different direction. Tariffs had been raised to unprecedented levels, and the Missouri Compromise had polarized the nation on the slavery issue. The planters of the Deep South thought that northern manufacturing interests and antislavery activists were striking at the heart of their livelihood and society. Calhoun followed their lead and became the leading theorist of states' rights (and the political leader of the South) in the antebellum period.

His involvement in the nullification crisis in the winter of 1832–33 was undoubtedly the defining moment of his career. He had served as vice president during Andrew Jackson's first term of office, but he fell out with the administration and returned to the capital as a U.S. senator. He developed the theory that states could both evaluate the constitutionality of federal laws and block (or "nullify") their implementation within the boundaries of the state. The nullification device was soundly rejected when South Carolina tried to use it to block the collection of tariff duties at the state's ports, but the state did manage to force Congress to compromise and set the country on the path to free trade. At the end of his life, Calhoun prepared two substantial treatises outlining his political and constitutional philosophy and offering proposals that he thought would ultimately be necessary to avoid secession and war. The key to his work was the idea of "concurrent majorities." Calhoun argued that it was insufficient to win the support of simple majorities to adopt deeply contested policies that affected fundamental interests. The policy should instead be supported by majorities of all the relevant, affected constituencies. The immediate application of the concept was to suggest that both the North and the South would have to agree before any change in federal policies regarding slavery or key economic issues could be made. More broadly, the theory was meant to develop a more effective constitutional check against the potential tyranny of the majority. His *Disquisition on Government* laid out the theory in more abstract form.

How does Calhoun's analysis of the problem of faction differ from Madison's? How does his solution differ from Madison's? To what degree is the principle of concurrent majorities reflected in the structure of the U.S. Constitution? Why might simple majority rule be insufficient as a guiding principle of politics? Why might existing systems of checks and balances, like the presidential veto and judicial review, be inadequate to protect minority rights? How would we go about identifying the relevant communities that would make up the concurrent majorities? Are there any public policies that should get the explicit buy-in of a majority of the state governments? Should farm policy, for example, need the approval of a majority of farmers?

In order to have a clear and just conception of the nature and object of government, it is indispensable to understand correctly what that constitution or law of our nature is, in which government originates; or, to express it more fully and accurately—that law, without which government would not, and with which, it must necessarily exist. Without this, it is as impossible to lay any solid foundation for the science of government, as it would be to lay one for that of astronomy, without a like understanding of that constitution or law of the material world, according to which the several bodies composing the solar system mutually act on each other, and by which they are kept in their respective spheres. The first question, accordingly, to be considered is—What is that constitution or law of our nature, without which government would not exist, and with which its existence is necessary?

In considering this, I assume, as an incontestable fact, that man is so constituted as to be a social being. His inclinations and wants, physical and moral, irresistibly impel him to associate with his kind; and he has, accordingly, never been found, in any age or country, in any state other than the social. In no other, indeed, could he exist; and in no other—were it possible for him to exist—could he attain to a full development of his moral and intellectual faculties, or raise himself, in the scale of being, much above the level of the brute creation.

I next assume, also, as a fact not less incontestable, that, while man is so constituted as to make the social state necessary to his existence and the full development of his faculties, this state itself cannot exist without government. The assumption rests on universal experience. In no age or country has any society or community ever been found, whether enlightened or savage, without government of some description.

Having assumed these, as unquestionable phenomena of our nature, I shall, without further remark, proceed to the investigation of the primary and important question—What is that constitution of our nature, which, while it impels man to associate with his kind, renders it impossible for society to exist without government?

The answer will be found in the fact (not less incontestable than either of the others) that, while man is created for the social state, and is accordingly so formed as to feel what affects others, as well as what affects himself, he is, at the same time, so constituted as to feel more intensely what affects him directly, than what affects him indirectly though others; or, to express it differently, he is so constituted, that his direct or individual affections are stronger than his sympathetic or social feelings. I intentionally avoid the expression, *selfish* feelings, as applicable to the former; because, as commonly used, it implies an unusual excess of the individual over the social feelings, in the person to whom it is applied; and, consequently, something depraved and vicious. My object is, to exclude such inference, and to restrict the inquiry exclusively to facts in their bearings on the subject under consideration, viewed as mere phenomena appertaining to our nature—constituted as it is; and which are as unquestionable as is that of gravitation, or any other phenomenon of the material world.

. . .

But that constitution of our nature which makes us feel more intensely what affects us directly than what affects us indirectly through others, necessarily leads to conflict between individuals. Each, in consequence, has a greater regard for his own safety or happiness, than for the safety or happiness of others; and, where these come in opposition, is ready to sacrifice the interests of others to his own. And hence, the tendency to a universal state of conflict, between individual and individual; accompanied by the connected passions of suspicion, jealousy, anger and revenge—followed by insolence, fraud and cruelty—and, if not prevented by some controlling power, ending in a state of universal discord and confusion, destructive of the social state and the ends for which it is ordained. This controlling power, wherever vested, or by whomsoever exercised, is GOVERNMENT.

It follows, then, that man is so constituted, that government is necessary to the existence of society, and society to his existence, and the perfection of his faculties. It follows, also, that government has its origin in this twofold constitution of his nature; the sympathetic or social feelings constituting the remote—and the individual or direct, the proximate cause.

. . .

But government, although intended to protect and preserve society, has itself a strong tendency to disorder and abuse of its powers, as all experience and almost every page of history testify. The cause is to be found in the same constitution of our nature which makes government indispensable. The powers which it is necessary for government to possess, in order to repress violence and preserve order, cannot execute themselves. They must be administered by men in whom, like others, the individual are stronger than the social feelings. And hence, the powers vested in them to prevent injustice and oppression on the part of others, will, if left unguarded, be by them converted into instruments to oppress the rest of the community. That, by which this is prevented, by whatever name called, is what is meant by CONSTITUTION. In its most comprehensive sense, when applied to GOVERNMENT.

Having its origin in the same principle of our nature, *constitution* stands to *government*, as *government* stands to *society*; and, as the end for which society is ordained, would be defeated without government, so that for which government is ordained would, in a great measure, be defeated without constitution. But they differ in this striking particular. There is no difficulty in forming government. It is not even a matter of choice, whether there shall be one or not. Like breathing, it is not permitted to depend on our volition. Necessity will force it on all communities in some one form or another. Very different is the case as to constitution. Instead of a matter of necessity, it is one of the most difficult tasks imposed on man to form a constitution worthy of the name; while, to form a perfect one—one that would completely counteract the tendency of government to oppression and abuse, and hold it strictly to the great ends for which it is ordained—has thus far exceeded human wisdom, and possibly ever will. From this, another striking difference results. Constitution is the contrivance of man, while government is of Divine ordination. Man is left to perfect what the wisdom of the Infinite ordained, as necessary to preserve the race.

With these remarks, I proceed to the consideration of the important and difficult question: How is this tendency of government to be counteracted? Or, to express it more fully—How can those who are invested with the powers of government be prevented from employing them, as the means of aggrandizing themselves, instead of using them to protect and preserve society? It cannot be done by instituting a higher power to control the government, and those who administer it. This would be but to change the seat of authority, and to make this bigger power, in reality, the government; with the same tendency, on the part of those who might control its powers, to pervert them into instruments of aggrandizement. Nor can it be done by limiting the powers of government, so as to make it too feeble to be made an instrument of abuse; for, passing by the difficulty of so limiting its powers, without creating a power higher than the government itself to enforce the observance of the limitations, it is a sufficient objection that it would, if practicable, defeat the end for which government is ordained, by making it too feeble to protect and preserve society. The powers necessary for this purpose will ever prove sufficient to aggrandize those who control it, at the expense of the rest of the community.

. . . Self-preservation is the supreme law, as well with communities as individuals. And hence the danger of withholding from government the full command of the power and resources of the state; and the great difficulty of limiting its powers consistently with the protection and preservation of the community. And hence the question recurs—By what means can government, without being divested of the full command of the resources of the community, be prevented from abusing its powers?

. . .

There is but one way in which this can possibly be done; and that is, by such an organism as will furnish the ruled with the means of resisting successfully this tendency on the part of the rulers to oppression and abuse. Power can only be resisted by power—and tendency by tendency. Those who exercise power and those subject to its exercise—the rulers and the ruled—stand in antagonistic relations to each other. . . .

. . .

The right of suffrage, of itself, can do no more than give complete control to those who elect, over the conduct of those they have elected. In doing this, it accomplishes all it possibly can accomplish. . . . But it is manifest that the right of suffrage, in making these changes, transfers, in reality, the actual control over the government, from those who make and execute the laws, to the body of the community; and, thereby, places the powers of the government as fully in the mass of the community, as they would be if they, in fact, had assembled, made, and executed the laws themselves, without the intervention of representatives or agents. The more perfectly it does this, the more perfectly it accomplishes its ends; but in doing so, it only changes the seat of authority, without counteracting, in the least, the tendency of the government to oppression and abuse of its powers.

If the whole community had the same interests, so that the interests of each and every portion would be so affected by the action of the government, that the laws which oppressed or impoverished one portion, would necessarily oppress and impoverish all others—or the reverse—then the right of suffrage, of itself, would be all-sufficient to counteract the tendency of the government to oppression and abuse of its powers; and, of course, would form, of itself, a perfect constitutional government. . . .

But such is not the case. . . .

. . . [A] struggle will take place between the various interests to obtain a majority, in order to control the government. If no one interest be strong enough, of itself, to obtain it, a combination will be formed between those whose interests are most alike—each conceding something to the others, until a sufficient number is obtained to make a majority. . . . When once formed, the community will be divided into two great parties—a major and minor—between which there will be incessant struggles on the one side to retain, and on the other to obtain the majority—and, thereby, the control of the government and the advantages it confers.

. . . The advantages of possessing the control of the powers of the government, and, thereby, of its honors and emoluments, are, of themselves, exclusive of all other considerations, ample to divide even such a community [as one with no inherent diversity of interests] into two great hostile parties.

. . .

As, then, the right of suffrage, without some other provision, cannot counteract this tendency of government, the next question for consideration is—What is that other provision? . . .

From what has been said, it is manifest, that this provision must be of a character calculated to prevent any one interest, or combination of interests, from using the powers of government to aggrandize itself at the expense of the others. Here lies the evil: and just in proportion as it shall prevent, or fail to prevent it, in the same degree it will effect, or fail to effect the end intended to be accomplished. There is but one certain mode in which this result can be secured; and that is, by the adoption of some restriction or limitation, which shall so effectually prevent any one interest, or combination of interests, from obtaining the exclusive control of the government, as to render hopeless all attempts directed to that end. There is, again, but one mode in which this can be effected; and that is, by taking the sense of each interest or portion of the community, which may be unequally and injuriously affected by the action of the government, separately, through its own majority, or in some other way by which its voice may be fairly expressed; and to require the consent of each interest, either to put or to keep the government in action. This, too, can be accomplished only in one way—and that is, by such an organism of the government—and, if necessary for the purpose, of the community also—as will, by dividing and distributing the powers of government, give to each division or interest, through its appropriate organ, either a concurrent voice in making and executing the laws, or a veto on their execution. It is only by such an organism, that the assent of each can be made necessary to put the government in motion; or the power made effectual to arrest its action, when put in motion—and it is only by the one or the other that the different interests, orders, classes, or portions, into which the community may be divided, can be protected, and all conflict and struggle between them prevented—by rendering it impossible to put or to keep it in action, without the concurrent consent of all.

Such an organism as this, combined with the right of suffrage, constitutes, in fact, the elements of constitutional government. The one, by rendering those who make and execute the laws responsible to those on whom they operate, prevents the rulers from oppressing the ruled; and the other, by making it impossible for anyone interest or combination of interests or class, or order, or portion of the community, to obtain exclusive control, prevents any one of them from oppressing the other. It is clear, that oppression and abuse of power must come, if at all, from the one or the other quarter. From no other can they come. It follows, that the two, suffrage and proper organism combined, are sufficient to counteract the tendency of government to oppression and abuse of power; and to restrict it to the fulfilment of the great ends for which it is ordained.

. . .

It may be readily inferred, from what has been stated, that the effect of organism is neither to supersede nor diminish the importance of the right of suffrage; but to aid and perfect it. The object of the latter is, to collect the sense of the community. The more fully and perfectly it accomplishes this, the more fully and perfectly it fulfils its end. But the most it can do, of itself, is to collect the sense of the greater number; that is, of the stronger interests, or combination of interests; and to assume this to be the sense of the community. It is only when aided by a proper organism, that it can collect the sense of the entire community—of each and all its interests; of each, through its appropriate organ, and of the whole, through all of them united. This would truly be the sense of the entire community; for whatever diversity each interest might have within itself—as all would have the same interest in reference to the action of the government, the individuals composing each would be fully and truly represented by its own majority or appropriate organ, regarded in reference to the other interests. In brief, every individual of every interest might trust, with confidence, its majority or appropriate organ, against that of every other interest.

It results, from what has been said, that there are two different modes in which the sense of the community may be taken; one, simply by the right of suffrage, unaided; the other, by the right through a proper organism. Each collects the sense of the majority. But one regards numbers only, and considers the whole community as a unit, having but one common interest throughout; and collects the sense of the greater number of the whole, as that of the community. The other, on the contrary, regards interests as well as numbers—considering the community as made up of different and conflicting interests, as far as the action of the government is concerned; and takes the sense of each, through its majority or appropriate organ, and the united sense of all, as the sense of the entire community. The former of these I shall call the numerical, or absolute majority; and the latter, the concurrent, or constitutional majority. I call it the constitutional majority, because it is an essential element in every constitutional government—be its form what it may. So great is the difference, politically speaking, between the two majorities, that they cannot be confounded, without leading to great and fatal errors; and yet the distinction between them has been so entirely overlooked, that when the term *majority* is used in political discussions, it is applied exclusively to designate the numerical—as if there were no other. Until this distinction is recognized, and better understood, there will continue to be great liability to error in properly constructing constitutional governments, especially of the popular form, and of preserving them when properly constructed. Until then, the latter will have a strong tendency to slide, first, into the government of the numerical majority, and, finally, into absolute government of some other form. . . .

The first and leading error which naturally arises from overlooking the distinction referred to, is, to confound the numerical majority with the people; and this so completely as to regard them as identical. This is a consequence that necessarily results from considering the numerical as the only majority. All admit, that a popular government, or democracy, is the government of the people; for the terms imply this. A perfect government of the kind would be one which would embrace the consent of every citizen or member of the community; but as this is impracticable, in the opinion of those who regard the numerical as the only majority, and who can perceive no other way by which the sense of the people can be taken—they are compelled to adopt this as the only true basis of popular government, in contradistinction to governments of the aristocratical or monarchical form. Being thus constrained, they are, in the next place, forced to regard the numerical majority, as, in effect, the entire people; that is, the greater part as the whole; and the government of the greater part as the government of the whole. It is thus the two come to be confounded, and a part made identical with the whole. And it is thus, also that all the rights, powers, and immunities of the whole people come to be attributed to the numerical majority; and, among others, the supreme, sovereign authority of establishing and abolishing governments at pleasure.

This radical error, the consequence of confounding the two, and of regarding the numerical as the only majority, has contributed more than any other cause, to prevent the formation of popular constitutional governments—and to destroy them even when they have been formed. It leads to the conclusion that, in their formation and establishment nothing more is necessary than the right of suffrage—and the allotment to each division of the community a representation in the government, in proportion to numbers. If the numerical majority were really the people; and if, to take its sense truly, were to take the sense of the people truly, a government so constituted would be a true and perfect model of a popular constitutional government; and every departure from it would detract from its excellence. But, as such is not the case—as the numerical majority, instead of being the people, is only a portion of them—such a government, instead of being a true and perfect model of the people's government, that is, a people self-governed, is but the government of a part, over a part—the major over the minor portion.

But this misconception of the true elements of constitutional government does not stop here. It leads to others equally false and fatal, in reference to the best means of preserving and perpetuating them, when, from some fortunate combination of circumstances, they are correctly formed. For they who fall into these errors regard the restrictions which organism imposes on the will of the numerical majority as restrictions on the will of the people, and, therefore, as not only useless, but wrongful and mischievous. And hence they endeavor to destroy organism, under the delusive hope of making government more democratic.

. . .

A written constitution certainly has many and considerable advantages; but it is a great mistake to suppose, that the mere insertion of provisions to restrict and limit the powers of the government, without investing those for whose protection they are inserted with the means of enforcing their observance, will be sufficient to prevent the major and dominant party from abusing its powers. Being the party in possession of the government, they will, from the same constitution of man which makes government necessary to protect society, be in favor of the powers granted by the constitution, and opposed to the restrictions intended to limit them. As the major and dominant party, they will have no need of these restrictions for their protection. . . .

The minor, or weaker party, on the contrary, would take the opposite direction—and regard them as essential to their protection against the dominant party. . . . But where there are no means by which they could compel the major party to observe the restrictions . . .

. . . But of what possible avail could the strict construction of the minor party be, against the liberal interpretation of the major, when the one would have all the powers of the government to carry its construction into effect—and the other be deprived of all means of enforcing its construction? In a contest so unequal, the result would not be doubtful. The party in favor of the restrictions would be overpowered. . . . The end of the contest would be the subversion of the constitution, either by the undermining process of construction—where its meaning would admit of possible doubt—or by substituting in practice what is called party-usage, in place of its provisions—or, finally, when no other contrivance would subserve the purpose, by openly and boldly setting them aside. By the one or the other, the restrictions would ultimately be annulled, and the government be converted into one of unlimited powers.

. . .

The necessary consequence of taking the sense of the community by the concurrent majority is, as has been explained, to give to each interest or portion of the community a negative on the others. It is this mutual negative among its various conflicting interests, which invests each with the power of protecting itself—and places the rights and safety of each, where only they can be securely placed, under its own guardianship. Without this there can be no systematic, peaceful, or effective resistance to the natural tendency of each to come into conflict with the others: and without this there can be no constitution. It is this negative power—the power of preventing or arresting the action of the government—be it called by what term it may—veto, interposition, nullification, check, or balance of power—which, in fact, forms the constitution. They are all but different names for the negative power. In all its forms, and under all its names, it results from the concurrent majority. Without this there can be no negative; and, without a negative, no constitution. The assertion is true in reference to all constitutional governments, be their forms what they may. It is, indeed, the *negative* power which makes the constitution—and the *positive* which makes the government. The one is the power of acting—and the other the power of preventing or arresting action. The two, combined, make constitutional governments.

. . .

It is, indeed, the single, or *one power*, which excludes the negative, and constitutes absolute government; and not the *number* in whom the power is vested. The numerical majority is as truly a *single power*, and excludes the negative as completely as the absolute government of one, or of the few. . . . And, hence, the great and broad distinction between governments is—not that of the one, the few, or the many—but of the constitutional and the absolute.

From this there results another distinction, which, although secondary in its character, very strongly marks the difference between these forms of government. I refer to their respective conservative principle—that is, the Principle by which they are upheld and preserved. This principle, in constitutional governments, is *compromise*—and in absolute governments, is *force*—as will be next explained.

. . .

[T]he government of the concurrent majority, where the organism is perfect, excludes the possibility of oppression, by giving to each interest, or portion, or order—where there are established classes—the means of protecting itself, by its negative, against all measures calculated to advance the peculiar interests of others at its expense. Its effect, then, is, to cause the different interests, portions, or orders—as the case lay be—to desist from attempting to adopt any measure calculated to promote the prosperity of one, or more, by sacrificing that of others; and thus to force them to unite in such measures only as would promote the prosperity of all, as the only means to prevent the suspension of the action of the government—and, thereby, to avoid anarchy, the greatest of all evils. . . .

. . .

The concurrent majority, then, is better suited to enlarge and secure the bounds of liberty, because it is better suited to prevent government from passing beyond its proper limits, and to restrict it to its primary end—the protection of the community. But in doing this, it leaves, necessarily, all beyond it open and free to individual exertions; and thus enlarges and secures the sphere of liberty to the greatest extent which the condition of the community will admit, as has been explained. The tendency of government to pass beyond its proper limits is what exposes liberty to danger, and renders it insecure; and it is the strong counteraction of governments of the concurrent majority to this tendency which makes them so favorable to liberty. On the contrary, those of the numerical, instead of opposing and counteracting this tendency, add to it increased strength, in consequence of the violent party struggles incident to them, as has been fully explained. And hence their encroachments on liberty, and the danger to which it is exposed under such governments.

. . .

THEODORE PARKER

LAW OF GOD AND THE STATUTES OF MEN (1854)

Theodore Parker was a Unitarian minister in Boston whose intellectual circle included William Lloyd Garrison, Ralph Waldo Emerson, and Elizabeth Cady Stanton. His 1854 sermon "The Law of God and the Statutes of Men" called on religious believers to resist the federal Fugitive Slave Act of 1850, which required private individuals to help recapture escaped slaves.

Parker was one of many antislavery northerners who championed active resistance to slavery. Henry David Thoreau, Parker's Massachusetts neighbor, urged citizens to disobey laws that immorally protected human bondage. Thoreau's most famous essay, "Civil Disobedience," condemned persons who preferred to preserve good social relations to violating unjust laws. Thoreau's "Slavery in Massachusetts" spoke directly on the obligation to disobey the Fugitive Slave Act:

> The judges and lawyers . . . and all men of expediency, try this case by a very low and incompetent standard. They consider, not whether the Fugitive Slave Law is right, but whether it is what they call constitutional. Is virtue constitutional, or vice? Is equity constitutional, or iniquity? In important moral and vital questions, like this, it is just as impertinent to ask whether a law is constitutional or not, as to ask whether it is profitable or not. They persist in being the servants of the worst of men, and not the servants of humanity. The question is, not whether you or your grandfather, seventy years ago, did not enter into an agreement to serve the Devil, and that service is not accordingly now due; but whether you will not now, for once and at last, serve God—in spite of your own past recreancy, or that of your ancestor—by obeying that eternal and only just CONSTITUTION, which He, and not any Jefferson or Adams, has written in your being.[5]

The excerpt from Parker's sermon below urges northerners to violate the Fugitive Slave Act. Later in life, Theodore Parker supported John Brown's more violent efforts to free slaves. Does the sermon suggest any limitations to the duty to obey the natural law? Do any limits exist to the moral duty to free slaves? How does Parker's assessment of relationship between individuals and government compare to Thoreau's?

. . .

Now see the relation of the individual to the Statutes of men. There is a natural duty to obey every statute which is just. It is so before the thing becomes a statute. The legislator makes a decree; it is a declaration that certain things must be done, or certain other things not done. If the things commanded are just, the statute does not make them just; does not make them any more morally obligatory than they were before. The legislator may make it very uncomfortable for me to disobey his command, when that is wicked; he cannot make it right for me to keep it when wicked. All the moral obligation depends on the justice of the statute, not on its legality; not on its constitutionality; but, on the fact that it is a part of the natural Law of God . . .

Now then, as it is a moral duty to obey a just statute because it is just, so it is a moral duty to disobey any statute which is unjust. . . . Here in disobedience, there are two degrees. First, there is passive disobedience, non-obedience, the doing nothing for the statute; and second, there is active disobedience, which is resistance, the doing something, not for the statute, but something against it. Sometimes the moral duty is accomplished by the passive disobedience, doing nothing; sometimes, to accomplish the moral duty, it is requisite to resist, to do something against the statute. However, we are to resist wrong by right, not wrong by wrong.

There are many statutes which relate mainly to matters of convenience. They are rules of public conduct indeed, but only rules of prudence, not of morals. Such are the statutes declaring that a man

5 Henry David Thoreau, *The Writings of Henry David Thoreau: Cape Cod and Miscellanies*, vol. 4 (Boston, MA: Houghton Mifflin Company, 1893), 401.

shall not vote till twenty-one; that he shall drive his team on the right hand side of the street . . . It is necessary that there should be such rules of prudence as these; and while they do not offend the conscience every good man will respect them; it is not immoral to keep them.

. . .

So the moral value of a statute is, that while it embodies justice it also represents the free conscience of the nation. Then also it is a monument of the nation's moral progress, showing how far it has got on. It is likewise a basis, for future progress, being a right rule for moral conduct. But when the statute only embodies injustice, and so violates the conscience, and is forced on men by bayonets, then its moral value is all gone; it is against the conscience. If the people consent to suffer it, it is because they are weak; and if they consent to obey it, it is because they are also wicked.

. . .

I know very well it is commonly taught that it is the moral duty of the officers of government to execute every statute, and of the people to submit thereto, no matter how wicked the statute may be. This is the doctrine of the Supreme Court of the United States of America, of the Executive of the United States; I know very well it is the doctrine of the majority of the Legislature in both Houses of Congress; it is the doctrine of the churches of Commerce;—God be praised, it is not the doctrine of the churches of Christianity, and there are such in every denomination, in many a town; even in the great centers of commerce there are ministers of many denominations, earnest, faithful men, who swear openly that they will keep God's Law, come what will of man's statute. This is practical piety; the opposite is practical atheism. I have known some speculative atheists. I abhor their doctrines; but the speculative atheists that I have known, all recognize a Law higher than men's passions and calculations; the Law of some Power which makes the Universe and sways it for noble purposes and to a blessed end.

Then comes the doctrine:—while the statute is on the books it must be enforced. It is not only the right of the legislator to make any constitutional statute he pleases, but it is the moral and religious duty of the magistrate to enforce the statute; it is the duty of the people to obey. So in Pharaoh's time it was a moral duty to drown the babies in the Nile; in Darius' time to pray to King Darius, and him only; in Herod's time to massacre the children of Bethlehem; in Henry the Eighth's time to cast your Bible to the flames. Iscariot only did a disagreeable duty.

It is a most dreadful doctrine; utterly false! Has a legislator, Pharaoh, Darius, Herod, Henry the Eighth, a single tyrant, any moral right to repudiate God, and declare himself not amenable to the moral Law of the Universe? You all answer, No! Have ten millions of men out of nineteen millions in America a right to do this? Has any man a moral right to repudiate justice and declare himself not amenable to conscience and to God? Where did he get the right to invade the conscience of mankind? Is it because he is legislator, magistrate, governor, president, king?

. . . It is only justified on the idea that there is no God, and this world is a chaos. But yet it is taught; and only last Sunday the minister of a "prominent church" taught that every law must be executed, right or wrong, and thanked the soldiers who, with their bayonets, forced an innocent man to slavery. No matter how unjust a statute is, it must be enforced and obeyed so long as it is on the Law Book!

. . .

. . . When the nation is willing to accept a statute which violates the nation's conscience, the nation is rotten. If a statute is right, I will ask how I can best obey it. When it is wrong, I will ask how I can best disobey it,—most safely, most effectually, with the least violence. . . .

. . .

III. CITIZENSHIP AND COMMUNITY

Major Developments

- Growth of social and political equality
- Nativist reaction to growing Catholic immigration
- Ideological polarization on slavery issue

In 1831, two young Frenchmen of minor aristocratic families traveled the United States, interviewing everyone from former presidents to frontiersmen. One of the foreign visitors, Alexis de Tocqueville, soon published his thoughts from the trip in a classic work of political sociology, *Democracy in America*. Tocqueville was intrigued by, among other things, the emergence of a new kind of person and a new kind of community in the young republic. The omnipresent state and the local nobility that were so familiar in Europe seemed to be largely absent in America. American democracy had "opened a thousand new roads to fortune and gave any obscure adventurer the chance of wealth and power." By comparison with Europeans, Americans had to deal with a startling "equality of conditions" in which "each man [can] entertain vast hopes" even while being "by himself weak." But the barriers to achieving true distinction had merely changed its shape, not disappeared. Individuals faced "the competition of all" and were always attempting to force their way through "the uniform crowd surrounding and hemming them in." Americans "form a habit of thinking of themselves in isolation and imagine that their whole destiny is in their own hands." At the same time, their individual impotence encouraged Americans to constantly campaign for influence and organize voluntary associations to achieve their social goals, societies that could be "something like a separate nation within the nation."[6]

What kind of community could be formed from these restless individuals? The answers varied. Some looked at the emerging American society with concern bordering on alarm, as Tocqueville did. Others looked on with hope and saw new possibilities for human flourishing. For many Whigs, social equality carried risks. The democratic masses needed leaders, and the challenge was to bring those natural leaders to the fore. For many Democrats, equality meant opportunity, and the challenge was to bring down the barriers that might still hamper individual achievement. Some reformers imagined new communities. Some flirted with anarchism, where individuals might connect only with communities of their own making; others with socialism, where individuals could be enmeshed in communal ties and share common resources.

The United States of the middle decades of the nineteenth century faced other political and social challenges as well. Vast numbers of immigrants flooded into the country, fleeing economic crisis and war in Europe. Nearly the entire American population was native born when Andrew Jackson was first elected president. By the time Abraham Lincoln was elected three decades later, more than a tenth of the population was foreign born. Moreover, the new waves of immigrants differed from the old. Large proportions came from

---

6 Alexis de Tocqueville, *Democracy in America*, trans. George Lawrence (Garden City, NY: Anchor Books, 1969), 11, 537, 508, 190.

Catholic countries, spoke languages other than English, or had difficult relations with Britain. Many native-born Protestants reacted with alarm, with nativist movements rising up to expel or subordinate the newcomers. Meanwhile, tensions between the slaveholding and non-slaveholding states increased. Abraham Lincoln eventually asked whether a nation half slave and half free could long survive, but he was hardly the first to question the viability of a union composed of such divergent economic and social societies. Lincoln's fellow Republican, New York's William Seward, famously argued that there was "an irrepressible conflict between opposing and enduring forces" in the United States, which would eventually come to a head and force the nation to become either all slave or all free. "Fanatical agitators" did not threaten the union; the union was riven at its core.[7]

7 William H. Seward, *Speech of William H. Seward, in the Senate of the United States, July 29, 1852* (Washington, D.C.: Buell & Blanchard, 1852), 2, 14.

SAMUEL F. B. MORSE

IMMINENT DANGERS TO THE FREE INSTITUTIONS OF THE UNITED STATES (1835)

Samuel Morse is best known for inventing a practical telegraph (and Morse code), but he had other pursuits, including an active career as a nativist in the 1830s. Many of his nativist writings began as newspaper essays under various pseudonyms, and they were frequently widely reprinted and collected into book form. At the core of this political writing was a warning that the wave of immigrants from Catholic countries threatened the stability of republican government in the United States. Like many nativists of the period, he believed that Catholics were ill suited to citizenship in a free society given the illiberal tendencies and strict hierarchical structure of the Catholic Church, and he questioned whether Catholics would ever reconcile themselves to the separation of church and state that had emerged in the United States. Morse also promoted conspiracy theories linking the political machinations of foreign states (where the Catholic Church was integrated with the government) and the migration of Catholic believers and priests to American shores; America was, in effect, being invaded by covert agents of foreign governments. Unlike some, Morse cautioned against anti-Catholic violence or the creation of an explicitly Protestant political party, preferring education and vigilance against antirepublican policies.

Are democracies particularly vulnerable to outside influences? Does the stability of republican institutions depend on a stable electorate? Why might rapid population change through immigration pose a threat to the political status quo? Why might immigration not have a significant effect on politics? Can all religions be regarded as equivalent by a republican government? Does Morse favor a separation of church and state, or the linkage of church and state? Why does Morse doubt the existence of a natural right to join the United States? Under what conditions should the United States turn away potential immigrants? Are an "oath" and a five-year residency requirement sufficient "checks" on political dangers posed by newly naturalized citizens? Does a long residency requirement before naturalization pose any problems for a free society?

. . .

Our country, in the position it has given to foreigners who have made it their home, has pursued a course in relation to them, totally different from that of any other country in the world. This course . . . subjects our institutions to peculiar dangers. In all other countries the foreigner, to whatever privileges he may be entitled by becoming a subject, can never be placed in a situation to be politically dangerous, for he has no share in the government of the country. . . .

. . .

This country on the contrary opens to the foreigner, without other check than an oath, that he has resided five years in the country, a direct influence on its political affairs.

. . .

. . . The mental elements . . . set in motion remotely by the *Protestant Revolution*, but more strongly agitated by *the American Revolution*, are yet working among the people of these governments to give the Tyrants of the earth uneasiness. . . . Can the example of Democratic liberty which this country shows, produce no uneasiness to monarchs? . . . And is there no danger of a *reaction* from Europe? Have we no interest in these changing aspects of European politics? . . .

There is danger of reaction from Europe; and it is the part of common prudence to look for it, and to provide against it. The great political truth has recently been promulgated at the capital of one of the principle courts of Europe, at Vienna . . . [that] the political revolutions to which European governments have been so long subjected, *from the popular desires for liberty, are the natural effects of the Protestant Reformation*. That *Protestantism* favors *Republicanism*, while *Popery* as naturally supports *Monarchical* power. . . . This country is designated directly to all her people, and to her allies despots, as the great *plague spot* of the world, the poisoned fountain whence flow all the deadly evils which threaten their own existence. . . . Austria has followed out her words with actions. . . . But how shall she attack us? She cannot send her armies, they would be useless. . . . How fitted then is Popery for her purpose! This she can send without alarming our fears. . . . She has set herself to work with all her activity to disseminate throughout the country the *Popish religion*. . . . [A] great society was formed in the Austrian capital, in Vienna, in 1829. . . . [W]hat is [its] purpose? Why, that *"of promoting the greater activity of Catholic missions in America;"* these are the words of their own reports. . . .

Let us examine the operations of this Austrian Society, for it hard at work all around us. . . . With its headquarters in Vienna, under the immediate direction and inspection of . . . [the] *great managing general of the diplomacy of Europe*, it makes itself felt already felt through the republic. Its emissaries are here. And who are these emissaries? They are JESUITS. . . .

These are the men at the moment ordered to America. And can they do nothing, Americans, to derange the free workings of your democratic institutions? Can they not, and do they not fan the slightest embers of discontent into a flame, those thousand little differences which must perpetually occur in any society, into riot. . . ? . . .

. . . Church and State must be forever separated, but it is the height of folly to suppose, that in political discussions, *Religion* especially, *the political character of any and every religious creed* may not be publicly discussed. The absurdity of such a position is too manifest to dwell a moment upon it. And in considering the materials in our society adapted to the purposes of hostile attack upon our Institutions, we must of necessity notice the Roman Catholic religion. *It is this form of religion* that is most implicated in the conspiracy against our liberties. . . . Americans will not be cowed into silence by the cries of *persecution, intolerance, bigotry, fanaticism*, and such puerile catchwords, perpetually uttered against those speak or write ever so calmly against the dangers of Popery. . . .

. . . And who are the members of the Roman Catholic communion? What proportion are natives of this land, nurtured under our institutions, and well versed in the nature of American liberty? Is it not notorious that the greater part are *Foreigners* from the various Catholic countries of Europe? . . . Whatever *the cause* of all this movement abroad to send to this country their poorer classes, the fact is certain, the class of emigrants is known, and the instrument, Austria, is seen in it. . . . They obey their priests as demigods, from the habit of their whole lives; they have been taught from infancy that their priests are infallible in the greatest matters, and can they, by mere importation to this country, be suddenly imbued with the knowledge that in civil matters their priests may err, and that they are not in these also their infallible guides? Who will teach them this? Will their priests? . . .

. . .

The Foreigner, when he arrives on these shores, finds a great insulated community; a large family, separated from all others; independent; each individual, in certain mutual and well settled relations. The foreigner presents himself at the door, and claims to be admitted into this community, and to equal rights with the rest of the family. On what ground? Why, on that of his *natural rights*, as set forth in our Declaration of Independence. . . . Let us examine the matter. . . . It is very clear then that Congress, in the Declaration of Independence, did not mean to allow of *any such construction of that instrument in regard to abstract equality, as should in effect be directly subversive of Independence*. They did not mean to allow of *any construction that must of necessity destroy the common rights of society*. . . . If we are indeed an independent nation, we surely have a right to regulate all *admission* into the nation. . . . [Independence] is an existence separate from all others, a disallowance of all foreign interference or control in its affairs. By independence, a State or community wins a right to arrange its own affairs, in its own way; not only to regulate its internal polity, among its own members, but to determine whether it will or will not admit others from foreign communities into the family; and if it chooses to admit them, on what terms they may come. . . .

. . .

. . . Each one in society, in order to constitute society, must of necessity surrender his *proper independence*, each one must consent *to yield so much of his natural right to be happy exclusively*; must consent to such an *expansion* of the right of happiness as shall embrace all in that society, whether it be composed of but two individuals, or hundreds of millions. . . . And here, true Democratic government, the government of the people begins, founded on the basis of *social compromise*; a compromise by which the natural right of each individual has been mutually restricted to produce the greater blessings of social right. If *natural rights* then are now insisted upon, it is evident that they can no longer be demanded in their original *unlimited* sense; they must ever be limited by the restrictions which society by power and authority conceded to it, in its formation, for the purpose of promoting the "greatest happiness of the greatest number for the longest time," has imposed on the original right. In short, *natural right*, which is the right of *the one*, has yielded to *social right*, which is the right of *the many*. . . . The *native citizen* is, *by his birth*, a member of this independent community. . . . The *foreigner*, on the contrary, *by his birth* belongs to another country, to a separate, independent community. . . . What right of admission can he claim? . . . [T]he people by the voice of their government may grant permission to enter the country, or withhold permission, and may prescribe their own conditions as they may think *expedient*, and without violating the rights natural or acquired of any human being. . . .

. . .

RALPH WALDO EMERSON

POLITICS (1844)

Ralph Waldo Emerson was an influential writer, speaker, and poet and the leading advocate of Transcendentalism, which held that man had the capacity to improve through good work and could access religious truths through intuition. His philosophy emphasized man's creative capacity and the need to free himself from the traditional and conventional. He embraced individualism and nonconformity: "no law can be sacred to me but that of my nature."[8] His essay on politics reflected his antislavery views and disappointment with the state of politics in the antebellum United States, but it also reflected his essential optimism about human progress.

What is his critique of civic republicanism? Why does Emerson distinguish between personal rights and property rights? Is he correct in thinking that not all rights are held equally? What are personal rights? Does he think free thought should—or will—be protected in a democratic society? Does he think the United States is ready for republican government? What political reforms are implied by his essay? How close is his vision of the state to Thoreau's? Is Emerson a kind of conservative?

. . .

In dealing with the State, we ought to remember that its institutions are not aboriginal, though they existed before we were born: that they are not superior to the citizen: that every one of them was once the act of a single man: every law and usage was a man's expedient to meet a particular case: that they all are imitable, all alterable; we may make as good; we may make better. Society is an illusion to the young citizen. It lies before him in rigid repose, with certain names, men, and institutions, rooted like oak-trees to the center, round which all arrange themselves the best they can. But the old statesman knows that society is fluid; there are no such roots and centers; but any particle may suddenly become the center of the movement, and compel the system to gyrate round it, as every man of strong will, like Pisistratus, or Cromwell, does for a time, and every man of truth, like Plato, or Paul, does forever. But politics rest on necessary foundations, and cannot be treated with levity. Republics abound in young civilians, who believe that the laws make the city, that grave modifications of the policy and modes of living, and employments of the population, that commerce, education, and religion, may be voted in or out; and that any measure, though it were absurd, may be imposed on a people, if only you can get sufficient voices to make it a law. But the wise know that foolish legislation is a rope of sand, which perishes in the twisting; that the State must follow, and not lead the character and progress of the citizen; the strongest usurper is quickly got rid of; and they only who build on Ideas, build for eternity; and that the form of government which prevails, is the expression of what cultivation exists in the population which permits it. The law is only a memorandum. . . .

The theory of politics, which has possessed the mind of men, and which they have expressed the best they could in their laws and in their revolutions, considers persons and property as the two objects for whose protection government exists. Of persons, all have equal rights, in virtue of being identical in nature. This interest, of course, with its whole power demands a democracy. Whilst the rights of all as persons are equal, in virtue of their access to reason, their rights in property are very unequal. One man owns his clothes, and another owns a county. This accident, depending, primarily, on the skill and virtue of the

8 Ralph Waldo Emerson, "Self-Reliance," in *Essays, Lectures, and Orations* (London: William S. Orr and Co., 1851), 23.

parties, of which there is every degree, and, secondarily, on patrimony, falls unequally, and its rights, of course, are unequal. Personal rights, universally the same, demand a government framed on the ratio of the census: property demands a government framed on the ratio of owners and of owning. Laban, who has flocks and herds, wishes them looked after by an officer on the frontiers, lest the Midianites shall drive them off, and pays a tax to that end. Jacob has no flocks or herds, and no fear of the Midianites, and pays no tax to the officer. It seemed fit that Laban and Jacob should have equal rights to elect the officer, who is to defend their persons, but that Laban, and not Jacob, should elect the officer who is to guard the sheep and cattle. And, if question arise whether additional officers or watch–towers should be provided, must not Laban and Isaac, and those who must sell part of their herds to buy protection for the rest, judge better of this, and with more right, than Jacob, who, because he is a youth and a traveler, eats their bread and not his own.

In the earliest society the proprietors made their own wealth, and so long as it comes to the owners in the direct way, no other opinion would arise in any equitable community, than that property should make the law for property, and persons the law for persons.

But property passes through donation or inheritance to those who do not create it. Gift, in one case, makes it as really the new owner's, as labor made it the first owner's: in the other case, of patrimony, the law makes an ownership, which will be valid in each man's view according to the estimate which he sets on the public tranquility.

It was not, however, found easy to embody the readily admitted principle, that property should make law for property, and persons for persons: since persons and property mixed themselves in every transaction. At last it seemed settled, that the rightful distinction was, that the proprietors should have more elective franchise than non-proprietors, on the Spartan principle of "calling that which is just, equal; not that which is equal, just."

That principle no longer looks so self-evident as it appeared in former times, partly, because doubts have arisen whether too much weight had not been allowed in the laws, to property, and such a structure given to our usages, as allowed the rich to encroach on the poor, and to keep them poor; but mainly, because there is an instinctive sense, however obscure and yet inarticulate, that the whole constitution of property, on its present tenures, is injurious, and its influence on persons deteriorating and degrading; that truly, the only interest for the consideration of the State, is persons: that property will always follow persons; that the highest end of government is the culture of men: and if men can be educated, the institutions will share their improvement, and the moral sentiment will write the law of the land.

If it be not easy to settle the equity of this question, the peril is less when we take note of our natural defenses. We are kept by better guards than the vigilance of such magistrates as we commonly elect. Society always consists, in greatest part, of young and foolish persons. The old, who have seen through the hypocrisy of courts and statesmen, die, and leave no wisdom to their sons. They believe their own newspaper, as their fathers did at their age. With such an ignorant and deceivable majority, States would soon run to ruin, but that there are limitations, beyond which the folly and ambition of governors cannot go. Things have their laws, as well as men; and things refuse to be trifled with. Property will be protected. Corn will not grow, unless it is planted and manured; but the farmer will not plant or hoe it, unless the chances are a hundred to one, that he will cut and harvest it. Under any forms, persons and property must and will have their just sway. They exert their power, as steadily as matter its attraction. . . .

. . .

The same necessity which secures the rights of person and property against the malignity or folly of the magistrate, determines the form and methods of governing, which are proper to each nation, and to its habit of thought, and nowise transferable to other states of society. In this country, we are very vain of our political institutions, which are singular in this, that they sprung, within the memory of living men, from the character and condition of the people, which they still express with sufficient fidelity,—and we ostentatiously prefer them to any other in history. They are not better, but only fitter for us. We may be wise in asserting the advantage in modern times of the democratic form, but to other states of society, in which religion consecrated the monarchical, that and not this was expedient. Democracy is better for us, because the religious sentiment of the present time accords better with it. Born democrats, we are nowise qualified to judge of monarchy, which, to our fathers living in the monarchical idea, was also relatively right. But our institutions, though in coincidence with the spirit of the age, have not any exemption from the practical defects which have discredited other forms. Every actual State is corrupt. Good men must not obey the laws too well. What satire on government can equal the severity of censure conveyed in the word politic, which now for ages has signified cunning, intimating that the State is a trick?

The same benign necessity and the same practical abuse appear in the parties into which each State divides itself, of opponents and defenders of the administration of the government. Parties are also founded on instincts, and have better guides to their own humble aims than the sagacity of their leaders. They have nothing perverse in their origin, but rudely mark some real and lasting relation. We might as wisely reprove the east wind, or the frost, as a political party, whose members, for the most part, could give no account of their position, but stand for the defense of those interests in which they find themselves. Our quarrel with them begins, when they quit this deep natural ground at the bidding of some leader, and, obeying personal considerations, throw themselves into the maintenance and defense of points, nowise belonging to their system. A party is perpetually corrupted by personality. Whilst we absolve the association from dishonesty, we cannot extend the same charity to their leaders. They reap the rewards of the docility and zeal of the masses which they direct. Ordinarily, our parties are parties of circumstance, and not of principle; as, the planting interest in conflict with the commercial; the party of capitalists, and that of operatives; parties which are identical in their moral character, and which can easily change ground with each other, in the support of many of their measures. Parties of principle, as, religious sects, or the party of free-trade, of universal suffrage, of abolition of slavery, of abolition of capital punishment, degenerate into personalities, or would inspire enthusiasm. The vice of our leading parties in this country (which may be cited as a fair specimen of these societies of opinion) is, that they do not plant themselves on the deep and necessary grounds to which they are respectively entitled, but lash themselves to fury in the carrying of some local and momentary measure, nowise useful to the commonwealth. Of the two great parties, which, at this hour, almost share the nation between them, I should say, that, one has the best cause, and the other contains the best men. The philosopher, the poet, or the religious man, will, of course, wish to cast his vote with the democrat, for free-trade, for wide suffrage, for the abolition of legal cruelties in the penal code, and for facilitating in every manner the access of the young and the poor to the sources of wealth and power. But he can rarely accept the persons whom the so-called popular party propose to him as representatives of these liberalities. They have not at heart the ends which give to the name of democracy what hope and virtue are in it. The spirit of our American radicalism is destructive and aimless: it is not loving; it has no ulterior and divine ends; but is destructive only out of hatred and selfishness. On the other side, the conservative party, composed of the most moderate, able, and cultivated part of the population, is timid, and merely defensive of property. It vindicates no right, it aspires to no real good, it brands no crime, it proposes no generous policy, it does not build, nor write, nor cherish the arts, nor foster religion, nor establish schools, nor encourage science, nor emancipate the slave, nor befriend the poor, or the Indian, or the immigrant. From neither party, when in power, has the world any benefit to expect in science, art, or humanity, at all commensurate with the resources of the nation.

I do not for these defects despair of our republic. We are not at the mercy of any waves of chance. In the strife of ferocious parties, human nature always finds itself cherished, as the children of the convicts at Botany Bay are found to have as healthy a moral sentiment as other children. Citizens of feudal states are alarmed at our democratic institutions lapsing into anarchy; and the older and more cautious among ourselves are learning from Europeans to look with some terror at our turbulent freedom. It is said that in our license of construing the Constitution, and in the despotism of public opinion, we have no anchor; and one foreign observer thinks he has found the safeguard in the sanctity of Marriage among us; and another thinks he has found it in our Calvinism. Fisher Ames expressed the popular security more wisely, when he compared a monarchy and a republic, saying, "that a monarchy is a merchantman, which sails well, but will sometimes strike on a rock, and go to the bottom; whilst a republic is a raft, which would never sink, but then your feet are always in water." No forms can have any dangerous importance, whilst we are befriended by the laws of things. . . . The fact of two poles, of two forces, centripetal and centrifugal, is universal, and each force by its own activity develops the other. Wild liberty develops iron conscience. Want of liberty, by strengthening law and decorum, stupefies conscience. 'Lynch-law' prevails only where there is greater hardihood and self-subsistency in the leaders. A mob cannot be a permanency: everybody's interest requires that it should not exist, and only justice satisfies all.

We must trust infinitely to the beneficent necessity which shines through all laws. Human nature expresses itself in them as characteristically as in statues, or songs, or railroads, and an abstract of the codes of nations would be a transcript of the common conscience. Governments have their origin in the moral identity of men. Reason for one is seen to be reason for another, and for every other. There is a middle measure which satisfies all parties, be they never so many, or so resolute for their own. Every man finds a sanction for his simplest claims and deeds in decisions of his own mind, which he calls Truth and Holiness. In these decisions all the citizens find a perfect agreement, and only in these; not in what is good to eat, good to wear, good use of time, or what amount of land, or of public aid, each is entitled to claim. This truth and justice men presently endeavor to make application of, to the measuring of land, the apportionment of service, the protection of life and property. Their first endeavors, no doubt, are very awkward. Yet absolute right is the first governor; or, every government is an impure theocracy. The idea, after which each community is aiming to make and mend its law, is, the will of the wise man. The wise man, it cannot find in nature, and it makes awkward but earnest efforts to secure his government by contrivance; as, by causing the entire people to give their voices on every measure; or, by a double choice to get the representation of the whole; or, by a selection of the best citizens; or, to secure the advantages of efficiency and internal peace, by confiding the government to one, who may himself select his agents. All forms of government symbolize an immortal government, common to all dynasties and independent of numbers, perfect where two men exist, perfect where there is only one man.

. . . I can see well enough a great difference between my setting myself down to a self-control, and my going to make somebody else act after my views: but when a quarter of the human race assume to tell me what I must do, I may be too much disturbed by the circumstances to see so clearly the absurdity of their command. Therefore, all public ends look vague and quixotic beside private ones. For, any laws but those which men make for themselves, are laughable. If I put myself in the place of my child, and we stand in one thought, and see that things are thus or thus, that perception is law for him and me. We are both there, both act. But if, without carrying him into the thought, I look over into his plot, and, guessing how it is with him, ordain this or that, he will never obey me. This is the history of governments,—one man does something which is to bind another. A man who cannot be acquainted with me, taxes me; looking from afar at me, ordains that a part of my labor shall go to this or that whimsical end, not as I, but as he happens to fancy. Behold the consequence. Of all debts, men are least willing to pay the taxes. What a satire is this on government! Everywhere they think they get their money's worth, except for these.

Hence, the less government we have, the better,—the fewer laws, and the less confided power. The antidote to this abuse of formal Government, is, the influence of private character, the growth of the Individual; the appearance of the principal to supersede the proxy; the appearance of the wise man, of whom the existing government, is, it must be owned, but a shabby imitation. That which all things tend to educe, which freedom, cultivation, intercourse, revolutions, go to form and deliver, is character; that is the end of nature, to reach unto this coronation of her king. To educate the wise man, the State exists; and with the appearance of the wise man, the State expires. The appearance of character makes the State unnecessary. The wise man is the State. He needs no army, fort, or navy,—he loves men too well; no bribe, or feast, or palace, to draw friends to him; no vantage ground, no favorable circumstance. He needs no library, for he has not done thinking; no church, for he is a prophet; no statute book, for he has the lawgiver; no money, for he is value; no road, for he is at home where he is; no experience, for the life of the creator shoots through him, and looks from his eyes. He has no personal friends, for he who has the spell to draw the prayer and piety of all men unto him, needs not husband and educate a few, to share with him a select and poetic life. His relation to men is angelic; his memory is myrrh to them; his presence, frankincense and flowers.

We think our civilization near its meridian, but we are yet only at the cock-crowing and the morning star. In our barbarous society the influence of character is in its infancy. As a political power, as the rightful lord who is to tumble all rulers from their chairs, its presence is hardly yet suspected. . . .

. . .

We live in a very low state of the world, and pay unwilling tribute to governments founded on force. There is not, among the most religious and instructed men of the most religious and civil nations, a reliance on the moral sentiment, and a sufficient belief in the unity of things to persuade them that society can be maintained without artificial restraints, as well as the solar system; or that the private citizen might be reasonable, and a good neighbor, without the hint of a jail or a confiscation. What is strange too, there never was in any man sufficient faith in the power of rectitude, to inspire him with the broad design of renovating the State on the principle of right and love. All those who have pretended this design, have been partial reformers, and have admitted in some manner the supremacy of the bad State. I do not call to mind a single human being who has steadily denied the authority of the laws, on the simple ground of his own moral nature. Such designs, full of genius and full of fate as they are, are not entertained except avowedly as air-pictures. If the individual who exhibits them, dare to think them practicable, he disgusts scholars and churchmen; and men of talent, and women of superior sentiments, cannot hide their contempt. Not the less does nature continue to fill the heart of youth with suggestions of this enthusiasm, and there are now men,—if indeed I can speak in the plural number,—more exactly, I will say, I have just been conversing with one man, to whom no weight of adverse experience will make it for a moment appear impossible, impossible, that thousands of human beings might exercise towards each other the grandest and simplest sentiments, as well as a knot of friends, or a pair of lovers.

GEORGE H. COLTON

RESPONSIBILITY OF THE BALLOT BOX (1846)

George H. Colton was the founder and editor of the *American Review*, based in New York City. Like many journals of the period, the *Review* freely mixed politics, literature, and the arts, and had a partisan editorial slant. The *Review* was closely associated with the Whig Party. Founded in 1844, as the Whig Henry Clay was going down in defeat to the Democratic James Polk, the journal was published for only three years under Colton's leadership. The journal survived its founder's early death by only two years. Colton had turned away from his first career as a teacher in order to become a writer, and published a lengthy narrative poem to celebrate William Henry Harrison's election as president, which attracted some attention. Besides being a reliable organ of Whig political arguments, the *Review* was most notable for publishing Edgar Allen Poe's poem "The Raven". The unsigned editorial here reflected typical Whig views about the nature of electoral politics in the mid-nineteenth century, while writing specifically about the upcoming ratification vote for the New York state constitution of 1846. Colton expressed the conservative inclination not to "disturb the reverence just beginning to gather around" the old constitution, but his primary concern in the essay was to call on the more intelligent and virtuous members of the community to do their duty at the ballot box to prevent the more democratic element from pursuing more radical change.

Why does Colton think that reverence for the laws is important? What does he think encourages reverence? Should we tolerate bad laws? What is the role of political leadership for Colton? Is this vision of leadership antidemocratic? Is Colton hostile to political parties generally? What are the responsibilities of voters in a republic? Do citizens have an obligation to vote? Under what circumstances?

. . .

The time has not come in this new country and in these recent States, when the value of the reserved power hoarded in a traditional reverence for the Constitution is capable of being estimated. Change is a comparatively small evil to us *now*, when the elements of prosperity are so large, that no possible instability of the Laws can repress them. Our Institutions are so superabundantly beneficent in their general character, that no abuse of them can, for the present, make them otherwise than benignant. . . . The laws press so lightly, taxes are so small, the avenues for enterprise and success so numerous, the propitiousness of soil and climate, the extent and cheapness of territory so great, that the People care very little in their hearts for a Constitution which ostensibly does little for them, and whose principle charm is, that it meddles so little with them in any way. The law is not a visible guardian presence in our country as yet. . . . There has been, as yet, little to call out the most dangerous passions of the people. . . . While this state of things lasts, it matters little what holds the Constitution has upon the love and veneration of the people. But this condition of things cannot be permanent. Nay, while we celebrate it, it is going and gone. . . . Already we have felt the need of that settled respect for the Constitution, which no shifting, changeable Charter of rights can secure! And, as our population becomes denser, the inequalities of fortune more marked, the difficulties of success greater, the more common and alarming will be the explosions of the ordinary political passions of our nature, and the greater the necessity for strong and energetic laws based upon a sacred and inviolable Constitution. It is the inevitable future, that we ought to be laying up a reserved fund of veneration for Law.

. . . We do not deny [the proposed constitution] is, in some respects, superior to the old. But that it has vital mistakes and most miserable innovations, is, we doubt not, the conviction of all those who *ought* to direct the *public* sentiment.

It is enough for us that the judges are made directly elective by the people—and for a limited and comparatively short period of time!

We had thought ourselves badly enough off, that our highest judges all left office at the very period of their greatest usefulness, when their passions had cooled and their judgment ripened, and just as the experience of the courts had brought their wisdom to the highest pitch; in short, at the time when other nations and other states are accustomed to think their judges at the very height of their usefulness! . . . This we thought quite too bad, and likely to bring unnecessary instability and disrespect to the office. But this we could bear. Our judges were firm, able, independent, and experienced men—raised above the influence of political party, and wholly beyond the caprice or resentment of the people they judged. But now, alas! A new element of insecurity and suspicion and instability is to be introduced into our Judiciary! . . . Hitherto, the people, justly suspicious of themselves and their own hasty and impulsive action, have voluntarily put it out of their power to disturb the sacred scale of justice with their excited hands. . . . And so, henceforth, our judges are to be the creatures of party; are to be tempted above the resistance of human nature, into unfairness and selfish biases, because the people are afraid to hold in reserve a particle of their power—though by voluntary restraint—and have got to think that they have somehow been juggled out of their rights by the Constitution. . . .

We have already said much more than we designed, in reference to the "new Constitution." After all! The main grievance is that it is *new*, and by its own provisions can never be *old*. Every twenty years is to see it plucked up by its still tender roots, and our liberties and rights and state attachments are never to know the shelter of anything better than a thrifty sapling! We had hoped to see a growing reluctance in our fellow-citizens to change in the laws. . . . They have not yet attained to any sense of the value of institutions and laws which share the reverence that belongs to the fathers and founders of the families that inherit them; which are woven in with the pride and affections—the instinctive, or earliest and latest emotions of the human heart. . . shared only by the religious faith they profess and the domestic affections they cherish!

. . . The change, emendation, or additions which the Constitution really required, lay rather in the feelings which the people were bound to bring around it than anywhere else! If it had been sacred enough in our eyes to make its principles binding and imperative; if the laws founded on it had been thoroughly carried out; if the rights and privileges under it had been fully availed of and cherished; if its duties had been faithfully done; there would, by this time, have grown up around it a feeling of confidence, respect, and attachment, which would have been infinitely more valuable to the character, happiness, and prosperity of our people, than any theoretical, or even practical, amendments of which it admits. . . .

One of the worst effects of disturbing the highest law of the State is the tendency it has to alienate the loyalty, interest, and activity of the best part of the people. . . . With the exception of the Senate of the United States, there is no political body that commands the respect of our people as being a representation of the highest intelligence, the loftiest patriotism, the purest wisdom of the nation, or any part of it. The sober sense, the high morality, the sound, practical conservatism of our community is not represented in our political assemblies, nor felt in its strength at the ballot box. There is a feeling, that it is idle to attempt to stem the current of a wild democracy. . . .

. . . The doctrine of political equality has been so perverted into a teaching of literal equality in endowments, competency, and political wisdom, that it is not easily understood how one head can be wiser than another, or more fit to govern. . . . But it is not strange that the people should believe the charlatans and knaves who take such pains to persuade them that they are as wise as they are free, as sagacious as they are privileged! . . . It is a great source of alarm and of evil to us, that so much ignorance, passion, and short-sightedness should be at the polls. We see not why the people should not manifest their weakness, blindness, and folly, in their political as much as in their other relations. We do not look for consummate wisdom among them on other subjects; why on this? But we can easily confess that we would sooner encounter and suffer the consequences of all this ignorance and folly than disfranchise a single citizen. . . . But we will not flatter and fawn upon the people. . . .

. . . What is now needed more than anything, is for the good and great men—the high-minded, honest, sensible and experienced men—to take hold of the politics of the country, and place themselves where they belong, at the head of the masses, to guide, teach and save them. But if the good and wise shrink from politics as from a pollution, let them not complain, that the people are deceived and betrayed! . . .

We contend earnestly, that the thinking and good men in our community shall not subtract their wisdom, experience, attention and activity from our politics, local, state, or general—that our politics shall not be abandoned to a class known as politicians. . . . The immense diversion of the best thought of the land to other enterprises and interests, leaves our politics in the hands of the unworthy. Just at a time when we need the greatest sagacity, prudence and principle, to shape our fluent or plastic destiny, we are under the hands of the weak and incompetent! Our offices of highest importance are filled with second and third-rate men . . . and our ballot box often empty of the votes of the best class of our people! . . .

We almost despair of bringing the intelligence and virtue of this nation, or of this State and community, to the ballot box. . . . The ignorant and misguided are sure to vote. All those who are creatures of imitation, of superficial excitement and gregarious tendencies, will of course vote, and vote as the wire-pullers of party shall direct. . . . [A]re wise and good men to see the country ruined, because they do not like everything about the measures or candidates of the party, whose cardinal principles they espouse? We detest the milk and water morality, which sacrifices to a scruple interests that have every general principle of duty and policy in their support! We have no patience with men who throw away their votes upon favorite candidates, while they suffer great principles of public policy to be stifled.

. . .

There seems to be a vague notion in the minds of a portion of the better part of the community that the country can be governed without parties . . . that they are not a legitimate part of the political machinery. . . . But this is mere indiscriminating sentiment. The very foundation of our government, its universal suffrage, its rotation in office, its free press, its frequent elections—all are fitted to create, and even designed to create, parties. . . . The only question is, what shall the character of these parties be, and who shall control them? . . .

. . .

. . . [A]nything short of immorality or untrustworthiness should be no bar to our voting for the party candidates. We should sacrifice preferences to principles, favorite candidates to important measures, men to policy, personal, local, or temporary interests, to national, general, and permanent interests. We should *vote with the party, exerting all our influence to make and keep it what it ought to be. . . .*

IV. EQUALITY AND STATUS

Major Developments

- Political empowerment of the working class
- Organization of women's rights movements
- Growth of antislavery and proslavery movements

Questions of equality were close to the heart of the Jacksonian Era. Scholars shaped by the New Deal tended to look back at this earlier age of Democratic Party dominance and saw a celebration of the common man. Western frontiersmen such as "Old Hickory" Andy Jackson himself and his home-state rival, Davy Crockett, seemed to define the spirit of the age. The old eastern establishment was being pushed aside by a new generation of self-made men. Scholars shaped by the civil rights movement were more likely to look back at the age of Jackson and see a white man's republic. Working-class, white males achieved new political and social status in the mid-nineteenth century, while the status of other groups was put very much into question. A serious women's rights movement emerged out of the various social reform causes that were blossoming during the period, and though their immediate gains were limited they were able to press issues of female equality harder than the previous generation of Americans had. American opinion was increasingly polarized by the slavery issue, with more extreme defenses of slavery and stronger advocacy of abolition taking center stage. Native Americans within the borders of the United States found their status unsettled, as they were physically pushed to the margins of the country.

The excerpts in this section reflect these core disagreements. Several competing strands of antislavery thought developed during this period. They are represented here by William Lloyd Garrison, Frederick Douglass, and Abraham Lincoln. Garrison was at one time a mentor to the former slave Douglass, but Douglass eventually split from him over the value of the U.S. Constitution and the means for achieving the end of slavery. Abraham Lincoln was a politician, not a social activist, but the antislavery cause was fundamental to his politics in the 1850s. Like Douglass, he drew from the American political tradition to condemn the continuation of the slave system. The growing proslavery position is represented by James Hammond and George Fitzhugh. Both tried to turn the table on northern critics of slavery, arguing that slavery was a positive good rather than a necessary evil (as it had been characterized by earlier generations) and that the slave system compared favorably with industrialization and the exploited wage laborers who filled northern cities. Elizabeth Cady Stanton and Sojourner Truth represent the emerging feminist movements of the period, which was entwined with and drew upon the antislavery movement.

WILLIAM LLOYD GARRISON

DECLARATION OF PRINCIPLES FOR THE LIBERATOR (1831)

A Massachusetts native, William Lloyd Garrison joined the growing social reform movement in the 1820s as a journalist and editor. Although involved in various causes, he soon settled on abolitionism as the cause that would become his life's work. In 1830, he founded *The Liberator* in Boston, and that journal immediately established itself as one of the most influential and uncompromising antislavery papers in the country. Like many antislavery activists of the period, he had initially favored gradual emancipation and African colonization, but by the time he founded *The Liberator* he had been converted to the cause of immediate emancipation. He was in active dialog with British antislavery activists and helped found the American Anti-Slavery Society. His brand of religiously influenced principles pointed not only to abolitionism but also to women's rights, pacifism, anarchism, and moral perfectionism. His call for "No Union with Slaveholders" insisted on political disengagement from the South, and his contention that the U.S. Constitution was a "covenant with death" and "an agreement with Hell" rejected political compromises with slave interests. Despite his general pacifism, he praised John Brown's 1859 raid on Harper's Ferry and supported Abraham Lincoln's war against the South. With the success of emancipation in the 1860s, Brown became a firm supporter of the Republican Party while largely retiring from public life.

Was Garrison right to focus on influencing specifically northern public opinion and writing off the South? Why might he have positioned himself as nonpartisan in 1831? Should he have remained nonpartisan in later years, or should he have supported efforts to create an antislavery political party? Why does he reject gradualism and support immediate emancipation? How are his commitments to pacifism and abolitionism linked? Does he offer a political strategy to achieve emancipation?

. . .

During my recent tour of the purpose of exciting the minds of the people by a series of discourses on the subject of slavery, every place that I visited gave fresh evidence of the fact, that a greater revolution in public sentiment was to be effected in the free states—and *particularly* in *New England*—than at the south. I found contempt more bitter, opposition more active, detraction more relentless, prejudice more stubborn, and apathy more frozen, than among slave owners themselves. Of course, there were individual exceptions to the contrary. This state of things afflicted, but did not dishearten me. I determined, at every hazard, to lift up the standard of emancipation in the eyes of the nation, within sight of Bunker Hill and in the birth place of liberty. That standard is now unfurled; and long may it float, unhurt by the spoliations of time or the missiles of a desperate foe—yea, till every chain be broken, and every bondmen set free! Let southern oppressors tremble—let their secret abettors tremble—let their Northern apologists tremble—let all the enemies of the persecuted blacks tremble.

I deem the publication of my original Prospectus unnecessary, as it has obtained a wide circulation. The principles therein inculcated will be steadily pursued in this paper, excepting that I shall not array myself as the political partisan of any man. In defending the great cause of human rights, I wish to derive the assistance of all religions and of all parties.

Assenting to the "self-evident truth" maintained in the American Declaration of Independence, "that all men are created equal, and endowed by the Creator with certain inalienable rights—among which are life, liberty and the pursuit of happiness," I shall strenuously contend for the immediate enfranchisement of our slave population. In Park-street Church, on the Fourth of July, 1829, in an address on slavery, I unreflectingly assented to the popular but pernicious doctrine of *gradual* abolition. I seize this opportunity to make a full and unequivocal recantation, and thus publicly to ask pardon of my God, of my country, and of my brethren the poor slaves, for having uttered a sentiment so full of timidity, injustice and absurdity. A similar recantation, from my pen, was published in the *Genius of Universal Emancipation* at Baltimore, in September, 1829. My conscience is now satisfied.

I am aware, that many object to the severity of my language; but is there not cause for severity? I *will be* as harsh as truth, and as uncompromising as justice. On this subject, I do not wish to think, or speak, or write, with moderation. No! no! Tell a man whose house is on fire to give a moderate alarm; tell him to moderately rescue his wife from the hands of the ravisher; tell the mother to gradually extricate her babe from the fire into which it has fallen;—but urge me not to use moderation in a cause like the present. I am in earnest—I will not equivocate—I will not excuse—I will not retreat a single inch—AND I WILL BE HEARD. The apathy of the people is enough to make every statue leap from its pedestal, and to hasten the resurrection of the dead.

. . .

In commencing this publication, we had but a single object in view—the total abolition of American slavery, and, as a just consequence, the complete enfranchisement of our colored countrymen. . . .

In entering upon our eighth volume, the abolition of slavery will still be the grand object of our labors, though not, perhaps, so exclusively as heretofore. There are other topics, which, in our opinion, are intimately connected with the great doctrine of inalienable human rights; and which, while they conflict with no religious sect, or political party, as such, are pregnant with momentous consequences to the freedom, equality and happiness of mankind. . . .

The motto upon our banner has been from the commencement of our moral warfare, "OUR COUNTRY IS THE WORLD—OUR COUNTRYMEN ARE ALL MANKIND." We trust that it will be our only epitaph. Another motto we have chosen is, "UNIVERSAL EMANCIPATION." Up to this time, we have limited its application to those who are held in this country, by southern taskmasters, as marketable commodities, goods and chattels, and implements of husbandry. Henceforth, we shall use it in its widest latitude: the emancipation of our whole race from the dominion of man, from the thralldom of self, form the government of brute force, from the bondage of sin—and bringing them under the dominion of God, the control of an inward spirit, the government of the law of love, and into the obedience and liberty of Christ, who is "*the same*, yesterday, TODAY, and forever."

[I]n consequence of the general corruption of all political parties and religious sects, and of the obstacles which they have thrown into the path of emancipation, we have been necessitated to reprove them all. Nor have we any intention . . . to assail or give the preference to any sect or party. . . . The abolition of American slavery we hold to be COMMON GROUND, upon which men of all creeds, complexions and parties, if they have true humanity in their hearts, may meet on amicable and equal terms. . . .

To the bigoted, the pharisaical, the time-serving, the selfish, the worshippers of expediency, the advocates of caste, the lovers of power, the enemies of liberty and equality, we make no appeal. . . .

Next to the overthrow of slavery, the cause of PEACE shall command our attention. The doctrine of non-resistance, as commonly received and practiced by Friends, and certain members of other religious denominations, we conceive to be utterly indefensible in its application to national wars—not that it "goes too far," but that it does not go far enough. If a nation may not redress its wrongs by physical force—if it may not repel or punish a foreign enemy who comes to plunder, enslave or murder its inhabitants—then it may not resort to arms to quell an insurrection, or send to prison or suspend upon a gibbet any transgressors upon its soil. If the slaves of the South have not an undoubted right to resist their masters in the last resort, then no man, or body of men, may appeal to the law of violence in self-defense—for none have ever suffered, or can suffer, more than they. . . . Now, the doctrine we shall endeavor to inculcate is, that the kingdoms of this world, are to become the kingdoms of our Lord and his Christ. . . . Its government is one of love, not of military coercion or physical restraint: its laws are not written upon parchment, but upon the hearts of its subjects. . . .

As to the governments of this world, whatever their titles or forms, we shall endeavor to prove, that, in their essential elements, and as present administered, they are all Anti-Christ; that they can never, by human wisdom, be brought into conformity with the will of God; that they cannot be maintained, except by naval and military power; that all their penal enactments being a dead letter without an army to carry them into effect, are virtually written in human blood; and that the followers of Jesus should instinctively shun their stations of honor, power and emolument—at the same time "submitting to every ordinance of man for the Lord's sake," and offering no *physical* resistance to any of their mandates, however unjust or tyrannical. . . .

. . . [I]f the kingdom of God is to come universally, and his will be done ON EARTH as it is IN HEAVEN . . . then why are not Christians obligated to come out NOW, and be separated from "the kingdoms of this world," which are all based upon the PRINCIPLE OF VIOLENCE, and which require their officers and servants to govern and be governed by that principle? How, then, is the wickedness of men to be overcome? Not by lacerating their bodies . . . but simply by returning good for evil, and blessing for cursing . . . committing the soul in well-doing, as unto a faithful Creator, and leaving it to God to bestow recompense—"for it is written, Vengeance is mine; I will repay, saith the Lord."

. . .

ELIZABETH CADY STANTON

SENECA FALLS DECLARATION OF SENTIMENTS (1848)

The Seneca Falls Convention was the first important gathering for women's rights held in the United States. Individual women demanded political equality before 1848. Abigail Adams and Priscilla Mason were among the many women who criticized the male monopoly on political power. Women did not organize to demand rights, however, during the Founding and Early National Eras. Gender politics in the United States changed after an international antislavery conference in London refused to seat a delegation of abolitionist women from the United States. Outraged, Elizabeth Cady Stanton and Lucretia Mott resolved to create a women's movement. Their goal was to obtain for women the same equal political and economic rights that radical abolitionists insisted persons of color should enjoy.

Compare the "Declaration of Sentiments" to the other Jacksonian readings in this chapter. The "Declaration of Sentiments" began by quoting verbatim from the Declaration of Independence. Stanton and her political allies inserted "women" at crucial points. To what extent might all the arguments below be described as conventional Jacksonian demands for equality, the only difference being that the equality being demanded was between men and women rather than between different classes of men? To what extent did Stanton and her political supporters make different kinds of equality arguments to justify gender equality?

. . .

We hold these truths to be self-evident: that all men and women are created equal; that they are endowed by their Creator with certain inalienable rights; that among these are life, liberty, and the pursuit of happiness; that to secure these rights governments are instituted, deriving their just powers from the consent of the governed. . . .

The history of mankind is a history of repeated injuries and usurpations on the part of man toward woman, having in direct object the establishment of an absolute tyranny over her. To prove this, let facts be submitted to a candid world.

He has never permitted her to exercise her inalienable right to the elective franchise.

He has compelled her to submit to laws, in the formation of which she had no voice.

He has withheld from her rights which are given to the most ignorant and degraded men—both natives and foreigners.

Having deprived her of this first right of a citizen, the elective franchise, thereby leaving her without representation in the halls of legislation, he has oppressed her on all sides.

He has made her, if married, in the eye of the law, civilly dead.

He has taken from her all right in property, even to the wages she earns.

He has made her, morally, an irresponsible being, as she can commit many crimes with impunity, provided they be done in the presence of her husband. In the covenant of marriage, she is compelled to promise obedience to her husband, he becoming, to all intents and purposes, her master—the law giving him power to deprive her of her liberty, and to administer chastisement.

He has so framed the laws of divorce, as to what shall be the proper causes, and in case of separation, to whom the guardianship of the children shall be given, as to be wholly regardless of the happiness of women—the law, in all cases, going upon a false supposition of the supremacy of man, and giving all power into his hands.

After depriving her of all rights as a married woman, if single, and the owner of property, he has taxed her to support a government which recognizes her only when her property can be made profitable to it.

He has monopolized nearly all the profitable employments, and from those she is permitted to follow, she receives but a scanty remuneration. He closes against her all the avenues to wealth and distinction which he considers most honorable to himself. As a teacher of theology, medicine, or law, she is not known.

He has denied her the facilities for obtaining a thorough education, all colleges being closed against her.

He allows her in Church, as well as State, but a subordinate position, claiming Apostolic authority for her exclusion from the ministry, and, with some exceptions, from any public participation in the affairs of the Church.

He has created a false public sentiment by giving to the world a different code of morals for men and women, by which moral delinquencies which exclude women from society, are not only tolerated, but deemed of little account in man.

He has usurped the prerogative of Jehovah himself, claiming it as his right to assign for her a sphere of action, when that belongs to her conscience and to her God.

He has endeavored, in every way that he could, to destroy her confidence in her own powers, to lessen her self-respect, and to make her willing to lead a dependent and abject life.

Now, in view of this entire disfranchisement of one-half the people of this country, their social and religious degradation—in view of the unjust laws above mentioned, and because women do feel themselves aggrieved, oppressed, and fraudulently deprived of their most sacred rights, we insist that they have immediate admission to all the rights and privileges which belong to them as citizens of the United States.

In entering upon the great work before us, we anticipate no small amount of misconception, misrepresentation, and ridicule; but we shall use every instrumentality within our power to effect our object. We shall employ agents, circulate tracts, petition the State and National legislatures, and endeavor to enlist the pulpit and the press in our behalf. We hope this Convention will be followed by a series of Conventions embracing every part of the country.

SOJOURNER TRUTH

AIN'T I A WOMAN (1851)

Sojourner Truth was born a slave in New York a decade after the drafting of the U.S. Constitution. In 1826, she escaped with her infant daughter, and the white family with whom she took refuge bought her freedom. She later successfully sued for the freedom of her young son, who had been illegally sold to an out-of-state owner. Like many others during this period, she became deeply religious, eventually joining a sect led by William Miller that anticipated the imminent earthly return of Jesus Christ. Upon her conversion in the early 1840s, she adopted the name Sojourner Truth and became a traveling preacher. Shortly thereafter, she became involved in the moral reform movement, taking a special interest in abolition and feminism. William Lloyd Garrison published her autobiography in 1850, and she spent the next two decades giving speeches at antislavery and feminist rallies, gaining substantial fame (meeting with two sitting presidents, Abraham Lincoln and Ulysses Grant). Her most famous speech was delivered to the Ohio Women's Rights Convention in 1851. The speech was extemporaneous, and the only accounts of it were published several years after the event. There is some reason to doubt the accuracy of this account, which first appeared in 1863, but Truth allowed it to be included in the second edition of her autobiography and it has become the standard.

What is the relationship between Truth's argument that women needed no special privileges and her argument for women's rights? What does she have to say about equality? To what extent does Truth argue from a religious standpoint?

Well, children, where there is so much racket there must be something out of kilter. I think that 'twixt the negroes of the South and the women at the North, all talking about rights, the white men will be in a fix pretty soon. But what's all this here talking about?

That man over there says that women need to be helped into carriages, and lifted over ditches, and to have the best place everywhere. Nobody ever helps me into carriages, or over mud-puddles, or gives me any best place, and ain't I a woman? Look at me! Look at my arm! I have ploughed and planted, and gathered into barns, and no man could head me—and ain't I a woman? I could work as much and eat as much as a man (when I could get it) and bear the lash as well—and ain't I a woman? I have borne thirteen children, and seen most all sold off to slavery, and when I cried out with my mother's grief, none but Jesus heard—and ain't I a woman?

Then they talk about this thing in the head; what's this they call it? ("Intellect," whispered someone near.) That's it, honey. What's that got to do with women's rights or negroes' rights? If my cup won't hold but a pint, and yours holds a quart, wouldn't you be mean not to let me have my little half measure full?

Then that little man in black there, he says women can't have as much rights as men, 'cause Christ wasn't a woman. Where did your Christ come from? Where did your Christ come from? From God and a woman! Man had nothing to do with Him. . . .

If the first woman God ever made was strong enough to turn the world upside down all alone, these [women] together ought to be able to turn it back and get it right side up again, and now they is asking to do it, the men better let them.

Obliged to you for hearing me, and now old Sojourner ain't got nothing more to say.

FREDERICK DOUGLASS

WHAT TO THE SLAVE IS THE FOURTH OF JULY? (1852)

Frederick Douglass was born a slave in Maryland just before the Missouri crisis. On his third attempt, he successfully escaped to New York City at the age of twenty. He married a free black woman from Baltimore who had helped in his escape, and they moved to Massachusetts, where he became a Methodist preacher. Soon he became an active speaker at antislavery gatherings under the tutelage of William Lloyd Garrison and published his first autobiography. After an international speaking tour, he returned to New York and established his own abolitionist newspaper, *The North Star*. He broke from Garrison's uncompromising critique of the U.S. Constitution and embraced the argument of Lysander Spooner and others that the Constitution could be read as an antislavery document. He attended the Seneca Falls Convention, speaking on behalf of female suffrage, and tried to discourage John Brown from making his raid on Harper's Ferry. His Independence Day speech to the Rochester Anti-Slavery Sewing Society, where he denounced the gap between American constitutional ideals and the practice of slavery, became one of his most famous.

Does Douglass claim the Fourth of July as his own? Is Douglass patriotic? How is American independence relevant to slavery? Is his argument here consistent with the Garrisonian view that the Constitution was a pact with the devil? What is his argument on behalf of the abolition of slavery? Is his argument more or less persuasive than Garrison's?

. . .

This, for the purpose of this celebration, is the 4th of July. It is the birthday of your National Independence, and of your political freedom. This, to you, is what the Passover was to the emancipated people of God. It carries your minds back to the day, and to the act of your great deliverance; and to the signs, and to the wonders, associated with that act, and that day. This celebration also marks the beginning of another year of your national life; and reminds you that the Republic of America is now 76 years old. I am glad, fellow-citizens, that your nation is so young. . . . [Y]ou are, even now, only in the beginning of your national career, still lingering in the period of childhood. I repeat, I am glad this is so. There is hope in the thought. . . .

. . . To say now that America was right, and England wrong, is exceedingly easy. Everybody can say it; the dastard, not less than the noble brave, can flippantly discant on the tyranny of England towards the American Colonies. It is fashionable to do so; but there was a time when to pronounce against England, and in favor of the cause of the colonies, tried men's souls. They who did so were accounted in their day, plotters of mischief, agitators and rebels, dangerous men. To side with the right, against the wrong, with the weak against the strong, and with the oppressed against the oppressor! here lies the merit, and the one which, of all others, seems unfashionable in our day. The cause of liberty may be stabbed by the men who glory in the deeds of your fathers. But, to proceed.

. . .

Oppression makes a wise man mad. Your fathers were wise men, and if they did not go mad, they became restive under this treatment. They felt themselves the victims of grievous wrongs, wholly incurable in their colonial capacity. With brave men there is always a remedy for oppression. Just here, the idea of a total separation of the colonies from the crown was born! It was a startling idea, much more so, than we, at this distance of time, regard it. The timid and the prudent (as has been intimated) of that day, were, of course, shocked and alarmed by it.

. . .

Their opposition to the then dangerous thought was earnest and powerful; but, amid all their terror and affrighted vociferations against it, the alarming and revolutionary idea moved on, and the country with it.

On the 2d of July, 1776, the old Continental Congress, to the dismay of the lovers of ease, and the worshipers of property, clothed that dreadful idea with all the authority of national sanction. . . .

Citizens, your fathers made good that resolution. They succeeded; and to-day you reap the fruits of their success. The freedom gained is yours; and you, therefore, may properly celebrate this anniversary. The 4th of July is the first great fact in your nation's history—the very ring-bolt in the chain of your yet undeveloped destiny.

Pride and patriotism, not less than gratitude, prompt you to celebrate and to hold it in perpetual remembrance. I have said that the Declaration of Independence is the ring-bolt to the chain of your nation's destiny; so, indeed, I regard it. The principles contained in that instrument are saving principles. Stand by those principles, be true to them on all occasions, in all places, against all foes, and at whatever cost.

. . .

Fellow Citizens, I am not wanting in respect for the fathers of this republic. The signers of the Declaration of Independence were brave men. They were great men too—great enough to give fame to a great age. It does not often happen to a nation to raise, at one time, such a number of truly great men. The point from which I am compelled to view them is not, certainly, the most favorable; and yet I cannot contemplate their great deeds with less than admiration. They were statesmen, patriots and heroes, and for the good they did, and the principles they contended for, I will unite with you to honor their memory.

They loved their country better than their own private interests; and, though this is not the highest form of human excellence, all will concede that it is a rare virtue, and that when it is exhibited, it ought to command respect. . . . In their admiration of liberty, they lost sight of all other interests.

They were peace men; but they preferred revolution to peaceful submission to bondage. They were quiet men; but they did not shrink from agitating against oppression. They showed forbearance; but that they knew its limits. They believed in order; but not in the order of tyranny. With them, nothing was "settled" that was not right. With them, justice, liberty and humanity were "final;" not slavery and oppression. You may well cherish the memory of such men. They were great in their day and generation. Their solid manhood stands out the more as we contrast it with these degenerate times.

. . .

We have to do with the past only as we can make it useful to the present and to the future. To all inspiring motives, to noble deeds which can be gained from the past, we are welcome. But now is the time, the important time. Your fathers have lived, died, and have done their work, and have done much of it well. You live and must die, and you must do your work. You have no right to enjoy a child's share in the labor of your fathers, unless your children are to be blest by your labors. . . .

. . .

Fellow-citizens, pardon me, allow me to ask, why am I called upon to speak here to-day? What have I, or those I represent, to do with your national independence? Are the great principles of political freedom and of natural justice, embodied in that Declaration of Independence, extended to us? and am I, therefore, called upon to bring our humble offering to the national altar, and to confess the benefits and express devout gratitude for the blessings resulting from your independence to us?

. . . I am not included within the pale of this glorious anniversary! Your high independence only reveals the immeasurable distance between us. The blessings in which you, this day, rejoice, are not enjoyed in common.—The rich inheritance of justice, liberty, prosperity and independence, bequeathed by your fathers, is shared by you, not by me. The sunlight that brought life and healing to you, has brought stripes and death to me. This Fourth [of] July is *yours*, not *mine*. *You* may rejoice, *I* must mourn. To drag a man in fetters into the grand illuminated temple of liberty, and call upon him to join you in joyous anthems, were inhuman mockery and sacrilegious irony. . . .

Fellow-citizens; above your national, tumultuous joy, I hear the mournful wail of millions! whose chains, heavy and grievous yesterday, are, to-day, rendered more intolerable by the jubilee shouts that reach them. If I do forget, if I do not faithfully remember those bleeding children of sorrow this day, "may my right hand forget her cunning, and may my tongue cleave to the roof of my mouth!" To forget them, to pass lightly over their wrongs, and to chime in with the popular theme, would be treason most scandalous and shocking, and would make me a reproach before God and the world. My subject, then fellow-citizens, is AMERICAN SLAVERY. I shall see, this day, and its popular characteristics, from the slave's point of view. . . . Standing with God and the crushed and bleeding slave on this occasion, I will, in the name of humanity which is outraged, in the name of liberty which is fettered, in the name of the constitution and the Bible, which are disregarded and trampled upon, dare to call in question and to denounce, with all the emphasis I can command, everything that serves to perpetuate slavery—the great sin and shame of America! "I will not equivocate; I will not excuse;" I will use the severest language I can command; and yet not one word shall escape me that any man, whose judgment is not blinded by prejudice, or who is not at heart a slaveholder, shall not confess to be right and just.

. . . I submit, where all is plain there is nothing to be argued. What point in the anti-slavery creed would you have me argue? On what branch of the subject do the people of this country need light? Must I undertake to prove that the slave is a man? That point is conceded already. Nobody doubts it. . . .

For the present, it is enough to affirm the equal manhood of the Negro race. Is it not astonishing that, while we are ploughing, planting and reaping, using all kinds of mechanical tools, erecting houses, constructing bridges, building ships, working in metals of brass, iron, copper, silver and gold; that, while we are reading, writing and cyphering, acting as clerks, merchants and secretaries, having among us lawyers, doctors, ministers, poets, authors, editors, orators and teachers; that, while we are engaged in all manner of enterprises common to other men, digging gold in California, capturing the whale in the Pacific, feeding sheep and cattle on the hill-side, living, moving, acting, thinking, planning, living in families as husbands, wives and children, and, above all, confessing and worshipping the Christian's God, and looking hopefully for life and immortality beyond the grave, we are called upon to prove that we are men!

Would you have me argue that man is entitled to liberty? that he is the rightful owner of his own body? You have already declared it. Must I argue the wrongfulness of slavery? Is that a question for Republicans? Is it to be settled by the rules of logic and argumentation, as a matter beset with great difficulty, involving a doubtful application of the principle of justice, hard to be understood? How should I look to-day, in the presence of Americans, dividing, and subdividing a discourse, to show that men have a natural right to freedom? . . . To do so, would be to make myself ridiculous, and to offer an insult to your understanding.—There is not a man beneath the canopy of heaven, that does not know that slavery is wrong *for him*.

What, am I to argue that it is wrong to make men brutes, to rob them of their liberty, to work them without wages, to keep them ignorant of their relations to their fellow men, to beat them with sticks, to flay their flesh with the lash, to load their limbs with irons, to hunt them with dogs, to sell them at auction, to sunder their families, to knock out their teeth, to burn their flesh, to starve them into obedience and submission to their masters? Must I argue that a system thus marked with blood, and stained with pollution, is *wrong*? No! I will not. I have better employments for my time and strength than such arguments would imply.

. . .

At a time like this, scorching irony, not convincing argument, is needed. O! had I the ability, and could I reach the nation's ear, I would, today, pour out a fiery stream of biting ridicule, blasting reproach, withering sarcasm, and stern rebuke. For it is not light that is needed, but fire; it is not the gentle shower, but thunder. We need the storm, the whirlwind, and the earthquake. The feeling of the nation must be quickened; the conscience of the nation must be roused; the propriety of the nation must be startled; the hypocrisy of the nation must be exposed; and its crimes against God and man must be proclaimed and denounced.

What, to the American slave, is your 4th of July? I answer: a day that reveals to him, more than all other days in the year, the gross injustice and cruelty to which he is the constant victim. To him, your celebration is a sham; your boasted liberty, an unholy license; your national greatness, swelling vanity; your sounds of rejoicing are empty and heartless; your denunciations of tyrants, brass fronted impudence; your shouts of liberty and equality, hollow mockery; your prayers and hymns, your sermons and thanksgivings, with all your religious parade, and solemnity, are, to him, mere bombast, fraud, deception, impiety, and hypocrisy—a thin veil to cover up crimes which would disgrace a nation of savages. There is not a nation on the earth guilty of practices, more shocking and bloody, than are the people of these United States, at this very hour.

. . .

Fellow-citizens! I will not enlarge further on your national inconsistencies. The existence of slavery in this country brands your republicanism as a sham, your humanity as a base pretense, and your Christianity as a lie. It destroys your moral power abroad; it corrupts your politicians at home. It saps the foundation of religion; it makes your name a hissing, and a bye-word to a mocking earth. It is the antagonistic force in your government, the only thing that seriously disturbs and endangers your *Union*. It fetters your progress; it is the enemy of improvement, the deadly foe of education; it fosters pride; it breeds insolence; it promotes vice; it shelters crime; it is a curse to the earth that supports it; and yet, you cling to it, as if it were the sheet anchor of all your hopes. Oh! be warned! be warned! a horrible reptile is coiled up in your nation's bosom; the venomous creature is nursing at the tender breast of your youthful republic; *for the love of God*, tear away, and fling from you the hideous monster, and *let the weight of twenty millions crush and destroy it forever*!

. . .

Fellow-citizens! there is no matter in respect to which, the people of the North have allowed themselves to be so ruinously imposed upon, as that of the pro-slavery character of the Constitution. In that instrument I hold there is neither warrant, license, nor sanction of the hateful thing; but, interpreted as it ought to be interpreted, the Constitution is a GLORIOUS LIBERTY DOCUMENT. Read its preamble, consider its purposes. Is slavery among them? . . . While I do not intend to argue this question on the present occasion, let me ask, if it be not somewhat singular that, if the Constitution were intended to be, by its framers and adopters, a slave-holding instrument, why neither slavery, slaveholding, nor slave can anywhere be found in it. . . . I hold that every American citizen has a right to form an opinion of the constitution, and to propagate that opinion, and to use all honorable means to make his opinion the prevailing one. . . .

Now, take the Constitution according to its plain reading, and I defy the presentation of a single pro-slavery clause in it. On the other hand it will be found to contain principles and purposes, entirely hostile to the existence of slavery.

. . .

Allow me to say, in conclusion, notwithstanding the dark picture I have this day presented of the state of the nation, I do not despair of this country. There are forces in operation, which must inevitably work the downfall of slavery. "The arm of the Lord is not shortened," and the doom of slavery is certain. I, therefore, leave off where I began, with hope. While drawing encouragement from the Declaration of Independence, the great principles it contains, and the genius of American Institutions, my spirit is also cheered by the obvious tendencies of the age. . . . No nation can now shut itself up from the surrounding world, and trot round in the same old path of its fathers without interference. The time was when such could be done. Long established customs of hurtful character could formerly fence themselves in, and do their evil work with social impunity. . . . But a change has now come over the affairs of mankind. Walled cities and empires have become unfashionable. The arm of commerce has borne away the gates of the strong city. Intelligence is penetrating the darkest corners of the globe. . . . The fiat of the Almighty, "Let there be Light," has not yet spent its force. No abuse, no outrage whether in taste, sport or avarice, can now hide itself from the all-pervading light. . . .

GEORGE FITZHUGH

CANNIBALS ALL!, OR, SLAVES WITHOUT MASTERS (1857)

George Fitzhugh was born during the Jefferson administration to a north Virginia surgeon. Trained as a lawyer, Fitzhugh was a rather bookish man, rarely straying far from his home and its library. He was an avid reader (including abolitionist literature) and was deeply influenced by the conservative Scottish writer Thomas Carlyle. His first book, *Sociology for the South,* may have been his most fully realized theoretical critique of capitalism and free labor, but his second book, *Cannibals All!,* was the more popular extension of his ideas. Many proslavery writers distanced themselves from Fitzhugh's wide-ranging critique of wage labor, but he received a great deal of attention from antislavery activists, including William Lloyd Garrison and Abraham Lincoln. For Carlyle, the mass of men were naturally "slaves," capable only of being led and not of providing heroic leadership; the indigent, he believed, would have been better off as serfs than as free laborers.[9] Rather than resting on racial ideas that justified slavery for blacks, Fitzhugh followed Carlyle in arguing that slavery was the natural condition of most of mankind and that capitalist democracies left most of society exploited and vulnerable.

What does Fitzhugh mean by the "White Slave Trade"? Why does he think that white wage laborers are worse off than black slaves? Does Fitzhugh think that democracy is sustainable? Why does he associate individualism with anarchy? What does Fitzhugh mean when he says that there is too much law and not enough government, and why does he think that?

We are, all, North and South, engaged in the White Slave Trade, and he who succeeds best, is esteemed most respectable. It is far more cruel than the Black Slave Trade, because it exacts more of its slaves, and neither protects nor governs them. We boast, that it exacts more, when we say, "that the *profits* made from employing free labor are greater than those from slave labor." The profits, made from free labor, are the amount of the products of such labor, which the employer, by means of the command which capital or skill gives him, takes away, exacts or "exploitates" from the free laborer. The profits of slave labor are that portion of the products of such labor which the power of the master enables him to appropriate. These profits are less, because the master allows the slave to retain a larger share of the results of his own labor, than do the employers of free labor. But we not only boast that the White Slave Trade is more exacting and fraudulent (in fact, though not in intention,) than Black Slavery; but we also boast, that it is more cruel, in leaving the laborer to take care of himself and family out of the pittance which skill or capital have allowed him to retain. When the day's labor is ended, he is free, but is overburdened with the cares of family and household, which make his freedom an empty and delusive mockery. But his employer is really free, and may enjoy the profits made by others' labor, without a care, or a trouble, as to their well-being. The negro slave is free, too, when the labors of the day are over, and free in mind as well as body; for the master provides food, raiment, house, fuel, and everything else necessary to the physical well-being of himself and family. The master's labors commence just when the slave's end. No wonder men should prefer white slavery to capital, to negro slavery, since it is more profitable, and is free from all the cares and labors of black slave-holding.

Now, reader, if you wish to know yourself—to "descant on your own deformity"—read on. But if you would cherish self-conceit, self-esteem, or self-appreciation, throw down our book; for we will

9 See, e.g., Thomas Carlyle, "Parliaments," in *Collected Works*, vol. 19 (London: Chapman and Hall, 1870), 299–300.

dispel illusions which have promoted your happiness, and show you that what you have considered and practiced as virtue, is little better than moral Cannibalism. But you will find yourself in numerous and respectable company; for all good and respectable people are "Cannibals all," who do not labor, or who are successfully trying to live without labor, on the unrequited labor of other people. . . .

. . .

"Property in man" is what all are struggling to obtain. Why should they not be obliged to take care of man, their property, as they do of their horses and their hounds, their cattle and their sheep. Now, under the delusive name of liberty, you work him, "from morn to dewy eve"—from infancy to old age—then turn him out to starve. You treat your horses and hounds better. Capital is a cruel master. The free slave trade, the commonest, yet the cruelest of trades.

. . .

. . . Slavery is an indispensable police institution;—especially so, to check the cruelty and tyranny of vicious and depraved husbands and parents. Husbands and parents have, in theory and practice, a power over their subjects more despotic than kings; and the ignorant and vicious exercise their power more oppressively than kings. Every man is not fit to be king, yet all must have wives and children. Put a master over them to check their power, and we need not resort to the unnatural remedies of woman's rights, limited marriages, voluntary divorces, and free love, as proposed by the abolitionists.

. . .

The true greatness of Mr. Jefferson was his fitness for revolution. He was the genius of innovation, the architect of ruin, the inaugurator of anarchy. His mission was to pull down, not to build up. He thought everything false as well in the physical, as in the moral world. He fed his horses on potatoes, and defended harbors with gun-boats, because it was contrary to human experience and human opinion. He proposed to govern boys without the authority of masters or the control of religion, supplying their places with Laissez-faire philosophy, and morality from the pages of Lawrence Sterne. His character, like his philosophy, is exceptional—invaluable in urging on revolution, but useless, if not dangerous, in quiet times.

We would not restrict, control, or take away a single human right or liberty, which experience showed was already sufficiently governed and restricted by public opinion. But we do believe that the slaveholding South is the only country on the globe, that can safely tolerate . . . rights and liberties. . . .

We are the friend of popular government, but only so long as conservatism is the interest of the governing class. At the South, the interests and feelings of many non-property holders, are identified with those of a comparatively few property holders. It is not necessary to the security of property, that a majority of voters should own property; but where the pauper majority becomes so large as to disconnect the mass of them in feeling and interest from the property holding class, revolution and agrarianism are inevitable. We will not undertake to say that events are tending this way at the North. The absence of laws of entail and primogeniture may prevent it; yet we fear the worst; for, despite the laws of equal inheritance and distribution, wealth is accumulating in few hands, and pauperism is increasing. We shall attempt hereafter to show that a system of very small entails might correct this tendency.

. . .

All modern philosophy converges to a single point—the overthrow of all government, the substitution of the untrammeled "Sovereignty of the Individual," for the Sovereignty of Society, and the inauguration of anarchy. First domestic slavery, next religious institutions, then separate property, then political government, and, finally, family government and family relations, are to be swept away. This is the distinctly avowed program of all able abolitionists and socialists; and towards this end the doctrines and the practices of the weakest and most timid among them tend. . . .

. . .

We do not agree with the authors of the Declaration of Independence, that governments "derive their just powers from the consent of the governed." The women, the children, the negroes, and but few of the non-property holders were consulted, or consented to the Revolution, or the governments that ensued from its success. As to these, the new governments were self-elected despotisms, and the governing class self-elected despots. Those governments originated in force, and have been continued by force. All governments must originate in force, and be continued by force. The very term, government, implies that it is carried on against the consent of the governed. Fathers do not derive their authority, as heads of families, from the consent of wife and children, nor do they govern their families by their consent. They never take the vote of the family as to the labors to be performed, the moneys to be expended, or as to anything else. Masters dare not take the vote of slaves, as to their government. If they did, constant holiday, dissipation and extravagance would be the result. Captains of ships are not appointed by the consent of the crew, and never take their vote, even in "doubling Cape Horn." If they did, the crew would generally vote to get drunk, and the ship would never weather the cape. Not even in the most democratic countries are soldiers governed by their consent, nor is their vote taken on the eve of battle. They have somehow lost (or never had) the "inalienable rights of life, liberty and the pursuit of happiness;" and, whether Americans or Russians, are forced into battle, without and often against their consent. The ancient republics were governed by a small class of adult male citizens, who assumed and exercised the government, without the consent of the governed. The South is governed just as those ancient republics were. In the county in which we live, there are eighteen thousand souls, and only twelve hundred voters. But we twelve hundred, the governors, never asked and never intend to ask the consent of the sixteen thousand eight hundred whom we govern. Were we to do so, we should soon have an "organized anarchy." The governments of Europe could not exist a week without the positive force of standing armies.

. . .

If the interests of the governors, or governing class, be not conservative, they certainly will not conserve institutions injurious to their interests. There never was and never can be an old society, in which the immediate interests of a majority of human souls do not conflict with all established order, all right of property, and all existing institutions. Immediate interest is all the mass look to; and they would be sure to revolutionize government, as often as the situation of the majority was worse than that of the minority. Divide all property to-day, and a year hence the inequalities of property would provoke a re-division.

In the South, the interest of the governing class is eminently conservative, and the South is fast becoming the most conservative of nations.

Already, at the North, government vibrates and oscillates between Radicalism and Conservatism; at present, Radicalism or Black Republicanism is in the ascendant.

The number of paupers is rapidly increasing; radical and agrarian doctrines are spreading; the women and the children, and the negroes, will soon be let in to vote; and then they will try the experiment of "Consent Government and Constituted Anarchy."

. . .

We think speculations as to constructing governments are little worth; for all government is the gradual accretion of Nature, time and circumstances. Yet these theories have occurred to us, and, as they are conservative, we will suggest them. In slaveholding countries all freemen should vote and govern, because their interests are conservative. In free states, the government should be in the hands of the landowners, who are also conservative. . . .

A word, at parting, to Northern Conservatives. A like danger threatens North and South, proceeding from the same source. Abolitionism is maturing what Political Economy began. With inexorable sequence "Let Alone" is made to usher in No-Government. North and South our danger is the same, and our remedies, though differing in degree, must in character be the same. "Let Alone" must be repudiated, if we would have any Government. We must, in all sections, act upon the principle that the world is "too little governed." You of the North need not institute negro slavery; far less reduce white men to the state of negro slavery. But the masses require more of protection, and the masses and philosophers equally require more of control. . . .

. . .

JAMES HAMMOND

SPEECH TO THE SENATE ON SLAVERY (1858)

James Henry Hammond was the son of a schoolteacher from Massachusetts. Hammond was going down the same path until he married a Charleston heiress in 1830 and became a wealthy planter. Almost immediately thereafter, he launched a successful political career as a Democrat that took him to the U.S. Senate and the South Carolina governor's mansion (but he was passed over for important positions in the government of the Confederacy). He never achieved the national prominence of John C. Calhoun, but he became an important home-state rival who positioned himself as a more forceful advocate of the slavery cause. He is best remembered for his proslavery arguments and his confidence that the economic clout of cotton would see the South through political crises. His 1858 speech to the Senate on the slavery debate in Kansas touched on both those themes, warning his colleagues from the North that "Cotton is king" and declaring that every society had a "mud-sill" at the bottom of the economic ladder and that republican society and government in the South benefitted from having this tier occupied by blacks rather than whites.

How does Hammond use the threat of secession to advance his policy goals? Why does he think southern independence would be viable? Does he anticipate the Civil War? Why does he think the South enjoys a unique "harmony of her political and political institutions"? Why does he think slavery is compatible with republican government? Why does he think republican government is more secure in the slave states than in the free states? How does his understanding of the relationship between slavery and government compare to Fitzhugh's?

. . .

[S]ir, the true object of the discussion on the other side of the Chamber, is to agitate the question of slavery. . . .

. . . [W]hat guarantee have we that you will not emancipate our slaves, or, at least, make the attempt? We cannot rely on your faith when you have the power. It has been always broken whenever pledged.

. . . I think it is not improper that I should attempt to bring the North and South face to face, and see what resources each of us might have in the contingency of separate organizations.

If we never acquire another foot of territory for the South, look at her. Eight hundred and fifty thousand square miles. As large as Great Britain, France, Austria, Prussia and Spain. Is not that territory enough to make an empire that shall rule the world? . . .

But, in this territory lies the great valley of the Mississippi now the real, and soon to be the acknowledged seat of the empire of the world. . . . [S]lave-labor will go over very foot of this great valley where it will be found profitable to use it, and some of those who may not use it are soon to be united with us by such ties as will make us one and inseparable. . . .

On this fine territory we have a population four times as large as that with which these colonies separated from the mother country, and a hundred, I might say a thousand fold stronger. . . . Upon our muster-rolls we have a million men. In a defensive war, upon an emergency, every one of them would be available. At any time, the South can raise, equip and maintain in the field, a larger army than any Power of the earth can send against her. . . .

. . .

But the strength of a nation depends in a great measure upon its wealth, and the wealth of a nation, like that of a man, is to be estimated by its surplus production. . . .

But if there were no other reason why we should never have war, would any sane nation make war on cotton? Without firing a gun, without drawing a sword, should they make war on us we could bring the whole world to our feet. The South is perfectly competent to go on, one, two, or three years without planting a seed of cotton. . . . What would happen if no cotton was furnished for three years? . . . England would topple headlong and carry the whole civilized world with her, save the South. No, you dare not make war on cotton. No power on earth dares to make war upon it. Cotton *is* king. . . .

But, sir, the greatest strength of the South arises from the harmony of her political and social institutions. This harmony gives her a frame of society, the best in the world, and an extent of political freedom, combined with entire security, such as no other people ever enjoyed upon the face of the earth. Society precedes government; creates it, and ought to control it. . . . In later centuries the progress of civilization and of intelligence has made the divergence so great as to produce civil wars and revolutions; and it is nothing now but the want of harmony between governments and societies which occasions all the uneasiness and trouble and terror that we see abroad. It was this that brought on the American Revolution. We threw off a Government not adapted to our social system, and made one for ourselves. The question is, how far have we succeeded? The South, so far as that is concerned, is satisfied, harmonious, and prosperous, but demands to be let alone.

In all social systems there must be a class to do the menial duties, to perform the drudgery of life. That is, a class requiring but a low order of intellect and but little skill. Its requisites are vigor, docility, fidelity. Such a class you must have, or you would not have that other class which leads progress, civilization, and refinement. It constitutes the very mud-sill of society and of political government; and you might as well attempt to build a house in the air, as to build either the one or the other, except on this mud-sill. Fortunately for the South, she found a race adapted to that purpose to her hand. A race inferior to her own, but eminently qualified in temper, in vigor, in docility, in capacity to stand the climate, to answer all her purposes. We use them for our purpose, and call them slaves. We found them slaves by the common "consent of mankind." . . . We are old-fashioned at the South yet; slave is a word discarded now by "ears polite;" I will not characterize that class at the North by that term; but you have it; it is there; it is everywhere; it is eternal.

The Senator from New York said yesterday that the whole world had abolished slavery. Aye, the name, but not the *thing*; all the powers of the earth cannot abolish that. God can only do it when he repeals the *fiat*, "the poor ye always have with you;" for the man who lives by daily labor, and scarcely lives at that, and who has to put out his labor in the market, and take the best he can get for it; in short, your whole hireling class of manual laborers and "operatives," as you call them, are essentially slaves. The difference between us is, that our slaves are hired for life and well compensated; there is no starvation, no begging, no want of employment among our people, and not too much employment either. Yours are hired by the day, not cared for, and scantily compensated, which may be proved in the most painful manner, at any hour in any street in any of your large towns. . . . We do not think that whites should be slaves either by law or necessity. Our slaves are black, of another and inferior race. The *status* in which we have placed them is an elevation. They are elevated from the condition in which God first created them, by being made our slaves. None of that race on the whole face of the globe can be compared with the slaves of the South. They are happy, content, unaspiring, and utterly incapable, from intellectual weakness, ever to give us any trouble by their aspirations. Yours are white, of your own race; you are brothers of one blood. They are not equals in natural endowment of intellect, and they feel galled by their degradation. Our slaves do not vote. We give them no political power. Yours do vote, and, being the majority, they are the depositories of all your political power. If they knew the tremendous secret, that the ballot-box is stronger than "an army with banners," and could combine, where would you be? Your society would be reconstructed, your government overthrown, your property divided, not as they have mistakenly attempted to initiate such proceedings by meeting in parks, with arms in their hands, but by the quiet process of the ballot-box. You have been making war upon us to our very hearthstones. How would you like for us to send lecturers and agitators North, to teach these people this, to aid in combining, and to lead them?

. . .

Transient and temporary causes have thus far been your preservation. The great West has been open to your surplus population, and your hordes of semi-barbarian immigrants, who are crowding in year by year. . . . The South have sustained you in a great measure. You are our factors. You bring and carry for us. . . . Suppose we were to discharge you; suppose we were to take our business out of your hands; we should consign you to anarchy and poverty. You complain of the rule of the South: that has been another cause that has preserved you. We have kept the Government conservative to the great purposes of Government. We have placed her, and kept her, upon the Constitution; and that has been the cause of your peace and prosperity. . . .

ABRAHAM LINCOLN

SPEECH AT NEW HAVEN (1860)

Abraham Lincoln had humble origins in Kentucky and Indiana before trying out several vocations in Illinois. He finally settled on law and politics, launching a successful legal practice and a less noteworthy political career, which included a brief stint in the U.S. House of Representatives as a Whig. His political fortunes took off after the passage of the controversial Kansas-Nebraska Act of 1854, which repealed the Missouri Compromise and opened the door to introducing slavery into the northern territories. He announced his opposition to the extension of slavery in 1854, and came close to securing election to the U.S. Senate that year. With the Whig Party collapsing, Lincoln threw himself into organizing the Republican Party in Illinois, nearly winning the party's vice presidential nomination in 1856, and unsuccessfully challenging Stephen Douglas for the U.S. Senate in 1858. In the spring of 1860, Lincoln launched a speaking tour of the northeast in preparation for the presidential campaign, and in May he outmaneuvered more established politicians to win the party nomination for the presidency. His March speech in New Haven helped launch his swing through New England and was a variation on the standard stump speech that he delivered in those stops. The speech was greeted by large, raucous crowds and won praise from the rhetoric professor at Yale, who lectured on the speech the very next day. Of particular note, the speech focused less on the question of slavery in the territories that had occupied Lincoln's attention in his speeches to western audiences than on the moral wrongness of slavery itself and offered a concise version of the "free labor" ideology promoted by the Republicans.

How does Lincoln think that the existence of slavery is a threat to whites? How does he justify preserving a "great moral wrong" where it already exists? In what sense does he endorse Seward's "irrepressible conflict"? Why does Lincoln not regard the Constitution as "an agreement with Hell"? Why does Lincoln believe that there is no conflict between whites and blacks? What does Lincoln see as the central feature of the northern economic system? How would he respond to Hammond's critique of northern wage slavery?

. . .

. . . To us it appears natural to think that slaves are human beings; men, not property; that some of the things, at least, stated about men in the Declaration of Independence apply to them as well as to us. I say, we think, most of us, that this Charter of Freedom applies to the slave as well as to ourselves, that the class of arguments put forward to batter down that idea, are also calculated to break down the very idea of a free government, even for white men, and to undermine the very foundations of free society. We think Slavery a great moral wrong, and while we do not claim the right to touch it where it exists, we wish to treat it as a wrong in the Territories, where our votes will reach it. We think that a respect for ourselves, a regard for future generations and for the God that made us, require that we put down this wrong where our votes will properly reach it. We think that species of labor an injury to free white men—in short, we think Slavery a great moral, social and political evil, tolerable only because, and so far as its actual existence makes it necessary to tolerate it, and that beyond that, it ought to be treated as a wrong.

Now these two ideas, the property idea that Slavery is right, and the idea that it is wrong, come into collision, and do actually produce that irrepressible conflict which Mr. Seward has been so roundly abused for mentioning. The two ideas conflict, and must conflict.

. . .

. . . Now, I don't wish to be misunderstood, nor to leave a gap down to be misrepresented, even. I don't mean that we ought to attack it where it exists. To me it seems that if we were to form a government anew, in view of the actual presence of Slavery we should find it necessary to frame just such a government as our fathers did; giving to the slaveholder the entire control where the system was established, while we possessed the power to restrain it from going outside those limits. From the necessities of the case we should be compelled to form just such a government as our blessed fathers gave us; and, surely, if they have so made it, that adds another reason why we should let Slavery alone where it exists.

. . .

. . . I venture to defy the whole [Democratic] party to produce one man that ever uttered the belief that the Declaration did not apply to negroes, before the repeal of the Missouri Compromise! Four or five years ago we all thought negroes were men, and that when "all men" were named, negroes were included. *But the whole Democratic party has deliberately taken negroes from the class of men and put them in the class of brutes*. . . .

. . . "In the struggle between the white man and the negro" assumes that there is a struggle, in which either the white man must enslave the negro or the negro must enslave the white. There is no such struggle! It is merely an ingenious falsehood, to degrade and brutalize the negro. Let each let the other alone, and there is no struggle about it. If it was like two wrecked seamen on a narrow plank, when each must push the other off or drown himself, I would push the negro off or a white man either, but it is not; the plank is large enough for both. This good earth is plenty broad enough for white man and negro both, and there is no need of either pushing the other off.

. . .

. . . *I am glad to see that a system of labor prevails in New England under which laborers can strike* when they want to, where they are not obliged to work under all circumstances, and are not tied down and obliged to labor whether you pay them or not! I *like* the system which lets a man quit when he wants to, and wish it might prevail everywhere. One of the reasons why I am opposed to Slavery is just here. What is the true condition of the laborer? I take it that it is best for all to leave each man free to acquire property as fast as he can. Some will get wealthy. I don't believe in a law to prevent a man from getting rich; it would do more harm than good. So while we do not propose any war upon capital, we do wish to allow the humblest man an equal chance to get rich with everybody else. When one starts poor, as most do in the race of life, free society is such that he knows he can better his condition; he knows that there is no fixed condition of labor, for his whole life. I am not ashamed to confess that twenty five years ago I was a hired laborer, mauling rails, at work on a flat-boat—just what might happen to any poor man's son! I want every man to have the chance—and I believe a black man is entitled to it—in which he can better his condition—when he may look forward and hope to be a hired laborer this year and the next, work for himself afterward, and finally to hire men to work for him! That is the true system. . . .

. . .

V. POLITICAL ECONOMY

Major Developments

- Partisan debate over maintenance of a national bank
- Partisan debate over free trade
- Growing government investment in infrastructure

The debates over political economy in the early republic were relatively short-lived. Many of the disagreements were constitutional, and the policy disputes settled into fairly modest sniping at the margins. The debates of the Jacksonian period were more dramatic and enduring. If the Jeffersonians soon accepted core features of the Hamiltonian program (even if in a more moderate form), the Jacksonian Democrats and the Whigs sustained more of a running battle over federal economic policy. If the government achieved some level of stability in its approach to political economy, that was largely because the Whigs could never wrest control of the government away from the Democrats. As a consequence, national policy tended to reflect Democratic priorities and values.

The core of the national debate revolved around Henry Clay's "American System." The American System drew upon Hamiltonian ideas, was embraced by nationalistic Jeffersonians after the War of 1812, and became the centerpiece of the Whig platform in the antebellum era. The System had three primary parts: protectionist tariffs, a national bank, and internal improvements (the building of roads, canals, and bridges). The Jacksonians opposed each of those components, favoring free trade, a system of state banks and an independent national treasury, and state-funded internal improvements. Land policy was also contested, with the Democrats favoring westward expansion and rapid settlement and the Whigs preferring a less aggressive settlement of western territories.

Local debates over the political economy were more wide-ranging. State politics was sometimes fought over the details of economic policy, and the fallout of unsuccessful policies such as the overinvestment of public funds in bankrupt infrastructure projects. But localities also debated more fundamental features of social and economic arrangements. Laborers began to organize to demand better working conditions and better pay. Ideas for utopian communities were floated that suggested the collectivization of property and living arrangements. Public (or "common") schools were established, both to assimilate immigrants into America and to produce productive workers and citizens.

The readings in this section reflect both sets of debates. Andrew Jackson and Henry Clay debate two aspects of the American System, with Jackson denouncing the Bank of the United States (and finance capital more broadly) and Clay defending protective tariffs (and government intervention in the economy more broadly). William Leggett and Orestes Brownson offer two different perspectives on the proper relationship between government and economic interests. Both happened to be Jacksonians, but they represent quite distinct ideological positions, with Leggett offering a more libertarian perspective on the role of government and Brownson worrying about the effects of the rise of industrialization on the common man.

ANDREW JACKSON

VETO OF THE BANK BILL (1832)

The Second Bank of the United States was given a twenty-year charter by Congress in 1816, in a bill signed by President James Madison. Madison had been a sharp critic of the creation of the First Bank of the United States during the Washington administration, but the financial difficulties of the War of 1812 and the sustained political support for the Bank convinced Madison to acquiesce. The Bank served as the fiscal agent of the federal government, as well as accepting deposits and issuing bank notes to the general public.

President Andrew Jackson was a fierce opponent of the Bank. The Bank had powerful friends, however, among Jackson's congressional opponents. Massachusetts Senator Daniel Webster had served as the attorney for the Bank. Kentucky Senator Henry Clay was a chief sponsor of the Bank. In the summer of 1832, the Whig-controlled Congress passed an early new charter for the Bank. Jackson was expected to veto the bill, but Clay hoped that the issue would advance his own campaign to win the presidential election in the fall. Jackson proved happy to run on the Bank issue and beat Clay in a landslide.

Jackson's veto message was written to serve as a campaign document, and it was widely circulated by Democratic leaders. Part of his veto message focused on constitutional issues, explaining why the charter was not a necessary and proper exercise of congressional powers. But much of his message focused on policy questions, where he denounced the Bank bill as a financial boon to the current shareholders in the northeast and abroad. By settling the future of the Bank, the bill was expected to immediately boost the value of the Bank's stock, enriching current shareholders. In exchange for the exclusive federal charter, the Bank was obliged to pay the federal government an annual sum of $200,000. The U.S. Supreme Court had earlier declared that the state governments could not tax the branches of the Bank of the United States or its deposits, which left only the shareholders of the Bank as potential sources of state tax revenue. In effect, Jackson argued, the national Bank drew wealth from the rest of the country (where loans were made) and consolidated it in the northeast (where the shareholders collected the profits).

. . .

The present corporate body, denominated the president, directors, and company of the Bank of the United States, will have existed at the time this act is intended to take effect twenty years. It enjoys an exclusive privilege of banking under the authority of the General Government, a monopoly of its favor and support, and, as a necessary consequence, almost a monopoly of the foreign and domestic exchange. The powers, privileges, and favors bestowed upon it in the original charter, by increasing the value of the stock far above its par value, operated as a gratuity of many millions to the stockholders.

. . . The act before me proposes another gratuity to the holders of the same stock, and in many cases to the same men, of at least seven millions more. . . . On all hands it is conceded that its passage will increase at least 20 or 30 per cent more the market price of the stock, subject to the payment of the annuity of $200,000 per year secured by the act, thus adding in a moment one-fourth to its par value. It is not our own citizens only who are to receive the bounty of our Government. More than eight millions of the stock of this bank are held by foreigners. By this act the American Republic proposes virtually to make them a present of some millions of dollars. For these gratuities to foreigners and to some of our own opulent citizens the act secures no equivalent whatever. They are the certain gains of the present stockholders under the operation of this act, after making full allowance for the payment of the bonus.

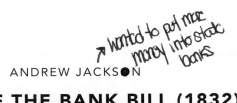

Every monopoly and all exclusive privileges are granted at the expense of the public, which ought to receive a fair equivalent. The many millions which this act proposes to bestow on the stockholders of the existing bank must come directly or indirectly out of the earnings of the American people. It is due to them, therefore, if their Government sell monopolies and exclusive privileges, that they should at least exact for them as much as they are worth in open market. . . .

It is not conceivable how the present stockholders can have any claim to the special favor of the Government. The present corporation has enjoyed its monopoly during the period stipulated in the original contract. If we must have such a corporation, why should not the Government sell out the whole stock and thus secure to the people the full market value of the privileges granted? Why should not Congress create and sell twenty-eight millions of stock, incorporating the purchasers with all the powers and privileges secured in this act and putting the premium upon the sales into the Treasury?

But this act does not permit competition in the purchase of this monopoly. It seems to be predicated on the erroneous idea that the present stockholders have a prescriptive right not only to the favor but to the bounty of Government. . . .

. . .

. . . As little stock is held in the West, it is obvious that the debt of the people in that section to the bank is principally a debt to the Eastern and foreign stockholders; that the interest they pay upon it is carried into the Eastern States and into Europe, and that it is a burden upon their industry and a drain of their currency, which no country can bear without inconvenience and occasional distress. . . . The branch bank at Mobile made last year $95,140, yet under the provisions of this act the State of Alabama can raise no revenue from these profitable operations, because not a share of the stock is held by any of her citizens. Mississippi and Missouri are in the same condition in relation to the branches at Natchez and St. Louis, and such, in a greater or less degree, is the condition of every Western State. . . .

. . .

Is there no danger to our liberty and independence in a bank that in its nature has so little to bind it to our country? The president of the bank has told us that most of the State banks exist by its forbearance. Should its influence become concentered, as it may under the operation of such an act as this, in the hands of a self-elected directory whose interests are identified with those of the foreign stockholders, will there not be cause to tremble for the purity of our elections in peace and for the independence of our country in war? Their power would be great whenever they might choose to exert it; but if this monopoly were regularly renewed every fifteen or twenty years on terms proposed by themselves, they might seldom in peace put forth their strength to influence elections or control the affairs of the nation. But if any private citizen or public functionary should interpose to curtail its powers or prevent a renewal of its privileges, it cannot be doubted that he would be made to feel its influence.

Should the stock of the bank principally pass into the hands of the subjects of a foreign country, and we should unfortunately become involved in a war with that country, what would be our condition? Of the course which would be pursued by a bank almost wholly owned by the subjects of a foreign power, and managed by those whose interests, if not affections, would run in the same direction there can be no doubt. All its operations within would be in aid of the hostile fleets and armies without. Controlling our currency, receiving our public moneys, and holding thousands of our citizens in dependence, it would be more formidable and dangerous than the naval and military power of the enemy.

If we must have a bank with private stockholders, every consideration of sound policy and every impulse of American feeling admonishes that it should be *purely American*. Its stockholders should be composed exclusively of our own citizens, who at least ought to be friendly to our Government and willing to support it in times of difficulty and danger. . . .

. . .

It is to be regretted that the rich and powerful too often bend the acts of government to their selfish purposes. Distinctions in society will always exist under every just government. Equality of talents, of education, or of wealth cannot be produced by human institutions. In the full enjoyment of the gifts of Heaven and the fruits of superior industry, economy, and virtue, every man is equally entitled to protection by law; but when the laws undertake to add to these natural and just advantages artificial distinctions, to grant titles, gratuities, and exclusive privileges, to make the rich richer and the potent more powerful, the humble members of society—the farmers, mechanics, and laborers—who have neither the time nor the means of securing like favors to themselves, have a right to complain of the injustice of their Government. There are no necessary evils in government. Its evils exist only in its abuses. If it would confine itself to equal protection, and, as Heaven does its rains, shower its favors alike on the high and the low, the rich and the poor, it would be an unqualified blessing. In the act before me there seems to be a wide and unnecessary departure from these just principles.

Nor is our Government to be maintained or our Union preserved by invasions of the rights and powers of the several States. In thus attempting to make our General Government strong we make it weak. Its true strength consists in leaving individuals and States as much as possible to themselves—in making itself felt, not in its power, but in its beneficence; not in its control, but in its protection; not in binding the States more closely to the center, but leaving each to move unobstructed in its proper orbit.

Experience should teach us wisdom. Most of the difficulties our Government now encounters and most of the dangers which impend over our Union have sprung from an abandonment of the legitimate objects of Government by our national legislation, and the adoption of such principles as are embodied in this act. Many of our rich men have not been content with equal protection and equal benefits, but have besought us to make them richer by act of Congress. By attempting to gratify their desires we have in the results of our legislation arrayed section against section, interest against interest, and man against man, in a fearful commotion which threatens to shake the foundations of our Union. It is time to pause in our career to review our principles, and if possible revive that devoted patriotism and spirit of compromise which distinguished the sages of the Revolution and the fathers of our Union. If we cannot at once, in justice to interests vested under improvident legislation, make our Government what it ought to be, we can at least take a stand against all new grants of monopolies and exclusive privileges, against any prostitution of our Government to the advancement of the few at the expense of the many, and in favor of compromise and gradual reform in our code of laws and system of political economy.

. . .

HENRY CLAY

SPEECH ON THE AMERICAN SYSTEM (1832)

Henry Clay was one of the leading Whig politics of the Jacksonian Era. He was born during the Revolutionary War in Virginia near the Kentucky border, and moved across the state line to launch his legal practice and (a decade later) start a tobacco and hemp plantation. He soon entered politics as a nationalist-minded Jeffersonian, and helped establish the Whig Party in opposition to President Andrew Jackson. His political ascent was meteoric, and his career was varied. At the age of twenty-nine (below the constitutional limit), he was selected to represent Kentucky in the U.S. Senate. Over the course of his career, he served as the Speaker of the U.S. House of Representatives, a U.S. senator, and U.S. Secretary of State. He ran three unsuccessful races for the presidency.

Clay's signature policy, which became the backbone of the Whig Party, was the "American System." The System built off the policies of Alexander Hamilton, and was later partly integrated into the platform of the Republican Party. The American System had three components: a protectionist tariff to encourage the growth of manufacturing, a national bank to facilitate finance and commerce, and federal support for "internal improvements" (or infrastructure construction) to connect farms to markets. Various pieces of the plan were opposed by states' rights–oriented Jeffersonians and, later, Jacksonians. Clay's three-day speech to the U.S. Senate in 1832 focused on the protective tariff (Clay had moved to eliminate all import duties on noncompeting goods, while retaining high duties on goods that were produced in the United States). The widely discussed speech was designed to help launch his second presidential campaign. Under pressure from South Carolina, the United States abandoned protectionist tariffs and shifted to a free trade regime after Jackson's 1832 reelection.

Why does Clay reject free trade? What does he set out as the goal of protective tariffs? Is it praiseworthy that there is "scarcely a vocation in society" not affected by the American System? Would it be more problematic if the tariffs were to reflect a narrow coalition of economic interests? Why does Clay regard free trade as equivalent to the recolonization of America? Are the arguments he offers for protectionism in the mid-nineteenth century equally compelling in the early twenty-first?

. . .

Eight years ago, it was my painful duty to present to the other House of Congress an unexaggerated picture of the general distress pervading the whole land. We must all yet remember some of its frightful features. We all know that the people were then oppressed, and borne down by an enormous load of debt; that the value of property was at the lowest point of depression; that ruinous sales and sacrifices were everywhere made of real estate; that stop laws, and relief laws, and paper money were adopted, to save the people from impending destruction; that a deficit in the public revenue existed, which compelled government to seize upon, and divert from its legitimate object . . . ; and that our commerce and navigation were threatened with a complete paralysis. *In short, sir, if I were to select any term of seven years since the adoption of the present Constitution which exhibited a scene of the most wide-spread dismay and desolation, it would be exactly that term of seven years which immediately preceded the establishment of the tariff of 1824.*

I have now to perform the more pleasing task of exhibiting an imperfect sketch of the existing state of the unparalleled prosperity of the country. On a general survey, we behold cultivation extended, the arts flourishing, the face of the country improved, our people fully and profitably employed, and the public countenance exhibiting tranquility, contentment, and happiness. . . . *If the term of seven years were to be selected, of the greatest prosperity which his people have enjoyed since the establishment of their present Constitution, it would be exactly that period of seven years which immediately followed the passage of the tariff of 1824.*

This transformation of the condition of the country from gloom and distress to brightness and prosperity, has been mainly the work of American legislation, fostering American industry, instead of allowing it to be controlled by foreign legislation, cherishing foreign industry. . . . Instead of the ruins of the public revenue, with which [critics] sought to deter us from the adoption of the American System, we are now threatened with its subversion, by the vast amount of the public revenue produced by that system. Every branch of our navigation has increased. . . . The truth is, [the growth of the cities] is the joint effect of both principles, the domestic industry nourishing the foreign trade, and the foreign commerce in turn nourishing the domestic industry. Nowhere more than in New York is the combination of both principles so completely developed. . . .

. . .

. . . Why, sir, there is scarcely an interest, scarcely a vocation in society, which is not embraced by the beneficence of the system.

It comprehends our coasting tonnage and trade, from which all foreign tonnage is absolutely excluded.

. . .

It embraces our fisheries, and all our hardy and enterprising fisherman.

It extends to almost every mechanic art. . . . The mechanics . . . enjoy a measure of protection adapted to their several conditions, varying from twenty to fifty percent. . . .

. . .

It affects the cotton planter himself, and the tobacco planter, both of whom enjoy protection.

. . .

Such are some of the items of this vast system of protection, which it is now proposed to abandon. We might well pause and contemplate, if human imagination could conceive the extent of mischief and ruin from its total overthrow, before we proceed to the work of destruction. . .

. . .

[T]his great system of protection [has] been gradually built, stone upon stone, and step by step, from the 4th of July, 1789, down to the present period. In every stage of its progress it has received the deliberate sanction of Congress. A vast majority of the people of the United States has approved and continue to approve it. Every chief magistrate of the United States, from Washington to the present, in some form or other, has given to it the authority of his name; and, however the opinions of the existing president are interpreted south of Mason and Dixon's line, on the north they are at least understood to favor the establishment of a judicious tariff.

The question, therefore, which we are now called upon to determine, is not, whether we shall establish a new and doubtful system of policy, just proposed, and for the first time presented to our consideration, but whether we shall break down and destroy a long established system, patiently and carefully built up and sanctioned, during a series of years, again and again, by the nation and its highest and most revered authorities. . .

. . .

When gentlemen have succeeded in their design of an immediate or gradual destruction of the American System, what is their substitute? Free trade! Free trade! The call for free trade is as unavailing, as the cry of a spoiled child in its nurse's arms, for the moon. . . . It never has existed, it never will exist. Trade implies at least two parties. To be free, it should be fair, equal, and reciprocal. But if we throw our ports wide open to the admission of foreign productions, free of all duty, what ports of any other foreign nation shall we find open to the free admission of our surplus produce? We may break down all barriers to free trade on our part, but the work will not be complete, until foreign powers shall have removed theirs. There would be freedom on one side, and restriction, prohibitions, and exclusions, on the other. The bolts and the bars and the chains of all other nations will remain undisturbed. . . .

Gentlemen deceive themselves. It is not free trade that they are recommending to our acceptance. It is, in effect, the British colonial system that we are invited to adopt; and, if their policy prevail, it will lead substantially to the recolonization of these States under the commercial dominion of Great Britain. . . .

. . .

The danger to our Union does not lie on the side of persistence in the American System, but on that of its abandonment. If, as I have supposed and believe, the inhabitants of all north and east of James river, and all west of the mountains, including Louisiana, are deeply interested in the preservation of that system, would they be reconciled to its overthrow? Can it be expected that two thirds, if not three fourths, of the people of the United States, would consent to the destruction of a policy, believed to be indispensably necessary to their prosperity? . . . What would be the condition of this Union, if Pennsylvania and New York, those mammoth members of our confederacy, were firmly persuaded that their industry was paralyzed, and their prosperity blighted, by the enforcement of the British colonial system, under the delusive name of free trade? . . . [L]et these vast portions of our country despair of any favorable change, and then indeed might we tremble for the continuance and safety of this Union.

. . .

WILLIAM LEGGETT

TRUE FUNCTIONS OF GOVERNMENT (1834)

William Leggett was a native New Yorker who became a professional writer and editor in his late twenties. During Andrew Jackson's first term as president, Leggett turned to writing political editorials, taking over the *New York Evening Post.* He became a leading voice of the Loco-Foco faction of Jacksonian Democrats, a New York reform group committed to free-market principles and working against the Tammany Hall political machine. The uncompromising Leggett proved to be a political lightning rod, even among the Jacksonians (among other things, he was antislavery), and he left journalism soon after the end of Jackson's presidency and died from lingering illnesses in 1839. His more significant editorials were collected and published as a book soon after his death. The editor of the collection hoped the reader would get past the "temporary controversies" that had surrounded Leggett and focus on his central merit, his "intense love of freedom."[10]

Does the idea that "there are no necessary evils in government" depart from or extend Jeffersonian principles? Why is "equal protection" emphasized here? How does "offering encouragements" violate the idea of equal protection? Can government avoid "discriminating between different classes of the community"? Is it problematic for government to distinguish between different groups and interests in society and provide favor to some? How does Leggett's vision of the government's involvement in society differ from Henry Clay's? Does Leggett's starting point necessarily lead to a policy of free trade?

"There are no necessary evils in Government. Its evils exist only in its abuses. If it would confine itself to *equal protection,* and, as heaven does its rains, shower its favors alike on the high and the low, the rich and the poor, it would be an unqualified blessing."

This is the language of our venerated President [Andrew Jackson], and the passage deserves to be written in letters of gold, for neither in truth of sentiment or beauty of expression can it be surpassed. We choose it as our text for a few remarks on the true functions of Government.

The fundamental principle of all governments is the protection of person and property from domestic and foreign enemies; in other words, to defend the weak against the strong. By establishing the social feeling in a community, it was intended to counteract that selfish feeling, which, in its proper exercise, is the parent of all worldly good, and, in its excesses, the root of all evil. The functions of Government, when confined to their proper sphere of action, are therefore restricted to the making of *general laws,* uniform and universal in their operation, for these purposes, and for no other.

Governments have no right to interfere with the pursuits of individuals, as guaranteed by those general laws, by offering encouragements and granting privileges to any particular class of industry, or any select bodies of men, inasmuch as all classes of industry and all men are equally important to the general welfare, and equally entitled to protection.

Whenever a Government assumes the power of discriminating between the different classes of the community, it becomes, in effect, the arbiter of their prosperity, and exercises a power not contemplated by any intelligent people in delegating their sovereignty to their rulers. It then becomes the great regulator of the profits of every species of industry, and reduces men from a dependence on their own exertions, to a dependence on the caprices of their Government. Governments possess no delegated right to tamper with individual industry a single hair's-breadth beyond what is essential to protect the rights of person and property.

10 Theodore Sedgwick, Jr., "Preface," in *A Collection of the Political Writings of William Leggett,* vol. 1 (New York: Taylor & Dodd, 1840), iii, vi.

In the exercise of this power of intermeddling with the private pursuits and individual occupations of the citizen, a Government may at pleasure elevate one class and depress another; it may one day legislate exclusively for the farmer, the next for the mechanic, and the third for the manufacturer, who all thus become the mere puppets of legislative cobbling and tinkering, instead of independent citizens, relying on their own resources for their prosperity. It assumes the functions which belong alone to an overruling Providence, and affects to become the universal dispenser of good and evil.

. . . Why is it that parties now exhibit excitement aggravated to a degree dangerous to the existence of the Union and to the peace of society? Is it not that by frequent exercises of partial legislation, almost every man's personal interests have become deeply involved in the result of the contest? In common times, the strife of parties is the mere struggle of ambitious leaders for power; now they are deadly contests of the whole mass of the people, whose pecuniary interests are implicated in the event, because the Government has usurped and exercised the power of legislating on their private affairs. . . .

. . .

Experience will show that this power has always been exercised under the influence and for the exclusive benefit of wealth. It was never wielded in behalf of the community. Whenever an exception is made to the general law of the land, founded on the principle of equal rights, it will always be found to be in favor of wealth. These immunities are never bestowed on the poor. They have no claim to a dispensation of exclusive benefits, and their only business is to *"take care of the rich that the rich may take care of the poor."*

Thus it will be seen that the sole reliance of the laboring classes, who constitute a vast majority of every people on the earth, is the great principle of Equal Rights; that their only safeguard against oppression is a system of legislation which leaves all to the free exercise of their talents and industry, within the limits of the GENERAL LAW, and which, on no pretense of public good, bestows on any particular class of industry, or any particular body of men, rights or privileges not equally enjoyed by the great aggregate of the body politic.

. . .

ORESTES BROWNSON

THE LABORING CLASSES (1840)

Orestes Brownson was an influential, and controversial, New England journalist and activist. His life was something of a spiritual journey: he was raised a Calvinist, baptized as a Presbyterian, preached as a Universalist and a Unitarian, founded his own church, and finally converted to Catholicism. His religious wanderings were closely connected to his political writing and social activism. He flirted for a time with the utopian socialism associated with Robert Dale Owen in New York, became an advocate of Transcendentalism in New England, and turned conservative after his conversion to Catholicism in 1844. He was a prolific editor and writer, founding multiple journals, including the influential *Boston Quarterly* and *The Dial*, and finally *Brownson's Quarterly Review*.

This essay was among his most significant publications (though Brownson later renounced many of the views he expressed in it). Written during his Transcendentalist phase and in the midst of one of the deepest recessions in American history, his essay on "The Laboring Classes" was structured as a review of a book by the conservative British writer Thomas Carlyle and was republished as a pamphlet. At the time, Brownson was a strong supporter of Democratic president Martin Van Buren, but this essay was used by Van Buren's opponents as evidence of Democratic radicalism and contributed to Van Buren's failure to win reelection in 1840, souring Brownson's own view of democratic politics.

Is Brownson an advocate of slavery? To what extent does he anticipate the proslavery writings of George Fitzhugh? Is there a connection between his arguments here and his earlier advocacy of socialism? How does Brownson's argument here fit within Jacksonian philosophy? How does his approach to political economy compare with William Leggett's? To what extent does Brownson think that moral and religious reform is necessary to improve social and economic conditions? How does he think that government policy can affect economic conditions?

. . .

Now we will not so belie our acquaintance with political economy, as to allege that these alone perform all that is necessary to the production of wealth. We are not ignorant of the fact, that the merchant, who is literally the common carrier and exchange dealer, performs a useful service, and is therefore entitled to a portion of the proceeds of labor. But make all necessary deductions on his account, and then ask what portion of the remainder is retained, either in kind or in its equivalent, in the hands of the original producer, the working-man? All over the world this fact stares us in the face, the working-man is poor and depressed, while a large portion of the non-workingmen, in the sense we now use the term, are wealthy. It may be laid down as a general rule, with but few exceptions, that men are rewarded in an inverse ratio to the amount of actual service they perform. Under every government on earth the largest salaries are annexed to those offices, which demand of their incumbents the least amount of actual labor either mental or manual. And this is in perfect harmony with the whole system of repartition of the fruits of industry, which obtains in every department of society, Now here is the system which prevails, and here is its result. The whole class of simple laborers are poor, and in general unable to procure anything beyond the bare necessaries of life.

In regard to labor two systems obtain; one that of slave labor, the other that of free labor. Of the two, the first is, in our judgment, except so far as the feelings are concerned, decidedly the least oppressive. If the slave has never been a free man, we think, as a general rule, his sufferings are less than those of the free laborer at wages. As to actual freedom one has just about as much as the other. The laborer at wages has all the disadvantages of freedom and none of its blessings, while the slave, if denied the blessings, is freed from the disadvantages. We are no advocates of slavery, we are as heartily opposed to it as any modern abolitionist can be; but we say frankly that, if there must always be a laboring population distinct from proprietors and employers, we regard the slave system as decidedly preferable to the system at wages, it is no pleasant thing to go days without food, to lie idle for weeks, seeking work and finding none, to rise in the morning with a wife and children you love, and know not where to procure them a breakfast, and to see constantly before you no brighter prospect than the almshouse. Yet these are no un-frequent incidents in the lives of our laboring population. . . . It is said there is no want in this country. There may be less than in some other countries. But death by actual starvation in this country is, we apprehend, no uncommon occurrence. . . .

We pass through our manufacturing villages, most of them appear neat and nourishing. The operatives are well dressed, and we are told, well paid. They are said to be healthy, contented, and happy. This is the fair side of the picture; the side exhibited to distinguished visitors. There is a dark side, moral as well as physical. Of the common operatives, few, if any, by their wages, acquire a competence. A few of what Carlyle terms not inaptly the body-servants are well paid, and now and then an agent or an overseer rides in his coach. But the great mass wear out their health, spirits, and morals, without becoming one whit better off than when they commenced labor. . . . We know no sadder sight on earth than one of our factory villages presents, when the bell at break of day, or at the hour of breakfast, or dinner, calls out its hundreds or thousands of operatives. We stand and look at these hard working men and women hurrying in all directions, and ask ourselves where go the proceeds of their labors? The man who employs them, and for whom they are toiling as so many slaves, is one of our city nabobs, reveling in luxury; or he is a member of our legislature, enacting laws to put money in his own pocket; or he is a member of Congress, contending for a high Tariff to tax the poor for the benefit of the rich or in these times he is shedding crocodile tears over the "deplorable condition" of the poor laborer, while he docks his wages twenty-five percent. . . . And this man too would fain pass for a Christian and a republican. He shouts for liberty, stickles for equality, and is horrified at a Southern planter who keeps slaves.

One thing is certain; that of the amount actually produced by the operative, he retains a less proportion than it costs the master to feed, clothe, and lodge his slave. Wages is a cunning device of the devil, for the benefit of tender consciences, who would retain all the advantages of the slave system, without the expense, trouble, and odium of being slave-holders.

. . .

Now the great work for this age and the coming, is to raise up the laborer, and to realize in our own social arrangements and in the actual condition of all men, that equality between man and man, which God has established between the rights of one and those of another. In other words, our business is to emancipate the proletaries, as the past has emancipated the slaves. This is our work. There must be no class of our fellow men doomed to toil through life as mere workmen at wages. If wages are tolerated it must be, in the case of the individual operative, only under such conditions that by the time he is of a proper age to settle in life, he shall have accumulated enough to be an independent laborer on his own capital,—on his own farm or in his own shop. Here is our work. How is it to be done?

Reformers in general answer this question, or what they deem its equivalent, in a manner which we cannot but regard as very unsatisfactory. They would have all men wise, good, and happy; but in order to make them so, they tell us that we want not external changes, but internal; and therefore instead of declaiming against society and seeking to disturb existing social arrangements, we should confine ourselves to the individual reason and conscience; seek merely to lead the individual to repentance, and to reformation of life ; make the individual a practical, a truly religious man, and all evils will either disappear, or be sanctified to the spiritual growth of the soul.

. . .

This theory, however, is exposed to one slight objection, that of being condemned by something like six thousand years' experience. . . .

. . .

The truth is, the evil we have pointed out is not merely individual in its character. . . . [T]he evil we speak of is inherent in all our social arrangements, and cannot be cured without a radical change of those arrangements. Could we convert all men to Christianity in both theory and practice, as held by the most enlightened sect of Christians among us, the evils of the social state would remain untouched. . . . The evils of slavery do not result from the personal characters of slave masters. They are inseparable from the system, let who will be masters. Make all your rich men good Christians, and you have lessened not the evils of existing inequality in wealth. The mischievous effects of this inequality do not result from the personal characters of either rich or poor, but from itself, and they will continue, just so long as there are rich men and poor men in the same community. You must abolish the system or accept its consequences. No man can serve both God and Mammon. If you will serve the devil, you must look to the devil for your wages; we know no other way.

. . . No man can be a Christian who does not begin his career by making war on the mischievous social arrangements from which his brethren suffer. . . .

. . . There is nothing in the actual difference of the powers of individuals, which accounts for the striking inequalities we everywhere discover in their condition. The child of the plebeian, if placed early in the proper circumstances, grows up not less beautiful, active, intelligent, and refined, than the child of the patrician; and the child of the patrician may become as coarse, as brutish as the child of any slave. So far as observation on the original capacities of individuals goes, nothing is discovered to throw much light on social inequalities.

. . .

Having, by breaking down the power of the priesthood and the Christianity of the priests, obtained an open field and freedom for our operations, and by preaching the true Gospel of Jesus, directed all minds to the great social reform needed, and quickened in all souls the moral power to live for it or to die for it; our next resort must be to government, to legislative enactments. Government is instituted to be the agent of society, or more properly the organ through which society may perform its legitimate functions. It is not the master of society; its business is not to control society, but to be the organ through which society effects its will. Society has never to petition government; government is its servant, and subject to its commands.

. . .

But again what legislation do we want so far as this country is concerned? We want first the legislation which shall free the government, whether State or Federal, from the control of the Banks. The Banks represent the interest of the employer, and therefore of necessity interests adverse to those of the employed; that is, they represent the interests of the business community in opposition to the laboring community. . . .

Following the distinction of the Banks, must come that of all monopolies, of all privilege. There are many of these. We cannot specify them all; we therefore select only one, the greatest of them all, the privilege which some have of being born rich while others are born poor. It will be seen at once that we allude to the hereditary descent of property, an anomaly in our American system, which must be removed, or the system itself will be destroyed. . . . A man shall have all he honestly acquires, so long as he himself belongs to the world in which he acquires it. But his power over his property must cease with his life, and his property must then become the property of the state, to be disposed of by some equitable law for the use of the generation which takes his place. . . .

VI. AMERICA AND THE WORLD

Major Developments

- Adoption of policy of forcible removal of Native American tribes
- Embrace of "manifest destiny" and westward expansion to the Pacific Ocean
- Growing threat of secession

The successful conclusion of the War of 1812 brought on the Era of Good Feelings. The good feelings and national unity did not last. The United States might have been shielded from the European powers by an ocean, but she nonetheless found herself in military conflicts and international entanglements in the Jacksonian Era.

These decades brought four distinct geostrategic challenges. The first carried over from the first years of the republic's existence: the threat posed by Native American tribes on the American frontier. The "frontier" was steadily advancing westward, and some tribes were incorporated into settled American territory. Both on the borders and along the boundaries between the states and these interior tribes, conflicts routinely arose. The most significant issues during the Jacksonian period were in the "southwest," in the regions that included Georgia, Alabama, Florida, and Tennessee. The Jackson administration's response to those challenges was to forcibly remove the Native American tribes beyond the perimeter of the settled country and west of the Mississippi River. The second challenge was new. The withdrawal of the Spanish empire from the immediate borders of the United States created new uncertainties and opportunities. Newly independent Mexico claimed vast tracts of largely unsettled land to the west of the United States. The annexation of the Republic of Texas in 1845 and the Mexican–American War in 1846 shifted much of that territory into the hands of the United States, creating a transcontinental nation. Third, the revolutionary movements in Latin America against Spanish rule created substantial political instability in the region. The United States looked on the instability with a great deal of interest, both because of the possible threat of the return of European powers to the region and because of the possible alliance of the newly independent countries with the United States. Multiple "filibuster" expeditions by American citizens into Latin American countries from Cuba to Nicaragua complicated official efforts of the United States to remain neutral to the political fates of those countries and invited schemes to expand the borders of the United States southward. Finally, the United States had to grapple repeatedly with the threat of the secession of the slaveholding states. After a brief flirtation with secessionist sentiments in New England during the War of 1812, the primary threat of disunion came from the South. The threat would become a reality in 1860, but in the antebellum years the threat alone was sufficient to complicate domestic politics.

These excerpts focus on the problem of Indian removal and westward expansion. These debates raised enduring questions of the principles that would guide American foreign policy, and their results helped shape American national identity. President Andrew Jackson was the most significant proponent of the forcible removal of Native American tribes from the boundaries of settled American territory. The Cherokee Nation was among the tribes most affected by Jackson's policy, and they were distinguished in part by having generally maintained friendly relations with the United States since American independence. Their formal protest to the removal policy raised questions about what principles should guide international relations. John O'Sullivan's editorials arguing for an American "manifest destiny" to expand westward helped set the tone for the politics of the 1840s.

ANDREW JACKSON

SPEECH ON INDIAN REMOVAL (1830)

Andrew Jackson won his initial fame as an Indian fighter. During the War of 1812, Jackson led an American military victory over a Creek Indian alliance in the southwest that resulted in a peace treaty renouncing Native American claims to much of the land in Georgia and Alabama. A few years later, he led American forces in the First Seminole War in Georgia, where he arguably exceeded presidential orders and seized the Spanish territory of Florida (which was a base of operations for the Seminoles). When Jackson won the presidency in 1828, he shifted American policy toward the Native Americans, especially in the southwest. As state governments in the region adopted an increasingly bellicose posture toward local tribes, Jackson offered no federal intervention to support treaty rights. Having dealt with Native American military resistance (often in association with European powers) in the region for the prior two decades, Jackson threw his support to a policy of forcible removal of Native American tribes from occupied American territory as the best way of avoiding future conflicts. He used his 1830 annual message to Congress to announce the policy that would eventually lead to the "Trail of Tears" and the removal of Native American tribes to American territory west of the Mississippi (what would eventually become the state of Oklahoma).

How does Jackson's characterization of government policy toward the Native Americans compare with Thomas Jefferson's? How does Jackson justify removal? How does he argue that the policy will benefit the tribes themselves? To what extent is removal framed as a national security measure? To what extent does the justification for his policy hinge on the superiority of European civilization? Is Jackson right to think that removal is a natural next step in American political development up to that point? Would Jackson's removal policy be more justifiable if it had been limited to the tribes that had pursued military resistance to the United States or that had allied themselves with European powers?

. . .

It gives me pleasure to announce to Congress that the benevolent policy of the Government, steadily pursued for nearly 30 years, in relation to the removal of the Indians beyond the white settlements is approaching to a happy consummation. Two important tribes have accepted the provision made for their removal at the last session of Congress, and it is believed that their example will induce the remaining tribes also to seek the same obvious advantages.

The consequences of a speedy removal will be important to the United States, to individual States, and to the Indians themselves. The pecuniary advantages which it promises to the Government are the least of its recommendations. It puts an end to all possible danger of collision between the authorities of the General and State Governments on account of the Indians. It will place a dense and civilized population in large tracts of country now occupied by a few savage hunters. By opening the whole territory between Tennessee on the north and Louisiana on the south to the settlement of the whites it will incalculably strengthen the southwest frontier and render the adjacent States strong enough to repel future invasions without remote aid. It will relieve the whole State of Mississippi and the western part of Alabama of Indian occupancy, and enable those States to advance rapidly in population, wealth, and power. It will separate the Indians from immediate contact with settlements of whites; free them from the power of the States; enable them to pursue happiness in their own way and under their own rude institutions; will retard the progress of decay, which is lessening their numbers, and perhaps cause them gradually, under the protection of the Government and through the influence of good counsels, to cast off their savage habits and become an interesting, civilized, and Christian community. These consequences, some of them so certain and the rest so probable, make the complete execution of the plan sanctioned by Congress at their last session an object of much solicitude.

Toward the aborigines of the country no one can indulge a more friendly feeling than myself, or would go further in attempting to reclaim them from their wandering habits and make them a happy, prosperous people. I have endeavored to impress upon them my own solemn convictions of the duties and powers of the General Government in relation to the State authorities. For the justice of the laws passed by the States within the scope of their reserved powers they are not responsible to this Government. As individuals we may entertain and express our opinions of their acts, but as a Government we have as little right to control them as we have to prescribe laws for other nations.

. . .

Humanity has often wept over the fate of the aborigines of this country, and Philanthropy has been long busily employed in devising means to avert it, but its progress has never for a moment been arrested, and one by one have many powerful tribes disappeared from the earth. To follow to the tomb the last of his race and to tread on the graves of extinct nations excite melancholy reflections. But true philanthropy reconciles the mind to these vicissitudes as it does to the extinction of one generation to make room for another. In the monuments and fortifications of an unknown people, spread over the extensive regions of the West, we behold the memorials of a once powerful race, which was exterminated or has disappeared to make room for the existing savage tribes. Nor is there anything in this which, upon a comprehensive view of the general interests of the human race, is to be regretted. Philanthropy could not wish to see this continent restored to the condition in which it was found by our forefathers. What good man would prefer a country covered with forests and ranged by a few thousand savages to our extensive Republic, studded with cities, towns, and prosperous farms, embellished with all the improvements which art can devise or industry execute, occupied by more than 12,000,000 happy people, and filled with all the blessings of liberty, civilization, and religion?

The present policy of the Government is but a continuation of the same progressive change by a milder process. The tribes which occupied the countries now constituting the Eastern States were annihilated or have melted away to make room for the whites. The waves of population and civilization are rolling to the westward, and we now propose to acquire the countries occupied by the red men of the South and West by a fair exchange, and, at the expense of the United States, to send them to a land where their existence may be prolonged and perhaps made perpetual.

Doubtless it will be painful to leave the graves of their fathers; but what do they more than our ancestors did or than our children are now doing? To better their condition in an unknown land our forefathers left all that was dear in earthly objects. Our children by thousands yearly leave the land of their birth to seek new homes in distant regions. Does Humanity weep at these painful separations from everything, animate and inanimate, with which the young heart has become entwined? Far from it. It is rather a source of joy that our country affords scope where our young population may range unconstrained in body or in mind, developing the power and faculties of man in their highest perfection.

These remove hundreds and almost thousands of miles at their own expense, purchase the lands they occupy, and support themselves at their new homes from the moment of their arrival. Can it be cruel in this Government when, by events which it cannot control, the Indian is made discontented in his ancient home to purchase his lands, to give him a new and extensive territory, to pay the expense of his removal, and support him a year in his new abode? How many thousands of our own people would gladly embrace the opportunity of removing to the West on such conditions! If the offers made to the Indians were extended to them, they would be hailed with gratitude and joy.

And is it supposed that the wandering savage has a stronger attachment to his home than the settled, civilized Christian? Is it more afflicting to him to leave the graves of his fathers than it is to our brothers and children? Rightly considered, the policy of the General Government toward the red man is not only liberal, but generous. He is unwilling to submit to the laws of the States and mingle with their population. To save him from this alternative, or perhaps utter annihilation, the General Government kindly offers him a new home, and proposes to pay the whole expense of his removal and settlement.

. . .

May we not hope, therefore, that all good citizens, and none more zealously than those who think the Indians oppressed by subjection to the laws of the States, will unite in attempting to open the eyes of those children of the forest to their true condition, and by a speedy removal to relieve them from all the evils, real or imaginary, present or prospective, with which they may be supposed to be threatened.

. . .

MEMORIAL OF THE CHEROKEE NATION (1830)

The Cherokee Nation had historically occupied lands in the lower Appalachia. After American independence, the Cherokees were one of the tribes that embraced the American "civilization" policy and shifted their society toward farming and crafts, individual land ownership, a written language, and in many cases conversion to Christianity, but they maintained their own independence as a sovereign nation. In the first two decades of the nineteenth century, the U.S. government entered into treaties with the Cherokees to establish reservations in the west (near the Mississippi River) in exchange for ceding lands in Georgia. This policy of voluntary removal had only limited success, and the Georgia government encouraged increasing encroachment on remaining Cherokee land within its borders. Finally, in 1830, Congress passed the Indian Removal Act, which required the resettlement of Native American tribes west of the Mississippi. The Memorial of the Cherokee Nation was a formal petition to Congress opposing the removal policy. It was written at the end of 1829 and published in both a Cherokee newspaper and a prominent American newspaper based in Baltimore in the spring of 1830. Shortly afterwards, Congress passed the Indian Removal Act.

Do the Cherokees appeal to Congress as Americans? As allies? Are the Cherokee positioned any differently relative to the United States than the British or the Spanish in the 1830s? What appeals do the Cherokees make to the United States? To what degree do they appeal to American self-interest? Is their appeal responsive to President Jackson's arguments for removal? On what points do the memorial and Jackson's message conflict?

. . .

The undersigned memorialists, humbly make known to your honorable bodies, that they are free citizens of the Cherokee nation. Circumstances of late occurrence have troubled our hearts, and induced us at this time to appeal to you, knowing that you are generous and just. As weak and poor children are accustomed to look to their guardians and patrons for protection, so we would come and make our grievances known. Will you listen to us? Will you have pity on us? You are great and renowned—the nation which you represent, is like a mighty man who stands in his strength. But we are small—our name is not renowned. You are wealthy, and have need of nothing; but we are poor in life, and have not the arm and power of the rich.

By the will of our Father in heaven, the governor of the whole world, the red man of America has become small, and the white man great and renowned. When the ancestors of the people of these United States first came to the shores of America, they found the red man strong—though he was ignorant and savage, yet he received them kindly, and gave them dry land to rest their weary feet. They met in peace, and shook hands in token of friendship. Whatever the white man wanted and asked of the Indian, the latter willingly gave. At that time the Indian was the lord, and the white man the suppliant. But now the scene has changed. The strength of the red man has become weakness. At his neighbors increased in numbers, his power became less, and now, of the many and powerful tribes who once covered these United States, only a few are to be seen—a few whom a sweeping pestilence has left. The north tribes, who were once so numerous and powerful, are now nearly extinct. Thus it has happened to the red man of America. Shall we, who are remnants, share the same fate?

Brothers—we address you according to the usage adopted by our forefathers, and the great and good men who have successfully directed the councils of the nation you represent—we now make known to you our grievances. We are troubled by some of your own people. Our neighbor, the state of Georgia, is pressing hard upon us, and urging us to relinquish our possessions for her benefit. We are told, if we do not leave the country, which we dearly love, and betake ourselves to the western wilds, the laws of the state will be extended over us. . . . When we first heard of this we were grieved and appealed to our father, the president, and begged the protection might be extended over us. But we were doubly grieved when we understood . . . that our father the president had refused us protection, and that he had decided in favor of the extension of the laws of the state over us. . . . We love, we dearly love our country, and it is due to your honorable bodies, as well as to us, to make known why we think the country is ours, and why we wish to remain in peace where we are.

The land on which we stand, we have received as an inheritance from our fathers, who possessed it from time immemorial, as a gift from our common father in heaven. We have already said, that when the white man came to the shores of America, our ancestors were found in peaceable possession of this very land. . . . This right of inheritance we have *never ceded*, nor ever *forfeited*. Permit us to ask, what better right ca a people have to a country, than the right of *inheritance* and *immemorial peaceable possession*? We know it is said of late by the state of Georgia, and by the executive of the United States, that we have forfeited this right—but we think this is said gratuitously. At what time have we made the forfeit? What crime have we committed, whereby we must forever be divested of our country and rights? Was it when we were hostile to the United States, and took part with the king of Great Britain, during the struggle for independence? If so, why was not this forfeiture declared in the first treaty of peace? . . . This was the proper time to assume such a position. . . . All that they have conceded and relinquished are inserted in the treaties open to the investigation of all people. We would repeat, then, the right of inheritance and peaceable possession which we claim, we have never ceded nor forfeited.

In addition that first of all rights, the right of inheritance and peaceable possession, we have the faith and pledge of the United States, repeated over and over again, in treaties made at various times. By these treaties our rights as a separate people are distinctly acknowledged, and guarantees given that they shall be secured and protected. So we have always understood the treaties. The conduct of the government towards us, from its organization until very lately, the talks given to our beloved men by the presidents of the United States . . . all concur to show that we are not mistaken in our interpretation—some of the beloved men who signed the treaties are still living, and their testimony tends to the same conclusion. . . . In what light shall we view the conduct of the United States and Georgia, in their intercourse with us, in urging us to enter into treaties, and cede lands? If we were but tenants at will, why was it necessary that our consent must be obtained before these governments could take lawful possession of our lands? The answer is obvious. These governments perfectly understood our rights—our right to the country, and our right to self-government. Our understanding of the treaties is further supported by the intercourse law of the United States, which prohibits all encroachments upon our territory. The undersigned memorialists humbly represent, that if their interpretation of the treaties has been different from that of the government, then they have ever been deceived as to how the government regarded them, and what she asked and promised. Moreover, they have uniformly misunderstood their own acts.

In view of the strong ground upon which their rights are founded, your memorialists solemnly protest against being considered as tenants at will, or as mere occupants of the soil, without possessing the sovereignty. We have already stated to your honorable bodies, that our forefathers were found in possession of this soil in full sovereignty, by the first European settlers; and as we have never ceded nor forfeited the occupancy of the soil and the sovereignty over it, we do solemnly protest against being forced to leave it, either direct or by indirect measures. To the land of which we are now in possession we are attached—it is our father's gift—it contains their ashes—it is the land of our nativity, and the land of our intellectual birth. We cannot consent to abandon it, for another *far inferior*, and which holds out to us no inducements. We do moreover protest against the arbitrary measures of our neighbor, the state of Georgia, in her attempt to extend her laws over us, in surveying our lands without our consent and in direct opposition to treaties and the intercourse law of the United States, and interfering with our municipal regulations in such a manner as to derange the regular operations of our own laws. To deliver and protect them from all these and every encroachment upon their rights, the undersigned memorialists do most earnestly pray your honorable bodies. Their existence and future happiness are at stake—divest them of their liberty and country, and you sink them in degradation, and put a check, if not a final stop, to their present progress in the arts of civilized life, and in the knowledge of the Christian religion. Your memorialists humbly conceive, that such an act would be in the highest degree oppressive. From the people of these United States, who perhaps, of all men under heaven, are the most religious and free, it cannot be expected. Your memorialists, therefore, cannot anticipate such a result. You represent a virtuous, intelligent and Christian nation. To you they willingly submit their cause for your righteous decision.

JOHN L. O'SULLIVAN

MANIFEST DESTINY (1839)

As Americans settled the territory acquired by the Louisiana Purchase, their eyes turned further westward. The territory to the west was claimed by Britain and the newly independent country of Mexico, but neither country had established a significant group of settlers in its territories and in many cases the effective possession of the land was in the hands of hostile Native American tribes. The secession of the state of Tejas from Mexico in 1836 seemed to destabilize the situation in the west and create opportunities for American advancement. Despite its popular appeal, westward expansion soon became a partisan issue. The most immediate question on the table was the fate of Texas. If the independent Republic of Texas were to join the union, it was expected not only to be slave state but also Democratic (the first president of Texas, Sam Houston, had previously served as a Jacksonian governor of Tennessee). But the Texas question encouraged further speculation on the American future in the far west.

The Democratic newspaper editor John L. O'Sullivan influentially encouraged western expansion. Born to an American diplomat in 1813, O'Sullivan briefly practiced law before becoming a newspaper editor and Democratic politician in New York. After his sister married a Cuban revolutionary, he became interested in the movement to liberate Cuba from Spanish rule (and potentially join it to the United States). In the 1850s, he was tried but not convicted of aiding Cuban revolutionaries in violation of American neutrality. During the Civil War, he lived in Europe and advocated for the Confederate cause. When he returned to New York in the 1870s, he found himself to be a political outcast. But his greatest claim to fame was in coining the term "manifest destiny" in a series of editorials advocating annexation of Texas, war with Mexico, and eventual American expansion to the Pacific coast.

What does O'Sullivan mean by "destiny"? How does O'Sullivan's vision of American destiny differ from other accounts of America's place in the world and in world history? What is an American, according to O'Sullivan? What is the correct foundation for national claims of control over territory? Is the likely future use of the territory a legitimate basis for resolving contested territorial claims? Are the preferences of those currently residing in the territory decisive? Is O'Sullivan's view of the relationship of the United States to Europe a natural outgrowth of the Monroe Doctrine? Is population destiny? How might O'Sullivan's arguments be applied to the American southwest today?

The American people having derived their origin from many other nations, and the Declaration of National Independence being entirely based on the great principle of human equality, these facts demonstrate at once our disconnected position as regards any other nation; that we have, in reality, but little connection with the past history of any of them, and still less with all antiquity, its glories, or its crimes. On the contrary, our national birth was the beginning of a new history, the formation and progress of an untried political system, which separates us from the past and connects us with the future only; and so far as regards the entire development of the natural rights of man, in moral, political, and national life, we may confidently assume that our country is destined to be *the great nation* of futurity.

It is so destined, because the principle upon which a nation is organized fixes its destiny, and that of equality is perfect, is universal. It presides in all the operations of the physical world, and it is also the conscious law of the soul—the self-evident dictate of morality, which accurately defines the duty of man to man, and consequently man's rights as man. Besides, the truthful annals of any nation furnish abundant evidence, that its happiness, its greatness, its duration, were always proportionate to the democratic equality of its system of government.

. . .

. . . The expansive future is our arena, and for our history. We are entering on its untrodden space, with the truths of God in our minds, beneficent objects in our hearts, and with a clear conscience unsullied by the past. We are the nation of human progress, and who will, what can, set limits to our onward march? Providence is with us, and no earthly power can. . . .

. . . American patriotism is not of soil; we are not aborigines, nor of ancestry, for we are of all nations; but it is essentially personal enfranchisement, for "where liberty dwells," said Franklin, the sage of the Revolution, "there is my country."

. . . We must onward to the fulfillment of our mission—to the entire development of the principle of our organization—freedom of conscience, freedom of person, freedom of trade and business pursuits, universality of freedom and equality. This is our high destiny, and in nature's eternal, inevitable decree of cause and effect we must accomplish it. All this will be our future history, to establish on earth the oral dignity and salvation of man—the immutable truth and beneficence of God. For this blessed mission to the nations of the world, which are shut out from the life-giving light of truth, has America been chosen; and her high example shall smite unto death the tyranny of kings, hierarchs, and oligarchs, and carry the glad tidings of peace and good will where myriads now endure an existence scarcely more enviable than that of beasts of the field. . . .

. . .

Away, then, with all idle French talk of *balances of power* on the American Continent. There is no growth in Spanish America! Whatever progress of population there may be in the British Canada, is only for their own early severance of their present colonial relation to the little island three thousand miles across the Atlantic; soon to be followed by Annexation, and destined to swell the still accumulating momentum of our progress. . . .

. . .

And yet after all, unanswerable as is the demonstration of our legal title in Oregon—and the whole of Oregon, if a rood!—we have a still better title than say that can ever be constructed out of all these antiquated materials of old black-letter international law. Away, away with all these cobweb tissues of rights of discovery, exploration, settlement, continuity, etc. To state the truth at once in its naked simplicity, we are free to say that were the respective cases and arguments of the two parties, as to all those points of history and law, reversed—had England all ours, and we nothing but hers—our claim to Oregon would still be best and strongest. And that claim is by the right of our manifest destiny to overspread and to possess the whole of the continent which Providence has given for the development of the great experiment of liberty and federative self-government entrusted to us. It is a right such as that of the trees to the space of air and earth suitable for the full expansion of its principle and destiny of growth—such as that of the stream to the channel required for the still accumulating volume of its flow. It is in our future far more than in our past, or in the past history of Spanish exploration or French colonial rights, that our True Title is to be found. Consider only the wonderful law of growth which has been thus far exhibited in the increase of our population from the commencement of our present system of government—namely, that of *doubling every quarter of a century*. Carry this forward for only a hundred years from the present day—to a period which thousands of children already born among us will live to witness. . . . *Three hundred millions*, within little more than the ordinary term of hale and healthy old age! The duty and right of providing the necessary accommodation for all this stupendous future of the American destiny—our existing position on this continent, led and established here as we have been by the finger of God himself—that pervading tendency westward, westward, which marks the slope of our national movement, and bears us ever on towards the Pacific. . . .

Were England in ours or a similar position in regard to that portion of the North American continent, she would have, in her degree, rights of a similar nature. But such is not, and can never become, her position. Oregon can never be to her or for her anything but a mere hunting ground for furs and peltries. There is no population there to be worked and ground and sweated and drained of tribute to pay for their own subjugation, and to minister to the aggrandizement of their conquerors. Nor can she ever colonize it with any sort of transplanted population of her own. It is far too remote and too ungenial for any such purpose. In her hands it is and must always remain wholly useless and worthless for any purpose of human civilization or society. In our hands on the contrary, it must fast fill in with a population destined to establish, within the life of the existing generation, a noble young empire of the Pacific, vying in all the elements of greatness with that already overspreading the Atlantic and the great Mississippi valley. The God of nature and of nations has marked it for our own; and with His blessing we will firmly maintain the incontestable rights He has given, and fearlessly perform the high duties He has imposed.

FOR FURTHER STUDY

Blau, Joseph L., ed. *Social Theories of Jacksonian Democracy: Representative Writings of the Period, 1825–1850* (Indianapolis, IN: Bobbs-Merrill, 1954).

Brownson, Orestes A. *Selected Essays*, ed. Russell Kirk (Chicago, IL: H. Regnery, 1955).

Calhoun, John C. *Union and Liberty: The Political Philosophy of John C. Calhoun*, ed. Ross M. Lence (Indianapolis, IN: Liberty Fund, 1992).

Douglass, Frederick. *The Oxford Frederick Douglass Reader*, ed. William L. Andrews (New York: Oxford University Press, 1996).

Emerson, Ralph Waldo. *The Political Emerson: Essential Writings on Politics and Social Reform*, ed. David M. Robinson (Boston, MA: Beacon Press, 2004).

Goodrich, Carter, ed. *The Government and the Economy, 1783–1861* (Indianapolis, IN: Bobbs-Merrill, 1967).

Howe, Daniel Walker. *The American Whigs: An Anthology* (New York: Wiley, 1973).

Leggett, William. *Democratick Editorials: Essays in Jacksonian Political Economy*, ed. Lawrence H. White (Indianapolis, IN: Liberty Fund, 1984).

Lowance, Mason I., Jr., ed. *A House Divided: The Antebellum Slavery Debates in America, 1776–1865* (Princeton, NJ: Princeton University Press, 2003).

Stanton, Elizabeth Cady. *The Elizabeth Cady Stanton-Susan B. Anthony Reader: Correspondence, Writings, Speeches*, ed. Ellen Carol DuBois (Boston, MA: Northeastern University Press, 1992).

Tocqueville, Alexis de. *Democracy in America*, ed. J. P. Mayer (New York: Perennial, 2000).

Webster, Daniel. *The Webster-Hayne Debate on the Nature of the Union: Selected Documents*, ed. Herman Belz (Indianapolis, IN: Liberty Fund, 2000).

SUGGESTED READINGS

Carpenter, Jesse T. *The South as a Conscious Minority, 1789–1861: A Study in Political Thought* (New York: New York University Press, 1930).

Davis, Sue. *The Political Thought of Elizabeth Cady Stanton: Women's Rights and the American Political Traditions* (New York: New York University Press, 2008).

Eaton, Clement. *The Mind of the Old South*, rev. ed. (Baton Rouge: Louisiana State University Press, 1967).

Ellis, Richard E. *The Union at Risk: Jacksonian Democracy, States' Rights, and the Nullification Crisis* (New York: Oxford University Press, 1987).

Faust, Drew Gilpin. *A Sacred Circle: The Dilemma of the Intellectual in the Old South, 1840–1860* (Baltimore, MD: Johns Hopkins University Press, 1977).

Fehrenbacher, Don E. *Constitutions and Constitutionalism in the Slaveholding South* (Athens: University of Georgia Press, 1989).

Foner, Eric. *Free Soil, Free Labor, Free Men: The Ideology of the Republican Party before the Civil War* (New York: Oxford University Press, 1970).

Graber, Mark E. *Dred Scott and the Problem of Constitutional Evil* (New York: Cambridge University Press, 2006).

Grant, Susan-Mary. *North over South: Northern Nationalism and American Identity in the Antebellum Era* (Lawrence: University Press of Kansas, 2000).

Horsman, Reginald. *Race and Manifest Destiny: Origins of American Racial Anglo-Saxonism* (Cambridge, MA: Harvard University Press, 1986).

Howe, Daniel Walker. *The Political Culture of the American Whigs* (Chicago, IL: University of Chicago Press, 1979).

Jaffa, Harry V. *The Crisis of the House Divided: An Interpretation of the Issues in the Lincoln-Douglas Debates* (Chicago, IL: University of Chicago Press, 1959).

Kateb, George. *Emerson and Self-Reliance*, new ed. (Lanham, MD: Rowman & Littlefield, 2002).

McCardle, John. *The Idea of a Southern Nation: Southern Nationalists and Southern Nationalism, 1830–1860* (New York: W.W. Norton, 1979).

McCoy, Drew R. *The Last of the Fathers: James Madison and the Republican Legacy* (New York: Cambridge University Press, 1989).

Mushkat, Jerome, and Joseph G. Rayback. *Martin Van Buren: Law, Politics, and Republican Ideology* (Lanham, MD: Rowman & Littlefield, 1997).

Myers, Peter C. *Frederick Douglass: Race and the Rebirth of American Liberalism* (Lawrence: University Press of Kansas, 2008).

Nagel, Paul C. *One Nation Indivisible: The Union in American Thought, 1776–1861* (New York: Oxford University Press, 1964).

O'Brien, Michael. *Conjectures of Order: Intellectual Life and the American South, 1810–1860* (Chapel Hill: University of North Carolina Press, 2003).

Perry, Lewis. *Radical Abolitionism: Anarchy and the Government of God in Antislavery Thought* (Ithaca, NY: Cornell University Press, 1973).

Peterson, Merrill D. *The Great Triumvirate: Webster, Clay, and Calhoun* (New York: Oxford University Press, 1987).

Read, James H. *Majority Rule versus Consensus: The Political Thought of John C. Calhoun* (Lawrence: University Press of Kansas, 2009).

Rose, Anne C. *Transcendentalism as a Social Movement, 1830–1850* (New Haven, CT: Yale University Press, 1981).

Scalia, Laura J. *America's Jeffersonian Experiment: Remaking State Constitutions, 1820–1850* (De Kalb: Northern Illinois University Press, 1999).

CHAPTER 6

SECESSION, CIVIL WAR, AND RECONSTRUCTION, 1861–1876

I. INTRODUCTION

In the summer of 1862, the influential Republican editor Horace Greeley published in the *New York Tribune* an open letter to President Abraham Lincoln contending that the president's supporters were "sorely disappointed and deeply pained" by Lincoln's apparent deference to the border states and apparent foot-dragging on the effort to emancipate the slaves. The war was not going particularly well, and the White House faced criticism from both its Republican allies, who thought the president was too conservative, and its Democratic foes, who thought the president was too radical. Lincoln tried to put out this brush fire by famously writing a letter to Greeley contending

> If there be those who would not save the Union, unless they could at the same time *save* slavery, I do not agree with them. If there be those who would not save the Union unless they could at the same time *destroy* slavery, I do not agree with them. My paramount object in this struggle *is* to save the Union, and is *not* either to save or to destroy slavery. If I could save the Union without freeing *any* slave I would do it, and if I could save it by freeing *all* the slaves I would do it; and if I could save it by freeing some and leaving others alone I would also do that.[1]

A few months later, Lincoln issued the Emancipation Proclamation, declaring that all slaves in the rebel states were free but without freeing slaves in the slaveholding states that were under the control of the Union army.

The secession of the southern states and its aftermath was the greatest crisis that Americans had faced since the Revolution. Those events raised questions about fundamental features of American politics and government, and, Lincoln insisted, called into question whether stable democratic government was even possible. Americans still held up the United States as the

---

1 Abraham Lincoln, *The Collected Works of Abraham Lincoln*, ed. Roy P. Basler, vol. 5 (New Brunswick, NJ: 1953), 388.

shining beacon of the future of mankind, but Europe was still uncertain about the prospects of the republican form of government. Monarchies had the longer track record, and the success of the democratic experiment was still uncertain.

Politics. Jacksonian politics was relatively stable for two decades, but the slavery issue put increasing strains on the established ways of doing things. The Democratic and Whig parties had attempted to finesse the slavery issue, but the "Conscience Whigs" of New England preferred a purer, more clearly antislavery stance. Some decamped to support the Free Soil Party in 1848 and 1852. Meanwhile, Southern "fire-eaters" pressed greater Southern unity and firmer proslavery commitments, particularly within the Democratic Party. The Whigs finally gave in to the pressure and splintered in 1856. The newly formed Republican Party picked up the pieces, claiming second place in the presidential election and eventually driving out such alternatives as the nativist "Know-Nothing" Party. The Democrats splintered in turn in 1860, with three separate candidates splitting the Democratic vote and allowing Abraham Lincoln to claim the White House with less than 40 percent of the vote and no significant support in the southern states. Unlike the Whigs, the Democrats managed to patch things up and survive as a competitive, organized party in both the North and the South.

Two issues dominated the agenda in these years: war and slavery. The Republicans largely inherited Whig views on issues such as the scope of national power and economic policy, but conflicts over economics were pushed into the background until the issues of union and slavery were settled. The Republicans were committed to war and the end of slavery but were divided over war aims and how far and how fast to drive toward emancipation. Northern Democrats had little interest in continuing the war or in freeing the slaves and stumped for a negotiated peace.

Once the South surrendered in the spring of 1865, northern politics quickly shifted toward defining the terms of the peace. An assassin's bullet brought Andrew Johnson to the presidency shortly after the end of the war, and the former border-state Democrat proved more interested in a quick return to a peaceful union than black civil rights. The formal abolition of slavery was a given by 1865, and the Thirteenth Amendment both reinforced and nationalized the Emancipation Proclamation. Beyond that, there was little agreement. As a practical matter, Johnson's plan of rapid restoration of the southern states to the Union meant the return of Democratic national majorities and limited racial or economic reform in the South. Congressional Reconstruction, launched in 1866 over the president's objections, kept the southern states under military occupation while working to create a viable Republican Party in the South composed of Union loyalists and former slaves. Political vulnerability, northern exhaustion, and growing interest in the western frontier eventually brought the era of southern Reconstruction to a close in 1877 with the withdrawal of northern troops and the return of "home" rule (white, Democratic rule) in the southern states.

Society. The Civil War touched society more deeply than any military conflict since the Revolution. More American soldiers were killed in single battles in the 1860s than had previously been lost in entire wars. The war was fought on American soil, especially in border states like

FIGURE 6-1 TIMELINE OF SECESSION, CIVIL WAR, AND RECONSTRUCTION

Events	Year	Writings
	1860	Charles Sumner's Barbarism of Slavery Speech
Abraham Lincoln wins presidency	1860	
South Carolina secedes from the Union	1860	
	1861	Abraham Lincoln's First Inaugural Address
	1861	Alexander H. Stephen's Cornerstone Address
Battle of Fort Sumter	1861	
Union capture of New Orleans	1862	
	1863	Abraham Lincoln's Emancipation Proclamation
Union capture of Vicksburg	1863	
	1863	Abraham Lincoln's Gettysburg Address
John Stuart Mill's Utilitarianism	1863	
Union capture of Atlanta	1864	
General Robert E. Lee surrenders at Appomotax	1865	
Abraham Lincoln assassinated	1865	
President Andrew Johnson vetoes Civil Rights Bill	1866	
Launch of Congresssional Reconstruction	1866	
	1867	Lysander Spooner's No Treason
President Andrew Johnson impeached	1868	
Fourteenth Amendment ratified	1868	
U.S. Grant wins presidency	1868	
National Woman Suffrage Association founded	1869	
	1870	Alexander H. Stephen's A Constitutional View of the Late War
Battle of Little Bighorn	1876	
Compromise of 1877 ends Reconstruction	1877	

Pennsylvania and southern states like Virginia and Georgia. For the first time, the federal government resorted to a military draft to fill the ranks of the army, sparking riots in northern cities. Industrial innovation and capacity were jumpstarted, generating significant fortunes for some and disrupting old economic patterns. At the same time, economic assets in the South were devastated and old economic relationships were upended by the abolition of slavery.

War and Reconstruction also created new opportunities for reconsidering social relations. Ending slavery was eventually put on par with saving the Union as a northern war aim. Antislavery activists, both black and white, were welcomed into the Republican White House. Blacks demanded, and received, new civil and political rights, but the goal was a moving target. In the early stages of the war, simple emancipation seemed unlikely. At the end of the war, black suffrage seemed improbable. By the end of Reconstruction, gains had been made but their durability was in doubt. But the war did not put just black civil rights in question. Advocates of female suffrage pushed to include women in the postwar expansion of rights. Moral reformers (often Protestant Christians) sought to build on the success of the antislavery movement and remake society more broadly.

Ideas. The secession crisis gave new urgency to ideas that had been circulating since the founding. American independence and the ratification of the U.S. Constitution did not fully settle the terms of union. Threats of secession, and worries about disunion, had been common in the decades between ratification and the Civil War. Southern fire-eaters were particularly vocal about calculating the price of continued union with the free states, but they had not been alone in considering the legitimacy and desirability of separation. As southern states declared their secession from the Union, their supporters drew on a tradition of Jeffersonian arguments favoring states' rights, while their critics drew on ideas of American nationalism. The internecine war that followed secession likewise raised questions about the inherited constitutional scheme. To what degree did the war represent a failure of American institutions and values? Was the war the result of tragic errors by the reigning political generation, or did it result from fundamental flaws in the American project?

The collapse of slavery rapidly pushed forward a debate about civil rights. Antebellum arguments surrounding African-Americans had focused on the problem of slavery and emancipation. The advent of emancipation raised a host of new issues that had previously been given little consideration. Did full legal and political equality follow naturally from emancipation, or were there multiple tiers of citizenship? At the same time, the reform movements that had been most concerned with advancing the cause of emancipation had gained sudden and dramatic success. What else could be put on the political agenda? How far had Americans gone in embracing the vision of a reformed society?

II. DEMOCRACY AND LIBERTY

Major Developments

- Debate over secession as expression of popular government
- Concern over willingness of electoral losers to acquiesce
- Concern over rise of regional parties
- Debate over imposition of martial law in the South

Secession and Reconstruction posed unprecedented challenges to inherited American commitments to democracy and liberty. The southern states claimed the right to "exit" the Union if the direction of American politics became too inhospitable to their critical interests. To support such a right, southerners appealed to the revolutionary principles of the Declaration of Independence, among other sources. It was, they contended, the "right of the people to alter or to abolish" a government that no longer advanced their political purposes. A free government resting on the consent of the people depended on the continued voluntary willingness of the people to support it and live under its laws. Lincoln responded that democracies were premised on the willingness of electoral losers to accede to the electoral winners. No matter the electoral count, Lincoln was not the northern or abolitionist president but was the American president, the president of all of the United States. Democracy would quickly fall apart and give way to anarchy and despotism if the citizens were not willing to embrace the legitimacy of their elected leaders. Others, like Sidney George Fisher, questioned the inherited institutions of democratic government. Perhaps the secession crisis reflected a fundamental failing in how our particular form of republican government operated. What would be necessary to design a republican government that was both accountable to the people and stable, capable of governing and of respecting diverse interests and freedoms?

The uneasy peace the followed the war opened a somewhat different set of questions about American democracy. Brother had made war on brother, and now one side had surrendered. How were the losers of the military conflict to be treated? What civil or political rights did they still possess? Did a "rebel" have any rights that a loyal Unionist was bound to respect? The emancipation of the slaves gave new salience to old antislavery arguments about the meaning of republican government in a multiracial society. Could the southern governments be considered to have a republican form of government if the former slaves could not vote? If the former Confederates could not vote? And when should military occupation properly end? Was military reconstruction consistent with democratic norms and aspirations? Could a more democratic government be expected to emerge from military rule? Congressional leader Thaddeus Stevens occupied one extreme on a spectrum of views in arguing that the southern states had been dissolved by the war and that their territories and peoples could be governed at the discretion of Congress.

ABRAHAM LINCOLN

FIRST INAUGURAL ADDRESS (1861)

Lincoln's arrival at the White House came in extremely unusual circumstances. He was the first candidate to win a presidential election with purely sectional support. The Republican Party did not even run presidential electors in most slaveholding states. Even in border states from Maryland to Missouri, the Republican candidate received a negligible number of votes. Lincoln made up the difference by winning solid majorities throughout the North. But Lincoln was not the only sectional candidate in the race. The Democratic Party had splintered in 1860, producing three separate presidential candidates. Illinois's Stephen Douglas competed with Lincoln in the North; Tennessee's John Bell and Kentucky's John Breckenridge competed with each other in the South. Lincoln won a majority of the electoral vote, but he received less than 40 percent of the popular vote.

The sectional splits reflected the Republican Party's explicitly antislavery stance. Where all previous major parties had obscured the slavery issue and competed for votes in both the slave and free states, the Republicans denounced the South's economic and social system as immoral and rallied the growing antislavery sentiment in the North. Several of the justices on the Supreme Court were sufficiently disturbed by the challenge the Republicans presented to the established political order that they hoped that their decision in the Dred Scott case would tar the party as operating outside the constitutional mainstream. As many had feared, Lincoln's election immediately set off a chain reaction of secessionist movements in the South. By the time of his inaugural address in March 1861, seven states had proclaimed their departure from the Union. Four more followed after Lincoln's inauguration.

Lincoln used his first inaugural address to appeal to the slaveholding states to remain in the Union and to try to reassure them that their established rights would be secure under a Republican administration. A key concern that Lincoln raised in his address was the stability of democratic government. Democracy implied contested elections and majority rule. If the electoral losers were not willing to accept the outcome of elections, then what future could democracy have, and what example was the South setting by attempting to withdraw from the polity rather than submitting to the will of the majority?

Can any president be tolerated for "the brief constitutional term of four years"? Why does Lincoln think that the Union is "perpetual"? Are there circumstances under which the Union might not be perpetual? Who are the parties that "made it"? Whose participation and consent might be necessary to unmake the Union? Are there any circumstances under which Lincoln would accept disunion? Why does Lincoln think the Union predates the Constitution? Is it possible for the states to separate? Does the possibility of secession undermine democracy?

. . .

I hold that in contemplation of universal law and of the Constitution the Union of these States is perpetual. Perpetuity is implied, if not expressed, in the fundamental law of all national governments. It is safe to assert that no government proper ever had a provision in its organic law for its own termination. Continue to execute all the express provisions of our National Constitution, and the Union will endure forever, it being impossible to destroy it except by some action not provided for in the instrument itself.

Again: If the United States be not a government proper, but an association of States in the nature of contract merely, can it, as a contract, be peaceably unmade by less than all the parties who made it? One party to a contract may violate it—break it, so to speak—but does it not require all to lawfully rescind it?

Descending from these general principles, we find the proposition that in legal contemplation the Union is perpetual confirmed by the history of the Union itself. The Union is much older than the Constitution. It was formed, in fact, by the Articles of Association in 1774. It was matured and continued by the Declaration of Independence in 1776. It was further matured, and the faith of all the then thirteen States expressly plighted and engaged that it should be perpetual, by the Articles of Confederation in 1778. And finally, in 1787, one of the declared objects for ordaining and establishing the Constitution was *"to form a more perfect Union."*

But if destruction of the Union by one or by a part only of the States be lawfully possible, the Union is *less* perfect than before the Constitution, having lost the vital element of perpetuity.

It follows from these views that no State upon its own mere motion can lawfully get out of the Union; that *resolves* and *ordinances* to that effect are legally void, and that acts of violence within any State or States against the authority of the United States are insurrectionary or revolutionary, according to circumstances.

I therefore consider that in view of the Constitution and the laws the Union is unbroken, and to the extent of my ability, I shall take care, as the Constitution itself expressly enjoins upon me, that the laws of the Union be faithfully executed in all the States. Doing this I deem to be only a simple duty on my part, and I shall perform it so far as practicable unless my rightful masters, the American people, shall withhold the requisite means or in some authoritative manner direct the contrary. I trust this will not be regarded as a menace, but only as the declared purpose of the Union that it *will* constitutionally defend and maintain itself.

In doing this there needs to be no bloodshed or violence, and there shall be none unless it be forced upon the national authority. The power confided to me will be used to hold, occupy, and possess the property and places belonging to the Government and to collect the duties and imposts; but beyond what may be necessary for these objects, there will be no invasion, no using of force against or among the people anywhere. Where hostility to the United States in any interior locality shall be so great and universal as to prevent competent resident citizens from holding the Federal offices, there will be no attempt to force obnoxious strangers among the people for that object. While the strict legal right may exist in the Government to enforce the exercise of these offices, the attempt to do so would be so irritating and so nearly impracticable withal that I deem it better to forego for the time the uses of such offices.

. . .

All profess to be content in the Union if all constitutional rights can be maintained. Is it true, then, that any right plainly written in the Constitution has been denied? I think not. Happily, the human mind is so constituted that no party can reach to the audacity of doing this. Think, if you can, of a single instance in which a plainly written provision of the Constitution has ever been denied. If by the mere force of numbers a majority should deprive a minority of any clearly written constitutional right, it might in a moral point of view justify revolution; certainly would if such right were a vital one. But such is not our case. All the vital rights of minorities and of individuals are so plainly assured to them by affirmations and negations, guaranties and prohibitions, in the Constitution that controversies never arise concerning them. But no organic law can ever be framed with a provision specifically applicable to every question which may occur in practical administration. No foresight can anticipate nor any document of reasonable length contain express provisions for all possible questions. Shall fugitives from labor be surrendered by national or by State authority? The Constitution does not expressly say. *May* Congress prohibit slavery in the Territories? The Constitution does not expressly say. *Must* Congress protect slavery in the Territories? The Constitution does not expressly say.

From questions of this class spring all our constitutional controversies, and we divide upon them into majorities and minorities. If the minority will not acquiesce, the majority must, or the Government must cease. There is no other alternative, for continuing the Government is acquiescence on one side or the other. If a minority in such case will secede rather than acquiesce, they make a precedent which in turn will divide and ruin them, for a minority of their own will secede from them whenever a majority refuses to be controlled by such minority. For instance, why may not any portion of a new confederacy a year or two hence arbitrarily secede again, precisely as portions of the present Union now claim to secede from it? All who cherish disunion sentiments are now being educated to the exact temper of doing this.

Is there such perfect identity of interests among the States to compose a new union as to produce harmony only and prevent renewed secession?

Plainly the central idea of secession is the essence of anarchy. A majority held in restraint by constitutional checks and limitations, and always changing easily with deliberate changes of popular opinions and sentiments, is the only true sovereign of a free people. Whoever rejects it does of necessity fly to anarchy or to despotism. Unanimity is impossible. The rule of a minority, as a permanent arrangement, is wholly inadmissible; so that, rejecting the majority principle, anarchy or despotism in some form is all that is left.

I do not forget the position assumed by some that constitutional questions are to be decided by the Supreme Court, nor do I deny that such decisions must be binding in any case upon the parties to a suit as to the object of that suit, while they are also entitled to very high respect and consideration in all parallel cases by all other departments of the Government. And while it is obviously possible that such decision may be erroneous in any given case, still the evil effect following it, being limited to that particular case, with the chance that it may be overruled and never become a precedent for other cases, can better be borne than could the evils of a different practice. At the same time, the candid citizen must confess that if the policy of the Government upon vital questions affecting the whole people is to be irrevocably fixed by decisions of the Supreme Court, the instant they are made in ordinary litigation between parties in personal actions the people will have ceased to be their own rulers, having to that extent practically resigned their Government into the hands of that eminent tribunal. Nor is there in this view any assault upon the court or the judges. It is a duty from which they may not shrink to decide cases properly brought before them, and it is no fault of theirs if others seek to turn their decisions to political purposes.

. . .

Physically speaking, we cannot separate. We cannot remove our respective sections from each other nor build an impassable wall between them. A husband and wife may be divorced and go out of the presence and beyond the reach of each other, but the different parts of our country cannot do this. They cannot but remain face to face, and intercourse, either amicable or hostile, must continue between them. Is it possible, then, to make that intercourse more advantageous or more satisfactory *after* separation than *before?* Can aliens make treaties easier than friends can make laws? Can treaties be more faithfully enforced between aliens than laws can among friends? Suppose you go to war, you cannot fight always; and when, after much loss on both sides and no gain on either, you cease fighting, the identical old questions, as to terms of intercourse, are again upon you.

This country, with its institutions, belongs to the people who inhabit it. Whenever they shall grow weary of the existing Government, they can exercise their *constitutional* right of amending it or their *revolutionary* right to dismember or overthrow it. I can not be ignorant of the fact that many worthy and patriotic citizens are desirous of having the National Constitution amended. While I make no recommendation of amendments, I fully recognize the rightful authority of the people over the whole subject, to be exercised in either of the modes prescribed in the instrument itself; and I should, under existing circumstances, favor rather than oppose a fair opportunity being afforded the people to act upon it. I will venture to add that to me the convention mode seems preferable, in that it allows amendments to originate with the people themselves, instead of only permitting them to take or reject propositions originated by others, not especially chosen for the purpose, and which might not be precisely such as they would wish to either accept or refuse. I understand a proposed amendment to the Constitution—which amendment, however, I have not seen—has passed Congress, to the effect that the Federal Government shall never interfere with the domestic institutions of the States, including that of persons held to service. To avoid misconstruction of what I have said, I depart from my purpose not to speak of particular amendments so far as to say that, holding such a provision to now be implied constitutional law, I have no objection to its being made express and irrevocable.

The Chief Magistrate derives all his authority from the people, and they have referred none upon him to fix terms for the separation of the States. The people themselves can do this if also they choose, but the Executive as such has nothing to do with it. His duty is to administer the present Government as it came to his hands and to transmit it unimpaired by him to his successor.

Why should there not be a patient confidence in the ultimate justice of the people? Is there any better or equal hope in the world? In our present differences, is either party without faith of being in the right? If the Almighty Ruler of Nations, with His eternal truth and justice, be on your side of the North, or on yours of the South, that truth and that justice will surely prevail by the judgment of this great tribunal of the American people.

. . .

. . . We are not enemies, but friends. We must not be enemies. Though passion may have strained it must not break our bonds of affection. The mystic chords of memory, stretching from every battlefield and patriot grave to every living heart and hearthstone all over this broad land, will yet swell the chorus of the Union, when again touched, as surely they will be, by the better angels of our nature.

THADDEUS STEVENS

SPEECH ON THE RECONSTRUCTION ACTS (1867)

Thaddeus Stevens had a mixed career as a lawyer and politician in Pennsylvania prior to the Civil War, serving briefly in Congress as a Whig. He remade himself as a Republican and returned to the U.S. House of Representatives in 1858. He served in Congress until 1868, when he fell ill and died. During the war and Reconstruction, Stevens emerged as the leader of the Radical Republicans in the House. He was a key figure in establishing congressional policy on the war and was on the leading edge of efforts to reconstruct the South after the war. He was the chief figure advancing the impeachment of President Andrew Johnson in 1867, and he grew increasingly frustrated with the moderation of the party in the last year of his life.

In January 1867, Stevens introduced a bill to establish congressional Reconstruction in the South. The proposal would disband the governments that had been established by President Johnson and impose martial law in the South. Supporters of the former Confederacy would be excluded from participating in the establishment of new civilian governments, and the former slaves would be given the vote. The proposals were adopted, launching congressional and military control over the southern governments that would last a dozen years. The Reconstruction Acts were passed over Johnson's presidential veto in March 1867.

Why might Stevens be unwilling to allow civilian courts to operate in the postbellum South? Under what circumstances would it be appropriate to suspend the operation of civilian courts? Does Stevens anticipate the exclusion of former Confederates from the postbellum government to be a temporary measure? Who should be reasonably excluded from holding office after the Civil War? Who should be excluded from voting? Is Stevens right to think that free government is defined by who participates in government rather than how the government behaves? Does Stevens' argument require female suffrage? Under what conditions should the states that joined the Confederacy be able to resume normal political relations with the federal government? Did the states that attempted to secede commit "suicide"? Could Congress treat them like unorganized territorial possessions?

. . . I desire that as early as possible, without curtailing debate, this House shall come to some conclusion as to what shall be done with the rebel States. This becomes more and more necessary every day; and the late decision of the Supreme Court of the United States has rendered immediate action by Congress upon the question of the establishment of governments in the rebel States absolutely indispensable.[2]

That decision, although in terms perhaps not as infamous as the *Dred Scott* decision, is yet far more dangerous in its operation upon the lives and liberties of the loyal men of this country. That decision has taken away every protection in every one of these rebel States from every loyal man, black or white, who resides there. That decision has unsheathed the dagger of the assassin, and places the knife of the rebel at the throat of every man who dares proclaim himself to be now, or to have been heretofore, a loyal Union man. . . .

Now, Mr. Speaker, unless Congress proceeds at once to do something to protect these people from the barbarians who are now daily murdering them . . . I ask you and every man who loves liberty whether we will not be liable to the just censure of the world for our negligence or our cowardice or our want of ability to do so?

2 In the spring of 1866, the U.S. Supreme Court decided in *Ex parte Milligan*, 71 U.S. 2, that citizens could not be tried by military tribunals where civilian courts were operating. The case arose in Indiana, but it had more immediate implications for the South, where civilian courts under the jurisdiction of the United States were being reopened. Stevens preferred that crimes in the South be tried in federal military courts rather than civilian state courts [ed.].

. . . This is a bill designed to enable loyal men, so far as I could discriminate them in these States, to form governments which shall be in loyal hands, that they may protect themselves from such outrages as I have mentioned. In States that have never been restored since the rebellion from a state of conquest, and which are this day held in captivity under the laws of war, the military authorities, under the decision and its extensions into disloyal States, dare not order the commanders of departments to enforce the laws of the country. . . .

. . .

. . . Possibly the people would not have inaugurated this revolution to correct the palpable incongruities and despotic provisions of the Constitution; but having it forced upon them, will they be so unwise as to suffer it to subside without erecting this nation into a perfect Republic?

Since the surrender of the armies of the confederate States of America a little has been done toward establishing this Government upon the true principles of liberty and justice; and but a little if we stop here. We have broken the material shackles of four million slaves. . . . But in what have we enlarged their liberty of thought? In what have we taught them the science and granted them the privilege of self-government? . . . By what civil weapon have we enabled them to defend themselves against oppression and injustice? Call you this liberty? Call you this a free Republic where four millions are subjects but not citizens? Then Persia, with her kings and satraps, was free; then Turkey is free! Their subjects had liberty of motion and of labor, but the laws were made without and against their will. . . . Think not I would slander my native land; I would reform it. . . .

The freedom of a Government does not depend upon the quality of its laws, but upon the power that has the right to enact them. During the dictatorship of Pericles his laws were just, but Greece was not free.

. . .

No Government can be free that does not allow all its citizens to participate in the formation and execution of her laws. There are degrees of tyranny. But every other government is a despotism. . . .

. . .

President Lincoln, Vice President Johnson, and both branches of Congress repeatedly declared that the belligerent States could never again intermeddle with the affairs of the Union, or claim any right as members of the United States Government until the legislative power of the Government should declare them entitled thereto. Of course the rebels claimed no such rights; for whether their States were out of the Union as they declared, or were disorganized and "out of their proper relations" to the Government, as some subtle metaphysicians contend, their rights under the Constitution had all been renounced and abjured under oath, and could not be resumed on their own mere motion. How far their liabilities remained there was more difference of opinion.

The Federal arms triumphed. The confederate armies and government surrendered unconditionally. The law of nations then fixed their condition. They were subject to the controlling power of the conquerors. No former laws, no former compacts or treaties existed to bind the belligerents. They had all been melted and consumed in the fierce fires of the terrible war. . . . No sane man believed that they had any organic or municipal laws which the United States were bound to respect. . . .

. . .

In this country the whole sovereignty rests with the people, and is exercised through their Representatives in Congress assembled. The legislative power is the sole guardian of that sovereignty. . . . No Government official, from the President and Chief Justice down, can do any one act which is not prescribed and directed by the legislative power. . . .

. . . Since, then, the President cannot enact, alter, or modify a single law; cannot even create a petty office within his own sphere of duties; if, in short, he is the mere servant of the people, who issue their commands to him through Congress, whence does he derive the constitutional power to create new States; to remodel old ones; to dictate organic laws; to fix the qualifications of voters; to declare that States are republican and entitled to command Congress to admit their Representatives? To my mind it is either the most ignorant and shallow mistake of his duties, or the most brazen and impudent usurpation of power. . . . How absurd that a mere executive officer should claim creative powers! . . .

. . .

To reconstruct the nation, to admit new States, to guaranty republican governments to old States are all legislative acts. The President claims the right to exercise them. Congress denies it and asserts the right to belong to the legislative branch. . . .

. . . The President is for exonerating the conquered rebels from all the expense and damages of the war. . . . He desires that the traitors . . . should be exempt from further fine, imprisonment, forfeiture, exile, or capital punishment, and be declared entitled to all the rights of loyal citizens. . . . He is determined to force a solid rebel delegation into Congress from the South, and together with Northern Copperheads, could at once control Congress and elect all future Presidents.

. . . Congress denies that any State lately in rebellion has any government or constitution known to the Constitution of the United States, or which can be recognized as part of the Union. . . . I know of no Republican who does not ridicule what Mr. Seward thought a cunning movement, in counting Virginia and other outlawed States among those which had adopted the constitutional amendment abolishing slavery.

It is to be regretted that inconsiderate and incautious Republicans should ever have supposed that the slight amendments already proposed to the Constitution, even when incorporated into that instrument, would satisfy the reforms necessary for the security of the Government. Unless the rebel States, before admission, should be made republican in spirit, and placed under the guardianship of loyal men, all our blood and treasure will have been spent in vain. . . . There are several good reasons for passage of this bill. In the first place, it is just. I am now confining my arguments to negro suffrage in the rebel States. Have not loyal blacks quite as good a right to choose rulers and make laws as rebel whites? In the second place, it is a necessity in order to protect the loyal white men in the seceded States. The white Union men are in a great minority in each of those States. With them the blacks would act in a body. . . .

Another good reason is, it would insure the ascendancy of the Union party. Do you avow the party purpose? Exclaims some horror-stricken demagogue. I do. For I believe, on my conscience, that on the continued ascendency of that party depends the safety of this great nation. . . .

But it will be said . . . "This is negro equality!" What is negro equality. . . ? It means, as understood by honest Republicans, just this much, and no more: every man, no matter what his race or color; every earthly being who has an immortal soul, has an equal right to justice, honesty, and fair play with every other man; and the law should secure him these rights. The same law which condemns or acquits an African should condemn or acquit a white man. . . . Such is the law of God and such ought to be the law of man. This doctrine does not mean that a negro shall sit on the same seat or eat at the same table with a white man. That is a matter of taste which every man must decide for himself. The law has nothing to do with it. If there be any who are afraid of the rivalry of the black man in office or in business, I have only to advise them to try and beat their competitor in knowledge and business capacity, and there is no danger that his white neighbor will prefer his African rival to himself. . . .

. . .

III. CITIZENSHIP AND COMMUNITY

Major Developments

- Debate over what political community is most fundamental
- Debate over requirements of political allegiance in a democratic government

Secession posed unusual problems for ideas about American national identity. The United States had sometimes been characterized as a "family" of states and as a voluntary federation of republics. In many cases, personal political identity was still often defined by the state of birth or residence as much or more than national citizenship. Secession tested those bonds. For communities, this meant deciding whether to separate and chart an independent political course. For individuals, this meant deciding where their loyalties lay. From a southern perspective, ultimate loyalty was to the state and region, and individuals had some obligation to follow the choices of those political communities. From a northern perspective, the secessionists were "rebels" and "traitors" who had violated their core political obligations and allegiances. During the secession crisis itself, these tensions forced individuals to choose sides. During the war, the problem of divided loyalties raised questions about how the federal government should treat Confederate soldiers and southern civilians. After the war, the government spent some months pondering whether to hold treason trials for the political and military leaders of the secessionist movement, eventually deciding not to risk such trials.

Mississippi Senator (and future Confederate president) Jefferson Davis was one of many southern politicians who faced a stark choice. Davis was a supporter of secession and chose to return home when his state announced its departure from the Union. The vice president of the Confederacy, Georgia's Alexander Stephens, did not favor secession but likewise chose to return home when his state left. By contrast, Tennessee's Andrew Johnson declined to follow his state into secession and remained in Washington, D.C., and Texas Governor Sam Houston refused to take an oath of loyalty to the Confederacy and was denounced as a traitor and immediately removed from office. After the war, southern apologists argued that no secessionist had been guilty of treason to the United States, and indeed federal officials were guilty of converting a republic into an empire by keeping the South in the Union at the point of a gun. Support came from an unexpected and idiosyncratic source when the abolitionist anarchist Lysander Spooner published a series of essays arguing that it was not possible to commit the crime of treason in a free government. In contrast to these appeals to individual consent and local community, Abraham Lincoln used the occasion of his second inaugural address to appeal to the common bonds of shared sacrifice and history that tied all Americans together.

JEFFERSON DAVIS

FAREWELL TO THE SENATE (1860)

Jefferson Davis was part of a new generation of Southern political leadership. Davis was born at the tail end of the presidential administration of his namesake in Kentucky, but his family moved to Mississippi soon thereafter. Davis graduated from the U.S. Military Academy at West Point and served at a fort in the Wisconsin frontier. After his military service, he started a plantation in his home state, and in the 1840s was drawn into politics and briefly served in the U.S. House of Representatives before resigning to join a group of volunteers to fight in the war with Mexico in 1846. At the conclusion of the war, he declined a commission as brigadier general in order to return to civilian life and politics, serving two separate terms in the U.S. Senate and as U.S. Secretary of War. He was a member of the Senate when Mississippi seceded from the Union in January 1861. He resigned from the Senate and was elected president of the Confederate States of America. His farewell address to the Senate did not offer an elaborate defense of the right of secession but briefly stated the claim that a state's departure from the voluntary federal union was a peaceful remedy to the threat of political abuses. To those who thought that Davis should have remained in the Senate after the secession vote (as Tennessee's Andrew Johnson did), Davis responded that a senator was nothing but "an ambassador from his State" and had no legitimate role to play in Congress once his state had withdrawn from the Union, and it would have been dishonorable to remain in the U.S. Senate only "for the purpose of crippling the Government" from within.[3]

What was the obligation of the citizen of a state that announced its separation from the United States? Did a loyal citizen have an obligation to return to his home state and aid its government? Did he have a higher obligation to remain within the borders of the Union? What was the obligation of a southern member of Congress after secession? Would it have been appropriate to continue to occupy a seat in Congress—and potentially cast votes against the effort to fight the Civil War and organize the Union government? If Davis had chosen to remain in Washington, D.C., would there be a seat in the Senate for him to fill?

I rise, Mr. President, for the purpose of announcing to the Senate that I have satisfactory evidence that the State of Mississippi, by a solemn ordinance of her people in convention assembled, has declared her separation from the United States. Under these circumstances, of course my functions are terminated here. It has seemed to me proper, however, that I should appear in the Senate to announce that fact to my associates, and I will say but very little more. . . .

It is known to Senators who have served with me here, that I have for many years advocated, as an essential attribute of State sovereignty, the right of a State to secede from the Union. Therefore, if I had thought that Mississippi was acting without sufficient provocation, or without an existing necessity, I should still, under my theory of the Government, because of my allegiance to the State of which I am a citizen, have been bound by her action. I, however, may be permitted to say that I do think she has justifiable cause, and I approve of her act. I conferred with her people before that act was taken, counseled them then that if the state of things which they apprehended should exist when the convention met, they should take the action which they have now adopted.

. . .

A great man who now reposes with his fathers, and who has often been arraigned for want of fealty to the Union, advocated the doctrine of nullification, because it preserved the Union. It was because of his deep-seated attachment to the Union, his determination to find some remedy for existing ills short of a severance of the ties which bound South Carolina to the other States, that Mr. Calhoun advocated the doctrine of nullification, which he proclaimed to be

3 Jefferson Davis, *The Rise and Fall of the Confederate Government*, vol. 1 (New York: Appleton Co., 1881), 225.

peaceful, to be within the limits of State power, not to disturb the Union, but only to be a means of bringing the agent before the tribunal of the States for their judgment.

Secession belongs to a different class of remedies. It is to be justified upon the basis that the States are sovereign. There was a time when none denied it. I hope the time may come again, when a better comprehension of the theory of our Government, and the inalienable rights of the people of the States, will prevent anyone from denying that each State is a sovereign, and thus may reclaim the grants which it has made to any agent whomsoever.

I therefore say I concur in the action of the people of Mississippi, believing it to be necessary and proper, and should have been bound by their action if my belief had been otherwise; and this brings me to the important point which I wish on this last occasion to present to the Senate. It is by this confounding of nullification and secession that the name of a great man, whose ashes now mingle with his mother earth, has been invoked to justify coercion against a seceded State. The phrase, "to execute the laws," was an expression which General Jackson applied to the case of a State refusing to obey the laws while yet a member of the Union. That is not the case which is now presented. The laws are to be executed over the United States, and upon the people of the United States. They have no relation to any foreign country. It is a perversion of terms, at least it is a great misapprehension of the case, which cites that expression for application to a State which has withdrawn from the Union. You may make war on a foreign State. If it be the purpose of gentlemen, they may make war against a State which has withdrawn from the Union; but there are no laws of the United States to be executed within the limits of a seceded State. A State finding herself in the condition in which Mississippi has judged she is, in which her safety requires that she should provide for the maintenance of her rights out of the Union, surrenders all the benefits, (and they are known to be many,) deprives herself of the advantages, (and they are known to be great,) severs all the ties of affection, (and they are close and enduring,) which have bound her to the Union; and thus divesting herself of every benefit, taking upon herself every burden, she claims to be exempt from any power to execute the laws of the United States within her limits.

. . .

It has been a conviction of pressing necessity, it has been a belief that we are to be deprived in the Union of the rights which our fathers bequeathed to us, which has brought Mississippi to her present decision. She has heard proclaimed the theory that all men are created free and equal, and this made the basis of an attack upon her social institutions; and the sacred Declaration of Independence has been invoked to maintain the position of the equality of the races. That Declaration of Independence is to be construed by the circumstances and purposes for which it was made. The communities were declaring their independence; the people of those communities were asserting that no man was born—to use the language of Mr. Jefferson—booted and spurred to ride over the rest of mankind; that men were created equal—meaning the men of the political community; that there was no divine right to rule; that no man inherited the right to govern; that there were no classes by which power and place descended to families, but that all stations were equally within the grasp of each member of the body politic. These were the great principles they announced; these were the purposes for which they made their declaration; these were the ends to which their enunciation was directed. They have no reference to the slave; else, how happened it that among the items of arraignment made against George III was that he endeavored to do just what the North has been endeavoring of late to do — to stir up insurrection among our slaves? . . . When our Constitution was formed, the same idea was rendered more palpable, for there we find provision made for that very class of persons as property; they were not put upon the footing of equality with white men—not even upon that of paupers and convicts; but, so far as representation was concerned, were discriminated against as a lower caste, only to be represented in the numerical proportion of three-fifths.

Then, Senators, we recur to the compact which binds us together; we recur to the principles upon which our Government was founded; and when you deny them, and when you deny us the right to withdraw from a Government which thus perverted threatens to be destructive of our rights, we but tread in the path of our fathers when we proclaim our independence, and take the hazard. This is done, not in hostility to others; not to injure any section of the country, not even for our own pecuniary benefit, but from the high and solemn motive of defending and protecting the rights we inherited, and which it is our duty to transmit unshorn to our children.

I find in myself, perhaps, a type of the general feeling of my constituents towards yours. I am sure I feel no hostility to you, Senators from the North. I am sure there is not one of you, whatever sharp discussion there may have been between us, to whom I cannot now say, in the presence of my God, I wish you well; and such, I am sure, is the feeling of the people whom I represent towards those whom you represent. I therefore feel that I but express their desire when I say I hope, and they hope, for peaceful relations with you, though we must part. They may be mutually beneficial to us in the future, as they have been in the past, if you so will it. The reverse may bring disaster on every portion of the country; and if you will have it thus, we will invoke the God of our fathers, who delivered them from the power of the lion, to protect us from the ravages of the bear; and thus, putting our trust in God, and in our firm hearts and strong arms, we will vindicate the right as best we may.

. . .

Mr. President, and Senators, having made the announcement which the occasion seemed to me to require, it only remains for me to bid you a final adieu.

ABRAHAM LINCOLN

SECOND INAUGURAL ADDRESS (1865)

Abraham Lincoln's election to a second term of office seemed far from certain. The Civil War, which was expected to be brief, instead turned into a drawn-out war of attrition. By the time of the 1864 elections, the war with the Confederacy had lasted longer than any previous American war since the American Revolution. The hundreds of thousands of dead just on the Union side of the war dwarfed anything that the nation had previously experienced, and the economic toll on the nation was severe. Union army victories had been limited and costly. Many in the North had doubted the value of the war to start with, and by 1864 many more were exhausted by it. The Democratic presidential nominee, General George McClellan, was running on a peace platform, and the still-new Republican Party was not yet well entrenched with the electorate. In the summer of 1864, even the president thought defeat at the polls was likely. The "National Union" party was invented in the summer of 1864 in order to try to build a bipartisan, pro-war coalition. The "War Democrat" Andrew Johnson of Tennessee was chosen as vice president as a show of national unity. All that changed with the fall of Atlanta in September. With military victory in sight, the National Union ticket swept to electoral victory. In March 1865, Lincoln celebrated his second inaugural. A month later, General Robert E. Lee surrendered the Confederate army, and less than a week after that Lincoln was assassinated and Andrew Johnson assumed the presidency.

In his second inaugural address, Lincoln looked forward to the postwar reconciliation with the South. He had been a war president in his first term. His second term promised to be a presidency dominated by the effort of restoring the peace. Rather than laying out a policy program in his inaugural address, Lincoln offered a retrospective vision of the meaning of the war and the terms of union moving forward.

How much attention does Lincoln give to the current and former slaves in this speech? Does he lay the groundwork for a reconstruction relating to slavery? To what extent does he treat the Confederate forces as (nearly defeated) enemies? How does he try to prepare the way for a reunification? How does he see the war in relation to American national identity? What is the role of religion in this speech?

. . .

On the occasion corresponding to this four years ago all thoughts were anxiously directed to an impending civil war. All dreaded it, all sought to avert it. While the inaugural address was being delivered from this place, devoted altogether to *saving* the Union without war, insurgent agents were in the city seeking to *destroy* it without war—seeking to dissolve the Union and divide effects by negotiation. Both parties deprecated war, but one of them would *make* war rather than let the nation survive, and the other would *accept* war rather than let it perish, and the war came.

One-eighth of the whole population were colored slaves, not distributed generally over the Union, but localized in the southern part of it. These slaves constituted a peculiar and powerful interest. All knew that this interest was somehow the cause of the war. To strengthen, perpetuate, and extend this interest was the object for which the insurgents would rend the Union even by war, while the Government claimed no right to do more than to restrict the territorial enlargement of it. Neither party expected for the war the magnitude or the duration which it has already attained. Neither anticipated that the *cause* of the conflict might cease with or even before the conflict itself should cease. Each looked for an easier triumph, and a result less fundamental and astounding. Both read the same Bible and pray to the same God, and each invokes His aid against the other. It may seem strange that any men should dare to ask a just God's assistance in wringing their bread from the sweat of other men's faces, but let us judge not, that we be not judged. The prayers of both could not be answered. That of neither has been answered fully. The Almighty has His own purposes. "Woe unto the world because of offenses; for it must needs be that offenses come, but woe to that man by whom the offense cometh." If we shall suppose that American slavery is one of those offenses which, in the providence of God, must needs come, but which, having continued through His appointed time, He now wills to remove, and that He gives to both North and South this terrible war as the woe due to those by whom the offense came, shall we discern therein any departure from those divine attributes which the believers in a living God always ascribe to Him? Fondly do we hope, fervently do we pray, that this mighty scourge of war may speedily pass away. Yet, if God wills that it continue until all the wealth piled by the bondsman's two hundred and fifty years of unrequited toil shall be sunk, and until every drop of blood drawn with the lash shall be paid by another drawn with the sword, as was said three thousand years ago, so still it must be said "the judgments of the Lord are true and righteous altogether."

With malice toward none, with charity for all, with firmness in the right as God gives us to see the right, let us strive on to finish the work we are in, to bind up the nation's wounds, to care for him who shall have borne the battle and for his widow and his orphan, to do all which may achieve and cherish a just and lasting peace among ourselves and with all nations.

LYSANDER SPOONER

NO TREASON (1867)

Lysander Spooner was raised on a small farm in Massachusetts and was trained as a lawyer. His legal practice was not particularly successful, and he spent part of his time challenging state education and licensing requirements for professionals as an unwarranted interference with ability of the less-well-off to pursue a career. He then questioned the federal government's postal monopoly and started his own mail delivery business, but the government eventually forced him to shut it down. After that, he dedicated most of his time to his extreme Jeffersonian writings. His greatest fame came as an abolitionist. Unlike such abolitionists as William Lloyd Garrison, Spooner contended that slavery was inconsistent with the U.S. Constitution, an argument that won over Frederick Douglass. His economic views left him at odds with many of the former Whigs who created the Republican Party, however. He found himself further isolated during the Civil War, which he denounced as an act of imperialism. For him, the same natural-rights principles supported both secession and free labor. After the war, as many Republicans called for treason trials against the leaders of the Confederacy, Spooner published a series of pamphlets elaborating his view that secession was consistent with the Constitution and the requirements of free government. His disagreements with American actions during the war and Reconstruction fueled further radicalism in his own views, and he spent his last years writing in anarchist intellectual circles.

Can the acts of the U.S. government during the Civil War be separated from the substantive issue of slavery? Is the desire to maintain union sufficient to justify fighting the Civil War? Is the actual accomplishment of the end of slavery necessary to justify American actions during the war? Are loyalty and allegiance strictly voluntary, or do citizens owe loyalty to the U.S. government? Can entire groups of citizens renounce their citizenship and establish a politically independent state within the geographic boundaries of the United States? How important is actual consent of the governed to political legitimacy? How do Spooner's views compare to Thoreau's?

The question of treason is distinct from that of slavery; and is the same that it would have been, if free States, instead of slave states, had seceded.

On the part of the North, the war was carried on, not to liberate the slaves, but by a government that had always perverted and violated the Constitution, to keep the slaves in bondage; and was still willing to do so, if the slaveholders could be thereby induced to stay in the Union.

The principle, on which the war was waged by the North, was simply this: That men may rightfully be compelled to submit to, and support, a government that they do not want; and that resistance, on their part, makes them traitors and criminals.

No principle, that is possible to be named, can be more self-evidently false than this; or more self-evidently fatal to all political freedom. Yet it triumphed in the field, and is now assumed to be established. If it be really established, the number of slaves, instead of having been diminished by the war, has been greatly increased; for a man, thus subjected to a government that he does not want, is a slave. . . .

Previous to the war, there were some grounds for saying that—in theory, at least, if not in practice—our government was a free one; that it rested on consent. But nothing of that kind can be said now, if the principle on which the war was carried on by the North, is irrevocably established.

If that principle be *not* the principle of the Constitution, the fact should be known. If it *be* the principle of the Constitution, the Constitution itself should be at once overthrown.

. . .

Notwithstanding all the proclamations we have made to mankind, within the last ninety years, that our government rested on consent, and that that was the only rightful basis on which any government could rest, the late war has practically demonstrated that our government rests upon force—as much so as any government that ever existed.

The North has thus virtually said to the world: It was all very well to prate of consent, so long as the objects to be accomplished were to liberate ourselves from our connection with England, and also to coax a scattered and jealous people into a great national union; but now that those purposes have been accomplished, and the power of the North has become consolidated, it is sufficient for us—as for all governments—simply to say: *Our power is our right.*

. . .

What, then, is implied in a government's resting on consent?

If it be said that the consent of the *strongest party,* in a nation, is all that is necessary to justify the establishment of a government that shall have authority over the weaker party, it may be answered that the most despotic governments in the world rest upon that very principle, viz: the consent of the strongest party. These governments are formed simply by the consent or agreement of the strongest party, that they will act in concert in subjecting the weaker party to their dominion. And the despotism, and tyranny, and injustice of these governments consist in that very fact. Or at least that is the first step in their tyranny; a necessary preliminary to all the oppressions that are to follow.

If it be said that the consent of the *most numerous party,* in a nation, is sufficient to justify the establishment of their power over the less numerous party, it may be answered:

First, That two men have no more natural right to exercise any kind of authority over one, than one has to exercise the same authority over two. A man's natural rights are his own, against the whole world; and any infringement of them is equally a crime, whether committed by one man, or by millions; whether committed by one man, calling himself a robber, (or by any other name indicating his true character,) or by millions, calling themselves a government.

Second. It would be absurd for the most numerous party to talk of establishing a government over the less numerous party, unless the former were also the strongest, as well as the most numerous; for it is not to be supposed that the strongest party would ever submit to the rule of the weaker party, merely because the latter were the most numerous. And as matter of fact, it is perhaps never that governments are established by the most numerous party. They are usually, if not always, established by the less numerous party; their superior strength consisting in their superior wealth, intelligence, and ability to act in concert.

Third. Our Constitution does not profess to have been established simply by the majority; but by "the people;" the minority, as much as the majority.

Fourth. If our fathers, in 1776, had acknowledged the principle that a majority had the right to rule the minority, we should never have become a nation; for they were in a small minority, as compared with those who claimed the right to rule over them.

Fifth. Majorities, *as such,* afford no guarantees for justice. They are men of the same nature as minorities. They have the same passions for fame, power, and money, as minorities; and are liable and likely to be equally—perhaps more than equally, because more boldly—rapacious, tyrannical and unprincipled, if entrusted with power. There is no more reason, then, why a man should either sustain, or submit to, the rule of a majority, than of a minority. . . .

. . .

The question, then, returns, What is implied in a government's resting on consent?

Manifestly this one thing (to say nothing of others) is necessarily implied in the idea of a government's resting on consent, viz: *the separate, individual consent of every man who is required to contribute, either by taxation or personal service, to the support of the government.* All this, or nothing, is necessarily implied, because one man's consent is just as necessary as any other man's. . . .

. . .

Clearly this individual consent is indispensable to the idea of treason; for if a man has never consented or agreed to support a government, he breaks no faith in refusing to support it. And if he makes war upon it, he does so as an open enemy, and not as a traitor—that is, as a betrayer, or treacherous friend.

. . .

[Imagine an agreement that says:] We, the people of the town of A—, agree to sustain a church, a school, a hospital, or a theatre, for ourselves and our children.

Such an agreement clearly could have no validity, except as between those who actually consented to it. If a portion only of "the people of the town of A—," should assent to this contract, and should then proceed to *compel* contributions of money or service from those who had not consented, they would be mere robbers; and would deserve to be treated as such.

Neither the conduct nor the rights of these signers would be improved at all by their saying to the dissenters: We offer you equal rights with ourselves, in the benefits of the church, school, hospital, or theatre, which we propose to establish, and equal voice in the control of it. It would be a sufficient answer for the others to say: We want no share in the benefits, and no voice in the control, of your institution; and will do nothing to support it.

. . .

One essential of a free government is that it rest wholly on voluntary support. And one certain proof that a government is not free, is that it coerces more or less persons to support it, against their will. All governments, the worst on earth, and the most tyrannical on earth, are free governments to that portion of the people who voluntarily support them. And all governments—though the best on earth in other respects—are nevertheless tyrannies to that portion of the people—whether few or many—who are compelled to support them against their will. A government is like a church, or any other institution, in these respects. There is no other criterion whatever, by which to determine whether a government is a free one, or not, than the single one of its depending, or not depending, solely on voluntary support.

. . .

IV. EQUALITY AND STATUS

Major Developments

- National commitment to abolition of slavery
- Scope of civil rights of freedmen
- Expansion of suffrage to African-American males

Perhaps surprisingly, the question of slavery and emancipation in the 1860s stirred less consideration of liberty than of equality. Slavery, as it was experienced in the United States in the mid-nineteenth century, was centrally about race. The condition of slavery, in turn, was a matter of legal, political, and social status. The crucial problem for white Americans thinking about the prospect of emancipation was whether and in what sense African-Americans could be regarded as their equals. Did racial inequality necessitate or justify slavery? Did emancipation from the status of slavery imply equality? Could freedom from slavery be made consistent with inequality of status?

Not surprisingly, the answers to such questions varied. Antislavery politicians like William Henry Seward and Charles Sumner thought the issue was stark. As Sumner declared, the system of slavery was a form of "barbarism" that could not be reconciled with a Christian civilization. Many in the South agreed that the issue was a stark one. Confederate Vice President Alexander Stephens asserted boldly that racial inequality was the "cornerstone" of the new Confederate government. As the war wound to a close, such divisions did not quickly go away. Radical Republicans pressed for greater legal and political equality for blacks. Southern politicians resisted giving much more than mere emancipation. Abraham Lincoln tried to bridge the divide, to the dissatisfaction of some.

If the problem of slavery was necessarily in the foreground of American politics in the 1860s and 1870s, there was disagreement over whether the rights and status of women should be in the background. The former slave Frederick Douglass had been a forceful advocate for women's rights in the antebellum era, but he joined other antislavery activists in arguing that the Reconstruction years were a time for an exclusive focus on the problems of the freedmen. At an 1869 women's rights convention, Douglass stated his case plainly:

> I must say that I do not see how any one can pretend that there is the same urgency in giving the ballot to woman as to the negro. With us, the matter is a question of life and death, at least, in fifteen States of the Union. When women, because they are women, are hunted down through the cities of New York and New Orleans; when they are dragged from their houses and hung upon lamp-posts . . . then they will have an urgency to obtain the ballot equal to our own.[4]

The abolitionist leader Wendell Phillips declared succinctly, "It is not the woman's but the negro's hour." Suffragists like Susan B. Anthony saw the postbellum years as a crucial opportunity for advancing the rights of women as well as African-Americans; she was not inclined to defer to her male colleagues in the reform movement.

---

4 *History of Woman Suffrage*, ed. Elizabeth Cady Stanton, Susan B. Anthony, and Matilda Joslyn Gage, vol. 2 (New York: Fowler & Wells, 1882), 382.

CHARLES SUMNER

THE BARBARISM OF SLAVERY (1860)

Charles Sumner was the senior statesman of the Republican Party. His father had been an early antislavery leader in Massachusetts, and as a young man Sumner established himself as an erudite lawyer and renowned orator. Eschewing the Whig Party, he helped organize the antislavery Free Soil Party in 1848 and with their support was sent to the U.S. Senate in 1851. Sumner was unusually personal in his attacks on slavery and in 1856 was severely beaten on the floor of the Senate by South Carolina congressman Preston Brooks. Sumner needed more than three years to recuperate from the attack and resume his seat in the Senate. His June 1860 speech on the barbarism of slavery rallied the Republican faithful for the presidential campaign and marked his return to public life. Over the course of the war and Reconstruction, he led the Radical Republicans in the Senate. Unlike other Radicals, however, Sumner supported efforts at national reconciliation, earning a censure from the Massachusetts state legislature.

Why does Sumner abandon "soft words"? Can public policy avoid taking up "moral questions"? Should political partisans be willing to denounce the other side as evil and illegitimate? What are the limits of partisanship? Is Sumner right to think that how many people engage in a practice makes no difference to evaluating the wrongness of the practice? Why does Sumner appeal to arguments about "practical results"? What does he mean by the "Africanization" of the Constitution?

. . .

This is no time for soft words or excuses. All such are out of place. They may turn away wrath; but what is the wrath of man? This is no time to abandon any advantage in the argument. Senators sometimes announce that they resist Slavery on political grounds only, and remind us that they say nothing of the moral question. This is wrong. Slavery must be resisted not only on political grounds, but on all other grounds, whether social, economical, or moral. Ours is no holiday contest; nor is it any strife of rival factions . . . but it is a solemn battle between Right and Wrong; between Good and Evil. . . .

. . .

It is natural that Senators . . . insensible to the true character of Slavery, should evince an equal insensibility to the true character of the Constitution. This is shown in the claim now made . . . that by virtue of the Constitution, the pretended property in man is placed beyond the reach of Congressional prohibition even within Congressional jurisdiction, so that the Slave-master may at all times enter the broad outlying Territories of the Union with the victims of his oppression, and there continue to hold them by lash and chain.

Such are the two assumptions, the *first* an assumption of fact, and the *second* an assumption of constitutional law, which are now made without apology or hesitation. I meet them both. To the first I oppose the essential Barbarism of Slavery, in all its influences, whether high or low, as Satan is Satan still, whether towering in the sky or squatting in the toad. To the second I oppose the unanswerable, irresistible truth, that the Constitution of the United States nowhere recognizes property in man. These two assumptions naturally go together. . . . It is only when Slavery is exhibited in its truly hateful character, that we can fully appreciate the absurdity of the assumption, which, in defiance of the express letter of the Constitution, and without a single sentence, phrase, or word, upholding human bondage, yet folds into this blameless text the barbarous idea that man can hold property in man.

. . .

It is the often-quoted remark of John Wesley, who knew well how to use words, as also how to touch hearts, that Slavery was "the sum of all villainies." . . . Look at it in the light of principles, and it is nothing less than a huge insurrection against the eternal law of God, involving in its pretensions the denial of all human rights, and also the denial of that Divine Law in which God himself is manifest, thus being practically the grossest lie and the grossest Atheism. Founded in violence, sustained only by violence, such a wrong must by a sure law of compensation blast the master as well as the slave; blast the lands on which they live; blast the community of which they are a part; blast the Government which does not forbid the outrage; and the longer it exists and the more completely it prevails, must its blasting influences penetrate the whole social system. . . .

. . .

. . . "Two civilizations!" Sir, in this nineteenth century of Christian light, there can be but one Civilization, and this is where Freedom prevails. Between Slavery and Civilization there is an essential incompatibility. If you are for the one, you cannot be for the other; and just in proportion to the embrace of Slavery is the divorce from Civilization. That Slave-masters should be disturbed when this is exposed, might be expected. . . .

. . .

. . . If the offense of Slavery were less extended; if it were confined to some narrow region . . . [it] would find little indulgence. All would rise against it, while religion and civilization would lavish their choicest efforts in the general warfare. But what is wrong, when done to one man, cannot be right when done to many. . . .

. . .

In considering the *practical results of Slavery*, the materials are so obvious and diversified that my chief care will be to abridge and reject. . . .

The States where this Barbarism now exists excel the Free States in all natural advantages. . . .

But Slavery plays the part of a Harpy, and defiles the choicest banquet. See what it does with this territory, thus spacious and fair.

An important indication of prosperity is to be found in the growth of *population*. In this respect the two regions started equal. . . . [T]he white population of the Free States had not only doubled, but commenced to triple that of the Slave States, although occupying a smaller territory. . . .

. . .

The Slave States boast of agriculture; but here again, notwithstanding their superior natural advantages, they must yield to the Free States on every point, in number of farms and plantations, in the number of acres of improved lands, in the cash value of farms, in the average value per acre, and in the value of farming implements and machinery. . . .

. . .

. . . Never was the saying of Montesquieu more triumphantly verified, that countries are not cultivated by reason of their fertility, but by reason of their liberty. To this truth the Slave States constantly testify by every possible voice. Liberty is the powerful agent which drives the plow, the spindle, and the keel; which opens avenues of all kinds; which inspires charity; which awakens a love of knowledge, and supplies the means of gratifying it. Liberty is the first of schoolmasters.

. . .

Can Barbarism further go? Here is an irresponsible power, rendered more irresponsible still by the seclusion of the plantation, and absolutely fortified by the supplementary law excluding the testimony of slaves. That under its shelter enormities should occur, stranger than fiction, too terrible for imagination, and surpassing any individual experience, is simply according to the course of nature and the course of history. . . . Slavery, in its recesses, is another Bastille, whose horrors will never be known until it all is razed to the ground. . . .

. . .

It is according to irresistible law that men are fashioned by what is about them, whether climate, scenery, life or institutions. Like produces like, and this ancient proverb is verified always. . . . If institutions generous and just ripen souls also generous and just, then other institutions must exhibit their influence also. Violence, brutality, injustice, barbarism, must be reproduced in the lives of all who live within their fatal sphere. . . .

Instead of "ennobling" the master, nothing can be clearer than that the slave drags his master down, and this process begins in childhood, and is continued through life. . . .

. . .

When Slavery is seen to be the Barbarism which it is, there are few who would not over it from sight, rather than insist upon sending it abroad with the flag of the republic. It is only because people have been insensible to its true character that they have tolerated for a moment its exorbitant pretensions. . . .

[The assumption of constitutional law] may be described as an attempt to *Africanize* the Constitution, by introducing into it the barbarous Law of Slavery, derived as we have seen originally from barbarous Africa; and then, though such *Africanization* of the Constitution, to Africanize the Territories, and to *Africanize* the National Government. . . .

Property implies an owner and a thing owned. On the one side is a human being, and on the other side a thing. But the very idea of a human being necessarily excludes the idea of property in that being, just as the very idea of a thing necessarily excludes the idea of a human being. . . .

If this property does exist, out of what title is it derived? Under what ordinance of Nature or of Nature's God is one human being stamped an owner and another stamped a thing? God is no respecter of persons. Where is the sanction for this respect of certain persons to a degree which becomes outrage to other persons? God is the Father of the Human Family, and we are all his children. Where then is the sanction of this pretension by which a brother lays violent hands upon a brother? To ask these questions is humiliating; but it is clear there can be but one response. There is no sanction for such pretension. . . .

The intrinsic feebleness of this pretension is apparent in the intrinsic feebleness of the arguments by which it is maintained. . . .

The first is the alleged inferiority of the African race; an argument which, while surrendering to Slavery a whole race, leaves it uncertain whether the same principle may not be applied to other races. . . .

. . .

. . . The sacred animosity between Freedom and Slavery can end only with the triumph of Freedom. This same Question will be soon carried before the high tribunal, supreme over Senate and Court, where the judges will be counted by millions, and where thejudgment rendered will be the solemn charge of an aroused people, instructing a new President, in the name of Freedom, to see that Civilization receives no detriment.

ALEXANDER H. STEPHENS

CORNERSTONE ADDRESS (1861)

Alexander H. Stephens was a Southern Whig and generally regarded as a moderate in the antebellum era. Unlike Jefferson Davis, Stephens had advised against secession as the final crisis was cresting. He served in the U.S. House of Representatives in the 1850s and was elected vice president of the Confederacy after Georgia's secession. He was arrested immediately after the war but released after a few months. The Georgia legislature chose him for the U.S. Senate in 1866, spurring outrage from the Republicans and the launch of congressional Reconstruction. He returned to the U.S. House of Representatives in the 1870s, resigning to assume the office of state governor in 1882. He died a few months later.

In March 1861, Stephens was the featured speaker at a public meeting in Savannah, Georgia. He gave a lengthy speech, only partly transcribed and reported in the local newspaper, laying out some features of the new Confederate government and relaying the current state of affairs with the United States. The address immediately became known as the "cornerstone speech," however, because of his statements on slavery (as one northern publication titled the speech, "African Slavery, the Corner-Stone of the Southern Confederacy"), and the speech was widely reprinted in the North as well as the South. After the war, Stephens produced a lengthy defense of secession, including a number of relevant documents as appendices. He did not include the text of this address but did defend parts of the speech against criticism. There he denied any originality in the cornerstone metaphor, saying that he simply borrowed it from the judicial opinion of a Supreme Court justice, who had stated that "the rights of property in slaves" represented a cornerstone of the U.S. government.[5]

Is there a consistency between Stephens' praise of the "perfect equality" of "honest labor and enterprise" and his endorsement of slavery? Is Stephens right that the U.S. Constitution was founded on the principle of the "equality of the races"? Does his belief that the Constitution secured "every essential guarantee" of slavery undermine the case for secession? Why would the inequality of the races be the "cornerstone" of the Confederacy? Does his focus on the inequality of the races respond to the suggestion of Sumner and others that "other races" could also be subjected to slavery? Is the commitment to racial inequality important to securing the claim of white equality? How does slavery, in his view, strengthen the ties among whites, regardless of class? Is Stephens right to argue that the North was implicated in slavery?

I was remarking that we are passing through one of the greatest revolutions in the annals of the world. Seven States have within the last three months thrown off an old government and formed a new. This revolution has been signally marked, up to this time, by the fact of its having been accomplished without the loss of a single drop of blood.

This new constitution, or form of government, constitutes the subject to which your attention will be partly invited. . . . It amply secures all our ancient rights, franchises, and liberties. All the great principles of Magna Charta are retained in it. No citizen is deprived of life, liberty, or property, but by the judgment of his peers under the laws of the land. The great principle of religious liberty, which was the honor and pride of the old constitution, is still maintained and secured. All the essentials of the old constitution, which have endeared it to the hearts of the American people, have been preserved and perpetuated. Some changes have been made. . . . Some of these I should have preferred not to have seen made. . . . But other important changes do meet my cordial approbation. They form great improvements upon

5 Alexander H. Stephens, *A Constitutional View of the Late War Between the States*, vol. 2 (Boston, MA: National Publishing Company, 1870), 86. The reference is to *Johnson v. Tompkins*, 13 F.Cas. 840 (C.C.E.D. Pa. 1833), where Justice Baldwin insisted on the need for the states to faithfully comply with the fugitive slave clause because "the whole structure must fall by disturbing the corner stones" of the constitutional settlement reached in 1787.

the old constitution. So, taking the whole new constitution, I have no hesitancy in giving it as my judgment that it is decidedly better than the old.

Allow me briefly to allude to some of these improvements. The question of building up class interests, or fostering one branch of industry to the prejudice of another under the exercise of the revenue power, which gave us so much trouble under the old constitution, is put at rest forever under the new. We allow the imposition of no duty with a view of giving advantage to one class of persons, in any trade or business, over those of another. All, under our system, stand upon the same broad principles of perfect equality. Honest labor and enterprise are left free and unrestricted in whatever pursuit they may be engaged. This old thorn of the tariff, which was the cause of so much irritation in the old body politic, is removed forever from the new.

. . .

But not to be tedious in enumerating the numerous changes for the better, allow me to allude to one other though last, not least. The new constitution has put at rest, forever, all the agitating questions relating to our peculiar institution—African slavery as it exists amongst us—the proper *status* of the negro in our form of civilization. This was the immediate cause of the late rupture and present revolution. Jefferson in his forecast, had anticipated this, as the "rock upon which the old Union would split." But whether he fully comprehended the great truth upon which that rock *stood* and *stands,* may be doubted. The prevailing ideas entertained by him and most of the leading statesmen at the time of the formation of the old constitution, were that the enslavement of the African was in violation of the laws of nature; that it was wrong in *principle,* socially, morally, and politically. It was an evil they knew not well how to deal with, but the general opinion of the men of that day was that, somehow or other in the order of Providence, the institution would be evanescent and pass away. This idea, though not incorporated in the constitution, was the prevailing idea at that time. The constitution, it is true, secured every essential guarantee to the institution while it should last, and hence no argument can be justly urged against the constitutional guarantees thus secured, because of the common sentiment of the day. Those ideas, however, were fundamentally wrong. They rested upon the assumption of the equality of races. This was an error. It was a sandy foundation, and the government built upon it fell when the "storm came and the wind blew."

Our new government is founded upon exactly the opposite idea; its foundations are laid, its cornerstone rests upon the great truth, that the negro is not equal to the white man; that slavery—subordination to the superior race—is his natural and normal condition. This, our new government, is the first, in the history of the world, based upon this great physical, philosophical, and moral truth. . . .

. . .

. . . Many governments have been founded upon the principle of the subordination and serfdom of certain classes of the same race; such were and are in violation of the laws of nature. Our system commits no such violation of nature's laws. With us, all of the white race, however high or low, rich or poor, are equal in the eye of the law. Not so with the negro. Subordination is his place. He, by nature, or by the curse against Canaan, is fitted for that condition which he occupies in our system. The substratum of our society is made of the material fitted by nature for it, and by experience we know that it is best, not only for the superior, but for the inferior race, that it should be so. It is, indeed, in conformity with the ordinance of the Creator. It is not for us to inquire into the wisdom of his ordinances, or to question them. For his own purposes, he has made one race to differ from another, as he has made "one star to differ from another star in glory." . . .

. . .

The surest way to secure peace, is to show your ability to maintain your rights. The principles and position of the present administration of the United States the republican party present some puzzling questions. While it is a fixed principle with them never to allow the increase of a foot of slave territory, they seem to be equally determined not to part with an inch "of the accursed soil." Notwithstanding their clamor against the institution, they seemed to be equally opposed to getting more, or letting go what they have got. They were ready to fight on the accession of Texas, and are equally ready to fight now on her secession. Why is this? How can this strange paradox be accounted for? There seems to be but one rational solution and that is, notwithstanding their professions of humanity, they are disinclined to give up the benefits they derive from slave labor. Their philanthropy yields to their interest. The idea of enforcing the laws, has but one object, and that is a collection of the taxes, raised by slave labor to swell the fund necessary to meet their heavy appropriations. The spoils is what they are after though they come from the labor of the slave.

. . .

ABRAHAM LINCOLN

GETTYSBURG ADDRESS (1863)

The Gettysburg Address is widely regarded as one of the most important documents in American history. The occasion was somber one. At the beginning of July 1863, the bulk of the Union and Confederate armies fought near Gettysburg, Pennsylvania. General Lee was looking to lead his forces into the North, and the Union army moved to block his advance. Lee charged the defensive positions of the larger Union army, but the northern lines held, forcing Lee to retreat to Virginia. Both armies suffered massive casualties, but the South took proportionally more and was forced to give ground. The North immediately celebrated the victory as the turning point in the war, though the South saw the loss as a more modest setback. In November, the Soldiers National Cemetery was dedicated at Gettysburg, receiving the remains of Union soldiers who had been killed in the conflict. President Lincoln made the trip to speak at the dedication ceremony and delivered a brief address. The contemporary reception was mixed, but Charles Sumner was among those who thought that the speech was "sanctified by the martyrdom of its author" less than two years later.[6]

What is the significance to Lincoln starting his speech with the events of 1776? What were the founding principles of the country, according to Lincoln? Is he correct in his identification of the founding principles? How does that identification of founding principles connect to the "cause for which they gave the last full measure of devotion"? What does Lincoln say is at stake in the war? How is the nation being reborn in the war?

Four score and seven years ago our fathers brought forth on this continent, a new nation, conceived in Liberty, and dedicated to the proposition that all men are created equal.

Now we are engaged in a great civil war, testing whether that nation, or any nation so conceived and so dedicated, can long endure. We are met on a great battle-field of that war. We have come to dedicate a portion of that field, as a final resting place for those who here gave their lives that that nation might live. It is altogether fitting and proper that we should do this.

But, in a larger sense, we cannot dedicate—we cannot consecrate—we cannot hallow—this ground. The brave men, living and dead, who struggled here, have consecrated it, far above our poor power to add or detract. The world will little note, nor long remember what we say here, but it can never forget what they did here. It is for us the living, rather, to be dedicated here to the unfinished work which they who fought here have thus far so nobly advanced. It is rather for us to be here dedicated to the great task remaining before us—that from these honored dead we take increased devotion to that cause for which they gave the last full measure of devotion—that we here highly resolve that these dead shall not have died in vain—that this nation, under God, shall have a new birth of freedom—and that government of the people, by the people, for the people, shall not perish from the earth.

6 Charles Sumner, "Eulogy of Hon. Charles Sumner," in *A Memorial of Abraham Lincoln* (Boston, MA: J.B. Parwell, 1865), 127.

RECONSTRUCTION AMENDMENTS TO THE U.S. CONSTITUTION

The Thirteenth, Fourteenth, and Fifteenth Amendments to the U.S. Constitution are commonly referred to as the Reconstruction Amendments. All three came out of the struggles of the Civil War, and they marked the first formal changes to the Constitution since the founding era. The Constitution was not amended again until the twentieth century.

The three Reconstruction Amendments were adopted in quick succession between 1865 and 1870, and they all reflected the effort to account for the end of slavery. The Thirteenth abolished slavery throughout the Union, in areas that had not been covered by the Emancipation Proclamation as well as those that were. The Fourteenth was an omnibus amendment, packaging several different proposals that had the general goal of constraining the political consequences of the return of the former Confederate states. The Fifteenth prohibited racial qualifications on voting, throughout the nation and for any office. The Thirteenth Amendment was the least controversial. By the conclusion of the war, the end of slavery was generally assumed to be a foregone conclusion. The Fourteenth and Fifteenth generated controversy in the North as well as the South and were generally resisted by Democratic politicians. The former Confederate states were required to ratify the amendments in order to secure their full inclusion in the Union, and those ratification votes proved to be important to the ratification of the Fourteenth Amendment in particular. The initial refusal of southern state governments to ratify the Fourteenth Amendment helped spur Congress to dissolve those governments and impose a more thorough Reconstruction.

Do these amendments reflect the "new birth of freedom" that Lincoln promised in the Gettysburg Address? In what ways do they modify the original constitutional design? How far do they go in establishing liberty and equality? Do they go far enough? To what extent do these amendments reflect enduring principles, and to what extent do they reflect immediate political needs?

THIRTEENTH AMENDMENT (1865)

Section 1. Neither slavery nor involuntary servitude, except as a punishment for crime whereof the party shall have been duly convicted, shall exist within the United States, or any place subject to their jurisdiction.

Section 2. Congress shall have power to enforce this article by appropriate legislation.

FOURTEENTH AMENDMENT (1868)

Section 1. All persons born or naturalized in the United States, and subject to the jurisdiction thereof, are citizens of the United States and of the state wherein they reside. No state shall make or enforce any law which shall abridge the privileges or immunities of citizens of the United States; nor shall any state deprive any person of life, liberty, or property, without due process of law; nor deny to any person within its jurisdiction the equal protection of the laws.

Section 2. Representatives shall be apportioned among the several states according to their respective numbers, counting the whole number of persons in each state, excluding Indians not taxed. But when the right to vote at any election for the choice of electors for President and Vice President of the United States, Representatives in Congress, the executive and judicial officers of a state, or the members of the legislature thereof, is denied to any of the male inhabitants of such state, being twenty-one years of age, and citizens of the United States, or in any way abridged, except for participation in rebellion, or other crime, the basis of representation therein shall be reduced in the proportion which the number of such male citizens shall bear to the whole number of male citizens twenty-one years of age in such state.

Section 3. No person shall be a Senator or Representative in Congress, or elector of President and Vice President, or hold any office, civil or military, under the United States, or under any state, who, having previously taken an oath, as a member of Congress, or as an officer of the United States, or as a member of any state legislature, or as an executive or judicial officer of any state, to support the Constitution of the United States, shall have engaged in insurrection or rebellion against the same, or given aid or comfort to the enemies thereof. But Congress may by a vote of two-thirds of each House, remove such disability.

Section 4. The validity of the public debt of the United States, authorized by law, including debts incurred for payment of pensions and bounties for services in suppressing insurrection or rebellion, shall not be questioned. But neither the United States nor any state shall assume or pay any debt or obligation incurred in aid of insurrection or rebellion against the United States, or any claim for the loss or emancipation of any slave; but all such debts, obligations and claims shall be held illegal and void.

Section 5. The Congress shall have power to enforce, by appropriate legislation, the provisions of this article.

FIFTEENTH AMENDMENT (1870)

Section 1. The right of citizens of the United States to vote shall not be denied or abridged by the United States or by any state on account of race, color, or previous condition of servitude.

Section 2. The Congress shall have power to enforce this article by appropriate legislation.

FREDERICK DOUGLASS

ORATION IN MEMORY OF ABRAHAM LINCOLN (1876)

By the time of Civil War, Frederick Douglass was one of the most influential abolitionists, and probably the most famous African-American, in the United States. As the war progressed, he continued to press the government to take steps to advance black freedom, from rapid emancipation to the enlistment of black soldiers to the extension of suffrage. Like some Radicals in Congress, he was sometimes frustrated with what he saw as the slow pace of change being promoted by the Lincoln administration.

In April 1876, with the Grant administration coming to an end and the Democratic South returning to the Union, the Freedman's Memorial was unveiled in Washington, D.C. The funds for the memorial were raised from former slaves, and Douglass was asked to deliver the keynote address at its dedication. Douglass's speech gave a complex view of Lincoln from an explicitly African-American perspective, criticizing his tardiness in accomplishing the goal of ending slavery while celebrating the achievement itself.

Why does Douglass call Lincoln the "white man's president"? Is that fair? Was Lincoln antislavery enough? Does Douglass portray Lincoln as strategic about how he accomplished a consistent set of antislavery goals, or as shifting over time in his own commitments? How does Douglass's view of Lincoln as a white man's president relate to his assessment of the U.S. Constitution? Is it appropriate to criticize Lincoln for his willingness to return fugitive slaves? Does Lincoln's ultimate achievement suggest that politicians generally deserve the "latitude of time" to pursue their objectives? Is it the statesman's duty to consult public sentiment? Is there a higher duty to be "swift" and "radical" in pursuit of what the statesman thinks is right?

. . .

Few facts could better illustrate the vast and wonderful change which has taken place in our condition as a people than the fact of our assembling here for the purpose we have today. Harmless, beautiful, proper, and praiseworthy as this demonstration is, I cannot forget that no such demonstration would have been tolerated here twenty years ago. The spirit of slavery and barbarism, which still lingers to blight and destroy in some dark and distant parts of our country, would have made our assembling here the signal and excuse for opening upon us all the floodgates of wrath and violence. That we are here in peace today is a compliment and a credit to American civilization, and a prophecy of still greater national enlightenment and progress in the future. . . .

. . .

For the first time in the history of our people, and in the history of the whole American people, we join in this high worship, and march conspicuously in the line of this time-honored custom. First things are always interesting, and this is one of our first things. It is the first time that, in this form and manner, we have sought to do honor to an American great man, however deserving and illustrious. I commend the fact to notice; let it be told in every part of the Republic; let men of all parties and opinions hear it; let those who despise us, not less than those who respect us, know that now and here, in the spirit of liberty, loyalty, and gratitude . . . we, the colored people, newly emancipated and rejoicing in our blood-bought freedom, near the close of the first century in the life of this Republic, have now and here unveiled, set apart, and dedicated a monument of enduring granite and bronze, in every line, feature, and figure of which the men of this generation may read, and those of aftercoming generations may read, something of the exalted character and great works of Abraham Lincoln, the first martyr President of the United States.

. . . It must be admitted, truth compels me to admit, even here in the presence of the monument we have erected to his memory, Abraham Lincoln was not, in the fullest sense of the word, either our man or our model. In his interests, in his associations, in his habits of thought, and in his prejudices, he was a white man.

He was preeminently the white man's President, entirely devoted to the welfare of white men. He was ready and willing at any time during the first years of his administration to deny, postpone, and sacrifice the rights of humanity in the colored people to promote the welfare of the white people of this country. In all his education and feeling he was an American of the Americans. He came into the Presidential chair upon one principle alone, namely, opposition to the extension of slavery. His arguments in furtherance of this policy had their motive and mainspring in his patriotic devotion to the interests of his own race. To protect, defend, and perpetuate slavery in the states where it existed Abraham Lincoln was not less ready than any other President to draw the sword of the nation. He was ready to execute all the supposed guarantees of the United States Constitution in favor of the slave system anywhere inside the slave states. He was willing to pursue, recapture, and send back the fugitive slave to his master, and to suppress a slave rising for liberty, though his guilty master were already in arms against the Government. The race to which we belong were not the special objects of his consideration. Knowing this, I concede to you, my white fellow-citizens, a pre-eminence in this worship at once full and supreme. First, midst, and last, you and yours were the objects of his deepest affection and his most earnest solicitude. You are the children of Abraham Lincoln. We are at best only his step-children; children by adoption, children by forces of circumstances and necessity. To you it especially belongs to sound his praises, to preserve and perpetuate his memory, to multiply his statues, to hang his pictures high upon your walls, and commend his example, for to you he was a great and glorious friend and benefactor. Instead of supplanting you at his altar, we would exhort you to build high his monuments; let them be of the most costly material, of the most cunning workmanship; let their forms be symmetrical, beautiful, and perfect, let their bases be upon solid rocks, and their summits lean against the unchanging blue, overhanging sky, and let them endure forever! But while in the abundance of your wealth, and in the fullness of your just and patriotic devotion, you do all this, we entreat you to despise not the humble offering we this day unveil to view; for while Abraham Lincoln saved for you a country, he delivered us from a bondage, according to Jefferson, one hour of which was worse than ages of the oppression your fathers rose in rebellion to oppose.

. . .

When, therefore, it shall be asked what we have to do with the memory of Abraham Lincoln, or what Abraham Lincoln had to do with us, the answer is ready, full, and complete. Though he loved Caesar less than Rome, though the Union was more to him than our freedom or our future, under his wise and beneficent rule we saw ourselves gradually lifted from the depths of slavery to the heights of liberty and manhood; under his wise and beneficent rule, and by measures approved and vigorously pressed by him, we saw that the handwriting of ages, in the form of prejudice and proscription, was rapidly fading away from the face of our whole country; under his rule, and in due time, about as soon after all as the country could tolerate the strange spectacle, we saw our brave sons and brothers laying off the rags of bondage, and being clothed all over in the blue uniforms of the soldiers of the United States . . . under his rule, assisted by the greatest captain of our age, and his inspiration, we saw the Confederate States, based upon the idea that our race must be slaves, and slaves forever, battered to pieces and scattered to the four winds; under his rule, and in the fullness of time, we saw Abraham Lincoln, after giving the slave-holders three months' grace in which to save their hateful slave system, penning the immortal paper, which, though special in its language, was general in its principles and effect, making slavery forever impossible in the United States. Though we waited long, we saw all this and more.

. . .

I have said that President Lincoln was a white man, and shared the prejudices common to his countrymen towards the colored race. Looking back to his times and to the condition of his country, we are compelled to admit that this unfriendly feeling on his part may be safely set down as one element of his wonderful success in organizing the loyal American people for the tremendous conflict before them, and bringing them safely through that conflict. His great mission was to accomplish two things: first, to save his country from dismemberment and ruin; and, second, to free his country from the great crime of slavery. To do one or the other, or both, he must have the earnest sympathy and the powerful cooperation of his loyal fellow-countrymen. Without this primary and essential condition to success his efforts must have been vain and utterly fruitless. Had he put the abolition of slavery before the salvation of the Union, he would have inevitably driven from him a powerful class of the American people and rendered resistance to rebellion impossible. Viewed from the genuine abolition ground, Mr. Lincoln seemed tardy, cold, dull, and indifferent; but measuring him by the sentiment of his country, a sentiment he was bound as a statesman to consult, he was swift, zealous, radical, and determined.

. . .

Had Abraham Lincoln died from any of the numerous ills to which flesh is heir; had he reached that good old age of which his vigorous constitution and his temperate habits gave promise; had he been permitted to see the end of his great work; had the solemn curtain of death come down but gradually—we should still have been smitten with a heavy grief, and treasured his name lovingly. But dying as he did die, by the red hand of violence, killed, assassinated, taken off without warning, not because of personal hate—for no man who knew Abraham Lincoln could hate him—but because of his fidelity to union and liberty, he is doubly dear to us, and his memory will be precious forever.

. . .

Fellow-citizens, I end, as I began, with congratulations. We have done a good work for our race today. In doing honor to the memory of our friend and liberator, we have been doing highest honors to ourselves and those who come after us; we have been fastening ourselves to a name and fame imperishable and immortal; we have also been defending ourselves from a blighting scandal. When now it shall be said that the colored man is soulless, that he has no appreciation of benefits or benefactors; when the foul reproach of ingratitude is hurled at us, and it is attempted to scourge us beyond the range of human brotherhood, we may calmly point to the monument we have this day erected to the memory of Abraham Lincoln.

SUSAN B. ANTHONY

IS IT A CRIME FOR A CITIZEN OF THE UNITED STATES TO VOTE? (1873)

Susan B. Anthony was perhaps the leading feminist in the mid- to late nineteenth century. Born into an activist Quaker family from Massachusetts, she had been involved in the antislavery movement from her teens. In her early thirties, she met and started working closely with Elizabeth Cady Stanton and quickly became a leader of the National Women's Rights Convention, a series of feminist assemblies that succeeded the Seneca Falls Convention. But she continued to dedicate much of her energy to the antislavery cause in the 1850s. As the war came to a conclusion and the Thirteenth Amendment was passed, Anthony threw herself into the cause of female suffrage, helping to found several organizations that worked for "universal suffrage." In doing so, she split with some other abolitionists and some suffragists who argued that Reconstruction, and eventually the Fifteenth Amendment, should focus on the more critical problems of the former slaves. Her primary postbellum organization, the National Woman Suffrage Association, adopted a litigation strategy to force the recognition of a female right to vote that was already implicit in federal and state constitutions. Anthony was arrested in Rochester, New York, for illegally voting in the presidential election of 1872, and she launched a speaking tour to advance her case. In a well-publicized trial in federal court, she was convicted and fined $100, which she refused to pay. The excerpt is from a published version of the speech she gave in her pretrial tour of the state.

Is voting a natural right, or is it a right that "governments can give"? What reasons does Anthony offer for considering voting to be an inalienable right? What is the case for female suffrage if voting is not a natural right? Does she think that the people in the early republic made a mistake about the implications of their commitment to natural rights, or that they also tacitly accepted a right of female suffrage? Was a constitutional amendment needed to establish female suffrage? How does Anthony understand the requirements of the "consent of the governed"? How does that compare with Spooner? Is the fate of female suffrage tied to the interests of other groups in society, or do women have a unique interest in that cause? Was Anthony right to push for female suffrage during the Reconstruction debates, or was Frederick Douglass right to argue that there was not "the same urgency" to enfranchise women in the 1870s?

Friends and Fellow-citizens: I stand before you to-night, under indictment for the alleged crime of having voted at the last Presidential election, without having a lawful right to vote. It shall be my work this evening to prove to you that in thus voting, I not only committed no crime, but, instead, simply exercised my *citizen's right,* guaranteed to me and all United States citizens by the National Constitution, beyond the power of any State to deny.

Our democratic-republican government is based on the idea of the natural right of every individual member thereof to a voice and a vote in making and executing the laws. We assert the province of government to be to secure the people in the enjoyment of their unalienable rights. We throw to the winds the old dogma that governments can give rights. Before governments were organized, no one denies that each individual possessed the right to protect his own life, liberty and property. And when 100 or 1,000,000 people enter into a free government, they do not barter away their natural rights; they simply pledge themselves to protect each other in the enjoyment of them, through prescribed judicial and legislative tribunals. They agree to abandon the methods of brute force in the adjustment of their differences, and adopt those of civilization.

. . .

> "All men are created equal, and endowed by their Creator with certain unalienable rights. Among these are life, liberty and the pursuit of happiness. That to secure these, governments are instituted among men, deriving their just powers from the consent of the governed."

Here is no shadow of government authority over rights, nor exclusion of any from their full and equal enjoyment. Here is pronounced the right of all men, and "consequently," as the Quaker preacher said, "of all women," to a voice in the government. And here, in this very first paragraph of the declaration, is the assertion of the natural right of all to the ballot; for, how can "the consent of the governed" be given, if the right to vote be denied. Again:

> "That whenever any form of government becomes destructive of these ends, it is the right of the people to alter or abolish it, and to institute a new government, laying its foundations on such principles, and organizing its powers in such forms as to them shall seem most likely to effect their safety and happiness."

Surely, the right of the whole people to vote is here clearly implied. For however destructive in their happiness this government might become, a disfranchised class could neither alter nor abolish it, nor institute a new one, except by the old brute force method of insurrection and rebellion. One-half of the people of this nation to-day are utterly powerless to blot from the statute books an unjust law, or to write there a new and a just one. The women, dissatisfied as they are with this form of government, that enforces taxation without representation,—that compels them to obey laws to which they have never given their consent,—that imprisons and hangs them without a trial by a jury of their peers, that robs them, in marriage, of the custody of their own persons, wages and children,—are this half of the people left wholly at the mercy of the other half, in direct violation of the spirit and letter of the declarations of the framers of this government, every one of which was based on the immutable principle of equal rights to all. By those declarations, kings, priests, popes, aristocrats, were all alike dethroned, and placed on a common level politically, with the lowliest born subject or serf. By them, too, men, as such, were deprived of their divine right to rule, and placed on a political level with women. By the practice of those declarations all class and caste distinction will be abolished; and slave, serf, plebeian, wife, woman, all alike, bound from their subject position to the proud platform of equality.

The preamble of the federal constitution says: "We, the people of the United States . . ."

It was we, the people, not we, the white male citizens, nor yet we, the male citizens; but we, the whole people, who formed this Union. And we formed it, not to give the blessings or liberty, but to secure them; not to the half of ourselves and the half of our posterity, but to the whole people—women as well as men. And it is downright mockery to talk to women of their enjoyment of the blessings of liberty while they are denied the use of the only means of securing them provided by this democratic-republican government—the ballot.

. . .

Article 1 of the New York State Constitution says: "No member of this State shall be disfranchised or deprived of the rights or privileges secured to any citizen thereof, unless by the law of the land, or the judgement of his peers."

. . .

. . . New York can get no power from that source to disfranchise one entire half of her members. . . . Clearly, then, there is no constitutional ground for the exclusion of women from the ballot-box in the State of New York, No barriers whatever stand to-day between women and the exercise of their right to vote save those of precedent and prejudice.

. . .

. . . To [women], this government has no just powers derived from the consent of the governed. To them this government is not a democracy. It is not a republic. It is an odious aristocracy; a hateful obligarchy of sex. The most hateful aristocracy ever established on the face of the globe. An obligarchy of wealth, where the rich govern the poor; an obligarchy of learning, where the educated govern the ignorant; or even an obligarchy of race, where the Saxon rules the African, might be endured; but this obligarchy of sex, which makes father, brothers, husband, sons, the obligarchs over the mother and sisters, the wife and daughters of every household; which ordains all men sovereigns, all women subjects, carries dissension, discord and rebellion into every home of the nation. And this most odious aristocracy exists, too, in the face of Section 4, of Article 4, which says: "The United States shall guarantee to every State in the Union a republican form of government."

What, I ask you, is the distinctive difference between the inhabitants of a monarchical and those of a republican form of government, save that in the monarchical the people are subjects, helpless, powerless, bound to obey laws made by superiors—while in the republican, the people are citizens, individual sovereigns, all clothed with equal power, to make and unmake both their laws and law makers, and the moment you deprive a person of his right to a voice in the government, you degrade him from the status of a citizen of the republic, to that of a subject, and it matters very little to him whether his monarch be an individual tyrant, as is the Czar of Russia, or a 15,000,000 headed monster, as here in the United States; he is a powerless subject, serf or slave; not a free and independent citizen in any sense.

. . .

[W]hatever there was for a doubt, under the old regime, the adoption of the fourteenth amendment settled that question forever, in its first sentence: "All persons born or naturalized in the United States and subject to the jurisdiction thereof, are citizens of the United States and of the state wherein they reside."

. . .

The only question left to be settled, now, is: Are women persons? And I hardly believe any of our opponents will have the hardihood to say they are not. Being persons, then, women are citizens, and no state has a right to make any new law, or to enforce any old law, that shall abridge their privileges or immunities. Hence, every discrimination against women in the constitutions and laws of the several states, is to-day null and void, precisely as is every one against negroes.

Is the right to vote one of the privileges or immunities of citizens? I think the disfranchised ex-rebels, and the ex-state prisoners will agree with me, that it is not only one of them, but the one without which all the others are nothing. Seek the first kingdom of the ballot, and all things else shall be given thee, is the political injunction.

. . .

Associate Justice Washington, in defining the privileges and immunities of the citizen, more than fifty years ago, said: "they included all such privileges as were fundamental in their nature. And among them is the right to exercise the elective franchise, and to hold office."

. . .

. . . We all know that American citizenship, without addition or qualification, means the possession of equal rights, civil and political. We all know that the crowning glory of every citizen of the United States is, that he can either give or withhold his vote from every law and every legislator under the government.

. . .

If we once establish the false principle, that United States citizenship does not carry with it the right to vote in every state in this Union, there is no end to the petty freaks and cunning devices, that will be resorted to, to exclude one and another class of citizens from the right of suffrage.

It will not always be men combining to disfranchise all women; native born men combining to abridge the rights of all naturalized citizens, as in Rhode Island. It will not always be the rich and educated who may combine to cut off the poor and ignorant; but we may live to see the poor, hardworking, uncultivated day laborers, foreign and native born, learning the power of the ballot and their vast majority of numbers, combine and amend state constitutions so as to disfranchise the Vanderbilts and A. T. Stewarts, the Conklings and Fentons. It is poor rule that won't work more ways than one. Establish this precedent, admit the right to deny suffrage to the states, and there is no power to foresee the confusion, discord and disruption that may await us. There is, and can be, but one safe principle of government—equal rights to all. And any and every discrimination against any class, whether on account of color, race, nativity, sex, property, culture, can but embitter and disaffect that class, and thereby endanger the safety of the whole people.

Clearly, then, the national government must not only define the rights of citizens, but it must stretch out its powerful hand and protect them in every state in this Union.

. . .

I admit that prior to the rebellion, by common consent, the right to enslave, as well as to disfranchise both native and foreign born citizens, was conceded to the States. But the one grand principle, settled by the war and the reconstruction legislation, is the supremacy of national power to protect the citizens of the United States in their right to freedom and the elective franchise, against any and every interference on the part of the several States. And again and again, have the American people asserted the triumph of this principle, by their overwhelming majorities for Lincoln and Grant.

The one issue of the last two Presidential elections was, whether the fourteenth and fifteenth amendments should be considered the irrevocable will of the people; and the decision was, they shall be—and that it is only the right, but the duty of the National Government to protect all United States citizens in the full enjoyment and free exercise of all their privileges and immunities against any attempt of any State to deny or abridge.

. . .

We no longer petition Legislature or Congress to give us the right to vote. We appeal to the women everywhere to exercise their too long neglected "citizen's right to vote." We appeal to the inspectors of election everywhere to receive the votes of all United States citizens as it is their duty to do. We appeal to United States commissioners and marshals to arrest the inspectors who reject the names and votes of United States citizens, as it is their duty to do, and leave those alone who, like our eighth ward inspectors, perform their duties faithfully and well.

We ask the juries to fail to return verdicts of "guilty" against honest, law-abiding, tax-paying United States citizens for offering their votes at our elections. Or against intelligent, worthy young men, inspectors of elections, for receiving and counting such citizens votes.

We ask the judges to render true and unprejudiced opinions of the law, and wherever there is room for a doubt to give its benefit on the side of liberty and equal rights to women, remembering that "the true rule of interpretation under our national constitution, especially since its amendments, is that anything for human rights is constitutional, everything against human right unconstitutional."

And it is on this line that we propose to fight our battle for the ballot—all peaceably, but nevertheless persistently through to complete triumph, when all United States citizens shall be recognized as equals before the law.

V. POLITICAL ECONOMY

Major Developments

- Adoption of free-labor ideology
- Renewed emphasis on economic opportunity

Matters of political economy were, for the most part, chained to the war effort. The most crucial question facing both the North and the South was how to harness available financial and material resources so as to strengthen the army in the field. In the darkest days of the war, this overriding priority led Confederate officials to intrude onto the slave system itself and led Union officials to replace gold coin with legal tender. In the aftermath of war, economic policy similarly focused on unwinding the economic consequences of the conflict.

Nonetheless, some more enduring issues emerged. A key part of the Republican critique of slavery was based on the valorization of "free labor." The free-labor ideology explained the superiority of the northern way of life to the southern way of life, justified the abolition of slavery, and underwrote the emerging industrial economy. From this perspective, the crucial freedom that slaves lacked and that free men possessed was the liberty to contract and to benefit from the fruits of their own labor. Freedom from slavery meant freedom to work for wages, or to work for oneself. Government policy could offer positive support for free labor through a variety of means, including the provision of vocational education and cheap land for farming. Abraham Lincoln gave voice to the free-labor philosophy on a variety of occasions. Writing to a northern labor group, Lincoln declared that property "is a positive good in the world" because it was ultimately "the fruit of labor" and provided "encouragement to industry and enterprise." Working people and the "owners of property" shared the same interests, and the example of the wealthy "shows that others may become rich" in turn.[7]

The dynamic possibility of individual advancement and economic opportunity was often central to American ideals. The belief in a wide expanse of opportunity for those willing to do what was necessary to take advantage of it received new support after the war. The popular lecturer and writer Russell Conwell celebrated this vision, pointing to the "acres of diamonds" that lay within reach of those who could find ways to better serve their fellows. In these postwar years, the writer Horatio Alger struck gold of his own with his stories of poor youths finding middle-class success.

---

7 Abraham Lincoln, "Reply to a Committee from the Workingmen's Association (1864)," in *The Writings of Abraham Lincoln*, ed. Arthur Brooks Lapsley, vol. 7 (New York: Lamb Publishing, 1906), 110.

ABRAHAM LINCOLN

FIRST ANNUAL MESSAGE (1861)

In March 1861, Abraham Lincoln was inaugurated as the sixteenth president of the United States. A month earlier, Jefferson Davis was inaugurated as the first president of the Confederacy, and a month after Lincoln's assumption of office, shots were fired at Fort Sumter in Charleston, South Carolina, starting the Civil War. In December 1861, Lincoln delivered his first annual message to Congress. Lincoln had already communicated with Congress about the special circumstances of the secession crisis and war, and so the annual message merely provided a progress report on the war effort. The bulk of the message reviewed more routine foreign and domestic issues, concluding with some thoughts on capital and labor. There he echoed some themes that he had expressed in speeches around the country over the past few years. In those speeches, he often recalled his own time as a "penniless boy" and "hired laborer" as he celebrated the possibilities of free labor and upward mobility. As president, Lincoln was less personal but no less emphatic on the opportunities offered to the common worker in the northern system of free labor.

What does Lincoln mean by an effort to place "capital on an equal footing" with labor? What does he mean by "labor"? What economic activity or class does Lincoln most celebrate? How does he respond to Hammond's "mud-sill" argument? Does he deny that working conditions can be poor in the North? How important is upward mobility to his economic vision? Is his free-labor economic vision still relevant today?

In the midst of unprecedented political troubles we have cause of great gratitude to God for unusual good health and most abundant harvests.

. . .

[T]here is one point, with its connections, not so hackneyed as most others, to which I ask a brief attention. It is the effort to place capital on an equal footing with, if not above, labor in the structure of government. It is assumed that labor is available only in connection with capital; that nobody labors unless somebody else, owning capital, somehow by the use of it induces him to labor. This assumed, it is next considered whether it is best that capital shall hire laborers, and thus induce them to work by their own consent, or buy them and drive them to it without their consent. Having proceeded so far, it is naturally concluded that all laborers are either hired laborers or what we call slaves. And further, it is assumed that whoever is once a hired laborer is fixed in that condition for life.

Now there is no such relation between capital and labor as assumed, nor is there any such thing as a free man being fixed for life in the condition of a hired laborer. Both these assumptions are false, and all inferences from them are groundless.

Labor is prior to and independent of capital. Capital is only the fruit of labor, and could never have existed if labor had not first existed. Labor is the superior of capital, and deserves much the higher consideration. Capital has its rights, which are as worthy of protection as any other rights. Nor is it denied that there is, and probably always will be, a relation between labor and capital producing mutual benefits. The error is in assuming that the whole labor of community exists within that relation. A few men own capital, and that few avoid labor themselves, and with their capital hire or buy another few to labor for them. A large majority belong to neither class—neither work for others nor have others working for them. In most of the Southern States a majority of the whole people of all colors are neither slaves nor masters, while in the Northern a large majority are neither hirers nor hired. Men, with their families—wives, sons, and daughters—work for themselves on their farms, in their houses, and in their shops, taking the whole product to themselves, and asking no favors of capital on the one hand nor of hired laborers or slaves on the other. It is not forgotten that a considerable number of persons mingle their own labor with capital; that is, they labor with their own hands and also buy or hire others to labor for them; but this is only a mixed and not a distinct class. No principle stated is disturbed by the existence of this mixed class.

Again, as has already been said, there is not of necessity any such thing as the free hired laborer being fixed to that condition for life. Many independent men everywhere in these States a few years back in their lives were hired laborers. The prudent, penniless beginner in the world labors for wages awhile, saves a surplus with which to buy tools or land for himself, then labors on his own account another while, and at length hires another new beginner to help him. This is the just and generous and prosperous system which opens the way to all, gives hope to all, and consequent energy and progress and improvement of condition to all. No men living are more worthy to be trusted than those who toil up from poverty; none less inclined to take or touch aught which they have not honestly earned. Let them beware of surrendering a political power which they already possess, and which if surrendered will surely be used to close the door of advancement against such as they and to fix new disabilities and burdens upon them till all of liberty shall be lost.

. . .

RUSSELL H. CONWELL

ACRES OF DIAMONDS (1870)

Russell H. Conwell grew up on a farm in Massachusetts. After serving in the Union army during the Civil War, he trained as a lawyer, eventually was ordained as a Baptist minister in Philadelphia, and from that post founded what became Temple University. He achieved his wealth and fame, however, as a public lecturer and popular writer. His most popular lecture was called "Acres of Diamonds." He traveled the world delivering versions of the speech for two decades, finally publishing it in 1890. He was, in essence, what we would call today a motivational speaker, and his Acres of Diamonds speech was designed to justify and encourage the common man to pursue a path of wealth. He began the lecture with a tale of two Arabs who sought their fortune (the "acres of diamonds"). One died penniless after traveling the world in a vain search for easy money, looking for the place where "you will always find diamonds." The other became rich by remaining at home and pursuing wealth in "his own wheat-fields." Conwell contended that too many thought that pursuing wealth was immoral or required something distant and unobtainable. His message was that "every man has the opportunity to make more of himself" by taking full advantage of his own environment and his own skill, and ultimately "you can measure the good you have done [by what is] paid you." The heroes of his stories were inventors and entrepreneurs.

Does Conwell think that opportunities are found or made? Does he portray America as an exceptional land of opportunity? What does he think causes poverty? In what way does he think that getting rich is a "godly duty"? In what way does he think being poor is immoral? How does his advice on the pursuit of wealth compare to Benjamin Franklin's? What are the political implications of his message?

. . .

I say again that the opportunity to get rich, to attain unto great wealth, is here in Philadelphia now, within the reach of almost every man and woman who hears me speak to-night, and I mean just what I say. I have not come to this platform even under these circumstances to recite something to you. I have come to tell you what in God's sight I believe to be the truth, and if the years of life have been of any value to me in the attainment of common sense, I know I am right; that the men and women sitting here, who found it difficult perhaps to buy a ticket to this lecture or gathering to-night, have within their reach "acres of diamonds," opportunities to get largely wealthy. There never was a place on earth more adapted than the city of Philadelphia to-day, and never in the history of the world did a poor man without capital have such an opportunity to get rich quickly and honestly as he has now in our city. . . .

I say that you ought to get rich, and it is your duty to get rich. How many of my pious brethren say to me, "Do you, a Christian minister, spend your time going up and down the country advising young people to get rich, to get money?" "Yes, of course I do." They say, "Isn't that awful! Why don't you preach the gospel instead of preaching about man's making money?" "Because to make money honestly is to preach the gospel." That is the reason. The men who get rich may be the most honest men you find in the community.

"Oh," but says some young man here to-night, "I have been told all my life that if a person has money he is very dishonest and dishonorable and mean and contemptible." My friend that is the reason why you have none, because you have that idea of people. The foundation of your faith is altogether false. Let me say here clearly, and say it briefly, though subject to discussion which I have not time for here, ninety-eight out of one hundred of the rich men of America are honest. That is why they are rich. That is why they are trusted with money. That is why they carry on great enterprises and find plenty of people to work with them. It is because they are honest men.

. . .

Money is power, and you ought to be reasonably ambitious to have it. You ought because you can do more good with it than you could without it. Money printed your Bible, money builds your churches, money sends your missionaries, and money pays your preachers, and you would not have many of them, either, if you did not pay them. I am always willing that my church should raise my salary, because the church that pays the largest salary always raises it the easiest. You never knew an exception to it in your life. The man who gets the largest salary can do the most good with the power that is furnished to him. Of course he can if his spirit be right to use it for what it is given to him.

I say, then, you ought to have money. If you can honestly attain unto riches in Philadelphia, it is your Christian and godly duty to do so. It is an awful mistake of these pious people to think you must be awfully poor in order to be pious.

. . . While we should sympathize with God's poor—that is, those who cannot help themselves—let us remember there is not a poor person in the United States who was not made poor by his own shortcomings, or by the shortcomings of someone else. It is all wrong to be poor, anyhow. Let us give in to that argument and pass that to one side.

. . .

. . . "The love of money is the root of all evil." He who tries to attain unto it too quickly, or dishonestly, will fall into many snares, no doubt about that. The love of money. What is that? It is making an idol of money, and idolatry pure and simple everywhere is condemned by the Holy Scriptures and by man's common sense. The man that worships the dollar instead of thinking of the purposes for which it ought to be used, the man who idolizes simply money, the miser that hordes his money in the cellar, or hides it in his stocking, or refuses to invest it where it will do the world good, that man who hugs the dollar until the eagle squeals has in him the root of all evil.

. . . . "A man has no right to keep a store in Philadelphia twenty years and not make at least five hundred thousand dollars even though it be a corner grocery up-town." You say, "You cannot make five thousand dollars in a store now." Oh, my friends, if you will just take only four blocks around you, and find out what the people want and what you ought to supply and set them down with your pencil and figure up the profits you would make if you did supply them, you would very soon see it. There is wealth right within the sound of your voice.

. . .

The statistics of Massachusetts showed that not one rich man's son out of seventeen ever dies rich. I pity the rich man's sons unless they have the good sense of the elder Vanderbilt, which sometimes happens. He went to his father and said, "Did you earn all your money?" "I did, my son. I began to work on a ferry-boat for twenty-five cents a day." "Then," said his son, "I will have none of your money," and he, too, tried to get employment on a ferry-boat that Saturday night. He could not get one there, but he did get a place for three dollars a week. Of course, if a rich man's son will do that, he will get the discipline of a poor boy that is worth more than a university education to any man. He would then be able to take care of the millions of his father. But as a rule the rich men will not let their sons do the very thing that made them great. As a rule, the rich man will not allow his son to work—and his mother! Why, she would think it was a social disgrace if her poor, weak, little lily-fingered, sissy sort of a boy had to earn his living with honest toil. I have no pity for such rich men's sons.

. . .

. . . Greatness consists not in the holding of some future office, but really consists in doing great deeds with little means and the accomplishment of vast purposes from the private ranks of life. To be great at all one must be great here, now, in Philadelphia. He who can give to this city better streets and better sidewalks, better schools and more colleges, more happiness and more civilization, more of God, he will be great anywhere. Let every man or woman here, if you never hear me again, remember this, that if you wish to be great at all, you must begin where you are and what you are, in Philadelphia, now. He that can give to his city any blessing, he who can be a good citizen while he lives here, he that can make better homes, he that can be a blessing whether he works in the shop or sits behind the counter or keeps house, whatever be his life, he who would be great anywhere must first be great in his own Philadelphia.

VI. AMERICA AND THE WORLD

Major Developments

- Struggle to maintain territorial integrity of the Union
- Diplomatic effort to preserve European neutrality in Civil War
- Pacification of Great Plains Indian tribes

The central geostrategic crisis for the United States during these years was the fate of the territorial integrity of the Union and whether the southern states would become a separate nation. Despite predictions to the contrary by advocates of secession, the effort to withdraw from the Union quickly degenerated into armed conflict. Predictions that any fighting would be brief were likewise proven false. Instead the nation mobilized for war as it had never done before. Throughout the war, Lincoln was dogged by doubts about the war. He repeatedly sought to justify the federal government's use of force against the southern states, starting with his Fourth of July Message to Congress in 1861, explaining the necessity of preserving the territorial integrity of the nation and the ultimate value of the Union to freedom.

Less pressing than events in the South were events in the West. Over the course of the 1860s, small conflicts with various Native American tribes had erupted along the western frontier. In 1867, Congress established the Indian Peace Commission to try to establish a sustainable peace with the Plains Indians. The Commission issued reports that were deeply critical of federal government actions in the region, which they contended had helped provoke violent uprisings. Having admitted to bad behavior in the past, the commissioners were able to negotiate a series of treaties that moved tribes to Indian Territory in modern Oklahoma, opening more of the Midwest to American settlement. At the same time, many Union army leaders were reassigned to the western frontier after the Civil War. General William T. Sherman, who had helped seal Northern victory with his march on Atlanta, reflected the view of many in the military in telling his brother, "All who cling to their old hunting grounds are hostile and will remain so till killed off." Peace would only come when the Native Americans accepted the reservations that had been provided for them (and Congress provided sufficient enticements to persuade the tribes to accept those terms) and the remaining resistance was "clean[ed] out" through scattered skirmishes.[8]

---

8 William T. Sherman, *The Sherman Letters*, ed. Rachel Sherman Thorndike (New York: Charles Scribner's Sons, 1894), 321.

ABRAHAM LINCOLN

FOURTH OF JULY MESSAGE TO CONGRESS (1861)

The Civil War began while Congress was out of session. In the nineteenth century, Congress was out of session for long stretches, but the Constitution empowers the president to call Congress into special session "on extraordinary occasions." Shortly after the battle of Fort Sumter, Lincoln issued a call for Congress to convene in special session on July 4, 1861. When the legislators arrived in Washington, D.C., Lincoln sent them a special message on the state of war and called upon them to support presidential actions with new legislation. The message also justified the actions that the president had already unilaterally taken and outlined his rejection of any right of secession.

Does Lincoln regard the situation with the Confederate States of America to be a foreign policy problem? Does he regard himself as fighting a war? What authority to act does he claim for the president? What does he suggest is the place of liberty in wartime? Does Lincoln provide a response to Spooner's argument in favor of a right of secession? What does he identify as the goals of the war? Does he leave room for a negotiated peace? Is democracy threatened by a right of secession? Would American national security have been threatened if the South had been able to peacefully secede and establish a separate nation?

. . .

At the beginning of the present Presidential term, four months ago, the functions of the Federal Government were found to be generally suspended within the several States of South Carolina, Georgia, Alabama, Mississippi, Louisiana, and Florida, excepting only those of the Post-Office Department.

. . .

. . . Simultaneously and in connection with all this the purpose to sever the Federal Union was openly avowed. In accordance with this purpose, an ordinance had been adopted in each of these States declaring the States respectively to be separated from the National Union. A formula for instituting a combined government of these States had been promulgated, and this illegal organization, in the character of Confederate States, was already invoking recognition, aid, and intervention from foreign powers.

. . .

. . . In this act [the firing on Fort Sumter], discarding all else, they have forced upon the country the distinct issue, "Immediate dissolution or blood."

And this issue embraces more than the fate of these United States. It presents to the whole family of man the question whether a constitutional republic, or democracy—a government of the people by the same people—can or cannot maintain its territorial integrity against its own domestic foes. It presents the question whether discontented individuals, too few in numbers to control administration according to organic law in any case, can always, upon the pretenses made in this case, or on any other pretenses, or arbitrarily without any pretense, break up their government, and thus practically put an end to free government upon the earth. It forces us to ask, Is there in all republics this inherent and fatal weakness? Must a government of necessity be too *strong* for the liberties of its own people, or too *weak* to maintain its own existence?

So viewing the issue, no choice was left but to call out the war power of the Government and so to resist force employed for its destruction by force for its preservation.

. . .

The forbearance of this Government had been so extraordinary and so long continued as to lead some foreign nations to shape their action as if they supposed the early destruction of our National Union was probable. While this on discovery gave the Executive some concern, he is now happy to say that the sovereignty and rights of the United States are now everywhere practically respected by foreign powers, and a general sympathy with the country is manifested throughout the world.

. . .

It is now recommended that you give the legal means for making this contest a short and a decisive one. . . .

A right result at this time will be worth more to the world than ten times the men and ten times the money. . . .

It might seem at first thought to be of little difference whether the present movement at the South be called "secession" or "rebellion." The movers, however, well understand the difference. At the beginning they knew they could never raise their treason to any respectable magnitude by any name which implies *violation* of law. They knew their people possessed as much of moral sense, as much of devotion to law and order, and as much pride in and reverence for the history and Government of their common country as any other civilized and patriotic people. They knew they could make no advancement directly in the teeth of these strong and noble sentiments. Accordingly, they commenced by an insidious debauching of the public mind. They invented an ingenious sophism, which, if conceded, was followed by perfectly logical steps through all the incidents to the complete destruction of the Union. The sophism itself is that any State of the Union may *consistently* with the National Constitution, and therefore *lawfully* and *peacefully*, withdraw from the Union without the consent of the Union or of any other State. The little disguise that the supposed right is to be exercised only for just cause, themselves to be the sole judge of its justice, is too thin to merit any notice.

With rebellion thus sugar coated they have been drugging the public mind of their section for more than thirty years, and until at length they have brought many good men to a willingness to take up arms against the Government the day *after* some assemblage of men have enacted the farcical pretense of taking their State out of the Union who could have been brought to no such thing the day *before*.

This sophism derives much, perhaps the whole, of its currency from the assumption that there is some omnipotent and sacred supremacy pertaining to a *State—to* each State of our Federal Union. Our States have neither more nor less power than that reserved to them in the Union by the Constitution, no one of them ever having been a State out of the Union. The original ones passed into the Union even *before* they cast off their British colonial dependence, and the new ones each came into the Union directly from a condition of dependence, excepting Texas; and even Texas, in its temporary independence, was never designated a State. The new ones only took the designation of States on coming into the Union, while that name was first adopted for the old ones in and by the Declaration of Independence. Therein the "United Colonies" were declared to be "free and independent States;" but even then the object plainly was not to declare their independence of *one another* or of the *Union*, but directly the contrary, as their mutual pledge and their mutual action before, at the time, and afterwards abundantly show. The express plighting of faith by each and all of the original thirteen in the Articles of Confederation, two years later, that the Union shall be perpetual is most conclusive. Having never been States, either in substance or in name, *outside* of the Union, whence this magical omnipotence of "State rights," asserting a claim of power to lawfully destroy the Union itself? Much is said about the "sovereignty" of the States, but the word even is not in the National Constitution, nor, as is believed, in any of the State constitutions. What is a "sovereignty" in the political sense of the term? Would it be far wrong to define it "a political community without a political superior"? Tested by this, no one of our States, except Texas, ever was a sovereignty; and even Texas gave up the character on coming into the Union, by which act she acknowledged the Constitution of the United States and the laws and treaties of the United States made in pursuance of the Constitution to be for her the supreme law of the land. The States have their status in the Union, and they have no other legal status. If they break from this, they can only do so against law and by revolution. The Union, and not themselves separately, procured their independence and their liberty. By conquest or purchase the Union gave each of them whatever of independence and liberty it has. The Union is older than any of the States, and, in fact, it created them as States. Originally some dependent colonies made the Union, and in turn the Union threw off their old dependence for them and made them States, such as they are. Not one of them ever had a State constitution independent of the Union. Of course it is not forgotten that all the new States framed their constitutions before they entered the Union, nevertheless dependent upon and preparatory to coming into the Union.

Unquestionably the States have the powers and rights reserved to them in and by the National Constitution; but among these surely are not included all conceivable powers, however mischievous or destructive, but at most such only as were known in the world at the time as governmental powers; and certainly a power to destroy the Government itself had never been known as a governmental—as a merely administrative power. This relative matter of national power and State rights, as a principle, is no other than the principle of *generality* and *locality*. Whatever concerns the whole should be confided to the whole—to the General Government—while whatever concerns *only* the State should be left exclusively to the State. This is all there is of original principle about it. Whether the National Constitution in defining boundaries between the two has applied the principle with exact accuracy is not to be questioned. We are all bound by that defining without question.

What is now combated is the position that secession is consistent with the Constitution—is *lawful* and *peaceful*. It is not contended that there is any express law for it, and nothing should ever be implied as law which leads to unjust or absurd consequences. The nation purchased with money the countries out of which several of these States were formed. Is it just that they shall go off without leave and without refunding? The nation paid very large sums (in the aggregate, I believe, nearly a hundred millions) to relieve Florida of the aboriginal tribes. Is it just that she shall now be off without consent or without making any return? The nation is now in debt for money applied to the benefit of these so-called seceding States in common with the rest. Is it just either that creditors shall go unpaid or the remaining States pay the whole? A part of the present national debt was contracted to pay the old debts of Texas. Is it just that she shall leave and pay no part of this herself?

Again: If one State may secede, so may another; and when all shall have seceded none is left to pay the debts. Is this quite just to creditors? Did we notify them of this sage view of ours when we borrowed their money? If we now recognize this doctrine by allowing the seceders to go in peace, it is difficult to see what we can do if others choose to go or to extort terms upon which they will promise to remain.

The seceders insist that our Constitution admits of secession. They have assumed to make a national constitution of their own, in which of necessity they have either *discarded* or *retained* the right of secession, as they insist it exists in ours. If they have discarded it, they thereby admit that on principle it ought not to be in ours. If they have retained it, by their own construction of ours they show that to be consistent they must secede from one another whenever they shall find it the easiest way of settling their debts or effecting any other selfish or unjust object. The principle itself is one of disintegration, and upon which no government can possibly endure.

If all the States save one should assert the power to drive that one out of the Union, it is presumed the whole class of seceder politicians would at once deny the power and denounce the act as the greatest outrage upon State rights. But suppose that precisely the same act, instead of being called "driving the one out," should be called "the seceding of the others from that one," it would be exactly what the seceders claim to do, unless, indeed, they make the point that the one, because it is a minority, may rightfully do what the others, because they are a majority, may not rightfully do. These politicians are subtle and profound on the rights of minorities. They are not partial to that power which made the Constitution and speaks from the preamble, calling itself "we, the people."

It may well be questioned whether there is to-day a majority of the legally qualified voters of any State, except, perhaps, South Carolina, in favor of disunion. There is much reason to believe that the Union men are the majority in many, if not in every other one, of the so-called seceded States. . . .

It may be affirmed without extravagance that the free institutions we enjoy have developed the powers and improved the condition of our whole people beyond any example in the world. . . . Whoever in any section proposes to abandon such a government would do well to consider in deference to what principle it is that he does it; what better he is likely to get in its stead; whether the substitute will give, or be intended to give, so much of good to the people. There are some foreshadowings on this subject. Our adversaries have adopted some declarations of independence in which, unlike the good old one penned by Jefferson, they omit the words "all men are created equal." Why? They have adopted a temporary national constitution, in the preamble of which, unlike our good old one signed by Washington, they omit "We, the people," and substitute "We, the deputies of the sovereign and independent States." Why? Why this deliberate pressing out of view the rights of men and the authority of the people?

This is essentially a people's contest. On the side of the Union it is a struggle for maintaining in the world that form and substance of government whose leading object is to elevate the condition of men; to lift artificial weights from all shoulders; to clear the paths of laudable pursuit for all; to afford all an unfettered start and a fair chance in the race of life. Yielding to partial and temporary departures, from necessity, this is the leading object of the Government for whose existence we contend.

. . .

Our popular Government has often been called an experiment. Two points in it our people have already settled—the successful establishing and the successful *administering* of it. One still remains—its successful *maintenance* against a formidable internal attempt to overthrow it. It is now for them to demonstrate to the world that those who can fairly carry an election can also suppress a rebellion; that ballots are the rightful and peaceful successors of bullets, and that when ballots have fairly and constitutionally decided there can be no successful appeal back to bullets; that there can be no successful appeal except to ballots themselves at succeeding elections. Such will be a great lesson of peace, teaching men that what they cannot take by an election neither can they take it by a war; teaching all the folly of being the beginners of a war.

Lest there be some uneasiness in the minds of candid men as to what is to be the course of the Government toward the Southern States *after* the rebellion shall have been suppressed, the Executive deems it proper to say it will be his purpose then, as ever, to be guided by the Constitution and the laws, and that he probably will have no different understanding of the powers and duties of the Federal Government relatively to the rights of the States and the people under the Constitution than that expressed in the inaugural address.

. . .

The Constitution provides, and all the States have accepted the provision, that "the United States shall guarantee to every State in this Union a republican form of government." But if a State may lawfully go out of the Union, having done so it may also discard the republican form of government; so that to prevent its going out is an indispensable *means* to the *end* of maintaining the guaranty mentioned; and when an end is lawful and obligatory the indispensable means to it are also lawful and obligatory.

It was with the deepest regret that the Executive found the duty of employing the war power in defense of the Government forced upon him. He could but perform this duty or surrender the existence of the Government. No compromise by public servants could in this case be a cure; not that compromises are not often proper, but that no popular government can long survive a marked precedent that those who carry an election can only save the government from immediate destruction by giving up the main point upon which the people gave the election. The people themselves, and not their servants, can safely reverse their own deliberate decisions.

As a private citizen the Executive could not have consented that these institutions shall perish; much less could he in betrayal of so vast and so sacred a trust as these free people had confided to him. He felt that he had no moral right to shrink, nor even to count the chances of his own life in what might follow. In full view of his great responsibility he has so far done what he has deemed his duty. You will now, according to your own judgment, perform yours. He sincerely hopes that your views and your action may so accord with his as to assure all faithful citizens who have been disturbed in their rights of a certain and speedy restoration to them under the Constitution and the laws.

And having thus chosen our course, without guile and with pure purpose, let us renew our trust in God and go forward without fear and with manly hearts.

ABRAHAM LINCOLN

LETTER TO JAMES C. CONKLING (1863)

For many years, Abraham Lincoln's wartime letter to James C. Conkling was regarded as one of his most important works. In the summer of 1863, the war had become a quagmire, absorbing men and treasure with few clear results to show for it. The Emancipation Proclamation that had been issued at the beginning of the year polarized northern opinion. A military draft had been introduced and had been met with rioting in the streets. Peace protests broke out throughout the North, and Republicans were going down in federal, state, and local elections. To try to shore up public support for the administration, Lincoln's close associates in his home state organized a mass rally of "unconditional Union men" to be held at Springfield, Illinois, on September 3. Lincoln was invited to attend but in the end was only able to send a letter to James C. Conkling, the chief organizer of the event. The letter was to be "read slowly" by Conkling to the huge assembled crowd, and it was published in newspapers throughout the country (a jumbled version was in fact printed early). Many Republicans thought that the letter secured for Lincoln the party nomination for a second term and helped put the opponents to the war on the defensive.

Who is Lincoln addressing as "you" in the letter? How does he characterize the goal of the war? Why does Lincoln claim that a negotiated peace is not possible? Are "refugees from the South" the relevant party with which to open negotiations? How does he defend emancipation? What vision of postbellum society does he offer? Is the Reconstruction that followed the war consistent with what Lincoln says here?

. . .

There are those who are dissatisfied with me. To such I would say: You desire peace, and you blame me that we do not have it. But how can we obtain it? There are but three conceivable ways: *First*—to suppress the rebellion by force of arms. This I am trying to do. Are you for it? If you are, so far we are agreed. If you are not for it, a *second* way is to give up the Union. I am against this. Are you for it? If you are you should say so plainly. If you are not for force nor yet for dissolution, there only remains some imaginable compromise.

I do not believe that any compromise embracing the maintenance of the Union is now possible. All that I learn leads to a directly opposite belief. The strength of the rebellion is its military, its army. That army dominates all the country and all the people within its range. Any offer of terms made by any man or men within that range, in opposition to that army, is simply nothing for the present; because such man or men have no power whatever to enforce their side of a compromise, if one were made with them.

To illustrate: Suppose refugees from the South and peace men of the North get together in convention, and frame and proclaim a compromise embracing a restoration of the Union. In what way can that compromise be made to keep Lee's army out of Pennsylvania? Meade's army can keep Lee's army out of Pennsylvania, and, I think can ultimately drive it out of existence. But no paper compromise to which the controllers of Lee's army are not agreed can at all affect that army. . . .

A compromise, to be effective, must be made either with those who control the rebel army, or with the people, first liberated from the domination of that army by the success of our own army. Now allow me to assure you that no word or intimation from that rebel army, or from any peace compromise, has ever come to my knowledge or belief. All charges and insinuations to the contrary are deceptive and groundless. . . . I freely acknowledge myself to be the servant of the people, according to the bond of service, the United States Constitution, and that, as such, I am responsible to them.

But, to be plain: You are dissatisfied with me about the negro. Quite likely there is a difference of opinion between you and myself upon that subject. I certainly wish that all men could be free, while you,

I suppose, do not. Yet, I have neither adopted nor proposed any measure which is not consistent with even your view, provided you are for the Union. I suggested compensated emancipation; to which you replied you wished not to be taxed to buy negroes. But I had not asked you to be taxed to buy negroes, except in such way as to save you from greater taxation to save the Union exclusively by other means.

You dislike the Emancipation Proclamation, and perhaps would have it retracted. You say it is unconstitutional. I think differently. I think the Constitution invests its commander-in-chief with the law of war in time of war. The most that can be said, if so much, is, that slaves are property. Is there, has there ever been, any question that by the law of war, property, both of enemies and friends, may be taken when needed? And is it not needed whenever it helps us and hurts the enemy? Armies, the world over, destroy enemies' property when they cannot use it, and even destroy their own to keep it from the enemy. Civilized belligerents do all in their power to help themselves or hurt the enemy, except a few things regarded as barbarous or cruel. Among the exceptions are the massacre of vanquished foes and non-combatants, male and female.

. . .

I know, as fully as one can know the opinions of others, that some of the commanders of our armies in the field, who have given us our most important victories, believe the emancipation policy and the use of colored troops constitute the heaviest blows yet dealt to the rebellion, and that at least one of those important successes could not have been achieved when it was but for the aid of black soldiers.

Among the commanders who hold these views are some who have never had any affinity with what is called "Abolitionism," or with "Republican party politics," but who hold them purely as military opinions. . . .

You say that you will not fight to free negroes. Some of them seem willing to fight for you; but no matter. Fight you, then, exclusively to save the Union. I issued the proclamation on purpose to aid you in saving the Union. Whenever you shall have conquered all resistance to the Union, if I shall urge you to continue fighting, it will be an apt time then for you to declare you will fight to free negroes. . . . But negroes, like other people, act upon motives. Why should they do anything for us if we will do nothing for them? If they stake their lives for us they must be prompted by the strongest motive, even the promise of freedom. And the promise, being made, must be kept.

. . .

Peace does not appear so distant as it did. I hope it will come soon, and come to stay, and so come as to be worth the keeping in all future time. It will then have been proved that among freemen there can be no successful appeal from the ballot to the bullet, and that they who take such appeal are sure to lose their case and pay the cost. And there will be some black men who can remember that with silent tongue, and clinched teeth, and steady eye, and well-poised bayonet, they have helped mankind on to this great consummation; while I fear there will be some white ones unable to forget that with malignant heart and deceitful speech they have striven to hinder it.

. . .

CHIEF SPOTTED TAIL

SPEECH TO THE SIOUX COMMISSIONERS (1876)

In 1874, General Armstrong Custer led an expedition into the Dakotas to investigate claims that gold had been discovered there. Custer did not discover much, but rumors of gold sparked a rush of white migration to the Black Hills, which paid particular dividends when a significant vein of gold was soon discovered there. In 1876, a commission was appointed to negotiate a modification of the existing treaties with the local Native American tribes and the concession of land in the Black Hills to the U.S. government. For some tribes, this would mean a significant relocation, and the government preferred that "Indian Territory" (future Oklahoma) be the destination. As the commissioner reported to the Secretary of Interior, the Indian Territory's "soil and climate are incomparably superior to those of the Dakota reservation. . . . There would seem to be scarcely a question that, if it is the purpose of the Government to undertake in earnest the civilization of the Sioux, the true policy is to locate them as rapidly as possible . . . where the conditions are the most favorable for rapid progress in the peaceful arts of agriculture and stock-raising." The negotiations with the Sioux were largely successful, winning concessions on the land in the Dakotas in exchange for new land elsewhere and subsistence provisions "until such time as they shall become self-supporting." The agreement with the Sioux would, however, require further negotiation with the Cherokees, who would need to be persuaded to give up land then lying in "an uprofitable and unimproved waste" in order to make room for the Sioux in the Indian Territory.[9]

Did the American government violate the spirit of its earlier treaties with the Sioux by seeking to renegotiate terms sooner than the fifty or thirty-five years agreed to earlier? How long should such treaties last? Why did these treaties provide for ongoing economic support for the Sioux? Is Chief Spotted Tail successful in arguing that the Sioux and the Americans were motivated by similar concerns and interests? Do the Sioux and the Americans have the same understanding of the value of land?

. . . I have considered the matter of these messages and words sent out by the Great Father to me. This is the fifth time that you have come. At the time of the first treaty that was made on Horse Creek—the one we call the "great treaty"—there was provision made to borrow the overland road of the Indians, and promises were made at the time of the treaty, though I was a boy at the time; they told me it was to last fifty years. These promises have not been kept. All the Dakotas that lived in this country were promised these things together at that time. All the words have proved to be false.

The next conference was the one held with General Maydear, where there was no promises made in particular, nor for any amount to be given us, but we had a conference with him and made friends and shook hands. Then after that there was a treaty made by General Sherman, General Sanborn, and General Harney. At that time the general told us we should have annuities and goods from that treaty for thirty-five years. He said this, but yet he didn't tell the truth. At that time General Sherman told me the country was mine, and that I should select any place I wished for my reservation and live in it. I told the general I would take the land from the headwaters of the White River to the Missouri, and he assented to it. My friends, I will show you well his words today. When he promised us we should have annuities for thirty-five years he told us there should be an issue of goods in the spring when the grass began to grow, and also another issue of goods every fall. He said we should raise cattle; that they would give us cows to raise

9 *Message from the President of the United States, Communicating the Report and Journal of Proceedings of the Commission Appointed to Obtain Certain Concessions from the Sioux Indians*, U.S. Senate, 44th Cong., 2nd Sess., Ex. Doc. No. 9 (1876), 3.

cattle with, and mares to raise horses with, and that they would give us yokes of oxen to haul logs with; that they would give us large wagons to haul goods with, in order that we might earn money in that way. He said also there should be issues of such things as we needed to learn the arts with, besides that there should be money given to everyone. . . . [B]ut it was not true.

When these promises failed to be carried out, I went myself to see the Great Father. . . . The Great Father told me to go home, to select any place in my country I choose, and to go there and live with my people. I came home and selected this place to move here and settle. Then persons came to me, after I had settled, and said I must move from this place, and I came back here again and located the agency. You told me to come here and locate the agency. . . . You gave me some very small cows, some very bad cattle, and some old wagons that were worn out.

Again: you came last summer to talk about the country, and we said we would consider the matter; we said we would leave the matter to the Great Father for settlement. In answer to that reply of ours, he has sent you out this summer. You have now come to visit our land, and we now ask you how many years there are for us to live! My friends, you that sit before me are traders and merchants. You have come here to trade. You have not come here to turn anything out the way without payment for it. When a man has a possession he values, and another party comes to buy it, he brings with him such good things as the people that own it desire to have. My friends, your people have both intellect and hearts. You use these to consider in what way you had best live. My people, who are here before you today, are precisely the same. If you have much of anything you use it for your own benefit and in order that your children shall have food and clothing, and my people are also the same. . . . [T]hey also live upon the earth and upon the things that come to them from above. We have the same thoughts and desires in that respect that white people have. The people that you see before you are not men of a different country, but this is their country, where they were born and where they have acquired all their property; their children, their horses, and other property were all raised here in this country. You have come here to buy this country of ours, and it would be well if you came with the things your propose to give us—the good price you propose to pay for it in your hands, so we could see the price you propose to pay for it, then our hearts would be glad.

My people have grown up together with these white men, who have married into our tribe. A great many of them have grown up with their children; a great many of us learned to speak their language; our children are with theirs in our school, and we want to be considered all one people with them. My friends, when you get back to the Great Father, we wish you to tell him to send us goods. . . .

My friends, this seems to me to be a very hard day. You have come here to buy our country, and there is, at the time you come, half our country at war, and we have come upon very difficult times. This war did not spring up here in our land; this war was brought upon us by the children of the Great Father who came to take our land from us without price, and who, in our land, do a great many evil things. The Great Father and his children are to blame for this trouble.

. . . It has been our wish to live here in our country peaceably, and do such things as may be for the welfare and good of our people, but the Great Father has filled it with soldiers who think only of our death. Some of our people who have gone from here in order they may have a change, and others who have gone north to hunt, have been attacked by soldiers from the other side, and now when they are willing to come back the soldiers stand between them to keep them from coming home. It seems to me that there is a better way than this. When people come to trouble, it is better for both parties to come together without arms and talk it over and find some peaceful way to settle it.

My friends, you have come to me today, and mentioned two countries to me. One of them I know of old—the Missouri River. It is not possible for me to go there. When I was there before we had a great deal of trouble. I left, also, one hundred of my people buried there. The other country you have mentioned is one I have never seen since I was born, but I agree to go and look at it. When men have a difficult business to settle it is not possible it should be well settled in one day; it takes at least twelve months to consider it. . . .

FOR FURTHER STUDY

Benedict, Michael Les, ed. *The Fruits of Victory: Alternatives in Restoring the Union, 1865–1877* (Lanham, MD: University Press of America, 1986).

Davis, Jefferson. *Jefferson Davis: The Essential Writings*, ed. William J. Cooper, Jr. (New York: Modern Library, 2003).

DeRosa, Marshall L., ed. T*he Politics of Dissolution: The Quest for a National Identity and the Civil War* (New Brunswick, NJ: Transaction Publishers, 1998).

Freehling, William W., and Craig M. Simpson, ed. *Showdown in Virginia: The 1861 Convention and the Fate of the Union* (Charlottesville: University of Virginia Press, 2010).

Hyman, Harold M., ed. *The Radical Republicans and Reconstruction, 1861–1870* (Indianapolis, IN: Bobbs-Merrill, 1967).

Lieber, Francis. *The Miscellaneous Writings of Francis Lieber* (Philadelphia: J.B. Lippincott, 1881).

Lincoln, Abraham. *Abraham Lincoln: Political Writings and Speeches*, ed. Terence Ball (New York: Cambridge University Press, 2012).

Mackey, Thomas C., ed. *A Documentary History of the American Civil War Era* (Knoxville: University of Tennessee Press, 2012).

Stephens, Alexander H. *A Constitutional View of the Late War between the States: Its Causes, Character, Conduct and Results* (Philadelphia, PA: National Publishing Co., 1868).

Stevens, Thaddeus. *The Selected Papers of Thaddeus Stevens*, ed. Beverly Wilson Palmer (Pittsburgh, PA: University of Pittsburgh Press, 1997).

SUGGESTED READINGS

Belz, Herman. *A New Birth of Freedom: The Republican Party and the Freedmen's Rights, 1861 to 1866* (Westport, CT: Greenwood, 1976).

Bernath, Michael T. *Confederate Minds: The Struggle for Intellectual Independence in the Civil War South* (Chapel Hill: University of North Carolina Press, 2010).

Brandon, Mark. *Free in the World: American Slavery and Constitutional Failure* (Princeton, NJ: Princeton University Press, 1998).

Calhoun, Charles W. *Conceiving a New Republic: The Republican Party and the Southern Question, 1869–1900* (Lawrence: University Press of Kansas, 2006).

Connelly, Thomas L. *The Marble Man: Robert E. Lee and His Image in American Society* (Baton Rouge: Louisiana University Press, 1977).

Dirck, Brian R. *Lincoln and Davis: Imagining America, 1809–1865* (Lawrence: University Press of Kansas, 2001).

Dudden, Faye E. *Fighting Chance: The Struggle over Woman Suffrage and Black Suffrage in Reconstruction America* (New York: Oxford University Press, 2011).

Escott, Paul D. *After Secession: Jefferson Davis and the Failure of Confederate Nationalism* (Baton Rouge: Louisiana State University Press, 1978).

Farber, Daniel A. *Lincoln's Constitution* (Chicago, IL: University of Chicago Press, 2003).

Foner, Eric. *Politics and Ideology in the Age of the Civil War* (New York: Oxford University Press, 1981).

Foner, Eric. *Reconstruction: America's Unfinished Revolution, 1863–1877* (New York: Harper & Row, 1988).

Fredrickson, George M. *The Inner Civil War: Northern Intellectuals and the Crisis of the Civil War* (New York: Harper & Row, 1965).

Guelzo, Allen C. *Abraham Lincoln as a Man of Ideas* (Carbondale: Southern Illinois University Press, 2009).

Hyman, Harold M. *A More Perfect Union: The Impact of the Civil War and Reconstruction on the Constitution* (New York: Knopf, 1973).

Lawson, Melinda. *Patriot Fires: Forging a New American Nationalism in the Civil War North* (Lawrence: University Press of Kansas, 2002).

McKitrick, Eric. *Andrew Johnson and Reconstruction* (Chicago, IL: University of Chicago Press, 1960).

Randall, James G. *Constitutional Problems under Lincoln* (Urbana: University of Illinois Press, 1951).

Stout, Harry S. *Upon the Altar of the Nation: A Moral History of the Civil War* (New York: Viking, 2006).

Trefousse, Hans L. *Thaddeus Stevens: Nineteenth-Century Egalitarian* (Chapel Hill: University of North Carolina Press, 1997).

Wills, Garry. *Lincoln at Gettysburg: The Words that Remade America* (New York: Simon and Schuster, 1992).

CHAPTER 7

THE GILDED AGE, 1877–1900

I. INTRODUCTION

"[T]he poor ought to be looked to; I tell my wife, that the poor must be looked to; if you can tell who are poor—there's so many imposters. And then, there's so many poor in the legislature to be looked after. . . . an uncommon poor lot this year, uncommon. Consequently an expensive lot. The fact is . . . that the price is raised so high on United States Senator now, that it affects the whole market; you can't get any public improvement through on reasonable terms."[1] A minor work of Mark Twain's—a collaborative effort satirizing the corruption of lobbyists and politicians and a culture that revolved more around speculation and government largesse than productive labor—gave the years between Reconstruction and the turn of the century its name. Estimating the price at which a politician could be bought, Twain feared, had displaced more honest pursuits. The "Gilded Age" was a period of booms and busts, of economic and social dislocation and of seemingly boundless opportunities. The frontier retreated in the West, and once isolated communities were knit together into a single national market. Vast interstate corporations, concerned with everything from railroads to sugar, grew to exploit that market. Political movements aspiring to reverse or transform those economic and social changes jostled with machine politicians skilled at mobilizing voters and operating the machinery of government.

The disagreements that had roiled mid-nineteenth-century politics were very self-consciously set aside. War and Reconstruction were replaced with national reunion and economic progress. The South, and the former slaves, were left to their own devices by the national government. Republicans "waved the bloody shirt" at election time and funneled pension money to an ever-expanding list of war veterans, but otherwise politics turned to new concerns of economic development and regulation.

1 Mark Twain and Charles Dudley Warner, *The Gilded Age: A Tale of Today* (Hartford, CT: American Publishing Company, 1874), 143.

Politics. The Compromise of 1877 gave the disputed presidential election to the Republican Rutherford B. Hayes but abandoned the fragile Republican parties in the southern states. American politics through the rest of the nineteenth century balanced on a knife's edge. The Democrats solidified their control over the U.S. House of Representatives, while the Republicans maintained their hold on the U.S. Senate. The presidential election largely turned on which party could swing New York. Control of the White House shuttled between the two parties, with neither capable of winning solid popular majorities.

For most of this period, the two major parties pursued surprisingly similar policies, necessitated by their struggle to win over a small number of swing states. A more radical agenda was promoted by a bevy of third parties that competed during this period. Those parties were more successful in state and local races, but they attracted votes in national contests as well. The Greenback Party resisted the return to the gold standard and "hard money," favoring more inflationary policies that would benefit farmers and debtors. The Prohibition Party advocated more explicit recognition of God in politics, the tighter regulation of vice, and female suffrage. The Union Labor Party argued for the restriction of immigration, nationalization of the railroads, and redistribution of land. The Populist Party, the most successful third party in the period, borrowed from some of the earlier movements but also emphasized the adoption of a graduated income tax, term limits, initiatives and referenda, and additional labor laws. In the midst of one of the worst depressions in American history, the Populists managed to capture the Democratic Party in 1896 and incorporate its candidates and platforms under the Democratic banner. In the process, the postbellum pattern of closely contested elections was broken and the Republican Party established a dominance that would last until the Great Depression.

Society. American society looked very different at the end of the nineteenth century than it did at the beginning. The basic boundaries of the United States were set in the Jacksonian Era, but most of that land was unpopulated by Americans. Over the course of the Gilded Age, new settlers flooded into those territories, drawn by the promise of gold and farmland, the pacification of hostile Native American tribes, and improved transportation and communication. By the end of the century, the government could declare the frontier closed; the territories had been settled. Laura Ingalls Wilder's childhood in the little house on the Kansas prairie immediately followed the Civil War. By the time her books were published in the early twentieth century, only nostalgic memories remained of that world.

The Midwest could be transformed in part because its vast harvest of grain could be transported and processed for distant markets. Corporations took on new size and shape in order to better exploit new technologies of production and make use of economies of scale. As early as 1870, the *Atlantic Monthly* was already complaining of "a race of trading sharks and wolves," "the aristocracy of swindling millionaires," who got rich not by the sword like the "robber barons of the Middle Ages" but by "dazzling and astonishing others into the hope of getting rich" and by enticing the "simple people" into speculating on enterprises that they did not understand and could not expect to master.[2] The "robber baron" comparison stuck

2 "Mr. Hardhack on the Sensational in Literature and Life," *Atlantic Monthly* 26 (August 1870): 199.

FIGURE 7-1 TIMELINE OF THE GILDED AGE

Events	Year	Writings
President Rutherford B. Hayes withdraws federal troops from South	1877	
	1879	Henry George's *Progress and Poverty*
Thomas Edison invents the electric light bulb	1879	
	1880	Henry Adams's *Democracy*
Congress passes the Chinese Exclusion Act	1882	
	1883	William Graham Sumner's *What Social Classes Owe to Each Other*
Friedrich Nietzsche's *Beyond Good and Evil*	1886	
American Federation of Labor founded	1886	
Haymarket Square Riot	1886	
Congress passes Interstate Commerce Act	1887	
Congress passes Sherman Antitrust Act	1890	
Census Bureau announces closing of western frontier	1890	
Adoption of literacy requirement for voting in Mississippi	1890	
	1892	James B. Weaver's *A Call to Action*
	1892	Booker T. Washington's Atlanta Exposition Address
Pullman Strike in Chicago	1894	
U.S. Supreme Court strikes down federal income tax	1895	
	1896	William Jennings Bryan's Cross of Gold Speech
	1898	Charlotte Perkins Gilman's *Women and Economics*
Congress declares war on Spain	1898	
American Anti-Imperialist League founded	1898	
	1899	Thorstein Veblen's *The Theory of the Leisure Class*

and was increasingly used to describe a new breed of industrialist. Men like Andrew Carnegie, Marshall Field, Jay Gould, J. P. Morgan, and John D. Rockefeller remade industries ranging from steel manufacturing to retailing to finance to oil production. As such companies grew and consolidated, individual workers increasingly moved from small shops and farms to seek employment in large factories. The economic transformation fed not only a "prairie revolt" of farmers' movements hostile to the commercial interests that controlled their access to markets but also often-violent labor strife in urban areas.

Ideas. New intellectual movements made themselves felt in the latter half of the nineteenth century. Some were adapted from other intellectual arenas and applied to politics. Charles Darwin's *On the Origin of Species* appeared in 1859 and quickly influenced not only scientific debates but also religious, social, and political thinking, especially once Darwin explicitly extended the logic of his argument to humans a dozen years later in *The Descent of Man*. Early interpretations of Darwin tended to emphasize the purposeful quality of evolution, suggesting a progressive improvement of both the natural world and of mankind. The English philosopher Herbert Spencer had already been integrating ideas about evolution into social thought by the time Darwin published his findings, and Spencer's version of "Social Darwinism" that posited the progressive improvement of civilizations over time through competition and adaptation found widespread influence.[3]

Religion also made itself felt, though in disparate ways. For many advocates of laissez-faire economics in the nineteenth century, Christian virtues of industry, honesty, and thrift provided the moral underpinnings for a free market. For some moral reformers emboldened by the success of the Civil War in banishing slavery, the years after the war were an opportune time to take additional steps to suppress vice and honor God. For other reformers, Christian values were at odds with laissez-faire economics. Teachers of the Social Gospel denounced the selfishness that they thought was at the heart of the market economy and urged a turn toward cooperation and charity rather than competition and profit-taking.

II. DEMOCRACY AND LIBERTY

Major Developments

- Close party competition in national elections
- Sustained period of divided government
- Rise of interest groups and third-party movements
- Growing class conflict and farmer unrest

The late nineteenth century brought new challenges to the American commitment to democracy. By the end of Reconstruction, the United States had at least formally adopted universal manhood suffrage, abandoning both the property and racial qualifications that had limited suffrage in the first decades of the American republic. The mass political parties that had been pioneered under the Jacksonians had been elevated to an art form by the late nineteenth century. Urban machines socialized and mobilized even the most downtrodden and illiterate citizens. Parties provided patronage to its operatives and services to its constituents, while voters embraced party labels and demonstrated their firm loyalty to

---

3 The classic study of Social Darwinism is Richard Hofstadter, *Social Darwinism in American Thought, 1860–1915* (Philadelphia: University of Pennsylvania Press, 1944). The significance of Hofstadter's Social Darwinism to turn-of-the-century social thinking is challenged in Robert C. Bannister, *Social Darwinism* (Philadelphia, PA: Temple University Press, 1979).

their favored parties. Voter participation rates hovered around 80 percent. Third parties and social movements flourished, and organized interest groups were formed to lobby legislatures.

As social conflicts intensified, this type of mass democratic mobilization seemed to carry risk as well as promise. Conservatives increasingly worried that democratic majorities posed a threat to traditional liberties. Whether from momentary passion or settled interest, the mass public could not be relied upon to respect the rights and concerns of political minorities. Other conservatives thought this democratic ferment tended to corrupt politics rather than elevate it. The image of party bosses driving unthinking voters to the polls like cattle resonated with a social elite who saw politics as a dirty business. At the same time, there were those on the left who doubted the efficacy of democratic institutions. If corruption were rampant and legislatures could be bought, perhaps the greatest risk to a well-functioning democracy came not from unruly popular majorities but from deep-pocketed business interests.

The readings in this section reflect these developing ideas about the tensions between democracy and liberty in the late nineteenth century. Just a few years after a group of "liberal" Republicans broke party ranks in order to oppose the corruption of the Grant administration, Francis Parkman expressed an elite contempt for the unpredictable "masses" who now held sway in American politics. Conservative jurists like Stephen Field were leaders in developing new ideas about legal rights in the postbellum world and an activist judiciary to enforce them. James Weaver led the Populist Party to its greatest electoral threat and set the stage for the ultimate conversion of the Democratic Party.

FRANCIS PARKMAN

THE FAILURE OF UNIVERSAL SUFFRAGE (1878)

Francis Parkman was the son of a distinguished minister in Boston and educated at Harvard in the 1840s. Immediately upon graduation, he chose the unusual pursuit of becoming a professional historian, focusing on the even more unusual topic of the western frontier. His substantial family wealth made such a vocation possible. He traveled through the West, living for a time with Native American tribes, and became a staunch advocate of manifest destiny and the civilizing influence of American westward expansion. During the Civil War, he began a monumental history of European discovery and colonization of North America, a project that occupied the rest of his life. Internationally renowned at the time, he is regarded as one of the most influential and respected American historians of the nineteenth century. Parkman was also aristocratic in his sensibilities and held a low opinion of American democracy. Although a Republican, he had little patience for the social reform movements of the day and resisted any expansion of the suffrage.

What evils does Parkman associate with popular sovereignty? Does he think democracy is more or less workable in the late nineteenth century? Does the expansion of suffrage alleviate or exacerbate the problems he sees in American politics? Is democratic government consistent with good government? What tensions are there between liberty and equality? What might improve the quality of public officials?

. . .

It is but lately . . . that crowns and scepters have been denounced as enemies of the rights of man; but the war against them has been waged so hotly, and has left such vigorous traditions behind it, that the same battle cry is still raised in quarters where the foe has been driven off the field and utterly annihilated; where the present danger is not above but beneath, and where the real tyrant is organized ignorance, led by unscrupulous craft, and marching, amid the applause of fools, under the flag of equal rights. . . . The transfer of sovereignty to the people, and the whole people, is proclaimed the panacea of political and social ills, and we are but rarely reminded that popular sovereignty has evils of its own, against which patriotism may exercise itself to better purpose. . . .

We speak, of course, of our own country, where no royalty is left to fear, except the many-headed one that bears the name of Demos, and its portentous concourse of courtiers, sycophants, and panders. . . .

. . .

Liberty was the watchword of our fathers, and so it is of ourselves. But, in their hearts, the masses of the nation cherish desires not only different from it, but inconsistent with it. They want equality more than they want liberty. Now, there is a facetious inequality and a real and intrinsic one. Rank, titles, privileges, and wealth, make up the first; and character, ability, and culture, the second. Excepting only distinctions of wealth, we have abolished the artificial inequality, and now we are doing what we can to abolish the real one. Vaguely and half unconsciously, but every day more and more, the masses hug the flattering illusion that one man is essentially about as good as another. . . .

. . . In his vague way, [Demos] fancies that aggregated ignorance and weakness will bear the fruits of wisdom. He begins to think that science, thought, and study, are old-time illusions; that everybody has a right to form his own opinion as to whether the world is round or flat, and that the votes of the majority ought to settle the question.

We have said that intrinsic equality is inconsistent with liberty. It is so because, in order to produce it, very unequal opportunities of development must be granted to different kinds of mind and character, and an even distributive justice refused to human nature. The highest must be repressed and the lowest stimulated in order to produce a level average. In such an attempt no political or social system can completely succeed; but in so far as it tends this way it is false and pernicious. If it could succeed, or approach to success, it would be an outrage upon humanity. . . .

A society where liberty was complete, and where all men had equal opportunities of development, according to their several qualities, would show immense diversities of all kinds. . . .

Shall we look for an ideal society in that which tends to a barren average and a weary uniformity, treats men like cattle, counts them by the head, and gives them a vote apiece without asking whether or not they have the sense to use it; or in that which recognizes the inherent differences between man and man, gives the preponderance of power to character and intelligence, yet removes artificial barriers, keeps circulation free through all its parts, and rewards merit whenever it appears with added influence? This, of course, is a mere idea, never to be fully realized; but it makes vast difference at what a republic aims, and whether it builds on numbers or on worth. . . .

The success of an experiment of indiscriminate suffrage hangs on the question whether the better part of the community is able to outweigh the worse. . . .

We are told that, to make a bad voter a good one, we have only to educate him. His defect, however, is not merely intellectual. It consists also in the want of feeling that his own interests are connected with those of the community, and in the weakness or absence of the sense of moral and political duty. . . .

There is an illusion, or a superstition, among us respecting the ballot. The means are confounded with the end. Good government is the end, and the ballot is worthless except so far as it helps to reach this end. Any reasonable man would willingly renounce his privilege of dropping a piece of paper into a box, provided that good government were assured to him and his descendants.

. . .

. . . Good government cannot be maintained or restored unless the instructed and developed intellect of the country is in good degree united with political habits and experience. The present tendency is to divorce it from them; and this process of separation, begun long ago, is moving on now more rapidly than ever. Within a generation the quality of public men has sunk conspicuously. . . . Young men of the best promise have ceased to regard politics as a career. This is not from want of patriotism. . . .

In fact, the people did not want them there. The qualities of the most highly gifted and highly cultivated are discarded for cheaper qualities, which are easier of popular comprehension, and which do not excite jealousy. Therefore the strongest incentive to youthful ambition, the hope of political fame, is felt least by those who, for the good of the country, ought to feel it most. The natural results follow. . . .

STEPHEN J. FIELD

THE CENTENARY OF THE SUPREME COURT OF THE UNITED STATES (1890)

As social reformers gained influence in the political arena, conservatives called on the courts to stop the menace. In the preface to his influential postbellum treatise on the limits of the constitutional authority of the states, Christopher Tiedeman called for "a full appreciation of the power of constitutional limitations to protect private rights against the radical experiments of social reformers."[4] This view was echoed across the country by the increasingly organized and vocal legal profession, which found strong support in the national legislature and executive.

In 1890, the New York Bar Association sponsored a centennial celebration of the U.S. Supreme Court. The public celebration had been suggested by Republican President Benjamin Harrison, and the festivities were presided over by Democratic former-President Grover Cleveland. Associate Justice Stephen Field was selected by his brethren to represent the Court at the event, and this reading is excerpted from his speech on that occasion. Field was at that point the most senior justice, aside from the ailing Samuel Miller. A conservative Democrat, Field had been appointed by the Republican Abraham Lincoln, and he had distinguished himself on the bench with his expansive view of the protections of the Fourteenth Amendment to include the "right to pursue an ordinary vocation" and the unconstitutionality of legal tender. In New York, he joined other speakers in emphasizing the importance of an "independent judiciary [as] the true and final custodian of the liberty of the subject."[5]

In 1901, the American Bar Association organized another celebration, this time of the centennial of the appointment of John Marshall to the Supreme Court. It became the occasion to emphasize the value of judicial review and John Marshall's contribution to throwing off "the doctrines and theories engendered by the French Revolution—the supreme and uncontrollable right of the people to govern."[6] As John F. Dillon, former state and federal judge, declared in his presidential address to the American Bar Association during this period, "It is the loftiest function and most sacred duty of the judiciary" to act as "the only breakwater against the haste and passions of the people—against the tumultuous ocean of democracy. It must, at all costs, be maintained."[7] Public education and political mobilization were essential parts of that task of maintaining an activist judiciary.

Who has the final say in interpreting the requirements of the Constitution? Why does Field think that judicial review is necessary? How should judges think about constitutional rules? Does Field think judges should be deferential to legislatures? Are there circumstances when judges should defer to the popular will?

. . .

No government is suited to a free people where a judicial department does not exist with power to decide all judicial questions arising under its constitution and laws.

. . .

The power of the court to pass upon the conformity with the constitution of an act of Congress, or of a State, and thus to declare its validity or invalidity, or limit its application, follows from the nature of the Constitution itself, as the supreme law of the land. . . .

. . .

The limitations upon legislative power, arising from the nature of the constitution and its specific restraints in favor of private rights, cannot be disregarded without conceding that the legislature can

4 Christopher G. Tiedeman, *A Treatise on the Limitations of Police Powers in the United States* (St. Louis, MO: F.H. Thomas Law Book Co., 1886), viii.

5 Former American Bar Association president Edward J. Phelps, quoted in Arnold M. Paul, *Conservative Crisis and the Rule of Law* (New York: Harper & Row, 1969), 63.

6 John F. Dillon, "Introduction," in *John Marshall*, ed. John F. Dillon, vol. 1 (Chicago, IL: Callaghan & Company, 1903), xvii.

7 John F. Dillon, "Address of the President," in *Report of the Fifteenth Annual Meeting of the American Bar Association* (Chicago, IL: American Bar Association, 1892), 211.

change at will the form of our government from one of limited to one of unlimited powers. Whenever, therefore, any court, called upon to construe an enactment of Congress or of a State, the validity of which is assailed, finds its provisions inconsistent with the constitution, it must give effect to the latter, because it is the fundamental law of the whole people, and, as such, superior to any law of Congress or any law of a State. Otherwise the limitations upon legislative power expressed in the constitution or implied by it must be considered as vain attempts to control a power which is in its nature uncontrollable.

. . .

. . . I hardly need say, that, to retain the respect and confidence conceded in the past, the court, whilst cautiously abstaining from assuming powers granted by the constitution to other departments of the government, must unhesitatingly and to the best of its ability enforce, as heretofore, not only all the limitations of the constitution upon the Federal and State governments, but also all the guarantees it contains of the private rights of the citizen, both of person and of property. As population and wealth increase—as the inequalities in the conditions of men become more and more marked and disturbing—as the enormous aggregation of wealth possessed by some corporations excites uneasiness lest their power should become dominating in the legislation of the country, and thus encroach upon the rights or crush out the business of individuals of small means—as population in some quarters presses upon the means of subsistence, and angry menaces against order find vent in loud denunciations—it becomes more and more the imperative duty of the court to enforce with a firm hand every guarantee of the constitution. Every decision weakening their restraining power is a blow to the peace of society and to its progress and improvement. It should never be forgotten that protection to property and persons cannot be separated. Where property is insecure the rights of persons are unsafe. Protection to the one goes with protection to the other; and there can be neither prosperity nor progress where either is uncertain.

. . . [I]t is not sufficient for the performance of his judicial duty that a judge should act honestly in all that he does. He must be ready to act in all cases presented for his judicial determination with absolute fearlessness. Timidity, hesitation, and cowardice in any public officer excite and deserve only contempt, but infinitely more in a judge than in any other, because he is appointed to discharge a public trust of the most sacred character. . . . If he is influenced by apprehensions that his character will be attacked, or his motives impugned, or that his judgment will be attributed to the influence of particular classes, cliques or associations, rather than to his own convictions of the law, he will fail lamentably in his high office.

To the intelligent and learned Bar of the country the judges must look for their most effective and substantial support. . . . Sustained by this professional and public confidence, the Supreme Court may hope to still further strengthen the hearts of all in love, admiration and reverence for the constitution of the United States, the noblest inheritance ever possessed by a free people.

JAMES B. WEAVER

A CALL TO ACTION (1892)

James B. Weaver was raised on a farm in Iowa and established a legal practice shortly before the secession crisis. He enlisted in the Union army as a private and by the end of the war had been promoted to brigadier general. He soon launched a political career, but his policy views were unacceptable to the leadership of the Republican Party. He won election to the U.S. House of Representatives under the banner of the Greenback Party in 1878. After a single term in the House, he was nominated for the presidency by his party in 1880, garnering just over three percent of the national vote. After serving two more terms in the House, he ran for president as the nominee of the Populist Party in 1892, winning nearly ten percent of the popular vote and claiming twenty-two electoral votes from Plains and Mountain states. He was, however, unable to win another election for a House seat. He was one of the key figures in organizing the Populist (or People's) Party, pulling together many of the elements of earlier radical parties. He helped orchestrate the nomination of the populist William Jennings Bryan by the Democratic Party in 1896, but the collapse of an independent Populist Party damaged his own political career. His book, *A Call to Action,* served a campaign document for his 1892 presidential bid.

How accurate is Weaver's description of the American constitutional system? How well does it describe the actual workings of that system? Is the American political system recognizable as "government by the people"? What is Weaver's proposed solution to the American democracy gap? Does he go far enough?

. . .

The revolt which brought on the American revolution was not so much against British institutions as against the tyranny of administration. England . . . had a House of Lords, therefore, it was argued, the young republic must have a similar body; the Lords were men of great wealth and represented the aristocracy of the realm, therefore our senators should be selected because of their holdings in order that they might represent the wealth of this country. . . It might be safe, they thought, to entrust the commonalty to select their State Legislators and national Representatives, but here their power must cease. It would be positively dangerous to go farther. Alexander Hamilton likened the method decided upon to a filter. . . . This removed them, with great prudence, far enough from the common herd to enable the wealthy classes to repose confidence in them. It was argued that this would afford a safe retreat from the excesses of the multitude and the follies of democracy. Hence they severed the legislative department and relegated the House to the vote holders and the Senate to the wealth holders.

When they reached the Executive, it was, of course, preposterous to think of electing that officer directly by the people. . . . Whoever heard of a British king being chosen by the multitude? Did he not wear his crown by divine authority? Our President could not hope to derive his office from so high a source, and yet it would never do to entrust his selection directly to the common people. . . . Hence the Electoral College was constructed. . . . [The Executive and the Senate] combined are at once prepared to resist with lordly and platonic firmness all radical innovations threatened by the multitude. We call this government by the people. If it were not for the label it would never be so recognized.

. . .

The immense volume of legislation . . . have given rise to a flood tide of litigation unequaled in any age or clime. . . . When the Supreme Court is in session it is a common thing to see the leading Senators leave their seats and pass into the courtroom, there to act as counsel for the leading corporations and other moneyed interests. Such things are incompatible with the faithful discharge of public duty. . . .

The august body is literally filled with splendid specimens of a bygone epoch—men whose only mission is to preserve the old order of things—to guard the embalmed corpse of the past from the touch of the profane reformer. . . . They are fit only to adorn museums and musty cabinets. . . .

The cure for this frightful public affliction cannot be applied too quickly. It should consist of a plain amendment to the Constitution which shall provide for the election of the United States Senators by the direct vote of the people of the respective States. . . .

. . .

Why should the American judiciary of today be exempted from elective control or hold their position for life? The idea was adopted in the old world, not because it was free from objection, but because it was less objectionable than any other under the peculiar circumstances by which they were environed. The conditions which called for these so-called safeguards have vanished even there; but the evils inherent in the system still remain both here and abroad to curse mankind and imperil the safety of society. It is not probable that any representative body of men, chosen by the people of the United States today, would seriously entertain a proposition to grant to our Supreme Court the powers now claimed by that tribunal. Nor would they for a moment think of appointing the judges for life. The growth of plutocratic spirit, the rapid rise of corporate influence, and the varied experiences of a Century under our Constitution, would imperatively forbid it. Power must of course be confided to human hands, but it is constantly subject to abuse. Those who exercise it should always be under the restraint of those from whom it was derived. Elective control is the only safeguard of liberty. If the history of the republics of the earth has in store for our race a single lesson of value, it is this.

. . . It is a startling fact that the people are only permitted to directly one out of the four [parts of the national government], the House, while the other three-fourths are exempt from elective control and popular supervision. . . .

. . .

. . . The bench, both State and National, must be supplied from eminent members of the bar, and practically all the so-called distinguished members of the profession are in the service of the corporations. . . . How can we construct a safe building from unsound timber? When we shall most need it as a refuge from the storm, it will prove to be our greatest point of danger, and fall upon and crush us. . . .

. . . The design of the Declaration [of Independence] was to assert the right of man to smite his oppressor and to break every chain. It boldly asserts the theory of human equality and justice. The Constitution is the Declaration enacted into law. It should enable the citizen to strike down, through the proper lawmaking bodies and the courts of justice, every assailant of individual rights or personal security. The internal foes of social order or personal liberty are more dangerous—more insidious than those which threaten from without. The Constitution should be so interpreted as to protect society from both. If it be not capable of such translation it is a broken reed and the most stupendous failure of the Century.

. . .

III. CITIZENSHIP AND COMMUNITY

Major Developments

- Reintegration of the South into national politics and society
- Concern over the completion of the settlement of the West
- Debate over suitability of immigrants from outside northern and western Europe

With the end of the Civil War and the return of the southern states to full status in the Union, some of the major issues regarding the nature of the American political community were apparently resolved. As the U.S. Supreme Court declared, the United States was now to be understood as an "indissoluble unity." The "separate and independent" states were part of a "perpetual" national community.[8]

New issues took their place. Most immediately, there was the question of how the South would be reintegrated into the Union and how the former slaves would be worked into the body of the people. The Fourteenth Amendment secured citizenship for all those born within the jurisdiction of the United States, but there was no firm benchmark as to what citizenship entailed. By the 1880s, the Court clarified that citizenship did not secure a right to be free from private racial discrimination, though Justice John Marshall Harlan argued in dissent that in many cases such discrimination had the effect of branding the freedmen with a continuing "badge of servitude."[9] Across politics and society as a whole, national reconciliation was read to mean minimizing the status of blacks within the community. The North was quick to believe that the "New South" had worked out a reasonable solution to the race problem.

By the end of the century, Americans were challenged by two, interrelated tests to their idea of American identity. The first was the "closing of the West." The historian Frederick Jackson Turner gave clearest voice to the ways in which the idea of the frontier had affected American society and politics and the late-century worries that settlement of the West might have deep consequences for the United States moving forward. Was the United States still part of a liberated and liberating "New World," and could Americans still be the high-spirited adventurers that they often celebrated without the West to provide the setting? The second was the beginning of a "new" kind of immigration. In an increasingly settled country, new immigrants could be expected to pool in the urban coasts rather than disperse to the frontier. Even so, immigration to the United States surged forward at the end of the nineteenth century, and the composition of the mass of new immigrants changed somewhat. Although most new immigrants continued to hail from northern and western Europe, a growing number came from southern and eastern Europe, Asia, and (less remarked upon) Latin America. The new Asian immigrants faced growing hostility on the west coast. The new European immigrants encountered anti-immigrant sentiments on the east coast. Congress responded to those feelings with legislation that for the first time significantly restricted immigration to the United States, such as the Chinese Exclusion Act of 1882 and, after some delay, a series of statutes aimed at restricting European immigration in the early twentieth century. Faced with these new residents, political elites began to debate what it means to be an American and which potential new Americans should be welcomed and which should be turned away.

---

8 *Texas v. White*, 74 U.S. 700, 725 (1869).

9 *Civil Rights Cases*, 109 U.S. 3 (1883).

HENRY W. GRADY

THE NEW SOUTH (1886)

Henry W. Grady was the editor of the *Atlanta Constitution* newspaper in the 1880s and the self-proclaimed spokesman for the "New South." A Georgia native, Grady was too young to have participated in the Civil War (his father was killed in action). As a journalist in Atlanta at the tail end of Reconstruction, Grady caught the attention of an emerging group of Democratic leaders in the state. Grady became a tireless advocate for investment and economic diversification as the solution to the South's postbellum problems. Economic development, fueled by northern investment, Grady promised, would overcome sectional and racial conflicts. As he sought to entice northern investment in the region, he strove to alleviate northerners' concerns over the emerging Jim Crow order and put into the past a nation divided between northern "Puritans" and southern "Cavaliers." This speech was delivered to the New England Society in New York, where the northern financial elite were gathered. The speech was widely reported as a great success in both the northern and southern newspapers, and his genial approach to national reconciliation helped make him a national celebrity. In 1889, he died of pneumonia after yet another successful speaking tour in the North.

How does Grady invoke Abraham Lincoln in his speech? How had the North and South made common sacrifice and spilled "common blood" for the republic? What did he mean by the "New South"? In what ways did it differ from the Old South? What place did the freedmen have in the New South? Was the South still a distinctive section, according to Grady? Is Grady's vision attractive? Is the path forward from the war that he suggested a reasonable one? To what degree can the race problem be solved through economic growth and development?

. . .

. . . Neither Puritan nor Cavalier long survived as such. The virtues and traditions of both happily still live for the inspiration of their sons and the saving of the old fashion. But both Puritan and Cavalier were lost in the storm of the first Revolution; and the American citizen, supplanting both and stronger than either, took possession of the Republic bought by their common blood and fashioned to wisdom, and charged himself with teaching men government and establishing the voice of the people as the voice of God.

. . . Great types like valuable plants are slow to flower and fruit. But from the union of these colonist Puritans and Cavaliers, from the straightening of their purposes and the crossing of their blood, slow perfecting through a century, came he who stands as the first typical American, the first who comprehended within himself all the strength and gentleness, all the majesty and grace of this Republic—Abraham Lincoln. He was the sum of Puritan and Cavalier, for in his ardent nature were fused the virtues of both, and in the depths of his great soul the faults of both were lost. He was greater than Puritan, greater than Cavalier, in that he was American [Renewed applause] and that in his homely form were first gathered the vast and thrilling forces of his ideal government—charging it with such tremendous meaning and so elevating it above human suffering that martyrdom, though infamously aimed, came as a fitting crown to a life consecrated from the cradle to human liberty. Let us, each cherishing the traditions and honoring his fathers, build with reverent hands to the type of this simple but sublime life, in which all types are honored; and in our common glory as Americans there will be plenty and to spare for your forefathers and for mine.

In speaking to the toast with which you have honored me, I accept the term, "The New South," as in no sense disparaging to the Old. Dear to me, sir, is the home of my childhood and the traditions of my people. I would not, if I could, dim the glory they won in peace and war, or by word or deed take aught from the splendor and grace of their civilization—never equaled and, perhaps, never to be equaled in its chivalric strength and grace. There is a New South, not through protest against the Old, but because of new conditions, new adjustments and, if you please, new ideas and aspirations. It is to this that I address myself. . . .

. . . Will you bear with me while I tell you of another army that sought its home at the close of the late war—an army that marched home in defeat and not in victory—in pathos and not in splendor, but in glory that equaled yours, and to hearts as loving as ever welcomed heroes home. Let me picture to you the footsore Confederate soldier, as, buttoning up in his faded gray jacket the parole which was to bear testimony to his children of his fidelity and faith, he turned his face southward from Appomattox in April, 1865. Think of him as ragged, half-starved, heavy-hearted, enfeebled by want and wounds; having fought to exhaustion, he surrenders his gun, wrings the hands of his comrades in silence, and lifting his tear-stained and pallid face for the last time to the graves that dot the old Virginia hills, pulls his gray cap over his brow and begins the slow and painful journey. What does he find—let me ask you, who went to your homes eager to find in the welcome you had justly earned, full payment for four years' sacrifice—what does he find when, having followed the battle-stained cross against overwhelming odds, dreading death not half so much as surrender, he reaches the home he left so prosperous and beautiful? He finds his house in ruins, his farm devastated, his slaves free, his stock killed, his barns empty, his trade destroyed, his money worthless; his social system, feudal in its magnificence, swept away; his people without law or legal status, his comrades slain, and the burdens of others heavy on his shoulders. Crushed by defeat, his very traditions are gone; without money, credit, employment, material or training; and, besides all this, confronted with the gravest problem that ever met human intelligence—the establishing of a status for the vast body of his liberated slaves.

. . . As ruin was never before so overwhelming, never was restoration swifter. The soldier stepped from the trenches into the furrow; horses that had charged Federal guns march before the plow, and fields that ran red with human blood in April were green with the harvest in June; women reared in luxury cut up their dresses and made breeches for their husbands, and, with a patience and heroism that fit women always as a garment, gave their hands to work. There was little bitterness in all this. Cheerfulness and frankness prevailed. . . .

But in all this what have we accomplished? What is the sum of our work? We have found out that in the general summary the free Negro counts more than he did as a slave. We have planted the schoolhouse on the hilltop and made it free to white and black. We have sowed towns and cities in the place of theories and put business above politics. . . . We have learned that one Northern immigrant is worth fifty foreigners, and have smoothed the path to southward, wiped out the place where Mason and Dixon's line used to be, and hung our latch-string out to you and yours.

. . .

But what of the Negro? Have we solved the problem he presents or progressed in honor and equity towards the solution? Let the record speak to the point. No section shows a more prosperous laboring population than the Negroes of the South; none in fuller sympathy with the employing and land-owning class. He shares our school fund, has the fullest protection of our laws and the friendship of our people. Self-interest, as well as honor, demand that he should have this. Our future, our very existence depend upon our working out this problem in full and exact justice. We understand that when Lincoln signed the Emancipation Proclamation, your victory was assured; for he then committed you to the cause of human liberty, against which the arms of man cannot prevail; while those of our statesmen who trusted to make slavery the cornerstone of the Confederacy doomed us to defeat as far as they could, committing us to a cause that reason could not defend or the sword maintain in the sight of advancing civilization. . . .

The relations of the Southern people with the Negro are close and cordial. . . . To his eternal credit be it said that whenever he struck a blow for his own liberty he fought in open battle, and when at last he raised his black and humble hands that the shackles might be struck off, those hands were innocent of wrong against his helpless charges, and worthy to be taken in loving grasp by every man who honors loyalty and devotion.

Ruffians have maltreated him, rascals have misled him, philanthropists established a bank for him, but the South, with the North, protects against injustice to this simple and sincere people. To liberty and enfranchisement is as far as law can carry the Negro. The rest must be left to conscience and common sense. It should be left to those among whom his lot is cast, with whom he is indissolubly connected and whose prosperity depends upon their possessing his intelligent sympathy and confidence. Faith has been kept with him in spite of calumnious assertions to the contrary by those who assume to speak for us or by frank opponents. Faith will be kept with him in the future, if the South holds her reason and integrity.

. . .

The Old South rested everything on slavery and agriculture, unconscious that these could neither give nor maintain healthy growth. The New South presents a perfect democracy, the oligarchs leading in the popular movements social system compact and closely knitted, less splendid on the surface but stronger at the core—a hundred farms for every plantation, fifty homes for every palace, and a diversified industry that meets the complex needs of this complex age.

The New South is enamored of her new work. Her soul is stirred with the breath of a new life. The light of a grander day is falling fair on her face. She is thrilling with the consciousness of growing power and prosperity. As she stands upright, full-statured and equal among the people of the earth, breathing the keen air and looking out upon the expanding horizon, she understands that her emancipation came because in the inscrutable wisdom of God her honest purpose was crossed and her brave armies were beaten.

. . .

This message, Mr. President, comes to you from consecrated ground. Every foot of the soil about the city in which I live is sacred as a battleground of the Republic. Every hill that invests it is hallowed to you by the blood of your brothers, who died for your victory, and doubly hallowed to us by the blood of those who died hopeless, but undaunted, in defeat—sacred soil to all of us rich with memories that make us purer and stronger and better, silent but stanch witnesses in its red desolation of the matchless valor of American hearts and the deathless glory of American arms—speaking an eloquent witness in its white peace and prosperity to the indissoluble union of American States and the imperishable brotherhood of the American people.

Now, what answer has New England to this message? Will she permit the prejudices of war to remain in the hearts of the conquerors, when it has died in the hearts of the conquered? . . . [I]f she accepts in frankness and sincerity this message of goodwill and friendship, then will the prophecy of Webster, delivered in this very Society forty years ago amid tremendous applause, be verified in its fullest and final sense, when he said: "Standing hand to hand and clasping hands, we should remain united as we have been for sixty years, citizens of the same country, members of the same government, united, all united now and united forever." . . .

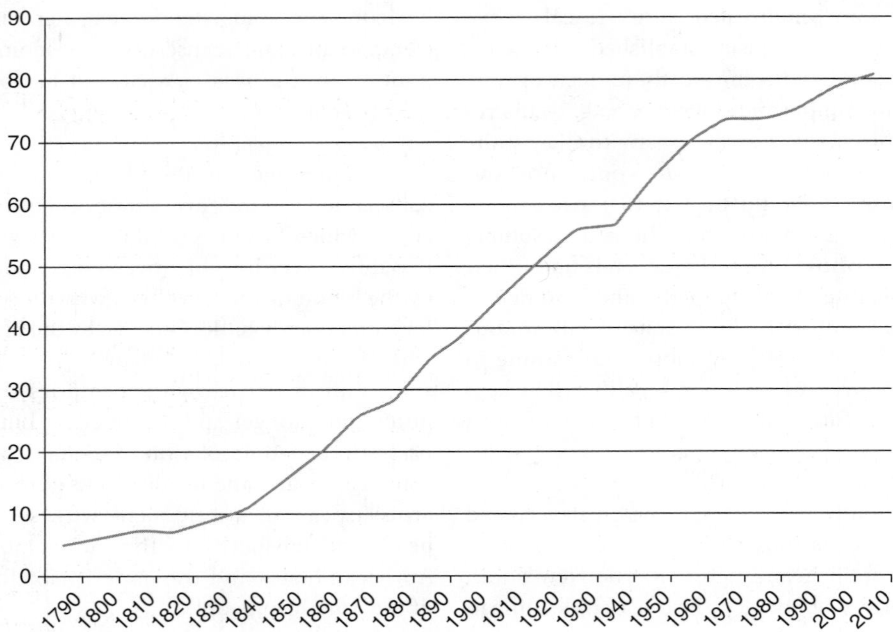

FIGURE 7-2 Percentage of Population in Urban Areas.

FREDERICK JACKSON TURNER

THE SIGNIFICANCE OF THE FRONTIER IN AMERICAN HISTORY (1893)

Frederick Jackson Turner was born during the Civil War to a middle-class family in Wisconsin. He was part of the first generation to enter academia with advanced degrees, graduating from the still-new University of Wisconsin and receiving a Ph.D. in history from Johns Hopkins University. He spent the bulk of his career at Wisconsin and Harvard University and established himself as one of the leading historians in the newly organizing profession at the turn of the century. His most influential intellectual contribution was the "frontier thesis," which argued for the significance of the frontier in shaping American democracy. Turner contended that the closer Americans stayed to the east coast, the more European they were in outlook and habits. It was on the western frontier that a distinctive American identity, habits, and practices were born. As Figure 7-2 indicates, the American population had become steadily more urbanized since the mid-nineteenth century, and by the end of the nineteenth century many had begun to wonder whether an urban America could still hold the distinctive virtues and values that had long defined the country.

How does Turner think that the frontier has shaped American development? What might be the consequence of losing the frontier? Are there "new frontiers" that can serve a similar purpose? Can immigrants be more or less effectively "Americanized" without a frontier of new settlements and farms? Is democracy less successful in crowded urban conditions than in rural conditions? Is economic, social, and political inequality inevitable without the frontier? Are American national borders now more like the European borders that Turner envisioned? Does the actual existence of large tracts of sparsely populated land in places like Nevada and Alaska counter Turner's worry?

. . . Up to our own day American history has been in a large degree the history of the colonization of the Great West. The existence of an area of free land, its continuous recession, and the advance of American settlement westward, explain American development.

Behind institutions, behind constitutional forms and modifications, lie the vital forces that call these organs into life and shape them to meet changing conditions. The peculiarity of American institutions is, the fact that they have been compelled to adapt themselves to the changes of an expanding people—to the changes involved in crossing a continent, in winning a wilderness, and in developing at each area of this progress out of the primitive economic and political conditions of the frontier into the complexity of city life. . . . Limiting our attention to the Atlantic coast, we have the familiar phenomenon of the evolution of institutions in a limited area, such as the rise of representative government; into complex organs; the progress from primitive industrial society, without division of labor, up to manufacturing civilization. But we have in addition to this a recurrence of the process of evolution in each western area reached in the process of expansion. Thus American development has exhibited not merely advance along a single line, but a return to primitive conditions on a continually advancing frontier line, and a new development for that area. American social development has been continually beginning over again on the frontier. This perennial rebirth, this fluidity of American life, this expansion westward with its new opportunities, its continuous touch with the simplicity of primitive society, furnish the forces dominating American character. The true point of view in the history of this nation is not the Atlantic coast, it is the Great West. . . .

The American frontier is sharply distinguished from the European frontier—a fortified boundary line running through dense populations. The most significant thing about the American frontier is, that it lies at the hither edge of free land. . . .

. . . The frontier is the line of most rapid and effective Americanization. The wilderness masters the colonist. It finds him a European in dress, industries, tools, modes of travel, and thought. It takes him from the railroad car and puts him in the birch canoe. It strips off the garments of civilization and arrays him in the hunting shirt and the moccasin. It puts him in the log cabin of the Cherokee and Iroquois and runs an Indian palisade around him. Before long he has gone to planting Indian corn and plowing with a sharp stick, he shouts the war cry and takes the scalp in orthodox Indian fashion. In short, at the frontier the environment is at first too strong for the man. He must accept the conditions which it furnishes, or perish, and so he fits himself into the Indian clearings and follows the Indian trails. Little by little he transforms the wilderness, but the outcome is not the old Europe . . . .

. . .

The effect of the Indian frontier as a consolidating agent in our history is important. From the close of the seventeenth century various intercolonial congresses have been called to treat with Indians and establish common measures of defense. Particularism was strongest in colonies with no Indian frontier. This frontier stretched along the western border like a cord of union. The Indian was a common danger, demanding united action. . . .

. . .

From the time the mountains rose between the pioneer and the seaboard, a new order of Americanism arose. The West and the East began to get out of touch of each other. The settlements from the sea to the mountains kept connection with the rear and had a certain solidarity. But the over-mountain men grew more and more independent. The East took a narrow view of American advance, and nearly lost these men. . . .

[W]e note that the frontier promoted the formation of a composite nationality for the American people. The coast was preponderantly English, but the later tides of continental immigration flowed across to the free lands. . . . In the crucible of the frontier the immigrants were Americanized, liberated, and fused into a mixed race, English in neither nationality nor characteristics. The process has gone on from the early days to our own. . . .

. . .

But the most important effect of the frontier has been in the promotion of democracy here and in Europe. As has been indicated, the frontier is productive of individualism. Complex society is precipitated by the wilderness into a kind of primitive organization based on the family. The tendency is anti-social. It produces antipathy to control, and particularly to any direct control. . . . The frontier States that came into the Union in the first quarter of a century of its existence came in with democratic suffrage provisions, and had reactive effects of the highest importance upon the older States whose peoples were being attracted there. An extension of the franchise became essential. It was *western* New York that forced an extension of suffrage in the constitutional convention of that State in 1821; and it was *western* Virginia that compelled the tide-water region to put a more liberal suffrage provision in the constitution framed in 1830, and to give to the frontier region a more nearly proportionate representation with the tide-water aristocracy. The rise of democracy as an effective force in the nation came in with western preponderance under Jackson and William Henry Harrison, and it meant the triumph of the frontier—with all of its good and with all of its evil elements. . . . So long as free land exists, the opportunity for a competency exists, and economic power secures political power. But the democracy born of free land, strong in selfishness and individualism, intolerant of administrative experience and education, and pressing individual liberty beyond its proper bounds, has its dangers as well as its benefits. Individualism in America has allowed a laxity in regard to governmental affairs which has rendered possible the spoils system and all the manifest evils that follow from the lack of a highly developed civic spirit. . . .

From the conditions of frontier life came intellectual traits of profound importance. The works of travelers along each frontier from colonial days onward describe certain common traits, and these traits have, while softening down, still persisted as survivals in the place of their origin, even when a higher social organization succeeded. The result is that to the frontier the American intellect owes its striking characteristics. That coarseness and strength combined with acuteness and inquisitiveness; that practical, inventive turn of mind, quick to find expedients; that masterful grasp of material things, lacking in the artistic but powerful to effect great ends; that restless, nervous energy; that dominant individualism, working for good and for evil, and withal that buoyancy and exuberance which comes with freedom—these are traits of the frontier, or traits called out elsewhere because of the existence of the frontier. Since the days when the fleet of Columbus sailed into the waters of the New World, America has been another name for opportunity. . . . He would be a rash prophet who should assert that the expansive character of American life has now entirely ceased. Movement has been its dominant fact, and, unless this training has no effect upon a people, the American energy will continually demand a wider field for its exercise. But never again will such gifts of free land offer themselves. For a moment, at the frontier, the bonds of custom are broken and unrestraint is triumphant. There is not *tabula rasa.* The stubborn American environment is there with its imperious summons to accept its conditions; the inherited ways of doing things are also there; and yet, in spite of environment, and in spite of custom, each frontier did indeed furnish a new field of opportunity, a gate of escape from the bondage of the past; and freshness, and confidence, and scorn of older society, impatience of its restraints and its ideas, and indifference to its lessons, have accompanied the frontier. What the Mediterranean Sea was to the Greeks, breaking the bond of custom, offering new experiences, calling out new institutions and activities, that, and more, the ever retreating frontier has been to the United States directly, and to the nations of Europe more remotely. And now, four centuries from the discovery of America, at the end of a hundred years of life under the Constitution, the frontier has gone, and with its going has closed the first period of American history.

HENRY CABOT LODGE

SPEECH TO THE SENATE ON LITERACY TESTS (1896)

A close political ally of Theodore Roosevelt, the Massachusetts Republican Henry Cabot Lodge became the party leader in the U.S. Senate in the early decades of the twentieth century. Like Roosevelt, Lodge was scholarly by nature and received a Ph.D. in political science from Harvard University. After serving in the U.S. House of Representatives, he was selected for the U.S. Senate in 1892. As a senator, he was known for his support for American military intervention abroad, restrictions on immigration, and opposition to the League of Nations. Just over a decade after his death in 1924, his son and namesake began his career in the U.S. Senate, becoming an important ally of Dwight Eisenhower. In the 1890s, Lodge was the chief sponsor of literacy tests for new immigrants, one of the more popular forms of immigration restriction under consideration at the time. His initial bill was vetoed by President Grover Cleveland but was incorporated into immigration bills in the early twentieth century.

Why does Lodge support literacy tests for new immigrants? Is language important in itself, or is it just a marker for some other trait? Is literacy important for deciding who should become an American? Does Lodge want to restrict the overall number of immigrants? Are immigration restrictions more appropriate to the condition of the country in the twentieth century than it was during most of the nineteenth century? Are closed borders consistent with American ideals? Is any mechanism of selecting among new immigrants consistent with American ideals? Should the United States be more welcoming to some kinds of immigrants than others? Should the rules for admittance into the country be significantly different than the rules for citizenship?

Mr. President, this bill is intended to amend the existing law so as to restrict still further immigration to the United States. Paupers, diseased persons, convicts, and contract laborers are now excluded. By this bill it is proposed to make a new class of excluded immigrants and add to those which have just been named the totally ignorant. The bill is of the simplest kind. The first section excludes from the country all immigrants who cannot read and write either their own or some other language. . . .

. . . It is found, in the first place, that the illiteracy test will bear most heavily upon the Italians, Russians, Poles, Hungarians, Greeks, and Asiatics, and very lightly, or not at all, upon English-speaking emigrants or Germans, Scandinavians, and French. In other words, the races most affected by the illiteracy test are those whose emigration to this country has begun within the last twenty years and swelled rapidly to enormous proportions, races with which the English-speaking people have never hitherto assimilated, and who are most alien to the great body of the people of the United States. On the other hand, immigrants from the United Kingdom and of those races which are most closely related to the English-speaking people, and who with the English-speaking people themselves founded the American colonies and built up the United States, are affected but little by the proposed test. These races would not be prevented by this law from coming to this country in practically undiminished numbers. These kindred races also are those who alone go to the Western and Southern States, where immigrants are desired, and take up our unoccupied lands. The races which would suffer most seriously by exclusion under the proposed bill furnish the immigrants who do not go to the West or South, where immigration is needed, but who remain on the Atlantic Seaboard, where immigration is not needed and where their presence is most injurious and undesirable.

. . . The committee's report proves that illiteracy runs parallel with the slum population, with criminals, paupers, and juvenile delinquents of foreign birth or parentage, whose percentage is out of all proportion to their share of the total population when compared with the percentage of the same classes among the native born. It also appears from investigations which have been made that the immigrants who would be shut out by the illiteracy test are those who bring least money to the country and come most quickly upon private or public charity for support. . . .

. . .

. . . There is no one thing which does so much to bring about a reduction of wages and to injure the American wage earner as the unlimited introduction of cheap foreign labor through unrestricted immigration. Statistics show that the change in the race character of our immigration has been accompanied by a corresponding decline in its quality. The number of skilled mechanics and of persons trained to some occupation or pursuit has fallen off, while the number of those without occupation or training, that is, who are totally unskilled, has risen in our recent immigration to enormous proportions. This low, unskilled labor is the most deadly enemy of the American wage earner, and does more than anything else toward lowering his wages and forcing down his standard of living. . . .

. . . The injury of unrestricted immigration to American wages and American standards of living is sufficiently plain and is bad enough, but the danger which this immigration threatens to the quality of our citizenship is far worse. . . .

This momentous fact is the one which confronts us to-day, and if continued, it carries with it future consequences far deeper than any other event of our times. It involves, in a word, nothing less than the possibility of a great and perilous change in the very fabric of our race. . . . The additions in this country until the present time have been from kindred people or from those with whom we have been long allied and who speak the same language. By those who look at this question superficially we hear it often said that the English-speaking people, especially in America, are a mixture of races. Analysis shows that the actual mixture of blood in the English-speaking race is very small, and that while the English-speaking people are derived through different channels, no doubt, there is among them none the less an overwhelming preponderance of the same race stock, that of the great Germanic tribes who reached from Norway to the Alps. They have been welded together by more than a thousand years of wars, conquests, migrations, and struggles, both at home and abroad, and in so doing they have attained a fixity and definiteness of national character unknown to any other people.

Mr. President, more precious even than forms of government are the mental and moral qualities which make what we call our race. While those stand unimpaired all is safe. When those decline all is imperiled. . . . In careless strength, with generous hand, we have kept our gates wide open to all the world. If we do not close them, we should at least place sentinels beside them to challenge those who would pass through. The gates which admit men to the United States and to citizenship in the great Republic should no longer be left unguarded.

GROVER CLEVELAND

LITERACY TEST VETO (1897)

Grover Cleveland was the first Democrat to be elected president after the Civil War and was the only president to serve two noncontiguous terms of office. Known as a reformer when he was New York's governor, Cleveland shared the hard money views of economic conservatives of both parties at the time but also emphasized more Democratic themes of fiscal restraint and free trade. Both of his elections, in 1884 and 1892, were won by razor-thin margins, and he did not win a majority of the popular vote in either contest. In 1888, he came out on the losing end of one of those contests, even though he won the plurality of the popular vote. He was a lame duck when Henry Cabot Lodge's literacy test bill reached his desk, but his veto was consistent with the historically pro-immigrant stand of the Democratic Party. Cleveland contended that the American borders were merely "an imaginary line" across which "neighbors" maintained "friendly intercourse." The effort to prevent aliens from sojourning across that line to seek work was "illiberal, narrow, and un-American."

What virtues of immigration does Cleveland emphasize? How does he think about the history and current circumstances of immigration differently than Lodge? Why is he skeptical of identifying undesirable immigrants? Would he be more open to immigration restrictions that did not attempt to separate low- and high-quality immigrants? Is Cleveland willing to restrict immigration for economic reasons? What rationale for immigration reform might he be willing to accept? Are there noneconomic reasons to worry about immigration? Are there circumstances under which immigration would be dangerous to American democracy?

. . .

A radical departure from our national policy relating to immigration is here presented. Heretofore we have welcomed all who came to us from other lands except those whose moral or physical condition or history threatened danger to our national welfare and safety. Relying upon the zealous watchfulness of our people to prevent injury to our political and social fabric, we have encouraged those coming from foreign countries to cast their lot with us and join in the development of our vast domain, securing in return a share in the blessings of American citizenship.

A century's stupendous growth, largely due to the assimilation and thrift of millions of sturdy and patriotic adopted citizens, attests the success of this generous and free-handed policy which, while guarding the people's interests, exacts from our immigrants only physical and moral soundness and a willingness and ability to work.

A contemplation of the grand results of this policy cannot fail to arouse a sentiment in its defense, for however it might have been regarded as an original proposition and viewed as an experiment its accomplishments are such that if it is to be uprooted at this late day its disadvantages should be plainly apparent and the substitute adopted should be just and adequate, free from uncertainties, and guarded against difficult or oppressive administration.

It is not claimed, I believe, that the time has come for the further restriction of immigration on the ground that an excess of population overcrowds our land.

It is said, however, that the quality of recent immigration is undesirable. The time is quite within recent memory when the same thing was said of immigrants who, with their descendants, are now numbered among our best citizens.

It is said that too many immigrants settle in our cities, thus dangerously increasing their idle and vicious population. This is certainly a disadvantage. It cannot be shown, however, that it affects all our cities, nor that it is permanent; nor does it appear that this condition where it exists demands as its remedy the reversal of our present immigration policy.

The claim is also made that the influx of foreign laborers deprives of the opportunity to work those who are better entitled than they to the privilege of earning their livelihood by daily toil. An unfortunate condition is certainly presented when any who are willing to labor are unemployed, but so far as this condition now exists among our people it must be conceded to be a result of phenomenal business depression and the stagnation of all enterprises in which labor is a factor. With the advent of settled and wholesome financial and economic governmental policies and consequent encouragement to the activity of capital the misfortunes of unemployed labor should, to a great extent at least, be remedied. If it continues, its natural consequences must be to check the further immigration to our cities of foreign laborers and to deplete the ranks of those already there. In the meantime those most willing and best entitled ought to be able to secure the advantages of such work as there is to do.

. . .

The best reason that could be given for this radical restriction of immigration is the necessity of protecting our population against degeneration and saving our national peace and quiet from imported turbulence and disorder.

I cannot believe that we would be protected against these evils by limiting immigration to those who can read and write in any language twenty-five words of our Constitution. In my opinion, it is infinitely more safe to admit a hundred thousand immigrants who, though unable to read and write, seek among us only a home and opportunity to work than to admit one of those unruly agitators and enemies of governmental control who can not only read and write, but delights in arousing by inflammatory speech the illiterate and peacefully inclined to discontent and tumult. Violence and disorder do not originate with illiterate laborers. They are, rather, the victims of the educated agitator. The ability to read and write, as required in this bill, in and of itself affords, in my opinion, a misleading test of contented industry and supplies unsatisfactory evidence of desirable citizenship or a proper apprehension of the benefits of our institutions. If any particular element of our illiterate immigration is to be feared for other causes than illiteracy, these causes should be dealt with directly, instead of making illiteracy the pretext for exclusion, to the detriment of other illiterate immigrants against whom the real cause of complaint cannot be alleged.

. . .

IV. EQUALITY AND STATUS

Major Developments

- Establishment of Jim Crow
- Emergence of separate African-American institutions
- Growing debate over political and social status of women

The Civil War freed the slaves, but Reconstruction did not resolve their status within the American constitutional system. The freedmen were recognized as citizens of the United States, but the implications of citizenship were not clearly defined. The Fifteenth Amendment to the U.S. Constitution prohibited the restriction of the franchise based on race, but suffragists failed to get women included in those constitutional reforms. As a formal matter, women were still widely excluded from the vote after Reconstruction, and as a practical matter, states and localities were already starting to experiment with ways to keep black men away from the ballot box. Republicans had hoped that black suffrage would make the Republican Party competitive in the South, but when that hope proved unavailing northern politicians lost interest in expending much political capital on the issue.

Over the course of the Gilded Age, the political fortunes of women and blacks moved in opposite directions. The gains African-Americans had made with emancipation and the Reconstruction amendments were qualified by the rise of Jim Crow segregation. In 1896, the U.S. Supreme Court gave its blessing to the growing welter of laws mandating the separation of the races, with only Justice John Marshall Harlan arguing in dissent that the "constitution is color-blind, and neither knows nor tolerates classes among citizens."[10] If the status of the freedmen was moving backward across the Gilded Age, the status of women was improving. After women were left out of the Fifteenth Amendment, suffragists turned their attention to a state-by-state campaign. The campaign paid dividends most quickly in the West. Western territories that were desperate to attract settlers, and particularly women, granted women suffrage, and those political rights carried over into statehood.

10 *Plessy v. Ferguson*, 163 U.S. 537, 559 (1896).

THOMAS E. WATSON

THE NEGRO QUESTION IN THE SOUTH (1892)

Tom Watson was a Georgia schoolteacher and lawyer. In 1882, he was elected to the state legislature as a Democrat, where he pursued a populist agenda attacking the railroads. In 1890, he was elected to the U.S. House of Representatives and helped organize the Populist Party. His time in the House was brief, however, and he turned his attention to journalism and party organization. After being passed over by William Jennings Bryan for a spot on the ticket in 1896, he recommitted himself to the populist cause, receiving the Populist Party presidential nomination in 1904. Over the next two decades, Watson's influence as a journalist grew, but he also became more focused on promoting anti-Catholicism, anti-Semitism, and white supremacy. In his earlier Populist phase, however, Watson had been a leading voice in favor of a cross-racial, class-based political coalition. Like some Populists at the time, and some Socialists in the early twentieth century, Watson argued that class, not race, was the most important dividing line in American society and politics.

Why might working-class whites and blacks have divergent interests? Why did Watson think that they had more in common than not? What were the implications of Watson's analysis for the political parties? What were the obstacles to the Republican Party attracting working-class voters in the South? To what degree has Watson's advice been followed by modern politicians and voters? Does Watson's argument suggest that a class-based party should ignore racial issues? What are the obstacles to a class-based party in the United States? Should voters and activists pursue a class-based party today?

The Negro Question in the South has been for nearly thirty years a source of danger, discord, and bloodshed. It is an ever-present irritant and menace.

Several millions of slaves were told that they were the prime cause of the civil war; that their emancipation was the result of the triumph of the North over the South; that the ballot was placed in their hands as a weapon of defense against their former interns; that the war-won political equality of the black man with the white, must be asserted promptly and aggressively, under the leadership of adventurers who had swooped down upon the conquered section in the wake of the Union armies.

No one, who wishes to be fair, can fail to see that, in such a condition of things, strife between the freedman and his former owner was inevitable. In the clashing of interests and of feelings, bitterness was born. . . .

In brief, the end of the war brought changed relations and changed feelings. Heated antagonisms produced mutual distrust and dislike—ready, at any accident of unusual provocation on either side, to break out into passionate and bloody conflict.

Quick to take advantage of this deplorable situation, the politicians have based the fortunes of the old parties upon it. Northern leaders have felt that at the cry of "Southern outrage" they could not only "fire the Northern heart," but also win a unanimous vote from the colored people. Southern politicians have felt that at the cry of "Negro domination" they could drive into solid phalanx every white man in all the Southern states.

. . .

Now consider: here were two distinct races dwelling together, with political equality established between them by law. They lived in the same section; won their livelihood by the same pursuits; cultivated adjoining fields on the same terms; enjoyed together the bounties of a generous climate; suffered together the rigors of cruelly unjust laws; spoke the same language; bought and sold in the same markets; classified themselves into churches under the same denominational teachings; neither race antagonizing the other in any branch of industry; each absolutely dependent on the other in all the avenues of labor and employment; and yet, instead of being allies, as every dictate of reason and prudence and self-interest and justice said they should be, they were kept apart, in dangerous hostility, that the sordid aims of partisan politics might be served!

So completely has this scheme succeeded that the Southern black man almost instinctively supports any measure the Southern white man condemns, while the latter almost universally antagonizes any proposition suggested by a Northern Republican. We have, then, a solid South as opposed to a solid North; and in the South itself, a solid black vote against the solid white.

. . .

Never before did two distinct races dwell together under such conditions.

And the problem is, can these two races, distinct in color, distinct in social life, and distinct as political powers, dwell together in peace and prosperity?

. . .

It is safe to say that the present status of hostility between the races can only be sustained at the most imminent risk to both. It is leading by logical necessity to results which the imagination shrinks from contemplating. And the horrors of such a future can only be averted by honest attempts at a solution of the question which will be just to both races and beneficial to both.

Having given this subject much anxious thought, my opinion is that the future happiness of the two races will never be assured until the political motives which drive them asunder, into two distinct and hostile factions, can be removed. There must be a new policy inaugurated, whose purpose is to allay the passions and prejudices of race conflicts and which makes its appeal to the sober sense and honest judgment of the citizen regardless of his color.

To the success of this policy two things are indispensable—a common necessity acting upon both races, and a common benefit assured to both—without injury or humiliation to either.

. . .

The white people of the South will never support the Republican Party. This much is certain. The black people of the South will never support the Democratic Party. This is equally certain.

. . .

Therefore a new party was absolutely necessary. It has come, and it is doing its work with marvelous rapidity.

Why does a Southern Democrat leave his party and come to ours?

Because his industrial condition is pitiably bad; because he struggles against a system of laws which have almost filled him with despair; because he is told that he is without clothing because he produces too much cotton, and without food because corn is too plentiful; because he sees everybody growing rich off the products of labor except the laborer; because the millionaires who manage the Democratic Party have contemptuously ignored his plea for a redress of grievances and have nothing to say to him beyond the cheerful advice to "work harder and live closer."

Why has this man joined the PEOPLE'S PARTY? Because the same grievances have been presented to the Republicans by the farmer of the West, and the millionaires who control that party have replied to the petition with the soothing counsel that the Republican farmer of the West should "work more and talk less."

Therefore, if he were confined to a choice between the two old parties, the question would merely be (on these issues) whether the pot were larger than the kettle—the color of both being precisely the same.

. . . The two races can never act together permanently, harmoniously, beneficially, till each race demonstrates to the other a readiness to leave old party affiliations and to form new ones, based upon the profound conviction that, in acting together, both races are seeking new laws which will benefit both. On no other basis under heaven can the "Negro Question" be solved.

. . .

The People's Party will settle the race question. First, by enacting the Australian ballot system. Second, by offering to white and black a rallying point which is free from the odium of former discords and strifes. Third, by presenting a platform immensely beneficial to both races and injurious to neither. Fourth, by making it to the interest of both races to act together for the success of the platform. Fifth, by making it to the interest of the colored man to have the same patriotic zeal for the welfare of the South that the whites possess.

. . .

The white tenant lives adjoining the colored tenant. Their houses are almost equally destitute of comforts. Their living is confined to bare necessities. They are equally burdened with heavy taxes. They pay the same high rent for gulled and impoverished land. They pay the same enormous prices for farm supplies. Christmas finds them both without any satisfactory return for a year's toil. Dull and heavy and unhappy, they both start the plows again when "New Year's" passes.

Now the People's Party says to these two men, "You are kept apart that you may be separately fleeced of your earnings. You are made to hate each other because upon that hatred is rested the keystone of the arch of financial despotism which enslaves you both. You are deceived and blinded that you may not see how this race antagonism perpetuates a monetary system which beggars both."

This is so obviously true it is no wonder both these unhappy laborers stop to listen. No wonder they begin to realize that no change of law can benefit the white tenant which does not benefit the black one likewise; that no system which now does injustice to one of them can fail to injure both. Their every material interest is identical. The moment this becomes a conviction, mere selfishness, the mere desire to better their conditions, escape onerous taxes, avoid usurious charges, lighten their rents, or change their precarious tenements into smiling, happy homes, will drive these two men together, just as their mutually inflamed prejudices now drive them apart.

Suppose these two men now to have become fully imbued with the idea that their material welfare depends upon the reforms we demand. Then they act together to secure them. Every white reformer finds it to the vital interest of his home, his family, his fortune, to see to it that the vote of the colored reformer is freely cast and fairly counted.

. . .

Let us draw the supposed teeth of this fabled dragon by founding our new policy upon justice—upon the simple but profound truth that, if the voice of passion can be hushed, the self interest of both races will drive them to act in concert. There never was a day during the last twenty years when the South could not have flung the money power into the dust by patiently teaching the Negro that we could not be wretched under any system which would not afflict him likewise; that we could not prosper under any law which would not also bring its blessings to him.

. . .

The question of social equality does not enter into the calculation at all. That is a thing each citizen decides for himself. No statute ever yet drew the latch of the humblest home—or ever will. Each citizen regulates his own visiting list—and always will.

The conclusion, then, seems to me to be this: the crushing burdens which now oppress both races in the South will cause each to make an effort to cast them off.

They will see a similarity of cause and a similarity of remedy. They will recognize that each should help the other in the work of repealing bad laws and enacting good ones. They will become political allies, and neither can injure the other without weakening both. It will be to the interest of both that each should have justice. And on these broad lines of mutual interest, mutual forbearance, and mutual support the present will be made the stepping-stone to future peace and prosperity.

BOOKER T. WASHINGTON

ATLANTA EXPOSITION ADDRESS (1895)

Booker T. Washington was perhaps the best-known African-American of the Gilded Age. Born a slave in Virginia just before the Civil War, he grew up free in West Virginia. He worked his way through a Virginia school established for freedmen (which later became Hampton University), and in 1881 he was asked to lead the new Tuskegee Institute (later Tuskegee University) in Alabama. Tuskegee was founded by the same missionary society that had established his alma mater and was designed as a teachers' college. Washington emphasized the work-study component of Tuskegee and the need for students to become self-reliant citizens in the largely agricultural economy that he served. Washington cultivated a national network of black advisors and white philanthropists, many of whom were particularly interested in his emphasis on industrial education. He took the opportunity as the designated African-American speaker to the 1895 Atlanta Cotton States and International Exposition to call for a reconciliation of black and white southerners. His willingness to accept racial segregation in exchange for black employment sparked debate across the country. For many whites, Washington was immediately recognized as the preeminent spokesman for the black community (though he was still denounced by the strongest segregationists). For a rising generation of African-Americans, Washington's willingness to compromise with Jim Crow was an increasing source of controversy. The speech was soon followed by best-selling memoirs, honorary degrees, and an invitation to the White House.

What does Washington mean by "cast down your bucket where you are"? How does he think reconciliation would benefit blacks? How does he think it would benefit whites? Why does he emphasize the practical arts? In what ways does Washington argue that blacks and whites should stand in solidarity? Does he offer a path toward breaking down Jim Crow? Does he accept the equality of blacks and whites? Does he endorse white supremacy? To what degree is Washington's approach to race relations time-bound?

One-third of the population of the South is of the Negro race. No enterprise seeking the material, civil, or moral welfare of this section can disregard this element of our population and reach the highest success. . . .

. . . Ignorant and inexperienced, it is not strange that in the first years of our new life we began at the top instead of at the bottom; that a seat in Congress or the state legislature was more sought than real estate or industrial skill; that the political convention or stump speaking had more attractions than starting a dairy farm or truck garden.

A ship lost at sea for many days suddenly sighted a friendly vessel. From the mast of the unfortunate vessel was seen a signal, "Water, water; we die of thirst!" The answer from the friendly vessel at once came back, "Cast down your bucket where you are." A second time the signal, "Water, water; send us water!" ran up from the distressed vessel, and was answered, "Cast down your bucket where you are." And a third and fourth signal for water was answered, "Cast down your bucket where you are." The captain of the distressed vessel, at last heeding the injunction, cast down his bucket, and it came up full of fresh, sparkling water from the mouth of the Amazon River. To those of my race who depend on bettering their condition in a foreign land or who underestimate the importance of cultivating friendly relations with the Southern white man, who is their next-door neighbor, I would say: "Cast down your bucket where you are"—cast it down in making friends in every manly way of the people of all races by whom we are surrounded.

Cast it down in agriculture, mechanics, in commerce, in domestic service, and in the professions. And in this connection it is well to bear in mind that whatever other sins the South may be called to bear, when it comes to business, pure and simple, it is in the South that the

Negro is given a man's chance in the commercial world, and in nothing is this Exposition more eloquent than in emphasizing this chance. Our greatest danger is that in the great leap from slavery to freedom we may overlook the fact that the masses of us are to live by the productions of our hands, and fail to keep in mind that we shall prosper in proportion as we learn to dignify and glorify common labor, and put brains and skill into the common occupations of life; shall prosper in proportion as we learn to draw the line between the superficial and the substantial, the ornamental gewgaws of life and the useful. No race can prosper till it learns that there is as much dignity in tilling a field as in writing a poem. It is at the bottom of life we must begin, and not at the top. Nor should we permit our grievances to overshadow our opportunities.

To those of the white race who look to the incoming of those of foreign birth and strange tongue and habits for the prosperity of the South, were I permitted I would repeat what I say to my own race, "Cast down your bucket where you are." Cast it down among the eight millions of Negroes whose habits you know, whose fidelity and love you have tested in days when to have proved treacherous meant the ruin of your firesides. Cast down your bucket among these people who have, without strikes and labor wars, tilled your fields, cleared your forests, builded your railroads and cities, and brought forth treasures from the bowels of the earth, and helped make possible this magnificent representation of the progress of the South. Casting down your bucket among my people, helping and encouraging them as you are doing on these grounds, and to education of head, hand, and heart, you will find that they will buy your surplus land, make blossom the waste places in your fields, and run your factories. While doing this, you can be sure in the future, as in the past, that you and your families will be surrounded by the most patient, faithful, law-abiding, and unresentful people that the world has seen. As we have proved our loyalty to you in the past, in nursing your children, watching by the sick-bed of your mothers and fathers, and often following them with tear-dimmed eyes to their graves, so in the future, in our humble way, we shall stand by you with a devotion that no foreigner can approach, ready to lay down our lives, if need be, in defense of yours, interlacing our industrial, commercial, civil, and religious life with yours in a way that shall make the interests of both races one. In all things that are purely social we can be as separate as the fingers, yet one as the hand in all things essential to mutual progress.

There is no defense or security for any of us except in the highest intelligence and development of all. If anywhere there are efforts tending to curtail the fullest growth of the Negro, let these efforts be turned into stimulating, encouraging, and making him the most useful and intelligent citizen. Effort or means so invested will pay a thousand percent interest. These efforts will be twice blessed—blessing him that gives and him that takes.

There is no escape through law of man or God from the inevitable: –

The laws of changeless justice bind
Oppressor with oppressed;
And close as sin and suffering joined
We march to fate abreast

Nearly sixteen millions of hands will aid you in pulling the load upward, or they will pull against you the load downward. We shall constitute one-third and more of the ignorance and crime of the South, or one-third [of] its intelligence and progress; we shall contribute one-third to the business and industrial prosperity of the South, or we shall prove a veritable body of death, stagnating, depressing, retarding every effort to advance the body politic.

. . .

The wisest among my race understand that the agitation of questions of social equality is the extremist folly, and that progress in the enjoyment of all the privileges that will come to us must be the result of severe and constant struggle rather than of artificial forcing. No race that has anything to contribute to the markets of the world is long in any degree ostracized. It is important and right that all privileges of the law be ours, but it is vastly more important that we be prepared for the exercise of these privileges. The opportunity to earn a dollar in a factory just now is worth infinitely more than the opportunity to spend a dollar in an opera-house.

In conclusion, may I repeat that nothing in thirty years has given us more hope and encouragement, and drawn us so near to you of the white race, as this opportunity offered by the Exposition; and here bending, as it were, over the altar that represents the results of the struggles of your race and mine, both starting practically empty-handed three decades ago, I pledge that in your effort to work out the great and intricate problem which God has laid at the doors of the South, you shall have at all times the patient, sympathetic help of my race; only let this he constantly in mind, that, while from representations in these buildings of the product of field, of forest, of mine, of factory, letters, and art, much good will come, yet far above and beyond material benefits will be that higher good, that, let us pray God, will come, in a blotting out of sectional differences and racial animosities and suspicions, in a determination to administer absolute justice, in a willing obedience among all classes to the mandates of law. This, coupled with our material prosperity, will bring into our beloved South a new heaven and a new earth.

HELEN KENDRICK JOHNSON

WOMAN AND THE REPUBLIC (1897)

Helen Kendrick Johnson grew up in New York and Georgia in the mid-nineteenth century. She married a politically active Republican editor and writer and became herself a prolific author. She gained particular success with her children's books and songbooks. In 1894, she assumed the editorship of a suffragist journal, which was her first substantial exposure to the movement. She soon became critical of the suffragist arguments and left the journal, becoming an active writer and speaker against female suffrage. Her most comprehensive work was *Woman and the Republic*. Her critique of the suffragist movement was far-reaching, questioning the social as well as the political consequences of a successful feminist movement, but a central argument against extending the franchise focused on the practical value of the ballot as an alternative to the use of force in civil disputes. As her husband wrote, the "philosophy of a popular election" was to peacefully determine which faction in society had the weight of arms behind it so that actual violence would not be necessary. The minority in democratic societies acquiesced to electoral results only because, and to the extent that, "they know that if they do not submit peaceably they will be compelled to do so."[11] Counting women (who were presumably irrelevant to the successful use of force) in such a vote would consequently muddy the result and vitiate the value of elections.

Is it inconsistent to argue for both female suffrage and literacy tests for the exercise of the franchise? What is the basis for arguing in favor of female suffrage (prior to its establishment under state and federal constitutions)? Is the strongest argument rooted in a claim about rights or a claim about good government? Why does Johnson think that the restriction of the franchise is consistent with government by "consent of the governed"? To what extent does the right to vote significantly add to the political power of women? Why does Johnson think that being able to cast a ballot is irrelevant to measuring Elizabeth Cady Stanton's actual political power? Is Johnson right to worry that if electoral outcomes do not accurately reflect societal pressures, then the political system will become unstable? Would Johnson's argument support the return of property qualifications on the right to vote? Would Johnson's argument support extending the franchise to resident aliens?

. . .

It seems to me quite . . . evident that what is now called universal manhood suffrage does not rest upon any belief by the state that this is "the first right of a citizen," because no one doubts that if the time came when a majority deemed that the preservation of the state depended upon disenfranchising a number of voters, they would be disenfranchised although they remain citizens. The Suffrage leaders have, in theory at least, also abandoned the claim to suffrage on the ground of their universal right as citizens. A proof of this is seen in the fact that at various times they have suggested the extension of suffrage under qualification [such literacy requirements]. . . . [Elizabeth Cady Stanton] must therefore believe that the Legislature has the *legal* right to qualify it for men; and to withhold it from women is but an extension of the right to qualify suffrage, because it only says: "We do not consider woman citizens qualified to be voters." Writing a year ago, Mrs. Stanton said: "It is the duty of the educated women of this Republic to protest against the extension of the suffrage to another man until they themselves are enfranchised!" Thus it would appear that Mrs. Stanton does not believe in universal suffrage. A Suffrage speaker in New York not long ago said naively: "We [the women when enfranchised] will vote to withhold the suffrage from the ignorant." . . . [She did not] appear to realize that she was practically admitting that the present voters have the right to withhold the suffrage from those whom *they* consider unfitted for it.

11 Rossiter Johnson, *The Blank-Cartridge Ballot* (New York: New York State Association Opposed to Women Suffrage, 1894), 2.

But it is not true that American women did not, and do not, "consent to be governed." They have always consented loyally and joyfully. From the time of the Boston Tea Party down to the Civil War . . . when the Government formally asked the assistance of its woman citizens, they showed their consent by their deeds. . . . And the Suffragists themselves consent to be governed every time they accept the protection of the law or invoke it against a debtor; for they thereby acknowledge its proper application to themselves if the case were reversed.

The second count in the list of political grievances runs: "He has compelled her to submit to laws in the formation of which she had no voice." This was not true, for the women who wrote that sentence were free to use their voices in regard to every law they desired to affect, and circumstances have proved that they were sure of being heard, and, if the law were just, and for the general good, of assisting materially to establish it. . . At the very time when Elizabeth Cady Stanton and Lucretia Mott were writing that indictment against the United States Government, Dorothea Dix was presenting a memorial to the National Congress asking for an appropriation of five hundred thousand acres of the public lands to endow hospitals for the indigent insane. . . . The right to petition is not only as open to women as to men, but because of the nonpartisan character of their claims and suggestions they find quicker hearing. . . . There was no unjust law which the Suffrage Association could not have changed during these fifty years, had it cared to try, and indeed its members make the boast that many of the changes are their own. Change and improvement of laws was not their aim. It was a vote upon changing or not changing laws that they sought for. The difference is world-wide.

. . . The Government laid aside all "attribute of education, or glamour of wealth, or prestige of birth," and committed its life to the keeping of its defenders. In this land, the vote is the "insignia of actual power," but it is only the insignia; the power to defend themselves and those who make country and home worth defending, lies with the individual defenders. To attempt to put it into the hands of those who are not physically fitted to maintain the obligations that may result from any vote or any legislative act, is to render law a farce, and to betray the trust imposed upon them by the constitution they have sworn to uphold. . . . If a government is not stable, it is of little consequence that it is full of noble ideals; and the most far-reaching thought has now grasped the idea that manhood strength is the natural and only defense of the state. This is the underlying theory of our Government, the one solid rock on which it rests. When any question of governmental policy comes up, we virtually decide it, sooner or later, by a manhood vote; and as the decision has a majority of the men of the country behind it, there is no power that can overthrow it. If we attempt to establish policies or execute laws to which a majority of the men are opposed, we throw away our one assurance of stability, and are in constant danger of revolution. . . . To give women a position of apparent power, without its reality, would be to make our Government forever unstable.

. . . So successful has our Government been in carrying out the benign purposes for which its heroes staked their lives, their fortunes, and their sacred honor, that in ordinary times we see little of the strength that stands quietly but firmly behind every law's enactment and every poll's decision. The "strong arm" of the law would lose its power to compel obedience if behind the decree of the judge, jury, and legislators there was not a sheriff or a body of militia ready to commit the unconsenting criminal to prison, or to take care of an unruly minority. At an election, the minority do not acquiesce in the decision of the majority because the outcome of the vote has convinced them that the majority were right, and they were wrong. . . . That decision, as recorded by the ballot, shows that if the minority do not keep their opinions in abeyance, there are men enough on the other side to compel them. . . .

. . .

CHARLOTTE PERKINS GILMAN

WOMEN AND ECONOMICS (1898)

Charlotte Perkins was born in Connecticut on the eve of the Civil War. Her father, a member of the Beecher family, abandoned her family soon after her birth, leaving them destitute. After separating from her own first husband and suffering an extended bout of depression, she moved to California in 1888 and took up a career writing (both fiction and nonfiction) and speaking (both in the United States and Europe) and became active in feminist and socialist circles. She had one daughter from her first marriage and ultimately sent her to live with her ex-husband and his new wife, sparking both public and private criticism. She eventually returned east and entered a second, more successful, marriage to George Gilman.

Women and Economics is now regarded as the most significant feminist work of the period, though it had fallen into obscurity for several decades. Much of her work focused on the organization of the household and women's place in the social and economic world and argued for the value of collectivized domestic arrangements, including childrearing, housing, and cooking. As she contended in a different work, "The mothers of the world are responsible for the children of the world."[12] Children should benefit from "social parentage" rather than be dependent on the biological parents they happen to have, and parents should be freed from domestic labors and responsibilities for which they might be ill suited.

What value does Gilman think that women currently provide to justify their place in society? Does Gilman advocate social change for the sake of women or for other reasons? Why is it necessary that women "justify" their economic status? Would Gilman's argument accept that marriage is a justifiable, or desirable, social institution? How does Gilman believe that collective childrearing would benefit society? Is Gilman's feminism separable from her socialism? Should families be allowed to raise their own children, given Gilman's argument? Should women (or men) be allowed to be stay-at-home moms (or dads)?

. . .

Without touching yet upon the influence of the social factors, treating the human being merely as an individual animal, we see that he is modified most by his economic conditions, as is every other animal. . . .

The human animal is no exception to this rule. Climate affects him, weather affects him, enemies affect him; but most of all he is affected, like every other living creature, by what he does for his living. . . .

In view of these facts, attention is now called to a certain marked and peculiar economic condition affecting the human race, and unparalleled in the organic world. We are the only animal species in which the female depends on the male for food, the only animal species in which the sex-relation is also an economic relation. With us an entire sex lives in a relation of economic dependence upon the other sex. . . . The economic status of the human female is relative to the sex-relation.

. . .

To take from any community its male workers would paralyze it economically to a far greater degree than to remove its female workers. The labor now performed by the women could be performed by the men, requiring only the setting back of many advanced workers into earlier forms of industry; but the labor now performed by the men could not be performed by the women without generations of effort and adaptation. Men can cook, clean, and sew as well as women; but the making and managing of the great engines of modern industry . . . could not be done so well by women in their present degree of economic development.

This is not owing to lack of the essential human faculties necessary to such achievements, nor to any inherent disability of sex, but to the present condition of woman, forbidding the development of this degree of economic ability. . . . Speaking collectively,

12 Charlotte Perkins Gilman, *Concerning Children* (Boston, MA: Small Maynard & Company, 1900), 288.

men produce and distribute wealth; and women receive it at their hands. . . .

. . . None can deny these patent facts—that the economic status of women generally depends upon that of men generally, and that the economic status of women individually depends upon that of men individually, those men to whom they are related. . . .

Women consume economic goods. What economic product do they give in exchange for what they consume? The claim that marriage is a partnership, in which the two persons married produce wealth would neither of them, separately, could produce, will not bear examination. A man happy and comfortable can produce more than one unhappy and uncomfortable . . . [b]ut those relatives who make him happy are not therefore his business partners, and entitled to share his income.

. . .

The labor which the wife performs in the household is given as part of her functional duty, not as employment. . . .

To take this ground and hold it honestly, wives, as earners through domestic service, are entitled to the wages of cooks, housemaids, nursemaids, seamstresses, or housekeepers, and to no more. This would of course reduce the spending money of the wives of the rich, and put it out of the power of the poor man to "support" a wife at all, unless, indeed, the poor man faced the situation fully, paid his wife her wages as house servant, and then she and he combined their funds in support of their children. . . . But nowhere on earth would there be "a rich woman" by these means. . . .

. . . Few women—or men either—care to face this condition. The ground that women earn their living by domestic labor is instantly forsaken, and we are told that they obtain their livelihood as mothers. This is a peculiar position. . . .

. . .

If this is so, if motherhood is an exchangeable commodity given by women in payment for clothes and food, then we must of course find some relation between the quantity or quality of the motherhood and the quantity and quality of the pay. This being true, then the women who are not mothers have no economic status at all; and the economic status of those who are must be shown to be relative to their motherhood. This is obviously absurd. . . . Visibly, and upon the face of it, women are not maintained in economic prosperity proportioned to their motherhood. Motherhood bears no relation to their economic status. . . .

. . . [W]hat remains to those who deny that women are supported by men? This (and a most amusing position it is)—that the function of maternity unfits a woman for economic production, and, therefore, it is right that she should be supported by her husband.

. . .

It is not motherhood that keeps the housewife on her feet from dawn till dark; it is house service, not child service. Women work longer and harder than most men, and not solely in maternal duties. . . .

In spite of her supposed segregation to maternal duties, the human female, the world over, works at extra-maternal duties for hours enough to provide her with an independent living, and then is denied independence on the ground that motherhood prevents her working!

. . .

. . . The women whose splendid extravagance dazzles the world, whose economic goods are the greatest, are often neither houseworkers nor mothers, but simply the women who hold most power over the men who have the most money. The female of genus homo is economically dependent on the male. He is her food supply.

. . .

Two things let us premise and agree upon before starting. First, that the duty of human life is progress, development; that we are here not merely to live, but to grow. . . . Just to live and bear children does not prove the relative superiority of any system, either in sex or economics. But, when we believe that life means progress, then each succeeding form of sex-relation or economic relation is to be measured by its effect on that progress.

. . . According to the general law of organic evolution, [human progress] may be defined as follows: such progress in the individual and in his social relations as shall maintain him in health and happiness and increase the organic development of society.

If we accept such a definition of human progress, if we agree that progress is the duty of society, and that all social institutions are to be measured by it, we may proceed to our second premise. . . .

The second premise is this: our enjoyment of a thing does not prove that it is right. . . . A thing may be right in one stage of evolution which becomes wrong in another. . . .

. . .

In our present method of home life, based on the economic dependence of woman in the sex-relation, the best calculated to maintain the individual in health and happiness, and develop in him the higher social faculties? The individual is not maintained in health and happiness—that is visible to all; and how little he is developed in social relation is shown in the jarring irregularity and wastefulness of our present economic system.

Economic independence for women necessarily involves a change in the home and family relation. But, if that change is for the advantage of individual and race, we need not fear it. It does not involve a change in the marriage relation except in withdrawing the element of economic dependence, nor in the relation of mother to child save to improve it. But it does involve the exercise of human faculty in women, in social service and exchange rather than in domestic service solely. This will of course require the introduction of some other form of living than that which now obtains. It will render impossible the present method of feeding the world by means of millions of private servants, and bringing up children by the same hand.

It is a melancholy fact that the vast majority of our children are reared and trained by domestic servants—generally their mothers, to be sure, but domestic servants by trade. To become a producer, a factor in the economic activities of the world, must perforce interfere with woman's present status as a private servant. . . .

. . . Marriage is not perfect unless it is between class equals. There is no equality in class between those who do their share in the world's work in the largest, newest, highest ways and those who do theirs in the smallest, oldest, lowest ways.

. . .

In reconstructing in our minds the position of woman under conditions of economic independence, it is most difficult to think of her as a mother.

. . .

[W]e have reached a stage where individual and racial progress is best served by the higher specialization of individuals and by a far wider sense of love and duty. This change renders the psychic conditions of home life increasingly disadvantageous. We constantly hear of the inferior manners of the children today. . . It is visibly not so easy to live at home as it used to be. Our children are not more perversely constituted than the children of earlier ages, but the conditions in which they are reared are not suited to develop the qualities now needed in human beings.

. . .

. . . The child learns more of the virtues needed in modern life—of fairness, of justice, of comradeship, of collective interest and action—in a common school than can be taught in the most perfect family circle. . . .

. . .

. . . The short range between effort and attainment, the constant attention given to personal needs, is bad for the man, worse for the woman, and worst for the child. It belittles his impressions of life at the start. It accustoms him to magnify the personal duties and minify the social ones, and it greatly retards his adjustment to larger life. This servant-motherhood, with all its unavoidable limitation and ill results, is the concomitant of the economic dependence of woman upon man, the direct and inevitable effect of the sexuo-economic relation.

. . . A baby who spent certain hours every day among other babies, being cared for because he was a baby, and not because he was "my baby," would grow to have a very different opinion of himself from that which is forced upon each new soul that comes among us by the ceaseless adoration of his own immediate family. What he needs to learn at once and for all, to learn softly and easily, but inexorably, is that he is one of many. . . .

. . . Some women there are, and some men, whose highest service to humanity is the care of children. Such should not concentrate their powers upon their own children alone . . . but should be so placed that their talent and skill, their knowledge and experience, would benefit the largest number of children. . . . Simply to bear children is a personal matter—an animal function. Education is collective, human, a social function.

. . .

V. POLITICAL ECONOMY

Major Developments

- Rise of industrialism
- Growth of large interstate corporations
- Rise of large labor unions
- Integration of local markets into national economy

The two major political parties agreed more than they disagreed on economic policy over the course of the Gilded Age. Both parties were committed to keeping the United States on the gold standard, paying down the national debt incurred during the Civil War, settling the West, maintaining labor peace, and integrating states and localities into a single national economy. Both parties largely accepted the growth of national corporations, individual fortunes, and economic fluctuations as natural features of the economic world. The role of government was simply to maintain the legal preconditions for economic productivity. For the Republicans, protective tariffs remained a valuable tool for securing domestic economic growth and employment and generous expenditures on veterans' pensions helped sustain party loyalty. The Democrats countered with calls for free trade and government frugality. William Graham Sumner and Andrew Carnegie represent the advocates of freer markets.

More radical suggestions were left to upstart parties. Farm and labor interests agitated for softer, more inflationary currency. Farmers' movements sought to insulate local economies from national forces and restrain the prices charged by railroads. Populists urged greater control of the wealthy and corporations through the adoption of progressive income taxes, land reform, immigration restrictions, and economic regulations. Labor unions argued for greater legal protection for their existence as organizations and for their tactics, and increasingly for government requirements implementing their preferences for working conditions. Congress sometimes coopted these programs when they became too popular or other vital interests were under pressure. In 1887, a bipartisan coalition initiated federal regulation of railroads. In 1890, a Republican Congress adopted the Sherman Antitrust Act to relieve pressure on protective tariffs (which were seen as a subsidy to big business). In 1894, a Democratic Congress adopted a federal income tax in order to buy Populist votes for lower protective tariffs (the Supreme Court struck the tax down the next year). Henry Lloyd represents those advocating for more government intervention.

WILLIAM GRAHAM SUMNER

WHAT SOCIAL CLASSES OWE TO EACH OTHER (1883)

William Graham Sumner was raised in modest circumstances in New Jersey and Connecticut. He graduated from Yale University in 1863 and embarked on a career as a Episcopalian minister, but within a decade he had returned to Yale as a popular but controversial teacher in the social sciences. He soon became a national leader of efforts to shift to a more professionalized and scientific approach to the study of human behavior. He was also perhaps the nation's leading advocate for laissez-faire economic policies in the late nineteenth century, producing works on everything from hard currency, free trade, and labor relations to political philosophy. During the Spanish-American War, he was a leader of the anti-imperialism movement, and in the decade before his death in 1910 he produced foundational work on social customs and served as one of the first presidents of the American Sociological Association (succeeding Lester Ward, one of the leading academic critics of laissez-faire policies).

What does Sumner mean by the "Forgotten Man"? What duties do individuals owe to another in a society? To what extent do duties vary depending on the economic circumstances of the individuals? On what basis might "some-of-us" make claims on "all-of-us"? How do we determine what class of ills results simply from "the struggle with nature for existence" and what result from "imperfections or errors of civil institutions"? To what degree do the successful have an obligation to aid those who are less successful in the "struggle with nature"? How great is the risk that the state will be turned to exploiting the "earnings of others" if redistribution is accepted as a valid use of government power?

. . . Who are those who assume to put hard questions to other people and to demand a solution of them? . . .

So far as I can find out what the classes are who are respectively endowed with the rights and duties of posing and solving social problems, they are as follows: Those who are bound to solve the problems are the rich, comfortable, prosperous, virtuous, respectable, educated, and healthy; those whose right it is to set the problems are those who have been less fortunate or less successful in the struggle for existence. The problem itself seems to be, How shall the latter be made as comfortable as the former? To solve this problem, and make us all equally well off, is assumed to be the duty of the former class; the penalty, if they fail of this, is to be bloodshed and destruction. If they cannot make everybody else as well off as themselves, they are to be brought down to the same misery as others.

. . .

If anybody is to benefit from the action of the state it must be Some-of-us. If, then, the question is raised, What ought the state to do for labor, for trade, for manufactures, for the poor, for the learned professions? etc.—that is, for a class or an interest—it is really the question . . . . What ought Some-of-us to do for Others-of-us? or, What do social classes owe to each other?

I now propose to try to find out whether there is any class in society which lies under the duty and burden of fighting the battles of life for any other class, or of solving social problems for the satisfaction of any other class; also, whether there is any class which has the right to formulate demands on "society"—that is, on other classes; also, whether there is anything but a fallacy and a superstition in the notion that "the State" owes anything to anybody except peace, order, and the guarantees of rights.

. . .

. . . We are absolutely shut up to the need and duty, if we would learn how to live happily, of investigating the laws of nature, and deducing the rules of right living in the world as it is. These are very wearisome and commonplace tasks. They consist in labor and self-denial repeated over and over again in learning and doing. When the people whose claims we are considering are told to apply themselves to these tasks they become irritated and feel almost insulted. They formulate their claims as rights against society—that is, against some other men. In their view they have a right, not only to *pursue* happiness, but to *get* it; and if they fail to get it, they think they have a claim to the aid of other men—that is, to the labor and self-denial of other men—to get it for them. They find orators and poets who tell them that they have grievances, so long as they have unsatisfied desires.

. . .

Certain ills belong to the hardships of human life. They are natural. They are part of the struggle with nature for existence. We cannot blame our fellow men for our share of these. My neighbor and I are both struggling to free ourselves from these ills. The fact that my neighbor has succeeded in this struggle better than I constitutes no grievance for me. Certain other ills are due to the malice of men, and to the imperfections or errors of civil institutions. These ills are an object of agitation, and a subject for discussion. The former class of ills is to be met only by manly effort and energy; the latter may be corrected by associated effort. The former class of ills is constantly grouped and generalized, and made the object of social schemes. We shall see, as we go on, what that means. The second class of ills may fall on certain social classes, and reform will take the form of interference by other classes in favor of that one. The last fact is, no doubt, the reason why people have been led, not noticing distinctions, to believe that the same method was applicable to the other class of ills. The distinction here made between the ills which belong to the struggle for existence and those which are due to the faults of human institutions is of prime importance.

. . .

The humanitarians, philanthropists, and reformers, looking at the facts of life as they present themselves, find enough which is sad and unpromising in the condition of many members of society. They see wealth and poverty side by side. They note great inequality of social position and social chances. They eagerly set about the attempt to account for what they see, and to devise schemes for remedying what they do not like. In their eagerness to recommend the less fortunate classes to pity and consideration they forget all about the rights of other classes; they gloss over all the faults of the classes in question, and they exaggerate their misfortunes and their virtues. . . . The man who by his own effort raises himself above poverty appears, in these discussions, to be of no account. The man who has done nothing to raise himself above poverty finds that the social doctors flock about him, bringing the capital which they have collected from the other class, and promising him the aid of the state to give him what the other had to work for.

In all these schemes and projects the organized intervention of society through the state is either planned or hoped for, and the state is thus made to become the protector and guardian of certain classes. The agents who are to direct the state action are, of course, the reformers and philanthropists. Their schemes, therefore, may always be reduced to this type—that A and B decide what C shall do for D. It will be interesting to inquire, at a later period of our discussion, who C is, and what the effect is upon him of all these arrangements. In all the discussions attention is concentrated on A and B, the noble social reformers, and on D, the "poor man." I call C the Forgotten Man, because I have never seen that any notice was taken of him in any of the discussions. . . . Here it may suffice to observe that, on the theories of the social philosophers to whom I have referred, we should get a new maxim of judicious living: poverty is the best policy. If you get wealth, you will have to support other people; if you do not get wealth, it will be the duty of other people to support you.

. . .

. . . A society based on contract is a society of free and independent men, who form ties without favor or obligation, and cooperate without cringing or intrigue. A society based on contract, therefore, gives the utmost room and chance for individual development, and for all the self-reliance and dignity of a free man. . . . It follows, however, that one man, in a free state, cannot claim help from, and cannot be charged to give help to, another. . . .

. . .

History is only a tiresome repetition of one story. Persons and classes have sought to win possession of the power of the state in order to live luxuriously out of the earnings of others. Autocracies, aristocracies, theocracies, and all other organizations for holding political power, have exhibited only the same line of action. It is the extreme of political error to say that if political power is only taken away from generals, nobles, priests, millionaires, and scholars, and given to artisans and peasants, these latter may be trusted to do only right and justice, and never to abuse the power; that they will repress all excess in others, and commit none themselves. They will commit abuse, if they can and dare, just as others have done. The reason for the excesses of the old governing classes lies in the vices and passions of human nature—cupidity, lust, vindictiveness, ambition, and vanity. . . . The only thing which has ever restrained these vices of human nature in those who had political power is law sustained by impersonal institutions. . . .

. . .

The notion of civil liberty which we have inherited is that of *a status created for the individual by laws and institutions, the effect of which is that each man is guaranteed the use of all his own powers exclusively for his own welfare*. It is not at all a matter of elections, or universal suffrage, or democracy. All institutions are to be tested by the degree to which they guarantee liberty. It is not to be admitted for a moment that liberty is a means to social ends, and that it may be impaired for major considerations. Anyone who so argues has lost the bearing and relation of all the facts and factors in a free state. A human being has a life to live, a career to run. He is a center of powers to work, and of capacities to suffer. What his powers may be—whether they can carry him far or not; what his chances may be, whether wide or restricted; what his fortune may be, whether to suffer much or little—are questions of his personal destiny which he must work out and endure as he can; but for all that concerns the bearing of the society and its institutions upon that man, and upon the sum of happiness to which he can attain during his life on earth, the product of all history and all philosophy up to this time is summed up in the doctrine, that he should be left free to do the most for himself that he can, and should be guaranteed the exclusive enjoyment of all that he does. If the society—that is to say, in plain terms, if his fellow men, either individually, by groups, or in a mass—impinge upon him otherwise than to surround him with neutral conditions of security, they must do so under the strictest responsibility to justify themselves. . . . [L]iberty for labor and security for earnings are the ends for which civil institutions exist, not means which may be employed for ulterior ends.

. . .

A free man in a free democracy has no duty whatever toward other men of the same rank and standing, except respect, courtesy, and goodwill. We cannot say that there are no classes, when we are speaking politically, and then say that there are classes, when we are telling A what it is his duty to do for B. In a free state every man is held and expected to take care of himself and his family, to make no trouble for his neighbor, and to contribute his full share to public interests and common necessities. If he fails in this he throws burdens on others. He does not thereby acquire rights against the others. On the contrary, he only accumulates obligations toward them; and if he is allowed to make his deficiencies a ground of new claims, he passes over into the position of a privileged or petted person—emancipated from duties, endowed with claims. This is the inevitable result of combining democratic political theories with humanitarian social theories. . . .

. . .

The aggregation of large fortunes is not at all a thing to be regretted. On the contrary, it is a necessary condition of many forms of social advance. If we should set a limit to the accumulation of wealth, we should say to our most valuable producers, "We do not want you to do us the services which you best understand how to perform, beyond a certain point." It would be like killing off our generals in war. . . .

. . .

Every man and woman in society has one big duty. That is, to take care of his or her own self. This is a social duty. For, fortunately, the matter stands so that the duty of making the best of oneself individually is not a separate thing from the duty of filling one's place in society, but the two are one, and the latter is accomplished when the former is done.

The common notion, however, seems to be that one has a duty to society, as a special and separate thing, and that this duty consists in considering and deciding what other people ought to do. . . .

The danger of minding other people's business is twofold. First, there is the danger that a man may leave his own business unattended to; and, second, there is the danger of an impertinent interference with another's affairs. The "friends of humanity" almost always run into both dangers. I am one of humanity, and I do not want any volunteer friends. I regard friendship as mutual, and I want to have my say about it. . . .

Yet we are constantly annoyed, and the legislatures are kept constantly busy, by the people who have made up their minds that it is wise and conducive to happiness to live in a certain way, and who want to compel everybody else to live in their way. Some people have decided to spend Sunday in a certain way, and they want laws passed to make other people spend Sunday in the same way. Some people have resolved to be teetotalers, and they want a law passed to make everybody else a teetotaler. Some people have resolved to eschew luxury, and they want taxes laid to make others eschew luxury. The taxing power is especially something after which the reformer's finger always itches. Sometimes there is an element of self-interest in the proposed reformation, as when a publisher wanted a duty imposed on books, to keep Americans from reading books which would unsettle their Americanisms; and when artists wanted a tax laid on pictures, to save Americans from buying bad paintings.

I make no reference here to the giving and taking of counsel and aid between man and man. . . . The very sacredness of the relation in which two men stand to one another when one of them rescues the other from vice separates that relation from any connection with the work of the social busybody, the professional philanthropist, and the empirical legislator.

. . .

. . . Society needs first of all to be freed from these meddlers—that is, to be let alone. Here we are, then, once more back at the old doctrine—*laissez faire*. Let us translate it into blunt English, and it will read, Mind your own business. It is nothing but the doctrine of liberty. Let every man be happy in his own way. If his sphere of action and interest impinges on that of any other man, there will have to be compromise and adjustment. Wait for the occasion. Do not attempt to generalize those interferences or to plan for them *a priori*. We have a body of laws and institutions which have grown up as occasion has occurred for adjusting rights. Let the same process go on. . . .

. . . We never supposed that *laissez faire* would give us perfect happiness. We have left perfect happiness entirely out of our account. If the social doctors will mind their own business, we shall have no troubles but what belong to nature. Those we will endure or combat as we can. What we desire is that the friends of humanity should cease to add to them. . . .

. . . When a millionaire gives a dollar to a beggar the gain of utility to the beggar is enormous, and the loss of utility to the millionaire is insignificant. Generally the discussion is allowed to rest there. But if the millionaire makes capital of the dollar, it must go upon the labor market, as a demand for productive services. Hence there is another party in interest—the person who supplies productive services. There always are two parties. The second one is always the Forgotten Man, and anyone who wants to truly understand the matter in question must go and search for the Forgotten Man. He will be found to be worthy, industrious, independent, and self-supporting. He is not, technically, "poor" or "weak"; he minds his own business, and makes no complaint. Consequently the philanthropists never think of him, and trample on him.

. . .

. . . The rights, advantages, capital, knowledge, and all other goods which we inherit from past generations have been won by the struggles and sufferings of past generations; and the fact that the race lives, though men die, and that the race can by heredity accumulate within some cycle its victories over nature, is one of the facts which make civilization possible. The struggles of the race as a whole produce the possessions of the race as a whole. Something for nothing is not to be found on earth.

. . .

. . . The greatest social evil with which we have to contend is jobbery. Whatever there is in legislative charters, watering stocks, etc., which is objectionable, comes under the head of jobbery. Jobbery is any scheme which aims to gain, not by the legitimate fruits of industry and enterprise, but by extorting from somebody a part of his product under guise of some pretended industrial undertaking. Of course it is only a modification when the undertaking in question has some legitimate character, but the occasion is used to graft upon it devices for obtaining what has not been earned. Jobbery is the vice of plutocracy, and it is the especial form under which plutocracy corrupts a democratic and republican form of government. The United States is deeply afflicted with it, and the problem of civil liberty here is to conquer it. It affects everything which we really need to have done to such an extent that we have to do without public objects which we need through fear of jobbery. Our public buildings are jobs—not always, but often. They are not needed, or are costly beyond all necessity or even decent luxury. Internal improvements are jobs. They are not made because they are needed to meet needs which have been experienced. They are made to serve private ends, often incidentally the political interests of the persons who vote the appropriations. Pensions have become jobs. In England pensions used to be given to aristocrats, because aristocrats had political influence, in order to corrupt them. Here pensions are given to the great democratic mass, because they have political power, to corrupt them. Instead of going out where there is plenty of land and making a farm there, some people go down under the Mississippi River to make a farm, and then they want to tax all the people in the United States to make dikes to keep the river off their farms. The California gold-miners have washed out gold, and have washed the dirt down into the rivers and on the farms below. They want the federal government to now clean out the rivers and restore the farms. The silver-miners found their product declining in value, and they got the federal government to go into the market and buy what the public did not want, in order to sustain (as they hoped) the price of silver. The federal government is called upon to buy or hire unsalable ships, to build canals which will not pay, to furnish capital for all sorts of experiments, and to provide capital for enterprises of which private individuals will win the profits. All this is called "developing our resources," but it is, in truth, the great plan of all living on each other.

The greatest job of all is a protective tariff. . . .

Now, the plan of plundering each other produces nothing. It only wastes. All the material over which the protected interests wrangle and grab must be got from somebody outside of their circle. The talk is all about the American laborer and American industry, but in every case in which there is not an actual production of wealth by industry there are two laborers and two industries to be considered—the one who gets and the one who gives. . . . [E]very such industry must be a parasite on some other industry. What is the other industry? Who is the other man? This, the real question, is always overlooked.

In all jobbery the case is the same. There is a victim somewhere who is paying for it all. The doors of waste and extravagance stand open, and there seems to be a general agreement to squander and spend. It all belongs to somebody. . . . Now, who is the victim? He is the Forgotten Man. If we go to find him, we shall find him hard at work tilling the soil to get out of it the fund for all the jobbery, the object of all the plunder, the cost of all the economic quackery, and the pay of all the politicians and statesmen who have sacrificed his interests to his enemies. We shall find him an honest, sober, industrious citizen, unknown outside his little circle, paying his debts and his taxes, supporting the church and the school, reading his party newspaper, and cheering for his pet politician.

. . .

It is the Forgotten Man who is threatened by every extension of the paternal theory of government. It is he who must work and pay. When, therefore, the statesmen and social philosophers sit down to think what the state can do or ought to do, they really mean to decide what the Forgotten Man shall do. What the Forgotten Man wants, therefore, is a fuller realization of constitutional liberty. He is suffering from the fact that there are yet mixed in our institutions medieval theories of protection, regulation, and authority, and modern theories of independence and individual liberty and responsibility. . . .

. . .

We each owe it to the other to guarantee rights. Rights do not pertain to *results*, but only to *chances*.

They pertain to the *conditions* of the struggle for existence, not to any of the results of it; to the *pursuit* of happiness, not to the possession of happiness. It cannot be said that each one has a right to have some property, because if one man had such a right some other man or men would be under a corresponding obligation to provide him with some property. Each has a right to acquire and possess property if he can. It is plain what fallacies are developed when we overlook this distinction. . . . We each owe it to the other to guarantee mutually the chance to earn, to possess, to learn, to marry, etc., against any interference which would prevent the exercise of those rights by a person who wishes to prosecute and enjoy them in peace for the pursuit of happiness. If we generalize this, it means that All-of-us ought to guarantee rights to each of us. . . .

. . .

. . . Instead of endeavoring to redistribute the acquisitions which have been made between the existing classes, our aim should be to *increase, multiply, and extend the chances.* Such is the work of civilization. . . . The yearning after equality is the offspring of envy and covetousness, and there is no possible plan for satisfying that yearning which can do aught else than rob A to give to B; consequently all such plans nourish some of the meanest vices of human nature, waste capital, and overthrow civilization. But if we can expand the chances we can count on a general and steady growth of civilization and advancement of society by and through its best members. In the prosecution of these chances we all owe to each other goodwill, mutual respect, and mutual guarantees of liberty and security. Beyond this nothing can be affirmed as a duty of one group to another in a free state.

ANDREW CARNEGIE

THE GOSPEL OF WEALTH (1889)

Andrew Carnegie was among the best-known and wealthiest of the new class of industrialists who rose to prominence in the Gilded Age. The son of poor Scottish weavers, Carnegie immigrated with his family to the United States in 1848. His working career began upon his arrival in America at the age of 13 in a textile mill in Pittsburgh. A few years later, he took a job at a railroad company, rose through the ranks, and began investing in stocks. During the Civil War, Carnegie took advantage of the local wartime economy to move into iron works and eventually launched a steel mill. In 1892, the Carnegie Steel Company was founded, taking maximum advantage of technological innovations and corporate efficiencies to soon dominate the domestic steel industry. In 1901, he sold his interests to the newly consolidated U.S. Steel Corporation and retired to philanthropy and writing. His 1889 essay on wealth stirred an international discussion, arguing that entrepreneurs should dedicate themselves first to generating wealth and then to distributing those earnings through philanthropic causes.

Why does Carnegie believe that an estate tax (a tax on assets at the time of death) is the best form of tax? Why might a high estate tax be preferable to a high income tax, from his perspective? Carnegie praised a ten percent estate tax; would he be equally happy with a more modern rate of forty percent? Why does he think that the entrepreneur should be free to accumulate and distribute great wealth? In what sense does he think the entrepreneur is a "trustee for his poorer brethren"? Steve Jobs, the founder of Apple Computers, died with most of his wealth intact; Bill Gates, the founder of Microsoft, has committed to distributing most of his wealth through charitable activities. Is there reason for preferring Gates's approach? Should the state actively discourage individuals from following the example of Jobs? Should either have been allowed to accumulate large fortunes in the first place? What alternatives might be available?

The problem of our age is the proper administration of wealth, so that the ties of brotherhood may still bind together the rich and poor in harmonious relationship. The conditions of human life have not only been changed, but revolutionized, within the past few hundred years. In former days there was little difference between the dwelling, dress, food, and environment of the chief and those of his retainers. The Indians are to-day where civilized man then was. When visiting the Sioux, I was led to the wigwam of the chief. It was just like the others in external appearance, and even within the difference was trifling between it and those of the poorest of his braves. The contrast between the palace of the millionaire and the cottage of the laborer with us to-day measures the change which has come with civilization.

This change, however, is not to be deplored, but welcomed as highly beneficial. It is well, nay, essential for the progress of the race, that the houses of some should be homes for all that is highest and best in literature and the arts, and for all the refinements of civilization, rather than that none should be so. Much better this great irregularity than universal squalor. . . .

. . .Today the world obtains commodities of excellent quality at prices which even the generation preceding this would have deemed incredible. In the commercial world similar causes have produced similar results, and the race is benefited thereby. The poor enjoy what the rich could not before afford. What were the luxuries have become the necessaries of life. The laborer has now more comforts than the landlord had a few generations ago. The farmer has more luxuries than the landlord had, and is more richly clad and better housed. The landlord has books and pictures rarer, and appointments more artistic, than the King could then obtain.

The price we pay for this salutary change is, no doubt, great. We assemble thousands of operatives in the factory, in the mine, and in the counting-house, of whom the employer can know little or nothing, and to whom the employer is little better than a myth. All intercourse between them is at an end. Rigid Castes are formed, and, as usual, mutual ignorance breeds mutual distrust. Each Caste is without sympathy for the other, and ready to credit anything disparaging in regard to it. Under the law of competition, the employer of thousands is forced into the strictest economies, among which the rates paid to labor figure prominently, and often there is friction between the employer and the employed, between capital and labor, between rich and poor. Human society loses homogeneity.

The price which society pays for the law of competition, like the price it pays for cheap comforts and luxuries, is also great; but the advantage of this law are also greater still, for it is to this law that we owe our wonderful material development, which brings improved conditions in its train. But, whether the law be benign or not, we must say of it, as we say of the change in the conditions of men to which we have referred: It is here; we cannot evade it; no substitutes for it have been found; and while the law may be sometimes hard for the individual, it is best for the race, because it insures the survival of the fittest in every department. We accept and welcome therefore, as conditions to which we must accommodate ourselves, great inequality of environment, the concentration of business, industrial and commercial, in the hands of a few, and the law of competition between these, as being not only beneficial, but essential for the future progress of the race. . . .

Objections to the foundations upon which society is based are not in order, because the condition of the race is better with these than it has been with any others which have been tried. Of the effect of any new substitutes proposed we cannot be sure. The Socialist or Anarchist who seeks to overturn present conditions is to be regarded as attacking the foundation upon which civilization itself rests, for civilization took its start from the day that the capable, industrious workman said to his incompetent and lazy fellow, "If thou dost not sow, thou shalt not reap," and thus ended primitive Communism by separating the drones from the bees. One who studies this subject will soon be brought face to face with the conclusion that upon the sacredness of property civilization itself depends—the right of the laborer to his hundred dollars in the savings bank, and equally the legal right of the millionaire to his millions. To these who propose to substitute Communism for this intense Individualism the answer, therefore, is: The race has tried that. All progress from that barbarous day to the present time has resulted from its displacement. Not evil, but good, has come to the race from the accumulation of wealth by those who have the ability and energy that produce it. . . . Our duty is with what is practicable now; with the next step possible in our day and generation. It is criminal to waste our energies in endeavoring to uproot, when all we can profitably or possibly accomplish is to bend the universal tree of humanity a little in the direction most favorable to the production of good fruit under existing circumstances. . . . Unequally or unjustly, perhaps, as these laws sometimes operate, and imperfect as they appear to the Idealist, they are, nevertheless, like the highest type of man, the best and most valuable of all that humanity has yet accomplished.

. . .

The growing disposition to tax more and more heavily large estates left at death is a cheering indication of the growth of a salutary change in public opinion. The State of Pennsylvania now takes—subject to some exceptions—one-tenth of the property left by its citizens. . . . Of all forms of taxation, this seems the wisest. Men who continue hoarding great sums all their lives, the proper use of which for public ends would work good to the community, should be made to feel that the community, in the form of the state, cannot thus be deprived of its proper share. By taxing estates heavily at death the state marks its condemnation of the selfish millionaire's unworthy life.

. . .

This policy would work powerfully to induce the rich man to attend to the administration of wealth during his life, which is the end that society should always have in view, as being that by far most fruitful for the people. Nor need it be feared that this policy would sap the root of enterprise and render men less anxious to accumulate, for to the class whose ambition it is to leave great fortunes and be talked about after their death, it will attract even more attention, and, indeed, be a somewhat nobler ambition to have enormous sums paid over to the state from their fortunes.

There remains, then, only one mode of using great fortunes; but in this we have the true antidote for the temporary unequal distribution of wealth, the reconciliation of the rich and the poor—a reign of harmony—another ideal, differing, indeed, from that of the Communist in requiring only the further evolution of existing conditions, not the total overthrow of our civilization. . . . Under its sway we shall have an ideal state, in which the surplus wealth of the few will become, in the best sense the property of the many, because administered for the common good, and this wealth, passing through the hands of the few, can be made a much more potent force for the elevation of our race than if it had been distributed in small sums to the people themselves. Even the poorest can be made to see this, and to agree that great sums gathered by some of their fellow-citizens and spent for public purposes, from which the masses reap the principal benefit, are more valuable to them than if scattered among them through the course of many years in trifling amounts.

. . .

This, then, is held to be the duty of the man of Wealth: First, to set an example of modest, unostentatious living, shunning display or extravagance; to provide moderately for the legitimate wants of those dependent upon him; and after doing so to consider all surplus revenues which come to him simply as trust funds, which he is called upon to administer, and strictly bound as a matter of duty to administer in the manner which, in his judgment, is best calculated to produce the most beneficial results for the community—the man of wealth thus becoming the mere agent and trustee for his poorer brethren, bringing to their service his superior wisdom, experience and ability to administer, doing for them better than they would or could do for themselves.

We are met here with the difficulty of determining what are moderate sums to leave to members of the family; what is modest, unostentatious living; what is the test of extravagance. . . . The verdict rests with the best and most enlightened public sentiment. The community will surely judge and its judgments will not often be wrong.

. . .

Thus is the problem of Rich and Poor to be solved. The laws of accumulation will be left free; the laws of distribution free. Individualism will continue, but the millionaire will be but a trustee for the poor; entrusted for a season with a great part of the increased wealth of the community, but administering it for the community far better than it could or would have done for itself. . . .

HENRY D. LLOYD

WEALTH AGAINST COMMONWEALTH (1894)

Henry Demarest Lloyd was part of a new breed of reform-minded, investigative journalists who in the early twentieth century became known as muckrakers. He was raised in modest circumstances in New York City by a minister-turned-bookshop-owner. After graduating from Columbia University and law school, he entered journalism, eventually becoming the lead editorial writer for the *Chicago Tribune* in the early 1880s. His investigation of "a great monopoly" for the *Atlantic Monthly* launched his career as a muckraker and political activist. In the 1890s, he became active in the Illinois Populist Party but abandoned politics when the Populists merged with the Democrats. He dedicated his final years to labor activism and the socialist movement. His most influential book, *Wealth against Commonwealth*, was an extended critique of John D. Rockefeller's Standard Oil Company and the business practices of large corporations.

Why does he think that monopoly is "Business at the end of its journey"? What does Lloyd see as the chief problem of the modern economy? To what degree does Lloyd object to Adam Smith? Is he right to think so? In what sense are modern industrialists like the kings of Europe? Is our wealth too great for the old political and social forms?

Nature is rich; but everywhere man, the heir of nature, is poor. Never in this happy country or elsewhere . . . has there been enough of anything for the people. Never since time began have all the sons and daughters of men been all warm, and all filled, and all shod and roofed. Never yet have all the virgins, wise or foolish, been able to fill their lamps with oil.

The world, enriched by thousands of generations of toilers and thinkers, has reached a fertility which can give every human being a plenty undreamed of even in the Utopias. But between this plenty ripening on the boughs of our civilization and the people hungering for it step the "cornerers," the syndicates, trusts, combinations, with the cry of "overproduction"—too much of everything. Holding back the riches of earth, sea, and sky from their fellows who famish and freeze in the dark, they declare to them that there is too much light and warmth and food. They assert the right, for their private profit, to regulate the consumption by the people of the necessaries of life, and to control production, not by the needs of humanity, but by the desires of a few for dividends. . . .

The majority have never been able to buy enough of anything; but this minority have too much of everything to sell. Liberty produces wealth, and wealth destroys liberty. . . . Our bignesses—cities, factories, monopolies, fortunes, which are our empires, are the obesities of an age gluttonous beyond its powers of digestion. Mankind are crowding upon each other in the centers, and struggling to keep each other out of the feast set by the new sciences and the new fellowships. Our size has got beyond both our science and our conscience. . . . [T]he people cannot reach across even a ward of a city to rule their rulers; Captains of Industry "do not know" whether the men in the ranks are dying from lack of food and shelter; we cannot clean our cities nor our politics. . . .

For those who like the perpetual motion of a debate in which neither of the disputants is looking at the same side of the shield, there are infinite satisfactions in the current controversy as to whether there is any such thing as "monopoly." "There are none," says one side. "They are legion," says the other. . . . Those who say "there are none" hold with the Attorney General of the United States . . . that no one has a monopoly unless there is a "disability" or "restriction" imposed by law on all who would compete. A syndicate that had succeeded in bottling for sale all the air of the earth would not have a monopoly in this view, unless there were on the statute books a law forbidding everyone else from selling air. . . .

Excepting in the manufacture of postage-stamps, gold dollars, and a few other such cases of a "legal restriction," there are no monopolies according to this definition. It excludes the whole body of facts which the people include in their definition, and dismisses a great public question by a mere play on words. . . .

. . .

What we call Monopoly is Business at the end of its journey. The concentration of wealth, the wiping out of the middle class, are other names for it. To get it is, in the world of affairs, the chief end of man.

There are no solitary truths, Goethe says, and monopoly—as the greatest business facts of our civilization, which gives to business what other ages gave to war and religion—is our greatest social, political, and moral fact.

. . .

The corn of the coming harvest is growing so fast that, like the farmer standing at night in his fields, we can hear it snap and crackle. We have been fighting fire on the well-worn lines of old-fashioned politics and political economy, regulating corporations, and leaving competition to regulate itself. But the flames of a new economic evolution run around us, and we turn to find that competition has killed competition, that corporations are grown greater than the State and have bred individuals greater than themselves, and that the naked issue of our time is with property becoming master instead of servant, property in many necessaries of life becoming monopoly of the necessaries of life.

We are still, in part, as Emerson says, in the quadruped state. Our industry is a fight of every man for himself. The prize we give the fittest is monopoly of the necessaries of life, and we leave these winners of the powers of life and death to wield them over us by the same "self-interest" with which they took them from us. In all this we see at work a "principle" which will go into the records as one of the historic mistakes of humanity. "Institutions stand or fall by their philosophy, and the main doctrine of industry since Adam Smith has been the fallacy that the self-interest of the individual was a sufficient guide to the welfare of the individual and society." Heralded as a final truth of "science" this proves to have been nothing higher than a temporary formula for a passing problem. It was a reflection in words of the policy of the day.

. . . "There is no hope for any of us, but the weakest must go first," is the golden rule of business. There is no other field of human associations in which any such rule of action is allowed. The man who should apply in his family or his citizenship this "survival of the fittest" theory as it is practically professed and operated in business would be a monster, and would be speedily made extinct, as we do with monsters. . . . In trade men have not yet risen to the level of the family life of the animals. The true law of business is that all must pursue the interest of all. In the law, the highest product of civilization, this has long been a commonplace. The safety of the people is the supreme law. We are in travail to bring industry up to this. . . .

. . . For a hundred years or so our economic theory has been one of industrial government by the self-interest of the individual. Political government by the self-interest of the individual we call anarchy. . . . Politically, we are civilized; industrially, not yet. . . .

. . .

Thousands of years' experience has proved that government must begin where it ends—with the people; that the general welfare demands that they who exercise the powers and they upon whom these are exercised must be the same, and that higher political ideals can be realized only through higher political forms. . . . We are calling upon [the] owners [of industrial power and property], as mankind called upon kings in their day, to be good and kind, wise and sweet, and we are calling in vain. We are asking them not to be what we have made them to be. We have put power into their hands and ask them not to use it as power. If this power is a trust for the people, the people betrayed it when they made private estates out of it for individuals. If the spirit of power is to change, institutions must change as much. Liberty recast the old forms of government into the Republic, and it must remold our institutions of wealth into the Commonwealth.

. . .

Industry and monopoly cannot live together. Our modern perfection of exchange and division of labor cannot last without equal perfection of morals and sympathy. Everyone is living at the mercy of everyone else in a way entirely peculiar to our times. Nothing is any longer made by a man; parts of things are made by parts of men, and become wholes by the luck of a good humor which so far keeps men from flying asunder. It takes a whole company to make a match. A hundred men will easily produce a hundred million matches, but not one of them could make one match. No farm gets its plough from the crossroads blacksmith, and no one in the chilled-steel factory knows the whole of the plough. . . . Never was there a social machinery so delicate. Only on terms of love and justice can men endure contact so close.

. . . No man can half understand or half operate the fullness of this big citizenship, except by giving his whole time to it. This the place hunter can do, and the privilege hunter. Government, therefore—municipal, State, national—is passing into the hands of these two classes, specialized for the functions of power by their appetite for the fruits of power. The power of citizenship is relinquished by those who do not and cannot know how to exercise it to those who can and do—by those who have a livelihood to make to those who make politics their livelihood.

These specialists of the ward club, the primary, the campaign, the election, and office unite by a law as irresistible as that of the sexes, with those who want all the goods of government—charters, contracts, rulings, permits. . . . There might come a time when the policeman and the railroad president would equally show that they cared nothing for the citizen, individually or collectively, because aware that they and not he were the government. . . . If we cannot find a remedy, all that we love in the word America must die. It will be an awful price to pay if this attempt at government of the people, by the people, for the people must perish from off the face of the earth to prove to mankind that political brotherhood cannot survive where industrial brotherhood is denied. . . .

. . . For as true as that a house divided against itself cannot stand, and that a nation half slave and half free cannot permanently endure, is it true that a people who are slaves to market-tyrants will surely come to be their slaves in all else, that all liberty begins to be lost when one liberty is lost, that a people half democratic and half plutocratic cannot permanently endure.

The secret of the history we are about to make is not that the world is poorer or worse. It is richer and better. Its new wealth is too great for the old forms. . . . The wonder of today is the modern multiplication of products by the union of forces; the marvel of tomorrow will be the greater product which will follow when that which is cooperatively produced is cooperatively enjoyed. . . .

Whether the great change comes with peace or sword, freely through reform or by nature's involuntary forces, is a mere matter of detail, a question of convenience—not of the essence of the thing. The change will come. . . .

. . .

. . . The possibility of regulation is a dream. As long as this control of the necessaries of life and this wealth remain private with individuals, it is they who will regulate, not we. The policy of regulation, disguise it as we may, is but moving to a compromise and equilibrium within the evil all complain of. It is to accept the principle of the sovereignty of the self-interest of the individual and apply constitutional checks to it. . . . [T]he weeding must be done at the roots. . . .

. . . We are to apply the cooperative methods of the post office and the public schools to many other common toils, to all toils in which private sovereignty has become through monopoly a despotism over the public, and to all in which the association of the people and the organization of processes have been so far developed that the profit-hunting Captain of Industry may be replaced by the public-serving Captain of Industry. But we are to have much more. . . .

. . . We are to become honest, giving when we get, and getting with the knowledge and consent of all. We are to become rich, for we shall share in the wealth now latent in idle men and idle land, and in the fertility of work done by those who have ceased to withstand but stand with each other. . . .

THORSTEIN VEBLEN

THE THEORY OF THE LEISURE CLASS (1899)

Thorstein Veblen was one of the most important, if unorthodox, American economists at the turn of the century. He was raised on farms in Wisconsin and Minnesota by his Norwegian parents. He first sought an academic appointment as a philosopher, but without success. He eventually pursued additional graduate work in economics, landing a fellowship at the University of Chicago. In a series of works beginning in the 1890s, he produced some of the foundational studies in institutional economics, which emphasized the significance of the institutional and social features of an economic system to its operation and development and the limitations of models of economic behavior that emphasize the pure rationality of market participants. His academic career, however, was rocky. After his death, his ideas enjoyed some renewed success during the New Deal. *The Theory of the Leisure Class*, the first of his notable books, introduced the importance of conspicuous consumption as a driver of economic behavior and the distinction between the effort to generate profits and the effort to produce useful goods.

What is the importance of "emulation" for Veblen? How important is esteem in driving economic and social behavior? Do Americans consume in the way that Veblen imagines? Is the idea of conspicuous consumption timeless, or is that a feature of particular social environments? Do the affluent aspire toward idleness? What might be the political consequences of conspicuous consumption? Does esteem as a driving force of individual behavior alter how we might think politics works?

. . .

. . . These lower classes can in any case not avoid labor, and the imputation of labor is therefore not greatly derogatory to them, at least not within their class. Rather, since labor is their recognized and accepted mode of life, they take some emulative pride in a reputation for efficiency in their work, this being often the only line of emulation that is open to them. For those for whom acquisition and emulation is possible only within the field of productive efficiency and thrift, the struggle for pecuniary reputability will in some measure work out in an increase of diligence and parsimony. . . .

But it is otherwise with the superior pecuniary class, with which we are here immediately concerned. For this class also the incentive to diligence and thrift is not absent; but its action is so greatly qualified by the secondary demands of pecuniary emulation, that any inclination in this direction is practically overborne and any incentive to diligence tends to be of no effect. The most imperative of these secondary demands of emulation, as well as the one of widest scope, is the requirement of abstention from productive work. . . .

In order to gain and to hold the esteem of men it is not sufficient merely to possess wealth or power. The wealth or power must be put in evidence, for esteem is awarded only on evidence. . . .

. . .

It has already been remarked that the term "leisure", as here used, does not connote indolence or quiescence. What it connotes is non-productive consumption of time. Time is consumed non-productively (1) from a sense of the unworthiness of productive work, and (2) as an evidence of pecuniary ability to afford a life of idleness. . . .

. . .

The quasi-peaceable gentleman of leisure, then, not only consumes of the staff of life beyond the minimum required for subsistence and physical efficiency, but his consumption also undergoes a specialization as regards the quality of the goods consumed. He consumes freely and of the best, in food, drink, narcotics, shelter, services, ornaments, apparel, weapons and accoutrements, amusements, amulets, and idols or divinities. In the process of gradual amelioration which takes place in the articles of his consumption, the motive principle and proximate aim of innovation is no doubt the higher efficiency of the improved and more elaborate products for personal comfort and well-being. But that does not remain the sole purpose of their consumption. The canon of reputability is at hand and seizes upon such innovations as are, according to its standard, fit to survive. Since the consumption of these more excellent goods is an evidence of wealth, it becomes honorific; and conversely, the failure to consume in due quantity and quality becomes a mark of inferiority and demerit.

This growth of punctilious discrimination as to qualitative excellence in eating, drinking, etc. presently affects not only the manner of life, but also the training and intellectual activity of the gentleman of leisure. He is no longer simply the successful, aggressive male,—the man of strength, resource, and intrepidity. In order to avoid stultification he must also cultivate his tastes, for it now becomes incumbent on him to discriminate with some nicety between the noble and the ignoble in consumable goods. . . .

Conspicuous consumption of valuable goods is a means of reputability to the gentleman of leisure. . . .

. . .

VI. AMERICA AND THE WORLD

Major Developments

- Spanish-American War
- Acquisition of overseas territories
- Debate over imperialism

After the Civil War, the volunteers returned home and the federal army was shrunk in size. The United States had over a million men under arms by the end of the war. Just a few years later, the American military was only somewhat larger than it had been before the war. Over the course of the 1880s, the United States could boast fewer than 40,000 military personnel. Once Reconstruction was brought to an end, the military was primarily occupied with pacifying Native American tribes on the Great Plains (a task that was largely completed before the end of the century) and with brief assignments to protect American embassies, citizens, and property in unstable countries (often in Latin America).

The situation changed dramatically in 1898. The sinking of the *USS Maine* in Havana Harbor in February 1898 prompted American intervention against Spanish imperial forces in the independence movement in Cuba. The war only lasted a few weeks but resulted in Spain withdrawing not only from Cuba but also from Puerto Rico, Guam, and the Philippine Islands. The war, and particularly its aftermath, set off a heated debate in the United States over the desirability of creating a far-flung American empire. As a result of the war, the United States came into possession of territories that were already populated and were unlikely to ever be incorporated into the body politic as full-fledged states and territories that extended into Asia, far beyond the traditional American sphere of influence. The United States occupied Cuba for four years before ceding sovereignty to the Cuban republic, held Guam and Puerto Rico as long-term territories, and fought a vicious war with revolutionary forces in the Philippines and then held the islands as a territory before transition to independence after World War II.

The extension of American sovereignty over foreign lands was anticipated in the years preceding the Spanish-American War, and the growing debate over the possible emergence of the United States as a world power is represented by Josiah Strong. The war itself brought the debate over imperialism to a head, as both advocates like Elihu Root and critics like William Graham Sumner sought to influence the direction of American foreign policy and contextualize the situation at the turn of the century within the American tradition.

JOSIAH STRONG

OUR COUNTRY (1885)

Josiah Strong grew up in Ohio during the Civil War and was ordained as a minister in 1871. His book, *Our Country*, was a national sensation. It issued a call for Protestant Christian reform of a country that Strong thought was in spiritual and social crisis and became a frequently reprinted bestseller. After the success of the book, he became a leader in the evangelical community and pressed for social reform. He was a key figure in the Social Gospel movement of the period, which advocated the advancement of social justice as a Christian duty. His emphasis on the importance of the Anglo-Saxon race in advancing civilization at this juncture in history both reflected and fueled arguments for a more expansive American role in the world.

What does "Anglo-Saxon" represent for Strong? To what extent is it a biological category? What does he mean by "spiritual Christianity"? What role does Darwinism play in his argument? Does Strong advocate militarism? What American role in the world would be most consistent with Strong's ideas? Is there still a place for his vision of America's contribution to the world today?

. . .

Every race which has deeply impressed itself on the human family has been the representative of some great idea—one or more—which has given direction to the nation's life and form to its civilization. . . . The Anglo-Saxon is the representative of two great ideas, which are closely related. One of them is that of civil liberty. Nearly all of the civil liberty in the world is enjoyed by Anglo-Saxons. . . .

The other great idea of which the Anglo-Saxon is the exponent is that of a pure *spiritual* Christianity. . . .

It is not necessary to argue to those for whom I write that the two great needs of mankind, that all men may be lifted up into the light of the highest Christian civilization, are, first, a pure, spiritual Christianity, and, second, civil liberty. Without controversy, these are the forces which, in the past, have contributed most to the elevation of the human race, and they must continue to be, in the future, the most efficient ministers to its progress. It follows, then, that the Anglo-Saxon, as the great representative of these two ideas, the depository of these two great blessings, sustains peculiar relations to the world's future, is divinely commissioned to be, in a peculiar sense, his brother's keeper. Add to this the fact of his rapidly increasing strength in modern times, and we have well nigh a demonstration of his destiny. . . . The mighty Anglo-Saxon race, though comprising only one-fifteenth part of mankind, now rules more than one-third of the earth's surface, and more than one-fourth of its people. . . .

This race is multiplying not only more rapidly than any other European race, but far more rapidly than *all* the races of continental Europe. . . . Heretofore, the great causes which have operated to check the growth of population in the world have been war, famine, and pestilence; but, among civilized peoples, these causes are becoming constantly less operative. Paradoxical as it seems, the invention of more destructive weapons of war renders war less destructive; commerce and wealth have removed the fear of famine, and pestilence is being brought more and more under control by medical skill and sanitary science. . . . Europe is crowded, and is constantly become more so, which will tend to reduce continually the ratio of increase; while nearly two-thirds of the Anglo-Saxons occupy lands which invite almost unlimited expansion. . . . [E]migration from Europe, which is certain to increase, is chiefly into Anglo-Saxon countries; while these foreign elements exert a modifying influence on the Anglo-Saxon stock, their descendants are certain to be Anglo-Saxonized. From 1870 to 1880, Germany lost 987,000 inhabitants by emigration; in one generation, their children will be counted Anglo-Saxons. . . .

. . . It is not unlikely that, before the close of the next century, this race will outnumber all the other civilized races of the world. Does it not look as if God were not only preparing in our Anglo-Saxon civilization the die with which to stamp the peoples of the earth, but as if he were also massing behind that die the mighty power with which to press it? . . . I look forward to what the world has never yet seen united in the same race; viz., the greatest numbers, *and* the highest civilization.

There can be no reasonable doubt that North America is to be the great home of the Anglo-Saxon, the principal seat of his power, the center of his life and influence. . . . Our continent has room and resources and climate, it lies in the pathway of the nations, it belongs to the zone of power, and already, among Anglo-Saxons, do we lead in population and wealth. . . . America is to have the great preponderance of numbers and of wealth, and by the logic of events will follow the scepter of controlling influence. . . .

. . .

[W]e are to have not only the larger portion of the Anglo-Saxon race for generations to come, we may reasonably expect to develop the highest type of Anglo-Saxon civilization. If human progress follows a law of development, if "time's noblest offspring is the last," our civilization should be the noblest; for we are "the heirs of all the ages in the foremost flies of time," and not only do we occupy the latitude of power, but *our land is the last to be occupied in that latitude*. There is no other virgin soil in the North Temperate Zone. If the consummation of human progress is not to be looked for here, if there is yet to flower a higher civilization, where is the soil that is to produce it? . . . Heretofore, war has been almost the chief occupation of strong races. England, during the past sixty-eight years, has waged some seventy-seven wars. . . . [B]ut the world is making progress, we are leaving behind the barbarism of war; as civilization advances, it will learn less of war, and concern itself more with the arts of peace. . . .

Mr. Darwin is not only disposed to see, in the superior vigor of our people, an illustration of his favorite theory of natural selection, but even intimates that the world's history thus far has been simply preparatory for our future, and tributary to it. He says: "There is apparently much truth in the belief that the wonderful progress of the United States, as well as the character of the people, are the results of natural selection; for the more energetic, restless, and courageous men from all parts of Europe have emigrated during the last ten or twelve generations to that great country, and have there succeeded best. . . ."

There is abundant reason to believe that the Anglo-Saxon race is to be, is, indeed, already becoming, more effective here than in the mother country. The marked superiority of this race is due, in large measure, to its highly mixed origin. Says Rawlinson: "It is a general rule, now almost universally admitted by ethnologists, that the mixed races of mankind are superior to the pure ones." . . . If the dangers of immigration, which have been pointed out, can be successfully met for the next few years, until it has passed its climax, it may be expected to add value to the amalgam which will constitute the new Anglo-Saxon race of the New World. . . .

It may be easily shown . . . that the two great ideas of which the Anglo-Saxon is the exponent are having a fuller development in the United States than in Great Britain. . . . Furthermore, it is significant that the marked characteristics of this race are being here emphasized most. Among the most striking features of the Anglo-Saxon is his money-making power—a power of increasing importance in the widening commerce of the world's future. . . .

Again, another marked characteristic of the Anglo-Saxon is what may be called an instinct or genius for colonizing. His unequaled energy, his indomitable perseverance, and his personal independence, made him a pioneer. He excels all others in pushing his way in to new countries. It was those in whom this tendency was strongest that came to America. . . .

. . . Moreover, our social institutions are stimulating. In Europe the various ranks of society are, like the strata of the earth, fixed and fossilized. There can be no great change without a terrible upheaval, a social earthquake. Here society is like the waters of the sea, mobile . . . that which is at the bottom today may one day flash on the crest of the highest wave.

Everyone is free to become whatever he can make of himself; free to transform himself from a rail-splitter or a tanner or a canal-boy, into the nation's President. Our aristocracy, unlike that of Europe, is open to all comers. Wealth, position, influence are prizes offered for energy. . . .

What is the significance of such facts? These tendencies infold the future; they are the mighty alphabet with which God writes his prophesies. . . . It seems to me that God, with infinite wisdom and skill, is training the Anglo-Saxon race for an hour sure to come in the world's future. . . . There are no more new worlds. The unoccupied arable lands of the earth are limited, and will soon be taken. The time is coming when the pressure of population on the means of subsistence will be felt here as it is now felt in Europe and Asia. Then will the world enter upon a new stage of its history—the final competition of races, for which the Anglo-Saxon is being schooled. . . . Then this race of unequaled energy, with all the majesty of numbers and the might of wealth behind it—the representative, let us hope, of the largest liberty, the purest Christianity, the highest civilization—having developed peculiarly aggressive traits calculated to impress its institutions upon mankind, will spread itself over the earth. . . . And can anyone doubt that the result of this competition of races will be the "survival of the fittest"? . . . To this result no war of extermination is needful; the contest is not one of arms, but of vitality and of civilization. . . .

Some of the stronger races, doubtless, may be able to preserve their integrity; but, in order to compete with the Anglo-Saxon, they will probably be forced to adopt his methods and instruments, his civilization and his religion. . . .

. . . Men of this generation, from the pyramid top of opportunity on which God has set us, *we look down on forty centuries!* We stretch our hand into the future with power to mold the destinies of unborn millions. . . .

WILLIAM GRAHAM SUMNER

THE CONQUEST OF THE UNITED STATES BY SPAIN (1899)

Illness had forced William Graham Sumner to maintain a lower public profile in the 1890s than he had in the 1880s, but he recovered in time to take a visible role in the debate over the annexation of the Philippines. Sumner joined the Anti-Imperialist League and spoke out against the Republican administration. Sumner likewise publicly declined to support the Republicans in the 1900 election, though he was unwilling to go so far as to support the populist Democratic challenger, William Jennings Bryan. His lecture before the Phi Beta Kappa Society at Yale University in the spring of 1899 was published and widely reprinted.

What is the basis for Sumner's opposition to the occupation of the Philippines? Are there any commonalities between Sumner's anti-imperialism arguments and his argument about class relations? In what sense does Sumner think that the United States was being "conquered" by Spain? Do we have experience to evaluate the kind of consequences that Sumner thought would follow from American activities abroad?

. . . Spain was the first, for a long time the greatest, of the modern imperialistic states. The United States, by its historical origins, its traditions and its principles, is the chief representative of the revolt and reaction against that kind of state. I intend to show that, by the line of action now proposed to us, which we call expansion and imperialism, we are throwing away some of the most important elements of the American symbol, and are adopting some of the most important elements of the Spanish symbol. We have beaten Spain in a military conflict, but we are submitting to be conquered by her on the field of ideas and policies. . . . Those philosophies appeal to national vanity and national cupidity. They are seductive. . . . They are delusions, and they will lead us to ruin unless we are hard-headed enough to resist them. . . .

. . .

. . . What comes to us in the evolution of our own life and interests, that we must meet; what we go to seek which lies beyond that domain, is a waste of our energy and a compromise of our liberty and welfare. If this is not sound doctrine, then the historical and social sciences have nothing to teach us which is worth any trouble.

. . . There is a set of men who have always been referred to, in our Northern States, for the last thirty years, with special disapproval. They are those Southerners who, in 1861, did not believe in secession, but, as they said, "Went with their States." They have been condemned for moral cowardice. Yet within a year it has become almost a doctrine with us that patriotism requires that we should hold our tongues whenever our rulers choose to engage in war, although out interests, our institutions, our most sacred traditions, and our best established maxims may be trampled underfoot. There is no doubt that moral courage is the virtue which is more needed than any other in the modern democratic state, and that truckling to popularity is the worst political vice. . . . Let us be well-assured that self-government is not a matter of flags and Fourth of July orations, nor yet of strife to get offices. Eternal vigilance is the price of that as of every other political good. The perpetuity of self-government depends on the sound political sense of the people, and sound political sense is a matter of habit and practice. . . .

There is not a civilized nation which does not talk about its civilizing mission just as grandly as we do. . . . Now each nation laughs at all the others when it observes these manifestations of national vanity. You may rely upon it that they are all ridiculous by virtue of these pretensions, including ourselves. The point is that each of them repudiates the standards of the others, and the outlying nations, which are to be civilized, hate all the standards of civilized men. We assume that what we like and practice, and what we think better, must come as a welcome blessing to Spanish-Americans and Filipinos. This is grossly and obviously untrue. They hate our ways. They are hostile to our ideas. Our religion, language, institutions, and manners offend them. . . . The most important thing which we shall inherit from the Spaniards will be the task of suppressing rebellions. If the United States takes out of the hands of Spain her mission, on the ground that Spain is not executing it well, and if this nation, in its turn, attempts to be school-mistress to others, it will shrivel up into the same vanity and self-conceit of which Spain now is an example. . . . Now, the great reason why all these enterprises, which began by saying to somebody else: We know what is good for you, better than you know yourself, and we are going to make you do it—are false and wrong, is that they violate liberty; or, to turn the same statement into other words: the reason why liberty, of which we Americans talk so much, is a good thing, is, that it means leaving people to live out their own lives in their own way, while we do the same. . . .

. . .

Everywhere you go on the Continent of Europe at this hour you see the conflict between militarism and industrialism. You see the expansion of industrial power pushed forward by the energy, hope, and thrift of men, and you see the development arrested, diverted, crippled, and defeated by measures which are dictated by military considerations. . . . It is militarism which is eating up all the products of science and art, defeating the energy of the population, and wasting its savings. It is militarism which forbids the people to give their attention to the problems of their own welfare, and to give their strength to the education and comfort of their children. It is militarism which is combating the grand efforts of science and art to ameliorate the struggle for existence.

The American people believe that they have a free country, and we are treated to grandiloquent speeches about our flag and our reputation for freedom and enlightenment. The common opinion is that we have these things because we have chosen and adopted them, because they are in the Declaration of Independence and the Constitution. We suppose, therefore, that we are sure to keep them, and that the follies of other people are things which we can hear about with complacency. People say that this country is like no other, that its prosperity proves its exceptionality, and so on. These are popular errors which in time will meet with harsh correction. The United States is in a protected situation. It is easy to have equality where land is abundant, and where the population is small. It is easy to have prosperity where a few men have a great continent to exploit. It is easy to have liberty when you have no dangerous neighbors, and when the struggle for existence is easy. There are no severe penalties, under such circumstances, for political mistakes. Democracy is not then a thing to be nursed and defended, as it is in an old country like France. It is rooted and founded in the economic circumstances of the country. . . . This protected position, however, is sure to pass away. As the country fills up with population, and the task of getting a living out of the ground becomes more difficult, the struggle for existence will become harder, and the competition of life more severe. Then liberty and democracy will cost something if they are to be maintained.

Now what will hasten the day when our present advantages will wear out, and when we shall come down to the conditions of the older and densely populated nations? The answer is: war, debt, taxation, diplomacy, a grand governmental system, pomp, glory, a big army and navy, lavish expenditures, political jobbery—in a word, imperialism. . . .

The great foe of democracy now and in the near future is plutocracy. . . . It is the social war of the twentieth century. In that war militarism, expansion, and imperialism will all favor plutocracy. In the first place, war and expansion will favor jobbery, both in the dependencies and at home. In the second place, they will take away the attention of the people from what the plutocrats are doing. In the third place, they will cause large expenditures of the people's money, the return for which will not go into the treasury, but into the hands of a few schemers. In the fourth place, they will call for a large public debt and taxes, and these things especially tend to make men unequal, because any social burdens bear more heavily on the weak than on the strong, and so make the weak weaker and the strong stronger. Therefore expansion and imperialism are a grand onslaught on democracy.

. . .

. . . My patriotism is of the kind which is outraged by the notion that the United States never was a great nation until in a petty three months' campaign it knocked to pieces a poor, decrepit, bankrupt old state like Spain. To hold such an opinion as that is to abandon all American standards, to put shame and scorn on all that our ancestors tried to build up here and to go over the standards of which Spain is a representative.

ELIHU ROOT

SPEECH AT CANTON, OHIO (1900)

Elihu Root graduated from Hamilton College at the end of the Civil War and went on to become one of the leading lawyers in New York City in the 1870s. He formed a relationship with Theodore Roosevelt in New York Republican circles in the 1880s and became a close ally. In 1899, President William McKinley appointed Root to be secretary of war at a time when the chief task to be confronted was the management of the new foreign territories. After a few months out of office, President Theodore Roosevelt tapped Root to become secretary of state in 1905, at a time when diplomatic and military tensions in Asia were particularly high. Root was later awarded the Nobel Peace Prize for his efforts in those two offices. After a term in the U.S. Senate, he was a vocal supporter of American intervention in World War I. Root was serving as secretary of war during the 1900 presidential campaign, and in October of that campaign season he delivered an address on the Philippines in the president's home town of Canton, Ohio. The widely discussed speech served as the formal Republican reply to Democratic attacks on American policy in the region.

How does Root reconcile American ideals with continued occupation of the Philippines? What role does Root stake out for the United States in foreign territories? Does Root embrace imperialism as such? What obligations does the United States owe to foreign peoples after a war? Are there circumstances in which the United States should attempt to create democratic institutions in a foreign territory?

. . .

Imperialism! The word has a familiar sound. The cry is one of the cheapest and most threadbare of the demagogue's stock, always certain to produce a sensation among a people alert for the protection of their liberties. . . . Is there any more in the cry now than there was in the days of Jefferson, or Lincoln and of Grant? Is the character of our institutions really about to be changed, or are our liberties really in danger? . . .

. . .

[W]e are told that, irrespective of agreements, irrespective of anything said or done by the Filipino leaders, or by ourselves, we ought to transfer to them sovereignty over the Philippine Islands, because government derives its just powers from the consent of the governed, and our maintenance of sovereignty is a violation of that great principle of the Declaration of Independence.

Nothing can be more misleading than a principle misapplied. . . . The doctrine that government derives its just powers from the consent of the governed was applicable to the conditions for which Jefferson wrote it, and to the people to whom he applied it. It is true wherever a people exists capable and willing to maintain just government, and to make free, intelligent and efficacious decision as to who shall govern. But . . . government does not depend upon consent. The immutable laws of justice and humanity require that people shall have government, that the weak shall be protected, that cruelty and lust shall be restrained, whether there be consent or not.

When I consider the myriads of human beings who have lived in subjection to the rule of force, ignorant of any other lot, knowing life only as the beast of the field knows it, without the seeds of progress, without initiative or capacity to rise, submissive to injustice and cruelty and perpetual ignorance and brutishness, I cannot believe that, for the external forces of civilization, to replace brutal and oppressive government, with which such a people in ignorance are content, by ordered liberty and individual freedom and a rule that shall start and lead them along the path of political and social progress, is a violation of the principle of Jefferson, or false to the highest dictates of liberty and humanity.

. . .

The testimony is absolutely overwhelming that the people inhabiting the Philippine archipelago are incapable of self-government, and that the fate here described [oscillating between anarchy and despotism] would have befallen these islands of the tropics had American sovereignty been withdrawn. There is no Philippine people. The hundreds of islands which compose the archipelago are inhabited by more than eighty different tribes, speaking more than sixty different languages. They have no common medium of communication, and they never had a government except the arbitrary rule of Spain. Most of them have not the first conception of what self-government means, or the first qualification for its exercise. Many of them have the capacity to learn, but they have never learned.

. . .

. . . A republic cannot have subjects and live, it is said. We have survived the government of Louisiana and the Northwest Territory and New Mexico and Alaska and many other territories in which the people of the United States as a whole have governed the people of the territory with as much authority and power as need be exercised in the Philippine Islands. The true proposition is the precise reverse of the charge which is made. The government of the Philippine Islands will not affect the character of our institutions, but the character of our institutions will determine and mold the government of the Philippine Islands. To govern as a despot would be fatal to the character of a republic, but to govern as Congress always has and always will govern in territory outside the limits of the States, in accordance with the spirit of our institutions, subject to all the great rules of liberty and right, and responsible for every act to a great liberty-loving people can but extend and strengthen our institutions.

. . .

It is charged that the present administration is in favor of increasing the regular army, and this is said to be *militarism*, a crime that endangers the liberty of the republic. . . .

. . .

Now does any sane American honestly believe that this [the maintenance of a standing army of 100,000 men] threatens the liberties or the institutions of our country? Why, President McKinley had 272,000 men in arms at the close of the Spanish war. Grant had an army of 1,052,000 on the 30th of April, 1865, and they melted away into the peaceable body of the people like snowflakes in May. But these are volunteers, it will be said. Well, all the soldiers of the regular army are volunteers. Never in the history of the army has there been a man drafted or forced into it against his will. Their term of enlistment is but three years, and at the end of that time they go back to the occupations of civil life. They are all Americans. They are intelligent Americans. None are admitted who cannot read and write. They are sound, wholesome Americans, of good habits and regular lives, for none are admitted who are not in perfect health. . . . They all swear allegiance, not to a Monarch or a President, but to the United States of America. . . . Where they go lawn and order and justice and charity and education and religion follow. . . . I challenge them to point to a single act of oppression, in all these one hundred and eleven years, to a single act of disloyalty on the part of the regular army, to the supremacy of civil law and the principles of our free constitutional government.

FOR FURTHER STUDY

Bryan, William Jennings. *William Jennings Bryan: Selections*, ed. Ray Ginger (Indianapolis, IN: Bobbs-Merrill, 1967).

Carnegie, Andrew. *The "Gospel of Wealth" Essays and Other Writings*, ed. David Nasaw (New York: Penguin, 2006).

Clark, Thomas Dionysius, ed. *The South since Reconstruction* (Indianapolis, IN: Bobbs-Merrill, 1973).

Cooley, Thomas M. *A Treatise on the Constitutional Limitations Which Rest Upon the Legislative Power of the State of the American Union* (Boston, MA: Little, Brown, 1927).

Filler, Louis, ed. *Late Nineteenth-Century American Liberalism: Representative Selections, 1880–1900* (Indianapolis, IN: Bobbs-Merrill, 1962).

George, Henry. *Progress and Poverty: An Inquiry into the Cause of Industrial Depressions and of Increase of Want with Increase of Wealth* (New York: Modern Library, 1938).

Gilman, Charlotte Perkins. *Herland and Related Writings*, ed. Beth Sutton-Ramspeck (New York: Broadview, 2012).

Gladden, Washington. *Applied Christianity: Moral Aspects of Social Questions* (New York: Arno Press, 1976).

Link, William A., and Susannah J. Link, eds. *The Gilded Age and Progressive Era: A Documentary Reader* (Malden, MA: Wiley-Blackwell, 2012).

Pollack, Norman, ed. *The Populist Mind* (Indianapolis, IN: Bobbs-Merrill, 1967).

Sumner, William Graham. *On Liberty, Society, and Politics: The Essential Essays of William Graham Sumner*, ed. Robert C. Bannister (Indianapolis, IN: Liberty Fund, 1992).

Ward, Lester. *Lester Ward and the Welfare State*, ed. Henry Steele Commager (Indianapolis, IN: Bobbs-Merrill, 1967).

Washington, Booker T. *Up from Slavery*, ed. William L. Andrews (New York: Oxford University Press, 1995).

SUGGESTED READINGS

Blight, David W. *Race and Reunion: The Civil War in American Memory* (Cambridge, MA: Harvard University Press, 2001).

Fine, Sidney. *Laissez Faire and the General-Welfare State: A Study in Conflict in American Thought, 1865–1901* (Ann Arbor: University of Michigan Press, 1956).

Foster, Gaines M. *Moral Reconstruction: Christian Lobbyists and the Federal Legislation of Morality, 1865–1920* (Chapel Hill: University of North Carolina Press, 2007).

Goldstene, Claire. *The Struggle for America's Promise: Equal Opportunity at the Dawn of Corporate Capital* (Jackson: University Press of Mississippi, 2014).

Gordon, Sarah Barringer. *The Mormon Question: Polygamy and Constitutional Conflict in Nineteenth-Century America* (Chapel Hill: University of North Carolina Press, 2002).

Hoffer, Williamjames Hull. *To Enlarge the Machinery of Government: Congressional Debates and the Growth of the American State, 1858–1891* (Baltimore, MD: Johns Hopkins University Press, 2007).

Keller, Morton. *Affairs of State: Public Life in Late Nineteenth Century America* (Cambridge, MA: Harvard University Press, 1977).

Kens, Paul. *Justice Stephen Field: Shaping American Liberty from the Gold Rush to the Gilded Age* (Lawrence: University Press of Kansas, 1997).

LaFeber, Walter. *The New Empire: An Interpretation of American Expansion, 1860–1898* (Ithaca: Cornell University Press, 1963).

McCloskey, Robert G. *American Conservatism in the Age of Enterprise, 1865–1910: A Study of William Graham Sumner, Stephen J. Field, and Andrew Carnegie* (New York: Harper & Row, 1964).

Meier, August. *Negro Thought in America, 1880–1915: Racial Ideologies in the Age of Booker T. Washington* (Ann Arbor: University of Michigan Press, 1963).

Ninkovich, Frank. *Global Dawn: The Cultural Foundation of American Internationalism, 1865–1890* (Cambridge, MA: Harvard University Press, 2009).

Palmer, Bruce. *"Man Over Money": The Southern Populist Critique of American Capitalism* (Chapel Hill: University of North Carolina Press, 1980).

Parrington, Vernon Louis. *Main Currents in American Thought, volume 3: The Beginnings of Critical Realism in America: 1860–1920* (New York: Harcourt, Brace & World, 1930).

Paul, Arnold M. *Conservative Crisis and the Rule of Law: Attitudes of Bar and Bench, 1887–1895* (Ithaca, NY: Cornell University Press, 1960).

Postel, Charles. *The Populist Vision* (New York: Oxford University Press, 2007).

Przybyszewski, Linda. *The Republic According to John Marshall Harlan* (Chapel Hill: University of North Carolina Press, 1999).

Sneider, Allison L. *Suffragists in an Imperial Age: U.S. Expansion and the Woman Question, 1870–1929* (New York: Oxford University Press, 2008).

Sullivan, Kathleen S. *Constitutional Context: Women and Rights Discourse in Nineteenth-Century America* (Baltimore, MD: Johns Hopkins University Press, 2007).

Swisher, Carl B. *Stephen Field: Craftsman of the Law* (Chicago, IL: University of Chicago Press, 1930).

Twiss, Benjamin R. *Lawyers and the Constitution: How Laissez Faire Came to the Supreme Court* (Princeton, NJ: Princeton University Press, 1942).

Wiebe, Robert H. *The Search for Order, 1877–1920* (New York: Hill and Wang, 1966).

CHAPTER 8

THE PROGRESSIVE ERA, 1901–1932

I. INTRODUCTION

It sometimes seemed that everyone was a Progressive in the first decades of the twentieth century. The political historian Richard Hofstadter labeled this the "age of reform" for a reason. These were the years when intellectuals, activists, and politicians from a variety of perspectives looked to reevaluate inherited institutions and modify America politics and society to better face the perceived challenges of the industrial age. Their actions, as Hofstadter concluded, "set the tone of American politics for the greater part of the twentieth century." Progressivism is not easily defined, however, in part because nearly everyone seemed to embrace it. Hofstadter referred to it simply as "the broader impulse toward criticism and change that was everywhere so conspicuous after 1900," with a "general theme" of restoring "economic individualism and political democracy" after the apparent corruption of large corporations and political machines.[1] Similarly, the intellectual historian Daniel Rodgers concluded that "the fundamental fact of the era is not reform in any traditional sense of the term, but the explosion of scores of aggressive, politically active pressure groups into the space left by the recession of traditional political loyalties."[2] There was a formal Progressive Party that ran candidates and offered a platform, but Progressives could be found in both major political parties and in a wide range of political and social movements.

The three- (or four-) way race for president in 1912 is emblematic of the period. William Howard Taft was the incumbent Republican president, the hand-picked successor to Theodore Roosevelt. Taft had earned a reputation (working in both the executive and judicial branches) as an efficient administrator and creative problem-solver, but Roosevelt soon decided that Taft was not bold enough in his thinking—and besides occupied the Oval Office that was Roosevelt's natural home. Woodrow Wilson was the Democratic challenger, the intellectual former president of Princeton University and governor of New Jersey who promised to save the

1 Richard Hofstadter, *The Age of Reform: From Bryan to F.D.R.* (New York: Vintage, 1955), 3, 5.
2 Daniel T. Rodgers, "In Search of Progressivism," *Reviews in American History* 10 (1982): 114.

Democratic Party from its Populist exile. Theodore Roosevelt, the "Bull Moose," had already served nearly eight years as president but was ready to try again under the Progressive Party banner. Marking out a more radical agenda than his competition, he declared that he believed in "pure democracy" and wanted to reform institutions to give the people more direct access to the levers of power. The long-time labor leader Eugene V. Debs once again ran for the presidency with the Socialist Party. Debs had his best showing in 1912, claiming nearly six percent of the popular vote. But the real battle was between Wilson, Roosevelt, and Taft, with the morose Taft primarily running with a goal of keeping Roosevelt from wrecking the Republican Party. Taft and Roosevelt split the traditional Republican vote, and Wilson squeaked into office with just over forty percent of the popular vote (but a landslide eighty-two percent of the electoral college). None of the candidates articulated the stand-pat views or small-government philosophy that was typical of the Gilded Age. The debate was not over whether to reform, but what to reform and by how much.

Politics. The Populist takeover of the Democratic Party in 1896 and the nomination of William Jennings Bryan for the presidency shook up the political landscape. The two major parties had been closely competitive in the Gilded Age and fought over a few, economically conservative, battleground states. Bryan tried to break the logjam by pulling together workers and farmers and unifying the Democrats and one or more of the large third parties under a single banner. The strategy backfired. Bryan took only forty-six percent of the popular vote in 1896, and the Democrats did even worse in subsequent elections (sometimes with Bryan at the top of the ticket). The Democrats snuck into the White House with Woodrow Wilson in 1912 and 1916, but by 1920 they were once again relegated to a distant second place. Third parties like the Socialists and the Prohibition Party were in no position to play spoiler, given the large Republican margins of victory in most races. The Progressive Party rallied around some popular individual candidates—Republicans Teddy Roosevelt in 1912 and Robert M. La Follette in 1924—but besides spoiling Taft's chances in 1912 had little effect on the party structure.

Republican electoral dominance did not mean political stagnation. The first decades of the twentieth century were a time of substantial political innovation. Electoral reforms like the adoption of party primaries and the Australian (or long-form) ballot were designed to break up the political machines. Suffrage reform like the widespread adoption of literacy tests and poll taxes for voters, voter registration, and female suffrage were intended to improve the quality of the electorate and reduce electoral fraud (while also having the effect of significantly reducing voter turnout). Institutional reforms like the spread of initiative and referenda mechanisms, city managers, civil service, and regulatory commissions and bureaus were intended to create more effective and efficient policy design and implementation. Policy reforms like the expansion of public schooling, economic regulation, immigration restrictions, eugenics, and alcohol prohibition were advanced as solutions to social ills. Constitutional reforms like the direct election of U.S. senators and the authorization of the income tax made significant changes in the U.S. Constitution for the first time since Reconstruction.

FIGURE 8-1 TIMELINE OF THE PROGRESSIVE ERA

Events	Year	Writings
	1903	W.E.B. Du Bois's *The Souls of Black Folk*
Max Weber's *The Protestant Ethic and the Spirit of Capitalism*	1905	Upton Sinclair's *The Jungle*
	1906	Emma Goldman's *Anarchism*
	1907	Herbert Croly's *The Promise of American Life*
	1909	
National Association for the Advancement of Colored People founded	1909	
Woodrow Wilson wins presidency against splintered Republican Party	1912	
Federal Income Tax Amendment ratified	1913	
United State declares war against Germany	1917	
Russian Revolution creates the Soviet Union	1917	
Prohibition Amendment ratified	1919	
U.S. Senate rejects the League of Nations treaty	1919	
American Civil Liberties Union founded	1920	
Women's Suffrage Amendment ratified	1920	
Gyorgy Lukacs's *History and Class Consciousness*	1923	
Establishment of national orign quotas for immigration to the United States	1924	
Scopes Trial for violation of ban on teaching of evolution in public schools in Tennessee	1925	
	1925	F. Scott Fitzgerald's *The Great Gatsby*
	1927	John Dewey's *The Public and Its Problems*
	1928	Herbert Hoover's "Rugged Individualism" Speech
Stock market crash marks beginning of Great Depression	1929	
Sigmund Freud's *Civilization and Its Discontents*	1930	

Society. In the early decades of the twentieth century, the United States became a more self-consciously urban nation. During the Gilded Age, populists like James Weaver, Ben Butler, Tom Watson, and William Jennings Bryan found their most natural constituency among the small farmers of the South and Midwest. During the Progressive Era, radicals and reformers were more likely to draw from and focus on the problems of the cities with their factories and slums. In 1900, over sixty percent of the population lived in rural areas. In 1930, nearly sixty percent lived in urban areas. The rural population grew hardly at all over those years, but the urban population exploded. African-Americans made the "Great Migration" from the countryside of the South to the cities of the North, and made places like Chicago and Harlem new cultural centers of black life. Immigrants from abroad, many from southern and eastern Europe, filed into port cities on the Atlantic coast. The federal government had declared the western frontier fully settled and closed. The new generation sought its fortunes in the city.

This was also a time of experimentation. Technological progress was rapid and profound. Innovations from the mass production of the automobile to the invention of the airplane, radio, the air conditioner, cornflakes, the zipper, and penicillin had immediate and dramatic effects on the average person's life. Muckrakers like Upton Sinclair and Lincoln Steffens exposed the unresolved problems of twentieth-century life. Modern architects like Frank Lloyd Wright remade the urban landscape. America popular music was transformed by new styles like ballroom orchestras, jazz, and musical theater. The political success of suffragists had its cultural accompaniment, from the growing numbers of women working outside the home to jazz-age flappers.

Ideas. In the arena of ideas, the new modernism was both embraced and challenged. The distinctly American tradition of pragmatism had its roots in the late nineteenth century and was influenced by the new science of evolution, but blossomed in the early twentieth. Hoping to cut through seemingly interminable philosophical debates, William James argued that "whenever a dispute is serious, we ought to be able to show some practical difference that must follow from one side or the other being right."[3] Truth was known by its instrumental value. John Dewey pushed such ideas forward, calling for a spirit of experimentation to learn what social arrangements and ways of living might be most valuable: "We live in a world that is changing, not settled and fixed." Little was to be gained by teaching that "our forefathers had finally determined all important social and political questions."[4] A different realist element was introduced into the public consciousness by psychologist Sigmund Freud. Men were not governed simply by reason; emotion and the unconscious must be given their due. Pointing to both Freud and the pragmatists, the journalist Walter Lippmann concluded we would be mistaken to divide the world of ideas into the true and the false and view ourselves as setting aside old errors. We must recognize that "reason serve[s] the irrational," has "always done" so, and "ought to always to do" so.[5]

Others were more reluctant to accept the quick dismissal of inherited verities. For these cultural critics, democracy and consumer capitalism were together undermining civilization. Henry Adams, grandson of President John Quincy Adams, complained of "our vast

---

3 William James, *Pragmatism* (New York: Longmans, Green, and Co., 1908), 45–46.

4 John Dewey, "Education and the Social Order," in *The Later Works of John Dewey*, ed. Jo Ann Boydston, vol. 9 (Carbondale: Southern Illinois University Press, 2008), 181.

5 Walter Lippmann, *A Preface to Politics* (New York: Mitchell Kennerley, 1914), 235.

crude democracy of trade" that favored the "cheap" and "the common" over the truly valuable.[6] The humanists did not necessarily reject the significance of emotions and irrationality, but they drew very different lessons from that observation. Irving Babbitt explained that the humanist, "as opposed to the humanitarian, is interested in the perfecting of the individual rather than in schemes for the elevation of mankind as a whole."[7] The democratic celebration of the "mass man," or the "yokels" as the journalist H. L. Mencken preferred, came at the expense of an appreciation for wisdom.

II. DEMOCRACY AND LIBERTY

Major Developments

- Adoption of new methods to restrict ballot access in North and South
- Debate over accountability of government officials
- Debate over establishing democratic control over corporations

The overriding challenge regarding democracy in the early twentieth century was reconciling free government with two unresolved problems from the late nineteenth century. Broadly speaking, the perceived inherited problems were the corruption of the political party machinery and the size and power of private corporations. Both problems had been the subject of periodic, piecemeal reforms in the Gilded Age, including the introduction of a civil service system in the federal bureaucracy in 1883, the clean-government "mugwump" revolt from the Republican Party that helped elect Democratic reformer Grover Cleveland in 1884, and the passage of the Sherman Antitrust Act of 1890 by a Republican-controlled Congress. But few regarded such reforms as adequate, and the early twentieth century was centrally concerned with reforming the institutions of democratic government to win back popular trust and reestablish popular control over society.

These two problems were related, but the proposed solutions were distinct. The reform of the institutions of democracy was seen as critical to overcoming entrenched political parties and their operatives. In the cities, neighborhood-based elected politicians were supplanted by professional managers and politicians elected in citywide elections. Long-tenured and trained civil servants replaced amateurish patronage appointees in government bureaucracies. Party primary systems shifted the choice of party nominees out of convention halls and into public elections. Initiative and referenda systems spread through the West, allowing ordinary citizens to make laws and bypass legislatures and their lobbyists. Civil groups like the League of Women Voters simultaneously pushed for the extension of the franchise to upper-class women and ballot reforms like literacy tests and voter registration that tended to suppress working-class voting. As Figure 8-2 illustrates, overall voter turnout fell dramatically from the Gilded Age to the Progressive Era, stabilizing at a lower level where it has remained ever since.

---

6 Henry James, *The American Scene* (New York: Harper & Brothers, 1907), 63.

7 Irving Babbitt, *Literature and the American College* (Cambridge, MA: Riverside Press, 1908), 8.

Cleaning up government was only half the battle. The other important question on the Progressive agenda was how best to subordinate business to government. For many reformers, empowering the people through democratic government meant not only securing popular control over government policy but also securing the effectiveness of government to achieve the desired goals. Democracy was meaningless if the government was toothless. In particular, big business was the other powerful player on the social stage, and reformers were concerned with finding ways to make sure that government occupied center stage and could, when necessary, dominate business.

The reform of democracy was closely associated with shifts in thinking about rights. For conservatives, radical movements and social tensions raised threats to traditional liberties. When Populists and Progressives called for a "pure democracy" that could implement the majority will, conservatives emphasized the importance of constitutional checks and balances to protect individuals and minorities from democratic majorities. Former Supreme Court Justice Charles Evans Hughes warned voters that Progressive proposals would put "everything you have, the security of your person and life . . . at the mercy of Congress."[8] Meanwhile, reform liberals questioned traditional understandings of liberty. The nineteenth-century British philosopher T. H. Green had taken the critical step, contending that when "we speak of freedom as something to be so highly prized, we mean a positive power

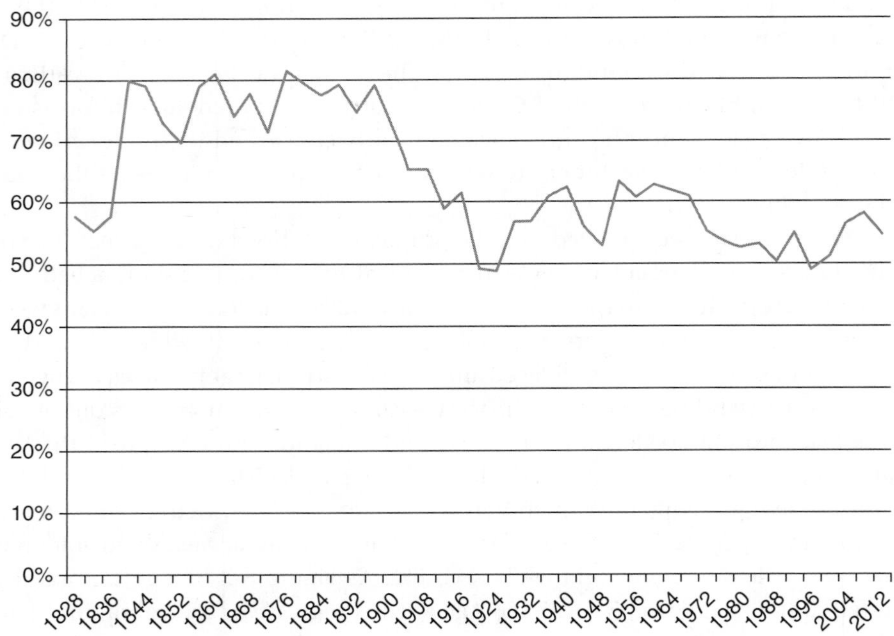

FIGURE 8-2 Voter Turnout in Presidential Elections.

8 "Hughes Answers Critics of Party," *New York Times* (October 5, 1924), E1.

or capacity of doing or enjoying something worth doing or enjoying."[9] The "mere" removal of constraints, in itself, makes "no contribution to true freedom." True or "positive" freedom empowered individuals to make "contributions to a common good." In the early twentieth century, British theorists like L. T. Hobhouse and Americans like John Dewey built on these ideas, arguing that liberalism, properly understood, is "aimed at securing the external and material conditions of [the] free and unimpeded development" of "inward growth and happiness."[10] For these new liberals, positive state action was essential to expanding liberty. The real threat to liberty could be found in the restrictions on democratic majorities that judges like Charles Evans Hughes or Thomas Cooley held dear.

9 Thomas Hill Green, "Liberal Legislation and Freedom of Contract," in *Works of Thomas Hill Green*, ed. R. L. Nettleship, vol. 3 (London: Longmans, Green, and Co., 1888), 371, 372.

10 L. T. Hobhouse, *Liberalism* (New York: Oxford University Press, 1964), 78.

THEODORE ROOSEVELT

THE NEW NATIONALISM (1910)

Theodore Roosevelt was elevated to the presidency when an anarchist's bullet killed President William McKinley just a few months after his second inaugural. Roosevelt was a popular reformer but had an uneasy relationship with the Republican Party regulars. As president, his signature policy initiative was a critique of large corporations. Promising a "square deal for every man," he sought to rein in corporate power and tamp down labor unrest while maintaining core Republican policies like protective tariffs and hard currency. He won a second term in his own right in 1904 and passed the White House to his hand-picked successor, William Howard Taft, with his personal popularity intact. Taft was unable to bridge the divisions within his party as successfully as Roosevelt had done. By 1910, Roosevelt had joined disaffected progressives within the Republican Party in calling for a change. In a speech in Osawatomie, Kansas, Roosevelt began to set the stage for another run at the White House. His proposal for a "New Nationalism" aligned fully with the progressive wing of the GOP, abandoning the more conservative wing, and called for direct national control over corporations. His 1912 campaign under the Progressive Party banner split the Republican Party, allowing a Democratic victory at the polls. Roosevelt became a vocal critic of Woodrow Wilson, regarding the president's foreign policy as insufficiently aggressive, and remained a possibility for another presidential campaign until ill health discouraged such talk.

How does Roosevelt see himself as following the legacy of Abraham Lincoln? What does Roosevelt mean by "equal opportunity"? What does he see as the relationship between the challenges of the early twentieth century and the challenges posed by slavery? Is it reasonable to simultaneously advocate "fair play" and changing the "rules of the game"? What does Roosevelt think is the alternative to public ownership of the large corporations? Is there a principled way to distinguish between those businesses that ought to be subject to such enhanced government control and those that should not? To what degree is Roosevelt abandoning "trust busting"—the use of antitrust laws to break up monopolies and block uncompetitive business practices? How does Roosevelt's approach to corporations differ from a regulatory approach? Is Roosevelt's approach preferable to a policy of regulation and antitrust enforcement?

. . . Our country—this great Republic—means nothing unless it means the triumph of a real democracy, the triumph of popular government, and, in the long run, of an economic system under which each man shall be guaranteed the opportunity to show the best that there is in him. . . .

. . .

In every wise struggle for human betterment one of the main objects, and often the only object, has been to achieve in large measure equality of opportunity. In the struggle for this great end, nations rise from barbarism to civilization, and through it people press forward from one stage of enlightenment to the next. One of the chief factors in progress is the destruction of special privilege. The essence of any struggle for healthy liberty has always been, and must always be, to take from some one man or class of men the right to enjoy power, or wealth, or position, or immunity, which has not been earned by service to his or their fellows. That is what you fought for in the Civil War, and that is what we strive for now.

At many stages in the advance of humanity, this conflict between the men who possess more than they have earned and the men who have earned more than they possess is the central condition of progress. In our day it appears as the struggle of freemen to gain and hold the right of self-government as against the special interests, who twist the methods of free government into machinery for defeating the popular will. At every stage, and under all circumstances, the essence of the struggle is to equalize opportunity, destroy privilege, and give to the life and citizenship of every individual the highest possible value both to himself and to the commonwealth. . . .

Practical equality of opportunity for all citizens, when we achieve it, will have two great results. First, every man will have a fair chance to make of himself all that in him lies; to reach the highest point to which his capacities, unassisted by special privilege of his own and unhampered by the special privilege of others, can carry him, and to get for himself and his family substantially what he has earned. Second, equality of opportunity means that the commonwealth will get from every citizen the highest service of which he is capable. No man who carries the burden of the special privileges of another can give to the commonwealth that service to which it is fairly entitled.

I stand for the square deal. But when I say that I am for the square deal, I mean not merely that I stand for fair play under the present rules of the games, but that I stand for having those rules changed so as to work for a more substantial equality of opportunity and of reward for equally good service. One word of warning, which, I think, is hardly necessary in Kansas. When I say I want a square deal for the poor man, I do not mean that I want a square deal for the man who remains poor because he has not got the energy to work for himself. If a man who has had a chance will not make good, then he has got to quit. . . .

Now, this means that our government, national and State, must be freed from the sinister influence or control of special interests. Exactly as the special interests of cotton and slavery threatened our political integrity before the Civil War, so now the great special business interests too often control and corrupt the men and methods of government for their own profit. We must drive the special interests out of politics. That is one of our tasks to-day. Every special interest is entitled to justice—full, fair, and complete—and, now, mind you, if there were any attempt by mob-violence to plunder and work harm to the special interest, whatever it may be, and I most dislike and the wealthy man, whomsoever he may be, for whom I have the greatest contempt, I would fight for him, and you would if you were worth your salt. He should have justice. For every special interest is entitled to justice, but not one is entitled to a vote in Congress, to a voice on the bench, or to representation in any public office. The Constitution guarantees protections to property, and we must make that promise good But it does not give the right of suffrage to any corporation. The true friend of property, the true conservative, is he who insists that property shall be the servant and not the master of the commonwealth; who insists that the creature of man's making shall be the servant and not the master of the man who made it. The citizens of the United States must effectively control the mighty commercial forces which they have themselves called into being.

There can be no effective control of corporations while their political activity remains. To put an end to it will be neither a short nor an easy task, but it can be done.

We must have complete and effective publicity of corporate affairs, so that people may know beyond peradventure whether the corporations obey the law and whether their management entitles them to the confidence of the public. It is necessary that laws should be passed to prohibit the use of corporate funds directly or indirectly for political purposes; it is still more necessary that such laws should be thoroughly enforced. Corporate expenditures for political purposes, and especially such expenditures by public-service corporations, have supplied one of the principal sources of corruption in our political affairs.

It has become entirely clear that we must have government supervision of the capitalization, not only of public-service corporations, including, particularly, railways, but of all corporations doing an interstate business. I do not wish to see the nation forced into the ownership of the railways if it can possibly be avoided, and the only alternative is thoroughgoing and effective regulation, which shall be based on a full knowledge of all the facts, including a physical valuation of property. This physical valuation is not needed, or, at least, is very rarely needed, for fixing rates; but it is needed as the basis of honest capitalization.

We have come to recognize that franchises should never be granted except for a limited time, and never without proper provision for compensation to the public. It is my personal belief that the same kind and degree of control and supervision which should be exercised over public-service corporations should be extended also to combinations which control necessaries of life, such as meat, oil, and coal, or which deal in them on an important scale. I have no doubt that the ordinary man who has control of them is much like ourselves. I have no doubt he would like to do well, but I want to have enough supervision to help him realize that desire to do well.

. . .

Combinations in industry are the result of an imperative economic law which cannot be repealed by political legislation. The effort at prohibiting all combination has substantially failed. The way out lies, not in attempting to prevent such combinations, but in completely controlling them in the interest of the public welfare. . . .

. . .

The absence of effective State, and, especially, national, restraint upon unfair money-getting has tended to create a small class of enormously wealthy and economically powerful men, whose chief object is to hold and increase their power. The prime need is to change the conditions which enable these men to accumulate power which is not for the general welfare that they should hold or exercise. We grudge no man a fortune which represents his own power and sagacity, when exercised with entire regard to the welfare of his fellows. . . . We grudge no man a fortune in civil life if it is honorably obtained and well used. It is not even enough that it should have gained without doing damage to the community. We should permit it to be gained only so long as the gaining represents benefit to the community. This, I know, implies a policy of a far more active governmental interference with social and economic conditions in this country than we have yet had, but I think we have got to face the fact that such an increase in governmental control is now necessary.

No man should receive a dollar unless that dollar has been fairly earned. Every dollar received should represent a dollar's worth of service rendered—not gambling in stocks, but service rendered. The really big fortune, the swollen fortune, by the mere fact of its size acquires qualities which differentiate it in kind as well as in degree from what is possessed by men of relatively small means. Therefore, I believe in a graduated income tax on big fortunes, and in another tax which is far more easily collected and far more effective—a graduated inheritance tax on big fortunes, properly safeguarded against evasion and increasing rapidly in amount with the size of the estate.

. . .

. . . Nothing is more true than that excess of every kind is followed by reaction; a fact which should be pondered by reformer and reactionary alike. We are face to face with new conceptions of the relations of property to human welfare, chiefly because certain advocates of the rights of property as against the rights of men have been pushing their claims too far. The man who wrongly holds that every human right is secondary to his profit must now give way to the advocate of human welfare, who rightly maintains that every man holds his property subject to the general right of the community to regulate its use to whatever degree the public welfare may require it.

But I think we may go still further. The right to regulate the use of wealth in the public interest is universally admitted. Let us admit also the right to regulate the terms and conditions of labor, which is the chief element of wealth, directly in the interest of the common good. The fundamental thing to do for every man is to give him a chance to reach a place in which he will make the greatest possible contribution to the public welfare. Understand what I say there. Give him a chance, not push him up if he will not be pushed. Help any man who stumbles; if he lies down, it is a poor job to try to carry him; but if he is a worthy man, try your best to see that he gets a chance to show the worth that is in him. No man can be a good citizen unless he has a wage more than sufficient to cover the bare cost of living, and hours of labor short enough so that after his day's work is done he will have time and energy to bear his share in the management of the community, to help in carrying the general load. We keep countless men from being good citizens by the conditions of life with which we surround them. . . .

National efficiency has many factors. It is a necessary result of the principle of conservation widely applied. In the end it will determine our failure or success as a nation. National efficiency has to do, not only with natural resources and with men, but is equally concerned with institutions. The State must be made efficient for the work which concerns only the people of the State; and the nation for that which concerns all the people. There must remain no neutral ground to serve as a refuge for lawbreakers, and especially for lawbreakers of great wealth, who can hire the vulpine legal cunning which will teach them how to avoid both jurisdictions. It is a misfortune when the national legislature fails to do its duty in providing a national remedy, so that the only national activity is the purely negative activity of the judiciary in forbidding the State to exercise power in the premises.

I do not ask for overcentralization; but I do ask that we work in a spirit of broad and far-reaching nationalism when we work for what concerns our people as a whole. We are all Americans. Our common interests are as broad as the continent. I speak to you here in Kansas exactly as I would speak in New York or Georgia, for the most vital problems are those which affect us all alike. The national government belongs to the whole American people, and where the whole American people are interested, that interest can be guarded effectively only by the national government. The betterment which we seek must be accomplished, I believe, mainly through the national government.

The American people are right in demanding that New Nationalism, without which we cannot hope to deal with new problems. The New Nationalism puts the national need before sectional or personal advantage. It is impatient of the utter confusion that results from local legislatures attempting to treat national issues as local issues. It is still more impatient of the impotence which springs from overdivision of governmental powers, the impotence which makes it possible for local selfishness or for legal cunning, hired by wealthy special interests, to bring national activities to a deadlock. This New Nationalism regards the executive power as the steward of the public welfare. It demands of the judiciary that it shall be interested primarily in human welfare rather than in property, just as it demands that the representative body shall represent all the people rather than any one class or section of the people.

. . .

WOODROW WILSON

THE NEW FREEDOM (1913)

Woodrow Wilson was one of the early recipients of a Ph.D. in political science in the United States, and after a few years he joined the faculty at Princeton University. As an academic, he was a leading theorist of the idea of a "living constitution," arguing that governments and constitutions were "living, organic thing[s]" that are necessarily "altered with the change of the nation's needs and purposes."[11] He was selected for the presidency of that school in 1902 and gained national prominence as an institutional reformer. In 1910, he entered electoral politics as a party outsider and managed to win the governorship in a largely Republican state. Riding a wave of favorable publicity, he joined a crowded field seeking the Democratic nomination for the presidency in 1912 and finally swung the national convention delegates in his favor when William Jennings Bryan decided that Wilson was the least beholden to Wall Street. Closely advised by labor lawyer Louis Brandeis, Wilson ran on a "New Freedom" platform that promised limited government and more aggressive antitrust enforcement aimed at shrinking the size of corporations. With the benefit of large Democratic majorities in Congress at the start of his term, he launched an ambitious legislative agenda that included the creation of the Federal Reserve, tariff reform, agricultural policy reform, antitrust reform, and labor legislation, winning plaudits from the progressive wing of the Republican Party as well. In 1916, Wilson narrowly retained his office by beating Charles Evans Hughes, who resigned from his seat on the U.S. Supreme Court to accept the Republican nomination but who could not unify his party.

Is the twentieth century a fundamentally new age in the American experience? To what degree are inherited values and institutions still useful given the socioeconomic changes? How does Wilson think it matters that most people are employees rather than self-employed? Are employees still citizens in the full sense that self-proprietors, or Jefferson's yeoman farmers, are? Should corporations be treated differently than other business enterprises? Is the problem with corporations one of abuse of power? Why does Wilson call his program the New Freedom? How does his vision contrast with Roosevelt's New Nationalism?

There is one basic fact which underlies all the questions that are discussed on the political platform at the present moment. That singular fact is that nothing is done in this country as it was done twenty years ago.

We are in the presence of a new organization of society. Our life has broken away from the past. The life of America is not the life that it was twenty years ago; it is not the life that it was ten years ago. We have changed our economic conditions, absolutely, from top to bottom; and, with our economic society, the organization of our life. The old political formulas do not fit the present problems; they read now like documents taken out of a forgotten age. The older cries sound as if they belonged to a past age which men have almost forgotten. Things which used to be put into the party platforms of ten years ago would sound antiquated if put into a platform now. We are facing the necessity of fitting a new social organization, as we did once fit the old organization, to the happiness and prosperity of the great body of citizens; for we are conscious that the new order of society has not been made to fit and provide the convenience or prosperity of the average man. The life of the nation has grown infinitely varied. It does not center now upon questions of governmental structure or of the distribution of governmental powers. It centers upon questions of the very structure and operation of society itself, of which government is only the instrument. Our development has run so fast and so far along the lines sketched in the earlier day of constitutional definition, has so crossed and interlaced those

11 Woodrow Wilson, *Constitutional Government in the United States* (New York: Columbia University Press, 1908), 60, 22.

lines, has piled upon them such novel structures of trust and combination, has elaborated within them a life so manifold, so full of forces which transcend the boundaries of the country itself and fill the eyes of the world, that a new nation seems to have been created which the old formulas do not fit or afford a vital interpretation of.

. . .

Why is it that we have a labor question at all? It is for the simple and very sufficient reason that the laboring man and the employer are not intimate associates now as they used to be in time past. Most of our laws were formed in the age when employer and employees knew each other, knew each other's characters, were associates with each other, dealt with each other as man with man. That is no longer the case. You not only do not come into personal contact with the men who have the supreme command in those corporations, but it would be out of the question for you to do it. Our modern corporations employ thousands, and in some instances hundreds of thousands, of men. The only persons whom you see or deal with are local superintendents or local representatives of a vast organization, which is not like anything that the workingmen of the time in which our laws were framed knew anything about. A little group of workingmen, seeing their employer every day, dealing with him in a personal way, is one thing, and the modern body of labor engaged as employees of the huge enterprises that spread all over the country, dealing with men of whom they can form no personal conception, is another thing. A very different thing. You never saw a corporation, any more than you ever saw a government. Many a workingman to-day never saw the body of men who are conducting the industry in which he is employed. And they never saw him. What they know about him is written in ledgers and books and letters, in the correspondence of the office, in the reports of the superintendents. He is a long way off from them.

So what we have to discuss is, not wrongs which individuals intentionally do,—I do not believe there are a great many of those,—but the wrongs of a system. . . . The truth is, we are all caught in a great economic system which is heartless. The modern corporation is not engaged in business as an individual. When we deal with it, we deal with an impersonal element, an immaterial piece of society. A modern corporation is a means of co-operation in the conduct of an enterprise which is so big that no one man can conduct it, and which the resources of no one man are sufficient to finance. . . .

. . .

. . . American industry is not free, as once it was free; American enterprise is not free; the man with only a little capital is finding it harder to get into the field, more and more impossible to compete with the big fellow. Why? Because the laws of this country do not prevent the strong from crushing the weak. That is the reason, and because the strong have crushed the weak the strong dominate the industry and the economic life of this country. . . .

. . .

There has come over the land that un-American set of conditions which enables a small number of men who control the government to get favors from the government; by those favors to exclude their fellows from equal business opportunity; by those favors to extend a network of control that will presently dominate every industry in the country, and so make men forget the ancient time when America lay in every hamlet . . . and eager men were everywhere captains of industry, not employees; not looking to a distant city to find out what they might do, but looking about among their neighbors, finding credit according to their character, not according to their connections, finding credit in proportion to what was known to be in them and behind them, not in proportion to the securities they held that were approved where they were not known. In order to start an enterprise now, you have to be authenticated, in a perfectly impersonal way, not according to yourself, but according to what you own that somebody else approves of your owning. You cannot begin such an enterprise as those that have made America until you are so authenticated, until you have succeeded in obtaining the good-will of large allied capitalists. Is that freedom? That is dependence, not freedom.

We used to think in the old-fashioned days when life was very simple that all that government had to do was to put on a policeman's uniform, and say, "Now don't anybody hurt anybody else." We used to say that the ideal of government was for every man to be left alone and not interfered with, except when he interfered with somebody else; and that the best government was the government that did as little governing as possible. That was the idea that obtained in Jefferson's time. But we are coming now to realize that life is so complicated that we are not dealing with the old conditions, and that the law has to step in and create new conditions under which we may live, the conditions which will make it tolerable for us to live.

. . . . [T]he treatment of labor by the great corporations is not what it was in Jefferson's time. Whenever bodies of men employ bodies of men, it ceases to be a private relationship. . . . This dealing of great bodies of men with other bodies of men is a matter of public scrutiny, and should be a matter of public regulation.

Similarly, it was no business of the law in the time of Jefferson to come into my house and see how I kept house. But when my house, when my so-called private property, became a great mine, and men went along dark corridors amidst every kind of danger in order to dig out of the bowels of the earth things necessary for the industries of a whole nation, and when it came about that no individual owned these mines, that they were owned by great stock companies, then all the old analogies absolutely collapsed and it became the right of the government to go down into these mines to see whether human beings were properly treated in them or not; to see whether accidents were properly safeguarded against; to see whether modern economical methods of using these inestimable riches of the earth were followed or were not followed. . . .

We are in a new world, struggling under old laws. As we go inspecting our lives to-day, surveying this new scene of centralized and complex society, we shall find many more things out of joint.

. . .

There are two theories of government that have been contending with each other ever since government began. One of them is the theory which in America is associated with the name of a very great man, Alexander Hamilton. A great man, but, in my judgment, not a great American. He did not think in terms of American life. Hamilton believed that the only people who could understand government, and therefore the only people who were qualified to conduct it, were the men who had the biggest financial stake in the commercial and industrial enterprises of the country.

That theory, though few have now the hardihood to profess it openly, has been the working theory upon which our government has lately been conducted. . . .

For indeed, if you stop to think about it, nothing could be a greater departure from original Americanism, from faith in the ability of a confident, resourceful, and independent people, than the discouraging doctrine that somebody has got to provide prosperity for the rest of us. And yet that is exactly the doctrine on which the government of the United States has been conducted lately. . . . The gentlemen whose ideas have been sought are the big manufacturers, the bankers, and the heads of the great railroad combinations. The masters of the government of the United States are the combined capitalists and manufacturers of the United States. . . .

. . .

. . . No group of men less than the majority has a right to tell me how I have got to live in America. I will submit to the majority, because I have been trained to do it,—though I may sometimes have my private opinion even of the majority. I do not care how wise, how patriotic, the trustees may be, I have never heard of any group of men in whose hands I am willing to lodge the liberties of America in trust.

. . . If I thought that the American people were reckless, were ignorant, were vindictive, I might shrink from putting the government into their hands. But the beauty of democracy is that when you are reckless you destroy your own established conditions of life; when you are vindictive, you wreak vengeance upon yourself; the whole stability of a democratic polity rests upon the fact that every interest is every man's interest.

. . .

What it liberty? You say of the locomotive that it runs free. What do you mean? You mean that its parts are so assembled and adjusted that friction is reduced to a minimum, and that it has perfect adjustment. We say of a boat skimming the water with light foot, "How free she runs," when we mean, how perfectly she is adjusted to the force of the wind, how perfectly she obeys the great breath out of the heavens that fills her sails. . . .

Human freedom consists in perfect adjustments of human interests and human activities and human energies.

Now, the adjustments necessary between individuals, between individuals and the complex institutions amidst which they live, and between those institutions and the government, are infinitely more intricate to-day than ever before. . . . Life has become complex; there are many more elements, more parts, to it than ever before. And, therefore, it is harder to keep everything adjusted,—and harder to find out where the trouble lies when the machine gets out of order.

You know that one of the interesting things that Mr. Jefferson said in those early days of simplicity which marked the beginnings of our government was that the best government consisted in as little governing as possible. And there is still a sense in which that is true. It is still intolerable for the government to interfere with our individual activities except where it is necessary to interfere with them in order to free them. But I feel confident that if Jefferson were living in our day he would see what we see: that the individual is caught in a great confused nexus of all sorts of complicated circumstances, and that to let him alone is to leave him helpless as against the obstacles with which he has to contend; and that, therefore, law in our day must come to the assistance of the individual. It must come to his assistance to see that he gets fair play; that is all, but that is much. Without the watchful interference, the resolute interference, of the government, there can be no fair play between individuals and such powerful institutions as the trusts. Freedom to-day is something more than being let alone. The program of a government of freedom must in these days be positive, not negative merely.

. . .

. . . I believe in human liberty as I believe in the wine of life. There is no salvation for men in the pitiful condescensions of industrial masters. Guardians have no place in a land of freemen. Prosperity guaranteed by trustees has no prospect of endurance. Monopoly means the atrophy of enterprise. If monopoly persists, monopoly will always sit at the helm of the government. I do not expect to see monopoly restrain itself. If there are men in this country big enough to own the government of the United States, they are going to own it; what we have to determine now is whether we are big enough, whether we are men enough, whether we are free enough, to take possession again of the government which is our own. . . .

. . .

Since their day the meaning of liberty has deepened. But it has not ceased to be a fundamental demand of the human spirit, a fundamental necessity for the life of the soul. And the day is at hand when it shall be realized on this consecrated soil,—a New Freedom,—a Liberty widened and deepened to match the broadened life of man in modern America . . . .

JOHN DEWEY

THE PUBLIC AND ITS PROBLEMS (1927)

John Dewey was raised in postbellum Vermont. He taught high school for a time before deciding to pursue a Ph.D. in philosophy at Johns Hopkins University and launching a successful academic career, eventually settling at Columbia University in 1904. While in New York, he also became active in broader intellectual and activist circles, becoming an outspoken activist for progressive causes and a frequent writer for journals such as *The New Republic*. Even after his retirement in 1930, he remained an active public figure and scholar for another two decades. He was a leading figure in the pragmatist movement, and his view was that the truth was identified not through logical argumentation but through its practical success. His social theory built on the same foundations, emphasizing the ways in which individuals existed within a social context and that social problems were best addressed through imaginative practical action. Democracy was best understood not as a set of political arrangements but as a commitment to communal experimentation in pursuit of the better satisfaction of social needs.

What does Dewey mean by democracy "as a social idea"? What forms of democracy "as a system of government" are compatible with the social idea of democracy? Is there a "sanctity" in universal suffrage and frequent elections? In what sense is the "cure for the ailments of democracy . . . more democracy"? What does Dewey take to be the criterion by which government activity is to be evaluated? Is this a controversial notion? Does Dewey recognize limits on democratic government? What does he mean by "liberty"?

. . .

We have had occasion to refer in passing to the distinction between democracy as a social idea and political democracy as a system of government. The two are, of course, connected. The idea remains barren and empty save as it is incarnated in human relationships. Yet in discussion they must be distinguished. The idea of democracy is a wider and fuller idea than can be exemplified in the state even at its best. To be realized it must affect all modes of human association, the family, the school, industry, religion. And even as far as political arrangements are concerned, governmental institutions are but a mechanism for securing to an idea channels of effective operation. It will hardly do to say that criticisms of the political machinery leave the believer in the idea untouched. For, as far as they are justified—and no candid believer can deny that many of them are only too well grounded—they arouse him to bestir himself in order that the idea may find a more adequate machinery through which to work. What the faithful insist upon, however, is that the idea and its external organs and structures are not to be identified. We object to the common supposition of the foes of existing democratic government that the accusations against it touch the social and moral aspirations and ideas which underlie the political forms. The old saying that the cure for the ills of democracy is more democracy is not apt if it means that the evils may be remedied by introducing more machinery of the same kind as that which already exists, or by refining and perfecting that machinery. But the phrase may also indicate the need of returning to the idea itself, of clarifying and deepening our apprehension of it, and of emphasizing our sense of its meaning to criticize and remake its political manifestations.

Confining ourselves, for the moment, to political democracy, we must, in any case, renew our protest against the assumption that the idea has itself produced the governmental practices which obtain in democratic states: General suffrage, elected representatives, majority rule, and so on. The idea has influenced the concrete political movement, but it has not caused it. The transition from family and dynastic government supported by the loyalties of tradition to popular government was the outcome primarily of technological discoveries and inventions working a change in the customs by which men had been bound together. It was not due to the doctrines of doctrinaires. The forms to which we are accustomed in democratic governments represent the cumulative effect of a multitude of events, unpremeditated as far as political effects were concerned and having unpredictable consequences. There is no sanctity in universal suffrage, frequent elections, majority rule, congressional and cabinet government. These things are devices evolved in the direction in which the current was moving, each wave of which involved at the time of its impulsion a minimum of departure from antecedent custom and law. The devices served a purpose; but the purpose was rather that of meeting existing needs which had become too intense to be ignored, than that of forwarding the democratic idea. In spite of all defects, they served their own purpose well.

. . .

Nevertheless the current has set steadily in one direction: toward democratic forms. That government exists to serve its community, and that this purpose cannot be achieved unless the community itself shares in selecting its governors and determining the policies, are a deposit of fact left, as far as we can see, permanently in the wake of doctrines and forms, however transitory the latter. They are not the whole of the democratic idea, but they express it in its political phase. Belief in this political aspect is not a mystic faith as if in some overruling providence that cares for children, drunkards and others unable to help themselves. It marks a well-attested conclusion from historic facts. We have every reason to think that whatever changes may take place in existing democratic machinery, they will be of a sort to make the interest of the public a more supreme guide and criterion of governmental activity, and to enable the public to form and manifest its purposes still more authoritatively. In this sense the cure for the ailments of democracy is more democracy. The prime difficulty, as we have seen, is that of discovering the means by which a scattered, mobile and manifold public may so recognize itself as to define and express its interests. This discovery is necessarily precedent to any fundamental change in the machinery. We are not concerned therefore to set forth counsels as to advisable improvements in the political forms of democracy. Many have been suggested. It is no derogation of their relative worth to say that consideration of these changes is not at present an affair of primary importance. The problem lies deeper; it is in the first instance an intellectual problem: the search for conditions under which the Great Society may become the Great Community. When these conditions are brought into being they will make their own forms. Until they have come about, it is somewhat futile to consider what political machinery will suit them.

In a search for the conditions under which the inchoate public now extant may function democratically, we may proceed from a statement of the nature of the democratic idea in its generic social sense. From the standpoint of the individual, it consists in having a responsible share according to capacity in forming and directing the activities of the groups to which one belongs and in participating according to need in the values which the groups sustain. From the standpoint of the groups, it demands liberation of the potentialities of members of a group in harmony with the interests and goods which are common. Since every individual is a member of many groups, this specification cannot be fulfilled except when different groups interact flexibly and fully in connection with other groups. A member of a robber band may express his powers in a way consonant with belonging to the group and be directed by the interest common to its members. But he does so only at the cost of repression of those of his potentialities which can be realized only through membership in other groups. The robber band cannot interact flexibly with other groups; it can act only through isolating itself. It must prevent the operation of all interests save those which circumscribe it in its separateness. But a good citizen finds his conduct as a member of a political group enriching and enriched by his participation in family life, industry, scientific and artistic associations. There is a free give-and-take: fullness of integrated personality is therefore possible of achievement, since the pulls and responses of different groups reinforce one another and their values accord.

. . .

Only when we start from a community as a fact, grasp the fact in thought so as to clarify and enhance its constituent elements, can we reach an idea of democracy which is not utopian. The conceptions and shibboleths which are traditionally associated with the idea of democracy take on a veridical and directive meaning only when they are construed as marks and traits of an association which realizes the defining characteristics of a community. Fraternity, liberty and equality isolated from communal life are hopeless abstractions. Their separate assertion leads to mushy sentimentalism or else to extravagant and fanatical violence which in the end defeats its own aims. Equality then becomes a creed of mechanical identity which is false to facts and impossible of realization. Effort to attain it is divisive of the vital bonds which hold men together; as far as it puts forth issue, the outcome is a mediocrity in which good is common only in the sense of being average and vulgar. Liberty is then thought of as independence of social ties, and ends in dissolution and anarchy. It is more difficult to sever the idea of brotherhood from that of a community, and hence it is either practically ignored in the movements which identify democracy with Individualism, or else it is a sentimentally appended tag. In its just connection with communal experience, fraternity is another name for the consciously appreciated goods which accrue from an association in which all share, and which give direction to the conduct of each. Liberty is that secure release and fulfillment of personal potentialities which take place only in rich and manifold association with others: the power to be an individualized self making a distinctive contribution and enjoying in its own way the fruits of association. Equality denotes the unhampered share which each individual member of the community has in the consequences of associated action. It is equitable because it is measured only by need and capacity to utilize, not by extraneous factors which deprive one in order that another may take and have.

. . .

The work of conversion of the physical and organic phase of associated behavior into a community of action saturated and regulated by mutual interest in shared meanings, consequences which are translated into ideas and desired objects by means of symbols, does not occur all at once nor completely. At any given time, it sets a problem rather than marks a settled achievement. We are born organic beings associated with others, but we are not born members of a community. The young have to be brought within the traditions, outlook and interests which characterize a community by means of education: by unremitting instruction and by learning in connection with the phenomena of overt association. Everything which is distinctly human is learned, not native, even though it could not be learned without native structures which mark man off from other animals. To learn in a human way and to human effect is not just to acquire added skill through refinement of original capacities.

To learn to be human is to develop through the give-and-take of communication an effective sense of being an individually distinctive member of a community; one who understands and appreciates its beliefs, desires and methods, and who contributes to a further conversion of organic powers into human resources and values. But this translation is never finished. . . .

. . . What are the conditions under which it is possible for the Great Society to approach more closely and vitally the status of a Great Community, and thus take form in genuinely democratic societies and state? What are the conditions under which we may reasonably picture the Public emerging from its eclipse?

. . .

Two essential constituents in that older theory, as will be recalled, were the notions that each individual is of himself equipped with the intelligence needed, under the operation of self-interest, to engage in political affairs; and that general suffrage, frequent elections of officials and majority rule are sufficient to ensure the responsibility of elected rulers to the desires and interests of the public. As we shall see, the second conception is logically bound up with the first and stands or falls with it. At the basis of the scheme lies what Lippmann has well called the idea of the "omni-competent" individual: competent to frame policies, to judge their results; competent to know in all situations demanding political action what is for his own good, and competent to enforce his idea of good and the will to effect it against contrary forces. Subsequent history has proved that the assumption involved illusion. . . . [C]urrent philosophy held that ideas and knowledge were functions of a mind or consciousness which originated in individuals by means of isolated contact with objects. But in fact, knowledge is a function of association and communication; it depends upon tradition, upon tools and methods socially transmitted, developed and sanctioned. Faculties of effectual observation, reflection and desire are habits acquired under the influence of the culture and institutions of society, not ready-made inherent powers. . . .

Habit is the mainspring of human action, and habits are formed for the most part under the influence of the customs of a group. The organic structure of man entails the formation of habit, for, whether we wish it or not, whether we are aware of it or not, every act effects a modification of attitude and set which directs future behavior. . . . The creation of a tabula rasa in order to permit the creation of a new order is so impossible as to set at naught both the hope of buoyant revolutionaries and the timidity of scared conservatives.

. . .

. . . Skill and ability work within a framework which we have not created and do not comprehend. Some occupy strategic positions which give them advance information of forces that affect the market; and by training and an innate turn that way they have acquired a special technique which enables them to use the vast impersonal tide to turn their own wheels. . . . But such knowledge goes relatively but little further than that of the competent skilled operator who manages a machine. It suffices to employ the conditions which are before him. Skill enables him to turn the flux of events this way or that in his own neighborhood. It gives him no control of the flux.

Why should the public and its officers, even if the latter are termed statesmen, be wiser or more effective? The prime condition of a democratically organized public is a kind of knowledge and insight which does not yet exist. . . . But some of the conditions which must be fulfilled if it is to exist can be indicated. . . . An obvious requirement is freedom of social inquiry and of distribution of its conclusions. . . .

There can be no public without full publicity in respect to all consequences which concern it. Whatever obstructs and restricts publicity, limits and distorts public opinion and checks and distorts thinking on social affairs. Without freedom of expression, not even methods of social inquiry can be developed. . . .

The belief that thought and its communication are now free simply because legal restrictions which once obtained have been done away with is absurd. Its currency perpetuates the infantile state of social knowledge. For it blurs recognition of our central need to possess conceptions which are used as tools of directed inquiry and which are tested, rectified and caused to grow in actual use. No man and no mind was ever emancipated by being left alone. Removal of formal limitations is but a negative condition; positive freedom is not a state but an act which involves methods and instrumentalities for control of conditions. . . .

Emotional habitations and intellectual habitudes on the part of the mass of men create the conditions of which the exploiters of sentiment and opinion only take advantage. Men have got used to an experimental method in physical and technical matters. They are still afraid of it in human concerns. . . . One of the commonest forms of a truly religious idealization of, and reverence for, established institutions; for example in our own politics, the Constitution, the Supreme Court, private property, free contract and so on. The words "sacred" and "sanctity" come readily to our lips when such things come under discussion. They testify to the religious aureole which protects the institutions. . . .

. . .

The smoothest road to control of political conduct is by control of opinion. As long as interests of pecuniary profit are powerful, and a public has not located and identified itself, those who have this interest will have an unresisted motive for tampering with the springs of political action in all that affects them. . . . Just as industry conducted by engineers on a factual technological basis would be a very different thing from what it actually is, so the assembling and reporting of news would be a very different thing if the genuine interests of reporters were permitted to work freely.

. . .

We have touched lightly and in passing upon the conditions which must be fulfilled if the Great Society is to become the Great Community; a society in which the ever-expanding and intricately ramifying consequences of associated activities shall be known in the full sense of that word, so that an organized, articulate Public comes into being. The highest and most difficult kind of inquiry and a subtle, delicate, vivid and responsive art of communication must take possession of the physical machinery of transmission and circulation and breathe life into it. When the machine age has thus perfected its machinery it will be a means of life and not its despotic master. Democracy will come into its own, for democracy is a name for a life of free and enriching communion. It had its seer in Walt Whitman. It will have its consummation when free social inquiry is indissolubly wedded to the art of full and moving communication.

. . .

[T]he question of what transactions should be left as far as possible to voluntary initiative and agreement and what should come under the regulation of the public is a question of time, place and concrete conditions that can be known only by careful observation and reflective investigation. For it concerns consequences; and the nature of consequences and the ability to perceive and act upon them varies with the industrial and intellectual agencies which operate. A solution, or distributive adjustment, needed at one time is totally unfitted to another situation. That "social evolution" has been either from collectivism to individualism or the reverse is sheer superstition. It has consisted in a continuous redistribution of social integrations on the one hand and of capacities and energies of individuals on the other. . . . They may think they are clamoring for a purely personal liberty, but what they are doing is to bring into being a greater liberty to share in other associations, so that more of their individual potentialities will be released and their personal experience enriched. Life has been impoverished, not by a predominance of "society" in general over individuality, but by a domination of one form of association, the family, clan, church, economic institutions, over other actual and possible forms. On the other hand, the problem of exercising "social control" over individuals is in reality that of regulating the doings and results of some individuals in order that a larger number of individuals may have a fuller and deeper experience. . . .

. . .

The strongest point to be made in behalf of even such rudimentary political forms as democracy has already attained, popular voting, majority rule and so on, is that to some extent they involve a consultation and discussion which uncover social needs and troubles. This fact is the great asset on the side of the political ledger. De Tocqueville wrote it down almost a century ago in his survey of the prospects of democracy in the United States. Accusing a democracy of a tendency to prefer mediocrity in its elected rulers, and admitting its exposure to gusts of passion and its openness to folly, he pointed out in effect that popular government is educative as other modes of political regulation are not. It forces recognition that there are common interests, even though the recognition of *what* they are is confused; and the need it enforces of discussion and publicity brings about some clarification of what they are. The man who wears the shoe knows best that it pinches and where it pinches, even fi the expert shoemaker is the best judge of how the trouble is to be remedied. Popular government has at least created public spirit even if its success in informing that spirit has not been great.

A class of experts is inevitably so removed from common interests as to become a class with private interests and private knowledge, which in social matters is not knowledge at all. The ballot is, as often said, a substitute for bullets. But what is more significant is that counting of heads compels prior recourse to methods of discussion, consultation and persuasion, while the essence of appeal to force is to cut short resort to such methods. Majority rule, just as majority rule, is as foolish as its critics charge it with being. But it never is *merely* majority rule. . . . No government by experts in which the masses do not have the chance to inform the experts as to their needs can be anything but an oligarchy managed in the interests of the few. And the enlightenment must proceed in ways which force the administrative specialists to take account of the needs. The world has suffered more from leaders and authorities than from the masses.

The essential need, in other words, is the improvement of the methods and conditions of debate, discussion and persuasion. That is *the* problem of the public. We have asserted that this improvement depends essentially upon freeing and perfecting the processes of inquiry and of dissemination of their conclusions. Inquiry, indeed, is a work which devolves upon experts. But their expertness is not shown in framing and executing policies, but in discovering and making known the facts upon which the former depend. They are technical experts in the sense that scientific investigators and artists manifest *expertise*. It is not necessary that the many should have the knowledge and skill to carry on the needed investigations; what is required is that they have the ability to judge of the bearing of the knowledge supplied by others upon common concerns.

. . .

III. CITIZENSHIP AND COMMUNITY

Major Developments

- Growing immigration from southern and eastern Europe
- Imposition of new immigration restrictions
- Development of conscious efforts to "Americanize" new immigrants

Immigration had spurred reactions at various points over the course of the nineteenth century, but the federal government did relatively little to stanch the flow of immigrants into the country (the 1882 Chinese Exclusion Act was the notable exception). With the closing of the frontier and a change in the composition of immigration to the United States, that began to change. In the early twentieth century, there was widespread concern that the number of immigrants entering the United States was significantly increasing, a larger proportion of them were coming from outside the traditional regions of western and northern Europe, and they were coming to rest in large ethnic enclaves in a small number of coastal cities. In the late nineteenth century, Grover Cleveland had held off legislative efforts to restrict immigration. In the early twentieth century, immigration reformers were better organized and more successful.

President McKinley's assassination spurred the immediate passage of the Anarchist Exclusion Act, which excluded immigrants who were political extremists. In 1906, Congress tightened rules on the naturalization of immigrants to citizenship, establishing the Bureau of Immigration and Naturalization to standardize and monitor the process, requiring that new citizens know English and be "free white persons" or persons of African descent. The next year, Congress created a bipartisan immigration commission under Senator William P. Dillingham to study the immigration problem and make recommendations for reforms. The final report in 1911 concluded that the new immigrants could not be easily assimilated and recommended a variety of restrictions. With the arrival of war in Europe in the 1910s, fears about immigration were further aroused by the tendency of various ethnic groups to rally around their nation of origin. After America entered the war, many states imposed restrictions on the speaking of German. The 1917 Immigration Act barred a wide range of "undesirables" (ranging from alcoholics to anarchists) and most Asians from entering the United States and required English literacy tests for all adult immigrants. That same year, the Department of the Interior created an Americanization Division charged with coordinating national efforts to assimilate the foreign-born into American society and values. The Immigration Act of 1924 imposed national origins quotas keyed to the size of that nationality group in 1890, which had the effect of sharply limiting the number of legal immigrants from eastern and southern Europe. Over much of the nineteenth century and early twentieth century, the percentage of the American population that had been born on foreign shores hovered in the teens. As Figure 8-3 shows, those numbers plunged after passage of the Immigration Act, bottoming out in the 1970s with over 95 percent of the American population being native born.

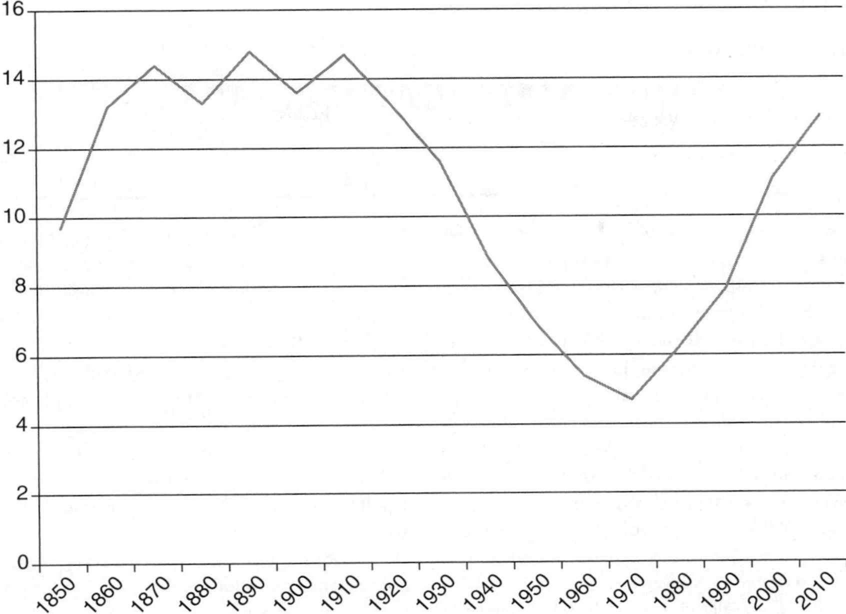

FIGURE 8-3 Foreign Born as Percentage of Population.

The debate over immigration was wide ranging. The economic, social, and political effects of the immigrant community were all unclear, and Americans began to more self-consciously consider what assimilation entailed and whether it was even necessary. The 1908 play *The Melting Pot* dramatized the challenges facing a newly arrived Russian-Jewish family, celebrating the idea that America was the "crucible" in which "all the races of Europe are melting and reforming" into a single, new race—the American. The play simultaneously popularized the term and spurred a debate about what was required to be an American.

LOUIS D. BRANDEIS

TRUE AMERICANISM (1915)

Louis D. Brandeis was born in Kentucky on the eve of the Civil War. His Jewish parents had fled Europe after the failure of the democratic revolutions of 1848. In 1878, he began his studies at Harvard Law School at the age of eighteen. Upon graduating he set up a practice in Boston, declining an offer to join the faculty at the law school. By his thirties, his practice was successful enough to allow him to begin doing legal work on behalf of various social and political causes. By the early twentieth century, he was a leading labor lawyer and pioneered new legal strategies to defend the growing number of labor laws. A close advisor to Woodrow Wilson, he was nominated for the U.S. Supreme Court in 1916, which provoked one of the more contentious confirmation battles to that point in American history. Over the next two decades, he was a reliable and creative progressive voice on a generally conservative Court. He was also a committed Zionist, and a few years after his death Brandeis University was named in his honor. As war broke out in Europe, Brandeis advocated Zionism to Jewish audiences in the United States, arguing that American ideals of democracy and social justice were central to the Zionist project as well. Brandeis's Zionism put the question of political identity in the foreground, and Brandeis resolved the dilemma by insisting that the advancement of American ideals abroad was the very height of loyalty to the United States.[12]

What is a "true American" for Brandeis? What does it mean to have the "national consciousness of an American"? Is it necessary that immigrants adopt "our ideals and aspirations"? Must they do so to become naturalized citizens? Must they do so to be resident aliens? Does Brandeis consider the possibility that immigrants will not seek naturalization? Is Brandeis right that we are necessarily "our brothers' keeper" for fellow citizens? What can the community reasonably demand of the individual living within it?

E pluribus unum—out of many one,—was the motto adopted by the founders of the Republic when they formed a union of the thirteen States. To these we have added, from time to time, thirty-five more. The founders were convinced, as we are, that a strong nation could be built through federation. They were also convinced, as we are, that in America, under a free government, many peoples would make one nation. Throughout all these years we have admitted to our country and to citizenship immigrants from the diverse lands of Europe. We had faith that thereby we could best serve ourselves and mankind. This faith has been justified. The United States has grown great. The immigrants and their immediate descendants have proved themselves as loyal as any citizens of the country. Liberty has knit us closely together as Americans. . . .

On the Nation's birthday it is customary for us to gather together for the purpose of considering how we may better serve our country. This year we are asked to address ourselves to the newcomers and to make this Fourth of July what has been termed Americanization Day.

What is Americanization? It manifests itself, in a superficial way, when the immigrant adopts the clothes, the manners and the customs generally prevailing here. Far more important is the manifestation presented when he substitutes for his mother tongue, the English language as the common medium of speech. But the adoption of our language, manners and customs is only a small part of the process. To become Americanized, the change wrought must be fundamental. However great his outward conformity,

12 See also, Melvin I. Urofsky, *Louis D. Brandeis: A Life* (New York: Schocken Books, 2009), 411–412. At the time of his nomination to the U.S. Supreme Court, political observers noted that the president was seeking to score points for nominating both a "German-American" (on the eve of American entry into World War I) and someone "of Jewish blood and a leader in the Zionist movement." "Brandeis Named for Highest Court; Will be Opposed," *New York Times* (January 29, 1916), 1.

the immigrant is not Americanized unless his interests and affections have become deeply rooted here. And we properly demand of the immigrant even more than this. He must be brought into complete harmony with our ideals and aspirations and cooperate with us for their attainment. Only when this has been done, will he possess the national consciousness of an American.

I say "he must be brought into complete harmony." But let us not forget that many a poor immigrant comes to us from distant lands, ignorant of our language, strange in tattered clothes and with jarring manners, who is already truly American in this most important sense; who has long shared our ideals and who, oppressed and persecuted abroad, has yearned for our land of liberty and for the opportunity of abiding in the realization of its aims.

What are the American ideals? They are the development of the individual for his own and the common good;—the development of the individual through liberty and the attainment of the common good through democracy and social justice.

Our form of government, as well as humanity, compels us to strive for the development of the individual man. Under universal suffrage (soon to be extended to women) every voter is a partner of the State. Unless the rulers have, in the main, education and character and are free men, our great experiment in democracy must fail. It devolves upon the State, therefore, to fit its rulers for their task. It must provide not only facilities for development, but the opportunity of using them. It must not only provide opportunity; it must stimulate the desire to avail of it. Thus we are compelled to insist upon observance of what we somewhat vaguely term the American standard of living; we become necessarily our brothers' keepers.

What does this standard imply? In substance, the exercise of those rights which our Constitution guarantees; the right to life, liberty, and the pursuit of happiness. . . . The essentials of American citizenship are not satisfied by supplying merely the material needs or even wants of the worker.

. . .

Such are our ideals and the standard of living we have erected for ourselves. But what is there in these ideals which is peculiarly American? Many nations seek to develop the individual man for himself and for the common good. Some are as liberty-loving as we. Some pride themselves upon institutions more democratic than our own. Still others, less conspicuous for liberty or democracy, claim to be more successful in attaining social justice. And we are not the only nation, which combines love of liberty, with the practice of democracy and a longing for social justice. But there is one feature in our ideals and practices which is peculiarly American. It is inclusive brotherhood.

. . . America . . . has always declared herself for equality of nationalities, as well as for equality of individuals. It recognized racial equality as an essential of full human liberty and true brotherhood, and that it is the complement of democracy. It has, therefore, given like welcome to all the peoples of Europe.

Democracy rests upon two pillars; One, the principle that all men are equally entitled to life, liberty, and the pursuit of happiness; and the other, the conviction that such equal opportunity will most advance civilization. Aristocracy on the other hand denies both these postulates. It rests upon the principle of the superman. It willingly subordinates the many to the few, and seeks to justify sacrificing the individual by insisting that civilization will be advanced by such sacrifices.

. . .

The movements of the last century have proved that whole peoples have individuality no less marked than that of the single person; that the individuality of a people is irrepressible, and that the misnamed internationalism which seeks the obliteration of nationalities or peoples is unattainable. The new nationalism adopted by America proclaims that each race or people, like each individual, has the right and duty to develop, and that only through such differentiated development will high civilization be attained. Not until these principles of nationalism, like those of democracy are generally accepted, will liberty be fully attained, and minorities be secure in their rights. Not until then can the foundation be laid for a lasting peace among the nations.

. . .

RANDOLPH S. BOURNE

TRANS-NATIONAL AMERICA (1916)

Randolph Bourne grew up in limited circumstances in New Jersey at the end of the nineteenth century. In 1913, he completed his studies at Columbia University with a M.A. in sociology. He turned to journalism, joining the newly established Progressive magazine *The New Republic*. Attracted to pacifism and socialism, Bourne broke with his associates at the journal over World War I, and he became a vocal critic of liberal intellectuals who supported the war effort. At the age of thirty-two, he died in the 1918 flu epidemic. His influential essays on American identity rejected the melting-pot metaphor. Instead of "Americanization," Bourne called for a "cosmopolitan America" that embraced diversity rather than assimilation.

Why does Bourne think that what assimilationists portray as "American" is really an "Anglo-Saxon tradition"? Are Anglo-Saxons just another competing nationality within the United States? Is there a distinctive American identity separate from its Anglo traditions? What does Bourne offer in place of assimilation? What is an "American" identity under this conception? Why does Bourne value the recent immigrants? How does Bourne's view of what it means to be a true American compare with Brandeis's?

No reverberatory effect of the great war has caused American public opinion more solicitude than the failure of the 'melting-pot.' The discovery of diverse nationalistic feelings among our great alien population has come to most people as an intense shock. It has brought out the unpleasant inconsistencies of our traditional beliefs. . . . We have had to listen to publicists who express themselves as stunned by the evidence of vigorous nationalistic and cultural movements in this country among Germans, Scandinavians, Bohemians, and Poles, while in the same breath they insist that the mien shall be forcibly assimilated to that Anglo-Saxon tradition which they unquestioningly label 'American.'

. . . We found that the tendency, reprehensible and paradoxical as it might be, has been for the national clusters of immigrants, as they became more and more firmly established and more and more prosperous, to cultivate more and more assiduously the literatures and cultural traditions of their homelands. Assimilation, in other words, instead of washing out the memories of Europe, made them more and more intensely real. Just as these clusters became more and more objectively American, did they become more and more German or Scandinavian or Bohemian or Polish.

To face the fact that our aliens are already strong enough to take a share in the direction of their own destiny, and that the strong cultural movements represented by the foreign press, schools, and colonies are a challenge to our facile attempts, is not, however, to admit the failure of Americanization. It is not to fear the failure of democracy. It is rather to urge us to an investigation of what Americanism may rightly mean. It is to ask ourselves whether our ideal has been broad or narrow—whether perhaps the time has not come to assert a higher ideal than the 'melting-pot.' Surely we cannot be certain of our spiritual democracy when, claiming to melt the nations within us to a comprehension of our free and democratic institutions, we fly into panic at the first sign of their own will and tendency. We act as if we wanted Americanization to take place only on our own terms, and not by the consent of the governed. All our elaborate machinery of settlement and school and union, of social and political naturalization, however, will move with friction just in so far as it neglects to take into account this strong and virile insistence that America shall be what the immigrant will have a hand in making it, and not what a ruling class, descendant of those British stocks which were the first permanent immigrants, decide that America shall be made. This is the condition which confronts us, and which demands a clear and general readjustment of our attitude and our ideal.

. . .

We are all foreign-born or the descendants of foreign-born, and if distinctions are to be made between us, they should rightly be on some other ground than indigenousness. The early colonists came over with motives no less colonial than the later. They did not come to be assimilated in an American melting pot. They did not come to adopt the culture of the American Indian. They had not the smallest intention of 'giving themselves without reservation' to the new country. They came to get freedom to live as they wanted to. They came to escape from the stifling air and chaos of the old world; they came to make their fortune in a new land. They invented no new social framework. Rather they brought over bodily the old ways to which they had been accustomed. Tightly concentrated on a hostile frontier, they were conservative beyond belief. Their pioneer daring was reserved for the objective conquest of material resources. In their folkways, in their social and political institutions, they were, like every colonial people, slavishly imitative of the mother country. So that, in spite of the 'Revolution,' our whole legal and political system remained more English than the English, petrified and unchanging, while in England law developed to meet the needs of the changing times.

It is just this English-American conservatism that has been our chief obstacle to social advance. We have needed the new peoples—the order of the German and Scandinavian, the turbulence of the Slav and Hun—to save us from our own stagnation. I do not mean that the illiterate Slav is now the equal of the New Englander of pure descent. He is raw material to be educated, not into a New Englander, but into a socialized American. . . . Let us cease to think of ideals like democracy as magical qualities inherent in certain peoples. Let us speak, not of inferior races, but of inferior civilizations. We are all to educate and to be educated. These peoples in America are in a common enterprise. It is not what we are now that concerns us, but what this plastic next generation may become in the light of a new cosmopolitan ideal.

. . .

. . . If there were to be any hyphens scattered about, clearly they should be affixed to those English descendants who had had centuries of time to be made American where the German had had only half a century. Most significantly has the war brought out of them this alien virus, showing them still loving English things, owing allegiance to the English Kultur, moved by English shibboleths and prejudice. It is only because it has been the ruling class in this country that bestowed the epithet that we have not heard copiously and scornfully of 'hyphenated English Americans.' . . .

. . .

If freedom means the right to do pretty much as one pleases, so long as one does not interfere with others, the immigrant has found freedom, and the ruling element has been singularly liberal in its treatment of the invading hordes. But if freedom means a democratic cooperation in determining the ideals and purposes and industrial and social institutions of a country, then the immigrant has not been free, and Anglo-Saxon element is guilty of just what every dominant race is guilty of in every European country: the imposition of its own culture upon the minority peoples. The fact that this imposition has been so mild and, indeed, semi- conscious does not alter its quality. And the war has brought out just the degree to which that purpose of 'Americanizing,' that is, 'Anglo-Saxonizing,' the immigrant has failed.

. . .

If we come to find this point of view plausible, we shall have to give up the search for our native 'American' culture. With the exception of the South and that New England which, like the Red Indian, seems to be passing into solemn oblivion, there is no distinctively American culture. It is apparently our lot rather to be a federation of cultures. . . .

. . .

The failure of the melting-pot, far from closing the great American democratic experiment, means that it has only just begun. Whatever American nationalism turns out to be, we see already that it will have a color richer and more exciting than our ideal has hitherto encompassed. In a world which has dreamed of internationalism, we find that we have all unawares been building up the first international nation. The voices which have cried for a tight and jealous nationalism of the European pattern are failing. . . . America is already the world-federation in miniature, the continent where for the first time in history has been achieved that miracle of hope, the peaceful living side by side, with character substantially preserved, of the most heterogeneous peoples under the sun. . . .

. . .

Only America, by reason of the unique liberty of opportunity and traditional isolation for which she seems to stand, can lead in this cosmopolitan enterprise. Only the American—and in this category I include the migratory alien who has lived with us and caught the pioneer spirit and a sense of new social vistas—has the chance to become that citizen of the world. America is coming to be, not a nationality but a trans-nationality, a weaving back and forth, with the other lands, of many threads of all sizes and colors. . . . Our question is, What shall we do with our America? How are we likely to get the more creative America—by confining our imaginations to the ideal of the melting-pot, or broadening them to some such cosmopolitan conception as I have been vaguely sketching?

. . .

IV. EQUALITY AND STATUS

Major Developments

- Growing challenges to Jim Crow
- National adoption of female suffrage

The Jim Crow system of racial apartheid was firmly in place by the end of the nineteenth century and had received the blessing of the U.S. Supreme Court in *Plessy v. Ferguson* (1896). Cracks began to form in that edifice early in the twentieth century, however. The challenge to Jim Crow developed slowly and did not achieve easy success. Woodrow Wilson's election brought with it new influence for the Southern Democrats; blacks were excluded from federal offices and federal departments were segregated. In the aftermath of World War I, the Ku Klux Klan was revived and for a few years was a significant force. As the Klan was gaining steam, race riots that left hundreds of blacks injured or killed swept the country. Lynchings continued to be a frequent occurrence, but at nearly half the rate that they had been in the late nineteenth century. It was in response to continued lynchings that a largely white group of liberal activists formed the National Association for the Advancement of Colored People (NAACP) in 1909. A few years before, W. E. B. Du Bois organized a group of African-American leaders at Niagara Falls to call for full equality in civil rights, and Du Bois was brought in as editor of the NAACP's new magazine, *The Crisis*. Du Bois was among the black leaders who increasingly called on African-Americans to take any necessary steps to defend themselves against white violence. Lobbying and litigation efforts began to show some signs of progress for black civil rights.

Activists for women's rights made more dramatic progress. In 1890, the women's rights movement was revitalized by the founding of the National American Woman Suffrage Association, which quickly won victories in western states, as shown in Figure 8-4. A more militant National Woman's Party led by Alice Paul was formed in 1916 and focused its efforts on passing a federal constitutional amendment. Four years later, the Nineteenth Amendment securing female suffrage was adopted. Women's rights activists were less successful with, and more divided over, other proposals. After the adoption of the Nineteenth Amendment, Paul turned her attention to a proposed Equal Rights (or "Blanket") Amendment, which would mandate full legal equality between men and women. Other feminists thought such an amendment was misguided, simultaneously ignoring the more serious problem of social norms while potentially subverting various protective legislation (such as "mother's pensions" and workplace requirements) that had been won in preceding years.

EDGAR GARDNER MURPHY

THE WHITE MAN AND THE NEGRO AT THE SOUTH (1900)

Raised in modest circumstances in postbellum Texas, Edgar Gardner Murphy was drawn to the ministry and was ordained as an Episcopalian priest in 1893. In his first post, in Laredo, Texas, he organized an antilynching protest. Influenced by the Social Gospel movement, he won a national reputation as a moderate southern Progressive. He was one of the central figures in organizing the national movement against child labor and in pressing for the expansion of public education in the South (where illiteracy was still common among both blacks and whites). He was possibly most famous for his work on race relations. Murphy's emphasis on incremental improvements in the social and economic conditions of blacks won plaudits from his friend Booker T. Washington. His arguments for the reasonableness of limits on the political and civil rights of blacks helped persuade northerners that Jim Crow was making an appropriate balance of competing interests. Increasingly hampered by illness, he died in 1913 at the age of forty-three.

Who does Murphy suggest is to blame for continuing racial problems in the South? What restriction on the franchise does Murphy think is necessary? Why does he support nonracial restrictions on suffrage? To what extent does Murphy think that whites and blacks have shared interests? Are there conditions in which universal suffrage would not be justified? Is literacy a reasonable basis on which to restrict suffrage? What are the concerns with literacy tests?

. . .

When we touch the problem of political privilege in relation to the Negro, we open up the questions that most deeply divide the opinions of Southern men. Never, to any people, has there been proposed a problem so terrible in all the alternatives which it presents. . . . Every man who knows the actual working conditions of the Southern county where the white voters are outnumbered by the Negroes six to one, knows also that the welfare of the Negroes themselves is contingent upon the supremacy of the forces of intelligence and property. It is simply a question of the preservation of those very economic and social conditions upon which, at the last, the Negro himself is dependent for his light and leading and welfare. . . . If you think he, the Negro, with his weaknesses and in his ignorance, would secure better representation, representation fairer to his own real interests, if permitted in every case the individual technical exercise of the suffrage, I can only say that you have forgotten the history of the reconstruction period.

As to the internal policy of the state itself toward the problem of Negro suffrage, I think Southern men are feeling the need, increasingly, for a limitation of the franchise by an education and property test. There are multitudes of us, however, who feel that this test—in justice to the welfare of the state, and in justice to the white man, even more than in justice to the Negro, should apply to the shiftless and the illiterate of both races. Under the provisions of the Fifteenth Amendment, such a test cannot technically be offered to the one element of the population without being offered to the other. But, through . . . subterfuges of legislation, such discretionary power is given to the judges of election, in the states which have adopted it, that the test in its enforcement bears chiefly upon the Negroes. . . . [I]n its application it carries with it all the moral odium of the practice of deceit and force. It is attended with the same heavy burdens, to the consciences of both the oppressor and the oppressed, as the more open employment of violence and wrong.

Southern sentiment will not approve the disenfranchisement of the illiterate Confederate soldier. In any civilization, there is a deep and rightful regard for the man who has fought in the armies of the State. But, with that exception, the state must eventually protect itself, and protect the interests of both races, by the just application of the suffrage-test to the whites and the blacks alike. . . . The South must, of course, secure the supremacy of intelligence and property. This we shall not secure, however, if we begin with the bald declaration that the Negro is to be refused the suffrage although he have both intelligence and property, and that the illiterate white man is to be accorded the suffrage although he have neither. Such a policy would, upon its face, sustain the charge that we are not really interested in the supremacy of intelligence and property, but solely in the selfish and oppressive supremacy of a particular race. Such a course, through its depressing influence upon the educational and industrial ambitions of the Negro, would but increase his idleness and his lawlessness, and work injustice to the Negro and to the State. Take out of his life all incentive to citizenship, and you will partly destroy his interest in the acquisition of knowledge and of property, because no people will, in the long run, accept as a working principle of life the theory of taxation without representation. . . . Put the rights of citizenship among the prizes of legitimate ambition, and you have blessed both the Negro and the State.

. . . [A false literacy test] leaves the white boy without such incentive, makes the ballot as cheap in his hands as ignorance and idleness, and through indifference to the God-given relation between fitness and reward, tempts the race which is supreme to base its supremacy more and more upon force rather than upon merit. To the white boy such a provision is an insult, as well as an injustice, for the reason that it assumes his need of an adventitious advantage over the Negro. For us to ask the Negro boy to submit to a test which we are unwilling to apply to our own sons, would be, in my judgment, a disgrace to the white manhood of the South. . . . The absolute supremacy of intelligence and property, secured through a suffrage test that shall be evenly and equally applicable in theory and in fact to white and black—this will be the ultimate solution of the South for the whole vexed problem of political privilege.

. . .

W. E. B. DU BOIS

THE SOULS OF BLACK FOLK (1903)

W. E. B. Du Bois was the most prominent African-American activist in the early twentieth century. Raised by his mother in a small Massachusetts town, he graduated from an integrated high school in 1884 and already had an established record of newspaper publications. He completed a Ph.D. in history at Harvard University in 1895. He immediately launched an ambitious series of scholarly projects focusing on problems of race in the United States. His 1903 book, *Souls of Black Folk*, was in part a critique of Booker T. Washington and a strategy of accommodation with Jim Crow. The next year he helped to organize the Niagara Movement, which called for an expansion of African-American civil and political rights, and soon thereafter he joined the newly formed NAACP, where he advocated for civil rights from his position as editor of *The Crisis*. In the 1930s, he turned toward Marxism and focused increasingly on economic issues and global affairs, eventually embracing Soviet communism. In the 1960s, he emigrated to Ghana and accepted citizenship there, dying there in 1963.

What does Du Bois mean by a "double self"? In what ways does Du Bois pose the challenges facing blacks in America as similar to the challenges faced by immigrants? How do they differ? Does Du Bois favor a melting pot for Americans of African descent as well? How does Du Bois disagree with Washington? Did Washington or Du Bois have a better strategy for addressing the problems of African-Americans in the South at the turn of the century?

Between me and the other world there is ever an unasked question: unasked by some through feelings of delicacy; by others through the difficulty of rightly framing it. All, nevertheless, flutter round it. They approach me in a half- hesitant sort of way, eye me curiously or compassionately, and then, instead of saying directly, How does it feel to be a problem? they say, I know an excellent colored man in my town; or, I fought at Mechanicsville; or, Do not these Southern outrages make your blood boil? At these I smile, or am interested, or reduce the boiling to a simmer, as the occasion may require. To the real question, How does it feel to be a problem? I answer seldom a word.

And yet, being a problem is a strange experience,—peculiar even for one who has never been anything else, save perhaps in babyhood and in Europe. . . . The shades of the prison-house closed round about us all: walls strait and stubborn to the whitest, but relentlessly narrow, tall, and unscalable to sons of night who must plod darkly on in resignation, or beat unavailing palms against the stone, or steadily, half hopelessly, watch the streak of blue above.

After the Egyptian and Indian, the Greek and Roman, the Teuton and Mongolian, the Negro is a sort of seventh son, born with a veil, and gifted with second-sight in this American world,—a world which yields him no true self-consciousness, but only lets him see himself through the revelation of the other world. It is a peculiar sensation, this double-consciousness, this sense of always looking at one's self through the eyes of others, of measuring one's soul by the tape of a world that looks on in amused contempt and pity. One ever feels his twoness,—an American, a Negro; two souls, two thoughts, two unreconciled strivings; two warring ideals in one dark body, whose dogged strength alone keeps it from being torn asunder.

The history of the American Negro is the history of this strife,—this longing to attain self-conscious manhood, to merge his double self into a better and truer self. In this merging he wishes neither of the older selves to be lost. He would not Africanize America, for America has too much to teach the world and Africa. He would not bleach his Negro soul in a flood of white Americanism, for he knows that Negro blood has a message for the world. He simply wishes to make it possible for a man to be both a Negro and an American, without being cursed and spit upon by his fellows, without having the doors of Opportunity closed roughly in his face.

This, then, is the end of his striving: to be a co-worker in the kingdom of culture, to escape both death and isolation, to husband and use his best powers and his latent genius. These powers of body and mind have in the past been strangely wasted, dispersed, or forgotten. The shadow of a mighty Negro past flits through the tale of Ethiopia the Shadowy and of Egypt the Sphinx. Through history, the powers of single black men flash here and there like falling stars, and die sometimes before the world has rightly gauged their brightness. Here in America, in the few days since Emancipation, the black man's turning hither and thither in hesitant and doubtful striving has often made his very strength to lose effectiveness, to seem like absence of power, like weakness. And yet it is not weakness,—it is the contradiction of double aims. The double-aimed struggle of the black artisan—on the one hand to escape white contempt for a nation of mere hewers of wood and drawers of water, and on the other hand to plough and nail and dig for a poverty-stricken horde—could only result in making him a poor craftsman, for he had but half a heart in either cause. By the poverty and ignorance of his people, the Negro minister or doctor was tempted toward quackery and demagogy; and by the criticism of the other world, toward ideals that made him ashamed of his lowly tasks. . . .

Away back in the days of bondage they thought to see in one divine event the end of all doubt and disappointment; few men ever worshipped Freedom with half such unquestioning faith as did the American Negro for two centuries. To him, so far as he thought and dreamed, slavery was indeed the sum of all villainies, the cause of all sorrow, the root of all prejudice; Emancipation was the key to a promised land of sweeter beauty than ever stretched before the eyes of wearied Israelites. . . .

. . .

. . .The Nation has not yet found peace from its sins; the freedman has not yet found in freedom his promised land. Whatever of good may have come in these years of change, the shadow of a deep disappointment rests upon the Negro people. . . .

. . . The ideal of liberty demanded for its attainment powerful means, and these the Fifteenth Amendment gave him. The ballot, which before he had looked upon as a visible sign of freedom, he now regarded as the chief means of gaining and perfecting the liberty with which war had partially endowed him. And why not? Had not votes made war and emancipated millions? Had not votes enfranchised the freedmen? Was anything impossible to a power that had done all this? A million black men started with renewed zeal to vote themselves into the kingdom. . . . Slowly but steadily, in the following years, a new vision began gradually to replace the dream of political power,—a powerful movement, the rise of another ideal to guide the unguided, another pillar of fire by night after a clouded day. It was the ideal of "book-learning"; the curiosity, born of compulsory ignorance, to know and test the power of the cabalistic letters of the white man, the longing to know. Here at last seemed to have been discovered the mountain path to Canaan; longer than the highway of Emancipation and law, steep and rugged, but straight, leading to heights high enough to overlook life.

. . .

A people thus handicapped ought not to be asked to race with the world, but rather allowed to give all its time and thought to its own social problems. But alas! while sociologists gleefully count his bastards and his prostitutes, the very soul of the toiling, sweating black man is darkened by the shadow of a vast despair. Men call the shadow prejudice, and learnedly explain it as the natural defense of culture against barbarism, learning against ignorance, purity against crime, the "higher" against the "lower" races. To which the Negro cries Amen! and swears that to so much of this strange prejudice as is founded on just homage to civilization, culture, righteousness, and progress, he humbly bows and meekly does obeisance. But before that nameless prejudice that leaps beyond all this he stands helpless, dismayed, and well-nigh speechless; before that personal disrespect and mockery, the ridicule and systematic humiliation, the distortion of fact and wanton license of fancy, the cynical ignoring of the better and the boisterous welcoming of the worse, the all-pervading desire to inculcate disdain for everything black, from Toussaint to the devil,—before this there rises a sickening despair that would disarm and discourage any nation save that black host to whom "discouragement" is an unwritten word.

But the facing of so vast a prejudice could not but bring the inevitable self-questioning, self-disparagement, and lowering of ideals which ever accompany repression and breed in an atmosphere of contempt and hate. Whisperings and portents came home upon the four winds: Lo! we are diseased and dying, cried the dark hosts; we cannot write, our voting is vain; what need of education, since we must always cook and serve? And the Nation echoed and enforced this self-criticism, saying: Be content to be servants, and nothing more; what need of higher culture for half-men? Away with the black man's ballot, by force or fraud,—and behold the suicide of a race! Nevertheless, out of the evil came something of good,—the more careful adjustment of education to real life, the clearer perception of the Negroes' social responsibilities, and the sobering realization of the meaning of progress.

. . . To be really true, all these ideals must be melted and welded into one. The training of the schools we need today more than ever,—the training of deft hands, quick eyes and ears, and above all the broader, deeper, higher culture of gifted minds and pure hearts. The power of the ballot we need in sheer self-defense,—else what shall save us from a second slavery? Freedom, too, the long-sought, we still seek,—the freedom of life and limb, the freedom to work and think, the freedom to love and aspire. Work, culture, liberty,—all these we need, not singly but together, not successively but together, each growing and aiding each, and all striving toward that vaster ideal that swims before the Negro people, the ideal of human brotherhood, gained through the unifying ideal of Race; the ideal of fostering and developing the traits and talents of the Negro, not in opposition to or contempt for other races, but rather in large conformity to the greater ideals of the American Republic, in order that someday on American soil two world-races may give each to each those characteristics both so sadly lack. We the darker ones come even now not altogether empty-handed: there are today no truer exponents of the pure human spirit of the Declaration of Independence than the American Negroes; there is no true American music but the wild sweet melodies of the Negro slave; the American fairy tales and folklore are Indian and African; and, all in all, we black men seem the sole oasis of simple faith and reverence in a dusty desert of dollars and smartness. Will America be poorer if she replace her brutal dyspeptic blundering with light-hearted but determined Negro humility? or her coarse and cruel wit with loving jovial good-humor? or her vulgar music with the soul of the Sorrow Songs?

Merely a concrete test of the underlying principles of the great republic is the Negro Problem, and the spiritual striving of the freedmen's sons is the travail of souls whose burden is almost beyond the measure of their strength, but who bear it in the name of an historic race, in the name of this the land of their fathers' fathers, and in the name of human opportunity.

. . .

Easily the most striking thing in the history of the American Negro since 1876 is the ascendancy of Mr. Booker T. Washington. It began at the time when war memories and ideals were rapidly passing; a day of astonishing commercial development was dawning; a sense of doubt and hesitation overtook the freedmen's sons,—then it was that his leading began. Mr. Washington came, with a simple definite program, at the psychological moment when the nation was a little ashamed of having bestowed so much sentiment on Negroes, and was concentrating its energies on Dollars. His program of industrial education, conciliation of the South, and submission and silence as to civil and political rights, was not wholly original; the Free Negroes from 1830 up to war-time had striven to build industrial schools, and the American Missionary Association had from the first taught various trades; and Price and others had sought a way of honorable alliance with the best of the Southerners. But Mr. Washington first indissolubly linked these things; he put enthusiasm, unlimited energy, and perfect faith into his program, and changed it from a by-path into a veritable Way of Life. And the tale of the methods by which he did this is a fascinating study of human life.

It startled the nation to hear a Negro advocating such a program after many decades of bitter complaint; it startled and won the applause of the South, it interested and won the admiration of the North; and after a confused murmur of protest, it silenced if it did not convert the Negroes themselves.

To gain the sympathy and cooperation of the various elements comprising the white South was Mr. Washington's first task; and this, at the time Tuskegee was founded, seemed, for a black man, well-nigh impossible. And yet ten years later it was done in the word spoken at Atlanta: "In all things purely social we can be as separate as the five fingers, and yet one as the hand in all things essential to mutual progress." This "Atlanta Compromise" is by all odds the most notable thing in Mr. Washington's career. . . .

. . .

. . . One hesitates, therefore, to criticize a life which, beginning with so little, has done so much. And yet the time is come when one may speak in all sincerity and utter courtesy of the mistakes and shortcomings of Mr. Washington's career, as well as of his triumphs, without being thought captious or envious, and without forgetting that it is easier to do ill than well in the world.

. . .

. . . Nearly all the former [leaders] had become leaders by the silent suffrage of their fellows, had sought to lead their own people alone, and were usually, save Douglass, little known outside their race. But Booker T. Washington arose as essentially the leader not of one race but of two,—a compromiser between the South, the North, and the Negro. Naturally the Negroes resented, at first bitterly, signs of compromise which surrendered their civil and political rights, even though this was to be exchanged for larger chances of economic development. The rich and dominating North, however, was not only weary of the race problem, but was investing largely in Southern enterprises, and welcomed any method of peaceful cooperation. Thus, by national opinion, the Negroes began to recognize Mr. Washington's leadership; and the voice of criticism was hushed.

Mr. Washington represents in Negro thought the old attitude of adjustment and submission; but adjustment at such a peculiar time as to make his program unique. This is an age of unusual economic development, and Mr. Washington's program naturally takes an economic cast, becoming a gospel of Work and Money to such an extent as apparently almost completely to overshadow the higher aims of life. Moreover, this is an age when the more advanced races are coming in closer contact with the less developed races, and the race-feeling is therefore intensified; and Mr. Washington's program practically accepts the alleged inferiority of the Negro races. Again, in our own land, the reaction from the sentiment of war time has given impetus to race-prejudice against Negroes, and Mr. Washington withdraws many of the high demands of Negroes as men and American citizens. In other periods of intensified prejudice all the Negro's tendency to self-assertion has been called forth; at this period a policy of submission is advocated. In the history of nearly all other races and peoples the doctrine preached at such crises has been that manly self-respect is worth more than lands and houses, and that a people who voluntarily surrender such respect, or cease striving for it, are not worth civilizing.

In answer to this, it has been claimed that the Negro can survive only through submission. Mr. Washington distinctly asks that black people give up, at least for the present, three things,—

First, political power,

Second, insistence on civil rights,

Third, higher education of Negro youth,—and concentrate all their energies on industrial education, and accumulation of wealth, and the conciliation of the South. This policy has been courageously and insistently advocated for over fifteen years, and has been triumphant for perhaps ten years. As a result of this tender of the palm-branch, what has been the return? In these years there have occurred:

1. The disfranchisement of the Negro.
2. The legal creation of a distinct status of civil inferiority for the Negro.
3. The steady withdrawal of aid from institutions for the higher training of the Negro.

These movements are not, to be sure, direct results of Mr. Washington's teachings; but his propaganda has, without a shadow of doubt, helped their speedier accomplishment. The question then comes: Is it possible, and probable, that nine millions of men can make effective progress in economic lines if they are deprived of political rights, made a servile caste, and allowed only the most meagre chance for developing their exceptional men? If history and reason give any distinct answer to these questions, it is an emphatic NO. And Mr. Washington thus faces the triple paradox of his career:

1. He is striving nobly to make Negro artisans business men and property-owners; but it is utterly impossible, under modern competitive methods, for workingmen and property- owners to defend their rights and exist without the right of suffrage.
2. He insists on thrift and self-respect, but at the same time counsels a silent submission to civic inferiority such as is bound to sap the manhood of any race in the long run.
3. He advocates common-school and industrial training, and depreciates institutions of higher learning; but neither the Negro common-schools, nor Tuskegee itself, could remain open a day were it not for teachers trained in Negro colleges, or trained by their graduates.

. . .

[Some critics] acknowledge Mr. Washington's invaluable service in counselling patience and courtesy in such demands; they do not ask that ignorant black men vote when ignorant whites are debarred, or that any reasonable restrictions in the suffrage should not be applied; they know that the low social level of the mass of the race is responsible for much discrimination against it, but they also know, and the nation knows, that relentless color-prejudice is more often a cause than a result of the Negro's degradation; they seek the abatement of this relic of barbarism, and not its systematic encouragement and pampering by all agencies of social power from the Associated Press to the Church of Christ. They advocate, with Mr. Washington, a broad system of Negro common schools supplemented by thorough industrial training; but they are surprised that a man of Mr. Washington's insight cannot see that no such educational system ever has rested or can rest on any other basis than that of the well-equipped college and university, and they insist that there is a demand for a few such institutions throughout the South to train the best of the Negro youth as teachers, professional men, and leaders.

This group of men honor Mr. Washington for his attitude of conciliation toward the white South; they accept the "Atlanta Compromise" in its broadest interpretation; they recognize, with him, many signs of promise, many men of high purpose and fair judgment, in this section; they know that no easy task has been laid upon a region already tottering under heavy burdens. But, nevertheless, they insist that the way to truth and right lies in straightforward honesty, not in indiscriminate flattery; in praising those of the South who do well and criticizing uncompromisingly those who do ill; in taking advantage of the opportunities at hand and urging their fellows to do the same, but at the same time in remembering that only a firm adherence to their higher ideals and aspirations will ever keep those ideals within the realm of possibility. They do not expect that the free right to vote, to enjoy civic rights, and to be educated, will come in a moment; they do not expect to see the bias and prejudices of years disappear at the blast of a trumpet; but they are absolutely certain that the way for a people to gain their reasonable rights is not by voluntarily throwing them away and insisting that they do not want them; that the way for a people to gain respect is not by continually belittling and ridiculing themselves; that, on the contrary, Negroes must insist continually, in season and out of season, that voting is necessary to modern manhood, that color discrimination is barbarism, and that black boys need education as well as white boys.

. . . The growing spirit of kindliness and reconciliation between the North and South after the frightful difference of a generation ago ought to be a source of deep congratulation to all, and especially to those whose mistreatment caused the war; but if that reconciliation is to be marked by the industrial slavery and civic death of those same black men, with permanent legislation into a position of inferiority, then those black men, if they are really men, are called upon by every consideration of patriotism and loyalty to oppose such a course by all civilized methods, even though such opposition involves disagreement with Mr. Booker T. Washington. We have no right to sit silently by while the inevitable seeds are sown for a harvest of disaster to our children, black and white.

. . .

. . . [W]hile it is a great truth to say that the Negro must strive and strive mightily to help himself, it is equally true that unless his striving be not simply seconded, but rather aroused and encouraged, by the initiative of the richer and wiser environing group, he cannot hope for great success.

In his failure to realize and impress this last point, Mr. Washington is especially to be criticized. His doctrine has tended to make the whites, North and South, shift the burden of the Negro problem to the Negro's shoulders and stand aside as critical and rather pessimistic spectators; when in fact the burden belongs to the nation, and the hands of none of us are clean if we bend not our energies to righting these great wrongs.

. . .

The black men of America have a duty to perform, a duty stern and delicate,—a forward movement to oppose a part of the work of their greatest leader. So far as Mr. Washington preaches Thrift, Patience, and Industrial Training for the masses, we must hold up his hands and strive with him, rejoicing in his honors and glorying in the strength of this Joshua called of God and of man to lead the headless host. But so far as Mr. Washington apologizes for injustice, North or South, does not rightly value the privilege and duty of voting, belittles the emasculating effects of caste distinctions, and opposes the higher training and ambition of our brighter minds,—so far as he, the South, or the Nation, does this,—we must unceasingly and firmly oppose them. By every civilized and peaceful method we must strive for the rights which the world accords to men, clinging unwaveringly to those great words which the sons of the Fathers would fain forget: "We hold these truths to be self-evident: That all men are created equal; that they are endowed by their Creator with certain unalienable rights; that among these are life, liberty, and the pursuit of happiness."

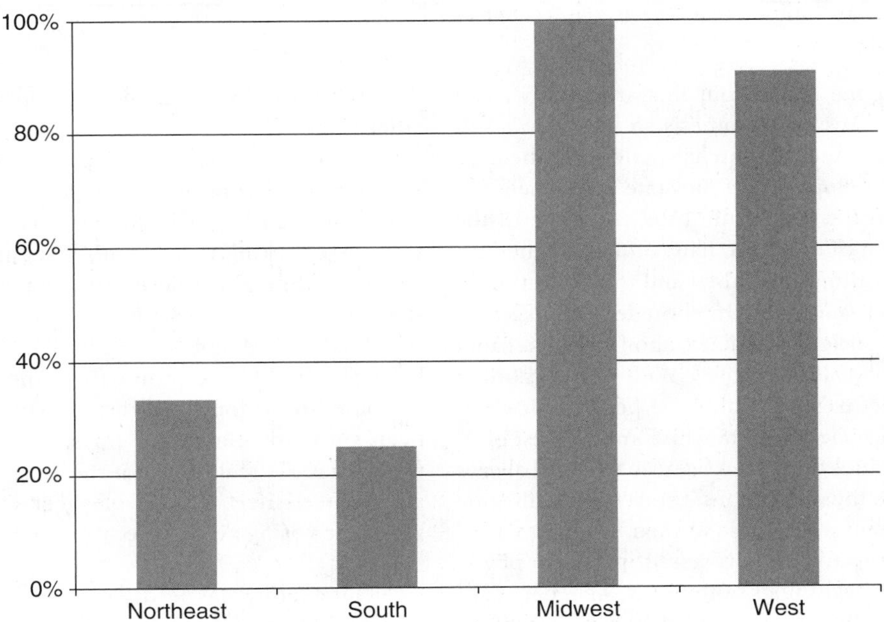

FIGURE 8-4 Percent of States by Region Allowing Women to Vote at Time of Nineteenth Amendment.

JANE ADDAMS

IF MEN WERE SEEKING THE FRANCHISE (1913)

Raised in a well-off Republican family in Illinois in the Civil War era, Jane Addams graduated from a women's college in 1881. Drawing on her own inheritance, she founded Hull House in a section of Chicago dominated largely by Italian immigrants. Hull House was a "settlement house," houses established in poor neighborhoods and occupied by middle-class residents who provided cultural education and social services for the neighborhood. Hull House soon became a center of social reform activism and feminism, and Addams herself became a prominent figure in a wide range of organizations, from the National American Woman Suffrage Association to the NAACP. In 1920, one of her causes was realized when the states ratified the Nineteenth Amendment barring restrictions on the right to vote based on sex. The amendment had the greatest effect in the older states of the Northeast and South; most of the newer states in the Midwest and West already allowed women to vote in many, if not all, elections.

With the outbreak of World War I, Addams broke from many Progressives and became an active pacifist, reducing her political influence in the United States and shifting her energies abroad. In 1931, she was awarded the Nobel Peace Prize for her efforts. By the time she passed away four years later, she was being celebrated by New Dealers. For a time she wrote a regular column in the popular magazine *Ladies' Home Journal*, which she often used to advance the cause of female suffrage.

What is the value of her hypothetical scenario of a matriarchal state? Given Addams's broader political views, could her arguments against male suffrage be taken sincerely? Is a concern about how a given group of citizens might vote and what policies they might favor ever be a justifiable reason for restricting the franchise? Is her essay well suited to persuading the somewhat conservative and well-off readership of the *Ladies' Home Journal*? Would her arguments be persuasive to those who actively opposed female suffrage? Is it necessary to accept the social reform agenda in order to favor female suffrage? Does Addams offer other reasons to support female suffrage? Is her argument more or less compelling than the type of argument offered by Susan B. Anthony?

Let us imagine throughout this article, if we can sustain an absurd hypothesis so long, the result upon society if the matriarchal period had held its own; if the development of the State had closely followed that of the Family until the chief care of the former, as that of the latter, had come to be the nurture and education of children and the protection of the weak, sick and aged. In short let us imagine a hypothetical society organized upon the belief that "there is no wealth but life." With this Ruskinian foundation let us assume that the political machinery of such a society, the franchise and the rest of it, were in the hands of women because they had always best exercised those functions. Let us further imagine a given moment when these women, who in this hypothetical society had possessed political power from the very beginnings of the State, were being appealed to by the voteless men that men might be associated with women in the responsibilities of citizenship.

Plagiarizing somewhat upon recent suffrage speeches let us consider various replies which these citizen women might reasonably make to the men who were seeking the franchise; the men insisting that only through the use of the ballot could they share the duties of the State.

First, could not the women say: "Our most valid objection to extending the franchise to you is that you are so fond of fighting—you always have been since you were little boys. You'd very likely forget that the real object of the State is to nurture and protect life, and out of sheer vainglory you would be voting away huge sums of money for battleships. . . ."

"Our educational needs are too great and serious to run any such risk. Democratic government itself is perilous unless the electorate is educated; our industries are suffering for lack of skilled workmen; more than half a million immigrants a year must be taught the underlying principles of republican government. Can we, the responsible voters, take the risk of wasting our taxes by extending the vote to those who have always been so ready to lose their heads over mere military display?"

Second, would not the hypothetical women, who would have been responsible for the advance of industry during these later centuries, as women actually were during the earlier centuries when they dragged home the game and transformed the pelts into shelter and clothing, say further to these disenfranchised men: "We have carefully built up a code of factory legislation for the protection of the workers in modern industry; we know that you men have always been careless about the house, perfectly indifferent to the necessity for sweeping and cleaning; if you were made responsible for factory legislation it is quite probable that you would let the workers in the textile mills contract tuberculosis through needlessly breathing the fluff, or the workers in machine shops through inhaling metal filings, both of which are now carried off by an excellent suction system which we women have insisted upon, but which it is almost impossible to have installed in a man-made State because the men think so little of dust and its evil effects. . . .

. . .

These wise women, governing the State with the same care they had always put into the management of their families, would further place against these men seeking the franchise the charge that men do not really know how tender and delicate children are, and might therefore put them to work in factories, as indeed they have done in man-made States during the entire period of factory production. . . .

Would not these responsible woman voters gravely shake their heads and say that as long as men exalt business profit above human life it would be sheer folly to give them the franchise; that, of course, they would be slow to make such matters the subject of legislation?

. . .

These conscientious women responsible for the State in which life was considered of more value than wealth would furthermore say: "Then, too, you men exhibit such curious survivals of the mere savage instinct of punishment and revenge. The United States alone spends every year five hundred million dollars more on its policemen, courts and prisons than upon all its works of religion, charity and education. The price of one trial expended on a criminal early in life might save the State thousands of dollars and the man untold horrors. And yet with all this vast expenditure little is done to reduce crime. Men are kept in jails and penitentiaries where there is not even the semblance of education or reformatory measure; young men are returned over and over again to the same institution until they have grown old and gray, and in all of that time they have not once been taught a trade, nor have they been in any wise prepared to withstand the temptations of life."

. . .

Did the enfranchised women evoked by our imagination speak thus to the disenfranchised men, the latter would at least respect their scruples and their hesitation in regard to an extension of the obligation of citizenship. But what would be the temper of the masculine mind if the voting women representing the existing State should present to them only the following half-dozen objections, which are unhappily so familiar to many of us: If the women should say, first, that men would find politics corrupting; second, that they would doubtless vote as their wives and mothers did; third, that men's suffrage would only double the vote without changing results; fourth, that men's suffrage would diminish the respect for men; fifth, that most men do not want to vote; sixth, that the best men would not vote?

I do not believe that women broadened by life and its manifold experiences would actually present these six objections to men as real reasons for withholding the franchise from their, unless indeed they had long formed the habit of regarding men not as comrades and fellow-citizens, but as a class by themselves, in essential matters really inferior although always held sentimentally very much above them.

Certainly no such talk would be indulged in between men and women who had together embodied in political institutions the old affairs of life which had normally and historically belonged to both of them. If woman had adjusted herself to the changing demands of the State as she did to the historic mutations of her own household she might naturally and without challenge have held the place in the State which she now holds in the family.

When Plato once related his dream of an ideal Republic he begged his fellow-citizens not to ridicule him because he considered the cooperation of women necessary for its fulfillment. He contended that so far as the guardianship of the State is concerned there is no distinction between the powers of men and women save those which custom has made.

V. POLITICAL ECONOMY

Major Developments

- Growth of economic and social regulation
- Establishment of the Federal Reserve system
- Emergence of radical movements
- Development of new corporate–government cooperative arrangements

Ideas about political economy were in flux in the early twentieth century, and a wide range of options for organizing the relationship between government and economic actors seemed to be on the table. The laissez-faire arguments that had been in ascendance in the Gilded Age were on the defensive throughout the early decades of the twentieth. The advent of the Soviet Union in 1917 and the establishment of a centralized planned economy indicated to many just how far it was possible to go—and possibly where the modern corporate economy was naturally headed. The Democratic Party had absorbed much of the policy platform of the Populists. The Socialists mounted credible presidential campaigns (and successful local campaigns) calling for public ownership of most industries. Progressives controlled much of the Republican Party and called for federal income taxes and robust federal regulation of corporations. The one successful Democratic candidate, Woodrow Wilson, pondered the possibility of breaking up the large corporations, until American entry into World War I brought with it a wartime economy that included direct federal control of key industries and extensive price and wage controls.

Even conservatives were open to a wide range of government interventions in the economy. The Progressive journalist Walter Lippmann complained that, unlike Theodore Roosevelt, President Calvin Coolidge was "no Hamiltonian Federalist," which seemed just fine to the business interests that "want to be left alone."[13] But though Coolidge famously declared that "the chief business of the American people is business," he was more interested in emphasizing that Americans were committed to "production" and "prospering in the world"—and all the material and cultural benefits that came in the wake of the economic growth—than suggesting that the role of government is simply to get out of the way.[14] After all, his technocratic commerce secretary, Herbert Hoover, was busily organizing the business community to improve labor conditions and produce more goods. As one of the preeminent American economists concluded at the end of the 1920s, economic policy was just a matter of "applying fresh intelligence to the day's work."[15] Government, business, workers, and social scientists were all pulling together to get things done.

These readings indicate the range of options that were driving intellectual debate. On the left, Eugene Debs and Emma Goldman advocated different forms of socialism. On the right, Herbert Hoover was trying to identify the distinctive American alternative to the socialism that seemed to be sweeping Europe. In between was Herbert Croly's influential call for a return to the economic and political philosophy of Alexander Hamilton.

---

13 Walter Lippmann, *Men of Destiny* (New York: Macmillan, 1927), 15.

14 Calvin Coolidge, "Address to the American Society of Newspaper Editors, January 17, 1925," in *Foundations of the Republic* (New York: Scribner's Sons, 1926), 187.

15 President's Conference on Unemployment, *Recent Economic Changes in the United States* (New York: McGraw-Hill, 1929), 867.

EUGENE V. DEBS

UNIONISM AND SOCIALISM (1904)

Eugene Debs was the son of an Indiana grocer. At the age of fourteen, he dropped out of school and went to work for a local railroad but was laid off in the Panic of 1873. Even though he was then working for a wholesale grocer, he became a leader in the local rail workers' benevolent association. He successfully ran for his first public office, as a Democrat for city clerk, in 1879. In 1893, he started the American Railway Union, which as an "industrial union" broke from the model of either the Knights of Labor or the American Federation of Labor in order to organize all workers within a single industry, regardless of their skill level or particular craft. Debs helped organize the Pullman strike of 1894, which became one of the largest and most violent labor actions of the period, resulting in his conviction for violating a court order. The strike and his trial catapulted Debs into the national spotlight. In 1896, he endorsed the Populists, and by 1897 he embraced socialism. By the 1910s, he was criticizing the revolutionary strategy of the Industrial Workers of the World for achieving worker control of the means of production and instead endorsed democratic efforts to advance socialism. He ran five times as the Socialist Party candidate for president, reaching a high-water mark in 1912. In 1918, he was convicted of violating the Espionage Act for his antiwar speeches. His sentence was commuted by President Warren G. Harding in 1921, and he died five years later. A popular public speaker, his best-known work was his pamphlet calling for both unionism and socialism.

Is Debs right that enslaving others is the "mainspring of human action"? Is he persuasive that the chief end of government is to maintain the oppression of the workers? Is that assessment of government more persuasive at the turn of the twentieth century than it might have been at other points in American history? How does he think that industrialism was a prerequisite for "social revolution"? What does Debs see as the purpose of unions? Why does he object to trade unions? Why does he think socialism and unionism are compatible? Why might there be tensions between unionism and socialism? Do the workers as such need political power to advance their interests? What is the best instrument for advancing the interests of the working class?

. . .

There has always been a labor question since man first exploited man in the struggle for existence, but not until its true meaning was revealed in the development of modern industry did it command serious thought or intelligent consideration, and only then came any adequate conception of its importance to the race.

Man has always sought the mastery of his fellowman. To enslave his fellow in some form and to live out of his labor has been the mainspring of human action.

. . .

The chief end of government has been and is to keep the victims of oppression and injustice in subjection.

The men and women who toil and produce have been and are at the mercy of those who wax fat and scornful upon the fruit of their labor.

The labor question was born of the first pang of protest that died unvoiced in unrequited toil.

. . .

A century ago a boy served his apprenticeship and became the master of his trade. The few simple tools with which work was then done were generally owned by the man who used them; he could provide himself with the small quantity of raw material he required, and freely follow his chosen pursuit and enjoy the fruit of his labor. But as everything had to be produced by the work of his hands, production was a slow process, meagre of results, and the worker found it necessary to devote from twelve to fifteen hours to his daily task to earn a sufficient amount to support himself and family.

. . .

There was no millionaire in the United States; nor was there a tramp. These types are the products of the same system. The former is produced at the expense of the latter, and both at the expense of the working class. They appeared at the same time in the industrial development and they will disappear together with the abolition of the system that brought them into existence.

The application of machinery to productive industry was followed by tremendous and far-reaching changes in the whole structure of society. First among these was the change in the status of the worker, who, from an independent mechanic or small producer, was reduced to the level of a dependent wage worker. The machine had leaped, as it were, into the arena of industrial activity, and had left little or no room for the application of the worker's skill or the use of his individual tools.

The economic dependence of the working class became more and more rigidly fixed—and at the same time a new era dawned for the human race.

The more or less isolated individual artisans were converted into groups of associated workers and marshalled for the impending social revolution.

. . .

The swift and vast concentration of capital and the unprecedented industrial activity which marked the close of the nineteenth century were followed by the most extraordinary growth in the number and variety of trades-unions in the history of the movement; yet this expansion, remarkable as it was, has not only been equaled, but excelled, in the first years of the new century, the tide of unionism sweeping over the whole country, and rising steadily higher, notwithstanding the efforts put forth from a hundred sources controlled by the ruling class to restrain its march, impair its utility or stamp it out of existence.

. . .

The more or less open enemies have inaugurated some interesting innovations during the past few years. The private armies the corporations used some years ago, such as Pinkerton mercenaries, coal and iron police, deputy marshals, etc., have been relegated to second place as out of date, or they are wholly out of commission. It has been found after repeated experiments that the courts are far more deadly to trades-unions, and that they operate noiselessly and with unerring precision.

. . .

The courts have found it in line with judicial procedure to strike every weapon from labor's economic hand and leave it defenseless at the mercy of its exploiter; and now that the courts have gone to the last extremity in this nefarious plot of subjugation, labor, at last, is waking up to the fact that it has not been using its political arm in the struggle at all; that the ballot which it can wield is strong enough not only to disarm the enemy, but to drive that enemy entirely from the field.

The courts, so notoriously in control of capital, and so shamelessly perverted to its base and sordid purposes is, therefore, exercising a wholesome effect upon trades-unionism by compelling the members to note the class character of our capitalist government and driving them to the inevitable conclusion that the labor question is also a political question and that the working class must organize their political power that they may wrest the government from capitalist control and put an end to class rule forever.

Trades-unionists for the most part learn slowly, but they learn surely, and fresh object lessons are prepared for them every day.

. . .

They have seen state legislatures, both Republican and Democratic, with never an exception, controlled bodily by the capitalist class and turn the committees of labor unions empty handed from their doors.

They have seen state supreme courts declare as unconstitutional the last vestige of law upon the statute books that could by any possibility be construed as affording any shelter or relief to the labor union or its members.

They have seen these and many other things and will doubtless see many more before their eyes are opened as a class but we are thankful for them all, painful though they be to us in having to bear witness to the suffering of our benighted brethren.

. . .

The "pure and simple" trade-union of the past does not answer the requirements of today, and they who insist that it does are blind to the changes going on about them, and out of harmony with the progressive forces of the age.

The attempt to preserve the "autonomy" of each trade and segregate it within its own independent jurisdiction, while the lines which once separated them are being obliterated, and the trades are being interwoven and interlocked in the process of industrial evolution, is as futile as to declare and attempt to enforce the independence of the waves of the sea.

A modern industrial plant has a hundred trades and parts of trades represented in its working force. To have these workers parceled out to a hundred unions is to divide and not to organize them, to give them over to factions and petty leadership and leave them an easy prey to the machinations of the enemy. The dominant craft should control the plant or, rather, the union, and it should embrace the entire working force. This is the industrial plan, the modern method applied to modern conditions, and it will in time prevail.

. . .

The members of a trade-union should be taught the true import, the whole object of the labor movement and understand its entire program.

They should know that the labor movement means more, infinitely more, than a paltry increase in wages and the strike necessary to secure it; that while it engages to do all that possibly can be done to better the working conditions of its members, its higher object is to overthrow the capitalist system of private ownership of the tools of labor, abolish wage-slavery and achieve the freedom of the whole working class and, in fact, of all mankind.

. . .

The cry, "no politics in the union," "dragging the union into politics," or "making the union the tail of some political kite," is born of ignorance or dishonesty, or a combination of both. It is echoed by every ward-heeling politician in the country. The plain purpose is to deceive and mislead the workers.

It is not the welfare of the union that these capitalist henchmen are so much concerned about, but the fear that the working class, as a class, organized into a party of their own, will go into politics, for well they know that when that day dawns their occupation will be gone.

. . .

The trades-union is not and cannot become a political machine, nor can it be used for political purposes. They who insist upon working class political action not only have no intention to convert the trades-union into a political party, but they would oppose any such attempt on the part of others.

The trades-union is an economic organization with distinct economic functions and as such is a part, a necessary part, but a part only of the Labor Movement; it has its own sphere of activity, its own program and is its own master within its economic limitations.

But the labor movement has also its political side and the trades-unionist must be educated to realize its importance and to understand that the political side of the movement must be *unionized* as well as the economic side; and that he is not in fact a union man at all who, although a member of the union on the economic side, is a non-unionist on the political side; and while striking for, votes against the working class.

The trades-union expresses the economic power and the Socialist party expresses the political power of the Labor movement.

The fully developed labor-unionist uses both his economic and political power in the interest of his class. He understands that the struggle between labor and capital is a class struggle; that the working class are in a great majority, but divided, some in trades-unions and some out of them, some in one political party and some in another; that because they are divided they are helpless and must submit to being robbed of what their labor produces, and treated with contempt; that they must unite their class in the trades-union on the one hand and in the Socialist party on the other hand; that industrially and politically they must act together as a class against the capitalist class and that this struggle is a class struggle, and that any workingman who deserts his union in a strike and goes to the other side is a scab, and any working man who deserts his party on election day and goes over to the enemy is a betrayer of his class and an enemy of his fellow man.

. . .

The workers . . . are poor as a rule, and ignorant as a class, *but they are in an overwhelming majority.*

In a word, they have the power, but are not conscious of it. This then is the supreme demand; to make them conscious of the power of their class, or class-conscious workingmen.

. . .

The working class alone—and by the working class I mean all useful workers, all who by the labor of their hands or the effort of their brains, or both in alliance, as they ought universally to be, increase the knowledge and add to the wealth of society—the working class alone is essential to society and therefore the only class that can survive in the world-wide struggle for freedom.

. . .

In the class struggle the workers must unite and fight together as one on both economic and political fields.

. . .

The union is educating the workers in the management of industrial activities and fitting them for co-operative control and democratic regulation of their trades,—the party is recruiting and training and drilling the political army that is to conquer the capitalist forces on the political battlefield; and having control of the machinery of government, use it to transfer the industries from the capitalists to the workers, from the parasites to the people.

. . .

It is of vital importance to the trades-union that its members be class-conscious, that they understand the class struggle and their duty as union men on the political field, so that in every move that is made they will have the goal in view, and while taking advantage of every opportunity to secure concessions and enlarge their economic advantage, they will at the same time unite at the ballot box, not only to back up the economic struggle of the trades-union, but to finally wrest the government from capitalist control and establish the working class republic.

EMMA GOLDMAN

ANARCHISM (1907)

Emma Goldman grew up in Lithuania and in 1885 emigrated to the United States while in her teens. She had already gotten involved in radical groups before leaving Europe, and in the United States she soon fell in with socialist and anarchist groups (she later admitted to helping plot the attempted murder of a factory manager). She was jailed for two years for inciting a riot, and in 1901 the assassin of President William McKinley credited Goldman as his inspiration. By the early twentieth century, Goldman had achieved international notoriety as a radical speaker but had renounced violence. Nonetheless, she was in and out of jail in the 1910s and was finally deported to the Soviet Union for her antiwar activities in 1919. After falling out with Soviet authorities, she fled to Europe and spent her last fifteen years moving from country to country, criticizing the communist movement while continuing to extol socialist anarchism. She died in Toronto in 1939 and was buried in Chicago.

What does Goldman mean by anarchism? Is she persuasive that anarchism is realistic and practical? What are the advantages of anarchism, according to Goldman? What does she take to be the critical social problems to be solved? What method of political change does she advocate in this essay? Is this preferable to the kind of democratic radicalism that Debs advocated?

. . .

The history of human growth and development is at the same time the history of the terrible struggle of every new idea heralding the approach of a brighter dawn. In its tenacious hold on tradition, the Old has never hesitated to make use of the foulest and cruelest means to stay the advent of the New, in whatever form or period the latter may have asserted itself. Nor need we retrace our steps into the distant past to realize the enormity of opposition, difficulties, and hardships placed in the path of every progressive idea. The rack, the thumbscrew, and the knout are still with us; so are the convict's garb and the social wrath, all conspiring against the spirit that is serenely marching on.

Anarchism could not hope to escape the fate of all other ideas of innovation. Indeed, as the most revolutionary and uncompromising innovator, Anarchism must needs meet with the combined ignorance and venom of the world it aims to reconstruct.

. . .

What, then, are the objections? First, Anarchism is impractical, though a beautiful ideal. Second, Anarchism stands for violence and destruction, hence it must be repudiated as vile and dangerous. . . .

A practical scheme, says Oscar Wilde, is either one already in existence, or a scheme that could be carried out under the existing conditions; but it is exactly the existing conditions that one objects to, and any scheme that could accept these conditions is wrong and foolish. The true criterion of the practical, therefore, is not whether the latter can keep intact the wrong or foolish; rather is it whether the scheme has vitality enough to leave the stagnant waters of the old, and build, as well as sustain, new life. In the light of this conception, Anarchism is indeed practical. More than any other idea, it is helping to do away with the wrong and foolish; more than any other idea, it is building and sustaining new life.

. . .

ANARCHISM: The philosophy of a new social order based on liberty unrestricted by man-made law; the theory that all forms of government rest on violence, and are therefore wrong and harmful, as well as unnecessary.

. . .

Anarchism is the only philosophy which brings to man the consciousness of himself; which maintains that God, the State, and society are non-existent, that their promises are null and void, since they can be fulfilled only through man's subordination. Anarchism is therefore the teacher of the unity of life; not merely in nature, but in man. There is no conflict between the individual and the social instincts, any more than there is between the heart and the lungs: the one the receptacle of a precious life essence, the other the repository of the element that keeps the essence pure and strong. The individual is the heart of society, conserving the essence of social life; society is the lungs which are distributing the element to keep the life essence—that is, the individual—pure and strong.

"The one thing of value in the world," says Emerson, "is the active soul; this every man contains within him. The soul active sees absolute truth and utters truth and creates." In other words, the individual instinct is the thing of value in the world. It is the true soul that sees and creates the truth alive, out of which is to come a still greater truth, the re-born social soul.

Anarchism is the great liberator of man from the phantoms that have held him captive; it is the arbiter and pacifier of the two forces for individual and social harmony. To accomplish that unity, Anarchism has declared war on the pernicious influences which have so far prevented the harmonious blending of individual and social instincts, the individual and society.

Religion, the dominion of the human mind; Property, the dominion of human needs; and Government, the dominion of human conduct, represent the stronghold of man's enslavement and all the horrors it entails. Religion! How it dominates man's mind, how it humiliates and degrades his soul. God is everything, man is nothing, says religion. But out of that nothing God has created a kingdom so despotic, so tyrannical, so cruel, so terribly exacting that naught but gloom and tears and blood have ruled the world since gods began. Anarchism rouses man to rebellion against this black monster. Break your mental fetters, says Anarchism to man, for not until you think and judge for yourself will you get rid of the dominion of darkness, the greatest obstacle to all progress.

Property, the dominion of man's needs, the denial of the right to satisfy his needs. Time was when property claimed a divine right, when it came to man with the same refrain, even as religion, "Sacrifice! Abnegate! Submit!" The spirit of Anarchism has lifted man from his prostrate position. He now stands erect, with his face toward the light. He has learned to see the insatiable, devouring, devastating nature of property, and he is preparing to strike the monster dead.

"Property is robbery," said the great French Anarchist Proudhon. Yes, but without risk and danger to the robber. Monopolizing the accumulated efforts of man, property has robbed him of his birthright, and has turned him loose a pauper and an outcast. Property has not even the time-worn excuse that man does not create enough to satisfy all needs. The A B C student of economics knows that the productivity of labor within the last few decades far exceeds normal demand. But what are normal demands to an abnormal institution? The only demand that property recognizes is its own gluttonous appetite for greater wealth, because wealth means power; the power to subdue, to crush, to exploit, the power to enslave, to outrage, to degrade. America is particularly boastful of her great power, her enormous national wealth. Poor America, of what avail is all her wealth, if the individuals comprising the nation are wretchedly poor? If they live in squalor, in filth, in crime, with hope and joy gone, a homeless, soilless army of human prey.

. . .

Real wealth consists in things of utility and beauty, in things that help to create strong, beautiful bodies and surroundings inspiring to live in. But if man is doomed to wind cotton around a spool, or dig coal, or build roads for thirty years of his life, there can be no talk of wealth. What he gives to the world is only gray and hideous things, reflecting a dull and hideous existence,—too weak to live, too cowardly to die. Strange to say, there are people who extol this deadening method of centralized production as the proudest achievement of our age. They fail utterly to realize that if we are to continue in machine subserviency, our slavery is more complete than was our bondage to the King. They do not want to know that centralization is not only the death-knell of liberty, but also of health and beauty, of art and science, all these being impossible in a clock-like, mechanical atmosphere.

Anarchism cannot but repudiate such a method of production: its goal is the freest possible expression of all the latent powers of the individual. Oscar Wilde defines a perfect personality as "one who develops under perfect conditions, who is not wounded, maimed, or in danger." A perfect personality, then, is only possible in a state of society where man is free to choose the mode of work, the conditions of work, and the freedom to work. One to whom the making of a table, the building of a house, or the tilling of the soil, is what the painting is to the artist and the discovery to the scientist,—the result of inspiration, of intense longing, and deep interest in work as a creative force. That being the ideal of Anarchism, its economic arrangements must consist of voluntary productive and distributive associations, gradually developing into free communism, as the best means of producing with the least waste of human energy. Anarchism, however, also recognizes the right of the individual, or numbers of individuals, to arrange at all times for other forms of work, in harmony with their tastes and desires.

Such free display of human energy being possible only under complete individual and social freedom, Anarchism directs its forces against the third and greatest foe of all social equality; namely, the State, organized authority, or statutory law,—the dominion of human conduct.

Just as religion has fettered the human mind, and as property, or the monopoly of things, has subdued and stifled man's needs, so has the State enslaved his spirit, dictating every phase of conduct. "All government in essence," says Emerson, "is tyranny." It matters not whether it is government by divine right or majority rule. In every instance its aim is the absolute subordination of the individual.

Referring to the American government, the greatest American Anarchist, David Thoreau, said: "Government, what is it but a tradition, though a recent one, endeavoring to transmit itself unimpaired to posterity, but each instance losing its integrity; it has not the vitality and force of a single living man. Law never made man a whit more just; and by means of their respect for it, even the well-disposed are daily made agents of injustice."

Indeed, the keynote of government is injustice. With the arrogance and self-sufficiency of the King who could do no wrong, governments ordain, judge, condemn, and punish the most insignificant offenses, while maintaining themselves by the greatest of all offenses, the annihilation of individual liberty. . . .

. . .

In fact, there is hardly a modern thinker who does not agree that government, organized authority, or the State, is necessary only to maintain or protect property and monopoly. It has proven efficient in that function only.

. . .

Unfortunately, there are still a number of people who continue in the fatal belief that government rests on natural laws, that it maintains social order and harmony, that it diminishes crime, and that it prevents the lazy man from fleecing his fellows. I shall therefore examine these contentions.

A natural law is that factor in man which asserts itself freely and spontaneously without any external force, in harmony with the requirements of nature. For instance, the demand for nutrition, for sex gratification, for light, air, and exercise, is a natural law. But its expression needs not the machinery of government, needs not the club, the gun, the handcuff, or the prison. To obey such laws, if we may call it obedience, requires only spontaneity and free opportunity. That governments do not maintain themselves through such harmonious factors is proven by the terrible array of violence, force, and coercion all governments use in order to live. Thus Blackstone is right when he says, "Human laws are invalid, because they are contrary to the laws of nature."

Unless it be the order of Warsaw after the slaughter of thousands of people, it is difficult to ascribe to governments any capacity for order or social harmony. Order derived through submission and maintained by terror is not much of a safe guaranty; yet that is the only "order" that governments have ever maintained. True social harmony grows naturally out of solidarity of interests. In a society where those who always work never have anything, while those who never work enjoy everything, solidarity of interests is non-existent; hence social harmony is but a myth. The only way organized authority meets this grave situation is by extending still greater privileges to those who have already monopolized the earth, and by still further enslaving the disinherited masses. Thus the entire arsenal of government—laws, police, soldiers, the courts, legislatures, prisons,—is strenuously engaged in "harmonizing" the most antagonistic elements in society.

. . .

Freedom, expansion, opportunity, and, above all, peace and repose, alone can teach us the real dominant factors of human nature and all its wonderful possibilities.

Anarchism, then, really stands for the liberation of the human mind from the dominion of religion; the liberation of the human body from the dominion of property; liberation from the shackles and restraint of government. Anarchism stands for a social order based on the free grouping of individuals for the purpose of producing real social wealth; an order that will guarantee to every human being free access to the earth and full enjoyment of the necessities of life, according to individual desires, tastes, and inclinations.

. . .

As to methods. Anarchism is not, as some may suppose, a theory of the future to be realized through divine inspiration. It is a living force in the affairs of our life, constantly creating new conditions. The methods of Anarchism therefore do not comprise an iron-clad program to be carried out under all circumstances. Methods must grow out of the economic needs of each place and clime, and of the intellectual and temperamental requirements of the individual. The serene, calm character of a Tolstoy will wish different methods for social reconstruction than the intense, overflowing personality of a Michael Bakunin or a Peter Kropotkin. Equally so it must be apparent that the economic and political needs of Russia will dictate more drastic measures than would England or America. Anarchism does not stand for military drill and uniformity; it does, however, stand for the spirit of revolt, in whatever form, against everything that hinders human growth. All Anarchists agree in that, as they also agree in their opposition to the political machinery as a means of bringing about the great social change.

. . .

What does the history of parliamentarism show? Nothing but failure and defeat, not even a single reform to ameliorate the economic and social stress of the people. . . .

. . . The State is the economic master of its servants. Good men, if such there be, would either remain true to their political faith and lose their economic support, or they would cling to their economic master and be utterly unable to do the slightest good. The political arena leaves one no alternative, one must either be a dunce or a rogue.

The political superstition is still holding sway over the hearts and minds of the masses, but the true lovers of liberty will have no more to do with it. Instead, they believe with Stirner that man has as much liberty as he is willing to take. Anarchism therefore stands for direct action, the open defiance of, and resistance to, all laws and restrictions, economic, social, and moral. But defiance and resistance are illegal. Therein lies the salvation of man. Everything illegal necessitates integrity, self-reliance, and courage. In short, it calls for free, independent spirits, for "men who are men, and who have a bone in their backs which you cannot pass your hand through."

. . .

. . . Direct action against the authority in the shop, direct action against the authority of the law, direct action against the invasive, meddlesome authority of our moral code, is the logical, consistent method of Anarchism.

Will it not lead to a revolution? Indeed, it will. No real social change has ever come about without a revolution. People are either not familiar with their history, or they have not yet learned that revolution is but thought carried into action.

Anarchism, the great leaven of thought, is today permeating every phase of human endeavor. Science, art, literature, the drama, the effort for economic betterment, in fact every individual and social opposition to the existing disorder of things, is illumined by the spiritual light of Anarchism. It is the philosophy of the sovereignty of the individual. It is the theory of social harmony. It is the great, surging, living truth that is reconstructing the world, and that will usher in the Dawn.

HERBERT CROLY

THE PROMISE OF AMERICAN LIFE (1909)

Herbert Croly was one of the most influential writers of the Progressive period. He grew up in a family of accomplished journalists in postbellum New York City. Between 1886 and 1899, he dropped in and out of Harvard University, repeatedly interrupting his studies with journalistic ventures and never completing a degree. His early journalism focused on cities and urban planning, but in 1909 he published his most important work, *The Promise of American Life,* which argued that industrial conditions required abandoning the Jeffersonian tradition and embracing a Hamiltonian theory of big government. The book was an immediate sensation and won the enthusiastic admiration of President Theodore Roosevelt. Croly leveraged his newfound fame to win financial backing for the launch of a new journal of opinion, *The New Republic,* which quickly became a significant outlet for liberal thought. Croly's own interests drifted, and he became disillusioned with the conservative direction of the country in the 1920s. He died of a stroke in 1928.

What does Croly believe is the central problem facing America? Why are Jeffersonian ideas inadequate for addressing them? What does he take from Hamilton? How does his Hamiltonianism contrast with Woodrow Wilson's New Freedom? What does Croly take to be the "democratic purpose"? To what degree has Croly's vision been realized? Are there risks to Croly's philosophy?

. . .

. . . There can be no democracy where the people do not rule; but government by the people is not necessarily democratic. The popular will must in a democratic state be expressed somehow in the interest of democracy itself; and we have not traveled very far towards a satisfactory conception of democracy until this democratic purpose has received some definition. In what way must a democratic state behave in order to contribute to its own integrity?

The ordinary American answer to this question is contained in the assertion of Lincoln, that our government is "dedicated to the proposition that all men are created equal." Lincoln's phrasing of the principle was due to the fact that the obnoxious and undemocratic system of negro slavery was uppermost in his mind when he made his Gettysburg address; but he meant by his assertion of the principle of equality substantially what is meant to-day by the principle of "equal rights for all and special privileges for none." Government by the people has its natural and logical complement in government for the people. Every state with a legal framework must grant certain rights to individuals; and every state, in so far as it is efficient, must guarantee to the individual that his rights, as legally defined, are secure. But an essentially democratic state consists in the circumstance that all citizens enjoy these rights equally. If any citizen or any group of citizens enjoys by virtue of the law any advantage over their fellow-citizens, then the most sacred principle of democracy is violated. On the other hand, a community in which no man or no group of men are granted by law any advantage over their fellow-citizens is the type of the perfect and fruitful democratic state. Society is organized politically for the benefit of all the people. Such an organization may permit radical differences among individuals in the opportunities and possessions they actually enjoy; but no man would be able to impute his own success or failure to the legal framework of society. Every citizen would be getting a "Square Deal."

. . .

But the principle of equal rights, like the principle of ultimate popular political responsibility, is not sufficient; and because of its insufficiency results in certain dangerous ambiguities and self-contradictions. American political thinkers have always repudiated the idea that by equality of rights they meant anything like equality of performance or power. The utmost varieties of individual power and ability are bound to exist and are bound to bring about many different levels of individual achievement. Democracy both recognizes the right of the individual to use his powers to the utmost, and encourages him to do so by offering a fair field and, in cases of success, an abundant reward. The democratic principle requires an equal start in the race, while expecting at the same time an unequal finish. But Americans who talk in this way seem wholly blind to the fact that under a legal system which holds private property sacred there may be equal rights, but there cannot possibly be any equal opportunities for exercising such rights. The chance which the individual has to compete with his fellows and take a prize in the race is vitally affected by material conditions over which he has no control. It is as if the competitor in a Marathon cross country run were denied proper nourishment or proper training, and was obliged to toe the mark against rivals who had every benefit of food and discipline. Under such conditions he is not as badly off as if he were entirely excluded from the race. With the aid of exceptional strength and intelligence he may overcome the odds against him and win out. But it would be absurd to claim, because all the rivals toed the same mark, that a man's victory or defeat depended exclusively on his own efforts. Those who have enjoyed the benefits of wealth and thorough education start with an advantage which can be overcome only in very exceptional men,—men so exceptional, in fact, that the average competitor without such benefits feels himself disqualified for the contest.

Because of the ambiguity indicated above, different people with different interests, all of them good patriotic Americans, draw very different inferences from the doctrine of equal rights. The man of conservative ideas and interests means by the rights, which are to be equally exercised, only those rights which are defined and protected by the law—the more fundamental of which are the rights to personal freedom and to private property. The man of radical ideas, on the other hand, observing, as he may very clearly, that these equal rights cannot possibly be made really equivalent to equal opportunities, bases upon the same doctrine a more or less drastic criticism of the existing economic and social order and sometimes of the motives of its beneficiaries and conservators. The same principle, differently interpreted, is the foundation of American political orthodoxy and American political heterodoxy. . . . Everybody seems to be clamoring for a "Square Deal" but nobody seems to be getting it.

The ambiguity of the principle of equal rights and the resulting confusion of counsel are so obvious that there must be some good reason for their apparently unsuspected existence. The truth is that Americans have not readjusted their political ideas to the teaching of their political and economic experience. For a couple of generations after Jefferson had established the doctrine of equal rights as the fundamental principle of the American democracy, the ambiguity resident in the application of the doctrine was concealed. The Jacksonian Democrats, for instance, who were constantly nosing the ground for a scent of unfair treatment, could discover no example of political privileges, except the continued retention of their offices by experienced public servants; and the only case of economic privilege of which they were certain was that of the National Bank. The fact is, of course, that the great majority of Americans were getting a "Square Deal" as long as the economic opportunities of a new country had not been developed and appropriated. . . . With the advent of comparative economic and social maturity, the exercise of certain legal rights became substantially equivalent to the exercise of a privilege; and if equality of opportunity was to be maintained, it could not be done by virtue of non-interference. . . .

. . .

Hence it is that continued loyalty to a contradictory principle is destructive of a wholesome public sentiment and opinion. A wholesome public opinion in a democracy is one which keeps a democracy sound and whole; and it cannot prevail unless the individuals composing it recognize mutual ties and responsibilities which lie deeper than any differences of interest and idea. No formula whose effect on public opinion is not binding and healing and unifying has any substantial claim to consideration as the essential and formative democratic idea. Belief in the principle of equal rights does not bind, heal, and unify public opinion. Its effect rather is confusing, distracting, and at worst, disintegrating. . . . The principle of equal rights encourages mutual suspicion and disloyalty. It tends to attribute individual and social ills, for which general moral, economic, and social causes are usually in large measure responsible, to individual wrong-doing; and in this way it arouses and intensifies that personal and class hatred, which never in any society lies far below the surface. Men who have grievances are inflamed into anger and resentment. In claiming what they believe to be their rights, they are in their own opinion acting on behalf not merely of their interests, but of an absolute democratic principle. Their angry resentment becomes transformed in their own minds into righteous indignation; and there may be turned loose upon the community a horde of self-seeking fanatics—like unto those soldiers in the religious wars who robbed and slaughtered their opponents in the service of God.

. . .

. . . Equality of rights is most in danger of being violated when the exercise of rights is associated with power, and any unusual amount of power is usually derived from the association of a number of individuals for a common purpose. The most dangerous example of such association is not, however, a huge corporation or a labor union; it is the state. . . . The power to legislate implies the power to discriminate; and the best way consequently for a good democracy of equal rights to avoid the danger of discrimination will be to organize the state so that its power for ill will be rigidly restricted. The possible preferential interference on the part of a strong and efficient government must be checked by making the government feeble and devoid of independence. The less independent and efficient the several departments of the government are permitted to become, the less likely that the government as a whole will use its power for anything but a really popular purpose.

. . . Even the meager social interest which Jefferson concealed under cover of his demand for equal rights could not be promoted without some effective organ of social responsibility; and the Democrats of today are obliged, as we have seen, to invoke the action of the central government to destroy those economic discriminations which its former inaction had encouraged. But even so the traditional democracy still retains its dislike of centralized and socialized responsibility. It consents to use the machinery of the government only for a negative or destructive object. Such must always be the case as long as it remains true to its fundamental principle. That principle defines the social interest merely in the terms of an indiscriminate individualism—which is the one kind of individualism murderous to both the essential individual and the essential social interest.

. . .

Thus the Jeffersonian principle of national irresponsibility can no longer be maintained by those Democrats who sincerely believe that the inequalities of power generated in the American economic and political system are dangerous to the integrity of the democratic state. To this extent really sincere followers of Jefferson are obliged to admit the superior political wisdom of Hamilton's principle of national responsibility, and once they have made this admission, they have implicitly abandoned their contention that the doctrine of equal rights is a sufficient principle of democratic political action. They have implicitly accepted the idea that the public interest is to be asserted, not merely by equalizing individual rights, but by controlling individuals in the exercise of those rights. The national public interest has to be affirmed by positive and aggressive fiction. The nation has to have a will and a policy as well as the individual; and this policy can no longer be confined to the merely negative task of keeping individual rights from becoming in any way privileged.

The arduous and responsible political task which a nation in its collective capacity must seek to perform is that of selecting among the various prevailing ways of exercising individual rights those which contribute to national perpetuity and integrity. Such selection implies some interference with the natural course of popular notion; and that interference is always costly and may be harmful either to the individual or the social interest must be frankly admitted. He would be a foolish Hamiltonian who would claim that a state, no matter how efficiently organized and ably managed, will not make serious and perhaps enduring mistakes; but he can answer that inaction and irresponsibility are more costly and dangerous than intelligent and responsible interference. The practice of non-interference is just as selective in its effects as the practice of state interference. It means merely that the nation is willing to accept the results of natural selection instead of preferring to substitute the results of artificial selection. In one way or another a nation is bound to recognize the results of selection. The Hamiltonian principle of national responsibility recognizes the inevitability of selection; and since it is inevitable, is not afraid to interfere on behalf of the selection of the really fittest. If a selective policy is pursued in good faith and with sufficient intelligence, the nation will at least be learning from its mistakes. It should find out gradually the kind and method of selection, which is most desirable, and how far selection by non-interference is to be preferred to active selection.

. . .

Impartiality is the duty of the judge rather than the statesman, of the courts rather than the government. The state which proposes to draw a ring around the conflicting interests of its citizens and interfere only on behalf of a fair fight will be obliged to interfere constantly and will never accomplish its purpose. In economic warfare, the fighting can never be fair for long, and it is the business of the state to see that its own friends are victorious. It holds, if you please, itself a hand in the game. The several players are playing, not merely with one another, but with the political and social bank. The security and perpetuity of the state and of the individual in so far as he is a social animal, depend upon the victory of the national interest—as represented both in the assurance of the national profit and in the domination of the nation's friends. . . . It must help those men to win who are most capable of using their winnings for the benefit of society.

Assuming, then, that a democracy cannot avoid the constant assertion of national responsibility for the national welfare, an all-important question remains as to the way in which and the purpose for which this interference should be exercised. Should it be exercised on behalf of individual liberty? Should it be exercised on behalf of social equality? Is there any way in which it can be exercised on behalf both of liberty and equality?

Hamilton and the constitutional liberals asserted that the state should interfere exclusively on behalf of individual liberty; but Hamilton was no democrat and was not outlining the policy of a democratic state. In point of fact democracies have never been satisfied with a definition of democratic policy in terms of liberty. Not only have the particular friends of liberty usually been hostile to democracy, but democracies both in idea and behavior have frequently been hostile to liberty. . . .

. . .

The desirable democratic object, implied in the traditional democratic demand for equality, consists precisely in that of bestowing a share of the responsibility and the benefits, derived from political and economic association, upon the whole community. . . .

. . .

No doubt the institution of private property, necessitating, as it does, the transmission to one person of the possessions and earnings of another, always involves the inheritance of unearned power and opportunity. But the point is that in the case of very large fortunes the inherited power goes far beyond any legitimate individual needs, and in the course of time can hardly fail to corrupt its possessors. The creator of a large fortune may well be its master; but its inheritor will, except in the case of exceptionally able individuals, become its victim, and most assuredly the evil social effects are as bad as the evil individual effects. The political bond which a democracy seeks to create depends for its higher value upon an effective social bond. Gross inequalities in wealth, wholly divorced from economic efficiency on the part of the rich, as effectively loosen the social bond as do gross inequalities of political and social standing. A wholesome social condition in a democracy does not imply uniformity of wealth any more than it implies uniformity of ability and purpose, but it does imply the association of great individual economic distinction with responsibility and efficiency. It does imply that economic leaders, no less than political ones, should have conditions imposed upon them which will force them to recognize the responsibilities attached to so much power. . . .

If the integrity of a democracy is injured by the perpetuation of unearned economic distinctions, it is also injured by extreme poverty, whether deserved or not. A democracy which attempted to equalize wealth would incur the same disastrous fate as a democracy which attempted to equalize political power; but a democracy can no more be indifferent to the distribution of wealth than it can to the distribution of the suffrage. In a wholesome democracy every male adult should participate in the ultimate political responsibility, partly because of the political danger of refusing participation to the people, and partly because of the advantages to be derived from the political union of the whole people. So a wholesome democracy should seek to guarantee to every male adult a certain minimum of economic power and responsibility. No doubt it is much easier to confer the suffrage on the people than it is to make poverty a negligible social factor; but the difficulty of the task does not make it the less necessary. It stands to reason that in the long run the people who possess the political power will want a substantial share of the economic fruits. A prudent democracy should anticipate this demand. Not only does any considerable amount of grinding poverty constitute a grave social danger in a democratic state, but so, in general, does a widespread condition of partial economic privation. The individuals constituting a democracy lack the first essential of individual freedom when they cannot escape from a condition of economic dependence.

The American democracy has confidently believed in the fatal prosperity enjoyed by the people under the American system. In the confidence of that belief it has promised to Americans a substantial satisfaction of their economic needs; and it has made that promise an essential part of the American national idea. The promise has been measurably fulfilled hitherto, because the prodigious natural resources of a new continent were thrown open to anybody with the energy to appropriate them. But those natural resources have now in large measure passed into the possession of individuals, and American statesmen can no longer count upon them to satisfy the popular hunger for economic independence. An ever larger proportion of the total population of the country is taking to industrial occupations, and an industrial system brings with it much more definite social and economic classes, and a diminution of the earlier social homogeneity. The contemporary wage-earner is no longer satisfied with the economic results of being merely an American citizen. His union is usually of more obvious use to him than the state, and he is tending to make his allegiance to his union paramount to his allegiance to the state. This is only one of many illustrations that the traditional American system has broken down. The American state can regain the loyal adhesion of the economically less independent class only by positive service. What the wage-earner needs, and what it is to the interest of a democratic state he should obtain, is a constantly higher standard of living. The state can help him to conquer a higher standard of living without doing any necessary injury to his employers and with a positive benefit to general economic and social efficiency. If it is to earn the loyalty of the wage-earners, it must recognize the legitimacy of his demand, and make the satisfaction of it an essential part of its public policy.

The American state is dedicated to such a duty, not only by its democratic purpose, but by its national tradition. So far as the former is concerned, it is absurd and fatal to ask a popular majority to respect the rights of a minority, when those rights are interpreted so as seriously to hamper, if not to forbid, the majority from obtaining the essential condition of individual freedom and development—viz. the highest possible standard of living. But this absurdity becomes really critical and dangerous, in view of the fact that the American people, particularly those of alien birth and descent, have been explicitly promised economic freedom and prosperity. The promise was made on the strength of what was believed to be an inexhaustible store of natural opportunities; and it will have to be kept even when those natural resources are no longer to be had for the asking. It is entirely possible, of course, that the promise can never be kept,—that its redemption will prove to be beyond the patience, the power, and the wisdom of the American people and their leaders; but if it is not kept, the American commonwealth will no longer continue to be a democracy.

We are now prepared, I hope, to venture upon a more fruitful definition of democracy. The popular definitions err in describing it in terms of its machinery or of some partial political or economic object. Democracy does not mean merely government by the people, or majority rule, or universal suffrage. All of these political forms or devices are a part of its necessary organization; but the chief advantage such methods of organization have is their tendency to promote some salutary and formative purpose. The really formative purpose is not exclusively a matter of individual liberty, although it must give individual liberty abundant scope. Neither is it a matter of equal rights alone, although it must always cherish the social bond which that principle represents. The salutary and formative democratic purpose consists in using the democratic organization for the joint benefit of individual distinction and social improvement.

. . .

The foregoing definition of the democratic purpose is the only one which can entitle democracy to an essential superiority to other forms of political organization. Democrats have always tended to claim some such superiority for their methods and purposes, but in case democracy is to be considered merely as a piece of political machinery, or a partial political idea, the claim has no validity. Its superiority must be based upon the fact that democracy is the best possible translation into political and social terms of an authoritative and comprehensive moral idea; and provided a democratic state honestly seeks to make its organization and policy contribute to a better quality of individuality and a higher level of associated life, it can within certain limits claim the allegiance of mankind on rational moral grounds.

. . .

The majority of good Americans will doubtless consider that the reconstructive policy, already indicated, is flagrantly socialistic both in its methods and its objects; and if any critic likes to fasten the stigma of socialism upon the foregoing conception of democracy, I am not concerned with dodging the odium of the word. The proposed definition of democracy is socialistic, if it is socialistic to consider democracy inseparable from a candid, patient, and courageous attempt to advance the social problem towards a satisfactory solution. It is also socialistic in case socialism cannot be divorced from the use, wherever necessary, of the political organization in all its forms to realize the proposed democratic purpose. On the other hand, there are some doctrines frequently associated with socialism, to which the proposed conception of democracy is wholly inimical; and it should be characterized not so much socialistic, as unscrupulously and loyally nationalistic.

A democracy dedicated to individual and social betterment is necessarily individualist as well as socialist. It has little interest in the mere multiplication of average individuals, except in so far as such multiplication is necessary to economic and political efficiency; but it has the deepest interest in the development of a higher quality of individual self-expression. There are two indispensable economic conditions of qualitative individual self-expression. One is the preservation of the institution of private property in some form, and the other is the radical transformation of its existing nature and influence. A democracy certainly cannot fulfill its mission without the eventual assumption by the state of many functions now performed by individuals, and without becoming expressly responsible for an improved distribution of wealth; but if any attempt is made to accomplish these results by violent means, it will most assuredly prove to be a failure. An improvement in the distribution of wealth or in economic efficiency which cannot be accomplished by purchase on the part of the state or by a legitimate use of the power of taxation, must be left to the action of time, assisted, of course, by such arrangements as are immediately practical. . . .

. . .

. . . The loyalty which a citizen owes to a government is dependent upon the extent to which the government is representative of national traditions and is organized in the interest of valid national purposes. National traditions and purposes always contain a large infusion of dubious ingredients; but loyalty to them does not necessarily mean the uncritical and unprotesting acceptance of the national limitations and abuses. Nationality is a political and social ideal as well as the great contemporary political fact. Loyalty to the national interest implies devotion to a progressive principle. It demands, to be sure, that the progressive principle be realized without any violation of fundamental national ties. It demands that any national action taken for the benefit of the progressive principle be approved by the official national organization. But it also serves as a ferment quite as much as a bond. It bids the loyal national servants to fashion their fellow-countrymen into more of a nation; and the attempt to perform this bidding constitutes a very powerful and wholesome source of political development. It constitutes, indeed, a source of political development which is of decisive importance for a satisfactory theory of political and social progress, because a people which becomes more of a nation has a tendency to become for that very reason more of a democracy.

. . .

Americans have always been both patriotic and democratic, just as they have always been friendly both to liberty and equality, but in neither case have they brought the two ideas or aspirations into mutually helpful relations. As democrats they have often regarded nationalism with distrust, and have consequently deprived their patriotism of any sufficient substance and organization. As nationalists they have frequently regarded essential aspects of democracy with a wholly unnecessary and embarrassing suspicion. They have been after a fashion Hamiltonian, and Jeffersonian after more of a fashion; but they have never recovered from the initial disagreement between Hamilton and Jefferson. If there is any truth in the idea of a constructive relation between democracy and nationality this disagreement must be healed. They must accept both principles loyally and unreservedly; and by such acceptance their "noble national theory" will obtain a wholly unaccustomed energy and integrity. The alliance between the two principles will not leave either of them intact; but it will necessarily do more harm to the Jeffersonian group of political ideas than it will to the Hamiltonian. The latter's nationalism can be adapted to democracy without an essential injury to itself, but the former's democracy cannot be nationalized without being transformed. . . . It must cease to be a democracy of indiscriminate individualism; and become one of selected individuals who are obliged constantly to justify their selection; and its members must be united not by a sense of joint irresponsibility, but by a sense of joint responsibility for the success of their political and social ideal. They must become, that is, a democracy devoted to the welfare of the whole people by means of a conscious labor of individual and social improvement; and that is precisely the sort of democracy which demands for its realization the aid of the Hamiltonian nationalistic organization and principle.

. . .

HERBERT HOOVER

AMERICAN INDIVIDUALISM (1922)

In the 1920s, Herbert Hoover was regarded as one of the foremost reformers in the country. Franklin D. Roosevelt confided, "I wish we could make him President . . . there could not be a better one," and the British economist John Maynard Keynes thought he was among the most impressive figures at the Paris peace talks at the end of World War I.[16]

Hoover was raised as a Quaker on farms in Iowa, but became an Episcopalian after he married. He sought his fortune, and found it, in California. He studied geology at Stanford University, launched a career as a mining engineer, and was wealthy with a global business by the start of World War I. At that point, he turned his attention to public service, earning high praise (and some bipartisan presidential talk) for organizing wartime relief efforts in Europe. He served as secretary of commerce through the 1920s, where he established himself as an activist reformer and strong advocate of greater government–business cooperation and economic planning through business associations. Over the objections of conservatives, Hoover took the Republican nomination for president in 1928 and handily won the general election. Once in office, he outlined a Progressive and activist agenda, but his program was immediately swamped by the stock market crash of 1929 and the onset of the Great Depression. Hoover proved unwilling to support direct aid to individuals and was slow to accept federal takeover of some traditional state initiatives. His political fate was sealed in the summer of 1932 when General Douglas MacArthur routed the "Bonus Army" of protesting veterans from their makeshift camp in Washington, D.C. His first political book, *American Individualism*, was published as he was beginning his service in the Department of Commerce and was intended as a response to the radicalism at home and abroad of the 1910s.

What traditions does Hoover draw upon to construct his ideal of American individualism? How does his vision compare with the New Nationalism or the New Freedom? Has he made a choice between Croly's Jeffersonian and Hamiltonian philosophies? Does he provide a response to the concerns raised by Debs or Goldman? Does he contradict the laissez-faire arguments of Gilded Age theorists like William Graham Sumner?

. . .

. . . Our individualism differs from all others because it embraces these great ideals: *that while we build our society upon the attainment of the individual, we shall safeguard to every individual an equality of opportunity to take that position in the community to which his intelligence, character, ability, and ambition entitle him; that we keep the social solution free from frozen strata of classes; that we shall stimulate effort of each individual to achievement; that through an enlarging sense of responsibility and understanding we shall assist him to this attainment; while he in turn must stand up to the emery wheel of competition.*

Individualism cannot be maintained as the foundation of a society if it looks to only legalistic justice based upon contracts, property, and political equality. Such legalistic safeguards are themselves not enough. In our individualism we have long since abandoned the laissez faire of the 18th Century—the notion that it is "every man for himself and the devil take the hindmost." We abandoned that when we adopted the ideal of equality of opportunity—the fair chance of Abraham Lincoln. We have confirmed its abandonment in terms of legislation, of social and economic justice—in part because we have learned that it is the hindmost who throws the bricks at our social edifice, in part because we have learned that the foremost are not always the best nor the hindmost the worst—and in part because we have learned that social injustice is the destruction of justice itself. We have learned that the impulse to production can only be maintained at a high pitch if there is a fair division of the product. We have also learned that fair division can only be

16 William J. Barber, *From New Era to New Deal* (New York: Cambridge University Press, 1985), 198.

obtained by certain restrictions on the strong and the dominant. . . .

. . .

That high and increasing standards of living and comfort should be the first of considerations in public mind and in government needs no apology. We have long since realized that the basis of an advancing civilization must be a high and growing standard of living for all the people, not for a single class; that education, food, clothing housing, and the spreading use of what we so often term non-essentials, are the real fertilizers of the soil from which spring the finer flowers of life. . . .

. . .

But those are utterly wrong who say that individualism has as its only end the acquisition and preservation of private property—the selfish snatching and hoarding of the common product. Our American individualism, indeed, is only in part an economic creed. It aims to provide opportunity for self-expression, not merely economically, but spiritually as well. Private property is not a fetish in America. The crushing of the liquor trade without a cent of compensation, with scarcely even a discussion of it, does not bear out the notion that we give property rights any headway over human rights. Our development of individualism shows an increasing tendency to regard right of property not as an object in itself, but in the light of a useful and necessary instrument in stimulation of initiative to the individual; not only stimulation to him that he may gain personal comfort, security in life, protection to his family, but also because individual accumulation and ownership is a basis of selection to leadership in administration of the tools of industry and commerce. It is when dominant private property is assembled in the hands of the groups who control the state that the individual begins to feel capital as an oppressor. . . . [L]arge capital is steadily becoming more and more a mobilization of the savings of the small holder—the actual people themselves—and its administration becomes at once more sensitive to the moral opinions of the people in order to attract their support. . . .

Large masses of capital can only find their market for service or production to great numbers of the same kind of the people that they employ and they must therefore maintain confidence in their public responsibilities in order to retain their customers. . . .

There has been in the last thirty years an extraordinary growth of organizations for advancement of ideas in the community for mutual cooperation and economic objectives—the chambers of commerce, trade associations, labor unions, bankers, farmers, propaganda associations, and what not. These are indeed variable mixtures of altruism and self-interest. Nevertheless, in these groups the individual finds an opportunity for self-expression and participation in the molding of ideas, a field of training and the stepping stones for leadership.

. . .

Today business organization is moving strongly toward cooperation. There are in the cooperative great hopes that we can even gain in individuality, equality of opportunity, and an enlarged field for initiative, and at the same time reduce many of the great wastes of over-reckless competition in production and distribution. Those who either congratulate themselves or those who fear that cooperation is an advance toward socialism need neither rejoice or worry. Cooperation in its current economic sense represents the initiative of self-interest blended with a sense of service. . . . Their only success lies where they eliminate waste either in production or distribution—and they can do neither if they destroy individual initiative. . . .

. . .

Our Government's greatest troubles and failures are in the economic field. Forty years ago the contact of the individual with the Government had its largest expression in the sheriff or policeman, and in debates over political equality. In those happy days the Government offered but small interference with the economic life of the citizen. But with the vast development of industry and the train of regulating functions of the national and municipal government that followed from it; with the recent vast increase in taxation due to the war—the Government has become through its relations to economic life the most potent force for maintenance or destruction of our American individualism.

. . .

To curb the forces in business which would destroy equality of opportunity and yet to maintain the initiative and creative faculties of our people are the twin objects we must attain. To preserve the former we must regulate that type of activity that would dominate. To preserve the latter, the Government must keep out of production and distribution of commodities and services. This is the deadline between our system and socialism. Regulation to prevent domination and unfair practices, yet preserving rightful initiative, are in keeping with our social foundations. Nationalization of industry or business is their negation.

. . .

VI. AMERICA AND THE WORLD

Major Developments

- Entry of the United States into World War I
- Defeat of the League of Nations proposal
- Debate over American disarmament after World War I

The United States started the twentieth century with new territorial and political commitments across the globe. As a result, political leaders were torn between the desire to flex American muscle and the desire to once again try to isolate themselves from foreign entanglements. Theodore Roosevelt was a strong voice in favor of the more muscular approach. National preparedness was essential in a dangerous world, he warned. Moreover, the United States had something to contribute—and interests to protect—by engaging with the wider world. European imperial powers were not hesitant about making a show of military force in order to advance their economic and political interests and ambitions. Roosevelt worried that the United States would be left behind and could no longer expect the oceans to provide an adequate barrier to world events. The horrors of World War I reinvigorated isolationist tendencies. Progressives like Senator William Borah, who had supported American ambitions earlier in the century, called for disarmament and withdrawal after the war. President Warren G. Harding promised voters a return to normalcy in the 1920 election. The time for heroics had passed.

American political leaders also disagreed over what principles ought to guide American foreign policy and define America's unique contribution to the world. Theodore Roosevelt emphasized the need to vindicate national interests. In his reading, the United States was not exceptional in the world—and the sooner Americans came to appreciate how their interests were threatened by foreign states and could be advanced by the strategic application of force, the better. Woodrow Wilson took a more idealistic and moralistic approach to evaluating world events. The civilized international community, he believed, should be grounded in ideals of democracy, respect for rights, and international law—essentially American values—and the United States should use its influence to actively vindicate those values.

These readings reflect those new debates. Theodore Roosevelt and Woodrow Wilson offer different approaches to thinking about American involvement in the war in Europe. William Borah provides one perspective on twentieth-century isolationism. Randolph Bourne raised a more radical voice against militarism in all of its forms.

THEODORE ROOSEVELT

SOCIAL VALUES AND NATIONAL EXISTENCE (1915)

As Theodore Roosevelt rose to prominence, he celebrated the virtues of manliness and a kind of energetic nationalism. His pre-established image as a big-game hunter and outdoorsman fit with the nickname for his volunteer cavalry regiment in the Spanish-American War, the "Rough Riders." As president, he inherited new territorial possessions, and he was determined to make the United States a player on the world stage. He helped orchestrate a revolution in Panama that facilitated the construction of the Panama Canal—and improved the ability of the United States to project its naval power in both the Pacific and Atlantic oceans. He insisted that the United States "provid[e] and keep[] the force necessary to back up a strong attitude" in order to move the world toward "the peace of justice," which in practice meant building up the navy to match those of the great imperial powers. Hoping to head off the European powers, he announced a corollary to the Monroe Doctrine that asserted that the United States would "exercise an international police power" in Latin American states that seemed unwilling or unable to pay their foreign creditors.[17] His work as a mediator in international peace negotiations earned him a Nobel Prize. Out of office, he remained keenly interested in foreign affairs and became a powerful voice in favor of American intervention in World War I. He kept up an active speaking schedule urging American resolve, which led him to take an increasingly belligerent view of ethnic groups in the United States that lobbied in favor of hostile foreign powers (notably Germany) and of those who worried about the effects of war. He was not averse to taking his arguments to skeptical audiences, as when he delivered this speech at a symposium on "war and militarism" at the annual meeting of the American Sociological Society.

Does Roosevelt advocate "militarism"? Why does he reject pacifism? Why is pacifism a prime alternative to war in the United States in 1915? Is there a "duty of national preparedness"? How far does such a duty extend? Is national preparedness consistent with democratic values? Are "men absorbed in money-getting" less valuable to a nation than its criminals?

[I]f an unscrupulous, warlike, and militaristic nation is not held in check by the warlike ability of a neighboring non-militaristic and well-behaved nation, then the latter will be spared the necessity of dealing with "moral and social values" because it won't be allowed to deal with anything. Until this fact is thoroughly recognized, and the duty of national preparedness by justice-loving nations explicitly acknowledged, there is very little use of solemnly debating the question "How war and militarism affect such social values as the sense of the preciousness of human life. . . ." It seems to me positively comic to fail to appreciate, with the example of [the 1914 invasion of] Belgium [by Germany] before our eyes, that the real question which modern peace-loving nations have to face is not how the militaristic or warlike spirit within their own borders will affect these "values," but how failure on their part to be able to resist the militarism of an unscrupulous neighbor will affect them. . . . [A]ll these "social values" existed in Belgium only up to the end of July, 1914. Not a vestige of them remains in 1915. To discuss them as regards present-day Belgium is sheer prattle, simply because on August 4, 1914, Belgium had not prepared her military strength. . . .

In the thirteenth century Persia had become a highly civilized nation, with a cultivated class of literary men and philosophers, with universities, and with great mercantile interests. These literary men and merchants took toward the realities of war much

17 Theodore Roosevelt, "Annual Message to Congress, December 6, 1904," in *A Compilation of the Messages and Papers of the Presidents*, ed. James D. Richardson, vol. 10 (New York: Bureau of National Literature and Art, 1908), 829.

the same attitude that is taken in our country by gentlemen of the stamp of . . . Henry Ford. Unfortunately for these predecessors of the modern pacifists they were within striking distance of Genghis Kahn and his Mongols; and, as of course invariably happens in such a case, when the onrush came, the pacifists' theories were worth just about what a tissue-paper barrier would amount to against a tidal wave. . . .

There are well-meaning people, utterly incapable of learning any lesson taught by history. . . . There are plenty of politicians, by no means so well meaning, who find it to their profit to pander to the desire common to most men to live softly and easily and avoid risk and effort. Timid and lazy men, men absorbed in money-getting, men absorbed in ease and luxury, and all soft and slothful people naturally hail with delight anybody who will give them high-sounding names behind which to cloak their unwillingness to run risks or to toil and endure. . . . It is questionable whether in the long run they do not form a less desirable national type than is formed by the men who are guilty of the downright iniquities of life; for the latter at least have in them elements of strength which, if guided aright, could be used to good purpose.

. . . But I believe that the bulk of our people are willing to follow duty, even though it be rather unpleasant and rather hard, if it can be made clearly evident to them. . . .

. . .

In the first place, we are dealing with a matter of definition. A war can be defined as violence between nations. . . . It is analogous to violence between individuals within a nation. . . . When this fact is clearly grasped, the average citizen will be spared the mental confusion he now suffers because he thinks of war as *in itself* wrong. Of course whether war is right or wrong depends purely upon the purpose for which, and the spirit in which, it is waged. . . . There are of course persons who believe that all force is immoral, that it is immoral to resist wrongdoing by force. I have never taken much interest in the individuals who profess this kind of twisted morality. . . . But of course, if they are right in theory, then it is wrong for a man to endeavor by force to save his wife or sister or daughter from rape or other abuse, or to save his children from abduction and torture. It is a waste of time to discuss with any man a position of such folly, wickedness, and poltroonery. . . .

. . .

. . . The task of getting all the policemen, all the college professors, all the businessmen and mechanics, and also all the professional crooks, in New York to abandon the reign of force and to live together in harmony would be undoubtedly very much easier than to secure a similar working agreement among the various peoples of Europe, America, Asia, and Africa. . . .

The really essential things for men to remember, therefore, in connection with war are, first, that neither war nor peace is immoral in itself, and secondly, that in order to preserve "social values" . . . it is absolutely essential to prevent the dominance in our country of the one form of militarism which is surely and completely fatal, that is, the military dominion of an alien enemy.

. . .

. . . There are dangers attendant on every course, dangers to be fought against in every kind of life, whether of an individual or of a nation. But it is not merely danger, it is death, the death of the soul even more than the death of the body, which surely awaits the nation that does not both cultivate the lofty morality which will forbid it to do wrong to others, and at the same time spiritually, intellectually, and physically prepare itself, by the development of the stern and high qualities of the soul and the will no less than in things material, to defend by its own strength its own existence. . . . At present, in this world, and for the immediate future, it is certain that the only way successfully to oppose the might which is the servant of wrong is by means of the might which is the servant of right.

. . .

WOODROW WILSON

ADDRESS TO THE SENATE ON THE TERMS OF PEACE (1917)

Foreign policy had not been a central interest of Woodrow Wilson's before he entered the White House, and his secretary of state, William Jennings Bryan, had spent his career focused on domestic issues. His administration began the process of shifting the status of the territorial possessions from the Spanish-American War—the Philippines toward independence, Puerto Rico toward formal territorial status. In his second inaugural, as World War I wound to a close, he emphasized the principled foundations of world peace: "peace cannot securely or justly rest upon an armed balance of power," and "governments derive all their just powers from the consent of the governed and . . . no other powers should be supported by the common thought, purpose or power of the family of nations."[18] However, supporting governments resting on the "consent of the governed" could sometimes mean American diplomatic or military intervention to help establish orderly and just governments. In 1914, he had urged American neutrality in the European war, but in the spring of 1917 he asked Congress for a declaration of war in response to German submarine attacks on American shipping. "The world must be made safe for democracy. Its peace must be planted upon the tested foundation of political liberty."[19] A year later, he began to outline his plan for a League of Nations that could maintain the emerging peace. Just a few months before his 1917 war message, Wilson laid down what he regarded to be the conditions of sustainable peace. Whether or not the United States committed troops to the war effort, it would, he insisted, have to play a prominent role in establishing a peaceful world order in the aftermath of the war. A stable peace would have to be a "just and secure peace."

Why should the United States play a part in the "great enterprise" of laying down a new plan of peace after the European war? Did the United States have any particular stake in European affairs in the early twentieth century? How does Wilson think that the American people have prepared themselves to play such a role? What is a peace "worth guaranteeing and securing"? Do Wilson's conditions of peace also establish the justifications for war? Does Wilson or Roosevelt outline the more active role for the United States to play in world affairs?

. . .

I have sought this opportunity to address you because I thought that I owed it to you, as the counsel associated with me in the final determination of our international obligations, to disclose to you without reserve the thought and purpose that have been taking form in my mind in regard to the duty of our Government in the days to come when it will be necessary to lay afresh and upon a new plan the foundations of peace among the nations.

It is inconceivable that the people of the United States should play no part in that great enterprise. To take part in such a service will be the opportunity for which they have sought to prepare themselves by the very principles and purposes of their polity and the approved practices of their government ever since the days when they set up a new nation in the high and honorable hope that it might, in all that it was and did, show mankind the way to liberty. They cannot in honor withhold the service to which they are now about to be challenged. They do not wish to withhold it. But they owe it to themselves and to the other nations of the world to state the conditions under which they will feel free to render it.

18 Woodrow Wilson, Second Inaugural Address, in *A Compilation of the Messages and Papers of the Presidents*, ed. James D. Richardson, supplement (New York: Bureau of National Literature, 1921), 8222.

19 Woodrow Wilson, War Message, April 2, 1917, in *A Compilation of the Messages and Papers of the Presidents*, ed. James D. Richardson, supplement (New York: Bureau of National Literature, 1921), 8231.

That service is nothing less than this, to add their authority and their power to the authority and force of other nations to guarantee peace and justice throughout the world. Such a settlement cannot now be long postponed. It is right that before it comes this Government should frankly formulate the conditions upon which it would feel justified in asking our people to approve its formal and solemn adherence to a League for Peace. I am here to attempt to state those conditions.

The present war must first be ended; but we owe it to candor and to a just regard for the opinion of mankind to say that, so far as our participation in guarantees of future peace is concerned, it makes a great deal of difference in what way and upon what terms it is ended. The treaties and agreements which bring it to an end must embody terms which will create a peace that is worth guaranteeing and preserving, a peace that will win the approval of mankind, not merely a peace that will serve the several interests and immediate aims of the nations engaged.

No covenant of cooperative peace that does not include the peoples of the New World can suffice to keep the future safe against war; and yet there is only one sort of peace that the peoples of America could join in guaranteeing. The elements of that peace must be elements that engage the confidence and satisfy the principles of the American governments, elements consistent with their political faith and with the practical convictions which the peoples of America have once for all embraced and undertaken to defend.

I do not mean to say that any American government would throw any obstacle in the way of any terms of peace the governments now at war might agree upon or seek to upset them when made, whatever they might be. I only take it for granted that mere terms of peace between the belligerents will not satisfy even the belligerents themselves. Mere agreements may not make peace secure. It will be absolutely necessary that a force be created as a guarantor of the permanency of the settlement so much greater than the force of any nation now engaged or any alliance hitherto formed or projected that no nation, no probable combination of nations could face or withstand it. If the peace presently to be made is to endure, it must be a peace made secure by the organized major force of mankind.

The terms of the immediate peace agreed upon will determine whether it is a peace for which such a guarantee can be secured. The question upon which the whole future peace and policy of the world depends is this: Is the present war a struggle for a just and secure peace, or only for a new balance of power? If it be only a struggle for a new balance of power, who will guarantee, who can guarantee the stable equilibrium of the new arrangement? Only a tranquil Europe can be a stable Europe. There must be, not a balance of power, but a community of power; not organized rivalries, but an organized common peace.

. . .

They imply, first of all, that it must be a peace without victory. It is not pleasant to say this. I beg that I may be permitted to put my own interpretation upon it and that it may be understood that no other interpretation was in my thought. I am seeking only to face realities and to face them without soft concealments. Victory would mean peace forced upon the loser, a victor's terms imposed upon the vanquished. It would be accepted in humiliation, under duress, at an intolerable sacrifice, and would leave a sting, a resentment, a bitter memory upon which terms of peace would rest, not permanently, but only as upon quicksand. Only a peace between equals can last. Only a peace the very principle of which is equality and a common participation in a common benefit. The right state of mind, the right feeling between nations, is as necessary for a lasting peace as is the just settlement of vexed questions of territory or of racial and national allegiance.

The equality of nations upon which peace must be founded if it is to last must be an equality of rights; the guarantees exchanged must neither recognize nor imply a difference between big nations and small, between those that are powerful and those that are weak. Right must be based upon the common strength, not upon the individual strength, of the nations upon whose concert peace will depend. Equality of territory or of resources there of course cannot be; nor any sort of equality not gained in the ordinary peaceful and legitimate development of the peoples themselves. But no one asks or expects anything more than an equality of rights. Mankind is looking now for freedom of life, not for equipoises of power.

And there is a deeper thing involved than even equality of right among organized nations. No peace can last, or ought to last, which does not recognize and accept the principle that governments derive all their just powers from the consent of the governed, and that no right anywhere exists to hand peoples about from sovereignty to sovereignty as if they were property. I take it for granted, for instance, if I may venture upon a single example, that statesmen everywhere are agreed that there should be a united, independent, and autonomous Poland, and that henceforth inviolable security of life, of worship, and of industrial and social development should be guaranteed to all peoples who have lived hitherto under the power of governments devoted to a faith and purpose hostile to their own.

I speak of this, not because of any desire to exalt an abstract political principle which has always been held very dear by those who have sought to build up liberty in America but for the same reason that I have spoken of the other conditions of peace which seem to me clearly indispensable-because I wish frankly to uncover realities. Any peace which does not recognize and accept this principle will inevitably be upset. It will not rest upon the affections or the convictions of mankind. The ferment of spirit of whole populations will fight subtly and constantly against it, and all the world will sympathize. The world can be at peace only if its life is stable, and there can be no stability where the will is in rebellion, where there is not tranquility of spirit and a sense of justice, of freedom, and of right.

So far as practicable, moreover, every great people now struggling towards a full development of its resources and of its powers should be assured a direct outlet to the great highways of the sea. Where this cannot be done by the cession of territory, it can no doubt be done by the neutralization of direct rights of way under the general guarantee which will assure the peace itself. With a right comity of arrangement no nation need be shut away from free access to the open paths of the world's commerce.

And the paths of the sea must alike in law and in fact be free. The freedom of the seas is the *sine qua non* of peace, equality, and cooperation. No doubt a somewhat radical reconsideration of many of the rules of international practice hitherto thought to be established may be necessary in order to make the seas indeed free and common in practically all circumstances for the use of mankind, but the motive for such changes is convincing and compelling. There can be no trust or intimacy between the peoples of the world without them. The free, constant, unthreatened intercourse of nations is an essential part of the process of peace and of development. It need not be difficult either to define or to secure the freedom of the seas if the governments of the world sincerely desire to come to an agreement concerning it.

It is a problem closely connected with the limitation of naval armaments and the cooperation of the navies of the world in keeping the seas at once free and safe. And the question of limiting naval armaments opens the wider and perhaps more difficult question of the limitation of armies and of all programs of military preparation. Difficult and delicate as these questions are, they must be faced with the utmost candor and decided in a spirit of real accommodation if peace is to come with healing in its wings, and come to stay. Peace cannot be had without concession and sacrifice. There can be no sense of safety and equality among the nations if great preponderating armaments are henceforth to continue here and there to be built up and maintained. The statesmen of the world must plan for peace and nations must adjust and accommodate their policy to it as they have planned for war and made ready for pitiless contest and rivalry. The question of armaments, whether on land or sea, is the most immediately and intensely practical question connected with the future fortunes of nations and of mankind.

. . . I hope and believe that I am in effect speaking for liberals and friends of humanity in every nation and of every program of liberty? I would fain believe that I am speaking for the silent mass of mankind everywhere who have as yet had no place or opportunity to speak their real hearts out concerning the death and ruin they see to have come already upon the persons and the homes they hold most dear.

And in holding out the expectation that the people and government of the United States will join the other civilized nations of the world in guaranteeing the permanence of peace upon such terms as I have named I speak with the greater boldness and confidence because it is clear to every man who can think that there is in this promise no breach in either our traditions or our policy as a nation, but a fulfilment, rather, of all that we have professed or striven for. I am proposing, as it were, that the nations should with one accord adopt the doctrine of President Monroe as the doctrine of the world: that no nation should seek to extend its polity over any other nation or people, but that every people should be left free to determine its own polity, its own way of development, unhindered, unthreatened, unafraid, the little along with the great and powerful.

I am proposing that all nations henceforth avoid entangling alliances which would draw them into competitions of power; catch them in a net of intrigue and selfish rivalry, and disturb their own affairs with influences intruded from without. There is no entangling alliance in a concert of power. When all unite to act in the same sense and with the same purpose all act in the common interest and are free to live their own lives under a common protection.

I am proposing government by the consent of the governed; that freedom of the seas which in international conference after conference representatives of the United States have urged with the eloquence of those who are the convinced disciples of liberty; and that moderation of armaments which makes of armies and navies a power for order merely, not an instrument of aggression or of selfish violence.

These are American principles, American policies. We could stand for no others. And they are also the principles and policies of forward looking men and women everywhere, of every modern nation, of every enlightened community. They are the principles of mankind and must prevail.

RANDOLPH S. BOURNE

THE STATE (1918)

Many intellectuals on the left adopted a bellicose stance as war broke out in Europe. From Progressives to radicals, war seemed both inevitable and just. Randolph Bourne was among the dissenters, and his resistance to the war movement wound up isolating him from his friends and colleagues and shutting him out of the journals to which he had contributed. At the time of his death, he was still working on what would be his last essay, an analysis of "the state" and its tendencies to war. The fragment was first included in a posthumous collection of essays appropriately titled "untimely papers." It gained new life, however, when it was republished in the 1960s and was taken up by radicals as a telling indictment of twentieth-century militarism.

What does Bourne mean by "the State"? Why does he think that "war is the health of the state"? Is Bourne against patriotism? Is he responsive to the concerns of Roosevelt and Wilson? What alternative does he offer?

To most Americans of the classes which consider themselves significant the war brought a sense of the sanctity of the State which, if they had had time to think about it, would have seemed a sudden and surprising alteration in their habits of thought. In times of peace, we usually ignore the State in favor of partisan political controversies, or personal struggles for office, or the pursuit of party politics. It is the Government rather than the State with which the politically minded are concerned. The State is reduced to a shadowy emblem which comes to consciousness only on occasions of patriotic holiday.

Government is obviously composed of common and unsanctified men, and is thus a legitimate object of criticism and even contempt. . . .

With a shock of war, however, the State comes into its own again. The Government, with no mandate from the people, without consultation with the people, conducts all the negotiations, the backing and filling, the menaces and explanations, which slowly bring it into collision with some other Government, and gently and irresistibly slides the country into war. . . . The result is that, even in those countries where the business of declaring war is theoretically in the hands of representatives of the people, no legislature has ever been known to decline the request of an Executive, which has conducted all foreign affairs in utter privacy and irresponsibility, that it order the nation into battle. Good democrats are wont to feel the crucial difference between a State in which the popular Parliament or Congress declares war, and the State in which an absolute monarch or ruling class declares war. But, put to the stern pragmatic test, the difference is not striking. In the freest of republics as well as in the most tyrannical of empires all foreign policy . . . are equally the private property of the Executive part of the Government, and are equally exposed to no check whatever from popular bodies, or the people voting as a mass themselves.

The moment war is declared, however, the mass of the people, through some spiritual alchemy, become convinced that they have willed and executed the deed themselves. They then . . . proceed to allow themselves to be regimented, coerced, deranged in all the environments of their lives, and turned into a solid manufactory of destruction toward whatever other people may have, in the appointed scheme of things, come within the range of the Government's disapprobation. . . .

The patriot loses all sense of the distinction between State, nation, and government. In our quieter moments, the Nation or Country forms the basic idea of society. We think vaguely of a loose population spreading over a certain geographical portion of the earth's surface, speaking a common language, and living in a homogeneous civilization. Our idea of

Country concerns itself with non-political aspects of a people, its ways of living, its personal traits, its literature and art, its characteristic attitudes toward life. . . . The Country, as an inescapable group into which we are born, and which makes us its particular kind of a citizen of the world, seems to be a fundamental fact of our consciousness, an irreducible minimum of social feeling.

Now this feeling for country is essentially non-competitive; we think of our own people merely as living on the earth's surface along with other groups, pleasant or objectionable as they may be, but fundamentally as sharing the earth with them. . . .

The State is the country acting as a political unit, it is the group acting as a repository of force, determiner of law, arbiter of justice, international politics is a "power politics" because it is a relation of States and That is what States infallibly and calamitously are, huge aggregations of human and industrial force that may be hurled against each other in war. When a country acts as a whole in relation to another country, or in imposing laws on its own inhabitants, or in coercing or punishing individuals or minorities, it is acting as a State. . . .

Government on the other hand is synonymous with neither State nor Nation. It is the machinery by which the nation, organized as a State, carries out its State functions. Government is the framework of the administration of laws, and the carrying out of the public force. Government is the idea of the State put into practical operation in the hands of definite, concrete, fallible men. . . .

. . . In times of peace the sense of the State flags in a republic that is not militarized. For war is essentially the health of the State. . . . The State is the organization of the herd to act offensively or defensively against another herd similarly organized. The more terrifying the occasion for defense, the closer will become the organization and the more coercive the influence upon each member of the herd. . . . All the activities of society are linked together as fast as possible to this central purpose of making a military offensive or a military defense, and the State becomes what in peacetimes it has vainly struggled to become—the inexorable arbiter and determinant of men's business and attitudes and opinions. . . .

War is the health of the State. It automatically sets in motion throughout society those irresistible forces for uniformity, for passionate cooperation with the Government in coercing into obedience the minority groups and individuals which lack the larger herd sense. The machinery of government sets and enforces the drastic penalties; the minorities are either intimidated into silence, or brought slowly around by a subtle process of persuasion which may seem to them really to be converting them. Of course, the ideal of perfect loyalty, perfect uniformity is never really attained. . . . Loyalty—or mystic devotion to the State—becomes the major imagined human value. Other values, such as artistic creation, knowledge, reason, beauty, the enhancement of life, are instantly and almost unanimously sacrificed, and the significant classes who have constituted themselves the amateur agents of the State are engaged not only in sacrificing these values for themselves but in coercing all other persons into sacrificing them.

. . .

It cannot be too firmly realized that war is a function of States and not of nations, indeed that it is the chief function of States. War is a very artificial thing. It is not the naïve spontaneous outburst of herd pugnacity. . . . War cannot exist without a military establishment, and a military establishment cannot exist without a State organization. . . . We cannot crusade against war without crusading implicitly against the State. And we cannot expect, or take measures to ensure, that this war is a war to end war, unless at the same time we take measures to end the State in its traditional form. The State is not the nation, and the State can be modified and even abolished in its present form, without harming the nation. . . . If the State's chief function is war, then the State must suck out of the nation a large part of its energy for its purely sterile purposes of defense and aggression. It devotes to waste or to actual destruction as much as it can of the vitality of the nation. . . .

. . .

The American Revolution began with certain latent hopes that it might turn into a genuine break with the State ideal. The Declaration of Independence announced doctrines that were utterly incompatible not only with the century-old conception of the Divine Right of Kings, but also with the Divine Right of the State. If all governments derive their authority from the consent of the governed, and if a people is entitled, at any time that it becomes oppressive, to overthrow it and institute one more nearly conformable to their interests and ideals, the old idea of the sovereignty of the State is destroyed. The State is reduced to the homely work of an instrument for carrying out popular policies. If revolution is justifiable, a State may even be criminal sometimes in resisting its own extinction. The sovereignty of the people is no mere phrase. It is a direct challenge to the history tradition of the State. . . .

For a while it seemed almost as if the State were dead. But men who are freed rarely know what to do with their liberty. In each colony the fatal seed of the State had been sown; it could not disappear. Rival prestiges and interests began to make themselves felt. Fear of foreign States, economic distress, discord between classes, the inevitable physical exhaustion and prostration of idealism which follows a protracted war—all combined to put the responsible classes of the new States into the mood for a regression to the State ideal. . . . and then, by one of the most successful *coups d'état* in history, turned their assembly [the Philadelphia Convention of 1787] into the manufacture of a new government on the strongest lines of the old State ideal.

. . .

WILLIAM E. BORAH

ON THE NEED FOR NAVAL DISARMAMENT (1919)

William Borah was born on an Illinois farm at the end of the Civil War. Although he did not finish high school, he apprenticed at a law practice and passed the bar exam in 1887. He earned a reputation as a successful criminal lawyer on the Idaho frontier and was drawn into Republican politics. A popular public speaker, he broke from the party and supported William Jennings Bryan in 1896. He did not fully reconcile with the party regulars until 1907, when he was awarded a seat in the U.S. Senate. A maverick in the Senate as well, he did not fully align with either the progressive or conservative wing of his party. He made his most significant contributions in foreign policy and served as the chair of the Senate Foreign Relations Committee through most of the 1920s. He was a strong supporter of entering World War I but did so on the basis of perceived American national interests. After the war, he played a crucial role in killing the League of Nations treaty, became critical of American military intervention abroad, and favored a dramatic postwar demobilization.

Why does Borah favor disarmament? Is Borah's argument in 1919 in conflict with Roosevelt's message in 1915? Are the military expenditures that Borah recounts a rebuke to Roosevelt's dismissal of the danger of militarism? Is rapid and complete disarmament the appropriate response to the end of a war? Are Borah's arguments equally applicable in 1945, or 1995?

Despite her military defeat, Germany, by reason of the shortsighted and blundering policies of the allied and associated powers, may yet secure economic dominance in Europe. Defeat has resulted in Germany's being deprived of her army and her navy. The burden of armaments has been forced from the backs of the German people. They may now devote their energies and their talents to agriculture, to industry, to the arts, to the things which constitute the real wealth and strength of a people. Their genius will find expression, not in arms, or on the military field, but in improved machinery and cooperative industry. . . .

On the other hand, the allied and associated powers are carrying a vast burden because of their great armies and navies. These burdens are being increased upon a stupendous scale. Hundreds of thousands of their people are to be engaged in lines which produce nothing, add no wealth to the community, make not for health, growth and happiness, but for display, parade and possibly for destruction and death. The German people are compelled to preserve their energies for things which count. The allied and associated powers are burying their people under intolerable taxes, discouraging industry, sterilizing human energy, and breeding discontent through their ever-enlarging plans for increased armaments.

. . .

[W]hile Germany has her billions of reparation, the allied and associated powers are spending their billions for their armies and navies—we alone expending as much for our army and navy as the entire reparation claims against Germany.

The business men of this country must realize, more keenly, perhaps, than anyone else just now, what these armament expenditures and the taxes thereby imposed mean to business of the future. There is little encouragement for men of business capacity to plan and strive for success when they realize, as they must, that their profits are to be taken for taxes, and that those taxes, when collected, are to be expended, not for things which make for wealth and development, but for sheer waste and sterility. We shall not enjoy that resiliency and revival in business which we are entitled to experience in this country until taxes are brought within reason. And taxes cannot be reduced until expenditures are brought within reason. And public expenditures cannot be reduced until outlays for armaments are brought within reason.

All that is being done and said just now about reducing the expenses of the Government in other departments and along other lines will amount to very little so far as lifting the burden of the taxpayer is concerned, unless we also cut most savagely the expenditures for armaments, for there is where the vast sum of money goes.

Neither can we wait, nor need we wait, until all questions about which nations may hold differing views are settled before we begin to limit our armament expenditures. There are now three nations in absolute dominance of the seas—the United States, Great Britain and Japan. These three nations are the only nations which are building vast navies. They are now actually engaged in a naval race. They are building navies with, mad speed and piling taxes upon the people at a rate and to an amount never before dreamed of in time of peace, and seldom in time of war. To say that these building programs shall go forward, that these taxes shall continue to be increased, and the burdens under which the people are breaking shall be augmented until all international questions about which nations and peoples may hold different views are settled, is to say that there is to be no disarmament.

Disarmament should not be postponed, or subordinated, or made incident to the settling and adjusting of all international questions. It should be made the controlling, dominating question. It is the most vital problem in the world today. Unless disarmament is effectuated, there is no possible relief from the economic conditions under which we are now suffering. And any plan, or any program, which makes the question of disarmament a subordinate, or incidental proposition, rather than the main and controlling proposition, will result in the future, as it has in the past, in no relief to the taxpayers and no relief from war.

[T]he obstacle which seems to me the greatest, the obstacle which seems to me the most difficult to master, is one which we will not admit exists, and that is the reliance which we have come to have on force as the only power left on earth with which to govern men.

. . .

The fact is that while we thought we had conquered militarism, it has apparently conquered us. The barbarous creed of Bernhardi has become the accepted rule of the parliaments and congresses and conferences of the new world, as well as the old. The thing which is paralyzing the energies and dissipating the moral forces of the whole human family today and retarding every effort toward peace, driving us to the very brink of chaos and barbarism, is the fact that governments are still worshipping at the throne of militarism. There is to them no God but force. Before the war we had great faith in the commanding influence of justice and the power of public opinion.

I have before me now an interesting editorial in which it is urged that it is useless to talk of disarming until the causes of war are removed. One of the most prolific causes of war is huge armaments. An armed world is a fighting world. Naval competition engenders suspicion, fear, hatred, war. If there should be twenty years of intense naval rivalry between the United States and Japan, any sterile, promontory or irrelevant rock in the Pacific might give rise to war.

There will always be questions of commercial rivalry, matters of difference between nations, and this rivalry and these differences will always lead easily to war when the nations are armed for war. If you wish to make it improbable that differences will lead to conflict, first reduce armaments, which always inspire war, and prevent naval competition which is a daily, ever-present, taunting suggestion of war.

I understand fully that there may be circumstances and conditions in which an appeal to force is not only necessary but righteous. But to deify force, to make it the dominating factor, to have it ever present, to sit at conference with your finger pointing back over your shoulder to your armies and navies, to intrude into every settlement, and to announce to the world that it is your ultimate reliance, is barbaric—and it is none the less barbaric when it is practiced by professedly Christian nations.

For myself, I refuse to concede that force is the only power left, or that it should be the dominating and controlling power. It cannot be possible. Reason and justice must still have their place in the affairs of the world, and if leaders and statesmen are strong enough to place their reliance upon them, they will go far. I venture to declare, in the face of professional militarists, that no nation can long defy the public opinion of the civilized world—and especially no government can long defy the public opinion of their own people. And if this conference is conducted as an appeal to the public opinion of the world and to the public opinions of the peoples of the respective countries, it will accomplish far more than if it is conducted under the constant threat of dominating armaments.

. . .

FOR FURTHER STUDY

Addams, Jane. *The Social Thought of Jane Addams*, ed. Christopher Lasch (Indianapolis, IN: Bobbs-Merrill, 1965).

Bourne, Randolph. *The Radical Will: Selected Writings, 1911–1918* (New York: Urizen Books, 1977).

Brandeis, Louis D. *Brandeis on Democracy*, ed. Philippa Strum (Lawrence: University Press of Kansas, 1995).

Commons, John R. *Legal Foundations of Capitalism* (New York: Macmillan, 1924).

Du Bois, W. E. B. *Writings* (New York: Library of America, 1996).

Eisenach, Eldon J., ed. *The Social and Political Thought of American Progressivism* (Indianapolis, IN: Hackett Publishing, 2006).

Filler, Louis, ed. *From Populism to Progressivism: Representative Selections* (Huntington, NY: R.E. Krieger, 1978).

Goldman, Emma. *Writings of Emma Goldman: Essays on Anarchism, Feminism, Socialism and Communism* (St. Petersburg, FL: Red and Black Publishers, 2013).

Lippmann, Walter. *Drift and Mastery: An Attempt to Diagnose the Current Unrest* (Madison: University of Wisconsin Press, 1985).

More, Paul Elmer. *The Essential Paul Elmer More: A Selection of His Writings*, ed. Byron C. Lambert (New Rochelle, NY: Arlington House, 1972).

Nock, Albert Jay. *The State of the Union: Essays in Social Criticism* (Indianapolis, IN: Liberty Press, 1987).

Resek, Carl, ed. *The Progressives* (Indianapolis, IN: Bobbs-Merrill, 1967).

Roosevelt, Theodore. *The Essential Theodore Roosevelt*, ed. John Gabriel Hunt (New York: Gramercy Books, 1994).

Taft, William Howard. *William Howard Taft: Essential Writings and Addresses*, ed. David H. Burton (Madison, NJ: Fairleigh Dickinson University Press, 2009).

Veblen, Thorstein. *A Veblen Treasury: From Leisure Class to War, Peace, and Capitalism*, ed. Rick Tilman (Armonk, NY: M.E. Sharpe, 1993).

Wilson, Woodrow. *Woodrow Wilson: Essential Writings and Speeches of the Scholar-President*, ed. Mario R. DiNunzio (New York: New York University Press, 2006).

SUGGESTED READINGS

Balfour, Katharine Lawrence. *Democracy's Reconstruction: Thinking Politically with W.E.B. DuBois* (New York: Oxford University Press, 2011).

Bannister, Robert C. *Sociology and Scientism: The American Quest for Objectivity, 1880–1940* (Chapel Hill: University of North Carolina Press, 1987).

Brick, Howard. *Transcending Capitalism: Visions of a New Society in Modern American Thought* (Ithaca, NY: Cornell University Press, 2006).

Cohen, Nancy. *The Reconstruction of American Liberalism, 1865–1914* (Chapel Hill: University of North Carolina Press, 2002).

Crunden, Robert Morse. *The Superfluous Men: Conservative Critics of American Culture, 1900–1945* (Austin: University of Texas Press, 1977).

Eisenach, Eldon J. *The Lost Promise of Progressivism* (Lawrence: University Press of Kansas, 1994).

Fink, Leon. *Progressive Intellectuals and the Dilemmas of Democratic Commitment* (Cambridge, MA: Harvard University Press, 1997).

Fried, Barbara. *The Progressive Assault on Laissez Faire: Robert Hale and the First Law and Economics Movement* (Cambridge, MA: Harvard University Press, 1998).

Hansen, Jonathan M. *The Lost Promise of Patriotism: Debating American Identity, 1890–1920* (Chicago, IL: University of Chicago Press, 2003).

Kloppenberg, James T. *Uncertain Victory: Social Democracy and Progressivism in European and American Thought, 1870–1920* (New York: Oxford University Press, 1986).

Nash, Roderick. *The Nervous Generation: American Thought, 1917–1930* (Chicago, IL: Rand McNally, 1971).

Reed, Adolph L. *W.E.B. Du Bois and American Political Thought: Fabianism and the Color Line* (New York: Oxford University Press, 1997).

Rodgers, Daniel T. *Atlantic Crossings: Social Politics in a Progressive Age* (Cambridge, MA: Harvard University Press, 1998).

Ryan, Alan. *John Dewey and the High Tide of American Liberalism* (New York: W.W. Norton, 1995).

Strum, Philippa. *Brandeis: Beyond Progressivism* (Lawrence: University Press of Kansas, 1993).

Vaughan, Leslie J. *Randolph Bourne and the Politics of Cultural Radicalism* (Lawrence: University Press of Kansas, 1997).

Westbrook, Robert B. *John Dewey and American Democracy* (Ithaca, NY: Cornell University Press, 1991).

White, Morton, *Social Thought in America: The Revolt Against Formalism* (New York: Viking Press, 1949).

CHAPTER 9

THE NEW DEAL ERA, 1933–1950

I. INTRODUCTION

In a radio address building up to his first presidential campaign, New York Governor Franklin D. Roosevelt compared the economic crisis with the outbreak of World War I, declaring

> these unhappy times call for the building of plans that rest upon the forgotten, the unorganized but the indispensable units of economic power, for plans like those of 1917 that build from the bottom up and not from the top down, that put their faith once more in the forgotten man at the bottom of the economic pyramid.

The crisis was going to require new thinking and new organization. Roosevelt warned against "the illusions of economic magic." Massive public works of the type that had already been supported by the Hoover administration could "be only a stopgap." The "real economic cure" could not simply treat "external symptoms" like unemployment; it would "go to the killing of the bacteria in the system."[1] But Roosevelt was optimistic. "The period of social pioneering is only at its beginning," and what was required was the vision "to bring under proper control the forces of modern society."[2] That effort—the effort to build up from the forgotten man and bring economic forces under government control—was to be the New Deal.

The New Deal era was in some ways a great departure and in other ways a continuation of what had come before. Roosevelt vocally committed the federal government to providing support for the needy and stability for the economy, and his administration dramatically expanded the size and scope of the federal government. But the New Dealers were

---

1 Franklin D. Roosevelt, "Radio Address from Albany, New York, April 7, 1932," in *The Public Papers and Addresses of Franklin D. Roosevelt*, ed. Samuel I. Rosenman, vol. 1 (New York: Random House, 1938), 625.

2 Franklin D. Roosevelt, "Address to the Young Democratic Club, April 13, 1936," in *The Public Papers and Addresses of Franklin D. Roosevelt*, ed. Samuel I. Rosenman, vol. 6 (New York: Random House, 1938), 165.

above all pragmatic experimenters. There was no single New Deal approach, either across time or across issues. Policy innovations were routinely launched and abandoned as the political winds and policy fortunes shifted. But many of those experiments were built on prior experience. The Progressives had for years called for the conscious mastery of the forces that had been unleashed by industrialism and urbanization, and federal, state, and local officials had responded with new budgetary and regulatory commitments. The alphabet soup of federal government agencies that were rapidly launched in the 1930s drew on the lessons of such earlier initiatives as the Interstate Commerce Commission, the Federal Trade Commission, and the Food, Drug and Insecticide Administration (later the Food and Drug Administration). Nonetheless, the United States emerged from the Depression (and World War II) transformed.

Politics. The New Deal upended the political order that had predominated since the turn of the century. The onset of the Great Depression had shaken many of its traditional supporters loose from the Republican Party. The Democratic Party picked up the pieces. Building on its longstanding base of support in the white South, the Democrats added a diverse coalition of religious and ethnic minorities, farmers, unions, and the urban working class. Franklin Roosevelt won an unprecedented four terms as president by landslides. The Republicans were reduced to small minorities in Congress.

The fissures in such a large coalition soon became evident. In Roosevelt's second term, the more conservative Southern Democrats began to ally with the Republicans in Congress. This "Conservative Coalition" created a limit on how far liberals could push policies in Congress from the late 1930s into the 1960s. In 1948, South Carolina's Strom Thurmond launched a "Dixiecrat" revolt from the national Democratic Party. He took over two percent of the popular vote in the 1948 presidential elections, but since his support was regionally concentrated he was able to claim thirty-nine electoral votes. Former Vice President Henry Wallace ran to Harry Truman's left on a Progressive Party ticket, claiming nearly as many votes as Thurmond but no electoral votes. The combination was not enough to deny Truman the election (despite the famous *Chicago Tribune* headline announcing "Dewey Defeats Truman"), but it did deny Truman a popular majority and emphasized to the Democratic leadership the difficulty of bridging the divide between liberals and conservatives and of putting race on the national political agenda.

Society. The New Deal era was overwhelmingly marked by the context of the Great Depression and World War II. The Depression was a global phenomenon but in the United States began with the stock market crash of October 1929 early in the administration of Herbert Hoover. At its worst the unemployment rate peaked in 1933 at roughly 25 percent of the civilian population, but unemployment hovered above 15 percent through the rest of the 1930s. The New Deal responded with a wide range of policies, from crop quotas and supports to public works programs to industrial planning to unionization.

World War II was well under way before the United States entered the scene. Germany invaded Poland in 1939, setting off war in Europe (Japan had begun fighting its neighbors

FIGURE 9-1 TIMELINE OF THE NEW DEAL ERA

Events	Year	Writings
	1932	Franklin Roosevelt's Commonwealth Club Address
Carl Schmitt's *The Concept of the Political*	1932	
Franklin D. Roosevelt inaugurated as president	1933	
FDR launches the New Deal	1933	
Adolph Hitler becomes Chancellor of Germany	1933	
National Prohibition repealed in United States	1933	
U.S. Supreme Court strikes down key components of New Deal on "Black Monday"	1935	
	1935	Huey Long's "Every Man a King" radio address
	1935	Sinclair Lewis's *It Can't Happen Here*
John Maynard Keynes's *The General Theory of Employment, Interest and Money*	1936	
FDR announces Court-packing plan	1937	
U.S. Supreme Court makes "switch in time"	1937	
United States declares war on Japan and Germany	1941	
	1942	A. Philip Randolp's March on Washington keynote address
Jean-Paul Sartre's *Being and Nothingness*	1943	
Friedrich Hayek's *The Road to Serfdom*	1944	
United States drops first atomic bombs in Japan	1945	
United Nations established	1945	
	1946	George Kennan's "Long Telegram"
	1947	Announcement of the Truman Doctrine
India and Pakistan gain independence	1947	
House Un-American Activities Committee's "Hollywood Ten" hearings	1947	
NATO established	1949	
George Orwell's *1984*	1949	

earlier). While the United States provided support for Britain, the United States did not commit to the war until the bombing of Pearl Harbor in December 1941. The war dramatically increased federal government spending and regulation of the economy, which only partly receded after the war. The mobilization for war resolved the persistent unemployment problem but left many fearful that the economy would return to its prewar, depressed state once peace was established. At the end of the war, many Americans still lived in poverty with no running water or central heat and most farms still lacked electricity. But rather than renewed recession, the postwar period launched an economic boom.

Ideas. In Europe, various radical philosophies flourished, having more indirect influence in the United States. The Soviet Union stood as a beacon and seeming success story in pulling an underdeveloped country into modernity, and Marxism flourished as an intellectual force. Adolf Hitler's *Mein Kampf* was published in 1925, and in 1933 he was appointed chancellor of Germany. Fascist nationalism had helped spur Benito Mussolini's rise to power in Italy. Such intellectual and political developments posed fundamental questions about the future direction that European societies would take and put liberal ideals on the defensive.

In the United States, the social sciences had emerged as an influential intellectual and social force. The social sciences established themselves as distinct disciplines and areas of professional scholarly inquiry in the late nineteenth century. The moral and religious teachings that dominated the writing and teaching of social activists in the early nineteenth century were displaced by a more empirical, scientific approach. Pragmatist philosophers like John Dewey drew the lesson from such developments that what once was the subject of moral absolutes should now be understood to be the subject of experimentation and empirical testing. Social scientists claimed better understanding of the operation of social forces. Legal Realists, centered particularly at Yale Law School, elaborated a growing skepticism about the determinacy of law and the neutrality of legal decision-makers. Many in these emerging schools of thought lent their talents to the federal government, especially when the United States began to prepare for war.

II. DEMOCRACY AND LIBERTY

Major Developments

- Formation of New Deal coalition of farmers, urban workers, and minorities
- Debate over independent judiciary and judicial review
- Reconstruction of constitutional law on individual rights
- Threat to existence of democratic governments in Europe

The period after World War I cast doubt the success of the democratic project. The Russian Revolution of 1917 was initially cheered as a further step away from monarchy, but the Bolshevik consolidation of power cast doubt on the direction of the Soviet regime. The fascist movement led by Benito Mussolini assumed power in Italy in 1922. Military coups swept across Europe in the 1920s and 1930s, including in Spain, Portugal, Poland, Lithuania, and Greece. The Nazi movement led by Adolf Hitler seized power in Germany in 1933. For many American observers, the future of democracy seemed far from certain. Moreover, many found the political and policy reforms being advanced by these new regimes to have their merits. The old joke that at least Mussolini made the trains run on time had its roots in prewar elite opinion. Praising how Mussolini had intervened to stop layoffs in automotive plants in Italy, the progressive magazine the *Christian Century* editorialized in 1929, "The hope of democracy will revive when it learns how to do the things that need to be done as efficiently as autocracy does them."[3]

Such worries were not lost on the Roosevelt administration, its allies, and its critics. A repeated theme of Roosevelt's rhetoric in the 1930s was the need to reform American democratic institutions so that they could be successful. Even as he tried to distance himself from the fascist governments to which the New Deal was being compared, Roosevelt echoed their complaints: "The real truth of the matter is that for a number of years in our country the machinery of democracy had failed to function." In contrast to those European examples, however, Roosevelt hoped that an "American method" could be devised, one that could make use of national cooperation and new representative institutions to reform society.[4]

The details of Roosevelt's approach to reviving the economy were often in flux, but the transformation he called for was potentially profound. Both government and businesses were to reorient themselves so as "to operate for the general welfare."[5] Among other things, this suggested the need to provide "security against the hazards and vicissitudes of life." Moving forward, it would be the government's "plain duty to provide for that security upon which welfare depends."[6] A democratic government was not merely government by the people; it was a government that worked for the people. "A democracy, the right kind of democracy, is bound together by the ties of neighborliness."[7] Federal taxing and spending never declined to prewar levels after the conclusion of World War I, but with the onset of the Depression, Congress began to ramp up federal spending to new peacetime highs. As Figure 9-2 indicates, the combination of the New Deal and World War II permanently transformed the federal government's size and significance in American life.

Franklin Roosevelt's democracy also called into question the relationship between majorities and individuals that had been established over the preceding decades. As the state and federal governments developed new policies to address the Great Depression, state and federal courts often reacted by declaring that those policy innovations violated inherited constitutional rules. Many of these decisions appealed to the rights of individuals to make contracts of their choosing, to pursue their vocations as they wished, and to use their

3 Quoted in Edward A. Purcell, Jr., *The Crisis of Democratic Theory* (Lexington: University Press of Kentucky, 1973), 122.

4 Franklin D. Roosevelt, "Address to the Representatives of Industry on N.R.A. Codes, March 5, 1934," in *The Public Papers and Addresses of Franklin D. Roosevelt*, ed. Samuel I. Rosenman, vol. 4 (New York: Random House, 1938), 124.

5 Ibid.

6 Franklin D. Roosevelt, "Message to Congress on the Objectives and Accomplishments of the Administration, June 8, 1934," in *The Public Papers and Addresses of Franklin D. Roosevelt*, ed. Samuel I. Rosenman, vol. 12 (New York: Random House, 1938), 291.

7 Franklin D. Roosevelt, "Address to the National Conference of Catholic Charities, October 4, 1933," in *The Public Papers and Addresses of Franklin D. Roosevelt*, ed. Samuel I. Rosenman, vol. 1 (New York: Random House, 1938), 380.

property as seemed most appropriate to them. President Roosevelt's eventual response to those decisions was to propose a plan to reorganize the federal judiciary, specifically by allowing the president to appoint additional justices so as to constitute an immediate, pro-New Deal majority. As the president explained to a Democratic gathering shortly after the proposal was announced, "In the United States democracy has not yet failed and does not need to fail. And we propose not to let it fail!"[8] The court-packing proposal launched a months-long debate, dividing more conservative and more liberal New Dealers. Roosevelt and his supporters argued that the Supreme Court was obliged to acquiesce to the expressed will of the majority. The opponents of the plan worried that it risked subordinating the courts to the will of the executive, to the ultimate detriment of political minorities and individual rights. By the time the plan was defeated in Congress, the Supreme Court had launched a revolution in constitutional law, acceding to the New Deal, abandoning judicial protection of the strong property rights of prior decades and beginning a quest to identify a new set of rights to protect.

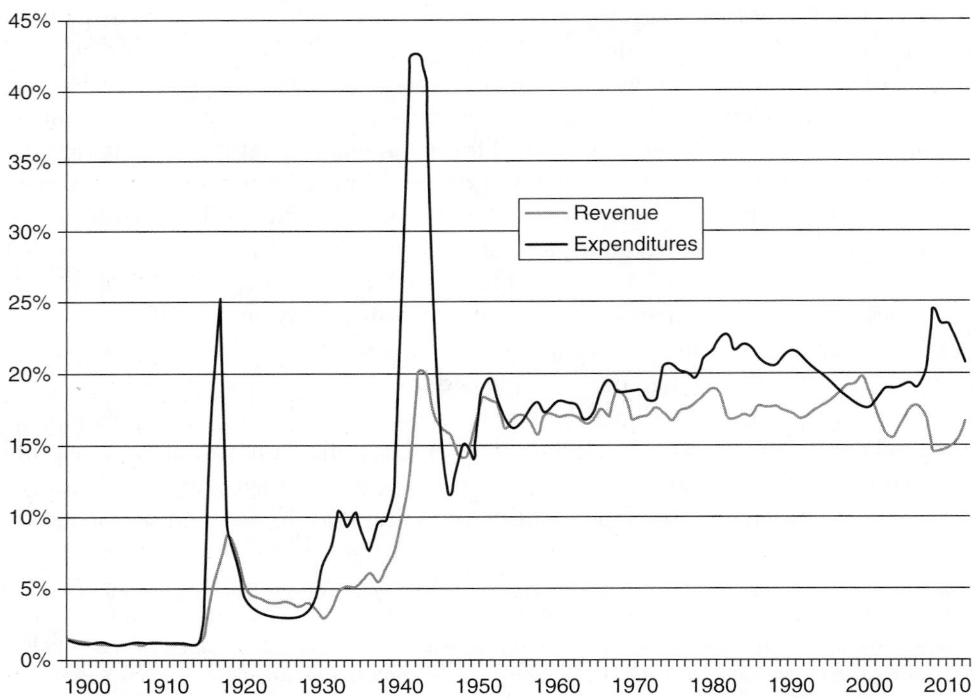

FIGURE 9-2 Federal Revenue and Expenditures as Percentage of GDP.

8 Franklin D. Roosevelt, "Address to the Democratic Victory Dinner, March 4, 1937," in *The Public Papers and Addresses of Franklin D. Roosevelt*, ed. Samuel I. Rosenman, vol. 7 (New York: Random House, 1938), 116.

HERBERT HOOVER

RUGGED INDIVIDUALISM SPEECH (1928)

Herbert Hoover's administration struggled through four years of the Great Depression, but it began on an optimistic note. His 1928 campaign speeches were gathered together and published in a single volume after his election in order to illuminate the "new liberalism" that the technocratic Hoover represented. "New conceptions of government" were needed in the twentieth century, and Hoover offered a way to balance the traditional "rights of individuals" and their emerging "duties and responsibilities to society."[9]

His speech to an overflow crowd at Madison Square Garden near the end of the campaign came to symbolize both Hoover and the Republican Party. It was a symbol that was cast in an increasingly negative light by the New Dealers in the 1930s. By the time of Franklin Roosevelt's rout of the incumbent President Hoover in 1932, this address was known, and derided, as the "rugged individualism"—or as some preferred "ragged individualism"—speech. The contemporary reaction was rather different, however. In 1928, it was known as the celebrated "Garden speech," and the primary Democratic reaction was to complain that Hoover had painted their candidate as a socialist when in fact he too firmly believed that "the trouble with the Federal Government is that there is too much interference with private business" and that Hoover had not drawn the natural conclusion that Prohibition should be repealed.[10] It was left to the Socialist candidate, Norman Thomas, to call out Hoover for his "rugged individualism" line, and Thomas's complaint was that the description was inaccurate: America already embraced government interventionism and a planned economy.[11]

To what degree does Hoover endorse laissez-faire in this speech? What does he see as the government's responsibility for the economy? Does he identify limitations on the government's role? What does he mean by "rugged individualism"? Is this a real American tradition? Is an ideal of rugged individualism still relevant?

. . .

It detracts nothing from the character and energy of the American people, it minimizes in no degree the quality of their accomplishments to say that the policies of the Republican Party have played a large part in recuperation from the war and the building of the magnificent progress which shows upon every hand today. I say with emphasis that without the wise policies which the Republican Party has brought into action during this period, no such progress would have been possible.

The first responsibility of the Republican administration was to renew the march of progress from its collapse by the war. The task involved the restoration of confidence in the future and the liberation and stimulation of the constructive energies of our people. It discharged that task. . . .

. . .

Nor do I need to remind you that government today deals with an economic and social system vastly more intricate and delicately adjusted than ever before. That system now must be kept in perfect tune if we would maintain uninterrupted employment and the high standard of living of our people. The government has come to touch their delicate web at a thousand points. Yearly the relations of government to national prosperity become more and more intimate. Only through keen vision and helpful cooperation by the government has stability in business and stability in employment been maintained. . . .

9 Ray Lyman Wilbur, "Introduction," in Herbert Hoover, *The New Day* (Stanford, CA: Stanford University Press, 1928).

10 "Comment is Varied on Hoover Speech," *New York Times* (October 24, 1928), 12.

11 "Thomas Uses Radio in his Final Appeal," *New York Times* (November 6, 1928), 19.

There always are some localities, some industries, and some individuals who do not share the prevailing prosperity. The task of government is to lessen these inequalities.

Never has there been a period when the Federal Government has given such aid and impulse to the progress of our people, not alone to economic progress but to the development of those agencies which make for moral and spiritual progress.

But in addition to this great record of contributions of the Republican Party to progress, there has been a further fundamental contribution—a contribution underlying and sustaining all the others—and that is the resistance of the Republican Party to every attempt to inject the government into business in competition with its citizens.

After the war, when the Republican Party assumed administration of the country, we were faced with the problem of determination of the very nature of our national life. During one hundred and fifty years we have builded up a form of self-government and a social system which is peculiarly our own. It differs essentially from all others in the world. It is the American system. It is just as definite and positive a political and social system as has ever been developed on earth. It is founded upon a particular conception of self-government in which decentralized local responsibility is the very base. Further than this, it is founded upon the conception that only through ordered liberty, freedom, and equal opportunity to the individual will his initiative and enterprise spur on the march of progress. And in our insistence upon equality of opportunity has our system advanced beyond all the world.

During the war we necessarily turned to the government to solve every difficult economic problem. . . . To a large degree we regimented our whole people temporarily into a socialistic state. However justified in time of war, if continued in peacetime it would destroy not only our American system but with it our progress and freedom as well.

When the war closed, the most vital of all issues both in our own country and throughout the world was whether governments should continue their wartime ownership and operation of many instrumentalities of production and distribution. We were challenged with a peace-time choice between the American system of rugged individualism and a European philosophy of diametrically opposed doctrines—doctrines of paternalism and state socialism. . . .

The Republican Party from the beginning resolutely turned its face away from these ideas and these war practices. . . . restored the government to its position as umpire instead of a player in the economic game. . . .

. . .

Commercial business requires a concentration of responsibility. Self-government requires decentralization and many checks and balances to safeguard liberty. Our Government to succeed in business would need become in effect a despotism. There at once begins the destruction of self-government.

. . . The hard practical fact is that leadership in business must come through the sheer rise in ability and character. . . . Political agencies are feeble channels through which to select able leaders to conduct commercial business.

. . .

The effect upon our economic progress would be even worse. Business progressiveness is dependent on competition. New methods and new ideas are the outgrowth of the spirit of adventure, of individual initiative, and of individual enterprise. Without adventure there is no progress. No government administration can rightly take chances with taxpayers' money.

. . .

[I do not] wish to be misinterpreted as believing that the United States is free-for-all and devil-take-the-hindmost. The very essence of equality of opportunity and of American individualism is that there shall be no domination by any group or combination in this republic, whether it be business or political. On the contrary, it demands economic justice as well as political and social justice. It is no system of laissez faire.

. . .

The American people from bitter experience have a rightful fear that great business units might be used to dominate our industrial life and by illegal and unethical practices destroy equality of opportunity.

Years ago the Republican administration established the principle that such evils could be corrected by regulation. It developed methods by which abuses could be prevented while the full value of industrial progress could be retained for the public. . . .

. . .

One of the great problems of government is to determine to what extent the government shall regulate and control commerce and industry and how much it shall leave it alone. No system is perfect. We have had many abuses in the private conduct of business. That every good citizen resents. It is just as important that business keep out of government as that government keep out of business.

. . .

We still have great problems if we would achieve the full economic advancement of our country. . . . We can assist in solving these problems by cooperation of our government. To the agricultural industry we shall need to advance initial capital to assist them to stabilize their industry. But this proposal implies that they shall conduct it themselves, and not by the government. It is in the interest of our cities that we shall bring agriculture and all industries into full stability and prosperity. . . .

. . .

To me the foundation of American life rests upon the home and the family. I read into these great economic forces, these intricate and delicate relations of the government with business and with our political and social life, but one supreme end—that we reinforce the ties that bind together the millions of our families, that we strengthen the security, the happiness, and the independence of every home.

. . .

Some may ask whether all this may lead beyond mere material progress. It leads to a release of the energies of men and women from the dull drudgery of life to a wider vision and a higher hope. . . . It leads to an America, healthy in body, healthy in spirit, unfettered, youthful, eager. . . .

FRANKLIN D. ROOSEVELT

COMMONWEALTH CLUB ADDRESS (1932)

Franklin D. Roosevelt grew up in a wealthy family in New York in the late nineteenth century. He graduated from Harvard, attended Columbia Law School, and spent a few years practicing law before winning a seat in the state legislature in 1910. His active support for the Woodrow Wilson campaign won him a position as an assistant secretary of the navy, where he helped build up the American naval fleet prior to World War I. In 1920, he was offered the vice presidential place on the national ticket, but the next year he contracted polio and suffered permanent paralysis. He served two terms as governor, from whence he launched his first presidential campaign in 1932. In the summer of 1932, he accepted the Democratic nomination, pledging "a New Deal for the American people." The content of the promised New Deal was left vague in 1932, but Roosevelt had already established himself as an aggressive leader who favored active government intervention to improve the economy.

His address to the Commonwealth Club in San Francisco in the fall of 1932 was one of Roosevelt's few forays into articulating a broad philosophy of government, and it was among his most important speeches. Drafted by the corporate law professor Adolf Berle, the speech helped establish a distinctive New Deal ideology and distance the Democratic Party of the 1930s from both its own recent past and from the Republican Party.

How does Roosevelt distinguish "politics" from "government"? To what extent does Roosevelt build on Herbert Croly (as found in Chapter 8)? How does he assess the importance of individualism in the American political tradition? Does he see challenges to the United States beyond the immediate crisis of the Great Depression? Is his agenda moving forward focused on social and economic structures, or the need for relief? What is the American "social contract"? In what ways does Roosevelt's political philosophy depart from Hoover's?

. . .

I want to speak not of politics but of Government. I want to speak not of parties, but of universal principles. They are not political, except in that larger sense in which a great American once expressed a definition of politics, that nothing in all of human life is foreign to the science of politics.

. . .

The issue of Government has always been whether individual men and women will have to serve some system of Government or economics, or whether a system of Government and economics exists to serve individual men and women. This question has persistently dominated the discussion of Government for many generations. On questions relating to these things men have differed, and for time immemorial it is probable that honest men will continue to differ.

. . .

When we look about us, we are likely to forget how hard people have worked to win the privilege of Government. The growth of the national Governments of Europe was a struggle for the development of a centralized force in the Nation, strong enough to impose peace upon ruling barons. In many instances the victory of the central Government, the creation of a strong central Government, was a haven of refuge to the individual. The people preferred the master far away to the exploitation and cruelty of the smaller master near at hand.

But the creators of national Government were perforce ruthless men. They were often cruel in their methods, but they did strive steadily toward something that society needed and very much wanted, a strong central State able to keep the peace, to stamp out civil war, to put the unruly nobleman in his place, and to permit the bulk of individuals to live safely. The man of ruthless force had his place in developing a pioneer country, just as he did in fixing the power of the central Government in the development of Nations. Society paid him well for his services and its development. When the development among the

Nations of Europe, however, had been completed, ambition and ruthlessness, having served their term, tended to overstep their mark.

There came a growing feeling that Government was conducted for the benefit of a few who thrived unduly at the expense of all. The people sought a balancing—a limiting force. There came gradually, through town councils, trade guilds, national parliaments, by constitution and by popular participation and control, limitations on arbitrary power.

Another factor that tended to limit the power of those who ruled, was the rise of the ethical conception that a ruler bore a responsibility for the welfare of his subjects.

The American colonies were born in this struggle. The American Revolution was a turning point in it. After the Revolution the struggle continued and shaped itself in the public life of the country. There were those who because they had seen the confusion which attended the years of war for American independence surrendered to the belief that popular Government was essentially dangerous and essentially unworkable. They were honest people, my friends, and we cannot deny that their experience had warranted some measure of fear. The most brilliant, honest and able exponent of this point of view was Hamilton. He was too impatient of slow-moving methods. Fundamentally he believed that the safety of the republic lay in the autocratic strength of its Government, that the destiny of individuals was to serve that Government, and that fundamentally a great and strong group of central institutions, guided by a small group of able and public spirited citizens, could best direct all Government.

But Mr. Jefferson, in the summer of 1776, after drafting the Declaration of Independence turned his mind to the same problem and took a different view. He did not deceive himself with outward forms. Government to him was a means to an end, not an end in itself; it might be either a refuge and a help or a threat and a danger, depending on the circumstances. . . . These people [the laboring class], he considered, had two sets of rights, those of "personal competency" and those involved in acquiring and possessing property. By "personal competency" he meant the right of free thinking, freedom of forming and expressing opinions, and freedom of personal living, each man according to his own lights. To insure the first set of rights, a Government must so order its functions as not to interfere with the individual. But even Jefferson realized that the exercise of the property rights might so interfere with the rights of the individual that the Government, without whose assistance the property rights could not exist, must intervene, not to destroy individualism, but to protect it.

. . .

. . . [I]ndividualism was made the great watchword of American life. The happiest of economic conditions made that day long and splendid. On the Western frontier, land was substantially free. No one, who did not shirk the task of earning a living, was entirely without opportunity to do so. Depressions could, and did, come and go; but they could not alter the fundamental fact that most of the people lived partly by selling their labor and partly by extracting their livelihood from the soil, so that starvation and dislocation were practically impossible. . . .

. . .

A glance at the situation today only too clearly indicates that equality of opportunity as we have known it no longer exists. Our industrial plant is built; the problem just now is whether under existing conditions it is not overbuilt. Our last frontier has long since been reached, and there is practically no more free land. More than half of our people do not live on the farms or on lands and cannot derive a living by cultivating their own property. There is no safety valve in the form of a Western prairie to which those thrown out of work by the Eastern economic machines can go for a new start. We are not able to invite the immigration from Europe to share our endless plenty. We are now providing a drab living for our own people.

. . .

Just as freedom to farm has ceased, so also the opportunity in business has narrowed. It still is true that men can start small enterprises, trusting to native shrewdness and ability to keep abreast of competitors; but area after area has been preempted altogether by the great corporations, and even in the fields which still have no great concerns, the small man starts under a handicap. The unfeeling statistics of the past three decades show that the independent business man is running a losing race. Perhaps he is forced to the wall; perhaps he cannot command credit; perhaps he is "squeezed out," in Mr. Wilson's words, by highly organized corporate competitors, as your corner grocery man can tell you. Recently a careful study was made of the concentration of business in the United States. It showed that our economic life was dominated by some six hundred odd corporations who controlled two-thirds of American industry. Ten million small business men divided the other third. More striking still, it appeared that if the process of concentration goes on at the same rate, at the end of another century we shall have all American industry controlled by a dozen corporations, and run by perhaps a hundred men. Put plainly, we are steering a steady course toward economic oligarchy, if we are not there already.

Clearly, all this calls for a re-appraisal of values. A mere builder of more industrial plants, a creator of more railroad systems, an organizer of more corporations, is as likely to be a danger as a help. The day of the great promoter or the financial Titan, to whom we granted anything if only he would build, or develop, is over. Our task now is not discovery or exploitation of natural resources, or necessarily producing more goods. It is the soberer, less dramatic business of administering resources and plants already in hand, of seeking to reestablish foreign markets for our surplus production, of meeting the problem of underconsumption, of adjusting production to consumption, of distributing wealth and products more equitably, of adapting existing economic organizations to the service of the people. The day of enlightened administration has come.

Just as in older times the central Government was first a haven of refuge, and then a threat, so now in a closer economic system the central and ambitious financial unit is no longer a servant of national desire, but a danger. I would draw the parallel one step farther. We did not think because national Government had become a threat in the 18th century that therefore we should abandon the principle of national Government. Nor today should we abandon the principle of strong economic units called corporations, merely because their power is susceptible of easy abuse. In other times we dealt with the problem of an unduly ambitious central Government by modifying it gradually into a constitutional democratic Government. So today we are modifying and controlling our economic units.

As I see it, the task of Government in its relation to business is to assist the development of an economic declaration of rights, an economic constitutional order. This is the common task of statesman and business man. It is the minimum requirement of a more permanently safe order of things.

Happily, the times indicate that to create such an order not only is the proper policy of Government, but it is the only line of safety for our economic structures as well. We know, now, that these economic units cannot exist unless prosperity is uniform, that is, unless purchasing power is well distributed throughout every group in the Nation. That is why even the most selfish of corporations for its own interest would be glad to see wages restored and unemployment ended and to bring the Western farmer back to his accustomed level of prosperity and to assure a permanent safety to both groups. That is why some enlightened industries themselves endeavor to limit the freedom of action of each man and business group within the industry in the common interest of all; why business men everywhere are asking a form of organization which will bring the scheme of things into balance, even though it may in some measure qualify the freedom of action of individual units within the business.

. . .

The Declaration of Independence discusses the problem of Government in terms of a contract. Government is a relation of give and take, a contract, perforce, if we would follow the thinking out of which it grew. Under such a contract rulers were accorded power, and the people consented to that power on consideration that they be accorded certain rights. The task of statesmanship has always been the redefinition of these rights in terms of a changing and growing social order. New conditions impose new requirements upon Government and those who conduct Government.

. . .

I feel that we are coming to a view through the drift of our legislation and our public thinking in the past quarter century that private economic power is, to enlarge an old phrase, a public trust as well. I hold that continued enjoyment of that power by any individual or group must depend upon the fulfillment of that trust. The men who have reached the summit of American business life know this best; happily, many of these urge the binding quality of this greater social contract.

The terms of that contract are as old as the Republic, and as new as the new economic order.

Every man has a right to life; and this means that he has also a right to make a comfortable living. He may by sloth or crime decline to exercise that right; but it may not be denied him. We have no actual famine or dearth; our industrial and agricultural mechanism can produce enough and to spare. Our Government formal and informal, political and economic, owes to everyone an avenue to possess himself of a portion of that plenty sufficient for his needs, through his own work.

Every man has a right to his own property; which means a right to be assured, to the fullest extent attainable, in the safety of his savings. By no other means can men carry the burdens of those parts of life which, in the nature of things, afford no chance of labor; childhood, sickness, old age. In all thought of property, this right is paramount; all other property rights must yield to it. If, in accord with this principle, we must restrict the operations of the speculator, the manipulator, even the financier, I believe we must accept the restriction as needful, not to hamper individualism but to protect it.

These two requirements must be satisfied, in the main, by the individuals who claim and hold control of the great industrial and financial combinations which dominate so large a part of our industrial life. They have undertaken to be, not business men, but princes of property. I am not prepared to say that the system which produces them is wrong. I am very clear that they must fearlessly and competently assume the responsibility which goes with the power. So many enlightened business men know this that the statement would be little more than a platitude, were it not for an added implication.

This implication is, briefly, that the responsible heads of finance and industry instead of acting each for himself, must work together to achieve the common end. They must, where necessary, sacrifice this or that private advantage; and in reciprocal self-denial must seek a general advantage. It is here that formal Government—political Government, if you chose—comes in. Whenever in the pursuit of this objective the lone wolf, the unethical competitor, the reckless promoter, the Ishmael or Insull whose hand is against every man's, declines to join in achieving an end recognized as being for the public welfare, and threatens to drag the industry back to a state of anarchy, the Government may properly be asked to apply restraint. Likewise, should the group ever use its collective power contrary to the public welfare, the Government must be swift to enter and protect the public interest.

The Government should assume the function of economic regulation only as a last resort, to be tried only when private initiative, inspired by high responsibility, with such assistance and balance as Government can give, has finally failed. As yet there has been no final failure, because there has been no attempt; and I decline to assume that this Nation is unable to meet the situation.

The final term of the high contract was for liberty and the pursuit of happiness. We have learned a great deal of both in the past century. We know that individual liberty and individual happiness mean nothing unless both are ordered in the sense that one man's meat is not another man's poison. We know that the old "rights of personal competency," the right to read, to think, to speak, to choose and live a mode of life, must be respected at all hazards. We know that liberty to do anything which deprives others of those elemental rights is outside the protection of any compact; and that Government in this regard is the maintenance of a balance, within which every individual may have a place if he will take it; in which every individual may find safety if he wishes it; in which every individual may attain such power as his ability permits, consistent with his assuming the accompanying responsibility.

All this is a long, slow talk. Nothing is more striking than the simple innocence of the men who insist, whenever an objective is present, on the prompt production of a patent scheme guaranteed to produce a result. Human endeavor is not so simple as that.

Government includes the art of formulating a policy, and using the political technique to attain so much of that policy as will receive general support; persuading, leading, sacrificing, teaching always, because the greatest duty of a statesman is to educate. But in the matters of which I have spoken, we are learning rapidly, in a severe school. The lessons so learned must not be forgotten, even in the mental lethargy of a speculative upturn. We must build toward the time when a major depression cannot occur again; and if this means sacrificing the easy profits of inflationist booms, then let them go; and good riddance.

Faith in America, faith in our tradition of personal responsibility, faith in our institutions, faith in ourselves demand that we recognize the new terms of the old social contract. We shall fulfill them, as we fulfilled the obligation of the apparent Utopia which Jefferson imagined for us in 1776, and which Jefferson, Roosevelt and Wilson sought to bring to realization. We must do so, lest a rising tide of misery, engendered by our common failure, engulf us all. But failure is not an American habit; and in the strength of great hope we must all shoulder our common load.

ALBERT JAY NOCK

LIFE, LIBERTY, AND . . . (1935)

The son of an Episcopalian minister, Albert Jay Nock entered the ministry himself in 1897. In 1909, he abruptly left the ministry and embarked on a new career in journalism. He initially expressed a generally Progressive political view, but he was transformed by the American entry into World War I. He already had pacifist leanings, but the Wilson administration's actions led him to embrace an individualist variety of anarchism. In 1920, he launched a new journal, *The Freeman*, which attracted an eclectic mix of writers but did not last long. He relied on patrons to subsidize his writing career, which included a biography of Thomas Jefferson, whose political philosophy influenced his own. Over the course of the 1930s, he was an often bitter critic of the New Deal and the growing influence of government on the economy and society. His autobiography, *Memoirs of a Superfluous Man*, was published near the end of his life during World War II and was subsequently embraced by the postwar conservative movement. His radical individualism was accepted as a precursor to the libertarian movement that arose in the 1950s and 1960s.

Is Nock's portrait of Jefferson the same as Roosevelt's, or Croly's? What does he see as the core components of the Jeffersonian inheritance? Are his disagreements with the direction of government primarily practical or philosophical? Does he offer a credible vision for the twentieth century? Does he think about the state in the same way as Progressive Era writers like Randolph Bourne or Emma Goldman? Should he have been pleased with Hoover's vision of rugged individualism?

For almost a full century before the Revolution of 1776, the classic enumeration of human rights was "life, liberty, and property." The American Whigs took over this formula from the English Whigs, who had constructed it out of the theories of their seventeenth-century political thinkers, notably John Locke. . . . But when the Declaration of Independence was drafted Mr. Jefferson wrote "life, liberty, and the pursuit of happiness" . . . .

It was a revolutionary change. "The pursuit of happiness" is of course an inclusive term. It covers property rights, because obviously if a person's property is molested, his pursuit of happiness is interfered with. But there are many interferences which are not aimed at specific property rights; and in so wording the Declaration as to cover all these interferences, Mr. Jefferson immensely broadened the scope of political theory—he broadened the idea of what government is for. The British and American Whigs thought the sociological concern of government stopped with abstract property rights. Mr. Jefferson thought it went further; he thought that government ought to concern itself with the larger and inclusive right to pursue happiness.

. . .

How, then, should the state act? What is the utmost that the state can do to raise the general level of happiness? Mr. Jefferson's answer to this question can be put in few words—that it should mind its own business. But what is its business? In Mr. Jefferson's view its business is to protect the individual from the aggressions and trespasses of his neighbors, and beyond this, to leave him strictly alone. The state's whole duty is, first, to abstain entirely from any positive regulation of the individual's conduct; and, second, to make justice easily and costlessly accessible to every applicant. . . . Its legitimate concern is with but two matters: first, freedom; second, justice.

This was Mr. Jefferson's notion of the state's part in bringing about an ideal social order. All his life was devoted to the doctrine that the state should never venture into the sphere of positive regulation. Its only intervention upon the individual should be the negative one of forbidding the exercise of rights in any way that interferes with the free exercise of the rights of others. According to this idea, one could see that the unhappiness and enervation which I was everywhere observing as due to state action were due to state action entirely outside the state's proper sphere. They were due to the state's not minding its own business but making a series of progressive encroachments on the individual's business. They were due to the state's repeated excursions out of the realm of negative coercion into the realm of positive coercion.

. . .

By way of consequence, two things are noticeable. The first one is that whatever the state has accomplished outside its own proper field has been done poorly and expensively. This is an old story, and I shall not dwell upon it. No complaint is more common, and none better founded, than the complaint against officialism's inefficiency and extravagance. Every informed person who is at the same time disinterested is aware—often by harassing experience—that as compared with the administration of private enterprise, bureaucratic administration is notoriously and flagrantly slow, costly, inefficient, improvident, unadaptive, unintelligent, and that it tends directly to become corrupt. . . .

The second noticeable consequence of the state's activity in everybody's business but its own is that its own business is monstrously neglected. According to our official formula expressed in the Declaration, as I have said, the state's business is, first, with freedom; second, with justice. In the countries I visited, freedom and justice were in a very dilapidated condition; and the striking thing was that the state not only showed complete indifference to their breakdown, but appeared to be doing everything it could to break them down still further. . . . Every few days brought out some new and arbitrary confiscation of individual rights. Labor was progressively confiscated, capital was progressively confiscated, even speech and opinion were progressively confiscated; and naturally, in the course of this procedure anything like freedom and justice was ignored.

In short, I thought the people might fairly be said to be living for the state. The state's fiscal exactions, necessary to support its incursions into everybody's business but its own, were so great that their payment represented the confiscation of an unconscionable amount of the individual's labor and capital. Its positive regulations and coercions were so many, so inquisitorial, and their points of incidence upon the individual were so various, as to confiscate an unconscionable amount of his time and attention. . . . Not daily but hourly, in the course of my travels, there occurred to me Mr. Henry L. Mencken's blunt characterization of the state as "the common enemy of all honest, industrious, and decent men."

So indeed it seemed. Putting the case in plain language, the individual was living in a condition of servitude to the state. The fact that he "furnished the means by which he suffered"—that he was a member of a nominally sovereign body—made his condition none the less one of servitude. Slavery is slavery whether it be voluntary or involuntary, nor is its character at all altered by the nature of the agency that exercises it. A man is in slavery when all his rights lie at the arbitrary discretion of some agency other than himself; when his life, liberty, property, and the whole direction of his activities are liable to arbitrary and irresponsible confiscation at any time—and this appeared to be the exact relation that I saw obtaining between the individual and the state.

. . .

Can any individual be happy when he is continually conscious of not being his own man? Can the pursuit of happiness be satisfactorily carried on when its object is prescribed and its course charted by an agency other than oneself? In short, is happiness compatible with a condition of servitude, whether the voluntary servitude of the "yes-than" or the involuntary servitude of the conscript? How far is happiness conditioned by character, by keeping the integrity of one's personality inviolate, by the cultivation of self-respect, dignity, independent judgment, a sense of justice; and how far is all this compatible with membership in a conscript society? . . .

What I have seen since I landed has made me think it is high time for Americans to wake up to what the state is doing, and ask themselves a few plain questions about it. There are plenty of examples to show what a conscript society is like—well, do they want to live in one? There are plenty of examples to show what sort of people a conscript society breeds—is that the sort of people they want to be? Do they like the idea of a slave-status with a coercive and militant state as their owner? If they do, I should say they are getting what they want about as fast as is reasonably possible; and if they do not, my impression is that they had better not lose much time about being heard from.

FRANKLIN D. ROOSEVELT

FIRESIDE CHAT ON THE REORGANIZATION OF THE JUDICIARY (1937)

President Roosevelt enjoyed large Democratic majorities in Congress and strong public support, which meant that there were few obstacles to the design and implementation of his New Deal program. But this did not mean his political dominance was perfect. Notably, Roosevelt was not able to appoint any justices to the U.S. Supreme Court during his first term of office, and he inherited a Court with a slim conservative majority. In a series of cases, major features of the early New Deal were struck down as unconstitutional. After his reelection, Roosevelt moved to tame the Court. His proposed "court-packing" plan would allow the president to appoint additional justices to the Supreme Court for every current justice over the age of 70, enough to give the president an immediate, reliable majority on the Court. The proposal sparked a firestorm of controversy. Opponents of the New Deal largely sat out the debate, leaving more conservative Democrats to lead the attack on the court-packing plan. The Senate Judiciary Committee recommended against the bill, and Roosevelt eventually conceded that he did not have the votes to pass the plan. Defeat of the bill was made easier by a "switch in time" on the Court, with a swing justice offering his support for the New Deal during the debate. Shortly after the court-packing debate, the conservative justices retired and the president was able to construct a pro-New Deal majority through the normal process of filling vacancies.

Should critical public policies depend on the possible switch of one vote on the Court? Should any individual right claim be able to trump what is necessary to achieve "an enduring Nation"? Do the Justices have an obligation to "pull in unison" if the other branches have a clear electoral mandate? How independent should courts be from the democratic will?

. . .

Tonight, sitting at my desk in the White House, I make my first radio report to the people in my second term of office.

I am reminded of that evening in March, four years ago, when I made my first radio report to you. We were then in the midst of the great banking crisis.

Soon after, with the authority of the Congress, we asked the Nation to turn over all of its privately held gold, dollar for dollar, to the Government of the United States.

Today's recovery proves how right that policy was.

But when, almost two years later, it came before the Supreme Court its constitutionality was upheld only by a five-to-four vote. The change of one vote would have thrown all the affairs of this great Nation back into hopeless chaos. In effect, four Justices ruled that the right under a private contract to exact a pound of flesh was more sacred than the main objectives of the Constitution to establish an enduring Nation.

In 1933 you and I knew that we must never let our economic system get completely out of joint again—that we could not afford to take the risk of another great depression.

We also became convinced that the only way to avoid a repetition of those dark days was to have a government with power to prevent and to cure the abuses and the inequalities which had thrown that system out of joint.

. . .

If we learned anything from the depression we will not allow ourselves to run around in new circles of futile discussion and debate, always postponing the day of decision.

The American people have learned from the depression. For in the last three national elections an overwhelming majority of them voted a mandate that the Congress and the President begin the task of providing that protection—not after long years of debate, but now.

The Courts, however, have cast doubts on the ability of the elected Congress to protect us against catastrophe by meeting squarely our modern social and economic conditions.

. . .

Last Thursday I described the American form of Government as a three horse team provided by the Constitution to the American people so that their field might be plowed. The three horses are, of course, the three branches of government—the Congress, the Executive and the Courts. Two of the horses are pulling in unison today; the third is not. Those who have intimated that the President of the United States is trying to drive that team, overlook the simple fact that the President, as Chief Executive, is himself one of the three horses.

It is the American people themselves who are in the driver's seat. It is the American people themselves who want the furrow plowed.

It is the American people themselves who expect the third horse to pull in unison with the other two.

I hope that you have re-read the Constitution of the United States in these past few weeks. Like the Bible, it ought to be read again and again.

It is an easy document to understand when you remember that it was called into being because the Articles of Confederation under which the original thirteen States tried to operate after the Revolution showed the need of a National Government with power enough to handle national problems. In its Preamble, the Constitution states that it was intended to form a more perfect Union and promote the general welfare; and the powers given to the Congress to carry out those purposes can be best described by saying that they were all the powers needed to meet each and every problem which then had a national character and which could not be met by merely local action.

But the framers went further. Having in mind that in succeeding generations many other problems then undreamed of would become national problems, they gave to the Congress the ample broad powers "to levy taxes . . . and provide for the common defense and general welfare of the United States."

That, my friends, is what I honestly believe to have been the clear and underlying purpose of the patriots who wrote a Federal Constitution to create a National Government with national power, intended as they said, "to form a more perfect union for ourselves and our posterity."

. . .

But since the rise of the modern movement for social and economic progress through legislation, the Court has more and more often and more and more boldly asserted a power to veto laws passed by the Congress and State Legislatures in complete disregard of this original limitation [that the judiciary should presume in favor of a statute's validity until its violation of the Constitution is proved beyond all reasonable doubt].

In the last four years the sound rule of giving statutes the benefit of all reasonable doubt has been cast aside. The Court has been acting not as a judicial body, but as a policy-making body.

When the Congress has sought to stabilize national agriculture, to improve the conditions of labor, to safeguard business against unfair competition, to protect our national resources, and in many other ways, to serve our clearly national needs, the majority of the Court has been assuming the power to pass on the wisdom of these Acts of the Congress—and to approve or disapprove the public policy written into these laws.

That is not only my accusation. It is the accusation of most distinguished Justices of the present Supreme Court. . . .

. . .

In the face of these dissenting opinions, there is no basis for the claim made by some members of the Court that something in the Constitution has compelled them regretfully to thwart the will of the people.

In the face of such dissenting opinions, it is perfectly clear, that as Chief Justice Hughes has said: "We are under a Constitution, but the Constitution is what the Judges say it is."

The Court in addition to the proper use of its judicial functions has improperly set itself up as a third House of the Congress—a super-legislature, as one of the justices has called it—reading into the Constitution words and implications which are not there, and which were never intended to be there.

We have, therefore, reached the point as a Nation where we must take action to save the Constitution from the Court and the Court from itself. We must find a way to take an appeal from the Supreme Court to the Constitution itself. We want a Supreme Court which will do justice under the Constitution—not over it. In our Courts we want a government of laws and not of men.

I want—as all Americans want—an independent judiciary as proposed by the framers of the Constitution. That means a Supreme Court that will enforce the Constitution as written—that will refuse to amend the Constitution by the arbitrary exercise of judicial power—amendment by judicial say-so. It does not mean a judiciary so independent that it can deny the existence of facts universally recognized.

How then could we proceed to perform the mandate given us? It was said in last year's Democratic platform, "If these problems cannot be effectively solved within the Constitution, we shall seek such clarifying amendment as will assure the power to enact those laws, adequately to regulate commerce, protect public health and safety, and safeguard economic security." In other words, we said we would seek an amendment only if every other possible means by legislation were to fail.

When I commenced to review the situation with the problem squarely before me, I came by a process of elimination to the conclusion that, short of amendments, the only method which was clearly constitutional, and would at the same time carry out other much needed reforms, was to infuse new blood into all our Courts. We must have men worthy and equipped to carry out impartial justice. But, at the same time, we must have Judges who will bring to the Courts a present-day sense of the Constitution—Judges who will retain in the Courts the judicial functions of a court, and reject the legislative powers which the courts have today assumed.

In forty-five out of the forty-eight States of the Union, Judges are chosen not for life but for a period of years. In many States Judges must retire at the age of seventy. Congress has provided financial security by offering life pensions at full pay for Federal Judges on all Courts who are willing to retire at seventy. . . .

What is my proposal? It is simply this: whenever a Judge or Justice of any Federal Court has reached the age of seventy and does not avail himself of the opportunity to retire on a pension, a new member shall be appointed by the President then in office, with the approval, as required by the Constitution, of the Senate of the United States.

That plan has two chief purposes. By bringing into the judicial system a steady and continuing stream of new and younger blood, I hope, first, to make the administration of all Federal justice speedier and, therefore, less costly; secondly, to bring to the decision of social and economic problems younger men who have had personal experience and contact with modern facts and circumstances under which average men have to live and work. This plan will save our national Constitution from hardening of the judicial arteries.

. . .

There is nothing novel or radical about this idea. It seeks to maintain the Federal bench in full vigor. It has been discussed and approved by many persons of high authority ever since a similar proposal passed the House of Representatives in 1869.

. . .

Those opposing this plan have sought to arouse prejudice and fear by crying that I am seeking to "pack" the Supreme Court and that a baneful precedent will be established.

What do they mean by the words "packing the Court"?

Let me answer this question with a bluntness that will end all honest misunderstanding of my purposes.

If by that phrase "packing the Court" it is charged that I wish to place on the bench spineless puppets who would disregard the law and would decide specific cases as I wished them to be decided, I make this answer: that no President fit for his office would appoint, and no Senate of honorable men fit for their office would confirm, that kind of appointees to the Supreme Court.

But if by that phrase the charge is made that I would appoint and the Senate would confirm Justices worthy to sit beside present members of the Court who understand those modern conditions, that I will appoint Justices who will not undertake to override the judgment of the Congress on legislative policy, that I will appoint Justices who will act as Justices and not as legislators—if the appointment of such Justices can be called "packing the Courts," then I say that I and with me the vast majority of the American people favor doing just that thing—now.

Is it a dangerous precedent for the Congress to change the number of the Justices? The Congress has always had, and will have, that power. The number of Justices has been changed several times before, in the Administrations of John Adams and Thomas Jefferson—both signers of the Declaration of Independence—Andrew Jackson, Abraham Lincoln and Ulysses S. Grant.

I suggest only the addition of Justices to the bench in accordance with a clearly defined principle relating to a clearly defined age limit. Fundamentally, if in the future, America cannot trust the Congress it elects to refrain from abuse of our Constitutional usages, democracy will have failed far beyond the importance to it of any kind of precedent concerning the Judiciary.

. . .

. . . Our difficulty with the Court today rises not from the Court as an institution but from human beings within it. But we cannot yield our constitutional destiny to the personal judgment of a few men who, being fearful of the future, would deny us the necessary means of dealing with the present.

This plan of mine is no attack on the Court; it seeks to restore the Court to its rightful and historic place in our system of Constitutional Government and to have it resume its high task of building anew on the Constitution "a system of living law." The Court itself can best undo what the Court has done.

. . .

It would take months or years to get substantial agreement upon the type and language of an amendment. It would take months and years thereafter to get a two-thirds majority in favor of that amendment in both Houses of the Congress.

Then would come the long course of ratification by three-fourths of all the States. No amendment which any powerful economic interests or the leaders of any powerful political party have had reason to oppose has ever been ratified within anything like a reasonable time. And thirteen States which contain only five percent of the voting population can block ratification even though the thirty-five States with ninety-five percent of the population are in favor of it.

. . .

And remember one thing more. Even if an amendment were passed, and even if in the years to come it were to be ratified, its meaning would depend upon the kind of Justices who would be sitting on the Supreme Court bench. An amendment, like the rest of the Constitution, is what the Justices say it is rather than what its framers or you might hope it is.

. . .

During the past half century the balance of power between the three great branches of the Federal Government, has been tipped out of balance by the Courts in direct contradiction of the high purposes of the framers of the Constitution. It is my purpose to restore that balance. You who know me will accept my solemn assurance that in a world in which democracy is under attack, I seek to make American democracy succeed. You and I will do our part.

III. CITIZENSHIP AND COMMUNITY

Major Developments

- Ascendance of a reform liberalism
- Acceptance of government obligation to provide for material security
- Debate over how to reconcile constitutional stability with political change

In accepting the 1932 Democratic Party nomination for the presidency, Franklin Roosevelt promised that the voters would face a choice, not an echo. The two parties would not be offering "the same reactionary doctrine. Ours must be a party of liberal thought, of planned action, of enlightened international outlook, and of the greatest good to the greatest number of our citizens." The Democratic Party was committed to a new "moral principle: the welfare and the soundness of a Nation depend first upon what the great mass of the people wish and need; and second, whether or not they are getting it."[12] In his famous "Four Freedoms" speech, President Roosevelt included as an "essential human freedom" the "freedom from want." There were, he contended, "basic things expected by our people of their political and economic systems." They included such goods as "jobs for those who can work" and "security for those who need it."[13] The old liberalism of individualism and limited government was to give way to a new liberalism concerned with liberating the individual from want.

To accomplish this new governmental mission, adjustments would have to be made in traditional political structures and expectations about individual rights. For a variety of reasons, the Roosevelt administration preferred not to seek constitutional amendments to bring the document up to date with the president's policy initiatives. Instead the New Dealers settled on an approach to constitutional interpretation that had been increasingly favored by Progressives and Legal Realists in the early twentieth century, the celebration of a "living constitution." Princeton constitutional scholar Edward S. Corwin, a former colleague of Woodrow Wilson and an advisor to Franklin Roosevelt, had long argued that "judges make law" and did so according to their own political inclinations and biases. As a result, the Constitution was best understood to be "a living statute, to be interpreted in the light of living conditions." "As a *document* the Constitution came from its framers . . . but as a *law* the Constitution comes from and derives all its force from the people of the United States of this day and hour."[14] Max Lerner, the editor of *The Nation* magazine, drew the natural conclusion: the Constitution was little more than a "totem" and "fetish." The Constitution was something on which citizens could "fix their emotions" and use to help bind their fractious community together, but it could not be understood to be a functional legislative device with specific binding content.[15] The New Deal made itself felt on the Constitution not by changing the text of the document, but by changing the judges and how they approached that text.

12 Franklin D. Roosevelt, "Address Accepting the Presidential Nomination at the Democratic National Convention in Chicago, July 2, 1932," in *The Public Papers and Addresses of Franklin D. Roosevelt*, ed. Samuel I. Rosenman, vol. 1 (New York: Random House, 1938), 657.

13 Franklin D. Roosevelt, "Annual Message to Congress on the State of the Union, January 6, 1941," in in *The Public Papers and Addresses of Franklin D. Roosevelt*, ed. Samuel I. Rosenman, vol. 10 (New York: Random House, 1938), 671.

14 Edward S. Corwin, "Constitution v. Constitutional Theory," *American Political Science Review* 19 (1925): 298, 303, 302.

15 Max Lerner, "Constitution and Court as Symbols," *Yale Law Journal* 46 (1937): 1294.

JOHN DEWEY

LIBERALISM AND SOCIAL ACTION (1935)

John Dewey established his philosophical and political reputation during the Progressive Era. By the time of the New Deal, he was a respected public figure and an influential voice on the left. Dewey himself, however, was more pessimistic about the future of capitalism in the 1930s than were most of the New Dealers. From his perspective, the Roosevelt administration was just "messing about" rather than launching the bold reconstruction of American society that was needed.[16] He spent the 1930s trying to find a position between New Deal reform and socialist revolution (which he still thought was too extreme). He had himself voted for Norman Thomas, the Socialist Party candidate, in the 1932 elections and hoped for the rise of a competitive new party to the left of Roosevelt's Democratic Party. He was not terribly clear about what program he wanted such a party to pursue, but his writings in the 1930s emphasized that the future of liberalism should focus on human "liberation" so that each person could fully realize his or her own individual "capacities." The "laissez-faire liberalism" that called for leaving individuals alone was "played out." The "humanitarian" liberalism of the future would focus instead on "the feeling that man is his brother's keeper."[17]

What does Dewey see as the challenges facing society? Why is liberalism the right approach to addressing those challenges? How should individuals ideally fit into society? How are conflicting interests to be resolved in a liberal community?

. . .

. . . Liberalism is committed to an end that is at once enduring and flexible: the liberation of individuals so that realization of their capacities may be the law of their life. It is committed to the use of freed intelligence as the method of directing change. In any case, civilization is faced with the problem of uniting the changes that are going on into a coherent pattern of social organization. The liberal spirit is marked by its own picture of that pattern that is required: a social organization that will make possible effective liberty and opportunity for personal growth in mind and spirit in all individuals. Its present need is recognition that established material security is a prerequisite of the ends which it cherishes, so that, the basis of life being secure, individuals may actively share in their wealth of cultural resources that now exist and may contribute, each in his own way, to their further enrichment.

. . .

. . . Civilization existed for most of human history in a state of scarcity in the material basis for a humane life. Our ways of thinking, planning and working have been attuned to this fact. Thanks to science and technology we now live in an age of potential plenty. The immediate effect of the emergence of the new possibility was simply to stimulate, to a point of incredible exaggeration, the striving for the material resources, called wealth, opened to men in the new vista. . . . The habits of desire and effort that were bred in the age of scarcity do not readily subordinate themselves and take the place of the matter-of-course routine that becomes appropriate to them when machines and impersonal power have the capacity to liberate man from bondage to the strivings that were once needed to make secure his physical basis. . . .

. . . The system that goes by the name of capitalism is a systematic manifestation of desires and purposes built up in an age of ever threatening want and now carried over into a time of ever increasing potential plenty. The conditions that generate insecurity for the many no longer spring from nature. They are

16 Alan Ryan, *John Dewey and the High Tide of American Liberalism* (New York: W.W. Norton, 1995), 246–247.

17 John Dewey, "The Future of Liberalism, or the Democratic Way of Change," in *The Later Works of John Dewey, 1925–1953*, ed. Jo Ann Boydston (Carbondale: Southern Illinois University Press, 1987), 282, 287.

found in institutions and arrangements that are within deliberate human control. Surely this change marks one of the greatest revolutions in that has taken place in all human history. . . .

. . .

[L]iberalism must now become radical, meaning by "radical" perception of the necessity of thoroughgoing activity to bring the changes to pass. For the gulf between what the actual situation makes possible and the actual state itself is so great that it cannot be bridged by piecemeal policies undertaken *ad hoc*. . . .

. . . It is foolish to regard the political state as the only agency now endowed with coercive power. Its exercise of this power is pale in contrast with that exercised by concentrated and organized property interests.

. . .

The argument drawn from past history that radical change must be effected by means of class struggle, culminating in open war, fails to discriminate between the two forces, one active, the other resistant and deflecting, that have produced the social scene in which we live. The active force is, as I have said, scientific method and technological application. The opposite force is that of older institutions and the habits that have grown up around them. . . .

. . .

. . . Of course, there are conflicting interests; otherwise there would be no social problems. The problem under discussion is precisely how conflicting claims are to be settled in the interest of the widest possible contribution to the interests of all—or at least of the great majority. The method of democracy—inasfar as it is that of organized intelligence—is to bring these conflicts out into the open where their special claims can be seen and appraised, where they can be discussed and judged in the light of more inclusive interest than are represented by either of them separately. . . . But what generates violent strife is failure to bring the conflict into the light of intelligence where the conflicting interests can be adjudicated in behalf of the interest of the great majority. . . .

. . .

The final argument in behalf of the use of intelligence is that as are the means used so are the actual ends achieved. . . . I know of no greater fallacy than the claim of those who hold to the dogma of the necessity of brute force that this use will be the method of calling genuine democracy into existence. . . . To profess democracy as an ultimate ideal and the suppression of democracy as a means to the ideal may be possible in a country that has never known even rudimentary democracy, but when professed in a country that has anything of a genuine democratic spirit in its traditions, it signifies desire for possession and retention of power by a class. . . . The one exception—and that apparent rather than real—to dependence upon organized intelligence as the method for directing social change is found when society through an authorized majority has entered upon the path of social experimentation leading to great social change, and a minority refuses by force to permit the method of intelligent action to go into effect. Then force may be intelligently employed to subdue and disarm the recalcitrant minority.

. . . The alternatives are continuation of drift with attendant improvisations to meet special emergencies; dependence upon violence; dependence upon socially organized intelligence. The first two alternatives, however, are not mutually exclusive, for if things are allowed to drift the result may be some sort of social change effected by the use of force, whether so planned or not. Upon the whole, the recent policy of liberalism has been to further "social legislation"; that is, measures which add performance of social services to the older functions of government. . . . It marks a decided move away from *laissez faire* liberalism, and has considerable importance in educating the public mind to a realization of the possibilities of organized social control. It has helped to develop some of the techniques that in any case will be needed in a socialized economy. But the cause of liberalism will be lost for a considerable period if it is not prepared to go further and socialize the forces of production, now at hand, so that the liberty of individuals will be supported by the very structure of economic organization.

. . .

Since liberation of the capacities of individuals for free, self-initiated expression is an essential part of the creed of liberalism, liberalism that is sincere must will the means that condition the achieving of its ends. . . . The eclipse of liberalism is due to the fact that it has not faced the alternatives and adopted the means upon which realization of its professed aims depends. Liberalism can be true to its ideals only as it takes the course that leads to their attainment. The notion that organized social control of economic forces lies outside the historic path of liberalism shows that liberalism is still impeded by remnants of its earlier laissez faire phase, with its opposition of society and the individual. . . . Earlier liberalism regarded the separate and competing economic action of individuals as the means to social well-being as the end. We must reverse the perspective and see that socialized economy is the means of free individual development as the end.

. . .

THURMAN ARNOLD

THE SYMBOLS OF GOVERNMENT (1935)

Thurman Arnold was raised on a Wyoming ranch at the turn of the twentieth century. After graduating from Harvard Law School in 1914, his legal career was interrupted by military service during World War I. He dabbled in Wyoming state politics as a Progressive Democrat before being pulled into legal academia, first as dean of West Virginia University law school and then as a faculty member at Yale. At Yale, he became an important contributor to the developing school of Legal Realism, which emphasized the indeterminacy of law. During the New Deal, he helped remake the Justice Department's approach to antitrust law, and later accepted an appointment to the influential U.S. Court of Appeals for the District of Columbia. His judicial tenure was brief, however, and in 1946 he established one of the most powerful Washington law firms of the mid-twentieth century. As a scholar, he highlighted the ways in which the "symbols of government" and the rule of law obscured the fallible and emotional humans who actually made political decisions that really governed society and called for government officials to be pragmatic problem solvers unconstrained by broader ideological commitments.

What does Arnold think causes people to lose faith in government? What role does he think ideology plays in government? Why does he compare governing to running an insane asylum? Is politics all just the obfuscation of the reality of governing? What is the relation between political leaders and ordinary citizens? Are political ideals meaningful? George H. W. Bush once dismissed "the vision thing" and the concern with larger themes that might organize a political agenda and policy proposals; should political leaders have a "vision"?

. . .

. . . Social institutions require faiths and dreams to give them morale. They need to escape from these faiths and dreams in order to progress. The hierarchy of governing institutions must pretend to symmetry, moral beauty, and logic in order to maintain their prestige and power. To actually govern, they must constantly violate those principles in hidden and covert ways. . . .

. . .

The present day is marked with a paralyzing lack of faith in both government institutions and their theories. The man on the street has lost confidence in the industrial feudalism which formerly gave him a job. The lack of faith is called radicalism. The businessman has lost faith that the National Government will serve as a buffer between him and the conflicting interests attacking his power. This is called a failure of business confidence. . . . Hopeful people today wave the flag of national power. Timid people wave the Constitution. Neither group is quite coherent as to specific objectives, but both feel better because of these respective ceremonies.

As a matter of fact the lack of faith in the future is not caused by specific legislation or the advocacy of specific objectives. It is the failure of practical institutions to function which has raised doubts in the hearts of conservatives. . . . Today we see before us both fascism and communism in actual operation, with their governments growing in power. Economic law no longer prevents such types of control. The only bulwark against change is the Constitution. But with the disappearance of the economic certainties, the actual words of the Constitution no longer appear like a bulwark. There is no settled faith in our form of government as the only workable type. Therefore the unified drive which accompanies settled faith is lacking. When belief in current symbols wavers, social unrest grows.

. . .

From a humanitarian point of view the best government is that which we find in an insane asylum.

In such a government the physicians in charge do not separate the ideas of the insane into any separate sciences such as law, economics, and sociology; nor then instruct the insane in the intricacies of these three sciences. Nor do they argue with the insane as to the soundness or unsoundness of their ideas. Their aim is to make the inmates of the asylum as comfortable as possible, regardless of their respective moral deserts. In this they are limited only by the facilities of the institution. . . . It is equally possible to adopt a point of view toward government where ideas are considered only in the light of their effect on conduct. . . .

The advantages of such a theory for purposes of thinking about government are that we escape the troublesome assumption that the human race is rational. We need not condemn policies which contradict each other solely on the ground that the action of government must be logically consistent. . . . The theory eliminates from our thinking the moral ideals which hamper us wherever a governmental institution takes practical action—ideals which create the necessity of a *sub rosa* political machine. It frees us from the necessity of worrying about names, and arguing about the respective merits of communism, fascism, or capitalism—arguments which have the unfortunate effect of creating phobias against practical and humanitarian measures. Such phobias are constantly preventing the day-to-day practical appraisals of a situation which is the essence of practical government.

. . .

. . . [T]he phobias against common-sense methods in this country added to the spiritual confusion. This confusion impeded organization. While Russia increased its industrial production from 1929 to date by 139 percent, our industrial income fell by almost one third in spite of a more efficient machine civilization. Yet it should be remembered that this same confusion prevented the intolerance and cruelty which follow when great people march in step to a single ideal.

In the confusion of present events we can observe that when societies become devoted to a single ideal—whatever it is—and pursue it with consistency and logic, marvels of human cooperation are accomplished. But there is a price to be paid in spiritual instability which sooner or later brings its reaction. . . .

. . .

And herein lies the greatness of the law. It preserves the appearance of unity while tolerating and enforcing ideals which run in all sorts of opposing directions. The judicial system loses its prestige and influence wherever great, popular, and single-minded ideals sweep a people off its feet. It rises in power and prestige when society again becomes able to tolerate contradictory ideals. . . .

Therefore the law is a barometer of the spiritual contentment of a people; and we can observe the rise and fall of that type of stability by observing the rise and fall and fall of the courts.

. . .

If by some magic we could convince the American people that the distribution of the equivalent of $200 in goods each month to every person was as important an ideal as winning a war, we would immediately turn every wheel in the country—not fearfully and reluctantly but with enthusiasm. . . . No one believes any longer that nations cannot afford to fight wars. They can fight so long as their goods last. In the same way they could distribute goods in peacetime so long as these goods lasted, if only the military spirit could be transferred to something constructive.

The question is whether the science of government, by understanding the function of symbols and ideals, can make men as enthusiastic about sensible things as they have been in the past about mad and destructive enterprises. There is no doubt about the desire of that great class of intelligent and conservative persons that production and distribution of comforts should be carried on at maximum efficiency and capacity. The chief problem is to rid ourselves of the paralyzing fears that if this be attempted in a direct and sensible way, by the type of organization which would work in a military emergency, it would lead to all sorts of indescribable dangers. . . .

. . .

The question which confronts the student of government is what kind of a social philosophy is required to make men free to experiment—to give them an understanding of the world, undistorted by the thick prismatic lenses of principles and ideals, and at the same time undamaged by the disillusionment which comes from the abandonment of ideals. . . .

. . .

The fundamental social axiom of the past was that man by working only for his personal profit, in the long run produced the most ideal social results. . . .

We suggest that the formula of the new social philosophy which is appearing may be the fundamental axiom that man works only for his fellow man. . . .

. . .

. . . The hope for this new humanitarian economic creed in America must be based on the belief that there exists a huge reservoir of technical skill, capable of running a great productive machine with new energy and efficiency, provided that social ideals can be accepted which permit this reservoir to be tapped.

. . .

. . . Fanatical devotion to principle on the part of the public still compels intelligent leaders to commit themselves, for political reasons, to all sorts of disorderly nonsense. So long as the public hold preconceived faiths about the fundamental principles of government, they will persecute and denounce new ideas in that science, and orators will prevail over technicians. So long as preconceived principles are considered more important than practical results, the practical alleviation of human distress and the distribution of available comforts will be paralyzed. . . .

IV. EQUALITY AND STATUS

Major Developments

- Growth of more militant civil rights movement
- Uncertainty over place of civil rights on political agenda

With Franklin Roosevelt's lengthy service as president, the Democrat Party finally succeeded in attracting a large segment of African-American voters. Over the course of the early twentieth century, a large number of blacks had moved from the rural South (where they were often excluded from the polls) to the urban North (where they were often able to freely vote). African-Americans had a long history of support for the Republican Party, which had not only fought for emancipation but had often been more friendly to their interests in the decades after Reconstruction. The Great Depression had shaken those partisan loyalties for blacks as they had for many whites. The Roosevelt administration brought in African-Americans for government offices in ways that previous Democratic administrations had not and aggressively courted their votes. What the New Deal did not offer was much progress on racially specific issues. The Southern Democrats, still the party of Jim Crow, remained a critical part of the New Deal coalition and Democratic congressional majorities as well. Not only did they draw the line against civil rights legislation, but they worked to exclude blacks from many New Deal benefits (agricultural and domestic labor did not build eligibility for social security benefits, for example).[18] President Roosevelt had little inclination to invest political capital in black civil rights at the potential cost of congressional support for his economic agenda.

If black civil rights remained off the national political agenda during the New Deal era, momentum was building for more aggressive action. The northern liberals who came to power with the New Deal increasingly were interested in black civil rights, which translated to, among other things, the appointment of favorably inclined federal judges. By the 1940s, Democratic politicians were starting to make calculations about the importance of African-Americans as a swing vote in the North and the need to do enough to keep them mobilized behind Democratic candidates. A new generation of black activists rose who were took their cues from relatively militant leaders like W. E. B. Du Bois. The economic and social dislocations of the Great Depression and World War II encouraged blacks to make more demands and gave them more leverage to have their demands met. The Swedish economist Gunnar Myrdal worked with black and white scholars in the United States to produce a landmark 1944 study of race in America, *An American Dilemma*, and President Harry Truman himself helped persuade V. O. Key, a native Texan and rapidly rising

---

18 For a defense of the thesis that the Southern Democrats limited the extension of New Deal policies to predominantly black industries, see Robert C. Lieberman, *Shifting the Color Line* (Cambridge, MA: Harvard University Press, 1998). For a critique emphasizing the lack of administrative capacity to incorporate those types of workers, see Larry DeWitt, "The Decision to Exclude Agricultural and Domestic Workers from the 1935 Social Security Act," *Social Security Bulletin* 70 (2010): 49.

political scientist, to produce the seminal 1949 study, *Southern Politics in State and Nation,* which began with the simple but bold observation that "the politics of the South revolves around the position of the Negro."[19] Truman was willing to shine a spotlight on racial issues and take policy steps such as the desegregation of the military. If the gains were still limited, a debate over the substance of black civil rights and the strategies for realizing them was rapidly developing.

19 V. O. Key, *Southern Politics in State and Nation* (New York: Alfred A. Knopf, 1949), 7.

JAMES WELDON JOHNSON

NEGRO AMERICANS, WHAT NOW? (1934)

James Weldon Johnson grew up in the black middle class of postbellum Florida. At the end of the nineteenth century, he briefly served as the principal of the African-American school in his hometown, but he soon abandoned that career for a diverse set of interests ranging from songwriting and poetry to serving as a diplomat under Roosevelt and Taft. He was a leader in the early NAACP. The younger radical sociologist E. Franklin Frazier paid Johnson the backhanded compliment of recognizing his 1934 book as exemplifying the thinking of the established group of black leaders of the day and admitted that Johnson "probably enjoys more prestige among Negroes and more authority among the whites as a spokesman for his race than any other Negro in America today." In short, Frazier thought Johnson was guilty of "intellectual 'Uncle Tomism'" for his failure to take seriously the possibility of more revolutionary action.[20]

What does Johnson think is the most realistic option for improving the situation of African-Americans? Why? Is "realistic" the most important consideration when considering strategies for moving forward? Does he underestimate the benefits or viability of other options? What obstacles does white racism put in the way of black progress? Why does Johnson not embrace Booker T. Washington's path of isolation?

The world today is in a state of semi-chaos. We Negro Americans as a part of the world are affected by that state. We are affected by it still more vitally as a special group. We are not so sanguine about our course and our goal as we were a decade ago. We are floundering. We are casting about for ways of meeting the situation, both as Americans and as Negroes. In this casting about we have discovered and rediscovered a number of ways to which we have given more or less consideration. Let us see if we cannot by elimination reduce confusion and narrow down the limits of choice to what might be shown to be the one sound and wise line to follow.

EXODUS

Exodus has for generations been recurrently suggested as a method for solving the race problem. At the present time there is being fomented by some person or persons in Chicago a plan based on the idea of colonization. The plan calls for the setting aside of a state or territory of the United States exclusively for Negro Americans.

. . .

A century and a quarter ago deportation of the free Negroes might have been feasible; a half century later *that* was not a practicable undertaking; today the deportation or exodus of the Negro American population is an utter impossibility. . . .

We may cross out exodus as a possible solution. We and the white people may as well make up our minds definitely that we, the same as they, are in this country to stay. . . .

PHYSICAL FORCE

Our history in the United States records a half-dozen major and a score of minor efforts at insurrection during the period of slavery. This, if they heard it, would be news to that big majority of people who believe that we have gone through three centuries of oppression without once thinking in terms of rebellion or lifting a finger in revolt. Even now there come times when we think in terms of physical force.

We must condemn physical force and banish it from our minds. But I do not condemn it on any moral or pacific grounds. The resort to force remains and will doubtless always remain the rightful recourse of oppressed peoples. Our own country was

20 E. Franklin Frazier, *"Quo Vadis?" Journal of Negro Education* 4 (1935): 130.

established upon that right. I condemn physical force because I know that in our case it would be futile.

We would be justified in taking up arms or anything we could lay hands on and fighting for the common rights we are entitled to and denied, if we had a chance to win. But I know and we all know there is not a chance. . . .

THE REVOLUTION

Those who look to the coming revolution (and why they should believe it is coming in the United States I see no good reason; it is obvious that the United States is going through revolutionary economic and social changes, but the changes do not point to Communism) seem to think it will work some instantaneous and magical transformation of our condition. It appears to me that this infinite faith in Communism indicates extreme *naïvete*. Those who hold this faith point to Soviet Russia as a land in which there is absolutely no prejudice against Negroes. This is an unquestioned fact, but I can see no grounds on which to attribute it to Communism. There was no prejudice against Negroes in Tsarist Russia. . . .

I hold no brief against Communism as a theory of government. I hope that the Soviet experiment will be completely successful. I know that it is having a strong influence on the principal nations of the world, including our own. I think it is a high sign of progress that Negro Americans have reached the point of holding independent opinions on political and social questions. What I am trying to do is to sound a warning against childlike trust in the miraculous efficacy on our racial situation of any economic or social theory of government—Communism or Socialism or Fascism or Nazism or New Deals. The solving of our situation depends principally upon an evolutionary process along two parallel lines: our own development and the bringing about of a change in the national attitude toward us. That outcome will require our persevering effort under whatever form the government might take on.

. . .

ISOLATION OR INTEGRATION?

By this process of elimination we have reduced choices of a way out to two. There remain, on the one hand, the continuation of our efforts to achieve integration and, on the other hand, an acknowledgment of our isolation and the determination to accept and make the best of it.

. . .

All along, however, majority opinion has held that the only salvation worth achieving lies in the making of the race into a component part of the nation, with all the common rights and privileges, as well as duties, of citizenship. This attitude has been basic in the general policy of the race—so far as it has had a general policy—for generations, the policy of striving zealously to gain full admission to citizenship and guarding jealously each single advance made.

. . .

The question is not one to be lightly brushed aside. Those who stand for making the race into a self-sufficient unit point out that after years of effort we are still Jim-Crowed, discriminated against, segregated, and lynched; that we are still shut out from industry, barred from the main avenues of business, and cut off from free participation in national life. They point out that in some sections of the country we have not even secured equal protection of life and property under the laws. They declare that entrance of the Negro into full citizenship is as distant as it was seventy years ago. And they ask: What is the Negro to do? Give himself over to wishful thinking? Stand shooting at the stars with a popgun? Is it not rather a duty and a necessity for him to face the facts of his condition and environment, to acknowledge them as facts, and to make the best use of them that he can? These are questions which the thinkers of the race should strive to sift clearly.

To this writer it seems that one of the first results of clear thinking is a realization of the truth that the making of the race into a self-sustaining unit, the creating of an *imperium in imperio*, does not offer an easier or more feasible task than does the task of achieving full citizenship. Such an *imperium* would have to rest upon a basis of separate group economic independence, and the trend of all present-day forces is against the building of any foundation of that sort.

Clear thinking reveals that the outcome of voluntary isolation would be a permanent secondary status, so acknowledged by the race. Such a status would, it is true, solve some phases of the race question. It would smooth away a good part of the friction and bring about a certain protection and security. The status of slavery carried some advantages of that sort. But I do not believe we shall ever be willing to pay such a price for security and peace.

. . .

Certainly, the isolationists are stating a truth when they contend that we should not, ostrich-like, hide our heads in the sand, making believe that prejudice is non-existent; but in so doing they are apostles of the obvious. Calling upon the race to realize that prejudice is an actuality is a needless effort; it is placing emphasis on what has never been questioned. The danger for us does not lie in a possible failure to acknowledge prejudice as a reality, but in acknowledging it too fully. We cannot ignore the fact that we are segregated, no matter how much we might wish to do so; and the smallest amount of common sense forces us to extract as much good from the situation as there is in it. Any degree of sagacity forces us at the same time to use all our powers to abolish imposed segregation; for it is an evil *per se* and the negation of equality either of opportunity or of awards. We should by all means make our schools and institutions as excellent as we can possibly make them—and by that very act we reduce the certainty that they will forever remain schools and institutions "for Negroes only." We should make our business enterprises and other strictly group under-takings as successful as we can possibly make them. We should gather all the strength and experience we can from imposed segregation. But any good we are able to derive from the system we should consider as a means, not an end. The strength and experience we gain from it should be applied to the objective of *entering into,* not *staying out of* the body politic.

Clear thinking shows, too, that, as bad as conditions are, they are not as bad as they are declared to be by discouraged and pessimistic isolationists. To say that in the past two generations or more Negro Americans have not advanced a single step toward a fuller share in the commonwealth becomes, in the light of easily ascertainable facts, an absurdity. Only the shortest view of the situation gives color of truth to such a statement; any reasonably long view proves it to be utterly false.

With our choice narrowed down to these two courses, wisdom and far-sightedness and possibility of achievement demand that we follow the line that leads to equal rights for us, based on the common terms and conditions under which they are accorded and guaranteed to the other groups that go into the making up of our national family. It is not necessary for our advancement that such an outcome should suddenly eradicate all prejudices. It would not, of course, have the effect of suddenly doing away with voluntary grouping in religious and secular organizations or of abolishing group enterprises—for example, Negro newspapers. The accordance of full civil and political rights has not in the case of the greater number of groups in the nation had that effect. Nevertheless, it would be an immeasurable step forward, and would place us where we had a fair start with the other American groups. More than that we do not need to ask.

. . .

RALPH J. BUNCHE

A CRITICAL ANALYSIS OF THE TACTICS AND PROGRAMS OF MINORITY GROUPS (1935)

Ralph Bunche was valedictorian at his hometown University of California at Los Angeles and went on to earn a Ph.D. in political science at Harvard in 1934 while he taught at Howard University in Washington, D.C. His early work focused on racial issues, and he was often critical of the Roosevelt administration for not pursuing more radical social and economic reform. In 1939, he entered government service, eventually shifting to a senior position at the newly created United Nations in 1946, but he remained active in the domestic civil rights movement. He was awarded the Nobel Peace Prize in 1950 (the first African-American so honored) and the U.S. Medal of Freedom in 1963 for his diplomatic efforts in the Middle East.

Does Bunche see democracy as conducive to civil rights? Does he see the middle class as allies to black interests? What does he see as the challenges facing black leaders? Are the interests of African-Americans in conflict with those of whites?

J.S. Mill in his fine treatise on *Representative Government* expressed the belief that it is virtually impossible to build up a democracy out of the intermingling of racially differentiated groups of men. It may be that historical experience has indicated the error of Mill's thesis insofar as different "racial" groups among the white peoples of the world are concerned, but there is apparently much evidence to substantiate it when related to the intermixture of white and black populations in the same society. Throughout the world today, wherever whites and blacks are present in any significant numbers in the same community, democracy becomes the tool of the dominant elements in the white population in their ruthless determination to keep the blacks suppressed. . . .

The responsibility, however, rests not with the institutions of democracy, *per se*, nor in the readily accepted belief that black and white simply cannot mix amicably. . . . Recent world history points out too clearly that modern democracy, conceived in the womb of middle-class revolutions, was early put to work in support of those ruling middle-class interests of capitalistic society which fathered it. . . .

. . .

The Negro group in the United States is characterized by the conditions of easy racial identification and severe economic competition with the dominant white population. In addition, the position of the Negro in this country is conditioned by the historical fact of his ancestral slavery. . . .

The factors of race and the slavery tradition do not fully explain the perpetuation of the "race problem," however. Much of what is called prejudice against the Negro can be explained in economic terms, and in the peculiar culture of the Southern states with their large "poor-white" populations. . . .

. . .

In reality the Negro population in the United States is a minority group only in the narrowly racial sense. In every other respect it is subject to the same divisive influences impinging upon the life of every other group in the nation. Economically, the Negro, in the vast majority, is identified with the peasant and proletarian classes of the country, which are certainly not in the minority. . . .

Negro leadership, however, has traditionally put its stress on the element of race; it has attributed the plight of the Negro to a peculiar racial condition. Leaders and organizations alike have had but one end in view—the elimination of "discrimination against the race." . . . They have not realized that so long as this basic conflict in the economic interests of the white and black groups persists, and it is a perfectly natural phenomenon in a modern industrial society, neither prayer, nor logic, nor emotional or legal appeal can make much headway against the stereotyped racial attitudes and beliefs of the masses of the dominant population. . . . The most that such organizations can hope to do is to devote themselves to the correction of the more flagrant specific cases of abuse, which because of their extreme nature may exceed even a prejudiced popular approval. . . .

. . .

Perhaps the favorite method of struggle for rights employed by minority groups is the political. Through the use of the ballot and the courts strenuous efforts are put forth to gain social justice for the group. Extreme faith is placed in the ability of these instruments of democratic government to free the minority from social prescription and civic inequality. The inherent fallacy of this belief rests in the failure to appreciate the fact that the instruments of the state are merely the reflections of the political and economic ideology of the dominant group, that the political arms of the state cannot be divorced from its prevailing economic structure, whose servant it must inevitably be.

. . .

The confidence of the proponents of the political method of alleviation is based on the protection which they feel is offered all groups in the society by that sacred document the Constitution. Particularly do they swear by the Bill of Rights and its three supplements, the Thirteenth, Fourteenth and Fifteenth amendments, as a special charter of the black man's liberties. The Constitution is thus detached from the political and economic realities of American life and becomes a sort of protective angel hovering above us and keeping a constant vigil over the rights of all America's children, black and white, rich and poor, employer and employee and, like impartial justice, blinded to their differences. This view ignores the quite significant fact that the Constitution is a very flexible instrument and that, in the nature of things, it cannot be anything more than the controlling elements in the American society wish it to be. In other words, this charter of the black man's liberties can never be more than our legislatures, and, in the final analysis, our courts, wish it to be. And, what these worthy institutions wish it to be can never be more than what American public opinion wishes it to be. . . .

It follows, therefore, that the policy of civil libertarianism is circumscribed by the dominant mores of the society. . . .

It is not surprising, therefore, that assertedly militant civil-libertarian organizations like the N.A.A.C.P. should employ tactics which are progressively less militant. Such organizations, if they remain constant in their faith, are forced into a policy of conciliation with the enlightened, i.e., the ruling interests, in the dominant group. . . . [T]hey must entreat, bargain, compromise and capitulate in order to win even petty gains. . . .

. . . The Negro has had countless experiences which sufficiently establish the fact that he has rights only as this august tribunal allows them, and even these are, more often than not, illusory. It is only inadvertently that the courts, like the legislatures, fail to reflect the dominant mass opinion. It must be futile, then, to expect these agencies of government to afford the Negro protection for rights which are denied to him by the popular will. . . . In the first place, American experience affords too many proofs that laws and decisions contrary to the will of the majority cannot be enforced. In the second place, the Supreme Court can effect no revolutionary changes in the economic order, and yet the status of the Negro, as that of other groups in the society, is fundamentally fixed by the functioning and demands of that order. . . .

. . .

. . . The only hope for the improvement in the condition of the masses of any American minority group is the hope that can be held out for the betterment of the masses of the dominant group. Their basic interests are identical and so must be their programs and tactics.

A. PHILIP RANDOLPH

MARCH ON WASHINGTON KEYNOTE ADDRESS (1942)

Raised in Florida by a minister in the African Methodist Episcopal church, Asa Philip Randolph moved to New York after graduating from Bethune-Cookman College in 1911. In New York, he became a socialist and an atheist and started to work in labor organizing. He founded the Brotherhood of Sleeping Car Porters, which vaulted him into national prominence. In the 1940s, he organized the March on Washington Movement, which was designed to stage a series of mass demonstrations calling for opening the defense industry to black workers, and later broadened his goals to include desegregation of the military and his tactics to include boycotts and civil disobedience. In the 1950s, he joined his efforts with Martin Luther King and expanded his agenda to include the integration of public schools, while forming a new organization to attack racial discrimination in the labor unions.

Why does Randolph believe that the March on Washington Movement should be a blacks-only organization? What does he think should be the aim of the war effort? What is an "economic democracy"? How does Randolph think a minority can advance its goals in a democracy? What distinguishes more militant figures like Bunche or Randolph from a more conservative black activist like Johnson? To what degree do African-Americans have distinct interests from whites? What does racial equality entail? What does "citizenship" require?

. . .

We have met at an hour when the sinister shadows of war are lengthening and becoming more threatening. As one of the sections of the oppressed darker races, and representing a part of the exploited millions of the workers of the world, we are deeply concerned that the totalitarian legions of Hitler, Hirohito, and Mussolini do not batter the last bastions of democracy. We know that our fate is tied up with the fate of the democratic way of life. And so, out of the depths of our hearts, a cry goes up for the triumph of the United Nations. But we would not be honest with ourselves were we to stop with a call for a victory of arms alone. We know this is not enough. We fight that the democratic faiths, values, heritages and ideals may prevail.

Unless this war sounds the death knell to the old Anglo-American empire systems, the hapless story of which is one of exploitation for the profit and power of a monopoly capitalist economy, it will have been fought in vain. Our aim then must not only be to defeat Nazism, fascism, and militarism on the battlefield but to win the peace, for democracy, for freedom and the Brotherhood of Man without regard to his pigmentation, land of his birth or the God of his fathers.

. . .

When this war ends, the people want something more than the dispersal of equality and power among individual citizens in a liberal, political democratic system. They demand with striking comparability the dispersal of equality and power among the citizen-workers in an economic democracy that will make certain the assurance of the good life—the more abundant life—in a warless world.

. . .

Thus our feet are set in the path toward equality—economic, political and social and racial. Equality is at the heart and essence of democracy, freedom and justice. Without equality of opportunity in industry, in labor unions, schools and colleges, government, politics and before the law, without equality in social relations and in all phases of human endeavor, the Negro is certain to be consigned to an inferior status. There must be no dual standards of justice, no dual rights privileges, duties or responsibilities of citizenship. No dual forms of freedom.

. . .

But our nearer goals include the abolition of discrimination, segregation and jim-crow in the Government, the [military] and defense industries; the elimination of discriminations in hotels, restaurants, on public transportation conveyances, in educational, recreational, cultural, and amusement and entertainment places such as theaters, beaches, and so forth.

We want the full works of citizenship with no reservations. We will accept nothing less.

. . .

. . . These rights will not be given. They must be taken.

Democracy was fought for and taken from political royalists—the kings. Industrial democracy, the rights of the workers to organize and designate the representatives of their own choosing to bargain collectively is being won and taken from the economic royalists—big business.

. . . The March on Washington Movement must be opposed to partisan political commitments, religious or denominational alliances. We cannot sup with the Communists, for they rule or ruin any movement. This is their policy. Our policy must be to shun them. . . .

As to the composition of our movement. Our policy is that it be all-Negro, and pro-Negro but not anti-white, or anti-semitic or anti-labor, or anti-Catholic. The reason for this policy is that all oppressed people must assume the responsibility and take the initiative to free themselves. . . .

. . . The essential value of an all-Negro movement such as the March on Washington is that it helps to create faith by Negroes in Negroes. It develops a sense of self-reliance with Negroes depending on Negroes in vital matters. It helps to break down the slave psychology and inferiority-complex in Negroes which comes and is nourished with Negroes relying on white people for direction and support. . . .

The problem of lynching is a specialized one and Negroes must take the responsibility and initiative to solve it, because Negroes are the chief victims of it just as the workers are the victims of law wages and must act to change and raise them.

But the problem of taxation, sanitation, health, a proper school system, an efficient fire department, and crime are generalized problems. They don't only concern the workers or Jews or Negroes or Catholics, but everybody and hence it is sound and proper social strategy and policy for all of these groups in the community to form a generalized or composite movement. . . .

Therefore, while the March on Washington Movement is interested in the general problems of every community and will lend its aid to help solve them, it has as its major interest and task the liberation of the Negro people, and this is sound social economy. . . .

. . .

. . . Without this type of organization, Negroes will never develop the mass power which is the most effective weapon a minority people can wield. Witness the strategy and maneuver of the people of India with mass civil disobedience and no-cooperation and the marches to the sea to make salt. . . . The central principle of the struggle of oppressed minorities like the Negro, labor, Jews, and others is not only to develop mass demonstration maneuvers, but to repeat and continue them. The workers don't picket firms today and quit. . . . They practice the principle of repetition. This principle is the basis of education. It is the key to shaping public opinion. . . .

We must develop huge demonstrations because the world is used to big dramatic affairs. . . . Nothing little counts.

Besides, the unusual attracts . . . to put our cause into the mainstream of public opinion and focus the attention of world interests. . . .

. . .

Now, let us be unafraid. We are fighting for big stakes. Our stakes are liberty, justice, and democracy. . . This is the hour of the Negro. It is the hour of the common man. May we rise to the challenge to struggle for our rights. Come what will or may, let us never falter.

V. POLITICAL ECONOMY

Major Developments

- Debate over structural reform to economic institutions
- Debate over relief and redistribution
- Debate over future of capitalism

The New Deal era was a time of great uncertainty about the future of economic arrangements within the United States and in much of the Western world. The Great Depression posed challenges to countries around the globe, sometimes exacerbating already difficult social and economic conditions. The launch of the New Deal was accompanied by substantial debate over what the best political response to the economic situation might be. Both the political and intellectual arenas seemed unusually open to the consideration of vastly different alternatives. In contrast to much of the nineteenth century, there was little consensus about how the economic system did or should work. One option that received relatively little consideration was the possibility of essentially sustaining the economic precepts that had guided policymakers in prior decades.

The New Dealers were themselves a varied group with different ideas about how reform should proceed, and they operated within a wider intellectual and political world where an even wider range of options were being actively debated. Developments in Europe suggested some of those possibilities. The communists in the Soviet Union claimed great success in increasing economic growth and eliminating poverty in Joseph Stalin's Soviet Union. The communist example called for the central planning of the production and consumption of goods and the elimination of private ownership of the means of production or a monetary economy. The Nazi and Fascist examples nationalized some industries and actively directed the operation of others, even if property remained in private hands. In the 1930s, those arrangements were often hailed as successful economic models, even if they were accompanied by some abuses. Even reformers who were reluctant to draw directly from those models often thought that capitalism itself was unlikely to survive in anything like its current form and would necessarily evolve in the same direction.

For those most central to the New Deal, the major questions facing politics in the 1930s and 1940s revolved around two basic issues. First was the question of how much relief should be provided and what form it should take. Even for the Republicans in the early days of the Depression, some form of emergency relief for the unemployed and impoverished seemed essential. For the Democratic administration, economic assistance to individuals should become a permanent feature of the new economy. But that still left important questions as to how much assistance should be offered, in what form, to whom, and under what conditions. Second was the question of what structural reforms should be made in the economy. Some advocated fundamental reforms, including central planning, nationalization, and direct government operation of some businesses. Others proposed more incremental reforms such as additional regulations of corporate behavior.

REXFORD G. TUGWELL

THE PRINCIPLE OF PLANNING AND THE INSTITUTION OF LAISSEZ FAIRE (1932)

Rexford Guy Tugwell was the son of a banker in upstate New York, earned a Ph.D. in economics from the University of Pennsylvania in 1922, and began teaching at Columbia University. He was a prolific author of both scholarly and public works on farm problems, the significance of technology, and industrial planning. Active in New York Democratic circles, he became a close advisor to Franklin D. Roosevelt and joined his administration. In the 1940s, he served as governor of Puerto Rico (a presidentially appointed position at the time), returning to academia for the rest of his career. He was a particularly significant advocate for centralized planning of the economy and a harsh critic of the free-market ideology that he thought had dominated American politics to that point.

What is "war in industry"? What does he mean by "planning"? Why does he think planning is necessary? In what sense is he calling for the end of "business"? What does he think is wrong with the profit motive? Does the profit motive still play any significant role in the economy? Does economic competition still serve useful purposes? Do corporations undermine the significance of competition? Should government play a stronger role in directing economic activity?

. . .

War in industry is just as ruinous as war among nations; and equally strenuous measures are taken to prevent it. The difficulty in the one case is precisely the difficulty in the other; so long as nations and industries are organized for conflict, wars will follow, and no elaboration of machinery for compromise will be altogether successful. There are vast, well-meaning endeavors being made in both fields which must necessarily be wasted. The disasters of recent years have caused us to ask again how the ancient paradox of business—conflict to produce order—can be resolved; the interest of the liberals among us in the institutions of the new Russia of the Soviets, spreading gradually among puzzled businessmen, has created wide popular interest in "planning" as a possible refuge from persistent insecurity; by many people it is now regarded as a kind of economic Geneva where all sorts of compromises may be had and where peace and prosperity may be insured.

. . . Most of those who say so easily that this is our way out do not, I am convinced, understand that fundamental changes of attitude, new disciplines, revised legal structures, unaccustomed limitations on activity, are all necessary if we are to plan. This amounts, in fact, to the abandonment, finally, of laissez faire. It amounts, practically, to the abolition of "business."

. . . In a romantic, risky, adventurous economy the business of managing industry can be treated as a game; the spoils can be thought of as belonging to the victor as spoils have always belonged to victors. But a mature and rational economy which considered its purposes and sought reasonable ways to attain them would certainly not present many of the characteristics of the present—its violent contrasts of well-being, its irrational allotments of individual liberty, its unconsidered exploitation of human and natural resources. It is better that these things be recognized early rather than late.

. . .

It is impossible to pursue a discussion of planning beyond the most elementary considerations without raising the question of motive. Most economists, even today, believe that Adam Smith laid his finger on a profound truth when he said that not benevolent feelings but rather self-interest actuated the butchers and bakers of this world; most of them believe, furthermore, that this self-interestedness requires an economy in which profit is the reward for characteristic virtue and lack of it the penalty of sin. . . . For persons with the usual intellectual contacts of our time to go on harboring these views, there has to be some violent rationalization. Surely they must be aware of the growing average size of our industrial organizations; and from this it is a simple conclusion that fewer persons all the time are profit-receivers in any direct sense. Surely they must be aware of the growing separation of ownership and control; and from this it seems a fairly simple inference that since profits go only to owners, control is effectively separated from its assumed motive. . . . The truth is that if industry could not run without this incentive it would have stopped running long ago.

It is even arguable that profits, instead of furnishing an indispensable actuating principle, tend to inject into industry many of those elements of uncertainty which we as economists unanimously deplore. . . . [T]hey are set aside as surplus reserves. . . . They are optimistically used for creating overcapacity in every profitable line . . . they are used, most absurdly of all, as investments in the securities of other industries.

. . .

It is clear that this institution does not, in any real sense, actuate our productive equipment. Furthermore its malign influence is reasonably obvious. Why is it, then, that we protect and argue for it with a violence and persistence out of all proportion to the gains we may expect? Because it seems to me, we are not genuinely interested in security, order, or rationality. Profits, in the sense in which we use the term, belong to a speculative age, one in which huge gambles are taken, and in which the rewards for success may be outstanding. When we speak of them as motives, we do not mean that the hope of making four percent induces to undertake an operation; we mean that we hope for some fabulous story-book success. These vast gambling operations are closer to the spirit of American business even yet, with all the hard lessons we have had, than are the contrasting ideas which have to do with constructive restraint and social control. In fact our businessmen have only a rudimentary conception of industry as a social function, as carrying a heavy responsibility of provision. Industry is thought of rather as a field for adventure, in which the creation of goods is a minor matter. . . .

The truth is that profits persuade us to speculate . . . they therefore have a considerable effect on the distribution of capital among various enterprises—an effect which seems clearly enough inefficient so that other methods might easily be better; but they have little effect in actually inducing or in supporting productive enterprises. . . . It would be untrue to maintain that profits do not supply one kind of motive for economic activity. . . . This is to emphasize, however, the speculative rather than the disciplined aspects of production. To say that this is one of the institutions which will have to be abandoned if planning is to become socially effective, is to make a sharp distinction among the effects to be expected from dependence upon alternative motives. . . . The question is whether we cannot well afford to dispense with it. It seems credible that we can. Industries now mature can be seen to operate without it; and new ones might be created and might grow from sheer workman-like proclivities and without the hope of speculative gains.

. . .

Most of us ought not to have been quite so free in our predictions that he institutions of Soviet Russia would break down from a failure of motive. Yet some of us have gone on saying that even in the face of evidence. . . . It ought rather to be a source of wonder that a society could operate at all when profits are allowed to be earned and disposed of as we do it. . . .

. . . It would be as unnatural for American businesses, which live by adventures in competition, to abdicate their privileges voluntarily, as it is to expect rival militarists to maintain peace, and for the same reasons. . . .

. . . [I]t seems altogether likely that we shall set up, and soon, such a consultative body [charged with the duty of planning the country's economic life, as suggested by the president of General Electric]. . . . [T]he day on which it comes into existence will be a dangerous one for business, just as the founding day of the League of Nations was a dangerous one for nationalism. . . . But it will be a clear recognition, one that can never be undone, that order and reason are superior to adventurous competition. It will demonstrate these day by day and year by year in the personnel of a civil service devoted to disinterested thinking rather than romantic hopes of individual gain. . . . Even if it does so little, and that so badly, as hardly to exist at all, it will still have had a different purpose: the achieving of order. . . .

. . .

. . . [W]e have a century and more of development to undo. The institutions of laissez faire have become so much a part of the fabric of modern life that the untangling and removing of their tissues will be almost like dispensing with civilization itself. We shall all of us be made unhappy in one way or another; for things we love as well as things that are only privileges will have to go. The protective vine makes the ruined wall seem beautiful; we dislike abandoning it for something different. . . .

The first series of changes will have to do with statutes, with constitutions, and with government. The intention of eighteenth and nineteenth century law was to install and protect the principle of conflict; this, if we begin to plan, we shall be changing once for all, and it will require the laying of rough, unholy hands on many a sacred precedent, doubtless calling on an enlarged and nationalized police power for enforcement. We shall also have to give up a distinction of great consequence, and very dear to many a legalistic heart, but economically quite absurd, between private and public or quasi-public employments. There is no private business, if by that we mean one of no consequence to anyone but proprietors; and so none exempt from compulsion to serve a planned public interest. Furthermore we shall have to progress sufficiently far in elementary realism to recognize that only the federal area, and often not even that, is large enough to be coextensive with modem industry; and that consequently the states are wholly ineffective instruments for control. All three of these wholesale changes are required by even a limited acceptance of the planning idea.

Planning is by definition the opposite of conflict; its meaning is aligned to coordination, to rationality, to publicly defined and expertly approached aims; but not to private money-making ventures; and not to the guidance of a hidden hand. . . .

The next series of changes will have to do with industry itself. It has already been suggested that business will logically be required to disappear. This is not an overstatement for the sake of emphasis; it is literally meant. . . . New industries will not just happen as the automobile industry did; they will have to be foreseen, to be argued for, to seem probably desirable features of the whole economy before they can be entered upon.

. . . We shall not, we never do, proceed to the changes here suggested all at once. Little by little, however, we may be driven the whole length of this road; once the first step is taken, which we seem about to take, that road will begin to suggest itself as the way to a civilized industry. For it will become more and more clear . . . that not very much is to be gained until the last step has been taken. . . . [T]he last link will almost imperceptibly find its place and suddenly we shall discover that we have a new world. . . .

. . .

There is no denying that the contemporary situation in the United States has explosive possibilities. The future is becoming visible in Russia; the present is bitterly in contrast; politicians, theorists, and vested interests seem to conspire ideally for the provocation to violence of a long-patient people. No one can pretend to know how the release of this pressure is likely to come. Perhaps our statesmen will give way or be more or less gently removed from duty; perhaps our constitutions and statutes will be revised; perhaps our vested interests will submit to control without too violent resistance. It is difficult to believe that any of these will happen; it seems just as incredible that we may have a revolution. Yet the new kind of economic machinery we have in prospect cannot function in our present economy. The contemporary situation is one in which all the choices are hard; yet one of them has to be made.

ADOLF A. BERLE, JR.

A HIGH ROAD FOR BUSINESS (1933)

Adolf Berle was raised in Massachusetts by a Congregational minister who was active in the Social Gospel movement. Upon graduation from Harvard Law School, he joined the law firm of Justice Louis Brandeis in Boston and later established his own Wall Street firm. He was an active writer in politics and economics and in 1927 began teaching corporate law at Columbia University. In 1932, he published with Gardiner C. Means the landmark work *The Modern Corporation and Private Property*, which argued that the rise of corporations marked a new phase in economics and politics and that corporate managers had a free hand to direct corporate resources as they wished without much control from shareholders or market forces. He became a close advisor to Franklin D. Roosevelt and New York Mayor Fiorello La Guardia and served for a time in the State Department. He remained an influential Cold War liberal and advisor to Democratic presidents until his death in 1971. This essay was directed to the business community in the early days of the Roosevelt presidency, encouraging business leaders to join in a policy of cooperative planning.

What does Berle have in mind by a "responsible, organized business community"? Is such a responsible and organized business community only appropriate in an economic crisis? Does Berle see any important differences between the economic reforms in Italy or Germany and those that would be followed in the United States? To what extent does Berle offer a different recommendation for reform than did Tugwell? What considerations does he think ought to drive economic decisions? Are there any important differences between corporate managers and civil servants? To what degree should corporate managers consider the needs and desires of corporate "stakeholders" other than shareholders—such as workers and consumers? To what degree should corporations focus on satisfying social needs rather than generating (or maximizing) profits? Should corporations continue to operate a manufacturing plant even if greater profits could be achieved by investing corporate assets in financial instruments or facilities overseas?

It is time we took account of stock. Apparently business life in America . . . is faced with two possibilities. . . . One of them is called collectivism, and appears under all guises, from the mild doctrines of government ownership to the extremes of communism and fascism. . . .

The alternative . . . is a thoroughly responsible, organized business community.

. . .

. . . A government faced with our present situation must find a solution if it is to survive. If the simplest and most viable method is that of tying the great services of supply into huge government corporations, that method will be followed sooner or later, quite irrespective of anyone's views as to the philosophical desirability of such a solution. At present there is little if any opposing philosophy in the field. Businessmen, so far from asserting their ancient right to run their own show, are apparently asking the government to take increasing responsibilities in their own field. The cry "less government in business" is today the slogan of a forgotten year. For you cannot raise that cry without at least a quaver, when you are at the same time asking the Reconstruction Finance Corporation for a loan, or requesting that the government purchase a large block of preferred stock in your bank in order to reopen it. . . .

And, if you look over the world, you will see that this experience, which we fondly believed to be unique, is happening in the entire western or industrialized areas. . . . In Italy, the state has already assumed responsibility for the industrial organization of things; in Germany the Nazi government is carrying out a series of steps called "coordination" which means collectivism, if ever anything did; in Russia . . . the experiment is already ten years old. Elsewhere the process tacks on to some intellectual current which was prevalent before the crisis broke; hence the names Communism, Fascism, National Socialism, and so forth. We have a different fortune. Intellectual currents were not popular in the United States, and were almost rigidly vetoed by the business district, so that there was no current of ideas to tack on to. Instead, we followed our instincts; and the result in the United States, when the tale is finally told, will not be called with any "ism," but will probably be called simply business.

. . .

It is not necessary either that there should be a collectivized state, or government intervention, to reach the goal which all of these various methods really seek—a unified, controlled, sensible operation of the system. You can get it by simply having group after group of men who operate the system realize that their first job is to make the system work; and that if this involves their working together instead of working at cross-purposes, then work together they must. . . .

. . .

. . . What exactly does it mean?

In the "control" activities such as commercial banking and investment banking, it means thinking not merely whether a bond issue or loan can be repaid, but whether the enterprise ought to be started at all. You recognize the danger. The banker might think that interests which he had in a company would be adversely affected if a competitor were to get the loan. This would be irresponsible thinking—thinking in terms of himself. Or he might consider whether the industry was not already overcrowded, and whether the new enterprise could offer anything additional which was really necessary. This would be responsible thinking. . . .

. . .

For one thing, commerce has now to think in terms not of a customer who can be parted from his money, but of a need which has to be satisfied. This means, among other things, that there is no justification in saying that the would-be customer is penniless and cannot buy. The need is there and the job of commerce is to supply that need somehow. . . .

. . .

. . . Were government tomorrow to assume control of the industrial system, we should still have to create a generation of responsible government servants—no small job either, and one taking almost as much time as that of making the business community responsible to the community at large. If responsible business is a dream, at least it is no more intangible the dreams we have been creating in the name of rugged individualism, of forced and strenuous competition, of high finance. To ask men to organize within their own industries for the common good is, after all, not materially different from asking them to organize in the interests of a great corporate empire which is certain to sink a good many of them in its rise. To ask a man to abandon a quick, easy, but unhealthy profit in business is not materially different from asking a government servant to decline to use his office for personal profit, a standard to decline to use his office for personal profit, a standard we have achieved with varying degrees of success, but on the whole fairly well, in our state and national governments. . . .

We have adhered to the idea of individualism because, intrinsically, there are values in it which we desire to preserve. These are values not of property or profits, but of a way of life: the integrity and pride of men, their aesthetics, their emotions, their fulfillments. We have, after all, no desire to sink all these into some formless organization whose end we cannot foresee. . . . [T]here is a middle course, this development of responsibility, this collectivism which involves no abandonment of our ancient heritage.

HUEY P. LONG

EVERY MAN A KING (1934)

Huey Long was raised on a farm in northern Louisiana at the turn of the twentieth century. He studied enough law to pass the state bar exam and in 1915 established a legal practice in his hometown, but he soon moved into politics. At the age of twenty-five, he won a seat on the state's powerful railroad commission, which regulated utilities and the oil and gas industry as well as railroads, cementing his reputation as a populist activist. In 1928, he rode the rural vote and a boisterous oratorical style to the governor's mansion. He quickly established a dominant political organization, earning him the nickname "Kingfish," and held office first as governor and then as U.S. senator from 1930 to 1935. He became a critic from the left of the New Deal, arguing that Roosevelt ought to focus more on economic redistribution. In 1934, he launched the Share Our Wealth Society, which called for a cap on personal income and wealth and guaranteed minimum incomes. Shortly after he announced his bid for the 1936 Democratic nomination for the presidency, he was shot and killed by a relative of a political opponent. Long's most famous speech was carried nationally by the NBC radio network, and a published version was distributed through his Share Our Wealth Society.

Why does Long think that there is "no difficult problem to solve in America"? How does he justify redistribution? Why does he think the redistribution of wealth is the key to addressing the economic problems of the day? Is his an emergency measure or a long-term plan? What is necessary to make "every man a king"? Is that the aspiration of a republican society? Does income inequality threaten democracy?

. . .

I contend, my friends, that we have no difficult problem to solve in America. . . .

It is not the difficulty of the problem which we have; it is the fact that the rich people of this country—and by rich people I mean the super-rich—will not allow us to solve the problems, or rather the one little problem that is afflicting this country, because in order to cure all of our woes it is necessary to scale down the big fortunes, that we may scatter the wealth to be shared by all of the people.

. . .

How many of you remember the first thing that the Declaration of Independence said? It said: "We hold these truths to be self-evident, that there are certain inalienable rights for the people, and among them are life, liberty, and the pursuit of happiness;" and it said further, "We hold the view that all men are created equal."

Now, what did they mean by that? Did they mean, my friends, to say that all men are created equal and that that meant that any one man was born to inherit $10,000,000,000 and that another child was to be born to inherit nothing?

Did that mean, my friends, that someone would come into this world without having had an opportunity, of course, to have hit one lick of work, should be born with more than it and all of its children and children's children could ever dispose of, but that another one would have to be born into a life of starvation?

That was not the meaning of the Declaration of Independence when it said that all men are created equal or "That we hold that all men are created equal."

Nor was it the meaning of the Declaration of Independence when it said that they held that there were certain rights that were inalienable—the right of life, liberty, and the pursuit of happiness.

Is that right of life, my friends, when the young children of this country are being reared into a sphere which is more owned by 12 men than it by 120,000,000 people?

. . .

Now let us see if we cannot return this Government to the Declaration of Independence and see if we are going to do anything regarding it. Why should we hesitate or why should we quibble or why should we quarrel with one another to find out what the difficulty is, when we know that the Lord told us what the difficulty is, and Moses wrote it out so a blind man could see it, then Jesus told us all about it, and it was later written in the Book of James, where everyone could read it?

I refer to the Scriptures, now, my friends, and give you what it says not for the purpose of convincing you of the wisdom of myself, not for the purpose, ladies and gentlemen, of convincing you of the fact that I am quoting the Scriptures means that I am to be more believed than someone else; but I quote you the Scripture, or rather refer you to the Scripture, because whatever you see there you may rely upon will never be disproved so long as you or your children or anyone may live; and you may further depend upon the fact that not one historical fact that the Bible has ever contained has ever yet been disproved by any scientific discovery or by reason of anything that has been disclosed to man through his own individual mind or through the wisdom of the Lord which the Lord has allowed him to have.

But the Scripture says, ladies and gentlemen, that no country can survive, or for a country to survive it is necessary that we keep the wealth scattered among the people, that nothing should keep the wealth scattered among the people, that nothing should be held permanently by any one person, and that 50 years seems to be the year of jubilee in which all property would be scattered about and returned to the sources from which it originally came, and every seventh year debt should be remitted.

. . .

I believe that was the judgment and the view and the law of the Lord, that we would have to distribute wealth ever so often, in order that there could not be people starving to death in a land of plenty, as there is in America today.

We have in America today more wealth, more goods, more food, more clothing, more houses than we have ever had. We have everything in abundance here.

. . .

We have trouble, my friends, In the country, because we have too much money owing, the greatest indebtedness that has ever been given to civilization, where it has been shown that we are incapable of distributing the actual things that are here, because the people have not money enough to supply themselves with them, and because the greed of a few men is such that they think it is necessary that they own everything, and their pleasure consists in the starvation of the masses, and in their possessing things they cannot use, and their children cannot use, but who bask in the splendor of sunlight and wealth, casting darkness and despair and impressing it on everyone else.

"So, therefore," said the Lord in effect, "if you see these things that now have occurred and exist in this and other countries, there must be a constant scattering of wealth in any country if this country is to survive."

"Then," said the Lord, in effect, "every seventh year there shall be a remission of debts; there will be no debts after 7 years." That was the law.

Now, let us take America today. We have in America today, ladies and gentlemen, $272,000,000,000 of debt. Two hundred and seventy-two thousand millions of dollars of debts are owed by the various people of this country today. Why, my friends, that cannot be paid. It is not possible for that kind of debt to be paid.

. . .

Both of these men, Mr. Hoover and Mr. Roosevelt, came out and said there had to be a decentralization of wealth, but neither one of them did anything about it. But, nevertheless, they recognized the principle. The fact that neither one of them ever did anything about it is their own problem that I am not undertaking to criticize; but had Mr. Hoover carried out what he says ought to be done, he would be retiring from the President's office, very probably, 8 years from now, instead of 1 year ago; and had Mr. Roosevelt proceeded along the lines that he stated were necessary for the decentralization of wealth, he would have gone, my friends, a long way already, and within a few months he would have probably reached a solution of all of the problems that afflict this country today.

But I wish to warn you now that nothing that has been done up to this date has taken one dime away from these big fortune-holders; they own just as much as they did, and probably a little bit more; they hold just as many of the debts of the common people as they ever held, and probably a little bit more; and unless we, my friends, are going to give the people of this country a fair shake of the dice, by which they will all get something out of the funds of this land, there is not a chance on the topside of this God's eternal earth by which we can rescue this country and rescue the people of this country.

. . .

Every man a king, so there would be no such thing as a man or woman who did not have the necessities of life, who would not be dependent upon the whims and caprices and *ipse dixit* of the financial barons for a living. What do we propose by this society? We propose to limit the wealth of big men in the country. There is an average of $15,000 in wealth to every family in America. That is right here today.

We do not propose to divide it up equally. We do not propose a division of wealth, but we propose to limit poverty that we will allow to be inflicted upon any man's family. We will not say we are going to try to guarantee any equality, or $15,000 to a family. No; but we do say that one third of the average is low enough for any one family to hold, that there should be a guarantee of a family wealth of around $5,000; enough for a home, an automobile, a radio, and the ordinary conveniences, and the opportunity to educate their children; a fair share of the income of this land thereafter to that family so there will be no such thing as merely the select to have those things, and so there will be no such thing as a family living in poverty and distress.

We have to limit fortunes. Our present plan is that we will allow no one man to own more that $50,000,000. We think that with that limit we will be able to carry out the balance of the program. It may be necessary that we limit it to less than $50,000,000. It may be necessary, in working out of the plans that no man's fortune would be more than $10,000,000 or $15,000,000. But be that as it may, it will still be more than any one man, or any one man and his children and their children, will be able to spend in their lifetimes; and it is not necessary or reasonable to have wealth piled up beyond that point where we cannot prevent poverty among the masses.

Another thing we propose is old-age pension of $30 a month for everyone that is 60 years old. Now, we do not give this pension to a man making $1,000 a year, and we do not give it to him if he has $10,000 in property, but outside of that we do.

We will limit hours of work. There is not any necessity of having overproduction. I think all you have got to do, ladies and gentlemen, is just limit the hours of work to such an extent as people will work only so long as it is necessary to produce enough for all of the people to have what they need. . . .

. . .

. . . You know what the trouble is. The man that says he does not know what the trouble is is just hiding his face to keep from seeing the sunlight.

God told you what the trouble was. The philosophers told you what the trouble was; and when you have a country where one man owns more than 100,000 people, or a million people, and when you have a country where there are four men, as in America, that have got more control over things than all the 120,000,000 people together, you know what the trouble is.

. . .

Now, my friends, we have got to hit the root with the ax. Centralized power in the hands of a few, with centralized credit in the hands of a few, is the trouble.

. . .

EARL BROWDER

WHAT IS COMMUNISM? (1936)

Earl Browder was the son of an impoverished schoolteacher in Populist Kansas. As a teenager, he joined the Socialist Party and became an activist but was politically restless. He was inspired by the 1917 Revolution in Russia, which incited him to move to New York and join the Communist Party. He was soon drawn into the international movement and became an ally of Joseph Stalin, which in turn led to his promotion to the post of general secretary of the Communist Party-USA in 1934. When he became too independent of Moscow, he was purged from the party in 1946 and forced into effective retirement. During those dozen years of leadership, he enjoyed both national celebrity and, during World War II, some measure of political influence. In the 1930s, he formally gave Communist Party support to Franklin Roosevelt and popularized a new slogan, "Communism is Twentieth Century Americanism."

Why does Browder expect communism to work better in the United States than in Russia? How does he expect economic conditions to improve under communism? What does he think limits human achievement in the United States? Does he appeal to American ideals to advance his cause? What does Browder expect to replace the profit motive? Does capitalism have a bias toward scarcity?

. . .

To what extent can we take the experience of the Soviet Union as a forecast of what a Soviet America would look like?

. . . The principles upon which a Soviet America would be organized would be the same, in every respect, as those which guided the Soviet Union. But in our case, these principles would be applied, not to the most backward but to the most advanced industrial country. This makes tremendous differences in the details of birth and growth of the new society.

. . .

In America most of our difficulties lie precisely in the achievement of power for the working class, in the establishment of the Soviet Government. After that has been accomplished, the American capitalists will have no great powerful allies from abroad to help them continue the struggle. It will already be clear that world capitalism has received the death blow. . . .

. . .

The question is, given the American working class in undisputed power, what would be the possible and probable course of development of the economic and social life of the country?

The new government would immediately take over and operate all the banks, railroads, water and air transport, mines and all major trustified industries. Minor industries, municipal public utilities and the distributive occupations would be reorganized as functions of local government or as cooperatives or, in some instances, as auxiliaries of major industries. Large-scale agriculture would be taken over and operated by the government, while the mass of small farmers would be encouraged and helped to combine into voluntary cooperatives for large-scale production with State aid.

All available manpower would be put to work immediately, first of all in the direct production of material wealth, second in its distribution, and third in the social services of health, education and entertainment.

Every able-bodied person would be required to go to work and for this receive wages according to a scale socially determined. . . .

. . . For the first time we could escape from the terrible housing of slum barracks imposed by capitalism and begin to get modern, decent homes for everybody. Even the first simple redistribution of existing housing would revolutionize the situation. We could smash the uniformity of clothing imposed by the combination of our own poverty and capitalist mass production. For the first time in our lives the majority could eat what their tastes dictate, because for the first time they could afford it. And for the first time, the human mind would be liberated from regimented mental slavery to Hollywood, Hearst & Co.

Why can we be sure that we would have all these desirable things? Because there would be nothing to prevent us from having them if we want them. We would have the power to form our lives the way we choose. . . .

. . .

We expect our socialist factories to produce at top speed, *because* the "profit motive" has been eliminated. That famous old profit motive, which used to open up factories in the youth of capitalism, operates in modern times mainly to close them down. The administrative apparatus of a socialist economy can never become a new ruling class, because it lacks that private ownership, that monopoly of the means of life of the masses, which is the foundation of class division in society.

. . .

What are the human motives to labor? The most primitive and almost the only ones under capitalism are the fear of hunger and want, the desire to escape poverty and starvation. . . . Under socialism, this most primitive motive will be applied mainly in the remaking of bourgeois elements into workers, as in the slogan "He who does not work, neither shall he eat." For the main mass of workers, socialism introduces new motives, social motives, the motives of social emulation, the honor and heroism of producers serving society and not private profit-takers.

. . .

Socialism is not only a revolution in economic life. It makes an entirely new human race. It takes this man who has been brutalized and degraded through the ages by the violence and oppression of the class societies, frees him from his woeful heritage, carries over from the past only the achievements of the human mind and not its crimes and stupidities, and remakes man, molding him in the heat of socialist labor into a new social being.

The rising socialist system in the Soviet Union has, for years now, demonstrated that in the expansion of material production it outdistances capitalism in the period of its youth by seven or eight-fold. In the production of superior types of human beings, the superiority of socialism is demonstrated a thousand times more decisively. . . .

VI. AMERICA AND THE WORLD

Major Developments

- Entry into World War II in 1941
- Establishment of the United Nations in 1945
- Establishment of the North Atlantic Treaty Organization in 1949

The United States faced two significant foreign policy challenges during the New Deal era that together reshaped Americans' conceptions of their role in the world. The first was World War II and its immediate aftermath. There was a significant isolationist sentiment that was reluctant to commit American forces to the wars in Europe and Asia. Japan's attack on Pearl Harbor and subsequent military clashes with German and Italy effectively ended that debate. Compared to the League of Nations fight after World War I, there was relatively little American resistance to joining the United Nations after World War II. American troops remained in occupied countries for a time after the war, slowing demobilization and emphatically demonstrating the impossibility of a rapid retreat from the problems on other continents. Two global wars in rapid succession and the myriad complications arising from World War II made the formation of the United Nations a more attractive option than the earlier proposal for an international organization.

The second challenge was the emergence of the Cold War and the obvious division of Europe between countries under Soviet influence and those outside of it. Bringing the fighting to an end in Europe had the result of dividing Europe up into zones controlled by the various armed forces of the Allied powers. The apparent reluctance of the Soviet Union to give up its territorial advantage and the rise of communist insurgencies elsewhere confronted the United States with a Europe divided into hostile camps. Quickly on the heels of World War II, the United States was faced with choices of whether to maintain some involvement in Europe or to withdraw, and with how to intervene in Europe if it chose to do so. The formation of the North Atlantic Treaty Organization (NATO) symbolized the American decision to remain closely tied to the countries of western Europe in a military alliance, the effective division of Europe into western and eastern blocs, and the beginning of the Cold War between the Soviet Union and the West.

The readings here illustrate the debates surrounding the beginning of the Cold War. The diplomat George Kennan laid out the containment policy that was soon adopted by President Harry Truman and became a key component of American foreign policy in the postwar period. The theologian Reinhold Niebuhr was among those considering the challenges of constructing a meaningful international community. Senator Robert A. Taft offered a revised isolationist impulse after World War II.

GEORGE F. KENNAN

THE SOURCES OF SOVIET CONDUCT (1947)

Raised in Wisconsin, George F. Kennan joined the diplomatic corps after graduating from Princeton University in 1925. He had various postings but gained expertise on the Soviet Union and was sent to Moscow for the second time during World War II. Frequently at odds with the direction of American foreign policy, his fame followed from his widely read "Long Telegram" to Washington in 1946 that outlined a new policy direction for U.S.–Soviet relations. In 1947, he published a version of the telegram's argument under the pseudonym "Mr. X." The telegram and article outlined what became known as containment policy, which soon became official U.S. policy. Kennan argued that the Soviet government was expansionistic and should be contained by the West within its current territorial borders. He subsequently moved in and out of government and became a popular author of books on foreign policy, eventually modifying his views on the desirability and scope of the containment policy.

Why does Kennan think the Soviet Union is a threat to American national interests? Is the Soviet Union distinctively threatening? Does he expect an imminent war with the Soviet Union? Why does he think containment is the best approach for dealing with the Soviet Union? What does containment imply for American foreign and military policy? Is the Vietnam War a natural extension of containment policy? Would withdrawal from European affairs be a plausible alternative? Is containment a reasonable approach to other foreign policy challenges?

The political personality of Soviet power as we know it today is the product of ideology and circumstances: ideology inherited by the present Soviet leaders from the movement in which they had their political origin, and circumstances of the power which they now have exercised for nearly three decades in Russia. There can be few tasks of psychological analysis more difficult than to try to trace the interaction of these two forces and the relative role of each in the determination of official Soviet conduct. Yet the attempt must be made if that conduct is to be understood and effectively countered.

It is difficult to summarize the set of ideological concepts with which the Soviet leaders came into power. Marxian ideology, in its Russian-Communist projection, has always been in process of subtle evolution. The materials on which it bases itself are extensive and complex. But the outstanding features of Communist thought as it existed in 1916 may perhaps be summarized as follows: (a) that the central factor in the life of man, the factor which determines the character of public life and the "physiognomy of society," is the system by which material goods are produced and exchanged; (b) that the capitalist system of production is a nefarious one which inevitably leads to the exploitation of the working class by the capital-owning class and is incapable of developing adequately the economic resources of society or of distributing fairly the material goods produced by human labor; (c) that capitalism contains the seeds of its own destruction and must, in view of the inability of the capital-owning class to adjust itself to economic change, result eventually and inescapably in a revolutionary transfer of power to the working class; and (d) that imperialism, the final phase of capitalism, leads directly to war and revolution.

. . . It must be noted that there was no assumption that capitalism would perish without proletarian revolution. A final push was needed from a revolutionary proletariat movement in order to tip over the tottering structure. But it was regarded as inevitable that sooner or later that push be given.

. . .

The circumstances of the immediate post-revolution period—the existence in Russia of civil war and foreign intervention, together with the obvious fact that the Communists represented only a tiny minority of the Russian people—made the establishment of dictatorial power a necessity. The experiment with "war Communism" and the abrupt attempt to eliminate private production and trade had unfortunate economic consequences and caused further bitterness against the new revolutionary regime. While the temporary relaxation of the effort to communize Russia, represented by the New Economic Policy, alleviated some of this economic distress and thereby served its purpose, it also made it evident that the "capitalistic sector of society" was still prepared to profit at once from any relaxation of governmental pressure, and would, if permitted to continue to exist, always constitute a powerful opposing element to the Soviet regime and a serious rival for influence in the country. . . .

Lenin, had he lived, might have proved a great enough man to reconcile these conflicting forces to the ultimate benefit of Russian society, though this is questionable. But be that as it may, Stalin, and those whom he led in the struggle for succession to Lenin's position of leadership, were not the men to tolerate rival political forces in the sphere of power which they coveted. Their sense of insecurity was too great. Their particular brand of fanaticism, unmodified by any of the Anglo-Saxon traditions of compromise, was too fierce and too jealous to envisage any permanent sharing of power. From the Russian-Asiatic world out of which they had emerged they carried with them a skepticism as to the possibilities of permanent and peaceful coexistence of rival forces. Easily persuaded of their own doctrinaire "rightness," they insisted on the submission or destruction of all competing power. . . .

. . .

Now the outstanding circumstance concerning the Soviet regime is that down to the present day this process of political consolidation has never been completed and the men in the Kremlin have continued to be predominantly absorbed with the struggle to secure and make absolute the power which they seized in November 1917. They have endeavored to secure it primarily against forces at home, within Soviet society itself. But they have also endeavored to secure it against the outside world. For ideology, as we have seen, taught them that the outside world was hostile and that it was their duty eventually to overthrow the political forces beyond their borders. The powerful hands of Russian history and tradition reached up to sustain them in this feeling. Finally, their own aggressive intransigence with respect to the outside world began to find its own reaction. . . . It is an undeniable privilege of every man to prove himself right in the thesis that the world is his enemy; for if he reiterates it frequently enough and makes it the background of his conduct he is bound eventually to be right.

. . . And this fact created one of the most basic of the compulsions which came to act upon the Soviet regime: since capitalism [was declared to have] no longer existed in Russia and since it could not be admitted that there could be serious or widespread opposition to the Kremlin springing spontaneously from the liberated masses under its authority, it became necessary to justify the retention of the dictatorship by stressing the menace of capitalism abroad.

This began at an early date. In 1924 Stalin specifically defended the retention of the "organs of suppression," meaning, among others, the army and the secret police, on the ground that "as long as there is a capitalist encirclement there will be danger of intervention with all the consequences that flow from that danger." In accordance with that theory, and from that time on, all internal opposition forces in Russia have consistently been portrayed as the agents of foreign forces of reaction antagonistic to Soviet power.

. . .

So much for the historical background. What does it spell in terms of the political personality of Soviet power as we know it today?

. . .

The first of these concepts is that of the innate antagonism between capitalism and Socialism. . . . It means that there can never be on Moscow's side any sincere assumption of a community of aims between the Soviet Union and powers which are regarded as capitalist. It must invariably be assumed in Moscow that the aims of the capitalist world are antagonistic to the Soviet regime. . . . If the Soviet government occasionally sets its signature to documents which would indicate the contrary, this is to be regarded as a tactical maneuver permissible in dealing with the enemy (who is without honor) and should be taken in the spirit of caveat emptor. . . . But we should not be misled by tactical maneuvers. These characteristics of Soviet policy [i.e., secretiveness, duplicity, suspiciousness], like the postulate from which they flow, are basic to the internal nature of Soviet power, and will be with us, whether in the foreground or the background, until the internal nature of Soviet power is changed.

This means that we are going to continue for a long time to find the Russians difficult to deal with. It does not mean that they should be considered as embarked upon a do-or-die program to overthrow our society by a given date. The theory of the inevitability of the eventual fall of capitalism has the fortunate connotation that there is no hurry about it. . . .

This brings us to the second of the concepts important to contemporary Soviet outlook. That is the infallibility of the Kremlin. . . .

. . .

. . . Kremlin has no compunction about retreating in the face of superior force. And being under the compulsion of no timetable, it does not get panicky under the necessity for such retreat. Its political action is a fluid stream which moves constantly, wherever it is permitted to move, toward a given goal. Its main concern is to make sure that it has filled every nook and cranny available to it in the basin of world power. But if it finds unassailable barriers in its path, it accepts these philosophically and accommodates itself to them. The main thing is that there should always be pressure, unceasing constant pressure, toward the desired goal. . . .

. . .

In these circumstances it is clear that the main element of any United States policy toward the Soviet Union must be that of a long-term, patient but firm and vigilant containment of Russian expansive tendencies. It is important to note, however, that such a policy has nothing to do with outward histrionics: with threats or blustering or superfluous gestures of outward "toughness." While the Kremlin is basically flexible in its reaction to political realities, it is by no means unamenable to considerations of prestige. Like almost any other government, it can be placed by tactless and threatening gestures in a position where it cannot afford to yield even though this might be dictated by its sense of realism. . . .

In the light of the above, it will be clearly seen that the Soviet pressure against the free institutions of the Western world is something that can be contained by the adroit and vigilant application of counterforce at a series of constantly shifting geographical and political points, corresponding to the shifts and maneuvers of Soviet policy, but which cannot be charmed or talked out of existence. . . .

. . .

It is clear that the United States cannot expect in the foreseeable future to enjoy political intimacy with the Soviet regime. It must continue to regard the Soviet Union as a rival, not a partner, in the political arena. It must continue to expect that Soviet policies will reflect no abstract love of peace and stability, no real faith in the possibility of a permanent happy coexistence of the Socialist and capitalist worlds, but rather a cautious, persistent pressure toward the disruption and weakening of all rival influence and rival power.

Balanced against this are the facts that Russia, as opposed to the western world in general, is still by far the weaker party, that Soviet policy is highly flexible, and that Soviet society may well contain deficiencies which will eventually weaken its own total potential. This would of itself warrant the United States entering with reasonable confidence upon a policy of firm containment, designed to confront the Russians with unalterable counterforce at every point where they show signs of encroaching upon the interest of a peaceful and stable world.

. . .

In would be an exaggeration to say that American behavior unassisted and alone could exercise a power of life and death over the Communist movement and bring about the early fall of Soviet power in Russia. But the United States has it in its power to increase enormously the strains under which Soviet policy must operate, to force upon the Kremlin a far greater degree of moderation and circumspection than it has had to observe in recent years, and in this way to promote tendencies which must eventually find their outlet in either the breakup or the gradual mellowing of Soviet power. For no mystical, messianic movement—and particularly not that of the Kremlin—can face frustration indefinitely without eventually adjusting itself in one way or another to the logic of that state of affairs.

. . . In the light of these circumstances, the thoughtful observer of Russian-American relations will find no cause for complaint in the Kremlin's challenge to American society. He will rather experience a certain gratitude to a Providence which, by providing the American people with this implacable challenge, has made their entire security as a nation dependent on their pulling themselves together and accepting the responsibilities of moral and political leadership that history plainly intended them to bear.

HARRY S. TRUMAN

ADDRESS BEFORE A JOINT SESSION OF CONGRESS (1947)

Raised on a Missouri farm, Harry Truman primarily worked on farms after graduating from high school until he joined the National Guard in 1917. Upon returning from the war, he opened a haberdashery in Kansas City, and when that business collapsed he won election to be a county court judge (more of an administrative than a judicial office). With the backing of the state's Democratic machine, Truman was elevated to the U.S. Senate in 1934, where he was a firm supporter of Roosevelt. Ten years later, he was brought onto the presidential ticket and was elevated to the Oval Office when President Roosevelt died shortly after his fourth inauguration. Soon after that, World War II was brought to an end, and the new president turned his attention to constructing the postwar peace. In this 1947 address to Congress, Truman formally embraced George Kennan's containment policy. The president was said to be following Senator Arthur Vandenberg's advice in trying to "scare hell out of the American people."[21] Seeking financial assistance for the governments of Greece and Turkey, Truman argued that continued American involvement in Europe was crucial to preventing the spread of revolutionary communism across the continent. The "Truman Doctrine" held that the United States should provide the necessary assistance to any democratic nation under threat from nondemocratic forces. The administration followed up with the Marshall Plan, providing funds for general European reconstruction.

To what degree does Truman echo Kennan? Is his vision of containment policy the same as Kennan's? Is Truman successful in establishing an American interest in the stability of the Greek and Turkish governments? Why should the Greek government's battle against a communist insurgency not be regarded as an internal Greek problem? Should the United States have instead withdrawn from Europe? Would Truman's argument justify more than just financial assistance? Would Truman's argument apply in other parts of the world?

The gravity of the situation which confronts the world today necessitates my appearance before a joint session of the Congress. The foreign policy and the national security of this country are involved.

One aspect of the present situation, which I wish to present to you at this time for your consideration and decision, concerns Greece and Turkey.

The United States has received from the Greek Government an urgent appeal for financial and economic assistance. Preliminary reports from the American Economic Mission now in Greece and reports from the American Ambassador in Greece corroborate the statement of the Greek Government that assistance is imperative if Greece is to survive as a free nation.

. . .

The very existence of the Greek state is today threatened by the terrorist activities of several thousand armed men, led by Communists, who defy the government's authority at a number of points, particularly along the northern boundaries. . . .

Meanwhile, the Greek Government is unable to cope with the situation. The Greek army is small and poorly equipped. It needs supplies and equipment if it is to restore the authority of the government throughout Greek territory. Greece must have assistance if it is to become a self-supporting and self-respecting democracy.

The United States must supply that assistance. We have already extended to Greece certain types of relief and economic aid but these are inadequate.

There is no other country to which democratic Greece can turn.

21 Eric F. Goldman, *The Crucial Decade* (New York: Knopf, 1956), 50.

. . .

The Greek Government has been operating in an atmosphere of chaos and extremism. It has made mistakes. The extension of aid by this country does not mean that the United States condones everything that the Greek Government has done or will do. We have condemned in the past, and we condemn now, extremist measures of the right or the left. We have in the past advised tolerance, and we advise tolerance now.

. . .

One of the primary objectives of the foreign policy of the United States is the creation of conditions in which we and other nations will be able to work out a way of life free from coercion. This was a fundamental issue in the war with Germany and Japan. Our victory was won over countries which sought to impose their will, and their way of life, upon other nations.

To ensure the peaceful development of nations, free from coercion, the United States has taken a leading part in establishing the United Nations, The United Nations is designed to make possible lasting freedom and independence for all its members. We shall not realize our objectives, however, unless we are willing to help free peoples to maintain their free institutions and their national integrity against aggressive movements that seek to impose upon them totalitarian regimes. This is no more than a frank recognition that totalitarian regimes imposed on free peoples, by direct or indirect aggression, undermine the foundations of international peace and hence the security of the United States.

The peoples of a number of countries of the world have recently had totalitarian regimes forced upon them against their will. . . .

At the present moment in world history nearly every nation must choose between alternative ways of life. The choice is too often not a free one.

One way of life is based upon the will of the majority, and is distinguished by free institutions, representative government, free elections, guarantees of individual liberty, freedom of speech and religion, and freedom from political oppression.

The second way of life is based upon the will of a minority forcibly imposed upon the majority. It relies upon terror and oppression, a controlled press and radio; fixed elections, and the suppression of personal freedoms.

I believe that it must be the policy of the United States to support free peoples who are resisting attempted subjugation by armed minorities or by outside pressures.

I believe that we must assist free peoples to work out their own destinies in their own way.

I believe that our help should be primarily through economic and financial aid which is essential to economic stability and orderly political processes.

The world is not static, and the status quo is not sacred. But we cannot allow changes in the status quo in violation of the Charter of the United Nations by such methods as coercion, or by such subterfuges as political infiltration. In helping free and independent nations to maintain their freedom, the United States will be giving effect to the principles of the Charter of the United Nations.

It is necessary only to glance at a map to realize that the survival and integrity of the Greek nation are of grave importance in a much wider situation. If Greece should fall under the control of an armed minority, the effect upon its neighbor, Turkey, would be immediate and serious. Confusion and disorder might well spread throughout the entire Middle East.

Moreover, the disappearance of Greece as an independent state would have a profound effect upon those countries in Europe whose peoples are struggling against great difficulties to maintain their freedoms and their independence while they repair the damages of war.

It would be an unspeakable tragedy if these countries, which have struggled so long against overwhelming odds, should lose that victory for which they sacrificed so much. Collapse of free institutions and loss of independence would be disastrous not only for them but for the world. Discouragement and possibly failure would quickly be the lot of neighboring peoples striving to maintain their freedom and independence.

. . .

This is a serious course upon which we embark.

I would not recommend it except that the alternative is much more serious. The United States contributed $341,000,000,000 toward winning World War II. This is an investment in world freedom and world peace.

The assistance that I am recommending for Greece and Turkey amounts to little more than 1 tenth of 1 per cent of this investment. It is only common sense that we should safeguard this investment and make sure that it was not in vain.

The seeds of totalitarian regimes are nurtured by misery and want. They spread and grow in the evil soil of poverty and strife. They reach their full growth when the hope of a people for a better life has died. We must keep that hope alive.

The free peoples of the world look to us for support in maintaining their freedoms.

If we falter in our leadership, we may endanger the peace of the world—and we shall surely endanger the welfare of our own nation.

Great responsibilities have been placed upon us by the swift movement of events.

I am confident that the Congress will face these responsibilities squarely.

REINHOLD NIEBUHR

THE CHILDREN OF LIGHT AND THE CHILDREN OF DARKNESS (1949)

Reinhold Niebuhr taught theology at Union Theological Seminary in New York. His mature philosophy became known as Christian Realism, which emphasized the intrinsic corruption of man. While Niebuhr adhered to many of the same goals of social justice and global peace that moved other Christian thinkers, his focus on human failings led him to be critical of utopian schemes. He was a vocal critic of pacifists in the lead-up to World War II and charted a course of liberal anticommunism after the war. In the aftermath of Nazism and in the context of the emerging Cold War, his realist critique of perfectionism and self-righteousness proved quite influential. His 1944 lectures at Stanford University offered a "realistic" defense of democracy that did not depend on "optimistic estimates of human nature" and concluded with a call for international cooperation. In both the domestic and international spheres, humanity confronted its own internal tension—its capacity for justice and its inclination to injustice. The "children of light" sought to discipline their pursuit of self-interest through recognition of a more universal law; the "children of darkness" "know no law beyond the self." Niebuhr argued that social progress depended on appreciating the extent of these egoistic impulses and seeking ways to constrain them.

What does Niebuhr see as the difference between individual countries and the international arena? Is there a universal human community? What are the limits of community? What are the challenges to the creation of a world community? Does a world community require a world government? Does the formation of the United States provide lessons for the formation of an international political order? What is America's international obligation?

. . . Beyond the national (and in a few cases the imperial) community lies international chaos, slightly qualified by minimal forms of international cooperation.

The problem of overcoming this chaos and of extending the principle of community to worldwide terms has become the most urgent of all the issues which face our epoch. The crisis of our age is undoubtedly due primarily to the fact that the requirements of a technical civilization have outrun the limited order which national communities have achieved, while the resources of our civilization have not been adequate for the creation of political instruments of order, wide enough to meet these requirements.

The special urgency under which we stand in dealing with the problem of the world community has been occasioned by the convergence of two forces of universality. . . . The old force of universality which challenges nationalistic particularism is the sense of universal moral obligation, transcending the geographic and other limits of historic communities. The new force of universality is the global interdependence of nations, achieved by a technical civilization.

. . . . Primitive society felt no strong sense of obligation to life outside of the tribal community, which was held together and limited by the principle of consanguinity. The early empires were achievements of human freedom over the limits of nature in the sense that they extended the boundaries of effective community beyond the limited force of consanguinity. . . .

. . .

In the more than two millennia between the rise of universalistic philosophies and religions and the present day, nations and empires have risen and fallen, and national and imperial cultures have competed, and been compounded, with one another in great profusion. But it seemed a fixed principle of history that the effective human community should be much smaller than the universal community which was implied in any rigorous analysis of man's obligation to his fellowmen. In this whole long period of history the national and imperial communities, which gave effective social cohesion to human life, drew a considerable part of their force of cohesion from the power of particularity. Geographic boundary, ethnic homogeneity and some common experience and tradition were the primary bases of their unity.

. . .

So matters stood until a technical civilization, developed during the past century, introduced a new force of universality into history. Its instruments of production, transport and communication reduced the space-time dimensions of the world to a fraction of their previous size and led to a phenomenal increase in the interdependence of all national communities. The new technical interdependence created a potential world community because it established complex interrelations which could be ordered only by a wider community than now exists.

. . .

The convergence of two forces of universality, one moral and the other technical, creates such a powerful impetus toward the establishment of a world community that the children of light regard it as a practically inevitable achievement. As always, they underestimate the power of particular forces in history. . . . Two world wars in one generation prove that the logic of history has less power over the recalcitrance of human wills than the children of light assume.

. . . The same technical situation which makes a universal community ultimately imperative, also arms particular nations, empires and centers of power with the instruments which make the unification of the world through imperialistic domination seem plausible, if not actually possible. . . .

. . . The great civilized nations are sufficiently children of light to refrain from efforts at the tyrannical unification of the world. But each of the great powers has sufficient strength to be tempted by the hope that it may establish its own security without too much concern for the security of others and without binding commitments to the common interests of all nations.

. . .

The children of light in our era might be divided into two schools, one more naïve and the other a little more sophisticated. The more naïve school of universalists believes that it would be sufficient to embody a moral imperative into a universally accepted law. They conceive human history, not as a vast realm of vitalities in which ideas and ideals are the instruments of conflict as well as tools for composing it; but rather as a realm of ideas in which ultimate ideals are bound to bring warring vitalities under their dominion. They imagine that nations insist upon absolute sovereignty only because we have had a "natural law" which justified such sovereignty; and that therefore a new definition of international law, which denied the principle of the absolute sovereignty of nations, would serve to annul the fact. They think that we lack an international government only because no one has conceived a proper blueprint of it. Therefore they produce such blueprints in great profusion. These pure constitutionalists have a touching faith in the power of a formula over the raw stuff of human history.

. . . Far more numerous is a school of more sophisticated idealists who recognize that power is required in the organization of all human communities. They would therefore create an international authority, associate an international court with the authority, and provide it with an international police force so that it would have power to enforce its decisions. With these constitutional instruments they would be ready to overcome international anarchy and solve all problems of the world community of nations. . . .

While a single sovereignty may be the final and indispensable instrument of a common community, it is not possible to achieve unity by the power of government alone. Government may be the head of the body, which without a single head could not be, or become, a single body; but it is not possible for a head to create a body. The communities of the world, imperial and national, which have achieved a high degree of integration, all have had some core of ethnic homogeneity, though various and heterogeneous elements may be on the periphery. . . . The authority of the government in such communities is not infrequently derived from the same history from which the community derived its unity. . . . Geographic limitation, ethnic and cultural uniqueness distinguishing this from other communities, and a common history, usually embodying comradeship in meeting a common foe, all contribute to the cohesion of communities. Governments develop to express and to perfect the unity thus achieved, but they do not create what they must presuppose.

America has produced so many pure constitutionalists in international political theory partly because American history encourages the illusion that the nation was created purely by constitutional fiat and compact. . . . Most modern nations do not have as clear a constitutional beginning as the United States. It is therefore the more significant that even in the history of the United States the real beginning is more organic and less constitutional than is usually assumed.

. . .

It may be regarded as axiomatic that the less a community is held together by cohesive forces in the texture of its life the more must it be held together by power. This fact leads to the dismal conclusion that the international community lacking these cohesive forces, must find its first unity through coercive force to a larger degree than is compatible with the necessities of justice. Order will have to be purchased at the price of justice. . . . For a long time to come the international community will have few elements of inner cohesion, or benefit from unity of a common culture or tradition. It will possess only two minimal forces of cohesion: a common overtone of universality in its moral ideals, and the fear of anarchy. The fear of anarchy will undoubtedly be the more potent of these two; but this fear is certainly not as powerful as the fear of a common and concrete foe.

. . .

. . . The international politics of the coming decades will be dominated by great powers who will be able to prevent recalcitrance among the smaller nations, but who will have difficulty in keeping peace between each other because they will not have any authority above their own powerful enough to bend or deflect their wills. . . .

While a balance between the great powers may be the actual consequence of present policies, it is quite easy to foreshadow the doom of such a system. No participant in a balance is ever quite satisfied with its own position. Every center of power will seek to improve its position: and every such effort will be regarded by the others as an attempt to disturb the equilibrium. There is sufficient mistrust between the great nations, even while they are still locked in the intimate embrace of a great common effort, to make it quite certain that a mere equilibrium between them will not suffice to preserve the peace.

. . .

The experience of Abraham Lincoln in dealing with national issues might well instruct us on the relative importance of order and justice in international politics. Facing civil conflict within the nation Lincoln declared: "My primary purpose is to save the union." Analogously our primary purpose must be to create a union. It was significant, however, that though Lincoln was prepared to save the union "half slave and half free" it soon became apparent that this could not be done. The union could be saved only by abolishing slavery. This is a nice symbol of the fact that order precedes justice in the strategy of government; but that only an order which implicates justice can achieve a stable peace. An unjust order quickly invites the resentment and rebellion which lead to its undoing.

While political strategies deal with outer and social checks upon the egoism of men and of nations and while no individual or collective expression of human vitality is ever moral enough to obviate the necessity of such checks, it is also true that outer checks are insufficient if some inner moral checks upon human ambition are not effective. Consistently egoistic individuals would require a tyrannical government for the preservation of social order. Fortunately individuals are not consistently egoistic. Therefore democratic government, rather than Thomas Hobbes' absolutism, has proved a possibility in national life. Nations are more consistently egoistic than individuals; yet even the collective behavior of men stands under some inner moral checks; and the peace of the world requires that these checks be strengthened.

Since no constitutional checks, which may be placed upon the power of the great hegemonic nations, will be fully adequate, it is particularly important that the strongest possible moral restraints be placed upon their power.

. . .

The so-called democratic and "Christian" nations have a culture which demands self-criticism in principle; and institutions which make it possible in practice. We must not assume, however, that any modern nation can easily achieve the high virtue of humility; or establish moral checks upon its power lusts. Britain has certain advantages over America in this realm for two reasons. The national interest of Britain is more completely identical with the interests of the nations than is the case with the United States; because Britain is more desperately in need of world security for its survival than America. Secondly, Britain has had longer experience in wielding power in the world affairs than America. Through the experience Britain has learned to exercise critical restraints upon its power impulses. . . .

Crude American criticisms of British policies are themselves a revelation of our moral problem. America is potentially more powerful than Britain; but it has had little moral consciousness of its own power. As a result it alternates between moods of complete irresponsibility and of cynicism. In the one mood it would disavow the responsibilities of power because it fears its corruption. In the other mood it displays an adolescent pride of power and a cynical disregard of its responsibilities.

. . . [I]f America achieves maturity, the primary mark of it must be the willingness to assume continuing responsibility in the world community of nations. We must seek to maintain a critical attitude toward our own power impulses. . . .

. . .

The world community, toward which all historical forces seem to be driving us, is mankind's final possibility and impossibility. The task of achieving it must be interpreted from the standpoint of a faith which understands the fragmentary and broken character of all historic achievements and yet has confidence in their meaning because it knows their completion to be in the hands of a Divine Power, whose resources are greater than those of men, and whose suffering love can overcome the corruption of man's achievements, without negating the significance of our striving.

ROBERT A. TAFT

A FOREIGN POLICY FOR AMERICANS (1951)

Robert Taft was the son of William Howard Taft, the president and chief justice. He graduated from Harvard Law School in 1913, just after his father lost the presidency to Woodrow Wilson. When war broke out, Taft went to work as an assistant for Herbert Hoover before entering electoral politics himself in 1920. He alternated between private practice and holding office in the Ohio state legislature, until he successfully ran as an anti-New Deal Republican for the U.S. Senate in 1938. He almost immediately became a contender for the Republican nomination for president but never managed to attract more progressive party members to his cause. As war broke out in Europe, Taft opposed American intervention until the United States was directly attacked. As the Cold War began, Taft was less supportive than the Republican leadership of embracing President Truman's call for continued American involvement in Europe. Taft opposed the creation of NATO but called for a more aggressive American policy in Asia. The isolationist Taft narrowly lost the Republican nomination to the more internationalist General Dwight Eisenhower in 1952. Taft died of cancer in 1953.

How does the foreign policy philosophy of Taft differ from the approach outlined by Truman? Does Taft support a return to a nineteenth-century foreign policy? How does he envision America's role in the postwar world? How does Taft's support for international law fit with his isolationist approach? How does he assess the communist threat? Would his approach have been preferable to the more muscular Cold War pursued by Truman? Would Taft's approach have been more viable for the post-Cold War period?

. . .

Fundamentally, I believe the ultimate purpose of our foreign policy must be to protect the liberty of the people of the United States. . . . To achieve that liberty we have gone to war, and to protect it we would go to war again.

Only second to liberty is the maintenance of peace. The results of war may be almost as bad as the destruction of liberty and, in fact, may lead, even if the war is won, to something very close to the destruction of liberty at home. War not only produces pitiful human suffering and utter destruction of many things worthwhile, but it is almost as disastrous for the victor as for the vanquished. . . . Much of the glamor has gone from it, and war today is murder by machine. . . . War, undertaken even for justifiable purposes, such as to punish aggression in Korea, has often had the principal results of wrecking the country intended to be saved and spreading death and destruction among an innocent civilian population. Even more than Sherman knew in 1864, "war is hell." War should never be undertaken or seriously risked except to protect American liberty.

Our traditional policy of neutrality and non-interference with other nations was based on the principle that this policy was the best way to avoid disputes with other nations and to maintain the liberty of this country without war. From the days of George Washington that has been the policy of the United States. It has never been isolationism; but it has always avoided alliances and interference in foreign quarrels as a preventative against possible war, and it has always oppose any commitment by the United States, in advance, to take any military action outside of our territory. It would leave us free to interfere or not interfere according to whether we consider the case of sufficiently vital interest to the liberty of this country. It was the policy of the free hand.

I have always felt, however, that we should depart from this principle if we could set up an effective international organization, because in the long run the success of such an organization should be the most effective assurance of world peace and therefore of American peace. . . .

We have now taken the lead in establishing the United Nations. The purpose is to establish a rule of law throughout the world and protect the people of the United States by punishing aggression the moment it starts and deterring future aggression through joint action of the members of such an organization.

I think we must recognize that this involves the theory of a preventative war, a dangerous undertaking at any time. If, therefore, we are going to join in such an organization it is essential that it be effective. . . .

The United Nations has failed to protect our peace, I believe, because it was organized on an unsound basis with a veto power in five nations and is based, in fact, on the joint power of such nations, effective only so long as they agree. I believe the concept can only be successful if based on a rule of law and justice between nations and willingness on the part of all nations to abide by the decisions of an impartial tribunal.

. . .

[E]xcept as such policies may ultimately protect our own security, we have no primary interest as a national policy to improve conditions or material welfare in other parts of the world or to change other forms of government. Certainly we should not engage in war to achieve such purposes. . . .

. . .

There are a good many Americans who talk about an American century in which America will dominate the world. They rightly point out that the United States is so powerful today that we should assume a moral leadership in the world to solve all the troubles of mankind. I quite agree that we need moral leadership not only abroad but also at home. We can take the moral leadership in trying to improve the international organization for peace. I think we can take leadership in the providing of example and advice for the improvement of material standards of living throughout the world. Above all, I think we can take the leadership in proclaiming the doctrines of liberty and justice and in impressing on the world that only through liberty and law and justice, and through socialism or communism, can the world hope to obtain the standards which we have attained in the United States. . . .

If we confine our activities to the field of moral leadership we shall be successful if our philosophy is sound and appeals to the people of the world. The trouble with those who advocate this policy is that they really do not confine themselves to moral leadership. . . . In their hearts they want to force on these foreign peoples through the use of American money and even, perhaps, American arms . . . .

. . .

The threat of communism against liberty is not by any means a purely military threat—in fact, if we had only to face the military strength of Soviet Russia I think there would not be any such concern as we see today. Communism is strong because it has developed a fanatical support and missionary ardor, which have spread throughout the world and appealed everywhere to some of those who are dissatisfied with their present condition. . . .

And so we have to consider the methods by which we can battle against the spread of communism and so weaken its spirit that its missionary ardor is destroyed. I believe that can only be done by a positive campaign in behalf of liberty. Liberty has always appealed to the minds of men and today is a far more appealing ideal than communism or material welfare can ever be. . . .

And when I say liberty I do not simply mean what is referred to as "free enterprise." I mean liberty of the individual to think his own thoughts and live his own life as he desires to thin and to live. . . .

. . . I believe that we should battle the principles of communism and socialism and convince the world that true happiness lies in the establishment of a system of liberty, that communism and socialism are the very antithesis of liberalism, and that only a nation conceived in liberty can hope to bring real happiness to its people or to the world.

. . .

In short, a war against communism in the world must finally be won in the minds of men. The hope of ultimate peace lies far more [in winning minds] than in a third world war, which may destroy civilization itself. . . . [T]here has never been a stronger case to present to the world, or a better opportunity to dissolve its darkness into light.

FOR FURTHER STUDY

Berle, Adolf A., Jr., and Gardiner C. Means. *The Modern Corporation and Private Property* (New Brunswick, NJ: Transaction Publishers, 1991).

Broderick, Francis L., and August Meier, eds. *Negro Protest Thought in the Twentieth Century* (Indianapolis, IN: Bobbs-Merrill, 1965).

Dewey, John. *The Essential Dewey*, eds. Larry A. Hickman and Thomas M. Alexander (Bloomington: Indiana University Press, 1998).

Hayek, Friedrich A. von. *The Road to Serfdom* (Chicago, IL: University of Chicago Press, 1994).

Jackson, Robert H. *The Struggle for Judicial Supremacy: A Study of a Crisis in American Power Politics* (New York: Alfred A. Knopf, 1941).

Lerner, Max. *It is Later than You Think: The Need for a Militant Democracy* (New Brunswick, NJ: Transaction Publishers, 1989).

Myrdal, Gunnar. *An American Dilemma: The Negro Problem and Modern Democracy* (New Brunswick, NJ: Transaction Publishers, 1996).

Niebuhr, Reinhold. *The Essential Reinhold Niebuhr: Selected Essays and Addresses*, ed. Robert McAfee Brown (New Haven, CT: Yale University Press, 1986).

Roosevelt, Franklin D. *Selected Speeches, Messages, Press Conferences, and Letters*, ed. Basil Rauch (New York: Rinehart, 1957).

Twelve Southerners. *I'll Take My Stand: The South and the Agrarian Tradition* (Baton Rouge: Louisiana State University Press, 2006).

Zinn, Howard, ed. *New Deal Thought* (Indianapolis, IN: Bobbs-Merrill, 1966).

SUGGESTED READINGS

Borgwardt, Elizabeth. *A New Deal for the World: America's Vision for Human Rights* (Cambridge, MA: Harvard University Press, 2005).

Brinkley, Alan. *The End of Reform: New Deal Liberalism in Recession and War* (New York: Alfred A. Knopf, 1995).

Cushman, Barry. *Rethinking the New Deal Court: The Structure of a Constitutional Revolution* (New York: Oxford University Press, 1998).

Frisch, Morton J. *Franklin D. Roosevelt, the Contribution of the New Deal to American Political Thought and Practice* (New York: Twayne Publishers, 1975).

Fusfeld, Daniel R. *The Economic Thought of Franklin D. Roosevelt and the Origins of the New Deal* (New York: Columbia University Press, 1956).

Hamby, Alonzo L. *Beyond the New Deal: Harry S. Truman and American Liberalism* (New York: Columbia University Press, 1973).

Hawley, Ellis W. *The New Deal and the Problem of Monopoly: A Study in Economic Ambivalence* (Princeton, NJ: Princeton University Press, 1966).

Karl, Barry D. *The Uneasy State: The United States from 1915 to 1945* (Chicago, IL: University of Chicago Press, 1983).

Katznelson, Ira. *Fear Itself: The New Deal and the Origins of Our Time* (New York: W.W. Norton, 2013).

Kleinman, Mark L. *A World of Hope, a World of Fear: Henry A. Wallace, Reinhold Niebuhr, and American Liberalism* (Columbus: Ohio State University Press, 2000).

Leuchtenburg, William E. *Franklin D. Roosevelt and the New Deal, 1932–1940* (New York: Harper & Row, 1963).

Parrish, Michael E. *Anxious Decades: America in Prosperity and Depression, 1920–1941* (New York: W.W. Norton, 1992).

Purcell, Edward A., Jr. *The Crisis of Democratic Theory: Scientific Naturalism and the Problem of Value* (Lexington: University Press of Kentucky, 1973).

Reagan, Patrick D. *Designing a New America: The Origins of New Deal Planning, 1890–1943* (Amherst: University of Massachusetts Press, 1999).

Rosenof, Theodore. *Economics in the Long Run: New Deal Theorists and their Legacies, 1933–1993* (Chapel Hill: University of North Carolina Press, 1997).

Sitkoff, Harvard. *A New Deal for Blacks: The Emergence of Civil Rights as a National Issue* (New York: Oxford University Press, 1978).

Weinstein, James. *Ambiguous Legacy: The Left in American Politics* (New York: New Viewpoints, 1975).

CHAPTER 10

CIVIL RIGHTS AND THE GREAT SOCIETY, 1951–1980

I. INTRODUCTION

In accepting the Democratic Party's presidential nomination in 1964, Lyndon Johnson characterized the coming contest as one

> Between courage and timidity. It is between those who have vision and those who see what can be, and those who want only to maintain the status quo. It is between those who welcome the future and those who turn away from its promises.
>
> This is the true cause of freedom. The man who is hungry, who cannot find work or educate his children, who is bowed by war—that man is not fully free.
>
> For more than 30 years, from social security to the war against poverty, we have diligently worked to enlarge the freedom of man. And as a result, Americans tonight are freer to live as they want to live, to pursue their ambitions, to meet their desires, to raise their families than at any time in all of our glorious history.[1]

In the middle of the twentieth century, liberals controlled the government and set the political agenda as they rarely had before in the United States. The liberal ascendance reached its peak with President Lyndon Johnson's landslide victory over Senator Barry Goldwater in 1964. Johnson not only won a term of his own as president, but he carried with him large, liberal Democratic majorities in Congress. The coalition that the New Dealers had pieced together between northern liberals and Southern Democrats was undone. The liberals had finally won on the most tender issue to the Southern Democrats—racial civil rights—and both the party and the nation were transformed.

The liberal victory that seemed so complete in 1964 already seemed like a distant dream by 1968. With the Southern Democrats in disarray, Republicans began to compete seriously in the South for the first time since the end of Reconstruction. The Vietnam War had become

---

1 Lyndon B. Johnson, "Remarks before the National Convention Upon Accepting the Nomination, August 27, 1964," in *Papers of the Presidents of the United States* (Washington, D.C.: Government Printing Office, 1965).

FIGURE 10-1 TIMELINE OF CIVIL RIGHTS AND THE GREAT SOCIETY

Events	Year	Writings
Korean War begins	1950	
	1951	Hannah Arendt's *The Origins of Totalitarianism*
	1952	Ralph Ellison's *Invisible Man*
	1954	Earl Warren's opinion in Brown v. Board of Education
	1956	J. Wright Mills's *The Power Elite*
Soviet *Sputnik* satellite launched	1957	
	1957	Ayn Rand's *Atlas Shrugged*
	1957	Jack Kerouac's *On the Road*
Isaiah Berlin's *Two Concepts of Liberty*	1958	
Students for a Democratic Society founded	1960	
Young Americans for Freedom founded	1960	
	1960	Harper Lee's *To Kill a Mockingbird*
Berlin Wall built	1961	
H.L.A. Hart's *The Concept of Law*	1961	
Michel Foucault's *Madness and Civilization*	1961	
	1962	Rachel Carson's *Silent Spring*
	1962	Milton Friedman's *Capitalism and Freedom*
Cuban Missile Crisis	1962	

deeply unpopular and weighed down the party as a whole. The various protest movements of the prior decade had coalesced to make a broad set of demands on the Democratic leadership but were themselves increasingly controversial with the general public. Johnson admitted defeat and withdrew from the race. Vice President Hubert Humphrey claimed the nomination at the national convention in Chicago but was unable to unite the party, symbolized by the "siege of Chicago" by antiwar protestors and another Dixiecrat bolt behind Alabama Governor George Wallace. The winning candidate, Republican Richard Nixon, claimed to speak for a "silent majority" but inherited a deeply divided nation.

Politics. The New Deal coalition was powerful but fragile. Union leaders and civil rights activists, liberals and conservatives sat uneasily with one another. It was usually enough to win elections and move federal legislation, but liberals often found themselves frustrated

Events	Year	Writings
	1963	Martin Luther King's "I Have a Dream" Speech
	1963	Betty Friedan's *The Feminine Mystique*
President John F. Kennedy assassinated	1963	
President Lyndon B. Johnson launches the Great Society	1964	
Congress passes Civil Rights Act	1964	
Congress passes Gulf of Tonkin Resolution	1964	
National Organization for Women founded	1966	
Black Panthers founded	1966	
Martin Luther King assassinated	1968	
	1969	Herbert Marcuse's *An Essay on Liberation*
Neil Armstrong becomes first person to walk on the moon	1969	
	1971	John Rawls's *A Theory of Justice*
United States withdraws from Vietnam	1973	
President Richard Nixon resigns	1974	
	1974	Robert Nozick's *Anarchy, State and Utopia*
Moral Majority founded	1979	
American embassy personnel taken hostage in Iran	1979	
Margaret Thatcher elected British prime minister	1979	

by powerful Southern Democrats in the 1950s. Political scientist James MacGregor Burns, a Kennedy insider, tellingly complained during the heady days of Camelot about the "deadlock of democracy" that would not simply let political majorities get their way. The Republicans returned to national office in 1952 for the first time since the Great Depression. But they did so by pushing aside their established and more conservative leaders and nominating the celebrated war hero Dwight Eisenhower, who had been courted by both parties, and they quickly lost their hold on Congress. The "New Republicanism" offered by Eisenhower had no coattails and only offered a more frugal version of the New Deal. Democrats returned to dominance with John F. Kennedy and Lyndon B. Johnson in the 1960s, until the coalition flew apart at the end of the 1960s. Democrats continued to hold Congress throughout the 1970s and passed landmark reform legislation like the Environmental Protection Act, even as Richard Nixon occupied the White House.

Society. The United States enjoyed an economic boom through much of the mid-twentieth century. Its industrial base emerged from World War II intact, and free trade predominated in the postwar world. American industry thrived as it produced goods for war-ravaged Europe and Asia. The Cold War meant continued defense spending at nearly wartime levels, constantly injecting funds into a growing defense industry. Even the manifesto of the Students for a Democratic Society recognized that the baby boomers who occupied college campuses in the 1960s had grown up "in at least modest comfort." Serious doubts about the idea of America as an affluent society did not arise until the "stagflation" of the 1970s, when both unemployment and inflation unexpectedly went up together.

General prosperity set the stage for social upheaval. The U.S. Supreme Court's declaration that segregated schools were unconstitutional set off sometimes violent conflicts across the South over whether, how, and how quickly to comply with judicial orders. The struggle to overcome the "massive resistance" of the school segregationists expanded into street demonstrations for a broader array of civil rights in the 1960s, culminating in landmark federal legislation aimed at tearing down Jim Crow. By the late 1960s, the movement for black civil rights had bled into an array of additional protest movements advocating against the military draft and on behalf of women's rights, antipoverty programs, and cultural change. Michael Harrington broke out of his socialist circle and won mainstream success with the publication in 1960 of *The Other America*, an exposé of continued poverty in the midst of plenty. The bright media spotlight shining on social ills from Appalachian poverty to southern racial violence both inspired and bolstered politicians and activists to push forward reform.

Ideas. The war had its effect on the course of intellectual development. Skepticism abounded in the 1920s and 1930s. The Legal Realist movement reflected those currents, casting doubt on the utility of legal rules and rights. Constitutional law was little more than the "common sense of the Supreme Court" at any given moment.[2] In the postwar period, such skepticism about the value of legal rules and rights seemed less attractive. New theories of human rights and constitutional rules occupied legal and political thought at midcentury. In philosophy, John Rawls launched a broad-based attack against utilitarianism, which similarly seemed to disparage rights. His work helped spark a sweeping resuscitation of interest in Kantian moral imperatives. The idea of individual rights as "side constraints" or "trumps" on the majority will or the public interest flourished. In contrast to the totalitarian regimes of Nazi Germany or communist Russia, American intellectuals emphasized their commitment to not only democracy but a democracy that respected liberty.

The rise of fascist regimes and subsequent war in Europe displaced many from their ancestral homes. Tens of thousands of Jewish immigrants settled in the United States; among them were a wide range of intellectuals who helped shape postwar American thought. Leo Strauss, for example, immigrated to the United States in 1937 and became an

---

2 Thomas Reed Powell, "The Logic and Rhetoric of Constitutional Law," *Journal of Philosophy, Psychology and Scientific Methods* 15 (1918): 653.

influential teacher at the University of Chicago in the postwar period, denouncing the moral relativism that he thought infested modern political philosophy and politics. Hannah Arendt arrived in the United States in 1941 and within a decade achieved public acclaim with her study of the origins of totalitarianism. Herbert Marcuse made his way to the United States in 1934, becoming a hero to the New Left in the 1960s for his Marxist- and Freudian-inflected utopian theorizing. Such Jewish intellectuals did not form a single school of thought, but they injected into American thinking a deep engagement with European intellectual traditions and the horrors of modern political repression.

The aftermath of World War II also brought the dissolution of the great European empires and with it new nationalist and pan-nationalist strains of thought that had repercussions in the United States. Indian independence from Britain gave new luster to Mahatma Gandhi's interwar doctrine of passive "noncooperation" as a moral principle and a political strategy. The French Caribbean native and advocate of Algerian independence Frantz Fanon developed a sustained critique of the racism that he thought was inherent in imperial Western thought. The Palestinian-American literary scholar Edward Said drew on emerging French philosophical work to expose the biases embedded in Western efforts to understand foreign peoples and cultures. Decolonization suggested both the possibility of political theory outside the Cold War and European-American context and the need to engage in political thinking from the particular perspective of the oppressed.

II. DEMOCRACY AND LIBERTY

Major Developments

- Civil liberties revolution
- Dissolution of the liberal consensus
- Emergence of the modern conservative movement

In 1938, the successful Democratic candidate for California attorney general, Earl Warren, explained what "liberalism" meant to him by shifting terms from liberal to "progressive" and explaining: "The progressive . . . realizes that democracy is a growing institution and that, if it is to succeed, we must make steady advances from day to day to constantly improve it and adapt it to human requirements on an ever-widening basis."[3] As Chief Justice of the United States from the mid-1950s to the end of the 1960s, Earl Warren did as much as anyone to try to improve and adapt democracy. The Warren Court, especially in its most activist phase in the 1960s, remade American constitutional law, launching what was subsequently called a civil rights and civil liberties revolution. Stocked with a solid liberal majority appointed by both Democratic and Republican presidents, the Warren Court offered a new vision of how to reconcile democracy and liberty. Democracy rested on a majoritarian base, and the Court took the lead in reapportioning legislatures, freeing speech, and extending voting rights. At the same time, the Court understood democracy

3 Quoted in Jim Newton, *Justice for All* (New York: Penguin, 2006), 216.

to require constitutional limits that respected individual liberty, and the liberty that the justices had in mind ranged from enhanced protections to criminal defendants, greater accommodation of religious minorities, and racial equality. The Court may have acted boldly, and often controversially, but it did not act alone. Politicians adopted their own measures to advance civil rights and professionalize police forces, and political activists took to the streets to demand social and political change.

Not everyone was in agreement about what reforms were necessary and how these changes should proceed. In 1949, the New Deal historian Arthur Schlesinger, Jr. had defended the liberal consensus as the "vital center," the moderate American path between communism and fascism. Advocacy organizations like Americans for Democratic Action (ADA) and the American Civil Liberties Union (ACLU) helped define what postwar liberalism would be. By the 1970s, America, and more particularly American liberalism, seemed to have come "unraveled."[4] Most visibly, a vocal New Left movement dissented from Cold War liberalism. Dissatisfied with the compromises and ambitions of mainstream liberals, these activists and intellectuals demanded not just rights but "liberation," not just welfare but a "humane" economy. Less visibly, a new conservative movement questioned the direction of liberalism from the right. William F. Buckley's new magazine, *National Review*, served as the vehicle for working out a new "fusionist" vision that tied together economic conservatives, social conservatives, and anticommunist hardliners. Conservatives maintained a steady drumbeat of criticism of the ways in which the Warren Court and Democratic politicians were redefining democracy and civil liberties, while calling for enhanced recognition for economic rights.

The postwar period also saw a growing body of scholarly work examining the meaning and functioning of democracy. The Harvard economist Joseph Schumpeter laid out what became known as the proceduralist or minimalist theory of democracy. Democracies were not to be understood as the expression and realization of the popular will, for that was unrealistic. Instead, democracies were characterized simply by a political process in which competing candidates gained political power by standing for popular election.[5] Fair procedures for holding government officials popularly accountable were both the necessary and sufficient condition for democratic governance. By contrast, more substantive or deliberative theories were emphasized by some normative theorists. From this perspective, as the philosopher and German émigré Hannah Arendt pointed out, "the trouble . . . is that politics has become a profession and a career." The minimalist approach to democracy "has achieved . . . a certain control of the rulers by those who are ruled," but it "has by no means enabled the citizen to become a 'participator' in public affairs" or necessarily secured the well-being of the public.[6] The longing for a more active form of citizenship was a growing theme of critiques of the democratic practices found in the United States.

---

4 See, Arthur Schlesinger, Jr., *The Vital Center* (Boston: Houghton Mifflin, 1949); Allen J. Matusow, *The Unraveling of America* (New York: Harper & Row, 1984).

5 Joseph Schumpeter, *Capitalism, Socialism and Democracy* (New York: Harper & Brothers, 1942).

6 Hannah Arendt, *On Revolution* (New York: Viking, 1963), 277, 268.

MILTON FRIEDMAN

CAPITALISM AND FREEDOM (1962)

Milton Friedman grew up in New Jersey and eventually completed a Ph.D. in economics at Columbia University in 1948 (interrupted by wartime service in the Treasury Department). He spent most of his academic career at the University of Chicago. Friedman made a variety of significant contributions to economics (for which he was awarded a Nobel Prize in 1976), most notably his work arguing that changes in the money supply affected economic growth. He was also a prominent public figure and political activist. With Friedrich Hayek, he helped to found the Mont Pelerin Society (an international group of intellectuals that promoted free-market economics) in 1947, wrote a regular column for *Newsweek* magazine for nearly two decades, wrote popular books on politics and economics, and served as a Republican presidential advisor.

Why does Friedman reject the idea of a "national purpose"? What does Friedman regard as the essential purpose of government? How important is democracy to his philosophy of government? What does he mean by economic freedom? Why does he regard economic freedom as an important component of freedom broadly? Is Friedman's argument consistent with the New Deal state?

In a much quoted passage in his inaugural address, President Kennedy said, "Ask not what your country can do for you—ask what you can do for your country." It is a striking sign of the temper of our times that the controversy about this passage centered on its origin and not on its content. Neither half of the statement expresses a relation between the citizen and his government that is worthy of the ideals of free men in a free society. The paternalistic "what your country can do for you" implies that government is the patron, the citizen the ward, a view that is at odds with the free man's belief in his own responsibility for his own destiny. The organismic, "what you can do for your country" implies that government is the master or the deity, the citizen, the servant or the votary. To the free man, the country is the collection of individuals who compose it, not something over and above them. He is proud of a common heritage and loyal to common traditions. But he regards government as a means, an instrumentality, neither a grantor of favors and gifts, nor a master or god to be blindly worshipped and served. He recognizes no national goal except as it is the consensus of the goals that the citizens severally serve. He recognizes no national purpose except as it is the consensus of the purposes for which the citizens severally strive.

The free man will ask neither what his country can do for him nor what he can do for his country. He will ask rather "What can I and my compatriots do through government" to help us discharge our individual responsibilities, to achieve our several goals and purposes, and above all, to protect our freedom? And he will accompany this question with another: How can we keep the government we create from becoming a Frankenstein that will destroy the very freedom we establish it to protect? Freedom is a rare and delicate plant. Our minds tell us, and history confirms, that the great threat to freedom is the concentration of power. Government is necessary to preserve our freedom, it is an instrument through which we can exercise our freedom; yet by concentrating power in political hands, it is also a threat to freedom. Even though the men who wield this power initially be of good will and even though they be not corrupted by the power they exercise, the power will both attract and form men of a different stamp.

. . .

. . . [A free economy] gives people what they want instead of what a particular group thinks they ought to want. Underlying most arguments against the free market is a lack of belief in freedom itself.

The existence of a free market does not of course eliminate the need for government. On the contrary, government is essential both as a forum for determining the "rules of the game" and as an umpire to interpret and enforce the rules decided on. What the market does is to reduce greatly the range of issues that must be decided through political means, and thereby to minimize the extent to which government need participate directly in the game. The characteristic feature of action through political channels is that it tends to require or enforce substantial conformity. The great advantage of the market, on the other hand, is that it permits wide diversity. It is, in political terms, a system of proportional representation. Each man can vote, as it were, for the color of tie he wants and get it; he does not have to see what color the majority wants and then, if he is in the minority, submit.

It is this feature of the market that we refer to when we say that the market provides economic freedom. But this characteristic also has implications that go far beyond the narrowly economic. Political freedom means the absence of coercion of a man by his fellow men. The fundamental threat to freedom is power to coerce, be it in the hands of a monarch, a dictator, an oligarchy, or a momentary majority. The preservation of freedom requires the elimination of such concentration of power to the fullest possible extent and the dispersal and distribution of whatever power cannot be eliminated—a system of checks and balances. By removing the organization of economic activity from the control of political authority, the market eliminates this source of coercive power. It enables economic strength to be a check to political power rather than a reinforcement.

. . .

. . . However attractive anarchy may be as a philosophy, it is not feasible in a world of imperfect men. Men's freedoms can conflict, and when they do, one man's freedom must be limited to preserve another's—as a Supreme Court Justice once put it, "My freedom to move my fist must be limited by the proximity of your chin."

The major problem in deciding the appropriate activities of government is how to resolve such conflicts among the freedoms of different individuals. In some cases, the answer is easy. There is little difficulty in attaining near unanimity to the proposition that one man's freedom to murder his neighbor must be sacrificed to preserve the freedom of the other man to live. In other cases, the answer is difficult. In the economic area, a major problem arises in respect of the conflict between freedom to combine and freedom to compete. . . .

. . .

The role of government just considered is to do something that the market cannot do for itself, namely, to determine, arbitrate, and enforce the rules of the game. We may also want to do through government some things that might conceivably be done through the market but that technical or similar conditions render it difficult to do in that way. These all reduce to cases in which strictly voluntary exchange is either exceedingly costly or practically impossible. . . .

. . .

BARRY GOLDWATER

ACCEPTANCE SPEECH FOR THE REPUBLICAN NOMINATION FOR PRESIDENT (1964)

Barry Goldwater was raised in Arizona, where his father had founded a department store. He spent the 1930s working at the store after his father's death but left to join the air force during World War II, eventually rising to the rank of brigadier general in the Air National Guard. After the war, he went into politics as a Republican, winning a seat in the U.S. Senate in 1952. In the Senate, he carved out a reputation as a staunch anticommunist and small-government conservative. His 1960 book *The Conscience of a Conservative* (ghost-written by his speechwriter, L. Brent Bozell) found a national audience, and he was recruited by conservative activists to run for president against the liberal incumbent, John F. Kennedy. Kennedy's successor, Lyndon B. Johnson, beat Goldwater in a landslide, but Goldwater's ability to win the Republican nomination over the liberal New York governor Nelson Rockefeller was seen as a significant battle for ideological control of the Republican Party. His nomination acceptance speech (to which a number of conservative activists contributed) helped galvanize the emerging conservative movement, including California Governor Ronald Reagan. He spent the remainder of his career in the U.S. Senate, retiring in 1986.

Why would Goldwater make freedom a central theme of his acceptance speech? What is the freedom that he has in mind? How does the vision of America that he sets out differ from Franklin Roosevelt's? What is the contrasting view of "man, his nature, and his destiny" on offer in the speech? Was it "dangerous, irresponsible, and frightening" (as Nelson Rockefeller said) for Goldwater to praise "extremism in the defense of liberty"?[7]

. . .

The good Lord raised this mighty Republic to be a home for the brave and to flourish as the land of the free—not to stagnate in the swampland of collectivism, not to cringe before the bully of communism.

Now, my fellow Americans, the tide has been running against freedom. Our people have followed false prophets. We must, and we shall, return to proven ways—not because they are old, but because they are true. We must, and we shall, set the tide running again in the cause of freedom. And this party, with its every action, every word, every breath, and every heartbeat, has but a single resolve, and that is freedom—freedom made orderly for this nation by our constitutional government; freedom under a government limited by laws of nature and of nature's God; freedom—balanced so that liberty lacking order will not become the slavery of the prison cell; balanced so that liberty lacking order will not become the license of the mob and of the jungle.

Now, we Americans understand freedom. We have earned it, we have lived for it, and we have died for it. This Nation and its people are freedom's model in a searching world. We can be freedom's missionaries in a doubting world. But, ladies and gentlemen, first we must renew freedom's mission in our own hearts and in our own homes.

. . .

Rather than useful jobs in our country, people have been offered bureaucratic "make work," rather than moral leadership, they have been given bread and circuses, spectacles, and, yes, they have even been given scandals. Tonight there is violence in our streets, corruption in our highest offices, aimlessness among our youth, anxiety among our elders and there is a virtual despair among the many who look beyond material success for the inner meaning of their lives. Where examples of morality should be set,

7 Richard Norton Smith, *On His Own Terms* (New York: Random House, 2014), 452.

the opposite is seen. Small men, seeking great wealth or power, have too often and too long turned even the highest levels of public service into mere personal opportunity.

. . .

Security from domestic violence, no less than from foreign aggression, is the most elementary and fundamental purpose of any government, and a government that cannot fulfill that purpose is one that cannot long command the loyalty of its citizens. History shows us—demonstrates that nothing—nothing prepares the way for tyranny more than the failure of public officials to keep the streets from bullies and marauders.

Now, we Republicans see all this as more, much more, than the rest: of mere political differences or mere political mistakes. We see this as the result of a fundamentally and absolutely wrong view of man, his nature and his destiny. Those who seek to live your lives for you, to take your liberties in return for relieving you of yours, those who elevate the state and downgrade the citizen must see ultimately a world in which earthly power can be substituted for divine will, and this Nation was founded upon the rejection of that notion and upon the acceptance of God as the author of freedom.

Those who seek absolute power, even though they seek it to do what they regard as good, are simply demanding the right to enforce their own version of heaven on earth. And let me remind you, they are the very ones who always create the most hellish tyrannies. Absolute power does corrupt, and those who seek it must be suspect and must be opposed. Their mistaken course stems from false notions of equality, ladies and gentlemen. Equality, rightly understood, as our founding fathers understood it, leads to liberty and to the emancipation of creative differences. Wrongly understood, as it has been so tragically in our time, it leads first to conformity and then to despotism.

Fellow Republicans, it is the cause of Republicanism to resist concentrations of power, private or public, which enforce such conformity and inflict such despotism. It is the cause of Republicanism to ensure that power remains in the hands of the people. And, so help us God, that is exactly what a Republican president will do with the help of a Republican Congress.

It is further the cause of Republicanism to restore a clear understanding of the tyranny of man over man in the world at large. It is our cause to dispel the foggy thinking which avoids hard decisions in the illusion that a world of conflict will somehow mysteriously resolve itself into a world of harmony, if we just don't rock the boat or irritate the forces of aggression—and this is hogwash.

It is further the cause of Republicanism to remind ourselves, and the world, that only the strong can remain free, that only the strong can keep the peace.

. . .

The Republican cause demands that we brand communism as a principal disturber of peace in the world today. Indeed, we should brand it as the only significant disturber of the peace, and we must make clear that until its goals of conquest are absolutely renounced and its rejections with all nations tempered, communism and the governments it now controls are enemies of every man on earth who is or wants to be free.

We here in America can keep the peace only if we remain vigilant and only if we remain strong. Only if we keep our eyes open and keep our guard up can we prevent war. And I want to make this abundantly clear—I don't intend to let peace or freedom be torn from our grasp because of lack of strength or lack of will—and that I promise you Americans.

I believe that we must look beyond the defense of freedom today to its extension tomorrow. I believe that the communism which boasts it will bury us will, instead, give way to the forces of freedom. And I can see in the distant and yet recognizable future the outlines of a world worthy our dedication, our every risk, our every effort, our every sacrifice along the way. Yes, a world that will redeem the suffering of those who will be liberated from tyranny. I can see and I suggest that all thoughtful men must contemplate the flowering of an Atlantic civilization, the whole world of Europe unified and free, trading openly across its borders, communicating openly across the world. This is a goal far, far more meaningful than a moon shot.

It's a truly inspiring goal for all free men to set for themselves during the latter half of the twentieth century. I can also see—and all free men must thrill to—the events of this Atlantic civilization joined by its great ocean highway to the United States. What a destiny, what a destiny can be ours to stand as a great central pillar linking Europe, the Americans and the venerable and vital peoples and cultures of the Pacific. I can see a day when all the Americas, North and South, will be linked in a mighty system, a system in which the errors and misunderstandings of the past will be submerged one by one in a rising tide of prosperity and interdependence. We know that the misunderstandings of centuries are not to be wiped away in a day or wiped away in an hour. But we pledge—we pledge that human sympathy—what our neighbors to the South call that attitude of "simpatico"—no less than enlightened self'-interest will be our guide.

I can see this Atlantic civilization galvanizing and guiding emergent nations everywhere.

I know this freedom is not the fruit of every soil. I know that our own freedom was achieved through centuries, by unremitting efforts by brave and wise men. I know that the road to freedom is a long and a challenging road. I know also that some men may walk away from it, that some men resist challenge, accepting the false security of governmental paternalism.

And I pledge that the America I envision in the years ahead will extend its hand in health, in teaching and in cultivation, so that all new nations will be at least encouraged to go our way, so that they will not wander down the dark alleys of tyranny or to the dead-end streets of collectivism. My fellow Republicans, we do no man a service by hiding freedom's light under a bushel of mistaken humility.

I seek an American proud of its past, proud of its ways, proud of its dreams, and determined actively to proclaim them. But our example to the world must, like charity, begin at home.

In our vision of a good and decent future, free and peaceful, there must be room for deliberation of the energy and talent of the individual—otherwise our vision is blind at the outset.

We must assure a society here which, while never abandoning the needy or forsaking the helpless, nurtures incentives and opportunity for the creative and the productive. We must know the whole good is the product of many single contributions.

I cherish a day when our children once again will restore as heroes the sort of men and women who—unafraid and undaunted—pursue the truth, strive to cure disease, subdue and make fruitful our natural environment and produce the inventive engines of production, science, and technology.

. . .

We Republicans see in our constitutional form of government the great framework which assures the orderly but dynamic fulfillment of the whole man, and we see the whole man as the great reason for instituting orderly government in the first place.

We see, in private property and in economy based upon and fostering private property, the one way to make government a durable ally of the whole man, rather than his determined enemy. We see in the sanctity of private property the only durable foundation for constitutional government in a free society. And beyond that, we see, in cherished diversity of ways, diversity of thoughts, of motives and accomplishments. We do not seek to lead anyone's life for him—we seek only to secure his rights and to guarantee him opportunity to strive, with government performing only those needed and constitutionally sanctioned tasks which cannot otherwise be performed.

We Republicans seek a government that attends to its inherent responsibilities of maintaining a stable monetary and fiscal climate, encouraging a free and a competitive economy and enforcing law and order. Thus do we seek inventiveness, diversity, and creativity within a stable order, for we Republicans define government's role where needed at many, many levels, preferably through the one closest to the people involved.

. . .

Back in 1858 Abraham Lincoln said this of the Republican party—and I quote him, because he probably could have said it during the last week or so: "It was composed of strained, discordant, and even hostile elements" in 1858. Yet all of these elements agreed on one paramount objective: To arrest the progress of slavery, and place it in the course of ultimate extinction.

Today, as then, but more urgently and more broadly than then, the task of preserving and enlarging freedom at home and safeguarding it from the forces of tyranny abroad is great enough to challenge all our resources and to require all our strength. Anyone who joins us in all sincerity, we welcome. Those who do not care for our cause, we don't expect to enter our ranks in any case. And let our Republicanism, so focused and so dedicated, not be made fuzzy and futile by unthinking and stupid labels.

I would remind you that extremism in the defense of liberty is no vice. And let me remind you also that moderation in the pursuit of justice is no virtue.

The beauty of the very system we Republicans are pledged to restore and revitalize, the beauty of this Federal system of ours is in its reconciliation of diversity with unity. We must not see malice in honest differences of opinion, and no matter how great, so long as they are not inconsistent with the pledges we have given to each other in and through our Constitution. Our Republican cause is not to level out the world or make its people conform in computer regimented sameness. Our Republican cause is to free our people and light the way for liberty throughout the world.

Ours is a very human cause for very humane goals.

This Party, its good people, and its unquestionable devotion to freedom, will not fulfill the purposes of this campaign which we launch here now until our cause has won the day, inspired the world, and shown the way to a tomorrow worthy of all our yesteryears.

. . .

HERBERT MARCUSE

AN ESSAY ON LIBERATION (1969)

Herbert Marcuse was raised in Germany by a wealthy Jewish family, and he earned a Ph.D. in literature in 1922, but his scholarly interests soon turned to philosophy and he joined a group of social scientists based at Frankfurt who were drawing on insights from G. W. F. Hegel and Karl Marx in developing a "critical theory" that could contribute to the transcendence of capitalist society (Marcuse himself added Sigmund Freud to the mix). In 1934, he fled Nazi Germany, becoming an American citizen in 1940 and working in intelligence during World War II. His work became increasingly influential over the course of the 1960s, and he became a significant figure in the student movement of the New Left when he was teaching at the University of California at San Diego.

What does Marcuse mean by "liberation"? Why does he think capitalism is inconsistent with a truly free society? What does he see as the problem with contemporary democracies? Can the "utopian possibilities" that he envisions be achieved democratically? What does he see as the limits of reform in a capitalist democracy? How does Marcuse's conception of the relationship between science, democracy, and freedom compare with John Dewey's in Chapter 8? Are there advantages to his ideal of a free society over liberal democracies?

. . .

Utopian possibilities are inherent in the technical and technological forces of advanced capitalism and socialism: the rational utilization of these forces on a global scale would terminate poverty and scarcity within a very foreseeable future. But we know now that neither their rational use nor—and this is decisive – their collective control by the "immediate producers" (the workers) would by itself eliminate domination and exploitation: a bureaucratic welfare state would still be a state of repression which would continue even into the "second phase of socialism," when each is to receive "according to his needs."

What is now at stake are the needs themselves. At this stage, the question is no longer: how can the individual satisfy his own needs without hurting others, but rather: how can he satisfy his needs without hurting himself, without reproducing, through his aspirations and satisfactions, his dependence on an exploitative apparatus which, in satisfying his needs, perpetuates his servitude? The advent of a free society would be characterized by the fact that the growth of well-being turns into an essentially new quality of life. . . .

. . .

This society is obscene in producing and indecently exposing a stifling abundance of wares while depriving its victims abroad of the necessities of life; obscene in stuffing itself and its garbage cans while poisoning and burning the scarce foodstuffs in the fields of its aggression; obscene in the words and smiles of its politicians and entertainers; in its prayers, in its ignorance, and in the wisdom of its kept intellectuals.

. . .

The so-called consumer economy and the politics of corporate capitalism have created a second nature of man which ties him libidinally and aggressively to the commodity form. The need for possessing, consuming, handling, and constantly renewing the gadgets, devices, instruments, engines, offered to and imposed upon the people, for using these wares even at the danger of one's own destruction, has become a "biological" need. . . . The second nature of man thus militates against any change that would disrupt and perhaps even abolish this dependence of man on a market ever more densely filled with merchandise—abolish his existence as a consumer consuming himself in buying and selling. The needs generated by this system are thus eminently stabilizing, conservative needs: the counterrevolution anchored in the instinctual structure.

. . .

For freedom indeed depends largely on technical progress, on the advancement of science. But this fact easily obscures the essential precondition: in order to become vehicles of freedom, science and technology would have to change their present direction and goals; they would have to be reconstructed in accord with a new sensibility—the demands of the life instincts. Then one could speak of a technology of liberation, product of a scientific imagination free to project and design the forms of a human universe without exploitation and toil. But this *gaya scienza* is conceivable only after the historical break in the continuum of domination as expressive of the needs of a new type of man.

. . .

Dialectics of democracy: if democracy means self-government of free people, with justice for all, then the realization of democracy would presuppose abolition of the existing pseudo-democracy. In the dynamic of corporate capitalism, the fight for democracy thus tends to assume anti-democratic forms, and to the extent to which the democratic decisions are made in "parliaments" on all levels, the opposition will tend to become extra-parliamentary. The movement to extend constitutionally professed rights and liberties to the daily life of the oppressed minorities, even the movement to preserve existing rights and liberties, will become "subversive" to the degree to which it will meet the stiffening resistance of the majority against an "exaggerated" interpretation and application of equality and justice.

An opposition which is directed, not against a particular form of government or against particular conditions within a society, but against a given social system as a whole, cannot remain legal and lawful because it is the established legality and the established law which it opposes. The fact that the democratic process provides for the redress of grievances and for legal and lawful changes does not alter the illegality inherent in an opposition to an institutionalized democracy which halts the process of change at the stage where it would destroy the existing system. By virtue of this built-in stabilizer or "governor," capitalist mass-democracy is perhaps to a higher degree self-perpetuating than any other form of government or society; and the more so the more it rests, not on terror and scarcity, but on efficiency and wealth, and on the majority will of the underlying and administered population. This new situation has direct bearing on the old question as to the right of resistance. Can we say that it is the established system rather than the resistance to it which is in need of justification? Such seems to be the implication of the social contract theories which consider civil society dissolved when, in its existing form, it no longer fulfills the functions for which it was set up, namely, as a system of socially necessary and productive repression, Theoretically, these functions were determined by the philosophers: the realistically minded defined the "end of government" as the protection of property, trade, and commerce; the idealists spoke of the realization of Reason, Justice, Freedom (without altogether neglecting or even minimizing the more material and economic aspects). In both schools, judgment as to whether a government actually fulfilled these "ends," and the criteria for judging, were usually limited to the particular nation-state (or type of nation-state) which the respective philosopher had in mind: that the security, growth, and freedom of the one nation-state involved the insecurity, destruction, or oppression of another did not invalidate the definition, nor did an established government lose its claim for obedience when the protection of property and the realization of reason left large parts of the population in poverty and servitude.

In the contemporary period, the questions as to the "end of government" have subsided. It seems that the continued functioning of the society is sufficient justification for its legality and its claim for obedience, and "functioning" seems defined rather negatively as absence of civil war, massive disorder, economic collapse. Otherwise anything goes: military dictatorship, plutocracy, government by gangs and rackets. Genocide, war crimes, crimes against humanity are not effective arguments against a government which protects property, trade, and commerce at home while it perpetrates its destructive policy abroad. And indeed, there is no enforceable law that could deprive such a constitutional government of its legitimacy and legality. But this means that there is no (enforceable) law other than that which serves the status quo, and that those who refuse such service are *eo ipso* outside the realm of law even before they come into actual conflict with the law.

. . .

For it is precisely the objective, historical function of the democratic system of corporate capitalism to use the Law and Order of bourgeois liberalism as a counterrevolutionary force, thus imposing upon the radical opposition the necessity of direct action and uncivil disobedience, while confronting the opposition with its vastly superior strength. Under these circumstances, direct action and uncivil disobedience become for the rebels integral parts of the transformation of the indirect democracy of corporate capitalism into a direct democracy in which elections and representation no longer serve as institutions of domination. As against the latter, direct action becomes a means of democratization, of change even within the established system. . . .

The alternative is, not democratic evolution versus radical action, but rationalization of the status quo versus change. As long as a social system reproduces, by indoctrination and integration, a self-perpetuating conservative majority, the majority reproduces the system itself—open to changes within, but not beyond, its institutional framework. Consequently, the struggle for changes beyond the system becomes, by virtue of its own dynamic, undemocratic in the terms of the system, and counter-violence is from the beginning inherent in this dynamic. Thus the radical is guilty—either of surrendering to the power of the status quo, or of violating the Law and Order of the status quo.

But who has the right to set himself up as judge of an established society, who other than the legally constituted agencies or agents, and the majority of the people? Other than these, it could only be a self-appointed elite, or leaders who would arrogate to themselves such judgment. Indeed, if the alternative were between democracy and dictatorship (no matter how "benevolent"), the answer would be non-controversial: democracy is preferable. However, this democracy does not exist, and the government is factually exercised by a network of pressure groups and "machines," vested interests represented by and working on and through the democratic institutions. These are not derived from a sovereign people. The representation is representative of the will shaped by the ruling minorities. Consequently, if the alternative is rule by an elite, it would only mean replacement of the present ruling elite by another; and if this other should be the dreaded intellectual elite, it may not he less qualified and less threatening than the prevailing one. True, such government, initially, would not have the endorsement of the majority "inherited" from the previous government—but once the chain of the past governments is broken, the majority would be in a state of flux, and, released from the past management, free to judge the new government in terms of the new common interest. . . .

. . .

What kind of life? We are still confronted with the demand to state the "concrete alternative." The demand is meaningless if it asks for a blueprint of the specific institutions and relationships which would be those of the new society: they cannot be determined a priori; they will develop, in trial and error, as the new society develops. . . .

The concept of the primary, initial institutions of liberation is familiar enough and concrete enough: collective ownership, collective control and planning of the means of production and distribution. This is the foundation, a necessary but not sufficient condition for the alternative: it would make possible the usage of all available resources for the abolition of poverty, which is the prerequisite for the turn from quantity into quality: the creation of a reality in accordance with the new sensitivity and the new consciousness. . . .

. . . [S]ocially necessary labor would be diverted to the construction of an aesthetic rather than repressive environment, to parks and gardens rather than highways and parking lots, to the creation of areas of withdrawal rather than massive fun and relaxation. . . .

Not regression to a previous stage of civilization, but return to an imaginary *temps perdu* in the real life of mankind: progress to a stage of civilization where man has learned to ask for the sake of whom or of what he organizes his society; the stage where he checks and perhaps even halts his incessant struggle for existence on an enlarged scale, surveys what has been achieved through centuries of misery and hecatombs of victims, and decides that it is enough, and that it is time to enjoy what he has and what can be reproduced and refined with a minimum of alienated labor: not the arrest or reduction of technical progress, but the elimination of those of its features which perpetuate man's subjection to the apparatus and the intensification of the struggle for existence—to work harder in order to get more of the merchandise that has to be sold. In other words, electrification indeed, and all technical devices which alleviate and protect life, all the mechanization which frees human energy and time, all the standardization which does away with spurious and parasitarian "personalized" services rather than multiplying them and the gadgets and tokens of exploitative affluence. In terms of the latter (and only in terms of the latter), this would certainly be a regression—but freedom from the rule of merchandise over man is a precondition of freedom.

. . . And there is an answer to the question which troubles the minds of so many men of good will: what are the people in a free society going to do? The answer which, I believe, strikes at the heart of the matter was given by a young black girl. She said: for the first time in our life, we shall be free to think about what we are going to do.

JOHN RAWLS

A THEORY OF JUSTICE (1971)

John Rawls was the son of a successful lawyer in Baltimore. After graduating from Princeton University in 1943, he fought in the Pacific in World War II. He returned to Princeton to earn a Ph.D. in philosophy in 1950 and spent most of his academic career at Harvard University. His work on social justice culminated in the landmark book *A Theory of Justice*, widely recognized as one of the most important works of political philosophy in the twentieth century. His argument for "justice as fairness" countered the then-dominant utilitarian argument that justice should be understand as advancing the greatest good for the greatest number. Rawls's approach instead emphasized the need to recognize individual liberties and redistribute wealth, conclusions that were grounded in an argument that a just society was fair to its least fortunate members. Among his critics was his Harvard colleague Robert Nozick, whose *Anarchy, State and Utopia* started from similar premises but concluded that only a minimal state could be justified. Rawls's work became a touchstone for political liberals, while Nozick's 1974 book became central to the libertarian movement.

What role does the hypothetical social contract serve in Rawls's theory? Why should a hypothetical agreement be informative of the principles of justice? What are the "circumstances of the original position"? Is Rawls persuasive on the terms under which we would agree to social cooperation? Why would we prefer to maximize (equal) liberty? Is Rawls persuasive in justifying redistribution? How extensive should redistribution be? How distant is Rawls's just society from the contemporary United States?

. . .

My aim is to present a conception of justice which generalizes and carries to a higher level of abstraction the familiar theory of the social contract as found, say, in Locke, Rousseau, and Kant. In order to do this we are not to think of the original contract as one to enter a particular society or to set up a particular form of government. Rather the guiding idea is that the principles of justice for the basic structure of society are the object of the original agreement. They are the principles that free and rational persons concerned to further their own interests would accept in an initial position of equality as defining the fundamental terms of their association. These principles are to regulate all further agreements; they specify the kinds of social cooperation that can be entered into and the forms of government that can be established. This way of regarding the principles of justice I shall call justice as fairness.

Thus we are to imagine that those who engage in social cooperation choose together, in one joint act, the principles which are to assign basic rights and duties and to determine the division of social benefits. Men are to decide in advance how they are to regulate their claims against one another and what is to be the foundation charter of their society. Just as each person must decide by rational reflection what constitutes his good, that is, the system of ends which it is rational for him to pursue, so a group of persons must decide once and for all what is to found among them as just and unjust. The choice which rational men would make in this hypothetical situation of equal liberty, assuming for the present that this choice problem has a solution, determines the principles of justice.

In justice as fairness the original position of equality corresponds to the state of nature in the traditional theory of the social contract. This original position is not, of course, thought of as an actual historical state of affairs, much less as a primitive condition of culture. It is understood as a purely hypothetical situation characterized so as to lead to a certain conception of justice. Among the essential features of this situation is that no one knows his place in society, his class position or social status, nor does anyone know his fortune in the distribution of natural assets and abilities, his intelligence, strength, and the like. I shall even assume that the parties do not know their conceptions of the good or their special psychological propensities. The principles of justice are chosen behind a veil of ignorance. This ensures that no one is advantaged or disadvantaged in the choice of principles by the outcome of natural chance or the contingency of social circumstances. Since all are similarly situated and no one is able to design principles to favor his particular condition, the principles of justice are the result of a fair agreement or bargain. For given the circumstances of the original position, the symmetry of everyone's relations to each other, this initial situation is fair between individuals as moral persons, that is, as rational beings with their own ends and capable of their own ends and capable, I shall assume, of a sense of justice. The original position is, one might say, the appropriate initial status quo, and thus the fundamental agreements reached in it are fair. This explains the propriety of the name "justice as fairness": it conveys the idea that the principles of justice are agreed to in an initial situation that is fair. The name does not mean that the concepts of justice and fairness are the same, any more than the phrase "poetry as metaphor" means that the concepts of poetry and metaphor are the same.

Justice as fairness begins . . . with one of the most general of all choices which persons might make together, namely, with the choice of the first principles of a conception of justice which is to regulate all subsequent criticism and reform of institutions. Then, having chosen a conception of justice, we can suppose that they are to choose a constitution and a legislature to enact laws, and so on, all in accordance with the principles of justice initially agreed upon. Our social situation is just if it is such that by this sequence of hypothetical agreements we would have contracted into the general system of rules which define it. . . . No society can, of course, be a scheme of cooperation which men enter voluntarily in a literal sense. . . . Yet a society satisfying the principles of justice as fairness come as close as a society can to being a voluntary scheme, for it meets the principles which free and equal persons would assent to under circumstances that are fair. . . .

. . .

I shall maintain that the person in the initial situation would choose two rather different principles: the first requires equality in the assignment of the basic rights and duties, while the second holds that social and economic inequalities, for example inequalities of wealth and authority, are just only if they result in compensating benefits for everyone, and in particular for the least advantaged members of society. These principles rule out justifying institutions on the grounds that the hardships of some are offset by a greater good in the aggregate. It may be expedient but it is not just that some should have less in order that others may prosper. But there is no injustice in the greater benefits earned by a few provided that the situation of persons not so fortunate is thereby improved. The intuitive idea is that since everyone's well-being depends upon a scheme of cooperation without which no one could have a satisfactory life, the division of advantages should be such as to draw forth the willing cooperation of everyone taking part in it, including those less well situated. Yet this can be expected only if reasonable terms are proposed. . . .

. . .

I shall now state in provisional form the two principles of justice that I believe would be chosen in the original position. . . .

The first statement of the two principles reads as follows.

First: each person is to have an equal right to the most extensive basic liberty compatible with a similar liberty for others.

Second: social and economic inequalities are to be arranged so that they are both (a) reasonably expected to be to everyone's advantage, and (b) attached to positions and offices open to all.

. . .

By way of general comment, these principles primarily apply . . . to the basic structure of society. They are to govern the assignment of right and duties and to regulate the distribution of social and economic advantages. As their formulation suggests, these principles presuppose that the social structure can be divided into two more or less distinct parts, the first principle applying to the one, the second to the other. They distinguish between those aspects of the social system that define and secure the equal liberties of citizenship and those that specify and establish social and economic inequalities. The basic liberties of citizens are, roughly speaking, political liberty (the right to vote and to be eligible for public office) together with freedom of speech and assembly; liberty of conscience and freedom of thought; freedom of the person along with the right to hold (personal) property; and freedom from arbitrary arrest and seizure as defined by the concept of the rule of law. These liberties are all required to be equal by the first principle, since citizens of a just society are to have the same basic rights.

The second principle applies, in the first approximation, to the distribution of income and wealth and to the design of organizations that make use of differences in authority and responsibility, or chains of command. While the distribution of wealth and income need not be equal, it must be to everyone's advantage, and at the same time, positions of authority and offices of command must be accessible to all. One applies the second principle by holding positions open, and then, subject to this constraint, arranges social and economic inequalities so that everyone benefits.

These principles are to be arranged in a serial order with the first principle prior to the second. The ordering means that a departure from the institutions of equal liberty required by the first principle cannot be justified, or compensated for, by greater social and economic advantages. The distribution of wealth and income, and the hierarchies of authority, must be consistent with both the liberties of equal citizenship and equality of opportunity.

. . . For the present, it should be observed that the two principles . . . are a special case of a more general conception of justice that can be expressed as follows.

> All social values—liberty and opportunity, income and wealth, and the RDbases of self-respect—are to be distributed equally unless an unequal distribution of any, or all, of these values is to everyone's advantage.

Injustice then, is simply inequalities that are not to the benefit of all. . . .

. . .

Now it is possible, at least theoretically, that by giving up some of their fundamental liberties men are sufficiently compensated by the resulting social and economic gains. The general conception of justice imposes no restrictions on what sort of inequalities are permissible; it only requires that everyone's position be improved. We need not suppose anything so drastic as consenting to a condition of slavery. Imagine instead that men forego certain political rights when the economic returns are significant and their capacity to influence the course of policy by the exercise of these rights would be marginal in any case. It is this kind of exchange which the two principles as stated rule out; being arranged in serial order they do not permit exchanges between basic liberties and economic and social gains. The serial ordering of principles expresses an underlying preference among primary social goods. . . .

. . .

Now the second principle insists that each person benefit from permissible inequalities in the basic structure. This means that it must be reasonable for each relevant representative man defined by this structure, when he views it as a going concern, to prefer his prospects with the inequality to his prospects without it. One is not allowed to justify differences in income or organizational powers on the ground that the disadvantages of those in another. Much less can infringements of liberty be counterbalanced in this way. Applied to the basic structure, the principle of utility would have us maximize the sum of expectations of representative men (weighted by the number of persons they represent, on the classical view); and this would permit us to compensate for the losses of some by the gains of others. Instead, the two principles require that everyone benefit from economic and social inequalities. . . .

. . .

. . . Assuming the framework of institutions required by equal liberty and fair equality of opportunity, the higher expectations of those better situated are just if and only if they work as part of a scheme which improves the expectations of the lead advantaged members of society. The intuitive idea is that the social order is not to establish and secure the more attractive prospects of those better off unless doing so is to the advantage of those less fortunate. . . .

. . .

. . . Those who have been favored by nature, whoever they are, may gain from their good fortune only on terms that improve the situation of those who have lost out. The naturally advantaged are not to gain merely because they are more gifted, but only to cover the costs of training and education and for using their endowments in ways that help the less fortunate as well. No one deserves his greater natural capacity nor merits a more favorable starting place in society. But it does not follow that one should eliminate these distinctions. There is another way to deal with them. The basic structure can be arranged so that these contingencies work for the good of the least fortunate. Thus we are led to the difference principle if we wish to set up the social system so that no one gains or loses from his arbitrary place in the distribution of natural assets or his initial position in society without giving or receiving compensating advantages in return.

. . .

Perhaps some will think that the person with greater natural endowments deserves those assets and the superior character that made their development possible. Because he is more worthy in this sense, he deserves the greater advantages that he could achieve with them. This view, however, is surely incorrect. It seems to be one of the fixed points of our considered judgments that no one deserves his place in the distribution of native endowments, any more than one deserves one's initial starting place in society. The assertion that a man deserves the superior character that enables him to make the effort to cultivate his abilities is equally problematic; for his character depends in large part upon fortunate family and social circumstances for which he can claim no credit. The notion of desert seems not to apply to these cases. Thus the more advantaged representative man cannot say that he deserves and therefore has a right to a scheme of cooperation in which he is permitted to acquire benefits in ways that do not contribute to the welfare of others. There is no basis for his making this claim. From the standpoint of common sense, then, the difference principle appears to be acceptable both to the more advantaged and to the less advantaged individual. Of course, none of this is strictly speaking an argument for the principle, since in a contract theory arguments are made from the point of view of the original position. . . .

. . .

III. CITIZENSHIP AND COMMUNITY

Major Developments

- Concern about mass society
- Launch of the Great Society
- Debate over patriotism

In 1956, the journalist William H. Whyte, Jr., stormed up the best seller lists with a book examining "the organization man." Americans might still retain their "old ethic" of rugged individualism, but the "current reality" was the "rat race" of life within large collective institutions, whether corporations, universities, public bureaucracies, or the military.[8] The year before, the popular novel (and subsequent movie) *The Man in the Gray Flannel Suit* dramatized the struggle to balance work and family in corporate America. More esoterically, the Beat poet Allen Ginsberg mourned the "best minds of my generation destroyed by madness," sacrificed to "Moloch whose blood is running money!"[9] The postwar boom brought prosperity and a cornucopia of new consumer goods, but it left in its wake fretting about the uniformity of mass society and frustration with the banality of the daily routine.

The wave of activism in the 1960s challenged the apparent conformity and anxiety of the 1950s. Americans of the 1950s were routinely characterized as continuing a tradition of the United States as a nation of "joiners," filling everything from fraternal orders to churches.[10] The activists of the 1960s were joiners of a different stripe. They parlayed their organizational memberships into a mobilization for reform. The apparent ideological consensus that had emerged out of the struggles of the New Deal gave way on both the right and the left. On the right, a new conservative movement pulling together libertarians, traditionalists, and anticommunists put the struggles of the New Deal behind it and sought a new path forward. From the other end of the political spectrum, the New Left borrowed elements from the socialist "Old Left" while expanding the agenda to include the concerns of the less economically oriented counterculture. Lyndon Johnson's Great Society program tried to marshal some of that energy, offering "community action" programs to fight poverty and a desire to rise above "a society of private satisfaction for some."[11]

---

8 William H. Whyte, Jr., *The Organization Man* (New York: Simon & Schuster, 1956), 5, 4.

9 Allen Ginsberg, *Howl and Other Poems* (San Francisco, CA: City Lights Books, 1956), 9, 21.

10 Murray Hausknecht, *The Joiners* (New York: Bedminster Press, 1962); Arthur M. Schlesinger, "Biography of a Nation of Joiners," *American Historical Review* 50 (1944): 1.

11 Lyndon B. Johnson, "Commencement Address at the University of Texas, May 30, 1964," in *Public Papers of the Presidents of the United States* (Washington, D.C.: Government Printing Office, 1965).

YOUNG AMERICANS FOR FREEDOM

THE SHARON STATEMENT (1960)

William F. Buckley, Jr., graduated from Yale University in 1950. The next year, he published his first book, *God and Man at Yale*, which offered a scathing critique of the liberalism of the faculty at Yale, and by extension in American higher education in the postwar period. In 1955, he founded *National Review*, which quickly became the leading journal of the modern conservative movement and the "fusion" of libertarians, traditional conservatives, and anticommunists. In the fall of 1960, Buckley hosted a large group of young conservative activists at his home in Sharon, Connecticut, to organize the Young Americans for Freedom (YAF). M. Stanton Evans, a recent Yale graduate and conservative journalist and editor, took the lead in drafting a statement of principles for both the organization and the emerging conservative movement. YAF established chapters on college campuses across the country and provided the energy behind the insurgent campaign to nominate Barry Goldwater for president in 1964 and a contrary voice to the radical student movements of the late 1960s.

What distinguishes these "conservative" principles from the basic tenets of twentieth-century liberalism? To what degree do these conservative principles build on the New Deal? To what degree do they depart from the New Deal? Does Barry Goldwater's acceptance speech touch all the same themes? Why develop a statement of principles for a youth organization?

In this time of moral and political crises, it is the responsibility of the youth of America to affirm certain eternal truths.

We, as young conservatives, believe:

That foremost among the transcendent values is the individual's use of his God-given free will, whence derives his right to be free from the restrictions of arbitrary force;

That liberty is indivisible, and that political freedom cannot long exist without economic freedom;

That the purpose of government is to protect those freedoms through the preservation of internal order, the provision of national defense, and the administration of justice;

That when government ventures beyond these rightful functions, it accumulates power, which tends to diminish order and liberty;

That the Constitution of the United States is the best arrangement yet devised for empowering government to fulfill its proper role, while restraining it from the concentration and abuse of power;

That the genius of the Constitution—the division of powers—is summed up in the clause that reserves primacy to the several states, or to the people, in those spheres not specifically delegated to the Federal government;

That the market economy, allocating resources by the free play of supply and demand, is the single economic system compatible with the requirements of personal freedom and constitutional government, and that it is at the same time the most productive supplier of human needs;

That when government interferes with the work of the market economy, it tends to reduce the moral and physical strength of the nation; that when it takes from one man to bestow on another, it diminishes the incentive of the first, the integrity of the second, and the moral autonomy of both;

That we will be free only so long as the national sovereignty of the United States is secure; that history shows periods of freedom are rare, and can exist only when free citizens concertedly defend their rights against all enemies;

That the forces of international Communism are, at present, the greatest single threat to these liberties;

That the United States should stress victory over, rather than coexistence with, this menace; and

That American foreign policy must be judged by this criterion: does it serve the just interests of the United States?

STUDENTS FOR A DEMOCRATIC SOCIETY

THE PORT HURON STATEMENT (1962)

Students for a Democratic Society (SDS) began as a student branch of the socialist movement. It adopted a new name at an organizational meeting near Port Huron, Michigan, in 1960 and issued a lengthy political manifesto that was initially drafted by Tom Hayden, a radical activist then at the University of Michigan. Leaders of the earlier socialist organization objected to the willingness of the SDS to accept communists. SDS expanded rapidly with the escalation of the Vietnam War (and, consequently, of the draft) in the mid-1960s. The SDS focused most of its efforts on antiwar activism, organizing the occupation of university buildings as well as marches and mass demonstrations. In 1969, the SDS splintered into various factions that disagreed over both goals and tactics (one prominent splinter group was the Weather Underground, which endorsed an armed struggle for revolutionary change).

Does the Port Huron Statement speak with the same voice and on behalf of the same subjects as the Sharon Statement? Do they appeal to the same abstract "American values"? How do their interpretations of common values differ? What is the generational split posited by the SDS? What is the SDS's concern with postwar society? What is the vision of democracy that SDS offers? How does it depart from the status quo? Why does SDS call for disciplined, polarized political parties? Would they be happy with the current partisan alignment?

We are people of this generation, bred in at least modest comfort, housed now in universities, looking uncomfortably to the world we inherit.

When we were kids the United States was the wealthiest and strongest country in the world: the only one with the atom bomb, the least scarred by modern war, an initiator of the United Nations that we thought would distribute Western influence throughout the world. Freedom and equality for each individual, government of, by, and for the people—these American values we found good, principles by which we could live as men. Many of us began maturing in complacency.

As we grew, however, our comfort was penetrated by events too troubling to dismiss. First, the permeating and victimizing fact of human degradation, symbolized by the Southern struggle against racial bigotry, compelled most of us from silence to activism. Second, the enclosing fact of the Cold War, symbolized by the presence of the Bomb, brought awareness that we ourselves, and our friends, and millions of abstract "others" we knew more directly because of our common peril, might die at any time. We might deliberately ignore, or avoid, or fail to feel all other human problems, but not these two, for these were too immediate and crushing in their impact, too challenging in the demand that we as individuals take the responsibility for encounter and resolution.

. . .

Making values explicit—an initial task in establishing alternatives—is an activity that has been devalued and corrupted. The conventional moral terms of the age, the politician moralities—"free world", "people's democracies"—reflect realities poorly, if at all, and seem to function more as ruling myths than as descriptive principles. But neither has our experience in the universities brought as moral enlightenment. Our professors and administrators sacrifice controversy to public relations; their curriculums change more slowly than the living events of the world; their skills and silence are purchased by investors in the arms race; passion is called unscholastic. The questions we might want raised—what is really important? can we live in a different and better way? if we wanted to change society, how would we do it?—are not thought to be questions of a "fruitful, empirical nature", and thus are brushed aside.

Unlike youth in other countries we are used to moral leadership being exercised and moral dimensions being clarified by our elders. But today, for us, not even the liberal and socialist preachments of the past seem adequate to the forms of the present. . . .

Theoretic chaos has replaced the idealistic thinking of old—and, unable to reconstitute theoretic order, men have condemned idealism itself. Doubt has replaced hopefulness—and men act out a defeatism that is labeled realistic. The decline of utopia and hope is in fact one of the defining features of social life today. The reasons are various: the dreams of the older left were perverted by Stalinism and never recreated; the congressional stalemate makes men narrow their view of the possible; the specialization of human activity leaves little room for sweeping thought; the horrors of the twentieth century, symbolized in the gas-ovens and concentration camps and atom bombs, have blasted hopefulness. To be idealistic is to be considered apocalyptic, deluded. To have no serious aspirations, on the contrary, is to be "tough-minded."

. . .

We regard men as infinitely precious and possessed of unfulfilled capacities for reason, freedom, and love. In affirming these principles we are aware of countering perhaps the dominant conceptions of man in the twentieth century: that he is a thing to be manipulated, and that he is inherently incapable of directing his own affairs. We oppose the depersonalization that reduces human beings to the status of things—if anything, the brutalities of the twentieth century teach that means and ends are intimately related, that vague appeals to "posterity" cannot justify the mutilations of the present. We oppose, too, the doctrine of human incompetence because it rests essentially on the modern fact that men have been "competently" manipulated into incompetence—we see little reason why men cannot meet with increasing skill the complexities and responsibilities of their situation, if society is organized not for minority, but for majority, participation in decision-making.

Men have unrealized potential for self-cultivation, self-direction, self-understanding, and creativity. It is this potential that we regard as crucial and to which we appeal, not to the human potentiality for violence, unreason, and submission to authority. The goal of man and society should be human independence: a concern not with image of popularity but with finding a meaning in life that is personally authentic: a quality of mind not compulsively driven by a sense of powerlessness, nor one which unthinkingly adopts status values, nor one which represses all threats to its habits, but one which has full, spontaneous access to present and past experiences, one which easily unites the fragmented parts of personal history, one which openly faces problems which are troubling and unresolved: one with an intuitive awareness of possibilities, an active sense of curiosity, an ability and willingness to learn.

This kind of independence does not mean egoistic individualism—the object is not to have one's way so much as it is to have a way that is one's own. Nor do we deify man—we merely have faith in his potential.

Human relationships should involve fraternity and honesty. Human interdependence is contemporary fact; human brotherhood must be willed however, as a condition of future survival and as the most appropriate form of social relations. Personal links between man and man are needed, especially to go beyond the partial and fragmentary bonds of function that bind men only as worker to worker, employer to employee, teacher to student, American to Russian.

Loneliness, estrangement, isolation describe the vast distance between man and man today. These dominant tendencies cannot be overcome by better personnel management, nor by improved gadgets, but only when a love of man overcomes the idolatrous worship of things by man.

As the individualism we affirm is not egoism, the selflessness we affirm is not self-elimination. On the contrary, we believe in generosity of a kind that imprints one's unique individual qualities in the relation to other men, and to all human activity. Further, to dislike isolation is not to favor the abolition of privacy; the latter differs from isolation in that it occurs or is abolished according to individual will. Finally, we would replace power and personal uniqueness rooted in possession, privilege, or circumstance by power and uniqueness rooted in love, reflectiveness, reason, and creativity.

As a *social system* we seek the establishment of a democracy of individual participation, governed by two central aims: that the individual share in those social decisions determining the quality and direction of his life; that society be organized to encourage independence in men and provide the media for their common participation.

In a participatory democracy, the political life would be based in several root principles:

> that decision-making of basic social consequence be carried on by public groupings;
>
> that politics be seen positively, as the art of collectively creating an acceptable pattern of social relations;
>
> that politics has the function of bringing people out of isolation and into community, thus being a necessary, though not sufficient, means of finding meaning in personal life;
>
> that the political order should serve to clarify problems in a way instrumental to their solution; it should provide outlets for the expression of personal grievance and aspiration; opposing views should be organized so as to illuminate choices and facilities the attainment of goals; channels should be commonly available to related men to knowledge and to power so that private problems—from bad recreation facilities to personal alienation—are formulated as general issues.

The economic sphere would have as its basis the principles:

> that work should involve incentives worthier than money or survival. It should be educative, not stultifying; creative, not mechanical; self-directed, not manipulated, encouraging independence; a respect for others, a sense of dignity and a willingness to accept social responsibility, since it is this experience that has crucial influence on habits, perceptions and individual ethics;
>
> that the economic experience is so personally decisive that the individual must share in its full determination;
>
> that the economy itself is of such social importance that its major resources and means of production should be open to democratic participation and subject to democratic social regulation.

Like the political and economic ones, major social institutions—cultural, education, rehabilitative, and others—should be generally organized with the well-being and dignity of man as the essential measure of success.

In social change or interchange, we find violence to be abhorrent because it requires generally the transformation of the target, be it a human being or a community of people, into a depersonalized object of hate. It is imperative that the means of violence be abolished and the institutions—local, national, international—that encourage non-violence as a condition of conflict be developed.

These are our central values, in skeletal form. It remains vital to understand their denial or attainment in the context of the modern world.

. . .

The American political system is not the democratic model of which its glorifiers speak. In actuality it frustrates democracy by confusing the individual citizen, paralyzing policy discussion, and consolidating the irresponsible power of military and business interests.

. . .

What emerges from the party contradictions and insulation of privately held power is the organized political stalemate: calcification dominates flexibility as the principle of parliamentary organization, frustration is the expectancy of legislators intending liberal reform, and Congress becomes less and less central to national decision-making, especially in the area of foreign policy. In this context, confusion and blurring is built into the formulation of issues, long-range priorities are not discussed in the rational manner needed for policymaking, the politics of personality and "image" become a more important mechanism than the construction of issues in a way that affords each voter a challenging and real option. The American voter is buffeted from all directions by pseudo-problems, by the structurally-initiated sense that nothing political is subject to human mastery. Worried by his mundane problems which never get solved, but constrained by the common belief that politics is an agonizingly slow accommodation of views, he quits all pretense of bothering.

A most alarming fact is that few, if any, politicians are calling for changes in these conditions. Only a handful even are calling on the President to "live up to" platform pledges; no one is demanding structural changes, such as the shuttling of Southern Democrats out of the Democratic Party. Rather than protesting the state of politics, most politicians are reinforcing and aggravating that state. While in practice they rig public opinion to suit their own interests, in word and ritual they enshrine "the sovereign public" and call for more and more letters. Their speeches and campaign actions are banal, based on a degrading conception of what people want to hear. They respond not to dialogue, but to pressure: and knowing this, the ordinary citizen sees even greater inclination to shun the political sphere. The politicians is usually a trumpeter to "citizenship" and "service to the nation", but since he is unwilling to seriously rearrange power relationships, his trumpetings only increase apathy by creating no outlets. Much of the time the call to "service" is justified not in idealistic terms, but in the crasser terms of "defending the free world from communism"—thus making future idealistic impulses harder to justify in anything but Cold War terms.

. . .

Every effort to end the Cold War and expand the process of world industrialization is an effort hostile to people and institutions whose interests lie in perpetuation of the East-West military threat and the postponement of change in the "have not" nations of the world. Every such effort, too, is bound to establish greater democracy in America. The major goals of a domestic effort would be:

1. America must abolish its political party stalemate. Two genuine parties, centered around issues and essential values, demanding allegiance to party principles shall supplant the current system of organized stalemate which is seriously inadequate to a world in flux. . . . What is desirable is sufficient party disagreement to dramatize major issues, yet sufficient party overlap to guarantee stable transitions from administration to administration. . . .
2. Mechanisms of voluntary association must be created through which political information can be imparted and political participation encouraged. Political parties, even if realigned, would not provide adequate outlets for popular involvement. Institutions should be created that engage people with issues and express political preference, not as now with huge business lobbies which exercise undemocratic power, but which carry political influence (appropriate to private, rather than public, groupings) in national decision-making enterprise. Private in nature, these should be organized around single issues (medical care, transportation systems reform, etc.), concrete interest (labor and minority group organizations), multiple issues or general issues. . . .
3. Institutions and practices which stifle dissent should be abolished, and the promotion of peaceful dissent should be actively promoted. . . .
4. Corporations must be made publicly responsible. It is not possible to believe that true democracy can exist where a minority utterly controls enormous wealth and power. . . . We are aware that simple government "regulation", if achieved, would be inadequate without increased worker participation in management decision-making, strengthened and independent regulatory power, balances of partial and/or complete public ownership, various means of humanizing the conditions and types of work itself, sweeping welfare programs and regional public government authorities. These are examples of measures to re-balance the economy toward public—and individual—control.
5. The allocation of resources must be based on social needs. . . .

All these tendencies suggest that not only solutions to our present social needs but our future expansion rests upon our willingness to enlarge the "public sector" greatly. Unless we choose war as an economic solvent, future public spending will be of a non-military nature—a major intervention into civilian production by the government.

. . .

America should concentrate on its genuine social priorities: abolish squalor, terminate neglect, and establish an environment for people to live in with dignity and creativeness.

. . .

The goals we have set are not realizable next month, or even next election—but that fact justifies neither giving up altogether nor a determination to work only on immediate, direct, tangible problems. Both responses are a sign of helplessness, fearfulness of visions, refusal to hope, and tend to bring on the very conditions to be avoided. Fearing vision, we justify rhetoric or myopia. Fearing hope, we reinforce despair.

The first effort, then, should be to state a vision: what is the perimeter of human possibility in this epoch? This we have tried to do. The second effort, if we are to be politically responsible, is to evaluate the prospects for obtaining at least a substantial part of that vision in our epoch: what are the social forces that exist, or that must exist, if we are to be at all successful? And what role have we ourselves to play as a social force?

. . .

These contemporary social movements—for peace, civil rights, civil liberties, labor—have in common certain values and goals. The fight for peace is one for a stable and racially integrated world; for an end to the inherently volatile exploitation of most of mankind by irresponsible elites; and for freedom of economic, political and cultural organization. The fight for civil rights is also one for social welfare for all Americans; for free speech and the right to protest; for the shield of economic independence and bargaining power; for a reduction of the arms race which takes national attention and resources away from the problems of domestic injustice. Labor's fight for jobs and wages is also one labor; for the right to petition and strike; for world industrialization; for the stability of a peacetime economy instead of the insecurity of the war economy; for expansion of the Welfare State. The fight for a liberal Congress is a fight for a platform from which these concerns can issue. And the fight for students, for internal democracy in the university, is a fight to gain a forum for the issues.

But these scattered movements have more in common: a need for their concerns to be expressed by a political party responsible to their interests. That they have no political expression, no political channels, can be traced in large measure to the existence of a Democratic Party which tolerates the perverse unity of liberalism and racism, prevents the social change wanted by Negroes, peace protesters, labor unions, students, reform Democrats, and other liberals. Worse, the party stalemate prevents even the raising of controversy—a full Congressional assault on racial discrimination, disengagement in Central Europe, sweeping urban reform, disarmament and inspection, public regulation of major industries; these and other issues are never heard in the body that is supposed to represent the best thoughts and interests of all Americans.

An imperative task for these publicly disinherited groups, then, is to demand a Democratic Party responsible to their interests. . . .

. . .

A new left must include liberals and socialists, the former for their relevance, the latter for their sense of thoroughgoing reforms in the system. The university is a more sensible place than a political party for these two traditions to begin to discuss their differences and look for political synthesis.

. . .

The bridge to political power, though, will be built through genuine cooperation, locally, nationally, and internationally, between a new left of young people, and an awakening community of allies. In each community we must look within the university and act with confidence that we can be powerful, but we must look outwards to the less exotic but more lasting struggles for justice.

. . .

To turn these possibilities into realities will involve national efforts at university reform by an alliance of students and faculty. They must wrest control of the educational process from the administrative bureaucracy. They must make fraternal and functional contact with allies in labor, civil rights, and other liberal forces outside the campus. They must import major public issues into the curriculum—research and teaching on problems of war and peace is an outstanding example. They must make debate and controversy, not dull pedantic cant, the common style for educational life. They must consciously build a base for their assault upon the loci of power.

. . .

LYNDON B. JOHNSON

REMARKS AT THE UNIVERSITY OF MICHIGAN (1964)

Lyndon Baines Johnson was a New Deal Democrat from Texas, winning election first to the U.S. House of Representatives in 1938 and then to the U.S. Senate in 1948, rising to the position of majority leader in 1955. Adept at bridging the gap between northern liberals and the more conservative Southern Democrats, Johnson was persuaded to accept the vice presidential nomination to add balance to the Kennedy ticket in 1960. Upon Kennedy's assassination in November 1963 Johnson assumed the Oval Office, defeating Barry Goldwater for a term of his own as president in 1964. His commencement speech at the University of Michigan in 1964 came just months after Kennedy's death. With the election looming on the horizon. Johnson used the occasion to announce a bold new domestic policy initiative to be known as the Great Society. It became one of the defining speeches of his presidency and launched the most significant period of reform since the 1930s.

How does Johnson characterize the difference between the challenges of the past and the challenges of the future? Why does he label his program the "Great Society"? How do the themes of his speech compare to those of Franklin Roosevelt's? How do his ambitions for America contrast with Goldwater's? Does he share any concerns with the SDS?

. . .

I have come today from the turmoil of your Capital to the tranquility of your campus to speak about the future of your country.

The purpose of protecting the life of our Nation and preserving the liberty of our citizens is to pursue the happiness of our people. Our success in that pursuit is the test of our success as a Nation.

For a century we labored to settle and to subdue a continent. For half a century we called upon unbounded invention and untiring industry to create an order of plenty for all of our people.

The challenge of the next half century is whether we have the wisdom to use that wealth to enrich and elevate our national life, and to advance the quality of our American civilization.

Your imagination, your initiative, and your indignation will determine whether we build a society where progress is the servant of our needs, or a society where old values and new visions are buried under unbridled growth. For in your time we have the opportunity to move not only toward the rich society and the powerful society, but upward to the Great Society.

The Great Society rests on abundance and liberty for all. It demands an end to poverty and racial injustice, to which we are totally committed in our time. But that is just the beginning.

The Great Society is a place where every child can find knowledge to enrich his mind and to enlarge his talents. It is a place where leisure is a welcome chance to build and reflect, not a feared cause of boredom and restlessness. It is a place where the city of man serves not only the needs of the body and the demands of commerce but the desire for beauty and the hunger for community.

It is a place where man can renew contact with nature. It is a place which honors creation for its own sake and for what it adds to the understanding of the race. It is a place where men are more concerned with the quality of their goals than the quantity of their goods.

But most of all, the Great Society is not a safe harbor, a resting place, a final objective, a finished work. It is a challenge constantly renewed, beckoning us toward a destiny where the meaning of our lives matches the marvelous products of our labor.

So I want to talk to you today about three places where we begin to build the Great Society—in our cities, in our countryside, and in our classrooms.

. . .

Aristotle said: "Men come together in cities in order to live, but they remain together in order to live the good life." It is harder and harder to live the good life in American cities today.

The catalog of ills is long: there is the decay of the centers and the despoiling of the suburbs. There is not enough housing for our people or transportation for our traffic. Open land is vanishing and old landmarks are violated.

Worst of all expansion is eroding the precious and time honored values of community with neighbors and communion with nature. The loss of these values breeds loneliness and boredom and indifference.

Our society will never be great until our cities are great. Today the frontier of imagination and innovation is inside those cities and not beyond their borders.

New experiments are already going on. It will be the task of your generation to make the American city a place where future generations will come, not only to live but to live the good life.

. . .

A second place where we begin to build the Great Society is in our countryside. We have always prided ourselves on being not only America the strong and America the free, but America the beautiful. Today that beauty is in danger. The water we drink, the food we eat, the very air that we breathe, are threatened with pollution. Our parks are overcrowded, our seashores overburdened. Green fields and dense forests are disappearing.

A few years ago we were greatly concerned about the "Ugly American." Today we must act to prevent an ugly America.

For once the battle is lost, once our natural splendor is destroyed, it can never be recaptured. And once man can no longer walk with beauty or wonder at nature his spirit will wither and his sustenance be wasted.

A third place to build the Great Society is in the classrooms of America. There your children's lives will be shaped. Our society will not be great until every young mind is set free to scan the farthest reaches of thought and imagination. We are still far from that goal.

. . .

In many places, classrooms are overcrowded and curricula are outdated. Most of our qualified teachers are underpaid, and many of our paid teachers are unqualified. So we must give every child a place to sit and a teacher to learn from. Poverty must not be a bar to learning, and learning must offer an escape from poverty.

But more classrooms and more teachers are not enough. We must seek an educational system which grows in excellence as it grows in size. This means better training for our teachers. It means preparing youth to enjoy their hours of leisure as well as their hours of labor. It means exploring new techniques of teaching, to find new ways to stimulate the love of learning and the capacity for creation.

These are three of the central issues of the Great Society. While our Government has many programs directed at those issues, I do not pretend that we have the full answer to those problems.

But I do promise this: We are going to assemble the best thought and the broadest knowledge from all over the world to find those answers for America. . . .

The solution to these problems does not rest on a massive program in Washington, nor can it rely solely on the strained resources of local authority. They require us to create new concepts of cooperation, a creative federalism, between the National Capital and the leaders of local communities.

. . .

. . . You can help build a society where the demands of morality, and the needs of the spirit, can be realized in the life of the Nation.

So, will you join in the battle to give every citizen the full equality which God enjoins and the law requires, whatever his belief, or race, or the color of his skin?

Will you join in the battle to give every citizen an escape from the crushing weight of poverty?

Will you join in the battle to make it possible for all nations to live in enduring peace—as neighbors and not as mortal enemies?

Will you join in the battle to build the Great Society, to prove that our material progress is only the foundation on which we will build a richer life of mind and spirit?

There are those timid souls who say this battle cannot be won; that we are condemned to a soulless wealth. I do not agree. We have the power to shape the civilization that we want. But we need your will, your labor, your hearts, if we are to build that kind of society.

Those who came to this land sought to build more than just a new country. They sought a new world. So I have come here today to your campus to say that you can make their vision our reality. So let us from this moment begin our work so that in the future men will look back and say: It was then, after a long and weary way, that man turned the exploits of his genius to the full enrichment of his life.

RALPH NADER

WE NEED A NEW KIND OF PATRIOTISM (1971)

The son of Lebanese immigrants, Ralph Nader grew up in Connecticut, graduated from Princeton University, and completed a law degree at Harvard in 1958. Daniel Patrick Moynihan shared Nader's budding interest in automobile safety and in 1965 hired Nader to do research on the subject for the Department of Labor. At the same time, Nader produced his most famous book, *Unsafe at Any Speed*, which argued that Detroit's auto manufacturers did not prioritize safety in the design of their automobiles. The book contributed to the creation of the National Highway Traffic Safety Administration in 1966. Nader subsequently launched a large number of consumer advocacy groups, most notably Public Citizen in 1971, which focused on investigatory work, followed by publicity, lobbying, and litigation on issues ranging from pollution to nuclear energy to food safety. Nader's organizational efforts were a model for the rise of "public interest" advocacy groups as a political force. He has, thus far, run for president three times under a variety of third-party banners, achieving greatest electoral success in 2000. His 1971 *Life* magazine article calling for a "new kind of patriotism" was in keeping with his efforts to draw students and young adults into nongovernmental political activism.

How does Nader understand "patriotism"? How does this differ from traditional understandings of patriotism? Is his argument consistent with traditional forms of patriotism? Why link his political commitments to the notion of patriotism? Is the concept of patriotism compatible with pursuing an "individual's own conscience and beliefs"? Would Henry David Thoreau or Randolph Bourne have thought of themselves as patriots? Is political dissent a form of patriotism? Is public advocacy a form of public service? Is Nader's strategy of lobbying and litigation preferable to the tactics favored by Herbert Marcuse or the SDS?

At a recent meeting of the national PTA, the idealism and commitment of many young people to environmental and civil rights causes were being discussed. A middle-aged woman who was listening closely stood up and asked, "But what can we do to make young people today patriotic?"

In a very direct way, she illuminated the tensions contained in the idea of patriotism. These tensions, which peak at moments of public contempt or respect for patriotic symbols such as the flag, have in the past few years divided the generations and pitted children against parents. Highly charged exchanges take place between those who believe that patriotism is automatically possessed by those in authority and those who assert that patriotism is not a pattern imposed but a condition earned by the quality of an individual's or a people's behavior. . . . It is time to talk of patriotism not as an abstraction steeped in nostalgia, but as behavior that can be judged by the standard of "liberty and justice for all."

Patriotism can be a great asset for any organized society, but it can also be a tool manipulated by unscrupulous or cowardly leaders and elites. The development of a sense of patriotism was a strong unifying force during the Revolution and its insecure aftermath. Defined then and now as "love of country," patriotism was an extremely important motivating force with which to confront foreign threats to the young nation. It was no happenstance that *The Star Spangled Banner* was composed during the War of 1812 when the Redcoats were not only coming but already here. For a weak frontier country beset by the competitions and aggressions of European power in the New World, the martial virtues were those of sheer survival. America produced patriots who never moved beyond the borders of their country. They were literally defenders of their home.

As the United States moved into the 20th century and became a world power, far-flung alliances and wars fought thousands of miles away stretched the boundaries of patriotism. "Making the world safe for democracy" was the grandiose way Woodrow Wilson put it. At other times and places (such as Latin America) it became distorted into "jingoism." World War II was the last war that all Americans fought with conviction. . . . When we became the most powerful nation on earth, the old insecurity that made patriotism into a conditioned reflex of "my country right or wrong" should have given way to a thinking process; as expressed by Carl Schurz, "Our country . . . when right, to be kept right. When wrong, to be put right." . . .

If we are to find true and concrete meaning in patriotism, I suggest these starting points. First, in order that a free and just consensus be formed, patriotism must once again be rooted in the individual's own conscience and beliefs. Love is conceived by the giver (citizens) when merited by the receiver (the governmental authorities). If "consent of the governed" is to have any meaning, the abstract ideal of country has to be separated from those who direct it; otherwise the government cannot be evaluated by its citizens. . . . Americans who consider themselves patriotic in the traditional sense do not usually hesitate to heap criticism in domestic matters over what they believe is oppressive or wasteful or unresponsive government handling of their rights and dignity. They should be just as vigilant in weighing similar government action which harnesses domestic resources for foreign involvements. Citizenship has an obligation to cleanse patriotism of the misdeeds done in its name abroad.

. . .

Second, patriotism begins at home. Love of country in fact is inseparable from citizen action to make the country more lovable. This means working to end poverty, discrimination, corruption, greed and other conditions that weaken the promise and potential of America.

Third, if it is unpatriotic to tear down the flag (which is a symbol of the country), why isn't it more unpatriotic to desecrate the country itself—to pollute, despoil and ravage the air, land and water? Such environmental degradation makes the "pursuit of happiness" ragged indeed. . . . Why isn't the systematic contravention of the U.S. Constitution and the Declaration of Independence in our treatment of minority groups, the poor, the young, the old and other disadvantaged or helpless people crassly unpatriotic? Isn't all such behavior contradicting the innate worth and the dignity of the individual in America? Is it not time to end the tragic twisting of patriotism whereby those who work to expose and correct deep injustices, and who take intolerable risks while doing it, are accused of running down America by the very forces doing just that? Our country and its ideals are something for us to uphold as individuals and together, not something to drape, as a deceptive cloak, around activities that mar or destroy these ideals.

Fourth, there is no reason why patriotism has to be so heavily associated, in the minds of the young as well as adults, with military exploits, jets and missiles. Citizenship must include the duty to advance our ideals actively into practice for a better community, country and world, if peace is to prevail over war. And this obligation stems not just from a secular concern for humanity but from a belief in the brotherhood of man—"I am my brother's keeper"—that is common to all major religions. . . . A patriotism manipulated by the government asks only for a servile nod from its subjects. A new patriotism requires a thinking assent from its citizens. If patriotism is to have any "manifest destiny," it is in building a world where all mankind is our bond in peace.

IV. EQUALITY AND STATUS

Major Developments

- Desegregation
- Sexual revolution
- Debate over women's rights

This period marked the emergence of the modern civil rights movement and the "Second Reconstruction." There had been precursors, but the 1950s and 1960s saw the legal collapse of segregation and the birth of a mass movement on behalf of black civil rights. Decisions by the U.S. Supreme Court, starting most notably with *Brown v. Board of Education* (1954), declared that the Jim Crow regime of racial segregation violated the U.S. Constitution. Congressional statutes, most importantly the Civil Rights Act of 1964 and the Voting Rights Act of 1965, committed the federal government to the dismantling of racial discrimination in everything from employment to elections. Thurgood Marshall and the NAACP won a string of legal victories in the courts from the 1940s through the 1960s, and Marshall himself was appointed by President Lyndon Johnson to the U.S. Supreme Court in 1967, the first African-American to hold that office. Martin Luther King, Jr., Bayard Rustin, James Farmer, Ralph Abernathy, and others organized marches, demonstrations, sit-ins, and boycotts in the 1960s calling for an end to segregation. While more conservative reformers like Thurgood Marshall had doubts about the tactics of demonstration leaders like Martin Luther King, Jr., King and his associates were likewise put under pressure by more militant activists like John Lewis and the Student Nonviolent Coordinating Committee, Malcolm X and the Nation of Islam, and Stokely Carmichael and the Black Panthers. Meanwhile, national Democratic Party leaders like Presidents John F. Kennedy and Lyndon B. Johnson faced challenges of how best to negotiate the increasingly pro-civil rights views of their northern constituents and the importance of the Southern Democratic voting bloc to national Democratic majorities.

The black civil rights movement was accompanied by and helped inspire others. In 1962, the Mexican-American labor organizer Cesar Chavez founded the United Farm Workers, which focused on the civil and economic conditions of primarily Latino farmworkers. In 1970, the La Raza Unida Party was established as a Chicano political movement. In 1966, the National Organization for Women (NOW) was established to advocate for women's rights. In 1969, the Gay Liberation Front was formed.

Undoubtedly the most immediately successful of these associated civil rights movements was the feminist movement. All of these movements struggled with their economic agenda for social reformation and justice. By the late 1960s, the women's movement was both the most visible and the most successful in making advances. Birth control pills had been approved for general use in 1960, opening the door to a broader revolution in sexual mores and a readjustment of the domestic and working life of women, and a prohibition on employment discrimination based on sex was incorporated into the Civil Rights Act of

1964, laying the legal foundations for elaborations and extensions of that basic principle. The Equal Rights Amendment was approved by Congress in 1972 but became bogged down in the state ratification process when Phyllis Schlafly's "STOP ERA" campaign emphasized the potential government benefits that women would lose if strict legal equality were required. Nonetheless, the U.S. Supreme Court, encouraged in part by the ACLU's Ruth Bader Ginsburg, gradually incorporated significant portions of the women's rights legal agenda into constitutional law over the course of the 1970s.

MARTIN LUTHER KING, JR.

LETTER FROM A BIRMINGHAM CITY JAIL (1963)

Martin Luther King, Jr. was the son of an African-American Baptist minister in Atlanta, Georgia (as was his father before him). He graduated from Morehouse College in 1948 and completed his Ph.D. in theology at Boston University in 1955. King had newly arrived at his first post in Montgomery, Alabama, when he was asked to help lead a boycott after the arrest of Rosa Parks in 1955. In 1957, he helped found the Southern Christian Leadership Conference (SCLC), which expanded civil rights protest activities across the South, before moving back to Atlanta in 1960. The 1963 mass demonstration in Birmingham, Alabama, was the largest to that date, provoking nationally publicized police brutality against the protestors and King's arrest (for violating a judicial order barring additional demonstrations) and putting pressure on President John F. Kennedy to take action on civil rights. Later that year, King delivered his speech at the Lincoln Memorial during the March on Washington. Violence at a march in Selma, Alabama, in 1964 pushed Congress to pass the Civil Rights Act of 1964. At the end of that year, he was awarded the Nobel Peace Prize. After 1964, King began to turn his attention to northern cities, where his leadership was increasingly challenged by both white politicians (who had often won the support of African-American constituents) and more militant black nationalists (like Malcolm X). In 1967, he formed the Poor People's Campaign to shift focus to economic issues. The next year, he was killed by a segregationist in Memphis, Tennessee, sparking riots throughout the nation. His letter from a Birmingham jail was framed as a response to a group of white southern ministers who had expressed concern about the civil unrest associated with the civil rights demonstrations and called for a focus on legal and political challenges to Jim Crow. King's "letter" was taken out of the jail in segments by his lawyers, and portions were printed in a number of national publications in the spring and summer of 1963. King himself republished the entire letter in a book in 1964.

Is it appropriate for those outside a community to lead protests within it? Does King's appeal to the example of Paul suggest that the right and obligation to protest against injustice are universal? Does the morality or efficacy of a protest depend on local support for it? Is there a logic to King's reference to "anyone who lives inside the United States"? What does King mean by "direct action"? When does he think it is justified? What are the limits to direct action in King's argument? Where are his disagreements with Malcolm X's assessment of the need for action?

My Dear Fellow Clergymen:

While confined here in the Birmingham city jail, I came across your recent statement calling my present activities "unwise and untimely." . . .

I think I should indicate why I am here in Birmingham, since you have been influenced by the view which argues against "outsiders coming in." . . . Several months ago the affiliate here in Birmingham asked us to be on call to engage in a nonviolent direct action program if such were deemed necessary. We readily consented, and when the hour came we lived up to our promise. So I, along with several members of my staff, am here because I was invited here. I am here because I have organizational ties here.

But more basically, I am in Birmingham because injustice is here. Just as the prophets of the eighth century B.C. left their villages and carried their "thus saith the Lord" far beyond the boundaries of their home towns, and just as the Apostle Paul left his village of Tarsus and carried the gospel of Jesus Christ to the far corners of the Greco Roman world, so am I compelled to carry the gospel of freedom beyond my own home town. Like Paul, I must constantly respond to the Macedonian call for aid.

Moreover, I am cognizant of the interrelatedness of all communities and states. I cannot sit idly by in Atlanta and not be concerned about what happens in Birmingham. Injustice anywhere is a threat to justice everywhere. We are caught in an inescapable network of mutuality, tied in a single garment of destiny. Whatever affects one directly, affects all indirectly. Never again can we afford to live with the narrow, provincial "outside agitator" idea. Anyone who lives inside the United States can never be considered an outsider anywhere within its bounds.

You deplore the demonstrations taking place in Birmingham. But your statement, I am sorry to say, fails to express a similar concern for the conditions that brought about the demonstrations. I am sure that none of you would want to rest content with the superficial kind of social analysis that deals merely with effects and does not grapple with underlying causes. It is unfortunate that demonstrations are taking place in Birmingham, but it is even more unfortunate that the city's white power structure left the Negro community with no alternative.

In any nonviolent campaign there are four basic steps: collection of the facts to determine whether injustices exist; negotiation; self-purification; and direct action. We have gone through all these steps in Birmingham. There can be no gainsaying the fact that racial injustice engulfs this community. Birmingham is probably the most thoroughly segregated city in the United States. Its ugly record of brutality is widely known. Negroes have experienced grossly unjust treatment in the courts. There have been more unsolved bombings of Negro homes and churches in Birmingham than in any other city in the nation. These are the hard, brutal facts of the case. On the basis of these conditions, Negro leaders sought to negotiate with the city fathers. But the latter consistently refused to engage in good faith negotiation.

. . .

You may well ask: "Why direct action? Why sit-ins, marches and so forth? Isn't negotiation a better path?" You are quite right in calling for negotiation. Indeed, this is the very purpose of direct action. Nonviolent direct action seeks to create such a crisis and foster such a tension that a community which has constantly refused to negotiate is forced to confront the issue. It seeks so to dramatize the issue that it can no longer be ignored. My citing the creation of tension as part of the work of the nonviolent resister may sound rather shocking. But I must confess that I am not afraid of the word "tension." I have earnestly opposed violent tension, but there is a type of constructive, nonviolent tension which is necessary for growth. Just as Socrates felt that it was necessary to create a tension in the mind so that individuals could rise from the bondage of myths and half truths to the unfettered realm of creative analysis and objective appraisal, so must we see the need for nonviolent gadflies to create the kind of tension in society that will help men rise from the dark depths of prejudice and racism to the majestic heights of understanding and brotherhood. The purpose of our direct action program is to create a situation so crisis packed that it will inevitably open the door to negotiation. I therefore concur with you in your call for negotiation. Too long has our beloved Southland been bogged down in a tragic effort to live in monologue rather than dialogue.

. . .

We know through painful experience that freedom is never voluntarily given by the oppressor; it must be demanded by the oppressed. Frankly, I have yet to engage in a direct action campaign that was "well timed" in the view of those who have not suffered unduly from the disease of segregation. For years now I have heard the word "Wait!" It rings in the ear of every Negro with piercing familiarity. This "Wait" has almost always meant "Never." We must come to see, with one of our distinguished jurists, that "justice too long delayed is justice denied."

We have waited for more than 340 years for our constitutional and God-given rights. The nations of Asia and Africa are moving with jetlike speed toward gaining political independence, but we still creep at horse and buggy pace toward gaining a cup of coffee at a lunch counter. Perhaps it is easy for those who have never felt the stinging darts of segregation to say, "Wait." But when you have seen vicious mobs lynch your mothers and fathers at will and drown your sisters and brothers at whim; when you have seen hate-filled policemen curse, kick and even kill your black brothers and sisters; when you see the vast majority of your twenty million Negro brothers smothering in an airtight cage of poverty in the midst of an affluent society; when you suddenly find your tongue twisted and your speech stammering as you seek to explain to your six-year-old daughter why she can't go to the public amusement park that has just been advertised on television, and see tears welling up in her eyes when she is told that Funtown is closed to colored children, and see ominous clouds of inferiority beginning to form in her little mental sky, and see her beginning to distort her personality by developing an unconscious bitterness toward white people; when you have to concoct an answer for a five-year-old son who is asking: "Daddy, why do white people treat colored people so mean?"; when you take a cross-county drive and find it necessary to sleep night after night in the uncomfortable corners of your automobile because no motel will accept you; when you are humiliated day in and day out by nagging signs reading "white" and "colored"; when your first name becomes "nigger," your middle name becomes "boy" (however old you are) and your last name becomes "John," and your wife and mother are never given the respected title "Mrs."; when you are harried by day and haunted by night by the fact that you are a Negro, living constantly at tiptoe stance, never quite knowing what to expect next, and are plagued with inner fears and outer resentments; when you are forever fighting a degenerating sense of "nobodiness"—then you will understand why we find it difficult to wait. There comes a time when the cup of endurance runs over, and men are no longer willing to be plunged into the abyss of despair. I hope, sirs, you can understand our legitimate and unavoidable impatience. You express a great deal of anxiety over our willingness to break laws. This is certainly a legitimate concern. Since we so diligently urge people to obey the Supreme Court's decision of 1954 outlawing segregation in the public schools, at first glance it may seem rather paradoxical for us consciously to break laws. One may well ask: "How can you advocate breaking some laws and obeying others?" The answer lies in the fact that there are two types of laws: just and unjust. I would be the first to advocate obeying just laws. One has not only a legal but a moral responsibility to obey just laws. Conversely, one has a moral responsibility to disobey unjust laws. I would agree with St. Augustine that "an unjust law is no law at all."

Now, what is the difference between the two? How does one determine whether a law is just or unjust? A just law is a man-made code that squares with the moral law or the law of God. An unjust law is a code that is out of harmony with the moral law. To put it in the terms of St. Thomas Aquinas: An unjust law is a human law that is not rooted in eternal law and natural law. Any law that uplifts human personality is just. Any law that degrades human personality is unjust. All segregation statutes are unjust because segregation distorts the soul and damages the personality. It gives the segregator a false sense of superiority and the segregated a false sense of inferiority. Segregation, to use the terminology of the Jewish philosopher Martin Buber, substitutes an "I it" relationship for an "I thou" relationship and ends up relegating persons to the status of things. Hence segregation is not only politically, economically and sociologically unsound, it is morally wrong and sinful. Paul Tillich has said that sin is separation. Is not segregation an existential expression of man's tragic separation, his awful estrangement, his terrible sinfulness? Thus it is that I can urge men to obey the 1954 decision of the Supreme Court, for it is morally right; and I can urge them to disobey segregation ordinances, for they are morally wrong.

Let us consider a more concrete example of just and unjust laws. An unjust law is a code that a numerical or power majority group compels a minority group to obey but does not make binding on itself. This is difference made legal. By the same token, a just law is a code that a majority compels a minority to follow and that it is willing to follow itself. This is sameness made legal. Let me give another explanation. A law is unjust if it is inflicted on a minority that, as a result of being denied the right to vote, had no part in enacting or devising the law. Who can say that the legislature of Alabama which set up that state's segregation laws was democratically elected? Throughout Alabama all sorts of devious methods are used to prevent Negroes from becoming registered voters, and there are some counties in which, even though Negroes constitute a majority of the population, not a single Negro is registered. Can any law enacted under such circumstances be considered democratically structured?

Sometimes a law is just on its face and unjust in its application. For instance, I have been arrested on a charge of parading without a permit. Now, there is nothing wrong in having an ordinance which requires a permit for a parade. But such an ordinance becomes unjust when it is used to maintain segregation and to deny citizens the First-Amendment privilege of peaceful assembly and protest.

I hope you are able to see the distinction I am trying to point out. In no sense do I advocate evading or defying the law, as would the rabid segregationist. That would lead to anarchy. One who breaks an unjust law must do so openly, lovingly, and with a willingness to accept the penalty. I submit that an individual who breaks a law that conscience tells him is unjust, and who willingly accepts the penalty of imprisonment in order to arouse the conscience of the community over its injustice, is in reality expressing the highest respect for law.

Of course, there is nothing new about this kind of civil disobedience. It was evidenced sublimely in the refusal of Shadrach, Meshach and Abednego to obey the laws of Nebuchadnezzar, on the ground that a higher moral law was at stake. It was practiced superbly by the early Christians, who were willing to face hungry lions and the excruciating pain of chopping blocks rather than submit to certain unjust laws of the Roman Empire. To a degree, academic freedom is a reality today because Socrates practiced civil disobedience. In our own nation, the Boston Tea Party represented a massive act of civil disobedience.

We should never forget that everything Adolf Hitler did in Germany was "legal" and everything the Hungarian freedom fighters did in Hungary was "illegal." It was "illegal" to aid and comfort a Jew in Hitler's Germany. Even so, I am sure that, had I lived in Germany at the time, I would have aided and comforted my Jewish brothers. If today I lived in a Communist country where certain principles dear to the Christian faith are suppressed, I would openly advocate disobeying that country's antireligious laws.

I must make two honest confessions to you, my Christian and Jewish brothers. First, I must confess that over the past few years I have been gravely disappointed with the white moderate. I have almost reached the regrettable conclusion that the Negro's great stumbling block in his stride toward freedom is not the White Citizen's Counciler or the Ku Klux Klanner, but the white moderate, who is more devoted to "order" than to justice; who prefers a negative peace which is the absence of tension to a positive peace which is the presence of justice; who constantly says: "I agree with you in the goal you seek, but I cannot agree with your methods of direct action"; who paternalistically believes he can set the timetable for another man's freedom; who lives by a mythical concept of time and who constantly advises the Negro to wait for a "more convenient season." Shallow understanding from people of good will is more frustrating than absolute misunderstanding from people of ill will. Lukewarm acceptance is much more bewildering than outright rejection.

I had hoped that the white moderate would understand that law and order exist for the purpose of establishing justice and that when they fail in this purpose they become the dangerously structured dams that block the flow of social progress. I had hoped that the white moderate would understand that the present tension in the South is a necessary phase of the transition from an obnoxious negative peace, in which the Negro passively accepted his unjust plight, to a substantive and positive peace, in which all men will respect the dignity and worth of human personality. Actually, we who engage in nonviolent direct action are not the creators of tension. We merely bring to the surface the hidden tension that is already alive. We bring it out in the open, where it can be seen and dealt with. Like a boil that can never be cured so long as it is covered up but must be opened with all its ugliness to the natural medicines of air and light, injustice must be exposed, with all the tension its exposure creates, to the light of human conscience and the air of national opinion before it can be cured.

. . .

I have tried to stand between these two forces, saying that we need emulate neither the "do nothingism" of the complacent nor the hatred and despair of the black nationalist. For there is the more excellent way of love and nonviolent protest. I am grateful to God that, through the influence of the Negro church, the way of nonviolence became an integral part of our struggle. If this philosophy had not emerged, by now many streets of the South would, I am convinced, be flowing with blood. And I am further convinced that if our white brothers dismiss as "rabble rousers" and "outside agitators" those of us who employ nonviolent direct action, and if they refuse to support our nonviolent efforts, millions of Negroes will, out of frustration and despair, seek solace and security in black nationalist ideologies—a development that would inevitably lead to a frightening racial nightmare.

Oppressed people cannot remain oppressed forever. The yearning for freedom eventually manifests itself, and that is what has happened to the American Negro. . . . If his repressed emotions are not released in nonviolent ways, they will seek expression through violence; this is not a threat but a fact of history. So I have not said to my people: "Get rid of your discontent." Rather, I have tried to say that this normal and healthy discontent can be channeled into the creative outlet of nonviolent direct action. . . .

. . .

I wish you had commended the Negro sit-inners and demonstrators of Birmingham for their sublime courage, their willingness to suffer and their amazing discipline in the midst of great provocation. One day the South will recognize its real heroes. . . . One day the South will know that when these disinherited children of God sat down at lunch counters, they were in reality standing up for what is best in the American dream and for the most sacred values in our Judaeo Christian heritage, thereby bringing our nation back to those great wells of democracy which were dug deep by the founding fathers in their formulation of the Constitution and the Declaration of Independence.

. . .

I hope this letter finds you strong in the faith. I also hope that circumstances will soon make it possible for me to meet each of you, not as an integrationist or a civil-rights leader but as a fellow clergyman and a Christian brother. Let us all hope that the dark clouds of racial prejudice will soon pass away and the deep fog of misunderstanding will be lifted from our fear drenched communities, and in some not-too-distant tomorrow the radiant stars of love and brotherhood will shine over our great nation with all their scintillating beauty.

MARTIN LUTHER KING, JR.

I HAVE A DREAM SPEECH (1963)

Just a few months after the events in Birmingham, Martin Luther King, Jr. joined the March on Washington for Jobs and Freedom in Washington, D.C. The march in 1963 followed the example of some earlier civil rights demonstrations, including the 1941 March on Washington organized by A. Philip Randolph in Chapter 9. The 1963 event was timed to coincide with the centennial of the signing of the Emancipation Proclamation, and it was scheduled to end on the mall in front of the Lincoln Memorial. The march was the joint effort of several civil rights organizations, including King's Southern Christian Leadership Conference. The idea for the march was initiated by Randolph and his Negro American Labor Council to put pressure on the Kennedy administration. Randolph had offered his support to King after the violence surrounding the 1961 "Freedom Rides," in which black and white civil rights activists took bus trips through the Deep South and acted in defiance of segregation rules along the way. With his own organization losing members, Randolph proposed a joint event in Washington, D.C. Randolph was focused on "job rights," but the joint march announced a broader agenda, including the desire for a "comprehensive civil rights bill," a voting rights bill, and public works programs. Although the march attracted a large number of civil rights organizations, Malcolm X was among those who kept their distance, and James Baldwin was deemed too militant to be given space at the podium. The event drew massive crowds, estimated at a quarter of a million people. King was positioned as a featured speaker near the end of the event. The event was heavily covered by the media, and King's speech became the focal point for much of that coverage. The event organizers met with President Kennedy in a scheduled meeting at the White House following the conclusion of the march.

How do the themes of the I Have a Dream speech compare with the themes of the Letter from a Birmingham Jail? What are the differences between King's approach and the view offered by Malcolm X? How does the speech compare with Randolph's earlier March on Washington keynote speech? To what degree is King's message about economics? What are the audiences for King's words, and does he have the same message for those different audiences? What does King's dream of the future entail? To what degree has it been realized? What would it take to satisfy King's demands in 1963? Is King's dream "deeply rooted in the American dream"?

. . .

Five score years ago, a great American, in whose symbolic shadow we stand today, signed the Emancipation Proclamation. This momentous decree came as a great beacon light of hope to millions of Negro slaves who had been seared in the flames of withering injustice. It came as a joyous daybreak to end the long night of captivity. But one hundred years later, the Negro still is not free. One hundred years later, the life of the Negro is still sadly crippled by the manacles of segregation and the chains of discrimination. One hundred years later, the Negro lives on a lonely island of poverty in the midst of a vast ocean of material prosperity. One hundred years later, the Negro is still languished in the corners of American society and finds himself in exile in his own land. So we have come here today to dramatize a shameful condition.

In a sense we've come to our nation's capital to cash a check. When the architects of our Republic wrote the magnificent words of the Constitution and the Declaration of Independence, they were signing a promissory note to which every American was to fall heir. This note was a promise that all men—yes, black men as well as white men—would be guaranteed the unalienable rights of life, liberty, and the pursuit of happiness. It is obvious today that America has defaulted on this promissory note insofar as her citizens of color are concerned. Instead of honoring this sacred obligation, America has given the Negro people a bad check; a check which has come back marked "insufficient funds."

But we refuse to believe that the bank of justice is bankrupt. We refuse to believe that there are insufficient funds in the great vaults of opportunity of this nation. So we have come to cash this check—a check that will give us upon demand the riches of freedom and the security of justice.

We have also come to this hallowed spot to remind America of the fierce urgency of now. This is no time to engage in the luxury of cooling off or to take the tranquilizing drug of gradualism. Now is the time to make real the promises of democracy. Now is the time to rise from the dark and desolate valley of segregation to the sunlit path of racial justice. Now is the time to lift our nation from the quicksands of racial injustice to the solid rock of brotherhood.

Now is the time to make justice a reality for all of God's children. It would be fatal for the nation to overlook the urgency of the moment. This sweltering summer of the Negro's legitimate discontent will not pass until there is an invigorating autumn of freedom and equality—1963 is not an end but a beginning. Those who hope that the Negro needed to blow off steam and will now be content will have a rude awakening if the nation returns to business as usual.

There will be neither rest nor tranquility in America until the Negro is granted his citizenship rights. The whirlwinds of revolt will continue to shake the foundations of our nation until the bright days of justice emerge. And that is something that I must say to my people who stand on the worn threshold which leads into the palace of justice. In the process of gaining our rightful place we must not be guilty of wrongful deeds. Let us not seek to satisfy our thirst for freedom by drinking from the cup of bitterness and hatred.

We must forever conduct our struggle on the high plane of dignity and discipline. We must not allow our creative protest to degenerate into physical violence. Again and again we must rise to the majestic heights of meeting physical force with soul force. The marvelous new militancy which has engulfed the Negro community must not lead us to a distrust of all white people, for many of our white brothers, as evidenced by their presence here today, have come to realize that their destiny is tied up with our destiny.

They have come to realize that their freedom is inextricably bound to our freedom. We cannot walk alone. And as we walk, we must make the pledge that we shall march ahead. We cannot turn back. There are those who are asking the devotees of civil rights, "When will you be satisfied!" We can never be satisfied as long as the Negro is the victim of the unspeakable horrors of police brutality.

We can never be satisfied as long as our bodies, heavy with the fatigue of travel, cannot gain lodging in the motels of the highways and the hotels of the cities.

We cannot be satisfied as long as the Negro's basic mobility is from a smaller ghetto to a larger one. We can never be satisfied as long as our children are stripped of their adulthood and robbed of their dignity by signs stating "For Whites Only."

We cannot be satisfied as long as a Negro in Mississippi cannot vote and a Negro in New York believes he has nothing for which to vote.

No, no, we are not satisfied, and we will not be satisfied until justice rolls down like waters and righteousness like a mighty stream.

. . .

I say to you today, my friends, though, even though we face the difficulties of today and tomorrow, I still have a dream. It is a dream deeply rooted in the American dream. I have a dream that one day this nation will rise up and live out the true meaning of its creed: "We hold these truths to be self-evident; that all men are created equal."

I have a dream that one day on the red hills of Georgia the sons of former slaves and the sons of former slave owners will be able to sit down together at the table of brotherhood. I have a dream that one day even the state of Mississippi, a state sweltering with the heat of injustice, sweltering with the heat of oppression, will be transformed into an oasis of freedom and justice.

I have a dream that my four little children will one day live in a nation where they will not be judged by the color of their skin but by the content of their character. I have a dream today. . . . I have a dream that one day in Alabama, with its vicious racists, with its governor having his lips dripping with the words of interposition and nullification, one day right there in Alabama little black boys and black girls will be able to join hands with little white boys and white girls as sisters and brothers.

I have a dream today. . . . I have a dream that one day every valley shall be exalted, every hill and mountain shall be made low. The rough places will be made plain, and the crooked places will be made straight. And the glory of the Lord shall be revealed, and all flesh shall see it together. This is our hope. This is the faith that I go back to the South with. With this faith we will be able to hew out of the mountain of despair a stone of hope. With this faith we will be able to transform the jangling discords of our nation into a beautiful symphony of brotherhood. With this faith we will be able to work together, to pray together, to struggle together, to go to jail together, to stand up for freedom together, knowing that we will be free one day.

This will be the day when all of God's children will be able to sing with new meaning. "My country 'tis of thee, sweet land of liberty, of thee I sing. Land where my fathers died, land of the pilgrims' pride, from every mountain side, let freedom ring." And if America is to be a great nation, this must become true. So let freedom ring from the prodigious hilltops of New Hampshire. Let freedom ring from the mighty mountains of New York. Let freedom ring from the heightening Alleghenies of Pennsylvania. Let freedom ring from the snowcapped Rockies of Colorado. Let freedom ring from the curvaceous slopes of California.

But not only that. Let freedom ring from the Stone Mountain of Georgia. Let freedom ring from Lookout Mountain of Tennessee. Let freedom ring from every hill and molehill of Mississippi, from every mountain side. Let freedom ring. . . .

When we allow freedom to ring—when we let it ring from every city and every hamlet, from every state and every city, we will be able to speed up that day when all of God's children, black men and white men, Jews and Gentiles, Protestants and Catholics, will be able to join hands and sing in the words of the old Negro spiritual, "Free at last, Free at last, Great God a-mighty, We are free at last."

MALCOLM X

THE BALLOT OR THE BULLET (1964)

Malcolm X was born Malcolm Little in Omaha, Nebraska. His parents were followers of the black nationalist Marcus Garvey. In 1946, he was sent to prison in Massachusetts for burglary. While incarcerated, he was drawn to Elijah Muhammad and the Nation of Islam. Upon his release he changed his name (with X representing his lost African name) and became a minister, quickly rising within the organization. His militancy and powerful oratory attracted attention in both the white and black communities. While Malcolm X led protests in the urban North, he was critical of the nonviolent strategies being advocated by Martin Luther King in the South. Malcolm X called for "revolution" and the pursuit of equality "by any means necessary." By the time of this speech in Cleveland at a conference organized by the Congress of Racial Equality (CORE), Malcolm X was seeking to unify the civil rights movement. At the same time, he split from the Nation of Islam leadership and in 1965 was killed by members of the Nation of Islam.

What doubts might Malcolm X have to overcome to persuade his audience that they all faced "a common problem"? How broad was that problem? What social issues could be reasonably addressed through that same agenda, and what issues would need to be set aside and dealt with separately? Does he explain why action was needed "by whatever means necessary"? What does that phrase imply in this speech? Was Malcolm X right to be wary of Lyndon Johnson and the Democratic Party in 1964? What are the strategic implications of holding such doubts? Is the willingness to turn to the bullet essential to gaining access to the ballot? Did the Jim Crow governments of the South in the 1960s have any claim to legitimate authority? Had the conditions for legitimate revolution been met? What does Malcolm X's philosophy of black nationalism imply for the post-civil rights era? Should African-Americans vote only for African-American politicians and spend their money only at stores owned by African-Americans?

. . . The question tonight, as I understand it, is "The Negro Revolt, and Where Do We Go From Here?" or "What Next?" In my little humble way of understanding it, it points toward either the ballot or the bullet.

. . . I myself am a minister, not a Christian minister, but a Muslim minister; and I believe in action on all fronts by whatever means necessary.

Although I'm still a Muslim, I'm not here tonight to discuss my religion. I'm not here to try and change your religion. I'm not here to argue or discuss anything that we differ about, because it's time for us to submerge our differences and realize that it is best for us to first see that we have the same problem, a common problem—a problem that will make you catch hell whether you're a Baptist, or a Methodist, or a Muslim, or a nationalist. Whether you're educated or illiterate, whether you live on the boulevard or in the alley, you're going to catch hell just like I am. We're all in the same boat and we all are going to catch the same hell from the same man. He just happens to be a white man. All of us have suffered here, in this country, political oppression at the hands of the white man, economic exploitation at the hands of the white man, and social degradation at the hands of the white man.

Now in speaking like this, it doesn't mean that we're anti-white, but it does mean we're anti-exploitation, we're anti-degradation, we're anti-oppression. And if the white man doesn't want us to be anti-him, let him stop oppressing and exploiting and degrading us. Whether we are Christians or Muslims or nationalists or agnostics or atheists, we must first learn to forget our differences. If we have differences, let us differ in the closet; when we come out in front, let us not have anything to argue about until we get finished arguing with the man. . . .

. . .

I'm not a politician, not even a student of politics; in fact, I'm not a student of much of anything. I'm not a Democrat, I'm not a Republican, and I don't even consider myself an American. If you and I were Americans, there'd be no problem. Those Hunkies that just got off the boat, they're already Americans; Polacks are already Americans; the Italian refugees are already Americans. Everything that came out of Europe, every blue-eyed thing, is already an American. And as long as you and I have been over here, we aren't Americans yet.

. . .

It was the black man's vote that put the present administration in Washington, D. C. Your vote, your dumb vote, your ignorant vote, your wasted vote put in an administration in Washington, D. C., that has seen fit to pass every kind of legislation imaginable, saving you until last, then filibustering on top of that. And your and my leaders have the audacity to run around clapping their hands and talk about how much progress we're making. And what a good president we have. If he wasn't good in Texas, he sure can't be good in Washington, D. C. Because Texas is a lynch state. It is in the same breath as Mississippi, no different. . . . And these Negro leaders have the audacity to go and have some coffee in the White House with a Texan, a Southern cracker—that's all he is—and then come out and tell you and me that he's going to be better for us because, since he's from the South, he knows how to deal with the Southerners. What kind of logic is that? . . .

In this present administration they have in the House of Representatives 257 Democrats to only 177 Republicans. They control two-thirds of the House vote. Why can't they pass something that will help you and me? In the Senate, there are 67 senators who are of the Democratic Party. Only 33 of them are Republicans. Why, the Democrats have got the government sewed up, and you're the one who sewed it up for them. And what have they given you for it? Four years in office, and just now getting around to some civil-rights legislation. Just now, after everything else is gone, out of the way, they're going to sit down now and play with you all summer long—the same old giant con game that they call filibuster. All those are in cahoots together. . . .

. . . It's got to be the ballot or the bullet. The ballot or the bullet. If you're afraid to use an expression like that, you should get on out of the country, you should get back in the cotton patch, you should get back in the alley. They get all the Negro vote, and after they get it, the Negro gets nothing in return. All they did when they got to Washington was give a few big Negroes big jobs. Those big Negroes didn't need big jobs, they already had jobs. That's camouflage, that's trickery, that's treachery, window-dressing. I'm not trying to knock out the Democrats for the Republicans, we'll get to them in a minute. But it is true—you put the Democrats first and the Democrats put you last.

. . .

If the black man in these Southern states had his full voting rights, the key Dixiecrats in Washington, D. C., which means the key Democrats in Washington, D. C., would lose their seats. The Democratic Party itself would lose its power. It would cease to be powerful as a party. When you see the amount of power that would be lost by the Democratic Party if it were to lose the Dixiecrat wing, or branch, or element, you can see where it's against the interests of the Democrats to give voting rights to Negroes in states where the Democrats have been in complete power and authority ever since the Civil War. You just can't belong to that party without analyzing it.

. . .

And now you're facing a situation where the young Negro's coming up. They don't want to hear that "turn-the-other-cheek" stuff, no. In Jacksonville, those were teenagers, they were throwing Molotov cocktails. Negroes have never done that before. But it shows you there's a new deal coming in. There's new thinking coming in. There's new strategy coming in. It'll be Molotov cocktails this month, hand grenades next month, and something else next month. It'll be ballots, or it'll be bullets. It'll be liberty, or it will be death. The only difference about this kind of death—it'll be reciprocal. . . .

. . .

You take the people who are in this audience right now. They're poor, we're all poor as individuals. Our weekly salary individually amounts to hardly anything. But if you take the salary of everyone in here collectively it'll fill up a whole lot of baskets. It's a lot of wealth. If you can collect the wages of just these people right here for a year, you'll be rich—richer than rich. When you look at it like that, think how rich Uncle Sam had to become, not with this handful, but millions of black people. Your and my mother and father, who didn't work an eight-hour shift, but worked from "can't see" in the morning until "can't see" at night, and worked for nothing, making the white man rich, making Uncle Sam rich.

This is our investment. This is our contribution—our blood. Not only did we give of our free labor, we gave of our blood. Every time he had a call to arms, we were the first ones in uniform. We died on every battlefield the white man had. We have made a greater sacrifice than anybody who's standing up in America today. We have made a greater contribution and have collected less. Civil rights, for those of us whose philosophy is black nationalism, means: "Give it to us now. Don't wait for next year. Give it to us yesterday, and that's not fast enough."

I might stop right here to point out one thing. Whenever you're going after something that belongs to you, anyone who's depriving you of the right to have it is a criminal. Understand that. Whenever you are going after something that is yours, you are within your legal rights to lay claim to it. And anyone who puts forth any effort to deprive you of that which is yours, is breaking the law, is a criminal. And this was pointed out by the Supreme Court decision. It outlawed segregation. Which means segregation is against the law. Which means a segregationist is breaking the law. A segregationist is a criminal. You can't label him as anything other than that. And when you demonstrate against segregation, the law is on your side. The Supreme Court is on your side.

Now, who is it that opposes you in carrying out the law? The police department itself. With police dogs and clubs. Whenever you demonstrate against segregation, whether it is segregated education, segregated housing, or anything else, the law is on your side, and anyone who stands in the way is not the law any longer. They are breaking the law, they are not representatives of the law. Any time you demonstrate against segregation and a man has the audacity to put a police dog on you, kill that dog, kill him, I'm telling you, kill that dog. I say it, if they put me in jail tomorrow, kill—that—dog. Then you'll put a stop to it. Now, if these white people in here don't want to see that kind of action, get down and tell the mayor to tell the police department to pull the dogs in. That's all you have to do. If you don't do it, someone else will.

If you don't take this kind of stand, your little children will grow up and look at you and think "shame." If you don't take an uncompromising stand—I don't mean go out and get violent; but at the same time you should never be nonviolent unless you run into some nonviolence. I'm nonviolent with those who are nonviolent with me. But when you drop that violence on me, then you've made me go insane, and I'm not responsible for what I do. And that's the way every Negro should get. Any time you know you're within the law, within your legal rights, within your moral rights, in accord with justice, then die for what you believe in. But don't die alone. Let your dying be reciprocal. This is what is meant by equality. What's good for the goose is good for the gander.

When we begin to get in this area, we need new friends, we need new allies. We need to expand the civil-rights struggle to a higher level—to the level of human rights. Whenever you are in a civil-rights struggle, whether you know it or not, you are confining yourself to the jurisdiction of Uncle Sam. No one from the outside world can speak out in your behalf as long as your struggle is a civil-rights struggle. Civil rights comes within the domestic affairs of this country. All of our African brothers and our Asian brothers and our Latin-American brothers cannot open their mouths and interfere in the domestic affairs of the United States. And as long as it's civil rights, this comes under the jurisdiction of Uncle Sam.

. . .

When you expand the civil-rights struggle to the level of human rights, you can then take the case of the black man in this country before the nations in the UN. You can take it before the General Assembly. You can take Uncle Sam before a world court. But the only level you can do it on is the level of human rights. Civil rights keeps you under his restrictions, under his jurisdiction. Civil rights keeps you in his pocket. Civil rights means you're asking Uncle Sam to treat you right. Human rights are something you were born with. Human rights are your God-given rights. Human rights are the rights that are recognized by all nations of this earth. And any time anyone violates your human rights, you can take them to the world court. Uncle Sam's hands are dripping with blood, dripping with the blood of the black man in this country. He's the earth's number-one hypocrite. He has the audacity—yes, he has—imagine him posing as the leader of the free world. The free world!—and you over here singing "We Shall Overcome." Expand the civil-rights struggle to the level of human rights, take it into the United Nations, where our African brothers can throw their weight on our side, where our Asian brothers can throw their weight on our side, where our Latin-American brothers can throw their weight on our side, and where 800 million Chinamen are sitting there waiting to throw their weight on our side.

Let the world know how bloody his hands are. Let the world know the hypocrisy that's practiced over here. Let it be the ballot or the bullet. Let him know that it must be the ballot or the bullet.

. . .

The political philosophy of black nationalism means that the black man should control the politics and the politicians in his own community; no more. The black man in the black community has to be re-educated into the science of politics so he will know what politics is supposed to bring him in return. Don't be throwing out any ballots. A ballot is like a bullet. You don't throw your ballots until you see a target, and if that target is not within your reach, keep your ballot in your pocket. . . . Black people are fed up with the dillydallying, pussyfooting, compromising approach that we've been using toward getting our freedom. We want freedom *now*, but we're not going to get it saying "We Shall Overcome." We've got to fight until we overcome.

The economic philosophy of black nationalism is pure and simple. It only means that we should control the economy of our community. Why should white people be running all the stores in our community? Why should white people be running the banks of our community? Why should the economy of our community be in the hands of the white man? Why? If a black man can't move his store into a white community, you tell me why a white man should move his store into a black community. The philosophy of black nationalism involves a re-education program in the black community in regards to economics. Our people have to be made to see that any time you take your dollar out of your community and spend it in a community where you don't live, the community where you live will get poorer and poorer, and the community where you spend your money will get richer and richer. Then you wonder why where you live is always a ghetto or a slum area. . . .

. . .

The social philosophy of black nationalism only means that we have to get together and remove the evils, the vices, alcoholism, drug addiction, and other evils that are destroying the moral fiber of our community. We ourselves have to lift the level of our community, the standard of our community to a higher level, make our own society beautiful so that we will be satisfied in our own social circles and won't be running around here trying to knock our way into a social circle where we're not wanted.

So I say, in spreading a gospel such as black nationalism, it is not designed to make the black man re-evaluate the white man—you know him already—but to make the black man re-evaluate himself. Don't change the white man's mind—you can't change his mind, and that whole thing about appealing to the moral conscience of America—America's conscience is bankrupt. She lost all conscience a long time ago. Uncle Sam has no conscience. They don't know what morals are. They don't try and eliminate an evil because it's evil, or because it's illegal, or because it's immoral; they eliminate it only when it threatens their existence. So you're wasting your time appealing to the moral conscience of a bankrupt man like Uncle Sam. If he had a conscience, he'd straighten this thing out with no more pressure being put upon him. So it is not necessary to change the white man's mind. We have to change our own mind. You can't change his mind about us. We've got to change our own minds about each other. We have to see each other with new eyes. We have to see each other as brothers and sisters. We have to come together with warmth so we can develop unity and harmony that's necessary to get this problem solved ourselves. . . .

. . .

Last but not least, I must say this concerning the great controversy over rifles and shotguns. The only thing that I've ever said is that in areas where the government has proven itself either unwilling or unable to defend the lives and the property of Negroes, it's time for Negroes to defend themselves. Article number two of the constitutional amendments provides you and me the right to own a rifle or a shotgun. It is constitutionally legal to own a shotgun or a rifle. This doesn't mean you're going to get a rifle and form battalions and go out looking for white folks, although you'd be within your rights—I mean, you'd be justified; but that would be illegal and we don't do anything illegal. If the white man doesn't want the black man buying rifles and shotguns, then let the government do its job. That's all. . . .

. . .

BETTY FRIEDAN

THE FEMININE MYSTIQUE (1963)

Bettye Goldstein was the daughter of Russian and Hungarian immigrants in southern Illinois. She graduated from Smith College in 1942 and studied psychology in the graduate program at the University of California at Berkeley. Rather than continuing in psychology, she decided to pursue journalism, initially focusing on the labor movement. She married Carl Friedan in 1947, and they moved from New York City to the nearby suburbs while she continued working in journalism and community activism. In 1963, she published her most important work, *The Feminine Mystique*, which helped jumpstart the modern feminist movement. After the book's publication, she shifted away from journalism and into political activism. In 1966, she helped found the National Organization for Women (NOW) and subsequently the National Association for the Repeal of Abortion Laws (NARAL) and the National Women's Political Caucus.

What is the "unspoken" problem? What does Friedan think is the "feminine mystique," the aspiration for women in the early 1960s? To what degree has that changed since the 1960s? To what degree is personal identity a political issue? How does Friedan think personal choices about career and lifestyle are socially structured? How can such identity issues be changed?

The problem lay buried, unspoken, for many years in the minds of American women. It was a strange stirring, a sense of dissatisfaction, a yearning that women suffered in the middle of the twentieth century in the United States. Each suburban wife struggled with it alone. As she made beds, shopped for groceries, matched slipcover material, ate peanut butter sandwiches with her children, chauffeured Cub Scouts and Brownies, lay beside her husband at night—she was afraid to ask even of herself the silent question—"Is this all?"

For over fifteen years there was no word of this yearning in the millions of words written about women, for women, in all the columns, books and articles by experts telling women their role was to seek fulfillment as wives and mothers. Over and over women heard in voices of tradition and of Freudian sophistication that they could desire no greater destiny than to glory in their own femininity. Experts told them how to catch a man and keep him, how to breastfeed children and handle their toilet training, how to cope with sibling rivalry and adolescent rebellion; how to buy a dishwasher, bake bread, cook gourmet snails, and build a swimming pool with their own hands; how to dress, look, and act more feminine and make marriage more exciting; how to keep their husbands from dying young and their sons from growing into delinquents. They were taught to pity the neurotic, unfeminine, unhappy women who wanted to be poets or physicists or presidents. They learned that truly feminine women do not want careers, higher education, political rights—the independence and the opportunities that the old-fashioned feminists fought for. Some women, in their forties and fifties, still remembered painfully giving up those dreams, but most of the younger women no longer even thought about them. A thousand expert voices applauded their femininity, their adjustment, their new maturity. All they had to do was devote their lives from earliest girlhood to finding a husband and bearing children.

. . .

The suburban housewife—she was the dream image of the young American woman and the envy, it was said, of women all over the world. The American housewife—freed by science and labor-saving appliances from the drudgery, the dangers of childbirth and the illnesses of her grandmother. She was healthy, beautiful, educated, concerned only about her husband, her children, her home. She had found true feminine fulfillment. . . .

In the fifteen years after World War II, this mystique of feminine fulfillment became the cherished and self-perpetuating core of contemporary American culture. . . . Their only dream was to be perfect wives and mothers; their highest ambition to have five children and a beautiful house, their only fight to get and keep their husbands. They had no thought for the unfeminine problems of the world outside the home; they wanted the men to make the major decisions. They gloried in their role as women, and wrote proudly on the census blank: "Occupation: housewife."

. . . Nobody argued whether women were inferior or superior to men; they were simply different. Words like "emancipation" and "career" sounded strange and embarrassing; no one had used them for years. . . .

If a woman had a problem in the 1950s and the 1960s, she knew that something must be wrong with her marriage, or with herself. Other women were satisfied with their lives, she thought. What kind of woman was she if she did not feel this mysterious fulfillment waxing the kitchen floor? . . . Even the psychoanalysts had no name for it. When a woman went to a psychiatrist for help, as many women did, she would say, "I'm so ashamed," or "I must be helplessly neurotic." "I don't know what's wrong with women today," a suburban psychiatrist said uneasily. . . .

. . .

Gradually I came to realize that the problem that has no name was shared by countless women in America. As a magazine writer I often interviewed women about problems with their children, or their marriages, or their houses, or their communities. But after a while I began to recognize the telltale signs of this other problem. . . . I think I understood first as a woman long before I understood their larger social and psychological implications.

Just what was this problem that has no name? What were the words women used when they tried to express it? Sometimes a woman would say "I feel empty somehow . . . incomplete." Or she would say, "I feel as if I don't exist." Sometimes she blotted out the feeling with a tranquilizer. . . .

. . .

I began to see in a strange new light the American return to early marriage and the large families that are causing the population explosion; the recent movement to natural childbirth and breastfeeding; suburban conformity, and the new neuroses, character pathologies and sexual problems being reported by the doctors. I began to see new dimensions to old problems that have long been taken for granted among women: menstrual difficulties, sexual frigidity, promiscuity, pregnancy fears, childbirth depression, the high incidence of emotional breakdown and suicide among women in their twenties and thirties, the menopause crises, the so-called passivity and immaturity of American men, the discrepancy between women's tested intellectual abilities in childhood and their adult achievement, the changing incidence of adult sexual orgasm in American women, and persistent problems in psychotherapy and in women's education.

If I am right, the problem that has no name stirring in the minds of so many American women today is not a matter of loss of femininity or too much education, or the demands of domesticity. It is far more important than anyone recognizes. . . . It may well be the key to our future as a nation and a culture. We can no longer ignore that voice within women that says: "I want something more than my husband and my children and my home."

. . .

It is my thesis that the core of the problem for women today is not sexual but a problem of identity—a stunting or evasion of growth that is perpetuated by the feminine mystique. It is my thesis that as the Victorian culture did not permit women to accept or gratify their basic sexual needs, our culture does not permit women to accept or gratify their basic need to grow and fulfill their potentialities as human beings, a need which is not solely defined by their sexual role.

. . .

There have been identity crises for man at all crucial turning points in human history, though those who lived through them did not give them that name. It is only in recent years that the theorists of psychology, sociology and theology have isolated this problem, and given it a name. But it is considered a man's problem.

It is defined, for man, as the crisis of growing up, of choosing his identity, "the decision as to what one is and is going to be," in the words of the brilliant psychoanalyst Erik H. Erikson. . . .

. . .

The search for identity is not new, however, in American thought—though in every generation, each man who writes about it discovers it anew. In America, from the beginning, it has somehow been understood that men must thrust into the future; the pace has always been too rapid for man's identity to stand still. In every generation, many men have suffered misery, unhappiness, and uncertainty because they could not take the image of the man they wanted to be from their fathers. The search for identity of the young man who can't go home again has always been a major theme of American writers. And it has always been considered right in America, good, for men to suffer these agonies of growth, to search for and find their own identities. . . .

. . .

But why have theorists not recognized this same identity crisis in women? In terms of the old conventions and the new feminine mystique women are not expected to grow up to find out who they are, to choose their human identity. Anatomy is woman's destiny, say the theorists of femininity; the identity of woman is determined by her biology.

But is it? More and more women are asking themselves this question. As if they were waking from a coma, they ask, "Where am I . . . what am I doing here?" For the first time in their history, women are becoming aware of an identity crisis in their own lives, a crisis which began many generations ago, has grown worse with each succeeding generation, and will not end until they, or their daughters, turn an unknown corner and make of themselves and their lives the new image that so many women now so desperately need.

In a sense that goes beyond any one woman's life, I think this is the crisis of women growing up—a turning point from an immaturity that has been called femininity to full human identity. I think women had to suffer this crisis of identity, which began a hundred years ago, and have to suffer it still today, simply to become fully human.

. . .

KATE MILLETT

SEXUAL POLITICS (1969)

Kate Millett was raised by her mother in St. Paul, Minnesota, and studied literature at the University of Minnesota and Oxford University. During the 1960s, she taught in a variety of positions while working as a sculptor, earning a Ph.D. in comparative literature at Columbia University in 1970. During the 1960s, she became active in the emerging feminist movement, studying educational institutions for the National Organization for Women. In 1969, she published her landmark work, *Sexual Politics*, which examined a number of literary works from a feminist perspective. Significantly, it emphasized the "politics" embedded in personal and sexual "power-structured relationships." She subsequently pursued a variety of artistic endeavors and writing projects, primarily memoirs.

What does Millett mean by "power-structured relationships"? In what sense are they "political"? What is gained by examining personal relationships from a political perspective? Should personal relationships be organized and evaluated in accordance with "agreeable and rational principles" similar to how political structures are evaluated? In what ways is power within personal relationships sexually structured? How does Millett challenge the significance of consent as a basis for evaluating institutions and practices? In what ways can the contemporary United States be considered a patriarchy?

. . .

. . . In introducing the term "sexual politics," one must first answer the inevitable question "Can the relationship between the sexes be viewed in a political light at all?" The answer depends on how one defines politics. This essay does not define the political as that relatively narrow and exclusive world of meetings, chairmen, and parties. The term "politics" shall refer to power-structured relationships, arrangements whereby one group of persons is controlled by another. By way of parenthesis one might add that although an ideal politics might simply be conceived of as the arrangement of human life on agreeable and rational principles from whence the entire notion of power *over* others should be banished, one must confess that this is not what constitutes the political as we know it, and it is to this that we must address ourselves.

. . .

The word "politics" is enlisted here when speaking of the sexes primarily because such a word is eminently useful in outlining the real nature of their relative status, historically and at the present. It is opportune, perhaps today even mandatory, that we develop a more relevant psychology and philosophy of power relationships beyond the simple conceptual framework provided by our traditional formal politics. Indeed, it may be imperative that we give some attention to defining a theory of politics which treats of power relationships on grounds less conventional than those to which we are accustomed. I have therefore found it pertinent to define them on grounds of personal contact and interaction between members of well-defined and coherent groups: races, castes, classes, and sexes. For it is precisely because certain groups have no representation in a number of recognized political structures that their position tends to be so stable, their oppression so continuous.

In America, recent events have forced us to acknowledge at last that the relationship between the races is indeed a political one which involves the general control of one collectivity, defined by birth, over another collectivity, also defined by birth. Groups who rule by birthright are fast disappearing, yet there remains one ancient and universal scheme for the domination of one birth group by another—the scheme that prevails in the area of sex. The study of racism has convinced us that a truly political state of affairs operates between the races to perpetuate a series of oppressive circumstances. The subordinated group has inadequate redress through existing political institutions, and is deterred thereby from organizing into conventional political struggle and opposition.

. . .

This is so because our society, like all other historical civilizations, is a patriarchy. The fact is evident at once if one recalls that the military, industry, technology, universities, science, political office, and finance—in short, every avenue of power within the society, including the coercive force of the police, is entirely in male hands. As the essence of politics is power, such realization cannot fail to carry impact. What lingers of supernatural authority, the Deity, "His" ministry, together with the ethics and values, the philosophy and art of our culture—its very civilization—as T. S. Eliot once observed, is of male manufacture.

. . .

Hannah Arendt has observed that government is upheld by power supported either through consent or imposed through violence. Conditioning to an ideology amounts to the former. Sexual politics obtains consent through the "socialization" of both sexes to basic patriarchal polities with regard to temperament, role, and status. As to status, a pervasive assent to the prejudice of male superiority guarantees superior status in the male, inferior in the female. The first item, temperament, involves the formation of human personality along stereotyped lines of sex category ("masculine" and "feminine"), based on the needs and values of the dominant group and dictated by what its members cherish in themselves and find convenient in subordinates: aggression, intelligence, force, and efficacy in the male; passivity, ignorance, docility, "virtue," and ineffectuality in the female. This is complemented by a second factor, sex role, which decrees a consonant and highly elaborate code of conduct, gesture and attitude for each sex. In terms of activity, sex role assigns domestic service and attendance upon infants to the female, the rest of human achievement, interest, and ambition to the male. The limited role allotted the female tends to arrest her at the level of biological experience. Therefore, nearly all that can be described as distinctly human rather than animal activity (in their own way animals also give birth and care for their young) is largely reserved for the male. Of course, status again follows from such an assignment. Were one to analyze the three categories one might designate status as the political component, role as the sociological, and temperament as the psychological—yet their interdependence is unquestionable and they form a chain. Those awarded higher status tend to adopt roles of mastery, largely because they are first encouraged to develop temperaments of dominance. That this is true of caste and class as well is self-evident.

. . .

Patriarchy's chief institution is the family. It is both a mirror of and a connection with the larger society; a patriarchal unit within a patriarchal whole. Mediating between the individual and the social structure, the family effects control and conformity where political and other authorities are insufficient. As the fundamental instrument and the foundation unit of patriarchal society the family and its roles are prototypical. Serving as an agent of the larger society, the family not only encourages its own members to adjust and conform, but acts as a unit in the government of the patriarchal state which rules its citizens through its family heads. Even in patriarchal societies where they are granted legal citizenship, women tend to be ruled through the family alone and have little or no formal relation to the state.

. . .

It is in the area of class that the caste-like status of the female within patriarchy is most liable to confusion, for sexual status often operates in a superficially confusing way within the variable of class. In a society where status is dependent upon the economic, social, and educational circumstances of class, it is possible for certain females to appear to stand higher than some males. Yet not when one looks more closely at the subject. This is perhaps easier to see by means of analogy: a black doctor or lawyer has higher social status than a poor white sharecropper. But race, itself a caste system which subsumes class, persuades the latter citizen that he belongs to a higher order of life, just as it oppresses the black professional in spirit, whatever his material success may be. In much the same manner, a truck driver or butcher has always his "manhood" to fall back upon. Should this final vanity be offended, he may contemplate more violent methods. . . .

. . .

One of the most efficient branches of patriarchal government lies in the agency of its economic hold over its female subjects. In traditional patriarchy, women, as non-persons without legal standing were permitted no actual economic existence as they could neither own nor earn in their own right. Since women have always worked in patriarchal societies, often at the most routine or strenuous tasks, what is at issue here is not labor but economic reward. In modern reformed patriarchal societies, women have certain economic rights, yet the "woman's work" in which some two thirds of the female population in most developed countries are engaged is work that is not paid for. In a money economy where autonomy and prestige depend upon currency, this is a fact of great importance. In general, the position of women in patriarchy is a continuous function of their economic dependence. Just as their social position is vicarious and achieved (often on a temporary or marginal basis) though males, their relation to the economy is also typically vicarious or tangential.

. . .

Since woman's independence in economic life is viewed with distrust, prescriptive agencies of all kinds (religion, psychology, advertising, etc.) continuously admonish or even inveigh against the employment of middle-class women, particularly mothers. The toil of working class women is more readily accepted as "need," if not always by the working-class itself, at least by the middle-class. And to be sure, it serves the purpose of making available cheap labor in factory and lower-grade service and clerical positions. Its wages and tasks are so unremunerative that, unlike more prestigious employment for women, it fails to threaten patriarchy financially or psychologically. Women who are employed have two jobs since the burden of domestic service and child care is unrelieved either by day care or other social agencies, or by the cooperation of husbands. The invention of labor-saving devices has had no appreciable effect on the duration, even if it has affected the quality of their drudgery. Discrimination in matters of hiring, maternity, wages and hours is very great. In the US. a recent law forbidding discrimination in employment, the first and only federal legislative guarantee of rights granted to American women since the vote, is not enforced, has not been enforced since its passage, and was not enacted to be enforced.

. . .

V. POLITICAL ECONOMY

Major Developments

- Acceptance of Keynesian welfare state
- Growth of postindustrialism
- Development of public choice economics

Even Milton Friedman, libertarian economic advisor to Barry Goldwater's presidential campaign, admitted that "We are all Keynesians now."[12] A general political consensus emerged out of the New Deal, and the British economist John Maynard Keynes was the symbol of it. Keynes had influentially argued that market forces were not always self-correcting and that government intervention would sometimes be needed to stabilize the economic system. In particular, Keynes emphasized the importance of consumer spending as the driver of economic growth (he had diagnosed the Depression as a problem of excessive savings) and "countercyclical" government deficit spending as an important mechanism for combating recessions. Programs like unemployment insurance and food stamps not only provided aid to the needy; they "primed the pump" of consumer spending, generating a ripple effect throughout the economy. Friedman spent much of his academic career overturning many of the core tenets of Keynesianism, but Keynes had set a new task for economists and a new role for government. The government was no longer concerned simply with establishing the rules of the economic game and enforcing compliance with them. The government was to be an active economic player that would constantly seek to manipulate the economic system to achieve socially desired results.[13]

The debates over Keynesianism occupied macroeconomists. Meanwhile, a new school of public choice economists were beginning to apply microeconomic analysis to political institutions and behavior. There were many branches to the emerging body of work, but a central feature of such work was to examine the behavior of actors in a nonprofit context (such as legislators and bureaucrats) and the types of incentives to which they responded and goals that they pursued. Rather than assuming that individuals who were not confronted with the profit incentive would simply work to advance the public welfare, these studies suggested that the behavior of these social actors were also often geared toward servicing private interests. Rather than viewing government as a "benevolent social guardian," this strain of economic thought increasingly emphasized the ways in which government officials and other political actors (including lobbyists) routinely engaged in "rent seeking"—the effort of generating a stream of income without doing anything to contribute to societal wealth. The analysis of "market failures"—which might call for government intervention to correct—was now paired with the analysis of "political failures"—instances

12 Friedman later clarified that his recognition of the dominance of Keynesianism was distinctly qualified. Milton Friedman and Rose D. Friedman, *Two Lucky People: Memoirs* (Chicago, IL: University of Chicago Press, 1998), 231.

13 The midcentury debates over Keynesianism are ably summarized in Mark Skousen, *The Making of Modern Economics*, 2nd ed. (Armonk, NY: M.E. Sharpe, 2009), 357–420.

in which special interests exploited control over the political process to enrich themselves at the expense of others.[14] While this literature was often cynical and pessimistic, other elements were more optimistic, hoping to find institutional solutions to the identified political failures. But on the whole, this emerging line of thought tended to deflate pressures for economic and social regulation and provoke deregulatory reforms.

These scholarly debates occurred against a background of postindustrialism. From a purely economic perspective, postindustrialism highlighted the rise of the service sector and information technology as important components of advanced economies. More broadly, postindustrialism (or its variant, postmaterialism) suggested economic conditions of general affluence and a shift of individual concerns and preferences away from the basics of material comfort and to a broader range of nonmaterial goods and values, from "objective welfare" to "subjective satisfaction."[15] A basically affluent society breeds an increasing preference for everything from environmental protection to artistic freedom to sexual liberation to organic farming.

14 Anne O. Krueger, "Economists' Changing Perceptions of Government," *Weltwirtschaftliches Archiv* 126 (1990): 417.

15 Ronald Inglehart, *The Silent Revolution* (Princeton, NJ: Princeton University Press, 1977), 136.

JOHN KENNETH GALBRAITH

AMERICAN CAPITALISM (1952)

A native of Canada, John Kenneth Galbraith came to the United States to receive his advanced training in agricultural economics. He remained in the United States through the Great Depression and World War II, joining the faculty of Harvard University in 1949. Over the course of his career, he moved in and out of government service and became a significant player in the liberal wing of the Democratic Party. As an academic economist, he favored the analysis of the institutional context of economic activity over the increasingly prominent mathematical models of economic behavior, and he often wrote for a popular audience in books, journalism, and novels (he was a frequent sparring partner with the conservative writer, William F. Buckley). At the heart of much of his economic writing was the assumption that economic competition and problems of scarcity no longer played a significant role in the operation of modern corporate economies. The key issues of the twentieth century were how to discipline large economic actors in the absence of market forces and how to ensure that desirable goods were widely distributed. The role of the state was to encourage "countervailing" forces in the economic arena that could check industrial power and to make public investments in science and education. The "industrial system" was an "essentially technical arrangement for providing convenient goods and services in adequate volume" and would "fall into its place as a detached and autonomous arm of the state," while the broader community turned to the "larger purposes of society."[16]

Are there any proponents of a free market within the American political system? Do businesses necessarily favor free markets? Under what conditions does Galbraith think that large corporations ought to be broken up? What does he see as the alternative to antitrust actions? What does he take to be the dangers of the accumulation of economic power? Does Galbraith give us reason to doubt that "countervailing power" is sufficient to sustain the American system? Is there an effective alternative to government support for weaker players in the economic system? Why does he characterize the role of conservatives as protectors of "positions of original power"? Should the government put a "thumb on the scale" to favor some economic actors over others? Should the rules of the economic game be neutral for all players, or should some players be handicapped? Are there other goals for state intervention in the economy beyond creating countervailing power?

In their relations with government, the American people have long shown a considerable ability to temper doctrine by pragmatism. The ruggedly conservative businessman who excoriates Statism, the Welfare State and the State Department, has never allowed his convictions to interfere with an approach to the government for a tariff if he really needs it. . . .

. . .

In fact, the support of countervailing power has become in modern times perhaps the major domestic peacetime function of the federal government. Labor sought and received it in the protection and assistance which the Wagner Act provided to union organization. Farmers sought and received it in the form of federal price supports to their markets—a direct subsidy of market power. Unorganized workers have sought and received it in the form of minimum wage legislation. . . . These measures, all designed to give a group a market power it did not have before, comprised the most important legislative acts of the New Deal. . . .

. . .

The role of countervailing power in the economy marks out two broad problems in policy for the government. In all but conditions of inflationary demand, countervailing power performs a valuable—indeed an indispensable—regulatory function in the modern economy. Accordingly it is incumbent upon government to give it freedom to develop and to determine how it may best do so. . . .

16 John Kenneth Galbraith, *The New Industrial State* (Boston, MA: Houghton Mifflin, 1967), 406.

. . . When, anywhere in the course of producing, processing or distributing a particular product, one or a few firms first succeed in establishing a strong market position they may be considered to be the possessors of original market power. They are able, as a result of their power over the prices they pay or charge, to obtain more than normal margins and profits. These are at the expense of the weaker suppliers or customers. . . . Countervailing power invades such positions of strength, whether they be held by suppliers or consumers, and redresses the position of the weaker group.

The role to be followed by government is, in principle, a clear one. There can be very good reason for attacking positions of original market power in the economy if these are not effectively offset by countervailing power. . . . There is no justification for attacking positions of countervailing power which leaves positions of original market power untouched. . . .

. . .

. . . Past efforts to extirpate economic power have been notably unavailing. One cannot suppose that they will be more successful in the future. Economic power may indeed be inherent in successful capitalism. We had better be content with restraints we have than to search or a never-never land in which they would be rendered unnecessary.

. . . [T]he government has subsidized with its own power the countervailing power of workers, farmers and others. . . . This assistance, clearly, explains some part of the self-confidence and well-being which these groups display today.

Yet few courses of policy have ever been undertaken more grudgingly and with a greater sense of guilt. . . .

. . . The reformer . . . has almost invariably been overtaken by the action. When the groups in question have developed enough influence to obtain government assistance on their own behalf they have simply gone ahead and got it without blessing or benefit of doctrine. As the role of countervailing power comes to be understood, we can expect that much of the anxiety that is evoked by government support to the process will disappear.

. . .

In the actual sequence of events, some measure of organization by the group themselves must precede any very important government subsidy to their developing market power. Not until farmers and workers achieved some organization on their own behalf were they able to get the state to reinforce their efforts. . . . Support to countervailing power is not endowed, *ad hoc,* by government. It must be sought.

. . . We can now see that a large part of the state's new activity . . . is associated with the development of countervailing power. As such it is neither adventitious nor abnormal; the government action supports or supplements a normal economic process. Steps to strengthen countervailing power are not, in principle, different from steps to strengthen competition. Given the existence of private market power in the economy, the growth of countervailing power strengthens the capacity of the economy for autonomous self-regulation and thereby lessens the amount of overall government control or planning that is required or sought.

. . . Increasingly, in our time, we may expect domestic political differences to turn on the question of supporting or not supporting efforts to develop countervailing power. Liberalism will be identified with the buttressing of weak bargaining positions in the economy; conservatism—and this may well be its proper function—will be identified with the protection of positions of original power. There will be debate over whether weak positions have been unduly strengthened. . . .

. . .

. . . It is only in light of history that our fear of the countervailing power of weaker groups dissolves, that their effort to establish their power in the market emerges as the stuff of which economic progress consists. It is by our experience, not our fears, that we should be guided.

GEORGE J. STIGLER

THE THEORY OF ECONOMIC REGULATION (1971)

George J. Stigler was a key figure in the Chicago School of Economics. In the postwar period, the University of Chicago attracted a large group of free-market economists whose interests ranged from monetary and fiscal policy to the economic foundations of social and political behavior. Stigler was trained at Chicago in the 1930s and went on to spend most of his career there. His best-known work focused on the economic theory of regulation, which won him a Nobel Prize in 1982. In the 1960s, a number of economists began to turn the tools and analytical frameworks of economics toward understanding how politics operated. Stigler emphasized the governmental monopoly on violence, or coercive force. Monopolistic power is always valuable, and Stigler contended that economic actors would look for ways to gain control over those levers of power and use them to advance their own private interests. Notably, he thought that economic regulations were most likely to be initiated and maintained by the regulated industries themselves, who could realize economic advantages from favorably designed regulations. Rather than serving a nebulous public interest, government action was most likely to serve concrete special interests.

Why does Stigler think that government regulation is more likely to serve private interests than public interests? Does his analysis suggest ways of reducing that risk? Does the rise of Nader-style public advocacy groups alter Stigler's analysis? Is such an economic analysis of policymaking corrosive of democracy? What are the implications of Stigler's analysis for the kind of economic policies that we should pursue? Can Stigler's analysis be extended to other political-economic systems besides the American-style democratic regulation of corporate capitalism?

The state—the machinery and power of the state—is a potential resource or threat to every industry in the society. With its power to prohibit or compel, to take or give money, the state can and does selectively help or hurt a vast number of industries. . . . The central tasks of the theory of economic regulation are to explain who will receive the benefits or burdens of regulation, what form regulation will take, and the effects of regulation upon the allocation of resources.

Regulation may be actively sought by an industry, or it may be thrust upon it. A central thesis of this paper is that, as a rule, regulation is acquired by the industry and is designed and operated primarily for its benefit. There are regulations whose net effects upon the regulated industry are undeniably onerous. . . . These onerous regulations, however, are exceptional. . . .

Two main alternative views of the regulation of industry are widely held. The first is that regulation is instituted primarily for the protection and benefit of the public at large or some large subclass of the public. . . . The second view is essentially that the political process defies rational expectation. . . .

. . .

. . . We assume that political systems are rationally devised and rationally employed, which is to say that they are appropriate instruments for the fulfillment of desires of members of the society. This is not to say that the state will serve any person's concept of the public interest: indeed the problem of regulation is the problem of discovering when and why an industry (or other group of likeminded people) is able to use the state for its purposes, or is singled out by the state to be used for alien purposes.

The state has one basic resource which in pure principle is not shared with even the mightiest of its citizens: the power to coerce. The state can seize money by the only method which is permitted by the laws of a civilized society, by taxation. The state can ordain the physical movements of resources and the economic decisions of households and firms without their consent. These powers provide the possibilities for the utilization of the state by an industry to increase its profitability. The main policies which an industry (or occupation) may seek of the state are four.

The most obvious contribution that a group may seek of the government is a direct subsidy of money. . . .

. . . [A]n industry with power to obtain governmental favors usually does not use this power to get money: unless the list of beneficiaries can be limited by an acceptable device, whatever amount of subsidies the industry can obtain will be dissipated among a growing number of rivals. . . .

The second major public resource commonly sought by an industry is control over entry by new rivals. . . .

We propose the general hypothesis: every industry or occupation that has enough political power to utilize the state will seek to control entry. In addition, the regulatory policy will often be so fashioned as to retard the rate of growth of new firms. . . .

A third set of general powers of the state which will be sought by the industry are those which affect substitutes and complements. Crudely put, the butter producers wish to suppress margarine and encourage the production of bread. . . .

The fourth class of public policies sought by an industry is directed to price-fixing. Even the industry that has achieved entry control will often want price controls administered by a body with coercive powers.

. . .

The industry which seeks regulation must be prepared to pay with the two things a party needs: votes and resources. The resources may be provided by campaign contributions, contributed services (the businessman heads a fund-raising committee), and more indirect methods such as the employment of party workers. The votes in support of the measure are rallied, and the votes in opposition are dispersed. . . .

. . .

VI. AMERICA AND THE WORLD

Major Developments

- Intensification of Cold War and detente
- Breakdown of bipartisan consensus on foreign policy
- Growing importance of postcolonial developing world

After World War I, the United States embarked on a program of demobilization and a return to "normalcy." There was no such respite after World War II. The United States moved rapidly from the shooting war in Europe and the Pacific to the global Cold War. The United States had roughly 334,000 troops on active duty in 1939, over 12 million in 1945, and nearly 1.5 million in 1950 (before the outbreak of the Korean War). As Figure 10-2 illustrates, the number of men (and women) under arms in the United States did not fall below two million again until after the fall of the Berlin Wall in 1989. The country maintained a perpetual war footing. The United States joined a series of collective security pacts, from the North Atlantic Treaty Organization (NATO) to the South East Asia Treaty Organization (SEATO). Advance bases put American troops on the frontlines of any potential conflict in Europe and Asia, and substantial defense expenditures helped fuel economic growth across the Sun Belt. President Kennedy promised that the United States would "pay any price, bear any burden, meet any hardship, support any friend, oppose any foe, in order to assure the survival and the success of liberty."[17] For much of the 1950s and 1960s, the Cold War heated up, with crises ranging from the Berlin blockade, to the Korean War, to the Soviet invasion of Hungary, to the Cuban Missile Crisis. By contrast, the 1970s marked a period of détente, as the United States withdrew from Vietnam, President Nixon visited China, and the United States negotiated new agreements with the Soviet Union, including the Helsinki Accords calling for recognition of existing territorial borders and respect for human rights.

Republican Senator Arthur Vandenberg popularized the aphorism that "politics stops at the water's edge" for the postwar world.[18] The slogan was always as much aspirational as descriptive. Vandenberg appealed to bipartisanship in order to encourage his fellow Republicans to join the White House in placing the United States in a more internationalist posture. Republicans who wanted to disengage from foreign entanglements and pull troops back home (or who wanted to blame President Truman for "losing" China to communism) were chided for politicizing foreign policy. Maintaining bipartisanship in foreign policy was an ongoing challenge, but presidents in the postwar period benefitted from a significant measure of support from across the aisle. Despite some dissenters, there was a broad political consensus in favor of a policy of containing communism within its current boundaries and maintaining American engagement overseas. That consensus broke down during the Vietnam War, with hardline cold warriors in both parties committed to resisting the expansion of communism and an increasingly vocal group of dissenters (primarily

---

17 John F. Kennedy, "First Inaugural Address, January 20, 1961," in *Public Papers of the President of the United States* (Washington, D.C.: Government Printing Office, 1966), 213.

18 The adage predated the Cold War and was exploited by both presidents Roosevelt, among others.

on the political left and in the Democratic Party) questioning basic features of the Cold War. From mainstream New Deal Democrats like Senator J. William Fulbright to radicals like the SDS, new doubts were being raised about the desirability of maintaining a hostile attitude toward the Soviet Union.

As the Cold War as an organizing principle of American foreign policy was collapsing, new emphasis was placed on the developing world. From a Cold War perspective, the developing world was primarily of concern as a theater for confronting the Soviet Union. But the collapse of colonialism and the rise of new nationalist movements and often unstable new governments changed the geostrategic landscape in the postwar period. The Vietnam War itself was part of the multi-decade fallout of the collapse of French Indochina. The New Left was more inclined to see capitalist exploitation and imperialism than communist insurgency as the key problem of the Third World. Upon assuming the presidency, Jimmy Carter declared that the new, postcolonial world required an American focus on "global questions of justice, equity, and human rights." Securing "social justice," not halting the advance of communism, was the new American priority.[19]

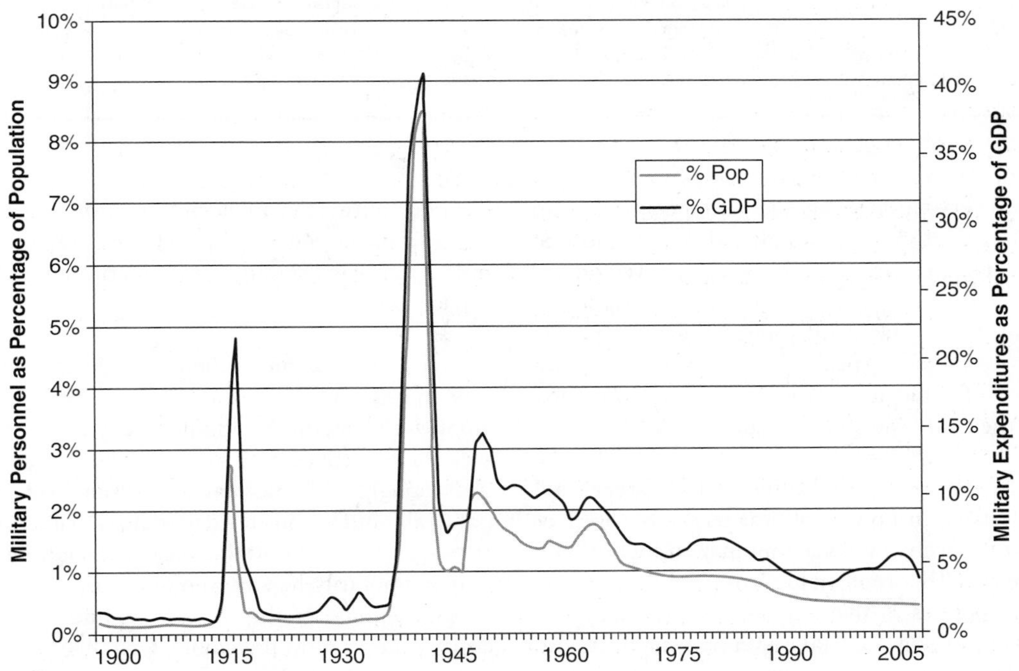

FIGURE 10-2 Military Personnel as Percentage of Population and Military Expenditures as Percentage of GDP.

19 Jimmy Carter, "Commencement Speech at Notre Dame University, May 22, 1977," in *Public Papers of the Presidents* (Washington, D.C.: Government Printing Office, 1978).

HANS J. MORGENTHAU

IN DEFENSE OF THE NATIONAL INTEREST (1952)

Hans Morgenthau was the son of a Jewish doctor in Germany. He studied the law in Frankfurt and began work writing briefs for the German supreme court but left Germany in 1931 due to the rise of Nazism. After teaching in Europe for a few years, he fled to the United States in 1937 and eventually found a stable job at the University of Chicago law school. His primary expertise was in international law and international relations, and in the postwar period he established himself as a leading advocate of a realist approach to foreign policy and served as a frequent consultant for the U.S. government. He became a critic of the Vietnam War, which he thought posed unacceptable strategic choices for the United States. His overriding concern, expressed in various works, was the importance of evaluating national interests in terms of maintaining power in the international arena.

Why does Morgenthau think that it is a mistake to imagine foreign policy decisions in "moralistic terms"? Is the United States mistaken to think that its actions sometimes reflect a moral vision, or is it mistaken to allow a moral vision to determine its actions? Is international conflict inevitable? Does the spread of democracy reduce the threat of conflict and war? Is it wrong for the United States to pursue a foreign policy designed to advance its own economic and political interests? Are national interests a sufficient justification for making foreign policy decisions? Is it a necessary condition that a foreign policy action be in the American national interests? Is it appropriate for democratic leaders to win public opinion by any means necessary in order to undertake otherwise desirable foreign policies? Should foreign policy be dependent on favorable public opinion?

. . . Until very recently the American people have appeared content to live in a political desert whose intellectual barrenness and aridity was relieved only by some sparse and neglected cases of insight and wisdom. What passed for foreign policy was either improvisation or—especially in our century—the invocation of some abstract moral principle in whose image the world was to be made over. . . .

. . .

. . . We have acted on the international scene, as all nations must, in power-political terms; but we have tended to conceive of our actions in non-political moralistic terms. This aversion to seeing problems of international politics as they are, and the inclination to view them in non-political and moralistic terms, can be attributed both to certain misunderstood peculiarities of the American experience in foreign affairs and to the general climate of opinion in the Western world during the better part of the nineteenth and the first decades of the twentieth centuries. Three of these peculiarities of the American experience stand out: the uniqueness of the American experiment; the actual isolation, during the nineteenth century, of the United States from the centers of world conflict; and the humanitarian pacifism and anti-imperialism of American ideology.

. . .

Yet while the foreign policy of the United States was forced, by circumstance if not by choice, to employ the methods, shoulder the commitments, seek the objectives, and run the risks, from which it had thought itself permanently exempt, American political thought continued to uphold that exemption at least as an ideal. And that ideal was supposed to be only temporarily beyond the reach of the American people, because of the wickedness and stupidity of either American or, preferably, foreign statesmen. In one sense, this ideal of a free, peaceful, and prosperous world, from which popular government had forever banished power politics, was a natural outgrowth of the American experience. In another sense, this ideal expressed in a particularly eloquent and consistent fashion the general philosophy that dominated the Western world during the better part of the nineteenth century. This philosophy rests on two basic propositions: that the struggle for power on the international scene is a mere accident of history, naturally associated with non-democratic government and therefore destined to disappear with the triumph of democracy throughout the world; and that, in consequence, conflicts between democratic and non-democratic nations must be primarily conceived not as struggles for mutual advantage in terms of power but as fights between good and evil, which can only end with complete triumph of good, and with evil wiped off the face of the earth.

. . .

The illusion that a nation can escape, if it wants to, from power politics into a realm where action is guided by moral principles rather than by considerations of power is deeply rooted in the American mind. . . .

. . .

The fundamental error that has thwarted American foreign policy in thought and action is the antithesis of national interest and moral principles. The equation of political moralizing with morality and of political realism with immorality is itself untenable. The choice is not between moral principles and the national interest, devoid of moral dignity, but between one set of moral principles divorced from political reality, and another set of moral principles derived from political reality.

. . .

. . . [A]bove the national societies there exists no international society so integrated as to be able to define for them the concrete meaning of justice or equality, as national societies do for their individual members. In consequence, the appeal to moral principles by the representative of a nation vis-à-vis another nation signifies something fundamentally different from a verbally identical appeal made by an individual to his relations to another individual member of the same national society. The appeal to moral principles in the international sphere has no concrete universal meaning. It is either so vague as to have no concrete meaning that could provide rational guidance for political action, or it will be nothing but the reflection of the moral preconceptions of a particular nation, and will by that same token be unable to gain the universal recognition it pretends to deserve.

. . . [N]o agency is able to promote and protect the interests of individual nations and to guard their existence—and that is emphatically true of the great powers—but the individual nations themselves. To ask, then, a nation to embark upon altruistic policies oblivious of the national interest is really to ask something immoral. For such disregard of the individual interest, on the part of nations as of individuals, can be morally justified only by the existence of social institutions, the embodiment of concrete moral principles, which are able to do what otherwise the individual would have to do. In the absence of such institutions it would be both foolish and morally wrong to ask a nation to forego its national interests. . . .

. . . Self-preservation both for the individual and for societies is . . . not only a biological and psychological necessity but, in the absence of overriding moral obligation, a moral duty as well. In the absence of an integrated international society, the attainment of a modicum of order and the realization of a minimum of moral values are predicated upon the existence of national communities capable of preserving order and realizing moral values within the limits of their power.

. . . A foreign policy derived from the national interests is in fact morally superior to a foreign policy inspired by universal moral principles. . . .

. . .

Foreign policy, like all politics, is in its essence a struggle for power, waged by sovereign nations for national advantage. . . . By its very nature this struggle is never ended, for the lust for power, and the fear of it, is never stilled. . . .

These stark and simple facts of the real political world have been replaced in the American mind by the picture of a political world that never existed, but whose reality . . . appears only too plausible. In that fictitious world the struggle for power is not a continuum, with each solved problem giving rise to a new one in a never ending succession. It is rather a kind of criminal disturbance, like a street brawl, disrupting a normalcy that knows only peaceful competition and cooperation. . . .

The United States flatters itself that in its dealings with other countries it seeks no selfish advantage but is inspired by universal moral principles. It is difficult for the United States to understand that other nations, in opposing American policies, may pursue their national interests, as legitimate at those which the United States denies pursuing but actually pursues just the same. . . . Since American foreign policy is by definition selfless and moral, the foreign policies of nations opposing it are by definition selfish and immoral. Since the United States is the policeman of the world seeking only peace and order and the welfare of all, only evil nations can dare oppose it. They are criminals when they act alone, conspirators when they act in union.

. . .

The kind of thinking required for the successful conduct of foreign policy must at times be diametrically opposed to the kind of considerations by which the masses and their representatives are likely to be moved The peculiar qualities of the statesman's mind are not always likely to find a favorable response in the popular mind. The statesman must think in terms of the national interest conceived as power among other powers. The popular mind, unaware of the fine distinctions of the statesman's thinking, reasons more often than not in the simple moralistic and legalistic terms of absolute good and absolute evil. The statesman must take the long view, proceeding slowly and by detours, paying with small losses for great advantages; he must be able to temporize, to compromise, to bide his time. The popular mind wants quick results; it will sacrifice tomorrow's real benefit for today's apparent advantage.

. . . A tragic choice often confronts those responsible for the conduct of foreign affairs. They must either sacrifice what they consider good policy upon the altar of public opinion, or by devious means gain popular support for policies whose true nature they conceal from the public.

. . .

JAMES BURNHAM

CONTAINMENT OR LIBERATION? (1953)

As a philosophy professor at New York University in the 1930s, James Burnham was a Trotskyite political activist. Burnham fell out from the radical movement, however, when the American socialist party purged the Trotskyites and the Soviet Union joined forces with Nazi Germany and invaded eastern Europe in 1939. By the time America entered World War II, he had renounced communism, left academia, and joined the precursor to the Central Intelligence Agency to work on political and psychological warfare. In the 1950s, he became a key figure in the formation of the modern conservative movement and a founding editor of *National Review*, injecting a central concern with an interventionist foreign policy into a movement that was initially focused on economics and culture and often embraced isolationism. He advocated an American policy aimed at the ultimate dissolution of the Soviet Union and the liberation of Eastern bloc countries from Russian control. He was convinced that if Russia could assimilate the territories and populations that it controlled in the aftermath of World War II, it would become the dominant global power. The best hope of the West was to use the tools of political and psychological warfare to encourage dissent and resistance within the Eastern bloc as part of a "protracted struggle" to encourage the eventual collapse of the Soviet empire. In 1983, President Ronald Reagan awarded Burnham the Presidential Medal of Freedom while praising the writer's influence on Reagan's own thinking.

Did the United States have a "foreign policy" in times of peace prior to the Cold War? Was it a mistake for the Cold War to define American foreign policy in the mid-twentieth century? Is Burnham right about the available options for approaching the Cold War? What does he mean by a policy of liberation? What would such a policy involve? Is that preferable to a policy of containment? How would we evaluate whether one strategic vision is preferable to another? Is a policy of liberation more or less dangerous to the United States than one of containment? Does liberation represent a more idealistic, Wilsonian approach to foreign policy?

. . . Heretofore in its history, the United States has had a foreign policy only in times of open war. Then . . . there has always been a policy, direct and unadorned: to win a military victory. At other times there has ordinarily been no foreign policy at all.

. . .

Since 1947 the United States has had a foreign policy, a deliberate policy consciously elaborated, with theoretical underpinnings and a perspective into the future. . . .

. . .

For the United States, foreign policy means policy toward world communism and the Soviet Union. The range is restricted to three possibilities: appeasement, containment, liberation. . . .

Besides these three, what policy could there even conceivably be? They empty the barrel. Your purpose can be to stand off the Soviet Empire by firmly bottling it up within its present boundaries (whatever these happen to be at the given moment). That is: *containment*. You can accept communism as a legitimate child of human civilization, and therefore wish to the bring the Soviet Empire within the family of nations. Because the Soviet imperial state is a totalitarian power which seeks world domination, this is equivalent to accepting the extension of Soviet control. In a word: *appeasement*. You can aim to get rid of Soviet rule, or at least reduce it to a scale which would no longer threaten all mankind. That is: *liberation*. You must either hold Soviet power where it is or let it advance or thrust it back.

. . .

I am inclined to think that the defenders of containment have sensed the historical vacuum upon which their position has rested. The containment period has brought into a kind of united front two groups with contrary perspectives which for a few years happened to intersect. One, partly out of ignorance, partly out of softness toward communism, believes at heart in appeasement. This group regards containment as a maneuver designed, on the one hand, to reach a better spot from which to negotiate with Moscow, and on the other, to quiet the more extreme anti-Soviet feelings at home, which might explode in the face of an open policy of appeasement. . . .

At the same time, others who went along with the policy of containment. . . . The second group has been by conviction or temperament for liberation, even if the name was not much used. It felt that so positive and sharp a policy as liberation could not be reached in a single jump from a friendly appeasement of war time and the post-war demobilization. . . . Containment, valueless for its own sake, was necessary as a bridge to the firm shore of liberation.

. . .

. . . The goal of liberation . . . includes freeing the subjects of the Soviet Empire as individuals, as workers, as worshippers, as members of families. If the Soviet subjects achieve liberation, this will mean not only that they have won national freedom but that they will be free from slave camps and the secret police, free to worship God as they see fit, free (if they so choose) to own and cultivate their own land and to work with their own tools, free to make peace with their fellow-men.

Second, liberation applies to the whole Soviet Empire, and is not limited to the regions which were seized at the end of the second World War and thereafter. Morally, such a restriction is indefensible. Practically, to make it would promote an irreconcilable hostility between the inhabitants of the original Soviet Union and those of the newly captive nations.

There is thus nothing mysterious about the policy of liberation. Its goal is freedom for the peoples and nations now enslaved by the Russian-centered Soviet state system. . . . For the United States to adopt the policy of liberation will mean in the first instance simply that a responsible decision by the government commits the country to that goal. The basic commitment must be open. . . .

Among those who accept the goal of liberation there will inevitably be disputes over means and methods. . . .

Following the commitment of the United States to the objective, the next act under a policy of liberation will be the communication of the decision to the inhabitants of the Soviet Empire, and to the world at large. . . . A genuine Resistance can develop only out of the conviction that the present state of affairs is temporary, that the system will not endure. This conviction must be shared by the masses, not confined to exceptional and perhaps eccentric individuals. . . . The policy of liberation addresses itself to entire nations and peoples: its goal is freedom, not subversion.

Words alone ("propaganda") will not be enough to convince the masses of the American commitment to liberation. This must be daily demonstrated in action. The content of the demonstration will be threefold: all-sided political warfare, auxiliary military and paramilitary actions where called for; adequate preparation for whatever military action may be required in the future. . . .

. . .

The goal of the policy of liberation is to free men from the totalitarian tyranny of communism. Communist power, and therefore anti-communist political warfare, operates outside as well as within the Soviet sphere. The liberation perspective suggests that the principle strategic aim in the non-Soviet nations should be the *outlawing* of the communist enterprise. I use this word in a double sense, meaning: to convince public opinion of the fact that communism is an intellectual and moral "outlaw"—outside the permissible boundaries of the civilized community; and, second, to draw the practical conclusion from this by illegalizing and suppressing the organized communist movement. . . .

. . .

. . . It is argued that liberation, though in itself good and to be wished for, is none of our business. . . . [W]e cannot be every man's keeper. Our task is to strengthen the liberty and well-being of our own land and people. So far as international conflict goes, our problem is our own national defense. . . .

Let us agree that national security and defense are the proper objective of a government's general strategy, and that any action in the field of foreign affairs which injures national security is wrong. . . .

The security of the United States, and of all nations that are still independent, is in the gravest peril. The danger, a mortal danger, is a reality of the present, not a vague possibility of the future. . . .

. . .

The peril can be summed up in a single sentence. If the communists succeed in consolidating what they have *already* conquered, then their complete world victory is certain. The threat does not come only from what the communists may do, but from what they have done. . . .

. . .

. . . Americans will not even be granted much longer the desperate comfort that as a last resort there are always the bombs to turn to. If the political offensive is long delayed, it will be too late for bombs.

J. WILLIAM FULBRIGHT

THE ARROGANCE OF POWER (1966)

A New Deal Democrat from Arkansas, J. William Fulbright was first elected to the U.S. Senate in 1944. The former football star and Rhodes Scholar had become the youngest person selected as president of the University of Arkansas, but he left after only two years to win a seat in the U.S. House of Representatives after the outbreak of World War II. During his lengthy political career, he became the longest-serving chair of the Senate Foreign Relations Committee. Although occupying a key policymaking role, he was a frequent critic of the foreign policies advanced by both Republican and Democratic administrations. Nonetheless, he sponsored the 1964 Gulf of Tonkin Resolution that initiated the Vietnam War. He soon emerged as a leading critic of the war, however, contributing to his defeat in the party primaries to a more hawkish Democrat in 1974. His book criticizing the war, *Arrogance of Power*, appeared alongside a series of televised hearings assessing the war effort and reevaluating presidential dominance of American foreign policymaking.

To what extent does Fulbright disagree with the aims of American foreign policy? Is he hostile to a "missionary" foreign policy? Does his argument point toward isolationism? Should the United States concern itself with the spread of democracy? Is military force an acceptable means for trying to spread (or preserve) democracies abroad? Could Fulbright's lessons derived from Vietnam have been extended to Greece in the early 1950s? To Afghanistan in the 2000s? Does Fulbright suggest that America's more idealistic goals are themselves inappropriate for the developing world?

. . .

For the most part America has made good use of her blessings, especially in her internal life but also in her foreign relations. Having done so much and succeeded so well, America is now at that historical point at which a great nation is in danger of losing its perspective on what exactly is within the realm of its power and what is beyond it. Other great nations, reaching this critical juncture, have aspired to too much, and by overextension of effort have declined and then fallen.

The causes of the malady are not entirely clear but its recurrence is one of the uniformities of history: power tend to confuse itself with virtue and a great nation is peculiarly susceptible to the idea that its power is a sign of God's favor, conferring upon it a special responsibility for other nations—to make them richer and happier and wiser, to remake them, that is, in its own shining image. Power confuses itself with virtue and tends also to take itself for omnipotence. . . .

I do not think for a moment that America, with her deeply rooted democratic traditions, is likely to embark upon a campaign to dominate the world in the manner of a Hitler or Napoleon. What I do fear is that she may be drifting into commitments which, though generous and benevolent in intent, are so far-reaching as to exceed even America's great capacities. . . .

The stakes are high indeed: they include not only America's continued greatness but nothing less than the survival of the human race in an era when, for the first time in human history, a living generation has the power of veto over the survival of the next.

When the abstractions and subtleties of political science have been exhausted, there remain the most basic unanswered questions about war and peace and why nations contest the issues they context and why they even care about them. . . .

. . . The more I puzzle over the great wars of history, the more I am inclined to the view that the causes attributed to them—territory, markets, resources, the defense or perpetuation of great principles—were not the root causes of all but rather explanations or excuses for certain unfathomable drives of human nature. For the lack of a clear and precise understanding of exactly what these motives are, I refer to them as the "arrogance of power"—as a psychological need that nations seem to have in order to prove that they are bigger, better, or stronger than other nations. Implicit in this drive is the assumption, even on the part of normally peaceful nations, that force is the ultimate proof of superiority—that when a nation shows that it has the stronger army, it is also proving that it has better people, better institutions, better principles, and, in general, a better civilization.

. . .

. . . [I]n all our souls there is a bit of the missionary. We all like telling people what to do, which is perfectly all right except that most people do not like being told what to do. . . .

. . .

There are signs of the arrogance of power in the way Americans act when they go to foreign countries. Foreigners frequently comment on the contrast between the behavior of Americans at home and abroad: in our own country, they say, we are hospitable and considerate, but as soon as we get outside our own borders something seems to get into us and wherever we are we become noisy and demanding and we strut around as if we owned the place. . . .

. . .

One reason Americans abroad may act of though they "own the place" is that in many places they very nearly do. . . .

I think that when any American goes abroad, he carries an unconscious knowledge of all this power with him and it affects his behavior, just as it once affected the behavior of Greeks and Romans, of Spaniards, Germans, and Englishmen, in their brief high noons of their respective ascendancies. . . .

. . .

Even when acting with the best of intentions, Americans, like other Western peoples who have carried their civilizations abroad, have had something of the same "fatal impact" on smaller nations that European explorers had on the Tahitians and the native Australians. We have not harmed people because we wished to; on the contrary, more often than not we have wanted to help people and, in some very important respects, we have helped them. . . . Bringing power without understanding, Americans as well as Europeans have had a devastating effect in less advanced areas of the world; without knowing they were doing it, they have shattered traditional societies, disrupted fragile economies and undermined peoples' self-confidence by the invidious example of their own power and efficiency. They have done this in many instances simply by being big and strong, by giving good advice, by intruding on people who have not wanted them but could not resist them.

. . .

The good deed above all others that Americans feel qualified to perform is the teaching of democracy. Let us consider the results of some American good deeds in various parts of the world.

. . .

For all our noble intentions, the countries which have had most of the tutelage in democracy by United States Marines have not been particularly democratic. . . .

Maybe, in light of this extraordinary record of accomplishment, it is time for us to reconsider our teaching methods. Maybe we are not really cut out for the job of spreading the gospel of democracy. Maybe it would profit us to concentrate on our own democracy instead of trying to inflict our particular version of it on all those ungrateful Latin Americans who stubbornly oppose their North American benefactors instead of the "real" enemies whom we have so graciously chosen for them. And maybe—just maybe—if we left our neighbors to make their own judgments and their own mistakes, and confined our assistance to matters of economics and technology instead of philosophy, maybe then they would begin to find the democracy and the dignity that have largely eluded them, and we in turn might begin to find the love and gratitude that we seem to crave.

. . .

FOR FURTHER STUDY

Arendt, Hannah. *On Revolution* (New York: Viking Press, 1963).

Bell, Daniel. *The End of Ideology: On the Exhaustion of Political Ideas in the Fifties* (Glencoe, IL: Free Press, 1960).

Carmichael, Stokely, and Charles V. Hamilton. *Black Power: The Politics of Liberation in America* (New York: Random House, 1967).
Carson, Rachel. *Silent Spring* (Boston, MA: Houghton Mifflin, 1962).
Commoner, Barry. *The Closing Circle: Nature, Man, and Technology* (New York: Alfred A. Knopf, 1971).
Harrington, Michael. *The Other America: Poverty in the United States* (New York: Macmillan, 1962).
Hayek, Friedrich. *The Constitution of Liberty* (Chicago, IL: University of Chicago Press, 1960).
Hoffman, Abbie. *Revolution for the Hell of It* (New York: Dial Press, 1968).
Marcuse, Herbert. *One Dimensional Man: Studies in the Ideology of Advanced Industrial Society* (Boston, MA: Beacon Press, 1964).
Meyer, Frank S. *In Defense of Freedom: A Conservative Credo* (Chicago, IL: H. Regnery Co., 1962).
Rand, Ayn. *Capitalism: The Unknown Ideal* (New York: New American Library, 1966).
Rothbard, Murray N. *Man, Economy, and State: A Treatise on Economic Principles* (Princeton, NJ: Van Nostrand, 1962).
Strauss, Leo. *Natural Right and History* (Chicago, IL: University of Chicago Press, 1953).
Walzer, Michael. *Obligations: Essays on Civil Disobedience, War, and Citizenship* (Cambridge, MA: Harvard University Press, 1970).

SUGGESTED READINGS

Allitt, Patrick. *Catholic Intellectuals and Conservative Politics in America, 1950–1985* (Ithaca, NY: Cornell University Press, 1993).
Bloom, Alexander. *Prodigal Sons: The New York Intellectuals and Their World* (New York: Oxford University Press, 1986).
Chappell, David L. *A Stone of Hope: Prophetic Religion and the Death of Jim Crow* (Chapel Hill: University of North Carolina Press, 2004).
Ciepley, David. *Liberalism and the Shadow of Totalitarianism* (Cambridge, MA: Harvard University Press, 2006).
Dyson, Michael Eric. *Making Malcolm: The Myth and Meaning of Malcolm X* (New York: Oxford University Press, 1995).
Echols, Alice. *Daring to be Bad: Radical Feminism in America, 1967–1975* (Minneapolis: University of Minnesota Press, 1989).
Geary, Daniel. *Radical Ambition: C. Wright Mills, the Left, and American Social Thought* (Berkeley: University of California Press, 2009).
Horowitz, Daniel. The *Anxieties of Affluence: Critiques of American Consumer Culture, 1939–1979* (Amherst: University of Massachusetts Press, 2004).
Jones, Daniel Stedman. *Masters of the Universe: Hayek, Friedman, and the Birth of Neoliberal Politics* (Princeton, NJ: Princeton University Press, 2012).
Lasch, Christopher. *The Agony of the American Left* (New York: Knopf, 1969).
Miller, James. *Democracy is in the Streets: From Port Huron to the Siege of Chicago* (Cambridge, MA: Harvard University Press, 1994).
Murphy, Paul V. *The Rebuke of History: The Southern Agrarians and American Conservative Thought* (Chapel Hill: University of North Carolina, 2001).

Nash, George H. *The Conservative Intellectual Movement in America, Since 1945* (New York: Basic Books, 1976).

Polsgrove, Carol. *Divided Minds: Intellectuals and the Civil Rights Movement* (New York: W.W. Norton, 2001).

Stears, Marc. *Demanding Democracy: American Radicals in Search of a New Politics* (Princeton, NJ: Princeton University Press, 2010).

Tomes, Robert R. *Apocalypse Then: American Intellectuals and the Vietnam War, 1954–1975* (New York: New York University Press, 1988).

Young, Cynthia. *Soul Power: Culture, Radicalism, and the Making of a U.S. Third World Left* (Durham, NC: Duke University Press, 2006).

CHAPTER 11

RECENT POLITICS, 1981–PRESENT

I. INTRODUCTION

Ronald Reagan used the occasion of his first inaugural address to declare that "government is not the solution . . . government is the problem." In doing so, he symbolically broke from the New Deal liberalism that had defined the boundaries of American politics for decades. The proclamation seemed bold, even radical, at the time. Nearly a dozen years later, the first Democrat to win the White House after Reagan accepted his party's nomination by practically complaining that the Republicans only "campaigned against big government" but had done too little to change it. President Clinton kept "big government" as a term of deprecation, repeatedly telling audiences that he was against it until finally announcing in his fourth State of the Union address that "the era of big government is over."[1]

The "Reagan Revolution" may have had more to do with politics and ideas than policy. Clinton was right that the Republicans in the 1980s had continued to "run this big government," symbolized not least by the continuation and expansion of the Department of Education that candidate Ronald Reagan had threatened to immediately abolish. Instead, such conservative favorites as Bill Bennett and Clarence Thomas cut their teeth on Education Department posts. Conservatives were learning to use government, rather than dismantle it. But Reagan ushered in a new skepticism of government that shifted the political debate at the turn of the twenty-first century and put "liberalism" on the defensive. Ultimately, the conservatives proved unable to weld together a political majority that could replace the New Deal coalition. Divided government and ideological polarization have instead characterized recent politics.

1 Ronald Reagan, "First Inaugural Address, January 20, 1981," in *Public Papers of the Presidents of the United States* (Washington, D.C.: Government Printing Office, 1982); Bill Clinton, "Address Accepting the Presidential Nomination, July 16, 1992," in *CQ Weekly* 50 (1992): 2128; Bill Clinton, "State of the Union Address, January 23, 1996," in *Public Papers of the Presidents of the United States* (Washington, D.C.: Government Printing Office, 1997).

FIGURE 11-1 TIMELINE OF THE RECENT POLITICS

Events	Year	Writings
Ronald Reagan inaugurated as president	1981	
Jurgen Habermas's *The Theory of Communicative Action*	1981	
The Federalist Society founded	1982	
Gay & Lesbian Alliance Against Defamation founded	1985	
Soviet General Secretary Mikhail Gorbachev launches *perestroika*	1987	
Fall of the Berlin Wall	1989	
Tiananmen Square Massacre	1989	
Nelson Mandela inaugurated as South African president	1994	
Republicans win both chambers of Congress for first time in fifty years	1994	
Destruction of World Trade Center	2001	
United States invades Afghanistan	2001	
United States invades Iraq	2003	
Start of "Great Recession"	2007	
Tea Party movement launched	2009	
Start of "Arab Spring"	2010	
Occupy Wall Street movement launched	2011	
Black Live Matter movement launched	2013	

Politics. The civil rights revolution of the 1960s set in motion a realignment of the two political parties that reached its final form in the 1990s. The "Solid South" had been the bedrock of the Democratic Party since the time of Andrew Jackson, but with the signing of the Civil Rights Act of 1964 Lyndon Johnson tossed it aside. Blue-collar "Reagan Democrats" and southern "Boll Weevils" abandoned the party in favor of the resurgent Republicans. A Reagan coalition of social conservatives, economic conservatives, and foreign policy hardliners helped redraw party lines, pulling in more conservative voters, pushing away more liberal voters, and shifting the center of gravity of the Republican Party from its historic home in New England toward the South and West. Both political parties withdrew toward their ideological wings, losing adherents who had once stood in the middle—or perhaps even with the other side. But neither party solidified its control over the government or popular majorities. Divided government became the rule, rather than the exception. Working majorities that could reach across the aisle became harder to come by.

Society. The 1980s and 1990s were riven by an often heated "culture war" that has cooled off since the turn of the twenty-first century. Evangelical Protestants and Catholics made common cause in the last years of the twentieth century and became politically active in a way that had not been true in earlier decades. The increasing party polarization on the abortion issue was illustrative of the general trends. When the U.S. Supreme Court decided *Roe v. Wade* in 1973, the abortion issue was still relatively quiet. The two parties were internally divided over how to approach the issue and as a consequence were disinclined to wade in. By the 1980s, the situation had changed. Activists had mobilized around the issue, the two parties had staked out contrasting positions on abortion rights, and voters with strong feelings on the issue were sorting themselves accordingly. At the 1992 Republican Party national convention, failed presidential candidate Pat Buchanan rallied his supporters with a stark claim that the coming election

> is about what we stand for as Americans. There is a religious war going on in our country for the soul of America. It is a culture war. . . . And in that struggle for the soul of America, Clinton and Clinton are on the other side, and George Bush is on our side.[2]

Other politicians might have been reluctant to adopt Buchanan's strident tone, but the issues he identified—from abortion to school prayer to pornography to gay marriage—were real and divisive ones. A more limited set of concerns, most notably gay marriage, continued to actively divide religious conservatives from secular liberals in the twenty-first century.

The economy cycled between boom and bust over the course of these decades, but structural changes were in some ways of more concern. Robert Reich, who became Clinton's labor secretary, called attention to the emerging global economy organized around fluid capital and high technology rather than manufacturing. In 1982, the Dow Jones Industrial Average rested on the back of such venerable blue-chip companies as Eastman Kodak, U.S. Steel, and General Motors. Three decades later, all were long gone from the index and were shadows of their former selves. In their place were new global leaders, including Cisco Systems, Goldman Sachs, and McDonald's. The rise of the information economy was disruptive and tended to render old public policies and old labor skills obsolete for the challenges ahead. Well before the Occupy movement focused attention on income inequality, commentators and analysts had been warning that the new economy would make stark distinctions between economic winners and losers, between the entrepreneurs at Google and the servers at McDonald's.

Ideas. The postwar philosophical defense of liberalism, rights, and individualism represented by writers like John Rawls came under attack from a variety of directions at the turn of the twenty-first century. The most direct response was offered by a loose group of communitarians. The communitarian critique was most concerned with the strong individualism offered by liberalism and countered that vision of self-directing individuals with a

---

2 Patrick J. Buchanan, *The Death of the West* (New York: St. Martin's Press, 2002), 7.

vision of individuals embedded within larger communities that helped shape their goals, values, and self-understandings. Such concerns had been advanced by religious and sociological thinkers but gained greater philosophical interest at the end of the twentieth century. Such arguments made their way into Bill Clinton's first presidential campaign, where he emphasized the need for a "New Covenant" that highlighted the duties individuals owed to their communities and not just their rights and desires.

More radical critiques of liberalism developed out of European thought in the late twentieth century. The postmodernist impulse denied the existence of a reality that could be understood as objective and separate from human perception. The human experience of the world is necessarily embedded in particular, historically specific, socially constructed frames of reference. Such arguments suggested that ideas about universal human rights, for example, just reflected a moment in Western thought rather than a deep feature of human society. By contrast, critical theory was often quite critical of both liberalism and postmodernism. Drawing most directly from twentieth-century Marxist thought, critical theory was focused on developing theoretical understanding of social systems specifically in order to overcome existing social and political arrangements and advance a goal of "human liberation."

II. DEMOCRACY AND LIBERTY

Major Developments

- Persistent divided government
- Rise of Reagan conservatism and ideological polarization
- Democratic third wave abroad

Commentators had been anticipating a "new Republican majority" since the late 1960s, but it did not materialize. Ronald Reagan's election to the presidency in 1980 spurred such talk again. Not only did Reagan return the Republicans to the White House after the debacle of Watergate, but he also carried the U.S. Senate with him for the first time since Eisenhower and made significant inroads into the Democratic majority in the House of Representatives. In the electorate, so-called Reagan Democrats buoyed Republican hopes of the erosion of the long-time Democratic advantage in voter identification. In Congress, so-called Boll Weevils (mostly conservative Southern Democrats) abandoned their party leaders (and sometimes their party label) to support the Reagan agenda. The sharp and deep recession of 1981 shored up Democratic support in the midterm elections, and the political system settled into a lengthy period of divided government. Republicans, with "issue ownership" of national defense and criminal justice, were thought to have an advantage in presidential elections, while Democrats, riding a persistent "incumbency advantage," had an apparent lock on Congress. The Clinton presidency in the 1990s scrambled that particular narrative but reinforced the apparent inability of either party to unite all the branches of government.

Reagan may not have been able to solidify a political majority, but he did help remake the Republican Party. His presidency marked the ascent of the modern conservative

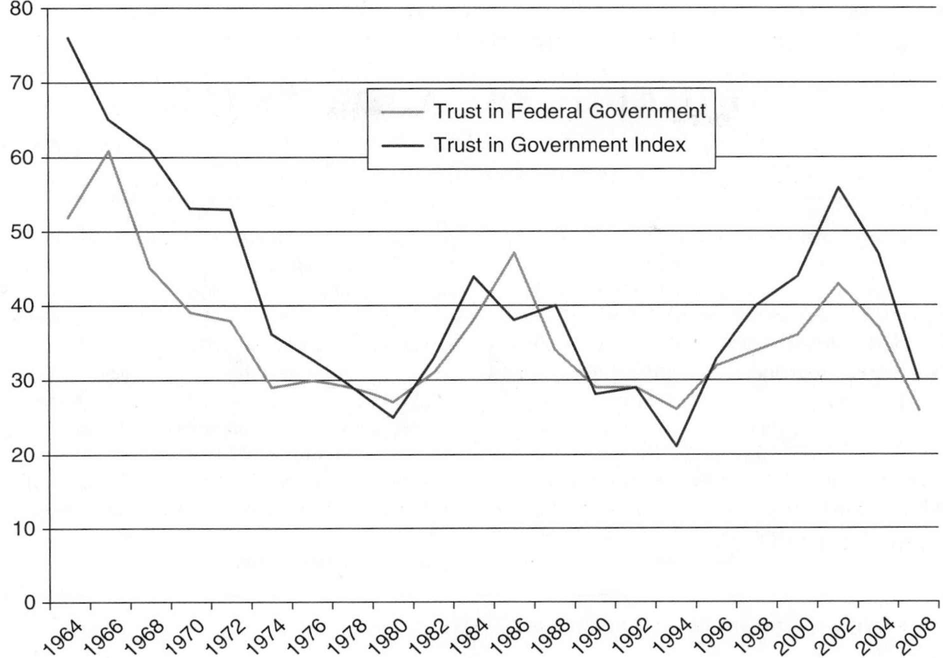

FIGURE 11-2 Trust in Government Index, 1964–2008.

movement. A coalition of religious activists, economic conservatives, and foreign policy hawks assumed control of electoral mobilization, the political agenda, and policy ideas within the party. Reagan was able to exploit the sharp decline in the public's trust in government (reflected in Figure 11-2) that destabilized the liberal politics of the mid-twentieth century. The Reagan era saw the acceleration of the ideological homogenization of the two parties. Conservative voters and politicians increasingly fled the Democratic Party (especially in the South), while liberal voters and politicians abandoned the Republican Party (especially in the Northeast). Rather than the "deadlock of democracy" brought on by fissures within the Democratic Party that disturbed 1960s liberals, partisan gridlock brought on by two ideologically polarized but closely matched parties became the concern at the turn of the twenty-first century.

The decades since 1980 also saw the "third wave" of democratization across the globe. The collapse of the Soviet Union gave space to new democratic movements in eastern Europe. Autocratic regimes from Latin America to eastern Asia transitioned into sometimes fragile democracies. Liberalizing pressures in the Middle East in the early twenty-first century have been somewhat less successful but further illustrate the depth and breadth of democratic ideals that spread across the globe. For the United States, such developments were not always entirely welcome, as they sometimes toppled allied American governments and substituted in their place less sympathetic political leaders. But in other instances, the spread of democracy was both welcomed and encouraged.

RONALD REAGAN

FIRST INAUGURAL ADDRESS (1981)

Raised in modest circumstances in rural Illinois, Ronald Reagan graduated from Eureka College in 1932 and started working in radio. Within a few years, he had shifted into film (and later television). An anticommunist Democrat, Reagan became active in the leadership of the Screen Actors Guild after the war, which encouraged a further interest in politics. By the 1960s, Reagan had switched political parties and become an active public speaker on political and economic topics, lending his talent to the failed Barry Goldwater campaign in 1964. Two years later, he ran a successful campaign for California governor as an economic and social conservative. He brought much the same philosophy to the presidency when he defeated incumbent Jimmy Carter in 1980. Pulling together a more robust version of the conservative coalition to which Goldwater had appealed in the 1960s, Reagan positioned himself as the leader of the modern conservative movement and the most conservative president since the Depression. His first inaugural address touched on many of the themes that he had been developing throughout his political career and that became core tenets of the post-Reagan Republican Party.

What does Reagan identify as the economic afflictions of the day? How does he diagnose them? Why does he think "government is the problem"? How does Reagan's attitude toward the government differ from that of the liberals of the New Deal and Great Society periods? How does Reagan's inaugural speech compare with Goldwater's acceptance speech? How does it compare with Herbert Hoover's?

To a few of us here today this is a solemn and most momentous occasion, and yet in the history of our nation it is a commonplace occurrence. The orderly transfer of authority as called for in the Constitution routinely takes place, as it has for almost two centuries, and few of us stop to think how unique we really are. In the eyes of many in the world, this every-4-year ceremony we accept as normal is nothing less than a miracle.

. . .

The business of our nation goes forward. These United States are confronted with an economic affliction of great proportions. We suffer from the longest and one of the worst sustained inflations in our national history. It distorts our economic decisions, penalizes thrift, and crushes the struggling young and the fixed-income elderly alike. It threatens to shatter the lives of millions of our people.

Idle industries have cast workers into unemployment, human misery, and personal indignity. Those who do work are denied a fair return for their labor by a tax system which penalizes successful achievement and keeps us from maintaining full productivity.

But great as our tax burden is, it has not kept pace with public spending. For decades we have piled deficit upon deficit, mortgaging our future and our children's future for the temporary convenience of the present. To continue this long trend is to guarantee tremendous social, cultural, political, and economic upheavals.

You and I, as individuals, can, by borrowing, live beyond our means, but for only a limited period of time. Why, then, should we think that collectively, as a nation, we're not bound by that same limitation? We must act today in order to preserve tomorrow. And let there be no misunderstanding: We are going to begin to act, beginning today.

The economic ills we suffer have come upon us over several decades. They will not go away in days, weeks, or months, but they will go away. They will go away because we as Americans have the capacity now, as we've had in the past, to do whatever needs to be done to preserve this last and greatest bastion of freedom.

In this present crisis, government is not the solution to our problem; government is the problem. From time to time we've been tempted to believe that society has become too complex to be managed by self-rule, that government by an elite group is superior to government for, by, and of the people. Well, if no one among us is capable of governing himself, then who among us has the capacity to govern someone else? All of us together, in and out of government, must bear the burden. The solutions we seek must be equitable, with no one group singled out to pay a higher price.

We hear much of special interest groups. Well, our concern must be for a special interest group that has been too long neglected. It knows no sectional boundaries or ethnic and racial divisions, and it crosses political party lines. It is made up of men and women who raise our food, patrol our streets, man our mines and factories, teach our children, keep our homes, and heal us when we're sick—professionals, industrialists, shopkeepers, clerks, cabbies, and truck drivers. They are, in short, "We the people," this breed called Americans.

Well, this administration's objective will be a healthy, vigorous, growing economy that provides equal opportunities for all Americans, with no barriers born of bigotry or discrimination. Putting America back to work means putting all Americans back to work. Ending inflation means freeing all Americans from the terror of runaway living costs. All must share in the productive work of this "new beginning," and all must share in the bounty of a revived economy. With the idealism and fair play which are the core of our system and our strength, we can have a strong and prosperous America, at peace with itself and the world.

So, as we begin, let us take inventory. We are a nation that has a government—not the other way around. And this makes us special among the nations of the Earth. Our government has no power except that granted it by the people. It is time to check and reverse the growth of government, which shows signs of having grown beyond the consent of the governed.

It is my intention to curb the size and influence of the Federal establishment and to demand recognition of the distinction between the powers granted to the Federal Government and those reserved to the States or to the people. All of us need to be reminded that the Federal Government did not create the States; the States created the Federal Government.

Now, so there will be no misunderstanding, it's not my intention to do away with government. It is rather to make it work—work with us, not over us; to stand by our side, not ride on our back. Government can and must provide opportunity, not smother it; foster productivity, not stifle it.

If we look to the answer as to why for so many years we achieved so much, prospered as no other people on Earth, it was because here in this land we unleashed the energy and individual genius of man to a greater extent than has ever been done before. Freedom and the dignity of the individual have been more available and assured here than in any other place on Earth. The price for this freedom at times has been high, but we have never been unwilling to pay that price.

It is no coincidence that our present troubles parallel and are proportionate to the intervention and intrusion in our lives that result from unnecessary and excessive growth of government. It is time for us to realize that we're too great a nation to limit ourselves to small dreams. We're not, as some would have us believe, doomed to an inevitable decline. I do not believe in a fate that will fall on us no matter what we do. I do believe in a fate that will fall on us if we do nothing. So, with all the creative energy at our command, let us begin an era of national renewal. Let us renew our determination, our courage, and our strength. And let us renew our faith and our hope.

We have every right to dream heroic dreams. Those who say that we're in a time when there are not heroes, they just don't know where to look. You can see heroes every day going in and out of factory gates. Others, a handful in number, produce enough food to feed all of us and then the world beyond. You meet heroes across a counter, and they're on both sides of that counter. There are entrepreneurs with faith in themselves and faith in an idea who create new jobs, new wealth and opportunity. They're individuals and families whose taxes support the government and whose voluntary gifts support church, charity, culture, art, and education. Their patriotism is quiet, but deep. Their values sustain our national life.

Now, I have used the words "they" and "their" in speaking of these heroes. I could say "you" and "your," because I'm addressing the heroes of whom I speak—you, the citizens of this blessed land. Your dreams, your hopes, your goals are going to be the dreams, the hopes, and the goals of this administration, so help me God.

We shall reflect the compassion that is so much a part of your makeup. How can we love our country and not love our countrymen; and loving them, reach out a hand when they fall, heal them when they're sick, and provide opportunity to make them self-sufficient so they will be equal in fact and not just in theory?

Can we solve the problems confronting us? Well, the answer is an unequivocal and emphatic "yes." To paraphrase Winston Churchill, I did not take the oath I've just taken with the intention of presiding over the dissolution of the world's strongest economy.

In the days ahead I will propose removing the roadblocks that have slowed our economy and reduced productivity. Steps will be taken aimed at restoring the balance between the various levels of government. Progress may be slow, measured in inches and feet, not miles, but we will progress. It is time to reawaken this industrial giant, to get government back within its means, and to lighten our punitive tax burden. And these will be our first priorities, and on these principles there will be no compromise.

On the eve of our struggle for independence a man who might have been one of the greatest among the Founding Fathers, Dr. Joseph Warren, president of the Massachusetts Congress, said to his fellow Americans, "Our country is in danger, but not to be despaired of . . . . On you depend the fortunes of America. You are to decide the important questions upon which rests the happiness and the liberty of millions yet unborn. Act worthy of yourselves."

Well, I believe we, the Americans of today, are ready to act worthy of ourselves, ready to do what must be done to ensure happiness and liberty for ourselves, our children, and our children's children. And as we renew ourselves here in our own land, we will be seen as having greater strength throughout the world. We will again be the exemplar of freedom and a beacon of hope for those who do not now have freedom.

To those neighbors and allies who share our freedom, we will strengthen our historic ties and assure them of our support and firm commitment. We will match loyalty with loyalty. We will strive for mutually beneficial relations. We will not use our friendship to impose on their sovereignty, for our own sovereignty is not for sale.

As for the enemies of freedom, those who are potential adversaries, they will be reminded that peace is the highest aspiration of the American people. We will negotiate for it, sacrifice for it; we will not surrender for it, now or ever.

. . .

RICHARD RORTY

THE PRIORITY OF DEMOCRACY TO PHILOSOPHY (1990)

Richard Rorty was raised in New York City in the anticommunist Left and completed a Ph.D. in philosophy at Yale University in 1956. He achieved his greatest influence in the 1980s and 1990s, writing on a wide range of topics. His greatest public influence came in his political writings, where he drew on the pragmatic tradition of democratic thinking. Rorty hoped to encourage a form of moderate liberalism that did not rely on universal or deep philosophical claims. Separating Rawlsian liberalism from Kantian philosophy, Rorty claimed that Rawls was "simply trying to systematize the principles and intuitions typical of American liberals." We did not need to see or justify our political beliefs "from a God's-eye point of view"; it was enough that that we were "acculturated as we were."[3]

How does Rorty see the separation of religion and politics as providing a model for other political concerns? What is his "Jeffersonian" perspective on politics? Why should we be liberals? Does Rorty offer an approach that can justify liberalism or define its content? Is it possible to form a liberal democracy with those who do not accept liberalism?

Thomas Jefferson set the tone for American liberal politics when he said "it does me no injury for my neighbor to say that there are twenty Gods or no God." His example helped make respectable the idea that politics can be separated from beliefs about matters of ultimate importance—that shared beliefs among citizens on such matters are not essential to a democratic society. Like many other figures of the Enlightenment, Jefferson assumed that a moral faculty common to the typical theist and the typical atheist suffices for civic virtue.

Many Enlightenment intellectuals were willing to go further and say that since religious beliefs turn out to be inessential for political cohesion, they should simply be discarded as mumbo jumbo—perhaps to be replaced (as in twentieth-century totalitarian Marxist states) with some sort of explicitly secular political faith that will form the moral consciousness of the citizen. Jefferson again set the tone when he refused to go that far. He thought it enough to privatize religion, to view it as irrelevant to social order but relevant to, and possibly essential for, individual perfection. Citizens of a Jeffersonian democracy can be as religious or irreligious as they please as long as they are not "fanatical." That is, they must abandon or modify opinions on matters of ultimate importance, the opinions that may hitherto have given sense and point to their lives, if these opinions entail public actions that cannot be justified to most of their fellow citizens.

This Jeffersonian compromise concerning the relation of spiritual perfection to public policy has two sides. Its absolutist side says that every human being, without the benefit of special revelation, has all the beliefs necessary for civic virtue. These beliefs spring from a universal human faculty, conscience—possession of which constitutes the specifically human essence of each human being. This is the faculty that gives the individual human dignity and rights. But there is also a pragmatic side. This side says that when the individual finds in her conscience beliefs that are relevant to public policy but incapable of defense on the basis of beliefs common to her fellow citizens, she must sacrifice her conscience on the altar of public expediency.

The tension between these two sides can be eliminated by a philosophical theory that identifies justifiability to humanity at large with truth. . . .

---

3 Richard Rorty, "Solidarity or Objectivity," in *Objectivity, Relativism and Truth: Philosophical Papers*, vol. 1 (New York: Cambridge University Press, 1991), 13.

In our century, this rationalist justification of the Enlightenment compromise has been discredited. Contemporary intellectuals have given up the Enlightenment assumption that religion, myth, and tradition can be opposed to something ahistorical, something common to all human beings qua human. . . . The result is to erase the picture of the self common to Greek metaphysics, Christian theology, and Enlightenment rationalism: the picture of an ahistorical nature center, the locus of human dignity, surrounded by an adventitious and inessential periphery.

The effect of erasing this picture is to break the link between truth and justifiability. This, in turn, breaks down the bridge between the two sides of the Enlightenment compromise. The effect is to polarize liberal social theory. If we stay on the absolutist side, we shall talk about inalienable "human rights" and about "one right answer" to moral and political dilemmas without trying to back up such talk with a theory of human nature. . . . But if we swing to the pragmatist side, and consider talk of "rights" an attempt to enjoy the benefits of metaphysics without assuming the appropriate responsibilities, we shall still need something to distinguish the sort of individual conscience we respect from the sort we condemn as "fanatical." This can only be something relatively local and ethnocentric—the tradition of a particular community, the consensus of a particular culture. . . .

. . .

. . . [W]e need to ask two questions. The first is whether there is any sense in which liberal democracy "needs" philosophical justification at all. Those who share Dewey's pragmatism will say that although it may need philosophical articulation, it does not need philosophical backup. On this view, the philosopher of liberal democracy may wish to develop a theory of the human self that comports with the institutions he or she admires. But such a philosopher is not thereby justifying these institutions by reference to more fundamental premises, but the reverse: He or she is putting politics first and tailoring a philosophy to suit. . .

The second question is one that we can ask even if we put the opposition between justification and articulation to one side. It is the question of whether a conception of the self that, as [Charles] Taylor says, makes "the community constitutive of the individual" does in fact comport better with liberal democracy than dos the Enlightenment conception of the self. . . .

. . . I shall answer "no" to the first question . . . and "yes" to the second. . . .

. . . [J]ust as the principle of religious toleration and the social thought of the Enlightenment proposed to bracket many standard theological topics when deliberating about public policy and constructing political institutions, so we need to bracket many standard topics of philosophical inquiry. For purposes of social theory, we can put aside such topics as an ahistorical human nature, the nature of selfhood, the motive of moral behavior, and the meaning of human life. We treat these as irrelevant to politics as Jefferson thought questions about the Trinity and about transubstantiation.

. . . [John] Rawls thinks that "philosophy as the search for truth about an independent metaphysical and moral order cannot . . . provide a workable and shared basis for a political conception of justice in democratic society." So he suggests that we confine ourselves to collecting "such settled convictions as the belief in religious toleration and the rejection of slavery" and then "try to organize the basic intuitive ideas and principles implicit in these convictions into a coherent conception of justice."

This attitude is thoroughly historicist and antiuniversalist. Rawls can wholeheartedly agree with Hegel and Dewey against Kant and can say that the Enlightenment attempt to free oneself from tradition and history, to appeal to "Nature" or "Reason," was self-deceptive. . . .

. . . Rawls echoes Dewey in suggesting that insofar as justice becomes the first virtue of a society, the need for such legitimation [by appeal to general philosophical principles] may gradually cease to be felt. Such a society will become accustomed to the thought that social policy needs no more authority than successful accommodation among individuals, individuals who find themselves heir to the same historical traditions and faced with the same problems. It will be a society that encourages the "end of ideology." . . . When such a society deliberates, when it collects the principles and intuitions to be brought into equilibrium, it will tend to discard those drawn from philosophical accounts of the self or of rationality. For such a society will view such accounts not as the foundations of political institutions, but as, at worst, philosophical mumbo jumbo, or, at best, relevant to private searches for perfection, but not to social policy.

. . .

[W]e heirs of Enlightenment think of enemies of liberal democracy like Nietzsche or Loyola as, to use Rawls's word, "mad." We do so because there is no way to see them as fellow citizens of our constitutional democracy, people whose life plans might, given ingenuity and good will, be fitted in with those of other citizens. They are not crazy because they have mistaken the ahistorical nature of human beings. They are crazy because the limits of sanity are set by what *we* can take seriously. This, in turn, is determined by our upbringing, our historical situation.

. . .

Just as Jefferson refused to let the Christian Scriptures set the terms in which to discuss alternative political institutions, so we either must refuse to answer the question, "What sort of human being are you hoping to produce?" or, at least, must not let our answer to this question dictate our answer to the question "Is justice primary?" . . . The idea that moral and political controversies should always be "brought back to first principles" is reasonable if it means merely that we should seek common ground in the hope of attaining agreement. But it is misleading if it is taken as a claim that there is a natural order of premises from which moral and political conclusions are to be inferred. . . .

. . .

Both Jefferson and Dewey described America as an "experiment." If the experiment fails, our descendants may learn something important. But they will not learn a philosophical truth, any more than they will learn a religious one. They will simply get some hints about what to watch out for when setting up their next experiment. Even if nothing else survives from the age of democratic revolutions, perhaps our descendants will remember that social institutions *can* be viewed as experiments in cooperation rather than as attempts to embody a universal and ahistorical order. It is hard to believe that this memory would not be worth having.

RICHARD A. EPSTEIN

SKEPTICISM AND FREEDOM (2003)

Richard Epstein was raised in New York, graduating from Yale Law School in 1968 and spending much of his career at the University of Chicago Law School. In the 1980s and 1990s, he established himself as perhaps the leading libertarian-oriented legal scholar in the country. In a series of publications that appeared during the Reagan administration, Epstein argued that key components of the New Deal were both unconstitutional and misguided and should be rolled back. In short, the constitutional revolution of the 1930s was "an intellectual and political mistake that ought to be undone if only we could find a way."[4] Although much of his work focused on property rights, it also included federalism, civil rights, and free speech. His more philosophical work defended a "night watchman state" limited to the functions endorsed by nineteenth-century liberal theory.

Why does Epstein think that state power is a "necessary evil rather than an unqualified blessing"? Why is state power "necessary"? Why is it nonetheless "evil"? What functions does Epstein assign to the state? What are the dangers of exceeding those functions? Is limited government necessarily weak government? Is it adequate to meeting public needs?

. . .

The functions of the state, then, are properly limited to the control of force and fraud on the one hand, and to the regulation and constraint of monopoly behavior on the other. The irony of this system is that the creation of the state poses risks of the very evil that it is supposed to negate. One need only think of those not-uncommon government regimes in the twentieth century alone that committed mass slaughter of individuals groups together by race, creed, or national origin. . . . Yet even when those massive failures are effectively checked, as they largely are in today's modern democracies, the dangers of state monopoly, factionalism, and favoritism are too large to be ignored. . . .

. . . The task is to develop a set of institutions that compel the state to respect the limitations on its use of force that are consistent with its role as a protector, not destroyer, of individual rights. The problem will be addressed only when we persuade ourselves that state power is a necessary evil rather than an unqualified blessing. That outlook, in turn, will come only when we recognize that the dark side of human nature does not disappear just because fallible human beings have assumed the trappings of public office. What are needed are clear rules that define the ends to which public force may be directed.

. . .

It is commonplace among liberal and progressive theorists to claim that the social contract behind laissez-faire economics fills an impoverished moral niche by stressing how each new right necessarily generates an equal and opposite correlative of duty. Garry Wills, for example, condemns the Lockean conception of the state for insisting that under it "we are faced with a zero-sum game. Any power given to the government is necessarily subtracted from the liberty of the governed." . . . The clear implication of his message is that defenders of laissez-faire necessarily condemn government to idleness, even as they shrink from the implication that it should be abolished.

Unfortunately, Wills misunderstands what zero-sum games are about. Every shift of rights between individuals, or from individuals to government, necessarily conserves the sum of legal rights. Two individuals cannot possess the same rights over the same thing at the same time. Likewise in politics, every accretion of government power necessarily shrinks rights left to individuals. Conceded. But to understand the social situation, we have to apply the zero-sum

4 Richard A. Epstein, "The Mistakes of 1937," *George Mason University Law Review* 11 (1988): 5.

concept not to *rights*, but to *utilities*. A transfer or reassignment of rights rarely, if ever, operates as a zero-sum game in the domain of utility. It is for just that a reason that people enter into voluntary exchanges: even though their rights as against the rest of the world are neither increased nor decreased, their joint utilities improve because of the exchange. To the Lockean social contract theorist . . . the ideal is to support only those forced transfers of legal rights that create positive-sum games in, of course, the domain of utility, while spurning proposed transfers that create negative or zero-sum results.

. . .

. . . The term "social" in the phrase "social contract" . . . is meant to sanction coercive arrangements fashioned by the state so long as they achieve the same distribution of ends—that is, mutual advantage—as the voluntary agreements on which they are modeled.

In order to achieve that goal, strong restrictions must be placed on the illicit use of government force while, at the same time, permitting the use of state force to constrain private acts of violence. . . . As individual and group preferences start to diverge, it becomes ever harder for state coercive behavior to replicate the win-win outcomes generated by the simple voluntary exchange. . . . The set of activities that satisfy the win-win constraint is more likely to be found only when the state confines itself to a minimal role that is consistent with the basic subjective preferences of all its members. Looking for the common elements across diverse peoples drives us back, inexorably, to the classical government roles: the preservation of order against foes, domestic and foreign, and the provision of familiar public goods, such as highways. . . . When the state supplies only these basics, then each individual or private group can treat those public services as an input for ends that it alone shares, without having to surrender its distinctive goals and objectives. . . .

. . .

. . . [I]t would be a mistake to assume that those who are in favor of limited government are necessarily in favor of weak government. Nothing could be further from the truth. The task here is to find ways to target government energies on clearly demonstrable tasks where public resources can do the most good. When that mission is well defined, several things happen at once. First, state enforcement enjoys the highest level of legitimacy, because it is directed against activities that everyone opposes in principle, no matter how much they may privately deviate from that principle in practice. . . . Second, the dangers of excessive taxation and regulation are effectively negated, because the state does not move into contentious areas (such as wage and price regulation) where public opinion and economic effects are likely to divide along various political and social axes. Political power is a scarce resource that must be husbanded for the few ends that it can serve best, for otherwise the level of care and attention that hard matters receive is diluted by the ever-expanding role of government authority.

. . .

DAVID GRAEBER

DIRECT ACTION, ANARCHISM, DIRECT DEMOCRACY (2009)

David Graeber grew up in the midst of radical politics in New York City, embracing anarchism early on. He completed his Ph.D. in anthropology at the University of Chicago in 1996. He has long been active in the international anarchist movement, and much of his writing has focused on the theory and practice of modern anarchism. He was a significant actor in the Occupy Wall Street movement, has called for a general cancellation of all existing debts, and is credited with coining "the 99 percent," referring to the income inequality between the very highest income earners and most others. In this essay, he advocates "direct action" as a strategy for implementing anarchism.

What is "direct action"? Why would anarchists prefer it to electoral or revolutionary approaches to political change? To what extent is direct action "democratic"? Under what conditions is this a viable political strategy? To what extent is direct action contrary to the workings of a liberal state? How does anarchy depart from liberalism? Does it pursue similar or different goals and values than liberalism? Does this vision of democracy have more in common with Martin Luther King, Jr. or Malcolm X? How does it contrast with the version of anarchism advocated by Lysander Spooner in the nineteenth century or Emma Goldman in the early twentieth century?

...

It should be easy enough to see why anarchists have always been drawn to the idea of direct action. Anarchists reject states and all those systematic forms of inequality states make possible. Neither do they seek to seize state power for themselves. Rather, they wish to destroy that power, using means that are—so far as possible—consistent with their ends, that embody them. . . . Direct action is perfectly consistent with this, because in essence direct action is the insistence, when faced with structures of unjust authority, on acting as if one is already free. . . . Insofar as one is capable, one proceeds as if the state does not exist.

This is the difference, in principle, between direct action and civil disobedience (though in practice there often is a good deal of overlap between the two). When one burns a draft card, one is withdrawing one's consent or cooperation from a structure of authority one deems illegitimate, but doing so is still a form of protest, a public act addressed at least partly to the authorities themselves. Typically, one practicing civil disobedience is also willing to accept the legal consequences of his actions. Direct action takes matters a step forward. The direct actionist does not just refuse to pay taxes to support a militarized school system, she combines with others to try to create a new school system that operates on different principles. She proceeds as she would if the state did not exist and leaves it to the state's representatives to decide whether to try to send armed men to stop her.

. . . When confrontations [with representatives of the state] occur, it is typically because those conducting a direct action insist on acting as if the state's representatives have no more right to impose their view of the rights or wrongs of the situation than anybody else. If a man is driving a truck full of toxic waste to dump in a local river, the direct actionist does not consider whether the corporation he represents is legally permitted to do so; he treats him as he would anyone else trying to dump a vat of poison in a local water source. (By this understanding, the fact that said direct actionist rarely simply attempts to physically overpower the culprit is a remarkable testimony to most activists' dedication to nonviolence.) . . . . The key point though is that one is still acting as if, at least as a moral entity, the state does not exist. At any rate it would be possible to have a secret direct action.

It is by definition impossible to conduct a secret act of civil disobedience.

. . .

A revolutionary strategy based on direct action can only succeed if the principles of direct action become institutionalized. Temporary bubbles of autonomy must gradually turn into permanent, free communities. However, in order to do so, those communities cannot exist in total isolation; neither can they have a purely confrontational relation with everyone around them. They have to have some way to engage with larger economic, social, or political systems that surround them. This is the trickiest question because it has proved extremely difficult for those organized on radically democratic lines to so integrate themselves in any meaningful way in larger structures without having to make endless compromises in their founding principles. For direct action-based groups, even working in alliance with radical NGOs or labor unions has often created what seem like insuperable problems. On a more immediate level, the strategy depends on the dissemination of the model: most anarchists, for example, do not see themselves as a vanguard whose historical role is to "organize" other communities, but rather as one community setting an example others can imitate. . . .

. . . There are thousands of Marxist academics but very few Anarchist ones. This is not because anarchism is anti-intellectual so much as because it does not see itself as fundamentally a project of analysis. It is more a moral project. . . . The basic principles of anarchism—self-organization, voluntary association, mutual aid, the opposition to all forms of coercive authority—are essentially moral and organizational.

. . .

How, then, do we think about a political movement in which the practice comes first and theory is essentially, secondary?

. . .

What I would like to argue is that "anarchism" is best thought of, not as any one of these things—not as a vision, but neither quite as an attitude or set of practices. It is, rather, best thought of as that very movement back and forth between these three. . . .

. . .

. . . One would be hard-pressed to find an anarchist whose instinct would not be to place himself more on the side of Malcolm X than with Martin Luther King or Gandhi; however, the fact remains that in terms of overall approach, Gandhi's "become the change you want to see" seems a thousand times more in keeping with the anarchist spirit than Malcolm X's "by all means necessary"—and Gandhi himself recognized a strong philosophical affinity of his own ideas and anarchism, which Malcolm X certainly did not. "By all means necessary," in fact, seems an awful lot like the very ends-justifies-the-means logic which anarchism has consistently rejected. Yet practical annoyances with pacifists, combined with the inevitable instinct to identify with the most radical option, tends to ensure that almost invariably, the anarchist will nonetheless identify with Malcolm X.

. . .

It is interesting to observe that historically, anarchism has thrived as a revolutionary movement most of all in times of peace, and in largely demilitarized societies. . . .

. . . The "short twentieth century" (which appears to have begun in 1914 and ended sometime around 1989 or 1991) was, by contrast, probably the most violent in human history. It was a century in which major powers were continually preoccupied with either waging world wars or preparing for them. Hardly surprising, then, that anarchism might come to seem unrealistic. . . . It makes perfect sense, then, that the moment the Cold War ended and violent conflict between industrialized powers again came to seem unthinkable, anarchism popped right back to where it had been at the end of the nineteenth century: an international movement at the very center of the revolutionary left. The surprising thing was that it happened almost instantly.

What's more, one could make a case that the effectiveness of more militant anarchist tactics tend to depend on the effective demilitarization of society. . . . In America, the police simply will not allow themselves to lose. If they decide to move in on a squat in force, that squat will be lost; the only reason to defend it is to make the police's job so difficult that they will hesitate before attacking other squats in the future. . . . Stand-up battles with the police are only possible in societies in which everyone, including the public, is aware that almost no one owns firearms, and therefore, police tactics appropriate to a society where most criminals can be assumed to be heavily armed—for example SWAT teams—seem wildly inappropriate. And certainly, in those parts of Europe where firearms and military know-how is much more broadly available (one thinks of Russia, Albania, the former Yugoslavia, or for that matter Iraq) classical anarchism and anarchist tactics do not find nearly as fertile ground [as they do in Italy or Japan].

. . .

III. CITIZENSHIP AND COMMUNITY

Major Developments

- Social fragmentation
- Growth of immigration from Latin America
- Discontent with global capitalism

The fictional lives of (real-life big band leader) Ozzie and Harriet Nelson in the long-running popular television sitcom have come to represent the uniformity and conformity of 1950s American suburbia. Perhaps the dramatized life of (real-life heavy metal singer) Ozzy and Sharon Osbourne in the short-lived reality television show suggested the change in American culture by the early twenty-first century. The homogenized vision of the 1950s has given way to a more fractured and diversified vision of the 2000s. "Mainline" religious denominations have been overshadowed by increasingly visible evangelical and fundamentalist churches. The middle-class cultural mainstream of the "big three" television networks and the Book-of-the-Month Club have given way to diverse offerings and narrow audiences of cable television and the Internet. The secure white majority of the postwar period has been overtaken by the growth of ethnic and racial minorities. Multiculturalism became both a rallying cry and an inescapable description of the contemporary United States.

A new wave of extensive immigration to the United States began in the 1970s and has continued with little pause since. The result has been the most dramatic influx of the foreign born since the early twentieth century. As a percentage of the American population, the foreign born now stand at over ten percent, rivalling their percentage of the population in 1910. The Progressive Era boom in immigration represented a shift in immigrants' region of origin from western and northern Europe to eastern and southern Europe. Similarly, the immigrants at the turn of the twenty-first century marked yet another new shift from historical patterns and the earlier makeup of the American population. In the first decade of the new century, individuals from Asia and Latin America made up three quarters of all legal immigrants into the country. The Census Bureau estimates that over half of the foreign-born residents of the United States are from Latin America.[5] Rather than entering the United States through cities on the eastern seaboard (and often settling there), the new immigrants were more likely to enter through the west and southwest. Unlike the largely unregulated immigration at the turn of the twentieth century, recent immigration has been characterized by a mix of documented and undocumented immigrants, further complicating the social, legal, and political landscape.

International trade is nothing new, but economic globalization has rapidly intensified in recent decades. The establishment of the World Trade Organization in 1995 was accompanied by a general reduction in trade barriers, and with it the expansion of international

5 Department of Homeland Security, *Yearbook of Immigration Statistics* (Washington, D.C.: Government Printing Office, 2014), Table 2; U.S. Census Bureau, *Current Population Survey* (Washington, D.C.: Government Printing Office, 2013), Table 2.1.

trade in goods and services. Financial markets are globally integrated, and direct foreign investment in domestic economic activities has grown. Multinational firms operate across national boundaries and are important conduits for moving goods and services across national boundaries. Transportation and communication costs have fallen dramatically. Measurements of globalization are complex, but the general tendency can be seen in the growth of international trade over time in the United States. Imports and exports accounted for four times as large of a percentage of gross national product in 2010 compared to 1970.[6] As globalization increased, social and economic disruptions followed. While globalization has been tied to a variety of positive social and economic outcomes (such as greater civil liberties and economic growth), it has also been linked to greater income inequality (both across individuals and across regions). Such developments have spurred protest and debate in the United States and abroad.

6 *Proquest Statistical Abstract of the United States* (Lanham, MD: Bernam, 2014), Table 695.

RICHARD JOHN NEUHAUS

WHAT THE FUNDAMENTALISTS WANT (1985)

Richard John Neuhaus was raised by a Lutheran minister in Canada but moved to the United States as a teen. He was ordained as a Lutheran minister himself in 1960 and became active in the antiwar and associated movements. But the emergence of the abortion issue in the 1970s led him toward more conservative politics, and in 1991 he was ordained as a Catholic priest. In the 1980s and 1990s, he helped found a variety of institutions that promoted religiously based political conservatism, including *First Things* magazine, and advised conservative politicians, including President George W. Bush. His writings and activism often focused on promoting religion in public life and building bridges among Protestant, Catholic, and Jewish political conservatives. Aimed at a neoconservative audience, this essay sought to reassure largely secular and Jewish conservatives about the rise of the conservative evangelical movement.

Why does Neuhaus think that there is a "shared moral reference" in the United States? How does Neuhaus link Protestants, Catholics, and Jews in this essay? In what sense is there a "Judeo-Christian" tradition? Does it matter to American politics that most Americans are actively religious? Is it dangerous to democratic commitment for social activists and citizens to speak from a religious perspective? Is it antidemocratic or illiberal to exclude religious arguments and speech from public debate? What explanation does Neuhaus offer for the rise of the religious right? Could similar explanations account for the activism of the religious left in the 1960s?

. . .

"When I hear the words 'Christian America' I see barbed wire," a notably liberal Reform rabbi tells me. I do not doubt him, but then he and a surprising number of others have a curious view of, among other things, Christianity. In this view the high points, sometimes the only points, of two millennia of Christian history are the blood curse upon the Jews, the Crusades, the Inquisition, and the Holocaust. This way of telling the Christian story is not unlike telling the story of America exclusively in terms of Salem witch-hunts, Indian massacres, slavery, the Ku Klux Klan, and alleged preparations for a nuclear first strike. Both stories, while highlighting some important truths, profoundly distort the tales they would tell.

Those who are most vocally anxious about Christian America usually have a special kind of Christian in mind. They do not worry about people who "happen to be" Lutheran, Episcopalian, Methodist, Catholic, or whatever. Even less worrisome are people who add that they happen to be whatever they happen to be "by background." These are the liberally acculturated who do not let their religion stick out or get in the way of living like normal people. They are, as Mort Sahl said of Adlai Stevenson, the sort of people who believe in the "Ten Suggestions" and who would—were they members of the Ku Klux Klan—burn a question mark on your lawn. With Christians like that, Christian America is no problem. But then there are those other Christians who do not just happen to be but really are. And what they really are frequently carries an off-brand name, such as Independent Baptist, Holiness, Pentecostal, or Assemblies of God.

. . .

In high schools and colleges across the country students are reading textbooks that state in a taken-for-granted manner that America is, or is rapidly becoming, a secular society. If religion is mentioned at all, it is said that people once found answers to their problems in religious teaching, but, of course, that is no longer possible in "our increasingly secular and pluralistic society."

Yet the proposition that America is, or is becoming, a secular society has everything going for it except the empirical evidence. The proposition is tied to a two-part dogma which has exercised an intellectual hegemony for nearly two hundred years.

The dogma states that as people become more enlightened (read, more educated) religion will wither away. The second part of the dogma states that, to the extent religion endures, it is a residual phenomenon that can be hermetically sealed off in the "private sphere" of life, safely removed from the public arena where, by the canons of secular "rationality," we debate and decide the ordering of our life together. This is a hypothesis about historical development. As such it is subject to historical confirmation or falsification. At least in America, it has been historically falsified.

. . .

. . . Most fundamentalists boiled their case down to insistence upon five "fundamentals": the inerrancy of Scripture (the Bible contains no errors in any subject on which it speaks); the virgin birth of Jesus (the Spirit of God conceived Jesus in Mary without human intervention); the substitutionary atonement of Jesus Christ (on the cross he bore the just punishment for the sins of the entire world); his bodily resurrection; the authenticity of the biblical miracles; and pre-millennialism.

The last point touches on the question of, among other things, Armageddon, a question which erupted in, of all places, the 1984 presidential campaign. All orthodox Christians believe in the return of Jesus in glory and the establishment of the kingdom of God as the consummation of history. Some Christian groups are pre-millennialist, others are post-millennialist, and some do not take a position on the question. Both post- and pre-millennialists believe there will be on earth a thousand-year reign of perfect peace, justice, and harmony with God's will. Pre-millennialists believe that Jesus will return first and then there will be that millennium; post-millennialists say the millennium will be established first and then Jesus will return in glory. The debate turns upon the interpretation of some marvelously obscure passages in the prophets Daniel and Ezekiel and the last book of the Christian Scriptures, Revelation.

In the past it was generally thought that pre-millennialist Christians would be politically passive, because there wasn't much point in trying to change the world before Jesus returns to set everything right. The important thing was not social reform but saving individual souls. . . . Post-millennialists, on the other hand, were avid social reformers, eager to put the world in order, establish the millennium, and thus hasten the return of Jesus. (The more modernist among them thought the last point to be an inspiring metaphor not to be taken literally.) But today the most aggressive political activism is being pushed by pre-millennialists.

The change is causing considerable consternation within the fundamentalist world. . . . The public platform and the pulpit platform engage two quite different worlds of discourse. The Moral Majority advertises and carefully nurtures its support from Catholics, Jews, and non-believers. But membership in the Moral Majority, it is made unmistakably clear, is not to be confused with membership in the company of the truly saved.

. . .

If a previously apolitical pre-millennialist fundamentalism has now turned in an activist direction, fundamentalist leaders did not just get together one day and decide to go political. They felt, and they feel, that they are responding to an assault upon their religious freedom. As Seymour Martin Lipset has put it, their activism may be viewed as an "aggressive defense." Their defense is against what they perceive as governmental actions dictated by the "secular humanists" in control of American public life. Ten years ago, before the religious Right was a major factor, Leo Pfeffer (then of the American Jewish Congress) saw the dynamic that would produce this response. "Matters which have long been considered private," he wrote, "are increasingly becoming the concern of government." He added, "The thirst for power is a potent force even in a democracy, and the state will be tempted and will yield to the temptation of seeking to exercise dominion over religion for no other reason than because it is there."

. . .

Even those who try to understand the religious Right sympathetically find themselves asking, "Yes, but what else do they want?" One useful answer is ACTV's list of ten issues in its campaign to "restore traditional moral and spiritual values" to American life. The list includes prayer and Bible reading in public schools, a "pro-life" amendment (or some other instrument for overruling *Roe* v. *Wade*), legal restrictions on pornography, an end to state "harassment" of Christian schools, resistance to feminist and gay-rights legislation, increased defense spending, and terminating social programs that, it is believed, only increase the dependency of the poor. Even some of the committed opponents of the religious Right might concede that most, if not all, of these items are legitimate issues for debate in a democratic society. Yet many people are alarmed, for they thought that all these issues had been "settled." Only now has it become evident that, at least on some of these issues, a majority of the American people had not consented to the settlement.

. . .

The activist fundamentalists want us to know that they are not going to go back to the wilderness. Many of them, being typical Americans, also want to be loved. They explain, almost apologetically, that they did not really want to bash in the door to the public square, but it was locked, and nobody had answered their knocking. Anyway, the hinges were rusty and it gave way under pressure that was only a little more than polite. And so the country cousins have shown up in force at the family picnic. They want a few rules changed right away. Other than that they promise to behave, provided we do not again try to exclude them from family deliberations. Surely it is incumbent on the rest of us, especially those who claim to understand our society, to do more in response to this ascendance of fundamentalism—and indeed of religion in general—than to sound an increasingly hysterical and increasingly hollow alarm.

MICHAEL WALZER

WHAT DOES IT MEAN TO BE AN "AMERICAN"? (1990)

Born in New York, Michael Walzer graduated in 1956 from Brandeis University, where he was brought into the world of public intellectuals, and he received his Ph.D. in government from Harvard University in 1961. While pursuing an academic career (retiring from the Institute for Advanced Study in 2005), he also maintained an active public profile. He was a long-time editor of *The New Republic* and *Dissent* magazines. His interests have been wide-ranging, but his work in the 1980s and 1990s often emphasized how moral judgments and political commitments were grounded in particular traditions and cultures rather than universal theories. He has characterized himself as a "soft multiculturalist," advocating for diverse and permeable local communities. This article, later expanded into a book, applies that sensibility to ideas about citizenship, patriotism, and ethnicity.

Why does Walzer not think that the United States is a "nation of nationalities"? What is the relationship between American identity and ethnic identity? Would Neuhaus agree that Americanism is "relatively unqualified by religion"? If Walzer is right about American identity, was the Moral Majority un-American? Is the American Jewish Congress? Is assimilation the price of citizenship in the United States? Is tolerance of diversity just a necessary evil? What does tolerance require?

There is no country called America. We live in the United States of America, and we have appropriated the adjective "American" even though we can claim no exclusive title to it. . . . Other countries, wrote the "American" political theorist Horace Kallen, get their names from the people, or from one of the peoples, who inhabit them. "The United States, on the other hand, has a peculiar anonymity." It is a name that doesn't even pretend to tell us who lives here. Anybody can live here, and just about everybody does—men and women from all the world's peoples. (*The Harvard Encyclopedia of American Ethnic Groups* begins with Acadians and Afghans and ends with Zoroastrians.) It is peculiarly easy to become an American. The adjective provides no reliable information about the origins, histories, connections, or cultures of those whom it designates. What does it say, then, about their political allegiance?

. . .

American politicians engage periodically in a fierce competition to demonstrate their patriotism. This is an odd competition, surely, for in most countries the patriotism of politicians is not an issue. There are other issues, and this question of political identification and commitment rarely comes up; loyalty to the *patrie*, the fatherland (or motherland), is simply assumed. Perhaps it isn't assumed here because the United States isn't a *patrie*. Americans have never spoken of their country as a fatherland (or a motherland). The kind of natural or organic loyalty that we (rightly or wrongly) recognize in families doesn't seem to be a feature of our politics. When American politicians invoke the metaphor of family they are usually making an argument about our mutual responsibilities and welfarist obligations, and among Americans, that is a controversial argument. One can be an American patriot without believing in the mutual responsibilities of American citizens—indeed, for some Americans disbelief is a measure of one's patriotism.

Similarly, the United States isn't a "homeland" (where a national family might dwell), not, at least, as other countries are, in casual conversation and unreflective feeling. It is a country of immigrants who, however grateful they are for this new place, still remember the old places. . . . To be "at home" in America is a personal matter: Americans have homesteads and homefolks and hometowns, and each of these is an endlessly interesting topic of conversation. But they don't have much to say about a common or communal home.

. . .

According to Kallen, the United States is less importantly a union of states than it is a union of ethnic, racial, and religious groups—a union of otherwise unrelated "natives." What is the nature of this union? The Great Seal of the United States carries the motto *E pluribus unum*, "From many, one," which seems to suggest that manyness must be left behind for the sake of oneness. Once there were many, now the many have merged or, in Israel Zangwell's classic image, been melted down into one. But the Great Seal presents a different image: the "American" eagle holds a sheaf of arrows. Here there is no merger or fusion but only a fastening, a putting together: many-in-one. Perhaps the adjective "American" describes this kind of oneness. We might say, tentatively, that it points to the citizenship, not the nativity or nationality, of the men and women it designates. It is a political adjective, and its politics is liberal in the strict sense: generous, tolerant, ample, accommodating—it allows for the survival, even the enhancement and flourishing, of manyness.

On this view, appropriately called "pluralist," the word "from" on the Great Seal is a false preposition. There is no movement from many to one, but rather a simultaneity, a coexistence—once again, many-in-one. . . .

In fact, the United States is not a "nation of nationalities" or a "social union of social unions." At least, the singular nation or union is not constituted by, it is not a combination or fastening together of, the plural nationalities or unions. In some sense, it includes them; it provides a framework for their coexistence; but they are not its parts. Nor are the individual states, in any significant sense, the parts that make up the United States. The parts are individual men and women. The United States is an association of citizens. . . . But on the pluralist view. Americans are allowed to remember who they were and to insist, also, on what else they are.

They are not, however, bound to the remembrance or to the insistence. Just as their ancestors escaped the old country, so they can if they choose escape their old identities, the "inwardness" of their nativity. Kallen writes of the individual that "whatever else he changes, he cannot change his grandfather." Perhaps not; but he can call his grandfather a "greenhorn," reject his customs and convictions, give up the family name, move to a new neighborhood, adopt a new "life-style."

. . .

But though these anonymous Americans were not better Americans for being or for having become anonymous, it is conceivable that they were, and are, better American citizens. If the manyness of America is cultural, its oneness is political, and it may be the case that men and women who are free from non-American cultures will commit themselves more fully to the American political system. Maybe cultural anonymity is the best possible grounding for American politics. From the beginning, of course, it has been the standard claim of British-Americans that their own culture is the best grounding. And there is obviously much to be said for that view. Despite the efforts of hyphenated Americans to describe liberal and democratic politics as a kind of United Way to which they have all made contributions, the genealogy of the American political system bears a close resemblance to the genealogy of the Sons and Daughters of the American Revolution—ethnic organizations if there ever were any! But this genealogy must also account for the flight across the Atlantic and the Revolutionary War. The parliamentary oligarchy of eighteenth-century Great Britain wasn't, after all, all that useful a model for America. When the ancestors of the Sons and Daughters described their political achievement as a "new order for the ages," they were celebrating a break with their own ethnic past almost as profound as that which later Americans were called upon to make. British-Americans who refused the break called themselves "Loyalists," but they were called disloyal by their opponents and treated even more harshly than hyphenated Americans from Germany, Russia, and Japan in later episodes of war and revolution.

Citizenship in the "new order" was not universally available, since blacks and women and Indians (Native Americans) were excluded, but it was never linked to a single nationality. "To be or to become an American," writes Philip Gleason, "a person did not have to be of any particular national, linguistic, religious, or ethnic background. All he had to do was to commit himself to the political ideology centered on the abstract ideals of liberty, equality, and republicanism." These abstract ideals made for a politics separated not only from religion but from culture itself or, better, from all the particular forms in which religious and national culture was, and is, expressed—hence a politics "anonymous" in Kallen's sense. . . . The adjective "American" named, and still names, a politics that is relatively unqualified by religion or nationality or, alternatively, that is qualified by so many religions and nationalities as to be free from any one of them.

It is this freedom that makes it possible for America's oneness to encompass and protect its manyness. Nevertheless, the conflict between the one and the many is a pervasive feature of American life. Those Americans who attach great value to the oneness of citizenship and the centrality of political allegiance must seek to constrain the influence of cultural manyness; those who value the many must disparage the one. The conflict is evident from the earliest days of the republic. . . .

. . .

[T]he symbols and ceremonies of American citizenship could not be drawn from the political culture or history of British-Americans. Our Congress is not a Commons; Guy Fawkes Day is not an American holiday; the Magna Carta has never been one of our sacred texts. American symbols and ceremonies are culturally anonymous, invented rather than inherited, voluntaristic in style, narrowly political in content: the flag, the Pledge, the Fourth, the Constitution. It is entirely appropriate that the Know-Nothing party had its origin in the Secret Society of the Star-Spangled Banner. And it is entirely understandable that the flag and the Pledge continue, every today, to figure largely in political debate. With what reverence should the flag be treated? On what occasions must it be saluted? Should we require school children to recite the Pledge, teachers to lead the recitation? Questions like these are the tests of a political commitment that can't be assumed, because it isn't undergirded by the cultural and religious commonalities that make for mutual trust. The flag and the Pledge are, as it were, all we have. One could suggest, of course, alternative and more practical tests of loyalty responsible participation in political life, for example. But the real historical alternative is the test proposed by the cultural pluralists: one proves one's Americanism, in their view, by living in peace with all the other "Americans," that is, by agreeing to respect social manyness rather than by pledging allegiance to the "one and indivisible" republic. . . .

. . .

Hence Kallen's program: assimilation "in matters economic and political," dissimilation "in cultural consciousness." The hyphen joined these two processes in one person, so that a Jewish-American (like Kallen) was similar to other Americans in his economic and political activity, but similar only to other Jews at the deeper level of culture. It is clear that Kallen's "hyphenates," whose spiritual life is located so emphatically to the left of the hyphen, cannot derive the greater part of their happiness from their citizenship. Nor, in a sense, should they, since culture, for the cultural pluralists, is far more important than politics and promises a more complete satisfaction. Pluralists, it seems, do not make good republicans—for the same reason that republicans, Rousseau the classic example, do not make good pluralists. The two attend to different sorts of goods.

Kallen's hyphenated Americans can be attentive and conscientious citizens, but on a liberal, not a republican model. This means two things. First, the various ethnic and religious groups can intervene in political life only in order to defend themselves and advance their common interests—as in the case of the NAACP or the Anti-Defamation League—but not in order to impose their culture or their values. They have to recognize that the state is anonymous (or, in the language of contemporary political theorists, neutral) at least in this sense: that it can't take on the character or the name of any of the groups that it includes. It isn't a nation-state of a particular kind and it isn't a Christian republic. Second, the primary political commitment of individual citizens is to protect their protection, to uphold the democratic framework within which they pursue their more substantive activities. This commitment is consistent with feelings of gratitude, loyalty, even patriotism of a certain sort, but it doesn't make for fellowship. . . . Here pluralism is straightforwardly opposed to republicanism: politics offers neither self-realization nor communion. All intensity lies, or should lie, elsewhere.

. . . . Kallen's more important point is simply that there is space and opportunity elsewhere for the emotional satisfactions that politics can't (or shouldn't) provide. And because individuals really do find this satisfaction, the groups within which it is found are permanently sustainable: they won't melt down, not, at least, in any ordinary (noncoercive) social process. Perhaps they can be repressed, if the repression is sufficiently savage; even then, they will win out in the end.

. . .

"An American nationality," writes Gleason, "does in fact exist." Not just a political status, backed up by a set of political symbols and ceremonies, but a full-blooded nationality, reflecting a history and a culture—exactly like all the other nationalities from which Americans have been, and continue to be, recruited. . . . Americans recognize one another, take pride in the things that fellow Americans have made and done, identify with the national community. So, while there no doubt are people plausibly called Italian-Americans or Swedish-Americans, spiritual (as well as political) life—this is Gleason's view—is lived largely to the right of the hyphen: contrasted with real Italians and real Swedes, these are real Americans.

. . .

The cultural pluralists come closer to getting the new order right than do the nativists and the nationalists and the American communitarians. Nonetheless, there is a nation and a national community and, by now, a very large number of native Americans. Even first- and second-generation Americans, as Gleason points out, have graves to visit and homes and neighborhoods to remember in this country, on this side of whatever waters their ancestors crossed to get here. What is distinctive about the nationality of these Americans is not its insubstantial character—substance is quickly acquired—but its nonexclusive character. Remembering the God of the Hebrew Bible, I want to argue that America is not a jealous nation. In this sense, at least, it is different from most of the others.

. . .

America is very different, and not only because of the eclipse of republicanism in the early nineteenth century. Indeed, republicanism has had a kind of afterlife as one of the legitimating ideologies of American politics. The Minute Man is a republican image of embodied citizenship. Reverence for the flag is a form of republican piety. The Pledge of Allegiance is a republican oath. But emphasis on this sort of thing reflects social disunity rather than unity; it is a straining after oneness where oneness doesn't exist. In fact, America has been, with severe but episodic exceptions, remarkably tolerant of ethnic pluralism (far less so of racial pluralism). I don't want to underestimate the human difficulties of adapting even to a hyphenated Americanism, nor to deny the bigotry and discrimination that particular groups have encountered. But tolerance has been the cultural norm.

Perhaps an immigrant society has no choice; tolerance is a way of muddling through when any alternative policy would be violent and dangerous. But I would argue that we have, mostly, made the best of this necessity, so that the virtues of toleration, in principle though by no means always in practice, have supplanted the single-mindedness of republican citizenship. . . .

. . .

One step more is required before we have fully understood this strange America: it is not the case that Irish-Americans, say, are culturally Irish and politically American, as the pluralists claim (and as I have been assuming thus far for the sake of the argument). Rather, they are culturally Irish American and politically Irish-American. Their culture has been significantly influenced by American culture; their politics is still, both in style and substance, significantly ethnic. With them, and with every ethnic and religious group except the American-Americans, hyphenation is doubled. It remains true, however, that what all the groups have in common is most importantly their citizenship and what most differentiates them, insofar as they are still differentiated, is their culture. Hence the alternation in American life of patriotic fevers and ethnic revivals, the first expressing a desire to heighten the commonality, the second a desire to reaffirm the difference.

. . .

. . . It isn't inconceivable that America will one day become an American nation-state, the many giving way to the one, but that is not what it is now; nor is that its destiny. America has no singular national destiny—and to be an "American" is, finally, to know that and to be more or less content with it.

IRVING KRISTOL

THE NEOCONSERVATIVE PERSUASION (2003)

Irving Kristol was raised by working-class Jewish immigrants in Brooklyn, graduating from City College of New York in 1940 with a Marxist orientation. After fighting in Europe in 1944, Kristol took up journalism, joining the editorial staff of *Commentary* magazine in 1947. Through the 1950s, Kristol was particularly active in the anticommunist left, but in 1965 he founded *Public Interest* magazine with Daniel Bell. *Public Interest* focused on domestic policy and was critical of the design and implementation of the Great Society programs, and in the 1970s Kristol identified with the Republican Party. At the end of the decade, the socialist writer Michael Harrington called Kristol the "godfather of neoconservatism," coining a label for a group of left-wing intellectuals who had moved to the right in the 1960s and 1970s. Neoconservatism became an important part of the modern conservative movement associated with Ronald Reagan, supplying policy ideas and government staffers if not electoral votes.

Are there differences between what Kristol sets as central features of neoconservatism and what other modern conservatives articulate as important values? Did American conservatism need to be converted in the 1970s into something "suitable to governing a modern democracy"? What does Kristol take to be foundational in "a modern democracy"? In what sense are neoconservatives "conservative"? Are such ideological shifts unifying or polarizing?

Journalists, and now even presidential candidates, speak with an enviable confidence on who or what is "neoconservative," and seem to assume the meaning is fully revealed in the name. Those of us who are designated as "neocons" are amused, flattered, or dismissive, depending on the context. It is reasonable to wonder: Is there any "there" there? . . .

[O]ne can say that the historical task and political purpose of neoconservatism would seem to be this: to convert the Republican party, and American conservatism in general, against their respective wills, into a new kind of conservative politics suitable to governing a modern democracy. That this new conservative politics is distinctly American is beyond doubt. There is nothing like neoconservatism in Europe, and most European conservatives are highly skeptical of its legitimacy. The fact that conservatism in the United States is so much healthier than in Europe, so much more politically effective, surely has something to do with the existence of neoconservatism. . . .

Neoconservatism is the first variant of American conservatism in the past century that is in the "American grain." It is hopeful, not lugubrious; forward-looking, not nostalgic; and its general tone is cheerful, not grim or dyspeptic. Its 20th-century heroes tend to be TR, FDR, and Ronald Reagan. Such Republican and conservative worthies as Calvin Coolidge, Herbert Hoover, Dwight Eisenhower, and Barry Goldwater are politely overlooked. Of course, those worthies are in no way overlooked by a large, probably the largest, segment of the Republican party, with the result that most Republican politicians know nothing and could not care less about neoconservatism. Nevertheless, they cannot be blind to the fact that neoconservative policies, reaching out beyond the traditional political and financial base, have helped make the very idea of political conservatism more acceptable to a majority of American voters. Nor has it passed official notice that it is the neoconservative public policies, not the traditional Republican ones, which result in popular Republican presidencies.

One of these policies, most visible and controversial, is cutting tax rates in order to stimulate steady economic growth. This policy was not invented by neocons, and it was not the particularities of tax cuts that interested them, but rather the steady focus on economic growth. Neocons are familiar with intellectual history and aware that it is only in the last two centuries that democracy has become a respectable option among political thinkers. In earlier times, democracy meant an inherently turbulent political regime, with the "have-nots" and the "haves" engaged in a perpetual and utterly destructive class struggle. It was only the prospect of economic growth in which everyone prospered, if not equally or simultaneously, that gave modern democracies their legitimacy and durability.

The cost of this emphasis on economic growth has been an attitude toward public finance that is far less risk averse than is the case among more traditional conservatives. Neocons would prefer not to have large budget deficits, but it is in the nature of democracy—because it seems to be in the nature of human nature—that political demagogy will frequently result in economic recklessness, so that one sometimes must shoulder budgetary deficits as the cost (temporary, one hopes) of pursuing economic growth. It is a basic assumption of neoconservatism that, as a consequence of the spread of affluence among all classes, a property-owning and tax-paying population will, in time, become less vulnerable to egalitarian illusions and demagogic appeals and more sensible about the fundamentals of economic reckoning.

This leads to the issue of the role of the state. Neocons do not like the concentration of services in the welfare state and are happy to study alternative ways of delivering these services. But they are impatient with the Hayekian notion that we are on "the road to serfdom." Neocons do not feel that kind of alarm or anxiety about the growth of the state in the past century, seeing it as natural, indeed inevitable. . . .

But it is only to a degree that neocons are comfortable in modern America. The steady decline in our democratic culture, sinking to new levels of vulgarity, does unite neocons with traditional conservatives—though not with those libertarian conservatives who are conservative in economics but unmindful of the culture. . . .

And then, of course, there is foreign policy, the area of American politics where neoconservatism has recently been the focus of media attention. This is surprising since there is no set of neoconservative beliefs concerning foreign policy, only a set of attitudes derived from historical experience. . . . These attitudes can be summarized in the following "theses" (as a Marxist would say): First, patriotism is a natural and healthy sentiment and should be encouraged by both private and public institutions. Precisely because we are a nation of immigrants, this is a powerful American sentiment. Second, world government is a terrible idea since it can lead to world tyranny. International institutions that point to an ultimate world government should be regarded with the deepest suspicion. Third, statesmen should, above all, have the ability to distinguish friends from enemies. This is not as easy as it sounds, as the history of the Cold War revealed. The number of intelligent men who could not count the Soviet Union as an enemy, even though this was its own self-definition, was absolutely astonishing.

Finally, for a great power, the "national interest" is not a geographical term, except for fairly prosaic matters like trade and environmental regulation. A smaller nation might appropriately feel that its national interest begins and ends at its borders, so that its foreign policy is almost always in a defensive mode. A larger nation has more extensive interests. And large nations, whose identity is ideological, like the Soviet Union of yesteryear and the United States of today, inevitably have ideological interests in addition to more material concerns. Barring extraordinary events, the United States will always feel obliged to defend, if possible, a democratic nation under attack from nondemocratic forces, external or internal. That is why it was in our national interest to come to the defense of France and Britain in World War II. That is why we feel it necessary to defend Israel today, when its survival is threatened. No complicated geopolitical calculations of national interest are necessary.

. . .

. . . With power come responsibilities, whether sought or not, whether welcome or not. And it is a fact that if you have the kind of power we now have, either you will find opportunities to use it, or the world will discover them for you. The older, traditional elements in the Republican party have difficulty coming to terms with this new reality in foreign affairs, just as they cannot reconcile economic conservatism with social and cultural conservatism. . . .

WENDELL BERRY

CITIZENSHIP PAPERS (2003)

Wendell Berry was raised on a farm in New Deal-era Kentucky, graduating with an M.A. from the University of Kentucky in 1957. He has subsequently made a career, primarily in Kentucky, of farming, teaching creating writing, and writing poetry, fiction, and nonfiction. He has often been involved in political activism, particularly promoting pacifism and environmentalism. He is one of the leading modern agrarians and a pioneer of the local food movement, which for him has political and economic significance as well as environmental. Only an autonomous "local economy" driven by "significant charity in just prices" and a focus on "subsistence" can protect individuals against the insecurities of global capitalism.[7]

In what sense does industrialism separate people and products from their histories? Why does Berry think this loss is significant? What does Berry mean by "satisfaction"? Is large-scale capitalism inherently unsatisfying? What is his vision of agrarianism? Is Berry right that agrarianism is the only credible alternative to the status quo? Is agrarianism more compatible with community than industrialism? Is it more supportive of individualism? Can participants in global capitalism be good citizens?

. . .

One of the primary results—and one of the primary needs—of industrialism is the separation of people and places and products from their histories. To the extent that we participate in the industrial economy, we do not know the histories of our meals or of our habitats of our families. This is an economy, and in fact of a culture, of the one-night stand. . . .

In this condition, we have many commodities, but little satisfaction, little sense of the sufficiency of anything. . . . and so we can say that the industrial economy's most-marked commodity is satisfaction, and that this commodity, which is repeatedly promised, bought, and paid for, is never delivered. On the other hand, people who have much satisfaction do not need many commodities.

. . . We do not cherish the memory of shoddy and transitory objects, and so we do not remember them. That is to say that we do not invest in them the lasting respect and admiration that make for satisfaction.

The problem with our dissatisfaction with all the things that we use is not correctable within the terms of the economy that produces those things. . . . [T]he origins of the products are typically too distant and too scattered and the process of trade, manufacture, transportation, and marketing too complicated. . . .

When there is no reliable accounting and therefore no competent knowledge of the economic and ecological effects of our lives, we cannot live lives that are economically and ecologically responsible. This is the problem that has frustrated, and to a considerable extent undermined, the American conservation effort from the beginning. . . .

. . .

That this nature-romanticism of the nineteenth century ignores economic facts and relationships has not prevented it from setting the agenda for modern conservation groups. . . . The giveaway is that when conservationists try to be practical they are likely to defend the "sustainable use of natural resources" with the argument that this will make the industrial economy sustainable. . . . Every human in the world cannot, now or ever, own the whole catalog of shoddy, high-energy industrial products, which cannot be sustainably made or used. . . .

. . .

7 Wendell Berry, "The Idea of a Local Economy," in *The Art of the Commonplace*, ed. Norman Wirzba (Berkeley, CA: Counterpoint, 2002), 260.

What, then, is the countervailing idea by which we might correct the industrial idea? We will not have to look hard to find it, for there is only one, and that is agrarianism. Our major difficulty (and danger) will be attempting to deal with agrarianism as "an idea"—agrarianism is primarily a practice, a set of attitudes, a loyalty, and a passion; it is an idea only secondarily and at a remove. . . .

The fundamental difference between industrialism and agrarianism is this: Whereas industrialism is a way of thought based on monetary capital and technology, agrarianism is a way of thought based on land.

Agrarianism, furthermore, is a culture at the same time that it is an economy. Industrialism is an economy before it is a culture. Industrial culture is an accidental by-product of the ubiquitous effort to sell unnecessary products for more than they are worth.

An agrarian economy rises up from the fields, woods, and streams. . . . The agrarian mind is therefore not regional or national, let alone global, but local. It must know on intimate terms the local plants and animals and local soils; it must know local possibilities and impossibilities, opportunities and hazards. It depends on and insists on knowing very particular local histories and biographies.

Because a mind so placed meets again and again the necessity for work to be good, the agrarian mind is less interested in abstract quantities than in particular qualities. It feels threatened and sickened when it hears people and creatures and places spoken of as labor, management, capital, and raw material. It is not at all impressed by the industrial legendry of gross national products. . . . It is interested—and forever fascinated—by questions leading toward the accomplishment of good work: What is the best location for a particular building or fence? What is the best way to plow *this* field? . . .

. . .

An agrarian economy is always a subsistence economy before it is a market economy. The center of an agrarian farm is the household. . . . A subsistence economy necessarily is highly diversified, and it characteristically has involved hunting and gathering as well as farming and gardening. These activities bind people to their local landscape by close, complex interests and economic ties. . . .

Agrarian people of the present, knowing that the land must be well cared for if anything is to last, understand the need for a settled connection, not just between farmers and their farms, but between urban people and their surrounding and tributary landscapes. Because the knowledge and know-how of good caretaking must be handed down to children, agrarians recognize the necessity of preserving the coherence of families and communities.

. . .

A major characteristic of the agrarian mind is a longing for independence—that is, for an appropriate degree of personal and local self-sufficiency. . . .

. . .

[One question] is whether or not agrarianism is simply a "phase" that we humans had to go through and then leave behind in order to get onto the track of technological progress toward ever greater happiness. The answer is that although industrialism has certainly conquered agrarianism, and has very nearly destroyed it altogether; it is also true that in every one of its uses of the natural world industrialism is in the process of catastrophic failure. . . .

The second question is whether or not by espousing the revival of agrarianism we will commit the famous sin of "turning back the clock." The answer to that, for present-day North Americans, is fairly simple. . . . We never yet have developed stable, sustainable, locally adapted land-based economies. . . . The possibility of an authentically settled country still lies ahead of us.

. . .

Whereas the corporate sponsors of the World Trade Organization, in order to promote their ambitions, have required only the hazy glamor of such phrases as "the global economy," "the global context," and "globalization," the local economists use a much more diverse and particularizing vocabulary that we can actually think with: "community," "ecosystem," "watershed," "place," "homeland," "family," "household."

. . .

. . . Agrarians would insist only that any manufacturing enterprise should be formed and scaled to fit the local landscape, the local ecosystem, and the local community, and that it should be locally owned and employ local people. . . .

. . .

[E]xperience seems increasingly to be driving us out of the categories of producer and consumer and into the categories of citizen, family member, and community member, in all of which we have an inescapable interest in making things last. . . .

. . .

IV. EQUALITY AND STATUS

Major Developments

- Disagreements over requirements of civil rights and racial equality
- Fragmentation of feminism
- Rise of multiculturalism
- Growth of gay rights movement

The political struggle over black civil rights in the 1950s and 1960s was intense. The 1954 *Brown* decision transitioned to "massive resistance" to President Lyndon Johnson's own use of the civil rights slogan "we shall overcome" in 1965. By the late twentieth century, support for Jim Crow had largely disappeared, but the debate over racial civil rights had hardly come to an end. The debate rapidly shifted to the terms for enforcing civil rights, the appropriate remedies for racial injustice, and the requirements of racial equality. For conservatives, civil rights were best understood in terms of "color-blind constitutionalism" and equal opportunity. For liberals, a commitment to eradicating the legacies of a racial caste system and the occasional use of race-conscious policies were essential to fully realizing racial civil rights.

While black civil rights were at the top of the agenda in the 1960s, by the 1980s the civil rights agenda had expanded to include a range of other ethnic and demographic groups. The use of affirmative action and minority set-asides as legal remedies for past discrimination necessitated the identification of groups eligible for such benefits. The black civil rights movement likewise inspired other groups to voice their own grievances and pursue legal, political, and social remedies. The rapidly changing demographics of American society further encouraged a reevaluation of inherited norms and expectations. The multiculturalism movement argued that at minimum a wider range of voices should be heard in society and politics. But it also suggested that mere tolerance of different (and often disadvantaged) groups was insufficient; equal respect for diverse groups required recognition and acceptance of differences. The more established feminist movement was affected by such debates as well. Having fought for and largely won legal equality, feminism fissured with the arrival of "third-wave feminism" that called for greater respect for difference and more concern with social and economic issues.

The gay rights movement was symbolically launched with the Stonewall riots of 1969 and achieved greater recognition when Harvey Milk won a seat on the San Francisco board of supervisors and advanced a civil rights ordinance providing legal protections for homosexuals in 1978. The movement gained greater prominence and organization with the onset of the AIDS epidemic in the 1980s. Groups like ACT UP and GLAAD mobilized the gay community to shift government policy and public perception, and both legal activism and political debate soon shifted from the politics of AIDS to a broader agenda of civil rights.

THOMAS SOWELL

CIVIL RIGHTS: RHETORIC OR REALITY? (1984)

Thomas Sowell grew up in modest circumstances in North Carolina and Harlem, becoming the first member of his family to attend high school. Nonetheless, he dropped out of school before graduation, completing a General Education certificate and taking night classes at Howard University only after serving in the Korean War. On the strength of his test scores and his performance at night school, he won admission to Harvard University and eventually completed a Ph.D. in economics at the University of Chicago in 1968. He spent a dozen years in academia before accepting a position at the Hoover Institution at Stanford University in 1980. He made his mark, however, with his public writings, authoring numerous books (primarily on race and economics) and a syndicated newspaper column. During the Reagan era, he was widely regarded as the leading black conservative in the nation (though it was not a label he preferred). His views on civil rights both reflected and shaped conservative thinking about the issue that extended from the Reagan administration through Justice Clarence Thomas.

What does Sowell characterize as the "civil rights vision"? Why does an expectation of equal results for different groups follow from it? How does Sowell depart from the civil rights vision? What does he think can affect group outcomes besides discrimination? Is Sowell's complaint about the substance of what civil rights are and equality requires, or about the techniques of implementing rules? How does this debate relate to the debates of earlier generations of black intellectuals?

. . .

The very meaning of the phrase "civil rights" has changed greatly since the *Brown* decision in 1954, or since the Civil Rights Act of 1964. Initially, civil rights meant, quite simply, that all individuals should be treated the same under the law, regardless of their race, religion, sex or other such social categories. For blacks, especially, this would have represented a dramatic improvement in those states where law and public policy mandated racially separate institutions and highly discriminatory treatment.

Many Americans who supported the initial thrust of civil rights . . . later felt betrayed as the original concept of equal individual *opportunity* evolved toward the concept of equal group *results*. The idea that statistical differences in results were weighty presumptive evidence of discriminatory processes was not initially an explicit part of civil rights law. But neither was it merely an inexplicable perversion, as many critics seem to think, for it followed logically from the civil rights *vision*.

If the causes of intergroup differences can be dichotomized into discrimination and innate ability, then non-racists and non-sexists must expect equal results from non-discrimination. Conversely, the persistence of highly disparate results must indicate that discrimination continues to be pervasive among recalcitrant employers, culturally biased tests, hypocritical educational institutions, etc. The early leaders and supporters of the civil rights movement did not advocate such corollaries, and many explicitly repudiated them. . . . But the corollaries were implicit in the vision—and in the long run that proved to be more decisive than the positions taken by the original leaders in the cause of civil rights. . . .

"Equal opportunity" laws and policies require that individuals be judged on their qualifications as individuals, *without regard* to race, sex, age, etc. "Affirmative action" requires that they be judged *with regard* to such group membership, receiving preferential or compensatory treatment in some cases to achieve a more proportional "representation" in various institutions and occupations.

. . . [A]s initially presented, affirmative action referred to various activities, such as monitoring subordinate decision makers to ensure the fairness of their hiring and promotion decisions, and spreading information about employment or other opportunities so as to encourage previously excluded groups to apply—after which the actual selection could be made *without regard* to group membership. Thus, it was both meaningful and consistent for President Kennedy's Executive Order to say that federal contractors should "take affirmative action to ensure that the applicants are employed, and that employees are treated during employment, without regard to their race, creed, color, or national origin."

. . .

The key development in this process was the creation of the Office of Federal Contract Compliance in the U.S. Department of Labor by President Lyndon Johnson's Executive Order No. 11,246 in 1965. In May 1968, this office issued guidelines containing the fateful expression "goals and timetables" and "representation." But as yet these were still not quotas. . . . By 1970, however, new guidelines referred to "results-oriented procedures," which hinted more strongly at what was to come. In December 1971, the decisive guidelines were issued, which made it clear that "goals and timetables" were meant to "increase materially the utilization of minorities and women." . . . The burden of proof—and remedy—was on the employer. "Affirmative action" was now decisively transformed into a numerical concept, whether called "goals" or "quotas."

. . .

Those who carry the civil rights vision to its ultimate conclusion see no great difference between promoting equality of opportunity and equality of results. . . . The fatal flaw in this kind of thinking is that there are many reasons, besides genes and discrimination, why groups differ in their economic performances and rewards. Groups differ by large amounts demographically, culturally, and geographically—and all of these differences have profound effects on incomes and occupations.

. . .

For example, mathematics preparation and performance differ greatly from one ethnic group to another and between men and women. A study of high school students in northern California showed that four-fifths of Asian youngsters were enrolled in the sequence of mathematics courses that culminate in calculus, while only one-fifth of black youngsters were enrolled in such courses. Moreover, even among those who began this sequence in geometry, the percentage that persisted all the way through to calculus was several times higher among the Asian students. Sex differences in mathematics preparation are comparably large. . . .

Mathematics is of decisive importance for many more professions than that of mathematician. Whole ranges of fields of study and work are off-limits to those without the necessary mathematical foundation. . . Cultural differences are real, and cannot be talked away by using pejorative terms such as "stereotypes" or "racism."

. . .

None of this disproves the existence of discrimination, nor is that its purpose. What is at issue is whether statistical differences mean discrimination, or whether there are innumerable demographic, cultural, and geographic differences that make this crucial automatic inference highly questionable.

. . .

THURGOOD MARSHALL

BICENTENNIAL SPEECH (1987)

Thurgood Marshall grew up in the black middle class in Baltimore, graduating from Howard University Law School in 1933. Three years later, his law school mentor, Charles Hamilton Houston, hired him as a staff attorney for the NAACP in New York. When Houston returned to Baltimore in 1938, Marshall took over as the lead attorney, a position he occupied until he was appointed to the federal circuit court in 1961. At the NAACP, Marshall spearheaded a systematic litigation campaign to undercut Jim Crow, which culminated in his victory in *Brown v. Board of Education* in 1954. In 1967, Marshall became the first African-American appointed to the U.S. Supreme Court. He held the seat until 1991. Although his tenure on the bench was overshadowed by some of his colleagues, he had been known as one of the most formidable litigators in the mid-twentieth century. While not an active public speaker during his time as a justice, he made headlines with his speech at a legal conference in Hawaii in 1987, the bicentennial of the drafting of the U.S. Constitution. The conservative Chief Justice Warren Burger had retired from the bench specifically to organize celebrations of the constitutional bicentennial, but Marshall sounded a more negative note about the achievements of the founders and what the Constitution represents.

What are Marshall's concerns about the U.S. Constitution? Why is he specifically critical of the bicentennial celebrations? How important was the founding to Marshall's conception of the Constitution? Should we celebrate what has sometimes been called the "second Founding"—the adoption of the Reconstruction Amendments—rather than events in Philadelphia in 1787? To what degree were the principles of the Constitution changed by the Reconstruction Amendments? Was the government designed by the framers "defective from the start"? Should the founders be celebrated—or reviled?

1987 marks the 200th anniversary of the United States Constitution. A Commission has been established to coordinate the celebration. The official meetings, essay contests, and festivities have begun.

The planned commemoration will span three years, and I am told 1987 is "dedicated to the memory of the Founders and the document they drafted in Philadelphia." we are to "recall the achievements of our Founders and the knowledge and experience that inspired them, the nature of the government they established, its origins, its character, and its ends, and the rights and privileges of citizenship, as well as its attendant responsibilities."

Like many anniversary celebrations, the plan for 1987 takes particular events and holds them up as the source of all the very best that has followed. Patriotic feelings will surely swell, prompting proud proclamations of the wisdom, foresight, and sense of justice shared by the Framers and reflected in a written document now yellowed with age. This is unfortunate—not the patriotism itself, but the tendency for the celebration to oversimplify, and overlook the many other events that have been instrumental to our achievements as a nation. The focus of this celebration invites a complacent belief that the vision of those who debated and compromised in Philadelphia yielded the "more perfect Union" it is said we now enjoy.

I cannot accept this invitation, for I do not believe that the meaning of the Constitution was forever "fixed" at the Philadelphia Convention. Nor do I find the wisdom, foresight, and sense of justice exhibited by the Framers particularly profound. To the contrary, the government they devised was defective from the start, requiring several amendments, a civil war, and momentous social transformation to attain the system of constitutional government, and its respect for the individual freedoms and human rights, we hold as fundamental today. When contemporary Americans cite "The Constitution," they invoke a concept that is vastly different from what the Framers barely began to construct two centuries ago.

For a sense of the evolving nature of the Constitution we need look no further than the first three words of the document's preamble: "We the People." When the Founding Fathers used this phrase in 1787, they did not have in mind the majority of America's citizens. "We the People" included, in the words of the Framers, "the whole Number of free Persons." On a matter so basic as the right to vote, for example, Negro slaves were excluded, although they were counted for representational purposes at three-fifths each. Women did not gain the right to vote for over a hundred and thirty years.

These omissions were intentional. The record of the Framers' debates on the slave question is especially clear: The Southern States acceded to the demands of the New England States for giving Congress broad power to regulate commerce, in exchange for the right to continue the slave trade. The economic interests of the regions coalesced: New Englanders engaged in the "carrying trade" would profit from transporting slaves from Africa as well as goods produced in America by slave labor. The perpetuation of slavery ensured the primary source of wealth in the Southern States.

Despite this clear understanding of the role slavery would play in the new republic, use of the words "slaves" and "slavery" was carefully avoided in the original document. Political representation in the lower House of Congress was to be based on the population of "free Persons" in each State, plus three-fifths of all "other Persons." Moral principles against slavery, for those who had them, were compromised, with no explanation of the conflicting principles for which the American Revolutionary War had ostensibly been fought: the self-evident truths "that all men are created equal, that they are endowed by their Creator with certain unalienable Rights, that among these are Life, Liberty and the pursuit of Happiness."

It was not the first such compromise. Even these ringing phrases from the Declaration of Independence are filled with irony, for an early draft of what became that Declaration assailed the King of England for suppressing legislative attempts to end the slave trade and for encouraging slave rebellions. The final draft adopted in 1776 did not contain this criticism. And so again at the Constitutional Convention eloquent objections to the institution of slavery went unheeded, and its opponents eventually consented to a document which laid a foundation for the tragic events that were to follow.

. . .

No doubt it will be said, when the unpleasant truth of the history of slavery in America is mentioned during this bicentennial year, that the Constitution was a product of its times, and embodied a compromise which, under other circumstances, would not have been made. But the effects of the Framers' compromise have remained for generations. They arose from the contradiction between guaranteeing liberty and justice to all, and denying both to Negroes.

The original intent of the phrase, "We the People," was far too clear for any ameliorating construction. Writing for the Supreme Court in 1857, Chief Justice Taney penned the following passage in the *Dred Scott* case, on the issue whether, in the eyes of the Framers, slaves were "constituent members of the sovereignty," and were to be included among "We the People":

> We think they are not, and that they are not included, and were not intended to be included. . . . They had for more than a century before been regarded as beings of an inferior order, and altogether unfit to associate with the white race . . .; and so far inferior, that they had no rights which the white man was bound to respect; and that the Negro might justly and lawfully be reduced to slavery for his benefit. . . . [A]ccordingly, a Negro of the African race was regarded . . . as an article of property, and held, and bought and sold as such. . . . [N]o one seems to have doubted the correctness of the prevailing opinion of the time.

And so, nearly seven decades after the Constitutional Convention, the Supreme Court reaffirmed the prevailing opinion of the Framers regarding the rights of Negroes in America. It took a bloody civil war before the 13th Amendment could be adopted to abolish slavery, though not the consequences slavery would have for future Americans.

While the Union survived the civil war, the Constitution did not. In its place arose a new, more promising basis for justice and equality, the 14th Amendment, ensuring protection of the life, liberty, and property of all persons against deprivations without due process, and guaranteeing equal protection of the laws. And yet almost another century would pass before any significant recognition was obtained of the rights of black Americans to share equally even in such basic opportunities as education, housing, and employment, and to have their votes counted, and counted equally. In the meantime, blacks joined America's military to fight its wars and invested untold hours working in its factories and on its farms, contributing to the development of this country's magnificent wealth and waiting to share in its prosperity.

What is striking is the role legal principles have played throughout America's history in determining the condition of Negroes. They were enslaved by law, emancipated by law, disenfranchised and segregated by law; and, finally, they have begun to win equality by law. Along the way, new constitutional principles have emerged to meet the challenges of a changing society. The progress has been dramatic, and it will continue.

The men who gathered in Philadelphia in 1787 could not have envisioned these changes. They could not have imagined, nor would they have accepted, that the document they were drafting would one day be construed by a Supreme Court to which had been appointed a woman and the descendent of an African slave. "We the People" no longer enslave, but the credit does not belong to the Framers. It belongs to those who refused to acquiesce in outdated notions of "liberty," "justice," and "equality," and who strived to better them.

And so we must be careful, when focusing on the events which took place in Philadelphia two centuries ago, that we not overlook the momentous events which followed, and thereby lose our proper sense of perspective. Otherwise, the odds are that for many Americans the bicentennial celebration will be little more than a blind pilgrimage to the shrine of the original document now stored in a vault in the National Archives. If we seek, instead, a sensitive understanding of the Constitution's inherent defects, and its promising evolution through 200 years of history, the celebration of the "Miracle at Philadelphia" will, in my view, be a far more meaningful and humbling experience. We will see that the true miracle was not the birth of the Constitution, but its life, a life nurtured through two turbulent centuries of our own making, and a life embodying much good fortune that was not.

Thus, in this bicentennial year, we may not all participate in the festivities with flag-waving fervor. Some may more quietly commemorate the suffering, struggle, and sacrifice that has triumphed over much of what was wrong with the original document, and observe the anniversary with hopes not realized and promises not fulfilled. I plan to celebrate the bicentennial of the Constitution as a living document, including the Bill of Rights and the other amendments protecting individual freedoms and human rights.

CORNEL WEST

RACE MATTERS (1994)

Cornel West grew up in California near the hotbed of the Black Panther movement. He graduated from Harvard University in 1973 and completed a Ph.D. in philosophy at Princeton University in 1980. He spent much of his career at Harvard and Princeton teaching religion and African-American studies. He also built a prominent public profile, quickly becoming involved in political activism on a range of issues, identifying himself as a democratic socialist, and working with presidential campaigns for Al Sharpton and Ralph Nader. His book of essays on racial issues, *Race Matters*, won a large public audience.

Why does West compare affirmative action policies to the GI Bill? Why does he doubt that affirmative action addresses the fundamental problems facing African-Americans? Why preserve affirmative action at all? Given West's diagnosis of the problem, are race-specific policies necessary? Does the condition of African-Americans provide an independent reason to support redistributionist policies? How does West's vision of civil rights compare with Sowell's?

. . .

The fundamental crisis in black America is twofold: too much poverty and too little self-love. The urgent problem of black poverty is primarily due to the distribution of wealth, power, and income—a distribution influenced by the racial caste system that denied opportunities to most "qualified" black people until two decades ago.

The historic role of American progressives is to promote redistributive measures that enhance the standard of living and quality of life for the have-nots and have-too-littles. Affirmative action was one such redistributive measure that surfaced in the heat of battle in the 1960s among those fighting for racial equality. Like earlier *de facto* affirmative action measures in the American past—contracts, jobs, and loans to select immigrants granted by political machines; subsidies to certain farmers; FHA mortgage loans to specific home buyers; or GI Bill benefits to particular courageous Americans—recent efforts to broaden access to America's prosperity have been based upon preferential policies. Unfortunately, these policies always benefit middle-class Americans disproportionately. The political power of big business in big government circumscribes redistributive measures and thereby tilts these measures away from the have-nots and have-too-littles.

Every redistributive measure is a compromise with and concession from the caretakers of American prosperity—that is, big business and big government. Affirmative action was one such compromise and concession achieved after the protracted struggle of American progressives and liberals in the courts and in the streets. Visionary progressives always push for substantive redistributive measures that make opportunities available to the have-nots and have-too-littles, such as more federal support to small farmers, or more FHA mortgage loans to urban dwellers as well as suburban home buyers. Yet in the American political system, where the powers that be turn a skeptical eye toward any program aimed at economic redistribution, progressives must secure whatever redistributive measures they can, ensure their enforcement, then extend their benefits if possible.

. . .

Progressives should view affirmative action as neither a major solution to poverty nor a sufficient means to equality. We should see it as primarily playing a negative role—namely, to ensure that discriminatory practices against women and people of color are abated. Given the history of this country, it is a virtual certainty that without affirmative action, racial and sexual discrimination would return with a vengeance. Even if affirmative action fails significantly to reduce black poverty or contributes to the persistence of racist perceptions in the workplace, without affirmative action, black access to America's prosperity would be even more difficult to obtain and racism in the workplace would persist anyway.

This claim is not based on any cynicism toward my white fellow citizens; rather, it rests upon America's historically weak will toward racial justice and substantive redistributive measures. This is why an attack on affirmative action is an attack on redistributive efforts by progressives unless there is a real possibility of enacting and enforcing a more wide-reaching class-based affirmative action policy.

. . .

Affirmative action is not the most important issue for black progress in America, but it is part of a redistributive chain that must be strengthened if we are to confront and eliminate black poverty. If there were social democratic redistributive measures that wiped out black poverty, and if racial and sexual discrimination could be abated through the good will and meritorious judgments of those in power, affirmative action would be unnecessary. Although many of my liberal and progressive citizens view affirmative action as a redistributive measure whose time is over or whose life is no longer worth preserving, I question their view because of the persistence of discriminatory practices that increase black social misery, and the warranted suspicion that good will and fair judgment among the powerful does not loom as large toward women and people of color.

If the elimination of black poverty is a necessary condition of substantive black progress, then the affirmation of black humanity, especially among black people themselves, is a sufficient condition of such programs. Such affirmation speaks to the existential issues of what it means to be a degraded African (man, woman, gay, lesbian, child) in a racist society. How does one affirm oneself without reenacting negative black stereotypes or overreacting to white supremacist ideals?

. . .

This paralysis takes two forms: black bourgeois preoccupation with white peer approval and black nationalist obsession with white racism.

The first form of paralysis tends to yield a navel-gazing posture that conflates the identity crisis of the black middle class with the state of siege raging in black working-poor and very poor communities. That unidimensional view obscures the need for redistributive measures that significantly affect the majority of blacks, who are working people on the edge of poverty.

The second form of paralysis precludes any meaningful coalition with white progressives because of an undeniable white racist legacy of the modern Western world. The anger this truth engenders impedes any effective way of responding to the crisis in black America. Broad redistributive measures require principled coalitions, including multiracial alliances. Without such measures, black America's sufferings deepen. White racism indeed contributes to this suffering. Yet an obsession with white racism often comes at the expense of more broadly based alliances to effect social change and borders on a tribal mentality. The more xenophobic versions of this viewpoint simply mirror the white supremacist ideals we are opposing and preclude any movement toward redistributive goals.

. . .

BARACK OBAMA

EULOGY AT THE FUNERAL SERVICE IN HONOR OF REVEREND CLEMENTA PINCKNEY (2015)

In June 2015, a gunman entered the Emanuel African Methodist Episcopal (AME) Church in Charleston, South Carolina, and killed nine African-American parishioners, including the senior pastor and state senator Clementa C. Pinckney. A young white man from North Carolina subsequently confessed to the murders, apparently with the desire to launch a race war.

Neither the timing nor the place of the incident was insignificant. The shooting came after several months of heated protest over episodes of police brutality against African-American suspects across the country. Just a few weeks before the shooting in Charleston, riots had raged in Baltimore in the aftermath of the death of an African-American man while in the custody of the city police. The treatment of African-Americans by law enforcement had leaped onto the political agenda. The church was also symbolic. It stood as one of the oldest African-American churches in the South. Before the Civil War, it had been embroiled in fears of a slave revolt. Since the war, it had become a center of African-American politics and civil rights organizing in the state and had hosted numerous national figures, including Martin Luther King. One immediate result of the shooting was a surge in public pressure to remove the Confederate Battle Flag from public spaces in South Carolina and elsewhere. The flag had been a source of intermittent controversy. It had been flying on a permanent basis at the South Carolina statehouse beginning with the 1961 centennial of the Civil War despite mounting pressure for its removal since the 1990s. Shortly after the shooting, the flag was removed from statehouse grounds in South Carolina, while debate continued in other states. While that debate was still ongoing, President Barack Obama visited the Emanuel AME Church in Charleston and delivered a eulogy for Pinckney. The eulogy was a major event, with several national political leaders from both parties in attendance and extended media coverage. The speech was hailed as one of Obama's most important during his presidency.

How does Obama use the concept of grace in the speech? How does Obama's religious framing of American racial history compare with Abraham Lincoln's in his second inaugural address? What political themes does he sound? To what degree is the speech specifically about race? Some black leaders criticized the president for being "afraid" to put "a spotlight on white supremacy." Is that a fair criticism of the speech? How does the president's efforts to speak to both a black and a white audience compare with Martin Luther King's in his I Have a Dream speech?

. . .

The Bible calls us to hope. To persevere and have faith in things not seen. "They were still living by faith when they died," Scripture tells us. "They did not receive the things promised; they only saw them and welcomed them from a distance, admitting that they were foreigners and strangers on Earth."

We are here today to remember a man of God who lived by faith. A man who believed in things not seen. A man who believed there were better days ahead, off in the distance. A man of service who persevered, knowing full well he would not receive all those things he was promised, because he believed his efforts would deliver a better life for those who followed.

. . .

Friends of his remarked this week that when Clementa Pinckney entered a room, it was like the future arrived; that even from a young age, folks knew he was special, anointed. He was the progeny of a long line of the faithful, a family of preachers who spread God's word, a family of protesters who sowed change to expand voting rights and desegregate the South. Clem heard their instruction, and he did not forsake their teaching.

. . .

As a senator, he represented a sprawling swath of the Lowcountry, a place that has long been one of the most neglected in America, a place still wracked by poverty and inadequate schools, a place where children can still go hungry and the sick can go without treatment—a place that needed somebody like Clem.

. . .

Reverend Pinckney embodied a politics that was neither mean, nor small. He conducted himself quietly and kindly and diligently. He encouraged progress not by pushing his ideas alone, but by seeking out your ideas, partnering with you to make things happen. He was full of empathy and fellow feeling, able to walk in somebody else's shoes and see through their eyes. . . .

Clem was often asked why he chose to be a pastor and a public servant. But the person who asked probably didn't know the history of the AME church. As our brothers and sisters in the AME church know, we don't make those distinctions. "Our calling," Clem once said, "is not just within the walls of the congregation, but . . . the life and community in which our congregation resides."

He embodied the idea that our Christian faith demands deeds and not just words; that the "sweet hour of prayer" actually lasts the whole week long; that to put our faith in action is more than individual salvation, it's about our collective salvation; that to feed the hungry and clothe the naked and house the homeless is not just a call for isolated charity, but the imperative of a just society.

. . .

To the families of the fallen, the Nation shares in your grief. Our pain cuts that much deeper because it happened in a church. The church is and always has been the center of African American life, a place to call our own in a too often hostile world, a sanctuary from so many hardships.

Over the course of centuries, Black churches served as "hush harbors" where slaves could worship in safety; praise houses where their free descendants could gather and shout, "Hallelujah"; rest stops for the weary along the Underground Railroad; bunkers for the foot soldiers of the civil rights movement. They have been and continue to be community centers where we organize for jobs and justice, places of scholarship and network, places where children are loved and fed and kept out of harm's way and told that they are beautiful and smart and taught that they matter. That's what happens in church.

That's what the Black church means. Our beating heart. The place where our dignity as a people is inviolate. And there's no better example of this tradition than Mother Emanuel, a church built by Blacks seeking liberty, burned to the ground because its founder sought to end slavery, only to rise up again, a Phoenix from these ashes.

When there were laws banning all-Black church gatherings, services happened here anyway, in defiance of unjust laws. When there was a righteous movement to dismantle Jim Crow, Dr. Martin Luther King, Jr., preached from its pulpit and marches began from its steps. A sacred place, this church. Not just for Blacks, not just for Christians, but for every American who cares about the steady expansion of human rights and human dignity in this country, a foundation stone for liberty and justice for all. That's what the church meant.

We do not know whether the killer of Reverend Pinckney and eight others knew all of this history. But he surely sensed the meaning of his violent act. It was an act that drew on a long history of bombs and arson and shots fired at churches, not random, but as a means of control, a way to terrorize and oppress; an act that he imagined would incite fear and recrimination, violence and suspicion; an act that he presumed would deepen divisions that trace back to our Nation's original sin.

Oh, but God works in mysterious ways. God has different ideas.

He didn't know he was being used by God. Blinded by hatred, the alleged killer could not see the grace surrounding Reverend Pinckney and that Bible study group, the light of love that shone as they opened the church doors and invited a stranger to join in their prayer circle. The alleged killer could have never anticipated the way the families of the fallen would respond when they saw him in court, in the midst of unspeakable grief, with words of forgiveness. He couldn't imagine that.

The alleged killer could not imagine how the city of Charleston, under the good and wise leadership of Mayor Riley, how the State of South Carolina, how the United States of America would respond: not merely with revulsion at his evil act, but with big-hearted generosity and, more importantly, with a thoughtful introspection and self-examination that we so rarely see in public life.

Blinded by hatred, he failed to comprehend what Reverend Pinckney so well understood: the power of God's grace. This whole week, I've been reflecting on this idea of grace: the grace of the families who lost loved ones; the grace that Reverend Pinckney would preach about in his sermons; the grace described in one of my favorite hymnals, the one we all know:

> Amazing grace! How sweet the sound,
> that saved a wretch like me!
> I once was lost, but now I'm found;
> was blind but now I see.

According to the Christian tradition, grace is not earned. Grace is not merited. It's not something we deserve. Rather, grace is the free and benevolent favor of God, as manifested in the salvation of sinners and the bestowal of blessings. Grace.

As a nation, out of this terrible tragedy, God has visited grace upon us, for he has allowed us to see where we've been blind. He has given us the chance, where we've been lost, to find our best selves. We may not have earned it, this grace, with our rancor and complacency and short-sightedness and fear of each other, but we got it all the same. He gave it to us anyway. He's once more given us grace. But it is up to us now to make the most of it, to receive it with gratitude and to prove ourselves worthy of this gift.

For too long, we were blind to the pain that the Confederate flag stirred in too many of our citizens. It's true, a flag did not cause these murders. But as people from all walks of life, Republicans and Democrats, now acknowledge—including Governor Haley, whose recent eloquence on the subject is worthy of praise—as we all have to acknowledge, the flag has always represented more than just ancestral pride. For many, Black and White, that flag was a reminder of systemic oppression and racial subjugation. We see that now. Removing the flag from this State's capitol would not be an act of political correctness; it would not be an insult to the valor of Confederate soldiers. It would simply be an acknowledgment that the cause for which they fought—the cause of slavery—was wrong. The imposition of Jim Crow after the Civil War, the resistance to civil rights for all people, was wrong. It would be one step in an honest accounting of America's history; a modest, but meaningful, balm for so many unhealed wounds. It would be an expression of the amazing changes that have transformed this State and this country for the better, because of the work of so many people of good will, people of all races striving to form a more perfect Union. By taking down that flag, we express God's grace.

But I don't think God wants us to stop there. For too long, we've been blind to the way past injustices continue to shape the present. Perhaps we see that now. Perhaps this tragedy causes us to ask some tough questions about how we can permit so many of our children to languish in poverty or attend dilapidated schools or grow up without prospects for a job or for a career.

Perhaps it causes us to examine what we're doing to cause some of our children to hate. Perhaps it softens hearts towards those lost young men, tens and tens of thousands caught up in the criminal justice system, and lead us to make sure that that system is not infected with bias; that we embrace changes in how we train and equip our police so that the bonds of trust between law enforcement and the communities they serve make us all safer and more secure.

Maybe we now realize the way racial bias can infect us even when we don't realize it, so that we're guarding against not just racial slurs, but we're also guarding against the subtle impulse to call Johnny back for a job interview, but not Jamal; so that we search our hearts when we consider laws to make it harder for some of our fellow citizens to vote. By recognizing our common humanity by treating every child as important, regardless of the color of their skin or the station into which they were born, and to do what's necessary to make opportunity real for every American—by doing that, we express God's grace.

. . .

We don't earn grace. We're all sinners. We don't deserve it. But God gives it to us anyway. And we choose how to receive it. It's our decision how to honor it.

None of us can or should expect a transformation in race relations overnight. Every time something like this happens, somebody says we have to have a conversation about race. We talk a lot about race. There's no shortcut. And we don't need more talk. None of us should believe that a handful of gun safety measures will prevent every tragedy. It will not. People of good will will continue to debate the merits of various policies, as our democracy requires. This is a big, raucous place, America is. And there are good people on both sides of these debates. Whatever solutions we find will necessarily be incomplete.

But it would be a betrayal of everything Reverend Pinckney stood for, I believe, if we allowed ourselves to slip into a comfortable silence again. Once the eulogies have been delivered, once the TV cameras move on, to go back to business as usual—that's what we so often do to avoid uncomfortable truths about the prejudice that still infects our society; to settle for symbolic gestures without following up with the hard work of more lasting change—that's how we lose our way again.

It would be a refutation of the forgiveness expressed by those families if we merely slipped into old habits, whereby those who disagree with us are not merely wrong, but bad, where we shout instead of listen, where we barricade ourselves behind preconceived notions or well-practiced cynicism.

Reverend Pinckney once said: "Across the South, we have a deep appreciation of history. We haven't always had a deep appreciation of each other's history." What is true in the South is true for America. Clem understood that justice grows out of recognition of ourselves in each other, that my liberty depends on you being free too, that history can't be a sword to justify injustice or a shield against progress, but must be a manual for how to avoid repeating the mistakes of the past, how to break the cycle. A roadway toward a better world. He knew that the path of grace involves an open mind, but more importantly, an open heart.

That's what I've felt this week, an open heart. That, more than any particular policy or analysis, is what's called upon right now, I think; what a friend of mine, the writer Marilynne Robinson, calls "that reservoir of goodness, beyond, and of another kind, that we are able to do each other in the ordinary cause of things."

That reservoir of goodness. If we can find that grace, anything is possible. If we can tap that grace, everything can change.

. . .

Through the example of their lives, they've now passed it on to us. May we find ourselves worthy of that precious and extraordinary gift as long as our lives endure. May grace now lead them home. May God continue to shed His grace on the United States of America.

V. POLITICAL ECONOMY

Major Developments

- Debate over free-market economics
- Retreat of socialist alternative
- Acceleration of economic globalization

"Reaganomics" offered less of a consistent remedy to the economic woes of the 1970s than a change in perspective. Unlike his more immediate predecessors, Ronald Reagan embraced the free market as an aspirational ideal. Unlike some, however, Reagan delivered the gospel of free markets as unalloyed good news. The neoconservatives who had joined the Reagan coalition could manage only "two cheers for capitalism," but Reaganism had little room for "ambivalent capitalism." The Reaganite George Gilder denounced the "dismal science of permanent poverty" and the Brahmin contempt for the vulgarities of a commercial culture that he saw at the heart of twentieth-century liberalism. Instead he celebrated "the miracle of human creativity" that could be unleashed through a combination of tax cuts and deregulation.[8] As the future

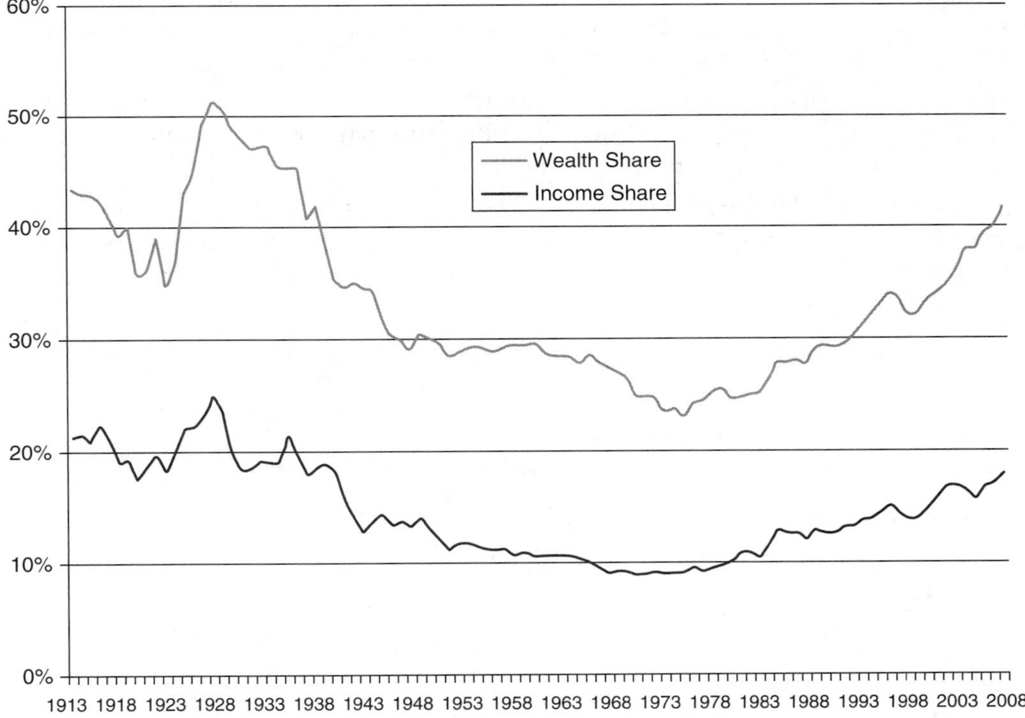

FIGURE 11-3 Share of Total Income and Total Wealth by Top 1% of Wealth Holders, 1913–2012.

8 George Gilder, *Wealth and Poverty* (New York: Basic Books, 1981), 5, 260, 268. Cf., Irving Kristol, *Two Cheers for Capitalism* (New York: Basic Books, 1978).

chairman of the Council of Economic Advisors concluded, "one of the most important achievements of the Reagan program has been a very considerable influence on the range of economic policies that are considered respectable."[9] Conservatives no longer positioned themselves as the dour "tax collectors for the welfare state," but rather as advocates of entrepreneurship and preachers of limited government. Economic conservatism (or "neoliberalism," as similar views were known in Europe) increasingly set the terms of debate.

The rise of free-market arguments was paralleled by the decline in obvious alternatives. By the 1980s, the bloom was largely off the communist rose. The economic miracles claimed by Soviet leaders were increasingly revealed as mirages, and the final collapse of the Soviet Union seemed to expose the failings of the Soviet economic system as much as anything. At the same time, the robust welfare states of Europe appeared to be unsustainable. The Tory Margaret Thatcher of England became the model rather than the Socialist François Mitterrand of France. Japan's deep and lengthy recession in the 1990s put on the shelf the model of managed capitalism that was thought to characterize "Japan, Inc." The "Washington consensus" of "market fundamentalism" often seemed to be the only game in town for both the developed and the developing world.

The conversation changed after the financial collapse of 2008. The deregulatory spirit of the Reagan years was put on the defensive. Alternatives to "market fundamentalism" won a new hearing. The value of a well-integrated global economy was cast into doubt. Simmering concerns about income inequality, which as Figure 11-3 indicates had been on the rise since the early 1980s, were put on the front burner. Where such debates go remains to be seen, but the confident neoliberalism of the last years of the twentieth century no longer claims the same political and intellectual dominance that it once did.

---

9 Michael J. Boskin, *Reagan and the U.S. Economy* (San Francisco, CA: International Center for Economic Growth, 1987), 10.

RICHARD A. POSNER

THE ECONOMICS OF JUSTICE (1981)

Richard Posner was born in New York City. Upon graduating from Harvard Law School in 1962, he worked as a law clerk for Justice William Brennan on the U.S. Supreme Court, a leader of the liberal wing of the Warren Court. Posner has spent most of his academic career at the University of Chicago Law School, where he became the leader of the emerging field of law and economics, which sought to apply economic analysis to legal doctrine and institutions. In 1981, he was appointed by President Ronald Reagan to a federal circuit court seat in Chicago, where he established himself as one of the most influential judges of the last quarter century. He has generally argued for a pragmatic approach to the law, and although generally regarded as a political conservative his positions are idiosyncratic. His book on the economics of justice argued on behalf of societal wealth maximization as the goal that ought to be pursued by political institutions and policies.

How does Posner's approach to justice compare with that offered by John Rawls? Does wealth maximization offer a distinctive approach to social ethics? Why should we value wealth maximization as a goal? How does wealth maximization help us resolve ethical dilemmas? Are property rights valuable?

. . .

What makes so many moral philosophers queasy about utilitarianism is that it seems to invite gross invasions of individual liberty. . . . But uncompromising insistence on individual liberty or autonomy regardless of the consequences for the happiness or utility of the people of the society seems equally misplaced and unacceptable. . . . The ethics of wealth maximization can be viewed as a blend of these rival philosophical traditions. Wealth is positively correlated, although imperfectly so, with utility, but the pursuit of wealth, based as it is on the model of the voluntary market transaction, involves greater respect for individual choice than in classical utilitarianism.

Compare . . . the man who is willing to pay $10,000 for a necklace with the man who has no money but is willing to incur a nonpecuniary disutility equivalent to that of giving up such a sum. The position of the first man is morally superior because he seeks to increase his welfare by conferring a benefit on another, namely the owner. Moreover, the buyer's $10,000 was in all likelihood accumulated through productive activity—that is, activity beneficial to other people besides himself, whether to his employer, customers, or his father's customers. If we assume that a person's income is less than the total value of his production, it follows that productive individual puts into society more than he takes out of it. Hence, not only does the buyer in our example confer a net benefit on the owner of the necklace . . . but at every stage in the accumulation of that money through productive activity, net benefits were conferred on other people besides the producer. The thief, in contrast, provides no benefit to the owner of the necklace or to anyone else. His "claim" to the necklace, which the utilitarian would honor, is based on a faculty—the capacity to experience pleasure—that may be worth nothing to other people. . . .

. . . But not all thefts are of this type. Consider [the] example of the person lost in the woods who breaks into an empty cabin and steals food that he must have to live. The cost of transacting with the owner would be prohibitive, and the theft is wealth maximizing because the food is worth in a strict economic sense to the thief than to the owner. It follows not that the thief should go unpunished in this case . . . but only that the punishment should be set at a level that deters stealing *unless* it is wealth maximizing. In contrast, if theft never had social value, the size of the penalty would be limited only by the costs of imposing it.

. . .

. . . [T]he wealth-maximization principle encourages and rewards the traditional "Calvinist" or "Protestant" virtues and capacities associated with economic progress. It may be doubted whether the happiness principle also implies the same constellation of virtues and capacities, especially given the degree of self-denial implicit in adherence to them. Utilitarians would have to give capacity for enjoyment, self-indulgence, and other hedonistic and epicurean values at least equal emphasis with diligence and honesty, which the utilitarian values only because they tend to increase wealth and hence *might* increase happiness.

Wealth maximization is a more defensible moral principle also in that it provides a firmer foundation for a theory of distributive and corrective justice. It has been argued that the source of rights exchanged in a market economy is itself necessarily external to the wealth-maximization principle. In fact the principle ordains the creation of a system of personal and property rights that ideally would extend to *all* valued things that are scarce—not only real and personal property but the human body and even ideas. Sometimes, to be sure, these rights have to be qualified because of the costs of protecting them . . . or because of transaction costs or because of the problems of conflicting use. . . . Nonetheless, the commitment of the economic approach to the principle of rights is stronger than that of most utilitarians—or, for that matter, of those Kantians who allow redistributive concerns to override property rights.

To many students of moral philosophy rights and economics seem incompatible concepts, but they are not. The theory of property rights is an important branch of modern microeconomic theory. A property right, in both law and economics, is a right to exclude everyone else from the use of some scarce resource. . . . The fact that the right cannot be extinguished or transferred without the owner's consent makes it absolute.

Absolute rights play an important role in the economic theory of the law. The economist recommends the creation of such rights . . . when the costs of voluntary transactions are low. . . . But when transaction costs are prohibitive, the recognition of absolute rights are inefficient. Hence I do not have an absolute property right against sound waves that penetrate my house or air pollution that deposits dirt on its window sills. . . . [In such examples] transaction costs preclude the use of voluntary transactions to thus move resources, and alternative allocative mechanisms to property rights must be found—such as liability rules, eminent domain, or zoning.

To make property rights, although absolute, contingent on transaction costs and subservient or instrumental to the goal of wealth maximization is to give rights less status than many "rights theorists" claim for them. . . . [T]hese rights are not transcendental or ends in themselves, and they operate, in general, only in settings of low transaction costs. Nevertheless, they are rights in a perfectly good sense of the term. . . .

. . .

NATIONAL CONFERENCE OF CATHOLIC BISHOPS

ECONOMIC JUSTICE FOR ALL (1986)

The religious right, prominently including evangelical Protestants, generally lined up in support of the economic as well as the social philosophy of the Reagan administration. The Moral Majority's Jerry Falwell argued that the "free enterprise system is clearly outlined in the Book of Proverbs in the Bible."[10] By contrast, the free-market economic principles of the new conservative movement were central to the opposition mobilized by the religious left. The landmark 1986 pastoral letter by the National Conference of Catholic Bishops became a central document in Catholic social teaching and a highly visible public rebuke to the Reagan administration.

Is there a distinctively religious perspective on political economy offered in the letter? Do the Catholic bishops have a particular authority to speak on economic issues? Are economic policies best judged "in light of what they do for the poor"? What does the "sacredness" of human beings imply for economics? What does economic justice require? Is economic inequality a particular concern in the letter?

...

Every perspective on economic life that is human, moral, and Christian must be shaped by three questions: What does the economy do *for* people? What does it do *to* people? And how do people *participate* in it? The economy is a human reality: men and women working together to develop and care for the whole of God's creation. All this work must serve the material and spiritual well-being of people. It influences what people hope for themselves and their loved ones. It affects the way they act together in society. If influences their very faith in God.

...

The quality of the national discussion about our economic future will affect the poor most of all, in this country and throughout the world. The life and dignity of millions of men, women, and children hang in the balance. Decisions must be judged in light of what they do *for* the poor, what they do *to* the poor, and what they enable the poor to do *for themselves*. The fundamental moral criterion for all economic decisions, policies, and institutions is this: They must be at the service of *all people, especially the poor.*

...

The basis for all that the Church believes about the moral dimensions of economic life is its vision of the transcendent worth—the sacredness—of human beings. The dignity of the human person, realized in community with others, is the criterion against which all aspects of economic life must be measured. All human beings, therefore, are ends to be served by the institutions that make up the economy, not means to be exploited for more narrowly defined goals. Human personhood must be respected with a reverence that is religious. . . . Similarly, all economic institutions must support the bonds of community and solidarity that are essential to the dignity of persons. Wherever our economic arrangements fail to conform to the demands of human dignity lived in community, they must be questioned and transformed. . . .

...

. . . Catholic social teaching, like much philosophical reflection, distinguishes three dimensions of basic justice: commutative justice, distributive justice, and social justice.

Commutative justice calls for fundamental fairness in all agreements and exchanges between individuals or private social groups. It demands respect for the equal human dignity of all persons in economic transactions, contracts, or promises. For example, workers owe their employers diligent work in exchange for

10 Jerry Falwell, *Listen, America!* (Garden City, NY: Doubleday, 1980), 13.

their wages. Employers are obligated to treat their employees as persons, paying them fair wages in exchange for the work done and establishing conditions and patterns of work that are truly human.

Distributive justice requires that the allocation of income, wealth, and power in society be evaluated in light of its effects on persons whose basic material needs are unmet. The Second Vatican Council stated: "The right to have a share of earthly goods sufficient for oneself and one's family belongs to everyone. . . . [W]e are obliged to come to the relief of the poor and to do so not merely out of superfluous goods." Minimum material resources are an absolute necessity for human life. If persons are to be recognized as members of the human community, then the community has an obligation to help fulfill these basic needs unless an absolute scarcity of resources makes this strictly impossible. . . .

Justice also has implications for the way the larger social, economic, and political institutions of society are organized. *Social justice implies that persons have an obligation to be active and productive participants in the life of society and that society has a duty to enable them to participate in this way.* This form of justice can be called "contributive," for it stresses the duty of all who are able to help create the goods, services, and other nonmaterial or spiritual values necessary for the welfare of the whole community. . . .

. . .

Economic conditions that leave large numbers of able people unemployed, underemployed, or employed in dehumanizing conditions fail to meet the converging demands of these three forms of basic justice. Work with adequate pay for all who seek it is the primary means for achieving basic justice in our society. . . .

Basic justice also calls for the establishment a floor of material well-being on which all can stand. . . .

. . . The concentration of privilege that exists today results far more from institutional relationships that distribute power and wealth inequitably than from differences in talent or lack of desire to work. These institutional patterns must be examined and revised if we are to meet the demands of basic justice. . . .

. . . There is certainly room for diversity of opinion in the Church and in U.S. society on *how* to protect the human dignity and economic rights of all our brothers and sisters. In our view, however, there can be no legitimate disagreement on the basic moral requirements.

. . .

The nation's founders took daring steps to create structures of participation, mutual accountability, and widely distributed power to ensure the political rights and freedoms of all. We believe that similar steps are needed today to expand economic participation, broaden the sharing of economic power, and make economic decisions more accountable to the common good. . . .

. . .

BILL CLINTON

REMARKS TO THE INTERNATIONAL BUSINESS COMMUNITY (1994)

William Jefferson ("Bill") Clinton was raised in modest circumstances in small-town Arkansas, attending the University of Oxford as a Rhodes Scholar and graduating from Yale Law School in 1973. He built a political career in Arkansas, becoming a leader of the "New Democrats" who urged the Democratic Party to shift to the right after the success of Ronald Reagan and to build a more centrist political coalition that could appeal to suburban voters. He won the presidency in 1992, when a central message of his campaign (in the words of his campaign advisor) was "the economy, stupid." His two terms as president were characterized by stable economic growth and an economic policy focused on support for economic globalization and fiscal restraint. Shortly after the midterm elections, when the Democrats lost control of the House of Representatives for the first time since the Eisenhower administration, President Clinton made a well-publicized trip to Jakarta, Indonesia, to attend a summit of the newly formed Asia-Pacific Economic Cooperation (APEC) forum, which promotes free trade on the Pacific Rim, and to finalize agreements on a host of lucrative joint business deals between the United States and Indonesia. The administration decoupled economic trade and cooperation from human rights concerns, arguing that "commercial engagement" would eventually result in improvements to the human rights record of Asian trading partners.

How big of a departure is the economic philosophy articulated by Clinton from that offered by Franklin Roosevelt? To what degree should government be in a "partnership" with business? Is free trade a matter of principle or a matter of pragmatism? Should the United States seek to "impose our vision of the world on others"? Is it consistent with American values to engage in economic cooperation with governments with a poor human rights record? On what basis does Clinton defend increasing economic ties with autocratic regimes?

. . .

Keeping America on the front lines of economic opportunity has been my first priority since I took office. We are pursuing a strategy to promote aggressive growth in the short run and in the long run. We began by putting our house in order. Our deficit was exploding; the public debt in America had quadrupled between 1981 and 1993. Now we're looking at a reduction in the deficit for the third year in a row. . . . Federal spending is the lowest it's been in more than a decade. We cut domestic and defense spending last year for the first time in 25 years. And the Federal work force is shrinking to its lowest level since President Kennedy was in office.

The second thing we are doing is working hard to expand trade and investment. That's what NAFTA was all about. That's what the GATT agreement is all about. . . .

The third thing we're working to do is to develop a system of lifelong learning for our people, from expanding preschool programs like Head Start to providing more affordable college education to our people, to changing the whole unemployment system in America to a continuous retraining system for people who must find new jobs in a rapidly changing global economy.

Lastly, we're trying to change the way our Government works. . . . There was, I think, a perception among American businesses when we took office that both parties, historically, were wrong in their approach to business, looking to the future, not to the past; that the Democratic Party sometimes tended to see the relationship between business and Government as adversarial and the Republican Party sometimes seemed to be philosophically committed to being inactive on the theory that anything the

Government did with the private sector would probably make things worse.

In a world in which all economics is global as well as local, clearly the important thing is partnership, efficiency, and good judgment. We have deregulated our banking and interstate trucking industries. We have changed our whole way of purchasing things in the Government. We have invested more in defense conversion and new technologies, in partnerships with the private sector. We have deregulated our relationships with our own local governments, permitting States to pursue their own reforms in health care and education and, most importantly, in changing our welfare system.

But perhaps over the long run the most significant thing we have done is to reorganize the way we relate to the private sector, requiring all of our departments to work together and to look outward in partnership. The key to making this strategy work is erasing the dividing line between domestic and foreign economics, between, therefore, domestic and foreign policy.

. . .

But the success of this ultimately rests on what our private sector does, on the productivity of our workers, the skill of our management, our continuing commitment to investment, to technologies, to enterprise, and to outreach.

. . .

Let me also say that I'm very often asked by our press, and sometimes by the global press as I travel around the world, whether or not our pursuit of economic engagement undermines our commitment to human rights throughout the world. And I have said many times, I will say again, I think it supports our commitment to human rights throughout the world. . . .

We do not seek to impose our vision of the world on others. Indeed, we continue to struggle with our own inequities and our own shortcomings. We recognize that in a world and in a region of such diverse and disparate cultures, where nations are at different stages of development, no single model for organizing society is possible or even desirable. And we respect the tremendous efforts being made throughout this region to meet the basic needs of people in all these countries.

At the same time, we remain convinced that strengthening the ties of trade among nations can help to break down chains of repression, that as societies become more open economically, they also become more open politically. It becomes in no one's interest to depress the legitimate aspirations and energies, the hopes, the dreams, and the voices of the many people who make up all of our nations. Commerce does tend to open more closed societies. . . .

. . .

Our Nation has sacrificed many of our sons and daughters for the cause of freedom around the world in this century. So we are moved and we will continue to be moved by the struggle for basic rights. But I will say again, even though we will continue to promote human rights with conviction and without apology, we reject the notion that increasing economic ties in trade and partnerships undermine our human rights agenda. We believe they advance together and that they must.

. . .

This is a remarkable time. And I am convinced that the increasing freedom of economic activity, rooted in your commitment to invest, your commitment to risk, your commitment to think and imagine and visualize what you might do and to mobilize human resources in this cause, is an absolutely pivotal part of continuing the march of freedom.

. . .

MICHAEL ALBERT

BEYOND CLASS RULE IS PARECON (2012)

An activist in Students for a Democratic Society (SDS) as an undergraduate at the Massachusetts Institute of Technology in the 1960s, Michael Albert became an important writer and editor in radical politics. In the 1970s, he helped found South End Press, which quickly became a leading publisher of books by scholars and activists on the political left. In the 1980s, he left to form *Z Magazine*, which focuses on left-wing politics and economics. Since the collapse of the Soviet Union, Albert has been the primary proponent of "participatory economics" (or "parecon") as an alternative to both capitalism and communism (or centrally planned socialism). Parecon would replace an economic system of money, prices, and property with a system of local, democratic councils that would jointly determine what should be produced and consumed and that would allocate goods based on the level of effort exerted by workers. Ultimately, "an economy should produce, allocate, and consume in ways that further people's values."[11] His ideas on political economy were a significant influence on the Occupy Wall Street movement.

What does Albert mean by a "solidarity economy"? How does he think economic institutions should be assessed? How does Albert's economic vision compare with the one laid out by the National Conference of Bishops? Should democratic values be applied to the workplace? What would a democratic economy look like? Is parecon more consistent with liberal values than a market economy? Should wealth maximization be sacrificed for the sake of "self-management"? Is some form of decentralized socialism the proper goal to pursue?

. . .

In contrast to the capitalist rat race, a good economy should be a solidarity economy generating sociality rather than anti-social greed. A good economy's institutions for production, consumption, and allocation should, therefore, by the roles they offer, propel even anti-social people into having to address other people's well-being if they are to advance their own well-being. . . .

. . .

Our second value has to do with the options people encounter in their economic lives. Capitalist market rhetoric trumpets opportunity but capitalist market discipline curtails satisfaction and development by replacing what is human and caring with what is commercial, profitable, and in accord with existing hierarchies of power and wealth. . . . We get Pepsi and Coke but we do not get soda that takes into account the well-being of soda producers, soda consumers, or the environment. The tremendous variety of tastes, preferences, and choices that humans naturally display are truncated by capitalism into conformist patterns imposed by advertising. . . .

Capitalism overwhelmingly rewards property and bargaining power. It says those who own productive property deserve profits based on the productivity of that property. . . .

Obviously real fairness entails eliminating the property and power roads to well-being. But, more positively, equitable economic institutions should not only not obstruct equity, they should propel it.

. . .

. . . [T]o be equitable, remuneration should be for effort and sacrifice in producing socially desired items.

If I work longer, in this view, I should get more reward. If I work harder, I should get more reward. And if I work in worse condition and at more onerous tasks, I should get more reward. However, I should not get ore for having better tools, or for producing something that happens to be valued more highly, or for having innate highly productive talents. Nor should I get more even for the output of learned skills. . . .

---

11 Michael Albert, *Parecon: Life after Capitalism* (New York: Verso Books, 2003), 20.

. . .

In capitalism, owners have tremendous say. Managers and high-level lawyers, engineers, financial officers, and doctors—each of whom monopolize empowering work and daily decision-making positions—are part of what we have called the coordinator class and have substantial say. However, people doing rote and obedient labor rarely even know what decisions are being made, much less influence them.

In contrast, we want a good economy to be a richly democratic economy where people have control over their own lives consistent with others doing likewise. . . .

. . .

What we hope to accomplish when we choose among all possible institutional means of discussing issues, setting agendas, sharing information, and, finally, making decisions, is that each person influences decisions in proportion to the degree he or she is affected by them. And that is our fourth participatory economic value, economic self-management.

. . .

Workers and consumers need a place to express their preferences if they are to self-manage their economic actions as our values advocate. Historically, when workers and consumers have attempted to seize control of their own lives, they have invariably created workers and consumers councils. This is true in a participatory economy as well. . . .

. . .

. . . [W]ho decides how hard we have worked? Clearly our workers councils decide—our fellow workers. . . .

. . .

In a parecon there won't be someone doing only surgery and someone else only cleaning bed pans. Instead people who do surgery will also help clean the hospital and perform other tasks so that the sum of all that they do incorporates a fair mix of conditions and responsibilities, and likewise for the person who used to only clean rooms.

. . .

. . . In participatory planning, worker and consumer councils propose their work activities and their consumption preferences in light of continually updated knowledge of the personal, local, and national implications of the full social benefits and costs of their choices.

. . .

Workers and consumers indicate in their councils their personal and group preferences. I say I want such and such. My workplace settles on a proposal that we wish to produce. We learn what preferences others have indicated as they learn ours. They, and we, alter and resubmit our preferences—keeping in mind the need to balance a personally fulfilling pattern of work and consumption with the requirements of a viable overall plan. . . . New information leads to new submissions in a sequence of cooperatively negotiated refinements, until settling on a plan.

. . .

VI. AMERICA AND THE WORLD

Major Developments

- Collapse of Soviet Union and Eastern bloc
- Rise of militant Islamist movement

The United States faced a transition in how it related to the world at the turn of the twenty-first century. When Ronald Reagan entered the White House, his administration saw communism and the Soviet threat as the defining feature of American foreign policy. The American relationship to the developing world was largely understood through the lens of U.S.–Soviet relations. The Cold War that had been self-consciously cooled off in the 1970s heated up again in the 1980s, only to come to a sudden end. The rapid collapse of the Soviet Union and the broader Eastern bloc suddenly made the Cold War framework for thinking about the world less useful and left the United States in an unaccustomed position on the world stage. Over the course of the Cold War, the United States had come to be seen and to see itself as one of two "superpowers" that competed to shape geopolitics. With the decline of the traditional great powers of Europe after World War II and the increasing reliance of the democratic industrial world on the American defense apparatus, a "bipolar" world divided between the "First World" of the West and the "Second World" of the communist states was locked into place. With the fall of the Berlin Wall in 1989, the United States was suddenly confronted with the possibility of being the sole remaining superpower. Addressing the United Nations in 1990, President George H. W. Bush looked forward to "a new world order and a long era of peace."[12] Some began to look forward to a fiscal "peace dividend" as the United States could finally demobilize the military forces that it had maintained since the bombing of Pearl Harbor. Others argued that the United States had an indispensable role to play in a new unipolar world.

Ironically, at the same time that the first President Bush was trying to develop a vision for a post-Cold War world, the United States found itself pulled into a war in the Middle East. In November 1989, the Berlin Wall fell, symbolizing the end of the division of Europe into hostile camps. Less than twelve months later, Iraq invaded Kuwait, putting troops on the doorstep of Saudi Arabia. For the elder Bush, the new world order ushered in by the events of 1989 made space for the emergence of "international collective security" that could repudiate "unprovoked aggression" and isolate aggressors and human rights violators like Iraq as rogue states. With the conclusion of "cold war's battle of ideas," the "epic battle" ahead was of the "civilized world" against those who would prefer to reside in the "Dark Ages." The attack on the World Trade Center in 2001 seemed to heighten the danger of a lawless and anarchic world. For President George W. Bush the actions of Islamic terrorists were on the same footing as the earlier actions of the secular Iraqi state, and both pitted the forces of civilization against the forces of "barbarism," the global community of nations against those who would deploy "inhumane weapons" against civilians.[13] To President George W. Bush, the United States had a new mission in the twenty-first century: "To answer these attacks and rid the world of evil."[14]

---

12 George Bush, "Address before the 45th Session of the United Nations General Assembly, October 1, 1990," in *Public Papers of the Presidents of the United States* (Washington, D.C.: Government Printing Office, 1991).

13 Bush, "United Nations Address," in *Public Papers of the Presidents of the United States* (Washington, D.C.: Government Printing Office, 1991); George W. Bush, "Remarks on Arrival at the White House and an Exchange with Reporters, September 16, 2001," in *Public Papers of the Presidents of the United States* (Washington, D.C.: Government Printing Office, 2002).

14 George W. Bush, "Remarks at the National Day of Prayer and Remembrance Service, September 14, 2001," in *Public Papers of the Presidents of the United States* (Washington, D.C.: Government Printing Office, 2002).

JEANE J. KIRKPATRICK

DICTATORSHIPS AND DOUBLE STANDARDS (1979)

Jeane Jordan was raised in the Depression-era Midwest and completed an M.A. in political science at Columbia University in 1950. In the 1950s, she worked for the State Department and married a colleague, Evron Kirkpatrick. In the 1960s, she completed her Ph.D. at Columbia and joined the faculty of Georgetown University. Her scholarly work was wide-ranging, but she became active in Democratic Party politics, urging a harder line on foreign policy. She was pulled into Ronald Reagan's 1980 presidential campaign as a foreign policy advisor, and in 1981 she was named the first female U.S. ambassador to the United Nations, returning to academia in 1985. Her most notable contribution to public discourse was her 1979 article in the neoconservative journal *Commentary* (later expanded into a book), which significantly affected conservative thinking about foreign policy in the 1980s. Characterized as the "Kirkpatrick Doctrine," she argued that traditional dictatorships were preferable, both for their own populations and for American national interests, to communist totalitarian states. As a consequence, she urged American policymakers to support even dictatorial governments against left-wing revolutionary movements.

Why does Kirkpatrick favor autocratic leaders over communist governments? Are there significant differences between different styles or ideological orientations of dictatorships? Is it ever consistent with American values and interests to support nondemocratic regimes? Under what circumstances should the United States support an incumbent dictator over a revolutionary movement? In more recent years, is it preferable for the United States to support a secular dictator over an Islamic insurgency? Under what conditions should the United States be willing to support revolutionary movements in other countries?

The failure of the Carter administration's foreign policy is now clear to everyone except its architects, and even they must entertain private doubts, from time to time, about a policy whose crowning achievement has been to lay the groundwork for a transfer of the Panama Canal from the United States to a swaggering Latin dictator of Castroite bent. In the thirty-odd months since the inauguration of Jimmy Carter as President there has occurred a dramatic Soviet military buildup, matched by the stagnation of American armed forces, and a dramatic extension of Soviet influence in the Horn of Africa, Afghanistan, Southern Africa, and the Caribbean, matched by a declining American position in all these areas. The U.S. has never tried so hard and failed so utterly to make and keep friends in the Third World.

. . .

[E]ven though Iran was rich, blessed with a product the U.S. and its allies needed badly, and led by a handsome king, while Nicaragua was poor and rocked along under a long-tenure president of less striking aspect, there were many similarities between the two countries and our relations with them. Both these small nations were led by men who had not been selected by free elections, who recognized no duty to submit themselves to searching tests of popular acceptability. Both did tolerate limited opposition, including opposition newspapers and political parties, but both were also confronted by radical, violent opponents bent on social and political revolution. Both rulers, therefore, sometimes invoked martial law to arrest, imprison, exile, and occasionally, it was alleged, torture their opponents. Both relied for public order on police forces whose personnel were said to be too harsh, too arbitrary, and too powerful. Each had what the American press termed "private armies," which is to say, armies pledging their allegiance to the ruler rather than the "constitution" or the "nation" or some other impersonal entity.

In short, both Somoza and the Shah were, in central ways, traditional rulers of semi-traditional societies. Although the Shah very badly wanted to create a technologically modern and powerful nation and Somoza tried hard to introduce modern agricultural methods, neither sought to reform his society in the light of any abstract idea of social justice or political virtue. Neither attempted to alter significantly the distribution of goods, status, or power (though the democratization of education and skills that accompanied modernization in Iran did result in some redistribution of money and power there).

Both Somoza and the Shah enjoyed long tenure, large personal fortunes (much of which were no doubt appropriated from general revenues), and good relations with the United States. The Shah and Somoza were not only anti-Communist, they were positively friendly to the U.S., sending their sons and others to be educated in our universities, voting with us in the United Nations, and regularly supporting American interests and positions even when these entailed personal and political cost. . . .

. . .

But once an attack was launched by opponents bent on destruction, everything changed. The rise of serious, violent opposition in Iran and Nicaragua set in motion a succession of events which bore a suggestive resemblance to one another and a suggestive similarity to our behavior in China before the fall of Chiang Kai-shek, in Cuba before the triumph of Castro, in certain crucial periods of the Vietnamese war, and, more recently, in Angola. In each of these countries, the American effort to impose liberalization and democratization on a government confronted with violent internal opposition not only failed, but actually assisted the coming to power of new regimes in which ordinary people enjoy fewer freedoms and less personal security than under the previous autocracy—regimes, moreover, hostile to American interests and policies.

. . .

[Whether through resignation or defeat of the incumbent leader], the U.S. will have been led by its own misunderstanding of the situation to assist actively in deposing an erstwhile friend and ally and installing a government hostile to American interests and policies in the world. At best we will have lost access to friendly territory. At worst the Soviets will have gained a new base. And everywhere our friends will have noted that the U.S. cannot be counted on in times of difficulty and our enemies will have observed that American support provides no security against the forward march of history.

. . .

Yet despite all the variations, the Carter administration brought to the crises in Iran and Nicaragua several common assumptions each of which played a major role in hastening the victory of even more repressive dictatorships than had been in place before. These were, first, the belief that there existed at the moment of crisis a democratic alternative to the incumbent government: second, the belief that the continuation of the status quo was not possible; third, the belief that any change, including the establishment of a government headed by self-styled Marxist revolutionaries, was preferable to the present government. Each of these beliefs was (and is) widely shared in the liberal community generally. Not one of them can withstand close scrutiny.

Although most governments in the world are, as they always have been, autocracies of one kind or another, no idea holds greater sway in the mind of educated Americans than the belief that it is possible to democratize governments, anytime, anywhere, under any circumstances. This notion is belied by an enormous body of evidence based on the experience of dozens of countries which have attempted with more or less (usually less) success to move from autocratic to democratic government. . . .

. . .

In the relatively few places where they exist, democratic governments have come into being slowly, after extended prior experience with more limited forms of participation during which leaders have reluctantly grown accustomed to tolerating dissent and opposition, opponents have accepted the notion that they may defeat but not destroy incumbents, and people have become aware of government's effects on their lives and of their own possible effects on government. Decades, if not centuries, are normally required for people to acquire the necessary disciplines and habits. . . .

Although there is no instance of a revolutionary "socialist" or Communist society being democratized, right-wing autocracies do sometimes evolve into democracies—given time, propitious economic, social, and political circumstances, talented leaders, and a strong indigenous demand for representative government. Something of the kind is in progress on the Iberian peninsula and the first steps have been taken in Brazil. Something similar could conceivably have also occurred in Iran and Nicaragua if contestation and participation had been more gradually expanded.

. . .

So far, assisting "change" has not led the Carter administration to undertake the destabilization of a *Communist* country. The principles of self-determination and nonintervention are thus both selectively applied. We seem to accept the *status quo* in Communist nations (in the name of "diversity" and national autonomy), but not in nations ruled by "right-wing" dictators or white oligarchies. . . .

. . .

. . . Traditional autocracies are, in general and in their very nature, deeply offensive to modern American sensibilities. The notion that public affairs should be ordered on the basis of kinship, friendship, and other personal relations rather than on the basis of objective "rational" standards violates our conception of justice and efficiency. The preference for stability rather than change is also disturbing to Americans whose whole national experience rests on the principles of change, growth, and progress. The extremes of wealth and poverty characteristic of traditional societies also offend us, the more so since the poor are usually very poor and bound to their squalor by a hereditary allocation of role. Moreover, the relative lack of concern of rich, comfortable rulers for the poverty, ignorance, and disease of "their" people is likely to be interpreted by Americans as moral dereliction pure and simple. The truth is that Americans can hardly bear such societies and such rulers. Confronted with them, our vaunted cultural relativism evaporates and we become as censorious as Cotton Mather confronting sin in New England.

. . .

The foreign policy of the Carter administration fails not for lack of good intentions but for lack of realism about the nature of traditional versus revolutionary autocracies and the relation of each to the American national interest. Only intellectual fashion and the tyranny of Right/Left thinking prevent intelligent men of good will from perceiving the *facts* that traditional authoritarian governments are less repressive than revolutionary autocracies, that they are more susceptible of liberalization, and that they are more compatible with U.S. interests. The evidence on all these points is clear enough.

. . .

[A] posture of continuous self-abasement and apology *vis-a-vis* the Third World is neither morally necessary nor politically appropriate. No more is it necessary or appropriate to support vocal enemies of the United States because they invoke the rhetoric of popular liberation. It is not even necessary or appropriate for our leaders to forswear unilaterally the use of military force to counter military force. Liberal idealism need not be identical with masochism, and need not be incompatible with the defense of freedom and the national interest.

SAMUEL P. HUNTINGTON

THE CLASH OF CIVILIZATIONS? (1993)

Raised in New York City, Samuel Huntington earned his Ph.D. in government in 1951 from Harvard University. He then spent most of his career at Harvard, becoming one of the most influential political scientists of his generation. He was a founder of the journal *Foreign Policy* and a frequent advisor to the federal government and Democratic politicians. His work was wide-ranging but often focused on national security issues and the politics of the developing world. His greatest public notoriety came with the publication of his article on the "clash of civilizations," subsequently expanded into a book. In contrast to Francis Fukuyama's argument that the end of the Cold War marked the ideological triumph of liberalism, Huntington argued that post-Cold War conflicts would shift from ideological to cultural divides. Rather than a bipolar conflict between communism and liberalism, or a series of merely national conflicts, future conflict would revolve around tensions between the several major cultures of the world.

What does Huntington mean by "cultural"? Why does he expect cultural conflicts to be predominant in the future? How does the United States fit within Huntington's "civilizations"? Does the United States share basic interests with other Western countries? Are those interests distinct from their shared characteristics as liberal democracies or capitalist economies? Does the United States have a commitment to advancing a universal civilization? Should the United States embrace a kind of "human rights imperialism"?

. . .

It is my hypothesis that the fundamental source of conflict in this new world will not be primarily ideological or primarily economic. The great divisions among humankind and the dominating source of conflict will be cultural. Nation states will remain the most powerful actors in world affairs, but the principal conflicts of global politics will occur between nations and groups of different civilizations. The clash of civilizations will dominate global politics. The fault lines between civilizations will be the battle lines of the future.

Conflict between civilizations will be the latest phase in the evolution of conflict in the modern world. For a century and a half after the emergence of the modern international system with the Peace of Westphalia, the conflicts of the Western world were largely among princes—emperors, absolute monarchs and constitutional monarchs attempting to expand their bureaucracies, their armies, their mercantilist economic strength and, most important, the territory they ruled. In the process they created nation states, and beginning with the French Revolution the principal lines of conflict were between nations rather than princes. . . . This nineteenth-century pattern lasted until the end of World War I. Then, as a result of the Russian Revolution and the reaction against it, the conflict of nations yielded to the conflict of ideologies, first among communism, fascism-Nazism and liberal democracy, and then between communism and liberal democracy. During the Cold War, this latter conflict became embodied in the struggle between the two superpowers, neither of which was a nation state in the classical European sense and each of which defined its identity in terms of its ideology.

These conflicts between princes, nation states and ideologies were primarily conflicts within Western civilization. . . . With the end of the Cold War, international politics moves out of its Western phase, and its centerpiece becomes the interaction between the West and non-Western civilizations and among non-Western civilizations. In the politics of civilizations, the peoples and governments of non-Western civilizations no longer remain the objects of history as targets of Western colonialism but join the West as movers and shapers of history.

. . .

. . . A civilization is thus the highest cultural grouping of people and the broadest level of cultural identity people have short of that which distinguishes humans from other species. It is defined both by common objective elements, such as language, history, religion, customs, institutions, and by the subjective self-identification of people. . . .

. . .

Westerners tend to think of nation states as the principal actors in global affairs. They have been that, however, for only a few centuries. The broader reaches of human history have been the history of civilizations. . . .

Civilization identity will be increasingly important in the future, and the world will be shaped in large measure by the interactions among seven or eight major civilizations. These include Western, Confucian, Japanese, Islamic, Hindu, Slavic-Orthodox, Latin American and possibly African civilization. The most important conflicts of the future will occur along the cultural fault lines separating these civilizations from one another.

Why will this be the case?

First, differences among civilizations are not only real; they are basic. Civilizations are differentiated from each other by history, language, culture, tradition and, most important, religion. . . . They are far more fundamental than differences among political ideologies and political regimes. Differences do not necessarily mean conflict, and conflict does not necessarily mean violence. Over the centuries, however, differences among civilizations have generated the most prolonged and the most violent conflicts.

Second, the world is becoming a smaller place. The interactions between peoples of different civilizations are increasing; these increasing interactions intensify civilization consciousness and awareness of differences between civilizations and commonalities within civilizations. . . .

Third, the processes of economic modernization and social change throughout the world are separating people from longstanding local identities. They also weaken the nation state as a source of identity. . . .

. . .

As people define their identity in ethnic and religious terms, they are likely to see an "us" versus "them" relation existing between themselves and people of different ethnicity or religion. The end of ideologically defined states in Eastern Europe and the former Soviet Union permits traditional ethnic identities and animosities to come to the fore. Differences in culture and religion create differences over policy issues, ranging from human rights to immigration to trade and commerce to the environment. . . .

The clash of civilizations thus occurs at two levels. At the micro-level, adjacent groups along the fault lines between civilizations struggle, often violently, over the control of territory and each other. At the macro-level, states from different civilizations compete for relative military and economic power, struggle over the control of international institutions and third parties, and competitively promote their particular political and religious values.

. . .

Conflict along the fault line between Western and Islamic civilizations has been going on for 1,300 years. . . .

This centuries-old military interaction between the West and Islam is unlikely to decline. It could become more virulent. The Gulf War left some Arabs feeling proud that Saddam Hussein had attacked Israel and stood up to the West. It also left many feeling humiliated and resentful of the West's military presence in the Persian Gulf, the West's overwhelming military dominance, and their apparent inability to shape their own destiny. Many Arab countries, in addition to the oil exporters, are reaching levels of economic and social development where autocratic forms of government become inappropriate and efforts to introduce democracy become stronger. Some openings in Arab political systems have already occurred. The principal beneficiaries of these openings have been Islamist movements. In the Arab world, in short, Western democracy strengthens anti-Western political forces. . . .

. . .

The West is now at an extraordinary peak of power in relation to other civilizations. Its superpower opponent has disappeared from the map. Military conflict among Western states is unthinkable, and

Western military power is unrivaled. Apart from Japan, the West faces no economic challenge. It dominates international political and security institutions and with Japan international economic institutions. Global political and security issues are effectively settled by a directorate of the United States, Britain and France, world economic issues by a directorate of the United States, Germany and Japan, all of which maintain extraordinarily close relations with each other to the exclusion of lesser and largely non-Western countries. Decisions made at the U.N. Security Council or in the International Monetary Fund that reflect the interests of the West are presented to the world as reflecting the desires of the world community. The very phrase "the world community" has become the euphemistic collective noun (replacing "the Free World") to give global legitimacy to actions reflecting the interests of the United States and other Western powers. . . .

. . .

That at least is the way in which non-Westerners see the new world, and there is a significant element of truth in their view. Differences in power and struggles for military, economic and institutional power are thus one source of conflict between the West and other civilizations. . . . Western concepts differ fundamentally from those prevalent in other civilizations. Western ideas of individualism, liberalism, constitutionalism, human rights, equality, liberty, the rule of law, democracy, free markets, the separation of church and state, often have little resonance in Islamic, Confucian, Japanese, Hindu, Buddhist or Orthodox cultures. Western efforts to propagate such ideas produce instead a reaction against "human rights imperialism" and a reaffirmation of indigenous values, as can be seen in the support for religious fundamentalism by the younger generation in non-Western cultures. The very notion that there could be a "universal civilization" is a Western idea, directly at odds with the particularism of most Asian societies and their emphasis on what distinguishes one people from another. . . .

. . .

NOAM CHOMSKY

UNDERSTANDING POWER (2002)

Raised in a middle-class Jewish family in Depression-era Philadelphia, Noam Chomsky was drawn to anarchism and socialism at an early age. He completed his Ph.D. in linguistics at the University of Pennsylvania in 1955 and began teaching at the Massachusetts Institute of Technology, where he has spent his academic career. In the 1960s, he published his path-breaking work in linguistic theory. By the late 1960s, however, he began to win a much more public audience for his political activism and political writings, beginning with antiwar protests. His political reputation and writings expanded in subsequent years, revolving around issues of foreign policy and global justice but extending to domestic politics and global capitalism as well. His book *Understanding Power* largely drew on a series of public discussions with political activists during the 1990s.

What does Chomsky thinks motivates American foreign policy? Why does he think that nationalism per se is a threat to perceived American interests? In what sense is the contemporary United States an "empire"? Does the United States have an interest in the economic development of other countries? Has Japan freed itself from "free-market discipline"? Should the United States encourage global economic cooperation? On what terms? Are American national interests best understood as economic, ideological, or something else?

Woman: Then is the basic goal of the United States when it intervenes in Third World countries to destroy left-wing governments in order to keep them from power?

No, the primary concern is to prevent *independence*, regardless of the ideology. Remember, we're the global power, so we have to make sure that all the various parts of the world continue serving their assigned functions in our global system. And the assigned functions of Third World countries are to be markets for American business, sources of resources for American business, to provide cheap labor for American business, and so on. I mean, there's no big secret about that—the media won't tell you and scholarship won't tell you, but all you have to do is look at declassified government documents and this is all explained very frankly and explicitly.

The internal documentary record in the United States goes way back, and it says the same thing over and over again. Here's virtually a quote: the main commitment of the United States, internationally in the Third World, must be to prevent the rise of nationalist regimes which are responsive to pressure form the masses of the population for improvement in low living standards and diversification of production; the reason is, we have to maintain a climate that is conducive to investment, and to ensure conditions which allow for adequate repatriation of profits to the West. Language like that is repeated year after year in top-level U.S. planning documents, like National Security Council reports on Latin America and so on—and that's exactly what we do around the world.

So the nationalism we oppose doesn't need to be *left-wing*—we're just as much opposed to *right-wing* nationalism. I mean, when there's a right-wing military coup which seeks to turn some Third World country on a course of independent development, the United States will also try to destroy that government. . . . So despite what you always hear, U.S. interventionism has nothing to do with resisting the spread of "Communism," it's *independence* we've always been opposed to everywhere—and for quite a good reason. If a country begins to pay attention to its own population, it's not going to be paying adequate attention to the overriding needs of U.S. investors. Well, those are unacceptable priorities, so that government's just going to have to go.

And the effects of this commitment throughout the Third World are dramatically clear: it takes only a moment's thought to realize that the areas that have been the most under U.S. control are some of the most horrible regions in the world. For instance, why is Central America such a horror-chamber? I mean, if a peasant in Guatemala woke up in Poland [i.e., under Soviet occupation], he'd think he was in heaven by comparison—and Guatemala's an area where we've had a hundred years of influence. Well, that tells you something. Or look at Brazil: potentially an extremely rich country with tremendous resources, except it had the curse of being part of the Western system of subordination. So in northeast Brazil, for example, which is a rather fertile area with plenty of rich land, just it's all owned by plantations, Brazilian medical researchers now identify the population as a new species with about 40 percent of the brain size of human beings, a result of generations of profound malnutrition and neglect. . . . Alright, that's a good example of the legacy of our commitments, and the same kind of pattern runs throughout former Western colonies.

In fact, if you look at the countries that have developed in the world, there's a simple fact which should be obvious to anyone on five minutes' observation, but which you never find anyone saying in the United States: every country that was colonized by the West is a total wreck. I mean, Japan was the one country that managed to resist European colonization, and it's the one part of the traditional Third World that developed. Okay, Europe conquered everything except Japan, and Japan developed. What does that tell you? . . .

But the point is, the Japanese-style development model works—in fact, it's how every country in the world that's developed has done it: by imposing high levels of protectionism, and by extricating its economy from free-market discipline. And that's precisely what the Western powers have been preventing the rest of the Third World from doing, right up to this moment.

. . .

. . . [I]f you ask, "Why have an empire?" . . . The empire is like every other part of social policy: it's a way for the poor to pay off the rich in their own society. So if the empire is just another form of social policy by which the poor are subsidizing the rich, that means that under democratic social planning, there would be very little incentive for it—let alone the obvious moral considerations that would become a factor at that point. In fact, all kinds of questions would just change, radically.

. . .

FOR FURTHER STUDY

Berman, Paul. *Terror and Liberalism* (New York: W.W. Norton, 2003).

Bloom, Allan D. *The Closing of the American Mind* (New York: Simon and Schuster, 1987).

Bookchin, Murray. *Post-Scarcity Anarchism*, 3rd ed. (Oakland, CA: AK Press, 2004).

Cole, David. *No Equal Justice: Race and Class in the American Criminal Justice System* (New York: New Press, 1999).

Gilder, George F. *Wealth and Poverty* (New York: Basic Books, 1981).

hooks, bell. *Ain't I a Woman: Black Women and Feminism* (Boston, MA: South End Press, 1981).

Krugman, Paul. *The Conscience of a Liberal* (New York: W.W. Norton, 2007).

Lind, Michael. *The Next American Nation: The New Nationalism and the Fourth American Revolution* (New York: Free Press, 1995).

Loury, Glenn C. *The Anatomy of Racial Inequality* (Cambridge, MA: Harvard University Press, 2002).

MacKinnon, Catharine A. *Feminism Unmodified: Discourses on Life and Law* (Cambridge, MA: Harvard University Press, 1987).

McKibben, Bill. *The End of Nature* (New York: Random House, 1989).

Morrison, Toni. *Playing in the Dark: Whiteness and the Literary Imagination* (Cambridge, MA: Harvard University Press, 1992).

Murray, Charles A. *Losing Ground: American Social Policy, 1950–1980* (New York: Basic Books, 1984).

Neuhaus, Richard John. *The Naked Public Square: Religion and Democracy in America* (Grand Rapids, MI: W.B. Eerdmans Publishing, 1984).

Reich, Robert B. *The Work of Nations: Preparing Ourselves for 21st Century Capitalism* (New York: Alfred A. Knopf, 1991).

Sandel, Michael J. *Democracy's Discontent: America in Search of a Public Philosophy* (Cambridge, MA: Harvard University Press, 1996).

Will, George F. *Statecraft as Soulcraft: What Government Does* (New York: Simon and Schuster, 1983).

Williams, Patricia J. *The Alchemy of Race and Rights* (Cambridge, MA: Harvard University Press, 1991).

Wills, Garry. *Under God: Religion and American Politics* (New York: Simon and Schuster, 1990).

Wilson, James Q., and Richard J. Hernstein. *Crime and Human Nature* (New York: Simon and Schuster, 1985).

SUGGESTED READINGS

Baker, Houston A. *Betrayal: How Black Intellectuals Have Abandoned the Ideals of the Civil Rights Era* (New York: Columbia University Press, 2008).

Courtwright, David T. *No Right Turn: Conservative Politics in a Liberal America* (Cambridge, MA: Harvard University Press, 2010).

Dawson, Michael C. *Black Visions: The Roots of Contemporary African-American Political Ideologies* (Chicago, IL: University of Chicago Press, 2001).

Ellis, Richard J. *The Dark Side of the Left: Illiberal Egalitarianism in America* (Lawrence: University Press of Kansas, 1998).

Farmer, Brian R. *American Political Ideologies: An Introduction to the Major Systems of Thought in the 21st Century* (Jefferson, NC: McFarland, 2006).

Fowler, Robert Booth. *Enduring Liberalism: American Political Thought since the 1960s* (Lawrence: University Press of Kansas, 1999).

Hoeveler, J. David, Jr. *The Postmodern Turn: American Thought and Culture in the 1970s* (New York: Twayne Publishers, 1996)

Lott, Eric. *The Disappearing Liberal Intellectual* (New York: Basic Books, 2006).

Robin, Corey. *The Reactionary Mind: Conservatism from Edmund Burke to Sarah Palin* (New York: Oxford University Press, 2011).

Rodgers, Daniel T. *Age of Fracture* (Cambridge, MA: Harvard University Press, 2011).

Skrentny, John D. *The Minority Rights Revolution* (Cambridge, MA: Harvard University Press, 2002).

Smith, Kimberly K. *Wendell Berry and the Agrarian Tradition: A Common Grace* (Lawrence: University Press of Kansas, 2003).

Smith, Mark A. *The Right Talk: How Conservatives Transformed the Great Society into the Economic Society* (Princeton, NJ: Princeton University Press, 2007).

Taylor, Bob Pepperman. *Our Limits Transgressed: Environmental Political Thought in America* (Lawrence: University Press of Kansas, 1992).

Teles, Steven M. *The Rise of the Conservative Legal Movement: The Battle for Control of the Law* (Princeton, NJ: Princeton University Press, 2008).

Troy, Gil. *Morning in America: How Ronald Reagan Invented the 1980's* (Princeton, NJ: Princeton University Press, 2007).

SOURCES

Chapter 2: Roger Williams, *The Bloudy Tenent, of Persecution, for Cause of Conscience* (London: J. Haddon, 1848). John Cotton, *An Exposition on the 13th Chapter of the Revelation* (London: Livewel Chapman, 1655). John Winthrop, *The History of New England from 1630 to 1649*, vol. 2 (Boston: Phelps and Farnham, 1826), 228–230. John Wise, *A Vindication of the Government of New-England Churches* (Boston: J. Allen, 1717). Thomas Paine, *The Writings of Thomas Paine*, vol. 1 (New York: G.P. Putnam's Sons, 1894). Jonathan Mayhew, *A Discourse Concerning Unlimited Submission and Non-Resistance to the Higher Powers* (Boston: D. Fowle, 1750). William Livingston, "Of Party Divisions," *The Independent Reflector* 13 (February 22, 1753): 51. William Henry Drayton, *Letters of Freeman, Etc.* (London: n.p., 1771). *Collections of the Massachusetts Historical Society*, 5th series, vol. 3 (1877): 432. Jonathan Boucher, *A View of the Causes and Consequences of the American Revolution* (London: G.C. and J. Robinson, 1797). *Collections of the Massachusetts Historical Society*, 3rd series, vol. 7 (1838): 33. Cotton Mather, *A Christian at His Calling: Two Brief Discourses* (Boston: B. Green and J. Allen, 1701). Benjamin Franklin, *Franklin's Way to Wealth; or, "Poor Richard Improved"* (New York: S. Wood and Sons, 1817). Joseph Doddridge, *Notes on the Settlement and Indian Wars of the Western Parts of Virginia and Pennsylvania, from 1763 to 1783, Inclusive* (Albany, NY: Joel Munsell, 1876). *Letters from a Farmer in Pennsylvania, to the Inhabitants of the British Colonies* (Philadelphia: D. Hall and W. Sellers, 1768). *Novanglus and Massachusettensis; or Political Essays published in the Years 1774 and 1775* (Boston: Hews and Goss, 1819).

Chapter 3: John Adams, *The Works of John Adams*, ed. Charles Francis Adams, vol. 4 (Boston: Little, Brown and Company, 1851). A Native of That Colony [Carter Braxton], *An Address to the Convention of the Colony and Ancient Dominion of Virginia* (Philadelphia: John Dunlap, 1776). Thomas Jefferson, *The Writings of Thomas Jefferson*, ed. H.A. Washington, vol. 8 (New York: H.W. Derby, 1861). *The Federalist: A Collection of Essays, Written in Favour of the New Constitution, as Agreed Upon by the Federal Convention, September 17, 1787, in two volumes* (New York: J. and A. McLean, 1788). *New York Journal* (October 18–November 1, 1787). *Observations Leading to a Fair Examination of the System of Government, Proposed by the Late Convention . . . In a Number of Letters from the Federal Farmer to the Republican* (New York: n.p., 1787). Thomas Jefferson, *Memoirs, Correspondence and Private Papers of Thomas Jefferson*, ed. Thomas Jefferson Randolph, vol. 2 (London: Henry Colburn and Richard Bentley, 1829). James Madison, *Letters and Other Writings of James Madison*, vol. 1 (Philadelphia: J.B. Lippincott & Co., 1865). J. Hector St. John de Crevecoeur, *Letter from an American Farmer Describing Certain Provincial Situations, Manners and Customs* (Philadelphia: M. Carey, 1793). Charles Francis Adams, ed., *Familiar Letters of John Adams, and His Wife Abigail Adams* (New York: Hurd and Hougton, 1876). Thomas Jefferson, *Notes on the State of Virginia* (Boston: David Carlisle, 1801). John H.B. Latrobe, *Memoir of Benjamin Banneker* (Baltimore: John D. Toy, 1845). Thomas Jefferson, *The Writings of Thomas Jefferson*, ed. H.A. Washington, vol. 3 (Washington, D.C.: Taylor & Maury, 1853). James Madison, *The Writings of James Madison*, ed. Gaillard Hunt, vol. 2 (New York: G.P. Putnam's Sons, 1901). William Tatham, "Speech of Onitositah," *Annual of Biography and Obituary* 4 (1820): 165.

Alexander Hamilton, *The Official and Other Papers of the Late Major-General Alexander Hamilton*, vol. 1 (New York: Wiley & Putnam, 1842). George Washington, "Circular Letter Addressed to the Governors of all the States on Disbanding the Army," in *The Writings of George Washington*, ed. Jared Sparks, vol. 8 (Boston: Hilliard, Gray, and Co., 1835).

Chapter 4: Thomas Jefferson, *The Writings of Thomas Jefferson*, ed. Henry Augustine Washington, vol. 9 (New York: Derby & Jackson, 1859). Fisher Ames, "For the Anthology," *Monthly Anthology and Boston Review* 2 (1805): 563. Thomas Jefferson, *The Writings of Thomas Jefferson*, ed. Henry Augustine Washington, vol. 8 (New York: Derby & Jackson, 1859). Marbury v. Madison, 5 U.S. 137 (1803). Lyman Beecher, *The Practicability of Suppressing Vice, by Means of Societies Instituted for That Purpose; A Sermon Delivered before the Moral Society in East-Hampton* (New London, CT: Samuel Green, 1804). Thomas Jefferson, *The Writings of Thomas Jefferson*, ed. Paul Leicester Ford, vol. 10 (New York: G.P. Putnam's Sons, 1899). *Reports of the Proceedings and Debates of the Convention of 1821, Assembled for the Purpose of Amending the Constitution of the State of New York*, ed. Nathaniel H. Carter and William L. Stone (Albany: E. and E. Horsford, 1821). George Washington, *The President's Address to the People of the United States, Announcing His Design of Retiring from Public Life* (Philadelphia: n.p., 1796). Thomas Jefferson, *The Writings of Thomas Jefferson*, ed. Paul Leicester Ford, vol. 9 (New York: G.P. Putnam's Sons, 1898). McCulloch v. Maryland, 17 U.S. 316 (1819). Judith Sargent Murray, *The Gleaner*, 3 vols. (Boston: I. Thomas and E.T. Andrews, 1798). U.S. House of Representatives, *Colonization of Free People of Color*, H. Rep. No. 101, 19th Cong., 2nd Sess. (March 3, 1827): 16. Alexander Hamilton, *The Works of Alexander Hamilton*, ed. Henry Cabot Lodge, vol. 2 (New York: G.P. Putnam's Sons, 1904). Alexander Hamilton, *The Works of Alexander Hamilton*, ed. Henry Cabot Lodge, vol. 4 (New York: G.P. Putnam's Sons, 1904). John Taylor, *Tyranny Unmasked* (Washington City: Davis and Force, 1822). Thomas Jefferson, *The Writings of Thomas Jefferson*, ed. Henry Augustine Washington, vol. 4 (New York: H.W. Derby, 1861). John Quincy Adams, *An Address Delivered at the Request of a Committee of the Citizens of Washington; on the Occasion of Reading the Declaration of Independence, on the Fourth of July, 1821* (Washington: Davis and Force, 1821). *The Addresses and Messages of the Presidents of the United States* (New York: Edward Walker, 1841).

Chapter 5: George Bancroft, *Literary and Historical Miscellanies* (New York: Harper & Brothers, 1857). Henry David Thoreau, *Anti-Slavery and Reform Papers*, ed. H.S. Salt (London: George Allen & Unwin Ltd., 1890). John C. Calhoun, *A Disquisition on Government* (Columbia, SC: A.S. Johnston, 1851). Theodore Parker, *Additional Speeches, Addresses, and Occasional Sermons*, vol. 2 (Boston, MA: Little, Brown and Co., 1855). Samuel F.B. Morse, *Imminent Dangers to the Free Institutions of the United States Through Foreign Immigration and the Present State of the Naturalization Laws* (New York: E.B. Clayton, 1835). Ralph Waldo Emerson, *Essays, Lectures and Orations* (London: William S. Orr and Co., 1851). "Responsibility of the Ballot Box; with an Illustration," *The American Review: A Whig Journal of Politics, Literature, Art, and Science*, 4:5 (November 1846): 435–446. William Lloyd Garrison, "To the Public," *The Liberator* (January 1, 1831): 1; "Prospectus of *The Liberator*," *The Liberator* (December 29, 1837): 1.Elizabeth Cady Stanton, Susan B. Anthony, and Matilda Joslyn Gage, eds., *History of Woman Suffrage*, 2nd ed., vol. I, (Rochester, NY: Charles Mann, 1889), 70–72.Sojourner Truth, *Narrative of Sojourner Truth: A Bonds-Woman of Olden Time* (Battle Creek, MI: n.p., 1878). Frederick Douglass, *Oration, Delivered in Corinthian Hall, Rochester* (Rochester, NY: Lee, Mann & Co., 1852). George Fitzhugh, *Cannibals All! Or, Slaves Without Masters* (Richmond, VA: A. Morris, 1857). James H. Hammond, *Selections from the Letters and Speeches of the Hon. James H. Hammond, of South Carolina* (New York: John F. Trow & Co., 1866). Abraham Lincoln, *The Writings of Abraham Lincoln*, ed. Arthur Brooks Lapsley, vol. 5 (New York: Lamb Publishing, 1906). Andrew Jackson, "Veto Message Regarding the Bank of the United States," (July 10, 1832), in *A Compilation of the Messages and Papers of the President, 1789–1897*, ed. James D. Richardson, vol. 2 (Washington, D.C.: Government Printing Office, 1896). Henry Clay, *The Speeches of Henry Clay*, ed. Calvin Colton, vol. 1 (New York: A.S. Barnes & Co., 1857). William Leggett, *A Collection of the Political Writings of William Leggett*, ed. Theodore Sedgwick Jr., vol. 1 (New York: Taylor & Dodd, 1840). Orestes A. Brownson, *The Laboring Classes, an Article from the Boston Quarterly Review*, 3rd ed. (Boston: Benjamin H. Greene, 1840). Andrew Jackson, "Second Annual Message," (December 6, 1830), in *A Compilation of the Messages and Papers of the President, 1789–1897*, ed. James D. Richardson, vol. 2 (Washington, D.C.: Government Printing Office, 1896). "Memorial of the Cherokee Indians," *Niles Weekly Register* (March 13, 1830): 53. John O'Sullivan,

"The Great Nation of Futurity," *The United States Democratic Review* 6:23 (November 1839): 426–430; John O'Sullivan, "Annexation," *The United States Democratic Review* 17:85 (July 1845): 5–10; John O'Sullivan, "The True Title," *New York Morning News* 3:110 (December 27, 1845): 2.

Chapter 6: Abraham Lincoln, *The Writings of Abraham Lincoln*, ed. Arthur Brooks Lapsley, vol. 5 (New York: Lamb Publishing, 1906). *Congressional Globe*, vol. 39, pt. 2 (January 3, 1867): 251. Jefferson Davis, *The Rise and Fall of the Confederate Government*, vol. 1 (New York: D. Appleton and Company, 1881). Abraham Lincoln, *The Writings of Abraham Lincoln*, ed. Arthur Brooks Lapsley, vol. 7 (New York: Lamb Publishing, 1906). Lysander Spooner, *No Treason* (Boston: Published by the author, 1867). Charles Sumner, *The Barbarism of Slavery: Speech of Hon. Charles Sumner, on the Bill for the Admission of Kansas as a Free State* (New York: Young Men's Republican Union, 1863). Henry Cleveland, *Alexander H. Stephens, in Public and Private: With Letters and Speeches, Before, During, and Since the War* (Philadelphia, PA: National Publishing Company, 1866). Frederick Douglass, *Life and Times of Frederick Douglass Written by Himself* (Hartford, CT: Park Publishing, 1882). Susan B. Anthony, *An Account of the Trial of Susan B. Anthony on the Charge of Illegal Voting* (Rochester, NY: Daily Democrat and Chronicle, 1874). Russell H. Conwell, *Acres of Diamonds: How Men and Women May Become Rich* (Philadelphia: John Y. Huber Company, 1890). Abraham Lincoln, *The Writings of Abraham Lincoln*, ed. Arthur Brooks Lapsley, vol. 6 (New York: Lamb Publishing, 1906). *Message from the President of the United States, Communicating the Report and Journal of Proceedings of the Commission Appointed to Obtain Certain Concessions from the Sioux Indians*, U.S. Senate, 44th Cong., 2nd Sess., Ex. Doc. No. 9 (1876).

Chapter 7: Francis Parkman, "The Failure of Universal Suffrage," *North American Review* 127 (July-August 1878): 1. Stephen Field, "The Centenary of the Supreme Court of the United States," *American Law Review* 24 (1890): 351. James B. Weaver, *A Call to Action: An Interpretation of the Great Uprising, Its Sources and Causes* (Des Moines: Iowa Printing Co., 1892). Henry W. Grady, *Life and Labors of Henry W. Grady* (Atlanta: H.C. Hudgins & Co., 1890). Frederick Jackson Turner, "The Significance of the Frontier in American History," *Annual Report of the American Historical Association for the Year 1893* (Washington: Government Printing Office, 1894). Henry Cabot Lodge, *Speeches and Addresses: 1884–1909* (Boston: Houghton Mifflin Company, 1909). *A Compilation of the Messages and Papers of the Presidents*, ed. James D. Richardson, vol. 14 (New York: Bureau of National Literature, 1897). Thomas E. Watson, "The Negro Question in the South," *The Arena* 6 (October 1892): 540. Booker T. Washington, *Up from Slavery: An Autobiography* (New York: Doubleday, Page & Co., 1907). Helen Kendrick Johnson, *Woman and the Republic: A Survey of the Woman-Suffrage Movement in the United States and a Discussion of the Claims and Arguments of its Foremost Advocates* (New York: D. Appleton & Co., 1897). Charlotte Perkins Stetson [Gilman], *Women and Economics: A Study of the Economic Relation Between Men and Women as a Factor in Social Evolution* (Boston: Small, Maynard & Co., 1898). William Graham Sumner, *What Social Classes Owe to Each Other* (New York: Harper & Brothers, 1884). Andrew Carnegie, "Wealth," *North American Review* 148 (June 1889): 653. Henry Demarest Lloyd, *Wealth Against Commonwealth* (New York: Harper & Brothers, 1894). Thorstein Veblen, *The Theory of the Leisure Class* (New York: Macmillan, 1899). Josiah Strong, *Our Country: Its Possible Future and Its Present Crisis* (New York: Baker & Taylor Co., 1885). William Graham Sumner, *The Conquest of the United States by Spain: A Lecture before the Phi Beta Kappa Society of Yale University, January 16, 1899* (Boston: Dana Estes & Company, 1899). Elihu Root, *Speech by the Hon. Elihu Root, Secretary of War, at Canton, Ohio, October 24, 1900* (n.p.: n.y.).

Chapter 8: Theodore Roosevelt, *The New Nationalism* (New York: Outlook Company, 1910). Woodrow Wilson, *The New Freedom: A Call for the Emancipation of the Generous Energies of a People* (New York: Doubleday, Page, and Company, 1913). John Dewy, *The Public and Its Problems* (New York: Henry Holt & Co., 1927). Louis Brandeis, "True Americanism," *Harper's Weekly* 61 (July 10, 1915): 31. Randolph Bourne, "Trans-National America," *Atlantic Monthly* 118 (July 1916): 86. Henry Pratt Fairchild, *The Melting-Pot Mistake* (Boston: Little, Brown, 1926). Edgar Gardner Murphy, *The White Man and the Negro at the South, an Address Delivered under Invitation of the American Academy of Political and Social Science* (Montgomery, AL: n.p., 1900). W.E.B. DuBois, *The Souls of Black Folk: Essays and Sketches* (Chicago: A.C. McClurg & Co., 1903). Jane Addams, "If Men Were Seeking the Franchise," *Ladies' Home Journal* 30 (June 1913): 21. Eugene V. Debs, *Unionism and Socialism: A Plea for Both* (Terre Haute, IN: Standard Publishing, 1904). Emma Goldman, *Anarchism and Other Essays* (New

York: Mother Earth Publishing, 1910). Herbert Croly, *The Promise of American Life* (New York: Macmillan, 1909). Herbert Hoover, *American Individualism* (Garden City, NY: Doubleday, Page & Company, 1922). Theodore Roosevelt, "Social Values and National Existence," *Papers and Proceedings of the Annual Meeting of the American Sociological Society* 10 (1915): 12. Woodrow Wilson, *President's Wilson's Great Speeches and Other History Making Documents* (Chicago: Stanton and Van Vliet, 1917). Randolph Bourne, *Untimely Papers* (New York: B.W. Huebsch, 1919). William Borah, "Disarmament," *Nation's Business* 9 (September 1921): 7. Courtesy of Hagley Museum and Library.

Chapter 9: Herbert Hoover, *The New Day: Campaign Speeches of Herbert Hoover, 1928* (Stanford, CA: Stanford University Press, 1928). Courtesy of Herbert Hoover Presidential Library and Museum. Albert Jay Nock, "Life, Liberty, and . . .," *Scribner's Magazine* 97 (March 1935): 150–154. Used by permission of Charles Scribner's Sons. John Dewey, *Liberalism and Social Action* (New York: G.P. Putnam's Sons, 1935). Used. By permission of G.P. Putnam's Sons, an imprint of Penguin Publishing Group, a division of Penguin Random House LLC. Thurman Arnold, *The Symbols of Government* (New Haven: Yale University Press, 1935). James Weldon Johnson, *Negro America, What Now?* (New York: Viking Press, 1934). Ralph J. Bunche, "A Critical Analysis of the Tactics and Programs of Minority Groups," *Journal of Negro Education* 4 (July 1935): 308–320. A. Philip Randolph, "Keynote Address to the Policy Conference of the March on Washington Movement, Detroit, Michigan," in *March on Washington Movement: Proceedings of Conference Held in Detroit, September 26–27, 1942* (n.p.: 1942). R.G. Tugwell, "The Principle of Planning and the Institution of Laissez Faire," *American Economic Review* 22:1 (March 1932): 75–92.A.A. Berle, Jr., "A High Road for Business," *Scribner's Magazine* 98 (June 1933): 325–331. Used by permission of Charles Scribner's Sons. Huey P. Long, *Share Our Wealth: Every Man a King* (Washington, D.C.: n.p., 1935), 7–17. Earl Browder, *What Is Communism?* (New York: Vanguard Press, 1936). X, "The Sources of Soviet Conduct," *Foreign Affairs* 25:4 (July 1947): 566–582. Copyright by the Council on Foreign Relations, Inc. www.Foreign Affairs.com Reinhold Niebuhr, *The Children of Light and the Children of Darkness* (New York: Charles Scribner's Sons, 1949). Robert A. Taft, *A Foreign Policy for Americans* (Garden City, NY: Doubleday & Company, 1951). Used by permission of Doubleday, an imprint of Knopf/Doubleday Publishing Group, a division of Random House LLC.

Chapter 10: Milton Friedman, *Capitalism and Freedom* (Chicago: University of Chicago Press, 1962). Used by permission of the publisher.Barry Goldwater, Acceptance Speech for the Republican Nomination for President, Senator Barry M. Goldwater Papers, Arizona Historical Foundation Collection, Arizona State University Libraries. Herbert Macuse, *An Essay on Liberation* (Boston: Beacon Press, 1969). Used by permission of Beacon Press, Boston. John Rawls, *A Theory of Justice* (Cambridge: Harvard University Press, 1971). Used by permission of the publisher. *Public Papers of the Presidents of the United States* (Washington, D.C.: Government Printing Office, 1965). Ralph Nader, "We Need a New Kind of Patriotism," *Life* 71 (July 9, 1971): 4. Martin Luther King, Jr., *Letter from a Birmingham City Jail* and *I Have a Dream*. Reprinted by Permission with the Heirs to the Estate of Martin Luther King, Jr., c/o Writers House as an agent of the proprietor New York, NY. Malcolm X, *Malcolm X Speaks: Selected Speeches and Statements*, ed. George Breitman (New York: Merit Publishers, 1965). Copyright by Betty Shabazz and Pathfinder Press. Reprinted by permission. Betty Friedan, *The Feminine Mystique* (New York: W.W. Norton, 1963). Used by permission of W.W. Norton & Company, Inc.Kate Millet, *Sexual Politics* (New York: Avon, 1969). Reprinted by permission of Georges Borchardt, Inc., on behalf of the author. John Kenneth Galbraith, *American Capitalism* (Boston: Houghton Mifflin, 1952). George J. Stigler, "The Theory of Economic Regulation," *Bell Journal of Economics and Management Science* 2 (Spring 1971): 3–21. Reprinted by permission of RAND Journal of Economics. Hans J. Morgenthau, *In Defense of the National Interest: A Critical Examination of American Foreign Policy* (New York: Alfred A. Knopf, 1952). James Burnham, *Containment or Liberation? An Inquiry into the Aims of United States Foreign Policy* (New York: John Day, 1953). Estate of James Burnham. J. William Fulbright, *The Arrogance of Power* (New York: Random House, 1966). Used by permission of Random House, an imprint of Random House LLC.

Chapter 11: Richard Rorty, *Objectivity, Relativism, and Truth: Philosophical Papers, Volume 1* (New York: Cambridge University Press, 1990). Richard A. Epstein, *Skepticism and Freedom: A Modern Case for Classical Liberalism* (Chicago: University of Chicago Press, 2003). David Graeber, *Direct Action: An Ethnography* (Oakland, CA: AK

Press, 2009). Richard John Neuhaus, "What the Fundamentalists Want," *Commentary* (May 1985): 41. Reprinted by permission. Michael Walzer, "What Does It Mean to Be an 'American'?" *Social Research* 57 (Fall 1990): 591. Irving Kristol, *The Neoconservative Persuasion: Selected Essays, 1942–2009* (New York: Basic Books, 2011). Reprinted by permission of Basic Books, a member of the Perseus Books Group. Wendell Berry, *Citizenship Papers* (Berkeley, CA: Shoemaker and Hoard, 2003). Thomas Sowell, *Civil Rights: Rhetoric or Reality?* (New York: William Morrow, 1984). Reprinted by permission of HarperCollins Publishers.Thurgood Marshall, "Reflections on the Bicentennial of the United States Constitution," *Harvard Law Review* 101 (1987): 1. Cornel West, *Race Matters* (New York: Vintage, 1994). Reprinted by permission of Beacon Press, Boston. Richard A. Posner, *The Economics of Justice* (Cambridge, MA: Harvard University Press, 1981). Reprinted by permission of the publisher. *Economic Justice for All: Pastoral Letter on Catholic Social Teaching and the U.S. Economy* (Washington, D.C.: National Conference of Catholic Bishops, 1986). Used with permission of the publisher.Michael Albert and Mark Evans, *Fanfare for the Future, Volume 2: Occupy Vision* (Woods Hole, MA: ZBooks, 2012). Jeane J. Kirkpatrick, "Dictatorships and Double Standards," *Commentary* (November 1979): 54. Used by permission of Commentary, Inc. Samuel P. Huntington, "The Clash of Civilizations?" *Foreign Affairs* (Summer 1993). Copyright by the Council on Foreign Relations, Inc. www.Foreign Affairs.com. Noam Chomsky, *Understanding Power: The Indispensable Chomsky*, ed. Peter R. Mitchell and John Schoeffel (New York: New Press, 2002).

INDEX

B

U